Dictionary of_____
Mexican
Literature

Dictionary of
Mexican
Literature

Edited by
Eladio Cortés

GREENWOOD PRESS
Westport, Connecticut • London

Library of Congress Cataloging-in-Publication Data

Dictionary of Mexican literature / edited by Eladio Cortés.
    p. cm.
    Includes bibliographical references and index.
    ISBN 0-313-26271-3 (alk. paper)
    1. Mexican literature—Dictionaries. 2. Mexican literature—20th
century—Dictionaries. I. Cortés, Eladio.
    PQ7106.D53 1992
    860.9'972'03—dc20   91-10529

British Library Cataloguing in Publication Data is available.

Library of Congress Catalog Card Number: 91-10529
ISBN: 0-313-26271-3

First published in 1992

Greenwood Press, 88 Post Road West, Westport, CT 06881
An imprint of Greenwood Publishing Group, Inc.

Printed in the United States of America

The paper used in this book complies with the
Permanent Paper Standard issued by the National
Information Standards Organization (Z39.48-1984).

10 9 8 7 6 5 4 3 2

Contents

Contributors

Ricardo Aguilar, Ph.D., is Associate Professor of Spanish at the University of Texas, El Paso and director of the Chicano Studies Program. He is a specialist on Mexican literature of the twentieth century, with the focus on the present era. He has published extensively about the latest generation of Mexican writers, in particular those living in the United States.

Robert K. Anderson, Ph.D., is a Professor of Spanish at California State University, Stanislaus. He has contributed articles and book reviews on Spanish and Mexican literature to *Hispanic Journal*, *Crítica Hispánica*, *Revista de Estudios Hispánicos*, and other publications. He has published numerous articles on the work of Elena Garro.

Melvin S. Arrington, Jr., is an Associate Professor of modern languages at the University of Mississippi, where he has taught since 1982. The holder of a Ph.D. in Spanish from the University of Kentucky, he has written primarily in the field of twentieth-century Spanish American prose fiction.

Teresa R. Arrington is Assistant Professor of Spanish at the University of Mississippi. He received her Ph.D. from the University of Kentucky. She has published articles about Spanish linguistics, foreign language teaching methology, transformational grammar, and Latin American feminist literature. She is currently the Executive Secretary-Treasurer of the Mississippi Foreign Language Association.

Mirta Barrea-Marlys is an Assistant Professor of Spanish at Rutgers University in Camden. She holds a Ph.D. from the University of Pennsylvania. Her major field of studies is nineteenth century literature. She has presented papers and published articles on the work of Gertrudis Gómez de Avellaneda and other women writers of that period.

Denise Guagliardo Bencivengo has completed her doctoral education at the University of Pennsylvania. She has studied at the Universidad Nacional Autónoma de México and at the Miguel de Cervantes Institute in Madrid. She currently chairs the Foreign Language Department at Princeton Day School in Princeton, New Jersey.

Carmen Blázquez Domínguez is a native of Jalapa, Veracruz, Mexico. Her doctorate is from El Colegio de México. Presently she is a full-time researcher at the Center of Historical Research of the Humanistic Research Institute of the Universidad Veracruzana in Xalapa, Mexico. She is the author of several books including *Miguel Lerdo de Tejada. Un liberal Veracruzano en la política nacional* (1976) and *Veracruz Liberal* (1986).

Peter G. Broad, Ph.D., is an Associate Professor of Spanish and Chairperson of the Department of Spanish and Classical Languages at Indiana University of Pennsylvania. He has recently published, among others, articles about a Chicano novel, *Suruma* by Sergio Elizondo, and also about the works of Carlos Fuentes.

Yolanda S. Broad, Ph.D., is Assistant Professor at Indiana University of Pennsylvania. She has written several articles on Latin American literature, the last one on the Mexican writer Josefina Vicens.

Alina Camacho-Gingerich, Ph.D., is Professor of Spanish American literature at St. John's University in New York. She is the author of *La cosmovisión poética de José Lezama Lima en Paradiso y Oppiano Licario* and numerous other studies on Carlos Fuentes, Elena Poniatowska, Alejo Carpentier, Gustavo Sáinz, Rogelio Sinán, and Vicente Huidobro. Her work has appeared in journals such as *Revista Iberoamericana, INTI: Revista de Literature Hispánica, Mundus Artium, Discurso Literario*, and *Hispania*.

Eladio Cortés is editor-in-chief of the *Dictionary of Mexican Literature*. He is also a Professor of Spanish at Rutgers University in Camden and co-editor with Emilio Carballido of *Tramoya*, a theater journal. He holds a Ph.D. from Rutgers University in New Brunswick, New Jersey. His major published works include *El teatro de los hermanos Machado* (1970), *El teatro de Francisco Villaespesa* (1972), *De literatura hispánica* (1988) as well as numerous articles on Elena Garro, Elena Santiago, Altair Tejeda de Tamez, Sabina Berman, José López Rubio, Ramón J. Sender, Salvador Novo, and others. He is presently finishing a critical edition of *La segunda Celestina* by Salazar y Torres.

Cynthia K. Duncan, Ph.D., teaches in the Department of Romance Languages at the University of Tennessee. She has published extensively on Mexican writers of the twentieth century, such as Emilio Carballido and Angeles Mastretta. She has also written about magical realism in Mexico.

Nora Eidelberg, Ph.D., is Associate Professor of Modern Languages at Wesleyan College. Among her publications are the books *Teatro experimental hispanoamericano, 1960-1980. La realidad social como manipulación* (1985) and *Voces en escena; Antología de dramaturgas latinoamericanas* (1991). She also does research on Latin American theater and translates such works to English.

Nora Erro-Peralta, a native of Salto, Uruguay, holds a Ph.D. from the University of Toronto. An Associate Professor at Florida Atlantic University in Boca Raton, Florida, she has co-authored two books: *Puerta abierta: la nueva escritora latinoamericana*, and *Beyond the Border: A New Age in Latin American Women's Fiction*. Her field of expertise is Latin American literature, on which she has written numerous articles.

Silka Freire holds a Ph.D. from Michigan State University. She is an Assistant Professor at Central Michigan State University. She has taught literature at the Instituto de Profesores "Artigas" in Montevideo, Uruguay. She has recently begun publishing articles and presenting papers on Latin American literature.

Mark Frisch is an Associate Professor of Modern Languages and Literatures at Duquesne University in Pittsburgh. He received his doctorate in 1985 from the University of Michigan. He has recently published the book, *La relación de Faulkner con La América Hispánica: Mallea, Rojas, Yáñez y García Márquez*. Recipient of a Fulbright Award, he lectured in Argentina in 1987. He has published articles on Elena Garro and has worked with the journal *Poe Studies* in compiling an international bibliography.

Barbara P. Fulks recently received her doctorate from the University of North Carolina, Chapel Hill where she teaches Spanish and Latin American literature. She has written articles about contemporary Mexican authors.

Delia Galván, Ph.D., a native of Mexico City, is an Assistant Professor at Cleveland State University. She has published and lectured on Elena Garro, Emilio Carballido, and others. She has published a book, *La ficción reciente de Elena Garro*, as well as articles on other Mexican writers.

Lino García, Ph.D., is a Professor of Spanish at Pan American University, Edinburg, Texas, where he chairs the Department of Foreign Languages. He has published extensively on the works of Rubén Darío, Carlos Fuentes, Agustín Yáñez, and other Mexican writers. He also has presented papers on contemporary Mexican literature.

Baudelio Garza, Ph.D., is Assistant Professor in the Department of Modern Languages at Baylor University in Waco, Texas. His main interest is on Mexican literature of the border. He has done research on contemporary Mexican writers.

Alfonso González is Professor of Spanish at California State University in Los Angeles. He holds a Ph.D. from the University of Kansas. He has published many books, including *Indice de la cultura en México 1962-1972* (1978), *26 autoras del México actual* (1979) (co-authored with Beth Miller), *Español para el hispanohablante en los Estados Unidos* (1987) (co-edited with Mirta. A. González), *Carlos Fuentes* (1988), and a revised edition of Bernardo de Balbuena's *El Siglo de Oro en las selvas Erífile*. He also has numerous articles on Cervantes, Juan Rulfo, Guillermina Bravo, and other authors.

Mirta A. González, Ph.D., is an Assistant Professor in the Department of Foreign Languages at California State University, San Bernardino. She has co-authored with Alfonso González the book, *Español para el hispanohablante en los Estados Unidos* (1987). She also has written articles on Spanish and Mexican Literature.

Patricia Hart, Ph.D., is an Associate Professor of Spanish at Purdue University where she chairs the Spanish and Portuguese section of the Department of Foreign Languages and Literatures. She is the author of *Narrative Magic in the Fiction of Isabel Allende*, and *The Spanish Sleuth*. She has collaborated on a dictionary of Cuban authors and has published articles on Carlos Fuentes and other writers. She has also written short stories.

Josef Hellebrandt is Assistant Professor of Spanish at Illinois State University-- Normal. He received the degree of Magister from the Ludwig Maximilians University in Munich and has a Ph.D. from Purdue University. His research is mainly in foreign language education.

Herlinda Hernández is a native of Silao, Guanajuato, Mexico. She holds a Ph.D. from the University of Pittsburgh. She is an Associate Professor of Spanish at Indiana University of Pennsylvania. She has studied and lived in Spain after receiving a fellowship from the Institute of Hispanic Culture. Her main research focuses on contemporary Mexican literature.

Esther Hernández-Palacios is a native of Jalapa, Veracruz, Mexico. She is a full-time researcher at the Institute of Humanistic Research of the University of Veracruz. She has done studies in modern language literature at La Université de Toulouse Le Mirail, France. She is a specialist in Mexican poetry and has published two books: *La poesía de Jaime Sabines* (1984) and *Antología de la Poesía Veracruzana* (1984).

Julie Greer Johnson is Associate Professor of Spanish at the University of Georgia. She is the author of *Women in Colonial Spanish American Literature: Literary Images*, and *The Book in the Americas: The Role of Books and Printing in the Development of Culture and Society in Colonial Latin America.* Her articles have appeared in *Hispania*, *Hispanic Journal*, *Hispanófila*, *Kentucky Romance Quarterly*, and other periodicals. She has been a fellow at the John Carter Brown Library of Brown University and a recipient of a Columbian Quincentennial Fellowship.

Janis L. Krugh, Ph.D., is an Assistant Professor of the Department of Foreign Languages at the University of Dayton, Ohio. She has published extensively on the works of Luisa Josefina Hernández, of whom she is a specialist, as well as other Mexican writers of today.

Michèle Muncy, a native of Paris, France, is Professor Emeritus at Rutgers University in Camden where she taught French, Spanish, and Latin American literature. She holds a Ph.D. in Spanish and French from Rutgers University in New Brunswick, New Jersey. She is a specialist in contemporary Mexican literature and author of two books on Salvador Novo and book chapters and articles on Elena Garro, Luisa Josefina Hernández, Emilio Carballido, Rosario Castellanos, Nellie Campobello, and many others. She is copy editor of the journal *Tramoya*.

Edna A. Rehbein received her Ph.D. from the University of Texas at Austin. She is an Associate Professor of Spanish and Mexican American Studies and serves as Assistant Vice President for Academic Affairs at Concordia Lutheran College in Austin, Texas. She is co-editor of the collection of essays titled, *Critical Approaches to Isabel Allende's Novels*, published in 1991. Her interests include the Latin American Avant-garde and its ties to contemporary Latin American literature, the literature of Mexican Americans, and contemporary Latin American women writers.

María A. Salgado, Ph.D., born in Tenerife, Spain, is Professor of Spanish American Literature at the University of North Carolina in Chapel Hill. She has published numerous articles on Hispanic literature with emphasis on Modernism and contemporary poetry. Her books deal with the works of Juan Ramón Jiménez and Rafael Arévalo Martínez.

Joan Saltz is an Assistant Professor of Spanish, currently teaching in the Department of Foreign Languages and Literature at St. Cloud State University, St. Cloud, Minnesota. She completed a doctorate in Latin American literature at the University of California, San Diego. She has written on the political elements in two works of Luisa Valenzuela as well as articles on José Emilio Pacheco, Elena Poniatowska and Josefina Vicens, and has translated the poems of Alberto Blanco.

Oscar Somoza, Ph.D., teaches at the University of Denver. His main research interest is contemporary Mexican literature about which he has published articles.

Anita K. Stoll, Ph.D., is a Professor of Spanish at Cleveland State University. Her major research interests are Spanish Golden Age drama and contemporary Mexican literature. She has published articles on these topics, on pedagogy, and a critical edition of Lope de Vega's *La noche de San Juan* (1988), and has edited two collections of essays: *A Different Reality: Studies on the Work of Elena Garro* (1990), and *The Perception of Women in the Spanish Theater of the Golden Age* (1991, with Dawn L. Smith).

Kenneth M. Taggart, Ph.D., is an Associate Professor of Spanish at Trinity University in San Antonio, Texas. His research interests are pedagogy and Latin American literature: a book on Yáñez, Rulfo, and Fuentes; a grammar review text; articles on Rulfo, García Márquez, José Luis González, Vargas Llosa, Isabel Allende, women writers, and feminist criticism.

Margarita Vargas, Ph.D., is an Assistant Professor at SUNY at Buffalo where she teaches Spanish and Latin American literature. She has done extensive research on various contemporary Latin American writers.

Joseph Vélez, Ph.D., is a Professor of Spanish and director of Latin American Studies at Baylor University in Waco, Texas. He has published or edited four books: *En la ruta de Pito Pérez, cuarenta años después* (1983), *Cinco ensayos sobre "Chambú"* (1984), *Escritores mexicanos según ellos mismos* (1990), and *Dramaturgos mexicanos según ellos mismos* (1990). He has published extensively on Chicano writers and has contributed various articles to such journals as *SCOLAS*, *La Chispa*, and others.

Jeanne C. Wallace is Assistant Professor of Spanish at Rutgers University in Camden. She holds a Ph.D. from Temple University, Philadelphia. She has published a book entitled, *The Figure of the Angel in Contemporary Spanish Poetry*. She has published articles on the theater of Emilio Carballido, Luisa Josefina Hernández, and Sabina Berman, as well as on the works of Cervantes and on the poetry of contemporary Spain.

Alicia G. Welden, Ph.D., a native of Valparaíso, Chile, teaches at the University of Tennessee. She is the author of many publications, including *Antología de romances, letrillas y sonetos de Luis de Góngora, Góngora, Antología clave*, and *Alta marea: introvisión crítica en ocho voces latinoamericanas*. She has written several books of poetry. Among them are *Jaula gruesa para el animal hembra* and *Oficio de mudanza*. She has been anthologized in *Palabra de mujer* by Jorge Boccanera, and in *Mujeres poetas de Hispanoamérica* by Ramiro Lagos.

Richard D. Woods, Ph.D., is a Professor of Spanish at Trinity University in San Antonio, Texas. He specializes in Mexican autobiography. One of his latest publications is *Mexican Autobiography: An Annotated Bibliography*. He is currently an associate editor of *Hispania*.

Filippa B. Yin, Ph.D., is Assistant Professor of Spanish at Cleveland State University, Ohio. Her major research interests are the contemporary Spanish novel and contemporary Spanish American literature. She has presented and published work in pedagogy, Mexican poetry and novel, the novel and film, and character development in the novel.

Preface

The *Dictionary of Mexican Literature* contains approximately 500 entries in English covering the most important writers, literary schools, and cultural movements in Mexican literary history. There is an emphasis on the figures of the twentieth century. The preparation of this volume is the result of the cooperation of American, Mexican, and Hispanic scholars as well as many of the authors themselves.

Specifically oriented toward the English-speaking public, the dictionary presents Mexican literature across the centuries in a sociocultural context. The entries are of varying length, determined by the relative importance of the writer or the literary movement. Each biographical entry contains factual information about the writer's life and works, plus a list of works and a secondary bibliography. The more extensive entries also provide a critical perspective of the writer. Translations are given for most Spanish titles.

The volume is divided into the following sections: List of Contributors, Preface, Abbreviations (General and for Journals, Periodicals and Supplements), Overview of Mexican Letters and Literature, Dictionary of Mexican Literature, Bibliography, and Index. The Overview discusses the development of Mexican literature within a cultural perspective. The entries place the author or the movement within the context of international literature.

Author entries are alphabetized by the writer's last name. Since most authors have two last names, the first is the one to be accepted. For instance, "Ramón López Velarde" would be found under "López." Writers listed as individual entries appear with their first last names in capital letters. Occasionally both last names are capitalized when the writer is publicly known accordingly, e.g., ABREU Gómez, Ermilo or CASTRO LEAL, Antonio. Cross-referencing of names is provided in the body of the text and in the index. The name is followed by the dates of birth and death, when known. Each entry contains both a biographical note and bibliographical information.

Citations of the author's works comprise the following information, when known: title of the work with an English translation, place of publication, publisher, date of publication and page numbers, where applicable. The works are listed in chronological order from the earliest to the latest dates.

Bibliographical information is in alphabetical order, by author. Each bibliographical entry follows basically the same format as the citations of the author's works. The entries selected are usually those which are most easily available in the United States. Also, for most of the authors, it is impossible to include all bibliographical material known; therefore, choices have had to be made. Accepted abbreviations are used in both types of listings.

This task would have been impossible without the help of the following people. I would like to thank the contributors who so generously gave of themselves to make this dictionary possible. I would like to express my gratitude to my friends and colleagues, Michèle Muncy and Jeanne C. Wallace for their unfailing help, as well as to Filippa B. Yin for her work in the writing of the "Overview" and to our departmental secretaries, Pennie Prete and Nancy Hoover, whose help has greatly facilitated the preparation of the manuscript. To my friends, Dr. Harold Rappaport, Dr. William Milligan, Mark Forrester, Mary Lou Coletta, Dr. Mirta Barrea-Marlys, Margaret Ryan, Dr. Rodney and Loretta Carlisle, Edwin Cosme-García, Emilio Carballido and Mercedes de la Cruz, goes my appreciation for their continual assistance. Special thanks to my Provost and friend, Walter K. Gordon, for his encouragement and constant support. Also to Dr. Joseph Held, for his advice and understanding. My deepest gratitude goes to Marilyn Brownstein and Terri R. Metz, of Greenwood Press for their tireless efforts and patience. As editor, I assume responsibility for whatever mistakes there may be in fact and judgment. All that is worthy and useful in these entries is the result of the excellence of the contributors.

Eladio Cortés

Abbreviations

GENERAL

Ant. Libr.	Antigua Librería (Old Bookstore)
BAM	Biblioteca de Autores Mexicanos
BEU	Biblioteca del Estudiante Universitario
Bibl.	Biblioteca (Library)
BMM	Biblioteca Mínima Mexicana
Bol.	Boletín (Newsletter, Journal)
ca.	hacia (circa)
Cía.	Compañía (company)
CEM	Colección de Escritores Mexicanos
Col.	Colección (collection)
Depto.	Departamento (department)
ed(s).	edición(es) (edition[s])
Ed.	Editor (edited by)
ed. rev.	edición revisada (revised edition)
Edit.	Editorial (Publishing Co.)
Edits.	Editores (Publishers)
estr.	estrenada (staged)
FCE	Fondo de Cultura Económica
Gráf.	Gráficos
ilustr(s).	ilustración(es) (illustration[s])
Imp.	Imprenta (Printers)
INAH	Instituto Nacional de Antropología e Historia
INBA	Instituto Nacional de Bellas Artes
INI	Instituto Nacional Indigenista
Introd.	Introducción (Introduction by)
Libr.	Librería (Book Store)
Linotip.	Linotipográficos (Linotypography)
Lit.	Literatura (Literature)
Ms.	Manuscrito (Manuscript)
n.d.	(no date)
n.p.	(no printer) (no place of publication)
núm(s).	número(s) (number[s])
O.C.	Obras completas (Complete Works)
Ofna	Oficina (Office)
prel.	preliminar (preliminary)
Pról.	Prólogo (Prologue)
Publ (s).	Publicación (es) (Publication [s])

Selec.	Selección (Selection)
SEP	Secretaría de Educación Pública
sg.	siguientes (following)
s/f.	sin fecha (no date)
s.p.i.	sin pie de imprenta (no printer)
Sría.	Secretaría (Government Office)
Sucs.	Sucesores (Successor)
Supl.	Suplemento (Supplement)
t.	tomo (volume)
Talls.	Talleres (Printing Shop)
Tip.	Tipográficos, tipografía (Typography)
trad.	traducción, traducido (translation, ed. by)
UNAM	Universidad Nacional Autónoma de México
vol (s).	volumen (s)

JOURNALS, PERIODICALS AND SUPPLEMENTS

Abside	Cultural Review, Mexico (Published since 1937)
Actual	Journal of the Universidad de los Andes, Mérida, Venezuela (Since 1967)
AIIE	Anales del Instituto de Investigaciones Estéticas, UNAM (Since 1937)
Alabastro	Literary Journal from Morelia, Mich. (since 1978)
Alero	Journal of the Universidad de San Carlos, Guatemala
Alcancía	Cultural Journal. Mexico (1933)
El Album Mexicano	Journal of Literature and arts, Mexico (1849)
Amaru	Journal of the Universidad Nacional de Lima, Perú
América	Journal of the SEP, Mexico (1942-1952, 1954-1960)
America Nuestra	Cultural Journal. Mexico (Since 1967)
Anábasis	Literary Magazine. Mexico (Since 1977)
El Anáhuac	Journal of the Sociedad Literaria Netzahualcóyotl (1869)
Anales	Annals of the University of Cuenca, Ecuador (Since 1944)
Anales de LH	*Anales de Literatura Hispanoamericana*. Universidad Complutense. Madrid (Since 1972)
Anales de la Literatura Española Contemporánea	Literary Journal. University of Colorado, Boulder, Col.
Antena	Monthly magazine, Mexico (1924)
Anuario Bibliográfico Colombiano	Yearly Journal of the Instituto Caro y Cuervo, Bogotá, Colombia (Since 1951)
Anuario CM	*Anuario del cuento mexicano*. Yearly publication of the INBA, Mexico (Since 1954)
Anuario de Filología	Philological Journal. Universidad del Zulia, Maracaibo, Venezuela (Since 1972)
Anuario de Letras	Journal of the College of Philosophy and Letters, UNAM, Mexico (Since 1963)
Anuario PM	*Anuario de la Poesía Mexicana*. Yearly Journal of the INBA. Mexico (1955-1963)

AP	*Acta Poética*. Journal of Poetics of UNAM, México (Since 1979)
Apolodionis	Cultural Magazine from Monterrey, N.L. (Since 1959)
Arbor	Research Journal. Consejo Superior de Investigaciones Científicas. Madrid. (Since 1945)
Armas y Letras	Journal of the University of Nuevo León, Monterrey, N.L. (Since 1944)
El Artista	Art Journal. Mexico (1874-1875)
Asomante	Journal of the University of Puerto Rico (Since 1945)
Atenea	Journal of the University of Concepción. Chile
El Ateneo Mexicano	Journal of the Ateneo mexicano. Mexico (1844)
Atlanta	Literary Magazine. Madrid (Since 1987)
BAM	*Boletín de la Academia Mexicana*. Bulletin of the Mexican Academy of the Language. Mexico (Since 1980)
Bandera de Provincias	Cultural Magazine. Guadalajara, Jal. (1929-1930)
BBH	*Boletín Bibliográfico de la Secretaría de Hacienda y Crédito Público*. Bibliographic Bulletin of the Treasury Department. Mexico (Since 1954)
BBM	*Boletín Bibliográfico Mexicano*. Bibliographic Bulletin of Editorial Porrúa. Mexico (Since 1940)
BBN	*Boletín de la Biblioteca Nacional*. Bulletin of the National Library. UNAM. Mexico (Since 1950)
BC	*Boletín Cultural*. Cultural Bulletin of the Dirección General de Relaciones Culturales. Madrid (Since 1981)
Bellas Artes	Journal of the INBA. Mexico (1956-1959)
Biblos	Weekly Bulletin from the National Library (1919-1922) and (1925-1926)
BIIB	*Boletín del Instituto de Investigaciones Bibliográficas*. Bulletin of the Institute of Bibliographical Research. UNAM. Mexico (Since 1969)
BM	*Bibliografía Mexicana*. Bibliographical Journal. UNAM. Mexico (Since 1967)
Bohemia Poblana	Journal of the Bohemia Poblana Association. Puebla (Since 1948)
Books Abroad	An International Literary Quarterly. Published by the University of Oklahoma Press, Norman, Okla.
La Brújula	Literary Magazine. Mexico (Since 1982)
El Búcaro	Literary Newspaper. Mexico (1875)
El Búho	Sunday Supplement of *Excelsior* (Since 1985)
Bulletin of the Comediantes	Theater Journal. University of Southern California. Los Angeles, Cal.
C.A.	*Cuadernos Americanos*. Mexico (Since 1942)
La Cabra	Bulletin of the Teatro Universitario. UNAM. Mexico (Since 1971)
El Caracol Marino	Literary Journal. Xalapa, Ver. (Since 1954)
Casa de las Américas	Journal of the Casa de las Américas. Havana, Cuba (Since 1960)
Cauce	Cultural Journal. Torreón, Coah. (Since 1948)

C. de B.A.	*Cuadernos de Bellas Artes*. Journal of the INBA. Mexico. (1960-1964)
La CD	*La Cultura al día*. Daily Cultural Supplement of *Excelsior*. Mexico (Since 1985)
La C. en M.	*La Cultura en Mexico*. Cultural Supplement of *Siempre!*. Mexico (Since 1962)
El Centavo	Literary Newsletter. Morelia, Mich. (Since 1954)
C.H.	*Cuadernos Hispanoamericanos*. Literary Journal from Cultura Hispánica. Madrid (Since 1948)
CL	*Cuadernos de Literatura*. Literary Magazine. Mexico (Since 1976)
CM	*Cuadernos de Marcha*. Literary Magazine. Mexico (Since 1979)
La C.N.	*La Cultura Nacional*. Daily Supplement of *El Nacional*. Mexico (1968)
Comunidad	Journal of the Iberoamerican University. Mexico (Since 1966)
Conjunto	Theater Journal from La Casa de las Américas. Havana (Since 1966)
Contemporáneos	Cultural Magazine. Mexico (1928-1931)
El Corno Emplumado	Bilingual Journal of Poetry. Mexico (Since 1962)
Creación	Literary Newsletter. Mexico (Since 1969)
Creación. RL	*Creación. Revista Literaria*. Literary Magazine. Guadalajara, Jal. (Since 1953)
Crítica Literaria	Literary Journal. Duquesne University. Pittsburgh, Penn.
CT	*Casa del Tiempo*. Journal of the Dirección de Difusión Cultural. UNAM. Mexico (Since 1980)
Cuadernos	Literary Journal from the Congress for Cultural Freedom (Congreso por la Libertad de la Cultura). Paris (Since 1953)
Cuadrante	Cultural Journal of the Universidad Autónoma de San Luis Potosí (Since 1952)
Cultura	Newsletter from the Education Department of El Salvador (Since 1955)
Cultura Norte	Cultural Newsletter of the Colegio de Sonora. Hermosillo, Son. (Since 1989)
Cultura Sur	Cultural Newsletter of the Consejo Nacional para la Cultura y las Artes. Mexico (Since 1989)
En la Cultura	Publication by the Instituto Tamaulipeco de Cultura. Ciudad Victoria, Tam. (Since 1989)
C.V.	*Cuadernos del Viento*. Cultural Magazine. Mexico (Since 1960)
CyC	*Creación y Crítica*. Literary Newsletter from Editorial Martín Casillas. Mexico (1982-1983)
D. de la C.	*Diorama de la Cultura*. Sunday Supplement of *Excelsior*. Mexico (Since 1917)
Deslinde	Literary Journal. UNAM. Mexico (Since 1968)
Deslinde UANL	Literary Journal. Universidad Autónoma de Nuevo León. Monterrey (Since 1982)

El Día	Daily Newspaper. Mexico (Since 1963)
Diagonales	Literary Magazine. Mexico (Since 1985)
Diálogos	Information Newsletter. El Colegio de Mexico. Mexico (1964-1985)
Diluvio de Pájaros	Literary Magazine. Mexico (Since 1963)
El Diario de México	Daily Newspaper. Mexico (1805-1817)
Discurso Literario	Literary Journal. Oklahoma State University. Stillwater, Okla.
El Domingo	Weekly Newspaper. Mexico (1871-1873)
Eco	Cultural Journal. Bogotá, Columbia (1958- 1985)
Estaciones	Literary Magazine. Mexico (1956-1960)
Estilo	Cultural Journal. San Luis Potosí. (Since 1945)
Estreno	Theater Journal. University of Cincinnati. Cincinnati, OH.
Et Caetera	Literary Magazine. Guadalajara, Jal. (Since 1966)
Examen	Literary Magazine. Mexico (1932)
Excelsior	Daily Newspaper. Mexico (Since 1917)
Fábula	Newsletter. Mexico (1934-1960)
La Falange	Cultural Journal. Mexico (1922-1923)
El Faro	Literary Magazine. Mexico (Since 1983)
El Federalista	Sunday Supplement of *El Federalista* (1872-1877)
FEM	Feminist Cultural Dissemination Journal. Mexico (Since 1976)
Filosofía y Letras	Journal of the College of Philosopfy and Letters. UNAM. Mexico (1941-1958)
El G. I.	*El Gallo Ilustrado.* Sunday Supplement of *El Día.* Mexico (Since 1962)
Gaceta de Cuba	Bulletin of the Association of Writers and Artists of Cuba. Havana (Since 1962)
Gaceta del FCE	*Gaceta del Fondo de Cultura Económica.* Mexico (Since 1954)
Gaceta UNAM	Bulletin of the UNAM. Mexico (Since 1954)
Gestos	Theater Journal. University of California. Irvine, Cal. (Since 1986)
Guía	Daily Cultural Supplement of *Novedades.* Mexico (1981-1985)
El H. C.	*El Heraldo Cultural.* Sunday Supplement of *El Heraldo de México.* Mexico (Since 1965)
Hemeroteca Literaria	Journal of the Hemeroteca Nacional. UNAM. Mexico (Since 1963)
Hispania	Journal of The American Association of Teachers of Spanish and Portuguese. (Since 1917)
HJ	*Hispanic Journal.* Journal of the Indiana University of Pennsylvania. Indiana, PA. (Since 1979)
Hojas Sueltas	Newsletter of the Universidad Autónona Metropolitana. Mexico (Since 1981)
La hora de México	Weekly Magazine. Mexico (Since 1956)
El H. P.	*El Hijo Pródigo.* Literary Journal. Mexico (1943-1946).
Horizontes	Bibliographical Newsletter from Librería Patria. México (1943-1946)

H. R.	*Hispanic Review*. University of Pennsylvania. Philadelphia, Penna. (Since 1932)
Humanitas	Yearly Journal of the University of Nuevo León. Monterrey (Since 1960)
Ideas de México	Cultural Magazine. Mexico (1953-1956)
La Ilustración Potosina	Publication from San Luis Potosí (1869-1879)
Incluso	Literary Magazine. Guadalajara, Jal. (Since 1978)
Indice	Literary Magazine. Madrid (Since 1945)
Indice UNAM	Bibliographical Index. UNAM. Mexico (Since 1974)
Insula	Literary Magazine. Madrid (Since 1945)
Inter Folia	Journal of the University Library "Alfonso Reyes." Monterrey, N.L. (Since 1953)
INTI	Literary Journal. Providence, Rhode Island (Since 1978)
JIAS	*Journal of Interamerican Studies*. Univ. of Miami. Coral Gables, FL, USA (Since 1959)
La Jornada	Daily Newspaper. Mexico (Since 1984)
La JL	*La Jornada. Libros*, Daily Supplement of *La Jornada*. Mexico (Since 1985)
La JS	*La Jornada Semanal*. Sunday Supplement of *La Jornada*. Mexico (Since 1984)
Juglar	Literary Magazine. Xalapa, Ver. (Since 1978)
LALR	*Latin American Literary Review*. University of Pittsburgh. Penna. (Since 1972)
LATR	*Latin American Theatre Review*. Theater Journal. University of Kansas, Lawrence, Kan. (Since 1967)
Lectura	Cultural Magazine. Mexico (Since 1936)
Letras de México	Literary Newsletter, Mexico (1937-1948)
Letras de Veracruz	Research Journal. Universidad Veracruzana. Xalapa, Ver. (Since 1973)
Letras Femeninas	Literary Journal. Now Published at The University of Nebraska. Lincoln, Neb. (Since 1974)
Letras Peninsulares	Literary Journal. Arizona State University. Tempe, Ariz.
Letras Potosinas	Cultural Newsletter. San Luis Potosí (Since 1943)
La LI	*La Letra y la Imagen*. Sunday Supplement of *El Universal*. Mexico (1979-1981)
LM	*Letras de México*. Cultural Bulletin. Mexico (1937-1948)
El L. y el P.,	El Libro y el Pueblo. SEP. Mexico (Since 1922)
Las L. P.,	*Las Letras Patrias*. Publication of the INBA. Mexico (1954-1959)
El LV	*El Libro y la Vida*. Bulletin of Information of *El Día*. Mexico (1969-1974)
El Maestro	Review of National Culture. Mexico (Since 1921)
MAM	*Memorias de la Academia mexicana de la Lengua*. Mexico (Since 1945)
M. en la C.	*México en la Cultura*. Sunday Supplement of Novedades. Mexico (Since 1949)
Metáfora	Literary Magazine. Mexico (1955-1958)
El Nacional	Daily Newspaper. Mexico (Since 1916)
Nivel	Cultural Journal. Mexico (Since 1959)

NNH	*Nueva Narrativa Hispanoamericana*. Adelphi University. Garden City, N.Y. (1971-1975)
Norte	Latin American Journal. Mexico (1929-1966)
Nosotros	Monthy Humanistic Publication. Buenos Aires (Since 1907)
Novedades	Daily Newspaper. Mexico (Since 1936)
NRFH	Nueva Revista de Filología Hispánica. Journal from El Colegio de México (Since 1947)
Nueva Estafeta	Literary Magazine. Madrid (Since 1978)
Nuevo Texto Crítico	Journal of Stanford University. Stanford. Cal. (Since 1989)
La Onda	Supplement of *Novedades*. Mexico (1973-1981)
Ovaciones	Sunday Supplement of *Ovaciones*. Mexico (Since 1962)
Pájaro Cascabel	Journal of Poetry. Mexico (1962-1967)
Papeles de Son Armadans	Literary Journal. Madrid-Palma de Mallorca. (1956-1979)
Perspectiva	Bulletin of tha UNAM. Mexico (Since 1980)
La PH	*La Palabra y el Hombre*. Journal of the Universidad Veracruzana. Xalapa, Ver. (Since 1957)
Plural	Monthly Literary Supplement of *Excelsior*. Mexico (Since 1971)
PMLA	Journal of the Modern Language Association of America. New York, N.Y. (Since 1883)
PP	*Pie de Página*. Bibliographical Journal. Mexico (Since 1982)
Punto de Partida	Student's Magazine. UNAM. Mexico (Since 1966)
Quimera	Literary Magazine. Barcelona (Since 1980)
El Rehilete	Literary Journal. Mexico (1961-1971)
Retablo	Literary Magazine. Mexico (Since 1966)
Rev. de B.A.	Journal of the INBA. Mexico (1965-1970, 1982-1983)
Rev. de la S.	*Revista de la Semana*. Sunday Supplement of *El Universal*. Mexico (1972-1974)
Rev. de la U. de Y.	Journal of the University of Yucatán, Mérida, Yuc. (1958)
Rev. de L.M.	*Revista de Literatura Mexicana*. Literary Journal. Mexico (1940)
Rev. H. M.	*Revista Hispánica Moderna*. Journal of the Instituto de las Españas. Columbia University. N.Y (Since 1934)
Rev. I.	*Revista Iberoamericana*. Publication of the Instituto Internacional de Literatura Iberoamericana. Pittsburgh, Penn. (Since 1939).
Rev. IB.	*Revista Interamericana de Bibliografía*. Publication of the Comité Interamericano de Bibliografía. Panamerican Union. Washington, D.C. (Since 1951)
Review	Journal of the Center for Inter-American Relations. New York, N.Y. (Since 1970)
Rev. I L.	*Revista Iberoamericana de Literatura*. Publication of the Universidad de la República de Montevideo.
Rev. Interamericana	Revista/Review Interamericana. Interamerican University of Puerto Rico. San Juan (Since 1970)

Rev. M. C.	*Revista Mexicana de Cultura*. Sunday Supplement of *El Nacional*. Mexico (Since 1947)
Rev. M. L.	*Revista Mexicana de Literatura*. Literary Journal. Mexico (1955-1965)
Revista Moderna	Literary Journal. Mexico. First epoch (1898-1903). Second epoch (1903-1911)
Rev. O.	*Revista de Occidente*. Literary Magazine. Madrid (1923-1936, since 1963)
Rev. Rev.	Weekly Literary Magazine. Mexico (Since 1910).
Rev. S.	*Revista de la Semana*. Sunday Supplement of *El Universal*. Mexico (1925-1979)
Rev. UAEM	*Revista de la Universidad Autónoma del Estado de Mexico*. Toluca (Since 1978)
Revueltas	Literary Magazine. Mexico (Since 1971)
Rev. UNAM	*Revista de la Universidad Nacional Autónoma de Mexico*. Mexico (1930-1933, 1946-1952, since 1952)
Rueca	Literary Magazine. Mexico (1941-1948)
Ruta	Monthly Literary Magazine. Mexico (Since 1938)
Sábado	Weekly Supplement of *Unomasuno*. Mexico (Since 1977)
La SBA	*La semana de Bellas Artes*. INBA. Mexico (1977-1982)
El SC	*El Semanario Cultural*. Sunday Supplement of *Novedades*. Mexico (Since 1982)
SECOLAS	Journal of the Southeastern Council on Latin American Studies (Since 1969)
Siempre!	Weekly Magazine. Mexico (Since 1951)
Siete	Journal of the Secretaría de Educación Pública. Mexico (Since 1973)
Sin Nombre	Literary Journal of the University of Puerto Rico. San Juan (Since 1970)
Sísifo	Literary Magazine. Mexico (1966-1970)
El SMC	*El Sol de México en la Cultura*. Sunday Supplement of *El Sol de México*. Mexico (Since 1974)
Taller	Journal of Poetry. Mexico (1938-1941)
Texto Crítico	Literary Journal. Universidad Veracruzana. Xalapa, Ver. (1975-1986)
El Telar	Literary Magazine. Mexico (Since 1978)
Thesaurus	Bulletin of the Instituto Caro y Cuervo. Bogotá, Colombia (Since 1944)
Thesis	Literary Journal. UNAM. Mexico (Since 1979).
Tiempo	Weekly Journal of Humanities, Mexico (Since 1940).
Tierra Nueva	Literary Journal, UNAM, Mexico (1940-1942).
La Torre	Publication of the University of Puerto Rico, San Juan de Puerto Rico (Since 1952).
Tramoya	Theater Journal of the Universidad Veracruzana. Xalapa, Ver. First Epoch (1975-1982), Second Epoch, published jointly with Rutgers University in Camden, N.J. (Since 1983)
U.	*Unión*. Journal of the Unión de Escritores y Artistas de Cuba. Havana Cuba (Since 1962)

Ulises	Literary Magazine. Mexico (1927-1928)
Un. de M.	*Universidad de México.* Publication of UNAM. Mexico (Since 1950)
Universidad	Biweekly Literary Journal. Universidad de Nuevo León. Monterrey (Since 1970)
Unomasuno	Daily Newspaper. Mexico (Since 1977)
La VL	*La vida Literaria.* Bulletin of Association of Writers of Mexico (Since 1970)
El VT	*El viejo topo.* Literary Magazine. Barcelona (Since 1976)
Vuelta	Monthly Literary Magazine. Mexico (Since 1976)
WLT	*World Literature Today.* University of Oklahoma. Norman, Okla. (Since 1977)
El Zaguán	Literary Magazine. Mexico (1975-1977)

Overview of Mexican Letters and Literature

Mexican literature is the creative effort of thousands of people who either lived in Mexico or spent the better part of their creative lives in Mexico. Initially several strands woven of Nahuatl, Maya, Cakchiquel, and other languages spoken in different regions, Mexican literature came to mean the corpus written in the particular Spanish evolved from the fusion of languages during the Spanish governance of Mexico. Consequently, there are at least three major historic, linguistic and cultural subdivisions upon which we must focus our investigation of the term "Mexican writing."

The greater part of literature prior to the Spanish presence in Mexico and surrounding areas has largely been lost to us. Usually of oral transmission, and occasionally by means of both pictographs and ideographs, the creations, which were designed to portray the cultures' myths, history, and customs, now exist only in fragmented and often distorted versions. Furthermore, this early literature was typically accompanied by song and dance, making the written versions pale in comparison with the original works. Of these, the major known works are Nahuatl poetry and religious discourses, the Mayan book *The Popol-Vuh* or *Book of Advice*, the *Annals of the Xahil* and the *Rabinal-Achí*, written in Cakchiquel.

Literature in Nahuatl flourished in the land of the Aztecs, that is, from the central plateau East and West to the coastal areas and extending North and South throughout the areas of Aztec conquest and trade. It dates, most probably, from about the middle of the thirteenth century. The literature reflected the concerns of this society of strong central government and religion.

Heroic poetry, as in the *Poema de Quetzalcóatl* (Poem of Quetzalcoatl), recounts the memorable events of the kings, plus the lineage and nobility of the dynasty. Religious poetry was abundant, dedicated to the celebration of the celestial gods, Coatlicue and Tlaloc; it also testified to the interrelationship of the gods with the lives of humankind in poetry depicting, for example, the power of Tlaloc and Xipe-Totec. At the same time, lyric poetry expressed, in rich images and ideas, the sense of the wonder of life, its ephemeral beauty, and the mystery of death. Stylistically, the plasticity of metaphors reflects the indigenous sentiment of nature. Refrains and synonymous word repetition are stylistic devices through which the makers of songs and poems showed the beauty of their work. Many of the ritual works were so codified from long use that they have no attribution of authorship, although the names of many poets have survived, including Axayacatzin, Xicoténcatl and the Poet King of Tezcoco, Netzahualcóyotl.

Religious theater was also performed in Nahuatl, spectacles which probably included dance, simulated battles, sacrificial rituals, song and music. Among these were the celebrations of Tlacaxipehualiztli and of Xochiquetzalli, the goddess of roses. Documentation for this can be found in the manuscript *Cantares mexicanos*

(Mexican Songs), in which there are poems of dramatic character, others with musical indications and other types as well. Another dramatic piece records Quetzalcóatl's leaving.

Prose literature included the *Huehuetlatolli*, or *Talks of the Old Ones*, didactic pieces for both young men and young women. These encompassed religious speeches, historic accounts extolling the virtues of kings, re-creations of the battles of conquest, and domestic material concerning traditional customs.

Though most of Nahuatl literature was lost in the turmoil of the Spanish conquest and by the zeal of the Catholic clergy, both historiographic and linguistic investigations have reclaimed valuable pieces of this tradition. For example, Fray Bernardino de *Sahagún (1499?-1590) collected the *Veinte poemas rituales* (Twenty Ritual Poems) between 1558 and 1560. The work of Del Paso and Troncoso, Icazbalceta, among others of the nineteenth century, has been added to by more recent projects in Mexico, headed by Drs. Miguel León-Portilla and Angel María Garibay.

The Mayas inhabited the southern portions of Mexico and some regions of what are today Guatemala, Honduras and El Salvador. Their cultural decline at the time of the arrival of the Spanish, plus the destruction by fire of some of the codices after the conquest, meant that little of their literature on paper was held in archives; the Paris, Dresden and Madrid codices today form the extant collection of this medium. The knowledge of Mayan hieroglyph writing has been immensely improved by recent scholarship, however, so that the cultural richness of the Mayan tradition is better appreciated. Monuments and associated stelae contain records of the historic events of reigns and religious events. Ceramic works contain many references to the traditional themes. And the codices contain, above all, scientific accounts relating to astronomy, calendrics, meteorology, hunting and agriculture. The great abundance of these documents testifies to the highly developed and literate society of the Mayas.

The *Popol Vuh*, the *Book of Advice*, may well have been written in glyphs on parchment. It was further conserved by oral tradition until it was anonymously transcribed in Quiché with Latin characters. This work includes four myths about the creation of the world and its people, and the second part is made up of the moral teachings through the history of the Hero Twins Hunahpú and Ixbalanque. Other important works include the *Libros de Chilam Balam* (Books of the Speaker of the Jaguar), written in Yucatecan Maya in Latin letters. A collection of religious, historic, medical, astrological and ritual texts, the work was written in Maya in 1782 and translated into Spanish in 1930. This work described, in addition to the categories mentioned above, the arrival of beings who would destroy the villages and disperse the Mayas.

Other works that may be considered of value to the consideration of pre-Hispanic culture are the *Anales de los Xahil* (Annals of the Xahil), which record legal documents relating to the rights of those who assisted the Spanish, probably in Pedro de Alvarado's campaign in Guatemala. The documents include the mythical origins and rights, historic dates and events of the Xahil and common customs. Another work is the *Rabinal Achi* (The Knight of Achi), a dramatic work in Cakchiquel, transcribed by Bartolo Zis in 1850. The work concretizes the tradition of theatrical literature among the early Mexican cultures and makes plausible the interest in liturgical plays that quickly became an instrument of Christian conversion. The *Rabinal Achi* is a dramatic work centering on two men, one of the Rabinal and one of the Quiché, whose death comes at the end of the play. As the bravery of this warrior is the main theme of the piece, it is sometimes called *K'iche Vinak* (Man of Quiche). Seen in their entirety, the pre-Hispanic works testify to cultures rich in tradition, advanced in scientific, legal, political and mathematical theory, and possessing levels of literacy throughout their societies that permitted a lively cultural appreciation.

FROM THE ARRIVAL OF THE SPANISH TO INDEPENDENCE

The Spanish presence, beginning in Mexico in 1519 and continuing until the Revolution in 1810, produced an immediate and irrevocable change in both Spanish and Mexican writing. The first works written in Spanish were descriptive and looked back to the Old World, chronicling the new land, its fauna and flora, its inhabitants and their customs, laws, and religious practices. The next works were prescriptive and communicative, providing the first links with the autochthonous traditions. The first works in Spanish by local Nahuatl writers provided another angle of access for knowledge and evaluation of the Mexican cultures. For the next three centuries the influx of European ideas, controlled by the Spanish Inquisition and the Council of the Indies, made its particular imprint on Mexican soil. Renaissance, Baroque, and Neoclassic ideals were manifested in Mexican modes. During this period also, religious and cultural integration was shown in original works of education, science, and literature.

The first to chronicle the events of the Spanish were the protagonists of these acts, beginning with Hernán Cortés (1485- 1547). His *Cartas de relación* (Letters of Relation) portray both his wonder at the events unfolding and his unwavering sense of mission and efforts to justify his course of action as he realizes the potential wealth available to the Spanish crown. Others followed, chief among them Bernal *Díaz del Castillo (1494?-1585). Although none were professional writers, their works portrayed the world through the criteria of Renaissance thinking, eager both to record and to communicate vividly the historical events taking place in the vast panorama of the situations they encountered.

With the *conquistadores* came the evangelists: Franciscan, Dominicans, Augustinians, and Jesuits. Writers among these included Friar Toribio de *Benavente, called Motolinia, Friar Bernadino de *Sahagún, Friar Juan de Torquemada, and Friar Bartolomé de las Casas (1474-1566), author of the *Historia de las Indias* (History of the Indies). His unflagging efforts brought the plight of the indigenous cultures into focus against the crushing zeal of the Spanish mission.

Writers who learned the Spanish language also wrote their own histories, in part to address historical inaccuracies, in part to express the natural sentiments of the vanquished cultures. These writings also form the base for a scholarly tradition through which pre-Hispanic Mexican culture and history were made known in Spanish. The *Códice de Aubin* (The Aubin Codex) and the *Manuscrito de Tlaltelolco* (The Tlaltelolco Manuscript) are examples of these. Later in the sixteenth century, Fernando de Alvarado Tezozomoc became preeminent among the bicultural, bilingual historians. Nephew of Montezuma Xocoytzin and brother-in-law of Antonio Valeriano, Sahagún's assistant, this writer's *Crónica mexicana* (Mexican Chronicle) (1598) revealed in 110 chapters the history and mentality of the Mexican culture. His *Crónica Mexicáyotl* (Mexican Chronicle) (1609) provided, in Nahuatl, many fragments of sagas and epic poems, unfortunately lost in subsequent editions. The genre, however, was followed by Fernando de *Alva Ixtlixóchitl, a descendant of the Poet King Netzahualcóyotl, in his *Historia chichimeca* (A Chichimeca History), written in Spanish around 1648, which is based on annals, paintings, songs and renderings of accounts from a number of informants.

Spanish language became the central tool of linguistic unification through the institution of teaching in both the monastic orders and in the University of Mexico. The diffusion of the written word through the printing press moved cultural unification forward.

The evangelists, who were charged, in 1523, with the education of the inhabitants of Mexico, wrote the first didactic literature in Spanish in Mexico. They developed and wrote two basic types of works: one to teach communication, as evidenced by the grammars and dictionaries, and one to communicate Catholic doctrine. The name of Friar Juan de Zumárraga, first bishop of Mexico, stands out for his *Breve y más compendiosa doctrina cristiana en lengua mexicana y castellana* (Brief and Most Complete Christian Doctrine in Mexican and Castilian Tongues). He also founded the Colegio de Santa Cruz de Tlaltelolco, in 1536. The indigenous Don Antonio Valeriano and Don Fernando de Alva Ixtlixóchtl attended this school, and illustrious Franciscans taught there, including Friar Andrés de Olmos, and Friar Juan Focher. Other schools were founded for various purposes in Mexico. San Juan de Letrán, established originally for the Mestizo children, soon became a teachers' preparatory school. The Augustinians started schools, such as that in Tiripitío, in Michoacán, for Creoles and Peninsular young mem. Private schools for young ladies were established. The Jesuits formed schools for higher education, such as the seminaries of San Miguel, San Bernardino, and San Gregorio in 1575 and 1576.

The University of Mexico was founded, by royal decree of Felipe II, in 1551. It became the center of intellectual life in Mexico for the following three centuries and continues to be the major center of higher education in Mexico. The first courses of study, inaugurated in 1553, included theology, sacred Scripture, canons, law, art, rhetoric and grammar. In 1582 medicine was added, followed by surgery in 1622 and, later, courses in Nahuatl and Otomí.

Upon the request of Friar Juan de Zumárraga to Felipe II, the first printing presses were established. In 1539 Juan Pablos made a contract with Juan Cromberger of Seville to set up a press in the capital. Soon thereafter the number of print shops increased, and some schools maintained their own facilities for printing. According to Joaquín de *Icazbalceta's *Bibliografía mexicana del siglo XVI* (Mexican Bibliography of the Sixteenth Century), compiled in 1886, more than seventy works had been printed by the end of the century.

While chronicles and didactic materials were the most prolific, other forms of literature were also present, in reduced number and for specific purposes. There were few works of prose overall produced during the sixteenth century. In addition to the expected works of doctrine and teaching, there were some texts of medicine, science, philosophy, and a few of prose literature, such as the *Diálogos latinos* (Latin Dialogues) by Francisco Cervantes de Salazar (1518?-1575). Born in Spain, Cervantes de Salazar went to Mexico as a young man, where he received religious orders. His subsequent positions included that of Canon of the Cathedral of Mexico, official chronicler of the City of Mexico and rector of the University, a post which he occupied at the time of his death. His *Diálogos* provides vivid pictures of life in Mexico city and its environs, particularly in the university. The work also gives insight into Mexican vocabulary and customs. In the field of pedagogy, the Jesuits provided a vigorous effort to maintain the study of the classical Latin literature.

Because most imported works were prohibited and approval by the Council of the Indies was required for the printing of new books, many manuscripts either were lost or were published only after considerable revision to satisfy the demands of the Council. This accounted for a chronic delay in the dissemination of these works. In spite of the above, however, a small number of copies of most works of the period, both in Spanish and in other languages, made their way to Mexico, where they circulated by hand among those avid for new ideas.

As the chronicle perhaps best expressed the tenor of the times, there were also poets who expressed the events around them in rhymed chronicles. The *Nuevo Mundo y conquista* (New World and Conquest) by Francisco de *Terrazas (1525?-1600?), the *Peregrino indiano* (The Indian Pilgrim) by Antonio de Saavedra Guzmán, and the *Historia de la Nueva México* (History of New Mexico) by Gaspar Pérez de Villagrá all exemplify this genre. Another, more pleasant form of epic poetry is found in the *Grandeza mexicana* (Mexican Grandeur) by Bernardo de *Balbuena (1561-1627). Born in Spain, he grew up in Mexico, where he did most of his writing. He later returned to Spain, then went to Jamaica and Puerto Rico as an abbot. *Grandeza mexicana* is a descriptive poem written in epistolary form, directed to Doña Isabel de Tovar y Guzmán. The Renaissance impulse to appreciate man in his world was given new impetus in Mexico by Balbuena's poetic imagery, and the abundance of descriptive elements. Balbuena's poetry is considered the best of its time.

Lyric poetry can be said to have arrived in Mexico via the mouths of the soldiers, who recited the Spanish *romances* (ballads), and who adapted them to their current situation, as cited by Bernal Díaz in his *Historia verdadera* (New History): "En Tacuba está Cortés / con su escuadrón esforzado, / triste estaba y muy penoso / triste y con un gran cuidado" (Cortés is in Tacuba / With his brave men, / Sad he was and suffering, / Sad and with great concern). Soon other poets, followers of the Sevillian school led by Fernando de Herrera, flourished in the shadows of the university and other schools. In 1577 an anthology of poems was published following the peninsular tradition. This *Flores de Varia Poesía* (Collection of Varied Poems) contains 359 compositions, of which 117 are anonymous and the rest are by 31 known poets. Among the poets writing during this period are Gutierre de *Cetina (1520-1557?), who was already famous in Spain, an author noted in anthologies for the sonnet "Ojos claros, serenos" (Eyes beautiful and serene), Juan de la *Cueva (1543-1610), brother of the archdeacon of Guadalajara and Francisco *Cervantes de Salazar, known better for his *Diálogos* (Dialogues) and *Crónica de la Nueva España* (Chronicle of New Spain). Francisco de Terrazas, mentioned above as one of the epic poets, born in Mexico around 1525, was well known in his time, both in Mexico and in Spain. His five sonnets in the *Flores de Varia Poesía* gave rise to his renown, and Miguel de Cervantes praised him in his novel *La Galatea*. The historian Fernando de Alva Ixtlixóchitl should also be related to these poets, as his translations, paraphrases and reworkings of a myriad of pre-Hispanic compositions show his affinity with the concerns of the humanist traditions as well as his penetrating nostalgic spirit.

Religious theater was developed to build on the Mexican tradition of the *mitote* (open air theater), presented for celebration and ritual. This tradition inspired the missionaries to utilize a theatrical performance to convey ideas of religious doctrine. On the grounds of temples, in the atriums of churches and convents and in the open air, productions such as the 1533 *Representación del fin del mundo*

(Depiction of the End of the World), the first known work so adapted (from the *Auto del juicio final* (Auto of Final Judgement). It closely resembled the medieval Spanish *auto*, both in purpose and technique. The plays used local actors, with boys playing the female roles. Generally anonymous in their authorship, few have survived; there are, however, references to them throughout the histories of the period.

The secular theater was nurtured by three elements: the performance of theatrical works in Spanish and in Latin in the Jesuit schools on commemorative occasions, the secularization of the tradition of local religous theater previously discussed and the existence in Spain of a vigorous theatrical tradition. Farces written by Lope de Rueda were imported and appreciated. Competitions were established to stimulate good writing and production, and the theaters gradually became separate houses for the interested minority. Spanish writers came to Mexico and composed both religious and secular works. Gutierre de Cetina, who died in Puebla in an *affaire du coeur*, and Juan de la Cueva, the celebrated pre-Classic writer in Spain (from 1579 to 1581), both gained fame in Mexico and elsewhere. Among the best-known Mexican writers of comedies were Fernán *González de Eslava, probably born in Seville around 1534, but assimilated into the new culture, and Juan Pérez Ramírez, son of a *conquistador*, born in Mexico in 1545.

The writer whose star shone brightest, however, finally made his home in Spain. Juan *Ruiz de Alarcón y Mendoza (1581-1639), born in the city of Mexico, felt compelled to compete with the Spanish playwrights. He succeeded, becoming one of the "four greats" of the Golden Age theater, beside Lope de Vega, Tirso de Molina, and Pedro Calderón de la Barca. However, many factors interfered with his success, making him the target of enmity among other playwrights and critics. Short, red-haired and hunchbacked, Juan Ruiz de Alarcón also exhibited excessive pride and had an overbearing manner. Furthermore, his condition of "Indian," the term for all who were identified with the Western Hemisphere, limited him considerably. His plays, on the other hand, showed his genius for construction and were a veritable gift. His Mexicanism, though, was evident in the Spanish productions and added to his extraordinary talents. His most famous works remain *Las paredes oyen* (The Walls Have Ears) and *La verdad sospechosa o el mentiroso* (The Truth Suspected or The Liar), which was later paraphrased in Corneille's *Le Menteur*.

As the world of Renaissance concerns yielded to complex ideas of the Baroque era, so the endlessly fertile grounds of literature bore new fruit, especially in the poetry and theater in Mexico. The Baroque, first an artistic and architectural manifestation, was also developed in Spanish literature. The Spanish *culteranismo* of Luis de Góngora and the *conceptismo* of Francisco de Quevedo brought literature to seemingly opposite heights. These Spanish currents, exaggeration of form and of ideas, also found expression in Mexico, especially in the poetry and plays of the period. In the cities of Mexico, elegant commemorative events invited poetry of circumstance, and prizes encouraged the invention of ever more complex devices. The elaboration of forms in poetry-- acrostics, anagrams, labyrinths, contradictory verses-- was due in large measure to the limitations imposed in the numerous literary contests. At the same time, a new sense of the fragility of man's existence gave rise to a more intimate poetry, which found its finest expression in the works of Sor Juana Inés de la *Cruz.

Writers whose works typically embrace the Baroque sensibility include those born in Spain but whose main works were written in Mexico. Arias de Villalobos (b. 1568) became the most celebrated poet of his time. He also wrote comedies, songs, epitaphs and elegies. Juan de Palafox (1600-1659), born in Navarre, became the archbishop of Mexico and the eighteenth viceroy of Mexico. He wrote many poems, grouped in *Poesías espirituales* (Spiritual Poems) and *Cánticos* (Canticles). Matías de *Bocanegra (1612-1668), born in Puebla, became a Jesuit and was known for his erudition and lively wit. His work included sermons, a comedy and several poetic works.

Carlos de Sigüenza y Góngora (1645-1700), born in Mexico City, was the nephew of the illustrious Don Luis de Góngora, to whom he was indebted for his lifelong involvement with poetry. By the age of seventeen, he had already published his *Primavera indiana* (Indian Spring). He became a member of the Jesuit order, but left it enter the University. Thereafter, he occupied the chair of astrology and mathematics. Named official cosmographer by King Carlos II of Spain, he participated in various expeditions to the north of Mexico and wrote important studies concerning these. Sigüenza y Góngora's many works included prize-winning poetry, in which the legacy of his uncle seems to have been continued and philosophical works written to deepen the understanding of the sciences and to combat superstition. Furthermore, he is considered the precursor of Mexican journalism for his *Mercurio Volante*, a literary periodical. Finally, Sigüenza y Góngora wrote the *Relación de los infortunios de Alonso Ramírez* (Story of the Misfortunes of Alonso Ramírez), an episodic narrative, in 1690. This single instance of the genre was permitted under the strict rules of the time because it was not "frivolous," rather, stated the censor, it should be read "for the common good." Sigüenza y Góngora was readmitted to the Jesuit order shortly before his death in 1700.

Juana de Asbaje y Ramírez de Santillana (1648-1695), who became Sor Juana Inés de la Cruz, known as the "Tenth Muse," was born in San Miguel Nepantla. Raised by her maternal grandparents, she showed a prodigious intelligence at an early age. Introduced in the court at the age of seventeen, she was examined by the most knowledgeable men of the times and acknowledged to be a genuine wonder. Between the stigma of having been born out of wedlock and her reluctance to join in courtly activities, she chose to withdraw to the Order of the Carmelites. Here, in spite of the duties of the order and the inconveniences of convent life, she made peace with herself and her world, producing a large body of written work. Always intelligently written, always based on profound understanding of human behavior and Catholic doctrine, her works were admired by her many friends and, through their publication, by countless others. Her works include three sacramental *autos*, two plays, several skits, farces, *loas* (commendatory introductions), and *villancicos* (Christmas carols). Her poetry reveals her dominance of the forms and ideas of Baroque poetry as well as her own inclinations and concerns. Finally, her prose, as in the *Respuesta a Sor Filotea* (Response to Sor Filotea), is a masterpiece of control and logic, exposition and passion in the service of religious vocation. In response to criticism of her scholarly activities within the religious order, Sor Juana, in sacrificial penitence, even renounced her substantial library and spent her final days in severe asceticism. She died in 1695 while caring for her sisters during a plague that desolated the convent.

The growth of scientific reasoning and tools during the eighteenth century was countered by a renewal of authoritarian ideas in government and in literature. The *Academia de la Lengua* (Academy of Language), established in Spain in 1713, was one manifestation of this philosophy, which sought to regulate the use of words and the rules of their usage. Renewed interest in Latin and Greek as the basis of higher studies led to a more strict aesthetic, in which the humanist ideal sought model philosophies in the classical cultures.

The advent of the Bourbon reign in Spain led to friction between the central government and the Jesuit congregations in Mexico, which had accumulated great political, economic, and cultural wealth. This clash culminated in the expulsion of the Jesuits in 1767. Throughout the century, in spite of material growth and greater communication with European currents, the ideals of government and the fine arts increasingly emphasized form over content, imitation over creation, and logic over passion. Thus Encyclopedism, Cartesian philosophy, and Neoclassicism showed their effects on Mexican culture and expressions in its writing. The *Poética* (Poetics) of Spain's Ignacio de Luzán, published in 1837, underscores the rational order, which he considered fundamental to all the best works of antiquity, to be the basis of "all kinds of arts and sciences."

The desire to inventory, catalog, rationalize, and compare all areas of science led to a wide variety of activities and comprehensive studies in many areas of Mexican life and the country itself: astronomical observations, geography, maps, highway and irrigation projects, examination of mines and the terrain, classification of the flora and fauna; in short, anything that curiosity could envision as material for scientific elaboration. Don Francisco Javier Gamboa in jurisprudence, Benito Díaz de Gamarra (1745-1783) in philosophy; Joaquín Velázquez y Cárdenas de León in mathematics and astronomy; José Agustín Aldama in indigenous languages; Antonio Alzate (1729-1790) in history, botany, and astronomy; and Juan José *Eguiara y Eguren (1696-1763) in bibliography all enriched the libraries and scholarly efforts of the epoch.

The Jesuits, teaching in the schools and seminaries, participated in the currents of widening knowledge. At Tepoztlán, scholars from all the Americas arrived to study Greek, Latin, philosophy and the natural sciences. With the expulsion of the Jesuits in 1767, they continued their work as refugees in Italy. This group's isolation enabled them to produce the first serious scholarly and literary efforts to describe, defend and exalt what they had left behind. In search of a Mexican spirit, they presaged the political revolution to come in the nineteenth century as they argued that any shortcomings in the products of Mexico were due to poor colonial organization, rather than to any defects of character of the Mexicans. Francisco Javier *Clavijero (1731- 1787) believed the state of Mexican culture when the Spanish arrived to exceed that of the Spanish when they were encountered by the Greeks, Romans and other invading groups. Other writers, such as Francisco Javier *Alegre, Diego José *Abad and Rafael *Landívar, continued to classify the knowledge they acquired on a great variety of subjects, including mathematics, anatomy, geography, industries, customs, and characteristics of the Mexican.

The Spanish *Academia de la Lengua* (Academy of Language) was a particular manifestation of the Neoclassic period, as it proposed rules of good taste, published the *Diccionario de Autoridades* (Dictionary of Authorities), and counted among its members the most prestigious writers of the period. Other appeals to critical taste resulted in the Spanish Academy of History and the *Arcadia romana* (Roman Arcady) in Italy, which advocated a bucolic simplicity in poetry against the excesses of the Baroque taste. In Mexico, as in Spain itself, the ideals of simplicity, rational construction and mathematical precision were embedded in the literature of the period, together with the new appreciation of the Classical Greek and Latin forms and themes. While there were those writers who could write well within these constrictions, most Neoclassic writing was lacking in vitality and artistic excellence, giving way to prosaic poetry, theater, and narrative. Theaters were built throughout Mexico at a great rate by both religious and secular groups; they served a social function better than they served literature. There were attempts to write plays in which Mexican customs and life were shown, and Neoclassic plays modeled after Fernando de Moratín's were performed. Essays and fables, both academic genres, were written. Poetry, however, enjoyed a measure of success and endured longer. José Agustín *Castro, Anastasio María de Ochoa and, especially, Friar José Manuel *Martínez de Navarrete (1768- 1809) best represent the period. At the same time, the poetry of the last mentioned extended beyond the classical patterns and displayed a deeper and more intimate sensibility, thus bridging the Neoclassic and Romantic periods. While a Franciscan teacher of Latin in Querétaro, he participated in commemorative events and literary contests. Martínez de Navarrete's poetry was not always of uniformly high quality, but exceptional pieces of religious poetry closely imitated that of Garcilaso de la Vega. In some of his late poetry, such as "L' inmortalidad" (Immortality), the melancholy tone and the sentimental landscap ', reflective of his own emotional state, were clearly early Romantic.

Distinct from the academic encyclopedic work, the essay found its public voic ' in the first daily publication of Mexico, the *Diario de México* (The Mexico Daily) (',805- 1817). This paper, founded by Jacobo de Villarrutia and Carlos Maria de *Bustamante, was comprehensive in its offerings, chronicling the transitic n from colonial Mexico to independent nation. Information of civil and religious c'aracter, governmental decrees and dispositions, arts and science sections, commercial advertisements, and literature were all printed. The Neoclassic poets' compositions were given a wide audience in the *Diario*, as were essays of a general and erudite nature.

Along with the development of the critical and humanist spirit of the late Neoclassic period, events in other parts of the world added tension to the final years of the colonial period. The French and North American battles for independence put into action the spirit of individual worth and collective fortune. The French presence on the Spanish throne accentuated the differences between Mexico and the mother country. In Mexico, the development of scientific knowledge, of the consciousness of what made Mexico unique, and of a nationalistic spirit helped prepare the people for independence.

FROM INDEPENDENCE TO THE PRESENT

In 1810, the cry for Mexican political independence acted as a catalyst for the search for national identity. Political turbulence, which lasted throughout the nineteenth century, was the backdrop for journalistic *tours de force* and other literary forms, and practically all writers were passionate adherents of political causes, either liberal or conservative. All of these elements contributed to the creation of what could then be truly designated a Mexican literature. From this point of evolution, all new literary currents, whether from the north, the Old World or other Spanish-speaking countries, were assimilated into the Mexican national character. And this literature, which continues to flourish, both contributes to and takes from contemporary movements, sharing Mexico's riches with the other literatures of the world today.

At the end of the eigtheenth century, a new activity for writers developed around the vital theme of independence: the political essay. The defenders of the monarchy, with more resources, circulated justifications and threats, while the insurgents, often in hiding from the authorities, counted on hastily printed leaflets and clandestine periodicals, often short-lived. The career of José Joaquín Fernández de Lizardi (1776-1827) exemplified the liberal publisher's dilemma. The Spanish Constitution of Cadiz, in 1812, decreed the liberty of the press. But as soon as the character of Lizardi's new weekly, *El Pensador Mexicano* (The Mexican Thinker), became known, he was the object of persecution and censorship. Other periodicals followed, but it seemed that a less overt form of social and political criticism would serve him better. Fernández de *Lizardi, who adopted the pen name "El Pensador," thus turned to the novel, legally prohibited earlier, to carry his message. In *El Periquillo Sarniento* (*The Itching Parrot*), Fernández de Lizardi utilized the picaresque tradition to document the discontent of Mexican society in transition. The press in general, however, which vigorously maintained various political stances, was both officially and privately subsidized and gradually became the vehicle of popular news, business dealings and occasional entertainment. Political journals inluded *El Despertador Americano* (1811) and *El Ilustrador Nacional* (1812) on the liberal side, Lucas Alamán's *El Tiempo, La Cruz*, and *El Eco Nacional*. Specifically literary periodicals included *La Revista Mexicana* (1835), *El Zurriago Literario* (1839) and *El Museo Mexicano* (1845). *El Siglo XIX* was published for fifty four years and disseminated the most advanced ideology of the Reform period. Another long-lived publication, was *El Monitor Republicano*, printed from 1844 to 1896, which advanced the ideas of the liberal progressive party.

From the beginning of the nineteenth century to 1867, that is, from the declaration of independence to the restoration of the Republic, most writers of all genres seemed sharply divided on their sources of inspiration and the stylistic models they chose to display. The poets of this period can be generally divided into traditionalist, conservative, Classical poets on the one hand, and, on the other, the unorthodox, liberal, Romantic ones. The Classicists, continuing the tradition of the end of the eighteenth century, were well educated in Greco-Latin humanist letters. The most prominent of these poets was José Joaquín *Pesado (1801-1861). Having received an excellent education and having independent means, he dedicated himself to the study of letters. Modeling his works stylistically after the Spanish poetry of the sixteenth century, he nevertheless was attracted to the indigenous theme, of which the poem "La princesa de Culhuacán" is a fine example. Other Classic poets include José *Sebastián Segura, Francisco de Paula *Guzmán, and Miguel Jerónimo Martínez.

The Romantic poets' lineage dates back to the final years of the eighteenth century, when the theme of independence inevitably changed the thrust of poetry. A classical calm gave way to a whirlwind of subjective exaltations and new themes of nationalism, injustice, and contemporary events. The works of Don Francisco Manuel Sánchez de Tagle (1782-1849), Andrés *Quintana Roo (1787-1851), and Francisco Ortega (1783-1849) exemplify this transitional period. They are superseded by poets of lesser education, perhaps because of the expulsion of the Jesuits. These poets found their primary inspiration in liberal causes. Their models of literature were Edgar Allan Poe, Lord Byron and some of the European Romantics, such as Johann Friedrich von Schiller and José Zorrilla (who visited Mexico in 1855). These poets included the blind Juan *Valle, Manuel *Flores, Isabel *Prieto de Landázuri, Ignacio Manuel *Altamirano and Guillermo *Prieto. The case of Ignacio *Ramírez (1818-1879) is of special interest. He represented the purest ideals of the liberal in the classical forms as well as in the newest genre, the newspaper. Throughout his life he fought with words and sword for independence and then for reform, obtaining powerful legislation and serving several administrations. In his poetry Ramírez sought the clearest expression of his themes in the classical models, even when his themes were as radical as that found in "Por los desgraciados" (On the Unfortunate).

The Academy of Letrán was formed in 1834 and was active until 1856. Many of the poets mentioned above, of both the Classical and the Romantic schools, belonged to the Academy. For the next twenty years, reciprocal criticism was given to assist the poets in their search for stylistic excellence and a sense of national self-expression. After the suppression of the Academy of Letrán on the eve of the War of Reform, this labor was carried on until 1882 at the Hidalgo Lyceum. Again, both liberal and conservative writers met in a spirit of mutual respect and literary excellence. Founded by Francisco *Zarco Mateos (1829-1869), and carried on by Ignacio Altamirano (1834-1893), the Hidalgo Lyceum counted among its members Vicente *Riva Palacio, Luis G. *Ortiz, José *Rosas Moreno, Guillermo Prieto, Manuel M. Flores, Manuel *Acuña, Justo *Sierra, and Juan de Dios *Peza, among others. The search for national excellence, after the Restoration, led to the formation of the *Academia Mexicana Correspondiente de la Española*, in 1875. Autonomous with regard to Mexican letters, it maintains a close relationship with the Spanish Academy, as do other Hispanic academies. The most important work of the Mexican Academy has been the fostering of intellectual activities and the promotion of studies of literary history and criticism.

In the nineteenth century theater, works were performed throughout Mexico, but were often of fleeting fame. Most plays were not published subsequent to their performance, attesting to the public's desire for constantly new entertainment. Of those writers whose works were published, the same transition seen in poetry from Neoclassic to Romantic ideas was evidenced. During the greater part of the nineteenth century, a shift in theme and in form could be observed. Prose replaced poetry as the dominant genre, with "costumbrismo" supplanting neoclassical tendencies. Manuel Eduardo de *Gorostiza (1789-1851) exemplifies the early theater of the period, writing plays in the style of Moratín which were, however, presented in Madrid. Exiled in London in 1821, he offered his services to the Mexican government and was one of the founders of the diplomatic service, in which he worked for many years. Engaged in these activities, he abandoned his dramatic writing, but returned to it later with the costumbrist prose play "Contigo pan y cebolla" (Bread, Onions, and You), which debuted in Mexico in 1833. Other playwrights of the period were better known as poets, including Fernando *Calderón. His plays included Classical and Romantic themes, the latter based on legendary or historic incidents that would delight the audience. His only comedy, "*A ninguna de las tres*" (None of the Three) was notable for its anti-Romantic sentiment and characters of local color. Others whose plays were performed throughout the country, but with little lasting literary success, are Ignacio *Rodríguz Galván, Carlos Hipólito Serán, Pantaleón *Tovar, José María *Vigil, and José Rosas Moreno. José *Peón y Contreras (1843-1907) achieved some lasting glory with his Romantic play "La hija del Rey" (The King's Daughter) in 1876. For it, he received a gold pen and a diploma designating him as the "restorer of the theater in the country of Alarcón and Gorostiza." Dramatic works in Mexico in the nineteenth century and into the twentieth, however, did not flourish as did other forms of literature.

The first history of Mexico's transition from colony to independent country was written by Friar Servando Teresa de* Mier (1764-1822), whose life was as extravagant as the period he chronicled. A Dominican priest, he was exiled to Spain after preaching a sermon on the Virgin of Guadalupe which made the Spanish claims to Mexico seem groundless. Because of political circumstances, he fled to London. Next he wrote the *Historia de la revolución de la Nueva España* (History of the Revolution of New Spain), using the pen name José Guerra. A passionate apology for the revolution, it details many events with which Teresa de Mier was familiar. Lucas Alamán 1792-1853) also wrote the history of the movement of independence, but from the conservative aspect, the *Historia de Méjico desde los primeros movimientos que prepararon su independencia en el año 1808 hasta la época presente* (History of Mexico from the First Movements that Prepared Its Independence in the Year 1808 until the Present Epoch). Other historians included Lorenzo de Zavala and Dr. José María Luis *Mora, whose influence was critical in the years of political reform that followed the initial independence movement.

Subsequent to the publication, in 1816, of *El Periquillo Sarniento* (*The Itching Parrot*), the novel emerged as an interesting combination of Romanticism and Realism, present to greater or lesser degrees in practically all the novelists of the period. Reasons commonly given for the previous lack of works in this genre include the edict against importing and printing novels, the censorship of "frivolous works" in the colony, the lack of a large literate, or appreciative, audience, and the scarcity of presses and the expense of publishing large works. It now appears more likely that the combined factors created the vacuum in prose fiction. Yet, novels popular in Europe were brought to Mexico, quickly circulating among the literate. In essence, though, the Mexican reading public was only a small percentage of the population.

The novel of the nineteenth century is commonly discussed in terms of its subthemes: the Romantic line gave rise to the sentimental and the historical novel, while the novel of customs was enhanced by that of social concerns. In turn, these were affected by the movements of realism and naturalism. The sentimental novel was initiated in Mexico by Fernando *Orozco y Berra (1822-1851), an unfortunate young man whose only work, *La Guerra de Treinta Años* (The Thirty Years' War), is a *roman à clef* detailing the author's many involvements with women in Mexico City. After this inauspicious beginning, the line is followed by Florencio M. del *Castillo (1828-1863) in a number of short novels, of which the most enduring is *Hermana de los Angeles* (Sister of the Angels) (1850), a study of self-sacrifice in a woman. Later, Pedro *Castera, in the shadow cast by the Columbian Jorge Isaacs' *María*, wrote *Carmen*, in 1882. And at the end of the century came other novelists, among them Don Pablo Zayas Guarneros, with *Amor sublime* (Sublime Love) (1899) and Don José Rafael *Guadalajara, with *Amalia, páginas del primer amor* (Amalia, Pages of First Love) (1899).

The historical novel was introduced in Mexico in imitation of the French novel of excitement and chivalry. Justo Sierra *O'Reilly (1814-1861) published *La hija del judío* (The Jew's Daughter) during 1848 and 1849. Juan *Díaz Covarrubias' (1837-1859) novel, *Gil Gómez el Insurgente* (Gil Gómez the Insurgent) (1858), defended the cause for independence and was one of the first to focus on the middle class. His execution at the age of twenty as one of the "Martyrs of Tacubaya" (1859) curtailed a promising literary career. Other historical novelists were Eligio *Ancona (1836-1893), Ireneo *Paz (1836-1924) and the eminent Vicente Riva Palacio (1832-1896), whose works were all written in the years from 1868 to 1870. A master of suspense, Riva Palacio wrote novels that depended on multiple plot twists and intriguing composite characters drawn in large part from the archives of the Inquisition.

The "costumbrista" (having to do with customs or manners) novel was initiated with *El fistol del diablo* (The Devil's Scarfpin) by Manuel *Payno (1810-1894), published serially in 1845-46. Payno's other works followed, including *Los Bandidos de Río Frío* (The Bandits of Río Frío) (1888-1891), in which the different societies of mid-century were depicted. Other novelists of this type included Luis G. *Inclán, José María *Roa Bárcena and José Tomás de *Cuéllar. By the end of the century, this novel of manners was raised to new heights by the works of Manuel *Sánchez Mármol: *Juanita Sousa* (1901), *Antón Pérez* (1903), and *Previvida* (A Life Foretold) (1906).

The novel of social intent came into being during the same period, drawing on the prior tradition and adding a heightened sense of social obligation. Pantaleón Tovar (1828-1876) initiated the genre with the novels *Ironías de la vida* (Ironies of Life) (1851) and *La hora de Dios* (God's Hour) (1863). Nicolás *Pizarro (1830-1895) drew on the Laws of Reform in his novel, *El monedero* (The Moneybag) (1861). And Ignacio M. Altamirano (1834-1893), his own literary career a direct result of the liberal policies promulgated during his youth, applied Mexican, moral and aesthetic concerns to works whose plot was usually historical. His first three novels continue to be valued both in Mexico and beyond. These works are *Clemencia*, in 1869; *El Zarco* (Blue-eyes), finished in 1888 and published in 1901; and *La navidad en las montañas* (*Christmas in the Mountains*), in 1870.

The realist novel was confined largely to the years 1880 to 1910, which coincided with the rule of Porfirio Díaz. While there were elements of all the prior novelistic types, the realist novel took as its motivation the investigation of causes and solutions to problems encountered. As in Spain and France, novelists concentrated on the descriptive elements of the characters and their problems, though each novelist presented clear differences of artistic temperament. Emilio *Rabasa (1856-1930), an eminent jurist, wrote four novels while still young, grouped under the title *Novelas mexicanas* (Mexican Novels). Rabasa's interests in the realist idiom, including his depiction of the middle class, its characteristics and ambitions and the social systems in which it necessarily moved, showed his affinities with the Spanish novelist Benito Pérez Galdós. Other realist novelists are José López *Portillo y Rojas (1850-1923), Rafael *Delgado (1853-1914), Angel de *Campo (1868-1908), Heriberto Frías (1870-1925) and Federico *Gamboa (1864-1939). Gamboa showed a clear tendency toward naturalism, known through the French novelists Emil Zola and the Goncourts. The title of his first work, *Del natural* (Of the Natural), is significant. Other works include *Apariencias* (Appearances), *Suprema Ley* (Supreme Law), *Metamorfosis* (Metamorphosis), and the most popular, *Santa* (Saint), on the life of a young prostitute and everything leading up to the death of the protagonist. While Gamboa applied a clinical eye to the many pathologies of life in the brothels of Mexico City, his deep belief in love, the "Supreme Law," is personified for Santa in Hipólito, a blind pianist, who saves her. The Mexican novel, by the end of this period, seems to have run its course, repeatedly describing the depressive aspects of Mexican society and history. The 1910 Revolution provided a break with history and a reason for new themes and philosophies of the novel.

Mexican poetry of the end of the nineteenth century embodies the transition to and emergence of Modernism, the most authentically Mexican literary movement until that time. As the predominant influence of Spain began to recede, Mexico's poets carried post-Romantic poetry into a period of self-examination and renewed vigor. The sources of Modernism included philosophy, as manifested in the Germans, Arthur Schopenhauer and Immanuel Kant, the French Impressionists and

Parnassians, other European and North American literary ideas, even the Japanese *haiku*. Modernism thus constituted an impressive statement of literary maturity, which showed the assimilation of all these sources and attempted to express enduring values that would supersede societal concerns. The Modernist movement began with the publication of the Nicaraguan Ruben Darío's *Azul* (Blue) and *Revista Azul* (Blue Journal) (1894- 1896), which the Mexican Manuel *Gutiérrez Nájera founded with Carlos *Díaz Dufoo. Writers in the other Spanish-speaking countries expanded the literature and its journals, a major tool of communication. The Modernist poets effected a rupture with the past and presented a kind of elite brotherhood whose influence was felt into the first decades of the twentieth century. Nonetheless, there was no great movement of solidarity; the poets' works stand by themselves as different manifestations of the Modernist concepts.

Among the precursors of the Modernist poets are Ignacio Altamirano and Justo Sierra. Ignacio Altamirano's search for a Mexican truth in his *Rimas* (Rhymes) (1880) points the way for an appreciation of a new sensibility. Justo Sierra (1848-1912), a disciple of Altamirano, began writing with the late Romantics, but the purification of his poetic writing shows a clear affinity with the Parnassian style. Luis G. Urbina (1868-1934) and Salvador *Díaz Mirón (1853-1928) also bridge these periods with their works.

Gutiérrez Nájera (1859-1895), publisher of the *Revista Azul*, also wrote poetry, published posthumously in 1896, subsequently augmented and published again in 1953. He also wrote short stories and literary and social criticism and is credited as being the creator of the chronicle in the Parisian style, which he wrote under the pen name El Duque Job (Duke Job). All his work was well-formed, of a grace and style that explain his far-reaching influence among his peers. His *Odas breves* (Brief Odes) and his *Cuentos frágiles* (Fragile Stories) both display an intimate delicacy characteristic of his work. Amado *Nervo (1870-1919), who wrote for *Revista Azul* while still a young man, had wanted to study theology; however, because of family difficulties, he began to earn his living with his pen. His volumes of poetry were abundant, and though he later carried out several diplomatic appointments, it was his poetry that led to his lasting fame. He was also a founder of the *Revista Moderna* (Modern Review), which enjoyed great prestige and long life (1898-1911) as a literary journal. Nervo's early poetry was influenced by the French symbolist elements, while his later poetry became simpler, almost mystic and ascetic. On his death in Montevideo at the age of forty nine, his remains were escorted back to Mexico by ships from several other countries, and his funeral was unprecedentedly lavish for a poet. Other Modernist poets, all of whom wrote in the *Revista Moderna*, include Manuel José *Othón, who also wrote drama and narrative, Jesús Urueta, Rafael *López, José Juan *Tablada and Enrique *González Martínez (1871-1952). Irritation with what he considered to be the excess superficiality of the Modernists led González Martínez in 1911 to write the sonnet "Tuérecele el cuello al cisne" (Twist the Swan's Neck). This appeal to intelligence over grace, to essence over appearance, capped the Modernist career. It also characterizes González Martínez' poetry, which continued to develop the themes of love, pain, death and an austere attitude toward life.

The 1910 Revolution not only was the central political fact for the period from 1910 to 1920, but also gave impetus to the literary forms of the day, providing the novel with its primary theme. Dr. Mariano *Azuela (1873-1952), a medical doctor, was both the most eloquent writer and the most prolific of the period. The publication of *Los* *de Abajo* (The Underdogs) exemplified the primary characteristics of the novel of the Revolution, of which there was a veritable flood. Using the Revolution as his theme, supported by economy of style, highly colloquial language and episodic plot, Azuela re-created that historical period for all to read. Azuela's sense of the novel evolved as he published subsequent ones approximately every two years until his death at the age of seventy nine. Other leading novelists of the Revolution include Rafael F. *Muñoz and Martín Luis *Guzmán, who was attracted to the figure of the *caudillo* (political boss) rather than that of the peasant.

The 1910 Revolution led to a vital interest in Mexico, past and present, its land and people. At least one manifestation of this interest, the indigenist novel, was not unique to Mexico, being even more pronounced in tone and importance in Ecuador, for example. In Mexico, just when the muralists Diego Rivera, José Clemente Orozco and David Alfaro Siqueiros began to dazzle the public with their artistic depiction of Mexico and its people, writers of the novel began to explore the indigenous theme. They documented the life of the Indian, portrayed the national figure as predominantly Indian or mestizo, and attempted to study and comprehend Indian mythology, psychology, poetry, and legend. Gregorio *López y Fuentes (1897-1966), who wrote *El indio* (The Indian), in 1935, initiated this theme. Other writers who have developed it were Miguel Angel *Menéndez, Mauricio *Magdaleno, Ermilo *Abreu Gómez, Lola Casanova, Ricardo *Pozas, and Rosario *Castellanos (1925-1974), whose novel *Balún Canán* (Nine Guardians) depicts both the landowners and the Indians of Chiapas as having problems of adjustment to modern politics and society.

Another theme of the novel dealt with social injustice on a broader scale, almost always political, sometimes sociological. José *Mancisidor (1895-1956) wrote *La ciudad roja* (The Red City), in 1932, *Frontera junto al mar* (Border by the Sea), in 1953, and *Alba en las simas* (Dawn in the Abyss), in 1953. Other authors of works of social concern include José *Revueltas, Rafael *Solana, and Luis *Spota, author of novels such as *La sangre enemiga* (Enemy Blood) (1959), who viewed in the abject living conditions of the inhabitants of the city the natural source of their spiritual poverty.

These themes continued into the fifties and sixties, but a new concern with the process of writing and reading the novel brought added emphasis to the aesthetic of the genre. Three authors are sufficient to exemplify this concern, and their works attest to the recent "Boom" in Latin American Literature. Agustín *Yáñez, whose novel *Al filo del agua* (The Edge of the Storm) was published in 1947; Juan Rulfo, with *Pedro Páramo*, in 1955; and Carlos *Fuentes, with *La muerte de Artemio Cruz* (The Death of Artemio Cruz), in 1962, all treat, to some degree, the Revolution, its causes, and its effects. But each writer brought new techniques to bear on the narration of the work, elevating the role of the reader to match that of the author. Interior monologue, multiple narrators, characters with shifting identities, planes of consciousness, achronological or antichronological development all mark these authors as active creators in the international literary movement. While Rulfo has published only one other work, a collection of short stories, Yáñez has written several novels, including *La tierra pródiga* (The Fruitful Earth) (1961) and *Las tierras flacas* (The Frail Lands) (1964). Carlos Fuentes has written essays, short stories and dramatic works in addition to his novels, including the hauntingly lovely short novel *Aura* (1962). In addition to *La muerte de Artemio Cruz*, other ambitious novels include *La región más transparente* (Where the Air is Clear) (1958) and *Cambio de* *piel* (A Change of Skin) (1967), for which Fuentes was awarded the prestigious Biblioteca Breve Prize for 1966.

The "Boom" presented the most comprehensive examination of national issues of the twentieth century, and already "Post-boom" novels and novelists are being discussed. As was the case with the modernists, there is a widespread internationality, so that representative authors include the Argentinean Julio Cortázar, the Colombian Gabriel García Márquez, the Cuban Alejo Carpentier, the Peruvian Mario Vargas Llosa, and the Guatemalan Miguel Angel Asturias as well as the Mexican novelists discussed earlier. The novel has continued to flourish in Mexico, and the number of good writers of novels is impressive, as is their concern for the social and aesthetic issues of these decades. The novels of Salvador *Elizondo, José Emilio *Pacheco, Carlos Montemayor, and Antonio Delgado present cases of diverse tendencies, expressions of their vision of the world in their own modes.

Other trends of the recent decades have included the thematic emphasis on the Cristero revolt of the late 1920s and the technical perspective of *magical realism, with which, for instance, Juan José *Arreola is strongly associated. Elena Garro's novel *Recuerdos del porvenir* (Remembrance of Things to Come) treats both of the above trends. With renewed interest in indigenous culture and history, under the auspices of the *Consejo Nacional para la Cultura y las Artes* (National Council for Culture and the Arts), there are regional efforts to produce works in various indigenous languages, including Nahuatl and Mayan. Another emphasis is feminist literature, as exemplified in the novels of Elena *Garro, Rosario Castellanos, and Elena *Poniatowska. Poetry and the theater also have feminist authors, such as María Luisa *Ocampo. Her work, *La virgen fuerte* (The Strong Virgin), presents a feminist subject: woman as decision-maker and her justification in contemporary society.

The theater in Mexico in the twentieth century continued many of the nineteenth-century traditions. While contemporary issues and characters began to make their appearance on the stage, there was not a sufficient change in the philosophy of the theater and its national significance. Actors still practiced the style and diction of the Spanish stage. A pessimistic combination of revolutionary themes and naturalistic influences competed with the continuing lighter works from the turn of the century to the 1930s. Dramatists whose works represented the former ideas include the naturalist and realist José Joaquín *Gamboa (1878-1931), author of *La carne (Teresa)* (The Flesh [Teresa]) and *El diablo tiene frío* (The Devil is Cold). Other playwrights are Francisco *Monterde and Víctor Manuel Díez Barroso. Lighter works were produced by Julio *Jiménez Rueda and Carlos *Noriega Hope. María Luisa Ocampo can be seen as a transition figure, since her early works seem to espouse turn-of-the-century ideas. But over a forty-year writing career, she caught the spirit of renovation and change in her later works. In 1923 the Society of Dramatic Authors was re-established. Through the efforts of José *Vasconcelos (1882-1959), then secretary of education, nonprofessional theaters and the *Comedia Mexicana* (Mexican Comedy) were organized. Around the same time, a group of poets published the journal *Ulises*, which lasted less than a year (May 1927 to February 1928), but gave rise to the experimental theatrical group, the *Teatro Ulises*. Those involved in both the magazine and the theater included Xavier *Villaurrutia (1903-1951), Salvador *Novo (1904-1974), Gilberto *Owen(1904-1952) and Celestino *Gorostiza (1904-1967). The playrights mentioned above are as well known for their poetry as for their theatrical works. This group provoked a vigorous national reaction, but it continued to be active and received state backing at the *Teatro Orientación*. Then, in 1933, Julio Bracho founded the *Teatro de la Universidad*, and in 1934 the Palace of Fine Arts was inaugurated. Works of national and international origin were presented in all these theaters, and a spirit of renewed vigor was felt. The patronage of the National Institute of Fine Arts has helped to put forward works of theatrical significance since 1948. Rodolfo *Usigli is of importance as a playwright, as creator of the *Teatro de Media Noche*, and as a professor of theatrical history at the National University. Here his students included Emilio *Carballido, Luisa Josefina *Hernández, Jorge *Ibargüengoitia and Sergio *Magaña, all of whom have made important contributions to the Mexican theater since the middle of the century. Their works can be characterized by technical excellence and Mexican themes. Emilio Carballido's works have progressed from realistic to several types of nonrealistic, including what he calls "psychological realism." Many of these have a classic basis but are brought into immediacy by modern settings and characters.

Among those whose works have recently influenced the Mexican theater is Carlos *Solórzano, who used concepts from the Brechtian spectacle in his play *Las manos de Dios* (The Hands of God). Luisa Josefina Hernández' play *La orgía del mulato* (The Mulatto's Orgy) is a work involving music, dance, and light as integral parts of the play. Her play *El orden de los factores* (The Order of Factors) takes a critical look at the devastating effects that social and personal problems have on people. A teacher at UNAM, Hernández uses many of her original plays as learning devices for her students. Another new development related to the theater is the play for television, initiated in the 1950s. Rafael *Bernal was among the first whose works were presented in this medium. Roberto Gómez Bolaños has written over 500 screenplays for television series, a genre whose relevance to the legitimate stage has not been thoroughly investigated. The fifteenth anniversary of the theatrical journal *Tramoya* (published originally by the Universidad Veracruzana) was celebrated in 1990. The distinguished Mexican playwright Emilio Carballido is coeditor along with Eladio Cortés of Rutgers University. Now published jointly by the Veracruzana and Rutgers University in Camden, *Tramoya* contains original plays.

The essay in recent decades reflects changes in purpose and in the writers themselves. As recently as the 1930s, writers dedicated themselves to the theme of Mexico in any of several aspects. José Vasconcelos (1899-1952) wrote about history, philosophy and politics; his *Ulisis Criollo* (Creole Ulysses) is a nationalistic philosophical autobiography. Alfonso *Reyes (1889-1959), considered by many as the dean of Mexican letters in the twentieth century, knew practically no limits within the arts, literary theory, and humanism. But since 1940, many writers have become specialists instead of generalists, devoting themselves almost exclusively to one theme or one philosophy. Jesús Silvia Herzog writes primarily on economic theory, while Alfonso Caso addresses anthropology. Elena Poniatowska has written essays concerning both feminism and the repression of the arts. This change in sensibility to a more narrow perspective has provided the reader with ample material in various genres and many different fields of study.

Along with the emergence of the Modernist poets, a number of other "isms" reflecting the need to change, progress and experiment made their presence felt in Mexico, including, to a greater or lesser degree: vanguardism, ultraism, dadaism, surrealism, creationism, cubism, and existentialism. Each of these had passionate adherents but did not achieve the pervasive influence of Modernism, constituting tendencies rather than movements. A new group, however, coalesced around the magazine *Contemporáneos*. Most of the members of this group had their first experiences in the Ateneo de Juventud (Youth Aetheneum), which had been modeled after El Ateneo de México (The Aetheneum of Mexico), the literary group of the previous generation, which included Pedro *Henríquez Ureña and Alfonso Reyes.

The editor of *Contemporáneos* was Bernardo *Ortiz de Montellano (1899-1949), and the principal contributors were Xavier Villaurrutia (1903-1950), Jaime *Torres Bodet (1902-1974), José *Gorostiza (1901-1973), Salvador *Novo, and Gilberto *Owen. This group's poetry tended to eschew politics, focusing instead on personal themes, or indeed, questions of universal expression that cut across the traditional boundaries of nationality or of the different arts. Ramón *López Velarde (1888-1921) provides the transition from the generation of the Ateneo to that of the Contemporáneos. His first book of poetry, *La sangre devota* (Devout Blood) (1916), is regional and intimate; throughout his poetic corpus he developed the conflict between material and ideal forces. Perhaps the most representative of the Contemporáneos poetry is "Muerte sin fin" (Endless Death), by José Gorostiza. In this long poem, the metaphysical themes of matter and existence, life and death, and the poem and the poet are presented in multiple levels within the imagery of a glass of water.

Two groups, so close in time that they may be seen as two aspects of the same period, coalesced at the end of the 1930s and into the 1940s. Their unifying aspect is that they represent the rebellion of the younger poets as compared to the Contemporáneos group, although there is some irony in this distinction, since many of the Contemporáneos had not yet made their most significant contributions to the literature of Mexico. The first of these rejected much of the Contemporáneos' aloofness for a more human-oriented stance; at the same time, they were more politically committed, being especially affected by the Spanish Civil War (1936-1939). They published and wrote in two literary magazines, *Taller poético* (1936-1938) and then *Taller* (1938- 1941). Representative members of Grupo *Taller* were Neftalí *Beltrán (1916-), Efraín *Huerta (1914-1982), Alberto Quintero Alvarez (1914-1944), and Rafael Solana (1915). The most famous member of *Taller* is Octavio *Paz, born in 1914 in Mexico City. He experienced the Spanish Civil War, was a member of the Mexican Foreign Service in both the United States and France, and later in India, a post he resigned in protest against the violence used against students, artists, and intellectuals in 1968. Since that time he has held a number of university positions and has continued to write. His poetic career was recognized with the awarding of the Nobel Prize in Literature in 1990. Specifically Mexican in his images, mythological and societal in most cases, he utilizes his wide vision of the world's cultures and history to search for new approaches to life and its meaning. He also has written numerous philosophical essays, including *El laberinto de la soledad* (*The Labyrinth of Solitude*), concerning the essence of Mexican character, plus studies on Mexican poetry and poets.

The second group to emerge in the 1940s were those initially of the review *Tierra Nueva* (1940-1942): Manuel *Calvillo (1918-), Wilberto *Cantón (1923-1979), Jorge *González Durán (1918-), and *Alí Chumacero (1918-). They were Akin to the Contemporáneos in their preoccupation with formal concerns, but only Alí Chumacero's poetry has led to serious evaluation. A more recent grouping, the Generation of 1954, presents a similar dichotomy in which some are more concerned with individual formation as poets and others with social themes. Among the more recent poets are women, both as members of groups and collaborators in the standard journals, and as members of feminist groups, generally apart from the ones alluded to above. Rosario Castellanos (1925-1974) published eight books of poetry. She is also known for her novels, such as *Oficio de Tinieblas* (Powers of Darkness). Her themes of feminist tendency and poetic expression intertwine in works of rich cultural and mythological imagery. Other poets include Jaime Sabines (1926-), Marco Antonio *Montes de Oca (1932-), and Manuel *Durán (1925-).

Another group of writers that enriched the cultural life of Mexico beginning in the 1940s were those Spanish artists exiled after the Civil War. Particularly numerous were the poets, such as Emilio *Prados, Luis *Cernuda, Manuel *Altolaguirre, Pedro *Garfías and especially León Felipe *Camino Galicia. Other writers included the novelist and critic Max *Aub, and the professor Enrique *Díez-Canedo.

Among the most recent poets, whose work dates from after the midpoint of the century, include those whose themes include the Mexican repression of the arts and intellectual freedom (1968), the American intervention in Vietnam and influence in Central America, and continuing Cuban revolutionary society. These include Juan *Bañuelos (1932-) and Jaime *Labastida (1939-). These two poets, along with Jaime Augusto *Shelley, Oscar *Oliva and Eraclio *Zepeda, joined together to form *La Espiga Amotinada* (The Spiked Sheaf) and published two controversial anthologies of socially committed poetry. Much of their work focuses on disturbing aspects of contemporary life and political reality. In particular, Zepeda deals with the indigenous theme. The above-named poets are concerned with aesthetics also, seeking to achieve a delicate balance between their message and its means of expression. Those whose poetry seems more preoccupied with subjective themes and technique include Homero *Aridjis (1940-) and José Emilio Pacheco. Both of these have published extensively in prose fiction as well as poetry, providing ample opportunity to view their different techniques and visions. Poetry itself is a flourishing genre, as attested to by the recent anthology *Asamblea de poetas jóvenes mexicanos* (Assembly of Young Mexican Poets), published in 1980.

There are many more writers today who are making their imprint on Mexican letters. Among the current group of influential authors are Cristina *Pacheco, a noted journalist; Miguel *González-Gerth, a poet and professor who now lives in Texas; Antonio *Argudín, a dramatist, poet, short story writer, and student, who was born in 1953; Sabina *Berman, a playwright whose work demonstrates that the theater is still flourishing; and Oscar *Villegas, another playwright whose dominant characteristic is experimentation with form.

So much more could be said about the history and state of Mexican letters. This essay serves merely as an introduction. For a more complete picture, it is necessary to take into account the lives and works of each individual author. The sheer volume of bibliographical information contained with the entries that follow indicates that there is an abiding interest in Mexican literature.

Dictionary of⎯⎯⎯⎯
Mexican
Literature

A

ABAD, Diego José (1727-1779). Abad was born in 1727 on an hacienda near Jiquilapán, Michoacán. He studied philosophy and literature at the Colegio de San Ildefonso and then entered the Jesuit order. He taught rhetoric, philosophy, and law in Jesuit seminaries and was rector of the seminary of San Francisco Javier de Querétaro when the Jesuits were expelled from New Spain. He spent the rest of his life in Italy and died in Bologna in 1779.

One of the great humanists who wrote in Latin, Abad left works of scientific character, and translated into Spanish some of the *Eclogues* of Virgil, but his greatest renown stems from his Latin poem *De Deo, Deoque Homine*. The first part is a theological treatise and the second, a life of Christ. Although begun before his exile in Italy, it was not published until shortly after his death, in 1780. He also wrote two poems in Spanish. One was a verse translation of the eighth Eclogue of Virgil and the other an original in Gongorine style written for the dedication of the Jesuit temple in Zacatecas.

WORKS: *Rasgo épico descriptivo de la fábrica y grandezas del Templo de la Compañía de Jesús de Zacatecas* (México, 1750; and in *Estilo* 34 [1955]: 119-35). *Egloga VIII, Pharmaceutia de Virgilio* (in José Antonio Alzate, *Observaciones sobre la física, historia natural y artes útiles)* (México, 1787). *De Deo, Deoque Homine Heroica* (Cesena; n.p., 1780).

BIBLIOGRAPHY: Alexander Davis V., "Diego José Abad" in *El Siglo de Oro de la Nueva España. Siglo XVIII* (México: Polis, 1945). Gabriel Méndez Plancarte, *Humanistas del Siglo XVIII* (México: UNAM, 1941). Arnold L. Kerson, "José Rafael Campoy and Diego José Abad: Two Enlightened Figures of Eighteenth-Century Mexico" in *Dieciocho: Hispanic Enlightenment, Aesthetics, and Literary Theory* 7, 2 (Fall 1984): 130-45. Benjamín Fernández Valenzuela, "'Canto noveno' of the 'Poema heróico' by Diego José Abad" in *Abside: Revista de Cultura Mejicana* 33 (1969): 133-51. "Diego José Abad y su Poema heróico," in *Abside* 33 (1969) 127-32.

ANITA K. STOLL

ABREU Gómez, Ermilo (1894-1971). Abreu Gómez was born in Mérida, Yucatán, on September 18, 1894, where he lived until he went to preparatory school in Puebla. Upon his return, he was employed by the *Revista de Mérida*, a position that enabled him to publish some of his early works. Much to his enjoyment, he also participated in the local theater company. His first writings are within the school of literary colonialism, and he was a part of the group of "colonialists" that disbanded around 1926.

In his early period, Abreu Gómez wrote plays and novels of traditional style. He later turned primarily to the critical essay, with special interest in indigenous and Mexican themes. He is particularly well-known for his erudite studies about Sor Juana Inés de la *Cruz, which brought both Abreu Gómez and Sor Juana added recognition.

He also has some highly creative works in the field of indigenous literature. For example, *Héroes mayas* (Mayan Heroes) (1942) has been cited as a book that expresses the soul of the Mayan people. Furthermore, the lyricism and artistic ingenuity with which it is written make it one of the finest examples of its type. One of its three sections, entitled *Canek*, is based upon an actual account dating from 1761 in Mérida. It has had more than thirty editions. *Canek* has been translated into several languages, including English. A work of impressionistic sketches, *Canek* intertwines two related stories of indigenous matters, told with prose, poetry, and mythical elements. Although fiction, the story brings Mayan history alive. The book is a continuous narrative, but with five separate, yet unified, sections, culminating in the chilling warfare of the Indians who have been humiliated, dominated, and treated with injustice. *Canek* is considered an architectural and verbal masterpiece.

Another book, *Quetzalcóatl, sueño y vigilia* (Quetzalcóatl, Dream and Vigil), published in 1947, combining a tender lyricism with the strength of the epic, is a poetic version of the story of the gentle god, Quetzalcóatl, spiritual hero of the indigenous peoples of the Mexican tableland. Abreu Gómez, whose prose is both fluid and tense, brings Quetzalcóatl to life, in all his beauty and vitality, making this one of his most excellent works, surpassing, for some critics, even *Canek*.

Naufragio de indios (Shipwreck of Indians), published in 1951, is an excellent novel about the protest of a Mexican village against the French invasion. Maximilian attempts to recruit troops for the army, but meets with heroic resistance. Anderson Imbert, reflecting on Abreu Gómez' style, remarks: "The episodes are like watercolors with incisive lines and variegated quantities of color." The novel ends tragically, with the sinking of a French ship, laden with Indian prisoners.

Tata Lobo (1952) is a type of picaresque novel, with the main character wandering from one adventure to another, relatively lost in turmoil and chaos. The work allows the author to critique society, much as did the early Spanish writers of picaresque novels. Abreu Gómez' well-developed protagonist, balanced by the novel's structure, binds the work together.

Abreu Gómez was also the biographer of Martín Luis *Guzmán. In 1968 he published a volume about Guzmán and his work, including a selection of his writings. He had previously published a number of critical essays and other studies in journals. Then, again in 1979, he produced an excellent anthology of Guzmán's work, arranged by genres.

In Mexico he contributed to the journal *Contemporáneos*, with which he became noted as a prolific literary critic, with impressive studies on Sor Juana Inés de la Cruz, *Ruíz de Alarcón, and others. A professor for many years, he also gave conferences and wrote many articles for journals. From 1947 to 1960 he lived and worked in Washington, D.C. In 1961, he returned to Mexico and secured a professorship in philosophy and letters at the Universidad Nacional de México. A nationally known and respected figure, he died in 1971, having contributed significantly to Mexican literature.

WORKS: Novels and Stories: *El corcovado* (The Hunchback) (México: n.p., 1924). *La vida del venerable Gregorio López* (The Life of the Venerable Gregorio López) (México: Talls. Linotip. "Carlos Rivadeneyra," 1925). *Cuentos de Juan Pirulero* (Stories of Juan Pirulero) (México: Ed. Letras de México, 1939). *Canek* (México: Eds. Canek, 1940); 2nd ed., in *Héroes mayas* (Mayan Heroes) (México: n.p., 1942); 3rd ed. (México: Manuel Altolaguirre, 1950); 4th ed. (1945); 5th ed., in *Cuatro siglos de literatura mexicana* (México: n.p., 1946); 6th ed. (1948); 7th ed. (Washington, D.C.: n.p., 1950); 8th ed. (México: Talls. Gráf. de la Nación, 1950); 9th ed. (México: Botas, 1959); ed. Col. "Lunes" no. 32 (México: n.p., 1963). *Héroes Mayas* (Mayan Heroes) (México: Cía. Gral. Editora, 1942). *Pirrimplín en la luna* (Pirrimplín on the Moon) (México: Ed. Mensaje, 1942). *Tres nuevos cuentos de Juan Pirulero* (Three New Stories of Juan Pirulero) (México: n.p., 1944). *Quetzalcóatl, sueño y vigilia* (Quetzalcóatl: Dream and Vigil) (México: n.p., 1947). *Naufragio de indios* (Shipwrecked Indians) (México: n.p., 1951). *Leyendas mexicanas* (Mexican Legends) (New York: n.p., 1951). *Tata Lobo* (Daddy Wolf) (México: FCE, 1952). *San Francisco* (St. Francis), story (México: n.p., 1954). *Cosas de mi pueblo* (Things about My Town) (México: n.p., 1957). *La Conjura de Xinum* (The Conspiracy of Xinum) (San Salvador, El Salvador: Ministerio de Cultura, Depto. Editorial, 1958). *Cuentos para contar junto al fuego* (Stories to Tell by the Fire) (México: B. Costa-Amic, 1959). *Leyendas y consejas del antiguo Yucatán* (Legends and Tales of Old Yucatán) (México: Botas, 1961). *San Francisco de Asís* (St. Francis of Assisi), poetic scenes from his life (México: Costa-Amic, 1964). Theater: *La Xtabay* (Mérida: n.p., 1919). *El cacique* (The Boss) (México: Imp. Italiana, 1921). *Máscaras* (Masks) (México: Imp. Italiana, 1921). *Muñecos* (Puppets), in *El Universal Ilustrado* 4, 213 (June 2, 1921): 19-41. *Viva el Rey* (Long Live the King) (México: Eds. Nosotros, Imp. del Comercio, 1921). *Humanidades* (Humanities) (México: Edit. Mendoza, Imp. del Comercio, 1923). *Romance de Reyes* (Ballads of Kings) (Madrid: Espasa-Calpe, 1926). *Pasos de Comedia* (Comedy Steps) (México: Herrero Hnos., Talls. Rivadeneyra, 1926). *Burla, burlando*, in *Sagitario* 14 (May 31, 1927). *Pirrimplín en la luna* (Pirrimplín on the Moon), in *Revista Mexicana de Cultura*, Mexico, 1942. *Un juego de escarnio* (A Play of Scorn) (México: Ed. Tiras de Colores, 1943); 2nd ed. (México: Castalia, 1963). *Un loro y tres golondrinas* (A Parrot and Three Swallows) (México: Eds. Letras de México, 1945); in *El Hijo Pródigo* 9, 28 (July 1945) 34-55. Memoirs: *La del alba sería...* (Day Was Dawning), vol. 1 (México: Eds. Botas, 1954). *Duelos y quebrantos* (Duels and Great Losses), vol. 2 (México: Botas, 1959). Essays, Studies, Criticism: *Guía de amantes* (Lovers' Guide) (México: Eds. Nieto, Talls. Gráf. de José Celorio Ortega, 1933). *Clásicos, románticos, modernos* (Classicists, Romantics, Modernists) (México: Botas, 1934). *Sor Juana Inés de la Cruz. Bibliografía y Biblioteca* (Sor Juana Inés de la Cruz, Bibliography and Library) (México: Imp. de la Sría. de Relaciones Exteriores, 1934). *Iconografía de Sor Juana* (Iconography of Sor Juana) (México: n.p., 1934). *Semblanza de Sor Juana Inés de la Cruz* (Portrait of Sor Juana Inés de la Cruz) (México: n.p., 1938). *La ruta de Sor Juana* (Sor Juana's Route) (México: Talls. Gráf. de la Nación, 1938). *Juan Ruiz de Alarcón, Bibliografía crítica* (Juan Ruiz de Alarcón, Critical Bibliography) (México: Botas, 1939). *Lecciones de literatura española* (Lessons about Spanish Literature) (México: Ed. Revista Musical Mexicana, Talls. Gráf. de la Nación, 1944). *Sala de retratos* (Room of Portraits) (México: Edit. Leyenda, 1946). "Breve historia de mis libros" (Brief History of My Books), in *El Hijo Pródigo* 11, 34 (Jan. 1946): 9-16. *Horacio Quiroga* (Washington, D.C.: Unión Panamericana, 1951). *Diálogo del buen decir y otros ensayos* (Dialogue of Good Speech and Other Essays) (San Salvador: Edit. Universitaria, 1961). *Diálogo del Quijote* (Dialogue of the Quijote) (San Salvador; n.p., 1961). *Discurso del estilo* (Speech on Style), in *Revista Mexicana de Cultura* 840 (May 5, 1963): 8-10. *Martín Luis Guzmán* (México: Empresas Editoriales, 1968), *Centenario de Don Francisco A. de Icaza* (One Hundredth Anniversary of Don Francisco A. de Icaza), in *CAM* 128, 3 (May-June 1963): 193-209. Anthologies: *Sor Juana Inés de la Cruz. Poesías completas*, ed. and prol. (México: Botas, 1941). *Claros versos españoles* (Clear Spanish Verses) (México: Edit. Delfín, 1944). *El Popol-Vuh* (México: BEP, 1944). *Rubén Darío, Poesías* (México: n.p., 1944). *Cuatro siglos de literatura mexicana* (Four Centuries of Mexican Literature), in collaboration (México: Edit. Leyenda, 1946). *Escritores de Costa Rica. Joaquín García Monge, Roberto Brenes Mesén y Carmen Lira* (Costa Rican Writers. . .) (Washington, D.C.: Unión Panamericana, 1950). *Antología de Martín Luis Guzmán* (México: Ediciones Oasis, 1970) Prologues: Arturo Peón Cisneros, *La espuma* (Mérida: n.p., 1915). Sor Juana Inés de la Cruz, *Respuesta a Sor Filotea de la Cruz* (México: n.p., 1929). Carlos Sigüenza y Góngora, *Poesía* (Madrid: n.p., 1931). Sor Juana Inés de la Cruz, *Carta Atenagórica* (México: n.p., 1934). Juan José Eguiara y Eguren, *Sor Juana Inés de la Cruz* (México: Ant. Libr. Robredo, 1936). Father Diego Calleja, S.J., *Vida de Sor Juana Inés de la Cruz* (México: n.p., 1936). *Sor Juana Inés de la Cruz. Liras* (México: n.p., 1937). José Mancisidor, *De una madre española* (México: Ed. México Nuevo, 1938). *Sor Juana Inés de la Cruz. Poesías* (México: n.p., 1940). Francisco Castillo Nájera, *El Gavilán* (México: n.p., 1940). Antonio Mediz Bolio, *La tierra del faisán y del venado*, 2nd ed. (México: n.p., 1940). José Mancisidor, *Diario de una madre* (México: n.p., 1942). Juan Francisco Molina Solís, *Historia del descubrimiento y conquista de Yucatán* (México: n.p., 1943). Justo Arosamena, *Ensayos morales* (México: n.p., 1949). *Rubén Darío, crítico literario* (México: n.p., 1951). Germán List Arzubide, *Ramón López Velarde y la Revolución* (México: Eds. Conferencias, 1963). Carmen Alardín, *Todo se deja así* (México: Eds. de Cuadernos del Viento, 1964).

BIBLIOGRAPHY: Fernando Alegría, *Breve historia de la novela hispanoamericana* (México: Eds. de Andrea, 1959), pp. 145-46; *Nueva historia de la novela hispanoamericana* (Hanover, N.H.: Ediciones del Norte, 1986), pp. 131, 132. Enrique Anderson Imbert, *Historia de la literatura hispanoamericana*, vol. 2 (México: FCE, 1957), pp. 114, 115, 116; *Spanish American Literature*, vol. 2, revised (Detroit: Wayne State University Press, 1969), pp. 512-13. Efraín Tomás Bo, "Memoria y creación de Ermilo Abreu Gómez" in *Letras de México* 4, 20 (Aug. 1, 1944). John S. Brushwood, *Mexico in Its Novel* (Austin: University of Texas Press, 1966), p. 185. Enrique Díez-Canedo, *Letras de América* (México: FCE, 1944), pp. 380-85. Jorge González Durán, review of *Héroes mayas* in *Cuadernos Americanos* (May-June 1943): 242-248. Andrés Henestrosa, Review of *Canek* in *Tierra Nueva* 2, 7-8 (Jan.-April 1941): 71-73. Ross Larson, *Fantasy and Imagination in the Mexican Narrative* (Tempe, Ariz.: Center for Latin American Studies, Arizona State University, 1977), p. 112. Luis Leal, *Breve historia del cuento mexicano* (México: Eds. de Andrea, 1956), pp. 115-16; *Bibliografía del cuento mexicano* (México: Eds. de Andrea, 1958), pp. 11-12; *Panorama de la literatura mexicana actual* (Washington, D.C.: Unión Panamericana, 1968), pp. 24, 32, 76, 112, 138. Antonio Magaña Esquivel, "Ermilo Abreu Gómez" in *Enciclopedia Yucatanense* V, pp. 679-82; in *Letras de México* 5, 119 (Jan. 1, 1946): 203. Antonio Magaña Esquivel and Ruth S. Lamb, *Breve historia del teatro mexicano* (México: Eds. de Andrea, 1958), pp. 118-19, 158. José Luis Martínez, *Literatura indígena moderna*

(México: Eds. Mensaje, 1942), pp. 18-20; *Literatura mexicana del siglo XX, 1910-1949)*, vol. 1 (México: Ant. Libr. Robredo, 1949), pp. 16-18, 53, 133, 218-20, 332-33; vol. 2 (1950), p. 13; *El ensayo mexicano moderno*, vol. 1 (México: FCE, 1958), pp. 373-74. Ernesto Mejía Sánchez, Review of *Diálogo del buen decir y otros ensayos* in *Anuario de Letras* 1 (México, 1961): 237-39. Isa Norman, Review of *La conjura de Xinum*, in *Revista Hispánica Moderna* 26, 3-4 (New York, July-Oct. 1960) 157. Aurora M. Ocampo de Gómez and Ernesto Prado Velázquez, *Diccionario de escritores mexicanos* (México: UNAM, 1967), pp. 2-4. José Emilio Pacheco, Review of *Discurso del estilo* in *La Cultura en México* 89 (Oct. 30, 1963): XVIII-XIX. Salvador Reyes Nevares, "Los pequeños recuerdos de Abreu Gómez," review of *Duelos y quebrantos*, in *México en la Cultura* 552 (Oct. 11, 1959): 4; Review of *Cuentos para contar junto al fuego* in *México en la Cultura* 590 (July 3, 1960): 4; Review of *Diálogo del buen decir y otros ensayos* in *México en la Cultura* 638 (June 4, 1961): 2. Laura de los Ríos, Review of *Héroes mayas* in *Revista Hispánica Moderna* 10 (1944): 270. Raúl Rogers, Review of *Héroes mayas* in *Hispania* 27, 1: 123-26. Isaac Rojas Rosillo, "Ermilo Abreu Gómez, novelista," in *México en la Cultura* 150 (Dec. 23, 1951): 7. George D. Schade, "Dos mexicanos vistos por sí mismos: Reyes y Abreu Gómez," in *Revista Iberoamericana* 55, 148-49 (July-Dec., 1989): 785-801. Sara Sefchovich, *México: país de ideas, país de novelas* (México: Edit. Grijalbo, 1987), pp. 84, 85, 235. Cynthia Steele, "Ideology and the Indigenista Novel in the Nineteenth-Century United States and in Twentieth-Century Mexico III" in *Balakian*, proceedings of the Xth Congress of the International Comparative Literature Association, New York, 1982. *El trato con escritores* (México: INBA, 1961), pp. 131, 132, 137, 153. *El trato con escritores*, 2nd series (México: INBA, 1964), pp. 25, 111, 133, 134, 156. Rafael Heliodoro Valle, "Ermilo Abreu Gómez, notas bibliográficas" in *Hispania* 33, 3: 230-32. Víctor Villela, "Entrevista a Ermilo Abreu Gómez" in *Cuadernos del Viento* 37-38, (Aug.-Dec. 1963): 559-95. Julia Whitsitt, "The Name of Canek Was Voice and Echo: Reading the Mosaic of Canek" in *Confluencia* Spring 2, 2 (1987): 100-107. Javier Wimer, "Perfil de Abreu Gómez" in *BBH* 9, 269 (April 15, 1963): 9. Jesús Zavala, "Notas cronológicas y bibliográficas" in *Sala de retratos* (México: Edit. Leyenda, 1946), pp. 305-08.

JEANNE C. WALLACE

ACEVEDO, Jesús T. (1892-1918). Born in Mexico City, Jesús T. Acevedo studied architecture at the Escuela Nacional Preparatoria and at the Academia de Bellas Artes. He was well-known for his collaboration with the major architects of his time. Due in part to his literary inclinations, he became a member of the Ateneo de la Juventud, although he wrote little. He died in the United States when he was twenty-six years old.

He authored only one book, *Disertaciones de un arquitecto* (Dissertations of an Architect), in which he gathered several of his studies and materials from various conferences whose main theme was architecture. In his essays, he speculated about the possibilities of an architecture national in scope, about the benefits to be derived from a career in architecture and about related matters.

Colonialism in literature, a current predominant in the 1930s, was guided by his work that began the study and reevaluation of the artistic and historical past of

Mexico. His essays are considered most valuable for the way in which he integrated innovative English and French aesthetic theories with Mexico's past. Alfonso Reyes noted that "His malicious insinuations, his aesthetic pleasure, the ease of his thought, his determined attitude toward life, made of him a kind of exception, a fruit of civilization superior to that of the world in which he lived." Therefore, even though Acevedo's contribution was small, it was, nonetheless, significant.

WORKS: *Disertaciones de un arquitecto* (Dissertations of an Architect) (México: Ediciones Mexico Moderno, 1920); 2nd ed. (México: INBA, Departamento de Literatura, 1967).

BIBLIOGRAPHY: Anon., "Escritores mexicanos contemporáneos, Jesús T. Acevedo" in *Biblos* 2, 85 (Sept. 1920): 137-38. Barbara Bockus Aponte, *Alfonso Reyes and Spain* (Austin: University of Texas Press, 1972), pp. 18, 21. Federico E. Mariscal, prologue to *Disertaciones de un arquitecto* in *Biblos*, 2, 85 (Sept. 1920). José Luis Martínez, *El ensayo mexicano moderno* (México: UNAM, 1958), vol. I, 39: 147-58. Alfonso Reyes, "Notas sobre Jesús Acevedo" *Obras completas* (México: FCE, 1955-1965), vol. IV, pp. 444-48. Manuel Toussaint, "Disertaciones de un arquitecto," in *Mexico Moderno* 1, (Aug. 1920): 62-63.

JEANNE C. WALLACE

ACEVEDO Escobedo, Antonio (1909-1985), short story writer, essayist, playwright, reviewer, prologues writer. Born in Aguascalientes, he was a typesetter, film reviewer and chief of information of *Renacimiento,* then a journalist at *El Universal Ilustrado, El Nacional, Revista de Revistas, Social, Fabula, Letras de Mexico, El hijo prodigo, Excelsior,* chief editorial member of *Universidad de México, Arquitectura,* and *Artes del libro,* underdirector of Editorial Ruta, organizer of over 150 events, including "Narrators Face the Readers," member of the Academy of the Language, head of the Department of Literature of the National Institute of Fine Arts, and member of the Mexican Seminary for Culture. He was first known for this short stories in *La sirena en el aula* (Siren in the Classroom), where he approaches sentimentality and tenderness, with social concerns.

WORKS: Narrative: *Sirena en el aula* (Tlalpam: Patricio Sáenz, 1935). *Mi caballito blanco* (My White Little Horse) (coauthored with Miguel N. Lira (México: SEP, 1943). *En la feria de San Marcos* (At the San Marcos Fair) (México: n.p., 1951). *Los días de Aguascalientes* (The Aguascalientes Days), prologue by Mariano Picón Salas (México: Stylo, 1952). *Al pie de la letra* (Literally Speaking) (México: n.p., 1953). Theater: *¡Ya viene Gorgonio Esparza! El matón de Aguascalientes* (Gorgonio Esparza Is Coming! The Killer of Aguascalientes) (México: n.p., 1944). Essay; *El azufre en México* (Sulphur in Mexico) (México: n.p., 1956). Editions and Prologues; *Aires de México* (Airs of Mexico) (México: UNAM, 1940). *Los cuatro poetas: Gutiérrez Nájera, Urbina, Icaza y Tablada* (The Four Poets) (México: SEP, 1944). Marquesa Calderón de la Barca: La vida en México (Fanny Calderón de la Barca: Life in Mexico) (México: SEP, 1944). *Poesía hispanoamericana contemporanea* (Contemporary Spanish-American Poetry). Juan Montalvo's *Siete tratados* (Seven Treaties) (México: SEP, 1947), Emilio Rabasa's *La bola y la conciencia* (The Revolution and Conscience) (México: Porrúa, 1948). Artemio de Valle Arizpe's *Obras completas*

(Complete Works) (México: Libreros Unidos Mexicanos, 1959). *Almanaque literario espejo del siglo XIX para 1960* (Literary Almanac Mirror of the Nineteenth Century for 1960) (México: INBA, 1959). *Letras sobre Aguascalientes* (Letters on Aguascalientes) (México: Stylo, 1963) Rafael López, *Prosas transeuntes* (Transient Proses). *Letras de los veintes* (Letters of the Twenties) (1966). *Entre prensas anda el juego* (The Game Is Among the Presses) (1967). *Asedios a Rojas Garcidueñas, escritor versatil* (Rojas Garcidueñas, Versatile Writer) (1970). *Cinco escritores en olvido* (Five Forgotten Writers) (Discurso de ingreso en la Academia) (1970). *Puertas a las curiosidad* (Doors to Curiosity) (1974). *Miscelánea literaria* (Literary Miscellany). Prologues: *Obras completas* (Complete Works) by Artemio de Valle-Arizpe. *El cristiano errante* (The Wandering Christian) by Antonio José de Irisarri. *Prosas transeuntes* (Transient Proses) by Rafael López (INBA, 1965). *Velero romantico* (Romantic Sailboat) by Alfredo Maillefert (FCE, 1967).

BIBLIOGRAPHY: Gastón García Cantu, "El azufre: Una historia a medias," *México en la Cultura* 369 (April 15, 1956): 2. Carlos González Peña, *Historia de la literatura mexicana* (México: Porrúa, 1966), p. 334. Walter M. Langford, *The Mexican Novel Comes of Age* (Notre Dame, Ind.: University of Indiana Press, 1972), p. 210. Luis Leal, *Breve historia del cuento mexicano* (México: Eds. de Andrea), pp. 125-26. Jorge Manach, Review of *La sirena en el auga* in *Revista Hispánica Moderna* 2 (1936): 28. José Luis Martínez, *Literatura* mexicana siglo XX, 1910-1949 (México: Ant. Libr. Robredo, 1949), vol. 1, pp. 65, 88, 125, 341; vol. 2 (1950), pp. 13-14; *El ensayo mexicano moderno*, vol. 2 (México: FCE, 1958), p. 266. José Emilio Pacheco, Review of *Letters on Aguascalientes* in *La Cultura en México* 88 (Oct. 23, 1963); xviii-xix.

DELIA GALVAN

ACUÑA, Manuel (1849-1873), poet. Together with Agustín F. *Cuenca, he founded the Nezahualcóyotl Literary Society, inspired by the nationalistic ideals of Ignacio *Altamirano. Born in Saltillo, Coahuila, on August 26, 1849, he went to Mexico City at age sixteen, where he studied first in the Colegio de San Ildefonso (along with Justo *Sierra and Agustín Cuenca), and later at the School of Medicine. His brief poetic career ended on December 6, 1873, when he committed suicide by swallowing cyanide at age twenty-four, citing as the cause the failure of his "muse," Rosario de la Peña (also a close friend of Manuel M. *Flores and José Martí), to return his affections.

Acuña's poetry consists of some humorous verse and romantic lyrics influenced strongly by Victor Hugo, Ramón de Campoamor, José de Espronceda, Mariano José de Larra, and especially Gustavo Adolfo Bécquer. The youthful verse, which suffers from prosaic turns of phrase, superficiality, and excess, is an exaggerated expression of romantic ideals, coupled with fervently positivistic attitudes, and treats typical themes of the period, including science as mankind's savior, doubt as to the existence of God, the perverse influence of faith as a substitute for science, fame, and of course, passion. Passion is the theme of his "Nocturno," written on the eve of his suicide, and considered one of his best pieces. "Ante un cadáver," another major poem, combines what Anderson Imbert has called a curious mixture of romantic lyricism and scientific materialism. He is generally considered a poet who would have been of much greater importance if he had lived and fulfilled his youthful promise. Publication came posthumously.

WORKS: Drama: *El pasado* (The Past) (México: Ira, 1872). *La Gloria* (Glory) (México: La Nación, Valle Brothers, 1873). Poetry: *Versos* (Verses) (México: Domingo R. Arellano, 1874). *Poesías* (Poetry) (Paris: Garnier, 1884). *Poesías* (Poetry) (México: Porrúa, 1919). General: *Obras* (Works) (Veracruz-Puebla-México-Paris: Ramón Laínez, 1891). *Historia de un pensamiento* (History of a Thought) (México: Imp. Universitaria, 1941). *Poesía, teatro, artículos y cartas* (Poetry, Theater, Articles, and Letters) (México: Porrúa, 1949).

BIBLIOGRAPHY: Carlos G. Amezaga, *Poetas mexicanos* (Buenos Aires: Pablo E. Coni and Sons, 1896). Joaquín Blanco, *Crónica de la poesía mexicana* (México: Libro de Bolsillo, 1983), pp. 26, 32, 33, 34. Martha Cándano, *Manuel Acuña* (Puebla: Ediciones de la Bohemia Poblana, 1955). Francisco Castillo Nájera, *Manuel Acuña* (México: Imp. Universitaria, 1950). José Castillo y Piña, *Mis recuerdos* (México: Castillo y Piña, 1941), pp. 224-35, 246-50. Frank Dauster, *Breve historia de la poesía mexicana* (México: Porrúa, 1972), vol. 2, pp. 80, 90, 108, 190. Salvador González Lobo, *Inspiración y muerte de Manuel Acuña*, Colección de Escritores Coahuilenses No. 5 (Saltillo: Eds. A.E.P.S., 1957). Carlos González Peña, *History of Mexican Literature* (Dallas: Southern Methodist University Press, 1968), pp. 202, 211, 261, 267, 272, 277-79, 391. Ernest S. Green, *Mexican and South American Poems* (New York: Gordon Press, 1977), pp. 73-78. Sergio Howland Bustamante, *Historia de la literatura mexicana* (México: F. Trillas, 1967), pp. 169, 183, 184. José López Portillo y Rojas, *Rosario, la de Acuña* (México: Librería Española, 1920). Armando de María y Campos, *Manuel Acuña en su teatro* (México: Compañía de Editores Populares, 1952). Roberto Núñez y Domínguez, *Cincuenta close-ups* (México: Botas, 1935), pp. 239-48. Aurora M. Ocampo de Gómez and Ernesto Prado Velázquez, *Diccionario de escritores mexicanos* (México: UNAM, 1967), pp. 4-5. Enrique de Olavarría y Ferrari, *Colección de los mejores autores: tomo XLV, poesías líricas mexicanas* (Madrid: Biblioteca Universal, 1878), pp. 119-22. José Emilio Pacheco, *La poesía mexicana del siglo XIX* (México: Empresas Editoriales, 1965), pp. 259-66. Agustín del Saz, *Antología general de la poesía mexicana* (Barcelona: Bruguera, 1972), pp. 109-17.

PATRICIA HART AND JOSEF HELLEBRANDT

AGRAZ García de Alba, Gabriel (1926-). He was born on March 23 March in Tecolotlán, Jalisco. In his early years he taught himself the history of Mexico and concentrated his studies on the history of his state, Jalisco. In 1956 he founded the newspaper *Ecos de provincia* in his hometown and was editor until 1958. In 1959 he founded in Guadalajara the Institute for Historical Research, which he directed until 1965. Under the auspices of the National University of Mexico he has prepared several bibliographical studies on Jaliscan authors.

WORKS: *Esbozos históricos de Tecolotlán (Jalisco)* (Historical Essays about Tecolotlán) (Guadalajara: El estudiante, 1950). *Jalisco y sus hombres. Compendio de*

Geografía, Historia y Biografías Jalicienses Jalisco and its men. Geography, History, and Biographies from Jalisco) (Guadalajara: Talls. Lin. Vera y Carrilo, 1958). *Jalisco a la vanguardia* (Jalisco in the Forefront) (Guadalajara: Departamento de Investigaciones Históricas de Tequila Sauza, 1966). *Bibliografía de los escritores de Jalisco* (Bibliography of Jaliscan Writers) (México: UNAM, 1980). *Bibliografía general de don José María Vigil* (General Bibliography of José María Vigil) (México: UNAM, 1981).

BIBLIOGRAPHY: Guadalupe Appendini, "340 escritores jaliscienses en el libro de Gabriel Agraz García de Alba," *Excelsior* (July 27, 1980): 1B-6B.

                                                                    . ELADIO CORTES

AGUAYO, Miguel (1934-). He was born in Mexico City but moved to Guadalajara, where he attended the Fine Arts School and became a painter. He has exhibited in many cities throughout the country. He has written novels and poetry and also has contributed to the journal *Abside*.

WORKS: *Cantares de sed* (Thirsty Songs) (México: Abside, 1964). *Los signos del silencio* (Signs of Silence) (México: Ed. Jus, 1967). *Trigo verde* (Green Wheat) (México: Jus, 1974). *Juego de espejos* (Game of Mirrors) (México: Jus, 1974). "El juego" *Abside* 1 (Jan.-Mar. 1978): 88.

BIBLIOGRAPHY: Heriberto García Rivas, *Historia de la literatura mexicana*, vol. 4 (México: Porrúa, 1974), pp. 364-65.

                                                                    MICHELE MUNCY

AGÜEROS, Victoriano (1854-1911), journalist and editor of the Biblioteca de Autores Mexicanos (Library of Mexican Authors). He was born in Tlalchapa, Guerrero, on September 4, 1854. Agüeros went to Mexico City at age twelve, and there he received certification as a teacher in 1870 and his law degree in 1881. He began his literary career as a journalist and contributed to various newspapers using the pseudonym José. His first book, *Ensayos de José* (Essays by Joseph), was a collection of articles he had written for the newspaper *La Iberia*. Agüeros also wrote for the newspaper *El Siglo XIX*, which published his *Dos leyendas* (Two Legends) and *Confidencias y recuerdos* (Confidential Remarks and Remembrances). His series of biographical and critical studies on Mexican literary figures for the Spanish magazine *La Ilustración Española y Americana* appeared in book form as *Escritores mexicanos contemporáneos* (Contemporary Mexican Writers). He served as editor of the newspaper *El Imparcial*, and he founded and directed the Catholic newspaper *El Tiempo*. He also founded the weekly *El Tiempo Ilustrado*. Agüeros was elected a corresponding member of the Academia Mexicana de la Lengua in 1902 and a regular member in 1911. He was an official representive to the coronation of George V of Great Britain. Subsequent to attending this ceremony, he died in Paris, France, on October 8, 1911.

The massive seventy-eight volume *Biblioteca de Autores Mexicanos* (Library of Mexican Authors), which he compiled and edited between 1896 and 1911, is a major source for Mexican writing of the second half of the nineteenth century. Although the collection does not fare well when judged by contemporary standards of literary scholarship, it was, at the time it was published, an important vehicle for the propagation of Mexican letters, and it remains, without question, his principal contribution to the literary life of the country.

WORKS: *Ensayos de José* (Essays by Joseph) (México: Imp. de Ignacio Escalante, 1874). *Dos leyendas* (Two Legends) (México: Eds. del Siglo XIX, 1877). *Escritores mexicanos contemporáneos* (Contemporary Mexican Writers) (México: Imp. de Ignacio Escalante, 1880).

BIBLIOGRAPHY: *Enciclopedia de México*, vol. 1 (México: SEP, 1987), p. 213. Carlos González Peña, *History of Mexican Literature* (Dallas, Texas: Southern Methodist University Press, 1968), p. 343. Julio Jiménez Rueda, *Historia de la literatura mexicana*, 3rd ed. (México: Botas, 1942), pp. 5, 235-36. Aurora M. Ocampo de Gómez and Ernesto Prado Velázquez, *Diccionario de escritores mexicanos* (México: UNAM, 1967), pp. 5-6. Alfonso Reyes, *Obras completas*, vol. 1 (México: FCE, 1955), pp. 283-89.

MELVIN S. ARRINGTON, JR.

AGUILAR, José Antonio (1943-). Born in Mexico City, Aguilar studied business administration and Spanish literature at the UNAM. After attending a short story workshop directed by the famous Julieta *Campos, he won the first prize in a short story contest from the magazine *Punto de Partida* for his "Juliano soñaba todas las noches" (Juliano dreamed every night). Besides his literary publications he has written business administration books. He also has been teaching at the National University.

His novel *El tiempo de Dios* is a profound study of the life of three generations of a family in Tabasco and their transformation from a rural setting to working in the oil industry.

WORKS: *Marina* (México: Eds. La Bolsa y la Vida, 1981). *El tiempo de Dios* (God's Time) (México: Ed. Terra Nova, 1982).

BIBLIOGRAPHY: Juana Armada Alegría, "*El tiempo de Dios*." in *El Heraldo Cultural* 894 (Jan. 2, 1983): 8. Raquel Díaz de León, "Remembranzas y malicia en la obra literaria de José Antonio Aguilar" (Review of *Marina*) *Excelsior* (Dec. 12, 1982): 17B, 22B. Agustín Monsreal, (Review of *El tiempo de Dios*) *Excelsior* (Oct. 30, 1982): 1 (Cult. Section).

ELADIO CORTES

AGUILAR Camín, Héctor (1946-). Novelist and political analyst, Aguilar Camín was born in Chetumal, Quintana Roo. He contributes to different journals such as *Unomasuno, La jornada semanal*, and *Nexos*, of which he is assistant director. His works, specially his political essays, deal mainly with social problems, class differences, and morals of the upper stratum of society.

WORKS: *La frontera nómada. Sonora y la Revolución mexicana* (The Nomad Fontier. Sonora and the Mexican Revolution) (México: Siglo XXI, 1977). *Con el filtro azul* (With a Blue Filter) (México: Premiá, 1979). *La decadencia del dragón* (The Dragon's Decline) (México: Océano, 1983). *Saldos de la Revolución (1910-1980)* (Revolution Results [1910-1980]) (México: Nueva Imagen, 1982). *Cuando los banqueros se van* (When the Banquers Leave) (México: Océano, 1982). Translation of Douglas Day's *Malcolm Lowry* (México: FCE, 1983).

BIBLIOGRAPHY: José Joaquín Blanco, "*La decadencia del dragón*," in *El Gallo Ilustrado* 1103 (Aug. 14, 1983): 15. Carlos Monsiváis, *Antología de la crónica en México* (México: UNAM, 1979), p. 182. José Emilio Pacheco, "Alvaro Obregón (1880-1928)," (Review of *La frontera nómada...*) in *Proceso* 174 (Mar. 3, 1980): 48-49.

ELADIO CORTES

AGUILAR Mora, Jorge (1946-   ), novelist, translator, critic, and poet, born in Chihuahua on January 9. After attending the University of México, where he obtained a degree in literature in 1974, he studied in Paris, and then back in his country, he earned a doctorate at the Colegio de México. Aguilar Mora belongs to the so-called Tlatelolco generation, and many of his works reflect that Mexican tragedy. He has taught literature at several institutions of higher learning and has contributed to *Revista de la Universidad de México* and *La cultura en México*.

The deep feelings of the students' revolution that ended in the "Plaza de las tres culturas" are portrayed in *Si muero lejos de ti*, in which the author studies the lives of the people that survived the events of Tlatelolco.

WORKS: Essays: *El texto de un juicio* (Text of a Hearing) (México: UNAM, 1974). *La divina pareja: historia y mito en Octavio Paz* (The Divine Couple: History and Myth in Octavio Paz) (México: Era, 1978). *Tránsito del cuerpo* (Body Transit) (México: La Máquina de Escribir, 1978). Novels: *Cadaver lleno de mundo* (Cadaver Full of People) (México: Mortiz, 1971). "Yoris y la prisionera de Amberes" (Frag.) in Margo Glantz, *Onda y escritura en México* (México: Siglo XXI, 1971), pp. 47-78. *Si muero lejos de tí* (If I Die Far Away from You) (México: Mortiz, 1979). "Don Juan" (Frag.) in Angel Rama, *Novísimos narradores hispanoamericanos en marcha. 1964-1980* (México: Marcha Eds. 1981), pp. 258-69. Poetry: *U.S. Postage Air Mail Special Delivery* (México: La máquina de Escribir, 1977). *No hay otro cuerpo* (There Is No Other Body) (México: Mortiz, 1978).

BIBLIOGRAPHY: Anon., "*Cadaver lleno de mundo*" in *La Cultura en México* 508 (Nov. 3, 1971); xii; "*U.S. Postage Air Mail. . .* in *Cambio* 8 (July-Sept. 1977); vii; also in *El Gallo Ilustrado* 797 (Oct. 2, 1977); p. 16; "*No hay otro cuerpo*" in *Cambio* 9 (Oct.-Dec. 1977); x. John S. Brushwood, *México en su novela* (México: FCE, 1973), pp. 125, 127-29. Emilio García Riera, *Historia Documental del cine mexicano* (México: Era, 1969), vol. 9, pp. 23, 159. Heriberto García Rivas, *Historia de la literatura mexicana* (México: Porrúa, 1971-1974), vol. 4, p. 541. Margo Glantz, *Onda y Escritura de México* (México: Siglo XXI, 1971), pp. 5-41, 42. Enrique Jaramillo Levi, *Poesía Erótica, 1889-1980* (México: Eds. Domés, 1982), vol. 2, p. 230. Elena Poniatowska, "Habla Jorge Aguilar Mora: Me da envidia el autor de un libro bien escrito" in *La Cultura en México* 525 (Mar. 1, 1972); vi-xix.

MICHELE MUNCY

AGUILERA Díaz, Gaspar (1947-), poet. Born in Parral, Chihuahua, Aguilera Diaz founded the literary workshop Pireni, where many youngsters developed their first writing abilities. He has received several poetry prizes. After teaching literature in Morelia, he became director of cultural activities at the University of San Nicolás. His poetic works, a combination of erotic and metaphoric elements, present a contradictory exposition of views of life.

WORKS: Poetry: *Informe de labores 1978* (Labor information 1978) (México: UNAM, 1981). *Pirénico* (Morelia: Int. Mich. de Cult., 1982). *Los siete deseos capitales* (The Seven Deadly Desires) (Morelia: Inst. Mich. de Cult., 1982). "Poemas" in *Plural* 147 (Dec. 1983): 48-49. *Zona de Derrumbe* (Distress Zone) (México: Katún, 1984).

BIBLIOGRAPHY: Anon., "La poesía debe hablar de todo lo que ocurre al escritor: Gaspar Aguilera Díaz" in *El Heraldo* (June 19, 1983); 11C. Saul Ibargoyen, "Poemario de Gaspar Aguilar Díaz" in *Excelsior* (June 13, 1981); 1C. Federico Patán, "*Zona de Derrumbe*, de Gaspar Aguilera Díaz" in *Sábado* 395 (May 11, 1985): 13.

MICHELE MUNCY

AGUILERA Malta, Demetrio (1909-1981), poet, short story writer, novelist, essayist, critic, journalist. Born in Ecuador, and married to the Mexican writer and journalist Velia Márquez, he has lived in Mexico since 1958. A law school graduate of the Universidad de Guayaquil, he held diplomatic positions in Ecuador, Brazil, and Chile. He was also undersecretary in the Ministry of Education in Ecuador, a director of the Quito Museum, and a film producer. He published extensively in newspapers, magazines, and journals in Latin America and the United States and with his wife produced several movies, among them *Cadena infinita* (Infinite Chain).

A member of the Guayaquil Group, he initiated a movement toward social and political realism. Fernando Alegría says he is a forerunner of *magical realism.

WORKS: Poetry: *El libro de los mangleros* (The Book of the Mangove People) (Guayaquil: published by author, 1929). *Primavera interior* (Interior Spring) (Guayaquil: Imp. de la Sociedad Filantrópica de Guayas, 1927). Narrative: *Los que se van, cuentos del Cholo y del Montuvio* (Those Who Leave, Stories of the Cholo and the Montuvio) (Ecuador: Gallegos y Gilbert, 1955). *Don Goyo* (Madrid: Cenit, 1933). *Canal Zone* (Chile: Ercilla, 1936); 2nd ed. (México: Eds. de Andrea, 1966; 3rd ed. (México: Mortiz, 1977). *La isla virgen* (The Virgin Island) (Guayaquil: Vera y Cía.,

1942). *Una cruz en la Sierra Maestra* (A Cross in Sierra Maestra) (Buenos Aires: Sophos, 1960). *La caballeresa del sol* (The Sun's Lady) (Madrid: Guadarrama, 1964). *El Quijote de El Dorado* (The Quixote of El Dorado) (Madrid: Guadarrama, 1964). *Siete lunas y siete serpientes* (Seven Moons and Seven Serpents) (México: FCE, 1970; Grijalbo, 1978). *El secuestro del general* (The General's Kidnapping) (México: Mortiz, 1973). *Jaguar* (México: Grijalbo, 1977). *Requiem para el diablo* (Requiem for the Devil) (México: Mortiz, 1978). *Un boleto, un sueño y diez centavos* (A Ticket, a Dream and Ten Cents) (1987). Theater: *España leal* (Loyal Spain), tragedy (México: Ministerio de Educación, 1938). *Lázaro* (Lazarus) (Guayaquil: Vicente Rocafuerte, 1940). *Sangre azul* (Blue Blood) (Guayaquil: Univ. de Guayaquil, 1944; 2nd ed. (Boston: Houghton Mifflin, 1950). *El pirata fantasma* (The Phantom Pirate) in *Dos Comedias fáciles* (Two Easy Comedies) (Boston: Houghton Mifflin, 1950). *No bastan los átomos* and *Dientes blancos* (Atoms Are Not Enough and White Teeth) (Quito: Casa de la Cultura Ecuatoriana, 1955). *El Tigre* (Quito: Casa de la Cultura Ecuatoriana, 1956); in Willis Knapp Jones, *Antología del teatro hispanoamericano* (México: Eds. de Andrea, 1958); in Carlos Solórzano, *El teatro hispanoamericano contemporáneo* (México: FCE, 1964), vol. 2. *Trilogía ecuatoriana* (Ecuadorian Trilogy) (México: Eds. de Andrea, 1959), includes *Honorarios, Dientes blancos*, and *El tigre*. *Un nuevo mar para el rey* (A New Sea for the King) (1965). *Infierno negro* (Black Inferno) (Xalapa: Univ. Veracruzana, 1967). *Una mujer para cada acto* (A Different Woman for Each Act) (1970). Teatro Completo (Complete Theater) (México: Finisterre, 1970). Essay: *Panamá; folklore* (Panamá: Star & Herald, 1930) *Leticia* (Panama: Ed. Benedetti Hnos., 1932) *Los generales de Bolívar* (Bolivar's Generals) (México: SEP, 1966). *El cuento actual latinoamericano* (Contemporary Latin American Short Story) (México: Eds. de Andrea, 1973). Films: *La cadena infinita* (The Infinite Chain) (1949). *Entre dos carnavales* (Between Two Carnivals) (1951).

BIBLIOGRAPHY: Ermilo Abreu Gómez, "Puro romanticismo," Review of *La caballeresa del sol* in *México en la Cultura* 815 (Nov. 1, 1964); 7; "Un autor y un libro," Review of *El Quijote de El Dorado* in *México en la Cultura* 824 (January 3, 1965) 8. Antonio Acevedo Escobedo, "Cardona Peña y Aguilera Malta," *El Nacional* (Feb. 14, 1965); 3, 8. Fernando Alegría, *Historia de la novela hispanoamericana* (México: Eds. de Andrea, 1965), pp. 261-62, 266-67. Richard E. Allen, "La obra literaria de Demetrio Aguilera Malta," *Mundo Nuevo* (Paris) 41 (1969); 52-62. Enrique Anderson Imbert, *Historia de la literatura hispanoamericana* (México: FCE, 1964), vol. 2, pp. 249, 251-52. Guiseppe Bellini, *Magia e realta nella narrativa di Demetrio Aguilera Malta* (Milan: Cisalpino-Goliardico, 1972). José María Benítez, Review of *La caballeresa del sol* in *Revista Mexicana de Cultura* 916 (Oct. 18, 1964); 15. Jorge Campos, "Demetrio Aguilera Malta y su saga mágica," *Insula* (Madrid) 27 (1972): 11, 15. E. D. A., "La epopeya de América en las novelas de Aguilera Malta," *El Gallo Ilustrado* 120 (Oct. 11, 1964); 4. Horacio Espinosa Altamirano, "Aguilera Malta, un hispanoamericano de pie," *México en la Cultura* 929 (Jan. 17, 1965); 5. Anthony Fama, "Compromiso y magia en la prosa de Demetrio Aguilera-Malta," *DAI* 37 (1976): 5160A (SUNY-Buffalo). Renan Flores Jaramillo, "Demetrio Aguilera Malta," *Cuadernos Hispanoamericanos* (Madrid) 348 (1979): 623-38. Lynn Carbon Gorell, "Demetrio Aguilera Malta (1909-1981)," *Latin American Theatre Review*, 2. Michael H. Handelsman, "El secuestro el general, El pueblo soy yo y la desmitificacion del caudillo," *Revista Interamericana* (San Juan) 2 (1980): 135-42.

Andrés Henestrosa, "La nota cultural," *El Nacional* (March 1, 1966); 3, 8; "La nota cultural," review of *Canal Zone* in *El Nacional* (Sept. 3, 1966) 3. Willis Knapp Jones, *Breve historia del teatro latinoamericano* (México: Eds. de Andrea, 1956), pp. 123-24, 195. Luis Leal, *Historia del cuento hispanoamericano* (México: Eds. de Andrea, 1966), p. 103. Gerardo A. Luzuriaga, "Demetrio Aguilera Malta dramaturgo," *DAI* 30 (1969): 3948A (University of Iowa), 1969; *Del realismo al expresionsimo: El teatro en America Latina* (Madrid: Plaza Mayor, 1971). William W. Megenney, "Problemas raciales y culturales en dos piezas de Demetrio Aguilera Malta," *Cuadernos Americanos* 176 (1971); 221-28. Seymour Menton, *El cuento hispanoamericano* (México: FCE, 1964), vol. 2, pp. 67, 69-70. Marta Morello-Frosch, "El realismo integrador de *Siete lunas y siete serpientes* de Demetrio Aguilera Malta," Festschrift article in *AN* 77-2-106 (1977): 387-92. Margaret Sayers Peden, "Aguilera Malta's Seven Serpents and Seven Moons," *Translation Review* (Richardson, Texas) 5 (1980): 37-41. Elide Pittarello, "Conversando con Demetrio Aguilera Malta," *Studi di Letteratura Ispano-Americana* (Milan) 12 (1982): 31-47. Clementine Christos Rabassa, "Demetrio Aguilera-Malta and Epic Tradition," *DAI* 34 (1970): 6603A (Columbia University); 2nd ed., *Demetrio Aguilera Malta and Social Justice: the Tertiary Phase of Epic Tradition in Latin American Literature* (Rutherford, N.J.: Fairleigh Dickinson University Press, 1980). Salvador Reyes Nevares, "Los episodios americanos de Aguilera Malta," *La cultura en México* 143 (Nov. 11, 1964); xix. Angel F. Rojas, *La novela ecuatoriana* (México, 1948). Gustavo Sáinz, "Escaparate de libros," review of *La caballeresa del sol* in *México en la Cultura* 809 (Sept. 20, 1964) 7. Mauricio de la Selva, "Demetrio Aguilera Malta" in *Diálogos con América* (México: Cuadernos Americanos, 1964), pp. 11-17. William L. Siemens, "The Antichrist-Figure in Three Latin American Novels," in *The Power of Myth in Literature and Film*, edited by Victor Carrabino (Tallahassee: University Presses of Florida, 1980). Carlos Solórzano, *El teatro hispanoamericano contemporáneo*, Antología, vol. 2 (México: FCE, 1964), p. 7.

DELIA GALVAN

AGUIRRE, Manuel J. (1893-1978). He was born on June 17, 1893, in Teoctiche, Jalisco, and lived in the area until he died in Guadalajara in November 1978. He attended school in his native village, then joining the "Partido Antirreeleccionista" of his local garrison. By age nineteen, he was already hard at work with the newspaper *El Regional* of Guadalajara, later adding the two papers *El Pueblo* and *El Demócrata*. He published *El Mensajero* in 1919, a newspaper focusing on revolutionary matters. *El Nacional Revolucionario* acquired him as a correspondent in 1929, a post he held for many years. He edited other papers as well, including *La Revanc* in Coahuila (1920-1921) and *El Jalisciense* (1932-1939). Until his death, he wrote weekly for *El Occidental* of Guadalajara and for the magazine *México Gráfico* of Mexico City.

A distinguished writer and a journalist of the revolution, Aguirre was interested in portraying in his articles the history, customs, and traditions of his native state. After careful and detailed research, he published the historical novel *Guadalajara, la ciudad errante* (Guadalajara, the Errant City), which earned him a gold medal, a special certificate, and honors. Although most of his publications were the many thousands of articles and essays he wrote for newspapers and journals, he did publish separately several books, including a volume of poetry, a play, two novels, and some essays.

WORKS: Essay: *Cananea, las garras del imperialismo en las entrañas de México* (Cananea, the Claws of Imperialism in the Bowels of Mexico) (México: Costa-Amic, 1958). José G. Zuno, *Un cura, un obispo y un virrey* (A Priest, a Bishop and a Viceroy), "Hombres de Jalisco: La personalidad polifacética del licenciado JGZ" (Men of Jalisco: The Many-Faceted Personality of the Lawyer JGZ), by Manuel J. Aguirre, Guadalajara, 1962, pp. 9-15. *Morelos, el inconmensurable* (Morelos, the Incommensurable) (Guadalajara: Eds. El Estudiante, 1965). Silvano Barba González, *Licenciado y General don Pedro Ogazón* (Lawyer and General don Pedro Ogazón), prologue by MJA (n.p.: Manuel Casa Impresor, 1967), pp. 11-17. *Mezcala. La isla indómita* (Mezcala. The Indomitable Island) (Guadalajara: n.p., 1970). *Ensayo histórico de Teocaltiche* (Historical Essay about Teocaltiche) (México: Costa-Amic, 1971). Novel: *Alma campera* (Country Soul) (México: Imp. de J. Jesús Covarrubias, 1940). *Guadalajara, la ciudad errante* (Guadalajara, the Errant City) (Guadalajara: n.p., 1951). Poetry: *Teocaltiche en mi recuerdo* (Teocaltiche in My Memory) (México: Costa-Amic, 1958). Theater: *Honra a tu madre* (Honor Your Mother) (Guadalajara, 1935).

BIBLIOGRAPHY: Pedro María Anaya Ibarra, "*Guadalajara, la ciudad errante*" in *El Nacional* (May 31, 1952). Alfonso Manuel Castañeda, presentation to *Ensayo histórico de Teocaltiche* (México: Costa Amic, 1971), p. 9. Juan N. Chávarri, prologue to *Cananea, las garras del imperialismo en las entrañas de México* (México: Costa-Amic, 1958), p. 509. Andrés Henestrosa, Review of *Cananea* in *El Nacional* (May 31, 1952). Guillermo de Luzuriaga, prologue to *Alma campera* (México: Imp. de J. Jesús Covarrubias, 1940), pp. vii-ix. Angel Moreno Ochoa, *Semblanzas revolucionarias* (Guadalajara, n.p., 1965), pp. 247-75. Luis Páez Brotchie, prologue to *Guadalajara* (Guadalajara: n.p., 1951), pp. 7-8. Jesús Romero Flores, *Maestro y amigos* (México: Costa-Amic, 1972), pp. 399-402. Felipe Sevilla del Río, prologue to *Teocaltiche en mi recuerdo* (México: Costa-Amic, 1958), pp. 7-8. José Guadalupe, Zuno, prologue to *Mezcala* (Guadalajara: n.p., 1970).

MICHELE MUNCY

AGUSTIN, José (1944-   ). Born José Agustín Ramírez on August 19, 1944, in Acapulco, Guerrero, he calls himself simply José Agustín. One of Mexico's most prolific and well-known writers today, Agustín studied at UNAM, then received a scholarship from the Centro Mexicano de Escritores in 1967. He also received one from the Guggenheim Foundation in 1977, and he was awarded a Fulbright in 1978.

He began his writing career with the publication of a novel, *La tumba* (The Tomb), in 1964, the "revelations of an adolescent." This was followed shortly thereafter with *De perfil* (From the Side). His play *Círculo vicioso* (Vicious Circle) (1974) won the prestigious Premio Juan Ruiz de Alarcón. One of his novels, *Ciudades desiertas* (Deserted Cities), won the Premio Colina in 1982. In addition to his theater and fiction, he has written essays such as *La nueva música clásica* (The New Classical Music) (1985) and an autobiography, *El rock de la cárcel* (The Rock of the Jail), also in 1985.

José Agustín lives the urban reality that he creates in most of his works. He breathes the atmosphere of the city, and is one of the leaders of the Onda, the youth movement, with its emphasis on rock music. He grew up during the Vietnam era, the time of the "flower children," the time of student protests, culminating in Tlatetolco in 1968. The Onda characteristics include drugs, violence, conflict, and corruption. The characters he creates often portray the generation of youth who live this type of reality. The language he uses, the situations he invents, and the techniques he employs all make most of his work easy to place chronologically.

José Agustín has been employed as a university professor, journalist, television commentator, dramatist, theater director, and song writer. He continues to write, to publish, and to produce intellectually stimulating and thought-provoking works.

WORKS: *La tumba* (The Tomb) (México: Eds. Mester, 1964); 2nd ed., enlarged (México: Edit. Novaro, 1966). *De perfil* (Profile) (México: Mortiz, 1966). *José Agustín*, prologue, Emmanuel Carballo (México: Empresas Editoriales, 1966). "Epílogo" in José Revueltas, *Obra literaria* (México: Empresas Editoriales, 1967), vol. 2, pp. 631-48. *Inventando que sueño* (Inventing That I Dream) (México: Mortiz, 1968). *Abolición de la propiedad* (Abolition of Property) (México: Mortiz, 1969). *Se está haciendo tarde: final en laguna* (It's Getting Late: Ending in a Lagoon) (México: Mortiz, 1973). *Círculo vicioso* (Vicious Circle), play (México: Mortiz, 1974). "Cuál es la onda," in *Diálogos* 55 (1974): 11-13. "*El luto humano*," in *Revista de Bellas Artes* 29 (1976): 61-64. *La mirada en el centro* (The Look in the Center) (México: Mortiz, 1977). "Quién soy, dónde estoy, qué me dieron," in his *La mirada en el centro* (México: Mortiz, 1977), pp. 13-59. *El rey se acerca a su templo* (The King Approaches His Temple) (México: Editorial Grijalbo, 1978). *Literature and Censorship in Latin America Today: Dream within a Dream*, edited by John Kirk and Don Schmidt (Denver: University of Denver, 1978). *Ciudades desiertas* (Deserted Cities) (México: Editorial Diana & Edivisión, 1982). *Ahí viene la plaga* (Here Comes the Plague), with José Buil and Gerardo Pardo (México: Mortiz, 1985). *Furor matutino* (Morning Fury) (México: Editorial Diana, 1985). *El rock de la cárcel* (The Rock of the Jail) (México: Editores Mexicanos Unidos, 1986). *Onda and Beyond*, edited by June C.D. Carter and Donald L. Schmidt (Columbia: University of Missouri Press, 1986).

BIBLIOGRAPHY: René Avilés Fabila, "Diálogo con José Agustín," in *La Cultura en México* 247 (Nov. 9, 1966): iv-vii. Héctor Gally, "José Agustín y los jóvenes de hoy," in *Ovaciones* 246, (Oct. 9, 1966): 3. Scott Hadley, "José Agustín y el lenguage coloquial literario: Una entrevista," in *Chasqui* 17, 2 (Nov. 1988): 75-82. John M. Kirk and Donald Schmidt, "José Agustín habla sobre la literatura latinoamericana," in *Chasqui* 9, 2-3 (Feb.-May, 1980): 65-70. Walter M. Langford, "José Agustín (1944)" in *The Mexican Novel Comes of Age* (Notre Dame, Ind.: University of Notre Dame Press, 1971), pp. 200-203. Francisco Pabón, "El viaje de José Agustín," in *Revista de Bellas Artes* 22 (1968): 60-61. Juan Tovar, "*Inventando que sueño*, de José Agustín," in *Revista de Bellas Artes* 22 (1968): 59-60. John H. Turner, "Se está haciendo tarde," in *Chasqui* 3, 3 (1974): 71-73. Ramón Xirau, "José Agustín, Navarreta, Del Paso," in *Diálogos* 14 (1967); 24-26.

ELADIO CORTES

AHUMADA, Herminio (1899-1983). Born on October 7, 1899, in Soyapa, Sonora, Herminio Ahumada started school in Hermosillo and went to grammar school in

Nogales. In Mexico City he studied in several settings, including the Free Law School
and the School of Law and Social Science. He took an early interest in politics,
becoming involved while still a student. The Sorbonne in France offered him a
unique opportunity to study international law and advanced sociology (1930-1931).
Sometime after the completion of his university studies, Ahumada accompanied José
*Vasconcelos, his mentor, during his five-year exile in Europe and South America.
Having returned to Mexico, Ahumada cofounded the University of Sonora in 1938.
An educator and politician, he filled many different posts in his lifetime. He served
the state of Sonora in the justice department and even made an unsuccessful bid to
be governor of that state. For a time, he was the president of the Congress of the
Union. His literary works are gathered in a volume entitled *Memoranda de Herminio
Ahumada*. He died in Mexico City on July 1, 1983.

   Most of his essays are dedicated to Vasconcelos; he does, however, have a number
of other outstanding narrative pieces which illustrate his abilities as a very prestigious
educator, writer, and citizen. He also translated from English a Langston Hughes
piece, "Yo soy también América" (I Am Also America) written in homage to Martin
Luther King, Jr. He also wrote several poems.

WORKS: Essays: *Fundamentos sociológicos de la raza, José Vasconcelos, Vasconcelos
poeta; Epistolario de José Vasconcelos* (México: Cuadernos de HA, 1959?). Poetry:
Tamiahua (México: Imp. Juan Pablos, 1952). *Pax Animae* (1954), *Sombra fiel*
(Faithful Shadow) (México: Imp. Taia, 1954). *El mundo acabará en lágrimas* (The
World Will End in Tears), in memory of Vasconcelos (México: Rabasa, 1964).
Cantares de San Miguel (Songs of St. Michael) (México: Finisterre, 1967). Translation:
Langston Hughes, *Yo también soy América* (I Am Also America) (homage to Martin
Luther King, Jr.) (México: Novaro, 1968).

BIBLIOGRAPHY: Guadalupe Appendini, "Por su valentía fue depuesto como
presidente del Congreso de la Unión el licenciado Herminio Ahumada," in *Excelsior*
(July 6, 1983). Esteban Durán Rosado, "San Miguel Allende en la poesía," review of
Cantares de San Miguel in *El Nacional* (Jan. 1969): 15; "Los restos de Herminio
Ahumada descansan en la Universidad sonorense que él fundó," in *Excelsior* (March
18, 1985). Ernesto Mejía Sánchez "Pellicer y Ahumada," in *Novedades* (Jan. 24, 1969):
5. Francisco Zendejas, "Yet...," Review of *Cantares de San Miguel* in *Excelsior* (Jan.
28, 1968): 1C, 5C.

                                                                MICHELE MUNCY

ALAMAN, Lucas (1792-1853), historian and politician. One of the most revealing,
public figures from the first half of the nineteenth century, he was considered the
leader of the Conservative party and the initiator of the industrialization project at
that time. Born in Guanajuato, October 18, 1792, he studied chemistry and
mineralogy at the Real Seminario de Minería. Later, he moved to Europe, living in
Freiberg and Gottinga, Germany, where he continued to learn about mining. After
that, he studied chemistry and natural science in Paris. From a very young age he was
interested in politics, later holding several public offices. He concentrated his efforts
to achieve economic progress in Mexico by organizing the Bank of Avío, by creating

textile industries in Celaya and Orizaba, by improving cattle raising, and by founding schools for the arts and agriculture. His most outstanding contribution was as minister of foreign relations. He worked to establish a political alliance among Latin American nations as a defense against U.S. expansion. In addition, he founded the General Record of the Nation, the Museum of Antiquities, and the Museum of Natural History. He died in Mexico City, June 2, 1853. His position and political ideology are reflected in his written work, in which he defined his conservative, monarchical ideas. He worked on behalf of the nation in its attempt to restore the power it had in colonial times, especially in the mining industry. He labored to promote new, profitable activities such as the textile industry. In addition to many articles, official reports and specific studies, he left two fundamental works to enhance the unsderstanding of the nation's historical process, which were published in the well-known newspaper *México Independiente*: "Disertaciones sobre la historia de la República Mexicana" (Dissertations on the History of the Mexican Republic) and his "Historia de México" (History of Mexico).

WORKS: *Disertaciones sobre la historia de la República Mexicana desde la época de la Conquista que los españoles hicieron a fines del siglo XV y principios del siglo XVI de las islas y continente americano hasta la independencia* (Dissertation on the History of the Mexican Republic from the Time of the Conquest, which the Spaniards Did at the End of the Fifteenth Century and the Beginning of the Sixteenth Century in the Islands and the American Continent until Independence) (México: Imp. of D. José Mariano Lara, 1844-1849). *Historia de México desde los primeros movimientos que prepararon su independencia en el año de 1808 hasta la época presente.* (History of Mexico from the First Movements, which Prepared its Independence in the Year 1808 until the Present Time) (México: Imp. of José Mariano Lara, 1849-1852). *Diccionario universal de historia y geografía, obra dada a luz en España por una sociedad de literatos distinguidos y refundida y aumentada considerablemente por su publicación en México con noticias históricas, geográficas, estadísticas, y biográficas sobre las Américas en general, especialmente sobre la Repúblic Mexicana,* por Lucas Alamán y otros (Universal Dictionary of History and Geography, a Work Printed in Spain by a Society of Distinguished Writers and Considerably Recast and Enlarged by its Publication in Mexico with Historical, Geographical, Statistical, and Biographical Information about the Americas in General, especially about the Mexican Republic, by Lucas Alamán and others) (México: Tip. by Rafael, 1853). *Dictamen sobre el importante ramo de la minería* (Report on the Important Branch of Mining) (s.p.i.). *Ensayo sobre las causas de la decadencia en la Nueva España* (Essay on the Causes of Decadence in New Spain) (s.p.i.).

BIBLIOGRAPHY: Lucas Alamán, *Documentos diversos inéditos y muy raros,* 4 vols. (México; Ed. Jus, 1945): *Documentos sobre historia de México, entre los años 1829 y 1852* (Austin: University of Texas, Latin American Collection, n.d.). Arturo Arnáiz y Freg, *Lucas Alamán, semblanza e ideario* (México: UNAM, 1939). Moisés González Navarro, *El pensamiento político de Lucas Alamán* (México: El Colegio de México, 1952). Alfonso López de Aparicio, *Alamán, primer economista de México* (México: Campeador, 1956). José C. Valadés, *Alamán estadistia e historiador* (México: UNAM, 1977).

CARMEN BLAZQUEZ DOMINGUEZ

ALARDIN, Carmen (1933-). A poet, she was born in Tampico, Tamaulipas, on July 5, 1933. Her early school years were spent in Nuevo León, where she earned her *bachillerato*. In Mexico City, she studied at the Instituto Francés and completed a degree in German letters in the School of Philosophy and Letters of the University.

Alardín first became known with her volume of poetry, *El canto frágil*, published in Monterrey. Three other volumes of poetry gained her a reputation as part of a Mexican group working on new poetic values. In addition to her books, she has contributed to literary journals such as *Letras Potosinas* and *Katarsis*, and to *El Nacional* and other literary supplements.

WORKS: Poetry: *El canto frágil* (The Fragile Song) (Monterrey, 1950). *Pórtico labriego* (Peasant Portal) (Monterrey: Ed. Parauque, 1953). *Celda de viento* (Cell of Wind), prologue by Tomás Díaz Bartlett (Veracruz: Edit. Veracruz, 1957). *Después del sueño* (After the Dream) (México: Cuadernos del Unicornio, 1960. *Todo se deja así* (All Remains Just So), presented by E. Abreu Gómez (México: Cuadernos del Viento, 1964).

BIBLIOGRAPHY: Ermilo Abreu Gómez, "Poesía femenina en México," in *México en la cultura* 814 (Oct. 25, 1964): 7. Huberto Batis, Review of *Todo se deja así* in *La cultura en México* 130 (Aug. 12, 1964): xviii. Alí Chumacero, Review of *Celda de viento* in *México en la cultura* 424 (May 5, 1957): 2. Tomás Díaz Bartlett, Prologue to *Celda de viento* (Veracruz: Edit. Veracruz, 1957). Aurora M. Ocampo de Gómez and Ernesto Prado Velázquez, *Diccionario de escritores mexicanos* (México: UNAM, 1967), p. 7.

                                                                    YOLANDA S. BROAD

ALATORRE, Antonio (1922-), educator, philologist, and essayist born in Autlin, Jalisco. Alatorre studied at the National University and at the Colegio de México. He has taught at the National University and the Colegio de México, among other institutions. Since 1953 Alatorre has served as secretary and director of the *Nueva Revista de Filología Hispánica*. He became director of the Centro de Estudios Linguísticos y Literarios of the Colegio de México in 1964.

WORKS: *Las Heroidas de Ovidio y su huella en las letras españolas* (México: Imp. Universitaria, 1950). "Los romances de Hero y Leandr," in *Libro jubilar de Alfonso Reyes* (México: UNAM, 1956), pp. 1-41. "Para la historia de un problema: La mexicanidad de Juan Ruiz de Alarcón" (The History of a Problem: The Mexicanity of Juan Ruiz de Alarcón) in *Anuario de Letras* (México: UNAM, 1964). "Avatares barrocos del romance: De Góngora a Sor Juana Inés de la Cruz" (The Baroque Avatars of the 'Romance': From Góngora to Sor Juana Inés de la Cruz) in *Nueva Revista de Filología Hispánica* 26 (1977): 341-459. *Los 1001 años de la lengua española* (The 1001 Years of the Spanish Language) (México: Bancomer, 1980).

BIBLIOGRAPHY: C. W. Atkinson, "Los romances de Hero y Leandro, *Modern Language Review* 53 (1958): 602-3. Gabriel Zaid, Review of "Los 1001 años," *Vuelta* 46 (1980): 38-39.

                                                                    ALFONSO GONZALEZ

ALATRISTE, Sealtiel (1949-   ). He was born in Mexico City on July 15, 1949. He received his primary and secondary instruction in Mexico and graduated from UNAM with a B.A. in business administration, granted by the School of Commerce in 1973, and a B.A. in Spanish letters, also in 1973, granted by the School of Philosophy and Letters. He went to England shortly thereafter, where he received a diploma in Latin American studies from Cambridge in 1976. In 1977, he became the business manager of the publishing house Nueva Imagen, a position he held until 1984. He is currently the coordinator for the institute for Hellenic studies, Difusión Cultural del Instituto Cultural Heléneco.

Although he has published several essays and other articles in area journals, Alatriste is most recognized in the literary field for his two novels, both of which give testimony to his love for the cinema. The first, entitled *Dreamfield*, is about a man who lives between reality and fantasy, unable to separate himself totally from his passion for the Hollywood-style motion picture. The man's actual reality, his dream life, and the cinema all get intermingled.

In his second work, *Por vivir en quinto patio* (By Living on the Fifth Patio), Alatriste creates a dependent character who relies heavily on the National Cinema and on Romantic Mexican songs of the 1940s. Exploring the intimate world of the middle-class protagonist in detail, the author provides a portrait of the typical Mexican of that class.

WORKS: Novel: *Dreamfield* (México: Nueva Imagen, 1981). *Por vivir en quinto patio* (By Living on the Fifth Patio) (México: Mortiz, 1985). Essays: "El desfile del amor" (The Parade of Love), in *Revista Universidad de México* 409-410 (Feb.-March 1985): 48-50. "Del carnaval al dolor. Crónica de la estética de José Chávez Morado," in *Revista Universidad de México* 416 (Sept. 1985): 25-32.

BIBLIOGRAPHY: Adolfo Martínez Solórzano, Review of "*Por vivir en quinto patio*," in *El Nacional* (Sept. 14, 1985), sec. 2, p. 7. Ariel Muñiz, "*Dreamfield*," in *Plural* 144 (Sept. 1983): 68. Saide Sesín, "*Por vivir en quinto patio*, rompe con la solemnidad de la literatura mexicana, dice Giner de los Ríos," in *Unomásuno* (Sept. 6, 1985): 20.

MICHELE MUNCY

ALBIÑANA, Asunción Izquierdo de (1914-   ), novelist. She has published under the pseudonyms Ana Mairena, Alba Sandoiz, and Pablo María Fonsalba as well as under her own name. Born in San Luis Potosí, she made her first appearance on the literary scene in 1938 with her novel *Andréida*, for which she used her own name. Her second novel, *Caos* (Chaos), was also published under her name, but for her third book, issued in 1945, she used the pseudonym Alba Sandoiz. This semi-autobiographical work presents an excellent analysis of psychological development. *Taetzani* was published one year later under the same pen-name. This was an evocation of the original inhabitants of Nayarit and their conquest by the Spaniards. For her fifth novel, *La ciudad sobre el lago* (The City on the Lake), published in 1949, she adopted the pseudonym Pablo María Fonsalba. She then published nothing until 1961, when *Los extraordinarios* (The Extraordinary Ones) was published under yet another pseudonym, Ana Mairena. This is the novel of a murder, or more exactly, of a murderer, in which the entire action takes place while the murderer is waiting for his victim. In 1964 she published a transcription of the oral traditions of the Cora Indians of western Mexico concerning the Creation of the Universe. This was issued in a bilingual edition with an English version by Elinor Randall.

WORKS: *Andréida, El tercer sexo* (Andréida, The Third Sex) (México: Botas, 1938). *Caos* (Chaos) (México: Botas, 1940). *La selva encantada* (The Enchanted Jungle) (México: Botas, 1945). *Taetzani*, Illustrated by Emilia Ortiz (México: Editorial Ideas, 1946). *La ciudad sobre el lago* (The City on the Lake) (México: 1949). *Los extraordinarios* (The Extraordinary Ones) (Barcelona: Seix-Barral, 1961). *El gran nayar* (The Great Nayar). *Majakuagymoukeia* (A transcription of Indian oral traditions according to the **Coras** tribus of Occidental Mexico), bilingual edition, English by Elinor Randall, Colección Acuario no. 1 (México: El Corno Emplumado, 1964).

BIBLIOGRAPHY: John S. Brushwood, *México en su novela* (México: FCE, 1973), pp. 81-82. Emmanuel Carballo, "La última novela de una escritora enmascarada: *Los extraordinarios*," in *México en la Cultura* 650 (Aug. 27, 1969): 2-9. Víctor Fuentes, Review of *Los extraordinarios* in Revista Hispánica Moderna 2-4 (April-Oct. 1962): 344-45. Manuel Pedro González, *Trayectoria de la novela en México* (México: Botas, 1951), pp. 339-50. Luis Leal, *Bibliografía del cuento mexicano* (México: Eds. de Andrea, 1958), p. 134. José Luis Martínez, *Literatura mexicana siglo* XX. 1910-1949 (México: Ant. Libr. Robredo, 1949), vol. 1, p. 66; vol. 2 (1950), p. 112. Aurora M. Ocampo de Gómez and Ernesto Prado Velázquez, *Diccionario de escritores mexicanos* (México: UNAM, 1967), p. 14. Lynn Ellen Rice Cortina, *Spanish-American Women Writers* (New York: Garland, 1983), p. 179.

PETER G. BROAD

ALEGRE, Francisco Javier (1729-1888). Born in Veracruz in 1729 Alegre studied rhetoric and philosophy and entered the Jesuit order at the age of seventeen. He was a professor of canon law and a historian and wrote *Historia de la Compañía de Jesús en España*. With the expulsion of the Jesuits in 1767 he went to Bologna, where this history was published. He died in Bologna in 1888 after writing eighteen books on theology published under the title *Instituciones teológicas*.

   Father Francisco Javier Alegre is considered the greatest Mexican Latinist and one of the important humanists of the eighteenth century. As well as the many treatises in Latin, he also translated some of Horace's satires and epistles and some of Nicolas Boileau's *Art of Poetry*. He is most remembered for the *Historia* mentioned earlier, which is useful for the historic data it provides, even though many believe that his descriptions are overly favorable to the Jesuit activities.

WORKS: *Historia de la Compañía de Jesús en Nueva España* (México: J.M. Lara, 1841-43). *Memorias para la historia de la provincia que tuvo la Compañía de Jesús en Nueva España* (México: Porrúa, 1940).

BIBLIOGRAPHY: Jorge García Icazbalceta, *Opúsculos inéditos, latinos y castellanos del padre Francisco Javier Alegre* (México: F. Díaz de León, 1889). Gabriel Méndez Plancarte, *Humanistas del Siglo XVIII* (México: UNAM, 1941). Bernabé Navarro, "Francisco Javier Alegre," in *Vidas de mexicanos ilustres del siglo XVIII* (México: Uñá, 1956, pp. 211-45. Víctor Ruiz González, *Historiadores mexicanos del siglo XVIII* (México: Instituto de Historia, UNAM, 1949). Arnold L. Kerson, "Francisco Javier Alegre, humanista mexicano del siglo XVIII," *Cuadernos Americanos* 160 (1968): 165-86.

ANITA K. STOLL

ALGARRA, María Luisa (1916-1957). Born in Barcelona, Spain, María Luisa Algarra was educated first at local schools, then studied at the University Autonomous of Catalonia. At age twenty she received her law degree, a rather uncommon occurrence for a woman at that time. She had already discovered, however, her true interest in the field of theater. While still in the university, she was awarded first prize in 1935 for her play *Judith*. It was performed in Barcelona in 1936. She left Spain for Mexico in 1939, at the conclusion of the Spanish Civil War. Marrying the artist José Reyes Meza, she became a naturalized Mexican citizen and lived there until her death in 1957.

Her 1944 play, *La primavera inútil* (Useless Spring), was successfully premiered by the Grupo Proa. By this time, she was fully apprised of Mexican dramatic techniques, which she incorporated in her play.

Algarra's themes and forms are more realistic than experimental. Her work was valued for its social message, expressed in a language readily understood by the audience. Although she was not very prolific, she won the Juan Ruiz de Alarcón Prize for her play *Los años de prueba* (The Testing Years). It is a work that deals with the issues faced by young people as they reconcile themselves to the society in which they live.

WORKS: *Judith*, performed in Barcelona, 1936. *La primavera inútil* (Useless Spring), performed in the Teatro del Sindicato Mexicano de Electricistas, 1944. *Casandra*, performed in the Teatro del Caballito, 1953. *Los años de prueba* (The Testing Years), in *Concurso Nacional de Teatro. Obras premiadas, 1954-1955* (México: INBA, 1956), pp. 1-105.

BIBLIOGRAPHY: *Concurso Nacional de Teatro. Obras premiadas, 1954-1955*, (México: INBA, 1956), pp. vii-viii, xi. Luisa Josefina Hernández, "Sobre María Luisa Algarra," in *México en la Cultura* 447 (Oct. 13, 1957): 8.

MICHELE MUNCY

ALMANZA, Héctor Raúl (1912-   ), diplomat, publisher, and novelist. Born August 20, 1912, in San Luis Potosí, he received a law degree from the UNAM and has held many diplomatic posts all over the world. He also published the review *El Heraldo* *del Estudiante.* All his novels deal with social and political problems of Mexico. In *Huelga blanca* (White Strike), he treats the problem of Mexican workers who cross the border into the United States looking for employment and who are exploited. In *Candelaria de los patos* (Candlemas of the Ducks), the action takes place in a barrio of that name, which is a typical slum with its consequent problems. *Brecha en la roca* (A Crack in the Rock) demonstrates the maturing of Almanza's novelistic technique as he deals with exploited workers in the oil fields of Huasteca. His most technically advanced novel, *Detrás del espejo* (Behind the Mirror), is reminiscent of Carlos *Fuentes' *La muerte de Artemio Cruz* in that each protagonist represents the cause of all the evils in contemporary Mexico: betrayal of the Revolution. In Almanza's novel we follow the life of Gabriel Sosa, who begins as a revolutionary but is gradually seduced by power and greed until he typifies the dominant, rich ruling class.

WORKS: *Huelga blanca* (White Strike) (San Luis Potosí: Academia Potosina de Artes y Ciencias, 1950). *Candelaria de los patos* (Candlemas of the Ducks) (San Luis Potosí: Academia Potosina de Artes y Ciencias, 1952). *Con polvo del camino* (With Dust from the Road), in *El Libro y el Pueblo* 7-8 (July-Aug. 1954): 83-96. *Brecha en la roca* (A Crack in the Rock) (México: Colección Ahuizote, 1955). *Pesca brava* (Brave Catch) (México: Eds. de Andrea, 1960). *Detrás del espejo* (Behind the mirror) (México: FCE, 1962).

BIBLIOGRAPHY: José Rogelio Alvarez, dir., *Enciclopedia de México* (México: SEP, 1987) vol. 1, p. 336. John S. Brushwood and José Rojas Garciadueñas, *Breve historia de la novela mexicana* (México: Eds. de Andrea, 1959), pp. 126-27. Aurora M. Ocampo de Gómez and Ernesto Prado Velázquez, *Diccionario de escritores mexicanos* (México: UNAM, 1967), pp. 9-10.

TERESA R. ARRINGTON

ALMAZAN, Pascual (1813-1886), novelist, lawyer, politician. He was born in Mexico City. He attended Colegio Carolino in Puebla. After receiving his law degree, he held several political posts. He was a representative in Puebla. He published a single historical novel under the pseudonym Natal del Palomar. He died in Puebla on October 12, 1886.

WORKS: *Un hereje y un musulmán* (A Heretic and a Muslim) (México: Luis G. Inclán, 1870).

BIBLIOGRAPHY: John S. Brushwood, *Mexico in Its Novel* (Austin: University of Texas Press, 1966), p. 100. Ralph E. Warner, *Historia de la novela mexicana en el siglo XIX* (México: Ant. Libr. Robredo, 1953).

JOSEPH VELEZ

ALTAMIRANO, Ignacio Manuel (1834-1893), novelist, short story writer, essayist, poet, and literary critic. A pure-blooded Indian, Ignacio Altamirano was born in the village of Tixtla (Guerrero) on November 13, 1834. Although his father was poor, illiterate, and spoke only an Indian language, he was highly respected in the village and was elected mayor soon after Ignacio's birth. In 1842, the senior Altamirano insisted that his son be allowed to attend school with the white children, and that young Ignacio learn to read Spanish. Out of respect for the mayor, the white schoolmaster agreed and, within a few years, Ignacio had established himself as an exceptionally intelligent student. In 1849, the governor of the state, in response to a request by Ignacio *Ramirez, professor of law at the Instituto Literario y Científico de Toluca, created some scholarships for Indian children who showed outstanding academic promise. Young Altamirano received one of these scholarships, and went to the Institute, where he attended classes with the sons of Mexico's richest families. He excelled in his studies of Spanish, French, Latin, and philosophy, and as a reward for his hard work, he was given a job in the Institute's library, where he was exposed to classic and contemporary European texts. His love for learning was equal only to his love for the liberal cause, a political stance which he acquired, at least in part, from his teacher, Ramírez. When political moderates gained control of the school in 1852, Ramírez, Altamirano, and other liberals were forced to leave. Altamirano joined a touring theater group, and traveled extensively throughout the Mexican provinces for two years. In 1854, he went to Mexico City to complete his studies, but politics once again intervened, and Altamirano left the Colegio de San Juan de Letrán to take part in a revolt against the dictator Santa Anna. The following year, Altamirano returned to Mexico City, where he studied law. He also taught in private schools and published articles in liberal newspapers in order to support himself while completing his studies. Altamirano received his law degree at the end of 1857, but shortly afterward, the War of the Reform broke out, and the Conservatives took control of the capital. Altamirano abandoned plans for a legal career in Mexico City and returned to Guerrero, where he fought for the liberal cause. In 1861, after the triumph of the liberals, Altamirano was elected representative to the national congress. He gained a reputation as a brilliant orator, and a staunch defender of Benito Juárez. Altamirano followed Juárez into exile when the French Intervention forced the Republicans out of the nation's capital in 1863. Not content to sit on the sidelines, Altamirano took an active part in several major battles against the French. He was named Colonel of Infantry in public recognition for his bravery in 1865. The capture and execution of the Emperor Maximillian in 1867 marked a turning point in the relationship between Altamirano and Juárez. Altamirano strongly opposed Juárez's decision to put Maximillian to death, for he felt that Maximilian had been the harmless pawn of the French. Juárez turned a deaf ear to Altamirano, which convinced Altamirano that Juárez was assuming autocratic powers. Juárez's announcement that he would put himself up for re-election in 1867 completely alienated Altamirano, and an obvious split occurred between the two. Altamirano was excluded from the circle of Juárez's advisers when the new government formed, and he was also denied the back pay due him, which brought him and his family to the point of bankruptcy.

By 1867, Altamirano had already acquired a following of younger writers who saw in him a great intellectual leader. When he founded *El Correo de México* (The Mexican Post) that year, it immediately became a vehicle for the liberal point of view. Altamirano, Ignacio Ramírez, Guillermo Prieto, Manuel Peredo, and José Tomás de Cuellar were regular contributors to the journal. Altamirano's literary salons, which also began in 1867, attracted some of the finest minds in Mexico. Justo *Sierra made his literary debut at one of Altamirano's soirees. In 1868, Altamirano's financial difficulties were temporarily assuaged when he was elected to the Supreme Court. His new position, however, did not deter him from holding his literary salons and from publishing literary criticism in *El Siglo* (The Century). In 1869, he founded the Sociedad de Autores Dramáticos (Society of Dramatic Authors) in Mexico City and reactivated the Hidalgo Lyceum, which had been founded by Francisco *Zarco Mateas a decade earlier and then abandoned. Under Altamirano's directorship, the Hidalgo Lyceum saw its greatest period of activity. He also founded the literary periodical *El Renacimiento* (The Renaissance), which, in a dramatic and revolutionary gesture, encouraged Mexican writers to put aside the political differences that had separated them for more than fifty years and to work together toward creating an authentic national literature. This journal was perhaps the most important vehicle for the literary production of Mexican writers in the second half of the nineteenth century. Altamirano, Sierra, and others founded the Sociedad de Libre Pensadores (The Society of Freethinkers) and created the society's journal, *El Libre Pensador* (The Free Thinker), in 1870. Altamirano also cofounded *El Federalista* (The Federalist) in 1871, *La Tribuna* (The Tribune) in 1875, and *La República* (The Republic) in 1880. He contributed on a regular basis to these and several other newspapers in the nation's capital. In 1871, Altamirano became secretary of the Mexican Geographical and Statistics Society. He later served as vice president of the Society and editor of its journal. In 1879, he assumed his chair as professor of the history of philosophy and eloquence at the School of Jurisprudence in Mexico City. In 1885, he set in motion plans for the Normal School of Mexico. Four years later, Altamirano was appointed consul-general to Spain. He was transferred to France in 1890, and he died at San Remo, Italy, on February 13, 1893. His ashes were placed in the Rotunda of Illustrious Men in Mexico City on the centenary of his birth.

Critics almost unanimously regard Altamirano as the greatest Mexican writer of his age. Although compared to his contemporaries he produced only a small body of work, he is one of the few nineteenth-century writers who continue to attract a large reading public today. Altamirano's prose fiction is remarkable for its self-control, its simplicity and directness of style, its concern for form, and its fine, delicate sensibility. In his works, he attempts to combine the best elements of Romanticism and Neo-Classicism, bringing the passion of the former school under the restrained control of the latter. There are also many costumbristic elements in Altamirano's work, which make it an accurate and colorful picture of the times in which he lived. In terms of literary technique, Altamirano was the first novelist in Mexico to concern himself with narrative control. His plots are carefully constructed, well proportioned, and easy to follow. His style is concise and clear. His heroes, often cast in the romantic mold, are sometimes idealized, but there is more character development in Altamirano's novels than in the works of most of his contemporaries. Altamirano felt very strongly that literature should teach the public moral values, and that it should encourage a sense of national pride. He incorporated liberal and Christian doctrines into his works, but never in a heavy-handed, didactic way. He felt that aesthetic concerns should under no circumstances be sacrificed. Altamirano strongly encouraged his contemporaries to use national material, national types, and national settings in their literature. He felt that Mexican writers should try to find a style, technique, and composition appropriate for the portrayal of Mexican reality, and that they should stop blindly following European literary trends. While he encouraged familiarity with European models, he warned of the dangers of imitation. Because he believed that art had a moral mission to guide the public in the formation of its attitudes and beliefs, and to teach patriotism and other virtues, he insisted that the novelist ground his work in material of national, not foreign, origin.

Altamirano's novel *Clemencia* (Clemency) has been praised as the best Mexican novel of its time. It was originally published in serial form in *El Renacimiento* in 1869 but, because of its immediate popularity, it was reprinted in Mexico and abroad at least seven times. The main action of Clemencia takes place during the French Intervention, and it is set primarily in the region of Guadalajara. Although historical detail abounds, it is merely the backdrop for what is, essentially, a romantic love story. Clemencia, of the title, is a sensuous, dark-haired beauty, who competes with her friend, the pale, angelic-looking Isabel, for the love of a young dandy named Enrique Flores. Enrique is an opportunistic army offer stationed in Guadalajara. He is blond, handsome, charming, and famous for his luck with women. But beneath his impressive good looks, he is a cowardly and unscrupulous liar. In contrast, his friend, Fernando Valle, is a dark, sickly, unattractive man, but a truly noble soul who turns out to be the hero of the novel. Enrique and Fernando both love Isabel, but Isabel loves only Enrique. Clemencia also loves Enrique, and the two women go to great lengths to attract the unworthy rogue. Eventually, Enrique disgraces himself in battle and, accused of treason, is sentenced to death. Fernando becomes the scapegoat, and dies in Enrique's place. Clemencia realizes at the last minute that Fernando is the better man, and she attempts to save him, but it is too late. Fernando dies, Clemencia goes into a convent, Isabel languishes in solitude, and Enrique goes on his merry way, undaunted by the experience. The story is saved from becoming a sentimental melodrama by the tone of artistic dignity that Altamirano manages to achieve throughout the work. The novel focuses on the sense of tragedy of human life, and the impossibility of human relationships. *La Navidad en las montañas* (Christmas in the Mountains) was published in 1871. It is a short novel about a traveling army officer who spends Christmas Eve in a small village in rural Mexico. It is a heart-warming portrait of life in the provinces, and it reinforces the notion that simple peasant values are the ones that give Mexico her true strength. *El Zarco* (The Blue-Eyed Bandit) was completed in 1888, but remained unpublished until 1901. It is a longer, more ambitious work than *La Navidad en las montañas*. Like *Clemencia*, it is also a historical novel, focusing on the years 1861-1863, when lawlessness and chaos reigned in the Mexican countryside, permitting the existence of large groups of roving bandits. El Zarco, of the title, is a romantic figure who captivates Manuela, a naive girl from the upper middle class. Manuela agrees to run away with El Zarco, an action that causes her mother to die of shame. Life among the bandits is not all Manuela dreamed it would be, however, and she comes to regret her rash behavior. When her lover is killed by vigilantes at the end of the novel, Manuela is left to face the cold reality that she will now become the communal property of the other bandits. Rather than accept this fate, Manuela gives into grief and dies. Despite the novel's obvious ties to Romanticism, it contains many realistic details, and deals with a social problem of some importance during the nineteenth century. Altamirano's prose style in this novel has been called "a model of elegance." Other novels by Altamirano include *Julia* (1870); *Antonia* (incomplete, published in part in 1872); *Beatriz* (incomplete, published in part in 1873-1874); and *Atenea* (incomplete, published in part in 1889).

Altamirano is also regarded as one of the major poets of nineteenth-century Mexico. He wrote his best poems early in his career, between 1854 and 1864. These include "Flor del alba" (Flower of the Dawn), "La salida de sol" (The Sunrise), "Los naranjos" (The Orange Trees), "Las amapolas" (The Poppies), and "Al Atoyac" (To the Atoyac River). They are descriptive poems, featuring the rural landscapes of Altamirano's childhood. His poems are sober in tone, harmonious in composition, and classic in style and versification, although occasional glimpses of romantic sentiment are visible.

WORKS: *Clemencia* (Clemency) (México: Tip. Literaria de Filomeno Mata, 1869; reprinted 1904, 1930, 1944, 1977). *Crónicas de la semana* (Chronicles of the Week), edited José Luis Martínez et al. (México: INBA, 1969). *Cuentos de invierno, Las tres flores* (Stories of Winter, The Three Flowers) (México: Tip. Literaria de Filomeno Mata, 1880). *La literatura nacional* (National Literature), edited by José Luis Martínez, 3 vols. (México: Porrúa, 1949). *La Navidad en las montañas* (Christmas in the Mountains) (México: Imp. de Ignacio Escalante y cía, 1871; reprinted 1917, 1948, 1966, 1972); *Obras* (Works) (México: Imp. de V. Agüeros, 1899). *Obras literarias completas* (Complete Literary Works), edited by Salvador Reyes Nevares (México: Oasis, 1959). *Obras completas* (Complete Works), edited by Moisés Ochoa Campos et al. (México: SEP, 1986). *Paisajes y leyendas, tradiciones y costumbres de México* (Landscapes and Legends, Traditions and Customs of Mexico) (México: Imp. Española, 1884; reprinted 1949). *Rimas* (Rhymes) (México: Tip. Literaria de Filomeno Mata, 1880); *El Zarco* (The Blue-Eyed Bandit) (México: J. Ballesca y cía, 1901); reprinted 1940, 1957, 1961, 1986).

BIBLIOGRAPHY: Pedro Pablo Figueroa, *Un poeta indigena* (Santiago de Chile: Imp. de B. Vicuna Mackenna, 1893). Carlos González Peña, *Historia de la literatura mexicana* (México: SEP, 1928), pp. 267-71; 311-13. Rafael Heliodoro Valle, *Bibliografía de Manuel Ignacio [sic] Altamirano* (México: Dapp, 1939). Luis Leal, *Breve historia del cuento mexicano* (México: Eds. de Andrea, 1956), pp. 52-53. Chris N. Nacci, *Ignacio Manuel Altamirano* (New York: Twayne, 1970). Moisés Ochoa Campos, *Ignacio Manuel Altamirano. El soplo de genio* (México: SEP, 1966). John Lloyd Read, *The Mexican Historical Novel* (New York: Instituto de las Españas en America, 1939), pp. 159-77. Víctor Ruiz Meza, *Altamirano* (México: Dept. de Bibliotecas, 1958). Various, *Homenaje a Ignacio M. Altamirano. Conferencias, estudios y bibliografia* (México: Imp. Universitaria, 1935). Ralph E. Warner, *Bibliografía de Ignacio Manuel Altamirano* (México: Imp. Universitaria, 1955); *Historia de la novela mexicana en el siglo XIX* (México: Imp. Universitaria, 1953).

CYNTHIA K. DUNCAN

ALTOLAGUIRRE, Manuel (1905-1959), poet, critic, and screenwriter. He was one of the editors of the journal *Litoral*. Born in Málaga, Spain on June 29, 1905, he completed law school but then pursued a career editing and publishing literary journals. He married another poet of his generation, Concha *Méndez and was also the closest friend of Emilio *Prados, another poet of the Spanish Generation of 1927. He lived in exile after the Spanish Civil War, in 1943 taking up permanent residence in Mexico, where he continued his publishing and writing. He was killed in an automobile accident while on a trip to Spain in 1959.

Altolaguirre was a key figure of the Spanish Generation of 1927; his literary journals, as well as his own considerable production, provided great impetus and cohesion to the group. *Litoral* is considered one of the finest examples of the literary production of the Generation of 1927. His greatest poetic influences are Juan Ramón Jiménez and Pedro Salinas. He considered the latter his poetic mentor. Solitude is a major theme, a characteristic he shares with Salinas and Prados. Clouds, a recurring metaphor, symbolize freedom. His poetic style is light and gentle, the final verses especially poetic. He is best known for his series *Las islas invitadas* (The Invited Islands). His most significant filmscript, which he wrote in collaboration with Juan de la *Cabada, is for Luis Buñuel's *Subida al cielo* (Highway to Heaven). Although his own poetic contributions to his generation are considerable, his primary role was that of publisher of poets.

WORKS: *Las islas invitadas* (Invited Islands) (Málaga: Imprenta Sur, 1926). *Ejemplo* (Example) (Málaga: Litoral, 1927). *Poesía (1930-31)* (Poetry) (Paris: n.p., 1931). *Un verso para una amiga* (A Poem for a Friend) (Paris: n.p., 1931). *Soledades juntas* (Solitudes Joined) (Madrid: Editorial Plutarco, 1931). *Nuevos poemas de las islas invitadas* (New Poems from the Invited Islands) (Madrid: Eds. Héroe, 1936). *La lenta libertad* (Slow Freedom) (Madrid: Eds. Héroe, 1936). *Nube temporal* (Temporary Cloud) (Havana: El Ciervo Herido, 1940). *Más poemas de las islas invitadas* (More Poems from the Invited Islands) (México: SEP, 1946). *Fin de un amor* (The End of a Love) (México: Editorial Isla, 1949). *Poemas en Amrica* (Poems in the New World) (Málaga: Imprenta Dardo, 1955). *Poesías completas 1926-1959* (Complete Works of Poetry 1926-1959) (México: FCE, 1960).

BIBLIOGRAPHY: María Luisa Alvarez Harvey, "La vida poética extraordinaria de Manuel Altolaguirre," *Cuadernos Americanos* 170, 3 (May-June 1970): 171-74. Aurora M. Ocampo de Gómez and Ernesto Prado Velázquez, *Diccionario de escritores mexicanos* (México: UNAM, 1967), p. 13. James Valender, ed., Manuel Altolaguirre, *Obras completas* (Madrid: Ediciones Istmo, 1986).

                                                                        KENNETH M. TAGGART

ALVA Ixtlixóchitl, Fernando de (1577-1648?), historian, interpreter, and statesman, was born in Mexico City. The son of a Spanish settler and an Indian noblewoman who was a descendant of the kings of Texcoco and Mexico, Alva Ixtlixóchitl distinguished himself as a student at the Colegio de Santa Cruz de Tlatelolco. He was governor of Texcoco in 1612 and of Tlamanalco in 1617. Alva Ixtlixóchitl based his accounts on several Indian codices that he owned and on testimonies he heard from his elders. He is regarded as the foremost authority of his time in the language and history of the Mexican Indians. He recorded some of the poems attributed to the legendary Mexican king-poet, Netzahualcóyotl, and to others. Alva Ixtlixóchitl has also given us a detailed account of theater in pre-Hispanic Mexico. His contribution to our understanding of life and culture in ancient Mexico is similar to the one made by Inca Garcilaso de la Vega in regard to Peru.

WORKS: *Relación histórica de la nación tolteca* (Historical Account of the Toltec Nation) (México: n.p., 1611). Also in *Obras históricas de don Fernando de Alva Ixtlixóchitl* (Historical Works of Don Fernando de Alva Ixtlixóchitl), edited by Alfredo Chavero (México: Tipografía de la Secretaría de Fomento, 1891-92); 2nd edited by J. Dávila Garibi (México: Ed. Nacional, 1952). *Historia chichimeca* (Chichimeca History) (México: n.p., 1648). Also in *Antiquities of Mexico*, edited by Lord Kingsborough. vol. 9 (London: Robert Havell, 1831, 1848); and in *Horribles crueldades de los conquistadores de México y de los indios que los auxiliaron para subyugarlos a la corona de Castilla* (The Horrible Cruelties of the Conquerors of Mexico and of the Indians That Helped Subjugate It) (México: Imp. Alejandro Valdés, 1829).

BIBLIOGRAPHY: José J. Arrom, *El teatro hispanoamericano colonial* (La Habana: Anuario Bibliográfico Cubano, 1956), pp. 16, 116. Eugene Bovan, *Documents pour servir a l'histoire du Mexique*, vol. 1 (Paris 1891). Francisco Javier Clavijero, *Historia antigua de México*, vol. 7 (México: Porrúa, 1958), p. 37. Angel María Garibay K., *Historia de la literatura náhuatl*, vol. 2 (México: Porrúa, 1954), pp.308-13.

ALFONSO GONZALEZ

ALVARADO, José (1911-1974), essayist and short story writer, born in Nuevo León. A lawyer from UNAM, a journalist interested in philosophy, art, and history, Alvarado was a follower of José *Vasconcelos, a teacher at the National Preparatory School, and a president of the Universidad de Nuevo León. He traveled to many countries and was a member of *Grupo Barandal*. A fine, evocative political writer, Alvarado published articles, essays, and short stories in *Excelsior, El Popular, El Nacional, Univesidad de México, Siempre!,* and other journals. An author of fine, keen perception in ironic style, he is strong, honest, and humorous. Considered an urban social writer within the Revolutionary ideal, he was one of the first to write on city alienation. Other themes are Mexican visions, Mexico City, history, politics, workers, peasants, books, authors, women, and characters. He is interested in creating characters. In *El personaje* (The Character), he shows developed narrative techniques. His chronicles reveal French influence and a polished style.

WORKS: Essay: "El cuento mexicano," in *Romance*, 3 (March 1, 1940): 18. Short Story: "La taberna de los musicos," in *Cuentalia* 1 (Dec. 1952): 47-50. "El acto de defuncion," in *Letras Patrias* 2, (April-June 1954): 91-100. Narrative: *Memorias de un espejo* (Memories of a Mirror) (México: Chimalistac, 1953). *El personaje* (The Character) (México: Los Presentes, 1955). *Luces de la ciudad: Antología en homenaje a José Alvarado* (City Lights: Homage Anthology to José Alvarado) (1978) was published posthumously by Raul Rangel Frías.

BIBLIOGRAPHY: Jesús Arellano, Review of *El personaje* in *Metáfora* 3 (July-August 1955). John S. Brushwood and Rojas Garcidueñas, *Breve historia* de la novela mexicana (México: Eds. de Andrea, 1959), p. 141. Gaston G. Cantu, ìeview of *El personaje* in *México en la Cultura* 24 (July 1955): 2. Henrique González Casanova, Review of *Memorias de un espejo* in *Universidad de México* 8 (1954): 30. Luis Leal,

Breve historia del cuento mexicano (México: Eds. de Andrea, 1956), p. 143. Elena Poniatowska, "Siluetas del periódico mexicano: José Alvarado, escritor político" in *Universidad de México* 5 (Jan. 1959): 14-16.

DELIA GALVAN

ALVARADO ZAVALA, José Antonio (1943-   ). He was born in Zacapu, Michoacán, on April 4, 1943. After completing his primary and secondary schooling, he attended the University of Michoacán for two years, then transferred to the School of Philosophy and Arts at UNAM. He supported himself for a while by working at the museum in Michoacán. Later, he moved to Xalapa, Veracruz, but he now resides in Morelia, Michoacán.

With regard to his literary production, Alvarado Zavala has published five volumes of poetry. In addition, he wrote the prologue for the book *Poesía joven de México* (1972). Several of his poems are published separately in individual journals and newspapers, especially in the late 1970s and early 1980s.

WORKS: Essay: *Poesía joven de México*, prologue and selection (Morelia, Michoacán: n.p., 1972). Poetry: *Habitación sin muros* (Room Without Walls) (Morelia, Michoacán: Balsal Edit., 1969). *Para la hora del té* (For Teatime) (Toluca: Casa de la Cultura del Estado de México, 1973). "La esperanza" (Hope), "¿El mundo?" (The World?), "El camino aquel" (That Road), in Raúl Arreola Cortés, *La poesía en Michoacán* (Morelia, Michoacán: n.p., 1949), pp. 544-47. *Ejercicio del sueño* (Dream Exercise) (Morelia: Gobierno del Estado, 1982). *Algo ha roto desde entonces* (Something Has Broken Since Then) (Morelia: Universidad Michoacana, 1983). *Respuesta a un interrogatorio de barandilla y otros textículos* (Answer to an Interrogation) (Morelia: Universidad Michoacana, 1984). "La noche del labrador" (The Night of the Worker), poem in *La Palabra y el Hombre* 27 (July-Sept. 1978): 54. "Debe ser noviembre" (It Must Be November), "Tu cuerpo" (Your Body), in *Plural* 130 (July 1982): 72.

BIBLIOGRAPHY: Raúl Arreola Cortés, *La poesía en Michoacán* (Morelia, Michoacán: n.p., 1949), p. 210. Raúl Hernández Vivero, "José Antonio Alvarado Zavala, un poeta joven," in *El Libro y el Pueblo* 62 (March 1970): 37-39. Francisco Prieto, "*Algo ha quedado roto desde entonces*," in *Proceso* 341 (May 16, 1983): 63.

MICHELE MUNCY

ALVAREZ, Griselda (1918-   ). Born in Guadalajara, Jalisco, on April 5, 1918, Alvarez began her sudies in Guadalajara and later obtained her teaching degree in Mexico City. Afterwards, she specialized in psychopathology at the Escuela Normal de Especialización. She was also in charge of archives at the General Hospital and chief of the Department of Social Work and Child Protection Agency beginning in 1953. She traveled extensively throughout the United States and South America.

Between 1951 and 1952, she was editor of the magazine *Acá*. Alvarez was also involved with the magazines *Revista de Revistas, Ovaciones, Excelsior, Novedades, El Rey del Hogar* and various medical journals.

Griselda Alvarez became known in 1956 with a book of love poems: *Cementerio de pájaros* (Bird Cemetery). In 1959 she published *Dos Cantos* (Two Songs) dedicated to maize and to her province. *Desierta compañía* (Deserted Friendship) (1961), her third volume, divided in two-part sonnets, explores the world and its environment and the author's preoccupation with her lonely being. Her latest works are *Letanía erótica para la paz* (Erotic Litany for Peace) (1963) and *La sombra niña* (The Sheltered Child) (1966).

WORKS: Poetry: *Cementerio de pájaros* (Bird Cemetery) (México: Cuadernos Americanos, 1956). *Dos Cantos* (Two Songs) (México: Escal, 1959). *Desierta compañía* (Deserted Friendship) (México: Ecuador, 1961). *Letanía erótica para la paz* (Erotic Litany for Peace) (México: Ecuador, 1963).

BIBLIOGRAPHY: Ma. Elvira Bermúdez, "La poesía de Griselda Alvarez" in *Nivel* 3 (March 25, 1963): 1-2. Guadalupe Dueñas, "Imaginaciones de Griselda Alvarez" in *Nivel* 3, (March 25, 1963): 2. Aurora M. Ocampo de Gómez and Ernesto Prado Velázquez, *Diccionario de escritores mexicanos* (México: UNAM, 1967), p. 15.

MIRTA BARREA-MARLYS

ALVAREZ Acosta, Miguel (1907-). Alvarez Acosta was born in the city of San Luis Potosí on September 29, 1907, and attended school there. He has been a director of primary and normal schools, a professor of sociology, civics, history and political economy, and secretary general of the Teachers' Union. The recipient of a law degree, he has served the Mexican government in a number of positions such as diplomat, judge, substitute governor of San Luis Potosí, sub-secretary of broadcasting and director general of the National Institute of Fine Arts.

Alvarez Acosta has also worked for a number of magazines and newspapers, gaining a reputation as a talented writer on a variety of subjects. Furthermore, he has garnered over fifty national prizes for his poems and narrative works. One of the literary creations that has brought him the most recognition is his prize-winning novel *Xilitla* (Place of the Snails), which portrays the national ills of México, particularly as they emanated from the Mexican Revolution. His poetry, bold and vivid, flowery and rhetorical, frequently provides a picturesque depiction of the provincial middle class.

WORKS: Poetry: *Romances* (Ballads) (San Luis Potosí: Valores Humanos, 1935). *Coloquio de los campos* (Dialogue with the Countryside) (San Antonio: Artes Gráficas, 1939). *Hogar adentro* (Within the Home) (San Antonio: n.p., 1940). *Nave de rosas antiguas* (A Vessel of Ancient Roses) (México: Eds. Cuadernos Americanos, 1952). *Los pozos sagrados* (The Sacred Wells) (México: Eds. Revista Mexicana de Cultura, 1952). Novels: *Xilitla* (Place of the Snails) (México: Ed. Mexicana, 1950). *Muro blanco en roca negra* (A White Wall on a Black Rock) (México: Eds. Cuadernos Americanos, 1952). *La frontera plural* (The Plural Border) (México: Mortiz, 1979). Short Stories: *Pausa breve* (A Brief Pause) (México: I.C.D., 1945). Play: *El forastero divino* (The Divine Stranger) (México: Ed. Domés, 1986). Other: *Hidalgo* (San

Antonio: Artes Gráficas, 1939). *Discursos* (Discourses), 2 vols. (México: SEP, 1956 and 1958). *El misterio de Juárez* (The Mystery of Juárez) (México: SEP, 1957). *Siembras y propagaciones* (Sowing and Propagation) (México: INBA, 1958). *Vestíbulos, prólogos y presentaciones* (Vestibules, Prologues and Presentations) (México: Imp. Araña, 1958). *Amistad y cultura: un mundo nuevo para el Nuevo Mundo* (Friendship and Culture: A New World for a New World) (México: Imp. Araña, 1960). *Juárez, cuatro estancias liberales* (Juárez, Four Liberal Sojourns) (México: Eds. Opic, 1964).

BIBLIOGRAPHY: Roderick A. Camp, *Mexican Political Biographies, 1935-1981*, 2nd ed. (Tucson: University of Arizona Press, 1982), pp. 12-13. Fernando Díaz de Urdanivia, interview with Miguel Alvarez Acosta, in *México en la Cultura* 684 (April 22, 1962): 5. Julia Hernández, *Novelistas de la Revolución* (México: Unidad Mexicana de Escritores, 1960), pp. 134-36. Jesús Medina Romero, ed., *Antología de poetas contemporáneos*, Biblioteca de Autores Potosinos, No. 1 (San Luis Potosí: Universidad Autónoma de San Luis Potosí, 1955), pp. 12 and 243. Jesús Silva Herzog, *Biografías de amigos y conocidos* (México: Cuadernos Amigos, 1980), pp. 26-31.

ROBERT K. ANDERSON

ALVAREZ Constantino, Jesús (1914-   ), novelist. Born in Chilchota, Michoacán, Alvarez Constantino has been an educator and editor as well as a novelist. He was an education professor, editor of the monthly periodical and annual pedagogy review *Renovación* (1953-1955), president of the Friends of Culture Club of La Piedad, Michoacán, and federal inspector of education in that same city. His two novels, *El centauro* (The Centaur) (1942) and *El Quijote adolescente* (The Adolescent Quixote) (1955), have social and psychological themes.

WORKS: Novels: *El centauro* (The Centaur) (Morelia: Fimax, 1942). *El Quijote adolescente* (The Adolescent Quixote) (Morelia: Fimax, 1955). Studies: *La educación de la comunidad* (Community Education), prologue by Rafael Ramírez (Morelia: n.p., 1952). *Memoria de las conferencias municipales de Morelia, Michoacán* (Proceedings of the Municipal Lectures of Morelia, Michoacán) (Morelia: 1952).

BIBLIOGRAPHY: Anon., "Comentarios de la obra literaria y pedagógica del profesor Jesús Alvarez Constantino," *Vida Nueva* (monthly publication of the Union of Professional Teachers and Students of La Cañada de Chilchota, Michoacán) 1, 2 (Sept. 1956): 4. Aurora M. Ocampo de Gómez and Ernesto Prado Velázquez, *Diccionario de escritores mexicanos* (México: UNAM, 1967), p. 16.

PETER G. BROAD

ALVAREZ Posada, José María or Celso Amieva (1911-1965?), poet and short story writer. Born in Llanes, Asturias, Spain, Alvarez Posada was a teacher in Asturias villages and a Republican soldier. From 1939 through 1944 he was in concentration camps in France, and then he worked in the Foreign Workers Companies in the

Pyrenees, in different types of work, and later as a peon at the shipyards in Saint Nazaire. In 1946 he was director of the Maison d'Enfants Espagnoles, and in 1948, teacher of the Maison d'Enfants Israelites. After having lived in Cuba, he moved to Mexico, where since 1953 he taught, as well as wrote for films. In 1959 he won an award for the script of his film *Pueblo en armas* (Armed People). He was a contributor to *Anuario de Letras de la UNAM* and the supplements of *El Nacional*, *El Día*, and *Excelsior*, He also published prose and poems in *El Eco de los Valles*, *El Pueblo*, *El Oriente de Asturias*, *El Noroeste*, *Region*, *Mundo Gráfico*, *Bohemia*, *Luz*, *Avance*, *Norte*, *Paso a la Juventud*, *Ataque*, *Ahora*, *L'Espagne Republicaine*, *Don Quijote*, *Norte*, *Hoy*, *Vanguardia Cubana*, and *La Ultima Hora*, publications of Spain, France, Cuba, and Mexico. He translated into French the poetry of Nicolás Guillén, and he also translated, from the French, Francis Jammes, Paul Eluard, Bertolt Brecht, Louis Aragon, and Hubert Juin among others. His poetry has been published in various anthologies.

WORKS: Poetry: *Poemas de Llanes* (Llanes Poems), prologue by Alfonso Camín (México: León Sánchez, 1955). *Versos del Maquís* (Maquís Verses) (México: Finisterre, 1960). *La almohada de arena* (The Sand Pillow) (México: Finisterre, 1961). *Poeta en la arena* (Poet on Sand) (includes prose) (México: Finisterre, 1964). Short stories: *El cura de Treviso* (The Treviso Priest) (México: León Sánchez, 1957). Prologues and Essays: Alfonso Camín, *La danza prima y otros poemas* (The Treble Dance and Other Poems) (Madrid: Author's ed., 1954). Felix Lunar, *A cielo abierto* (In Open Sky) (México: n.p. 1956). Emilio Palacios, *Lenguateras* (Buenos Aires: n.p., n.d.). "Alfonso Camín y la poesía negra," in Alfonso Camín, *El collar de la emperatriz* (Madrid: Author's ed., 1962). *Los vencedores de Negrín* (Negrín's Conquerors) (México: Roca, 1976).

BIBLIOGRAPHY: Anon., Review of *La almohada de arena* in *Tiempo* (April 17, 1961); Review of *Poemas de Llanes* in *Norte* (Feb. 1955): 7. Jesús Arellano, Review of *La almohada de arena* in *Nivel* 28 (April 25, 1961): 6. Emilio Criado y Romero, Review of *Versos del Maquis* in *Claridades* (Jan. 10, 1960). Manuel Díaz Martínez, Review of *Poemas de Llanes* in *Ideales y Renovación* (Havana) (Dec. 1956). Heriberto García Rivas, *Historia de la literatura mexicana*, vol. 4 (México: Porrúa, 1974), pp. 321-22. Pedro Gringoire, Review of *La almohada de arena* in *Excelsior* (March 18, 1961). Leopoldo de Luis, Review of *Poemas de Llanes* in *Poesía española* (Madrid) (Feb. 1956). Gilberto Rod, Review of *Poemas de Llanes* in *Ultimas Noticias* (May 1955). Federico Carlos Sáinz de Robles, *Diccionario de literatura* (Madrid, 1964), José Sanjurdo, Review of *Poemas de Llanes* in *Diario Ataja* (Havana) (July 1956). Mauricio de la Selva, Review of *Poeta en la arena* in *Excelsior* (May 24, 1964); *Cuadernos Americanos* 135, 4 (July-Aug. 1964): 291. Francisco Zendejas, Review of *Poeta en la arena* in *Excelsior* (May 26, 1964).

DELIA GALVAN

AMIEVA, Celso. See ALVAREZ POSADA, José María.

ANAYA, José Vicente (1947-). Anaya was born in Villa Coronado, Chihuahua, on January 22, 1947. He has been director of the Dirección General de Publicaciones at the Universidad Autónoma del Estado de México. His work as an editor is widely recognized among Mexico City and national literary circles. He is a distinguished translator of such figures as Allen Ginsberg, William Carlos Williams, Jack Kerouac, and Yukio Mishima. His critical articles on Mexican poetry constitute an important basis for study. He has recently undertaken further work in this area, focusing on the poetry produced by young writers in northern Mexico, especially those living along the border. During a period of his life he traveled extensively throughout Mexico and the United States and lived with the Tarahumara Indians in the high Sierra of the State of Chihuahua, where he was initiated into the ritual of Peyote. He is presently a free-lance writer and an editor with the Mexican literary review *Cultura Norte*.

Anaya's poetry is steeped in a gargantuan scope of readings. His work is heavily influenced by the poets of the Beat Generation. His own experience constitutes the basis for his highly experimental verse. *Híkuri*, a book-length rendition of visual and auditory imagery depicting the initiation into the ritual of Peyote is generated from a dream perspective and develops in an alternating sequence of rhythmic references from oneiric to contemporary Mexican reality.

WORKS: *Los valles solitarios nemorosos* (México: UNAM, 1976). *Punto negro* (Black Point) (Xalapa: Universidad Veracruzana, 1980). *Morque* (Toluca: UAEM, 1981). *En la mano desvanecida del tiempo* (In the Fainted Hand of the Time) (Toluca: UAEM, 1982). *Híkuri* (Puebla: Universidad Autónoma de Puebla, 1987).

BIBLIOGRAPHY: José Joaquín Blanco, *Crónica de la poesia mexicana* (México: Katún, 1981), pp. 264-70. Sandro Cohen, *Palabra nueva: Dos décadas de poesía en México* (México: Premiá, 1981), pp. 16, 115-19. Alferdo Espinosa and Rubén Mejía, *Muestra de poesía chihuahuense (1976-1986)* (Chihuahua, 1986). Jaime Moreno Villareal, *La línea y el círculo* (México: Universidad Autónoma Metropolitana, 1981).

RICARDO AGUILAR

ANAYA B., Alfonso (1926-   ), lawyer, playwright, and scriptwriter for radio and television programs. Born in Monterrey, on April 29, 1926, Anaya studied law and practiced for several years until in 1955 he decided to quit and dedicate himself to writing. His play *Despedida de Soltera* (The Departure of a Spinster) (1955) was a success and motivated the big change in his life. His plays show his ability to create natural dialogue together with involved plots and a humorous atmosphere. It is the jocose "costumbrismo" found in his plays that has made them so popular. Many of his works have been adapted to the cinema and to television, among them *Despedida de soltera*, *Lío de faldas*, *Las golfas*, and *Las del talón*. His technique is very similar to that of the Spaniard Alfonso Paso.

WORKS: Theater: *Despedida de soltera* (Departure of a Spinster), theatrical debut, 1955. *Y ahora...¿qué hacemos?* (And Now...What Do We Do?), theatrical debut, 1955. *Mis tres amantes* (My Three Lovers), theatrical debut, 1956. *¡Viva la paz!* (Long Live Peace!), theatrical debut, 1960. *Lío de faldas* (The Mix-up of the Skirts), theatrical debut, 1962. *Viuda...y tres millones* (Widowed...and Three Million), theatrical debut, 1963. *El presidente mañozo* (The Handy President), theatrical debut, 1963. *Sin* *novedad en el segundo frente* (All is Quiet in the Second Front), theatrical debut, 1964. *El piso de las sirenas* (The Floor of the Sirens), theatrical debut, 1965. Las mangas del chaleco (The Sleeves of the Vest), theatrical debut, 1966. *Pares o nones* (Odds and Evens), theatrical debut, 1966. *Baby shower o una fiesta embarazosa* (Baby Shower or an Embarrassing Party), debut, 1967. *Las golfas* (The Guttersnipers), debut, 1968. *La Godiva se nos fue viva* (Lady Godiva Left Alive), debut, 1968. *Un minuto de silencio* (A Minute of Silence), debut, 1968. *El adulterios es para adultos* (Adultery Is for Adults), debut, 1970. *Simplemente norteños* (Simply from the North), debut, 1971. *Historia de un par de piernas* (History of a Pair of Legs), debut, 1972. *A oscuras y en la alcoba* (In the Dark and in the Bedroom), debut, 1972. *Las del talón* (The Ones of the Heel), debut, 1974. *Vírgenes de medianoche* (Midnight Virgins), debut, 1976. *¡A qué buena está mi ahijada!* (How Sexy Is My Goddaughter!), debut, 1979. *Nadie es profeta en su cama* (Nobody Is a Prophet in His Bed), debut, 1981. *Sábanas calientes* (Warm Bedsheets), debut, 1982. *Señoritas divorciadas* (Divorced Single Girls), debut, 1983.

BIBLIOGRAPHY: Alberto Catani, "Alfonso Anaya B.: se puede vivir como escritor, si se vive modestamente," in *El Día* (México, Jan. 24, 1964): 11. Heriberto García Rivas, *Historia de la literatura mexicana*, vol. 4 (México: Porrúa, 1974), p. 469. Ruth S. Lamb, *Bibliografía del teatro mexicano del siglo XX* (México: Eds. de Andrea, 1962), p. 153. Antonio Magaña Esquivel, "Un nuevo comediógrafo mexicano triunfa en la Sala Chopín," in *El Nacional* (México, Aug. 24, 1955). Luis Reyes de la Maza, "Los actores de *Las mangas del chaleco*," in *El Nacional* (México, March 2O, 1966).

MIRTA BARREA-MARLYS AND ELADIO CORTES

ANCONA, Eligio (1835-1893), novelist, historian. Born in Mérida, Yucatán on November 30, 1835, Ancona became one of the most distinguished liberal politicians of his native state, as well as its most famous man of letters during the second half of the nineteenth century. He received his law degree from the Universidad Literaria del Estado in Yucatán in 1862, and was elected to the city council of Mérida, where he served until Maximilian ascended the throne in 1864. Ancona then left politics to write fiery attacks against the Empire, which were published in the liberal newspapers *La píldora* (The Bad News) and *Yucatán.* He was imprisoned in 1866 for his outspoken views; when released a year later, he joined the liberal troops of Juárez and became actively involved in the political life of Yucatán once more. Ancona served at different times as the governor of Yucatán, a member of the national Congress, a circuit court judge, and a judge on the Sumpreme Court in Mexico City. He died in the nation's capital on April 3, 1893.

Ancona is the author of six novels: *El filibustero* (The Patriot), *La cruz y la espada* (The Cross and the Sword), *Los mártires del Anáhuac* (The Martyrs of Anahuac), *El conde de Peñalva* (The Count of Peñalva), *Memorias de un alférez* (Memories of an Ensign), and *La mestiza* (The Half-Breed). All but the latter are in the historical vein. *La mestiza* is a Realistic novel, focusing on the conflicts between whites, Indians, and persons of mixed blood in Mexico. *Los Mártires del Anáhuac* deals with Cortés' conquest of Mexico and the establishment of a Spanish colony in the New World.

The other novels are set in colonial Yucatán. *Memorias de un alférez* is considered to be Ancona's best work. It is an entertaining mixture of love, adventure, and mystery, with characters who capture the reader's interest and engage his sympathy. Antonio Castro Leal calls it "one of the best-Mexican novels dealing with the colonial theme." Ancona also wrote two lengthy histories of his native state: *Compendio de la historia de Yucatán* (Compendium of the History of Yucatan) and *Historia de Yucatán desde la epoca más remota hasta nuestros días* (History of Yucatán from the Most Remote Past to the Present Day). Both works earned Ancona considerable praise as a scholar.

WORKS: *La cruz y la espada* (The Cross and the Sword), 2 vols. (Paris: Lib. de Rosa y Bouret, 1866). *El filibustero* (The Patriot) 2 vols. (Paris: Lib. de Rosa y Bouret, 1866). *Los mártires del Anáhuac* (The Martyrs of Anahuac), 2 vols. (México: Imp. de José Batiza, 1870). *La mestiza* (The Half-Breed) (Mérida, 1891). *Memorias de un alférez* (Memories of an Ensign), 2 vols. (Mérida: El Peninsular, 1904). *Compendio de la historia de Yucatán* (Compendium of the History of Yucatán) (Mérida, 1881). *Historia de Yucatán desde la epoca más remota hasta nuestros días* (History of Yucatán from the Most Remote Past to the Present Day), 4 vols. (Mérida, 1877-1880).

BIBLIOGRAPHY: Antonio Castro Leal, *La novela del México colonial* (México: Aguilar, 1964), vol. 1, pp. 397-99. María del Carmen Millán, *Literatura mexicana* (México: Edit. Esfinge, 1962), p. 166. John Lloyd Read, *The Mexican Historical Novel* (New York: Instituto de Las Españas, 1939), pp. 140-59.

CYNTHIA K. DUNCAN

ANDA, José Guadalupe de (1880-1950), novelist. He was born on December 12, 1880, in San Juan de los Lagos, Jalisco. He worked for the National Railroad Company as a railroad station manager until 1914, when he joined the revolutionary struggle by entering the political arena. In 1918 he was elected representative of his district, Los Altos. Twelve years later he was elected state senator.

Between 1926 and 1929, there were many confrontations between the Catholic Church and the national government headed by President Plutarco Elís Calles. This period of violence in Mexico's history, known as "the *cristero* movement," is the subject matter of de Anda's novel *Los cristeros* (Christ's Followers). This novel, unlike similar ones, is impartial and criticizes the excesses and cruelties of both sides. Because of its literary qualities and original point of view, *Los cristeros* is considered one of the principal novels of its time. His second work, *Los bragados* (The Valiant Ones), has a similar theme and characters. However, this time the struggle is not against government soldiers but against schoolteachers, many of whom were, if not killed, mutilated by having their ears cut off. The author is perceived as a vigorous novelist who shows improved literary techniques over his first work and gives us some beautiful prose pages on the subject of Mexico's revolutionary period. His third work, *Juan del riel* (Railroad John), moves quickly as it documents with realism and forceful descriptions the daily problems faced by railroad workers.

WORKS: *Los cristeros*: *La guerra santa en Los Altos* (Christ's Followers: The Holy War in The Highlands), foreword by Octavio G. Barreda and introduction by Alvaro

Ruiz Abreu (México: Ed. Hexagono, 1986, c. 1937). *Los bragados* (The Valiant Ones), foreword by José Carner (México: Cía. General Editora, 1942). *Juan del Riel* (Railroad John) (México: Cía. General Editora, 1942).

BIBLIOGRAPHY: Ermilo Abreu Gómez, "J. Guadalupe de Anda," *Letras de México* 3, 15 (April 1942). Mariano Azuela, *Obras completas*, vol. 3 (México: FCE, 1960), pp. 682-83. John S. Brushwood and José Rojas Garcidueñas, *Breve historia de la novela mexicana* (México: Eds. de Andrea, 1959), pp. 110-12. Julia Hernández, *Novelistas y cuentistas de la Revolución mexicana* (México: Unidad Mexicana de Escritores, 1960), pp. 25-26.

                                                        HERLINDA HERNANDEZ

ANDUJAR, Manuel (1913-), journalist, public official, and novelist. Born in La Carolina (Jaén), Spain, he studied in Málaga, then lived in Madrid, Lérida, and Barcelona, where he worked as a journalist and public official. In 1939 he moved to Mexico where he founded the review *Las Españas* (Spains) with José Ramón Arana. He has worked for the Fondo de Cultura Económica and the Editorial Joaquín Mortiz. He moved back to Spain in 1967.

  Andújar began his literary career in exile in Mexico, and his principal theme has been the problem of Spain, like his predecessors in the Spanish Generation of 98. All of his novels revolve around different aspects of the causes and results of the Spanish Civil War: *Partiendo de la angustia* (Starting with Anguish), *Cristal herido* (Wounded Glass), as well as his later trilogy, *Vísperas* (Eves), whose three volumes describe life in the country, the mines, and the port, respectively: *Llanura* (The Plain), *El vencido* (The Conquered), and *El destino de Lázaro* (The Fate of Lazarus).

WORKS: *Saint Cyprien, plage.* Campo de concentración (St. Cyprien, the Beach, Concentration Camp) (México: Cuadernos del Destierro, 1942). *Partiendo de la angustia* (Starting with Anguish) (México: Moncayo, 1944). *Cristal herido* (Wounded Glass) (México: Eds. Isla, 1945). *Llanura* (The Plain) (México: Editorial Centauro, 1947). *El vencido* (The Conquered) (México: Editorial Almendros, 1949). *El destino de Lázaro* (The Fate of Lazarus) (México: FCE, 1959). *El primer juicio final. Los aniversarios. El sueño robado. Tres piezas de teatro.* (The First Last Judgement. The Anniversaries The Stolen Dream) (México: Eds. de Andrea, 1962).

BIBLIOGRAPHY: José Rogelio Alvarez, ed., *Enciclopedia de México.* vol. 1 (México: SEP, 1987), p. 423. Aurora M. Ocampo de Gómez and Ernesto Prado Velázquez, *Diccionario de escritores mexicanos* (México: UNAM, 1967), p. 19.

                                                        TERESA R. ARRINGTON

"ANTONIORROBLES." See ROBLES, Antonio.

ARANGO y Escandón, Alejandro (1821-1883). Born in Puebla on July 10, 1821, Alejandro Arango y Escandón, from a well-to-do family, was sent as a boy for schooling in Spain. Upon his return to Mexico, he furthered his education, graduating as a lawyer in 1844. Throughout his lifetime, he held a number of important positions of public trust. In addition to his work in the legal profession, Arango y Escandón dedicated himself to the pursuit of literature, becoming a member of the Academia de Letrán, the Academia Mexicana de la Lengua, and other prestigious associations. A political conservative, he supported the government of Maximilian as one of his advisors. Following the downfall of the French emperor, he spent three months in prison and then was exiled again. When he returned to Mexico in 1877, he, as a founding member, accepted the position of director of the Academia Mexicana de la Lengua, a post he held for six years. He died February 28, 1883.

Arango y Escandón possessed a rare knowledge of both living and dead languages, an attribute he used to help disseminate selected foreign classical literature in Spanish. He also promoted Eastern studies, attempting to spark interest in Mexico, especially in the Hebrew and Greek languages and literatures. A devout man, he wrote religious poetry along classical lines, especially on the theme of the Immaculate Conception. He also penned an excellent essay entitled *Ensayo histórico sobre Fray Luis de León* (Historical Essay on Fray Luis de León), on the noted poet, scholar, and theologian of the Spanish Golden Age.

WORKS: *Ensayo histórico sobre Fray Luis de León*, lst ed., 1855; Prologue to *Officium Parvum Beatae Mariae Virginia*, by José Mariano Lara (México: n.p., 1870). "En la Inmaculada Concepción de Nuestra Señora" (On the Immaculate Conception of Our Lady), in *Memorias de la Academia Mexicana Correspondiente de la Real Española* (México: Imp. de F. Díaz de León, 1878), vol. 1, no. 3, pp. 205-07. "Invocación a la bondad divina" (Invocation to Divine Goodness), ibid. pp. 208-09. *Algunos versos* (Some Verses) (México: Imp. de Ignacio Escalante, 1879). "Seis sonetos inéditos" (Six Unpublished Sonnets), publ. by Jesús García Gutiérrez, in *Abside*, vol. 5, 7 (July 1941): 469-73.

BIBLIOGRAPHY: Victoriano Agüeros, *Escritores mexicanos contemporáneos* (México: Imp. de Ignacio Escalante, 1880), pp. 25-34. Jesús García Gutiérrez, *La poesía religiosa en México (Siglos xvi a xix)*, vol. 11, no. 1 (México: Cultura, 1919), p. 130. Joaquín Márquez Montiel, *Hombres célebres de Puebla*, vol. 1 (México: Edit. Jus, 1952), pp. 30-37, 373. Marcelino Menéndez y Pelayo, *Historia de la poesía hispano-americana*, vol. 1 (Madrid: Libr. General de Victoriano Suárez, 1911), p. 152. Aurora M. Ocampo de Gómez and Ernesto Prado Velázquez, *Diccionario de escritores mexicanos* (México: UNAM, 1967), pp. 19-20. Joaquín Arcadio Pagaza, sonnet, "A la memoria del Sr. D. Alejandro Arango y Escandón," in *Memorias de la Academia Mexicana correspondiente a la Real Española*, vol. 2, no. 3 (México: Imp. de F. Díaz de León, 1883), p. 355. Octaviano Valdés, *Poesía neoclásica y académica* (México: UNAM, 1946), pp. xxvi-xxvii. José Zorrilla, *México y los mexicanos* (México: Eds. de Andrea, 1955), pp. 107-09.

JEANNE C. WALLACE

ARELLANO, Jesús (1919-1979). Born in Ayo el Chico, Jalisco, on September 5, 1919, Jesús Arellano was schooled in both Mexico and the United States, studying primarily law and literature. He died December 2, 1979, in Mexico City. With an interest in the study and dissemination of modern Mexican poetry, Arellano produced *Antología de los 50* (Anthology of the Fifty) in 1952 and *Poetas jóvenes de México* (Young Poets of Mexico) in 1955. Founder and director of *Fuensanta, Litterae, Poesía y Letras,* and *Metáfora*, all literary magazines of cultural importance, he invested both time and energy in his endeavor to bring greater cultural and poetic awareness to the Mexican public.

A member of various national and international organizations, such as the Centre International D'Etudes Poétiques de la Maison Internationale de la Poésie, Arellano was very active both as a poet and as a critic. He wrote many essays reviewing and critiquing the poetry of contemporary writers in Mexico, such as *Bonifaz Nuño, Alí *Chumacero, Efraín *Huerta, and others, publishing them in a variety of well-known journals and magazines, among them *Nivel, El Día, Cuadernos del Viento,* and *Letras de Ayer y de Hoy* (which he codirected). One of the leaders of his poetic generation, Arellano also was very involved with the review *Metáfora*, as were others of his group. In his critical essays about the poetry of his contemporaries especially, Arellano often launched into sharp attacks, but also lauded what he saw as authentic and truthful.

José Arellano stands out as a poet, having been translated and edited in France and Portugal, and he published quite a few volumes of poetry, several anthologies, and books of stories. *La señal de la luz* (The Signal of Light), published in 1950, was his first book of poetry, reminiscent of Ramón *López Velarde. He was awarded the Premio Margot Valdés Peza for this endeavor. With an acute sense of melancholy disclosed through language, style, and structure, he expresses the anguish of living in *Ahora y en la aurora* (Now and in the Dawn), published in 1951. He continues along the same vein in *Poemas de la amarga posesión* (Poems of Bitter Possession) (1953). But, since *Nuevo día* (New Day) (1956), his sense of isolation, desolation, and bitterness has given way to a spirit of rebellion, opposing injustice, lauding the wonders of nature, and exploring the dimensions of life's vital problems. In some later work, Arellano also sings to his beloved, much in a traditional manner, although with a certain degree of originality.

WORKS: Poetry: *La señal de la luz* (The Signal of Light) (México: viñetas de Leopoldo Aréchiga Barba, 1950). *Ahora y en la aurora* (Now and in the Dawn) (México: Eds. Fuensanta, 1951). *Poemas de la amarga posesión* (Poems of Bitter Possession) (México: Eds. GEAR, 1953). *Nuevo día* (New Day) (México: Eds. Metáfora, 1956). *Desatadura* (Absolver) (México: Eds. Metáfora, 1958). *Diálogo* (Dialogue) (México: Eds. Metáfora, 1960). *Poemas choisis* (Brussels: Profils Poétiques des Pays Latins, 1961). *Camino libre* (Free Path) (México: Cuadernos del Viento, 1962). *A golpes de palavra* (Lison: Panorámica Poética Luso-Hispánica, 1962). *Limpia la madrugada* (Clean the Early Morning) (México: Eds. Metáfora, 1965). *Palabra de hombre* (Word of Man) (México: UNAM, 1966). Anthologies: *Antología de los 50 poetas contemporáneos de México* (Anthology of the 50 Contemporary Poets of México) (México: Eds. Alatorre, 1952). *Poetas jóvenes de México* (Young Poets of México), BMM, no. 23 (México: Eds. Libro-Mex, 1955). Short Story: *Por un vaso de agua* (For a Glass of Water) (México: n.p., 1950). Essays: "Poesía mexicana en 1956," in *Metáfora* 14 (May-June 1957). *Algunos académicos de la lengua* (Some Scholars of the Language) (México: Eds. Metáfora, 1958). "Raíces poéticas de Jaime Sabines," in *Nivel* 33 (Sept. 1961): 2, 6. "Drama poético en la obra de Rubén Bonifaz Nuño," in *Nivel*, 2nd epoch, 4 (May 1963): 5. "El poeta proscrito: Efraín Huerta," in *Nivel* 43

(July 1962): 5. Prologue to Rafael Cuevas, *Panorámica de las letras* (Panorama of Literature), 3 vols. (México: Ed. of the Revista de Bellas Artes, 1956).

BIBLIOGRAPHY: Huberto Batis, "Los libros al día," Review of *Limpia la madrugada* in *La Cultura en México* (July 21, 1965). Salvador Calvillo Madrigal, "Madrugada en mediodía," in *México en la Cultura* 866 (Oct. 24, 1965): 3. Boyd G. Carter, *"Limpia la madrugada* de Arellano," in *Revista de la Semana* (Nov. 7, 1965): 8. Antonio Castro Leal, *La poesía mexicana moderna* (México: FCE, 1953), p. 477. Frank Dauster, *Breve historia de la poesía mexicana* (México: Eds. de Andrea, 1956), p. 180; *The Double Strand* (Lexington: University of Kentucky Press, 1987), pp. 50, 64, 82, 105, 169. Gloria Espejel Mendoza, "La poesía de Arellano," in *Letras de Ayer y de Hoy* 11 (July 1966): 18-19. Horacio Espinosa Altamirano, "Breve semblanza de Jesús Arellano," in *Revista Mexicana de Cultura* (April 22, 1962); "Jesús Arellano o la levantada autonomía," in *BBH* 11, 327 (Sept. 1965): 18-19. Raúl Leiva, *Imagen de la poesía mexicana contemporánea* (México: UNAM, 1959): 313-19, 357; Review of *Camino libre* in *Nivel* 41 (May 25, 1962): 3; "Un poeta mexicano editado en Portugal," in *Nivel* 44, (Aug. 26, 1962): 3; Review of *Limpia la madrugada* in *México en la Cultura* 850 (July 4, 1965): 8; Review of *Palabra de hombre* in *México en la Cultura* 908 (Aug. 14, 1966): 6. Leopoldo de Luis, "La poesía de Jesús Arellano," in *Nivel* 10 (Oct. 25, 1963): 1. Antonio Magaña Esquivel, "Poeta mexicano en francés," in *Tiempo* 1010 (Sept. 1961); Review of *Limpia la madrugada,* in *Novedades* (July 31, 1965): 4; Review of *Palabra de hombre,* in *Novedades* (Sept. 3, 1966). Rafael Melero, Review of *Camino libre,* in *Nivel* 10, (Oct. 25, 1963): 1. Javier Morente, Review of *Limpia la madrugada,* in *Diorama de la Cultura* (Sept. 26, 1965). Thelma Nava, Review of *Limpia la madrugada,* in *El Día* (July 29, 1965). Aurora M. Ocampo de Gómez and Ernesto Prado Velázquez, *Diccionario de escritores mexicanos* (México: UNAM, 1967), pp. 20-21. Javier Peñalosa, Review of *Limpia la madrugada,* in *Nivel* 32 (Aug. 25, 1965): 4. Joaquín Antonio Peñalosa, Review of *Limpia la madrugada* in *Abside* 4 (Oct.-Dec., 1965): 486-88. René Rebetez, Review of *Palabra de hombre,* in *El Heraldo de México* (Sept. 3, 1966). Salvador Reyes Nevares, Review of *Desatadura,* in *México en la Cultura* 493 (Aug. 25, 1957): 4. Luis Mario Schneider, Review of *Limpia la madrugada,* in *La Palabra y el Hombre* 35 (July-Sept. 1965): 539-42. Mauricio de la Selva, Review of *Limpia la madrugada,* in *Diorama de la Cultura* (Sept. 5, 1965): 7. A. Silva Villalobos, *"Diálogo* de Jesús Arellano," in *Nivel* 16 (April 25, 1960): 5. Julio C. Treviño, Review of *Poemas de la amarga posesión,* in *Ideas de México* 2 (Sept.-Oct. 1953): 93-94.

JEANNE C. WALLACE

ARGUDIN, Antonio (1953-). Born on June 9, 1953, in Veracruz, Antonio Argudín has already enjoyed an active career in theater arts, while still studying drama at the UNAM. His first public recognition came in 1976 when he received honorable mention for a story he submitted to the National Story Contest. He has worked as an actor, a director, and a theater teacher at the Universidad Veracruzana. One of the most promising young playwrights and educators, Antonio Argudín has been significantly influenced by both Emilio *Carballido and Luisa Josefina *Hernández. He also has served on the board of *Tramoya,* a theatrical journal.

Although he has written some stories and a few poems, Argudín is most noted for his plays. He is featured in Emilio Carballido's anthologoy, *Teatro joven de México*, with the publication of *Las peripecias de un costal o la corona de hierro* (The Vicissitudes of a Frame or the Crown of Iron), performed in 1979.

WORKS: Story: *Ríos que vienen del mar* (Rivers Which Come from the Sea) (Xalapa: Universidad Veracruzana, 1983). Poetry: "Encrucijada" (Cross-Roads), in *La Palabra y el Hombre* 35 (July-Sept. 1980): 33-34. "Fragmento," in *Poesía joven de México*, pp. 34-35. "La luna y la tinta" (The Moon and Ink), in *Cuadernos del Caballo Verde* (Xalapa: Universidad Veracruzana, 1976). Theater: "Las peripecias de un costal o la corona de hierro" (The Vicissitudes of a Frame or the Crown of Iron), in Emilio Carballido, *Teatro joven de México*, vol. 2 (México: Editores Mexicanos Unidos, 1979), pp. 323-43. "Sueldo según capacidades" (Salary According to Capability), in Emilio Carballido, *Más teatro joven* (México: Editores Mexicanos Unidos, 1982), pp. 57-62. "La manzana" (monologue), in *Revista de Bellas Artes* 26 (March-April 1976): 59-60. "Comala," in *Diorama de la Cultura* (July 8, 1979): 2. "Cipris," in *Tramoya* 18 (Jan.-March 1980): 19-27. "Instinto maternal" (Maternal Instinct), in *Diograma de la Cultura* (May 11, 1980): 2. "La comadreja y sus comadres" (The Weasel and Her Friends), in *El Gallo Ilustrado* 985 (May 3, 1981): 18-21. "Trayecto," in *El Gallo Ilustrado* 1050 (Aug. 8, 1982): 11-12. Translations: John Kenneth Knowles, *Luisa Josefina Hernández: Teoría y práctica del drama* (Theory and Practice of Drama) (México: UNAM, 1980). Essay: "Mrozeck en México. Una entrevista" (Mrozeck in Mexico. An Interview), in *Tramoya* 17 (Oct.-Dec. 1979) 44-46.

BIBLIOGRAPHY: Emilio Carballido, notes, in *Teatro joven de México* vol. 2 (México: Editores Mexicanos Unidos, 1979), p. 349; and in *Más teatro joven en México* (México: Editores Mexicanos Unidos, 1982), pp. 62-63. Laura Reinking, "*Ríos que vienen del mar*, traen sueños amargos," in *Punto* 68 (Feb. 20-26, 1984): 2. Gonzalo Valdés Medellín, "El cuento, un universo cerrado," in *Sábado* 328 (Feb. 11, 1984): 9.

MICHELE MUNCY

ARGÜELLES, Hugo (1932-   ), dramatist. Born in Veracruz on January 2, 1932, Argüelles studied five years of surgery at the Medical School of UNAM in Mexico City. However, his true vocation was the theater, and in 1956 he enrolled at the School of Dramatic Arts of INBA, where he studied for three years. He won two awards for his play *Los prodigiosos* (The Prodigies) (1956). He also received the Juan Ruiz de Alarcón award for his play *El velorio en turno* (The Wake in Shifts), later changing the title to *Los cuervos están de luto* (The Crows Are in Mourning). He taught at the School of Dramatic Arts of INBA and was founder of the School of Fine Arts in Puebla. He founded in his home a workshop of dramatic literature in 1979.

The plays written by Argüelles capture the national Mexican spirit and its degeneration as a result of fanaticism and ancient customs of the native people. *Los cuervos están de luto* has been described as the first Mexican play to have "black humor" and to capture the Mexican spirit of mockery, even when the subjects are the sacred and lugubrious.

WORKS: *Los prodigiosos* (The Prodigies), won the award given by *Estaciones* in 1957 and the Premio Juan Ruiz de Alarcón de la Asociación de Críticos, 1961. *Los cuervos están de luto* (The Crows Are in Mourning), Premio Nacional de Teatro, 1958, and the Bellas Artes award, 1959; the movie version won the Premio Pecime for picture of the year, 1963. *El tejedor de Milagros* (The Miracle Weaver), Premio Pecime award for best picture of the year, 1962; theatrical debut, 1963. *Doña Macabra* (Madame Macabre), won all awards for 1963 for best television series and movie production, 1970. *La galería del silencio* (The Gallery of Silence), theatrical debut, 1967. *La ronda de la hechizada* (The Night-Song of the Bewitched), theatrical debut, 1973. *Medea y los visitantes del sueño* (Medea and the Dream Visitors), theatrical debut, Havana, Cuba, 1970. *La Dama de la luna roja* (The Woman of the Red Moon), theatrical debut, 1970. *El gran inquisidor* (The Great Interrogator), theatrical debut, 1973; also in Antonio Magaña Esquivel, ed., *Teatro mexicano del siglo XX*, vol. 5 (México: FCE, 1970), pp. 328-416, and in *Teatro mexicano, 1973* (México: Aguilar, 1977), pp. 33-77. *El ritual de la salamandra* (The Ritual of the Salamander), theatrical debut, 1981. *El retablo del gran relajo* (The Altar-Piece of the Great Degeneration), theatrical debut, 1981. *Concierto para guillotina y cuarenta cabezas* (Concert for the Guillotine and Forty Heads), Premio Nacional de Teatro, award from INBA, 1981. *El cocodrilo solitario del panteón rococó* (The Solitary Crocodile of the Rococo Pantheon), theatrical debut, 1982. *Los amores criminales de las vampiras morales* (The Criminal Loves of the Moral Vampires), Premio Sor Juana Inés de la Cruz award from the Theater Critics Union, 1983 (México: Editores Mexicanos Unidos, 1986). *Los gallos salvajes* (The Wild Roosters), theatrical debut, 1986 (México: Editores Mexicanos Unidos, 1986).

BIBLIOGRAPHY: Anon. "Hugo Argüelles, *Los prodigiosos*" in *Festival de teatro latinoamericano* (Havana: Casa de las Américas, 1965). Luis G. Basurto, "Hugo Argüelles, *Obras completas*," in *Excelsior* (Sept. 19 1983): 7A, 10A. Emilio García Riera, *Historia documental del cine mexicano* (México: Era, 1978), vol. 8, pp. 81-83, vol. 9, pp. 233-235. Heriberto García Rivas, *Historia de la literatura mexicana*, vol. 4 (México: Porrúa, 1974), pp. 478-79. Alyce Golding Cooper, *Teatro mexicano contemporáneo, 1940-1962* (México: UNAM, 1962), pp. 44-45. Ruth S. Lamb, *Bibliografía del teatro mexicano del siglo XX* (México: Eds. de Andrea, 1962), p. 28. Ruth S. Lamb and Antonio Magaña Esquivel, *Breve historia del teatro mexicano* (México: Eds. de Andrea, 1958), p. 161. Antonio Magaña Esquivel, "Reposición de *Los cuervos están de luto*," in *El Nacional* (México, Aug. 21, 1964), p. 5. and in *Teatro mexicano, 1973* (México: Aguilar, 1977), pp. 36, 37. Rafael Solana, "Teatro," Review of *El tejedor de milagros* (The Weaver of Miracles), in *Siempre!* 563 (México, April 8, 1964): 50-52, also prologue to *El teatro de Hugo Argüelles* (México: Oasis, 1961).

                                                            MIRTA BARREA-MARLYS

ARGÜELLES Bringas, Roberto (1875-1915), poet. Born in Veracruz, he occupied various public posts, among them secretary of the National Museum. His early death cut short his literary career, which had been heralded as promising.

Argüelles Bringas published his work in such journals as *Revista Moderna, Savia Moderna,* and *Nosotros.* His poems have been described as pessimistic and tortured in tone and innovative in syntax and alliteration.

WORKS: *Fuerza y dolor* (Power and Pain), anthology (México: SEP, 1975).

BIBLIOGRAPHY: Luis Castillo Ledón, "Roberto Argüelles Bringas," *Vida Moderna* (Nov. 25, 1915). Antonio Castro Leal, *La poesía mexicana moderna,* Col. Letras Mexicanas no. 12 (México: Fondo de Cultura Econónica, 1953), p. 150. Frank Dauster, *Breve historia de la poesía mexicana* (México: Eds. de Andrea, 1956), pp. 132-33. Genero Estrada, *Poetas nuevos de México* (México: Ed. Porrúa, 1916), pp. 1-2. Rafael López, "Laude," *Revista de Revistas* (Jan. 16, 1916); "Perfil," *Crónica* (Gaudalajara) (Apr. 15, 1907). José Luis Martínez, *La expresión nacional* (México: Imp. Universitaria, 1955), pp. 433-34. M. Parra, "Roberto Argüelles Bringas," *El Nacional* (Aug. 11, 1916). José Juan Tablada, "Poetas nuevos, Roberto Argüelles Bringas," *Revista Moderna* (Nov. 1905): 180-81.

BARBARA P. FULKS

ARIDJIS, Homero (1940-   ). Homero Aridjis was born on April 6, 1940, in Contepec, Michoan, of Greek and Mexican parentage. As a child, he attended school in Morelia, demonstrating an early inclination toward poetry and journalism. He later studied journalism in Mexico City. He has lived in Spain and France, and now resides in Mexico with his American wife. He has published in such journals and reviews as *Cuadernos del Viento, Pájaro Cascabel, S. Nob, La Palabra y el Hombre, La Cultura en México,* and in several jouranls in South America as well as in the United States and elsewhere. He was highlighted in a 1959-1960 issue of the *Revista Mexicana de Literatura.*

He was a fellow of the Centro Mexicano de Escritores in 1959-1960, publishing *Los ojos desdoblados* (The Split Eyes), which he wrote during that year. In 1961, he published *La tumba de Filidor* (Filidor's Tomb). He was awarded the Xavier Villaurrutia Prize in 1964 for *Mirándola dormir.* As a Guggenheim Fellow in 1966-1967, he traveled widely throughout Europe and the United States. Also in 1966, he edited the reviews *Correspondencias* and *Diálogos.* He represented Mexico in a Congress of the PEN Club of New York in 1966, also taking part in a symposium at Harvard University around that time. In addition, he gave lectures in universities such as George Washington, Yale, Wesleyan, and Fordham. During the 1967-1968 academic year, he was a visiting professor at the University of Indiana in Bloomington. In 1967, he read poems at the Festival of Two Worlds in Spoleto, Italy. From 1969 to 1971, he was employed in the same capacity at New York University. In 1975, he gave conferences in Leiden, Amsterdam, and Bristol. He was again a Guggenheim Fellow in 1979-1980. He has been a poet in residence at Columbia University's Translation Center. He has also served as Mexico's ambassador to Switzerland and the Netherlands. Homero Aridjis continues to work and write, producing critically acclaimed volumes of poetry and participating actively in the cultural life of the literary community.

Aridjis has been influenced significantly by several powerful sources: the poetry of San Juan de la Cruz and Luis de Góngora and James Joyce, plus the mystical Nahautl chants of the indigenous culture and some contemporary songs of the Huichol Indians. Considered a visionary poet, he sings of love, infinite spaces and pure bliss on the one hand, and of horror, apocalypse, and mass destruction on the other. Some of his works are highlighted below.

Aridjis began his literary career in earnest with the publication of the poetic volume *Los ojos desdoblados* (The Split Eyes) in 1960. Although still working to perfect his poetic techniques, he exhibits in *Los ojos desdoblados*, nonetheless, an elegance and grace, combined with artistic freshness.

Another of his early pieces, *Antes del reino* (Before the Kingdom) (1963), is a long, beautiful love poem, made of several smaller compositions, linked by a common atmosphere, a poetic climate of stunning imagery. The following year, he published *Mirándola dormir*, poetic prose so elegant and complex that it seems the work of a very experienced and mature writer. Highly erotic experiences are seen as a vital component of life. The poet, using hallucinatory and inconsonant images, evokes a picture of the sleeping lover, paving the way for a journey to the realm of the subconscious, which evolves from this juncture.

Perséfone, a 1967 publication later translated into English by Aridjis' wife, Betty Aridjis, is considered either a novelistic erotic poem or a poetic erotic novel. *Perséfone* retells the myth of Persephone, a virgin and whore, the goddess of fertility and queen of the underworld. With exquisite lyricism, Aridjis takes this myth and projects it onto the seamy underside of contemporary Mexican life, relentlessly exploring and exposing sexual passion.

El poeta niño (The Child Poet), published in 1971, is a three part work, beginning with an autobiography of the author's first eighteen years in Contepec, Michoacán. The second part is a superb collection of prose and verse. The third narrates the story of the death, wake, and burial of Susi, a Mexico City prostitute.

Espectáculo del año dos mil (Spectacle of the Year Two Thousand), with many theatrical elements, especially mythical and absurd ones, was published in 1981. Aridjis provides an apocalyptic treatment of end-of-the-millennium characteristics, using historical references to what happened in the past. In the text "Moctezuma," he shows the change from Aztec rule to Spanish domination, illustrating how the world continues as always, regardless of the changes.

Construir la muerte (Constructing Death) was published in 1982, its point of departure being a sentence by Montaigne that the continuous work of life is to construct death. Like a wandering minstrel, the poet meanders through specific spaces and time, reflecting on what cannot be changed--the past and, on the problems of the present day and the prospects for the future. Both bright and bleak, the poems, brief and succinct, directly express sensatory imagery contrasting light, colors and shadows.

In 1985, Aridjis published the novel *1492 vida y tiempos de Juan Cabezón de Castilla*, based on contemporary sources about the facts that he relates. Considered one of the most ambitious novels in recent times, it draws together both fiction and history from the fiftheenth century in Spain. The protagonist who links the story together is Juan Cabezón, a descendant of converts, a man in search of his lost love, Isabel de la Vega. Emerging as a truly fascinating and striking character, she is a convert from Ciudad Real whom the Inquisition has condemned to being burned alive. A journey through medieval towns and cities, coupled with keen observations about the daily lives of ordinary people, the novel creates unforgettable impressions about what it was like to live in 1492. Of particular interest is a vivid and emotional description of the exodus of the Jews, expelled by the Inquisition. The novel shows the Spain of the three religions, where enduring scenes ranging from acts of love and processions by penitents to public horrors by the Inquisition impress upon the reader.

One of his most recent works is *El último Adán* (The Last Adam) (1986). Eve has disappeared and there is Adam, running around through thick smoke, under a dark sky. He is searching for life, for anyone, but all he comes upon are destroyed cities, barren lands, and terrified groups of people whose skin and eyebrows are burned, their flesh hanging, their eyes out. Volcanos, spewing fire and ash, and deep fissures in the earth make his path doubly difficult, as he picks his way around rotting bodies. The lasting impression, however, is of the terrible stench produced by death and destruction. *El último Adán* is typical of some apocalyptical literature, but made all the more a possibility by the nuclear age. Aridjis Homero has been internationally recognized as the premier poet of his generation in Mexico. His sometimes stunning, sometimes horrifying lyricism soars to poetic heights. Even his prose has extraordinary poetic qualities, transmiting the essence of reality through language and technique. Octavio Paz observes that in the poetry of Homero Aridjis beats the pulse of the poet, the truth of the poet.

WORKS: Essays: "Encuentro," *El Corno Emplumado* (July 7, 1963): 108-10. "Homenaje a T.S. Elliot," El Corno Emplumado (April 14, 1965): 88. "La creación," *Diálogos* 52 (July-Aug. 1973): 19. Novel: *1492. Vida y tiempos de Juan Cabezón de Castilla* (México: Siglo XXI, 1985). Poetry: *La musa roja* (The Red Muse), private edition, México, 1958. "Poemas," *Revista Mexicana de Literatura* 6-7 (Dec. 1959-Jan. 1960): 5-11. *Los ojos desdoblados* (The Split Eyes) (México: Ediciones La Palabra, 1960). "La tumba de Filidor" (Filidor's Tomb) in *La Palabra*, México, 1961. *La difícil ceremonia* (The Difficult Ceremony) (México: Pájaro Cascabel, 1963). *Antes del reino* (Before the Kingdom) (México: Eds. Era, 1963). "Pavana a la amada difunta," in *Revista Mexicana de Literatura* 7-8 (July-Aug. 1963): 3-8. *Mirándola dormir* (Watching Her Sleep) (México: Mortiz, 1964). *Ajedrez/Navegaciones* (Chess/Navegations) (México: Siglo XXI, 1969). *Los espacios azules* (Blue Spaces), selected poems of Homero Aridjis, edited with an introduction by Kenneth Rexroth (New York: Seabury Press, 1969). *New Poetry of Mexico*, edited by Aridjis et al., bilingual edition by Mark Strand (New York: E. P. Dutton, 1970). *Perséfone* (México: Editions Gallimard, 1970). *El poeta niño* (The Child Poet) (México: FCE, 1971). *El encantador solitario* (The Solitary Enchanter) (México: FCE, 1972). *Seis poetas latinoamericanos de hoy*, ed. (New York: Harcourt Brace Jovanovich, 1972). *Quemar las naves* (To Burn One's Boats) (México: Mortiz, 1975). *Antología poética* (Poetic Anthology) (Madrid: Akal Editor, 1977). *Noche de independencia* and *Mirándola dormir* (Madrid: Ultramar Editores, 1978). *Antología*, 1st Festival Internacional de Poesía, Morelia, Mexico, 1981. Eliot Weinberger, ed. and trans., *Exaltation of Light* (Brockport, N.Y.: Boa Editions, 1981). *Construir la muerte* (Constructing Death) (México: Mortiz, 1982). Five poems translated into English, in *The Borzoi Anthology of Latin American Literature*, vol. 2, edited by Emir Rodríguez Monegal (New York: Alfred A. Knopf, 1986), pp. 855-57. Barry J. Luby and Wayne H. Finke, eds., *Anthology of Contemporary Latin American Literature 1960-1981* (Cranbury, N.J.: Associated University Presses, 1986), p. 48, contains two poems translated into English. *Obra poética* (1960-1986) (Poetic Work) (México: Mortiz, 1987). *Antología del Festival*

Internacional de Poesía de la Ciudad de México, 1987 (Anthology of the International Poetry Festival in Mexico City, 1987), edited with Betty Aridjis, incl. poems by Aridjis (México: Fundación Gutman, 1988), pp. 13-23. "Mi tía Inés" in *Acechando al unicornio, la virginidad en la literatura mexicana,* selection, study, and notes by Brianda Domeca (México: FCE, 1988), pp. 355-56. Theater: *Espectáculo del año dos mil* (Spectacle of the Year Two Thousand) (México: Mortiz, 1981). "Adiós mamá Carlota," frag. from *Gran teatro del fin del mundo,* in *México en el Arte* 3 (Winter 1983): 25-31. "Cristóbal Colón desembarca en el otro mundo," frag. from *Gran teatro del fin del mundo,* in *Revista de la UNAM* 32 (Dec. 1983): 30-38.

BIBLIOGRAPHY: Roland Barthes, *El grado cero de la escritura,* translation to Spanish by Nicolás Rosa (Argentina: Siglo XXI, 1973), p. 48. Sandro Cohen, "Poesía nueva en México," in *Lugar de encuentro* edited by Norma Klahn and Jesse Fernández (México: Editorial Katún, 1987), p. 221. Frank Dauster, *The Double Strand* (Lexington: University of Kentucky Press, 1987), pp. 32-33. Manuel Durán, "Música en sordina: Tres poetas mexicanos: Bonifaz Nuño, García Terres, Aridjis," in *Plural* 8 (1972): 29-31. Jesse Fernández, "La poesía de Homero Aridjis: La salvación por la palabra," in *Lugar de encuentro* edited by Norma Klahn and Jesse Fernández (México: Katún, 1987), pp. 179-90. David William Foster, *A Dictionary of Contemporary Latin American Authors* (Tempe: Center for Latin American Studies, Arizona State University, 1975), p. 7. Luis Leal, *Panorama de la literatura mexicana actual* (Washington, D.C.: Unión Panamericana, 1968), pp. 151, 155, 157. Manuel Lerín, Review of *Antes del reino,* in *Revista Mexicana de Cultura* 873 (Dec. 29, 1963): 15. José Muñoz Cota, "Dos notas sobre libros," review of *Mirándola dormir,* in *Revista Mexicana de Cultura* 899 (June 21, 1964): 10. Aurora M. Ocampo de Gómez and Ernesto Prado Velázquez, *Diccionario de escritores mexicanos* (México: UNAM, 1967), p. 22. Octavio Paz, *Poesía en movimiento,* selection and notes by Octavio Paz, Alí Chumacero, José Emilio Pacheco, and Homero Aridjis (México: Siglo XXI, 1966), p. 27. Javier Peñalosa, "Nombres, títulos y hechos," review of *Antes del reino,* in *México en la Cultura* 772 (Jan. 5, 1964): 3; "5 noticias literarias importantes del mes," review of *Mirándola dormir* in *Nivel* 20 (Aug. 25, 1964): 4. Gustavo Sáinz, Review of *Antes del reino,* in *México en la Cultura* 768 (Dec. 8, 1963): 5; "Un joven poeta encuentra un lenguaje y un tono singulares para hablar del amor y la mujer," in *México en la Cultura* 794 (June 7, 1964): 9. Linda Scheer and Miguel Flórez Ramírez, eds, *Poetry of Transition: Mexican Poetry of the 1960's and 1970's* (Ann Arbor, Mich.: Translation Press, 1984). Sara Sefchovich, *México: país de ideas, país de novelas* (México: Editorial Grijalbo, 1987), p. 153. Guillermo Sucre, "La nueva profundidad; superficies nítidas," in *Plural* 50 (México, Nov. 1975): 78. Ramón Xirau, *Mito y poesía* (México: UNAM, 1973), p. 79.

JEANNE C. WALLACE

ARREDONDO, Inés (1928-1989). Arredondo was born in Culiacán, Sinaloa, on March 20. She studied Spanish and Latin American literature at the National University of Mexico where she graduated with a master's degree. Upon receiving scholarships from the Center of Mexican Writers and the Farfield Foundation in 1962, she went to New York to study. During her stay in the United States she gave a series of lectures at Indiana University. Early in her career she traveled to Europe and resided in Montevideo, Uruguay, for two years (1963-1964). She contributed critical essays and short stories to many magazines and newspapers in Mexico: *Universidad de México, Revista de Bellas Artes, Revista Mexicana de Literatura, La cultura en México, Siempre!*, etc.

Arredondo's first work was a volume of short stories entitled *La señal* (The Sign). It consists of fourteen short stories in which the author examines the personal lives of her female protagonists. Two of the stories in this book, "La sunamita," considered a bestseller, and "Mariana," were made into films by Héctor *Mendoza and Juan Guerrero respectively.

Inés Arredondo received the Villaurrutia Prize for narrative in 1979 for her second collection of short stories, *Río subterráneo* (Subterranean River), in which she continues to analyze the innermost feelings of women. In her works Arredondo focuses on women and explores the themes of love and solitude. Her fiction is a profound inquiry into human relationships. Although Arredondo's literary production includes only two books of short stories, she is considered one of the Mexico's finest short story writers.

WORKS: Short Stories: *La señal* (México: Era, 1965). *Río subterráneo* (México: Mortiz, 1979). Essays: *Opus 1 2 3* (México: Oasis, 1983). *Acercamiento a Jorge Cuesta* (México: SepSetentas-Diana, 1982).

BIBLIOGRAPHY: Fabienne Bradu, *Señas particulares: escritora* (México: FCE, 1987), pp. 29-49. *Confrontaciones. Narradores ante el público* (México: Mortiz, 1966), pp. 121-26. Aurora M. Ocampo de Gómez and Ernesto Prado Velázquez, *Diccionario de escritores mexicanos* (México: UNAM, 1967), p. 22.

                                                                            NORA ERRO-PERALTA

ARREOLA, Juan José (1918-). An autodidactic (he never finished elementary school), short story writer, novelist, journalist, traveling salesman, teacher, and actor, Arreola was born in Ciudad Guzmán, Jalisco, previously known as Zapotlán El Grande, a town near Guadalajara. Arreola documents its history very well in his novel *La feria* (The Fair) (1963).

Arreola worked some time as a professional actor, starting his
career in Mexico City with Rodolfo *Usigli and Xavier *Villaurrutia. Later he traveled to Paris to study acting with Louis Jouvet under a scholarship from the French government (1945), a not very successful trip. As a result of World War II, financial need, and ill health, he returned to Mexico City, where in 1946 he began working for the Fondo de Cultura Económica as a proofreader and writing short introductory essays for book jackets. At the same time he continued to write and to publish his own short stories. In 1950 he received a Rockefeller Foundation scholarship for creative writing. In 1958 through *Cuadernos del Unicornio* (The Unicorn's Notebook), he was very active as a teacher of creative writing, supervising the publication of his students' work. By 1973 Arreola had already become very popular for his television program in which he presents, discusses, and analyzes different literary subjects. Presently he continues to host this same program.

He is a well traveled-writer, speaks several languages, and is familiar with universal literary movements. Arreola has published several of his stories in different anthologies with different titles. *Confabulario personal* (Personal Confabulary) (1979) is an anthology that includes short pieces from most of his works. An excellent narrator, Arreola is known more as a short story writer than as a novelist. He began his literary career in Guadalajara by editing two literary magazines, *Eos* and *Pan* (1942-1945). "Hizo el bien mientras vivió" (1943) is the short story that established his reputation as a careful and methodical writer. *Confabulario total* (Total Confabulary) (1962) is a publication which brings together two previous collections of short stories, *Varia invención* (Various Inventions) (1949) and *Confabulario* (Confabulary) (1952), and a one-act play, *La hora de todos* (Moment of Truth) (1954). In 1963 he won the prestigious Xavier Villaurrutia prize. Satire and irony are two predominant themes that bring together most of the stories from these collections. "El Guardagujas" (The Switchman) (1952) is one of his most anthologized stories. Here the basic idea is to satirize the railroad system in Mexico. But, as soon as the story unfolds, there is a very interesting turn of events. There is a fusion of reality and fantasy throughout the narration. Because Arreola refuses to follow conventional methods in creative writing, his stories generally contain more philosophical commentary than the physical, everyday narration of events. The strong realistic base within *Magical Realism is evident from Arreola's point of departure which, in this story, is based on a small Mexican train terminal, the inefficiencies of the Mexican railroad system, the timetables that are not kept, the better service provided to first-class passengers, etc. On the philosophical side, there is the question of boarding the train, the train of life in this case. A decision has to be made by the passengers whether to board the train or be left behind. The decision has to be made to board it and not to have any fixed destinations. The message is to live life fully and not worry about obstacles along the way.

Women have an important place in Arreola's narrative. Personally, he has said that he holds a contradictory feeling of attraction to and rejection of women. This theme is developed in several short stories such as "Pueblerina" (Small Town Tale), "Una mujer amaestrada" (A Trained Woman), and "El Rinoceronte" (The Rhinoceros). In these stories he is very hard on women describing them as insatiable and destructive, and he expresses a sigh of relief upon finally escaping from them. *Bestiario* (Bestiary) (1972) is Arreola's contribution to allegory that uses animals as characters. The similarity with others stops here, since Arreola is very adept at using irony and witticism in his efforts to better understand human beings and their behavior. His literary influences come from Franz Kafka (1883-1924), Albert Camus (1913-1960), and Jorge Luis Borges (1899-1986), among others. Arreola's excellent technique in the craft of short story writing, and his ability to go from the logical to the absurd, his careful style, and the expressive ability and economy of language, has placed him, along with Juan *Rulfo and Jorge Luis Borges, as one of the most outstanding short story writers in the Spanish-speaking world.

WORKS: *Gunther Stapenhorst* (México: Costa-Amic, 1946). *Varia invención* (Varied Invention) (México: FCE, 1949). *Cinco Cuentos* (Five Short Stories) (México: Los Presentes, 1951). *Confabulario* (Confabulary) (México: FCE, 1952). *La hora de todos* (Drama) (Moment of Truth) (México: Los Presentes, 1954). *Confabulario y Varia invención* (México: FCE, 1955); *Confabulario and Other Inventions*, translated by George D. Schade (Austin: University of Texas Press, 1964). *Punta de plata*

(Silverpoint) (México: UNAM, 1958). *Confabulario total* (Total Confabulary) (México: FCE, 1962). *La feria* (México: Mortiz, 1963); *The Fair*, translated by John Upton (Austin: University of Texas Press, 1977). *Confabulario* (México: FCE, 1966), includes most of Arreola's published work. *Lectura en voz alta* (Reading Aloud) (Anthology of world literature for oral presentation) (México: Colección Sepan Cuantos, 1968). *Palindroma* (Palindrome) (México: Mortiz, 1971). *Bestiario* (Bestiary) (México: Mortiz, 1972). *La palabra educación*, compiled by Jorge Arturo Ojeda (The Word Education) (México: SEP/Setentas, 1973), a book of Arreola's reflections on different subjects. *Y ahora, la mujer . . .* (And Now, Woman), compiled by Jorge Arturo Ojeda (México: Utopía, 1975), epigrams on Arreola's favorite subject, women. *Inventario* (Inventory) (México: Editorial Grijalbo, 1976). *Confabulario personal* (Personal Confabulary) (Barcelona: Bruguera, 1979).

BIBLIOGRAPHY: John S. Brushwood, *Mexico in Its Novel* (Austin: University of Texas Press, 1966). Emmanuel Carballo, *Diecinueve protagonistas de la literatura mexicana del siglo XX*, (México: Empresas Editoriales, 1965). Read G. Gilgen, "Absurdist Techniques in the Short Stories of Juan José Arreola," *Journal of Spanish Studies: Twentieth Century* 8: 67-77. Paula R. Heusinkveld, "La nueva ideología de Juan José Arreola," *Revista de Crítica Literaria Latinoamericana* 11, 23 (1986): 45-52. Walter M. Langford. *The Mexican Novel Comes of Age* (Notre Dame, Ind.: University of Notre Dame Press, 1971). Luis Leal, *El cuento mexicano* (México: Eds. de Andrea, 1955). Vicente Leñero, "¿Te acuerdas de Rulfo, Juan José Arreola?" in *Tramoya* 9 (Nueva Epoca), 1987 (Universidad Veracruzana-Rutgers University-Camden): 114-118. George R. McMurray, "Albert Camus' Concept of the Absurd and Juan José Arreola's 'The Switchman,'" *Latin American Literary Review* 11 (1977): 30-35. María del Carmen Millán, *Antología de cuentos mexicanos*, vol. 1 (México: Editorial Nueva Imagen, 1977). Cristina Peri Rossi, "Yo, Señores, soy de Zapotlán el Grande," Interview with J. J. Arreola in *Quimera: Revista de Literatura* 1 (Nov. 1980): 23-27. Yulan M. Washburn, *Juan José Arreola* (Boston: Twayne, 1983).

OSCAR SOMOZA

ARREOLA Cortés, Raúl (1917-), poet and essayist. Arreola Cortés was born in Pátzcuaro, Michoacán, in 1917. He studied at the Escuela Normal de Morelia and is a member of the Seminario de Cultura Mexicana and the Academia Mexicana de la Educación. He was editor of *Cuadernos de Literatura Michoacana* and *Pliego*, a literary magazine, and director and editor of *Cantera*, a cultural magazine (1946-1948). In 1940 he began publishing his poetry, which later appeared in magazines such as *Hispánica Moderna*, *Novedades*, and *El Universal*. He also wrote essays pertaining to literary criticism, especially about José Rubén *Romero and Miguel N. *Lira.

WORKS: Poetry: *Apuntes de un aprendiz* (Notes of an Apprentice) (Michoacán: n.p., 1940). *Ofrenda lírica al poeta César L. Bonequi* (Lirical Offering to the Poet César L. Bonequi) (Michoacán: n.p., 1940). Essays: "La influencia lorquiana en Miguel N. Lira" (The Lorquian Influence on Miguel N. Lira), in *Revista Hispánica Moderna* (México, Oct. 1942). "José Rubén Romero: vida y obra" (José Rubén Romero: Life and Works), in *Revista Hispánica Moderna* 1-2 (México, Jan.-Apr. 1946): 7-34. *Letras michoacanas contemporáneas* (Contemporary Michoacanas Letters) (Michoacán: n.p., 1949). "Notas sobre la obra poética de Miguel N. Lira" (Notes on the Poetic Work of Miguel N. Lira), in *Humanitas* 4 (Mexico, 1963): 257-68. Studies: *Historia de la Escuela Normal de Morelia* (History of the Normal School of Morelia) (Michoacán: n.p., 1947). *Hidalgo* (Nobleman) (Michoacán: n.p., 1955). *Historia del Colegio de San Nicolás de Hidalgo* (History of the College of Saint Nicholas of Hidalgo) (Michoacán: Ed. de la Universidad, 1958). *Morelos*, historical drama (Michoacán: n.p., 1959). *El maestro Rébsamen y la educación en Michoacán* (The Teacher Rébsamen and Education in Michoacán) (Michoacán: Escuela Normal Urbana Federal, 1962). *La influencia del maestro Enrique C. Rébsamen en la educación de Michoacán* (Influence of Teacher Enrique C. Rébsamen on the Educational System of Michoacán) (Xalapa: Univ. Veracruzana, 1964). *La obra científica y literaria de don Melchor Ocampo* (The Scientific and Literary Work of Melchor Ocampo) (Morelia: Universidad Michoacana, 1966). *Epitacio Huerta, soldado y estadista liberal* (Epitacio Huerta, Soldier and Liberal Politician) (México: SEP, 1967). *Miguel N. Lira. Vida y obra* (Miguel N. Lira. Life and Works) (México: INBA, 1967). *Jesús Sansón Flores, poeta revolucionario* (Jesús Sansón Flores, Revolutionary Poet) (México: SEP, 1968). *Melchor Ocampo, paladín de la revolución liberal* (Melchor Ocampo, Leader of the Liberal Revolution) (México: SEP, 1968). *Pablo Neruda en Morelia* (Morelia: Casa de San Nicolás, 1972). *Infancia y juventud de Juárez* (Juárez' Childhood and Youth) (Morelia: n.p., 1972). *Melchor Ocampo* (México: SEP, 1975). *Miguel N. Lira, el poeta y el hombre* (Miguel N. Lira, the Poet and the Man) (México: Jus, 1977). *Alfredo Maillefert: soledades y silencio* (Alfredo Maillefert: Solitude and Silence) (México: Jus, 1978). *La poesía en Michoacán* (The Poetry in Michoacán) (Morelia: Fimax, 1979). Prologues: Antonio Salas León, *Pátzcuaro, cosas de antaño y hogaño* (n.p., n.d.). José Santos Valdés, *La participación de los maestros mexicanos en la Revolución de 1910* (Michoacán: n.p., 1959). Alfredo Gálvez Bravo, *De la pedagogía y otros problemas* (n.p., n.d.). Gonzalo Mendoza Herrera, *Su nombre en un libro* (Michoacán: Ed. de la Escuela Normal, 1961).

BIBLIOGRAPHY: Salvador Calvillo Madrigal, *La literatura en Michoacán* (Morelia: Gobierno del Estado, n.d.), pp. 21-22. Heriberto García Rivas, *Historia de la literatura mexicana*, vol. 4 (México: Porrúa, 1974), p. 444. Aurora M. Ocampo de Gómez and Ernesto Prado Velázquez, *Diccionario de escritores mexicanos* (México: UNAM, 1967), p. 24.

                                                              MIRTA BARREA-MARLYS

ARRIOLA, Juan José de (1698-1768), poet and teacher, born in Guanajuato. He studied at the Colegio de San Idelfonso in Mexico City, joined the Jesuit Order in 1715, and became professor of humanities and rhetoric at the Royal and Pontifical University in Mexico City. Juan José de Arriola is known for his philosophical and religious poems. Though most of them remain in manuscript form, several were printed. One of his poems, "Canción a un desengaño" (Song upon a Deception) is based on a work by Matías de *Bocanegra, "Canción a la vista de un desengaño." He is also known for a fourteen-sonnet commentary on the poem "No me mueve mi Dios

...," attributed to Miguel de *Guevara. His claim to excellence in creative literature rests with the lyrical- biographical poem, "Vida y virtudes de . . . Santa Rosalía" (Life and Virtues of . . . Saint Rosalia).

WORKS: *La cátedra de Cristo* (The Lesson of Christ) (México, 1748). *Canción famosa a un desengaño* (Famous Song to a Deception) (Mexico, 1724). *Vida y virtudes de ... Santa Rosalía* (Life and Virtues of ... Saint Rosalia). (México, 1766); reprinted as *Décimas de Santa Rosalía* (Verses to Saint Rosalia); edited by Alfonso Méndez Plancarte (México: Los presentes, 1955), pp. 7-87. *Glosa en catorce sonetos ...* (Glossary in Fourteen Sonnets ...) (México: n.p., n.d.). *Panegírico de San Ignacio de Loyola* (Panegyric of San Ignacio de Loyola) (México 1748). *No hay mayor mal que los celos* (Jealously Is the Worst Evil) (Lost).

BIBLIOGRAPHY: José Mariano, Beristáin de Souza. *Biblioteca Mexicana Septentrional* (México, 1883), pp. 176-77. Alfonso Méndez Plancarte, "Nota," *Décimas de Santa Rosalía* (México: Los presentes, 1955), 89-111.

ALFONSO GONZALEZ

ARRONIZ, Marcos (?-1859?). Little is known about the early years of Marcos Arróniz, including the date of his birth, estimated to be somewhere around the beginning of the nineteenth century. It is believed that he was from Orizaba, Veracruz, and that he studied for a while in Mexico City. A conservative militant, he served under Santa Anna, taking part in active battle. In either 1858 or 1859, his body was found along the road in Puebla. Whether he committed suicide or was killed by bandits has not been ascertained. There is historical evidence, though, that he had become mentally deranged some months before his death, a factor contributing to the possibility of a suicide.

Arróniz was considered an authentic representative of the Romantic school in México. In 1857, the noted Spanish writer José Zorrilla declared that he was a poet of "doubt, delirium and desperation," characteristics which fit in with the Romantic outlook on life. He did write and publish some original poetry, apparently in journals of his day, but he never actually published a book. He also translated into Spanish the poetry of some French and English writers, including Lord George Byron, from whom he drew inspiration. In addition to his poetic endeavors, Arróniz wrote books pertaining to biography, history, and related fields, a couple of which were published.

WORKS: *Manual de biografía mexicana* (Manual of Mexican Biography) (Paris: Rosa and Bouret, 1857). *Manual de historia y cronología de México* (Paris: Rosa and Bouret, 1858).

BIBLIOGRAPHY: Ignacio M. Altamirano, *La literatura nacional*, vol. 3 (México: Edit. Porrúa, 1949), pp. 70-72. Francisco R. Illescas and Juan Bartolo Hernández, *Escritores veracruzanos* (Veracruz: n.p., 1945), p. 82. Alberto Leduc, Luis Lara Pardo, and Carlos Roumagnac, *Diccionario de geografía, historia y biografía mexicanas* (Paris and México: Vda. de Ch. Bouret, 1910). Aurora M. Ocampo de Gómez and Ernesto Prado Velázquez, *Diccionario de escritores mexicanos* (México: UNAM, 1967), p. 25.

52   ATL, Dr.

Francisco Pimentel, *Historia crítica de la literatura y de las ciencias en México desde la Conquista hasta nuestros días* (México: Libr. de la Enseñanza, 1890), pp. 677-79. José Zorrilla, *México y los mexicanos* (México: Eds. de Andrea, 1955), p. 150.

JEANNE C. WALLACE

ATL, Dr. See MURILLO, Gerardo.

ATTOLINI, José (1916-1957), poet, dramatist, short story writer, economist. Attolini was born in Mexico City on March 9, 1916, and died there on October 15, 1957. His formal education included a master's degree in economics and a doctorate in letters. Attolini was a professor at the Escuela Normal Superior, the Facultad de Economía, and the Escuela Nacional de Bellas Artes. He was also a permanent member of the Secretaría de Bienes Nacionales of the Comisión Nacional de Inversiones, and director of Control de Requisiciones of the Secretaría de Bienes Nacionales e Inspección Administrativa (1949); he became general technical director of organization in the same Secretaría, from 1950 to 1951, and was acting as general manager of Almacenes de Depósito when he died. He was a contributor to journals in both literature and economics.

Attolini began his literary career writing "vanguardista" poetry (1938-1940), the theme of which was the desperation and anguish of the poor. He also wrote dramatic works and narratives based on a social problematic. *Vagido* is a story inspired by the dark, turbulent atmosphere of the barrios of Mexico City. His essays, perhaps the most valuable of his work, examine literary problems within a framework of historical materialism.

WORKS: Poetry: *Desamor, Seis poemas* (Indifference, Six Poems) (México, 1938). *Saudades* (Nostalgia) (México: Private Edition, 1939). Leopoldo Ramos, (México: Ed. Canek, 1941). *Mito* (Myth) (México: Firmamento, 1942). *Testimonio* (Testimony) (México, 1957). Poetry and Short Stories: *Vagido* (Wail) (México: Encrucijada, 1958). Short Stories: *Honor y gloria* (Honor and Glory) (México: Encrucijada, 1957). Theater: *Kupra*, play in three acts (México: Tiras de Colores, 1944). *Vertedero* (Sewer), play in three acts (México: Tiras de Colores, 1944). Essays: *Fundamentos para una nueva interpretación de la historia del arte y de la literatura* (Foundation for a New Interpretation of the History of Art and Literature), master's thesis (México: UNAM, 1944). Studies: *Problemas economico sociales de Veracruz* (Socioeconomic Problems of Veracruz) (México: Encrucijada, 1947). *Breve historia de la Linguistica* (A Brief History of Linguistics), doctoral dissertation in Humanities (México: Encrucijada, 1948). *Economía de la Cuenca del Papaloapán: Agricultura* (Economy of the Valley of the Papaloapan: Agriculture) (México: Inst. de Investigación Económica, 1949). *Economía de la Cuenca de Papaloapán: bosques, fauna, pesca, ganadería e industria* (Economy of the Valley of Papaloapan: Forests, Fauna, Fish, Cattle, and Industry) (México: Instituto de Investigación Económica, 1950). *Las finanzas de la Universidad a través del tiempo* (Finances of the University over the

Years) (México: Escuela Nacional de Economía, UNAM, 1951). Prologue: Ermilio Abreu Gómez, *Héroes mayas, advertencia de...* (Mayan Heroes, Warnings of. . .) (México: General Editores, 1942).

BIBLIOGRAPHY: Ermilo Abreu Gómez, *Sala de retratos* (México: Ed. Leyenda, 1946). Ruth S. Lamb, *Bibliografía del teatro mexicano del siglo XX*, Col. Studium no. 33 (México: Eds. de Andrea, 1962), pp. 28-29. Luis Leal, *Bibliografía del cuento mexicano*, Col. Studium no. 21 (México: Eds. de Andrea, 1958), p. 16. Antonio Magaña Esquivel and Ruth S. Lamb, *Breve historia del teatro mexicano* (México: Eds. de Andrea, 1958), p. 157. José Luis Martínez, *Literatura mexicana siglo XX. 1910-1949* (México: Ant. Libr. Robredo, 1950), vol. 1, pp. 51, 85, 109, 131; vol. 2, p. 18. Aurora M. Ocampo de Gómez and Ernesto Prado Velázquez, *Diccionario de escritores mexicanos* (México: UNAM, 1967), pp. 25-26. Carlos J. Sierra, "Fuentes para el estudio del pensamiento contemporáneo: José Attolini Aguirre," in *Boletín Bibliográfico Hispánico* 303 (Sept. 15, 1964): 12-15, 16.

                                                                    JOAN SALTZ

AUB, Max (1903-1972), teacher, playwright, novelist, and essayist born in Paris, France. He was educated in Spain and was incarcerated for three years by the Franco regime. In 1942 Aub moved to Mexico City where he wrote most of his work, and where he died. He taught theater and cinema at the National University in Mexico, and also taught and/or delivered papers at the universities of Brussels, Paris, Harvard, and Yale. He was a member of the Real Academia de la Lengua. After a thirty-year absence, he returned to Spain in 1969. Max Aub was a prolific and experimental writer. While some of his writings are what he called "literary jokes," several of his books combine fiction, theater, and poetry. Some of his novels focus on the atrocities and indignities to which man is subject in a concentration camp. His essays deal with many topics including literary history and criticism.

WORKS: Poetry: *Los poemas cotidianos* (The Daily Poems) (Barcelona: Imp. Omega, 1925). *Diario de Djelfa* (Diary of Djelfa) (México: U.D. de Ediciones, 1944). *Canciones de la esposa ausente* (Songs of the Absent Wife) (México: Private Edition, 1953). *Lira Perpetua* (Perpetual Lyre) (México: Private Edition, 1959). *Antología traducida* (Translated Anthology) (México: UNAM, 1963). *Subversiones* (Subversions) (Madrid: Helios, 1971). Short Stories: *Fábula verde* (Green Fable) (Valencia: n.p., 1933). *No son cuentos* (They're Not Lies) (México: Tezontle, 1944). *Algunas Prosas* (Some Prose) (México: Los presentes, 1954). *Cuentos ciertos* (True Fictions) (México: Ant. Libr. Robredo, 1954). *Ciertos cuentos* (Certain Stories) (México: Ant. Libr. Robredo, 1956). *Crímenes ejemplares* (Exemplary Crimes) (México: Ant. Libr. Robredo, 1957). *Cuentos mexicanos con pilón* (Mexican Stories with a Small Gift) (México: Imp. Universitaria, 1959). *La verdadera historia de la muerte de Francisco Franco y otros cuentos* (The True Story of the Death of Francisco Franco and Other Stories) (México: Libro Mexicano Ed., 1960). *El remate* (The Sale) (México: Avándaro, 1961). *Juego de naipes; opúsculo* (Card Game; A Kiss) (México: Ecuador, 1964). *El Zopilote y otros cuentos mexicanos* (The Buzzard and Other Mexican Stories) (México: EDHA, 1964). *Historias del 36* (Stories from 1936) (Madrid: Ed.

Veintinueve, 1965). *Historias de mala muerte* (Stories of Undignified Deaths) (México: Mortiz, 1965). *La uña y otras narraciones* (The Fingernail and Other Stories) (Barcelona: Picazo, 1972). *Los pies por delante y otros cuentos* (Feet First and Other Stories) (Barcelona: Seix Barral, 1975). Novels: *Geografía* (Geography) (Madrid: Cuadernos Literarios de Lectura, 1929; México: Era, 1964). *Luis Alvarez Petreña* (Barcelona: Miracle, 1934). *Campo cerrado* (Closed Camp) (México: Tezontle, 1943). *Campo de sangre* (Blood Camp) (México: Tezontle, 1945). *Campo abierto* (Open Camp) (México: Tezontle, 1951). *Yo vivo* (I'm Alive) (México: FCE, 1953). *Las buenas intenciones* (Good Intentions) (México: FCE, 1954). *Jusep Torres Campalans* (Jusep Torres Campalans) (México: FCE, 1958). *La calle de Valverde* (Valverde's Street) (México: Universidad Veracruzana, 1961). *Campo del moro* (Camp of the Moor) (México: Mortiz, 1963). *Campo francés* (French Camp) (Paris: Ruedo Ibérico, 1965). *Vida y obra de Luis Alvarez Petreña* (Life and Works of Luis Alvarez Petreña) (Barcelona: Seix Barral, 1971). Theater: *Narciso* (Narcissus) (Barcelona: Altis, 1928). *Teatro incompleto* (Incomplete Theater) (Madrid: Sociedad General Española de Librerías, 1931). *Espejo de avaricia* (Mirror of Avarice) (Madrid: Cruz y Raya, 1935). *San Juan* (Saint John) (México: Tezontle, 1943). *Morir por cerrar los ojos* (To Die for Not Paying Attention) (México: Tezontle, 1944). *La vida conyugal* (Married Life) (México: Letras de México, 1945). *El rapto de Europa o siempre se puede hacer algo* (The Abduction of Europe or You Can Always Do Something) (México: Tezontle, 1946). *Cara y cruz* (Heads and Tails) (México: Soc. Grl. de Autores Mexicanos, 1948). *De algún tiempo a esta parte* (For Some Time Now) (México: Tezontle, 1949). *Deseada* (A Wished Woman) (México: Tezontle, 1950). *No* (No) (México: Tezontle, 1952). *Tres monólogos y uno solo verdadero* (Three Monologues and Only One Truthful) (México: 1956). *Del amor* (About Love) (México: Ecuador, 1960). *Obras en un acto I* (One Act Works I) (México: Imp. Universitaria, 1960). *Obras en un acto II* (One Act Works II) (México: Imp. Universitaria, 1960). *Las vueltas* (The Returns) (México: Mortiz, 1965). *Teatro Completo* (Complete Theater) (México: Aguilar, 1968). *Teatro* (Theater) (Madrid: Taurus, 1971). *El desconfiado prodigioso* (The Prodigious Diffident) (Madrid: Taurus, 1971). Theater, Prose, Poetry: *Sala de espera I* (Waiting Room I) (México: Gráficos Guanajuato, 1949). *Sala de espera II* (Waiting Room II) (México; Gráficos Guanajuato, 1950). *Sala de espera III* (Waiting Room III) (México; FCE, 1951). Essays: *La poesía española contemporánea* (Contemporary Spanish Poetry) (México: Imp. Universitaria, 1954). *Poesía mexicana 1950-1960* (Mexican Poetry 1950-1960) (México: Aguilar, 1960). *Pruebas* (Proofs) (Madrid: Ciencia Nueva, 1967). Collection of essays and prologues. *Diario español de Max Aub* (Spanish Diary of Max Aub) (México: Mortiz, 1969). *Pequeña y vieja historia marroquí* (Brief and Old Moroccan History) (Palma de Mallorca: Ed. Papeles de Son Armadans, 1971). *Ensayos mexicanos* (Mexican Essays) (México: UNAM, 1974). *Conversaciones con Buñuel.* (Conversations with Buñuel) (Madrid: Aguilar, 1985). Axioms and Epitaphs: *Crímenes ejemplares* (Exemplary Crimes) (México: Finisterre, 1969; Barcelona: Lumen, 1972).

BIBLIOGRAPHY: José Luis Alborg. *Hora Actual de la novela española, vol. 2* (Madrid: Taurus, 1962): pp. 75-132. Angelo Borris, *El teatro del exilio de Max Aub* (Sevilla: Universidad de Sevilla, 1975). Antonio Carreño, "Twentieth Century Spanish Drama: In Defense of Liberty," *The Theater and Hispanic Life: Essays in Honour of Nealy H. Taylor* (Waterloo: Wilfrid Laurier University Press, 1982), pp. 55-76; "Antología traducida de Max Aub: La alegoría de las máscaras múltiples," *Insula 35,*

406 (1980): 1, 10; *La dialéctica de la identidad en la poesía contemporánea* (Madrid: Gredos, 1982). Claude Couffon, "Un livre des bonnes intentions," *Les Lettres Francaises* 985 (1963): 4. Janet W. Díaz, "Spanish Civil War and Exile in the Novels of Aub, Ayala, and Sender," *Latin America and the Literature of Exile* (Heidelberg: Winter 1983), pp.207-31. Manuel Durán, "Max Aub o la vocación de escritor," *Siempre!* 14 (Aug. 1963): 6-7. Mikel de Epalsa, "Max Aub et les ecrivains espagnols 'exiles' en Algerie," *Espagne et Algérie au XXe siècle: Contacts culturels et création littéraire* (Paris: L'Harmattan, 1985), pp.125-39. I. González Pozuelo, "El laberinto mágico: Max Aub entre la novela y la historia," *Insula* 39, 449 (1984); 3. Rosario Hiriart, "Un estudio sobre las bromas literarias," *Insula* 37, 432 (1982): 12. Estelle Irizarry, et al., eds. "Cuatro bromas literarias de nuestros tiempos," *Actas del Sexto Congreso Internacional de Hispanistas celebrado en Toronto del 22 al 26 de agosto de 1977* (Toronto: Department of Spanish and Portuguese, University of Toronto, 1980), pp. 402-05. *Writer-Painters of Contemporary Spain* (Boston: Twayne, 1984). Amando C. Isasi Angulo, *Diálogos, entrevistas con Max Aub* (Madrid: Ed. Ayuso, 1974). Pilar Moraleda, "El teatro de Max Aub," *Cuadernos Hispanoamericanos* 411 (1984): 148-58. José Monleón, *El teatro de Max Aub* (Madrid: Taurus, 1971). Silvia Monti, "La comunicazione come problema nel primo teatro di Max Aub," *Quaderni di Lingue e Letterature* (Verona) 3-4 (1978-79): 267-83. Ignacio Soldevilla Durante, "El español de Max Aub," *La Torre* (Jan.-Mar. 1960): 103-20. *La obra narrativa de Max Aub 1929-1969* (Madrid: Gredos, 1973). Michael Ugarte, "Max Aub's Magical Labyrinth of Exile," *Hispania* 68, 4 (1985): 733-39. Lucinda W. Wright, "A Study of *Cara y Cruz* and San Juan," *DAI* 47, 5 (1986): 1745A, University of North Carolina, Chapel Hill. Wladyslaw Zaworski, "Tresc i forma w opowiadaniach Mikhala Szolochowa, Maxa Auba i Juana Rulfa: Zagadnienia wybrane." *Slavia Orientalis* (Warsaw) 33, 2 (1984): 191-98.

MIRTA A. GONZALEZ

AURA, Alejandro (1944-). Aura was born in Mexico City on March 2, 1944. Apart from being a renowned poet, he is also a consummate actor and playwright. He and poet-wife Carmen *Boullosa are co-owners of an exciting avant-garde Mexico City (Coyoacán) dinner theater called "El hijo del cuervo" where they are also cooks, waiters, and actors. He is presently host of one of Mexico's most popular television talk shows, "Entre amigos." He has traveled extensively through Mexico and Latin America and has been invited to lecture on contemporary Mexican theater and poetry at several American universities.

Aura started as a poet. In the collective work *Poesía joven de México*, with Leopoldo Ayala, José Carlos Becerra, and Raúl Garduño, Aura's "Cinco veces la flor" (Five Times the Flower) initiates the rendering of a demythified vision of Mexico City life within a tradition of Mexican poetry which is now well established and respected, especially after recognition of the work of such Mexican poetic giants as Efraín *Huerta and Jaime Sabines. It is a poetry concerned with presenting contemporary reality through simplicity of language, poignant love scenes, childhood images, reference to well-known places and people and a general reconstruction of what seems to be a life dismembered, chaotic, and absurd as compared to an orderly, aesthetic past. This vision continues to develop into a love for living and for what is truly human in later poetry and becomes crystallized in his last published work, *La patria vieja.*

WORKS: *Cinco veces la flor* (Five Times the Flower) (México: Siglo XXI, 1967). *Alianza para vivir* (Alliance to Live) (México: UNAM, 1969). *Various desnudos y dos docenas de naturalezas muertas* (Monterrey: Ediciones Poesía en el Mundo, 1971). *Los baños de Celeste* (Celeste's Baths) Premio Latinoamericano de cuento, 1972. *Volver a casa* (Coming Back Home), Premio Nacional de Poesía Aguascalientes, 1973 (México: Mortiz, 1974). *Tambor interno* (Internal Drum) (Toluca: Casa de la Cultura del Estado de México, 1975). *Hemisferio sur* (South Hemisphere) (México: Papeles Privados, 1982). *Salón calavera, Las visitas y Bang* (Skull Saloon, The Visits and Bang) (México: Océano, 1986). *Patria vieja* (Old Country) (Puebla: Universidad Autónoma de Puebla, 1986).

BIBLIOGRAPHY: José Joaquín Blanco, *Crónica de la poesía mexicana* (México: Katún, 1981), pp. 264-70. Sandro Cohen, *Palabra nueva: Dos décadas de poesía en México* (México: Premiá, 1981), pp. 15-16 and 56-61. Enrique R. Lamadrid and Mario Del Valle, *Un ojo en el muro/An Eye Through the Wall: Mexican Poetry: 1970-1985* (Santa Fe, N.M.:   Tooth of Time Books, 1986) pp. 33-43. Sergio Mondragón, *República de poetas* (México: Martín Casillas, 1985), pp.36-45. Jaime Moreno Villareal, *La línea y el círculo* (México: Universidad Autónoma Metropolitana, 1981). Alejandro Sandoval, *Veinte años de poesía en México: El premio de poesía de Aquascalientes, 1968-1988* (México: Mortiz, 1988), pp. 67-75.

RICARDO AGUILAR

AVELEYRA Arroyo de Anda, Teresa (1920-), critic, poet, and author of short stories. Born on March 7, 1920, in Mexico City, she received her bachelor's degree from UNAM, where she studied French, English, and Italian. While in Europe (1955), she took courses in literature at the Sorbonne and at the Alliance Française. She has dedicated her life to teaching and writing on Miguel de Cervantes, which won first prize at the second Cervantes Literary Contest sponsored by the Technological Institute of Monterrey. Subsequent works also manifest her love of Cervantine literature. In addition, she has published poetry, *Al viento submarino* (On the Underwater Wind), and a novelesque collection of short stories, *Pueblo limpio.*

WORKS: *El humorismo de Cervantes en sus obras menores* (Cervantes Humor in His Minor Works), thesis (México: Facultad de Filosofía y Letras, UNAM, 1962). *Pueblo limpio: cuentos de la montaña* (Clean Village: Mountain Stories) (México: Costa-Amic, 1962). *Trabajos premiados en el segundo concurso literario Cervantes* (Prize-winning Works in the Second Cervantes Literary Contest) (Monterrey, 1963). *Al viento submarino: libro del mar por dentro* (On the Underwater Wind: A Book of the Sea Inside) (Monterrey, N.L., México: Instituto Tecnológico y de Estudios Superiores, 1966). *Autobiografía sentimental de Alonso Quijano* (Sentimental Autobiography of Alonso Quijano) (Monterrey: Instituto Tecnológico y de Estudios Superiores, 1970).

BIBLIOGRAPHY: Anon., Review of *Pueblo limpio*, in *Tiempo* 53, 1100 (June 3, 1963): 40; Review of *Pueblo limpio*, in *Vida Universitaria*, 671 (Feb. 2, 1964). María Elvira Bermúdez, "Dos escritoras mexicanas," review of *Pueblo limpio*, in *Diorama de la Cultura* (May 26, 1963): 8; "La novela mexicana en 1963," in *Diorama de la Cultura* (Jan. 19, 1964): 8. Mario Calleros, "Las mesas de plomo. Dos libros de cuentos," review of *Pueblo limpio*, in *Ovaciones*, suppl. no. 114 (March 1, 1964): 8. J. Gibbs, Review of *El humorismo de Cervantes en sus obras menores*, in *Bulletin of Hispanic Studies* 41, 1 (Jan. 1964): 68-69. Pedro Gringoire, "Bibliogramas," review of *Pueblo limpio*, in *Excelsior* (April 16, 1963). Javier Morente, "Sala de lectura," review of *Pueblo limpio*, in *Diorama de la Cultura* (March 31, 1963): 8-B. Aurora M. Ocampo de Gómez and Ernesto Prado Velázquez, *Diccionario de escritores mexicanos* (México: UNAM, 1967), p. 27. Otto Olivera, Review of *El humorismo de Cervantes en sus obras menores*, in *Hispania* 46, 4 (Dec. 1963): 847. T., Review of *El humorismo de Cervantes en sus obras menores*, in *Cuadernos Hispanoamericanos* 170 (Feb. 1964): 428-29. Francisco Zendejas, "Multilibros," review of *Pueblo limpio*, in *Excelsior* (March 5, 1963).

JANIS L. KRUGH

AYALA Anguiano, Armando (1928-), novelist and essayist. He was born in León, Guanajuato. His life has been rich and varied. At the age of eight, he worked as a radio operator at the Tijuana Airport. As a journalist and correspondent for *Visión*, he traveled through Europe and the United States. His experience in the border town gave rise to *Las ganas de creer* (Desire to Believe). His experiences in Europe led to *El paso de la nada* (The Step from Nothingness). He has also published a number of historical and political essays such as *México antes de los Aztecas* (Mexico before the Aztecs) and *México en crisis* (Mexico in Crisis), as well as another novel, *Unos cuantos días* (A Few Days).

Ayala Anguiano's first novel, *Las ganas de creer* (Desire to Believe), is set in a border town like Tijauna. Like *Juan Rulfo and Agustín *Yáñez, he uses a specific point in space and time to try to capture a universal vision in this work. While his second fictional work, *El paso de la nada* (The Step from Nothingness), is set in Europe, he returns to Mexico for the setting of his third novel, *Unos cuantos días* (Some Few Days). He writes in a crisp, journalistic style. The characters in the last novel are down to earth and yet complex. Most of the action occurs in a small village, Guanjuatillos. The plot centers around the return of protagonist, Ramon, to his birthplace.

WORKS: Novels: *Las ganas de creer* (Desire to Believe) (México: Libro Mex, 1958). *El paso de la nada* (The Step from Nothingness) (Buenos Aires: Editorial Goyanarte, 1960). *Unos cuantos días* (Some Few Days) (México: Mortiz, 1965). Essays: *La aventura de México* (The Mexican Adventure) (México: AAA Publicaciones, 1967). *México antes de los aztecas* (Mexico before the Aztecs) (México: Organización Editorial Novaro, 1967). *México de carne y hueso* (Mexico of Meat and Bones) (México: Editorial Contenido, 1967). *México en crisis: el fin del sistema* (Mexico in Crisis: The End of the System) (México: Ediciones Océano, 1982). *Zapata y las grandes mentiras de la Revolución Mexicana* (Zapata and the Great Lies of the Mexican Revolution) (México: Editorial Vid, 1985).

BIBLIOGRAPHY: Emmanuel Carballo, "Un novelista en que hay que creer," *México en la Cultura* 509 (Dec. 14, 1958): book section; Review of *El Paso de la nada*," *México en la Cultura* 590 (July 3, 1960): 4. Heriberto García Rivas, *Historia de la literatura mexicana*, vol. 4 (México: Textos Universitarios, 1971), p. 417. Carlos González Peña, *History of Mexican Literature*, Translated by Gusta Barfield Nance and Florence Johnson Dunstan (Dallas, Texas: Southern Methodist University Press, 1968), p. 440. Aurora M. Ocampo de Gómez and Ernesto Prado Velázquez, *Diccionario de escritores mexicanos* (México: UNAM, 1967), pp. 227-28. Alberto Ramírez de Aguilar, "Un novelista con la vida por delante," *Diorama de la Cultura* (Aug. 17, 1958): 3.

MARK FRISCH

AZAR, Héctor (1930-), playwright, theater and movie director, drama teacher, and critic. Born in Atlixco, Puebla, on October 17, 1930, he is a professor of Spanish and French literature at the Universidad Nacional Autónoma of Mexico. He has been professor of dramatic arts and chairman of the Theater Department (1954-1972) at the university. He directed the theater El caballito, the theater of the Ciudad Universitaria, the Centro Universitario de Teatro, and the Compañía de Teatro Universitario. This last group obtained first world prize at the 1964 theater festival at Nancy, France. Azar directed several experimental groups at the Foro Isabelino, Teatro del Espacio 15, and Espacio C, all established by him. He edited a collection of playtexts with the purpose of divulging theater arts. During his tenure as chairman of the Theater Department of the Instituto Nacional de Bellas Artes y Literatura (1965-1972), he organized the Compañía Nacional de Teatro. In 1972 he created the theater magazine *La cabra*, and in 1973 he opened a private theater, the Centro de Arte Dramático, A.C. (CADAC). He has published in various national and foreign periodicals: *Conjunto* (Cuba), *Le Monde* (France), *Revista Hispanae* (United States), and *Insula* (Spain). He received the Xavier Villaurrutia Prize on five different occasions and the Academic Palms of France. Until 1986, he directed eighteen short films in Cine Verdad (Truthful Films) and sixty-three stagings. He staged an adaptation of *El periquillo sarniento* and translated into Spanish, in verse form, Molière's *Le Malade imaginaire*, *El amor médico*. In May 1987 he was elected member of the Academia Mexicana de la Lengua (Mexican Academy of Languages). Azar has written one-act plays, experimenting with language distortion and compelling the reader/spectator to submit to the ingenious and challenging games he introduces. His best-known play is *Olímpica* (in three acts), which has had several stagings and has been translated into German. This play deals with a mythical character, a Mexican youth who personifies all adolescents and has Greek and pre-Hispanic echoes embodied in oneiric and atavistic language.

WORKS: Poetry: *Estancias* (Stages) (Puebla: Imp. de Rodolfo S. Peralta, 1951). *Ventanas de Francia* (Windows of France) (Puebla: Imp. de Rodolfo S. Peralta, 1951). *Días santos* (Holy Days) (México: Impresores Modernos, 1954). Theater: *La appassionata* (México: Libros del Unicornio, no. 1, Col. Literaria de Juan José Arreola, 1958), reprinted in *Antología de obras en un acto* (México: Col. Teatro Mexicano, 1960). *El alfarero* (The Potter) (México: Imp. Universitaria, UNAM, 1959).

Olímpica (México: Col. Letras Mexicanas, no. 73, 1962, and Ed. Samo, 1972). *Los juegos del azar* (Azar's Games) [*Azar* means *chance* in Spanish, hence the play on words], containing six one-act plays, ranging from Athenian to biblical and modern urban themes. They are "La copa de plata" (The Silver Cup), "La cabeza de Apolo" (Apollo's Head), "La seda mágica" (Magic Silk), "Doña Abelarda de Francia," "Las vacas flacas" (The Skinny Cows), and "La cantata de los emigrantes" (The Song of the Emigrants) (México: SEP/Setentas, 1973). *Teatro breve* (Brief Plays), which contains "La appassionata," "El alfarero," "El milagro y su retablo" (The Miracle and Its Manger), "El corrido de Pablo Damián" (The Dance of Pablo Damián), and "El premio de excelencia" (Excellence Prize) (México: Ed. Jus, 1975). *Olímpica e inmaculada*, 3rd reprint (México: FCE, 1986). Essays: *La Universidad y el teatro* (1970). *Teatro y educacion* (1971). *El espacio C, una proposición escénica* (Space C, a Scenic Proposal) (1977). *Zoon Theatrikon (Teoría CADAC)* (México: UNAM, 1977). *Ocios, almanaques y meditaciones* (Pastimes, Almanacs and Meditations) (1978). *El teatro con adolescentes* (1979). *Arte y política, materias racionales* (Art and Politics, Rational Subjects) (1981).

BIBLIOGRAPHY: Some reviews of Azar's works are Fausto Castillo, review regarding the First Prize at Nancy, France, in *El día* (April 28, 1964): 11. José García Lora, "Carta de México. Alfombra Mágica del Teatro Mexicano (por Azar a Valle lnclán)," in *Insula* 212-13, (July-Aug. 1964): 21. Luisa Josefina Hernández, "Teatro Universitario," in *Ovaciones*, suppl. no. 151 (Nov. 15, 1964): 7. María del Carmen Millán, Prologue to *Los juegos del azar* (México: SEP/Setentas, 1973), pp. 5-20.

NORA EIDELBERG

AZUELA, Mariano (1873-1952), novelist, short story writer, dramatist, biographer. Born in Lagos de Moreno, Azuela studied medicine and literature in Guadalajara. After receiving his medical degree, he returned to Lagos to practice. When Madero was elected president, Azuela was named political leader of Lagos until Madero's assassination, at which time Azuela joined the revolution, serving with Pancho Villa and General Julián Medina. When Villa was defeated, Azuela escaped to El Paso, Texas. In 1916 he returned to Mexico City and withdrew from politics. In the capital, he worked in public clinics with the poor, wrote his novels, and lectured on Mexican, French, and Spanish novelists at the Colegio Nacional. In 1949 he received the Premio Nacional de Artes y Ciencias. He died of a heart attack in 1952 and was buried in the Rotonda de Hombres Ilustres in Mexico City.

Azuela is best known as a novelist. In his early work his style resembles that of the French Naturalists, in particular, Emil Zola. This stage covers the span from *María Luisa* to *Sin Amor*. characters are typically from the lower classes, and there is an abundance of regional color in the descriptions. Between 1911 and 1918 Azuela wrote the novels that were to secure his fame, the novels of the Revolution. The scope of the work changed from small village life to the national struggle. In point of view, Azuela dropped omniscience for first-person narration. Also, dialogue began to predominate over description. His most famous novel, *Los de abajo* (The Underdogs), is from this time period. After 1918, Azuela experimented with a new technique characterized by a more fragmentary style, distorted images like those of surrealism, and verbless series. His last stage, from 1937, included political novels that exposed corruption in public life.

Throughout his work, Azuela demonstrated an abiding interest in themes of the injustice of the rich and the suffering of the poor. He felt that the novel was the art form of the masses and wrote his novels in the people's language. His prose was a distinct break from the refinement and escapism of Modernism. Typical of his style are short paragraphs, simplicity of sentence structure and vocabulary, common language in Mexican Spanish, and dialogue predominating over description. His style has been described as cinematographic. Some of his novels have been made into films.

WORKS: *María Luisa* (Lagos de Moreno: López Arce, 1907). *María Luisa y otros cuentos* (María Luisa and Other Stories) (México: Botas, 1938). *Los fracasados* (The Failures) (Lagos de Moreno: Miller Hnos., 1908; Mexico: El Pueblo, 1918; México: Botas, 1939). *Mala yerba* (Marcela; a Mexican Love Story) (Jalisco: Gaceta de Guadalajara, 1909; México: Rosendo Terrazas, 1924; New York: Farrar and Rinehart, 1932; México: Botas, 1945). *Andrés Pérez, maderista* (Andrés Pérez, Partisan of Madera) (México: Blanco y Botas, 1911). *Sin amor* (Without Love) (México: Botas, 1945). *Los de abajo* (The Underdogs) (México: Botas, 1941, 1944, 1946, 1949; New York: Brentano's, 1929; London: Jonathan Cape, 1930; New York: Signet Classics, 1962; San Antonio: Trinity University Press, 1979). *Los caciques* (The Bosses) (México: Cía. Periodística Nacional, 1917; Los Angeles: University of California Press, 1956). *Las moscas* (The Flies) (México: A. Carranza e Hijos, 1918; La Razón, 1931; Los Angeles: University of California Press 1956). *Domitilo quiere ser diputado* (Domitilo Wants To Be Deputy) (México: A. Carranza e Hijos, 1918; Botas, 1945). *Las tribulaciones de una familia decente* (The Trials of a Respectable Family) (Tampico: El Mundo, 1918; San Antonio: Trinity University Press, 1963, 1979). *La Malhora* (The Evil One) (México: Rosendo Terrazas, 1923; Botas, 1941). *El desquite* (Revenge) (México: El Universal Ilustrado, 1925; Botas, 1941). *La luciérnaga* (The Firefly) (Madrid: Espasa-Calpe, 1932; México: Novaro, 1955; San Antonio: Trinity University Press, 1979). *Pedro Moreno, el insurgente* (Pedro Moreno, the Insurgent) (Santiago: Ercilla, 1935; México: Botas, 1937). *Precursores* (Precursors) (Santiago: Ercilla, 1935). *El camarada Pantoja* (Comrade Pantoja) (México: Botas, 1937, 1951). *San Gabriel de Valdivias, comunidad indígena* (San Gabriel de Valdivias, Indigenous Community) (Santiago: Ercilla, 1938). *Avanzada* (Advance) (México: Botas, 1940). *Nueva burguesía* (New Bourgeoisie) (Buenos Aires: Club del Libre, 1941). *La marchanta* (The Street Vender) (México: Seminario de Cultura Mexicana, 1944; Botas, 1951). *La mujer domada* (The Tamed Woman) (México: El Colegio, 1946). *Sendas perdidas* (Lost Paths) (México: Botas, 1949). *La maldición* (The Curse) (México: Letras Mexicanas, 1955). *Esa sangre* (That Blood) (México: Letras Mexicanas, 1956). *Obras Completas* (Complete Works) (México: FCE, 1958). Essay: "Azares de mi novela *Los de abajo*," *Revista de la Universidad de México* 1, 2 (1946): 1-4.

BIBLIOGRAPHY: Alfonso de Alba, "Mariano Azuela," *La provincia oculta; su mensaje literario* (México: Cultura, 1949), pp. 97-100. Victor Alba, "Mariano Azuela," *Mexicanos para la historia* (México: Libro-Mex, 1955), pp. 5-16. Carlos Alvarez, "Mariano Azuela: versión teatral de Los de abajo," *Papeles de Son Armadans* 247 (1976): 13-28. Manuel Antonio Arango, "Correlación simbólica en la estructura tripartita con el tono épico en *Los de abajo*, de Mariano Azuela," *Anales de Literatura Hispanoamericana* 5 (1976): 155-63; "Lo social en dos novelas de Mariano Azuela: *Mala yerba* y *Los de abajo*," *Explicación de Textos Literarios* 1 (1973): 135-41. Salvador Azuela, "De la vida y del pensamiento de Mariano Azuela," *Revista de la Universidad de México* 6, 6 (1952): 3, 29; also in *Universidades* 15 (1952): 55-56; "Sobre la obra literaria de Zola en el juicio de Mariano Azuela," *El libro y el pueblo* 13 (1964): 5-7. María Azuela Arriaga, *Mariano Azuela, novelista de la revolución mexicana* (México: UNAM, 1955). Peggy Baird, "Marcela," *New Republic* 73 (1932): 143. Juan F. Bazán, "Los de abajo," *Narrativa paraguaya y latinoamericana* (Asunción, 1976): 469-75. Antonio Benítez Rojo, "Los de abajo: Honestidad y desesperanza," *Recopilación de textos sobre la novela de la revolución mexicana* (Havana: Casa de las Américas, 1975) pp. 218-23. Beatrice Berler, "Azuela y la veracidad histórica," *Revista iberoamericana* 62 (1966): 289-305; "Preliminar," in *Mariano Azuela, Epistolario y archivo* (México: UNAM, 1969) pp. 9-11. Maryse Bertrand de Muñoz, "Un paralelismo estructural: *Los de abajo* de Mariano Azuela y *For Whom the bell tolls* de Ernest Hemingway," *La torre* 73-74 (1971): 237-46. Frans Blom, "The Underdogs," *Saturday Review of Literature* 6 (1929): 179. Anita Brenner, "Blood and Struggle of Mexico Incarnate in Underdogs," *New York Evening Post* (Aug. 31, 1929). Salvador Bueno, "Tres escritores de México: E. González Martínez, Mariano Azuela, José Rubén Romero," *Lyceum* 32 (1952): 106-53; "Mariano Azuela: médico de su desencanto," *La letra como testigo* (Santa Clara, Cuba: Universidad Central de las Villas, 1957), pp. 35-60. Salvador Calvillo Madrigal, "La obra novelística de Mariano Azuela," *Nueva democracia* 42, 4 (1962): 38-40. Enrique Caracciolo Trejo, "¿El suidicio de Demetrio?" *Revista de la Universidad de México* 23 (1969): 8-9. Emmanuel Carballo, "Apogeo y muerte y resurrección del latifundio," *Revista de la Universidad de México* 10, 8 (1956): 4. Olga Carreras González, "La naturaleza y el hombre en *Los de abajo*." *Norte* (Amsterdam) 14, 6 (1973): 136-42. Alfonso Caso, "Mariano Azuela," *Memoria de El Colegio Nacional de México* 2, 8 (1953): 155-64. Luis Arturo Castellanos, "Azuela, testigo insobornable," *Cauce* (Argentina) 1 (1963): 38-42. Borje Cederholm, "Elementos de un estilo novelesco. Estudio estilístico-lingüístico de *Los de abajo* y *Sendas perdidas*," unpublished thesis, Mexico City College, 1950. Eduardo Colín, "*Los de abajo* por Mariano Azuela," *Rasgos* (México: Manuel León Sánchez, 1934) pp. 79-86. Octavio Corvalán, "Mariano Azuela," *El postmodernismo* (New York: Las Américas, 1961) 91-104. G. Cotto-Thorner, "Mariano Azuela, el poeta en el novelista," *Nueva Democracia* 31, 4 (1951): 76-83. Santiago Daydi, "Characterization in *Los de abajo*," *American Hispanist* 11 (1976): 9-11. Jaime Delgado, "Las novelas de Mariano Azuela," *Revista de Literatura* 11-12 (1954): 315-33. Adalbert Dessau, "*Los de abajo*: una valoración objetiva," *Recopilación de textos sobre la novela de la revolución mexicana* (Havana: Casa de las Américas, 1975), pp. 201-17. Enrique Díez-Canedo, "Dos novelas mexicanas," *Letras de América* (México: El Colegio de México, 1944), pp. 373-79. Bernard M. Dulsey, "The Mexican Revolution as Mirrored in the Novels of Mariano Azuela," *Modern Language Journal* 35 (1951): 382-86; "The Mexican Revolution as Mirrored in the Novels of Mariano Azuela," unpublished Ph.D. dissertation, University of Illinois, 1950. Orlando Edreira, "Una cala en la técnica literaria de Mariano Azuela," *Cuadernos Americanos* 178 (1971): 229-36. John Eugene Englekirk, "The Discovery of *Los de abajo*," *Hispania* 18 (1935): 53-62; also as "El 'descubrimiento' de la novela mexicana *Los de abajo*," *Atenea* 31 (1935): 415-32; also in *Reportorio Americano* 35 (1938): 177-80; also in *De lo nuestro y lo ajeno* (México: Cultura, 1966), pp. 53-63; "Mariano Azuela: A Summing Up (1873-1952)," *South*

Atlantic Studies for Sturgis E. Leavitt (Washington, D.C.: Scarecrow Press, 1953), pp. 127-35. Ernestine Evans, "In the Days of Díaz: *Marcela* by Mariano Azuela," *New York Herald Tribune Book Review* (Sept. 25, 1932): 8. J. Fernández-Arias Campoamor, "Segunda época realista. Mariano Azuela," *Novelistas de México* (Madrid, 1952) 101-18. Jorge Ferretis, "Mariano Azuela," *Crisol* 13 (1935): 154-58; "Mariano Azuela, prototipo," *Letras* (México) 64 (1938): 1-2. Angel Flores, "Mariano Azuela," *Panorama* 17 (1941): 5-9. Waldo Frank, "The Underdogs," *New Republic* (Oct. 23, 1929): 275-76. Newton Freitas, "*Los de abajo*," *Ensayos americanos* (Buenos Aires: Schapire, 1942), pp. 133-51. Hilda Gladys Fretes, "La revolución mexicana a través de una novela," *Revista de Literatura Argentina y Latinoamericana* 1, 1 (1959): 83-92. Lewis Gannett, "The Underdogs," *New York Herald Tribune Book Review* (Aug. 25, 1929); also *Mexican Life* (Sept. 1929). Luis Garrido, "Despedida al doctor Mariano Azuela," *Revista de la Universidad de México* 6, 3 (1952): 1, 4. Elliott S. Glass, "La actitud de Mariano Azuela e Isaac Babel hacia la revolución," *Cuadernos Americanos* 195 (1974): 160-64. Isaac Goldberg, "The Underdogs," *New World Monthly* (Jan. 1930): 66-68. Manuel Pedro González, "Bibliografía del novelista Mariano Azuela," *Revista Bimestre Cubana* 48 (1941); also (Havana: Molina, 1941). Manuel Pedro González, "Mariano Azuela, crítico y epistológrafo," *Atenea* 418 (1967): 165-77; "Cien años de novela mexicana," *Revista Iberoamericana* 27 (1948): 23-29; "Significación del doctor Mariano Azuela," *Trayectoria de la novela en México* (México: Botas, 1951), pp. 108-99. José María González de Mendoza, "Mariano Azuela y lo mexicano," *Cuadernos Americanos* 133 (1952): 282-85. J. González de Mendoza, "Prólogo de *Mala hierba*," *Universidad* (México) 20 (1937): 13-16. Francisco González Guerrero, "Mariano Azuela: su última novela y su labor total," *En torno a la literatura mexicana* (México: SepSetentas, 1976) 151-54; "*La mujer domada*," *Los libros de los otros (recensiones)*; 1st series (México: Chapultepec, 1947), pp. 115-22. Raymond L. Grismer and Mary B. MacDonald, "Mariano Azuela," *Vida y obras de autores mexicanos* (Havana: Alfa, 1945), pp. 9-11. Ernest Gruening, "*The Underdogs*," *Nation* 129 (1929): 689-90. Manuel H. Guerra, "*La maldición*," *Books Abroad* 30 (1956): 288. Edenia Guillermo and Juana Amelia Hernández, "*Los de abajo*," *Quince novelas hispanoamericanas* (Long Island City: Las Américas, 1971), pp. 53-63. Frances Kellam Hendricks, Introduction, in *Mariano Azuela, Las tribulaciones de una familia decente* (New York: Macmillan, 1966), pp. 1-30. Gerhard Raymond Herbst, "Mexican Society as Seen through the Literary works of Mariano Azuela," *DAI* 34 (1973): 2628A; also (New York: Abra, 1977). Julia Hernández, "Mariano Azuela," *Novelistas y cuentistas de la revolución mexicana* (México: Universidad Mexicana de Escritores, 1960, pp. 39-40. Henry Holmes, "A Tea-Time Chat with Mariano Azuela in Mexico City," *Hispania* 29 (1946): 557-58. Feliciano Huerga, "El hombre de Azuela," *América Narra* (Buenos Aires: Rodolfo Alonso, 1975), pp. 57-60. Alfredo Hurtado, *Mariano Azuela, novelista de México* (Guadalajara: Xallixtlico, 1951). Andrés Iduarte, "*La mujer domada*," *Revista Hispánica Moderna* 13 (1947): 59-60. Richard L. Jackson, "Notas sobre *Los de abajo y La negra Angustias*," *Annali*, (Instituto Universitario, Napoli) 8 (1966): 261-64. Didier T. Jaén, "Realidad ideal y realidad antagónica en *Los de abajo*," *Cuadernos Americanos* 183 (1972) 231-43. Dewey R. Jones, "El doctor Mariano Azuela, médico y novelista," unpublished thesis, UNAM, 1960. Jerome Judson, "Mariano Azuela's *Los de abajo*," *Rediscoveries* (New York: Crown, 1971) pp. 179-89. R. Kelly, "Estudio Crítico de *Los de abajo*," *Universidad de México* 70 (1952): 16. Francis M. Kercherville, "El liberalismo de Azuela," *Revista Iberoamericana* 6 (1941): 381-98. Andris Keinbergs, "Función de la naturaleza en *Los de abajo*,"

Cuadernos Americanos 169 (1970): 194-201. Alyce de Kuehne, "Los dos aspectos del humor en *Los de abajo*," *La novela iberoamericana contemporánea* (Caracas: Universidad Central de Venezuela, 1968), pp. 223-38; also *Duquesne Hispanic Review* 8 (1969): 1-8. Walter M. Langford, "Mariano Azuela: A Break with the Past," *The Mexican Novel Comes of Age* (Notre Dame, Ind.: University Notre Dame Press, 1971), pp. 14-35. Ricardo Latcham, "El realismo mexicano de Mariano Azuela," *Carnet Crítico* (Montevideo: Alfa, 1962), pp. 9-16. Mariano Latorre, "*Tirano Banderas* y *Los de abajo*, dos novelas sobre la revolución mexicana," *Atenea* 5, 5 (1928): 448-52. Luis Leal, *Mariano Azuela* (Buenos Aires: Centro Editor de América Latina, 1967); *Mariano Azuela* (New York: Twayne, 1971); "Mariano Azuela, novelista médico," *Revista Hispánica Moderna* 28 (1962): 295-303; *Mariano Azuela, vida y obra* (México: Eds. de Andrea, 1961). Alfredo Leal Cortés, "Elogio de Mariano Azuela," *Filosofía y letras* 53-54 (1954): 253-56. Kurt L. Levy, "*La luciérnaga*: title, leitmotif, and structural units," *Hispanic Studies in Honor of Edmund de Chasca* (Iowa City: University of Iowa, 1972), pp. 321-28. Robert E. Luckey, "Mariano Azuela: 1873-1952," *Books Abroad* 27 (1953): 368-70; "Mariano Azuela as Thinker and Writer," unpublished Ph.D. dissertation, Stanford University, Stanford, Calif., 1951. Carlos R. Luis, "*Los de abajo*, narrativa crítica," *Filología* 15 (1971): 125-33. Julio Machuca, "Geografía física y humana de *Los de abajo*," *Ensayos* (San Juan: Venezuela, 1943), pp. 77-86. Antonio Magaña Esquivel, "[Azuela], *La novela de la revolución*" (México: Porrúa, 1974), pp. 69-96. Alfredo Maillefert, "Novelas de Azuela," *Los libros que yo leí* (México: Universitaria, 1942), pp. 107-13. Angélica Malagamba, "La novela de Mariano Azuela," unpublished thesis, UNAM, 1951. *Mariano Azuela y la crítica mexicana: estudios, artículos y reseñas* (México: SepSetentas, 1973). Juan Carlos Mariátegui, "*Los de abajo*, de Mariano Azuela," *Temas de Nuestra América* (Lima: Biblioteca Amauta, 1960), pp. 84-88. Rubén Marín, "Añoranza para don Mariano," *Abside* 37 (1973): 144-46. Eliud Martínez, *The Art of Mariano Azuela: Modernism in La malhora, El desquite, La luciérnaga* (Pittsburgh, Penn.: Latin American Literary Review Press, 1979); "Azuela's *La malhora* (The Evil One): From the Novel of the Mexican Revolution to the Modern Novel," *Latin American Literary Review* 8 (1976): 23-34; "Mariano Azuela and 'The Height of the Times': A Study of *La luciérnaga*," *Latin American Literary Review* 5 (1974): 113-30. Antonio Melis, "*Los de abajo*," in *Crítica Literaria* (Buenos Aires: Jorge Alvarez, 1969), pp. 209-12. Seymour Menton, "La estructura épica de *Los de abajo* y un prólogo especulativo," *Hispania* 50 (1967): 1001-11. Franco Meregalli, "Azuela," in *Narratori messicani* (Milano: La Goliardica, 1957), pp. 84-102. Domingo Miliani, "Azuela, renovador más allá de la revolución," in *La realidad mexicana en su novela de hoy* (Caracas: Monte Avila, 1968), pp. 45-49. María del Rosario Mondragón López, "Portrayals of Children in Mexican Literature," unpublished thesis, University of North Carolina, Chapel Hill, 1986. Francisco Monterde García Icazbalceta, *En defensa de una obra y de una generación* (Mexico, 1935); "En torno a *Los de abajo*," *Filosofía y Letras* 45-46 (1952): 265-69; "La etapa del hermetismo en la obra del Dr. Mariano Azuela," *Cuadernos Americanos* 63 (1952): 286-88; *Mariano Azuela y la crítica mexicana* (México: SEP, 1973); "Prólogo," *Obras completas* (México: FCE, 1958-60), pp. i-xxii. Ernest Richard Moore, "Biografía y bibliografía de don Mariano Azuela," *Abside* 4, 2 (1940): 53-62; 4, 3 (1940): 50-64; "Mariano Azuela," *Mexican Life* 16, 8 (1940): 50-64. Agustín Moral, "Un novelista de la revolución. Forma y estilo de Mariano Azuela," *El libro y el Pueblo* 21-23 (1966): 53-55. F. Rand Morton, "Mariano Azuela," in *Los novelistas de la revolución mexicana* (México: Cultura, 1949), pp. 29-69. Edward J. Mullen,

"Towards a prototype of Mariano Azuela's *La luciérnaga*," *Romance Notes* 11 (1970): 518-21. Timothy Murad, "Animal Imagery and Structural Unity in Mariano Azuela's *Los de abajo*," *Journal of Spanish Studies: Twentieth Century* 7 (1979): 207-22. Mary Nemztow, "*Esa sangre*, una novela inédita del Dr. Mariano Azuela," *Revista Iberoamericana* 37 (1953): 65-70. Madaline W. Nichols, "*La luciérnaga*," *Books Abroad* 8 (1934): 459-60. Aurora M. Ocampo de Gómez, "Paralelo entre *Los de abajo* y *El águila y la serpiente*," *Letras Nuevas* 1 (1957): 20-24. Harriet de Onís, Foreword, in *The Underdogs, a Novel of the Mexican Revolution* (New York: New American Library, 1962), pp. v-xi. Febriano Ortega, "Mariano Azuela," in *Hombres, mujeres* (México: INBA, 1966), pp. 85-89. Arthur Owen, "*Los de abajo*," *Books Abroad* 5 (1931): 264-65. José Emilio Pacheco, "[*La mujer domada*]," *Estaciones* 7 (1957): 362-63. Emmanuel Palacios, *Mariano Azuela, un testimonio literario* (Guadalajara, 1952); "Mariano Azuela: un testimonio literario," *Xallixtlico* 9 (1952): 5-17; *Mariano Azuela y su obra* (Los Altos, 1954). José Pichel, "Viendo actuar a Azuela," *Claridades literarias* (May 7,1959): 5. Marta Portal, "Mariano Azuela," in *Proceso narrativo de la revolución mexicana* (Madrid: Cultura Hispánica, 1977), pp. 73-81. Enrique Pupo-Walker, "Algo más sobre la creación de personajes en *Los de abajo*," *Romance Notes* 12 (1970): 50-54; "*Los de abajo* y la pintura de Orozco: un caso de correspondencias estéticas," *Cuadernos Americanos* 154 (1967): 237-54; "El protagonista en la evolución textual de *Los de abajo*," in *Estudios de literatura hispanoamericana en honor a José J. Arrom* (Chapel Hill: University of North Carolina Press, 1974), pp. 155-66. Angel Rama, "El perspectivismo social en la novela de Mariano Azuela," *Revista Iberoamericana de Literatura* 1, 1 (1966): 63-94. Raymundo Ramos, "Tres novelas de Mariano Azuela," in *3 novelas* (México: FCE, 1968), pp. 7-18. Ronald Paul Redman, "Political alienation in the novels of Mariano Azuela," DAI 35 (1974): 2293A. Thomas W. Renaldi, "Daudet's Petite Bougeoisie as Reflected in *Sin amor*," in *Romance Literary Studies; Homage to Harvey L. Johnson* (Potomac Md.: José Porrúa Turanzas, 1979), pp. 85-93. W.A.R. Richardson, "Introduction," in *Los de abajo* (London: Harrap, 1973), pp. 9-70. Stanley Linn Robe, *Azuela and the Mexican Underdogs* (Berkeley: University of California Press, 1979); "Dos comentarios de 1915 sobre *Los de abajo*," *Revista Iberoamericana* 91 (1975): 267-72. Celia Robledo Esparza, "Expresión de la realidad mexicana en las obras de Mariano Azuela," *Armas y Letras* 5, 1-2 (1962): 25-45. Hugo Rodríguez Alcalá, "El interés artístico de las riñas de gallo en *Los de abajo*, *La vorágine* y *Don Segundo Sombra*," *Romanische Forschungen* 76 (1964): 163-82; "Mariano Azuela y las antítesis de *Los de abajo*," in *Ensayos de norte a sur* (México: Eds. de Andrea, 1960), pp. 81-89. Emir Rodríguez Monegal, "Mariano Azuela: testigo y crítico," in *Narradores de esta América* (Montevideo: Alfa, 1974), pp. 50-66; "Mariano Azuela y la novela de la revolución mexicana," *Número* 20 (1952): 199-210. José Rojas Garcidueñas, "Notas sobre tres novelas mexicanas," *Anales del Instituto de Investigaciones Estéticas* 16 (1948): 5-26; also *América* 59 (1949): 237-61. Jesús Romero Flores, "El novelista Mariano Azuela," in *Maestros y amigos* (México: Costa-Amic, 1971), pp. 67-71. Harry L. Rosser, "Consequences of Agrarian Reform: Mondragón, Magdaleno, Barriga Rivas, Azuela," in *Conflict and Transformation in Rural Mexico* (Boston: Crossroads Press, 1980), pp. 47-79. Jorge Ruffinelli, *Literatura e ideología: el primer Mariano Azuela, 1896-1918* (México: Premia, 1982). Samuel G. Saldívar, "El desarrollo del personaje femenino en la novela mexicana contemporánea: Azuela, Yáñez y Fuentes," DAI 39 (1978): 3615A. Luis Alberto Sánchez, "Mariano Azuela," *Revista Nacional de Cultura* 151-52 (1962): 117-27; also in *Escritores Representativos de América; segunda serie* (Madrid: Gredos, 1963-64), pp.

189-201. Porfirio Sánchez, "La deshumanización del hombre en *Los de abajo*," *Cuadernos Americanos* 192 (1974): 179-91. Enrique Marcos Santamaría, "El machismo en México y tres novelas de Mariano Azuela," DAI 37 (1976): 2925A. Jorge A. Santana, "El oportunista en la narrativa de Mariano Azuela," *Cuadernos Hispanoamericanos* 275 (1973): 297-330. Mauricio de la Selva, "Obras completas," *Cuadernos Americanos* 18, 2 (1959): 271-73. Alfredo M. Sharpe, "El valor socio-histórico y el valor literario de algunas novelas de Mariano Azuela," *College Language Association Journal* 3 (1960): 193-99. Jefferson Rea Spell, "Mariano Azuela, Portrayer of the Mexican Revolution," in *Contemporary Spanish-American Fiction* (Chapel Hill: University of North Carolina Press, 1944), pp. 64-109; "Mexican Society of the Twentieth Century as Portrayed by Mariano Azuela," in *Inter-American Intellectual Exchange* (Austin: University of Texas Press, 1943), pp. 49-61. Oscar Byrne Tinney, "The Mask Motif in *Los de Abajo* and *La muerte de Artemio Cruz*," unpublished thesis, University of North Carolina, Chapel Hill, 1983. Moisés Tirado, "La sociedad mexicana en las novelas revolucionarias de Mariano Azuela," in *Literatura ibreroamericana; influjos locales* (México, 1965), pp. 117-21. Arturo Torres-Ríoseco, "Mariano Azuela," *Revista Cubana* 31 (1938): 44-72; also in *Novelistas contemporáneos de América hispana* (Santiago: Nascimento, 1939), pp. 11-44, and *Grandes novelistas de la América hispana* (Berkeley: University of California Press, 1949), pp. 3-40; "Tres grandes novelistas," in *Expressao literária do Novo Mundo* (Rio de Janeiro: Brasileira, 1945), pp. 306-29. Carl A. Tyre, "*El camarada Pantoja*," *Books Abroad* 12 (1938): 361-62. Edmundo Valadés, "La maldición de Azuela," *Novedades* (July 12, 1955). José Angel Valente, "La revolución mejicana y el descubrimiento de *Los de abajo*," *Insula* 114 (1955): 3, 5. José Vázquez Amaral, "*The Underdogs*: A Novel of the Mexican Revolution," in *The Contemporary Latin American Narrative* (New York: Las Américas, 1970), pp. 16-28. Xavier Villaurrutia, "Sobre la novela, el relato y el novelista Mariano Azuela," *Rueca* 5 (1942): 12-16; also in *Obras* (México: FCE, 1953), pp. 799-801. Donald D. Walsh, "*La mujer domada*," *Books Abroad* 21 (1947): 300. Cecil G. Wood, "Nuevas técnicas novelísticas en *La luciérnaga* de Mariano Azuela," *Revista Canadiense de Estudios Hispánicos* 1 (1977): 185-96. A. W. Woolsey, "Los protagonistas de algunas novelas de Manuel [sic] Azuela," *Hispania* 23 (1970): 341-48. Richard A. Young, "Narrative Structure in Two Novels by Mariano Azuela: Los caciques and *Los de abajo*," *Revista Canadiense de Estudios Hispánicos* (1978): 169-81.

BARBARA P. FULKS

B

BAEZ, Carmen (1908-). Carmen Báez was born in Morelia, Michoacán. She studied to be a teacher but soon abandoned the idea to become a reporter for *El nacional*. She is the author of *La roba-pajaros* (The Bird Thief) and *El cancionero de la tarde* (Evening Song Book). From 1962 to 1964 she was in charge of the Dirección General de Cinematografía.

La roba-pájaros (The Bird Thief) is a collection of twenty short stories. The second one lends its title to the book. Some of the characters are a rural teacher, the village doctor, the invalid girl, some caring and hardened women, and poor children who spend most of their time playing mischievously in the streets. They are all common people that live simple and routine lives. It is in this microcosmi that the anecdote acquires depth and transcendence. All of the stories have ethical and human values. Liberty is claimed to be more important than life. In *La roba-pájaros*, Chucha is a woman with a compulsion to cage birds. She snatches from the hands of a child a young bird that is attempting to fly. The clamor of the children is described. Lolita, the town's old woman, invariably repeats that when birds see their chicks caged they bring them--on the third day--a herb that ends their lives. The prediction comes true. "Yo hubiera hecho lo mismo" (I would have done the same thing), says Lolita, who had lost two sons in the Spanish Civil War.

El cancionero de la tarde (Evening Song Book) is divided into three parts: "La canción de las rosas" (The Song of the Roses), "La canción de los sueños" (The Song of the Dreams), and "La canción de la vida" (The Song of Life). An Impressionist vision is presented with exquisite coloring and light, and with simplicity of expression. In the first part the topic of the *memento mori* is evoked: the passage of time, the fragile condition of beauty, and death. Hopes and dreams are thematically predominant in the second part: life is a constant pursuit of chimeras and illusions. The third part expresses a yearning for life, for open spaces, and the thirst for liberty. The poem "Abre un poquito" (Open a Little) is reminiscent of Alfonsina Storni's "Hombre pequeñito" (Little Man). All the poems in *El cancionero de la tarde* are brief and simple, similar to songs. Fantasy, the use of color, and a certain Romantic tone, recall Gustavo Adolfo Bécquer and Rubén Darío. These similarities do not detract from the author's authentic and original voice.

WORKS: *El cancionero de la tarde* (Evening Song Book) (Morelia: n.p., 1928). *La roba-pájaros* (The Bird Thief) (México: FCE, 1957); 2nd ed. (1975); 3rd ed. (1979).

BIBLIOGRAPHY: Emmanuel Carballo, "Estampas, relatos, fábulas y cuentos," review of *La roba-pájaros* in *México en la Cultura* 432 (June 30, 1957): p. 4. Mauricio de la Selva, Review of *La roba-pájaros* in *Cuadernos Americanos* (Sept. 1957); 283-84.

ALICIA G. WELDEN

BAEZ, Edmundo (1914-   ), poet and playwright. Born in Aguascalientes on the 4th of August, Báez did his early schooling in his native state and in San Luis Potosí, from 1929 to 1932, the period from which dates his initiation into poetry. He finished his *bachillerato* in Monterrey, Nuevo León. In Mexico he took courses through the fifth year in medicine. He cofounded, with Dr. Alfonso Millón, the Sanatorio Floresta for the mentally ill. In 1940 he abandoned his studies to dedicate himself to literature, first becoming known as a poet, and later as a playwright. In 1945 he received a fellowship to go to Hollywood to specialize in the techniques of filmscript writing. After his return to Mexico he devoted himself to the writing of scenarios for various movie studios. Between original subjects and adaptations he has written more than thirty works, of which *Doña Diablo* earned him the Spanish Don Quijote trophy; for his adaptation of *El niño y la niebla* he won an Ariel, and the Agrupación de Periodistas Cinematográficos Mexicanos awarded him the Aguila de Plata for *Mi esposa y la otra*. As a poet, he became known through the journals *Rueca, Taller poético, Letras de México,* and *El hijo pródigo*. Later on he published his only book of poetry: *Razón del sueño,* where he achieves pages of impeccable verse in which he joins concept and emotion. As a dramatist, he stands out in *El rencor de la tierra* for his interweaving of strange, learned forms and thoughts and emotion grounded in the land, in the countryside, in the provinces, all typically Mexican. In *Un alfiler en los ojos,* considered his best work, tyrannical passions play an important role. *¡Un macho!* owes much to his background as a scenario writer.

WORKS: Poetry: *Razón del sueño* (México, 1949). Theater: *Los ausentes,* written in 1940, premiered in 1942, published in a special edition of *Pan, Revista de Literatura* 1, 7 (Jan.-Feb. 1946): 15-31. *El rencor de la tierra,* two-act tragedy, written in 1942, premiered in 1943, published in *Cuatro siglos de literatura mexicana* (México: Edit. Leyenda, 1946), pp. 343-50. *Un alfiler en los ojos,* three-act drama, written in 1950, premiered in 1952, published in Revista Mexicana de Cultura (Oct. 5, 1952): 11; in *Teatro mexicano del siglo XX,* vol. 2, pp. 650-701. *¡Un macho!,* three act farce, premiered in 1959.

BIBLIOGRAPHY: Fausto Castillo, Review of *¡Un macho!,* in *México en la Cultura* 560 (Dec. 6, 1959): 8. Alyce Golding Cooper, *Teatro mexicano contemporáneo, 1940-1962,* thesis (México: UNAM, 1962), pp. 24, 31, 61. Ruth S. Lamb, *Bibliografía del teatro mexicano del siglo XX* (México: Eds. de Andrea, 1962), p. 30. Antonio Magaña Esquivel, *Teatro mexicano del siglo XX* (México: FCE, 1956), vol. 2, pp. 648-49; *Medio siglo de teatro mexicano 1900-1961* (México: INBA, 1964), pp. 82-84, 94, 95. Antonio Magaña Esquivel and Ruth S. Lamb, *Breve historia* del teatro mexicano (México: Eds. de Andrea, 1958), p. 157.José Luis Martínez, *Literatura* mexicana siglo XX. 1910-1949 (México: Ant. Libr. Robredo, 1949), vol. 1, pp. 86, 136; vol. 2 (1950), p. 19. Jesús Medina Romero, *Antología* de poetas contemporáneos, 1910-1953 (San Luis Potosí: Universidad Autónoma de San Luis Potosí, 1953), pp. 14, 243. Aurora M. Ocampo de Gómez and Ernesto Prado Velázquez, *Diccionario de escritores mexicanos* (México: UNAM, 1967), pp. 31-32.

PETER G. BROAD

BALBUENA, Bernardo de (1562?-1627), poet and prelate. Balbuena was born in Valdepeñas, Spain. He came to the New World in 1584 and promptly enrolled at the

University in Mexico City, where he obtained a bachelor's degree in theology in 1586. Between 1585 and 1590 he participated in several literary contests, winning first prize in three of them. Soon after receiving his bachelor's, he was assigned to the parish of San Pedro Lagunillas in Nueva Galicia (what is now Jalisco and Nayarit). During his years in Nueva Galicia he wrote the pastoral novel *Siglo de oro en las selvas de Erífile* (Golden Age in the Forests of Erífile). Spurred perhaps by his early literary successes, he traveled to Mexico City in 1602 hoping to secure a better position in the Church and publish some of his works. While in the capital city he wrote the epistolary poem *Grandeza Mexicana* (Mexican Greatness), his best-known work. Dedicated to doña Isabel de Tovar, a young widow about to enter a convent in Mexico City, the epistolary poem is a hymn to the city. It is a forerunner to Rafael *Landívar's *Rusticatio Mexicana* and Andrés Bello's *Oda a la agricultura de la zona tórrida*. Though he failed to get a promotion, he did publish *Grandeza Mexicana*, along with a treatise on poetics, *Compendio apologético en defensa de la poesía* (Apologetic Compendium in Defense of Poetry).

Still seeking a higher rank, Balbuena traveled to Spain in 1607 where he obtained a doctorate in theology at the University of Sigüenza. Though he didn't sail back to the New World until two years later, he finally got his wish in 1608 when he was named Abbot of Jamaica. During this year his pastoral novel appeared in print. Inspired by Sannazaro's *Arcadia*, *Siglo de Oro* is one of only two pastoral novels written in America. While in Jamaica, Balbuena wrote the epic poem, *El Bernardo o la victoria de Roncesvalles* (The Bernardo or the Victory of Roncesvalles). Along with *La araucana* of Alonso de Ercilla y Zúñiga, this poem is representative of the Renaissance epic written in America. His two first major works have classified as samples of early baroque in New Spain. In 1622 he was named bishop of Puerto Rico, a post he held until his death in 1627.

WORKS: *Grandeza mexicana and Compendio apologético en defensa de la poesía* (Mexican Greatness and Apologetic Compendium in Defense of Poetry) (México, 1604); edited by Luis Adolfo Domínguez (México: Porrúa, 1985). *Siglo de oro en las selvas de Erífile* (Golden Age in the Forests of Erifile) (Madrid, 1608); Sidney James Williams, Jr., "A Critical Edition of *Siglo de oro en las selvas de Erífile*." Ph.D. Diss. University of North Carolina, Chapel Hill, 1966. *El Bernardo o la victoria de Roncesvalles.* (The Bernardo or the Victory of Roncesvalles) (Madrid, 1624); Cayetano Rossel; ed., *Poemas Épicos* (Madrid: Biblioteca de Autores Españoles, 1851).

BIBLIOGRAPHY: Juan Bautista Avalle Arce, "Bernardo de Balbuena," *La novela pastoril española* (Madrid: Istmo, 1974), pp. 209-14. Russel Banks, "The New World," *Ploughshares* 3 (1976): 8-35. José Pascual Bux, "Bernardo de Balbuena y el manierismo novohispano," *Studi Ispanici* (Pisa) (1977): 143-62. Maxime Chevalier, "Sur les elements marveilleux du Bernardo de Balbuena," *Etudes de Philologie Romane et D'Histoire Littéraire offerts a Jules Horrent,* edited by Jean M. D'Heur and Nicoletta Cherubini (Tournai: Gedit, 1980). Chester C. Christian, Jr., "Poetic and Prosaic Descriptions of Colonial Mexico City," *Exploration* (Dec. 1981): 1-21. Junco Manuel Fernández, *Don Bernardo de Balbuena, Obispo de Puerto Rico: Estudio Bibliográfico y Crítico,* (Puerto Rico, 1884). Joseph G. Fucilla, "Bernardo de Balbuena's Siglo de Oro and Its Sources," *Hispanic Review* 15 (1947): 101-19. Joaquín García Icazbalzeta, "La Grandeza Mexicana de Balbuena: Nota bibliográfica," *Obras,* vol. 2 (México: Agüeros, 1904). Felix Karlinger, "Ammerkungen zur 'El Bernardo' (libro nono) von Bernardo de Balbuena," in *Aureum Saeculum Hispanium: Beitage zu Texten des Siglo de Oro*, Karl Hermann and Dietrich Briesenmeister (Weisbaden: Steiner, 1983), pp. 117-23. Luis Leal, "El Siglo de Oro de Balbuena: Primera novela americana," in *Homenaje a Andrés Iduarte*, edited by J. Alazraki, R. Grass, and R. O. Salmon (Clear Creek, Ind.: American Hispanist, 1976), pp. 217-28. Angel Rama, "Fundación del manierismo hispanoamericano por Bernardo de Balbuena," *University of Dayton Review* 16, 2 (1983): 13-22. Alfredo A. Roggiano, "Instalación del barroco hispánico en América: Bernardo de Balbuena," *Homage to Irving A. Leonard*, edited by Raquel Chang Rodríguez and Donald Yates (East Lansing, Mich.: L.A. Studies Center, 1977), pp. 61-73. José Rojas Garcidueñas, *Bernardo de Balbuena: la vida y la obra* (México: UNAM, 1982). Georgina Sabat Rivers, "Balbuena: Géneros poéticos y la epístola épica a Isabel de Tobar," *Texto Crítico* 10, 28 (1984): 41-66. Josefa Salmón, "El paisaje en Berceo, Garcilaso y Balbuena: Tres conceptos del universo," *Prismal/Cabral* 7-8 (1982): 57-73. Gilberto Triviños, Gilberto. "Nacionalismo y desengaño en *El Bernardo* de Balbuena," *Acta Literaria* 6 (1981): 93-117. John Van Horne, *Bernardo de Balbuena: Biografía y Crítica* (Guadalajara: Font, 1940); Introduction. *'El Bernardo' of Bernardo de Balbuena* (Urbana: University of Illinois Studies in Language and Literature, 1927; Introduction. *La 'Grandeza Mexicana' de Bernardo de Balbuena* (Urbana: University of Illinois Studies in Language and Literature, 1930). Harald Weinreich, ed., *Spanische Sonette des 'Siglo de Oro': Zur vergleichenden Interpretation Zusamengestelt* (Tubingen: Niemayer, 1961). Sidney James Williams, Jr., Introduction. "A Critical Edition of *Siglo de Oro en las selvas de Erífile*." Ph.D. Diss. University of North Carolina at Chapel Hill, 1966.

ALFONSO GONZALEZ

BANDA Farfán, Raquel (1928-), short story writer and novelist. Banda Farfám was born March 10 in San Luis Potosí, where she lived for a number of years. Her experience in that region gave her material that she employed in many of her stories and novels. She taught for a number of years at various places in the state and has studied at the National University.

Banda Farfán's short stories are often set in rural areas or deal with characters who live in such regions. She demonstrates throughout her stories a unique ability to capture both the simplicity and complexity of the human soul in a direct and concise way. Her endings are often unexpected and at times quite powerful. She is a very effective storyteller who can draw readers in quickly and hold their attention to the end. Her collection of stories *Amapola* is a good example of her varied techniques and effects. She captures and at times criticizes the beliefs and visions of her characters and is also a critic of the social conditions under which they live. That is especially true of her novel *Cuesta abajo* (Downhill).

WORKS: Stories: *Escenas de la vida rural* (Scenes of Rural Life) (México: n.p., 1953). *La cita, cuentos* (The Appointment, Short Stories) (México: Eds. de Andrea, 1957). *Un pedazo de vida* (A Slice of Life) (Naucalpán, México: Comaval, 1959). *El secreto* (The Secret) (México: Editorial Diana, 1960). *Amapola* (México: Costa-Amic, 1964).

Novels: *Valle verde* (Green Valley) (México: Eds. de Andrea, 1957). *Cuesta abajo* (Downhill) (México: Eds. de Andrea, 1958). *106 cuentos mexicanos* (One Hundred and Six Mexican Short Stories) (México: Editores Mexicanos Modernos, 1968). *La luna de Ronda, catorce cuentos* (Ronda's Moon, Fourteen Short Stories) (México: Costa-Amic, 1971). Chronicle: *La tierra de los geranios* (The Land of the Geranium) (1966).

BIBLIOGRAPHY: Esteban Durán Rosado, "Nuevos cuentos de Raquel Banda Farfán," review of *Amapola* in *Revista Mexicana de Cultura* 900 (June 28, 1964);, 15. Román Fontán Lemes, *La cuentística de Raquel Banda Farfán* (Paysandu, Uruguay: Cuadernos Literarios "El Chucaro," no. 8, 1963). Heriberto García Rivas, *Historia de la literatura mexicana*, vol. 4 (México: Textos Universitarios, 1971), pp. 518-19. Eliana Godoy Godoy, *Raquel Banda Farfán en su obra* (Rome: Edicion Alleanza Internazionale dei Giornaliste e Scrittori Latini, 1961). Celia E. Lúquez, Review of *Cuesta abajo, Revista de Literatura Argentina e Iberoamericana* (Universidad Nacional de Cuyo, Mendoza, Argentina) 2, 2 (Dec. 1960): 145-46. Aurora M. Ocampo de Gómez and Ernesto Prado Velázquez, *Diccionario de escritores mexicanos* (México: UNAM, 1967), p. 32. Gregory Rabassa, Review of *El secreto, Revista Hispánica Moderna* 28, 1 (Jan. 1962): 61-62. Pedro Shimose, ed., *Diccionario de autores iberoamericanos* (Madrid: Ministerio de Asuntos Exteriores, 1982), p. 53A. Silva Villalobos, "El secreto de la cuentista Banda Farfán," *Nivel* 26 (Feb. 25, 1961): 5.

MARK FRISCH

BAÑUELOS, Juan (1932-), poet. Bañuelos was born in Tuxtla Gutiérrez, Chiapas, on October 6, 1932. At UNAM he studied at the Schools of Law, Political Science, and Philosophy and Letters. He was a member of the cultural club of Chiapas and belonged to the group La Espiga amontinada. He was also coordinator of poetry workshops at UNAM and the Universities of Guerrero, Querétaro, Sinaloa, and Chiapas. He has contributed to in the magazines *Estaciones, Revista Mexicana de Literatura, Revista Mexicana de Cultura, Triquarterly* (United States) *Poetmeat* (England), and *Carte Segrete* (Italy). He directs the literature section of the journal *Plural*. The BBC of London has broadcast readings of his poems.

In 1984, he received the Premio Chiapas for Mexican poetry. His work has been translated in many different languages and has been recorded in the collection of Voz Viva de México of the UNAM.

WORKS: Poetry: "Puertas del mundo" (Doors of the World), in *La Espiga amontinada* (México: FCE, 196O). "Escribo en las paredes" (I Write on the Walls), in *Ocupación de la palabra* (México: FCE, 1965). *Espejo humeante* (Steamy Mirror), winner of the Premio Nacional de Poesía Aguascalientes 1968 (México: INBA-Joaquín Mortiz, 1969). *No consta en actas* (It Is Not Recorded in the Minutes) (México: IPN, 1971). *Destino arbitrario* (Arbitrary Destiny) (México: Papeles Privados, 1982). *La guitarra azul* (The Blue Guitar), an anthology (México: Moriz Planeta, 1986). *Poesías* (Poems), selections by the author and Carmen Alardín (México: UNAM, 1987).

BIBLIOGRAPHY: Anon., biographical note in *Anuario de la poesía mexicana 1962* (México: INBA, 1963), pp. 22-23; Review of *Ocuapación de la palabra* in *La Gaceta* (FCE) 129 (May 1965): 4, 8. Jesús Arellano, "Las Ventas de don Quijote," in *Nivel* 33 (Sept. 25, 1965): 5. Marcos Ricardo Barnatán, "Poesía de Américca. Lezama, Liscano, Bañuelos" in *Insula* 282 (May 1970): 12. Rosario Castellanos, "Los jóvenes poetas mexicanos," in *El Gallo Ilustrado* 310 (June 2, 1968): 2, 3; "Espejo humeante. La conciencia y la palabra," in *Excelsior*, (Jan. 11, 1969): 6A-8A. Andrew P. Debicki, *Poetas hispanoamericanos contemporáneos* (Madrid: Gredos, 1976). Heriberto García Rivas, *Historia de la literatura mexicana*, vol. 4 (México: Porrúa, 1974), p. 363. Carlos Monsiváis, *La poesía mexicana del siglo XX* (México: Empresas Editoriales, 1966), pp. 71, 763; also in *Poesía mexicana*, vol. 2 (México: Promexa, 1979), pp. xlvii, 435-36. Ramón Xirau, Review of *Ocupación de la palabra*, in *Diálogos* 6 (Mexico, Sept.-Oct. 1965): 43.

MIRTA BARREA-MARLYS

BARAZABAL, Mariano (1772-1807), poet and satirist. Born in Taxco during the waning years of the Spanish Empire in the Americas, Barazábal wrote works in praise of royal officials as well as in support of the independence movement. His most notable contribution to Mexican literature lies in the cultivation of the classical fable, a genre that enjoyed a revival during the eighteenth century. By devising dialogue to be spoken by animal characters, he presented his views of man and society, and thus revealed the current problems of Mexican life and aspects of it that needed reform. His best fables were published in the *Diario de México* (Mexican Daily), and they may be found in May and September issues of 1807 and an August issue of 1808.

WORKS: *Colección de poesías* (Collection of Poems) (México: Fernández de Jaureguí, 1809). *Poesías* (Poems) (México: Oficina de Don Mariano de Zúñiga y Ontiveros, 1818). *El patriotismo en la jura del imperio mexicano* (Patriotism in the Oath of the Mexican Empire) (México: Oficina de Don Mariano de Zúñiga y Ontiveros, 1821).

BIBLIOGRAPHY: Orlando Gómez-Gil, *Historia crítica de la literatura hispanoamericana* (New York: Holt, Rinehart and Winston, 1968), pp. 215-16.

JULIE GREER JOHNSON

BARBACHANO Ponce, Miguel (1930-), playwright, novelist, movie critic, and television producer and director. Barbachano Ponce was born in Mérida, Yucatán, on May 12, 1930. His first play, *El hacedor de dioses* (The Maker of Gods) (1954), is based on a short story, *El diosero*, by Francisco *Rojas González. In 1964 he wrote the novel *El diario de José Toledo* (The Diary of José Toledo), the first Mexican novel dealing with homosexuality. *Los desterrados del limbo* (The Outcasts from Limbo)

(1971) deals with the fantastic and black humor. He was director of the news reel Cine-Verdad (Cinema-Truth) (1955-1974) and Tele Revista (Tele Review) (1956-1977). He has been a University professor and movie critic of *Excelsior* (1976-1979 and 1985).

WORKS: Theater: *El hacedor de dioses* (Maker of Gods), staged in 1954. *Examen de muertos* (Examination of the Dead) (1955). *Once lunas y una calabaza* (Eleven Moons and a Gourd), staged in 1958, obtained Honorable Mention at the Festival Dramático of the D.F. (Federal District). *Las lanzas rotas* (The Broken Spears) (México: Col. Teatro Mexicano, 1959). *Los pájaros* (The Birds), a collection of five plays (México: Eds. Era, 1961). Narratives: *El diario de José Toledo* (The Diary of José Toledo) (México: Talls. de la Libr. Madero, 1964). *Los desterrados del limbo* (The Exiled of Limbo) (México: Mortiz, 1971). *La utopía domestica* (The Domestic Utopia) (México: Oasis, 1981). Produced the following films: *Lola de mi vida* (Lola of My Life) (1965), in collaboration with Gabriel García Márquez, scriptwriter for the films *Raíces, Torero y Nazarín* (Roots, Bullfighter and Nazarín) (1963); with Cesare Zavattini, *El anillo* (The Ring), *México mío* (My Mexico), and *El petróleo* (The Oil); and with García Márquez and Sergio Pitol on the script of *El acoso* (The Persecution), unedited.

BIBLIOGRAPHY: Marco Antonio Acosta, *"Los pájaros," El Nacional* (Nov. 9, 1977): 16. Federico Alvarez, Review of *El diario de José Toledo,* in *La Cultura en México* 136 (Sept. 23, 1964): xvi-xvii. Salvador Reyes Nevares, Review of *Las lanzas rotas,* in *México en la cultura* 564 (Jan. 3, 1960): 4. Francisco Zendejas, *"Los desterrados del limbo," Excelsior* (March 13, 1971).

NORA EIDELBERG

BAROQUE POETRY. The Baroque style that gradually evolved from Renaissance tradition was the dominant influence to shape the poetry written in New Spain during the seventeenth century and the first half of the eighteenth. Composed for an intellectual elite, Baroque verse, like the other genres molded by this extravagant literary mode, was intricate and obscure and resulted in the creation of poetic ornamentation and the exaltation of artificiality. Poets, who found little inspiration in the well-worn language and imagery of Renaissance models, sought to renew the process of poetic invention, and they did so by extensively embellishing existing conventions. Disrupting the clarity, symmetry, and natural flow of sixteenth-century poetry, they emphasized complexity and erudition to the point of obstructing the reader's understanding and, at times, rendering their verses devoid of any meaning.

Just as the Baroque style followed two different tendencies in Spain, so too it did in Spanish America. Poets who sought to overwhelm the reader with technical devices imitated the poetry of *culteranismo,* whose remarkable leader, Luis de Góngora, had left an indelible impression on the Spanish Baroque with the publication of his *Soledades* (Solitudes). Often emulating aspects of classic Latin poetry, the *culteranos* invented new words or used words in an innovative way and distorted syntax and word order. They also devised striking imagery based on the sensory, created sharp contrasts such as juxtaposing the beautiful with the ugly, and delighted in the arrangement of profuse allusions to classic mythology. *Conceptismo*, or the counterpart of *culteranismo* and its occasional complement, lacked the extreme complexity of form and emphasized content and meaning through the ingenious effusion of ideas or the striking juxtaposition of opposing concepts. Although the poets of New Spain were influenced by both trends, their preference clearly rested with the more intense *culteranismo*, or *Gongorismo*, as it was more popularly known. Immersing themselves in this ornate mode of writing, therefore, they endeavored to explore every facet of its expression in a multitude of ways. Such enthusiasm and determination are evident in the myriad of works that they produced; their success, however, was limited, and their efforts often ended in exaggerated poetic exercises of questionable artistic taste.

The transfer of the Baroque from Spain to the New World viceroyalty of New Spain was quite predictable, but the zeal with which poets there embraced the new style was overwhelming and permitted it to persist years after it had ceased to be fashionable on the Peninsula. Because the Spanish- or American-born Spaniards dominated colonial society, the Baroque was readily accepted, and the aristocratic and learned element among them actively subscribed to this innovative literary movement both as readers and as writers. It flourished at the prestigious viceregal court in Mexico City and pervaded the academic circles of the capital's university. Members of the clergy as well participated in its growth and development, as the Church was a powerful institution during the colonial period and an enclave of educated individuals. Ceremonious occasions were the most frequent themes of Baroque poetry, as elaborate verses marked the marriage or death of a monarch, the birth of a prince, the arrival of a viceroy, or the celebration of a saint or the virgin. The university especially encouraged the composition of poetic tributes, and it sponsored contests, or *certámenes*, to challenge the viceroyalty's most accomplished poets to demonstrate their verbal dexterity. Although this literary activity was quite commendable for a society that had scarcely one hundred years to evolve, it unfortunately occurred, for the most part, in a vacuum, as New Spain was isolated from the rest of Europe and its social structure lacked the fluidity of the years following the conquest. In view of these circumstances, the viceroyalty's poetic artistry was a reflection of Spain's decadence that permeated the empire and was symptomatic of New Spain's own intellectual and literary stagnation.

One of the earliest poets to be influenced by the Baroque in New Spain was Bernardo de *Balbuena. His *Grandeza mexicana* (Mexican Grandeur), which was published in 1604, contains an eloquent description of Mexico City at the close of the sixteenth century. The language and imagery that he uses are indicative of the transitional period in which this affected style gained momentum, as his continual presentation of imaginative scenes filled with color and movement does not obstruct the clarity of his elegant poetic design.

In 1682 the University of Mexico held a literary competition in honor of the Immaculate Conception. An account of the event as well as many of the poetic entries is contained in Don Carlos de Sigüenza y Góngora's work, *Triunfo Parthénico* (Parthenic Triumph), a compilation that is representative of the garish gamut of Baroque poetry of New Spain. Few of the five hundred compositions are worthy of note, and their manner of expression ranqes from mere verbal exuberance to outright bombast. As participants deliberately distorted poetic form, innumerable meaningless verses emerged exposing the shallow intellectual content of this intricate style and engendering bizarre meter and rhyme, which serve now only as documentation of the oddities of the Baroque Age.

There are, however, several exceptions to the generally inferior verses found in Sigüenza's *Triunfo Parthénico*. Among them are Luis de Sandoval y Zapata's poetry to Our Lady of Guadalupe and Juan de Guevara's poems to the Virgin Mary. Unfortunately, the contributions of Sigüenza himself may not be counted among the most outstanding of his collection. Prose would be the genre in which he would excel, and his empty verses in the Baroque mode add nothing to his brilliant reputation as a writer and historian. Two literary figures, however, do emerge from the darkness of New Spain's Baroque period, and both were members of its religious community. The first, the Jesuit Matías de *Bocanegra, is distinguished for his poetic description of monastic life in his *Canción a la vista de un desengaño* (Allegorical Song of Disillusion), and the second is the famous poet Sor Juana Inés de la *Cruz, of the Hieronymite Order, whose works exemplify the artistic excellence of colonial letters.

Much of the poetry of Mexico's "Tenth Muse," as Sor Juana was appropriately called, is encomiastic or ceremonial, like that of her male counterparts, and was written in honor of the most important people of her day or in observance of special religious holidays. Before entering the convent, she had been a lady-in- waiting at the viceregal court, and it was there that she complied with numerous requests of nobles for poems of a secular nature.

Her "Laura" and "Lysi" poems, written to the vicereines Doña Leonor María de Carreto, the wife of the Marquis of Mancera, and Doña María Luisa Gonzaga y Manrique de Lara, the wife of the Marquis of La Laguna, are particularly graceful and elegant compositions and demonstrate her fondness for both of these women, who were her devoted admirers. Other exceptional poems by Sor Juana, which follow the conventions of Baroque style, are those written in a philosophical or amorous vein. Her sonnet "Este, que ves" (This [portrait] that you see) and her *redondillas*, or seven-syllable quatrains with alternate rhyme, entitled "Este amoroso tormento" (This Amorous Torment) are considered to be among the best examples of lyric poetry produced during the entire colonial period.

Although Sor Juana dominated the Baroque style and elevated it to its highest level of expression, she also saw a need for the renewal of metaphorical language to restore originality and creativity to the poetry of her time. In her satiric poem "El pintar de Lisarda la belleza" (The Painting of Lisarda's Beauty), she protests the use of conventional imagery in feminine portraiture and calls for the reevaluation of woman's role in society as well.

Sor Juana's longest and most complex work is her *Primero sueño* (First Dream), which is often considered to be the epitome of Baroque style devised by a New World poet. This poem contains a description of night as it comes over the earth and offers a philosophical view of nature and man's place within God's earthly hierarchy. Her verses are distinguished by the use of nocturnal imagery, mythological allusions, and references to seventeenth- century scientific concepts, which she blends together to create a spectacular poetic vision. Because of her splendid achievements within the realm of the Baroque, Sor Juana is viewed not only as the most eminent poet of seventeenth-century Mexico but a paragon of poetic creativity in the history of colonial Spanish American literature as well. Her remarkable talent effectively permitted her to avoid many of the excesses, which characterized much of the poetry of her contemporaries, and this enabled her to successfully transform its technical intricacies and obscure erudition into a poetic outpouring of sheer brilliance.

BIBLIOGRAPHY: Emilio Carilla, *El gongorismo en America* (Buenos Aires: Facultad de Filosofía y Letras de la Universidad de Buenos Aires, 1946); *La literatura barroca en Hispanoamérica* (New York: Anaya, 1972). Sor Juana Inés de la Cruz, *Obras completas*, edited by Alfonso Méndez Plancarte and Alberto G. Salceda, 4 vols. (México: Imprenta Nuevo Mundo, 1955; FCE, 1957). Irving A. Leonard, *Baroque Times in Old Mexico* (Ann Arbor: University of Michigan Press, 1966). Octavio Paz, *Sor Juana Inés de la Cruz o las trampas de la fe* (Barcelona: Ed. Seix Barral, 1982).

JULIE GREER JOHNSON

BARRIGA Rivas, Rogelio (1912-1961), novelist. Born in Tlacolula, Oaxaca, on March 15, 1912, Barriga Rivas died in Mexico City on January 9, 1961. He was a lawyer for the State Institute of Arts and Sciences in Oaxaca as well as an agent for the Federal Public Ministry. His first novel, *Guelaguetza* (Guelaguetza), concerned the abuses of power of local bosses. This was followed by *Río humano* (The Human River), about the plight of the urban poor, and later by an indigenista novel, *La mayordomía* (Stewardship), which was filmed under the title *Animas Trujano* (Trujano Souls). Another work, *Si yo fuera diputado* (If I Were a Congressman), was also brought to the screen, starring Cantinflas (Mario Moreno). His works are full of local color, which is what has attracted the attention of filmmakers.

WORKS: *Novels: Guelaguetza* (Guelaguetza) (México: Cortés, 1947). *Río humano* (The Human River) (México: Botas, 1949). *La mayordomía* (Stewardship) (México: Botas, 1952). *Juez letrado* (Learned Judge) (México: Botas, 1952). Screenplay: *Si yo fuera diputado* (If I Were a Congressman), n.d.

BIBLIOGRAPHY: Aurora M. Ocampo de Gómez and Ernesto Prado Velázquez, *Diccionario de escritores mexicanos* (México: UNAM, 1967), p. 36. José Rogelio Alvarez, dir., *Enciclopedia de México*, vol. 2 (México: SEP, 1987), p. 887. John S. Brushwood and José Rojas Garcidueñas, *Breve historia de la novela mexicana* (México: Eds.de Andrea, 1959), pp. 117-18. Manuel Pedro González, *Trayectoria de la novela en México* (México: Botas, 1951), pp. 399-400.

TERESA R. ARRINGTON

BARTRA, Agustí (1908-1982). Bartra was born in Barcelona, Spain. In 1931 he obtained an award for his short stories and later for his poetry on war. In 1937 he published *L'oasi perdut*, a first book of short stories, and in 1938 a book of poetry, *Cant corporal*. A participant in the Spanish Civil War, he was held in a concentration camp and later lived in exile in the Dominican Republic and in Cuba, finally settling in Mexico.

Some of the elements found in his poetry are Greek and Mexican mythology, a universe dominated by telluric forces, the anguish of contemporary man, the ocean (a recurrent topic), experiences of the civil war, and the denial of war and discrimination. It is a poetry of strong images, reminiscent of Surrealism. *El árbol de fuego* (The Tree of Fire) was originally written in Catalan and translated into Spanish by the author. The subjects of the poems are tragic: a son going to war, weapons, martyrs, crying mothers, the dead, concentration camps, tragic love, remembrances. At the same time there is a yearning for fullness and hope for beauty. The images are dramatic and the language is lyrical.

WORKS: Poetry: *El árbol de fuego* (The Tree of Fire) (Ciudad Trujillo: Librería Dominicana, 1940). *Odiseo* (Odysseus) (México: Tezontle, 1955). *Quetzalcóatl* (Song) (México: Tezontle, 1960). *Deméter* (Jalapa: Universidad Veracruzana, 1961). *Marsias i Adila* (México: Ed. El Corno Emplumado, 1962). *La luz en el yunque* (The Light on the Anvil) (México: Era, 1965). *La lechuza ciega* (The Blind Owl) (México: Mortiz, 1966). *Antología de la poesía mística* (Anthology of Mystical Poetry) (México: Editorial Pax, 1966). *Antología poética de la muerte* (Poetical Anthology of Death) (México: Editorial Pax, 1967). *Antología del amor* (Anthology of Love) (México: Editorial Pax, 1975). *Ecce homo* (Barcelona: Edicions 62, 1982). *El gallito canta para los dos* (The Rooster Sings for Both of Us) (Puebla: Universidad Autónoma de Puebla, 1984). *El tren de cristal* (The Crystal Train) (Barcelona: Ediciones Robrenyo de Teatre de Tots els Temps, 1979). *La noia del gira-sol* (Barcelona: Antonio Picazo Editor, 1982). Essay and Other Nonfiction: *Antología de la poesía norteamericana* (Anthology of North American Poetry), selection and notes (México: UNAM, 1959). *Panorama de la literatura española* (Panorama of Spanish Literature) (New York: Harcourt, Brace and World, 1967). *Cartes a Agusti Bartra* (Letters for Agusti Bartra) (Barcelona: n.p., 1972). *Diccionario de mitología* (Dictionary of Mythology) (México: Grijalbo, 1982). Novels: *Cristo de 200.000 brazos* (Christ of 200,000 Arms) (Barcelona: M. Roca, 1968). *La luna muere con agua* (The Moon Dies With Water) (Barcelona: Biblioteca Picazo, 1973). Stories: *Relatos maestros del crimen* (Master Stories of Crime) (Barcelona: Martínez Roca, 1977). *Relatos maestros policíacos* (Master Police Stories) (Barcelona: Martínez Roca, 1977).

BIBLIOGRAPHY: José de la Colina, Review of *Odiseo*, in *Universidad de México* 10, 2 (Oct. 1955): 30. Cecilia Gironella, *El ojo de Polifemo. Visión de la obra de Agustín Bartra* (México: Costa-Amic, 1957). José R. Marra-López, *Narrativa española fuera de España, 1939-1961* (Madrid: Guadarrama, 1962). Anna Muria, *Crónica de la vida d'Agustí Bartra* (Barcelona: Edicions Martínez Roca, 1967).

ALICIA G. WELDEN

BASSOLS Batalla, Angel (1925-). Born in Mexico City on February 7, 1925, Angel Bassols Batalla grew up in the city, studying at a local school. In 1945, he went to the former Soviet Union, where he studied at the University of Lomonosov in Moscow. He graduated in 1949 with a degree in economic geography. Upon the completion of his studies, he returned to Mexico to occupy the first of a number of important positions. From 1950 to 1957, he worked in the field of geography and meteorology as a technician. He has also been employed as a translator, a professor, and a journalist. He has taken many trips throughout the world, including visits to the Near East, Northern Africa, China, Europe, and various countries in the Americas. His many and varied experiences provide much of the basis for his literary work, which includes mostly stories and studies, often published in magazines and journals. Noted for his realism, his compassion for the problems of the masses, in particular, and his didactic manner of writing, Angel Bassols Batalla has made a small but important impact on Mexican letters.

WORKS: Stories and Accounts: *Cinco años en la URSS* (Five Years in the USSR) (México: n. p., 1950). *Caravana de Hombres Libres* (Caravan of Free Men) (México: n. p., 1951). *Relatos Mexicanos* (Mexican Tales) (México: Eds. de Andrea, 1954). *Mi teniente Ambrosio y otros cuentos* (My Lieutenant Ambrosio and Other Stories) (México: Eds. de Andrea, 1960). Studies: *El Estado Baja California* (The State of Baja California) (México: Edit. Stylo, 1955). *Viajes geográficos en Europa* (Geographical Journeys in Europe) (México: Sociedad Mexicana de Geografía y Estadística, 1965). *Las Huastecas en el desarrollo regional de México* (México: Trillas, 1977). *México. Formación de regiones económicas* (México: UNAM, 1979). La República socialista de Vietnam (México: UNAM, Instituto de Investigaciones Económicas, 1981).

BIBLIOGRAPHY: Andrés Iduarte, Review of *Mi teniente Ambrosio y otros cuentos*, in *Revista Hispánica Moderna* 27, 3-4 (June-Oct. 1961): 355. Aurora M. Ocampo de Gómez and Ernesto Prado Velázquez, *Diccionario de escritores mexicanos* (México: UNAM, 1967), pp. 37-38. Salvador Reyes Nevares, Review of *Viajes geográficos en Europa*, in *La Cultura en México* 196 (Nov. 17, 1965): xv.

MICHELE MUNCY

BASURTO, Luis G. (1920-), playwright, director, television commentator and lawyer. Born in Mexico City on March 11, 1920, Luis Basurto went to the UNAM, where he studied philosophy and letters and, like many of his contemporaries, also received a law degree. He began his literary and theatrical career at age nineteen, by publishing articles and chronicles in newspapers and magazines. He went to Hollywood in 1942 to pursue further studies in the technical aspects of the theatrical arts. After a short stay, he returned to work with Xavier *Villaurrutia, the noted dramatist. In the late 1940s, he dedicated himself almost exclusively to the professional theater. Basurto celebrated a successful theatrical tour of Spain in 1949 with an exclusive Mexican company. Upon his return to Mexico, he, as its artistic director, organized the first season of the new Unión Nacional de Actores, effectively launching his own career in Mexico. He has had a most distinguished affiliation with several theatrical enterprises in Mexico, including the Compañía de Repertorio del INBA, of which he has served as a director. He has also continued with his journalistic work, particularly with *El Heraldo de México* and *Excelsior*. He has been a popular television personality since 1975, currently being in charge of "Tribuna Pública" (Public Tribune). Since 1979 he has held the position of general advisor of the Dirección de Corporación Méxicana de Radio y Televisión.

Basurto has written more than twenty theatrical works, the first of which, *Los diálogos de Suzette* (The Dialogues of Suzette), was performed in 1940 by Rodolfo Usigli and the Teatro de Media Noche. As a dramatist, Basurto generally adheres to the classical, traditional methods. His works often deal with social issues and religious considerations. The everyday language he uses, the realistic characterization, and the balanced construction of the plays place most of them within the realism of tradition. Aesthetically pleasing and occasionally didactic, works such as *Cada quien su vida* (Each His Own Life) and *Miércoles de ceniza* (Ash Wednesday) are appealing both for their simplicity and for their social value. Basurto has distinguished himself in the field of theater for many years, both in Mexico and elsewhere, as a director, businessman, and promotor. On the twenty-fifth anniversary of his career, Basurto, in response to criticism, spoke in an interview about his theater, his faults, and ways to correct his faults. Nonetheless, he has, throughout his career, received more than thirty prizes, including the prestigious Premio Juan Ruiz de Alarcón for *Con la frente en el polvo* (With the Forehead in the Dust) in 1967. His plays have often been performed to critical acclaim, as have those which he has directed.

WORKS: *Los diálogos de Suzette* (The Dialogues of Suzette), performed in 1940. *Laberinto*, performed in 1941. *Faustina*, performed in 1942. *Voz como sangre* (Voice like Blood), performed in 1942. *El anticristo*, performed in 1942. *Bodas de plata* (Silver Weddings), 1943, performed in 1960. *La que se fue* (The One Who Went Away), 1945, performed in 1946. *Frente a la muerte* (In the Face of Death), performed in 1952 (México: Eds. de la Unión Nacional de Autores, 1954). *Toda una dama* (A Real Lady), performed in 1954, and in *Panorama del Teatro en México* (Feb. 7, 1955). *Cada quien su vida* (Each His Own Life), performed in 1955, in Antonio Magaña Esquivel *Teatro mexicano del siglo XX* (México: FCE, 1956), pp. 563-647. *Miércoles de ceniza* (Ash Wednesday), performed in 1956, published in Colección Panoramas (México: Costa-Amic, 1957). *La locura de los ángeles* (The Craziness of the Angels), performed in 1957. *Teatro mexicano 1958*, anthology, selection and prologue by Basurto (México: Aguilar, 1958). *Los reyes del mundo* (The Kings of the World), performed in 1959. *El escándalo de la verdad* (The Scandal of Truth), performed in 1960. *Olor de santidad* (Scent of Saintliness), performed in 1961. *Intimas enemigas* (Intimate Enemies), performed in 1962. *La gobernadora* (The Governess), performed in 1963. *Y todos terminaron ladrando* (And All Ended Up Barking), performed in 1964. *Cadena perpetua* (Perpetual Chain), performed in 1965. *Con la frente en el polvo* (With the Forehead in the Dust), performed in 1967. *Mañana será otro día* (Tomorrow Will Be Another Day), performed in 1968. *Asesinato de una conciencia* (Assassination of a Consciousness), performed in 1969. *La vida difícil de una mujer fácil* (The Difficult Life of a Loose Woman), performed in 1970. *Piedra de escándalo* (Stone of Scandal), performed in 1977. In addition, he has published a myriad of articles in journals such as *México en la Cultura, Excelsior, El Heraldo de México*, etc.

BIBLIOGRAPHY: Anon., "Basurto y sus 25 años de autor," in *El Nacional* (Sept. 5, 1965): 5; "*Con la frente en el polvo*," in *Siempre!* 751 (Nov. 15, 1967): 47-48. Tomás Espina, "Teatro de la Nación. Ciclo Los Clásicos. *El mercader de Venecia*," directed by Basurto, in *Tramoya* 9 (Oct.-Dec. 1977): 43-45. Beatriz Reyes Nevares, "Al cumplir 25 años como dramaturgo, Basurto habla sobre teatro, explica sus fallas y cómo corregirlas," in *Siempre!* 640 (Sept. 29, 1965): 42-43. Rafael Solana, "Los 40 años de

Basurto," in *Siempre!* 1439 (Jan. 21, 1981): 14, 70. Carlos Solórzano, *"Intimas enemigas,"* in *Ovaciones* 47 (Nov. 18, 1962): 5; "La crítica, como el champaña, golpea y acaricia a Basurto," in *La Cultura en México* 189 (Sept. 29, 1965): xvii.

JEANNE C. WALLACE

BATIS Martínez, Huberto (1934-). Batis was born in Guadalajara, Jalisco, on December 29, 1934. He graduated from the University of Mexico and worked as a researcher in the same university. He collaborates on various literary and cultural newspapers and journals, doing reviews and bibliographic criticism. In 1960, he was the founder and director, along with Carlos Valdés, of the review *Cuadernos del Viento,* and in so doing, brought to light new literary lights. His short stories have appeared in reviews, supplements, and yearbooks, and since 1965, he has been on the staff of the *Revista de Bellas Artes.*

Huberto Batis got his start in literary journals with the publication of tales, short stories and literary criticism articles. His editorial work has opened the doors to younger writers. His book *Indices de "El Renacimiento,"* is distinguished by the seriousness of its scholarship and its diligent research. Brushwood considers it to be a masterpiece of literary history and criticism. In 1985 he was awarded the prestigious prize "Abriles de Ensayo" for his essay "Lo que *Cuadernos del Viento* nos dejó," a very interesting chronicle about that journal.

WORKS: Short Stories: *En las ataduras* (In Binding), offprint from the journal *Cuadernos del Viento* 5 (Dec. 1960). Essays: *Indices de "El Renacimiento"* (Indexes of "El Renacimiento"), with a preliminary study (México: UNAM, 1963). "La revista literaria *El Renacimiento* (1869)," in *La vida y la cultura en México al triunfo de la República* (México: INBA, 1968), pp. 79-104. "José Pirómano," *Metáfora* 12 (Jan-Feb. 1957): 30-32. "Elena Garro, *Los recuerdos del porvenir,"* in *La Cultura en México* 103 (Feb. 5, 1964): xviii. *Lo que cuadernos del viento nos dejó* (México: Diógenes, 1984).

BIBLIOGRAPHY: Federico Alvarez, "El ensayo literario, 1963," in *La Cultura en México* 99 (Jan. 8, 1964): v; "Los libros al día," review of *Indices de "El renacimiento,"* in *La Cultura en México* 102 (Jan. 29, 1964): xviii. Anon., Bibliographic notes in *Anuario del cuento mexicano 1960* (México: INBA, 1961), p. 19. Jesús Arellano, *"Los índices de 'El renacimiento'* y Huberto Batis," in *México en la Cultura* 781 (Mar. 8, 1964): 7. Gabriel Agraz García de Alba, *Bibliografía de los escritores de Jalisco* (México: UNAM, 1980), pp. 114-15. Heriberto García Rivas, *Historia de la literatura mexicana,* vol. 4 (México: Porrúa, 1974), p. 524. Carlos González Peña, *History of Mexican Literature,* translated by Gusta Barfield Nance and Florene Johnson Dunstan (Dallas, Texas: Southern Methodist University Press, 1968), p. 450. Henrique González Casanova, "Textos y autores," review of *Indices de "El Renacimiento"* and of his work as director of *Cuadernos del Viento,* in *Ovaciones,* suppl. no. 59 (Feb. 10, 1963): 4. Javier Morente, "Sala de lectura," review of *Indices de "El Renacimiento,"* in *Diorama de la Cultura* (Feb. 9, 1964): 8. Angelina Muñiz, Review of *Indices de "El Renacimiento,"* in *Universidad de México* 18, 8 (1964): 31. Aurora M. Ocampo de Gómez and Ernesto Prado Velázquez, *Diccionario de escritores mexicanos* (México: UNAM, 1967), p. 39. Luis Guillermo Piazza, "Su mesa de redacción," review of *Indices de "El Renacimiento,"* in *Diorama de la Cultura* (Jan. 19, 1964): 4. Gustavo

Sáinz, "Escaparate," Review of *Indices de "El Renacimiento,"* in *México en la Cultura* 774 (1964): 5.

YOLANDA S. BROAD

BELTRAN, Neftalí (1916-), poet, playwright, radio and television scriptwriter. Beltrán was born in Alvarado, state of Veracruz, May 16, 1916, and lived and studied law in Mexico City as a youth. He was part of the *Grupo Taller*, and was editor of the magazine *Poesía* (1938), published by Angel Chapero. He also held a diplomatic post in the Mexican embassy in Brazil.

Noted for his sonnets, Beltrán published his first book, *Veintiún poemas* (1936), at the age of twenty. The book includes fourteen sonnets about love and solitude, and seven with a nautical theme. *Soledad enemiga* (Enemy Solitude), a book of sonnets which was expanded and reprinted, includes poems that deal with the theme of the poet's own death. Beltran's theatrical works include *A las siete en punto* and *La muralla*.

WORKS: Poetry: *Veintiún poemas* (Twenty One Poems), biog. sketch by Angel Chapero (México: Edit. Barco, 1936). *Poesía* (Poetry) (México: Canek, 1941). *Soledad enemiga* (Enemy Solitude) (México: Firmamento, 1944); expanded ed., Tals. Graf., no. 1 (México: SEP, 1949). *Algunas canciones de Neftalí Beltrán*, (Songs by Neftalí Beltrán) portrait and biog. sketch by Salvador Elizondo, Jr. (México: Imp. Veracruz, 1953). *Poesía, 1936-1977* (Poetry, 1936-1977) (México: FCE, 1978). *Poesía completa 1936-1964* (Complete Poetry 1936-1964) (México: FCE, 1966). Theater: *A las siete en punto* (At Seven O'Clock Sharp), premiere México 1938; in Ermilio Abreu Gómez et al., *Cuatro siglos de literatura mexicana* (México: Ed. Leyenda, 1946), pp. 330-42. *La muralla* (The Wall), play in three acts (México, 1944). *La Señora Narciso* (Mrs. Narcissus), play in three acts, Act I, *Rueca* 4, 13 (Winter 1944-45): 29-55. *México y los grabadores europeos* (Mexico and the European Engravers) (México: Artes de México, 1960).

BIBLIOGRAPHY: Anon., Biobibl. note in *Anuario de la poesía mexicana 1962* (México: INBA, 1963), p. 23. Santiago Salvador Baz, "La poesía de Neftalí Beltrán," *Nivel* 5 (May 25, 1963): 1-2, 11. Antonio Castro Leal, *La poesía mexicana moderna*, no. 12 (México: FCE, 1953), xxix, 422. Alí Chumacero, Review of *Soledad enemiga*, in *El Hijo Pródigo* 5, 16 (July 15, 1944): 56. Frank Dauster, *Breve historia de la poesía mexicana* (México: Eds. de Andrea, 1956), p. 175. Ruth S. Lamb, *Bibliografía del teatro mexicano del siglo XX* (México: Eds. de Andrea, 1956), p. 31. Raúl Leiva, *Imagen de la poesía mexicana contemporánea* (México: UNAM, 1959), pp. 244-55, 357. José Luis Martínez, *Literatura mexicana siglo XX*, vol. 1 (México: Ant. Libr. Robredo, 1949), pp. 77-78, 181; vol. 2 (1950), p. 21. Aurora M. Ocampo de Gómez and Ernesto Prado Velázquez, *Diccionario de escritores mexicanos* (México: UNAM, 1967), p. 39.

JOAN SALTZ

BENAVENTE, Fray Toribio de (? -1569). Believed to have been born in the Villa de Benavente, Zamora, Spain, Fray Toribio de Benavente, whose date of birth is unknown, was a friar living in Santiago when he received orders in 1524 to go to Mexico as one of the first few clergy to do so. With the others, he arrived in Veracruz on May 13, 1524. The whole group walked barefoot to Mexico City, observing as they went the humility and manner of dress of the Indian masses. They heard repeatedly the word "motolinía," meaning "poor." Fray Toribio decided to use it as his own name from that point on. Fray Toribio Motolinía, as he was hence known, sought, along with the others in his Franciscan Order, to protect the Indians, often experiencing legal and other difficulties with the authorities.

Among Fray Toribio's many duties as a Franciscan, he founded convents, churches, monasteries, and the city of Puebla. In 1529, he was sent to both Guatemala and Nicaragua to evangelize the Indians. His exceptionally good command of several Indian languages enabled him to establish more than adequate rapport with the Indians, whom he respected and wanted to help. Again, in 1533, he was returned to Guatemala in order to found convents. Over the years, he occupied more and more important positions in his order. By the time he died in Mexico City, in 1569, many people already considered him a saint.

Most of his written works have to do with histories of the indigenous peoples and letters to Emperor Charles V, with regard to his disputes with Fray Bartolomé de las Casas. His *Memoriales* constitutes, in essence, the first real history of the Mexican Indians written by a Spaniard. Most of what he wrote was not made public until the nineteenth century. It is, nonetheless, of utmost historical and cultural value today.

WORKS: *Ritos antiguos, sacrificios e idolatrías de los indios de la Nueva España, y de su conversión a la fe, y quiénes fueron los primeros que la predicaron* (Ancient Rites, Sacrifices and Idolatries of the Indians of New Spain, and of Their Conversion to the Faith, and Who Were the First to Preach It to Them), in *Antiquities of Mexico*, by Lord Kingsborough, vol. 9 (London: Robert Havell, 1848). *Historia de los indios de Nueva España* (History of the Indians of New Spain), vol. 1 (México: J. García Icazbalceta, 1858), pp. 1-249. *Historia de los indios de Nueva España* (México: Edit. Salvador Chávez Hayhoe, 1941). *Carta al Emperador, Refutación a Las Casas sobre la colonización española* (Letter to the Emperor, Refutation to Las Casas about Spanish Colonization), edited by José Bravo Ugarte (México: Jus, 1949).

BIBLIOGRAPHY: Víctor Adib, "Los indios en la 'Historia' de Motolinía," in *Abside* (México) 13, 1 (1949). Joaquín García Icazbalceta, "Carta de don Joaquín García Icazbalceta a don José Fernando Ramírez sobre los padres Las Casas y Motolinía," in *Carta al Emperador, Refutación a Las Casas sobre la colonización española*, edited by José Bravo Ugarte (México: Jus, 1949), pp. 106-11. José Fernando Ramírez, "Noticias de la vida y escritos de fray Toribio de Benavente o Motolinía," in *Obras*, vol. ' (México: Imp. de V. Agüeros, 1898), pp. 1-290.

MICHELE MUNCY

BENAVIDES, Rodolfo (1907-). Born in Pachuca, Hidalgo, to a fairly poor family, Rodolfo Benavides grew up without the benefit of much schooling. At an early age, he was obligated to work in the silver mines of his native area. This experience provided the background for his first novel, *El doble nueve* (The Double Nine), published in 1949, a book that reflects what the author observed and felt. The voice of protest is both strong and personal in this novel, which cannot be easily categorized as belonging to any particular narrative school or tendency. He later went to the United States, where he discovered his desire to commit his experiences and thoughts on paper. Unfortunately, he encountered the same miseries, the same injustices in the United States as he had in Mexico. When he returned to Mexico, he became very active in labor unions and other similar organizations. In 1950, he published *Las cuentas de mi rosario* (The Beads of My Rosary), a novel dealing with the French intervention in the days of Benito Juárez.

WORKS: *El doble nueve* (The Double Nine) (México: n.p., 1949). *Las cuentas de mi rosario* (The Beads of My Rosary) (México: n.p., 1950). *Rumbos humanos* (Human Directions), memoirs (México: n.p., 1954). *Dramáticas profecías de la gran pirámide* (Dramatic Prophecies of the Great Pyramid), essay, 2nd ed. (México: Libro-Mex, 1964).

BIBLIOGRAPHY: Enrique Anderson-Imbert, *Spanish American Literature*, vol. 2 (Detroit: Wayne State University Press, 1969), p. 626. John S. Brushwood, *Mexico in Its Novel* (Austin: University of Texas Press, 1966), p. 22n. John S. Brushwood and José Rojas Garciduenas, *Breve historia de la novela mexicana* (México: Eds. de Andrea, 1959), p. 124. Manuel Pedro González, *Trayectoria de la novela en México* (México: Botas, 1951), pp. 405-07. José Luis Martínez, *Literatura mexicana siglo XX 1910-1949*, vol. 1 (México: Ant. Libr. Robredo, 1949), p. 66; vol. 2 (1950), p. 21.

LINO GARCIA

BENITEZ, Fernando (1912-   ), journalist and prose writer. Born in Mexico City in 1912, Benitez was a reporter for, then editor of *El Nacional* (1936-1947), after which he founded and published several other newspapers and supplements: the *Daily News, México en la Cultura, Diario de la tarde*, and *Sábado*. He also taught journalism at the UNAM, traveled widely around the world, writing accounts of his travels, and was a member of the National Institute of Indigenous Affairs. The topics of his books, both fictional and historical, have ranged from the colonial period to the contemporary situation in Indian communities. These works include *Vida criolla del siglo XVI (The Century after Cortés)*, *La ruta de Hernán Cortés* (The Route of Hernán Cortés), a multivolume set entitled *Los indios de México* (The Indians of Mexico), which comprises *Viaje a la Tarahumara* (Trip to Tarahumara), *La última trinchera* (The Last Trench), and *En el país de las nubes* (In Cloud Country). Benítez has also written documentaries such as *K: El drama de un pueblo y de una planta* (K: The Drama of a People and a Plant), about henequen and exploited Indians, and *Los hongos alucinantes* (Hallucinogenic Mushrooms). Many of these books have been translated into other languages.

Benítez' fictional works include a collection of short stories, *Caballo y Dios* (Horse and God), as well as the novels *El rey viejo* (The Old King), about the life of Venustiano Carranza, and *El agua envenenada* (Poisoned Water), based on a real-life incident of rebellion against a local boss. The uprising and murder took place in Michoacán in 1959, but the novel may be interpreted as an attack on tyranny everywhere.

WORKS: *Caballo y Dios: relatos sobre la muerte* (Horse and God: Short Stories about Death) (México: Editorial Leyenda, 1945). *La ruta de Hernán Cortés* (The Route of Hernán Cortés) (México: FCE, 1950). *Cristóbal Colón* (México: FCE, 1951). *China a la vista* (China at a Glance) (México: Cuadernos Americanos, 1953). *Vida criolla del siglo XVI (The Century after Cortés)* (México: El Colegio de México, 1953). *K: El drama de un pueblo y de una planta* (K: The Drama of a People and a Plant) (México: FCE, 1956). *El rey viejo* (The Old King) (México: FCE, 1959). *La batalla de Cuba* (The Battle of Cuba) (México: Ediciones Era, 1960). *Viaje a la Tarahumara* (Trip to Tarahumara) (México: Biblioteca Era, 1960). *El agua envenenada* (Poisoned Water) (México: FCE, 1961). *La última trinchera* (The Last Trench) (México: Ediciones Era, 1963). *Los hongos alucinantes* (Hallucinogenic Mushrooms) (México: Ediciones Era, 1964). *The Century after Cortes*, translated by Joan MacLean (Chicago: University of Chicago Press, 1965). *En el país de las nubes* (In Cloud Country) (1967). *Los indios de México* (The Indians of Mexico) (México: Era, 1967). *En la tierra mágica del peyote* (In the Magic Land of Peyote) (México: Era, 1968). *Historia de un chamán cora* (History of a Chaman Cora) (México: Era, 1973). *Viaje al centro de México* (Trip to the Center of Mexico) (México: FCE, 1975). *Lázaro Cárdenas y la Revolución Mexicana* (Lázaro Cárdenas and the Mexican Revolution), 3 vols. (México: FCE, 1977-1978). *Historia de la Ciudad de México 1325-1982*, 9 vols. (History of Mexico City 1325-1982) (México: Salvat, 1982-1984). *Los demonios en el convento* (The Devils in the Convent) (México: Era, 1985).

BIBLIOGRAPHY: Jaime Acosta, "Fernando Benítez y los demonios del sexo," interview in *Contenido* (Oct. 1983): 3. Ross Larson, *Fantasy and Imagination in the Mexican Narrative* (Tempe, Ariz.: Center for Latin American Studies, Arizona State University, 1977), pp. 20-21, 41. Manuel Llerín, Review of *Caballo y Dios* in *América* 47 (April 15, 1946): 88-89. Aurora M. Ocampo de Gómez and Ernesto Prado Velázquez, *Diccionario de escritores mexicanos* (México: UNAM, 1967), pp. 41-42. José Emilio Pacheco, "*El rey viejo*," in *Revista de la UNAM* (Dec. 4, 1959): 30. José Rogelio Alvarez, dir., *Enciclopedia de México*, vol. 2 (México: SEP, 1987), p. 936. Jorge Ruffinelli, "Fernando Benítez: días de traición y de ira," in *Sábado 368* (Nov. 3, 1984): 8. Kessel Schwartz, *A New History of Spanish American Fiction*, vol. 2 (Coral Gables, Fla: University of Miami Press, 1971), pp. 285-86; 298.

TERESA R. ARRINGTON

BENITEZ, Jesús Luis (1949-1980), journalist and novelist. Benítez was born June 1, 1949, in Mexico City, where he resided during his short life. He learned to write very early, and his first essays were published in *El día* and *El Nacional*. A self-made man, he perfected his style by attending seminars under famous masters like Augusto *Monterroso for narrative, Emilio *Carballido for dramatic composition, and Juan *Tovar in criticism techniques, among others.

Benítez continued writing for the *Revista Mexicana de Cultura, La Onda, México en la Cultura, Plural*, and *Revista de Bellas Artes*. His short stories that appeared in these magazines were widely accepted. He deals with the life of middle-class young people and satirizes their customs and antisocial way of life. The characters in his works rebel against anything established and live marginal lives. His unpublished work follows the same line as the short stories.

WORKS: *A control remoto y otros rollos* (On Remote Control and Other Stories) (México: Lamo, 1974). *La mesa se va haciendo chiquita* (The Table Is Becoming Smaller) (México: Delambo, 1980). *Las motivaciones del personal* (The Personnel's Motivations) (Xalapa: Universidad Veracruzana, 1980). "Del color de ayer" (About the Color of Yesterday), in *Revista Mexicana de Cultura* 73 (June 21, 1970): 8. "Fin de semana del maese Drácula" (The Weekend of Master Dracula), in *La Onda* 51 (June 2, 1974): 8-9. "Fin de fiesta" (The End of the Party), in *Revista Mexicana de Cultura* 289 (Aug. 11, 1974): 8. "Naturaleza muerta con navaja" (Kill Life with Knife), in *Revista de Bellas Artes* 26 (March-April 1976): 61-64. "Tocando (en silencio) el piano" (Playing the piano silently), in *Revista Mexicana de Cultura* 6 (Feb. 12, 1978): 4. "Sí hay tos" (Yes, There Is Coughing), in *Plural* 100 (Jan. 1980): 7-12. "Mirando el día de noche" (Looking the Day at Night), in *Plural* 105 (June 1980): 14-18. Unpublished novel: "Alucinación constante" (Constant Allucination).

BIBLIOGRAPHY: Anon., "Un escritor joven: Jesús Luis Benítez," in *El Nacional* (March 4, 1972): 5. José Agustín, "Vivo para contar y cuento para vivir," review of *A control remoto*, in *La Onda* 53 (June 16, 1974): 10. Juan Cervera, "Conversación con Jesús Luis Benítez," in *Revista Mexicana de Cultura* 310 (Jan. 12, 1975): 2. José de Jesús Sampedro, "Notas sobre la narrativa mexicana (1965-1976)," in *Tierra Adentro* 11 (July 1977): 6. Marco Tulio Garamuño, "Algunas pesadillas más," review of *Las motivaciones del personal*, in *La Palabra y El Hombre* 33 (Jan.-Mar. 1980): 74-75.

ELADIO CORTES

BENITEZ, José María (1888-1967), poet and novelist. Born in Huanusco, Zacatecas, on June 19, 1888, Benítez first studied business in Zacatecas and continued his education at the National Preparatory School in Mexico City. He taught literature and history in high schools, and he worked in administrative and union positions. He died on September 11, 1967, in Mexico City.

Benítez started as a poet. His first book, *Gesto de Hierro* (Iron Expression), was published in 1822; and in the following years he developed into an important novelist. His novel *Ciudad* (City) won the prize Lanz Miguel Duret and is recognized as one of the most valuable documents about the Mexican Revolution. His greatest concern was to show the relationship between humanity and the environment through the technique of realism. This concern is demonstrated in his last book, *Lo que vio mi gato* (What My Cat Saw), which is composed of several short stories, among them "Al amanecer" (The Dawning), which is also included in the German anthology *Llano grande* (Big Plain) (México: Horst Erdnann, 1862).

WORKS: *Gesto de hierro* (Iron Expression) (Guadalupe, Zacatecas: n.p., 1922). *Ciudad* (City) (México: Botas, 1942). *Lo que vio mi gato* (What My Cat Saw) (México: Prisma, 1944). Hundreds of essays and reviews in literary magazines and journals.

BIBLIOGRAPHY: Rafael Carrasco Puente, *Hemerografía de Zacatecas (1825-1950)* (México: Secretaría de Relaciones Exteriores, 1951). Alí Chumacero, "Otra novela mexicana." *Letras de México* 18 (1942): 6. José Luis Martínez, *Literatura mexicana siglo XX. 1910-1949*, vol. 1 (México: Ant. Libr. Robredo, 1949), pp. 51, 123, 132, 142, 233, 239; vol. 2 (1950), p. 21. V.M., "En la novela procuro el realismo social y humano." *México en la Cultura* 721 (1963): 2.

SILKA FREIRE

BERISTAIN de Souza, José Mariano (1756-1817), ecclesiastic and bibliographer. The heir to the massive bibliographical project begun by Juan José de *Eguiara y Eguren, Beristáin was born in Puebla on May 22, 1756. There, in his birthplace, he began his studies and later received a bachelor's degree in philosophy from the University of Mexico. As a close friend of Fabián y Fuero, Puebla's bishop, he was invited to accompany the church official to Spain when he was appointed to the archbishopric of Valencia. Beristáin attended the university in Spain where he received a doctorate in theology, and he subsequently became a professor in his chosen field at the University of Valladolid. When he returned to Mexico, he was awarded numerous academic honors, and he dutifully served in prestigious posts within the Church as well as in academia.

Beristáin de Souza's greatest contribution to Mexican letters rests upon his *Biblioteca Hispano-Americana Septentrional* (Library of Northern Spanish America), an extensive catalog of New Spain's literary figures along with valuable commentary on the life and works of each one. Still considered an authority on some of Mexico's earliest writers and poets, it represents a marked improvement over the work of his precedessor, *Eguiara y Eguren, whose *Biblioteca Mexicana* (Mexican Library) was written in Latin and arranged alphabetically according to the authors' first names instead of their last. Beristáin's bibliographical project, which contains profiles of some four thousand writers, was published in three volumes in 1816, 1819, and 1821, respectively, and reprinted in 1883.

WORKS: *Biblioteca Hispano-Americana Septentrional* (Library of Northern Spanish America), 3 vols. (México: A. Valdés, 1816-1821).

BIBLIOGRAPHY: Joaquín García Icazbalceta, *La biblioteca de Beristáin de Souza* (México: Impr. de V. Agüeros, 1898); *Las "Bibliotecas" de Eguiara y de Beristáin* (México: Imp. de V. Agüeros, 1896) (Vol. 2 of Biblioteca de Autores Mexicanos), pp. 119-46. José Toribio Medina, *D. José Mariano Berstáin de Souza, estudio bio-bibliográfico* (Santiago de Chile; Imp. Elseviriana, 1897).

JULIE GREER JOHNSON

BERMAN, Sabina (1953-   ). Born in Mexico City on August 21, 1953, Sabina Bermana received her degree in psychology from the Universidad Iberoamericana and later studied dramatic arts, to which she has truly dedicated herself. Berman belongs to the movement Nueva Dramaturgia Mexicana (New Mexican Dramaturgy), under the leadership of Abraham Oceransky, her teacher and friend, with whom she learned acting, directing, and writing. She worked as an assistant director under Oceransky, responsible for such plays as Emilio *Carballido's *El día que se soltaron los leones*, and also as an actress in several montages. Her role as Poncia in the performance of Lorca's *La casa de Bernarda Alba* was outstanding.

Perhaps the most interesting aspect of her literary personality is her capacity as a lyrical poet, which gives her theater special literary merit. The ability to elevate realism to an aesthetic plane and the general overall quality of her works are contributing factors to her success. Four times she has received the National Prize in the competitions sponsored by Bellas Artes. Sabina Berman is the only person in Mexican literary history to have done this. Her play for children, *La historia del Chiquito Pingüica* (The Story of Little Pingüica), which is a version of an episode from the *Popol-Vuh*, won the first time. The second award was for her work *Bill*, later entitled *Yankee*, a frequently performed play. She was awarded the other two prizes, first with *Herejía* (Heresy), which exemplified the faith of the Carvajal family, and then with *Rompecapezas* (Puzzle), about the death of Trotsky.

The theater of Berman does not propose solutions to the complex problems that she illuminates, but does express a strong faith in the ability of women, in particular, to take a positive attitude toward resolution. Even in the absurd works, such as *El jardín de las delicias* (The Garden of Delights) and *El polvo del tiempo* (The Dust of Time), one can see a rebirth of hope, a sense of the future, and even an optimistic view of life.

An example of her theater is the play *Herejía*, written in 1983 and produced in 1984 at the Teatro Wilberto Cantón in Mexico City. It was an unqualified success both for its staging by Oceransky and for its controversial theme: the metaphor of contradiction in the Church's commandments. It focuses on "Thou shalt not kill" versus all those burned alive because they didn't follow the Church's dictates. The play became an act of rebellion against all persecution. *Herejía*, in reality, portrays any minority persecuted by a majority, whether for its ideas, politics, sexual conduct, or religion.

Despite the controversy and heaviness of some of her themes (including reactions to the Vietnam War, activities of the KGB, violence, etc.), Berman also alleviates her drama by use of humor, irony, and satire. Extraordinary characterizations and the use of the most advanced technical means also contribute to the success of Berman's theater.

Berman also has written some stories and a few poems. She participated in the poetry workshop led by Alicia Reyes in the Capilla Alfonsina. In 1975, she won first prize for a story, given by the Concurso Latinamericano de Cuento del Año Internacional de la Mujer (Latinamerican Story Contest in the International Year of the Woman). Likewise, she garnered a second prize for poetry in the Floral Games, sponsored by the states of Chiapas. Again, she won the Concurso de Poesía Pluridimensional "Máscara," with *Ocho cuartos igual a dos humores* (Eight Quarts Equal to Two Moods), which was followed in 1976 by her prize for *Mariposa* (Butterfly). She has also published in several journals and newspapers, including *Aquí Estamos*, *El Zaguan*, *Taller*, and others.

WORKS: Poetry: "Provengo de una larga cadena de extranjeros" (I Come from a Long Line of Foreigners), in *El Zaguán* (March 6, 1977): 66. Poems, in *Punto de Partida* 55-56 (April-May 1977): 40-45. "Poema en dos tiempos" (Poem in Two Tempos), in *Aquí Estamos* 1 (July-Aug. 1977). "Dentro de mí un capullo se abre" (Within Me a Bud Unfolds), in *La Semana de Bellas Artes* 52 (Nov. 29, 1978): 5. Poems in *Poemas y cuentos* (México: UNAM, 1978). "Con rabia, amor" (With Rage, Love), in Gabriel Zaid, *Asamblea de poetas jóvenes de México* (México: Siglo XXI, 1980), p. 202. Poems, in Enrique Jaramillo Levi, *Poesía erótica mexicana 1889-1980*, vol. 2 (México: Edit. Domés, 1982), pp. 540-43. Poems, in Xorge del Campo, *Cupido de lujuria* (Cupid of Lust) (México: Edit. Signos, 1983), pp. 139-40. Theater: "El jardín de las delicias" (The Garden of Delights), performed in Mexico, 1979. "Esto no es una obra de teatro" (This Is Not a Theatrical Work), in *Tierra Adentro* 30 (April-June 1982): 57-60. "De la maravillosa historia del Chiquito Pingüica. De cómo supo de su gran destino y de cómo comprobó su grandeza" (About the Marvelous Story of Chiquito Pingüica. About How He Learned of His Great Destiny and How He Proved His Greatness), in *Tierra Adentro* 31-32 (July-Dec. 1982): 62-63. "Bill," in Emilio Carballido, *Más teatro joven* (México: Editores Mexicanos Unidos, 1982), pp. 123-71; in Emilio Carballido, *Avanzada* (México: EDIMUSA, 1984), pp. 113-61. *Anatema* (Anathema), 1983. *Herejía* (Heresy), performed in 1984. *Un actor se repara* (An Actor Restrains Himself), performed in 1984. "Pingüica," in Emilio Carballido, *Jardín con animales*, pp. 257-96. *El Teatro de Sabina Berman*, prologue and notes by Hugo Argüelles and Alejandro Hermida Ochoa (México: EDIMUSA, 1985). *Muerte súbita* (México: Katún, 1988). Story: "De repente el grito" (Suddenly the Cry), in *Comunidad* (May-July 1977): 273-74. *El polvo del tiempo* (The Dust of Time), in *Tramoya* 9 (2nd. Epoch) (Jan.-Mar. 1987): 98-113.

BIBLIOGRAPHY: Hugo Argüelles and Alejandro Hermida Ochoa, prologue and notes, *El teatro de Sabina Berman* (México: EDIMUSA, 1985). Ronald D. Burgess, "Sabina Berman's Act of Creative Failure: *Bill*," in *Gestos* 2, 3 (1987): 103-13. Emilio Carballido, introduction, *Muerte súbita* (México: Katún, 1988); "Presentación," and Biographical Note, in *Avanzada, más teatro joven* (México: EDIMUSA, 1985), pp. 5-9, 161.

ELADIO CORTES

BERMUDEZ, María Elvira (1916-1988), detective story writer and essayist. Bermúdez was born in Durango, Durango, November 27, 1916, but resided in Mexico City from infancy on. She received a law degree from the Escuela Libre de Derecho in 1939. In 1948 she began to publish detective stories in *El Nacional* and *Selecciones Policiacas y de Misterio*. Bermúdez was also been a contributor of stories and essays to *México en la Cultura* from *Novedades*, in *Mujeres*, *Excelsior*, *Nivel*, and *Cuadernos Americanos*. In 1953 she received honorable mention in the Juegos Florales de Irapuato for her short story "Así es morir" (So It Is to Die). Since 1954 Bermúdez preferred to write criticism of contemporary literary works, essays which primarily appeared in the supplements of *Excelsior* and *El Nacional*. She gave lectures on literature, especially on the novel, participated in roundtable discussions of literary criticism, and publicly read her short stories. Her writing appears in anthologies in

English, Russian, French, and Italian, as well as in publications in Mexico and Latin America.
Bermúdez is representative of the few Mexican writers with an interest in detective novels and short stories, and authored critical studies about detective stories in Mexico, along with reviews of contemporary Mexican writings.

WORKS: Narrative: *Soliloquio de un muerto* (Soliloquy of a Corpse) (México: Col. Los Epígrafes, no. 10, 1951). *Diferentes razones tiene la muerte* (Death Has Different Reasons) (México: Talls. Graf. de la Nación, 1953; México: Plaza y Valdés, 1987). "La clave literaria" (The Literary Key), in *Los mejores cuentos policíacos mexicanos*, edited and introduction no. 15 (México: Libro Mex., 1955). "Cuando el río suena" (When the River Sings), in *Anuario del cuento mexicano 1954* (México: INBA, 1955), pp. 53-71. "Antea" (Buff), in *Anuario del cuento mexicano 1960* (México: INBA, 1961), pp. 38-40. "Detente sombra" (Wait Darkness), in *Anuario del cuento mexicano 1961* (México: INBA, 1962), pp. 30-55; (México: UNAM, 1984). *Alegoría presuntuosa y otros cuentos* (Insolent Allegory and Other Stories) (México: Federación Editorial Mexicana, 1971). *Cinco semanas en globo* (Five Weeks in a Balloon) (México: Porrúa, 1971). *Narraciones extraordinarias; Aventuras de Arturo Gordon Pym; El Cuervo* (Extraordinary Narrations; Adventures of Arturo Gordon Pym; The Crow) (México: Porrúa, 1972). *Aventuras de Sherlock Holmes* (Adventures of Sherlock Holmes) (México: Porrúa, 1982, 1984). *Viajes* (Journeys) (México: Porrúa, 1982). *Cuentos herejes,* (Heretical Stories) (México: Impresora Eficiencia, 1984). *Corazón: diario de un niño* (Heart: Diary of a Boy) (México: Porrúa, 1985). *Muerte a la zaga* (Death Follows) (México: Premiá, 1985); (México: SEP, 1986). Anthologies and Introductions: *Los mejores cuentos policíacos mexicanos* (The Best Mexican Police Stories), edited and introduction, no. 15, (México: Libro-Mex. Eds., 1955). *Cuentos fantásticos mexicanos,* (Fantastic Mexican Stories), edited and introduction (México: Eds. Oasis, 1963). Essays: *La vida familiar del mexicano* (Family Life of the Mexicans), Col. Mexico y lo mexicano, no. 20 (México: Ant. Libr. Robredo, 1955). *La Familia,* addendum to *México, 50 años de Revolución* (México: FCE, 1962). "Juana de Asbaje, poetisa barroca mejicana" (Juana de Asbaje, Barroque Mexican Poet), XVII Cong. Inst. Internac. de Lit. Iberoam.: El barroco en América: Literatura Hispanoamericana (Madrid: Cult. Hisp. del Centro Iberoam. de Coop.; Universidad Complutense de Madrid, 1973), pp. 173-86. *Narrativa mexicana revolucionaria* (Revolutionary Mexican Narrative) (México: Editorial ECOMA, 1974). "La fantasía en la literatura mexicana" (Fantasy in Mexican Literature), in *Otros mundos otros fuegos: Fantasía y realismo mágico en Iberoamérica,* edited by Donald R. Yated, XVI Intl. Cong. of Iberoam. Lit. (East Lansing: Michigan State University, Latin American Studies Center, 1975), pp. 6S-73. "El amor en la obra de Mario Benedetti," in *Recopilación de textos sobre Mario Benedetti,* edited by Ambrosio Fornet (Havana: Casa de las Américas, 1976), pp. 159-63.

BIBLIOGRAPHY: Anon., Biobibliographical note in *Anuario del cuento mexicano 1960* (México: INBA, 1961), p. 38; *Anuario del cuento mexicano 1961* (México: INBA, 1962), p. 30. Jesús Arellano, review of *Los mejores cuentos policíacos mexicanos*, in *Metáfora* 5 (Nov.-Dec. 1955): 36. Alberto Bonifaz Nuño, Review of *Los mejores cuentos policacos mexicanos*, in *Universidad de México* 10 (Dec. 4, 1955): 29. John S. Brushwood and José Rojas Garcidueñas, *Breve historia de la novela mexicana* (México: Eds. de Andrea, 1959), p. 143. Henrique González Casanova, "El libro de la semana: Las razones de la muerte," in *México en la Cultura* 189 (Nov. 2, 1952): 7. Luis Leal, *Breve historia del cuento mexicano* (México: Eds. de Andrea, 1956), pp. 135-36; *Bibliografía del cuento mexicano* (México: Eds. de Andrea, 1958), p. 22. Aurora M. Ocampo de Gómez and Ernesto Prado Velázquez, *Diccionario de escritores mexicanos* (México: UNAM, 1967), pp. 43-44. Donald A. Yates, ed., *El cuento policial latinoamericano*, introduction, and bibliography, no. 2 (México: Eds. de Andrea, 1964).

JOAN SALTZ

BERNAL, Rafael (1915-1972), poet, novelist, short story writer, and playwright. Bernal, who was born in Mexico City on June 28, studied at Loyola College in Montreal, Canada, the Colegio Francés de San Francisco de Borja, and at the Instituto de Ciencia y Letras in Mexico City for an undergraduate degree in the humanities. From 1930 to 1938 he traveled to Europe, the United States, and Canada; from 1956 to 1960 to Venezuela, Colombia, and Cuba; in 1960 to Central America, and since 1961 to the Orient. In the late 1960s he served in the Mexican embassy in the Philippines. He received two prizes, Flores Naturales, for his poetry. Bernal's work includes radio and television scripts as well as poems and stories that have appeared in newspapers and magazines such as *Novedades*, *La Prensa Gráfica*, *Revista de América*, *Excelsior*, *Comment*, and *Unitas*, both in Mexico and abroad.

Bernal is the author of poetry, theatrical works, short stories and novels of diverse themes. *Federico Reyes, el cristero* (Federico Reyes, the Cristero) and *Memorias de Santiago Oxtotilpan* (Memoirs of Santiago Oxtotilpan) treat a social problematic. *Un muerto en la tumba* (A Dead Man in the Grave), *Su nombre era muerte* (His Name Was Death), the novella *El extraño caso de Aloysus Hands* (The Strange Case of Aloysus Hands), the book of short stories *Trópico* (Tropics), and *Tres novelas policiacas* (Three Police Novels) are of the detective and fantasy genres. In them Bernal has created Detective Teófilo Batanes, a character who, acccording to María Elvira *Bermúdez, embodies a type of G. K. Chesterton's Father Brown, "the infallible instrument by which divine providence punishes delinquents." A novel, *Tierra de gracia* (Land of Grace), is played out in the environs of the River Orinoco and in the city of Caracas, Venezuela, during the reign of the dictator Pérez Jiménez. The story allows Bernal to describe the "civilized" and "savage" life. As a playwright, Bernal was an initiator of theater for television. His script, *La carta* (The Letter), was one of the first theatrical works broadcast by Mexican television. He also wrote *Antonia*, a play that received a prize in the competition of the Fiestas de Primavera. His works have been staged by professional and experimental groups.

WORKS: Poetry: *Federico Reyes: el cristero* (Federico Reyes: The Cristero) (México: Ed. Canek, 1941). *Improperio a Nueva York y otros poemas* (Insult to New York and Other Poems), five poems (México: Quetzal, 1943). Narrative: *El fresco al oleo de Juan José Segura* (The Oil Fresco of Juan José Segura) (México: Ediciones Canek, 1941). *Memorias de Santiago Oxtotilpan* (Memoirs of Santiago Oxtotilpan) (México: Ed. Polis, 1945). *Un muerto en la tumba* (A Dead Man in the Grave) (México: Edit. Jus, 1946.) *El extraño caso de Aloysus Hands* (The Strange Case Of Aloysus Hands), novella (México: 1947). *Su nombre era muerte* (His Name Was Death) (México: Edit.

Jus, 1947). *El fin de la esperanza* (The End of Hope) (México: Ed. Calpulli, 1948). Caribal (From the Carribean) (México: Eds. La Prensa, 1956). *Tierra de gracia* (Land of Grace) (México: FCE, 1963). *En diferentes mundos* (In Different Worlds) (México: FCE, 1967). *El complot mongol* (México: Mortiz, 1969; México: Mortiz, SEP Cultura, l985). Short Stories: *Trópico* (Tropics), six short stories (México: Edit. Jus, 1946). *Tres novelas policíacas* (Three Police Novels) (México: Eds. Jus, 1946). (Others appearing in anthologies, newspapers, magazines, and supplements). Theater: *El cadáver del señor García* (Mr. Garcia's Cadaver), in the magazine *Cuit Poulet*, 1947. *La carta* (The Letter), first theatrical work brocdast by television in Mexico, Aug. 8, 1950. *Antonia*, play in three acts, premiere, 1950, prize at the Fiestas de la Primavera, 1950 same year, in *Panorama del Teatro en México*; 1, 4 (Oct.-Nov. 1954): 31-58; with "El maíz in la casa" (Corn in the House) and "La paz contigo" (Peace with You) (México: Edit. Jus, 1961). *Soledad* (Solitude), dramatic poem in three acts, in suppl. of *América* 62 (1950): 263-88. *El Idolo* (The Idol), comedy in three acts, premiere, 1952. *La paz contigo o el martirio del Padre Pro* (Peace with You or the Martyrdom of Father Pro), play in three acts, divided into ten scenes, premiere, 1955 (México: Edit. Jus, 1961). *Nancy Brown*, adaptation of a story of W. Somerset Maugham, premiere, 1956. *El maíz en la casa* (Corn in the House), rural tragedy (México: Edit. Jus, 1961). Essay: *México en Filipinas; Estudio de una transculturación* (Mexico in the Philippines: A Study of Transculturation) (México: UNAM, 1965). *Prologue to Philippine History* (Solidaridad Pub. House, 1967). Biography: *Gente de mar* (People of the Sea) (México: Edit. Jus, 1950).

BIBLIOGRAPHY: Anon., Review of *El fin de la esperanza* (The End of Hope), in *Fuensanta* 1, 3 (Feb. 3, 1949): 4. María Elvira Bermúdez, Intro. to *Los mejores cuentos policiacos mexicanos* (The Best Mexican Police Stories), no. 15 (México: Libro-Mex., 1955). "La novela mexicana en 1963" (The Mexican Novel in 1963), in *Diorama de la Cultura* (Jan. 19, 1964): 8. Rafael Bernal, "El teatro en televisión," in *Panorama del teatro mexicano* 1, 1 (July, 1954): 84. John S. Brushwood and José Rojas Garcidueñas, *Breve historia de la novela mexicana* (México: Eds. de Andrea, 1959), pp. 143-44. Emmanuel Carballo, "Entre libros. *Tierra de gracia*," in *Nivel* 14 (Feb. 25, 1964): 3. Alyce Golding Cooper, "Teatro mexicano contemporáneo, 1940-1962" Diss., Facultad de Filosofía y Letras, UNAM (México, 1962), pp. 37, 58. Gilberto González Contreras, "Las letras mexicanas de 1947 a 1952," in *México en el mundo de hoy* (México: Ed. Guaranía, 1952), p. 449. Miguel Guardia, "El teatro en México," review of *Antonia* and *Los de abajo*, in *México en la Cultura* 66 (May 7, 1950): 4, 7. Ruth S. Lamb, *Bibliografía del teatro mexicano del siglo xx* (México: Eds. de Andrea, 1956), p. 32. Luis Leal, *Breve historia del cuento mexicano* (México: Eds. de Andrea, 1956), pp. 134, 135; *Bibliografía del cuento mexicano* (México: Eds. de Andrea, 1958), p. 22. Antonio Magaña Esquivel and Ruth S. Lamb, *Breve historia del teatro mexicano* (México: Eds. de Andrea, 1958), p. 152. José Luis Martínez, *Literatura* mexicana siglo XX. 1910-1949 (México: Ant. Libr. Robredo, 1949), vol. 1, pp. 67, 247-50, vol. 2 (1950), p. 21. Daniel Moreno, "Hombre y letras," review of *Tierra de gracia*, in *Revista Mexicana de Cultura* 866 (Nov. 3, 1963): 2. Javier Morente, "Sala de lectura," review of *Tierra de gracia*, in *Diorama de la Cultura* (Nov. 3, 1963): 6. Aurora M. Ocampo de Gómez and Ernesto Prado Velázquez, *Diccionario de escritores mexicanos* (México: UNAM, 1967), pp. 44-45. Gustavo Sáinz, "Escaparate," review of *Tierra de gracia* in *México en la Cultura* 762 (Oct. 27, 1963): 5. Mauricio de la Selva, Review of *Tierra de gracia* in *Diorama de la Cultura* (Dec. 10, 1963): 3.

Xavier Sorondo, "Glosarios de cada día: *Antonia* ante la crítica," in *Panorama del teatro en México* 1, 4 (Oct.-Nov. 1954): 29-30.

JOAN SALTZ

BETETA Quintana, Ramón (1901-1965). Born in Hermosillo, Sonora, and educated both in Mexico and the United States with degrees in economics, law and social science, Beteta taught at UNAM from 1924 to 1942. Yet his career as a statesman spanned the years 1934-1958 with important positions under presidents Cárdenas, Avila Camacho, Alemán, and Ruiz Cortines. Perhaps his top post was secretary of the treasury from 1946 to 1953. As ambassador he served in Italy and Greece in the 1950s. Both a scholar and a journalist, he headed two periodicals, *Novedades* and *Diario de la Tarde*. Although several titles indicate Beteta's interest in the social sciences especially from the vantage point of public office, his best-written, most personal, and most enduring are his autobiographies. *Camino a Talxcalantongo* details one year of his life as a Carrancista and follows the structure of the novel. *Jarano*, of a larger time frame and with more focus on the family, is one of Mexico's best autobiographies.

WORKS: *La mendicidad en México* (México: Departamento de Acción Educativa, 1930). *Economic and Social Programs of Mexico* (México: n.p., 1935). *The Mexican Revolution, a Defense* (México: n.p., 1937). *Tierra del chicle* (México: Editorial México Nuevo, 1951). *Tres años (1947-1948-1949) de política hacendaria, perspectiva y acción* (México: Secretaría de Hacienda, 1951). *Camino a Tlaxcalantongo* (México: FCE, 1961). *Entrevistas y pláticas* (México: Editorial Renovación, 1961). *Jarano* (México: FCE, 1961).

BIBLIOGRAPHY: Roderic A. Camp, *Mexican Political Biographies, 1935-1981* (Tucson: University of Arizona Press, 1982), p. 33. *Diccionario Porrúa: Historia, biografía y geografía de México, Suplemento* (México: Porrúa, 1966), pp. 40-41. Felipe Morales, *200 personajes mexicanos* (México: Ediciones "Ateneo," 1952), pp. 51-52. Moisés Ochoa Campos, *La oratoria en México* (México: F. Trillas, 1963). James W. Wilkie, *México visto en el siglo XX: Entrevistas de historia oral* (México: Instituto Mexicano de Investigaciones Económicas, 1969), pp. 23-71. Richard D. Woods, *Mexican Autobiography: An Annotated Bibliography* (Westport, Conn.: Greenwood Press, 1988), pp. 18-19.

RICHARD D. WOODS

BLANCO, Alberto (1951-   ). Blanco was born in Tijuana, Baja California Norte on February 18, 1951. He studied physics at the Universidad Nacional Autónoma de México. He is a painter in his own right and is responsible for the design of a number of covers for the Letras Mexicanas series of the Fondo de Cultura Económica. He is a composer and musician who directs and plays with avant-garde groups in Mexico

City such as the now dissolved Las Plumas atómicas. He is also an excellent literary translator.

Blanco has delved into the many forms of poetry as few young Mexican poets have. He has developed his style and mastery of language and structure to an unprecedented degree. He is constantly experimenting, seeking new artistic experiences that will make him grow. His texts are witness to the extensive range and quality he has achieved. In *Giros de Faros* (Premio Carlos Pellicer) he dazzles the readers' imagination with the creation of brilliant, surprising metaphors such as a bird fair whirling around a crank organ in a Mexico City park. In *Antes de nacer* he works at establishing a long and complicated flowing structure that stands for the DNA molecule. But his foremost achievement to date is *Cromos*, an artistic work of very high aesthetic value which, presents the reader with a great number of world-renouned artworks, each followed by Blanco's own poem that extends or interprets its meaning.

WORKS: *Giros de faros* (México: FCE, 1979). *Antes de nacer* (Before Birth) (México: Penélope, 1983). *Tras el rayo* (After the Lightning) (Guadalajara, Jalisco: Cuarto Menguante Editores, 1985). *Cromos* (Cards) (México: INBA, 1987) (Premio Carlos Pellicer). *Canto a la sombra de los animales* (México: Galería López Quiroga, 1988).

BIBLIOGRAPHY: José Joaquín Blanco, *Crónica de la poesía mexicana* (México: Katún, 1981), pp. 264-70. Sandro Cohen, *Palabra nueva: Dos décadas de poesía en México* (México: Premiá, 1981), pp. 29, 222-27. Margo Glantz, *Ondas y escritura en México* (México: Siglo XXI, 1971), pp. 3, 41, 42. Efraín Gutiérrez, "¿Historia para qué?," *El Nacional* (Feb. 23, 1981), p. 17. Enrique Jaramillo Levi, *Poesía erótica mexicana 1889-1980*, vol. 2 (México: Edit. Domés, 1982), p. 370. Sergio Mondragón, *República de poetas* (México: Martín Casillas, 1985), pp. 59-71. Jaime Moreno Villareal, *La línea y el círculo* (México: UAM, 1981). Gonzalo Valdés Medellín, "Una casi frustrada entrevista con José Joaquín Blanco," *Revista Mexicana de Cultura* 98 (Jan. 13, 1985): 5. Rafael Vargas, "La vida es larga y transcuree entre aciertos y fallas," *Revista UNAM* (July 11, 1979): 42-44.

RICARDO AGUILAR

BLANCO Moheno, Roberto (1920-) journalist, novelist, and short story writer. Blanco was born on December 16, 1920, in Cosautlán, Veracruz. He received his elementary education there, but finished his studies in Mexico City. Forced to earn a living as a child, he sold newspapers on the streets. He held a variety of jobs until 1940, when he devoted his energies to journalism.   Widely traveled, he has collaborated in numerous periodicals, including *Siempre!*.

Some of his work (e.g., *Jicaltepec*) reflects his exposure to rural life in Veracruz. Most of his books, however, deal with Mexican historical figures and events, focusing on political, social, and revolutionary themes.

WORKS: *Jicaltepec: casi una novela* (Jicaltepec: Almost a Novel) (México, 1943; México: Libro-Mex, 1959, 1966; Ed. Diana, 1973). *Salvador Díaz Mirón* (México:

SEP, 1947). *Antología de Renato Leduc* (Anthology of Renato Leduc) (México: SEP, 1948). *Cuando Cárdenas nos dio la tierra, casi novela* (When Cárdenas Gave Us the Land, Almost a Novel) (México: Porrúa, 1952; Cía. General de Ediciones, 1958, 1960, 1966; Ed. Diana, 1970; Ed. Bruguera, 1980). *Crónica de la Revolución Mexicana* (Chronicle of the Mexican Revolution) (México: Libro-Mex, 1957, 1958, 1959, 1961, 1965; Ed. Diana, 1967, 1968). *Un son que canta en el río* (A Sound Singing in the River) (México: Libro-Mex, 1962, 1964; Ed. Diana, 1975; Bruguera Mexicana de Ediciones, 1981). *¡Este México nuestro! ¿Novela?* (This Mexico of Ours! Novel?) (México: Libro-Mex, 1960; Ed. Diana, 1976). *México, S.A.* (México: Libro-Mex, 1958, 1959, 1961). *Juárez ante Dios y ante los hombres* (Juárez before God and Men) (México: Libro-Mex, 1959, 1964, 1966; Ed. Diana, 1967, 1969, 1972). *Autopsia del periodismo mexicano* (An Autopsy of Mexican Journalism) (México: Libro-Mex, 1961). *El cardenismo* (Cardenism) (México: Libro-Mex, 1963). *Memorias de un reportero* (Memoirs of a Reporter) (México: Libro-Mex, 1965; Ed. V Siglos, 1975). *La noticia detrás de la noticia* (The News behind the News) (Zacatecas: Litográfica Zacatecana, 1966; México: Ed. V Siglos, 1975). *Pancho Villa, que es su padre* (Pancho Villa, Who Is Its Father) (México: Ed. Diana, 1969, 1971, 1975). *Tlatelolco: historia de una infamia* (Tlatelolco: An Infamous Story) (México: Ed. Diana, 1969, 1970, 1976, 1979). *Zapata* (México: Ed. Diana, 1970, 1973). *Tata Lázaro: vida obra y muerte de Cárdenas, Múgica y Carrillo Puerto* (Daddy Lázaro: The Life, Work and Death of Cárdenas, Múgica, and Carrillo Puerto) (México: Ed. Diana, 1972). *Historia de dos curas revolucionarios: Hidalgo y Morelos* (Story of Two Revolutionary Priests: Hidalgo and Morelos) (México: Ed. Diana, 1973). *Historia de la estupidez política* (History of Political Stupidity) (México: Ed. Diana, 1974:). *¡...pero contentos!: periodismo, 1968-1975* (...but Happy!: Journalism, 1968-1975) (México: Ed. Diana, 1976). *En este pueblo no pasa nada: medio novela* (Nothing Happens in This Town, Semi-novel) (México: Ed. Diana, 1978; Bruguera, 1981). *¡Puro cuento!* (Just Stories) (México: Ed. V. Siglos, 1978). *La corrupción en México* (Corruption in Mexico) (México: Bruguera Mexicana de Ediciones, 1979). *La "otra" política de México* (Mexico's "Other" Politics) (México: Bruguera Mexicana de Ediciones, 1981). *Díaz Ordaz, Echeverría, López Portillo: si Zapata y Villa levantaran la cabeza* (Díaz Ordaz, Echeverría, López Portillo: If Zapata and Villa Raised Their Heads) (México: Bruguera Mexicana de Ediciones, 1982). *Ya con ésta me despido mi vida, pero la de los demás* (And with This I Say Goodby to Life, but the Others') (México: Grijalbo, 1986).

BIBLIOGRAPHY: Anon., "*Cuando Cárdenas nos dio la tierra*," *Insula* 413 (April 1981): 17. Miguel Bustos Cerecedo, *La creación literaria en Veracruz* (Xalapa: Editora del Gobierno de Veracruz, 1977), pp. 230-34. Fausto Castillo, "Invitación a leer," review of *Memorias de un reportero* in *El Gallo Ilustrado* 153 (May 30, 1965); 4. Heriberto García Rivas, *Historia de la literatura mexicana*, vol. 1 (México: Porrúa, 1971-1974), pp. 228, 414. Alfredo Jiménez, "Acusa la editora Bruguera a Roberto Blanco Moheno de fraude," *Excelsior* (May 17, 1983): 27A. Carlos Monsiváis, *A ustedes les consta* (México: Era, 1980), pp. 59-61. Aurora M. Ocampo de Gómez and Ernesto Prado Velázquez, *Diccionario de escritores mexicanos* (México: UNAM, 1967), p. 45. Alberto Ramírez de Aguilar, "Blanco Moheno," *Diorama de la Cultura* (July 13, 1958); 3. Salvador Reyes Nevares, Review of *Juárez ante Dios y ante los hombres* in *México en la Cultura* 534 (May 24, 1959); 4.

JANIS L. KRUGH

BOCANEGRA, Matías de (1612-1668), Jesuit priest, poet, dramatist, and historian. Bocanegra was born in Puebla, Mexico. As the official historian of the most extensive Auto de Fe in the New World, Bocanegra has left us with an important sociohistorical document, *Historia del auto público y general de fé celebrado en México en 11 de abril de 1649* (History of the General and Public 'Auto de Fe' Celebrated in Mexico on April ll, 1649). It gives a detailed account of the genealogy and biography of 109 accused persons, and it manifests the attitudes of the clergy toward non- believers. He also wrote two dramas, *Comedia de San Francisco de Borja* (Comedy of San Francisco de Borja) and *Teatro jerárquico de la luz* (Hierarchical Theater of Light). A third, *Sufrir para merecer* (Suffering Before Deserving), has been attributed to him. Matías de Bocanegra, however, is better known as the author of the poem "Canción a la vista de un desengaño" (Song upon the Realization of a Deception), a fable about the ephemeral nature of human life, and a contrast between worldly and religious life. Inspired by Antonio Mira de Amezcua's "El jilguerillo" (The Little Goldfinch), it became one of the most imitated poems during the colonial period in New Spain.

WORKS: *Teatro jerárquico de la luz* (Hierarchical Theater of Light) México, 1642. "Canción a la vista de un desengaño" (Song upon the Realization of a Deception), in *Las cien mejores poesías mexicanas,* edited by Antonio Castro Leal (México, 1935). *Historia del auto público y general de fé celebrado en México en 11 de abril de 1649* (History of the Public and General Auto de Fe Celebrated in Mexico on April 11, 1649) (México, 1649), translated by Seymour B. Liebman as *Jews and the Inquisition of Mexico: The Great Auto de Fe of 1649* (Lawrence, Kansas: Coronado Press, 1974). "Comedia de San Francisco de Borja" (Comedy of San Francisco de Borja) (México, 1641); in *Tres piezas teatrales del virreinato,* edited by José Rojas Garcidueñas and José Juan Arróm (México: UNAM, 1976): pp. 237-379.

BIBLIOGRAPHY: José J. Arrom, "Una desconocida comedia mexicana del siglo XVII," *Revista Iberoamericana* 19, 37 (1953): 79-103; "*Sufrir para merecer,* comedia atribuida a Bocanegra," *Boletín del Archivo General de la Nación* 20. 3 (1949): 379-459; "El teatro de hispanoamerica en la época colonial," *Anuario Bibliográfico Cubano* (La Habana) (1956): 94-103. José Mariano Beristáin de Souza, *Biblioteca Mexicana.* vol. 1 (México: 1755), p. 273. Marcelino Menéndez y Pelayo, *Historia de la poesía hispanoamericana,* vol. 1 (Madrid: n.p., 1911), pp. 68-70. Alfonso Méndez Plancarte, *Poetas novohispanos, segundo siglo (1621-1721)* (México: Imp. Universitaria, 1943), pp. xlix-li, lxxv, 93-102. Francisco Pimentel. *Historia crítica de la literatura y de la ciencia* (México: n.p., 1870), 125-32. Carlos Miguel Suárez Radillo, *El teatro barroco hispanoamericano,* vol. 1 (Madrid: J. P. Turranzas, 1981), pp. 70-80.

ALFONSO GONZALEZ

BOJORQUEZ, Juan de Dios (1892-1967). Born March 8, 1892, in San Miguel Horcasitas, Sonora, Juan de Dios Borjórquez, an agricultural engineer and businessman by profession, he served in a wide variety of capacities, including military, political, agricultural and social. A worldwide traveler, he journeyed to many different lands, including the United States, several European countries, and other places.

A talented journalist, he directed and contributed to many newspapers and magazines. He founded *El Sector*, in 1915, with officials from the Mexican army of General Obregón. He was concurrently the director of *El Instante* and a contributor to several others. He also established the monthly magazine *Crisol*, a journal of the Bloque de Obreros Intelectuales (Block of Intellectual Workers). It lasted more than eight years. In 1931, he became the editor of *El Nacional*, and later founded *Matinal*, the first morning newspaper in Sonora. He was an important contributor to *Excelsior* and *El Universal*.

In addition to all the above-mentioned capacities, Juan de Dios Bojórquez, often using the pseudonym Djed Bórquez, also dedicated himself to literature. One of his most noteworthy literary contributions is the novel *Yórem Tamegua*, published in 1923. With an indigenous theme, the novel has been considered within the realm of the novel of the Revolution. Altogether, he published more than a dozen books on the Revolution. In addition, he wrote stories, chronicles, and biographies.

WORKS: *Sonot* (Sonora: Talleres de Orientación, 1917). *Apuntes sobre la vida del General Jesús M. Garza* (Notes on the Life of General Jesús M. Garza) (México: Lithographic and Typographic Co., S.A., 1923). *Calles* (Streets) (Guatemala: Talleres Sánchez and de Guise, 1923); 2nd ed. (México: Botas, 1925). *Yórem Tamegua* (Guatemala: Talleres Sánchez and De Guise, 1923). *El héroe de Nacozari* (The Hero of Nacozari) (Havana: Siglo XX, 1925). *Pasando por París* (Going through Paris) (México: n.p., 1929). *El mundo es igual* (The World Doesn't Matter) (México: n.p., 1930). *Champ* (México: n.p., 1932). *La inmigración española en México* (Spanish Immigration in Mexico), conference given in the Centro Asturiano, Sept. 25, 1932, special edition of *Crisol*, México, 1932. *Prologue: Ramón López Velarde, El son del corazón* (The Sound of the Heart) (México: Tall. Tip. de Alfredo del Bosque, 1932). *Obregón, aspectos de su vida* (Obregón, Aspects of His Life), in collaboration with Juan de Dios Robledo et al. (México: Ed. Cultura, 1935). *María Madre, del archipiélago Islas Marías en el Océano Pacíficoo* (Mother Mary, of the Archipelago Islas Marías in the Pacific Ocean) (México: n.p., 1937). *Crónica del Constituyente* (Chronicle of the Constituent) (México: n.p., 1938). *Forjadores de la Revolución Mexicana* (Forgers of the Mexican Revolution) (México: Biblioteca del Instituto Nacional de Estudios Históricos de la Revolución Mexicana, 1960). *Hombres y aspectos de México en la tercera etapa de la Revolución* (Men and Aspects of Mexico in the Third Period of the Revolution) (México: n.p., 1963).

BIBLIOGRAPHY: Andrés Henestrosa, Review of *Hombres y aspectos de México en la tercera etapa de la Revolución*, in *El Nacional* (Aug. 20, 1964): 3. Ross Larson, *Fantasy and Imagination in the Mexican Narrative* (Tempe, Ariz.: Center for Latin American Studies, Arizona State University, 1977), p. 47. José Luis Martínez, *Literatura mexicana siglo XX, 1910-1949*, vol. 2 (México: Ant. Libr. Robredo, 1950), pp. 21-22. Aurora M. Ocampo de Gómez and Ernesto Prado Velázquez, *Diccionario de escritores mexicanos* (México: UNAM, 1967), pp. 45-46. Enriqueta de Parodi, "Juan de Dios Bojórquez," in *El Nacional* (Sept. 3, 1964): 3. César Rodríguez Chicharro, "La novela indigenista mexicana," in *Estudios Literarios* 20 (1963): 146. Carlos J. Sierra, Review of *La inmigración española en México*, in *Boletín bibliográfico de la Secretaria de Hacienda y Crédito Público* 292 (April 1, 1964): 21.

JEANNE C. WALLACE

BONIFAZ Nuño, Alberto (1911-), short story writer, novelist, playwright and critic. Born in Niltepec, Oaxaca, on December 15, 1911, Bonifaz was first known for his short stories and articles on criticism and later by his novels. *El Nacional* awarded him a prize in 1959 for a piece of theater, and he contributes works to cultural journals like *Revista Mexicana de Cultura, La Cultura en México,* and *Revista de la Universidad.* A member of the editorial office of UNAM, he has done translation from French and English. In his works he shows human subjection, corruption, and opulence, and he combines dream and reality. He has baroque traits and is careful with detail; his dialogues flow.

WORKS: Novels: *La cruz del sureste* (The Southeast Cross) (México: FCE, 1954). *El derecho del señor* (The Right of the Master), comedy in three acts (México: UNAM, 1960). *Las cinco ciudades* (The Five Cities) (México: FCE, 1969). *El alba de oro* (The Golden Dawn) (México: UNAM, 1980). Short Stories: *La cachucha de armiño,* in *Ideas de México* 12 (July-Aug. 1955). *La tercer copia,* in *Bellas Artes* (Feb. 2, 1956): 38-39. *Juego de espejos* (Mirror Game) (México: UNAM, 1959). *El último castillo* (The Last Castle) (México: Imp. Universitaria, 1972). Essay: *El paraíso vendido* (Sold Paradise) (México: Imp. Universitaria, 1976). "Guillermo Francovich, *El pensamiento bolivariano en el siglo XX,*" in Francisco Monterde, *Teatro mexicano del siglo XX.* Translations: From French archives, "A cien años del 5 de mayo de 1862" (One Hundred Years After May 5th, 1862) (1962). From English, Lord Kingsborough's appendix to *Antiguedades de México* (Mexican Antiquities) (1964). Olen E. Leonard's *El cambio económico y social en cuatro comunidades del altiplano de Bolivia* (Economic and Social Change in Four Communities of the Bolivian Highlands) (1966).

BIBLIOGRAPHY: Leticia Algaba Martínez, "Notas sobre la novela mexicana en los últimos quince años," in *Armas y Letras* 1-2 (Jan.-Jun. 1962): 5-24. Juan Cervera, *"El alba de oro,"* in *Revista Mexicana de Cultura* 75 (May 17, 1981): 6. Carlos González Peña, *Historia de la literatura mexicana* (México: Porrúa, 1966), p. 306. Luis Leal, *Bibliografía del cuento mexicano* (México: Eds. de Andrea, 1958), p. 22. Bernardo Ruiz, "La tumba de los héroes," review of *El alba de oro,* in *La Cultura al Día* (June 8, 1985): 4.

DELIA GALVAN

BONIFAZ NUÑO, Rubén (1923-). Born November 12, 1923, in Córdoba, Veracruz, Rubén Bonifaz Nuño completed law school, but his literary calling became his career. Among a myriad of other activities, he has been the director of publications at UNAM and a Latin professor. Primarily a very unique and original poet, he has contributed to such literary journals and periodicals as *El Nacional, Universidad de México, Excelsior,* and others. Some of his works have been translated into English and French. He also translated some of the works of Classical Latin literature.

Rubén Bonifaz Nuño has successfully combined classicism, Greek and Latin traditions, and Náhuatl in one poetry. *Imágenes* (Images), constituting poems written between 1946 and 1951, is an impeccable example of his classicism. Revolving around the central themes of solitude and death, the poems in *Imágenes* demonstrate remarkable qualities of artistic maturity, but were composed during what Bonifaz Nuño called his period of "apprenticeship." *Los demonios y los días* (Demons and Days), published in 1956, with a decidedly social orientation, is poetry bordering on prose. A collection of forty-two poems rather tightly structured, *Los demonios y los días* belongs to what the author termed his creative period. His poem *El manto y la corona* (The Cloak and the Crown), published in 1958, is considered by a few critics to be one of his most perfect books, balancing classicism with social poetry, but the author later reconsidered his creation, feeling somewhat chagrined by its content. It is an unbalanced love story, unbalanced because it is one-sided, as all the poems represent the author's perspective, his feelings, his adoration, etc. Much of his poetry is bittersweet because, although always the eternal optimist, man, often in solitude, must deal with the evils of contemporary civilization that threaten to consume him. But man, he affirms, will rise up and create a new and better world in which both poetry and life are one and beautiful. In *Fuego de pobres* (Fire of the Poor) (1961), he deepens his sensitivity to social problems, freeing his voice to acknowledge his experiences, fears, hopes, and dreams without sacrificing poetic beauty. Greatly influenced by the pre-Hispanic world, *Siete de espadas* (Seven of Spades) (1966), is a tribute to the ancient spirit. It is not social poetry, but a poetry that recognizes the duel heritage of the Mexicans. It includes, among other things, visions of horror and poetic symbols, set in an intricate poetic structure. *El ala del tigre* (The Wing of the Tiger) (1969) deals with both the indigenous Mexican culture and the world of the Mediterranean. *La flama en el espejo* (The Flame in the Mirror) (1971) is an erotic, lyrical poem, highly acclaimed by critics. In 1979, he published *De otro modo lo mismo* (Otherwise the Same Thing) a collection of poetry from his earlier books and included some hitherto unpublished verses. *As de oro* (Ace of Gold) (1980) and *El corazón del espiral* (The Heart of the Spiral) (1983) attest to his poetic maturity and grace.

Bonifaz Nuño was awarded a scholarship by the Centro Mexicano de Escritores for the 1951-1952 academic period. He also received a Guggenheim fellowship for 1984-1985 in order to pursue Aztec studies. He has received quite a number of prizes and other distinctions for his original work and his outstanding contribution to Mexican letters. In 1985, he was awarded an honorary doctorate, given by the Universidad de Colima. He also received the distinguished Alfonso Reyes international prize the same year. The Universidad Nacional Autónoma de México recognized him with an honorary doctorate and the Jorge Cuesta Prize, in 1985. Although translations, essays, and poetry constitute his literary work, Bonifaz Nuño's major contribution is his poetry, a coherent and inspired work shaped by his humanistic spirit.

WORKS: *La muerte del ángel* (The Death of the Angel) (México: Edit. Firmamento, 1945). *Poética* (México: Los Presentes, 1951). *Ofrecimiento romántico* (Romantic Offering), no. 8 (México: Los Epígrafes 1951). *Imágenes* (Images) (México: FCE, 1953). *Los demonios y los días* (Demons and Days) (México: FCE, 1956). *Antología de la poesía latina* (Anthology of Latin Poetry), with Amparo Gaos (México: UNAM, 1957). *El manto y la corona* (The Cloak and the Crown) (México: UNAM, 1958). *Canto llano a Simón Bolívar* (Plain Chanting to Simón Bolívar) (México: Cuadernos del Unicornio, 1958). *El dolorido sentir* (Pained Emotion) (México: Edit. Cuadernos de El Cocodrilo, 1959). *Fuego de pobres* (Fire of the Poor) (México: FCE, 1961). *Siete de espadas* (Seven of Spades) (México: Mortiz, 1966). *El ala del tigre* (The Wing of the Tiger) (México: FCE, 1969). *La flama en el espejo* (The Flame in the Mirror) (México: FCE, 1971). *Tres poemas de antes* (Three Poems from Before) (México: UNAM, 1978). *De otro modo lo mismo* (Otherwise the Same Thing) (México: FCE, 1979). As de oro (Ace of Gold) (Sevilla: Calle del Aire, 1980; México: UNAM, 1981). *El corazón de la espiral* (The Heart of the Spiral) (México: Porrúa, 1983). Translations: Publio Virgilio Marón, *Geórgicas* (Georgics) (México: UNAM, 1963). Dante Alighieri, *Eglogas* (Eclogues) (México: n.p., 1965). Essay: *Destino del canto* (Destiny of the Song) (México: UNAM, 1963). *Ricardo Martínez* (México: UNAM, 1965). "El eterno retorno" (The Eternal Return), the *Metamorfosis* of Ovid, in *Diálogos* 76 (July-Aug. 1977): 42. "Invocación de Venus" (Invocation of Venus), *Cuadernos de Literatura* 1 (May 1982): 68-69.

BIBLIOGRAPHY: Ermilo Abreu Gómez, Review of *Geórgicas*, in *Revista Mexicana de Cultura* 857 (Sept. 1, 1963): 7; "Mi amigo Rubén Bonifaz Nuño," in *Revista Mexicana de Cultura* 863 (Oct. 13, 1963): 6. René Acuña, "Rubén Bonifaz Nuño: Una aproximación a *Fuego de pobres*," in *Mester* 4, 1 (Nov. 1973): 41-53. Federico Alvarez, Review of *Fuego de pobres*, in *México en la Cultura* 650 (Aug. 27, 1961): 4, 8. Enrique Anderson Imbert, *Historia de la literatura hispanoamericana*, vol. 2 (México: FCE, 1957), pp. 280-81. María Andueza, Review of *Tres poemas de antes*, in *Revista Universidad de México* 29, 5 (Feb. 1979): 39-41. Jesús Arellano, Review of *Los demonios y los días*, in *Metáfora* 14 (May-June, 1957): 10-16; "Drama poético en la obra de Bonifaz Nuño," in *Nivel* 4 (April 25, 1963): 5. Huberto Batis, Review of *Fuego de pobres*, in *Cuadernos del Viento* 13 (Aug. 1961): 206; Review of *Dante Alighieri: Eglogas*, in *La Cultura en México* 177 (July 7, 1965): xiv; Review of *Ricardo Martínez*, in *La Cultura en México* 208 (Feb. 9, 1966): xvii; "*Siete de espadas*: épica amorosa de Rubén Bonifaz Nuño," in *El Heraldo Cultural* 21 (April 3, 1966): 14; in *La Cultura en México* 216 (April 6, 1966): xiv. María Elvira Bermúdez, Review of *Siete de espadas*, in *Diorama de la Cultura* (April 30, 1966): 5, 6. Emmanuel Carballo, Review of *Imágenes*, in *México en la Cultura* 238 (Oct. 11, 1953): 2; "Rubén Bonifaz Nuño, *Los demonios y los días*," in *México en la Cultura* 379 (June 25, 1966): 2. Antonio Castro Leal, *La poesía mexicana moderna* (México: FCE, 1953), p. 479. Sandro Cohen, "Bonifaz Nuño: La íntima guerra fría," in *Revista de la Universidad de México* 34, 9 (May 1980): 44-45. Sabás Cruz García, Review of *Los demonios y los días*, in *Metáfora* 12 (Jan.-Feb. 1957): 35-36. Frank Dauster, *Breve historia de la poesía mexicana* (México: Eds. de Andrea, 1956), p. 181; *The Double Strand* (Lexington; University of Kentucky Press, 1987), pp. 103-33. Héctor Fontanar, "Nombres de México. Rubén Bonifaz Nuño, poeta," in *El Día* (Aug. 21, 1964): 9. Margarita García F., "Fines de la Editorial Universitaria," interview in *El Día* (Oct. 15, 1964): 9. Henrique González Casanova, "Rubén Bonifaz Nuño," in *La Cultura en México* 77 (Aug. 7, 1963): v-vii; "Textos y autores," review of *Geórgicas*, in *Ovaciones*, 85 (Aug. 11, 1963): 2. Raúl Leiva, "Rubén Bonifaz Nuño, *El manto y la corona*," in *La Palabra y el Hombre*, 10 (April-June 1959): 326-31; *Imagen de la poesía contemporánea* (México: UNAM, 1959), pp. 301-11; Review of *Geórgicas*, in *El Gallo Ilustrado* 69 (Oct. 20, 1963): 4; Review of *Siete de espadas*, in *México en la Cultura* 889 (April 3, 1966): 7; "La poesía de Rubén Bonifaz Nuño: Desde *Fuego de pobres* hasta *El ala del tigre*," in *Cuadernos Americanos* 30, 2 (March-April 1971): 167-83; "La poesía de Rubén Bonifaz Nuño: Desde *Imágenes* hasta *El manto y la corona*," in *Cuadernos Americanos* 30, 1 (Jan.-Feb. 1971): 165-86. Ernesto Mejía Sánchez, "*El manto y la corona*, ¿poesía prosaica?" in *Universidad de México* 13, 5 (Jan. 1959): 29-30. Víctor

Manuel Mendiola, "Bonifaz Nuño: Tres poemas de antes," in *La Semana de Bellas Artes* 180 (May 13, 1981): 14. Manuel Michel, "Un nuevo libro de Rubén Bonifaz Nuño," in *Universidad de México* 10, 11 (Aug. 1956): 30-31. Carlos Monsiváis, *La poesía mexicana del siglo XX* (México: Empresas Editoriales, 1966), pp. 67, 683. Rafael Moreno, "Nuevo Virgilio Mexicano," review of *Geórgicas*, in *La Cultura en México* 81 (Sept. 4, 1963): v-viii; in *Nivel* 25 (Jan. 25, 1965): 6-7, 8. Aurora M. Ocampo de Gómez and Ernesto Prado Velázquez, *Diccionario de escritores mexicanos* (México: UNAM, 1967), pp. 46-48. José Emilio Pacheco, Review of *Fuego de pobres*, in *México en la Cultura* 650 (Aug. 27, 1961): 4, 8. Octavio Paz et al., *Poesía en movimiento. México, 1915-1966* (México: Siglo XXI Editores, 1966), p. 188. Javier Peñalosa, Review of *Geórgicas*, in *México en la Cultura* 752 (Aug. 18, 1963): 7. Mario Puga, "Rubén Bonifaz Nuño," in *Universidad de México* 10, 10 (June, 1956): 19-20. Luis Rius, "Rubén Bonifaz Nuño," in *Universidad de México* 10, 11 (July, 1966): 31. César Rodríguez Chicharro, Review of *Imágenes*, in *Ideas de México* 2 (Sept.-Oct. 1953): 92-93. Mauricio de la Selva, Review of *Geórgicas*, in *Diorama de la Cultura* (Aug. 11, 1963): 7; Review of *Siete de espadas*, in *Diorama de la Cultura* (April 17, 1966): 5; *Algunos poetas mexicanos* (México: Finisterre, 1971). Carlos Valdés, Review of *Fuego de pobres*, in *Universidad de México* 16, 3 (Nov. 1961): 31. Various, "Hablan del admirable libro de Rubén Bonifaz Nuño. *Siete de espadas*," in *La Cultura en México* 221 (May 11, 1966): ii-v. Fausto Vega, "Aproximaciones," in *Nivel* 34 (Oct. 25, 1961): pp. 1, 2. Roberto Venegas, "Poetas mexicanos. Rubén Bonifaz Nuño," in *Diorama de la Cultura* (Aug. 2, 1964): 8. Víctor Villela, Review of *Destino del canto*, in *La Cultura en México* 96 (Dec. 18, 1963): xviii-xix; "Octavio Paz. Bonifaz Nuño. Informes estrictamente subjetivos," in *El Heraldo Cultural* 34 (July 3, 1966): 2; Review of *El ala del tigre*, in *Revista de Bellas Artes* 321 (Jan.-Feb. 1970): 62-63. Ramón Xirau, "The New Poetry of México. IV. Rubén Bonifaz Nuño," in *Bulletín of the Centro Mexicano de Escritores* 10, 2 (Jan. 15, 1963): 1-3. Agustín Yáñez, "Rubén Bonifaz Nuño, amante de Coatlicue," in *México en la Cultura* 755 (Sept. 8, 1963): 3; "Contestación," in *Destino del canto* (México: UNAM, 1963). Armando Zarate, Review of *Siete de espadas*, in *Revista de Bellas Artes* 9 (May-June 1966): 102.

JEANNE C. WALLACE

BOULLOSA, Carmen (1954-). Boullosa was born in Mexico City on September 4, 1954. Together with Alejandro *Aura, she is founder and co-owner of the avant-garde Coyoacán dinner theater El hijo del cuervo, where she is also a cook, waitress, and actress. She acts both in her own plays as well as in those of other authors. She has developed into a renowned woman poet who is also a bookmaker. She holds frequent expositions of very limited art object/book editions, which she makes from scratch in her workshop at home and which range from anthologies in the shape of wallets to hand-sewn handwritten plays. Aside from this, she also writes children's literature and has a record of children's stories called *La midas*.

Boullosa started as an actress and developed into a poet and novelist through her association with creative writers, printers, and artists. Since the publication of her first poetry chapbook *La memoria vacía*, her poetry has been concerned with the creation of a "feminine" mystique. Her brilliant images often deal with lost innocence, woman's discovery of her body, the sensuality inherent in sexual foreplay and intercourse yet never through coarse description but through subtle nuance, reference to limbs and body as plants, waterfalls, rivers, seas and suggestion, pain and pleasure as cosmic happenings. She is intrigued by traditional feminine symbols such as witches and mermaids and by storybook characters such as wolves, fairies, and maidens. Her most recent work, *Mejor desaparece*, is a macabre prose-poetry (novel) rendition of a suicide within a "happy family."

WORKS: *El hilo olvida* (The Thread Forgets) (México: La máquina de escribir, 1978). *Ingobernable* (Ungovernable) (México: UNAM, 1979). *La voz* (The Voice) (México: Martín Pescador, 1981). *Abierta* (Opened) (México: Práctica de vuelo, 1983). *La midas* (The Midas) (México: La hormiga de oro, 1986). *Mejor desaparece* (Better to Disappear) (México: Océano, 1987).

BIBLIOGRAPHY: Sandro Cohen, *Palabra nueva: Dos décadas de poesía en México* (México: Premiá, 1981), pp. 15, 305-309. José Joaquín Blanco, *Crónica de la poesía mexicana* (México: Katún, 1981), pp. 264-70. Jaime Moreno Villareal, *La línea y el círculo* (México: Universidad Autónoma Metroplitana, 1981). Sergio Mondragón, *República de poetas* (México: Martín Casillas, 1985), pp. 74-83.

RICARDO AGUILAR

BURNS, Archibaldo (1914-). Born in Mexico City on April 7, 1914, he studied in Europe, traveling through many countries. His first book, a short novel, published in 1954, allowed him, as he put it, to recover his language. *En presencia de nadie* (In the Presence of Nobody) (1964) is a fictionalized autobiography in which the author reflects on his youth from the perspective of the present. His 1966 book *El cuerpo del delito* (The Body of the Crime) is a collection of more or less satirical stories that also have an autobiographical aspect to them. He has distinguished himself as a movie producer and script adapter from his first collaboration on *Refugiados en Madrid* (Refugees in Madrid) in 1938 to the adaptation to the movies of Rosario *Castellanos' *Oficio de Tinieblas* (1980). In 1968 he was awarded the Film Prize of the German Institute for his documentary *El agujero en la niebla* (Hole in the Fog).

WORKS: *Fin* (End) (México: Eds. Los Presentes, 1954). *En presencia de nadie* (In the Presence of Nobody) (México: Mortiz, 1964). *El cuerpo del delito* (The Body of the Crime) (México: Porrúa, 1966). "Testimonios sobre Jorge Portilla," in *Revista Mexicana de Cultura* 26 (Aug. 26, 1983): 9. Movie adaptations: Elena Garro's *Perfecto Luna*, 1959. Elena Garro's *El árbol*, with the title *Juego de mentiras*, 1968. Ricardo Pozas' *Juan Pérez Jolote*, 1976. Rosario Castellanos' *Oficio de Tinieblas*, 1980.

BIBLIOGRAPHY: Anon., "Nombres, títulos, hechos," Review of *El cuerpo del delito* in *México en la Cultura* 879 (Jan. 1966): 3. Huberto Batis, Review of *En presencia de nadie* in *La Cultura en México* 150 (Dec. 30, 1964): xix; "Del escritor más transparente al fariseo," review of *El cuerpo del delito* in *El Heraldo Cultural* 11 (Jan. 23 1966), and *La Cultura en México* 206 (Jan. 26, 1966): xvi. María Elvira Bermúdez, Review of *Fin*,

Metáfora 3 (July-Aug. 1955): 38-39; "Otras novelas de 1964," *Diorama de la Cultura* (Jan. 10, 1965): 3. Emilio García Riera, *Historia documental del cine mexicano* (México: Era, 1978), vol. 1, pp. 179-80, 238-39; vol. 7, pp. 207-08. Heriberto García Rivas, *Historia de la literatura mexicana,* vol. 4 (México: Porrúa, 1974), p. 502. María Luisa Mendoza, "La O por lo redondo," review of *En presencia de nadie, El Día* (Dec. 31, 1964): 2. Aurora M. Ocampo de Gómez and Ernesto Prado Velázquez, *Diccionario de escritores mexicanos* (México: UNAM, 1967), p. 48. Margarita Peña, "Libro de memorias," *Ovaciones,* suppl. no. 166 (March 8, 1965): 8. Salvador Reyes Nevares, "Archibaldo Burns y sus espectros tutelares," *La Cultura en México* 155 (Feb. 3, 1965): xvi-xvii. Carlos Valdés, Review of *Fin,* in *Universidad de México* 9, 7 (March 1955): 30. Ramón Xirau, Review of *El cuerpo del delito,* in *Diálogos* 2, 3 (March-April 1966): 46.

                                                                    PETER G. BROAD

BUSTAMANTE, Carlos María de (1774-1884), publicist and writer. He was born in Oaxaca. He studied Latin grammar and philosophy at the Seminary of Oaxaca. He received a bachelor of arts degree in Mexico. Later, he was admitted to law school where he received his law degree from the Royal Tribunal of Guadalajara in 1801. Years later, he started the publication of *Diario de México* (Daily of Mexico). A supporter of the Insurgente Movement, he collaborated with José María Morelos y Pavón and continued writing *Correo del Sur* (Mail from the South), which contains the speech that the rebel "caudillo" read at the opening of the Congress of Chilpancingo. He created the "Acta solemne de la Declaración de Independencia de América Septentrional" (Solemn Affidavit of the Declaration of Independence of Septentrional America). After Mexico achieved independence, he practiced law. He got involved in political activities that led occasionally to his arrest and imprisonment. He was the legislator of Oaxaca several times. Opposed to federalism, he was designated as one of the five members of the Supreme Conservative Power, created in 1836. He died in Mexico City in 1848.

According to Manuel Orozco y Berra in his *Diccionario Universal de Historia y Geografía* (Universal Dictionary of History and Geography), Bustamante published 19,142 pages and left unpublished, among other works, a diary of remarkable events in several volumes. His overall production proves him to be a timely writer, a sharp observer of reality, and an interested politician. His editorial work is extensive. It can be classified as original work, which he published in newspapers and pamphlets.

WORKS: *Cuadro histórico de la revolución mexicana comenzada el 15 de septiembre de 1810 por el ciudadano Miguel Hidalgo y Costilla* (Historical Sketch of the Mexican Revolution Started on September 15, 1810, by the Citizen Miguel Hidalgo y Costilla) (México: Imp. de Mariano Lara, 1843). *Campañas del general D. Félix María Callejas, comandante en jefe del ejército real de operaciones llamado del centro* (Campaigns of General D. Félix María Callejas, Commander-in-Chief of the Royal Army for Operations Called from the Center) (México: Aguila, 1828). *Mañanas de la Alameda de México* (Mornings from the Alameda of Mexico) (México: Valdés, 1835-1836). *Diario Histórico de México* (Historical Newspaper of Mexico) (Zacatecas: Tipografía de la Escuela de Artes y Oficios de la Penitenciaria, 1896). *Hay tiempos de hablar y tiempos de callar* (There Is a Time to Talk and a Time to Keep Quiet) (México: Valdés, 1833). *La constitución de Apatzingán* (The Constitution of Apatzingan) (México: Empresas Editoriales, 1960). *El Congreso de Chilpancingo* (The Congress of Chilpancingo) (México: Empresas Editoriales, 1958).

BIBLIOGRAPHY: Even though he was an author with an extensive production, there are few studies about his work and his activities. *Enciclopedia de México* (México: Compañía Editora de Enciclopedias de México, 1987), vol. 2. Manuel Navarrete, *Poemas Inéditos*; *apuntes biográficos de D. Carlos María Bustamante* (México: Sociedad de Bibliografos Mexicanos, 1929). Manuel Orozco y Berra, *Diccionario Universal de Historia y Geografía* (México: n.p., 1853), vol. 1.

CARMEN BLAZQUEZ DOMINGUEZ

BUSTAMANTE, Octaviano N. (1903-1966), novelist, dramatist, short story writer, and critic. Bustamante was born in Mexico City on September 10, 1903. Although he pursued the study of law, he gained fame for his literary efforts during his university period, identifying himself with the Group of 29. He died in Mexico City on June 2, 1966.

Bustamente represents a departure from realism and neo-realism and an orientation toward a treatment of universal problems of man's psychological reality. His style is innovative and rich in humor and irony. His *Seis novelas iguales entre sí* (Six Repeated Novels) treats a single theme from six different national perspectives, satirizing different cultural reactions to the same problem.

WORKS: *Invitación al dancing* (Invitation to a Party) (México: Editoriales del Gobierno de Tlaxcala, 1927). *Teoría general de Cagancho* (General Theory of Cagancho) (México: Editorial Fábula, 1944). *Seis novelas iguales entre sí* (Six Repeated Novels) (México: Editorial Stylo, 1944). *El fracaso de la U*[nión] *S*[indical de] *P*[ersonajes], *nueva tragedia de Romeo y Julieta* (The Failure of the Character Actors' Guild, a New Tragedy of Romeo and Juliet) (México: Eds. de América, SEP, 1948).

BIBLIOGRAPHY: John S. Brushwood and José Rojas Garciadueñas, *Breve historia de la novela mexicana* (México: Eds. de Andrea, 1959), p. 144. Luis Leal, *Breve historia del cuento mexicano* (México: Eds. de Andrea, 1956), pp. 136-37. Aurora M. Ocampo de Gómez and Ernesto Prado Velázquez, *Diccionario de escritores mexicanos* (México: UNAM, 1967), p. 49.

KENNETH M. TAGGART

BUSTOS Cerecedo, Miguel (1912-), teacher and poet. Born September 29, 1912, in Chicontepec, Veracruz, Bustos Cerecedo has been a teacher of literature in secondary schools in Mexico City as well as a writer since 1933. Bustos Cerecedo began publishing in the review *Ruta* and later edited the reviews *Cono* and *Momento* and coedited *Letras de Ayer y de Hoy* and *El Ojo Literario*. He worked for the Department of Public Education and the Social Security Administration in Mexico before retiring in 1973.

In his poetry Bustos Cercedo expresses his sympathy for the liberation of man and society as well as his own personal experiences. His volumes of poetry include *La noche arrodillada* (Night on Its Knees), *Cauce* (Riverbed), *Tres poemas revolucionarios* (Three Revolutionary Poems), and *Cicatrices del viento* (Scars on the Wind). Books of short stories are *Un sindicato escolar* (A Student Union), *Un camino abierto* (An Open Way), and *En los cuernos de un cacique* (On the Horns of the Boss). Bustos Cercedo has also written several works of nonfiction such as *Adolfo Ruiz Cortines o la responsabilidad inexorable* (Adolfo Ruiz Cortines or the Unavoidable Responsibility), *La creación literaria en Veracruz* (Literary Creation in Veracruz), and *La ciudad que regresa* (The City That Returns).

WORKS: *La noche arrodillada* (Night on Its Knees) (Xalapa: "Momento," 1933). *Cauce* (Riverbed) (Xalapa: "Momento," 1934). *Tres poemas revolucionarios* (Three Revolutionary Poems) (México: LEAR, 1935). *Un sindicato escolar* (A Student Union), a children's novel (México: SEP, 1936). *Adolfo Ruiz Cortines o la responsabilidad inexorable* (Adolfo Ruiz Cortines or the Unavoidable Responsibility) (México: Acción Social, 1951). *Un camino abierto* (An Open Way) (México: SEP, 1957). *Cicatrices del viento* (Scars on the Wind) (México: UNAM, 1977). *La creación literaria en Veracruz* (Literary Creation in Veracruz) (Xalapa: Gobierno de Verzcruz, 1977). *En los cuernos de un cacique* (On the Horns of the Boss) (Xalapa: Gobierno de Veracruz, 1978). *La ciudad que regresa* (The City That Returns) (Xalapa: Gobierno de Veracruz, 1979).

BIBLIOGRAPHY: Aurora M. Ocampo de Gómez and Ernesto Prado Velázquez, *Diccionario de escritores mexicanos* (México: UNAM, 1967), p. 49. José Rogelio Alvarez, dir., *Enciclopedia de México*, vol. 2 (México: SEP, 1987), p. 1097.

                                                                 TERESA R. ARRINGTON

C

CABADA, Juan de la (1903-1987), short story writer and scriptwriter born in Campeche. Cabada's early writing was influenced by his experiences of traveling extensively in Cuba and throughout Mexico as a young man. His first short stories were predominantly of a social focus and were published in *El Machete*, which was the journal of the Mexican Communist party. He has been a prolific writer, producing over thirty books and screen scripts, in addition to many short stories published separately. He is also an active member of the editorial board of *Plural*, the literary Sunday magazine of *Excelsior*.

Cabada has contributed to a development of narrative style that has undoubtedly influenced other Mexican writers. His attempt to evoke a dialogue that is truly representative of his humble characters and, at the same time, highly poetic seems to foreshadow that of Juan *Rulfo. Other aspects of his style are worthy of note because of their innovative nature and contritbution to the development of Mexican fiction writing: use of multiple narrators, independent episodes within a story, and silence and ellipses as narrative technique. His efforts to evoke a vivid portrayal of the actual scenes in his short stories shows the influence of his scriptwriting experience.

WORKS: *Paseo de mentiras* (A Promenade of Lies), Colección Lunes (México: Edición Séneca, 1940); 2nd ed. (México: Imp. Universitaria, 1959). *Incidentes melódicos del mundo irracional* (Melodic Incidents from an Irrational World) (1944); 2nd ed. (México: UNAM, 1954). *El Brazo Fuerte* (The Strong Arm), Colección Ficción, no. 51 (Xalapa: Universidad Veracruzana, 1963).

BIBLIOGRAPHY: José Alvarado, "Los cuentos de Juan de la Cabada," in *Las Letras Patrias* 3 (July-Sept. 1954): 52. A. Sánchez Barbudo, "Aparición de un novelista," in *Romance* 1, 15 (Sept. 1, 1940): 18. Juan José Barrientos, "Encuentros cercanos de Borges a Juan de la Cabada," in *México en el arte* 9 (Summer 1985): 49-52. Alí Chumacero, "Juan de la Cabada, un cuentista notable," in *México en la Cultura* 561 (Dec. 13, 1959): 4. Luis Leal, *Breve historia del cuento mexicano* (México: Eds. de Andrea, 1956), pp. 139-40. Aurora M. Ocampo de Gómez and Ernesto Prado Velázquez, *Diccionario de escritores mexicanos* (México: UNAM, 1967). Margarita León, "Juan de la Cabada: testimonio vivo," *Plural* 15, 174 (March 86)): 12-16.

KENNETH M. TAGGART

CABRERA, Rafael (1884-1943). Cabrera was born in Puebla on May 5, 1884. He was educated in Puebla, where he attended the School of Medicine, from which he received a medical degree. While still a student he published poetry in local newspapers. In 1908 he founded the literary magazine *Don Quijote*. Ten years later, in 1918, he entered the diplomatic corps, serving as secretary of the Mexican delegation in Italy, Belgium, France, Holland, El Salvador, and Argentina. He resigned in 1935 and returned to Mexico. From 1939 he was the president of the Pension Plan Council, a post he held until his death in Mexico City on February 21, 1943.

Cabrera, a member of the prestigious group Atheneum, won a prize with one of his first poems, "Ojos negros," in 1902. He wrote only one book of poetry, *Presagios* (Omens), which was published in 1912. This volume merited him the reputation of a great poet. His poetry, influenced by Gustavo Adolfo Bécquer, José Zorrilla de San Martín, and Manuel *Gutiérrez-Nájera dealt with feelings and emotions yet was elegant and precise.

WORKS: Poetry: *Presagios* (Puebla: n.p., 1912; Puebla: La Enseñanza, 1935; México: n.p., 1950). "De la necesidad de tener una leyenda," in *Pegaso* 4 (March 29, 1917): 1. "Poemas," in *Pegaso* 9 (May 4, 1917): 8. "¡Azrael!" in *Pegaso* 10 (May 17, 1917).

BIBLIOGRAPHY: Aurora M. Ocampo de Gómez and Ernesto Prado Velázquez, *Diccionario de escritores mexicanos* (México: UNAM, 1967), p. 50. Carlos González Peña, *Historia de la literatura mexicana* (México: Porrúa, 1981), p. 270.

NORA ERRO-PERALTA

CALDERON, Fernando (1809-1845), playwright, lawyer, and poet. Calderón was born in Guadalajara, Jalisco, on July 20, 1809. Like most people who want to be where the action is, Calderón moved to Mexico City and soon joined the Liberal party. He became a frequent participant in the literary gathering at the San Juan de Letrán Academy, where poets and writers of the period met to read and comment on their own works. He died in Ojocaliente on January 18, 1845.

Calderón wrote dramatic essays and plays as well as plays of local color. At the age of eighteen he presented his first play in Guadalajara, *Reinaldo y Elvira*. Between 1827 and 1836, eight plays by Calderón were presented either in Guadalajara or in Zacatecas. He wrote chivalry plays such as *El Torneo* (The Tournament); historical plays such as *Ana Bolena* (Anne Boleyn), possibly his best-known play; and local color plays such as *A ninguna de las tres* (To None of the Three).

WORKS: *Zadio* (n.d.). *Leila o la esclava indiana* (Leila or the Indian Slave) (n.d.). *Armandina* (n.d.). *Los políticos al día* (Politicians of the Day) (n.d.) *Efigenia* (Ifigenie) (n.d.). *Hersilia y Virginia* (All the previous plays presented either in Guadalajara or in Zacatecas between 1827 and 1836.) *Reinaldo y Elvira*, presented in Guadalajara (1827). *El Torneo* (The Tournament) (1839). *Herman o La vuelta del cruzado* (Herman or the Return of the Crusader) (1842). *Ana Bolena* (Anne Boleyn) (1842). *El soldado de la libertad* (The Soldier of Liberty), an imitation of Espronceda's *La Canción del Pirata* (The Pirate's Song) (n.d.). *El sueño del tirano* (The Tyrant's Dream) (n.d.). *La vuelta del desterrado* (The Return of the Exiled) (n.d.). *Obras completas* (Complete Works) (Zacatecas: n.p., 1882). *Muerte de Virginia por la libertad de Roma* (Virginia's Death for the Libety of Rome) (n.d.).

BIBLIOGRAPHY: Enrique Anderson Imbert and Eugenio Florit, *Literatura Hispanoamericana. Antología e Introducción Histórica* (New York: Holt, Rinehart and Winston, 1960), p. 274. Frank N. Dauster, *Historia del teatro hispanoamericano, Siglos XIX y XX*, 2nd ed. (México: Eds. de Andrea, 1973), pp. 12-13. Orlando Gómez-Gil, *Historia Crítica de la Literatura Hispanoamericana* (New York: Holt, Rinehart and Winston, 1968), pp. 354-55. Julio Jiménez Rueda, *Historia de la Literatura Mexicana* (México: Botas, 1960), p. 222. Julio Jiménez Rueda, *Letras mexicanas en el siglo XIX* (México: FCE, 1944), p. 93. Raimundo Lazo, *Historia de la literatura hispanoamericana. El siglo XIX* (México: Porrúa, 1976), pp. 14, 34, 48, 60. Enrique de Olavarria y Ferrari, *Reseña Histórica del Teatro de México*, vol. 1 (México: Porrúa, 1961), pp. 391, 438-40, 654. Francisco Sosa, *Biografías de mexicanos distinguidos* (México: Oficina Tipográfica de la Secretaría de Fomento, 1884), pp. 183-85.

JOSEPH VELEZ

CALVILLO, Manuel (1918-   ), poet and critic. Calvillo was born in San Luis Potosi, San Luis Potosí, on January 29, 1919. Along with Alí *Chumacero and Jorge *González Durán he formed part of the group of writers who made up the journal *Tierra Nueva*. He also contributed to *Abside* and *Cuadernos Americanos*. He attended law school at the Universidad Nacional Autónoma de México and has practiced law since 1946.

His first collection of poetry, *Estancia en la voz* (Stanza in the Voice), was published in 1942. Two other works followed: *Primera vigilia terrestre* (First Terrestrial Vigil) and *Libro del emigrante* (Emigrant's Book). In general, his poetry lacks cohesion, but he is able to orchestrate the images he uses with dexterity. *Estancia en la voz* (Stanza in the Voice) is a collection of six erotic poems that focus on nature and childhood memories. The poems create an atmosphere of solitude that is harsh yet tender, quiet, and soothing. His second book, *Primera vigilia terrestre* (First Terrestrial Vigil), is one long poem made up of eight **cantos** in which he re-creates the conflict of the mestizo and the birth of the American being.

WORKS: Poetry: *Estancia en la voz* (Stanza in the Voice) (México: Eds. "Tierra Nueva," 1942). *Primera vigilia terrestre* (First Terrestrial Vigil) (México: FCE, 1953). *Libro del emigrante* (Emigrant's Book), in *Revista de la Universidad de México* 11, 9 (May 1957) (poema dividido en cuatro cantos-poem divided in four cantos). Essay: Introduction, prologue, and selection to Manuel José Othón's *Paisaje* (View) (México: UNAM, 1944), pp. ix-xxxv. Prologue to Manuel José Othón's *Manuel José Othón* (Poemas y cuentos) (México: SEP, 1945), pp. vii-xxvii. "Notas sobre Manuel José Othón," *Revista de la Universidad de México* 13, 1 (1958): 21. *Francisco Suárez* (Mexico City, 1945). Prologue to Servando Teresa de Mier's *Cartas de un americano, 1811-1812* (México: SEP, 1987).

BIBLIOGRAPHY: Bernardo Casanueva, Review of *Estancia en la Voz*, in *Tierra Nueva* 3, 15 (Dec. 1942): 169-71. Antonio Castro Leal, ed., *La poesía mexicana moderna* (México: FCE, 1953), p. 441. E.G.R., Review of *Primera vigilia terrestre*, in *Revista de la Universidad de México* 8, 6 (Feb. 1954): 25. Raúl Leiva, *Imagen de la poesía mexicana contemporánea* (México: UNAM, 1959), pp. 277-81. Jesús Medina

Romero, *Antología de poetas contemporáneos (1910-1953)* (México: Universidad Autónoma San Luis Potosí, 1953), pp. 26, 243. Rafael del Río, *Poesía mexicana contemporánea* (Torreón: Coahuila, 1955), p. 29. José Luis Martínez, *Literatura mexicana: Siglo XX. 1910-1949* (México: Ant. Libr. Robredo, 1950), p. 24. Angel M. Ocampo de Gómez and Ernesto Prado Velázquez, *Diccionario de escritores mexicanos* (México: UNAM, 1967), p. 51.

MARGARITA VARGAS

CALVILLO Madrigal, Salvador (1901-   ), journalist, fiction writer, and essayist. Calvillo Madrigal was born in Morelia, Michoacán, but has lived in Mexico City since 1917. He directed the cultural supplement of *El Nacional* and contributed a weekly column to *El Día* and *El Nacional*. His essays can also be found in journals such as *Nivel* and *Revista de la Universidad de México*. He became a corresponding member of the Academia Mexicana de la Lengua in 1968.

WORKS: Short Story: *Estas cosas* (These Things) (México: Ed. Prisma, 1944). *¿Una copa conmigo?* (Have a Drink with Me?) (México: Los Epígrafes, 1951). *Adán el importante* (Adam the Important One) (México: Ed. Stylo, 1952). *A las tres de la mañana* (At Three in the Morning) (México: Novaro, 1971). Novel: *Una rama en la hoguera* (A Branch in the Fire) (México: Ed. Novaro, 1966). Theater: *Amanecer* (Dawn), in *El hijo pródigo* 10, 33 (1945): 171-78. Essay: *Platería mexicana* (Mexican Silversmith) (México: Ed. de Arte, 1948). *La revolución que nos contaron* (The Revolution as It Was Told to Us) (México: Metáfora, 1950). *Dilucidario* (Dilucidario) (México: Los presentes, 1956). *Una hora de tres minutos* (A Three Minute Hour) (México: Ecuador, 1959). *El campesino y la reforma agraria* (The Farmer and the Agrarian Reform) (México: Ed. de Michoacán, 1960).

BIBLIOGRAPHY: Luis Leal, *Bibliografía del cuento mexicano* (México: Eds. de Andrea, 1958). José Luis Martínez, *Literatura mexicana, siglo xx, 1910-1949*, vol. 1 (México: Ant. Libr. Robredo, 1949), pp. 85-86.

MIRTA A. GONZALEZ

CAMARILLO y Roa de Pereyra, María Enriqueta (1872-1968), novelist and poet. She was born in Coatepec, Veracruz. She came from an upper middle class family and conservative lineage. At six, she started to write and to draw. At seven, she moved to Mexico City, where she entered the National Conservatory in 1887. She received a diploma as a pianist six years later. In 1894, at twenty-two, she was publishing in most magazines and newspapers of her time, such as *El Universal Ilustrado* and *La Revista Azul*. At first, she signed with the pseudonym of Iván Moskowski, but soon she discarded it to use her surname, which she used to sign her entire production. In 1896, she moved with her family to Nuevo Laredo and married the historian Carlos Pereyra on May 7 of that year. Her husband became a member of the Mexican Diplomatic Service in 1910. He was in charge of Mexican affairs in the Republic of Cuba. For the next thirty-eight years, the couple lived overseas:

Washington, Brussels, Laussane, and later Madrid. In the Spanish capital, María Enriqueta wrote and published most of her work. She was widely recognized by the critics and the public in general. Most of her work was translated to French, Portuguese, and Italian. In 1948, she moved back to Mexico, where she died twenty years later. Her work covers almost all of literary genres: poetry, short story, novel, memoirs, literary criticism, didactic books for children, music, and drawings. She was a modernist with romantic sensibility. Her short stories are romantic, but her novels are influenced by the Spanish realistic movement and are full of sentimentalism and moral eagerness. *El Secreto* (The Secret) was considered in France as the best foreign novel in 1922. It was the first Mexican novel to be translated into French. This work is about a suffering teenager who manages to escape his difficulties through the sensible development of artistic expression. Her *Rosas de la Infancia* (Roses from Childhood) was a required textbook in the elementary schools in Mexico for several decades. It became the first literary experience for many generations. Her poetry is fragile and moderate, with colloquial simplicity.

WORKS: Poetry: *Las consecuencias de un sueño* (Consequences of a Dream) (México: Tip. Carpeta, 1902). *Rumores de mi huerto* (Sounds of My Orchard) (México: Casa Ballescá, 1908). *Antología general de María Enriqueta* (General Anthology) (México: Porrúa, 1920). *Rumores de mi huerto. Rincones románticos.* (Sounds of My Orchard. Romantic Nooks) (Madrid: Imp. de Juan Pueyo, 1922). *Album sentimental* (Sentimental Album) (Madrid: Espasa-Calpe, 1926). *Fantasía y realidad* (Fantasy and Reality) (Madrid: Espasa-Calpe, 1933). *Poemas del campo* (Poems of the Countryside) (Madrid: Espasa-Calpe, 1935). *Recordando dulcemente* (Sweetly Remembering) (Madrid: Imp. Sap., 1946). *Hojas dispersas* (Scattered Pages) (México: Ed. Patria, 1950). Short Stories and Novellas: *Sorpresas de la vida* (Life's Surprises) (Barcelona: Biblioteca Nueva, 1921; Buenos Aires: Casa Virtus, 1924). *Entre el polvo de un castillo* (In the Dust of a Castle) (Buenos Aires: Casa Virtus, 1924). *El misterio de su muerte* (The Mystery of His Death) (Madrid: Espasa-Calpe, 1926). *Enigma y símbolo* (Enigma and Symbol) (Madrid: Espasa-Calpe, 1926). *Lo irremediable* (The Irremediable) (Madrid: Espasa-Calpe, 1927). *La torre de seda* (The Silk Tower) (México: Libr. Guadalupana, 1927). *Cuentecillos de cristal* (Crystal Tales) (Barcelona, Editorial Araluce, 1928). *El arca de colores* (The Colored Coffer) (Madrid: Espasa-Calpe, 1929). Novels: *Mirlitón* (Blackbird) (Madrid: Imprenta Juan Pueyo, 1918). *Jirón del mundo* (Piece of the World) (Madrid: Editorial América, 1919; México: Ed. Patria, 1952). *El secreto* (The Secret) (Madrid: Editorial América, 1922). Juvenile Readers: *Rosas de la infancia* (Roses of Infancy, five readers) (Paris and México: Casa Bouret, 1914). *Rosas de la infancia* (Roses of Infancy, sixth reader) (México: Ed. Patria, 1950). *Nuevas rosas de la infancia* (New Roses of Infancy, three readers) (México; Ed. Patria, 1953). Memoirs and Travel Books: *Brujas, Lisboa, Madrid* (Bruges, Lisbon, Madrid) (Madrid: Espasa-Calpe, 1930). *Del tapiz de mi vida* (From the Tapestry of My Life) (Madrid: Espasa-Calpe, 1931).

BIBLIOGRAPHY: José de Alba, "*Rosas de la infancia*: los libros en que aprendimos a leer," *Cuadernos* (Paris) April 1964: 92-93. Anon., "Escritores mexicanos contemporáneos," *Biblos* 2 (1920): 57-58. John S. Brushwood and José Rojas Garciduéñas, *Breve historia de la novela mexicana* (México: Eds. de Andrea, 1959) p. 76. Frank Dauster, *Breve historia de la poesía mexicana* (México: Eds. de Andrea, 1956) pp. 131-32. Angel Dotor, *María Enriqueta y su obra* (Madrid: Edit. Aguilar,

1943). Carlos González Peña, *Historia de la literatura mexicana* (History of Mexican Literature) (México: Porrúa, 1966) pp. 333, 356. Luis Leal, *Breve historia del cuento mexicano* (México: Eds. de Andrea, 1956), pp. 68-69. *Bibliografía del cuento mexicano* (México; Eds. de Andrea, 1958) pp. 25-27. José López Portillo y Rojas, *María Enriqueta* (pamphlet) April 15, 1909. María Elizabeth Sáenz Páez, "La escritora mexicana María Enriqueta," Diss. (México, UNAM, 1964). Angeles Mendieta Alatorre, "La limpia estirpe literaria de María Enriqueta," *El Nacional* (Jan. 29, 1964): 3. José Luis Rublúo, "María Enriqueta," *Revista de la Semana* (Jan. 19, 1964): 8. Valentín Yakovlev Baldín, "María Enriqueta Camarillo y Roa de Pereyra. Su vida y su obra," thesis (México: UNAM, 1956), and "María Enriqueta Camarillo y Roa de Pereyra. Su poesía y su prosa," Diss. (México: UNAM, 1957).

ESTHER HERNANDEZ-PALACIOS

CAMINO Galicia, León Felipe (1884-1968). Felipe Camino was born in Tábara, Zamora, Spain, on April 11, 1884. He spent his childhood in Sigüeras, Salamanca. After completing his studies in Santander, Valladolid, and Madrid, he earned his living as an actor in Spain and as a pharmacist in Africa.

Felipe Camino began his literary career in 1920 with a book of poetry entitled *Versos y oraciones de caminante* (Verses and Prayers of a Traveler). His first collection of poetry was warmly received by his contemporaries, who saw him as an original and authentic poet. Prior to 1940 he worked in Spanish Guinea and traveled extensively throughout Mexico and the United States, where he lectured at several universities: Cornell, Mexico and New Mexico. After Franco's dictatorship was established in Spain, he went into exile in Mexico, where he continued his career as a writer, poet, and professor. In Mexico, he contributed to many journals and magazines such as *Letras de México, Contemporáneos, Taller, España Peregrina, Romance, Universidad de México, Tierra Nueva*, and *Las Españas*. In conjunction with Jesús Silva Herzog, Bernardo *Ortiz de Montellano, Juan Larrea and others, he was instrumental in the founding of the magazine *Cuadernos Americanos*. Mexico was his residence from 1940 until his death in 1968. After World War II, he traveled and lectured extensively throughout South America, residing briefly in Argentina and Uruguay.

Although Camino wrote poetry, prose, and drama he is recognized primarily as a poet. He is the author of several books of poetry: *La insignia* (The Insignia) (1937), *El payaso de las bofetadas y el pescador de caña* (The Clown with the Buffets and the Fisherman with the Pole) (1938), *Llamadme publicano* (Call me Publican) (1950), *¡Oh, este viejo y roto violín!* (Oh, This Old and Broken Down Violin!) (1962). In his poetry Camino reveals a profound empathy for humanity. After his first book of poetry, *Versos y oraciones de caminante*, his poetry changed, acquiring a simpler form and a more revolutionary tone. His later volumes of poetry, *El español del éxodo y del llanto* (The Spaniard of the Exodus and of Weeping) (1939), *El hacha* (The Axe) (1939) and *El poeta prometéico* (The Promethean Poet) (1942), reveal his preocupation with the political situation in his country, the injustice and the opression that people must suffer, and his progression toward simplicity.

In addition to his work as a creative writer, Camino also wrote plays and prologues and translated works of T.S. Eliot, Waldo Frank, John Dos Passos, and Walt

Whitman into Spanish. But above all, he will be remembered for the profound, compassionate, and prophetic verses that he sang of the tragedy of his homeland.

WORKS: Poetry: *Versos y oraciones de caminante* (Poems and Prayers of Pilgrims) (Madrid: Imp. Juan Pérez Torres, 1920; New York: Instituto de las Españas, 1930; Madrid: Visor, 1981). *Drop a Star* (Madrid: Imp. Celorio, 1933; Madrid: Finisterre, 1974). *La insignia* (The Shield) (Valencia: n.p., 1938; Buenos Aires: Imán, 1939). *El payaso de las bofetadas y el pescador de caña* (The Clown with the Buffets and the Fisherman with the Pole) (México: FCE, 1938). *El Hacha* (The Ax) (México: El Colegio de México, 1939). *Español del éxodo y del llanto* (México: La Casa de España, 1939; Madrid: Finisterre, 1974). *El gran responsable* (México: FCE, 1940). *Ganarás la luz* (México: Editorial Cuadernos Americanos, 1942; Madrid: Finisterre, 1974). *Antología rota (1920-1947)* (Broken Anthology [1920-1947]) (Buenos Aires: Pleamar, 1947). *Nueva antología rota* (New Broken Anthology) (Madrid: Finisterre, 1974; Madrid: EDIMUSA, 1983). *¿Qué se hizo del rey don Juan?* (México: Ecuador, 1962). *Antología poética* (Madrid: Alianza, 1981). Theater: *La manzana* (The Apple) (México: FCE, 1951). *Macbeth o el asesino del sueño* (Macbeth or the Dream Murderer) (México: Lib. Madero, 1954; Madrid: Júcar, 1983). *El Juglarón* (The Big Troubador) (Madrid: Finisterre, 1961; 1974).

BIBLIOGRAPHY: Enrique Azcoaga, *Panorama de la poesía moderna española* (Buenos Aires: Periplo, 1953). Germán Bleiberg, "Felipe León (1884)," in *Diccionario de literatura española* (Madrid: Rev. de Occidente, 1953), p. 266. Max Aub, *La poesía española contemporánea* (México: Imp. Universitaria, 1954), pp. 206-16,224-25. Electra Arenal de Rodríguez, "La obra poética de León Felipe," Diss. at Columbia University, 1961. Luisa Josefina Hernández, "*El Juglarón* teatro didáctico," in *Ovaciones* 138 (Aug. 16, 1964); 8. María Luisa Capella, *La huella mexicana en la obra de León Felipe* (Madrid: Finisterre, 1975). Felix Córdova Iturregui, "La personalidad poética de León Felipe," Diss., Princeton University, 1979. Leopoldo de Luis, *Aproximaciones a la vida y obra de León Felipe* (Madrid: Instituto de España, 1984). Carlos González Peña, *Historia de la literatura mexicana* (México: Porrúa, 1981), pp. 289-90.

NORA ERRO-PERALTA

CAMPO, Angel del (1868-1908), journalist. He was born in Mexico City on July 9 and remained there until he died on February 8. Ignacio Manuel *Altamirano was his teacher in the Escuela Nacional Preparatoria. During his first year as a medical student (1890), his mother passed away. He interrupted his studies in order to take care of his family. His main professional activity was as a journalist and as a teacher. In order to support his family he kept a job in the Secretaria de Hacienda during the regime of Porfirio Díaz. With the pen names Micros and Tick-Tack, he began writing short stories, articles, and sketches for *El Imparcial*, a Mexico City newspaper. He occasionally wrote for the magazines *Revista Moderna* and *Revista Azul*.

El Imparcial published his series of articles, short stories, and sketches in a section entitled La Semana Alegre (The Happy Week). This section was very well received by Mexico City's readers. In 1890 *El Nacional* newspaper started the publication of his novel *La rumba*, which is considered his first and only published novel.

Angel del Campo's articles and sketches made him known as a "costumbrista" (person who writes about customs or habits). His topics, characters, and situations were extracted from the real daily life of the capital of Mexico. More than a writer who portrays popular characters and customs, Campo shows a very delicate sensitivity to and love for his characters, as seen by his treatment of "El Chato Barrios" (fictional character of a "barrio") and "El fusilado," two of his short stories. "La cobija" (The Blanket) and "El jarro" (The Clay Jug) are examples of sketches in which he makes his readers reflect on objects that constitute the only treasure of the poor people. The writer calls the attention of his readers to old customs that are disappearing in "Los nacimientos" (The Nativity Scenes) and "Las verbenas antiguas" (The Old Fashioned Gatherings). His works, once disseminated in newspapers and literary magazines, were collected in three volumes.

WORKS: *Ocios y apuntes* (Leisure Moments and Sketches) (México: Imp. de Ignacio Escalante, 1890). *Cosas vistas* (Things Seen) (México: El Nacional, 1894). *Cartones* (Sketches) (México: Imp. de la Librería Madrilene, 1897). *La rumba* (México: Ed. de Elizabeth Hellen Miller, 1951). *Pueblo y canto* (People and Song), prologue and selection by Mauricio Magdaleno (México: UNAM, 1973).

BIBLIOGRAPHY: John S. Brushwood, *Mexico in Its Novel* (Austin: Univeristy of Texas Press, 1966), pp. 133-34. Pedro Henríquez Ureña, *Las corrientes literarias en la America Hispanica* (México: FCE, 1954), p. 244. Julio Jiménez Rueda, *Historia de la Literatura Mexicana* (México: Botas, 1957), pp. 300-302. *Antología de la prosa en México*, edition and notes by Julio Jiménez Rueda (México: UNAM, 1973), pp. vi-xxii. Francisco Monterde, *Historia de la Literatura Mexicana* (México: Porrúa, 1960), p. 565.

BAUDELIO GARZA

CAMPOBELLO, Nellie Francisca Ernestina (1909-), novelist, poet (née, Francisca Moya Luna). Born November 7, 1909, in the northern part of the state of Durango in a small town, Villa Ocampo, which her family had helped to settle in the seventeenth century. In her own words, as a child she had two main occupations, riding horseback and suffering the winters and the Revolution. Soon after this terrible upheaval, Nellie's family, who had owned considerable landed property in the region since 1680, supported Francisco I. Madero's cause. Her father, Jesús Felipe Moya Luna, became one of the last generals and died in battle in 1914. Her mother, Rafaela, for whom Nellie was to profess a deep love and lasting admiration, remarried, to a doctor from Boston, Stephen Campbell, whose name Nellie adopted, changing it to Campobello. She never attended grade school, having to move around so much because of the Revolution. She learned to read and write with her mother. In 1922, after her mother's death, she went to Mexico City and was able to enter the very prestigious Escuela Inglesa, where besides regular clases she learned ballet. Even though in 1929 she published her first book, a collection of poems, *¡Yo!* (I!), writing was never to become her primary vocation. She dedicated herself to dancing, touring the country to do research and teach indigenous dances of which she is considered an authority. She created the Ballet of Mexico City, the National School of Dance, and the Ballet Folklórico de México. She wrote, in 1940, one of the first books on the subject of the authenticity and techniques of folkloric dancing, *Ritmos indígenas de México* (Native Rhythms of Mexico).

As a novelist she is the author of only two books, *Cartucho* (Cartridge, 1931), and *Las manos de mamá* (My Mother's Hands, 1937). Both describe life during the Revolution as she knew it, and are based on her memories, constituting a testimony from a child's point of view. She wrote the first one to narrate the tragedy of Cartucho, the prototype of a soldier of the Revolution, and to avenge an injury, that done to the real person of Francisco Villa, too often described as a cold-blooded military tyrant. The second novel is a sentimental and moving account of her mother's life, her love and sacrifice, not only for her children but for the suffering victims of the war.

In 1940, she wrote another book, *Apuntes sobre la vida militar de Francisco Villa* (Notes about the Military Life of Francisco Villa), a researched account of the military campaigns of the "guerrillero" from the North.

WORKS: Poetry: *¡Yo!* (I!) (México: Ed. L.I.D.N., 1928); a second edition had the title "Yo, versos por Francisca." "Ocho poemas de mujer," in *Revista de La Habana* 10 (Nov. 1930): 14. *Tres Poemas* (Three Poems) (México: Cía. General de Ediciones, 1957). Novels: *Cartucho* (Cartridge) (Xalapa: Eds. Integrales, 1931); 2nd ed. (México: EDIAPSA, 1940). *La manos de mamá* (My Mother's Hands) (México: Ed. Juventudes de Izquierda, 1937); 2nd ed., with drawings by José Clemente Orozco (México: Ed. Villa Ocampo, 1949). *Mis libros* (My Books) (México: Cía. General de Ediciones, 1960), contains "Yo, por Francisca," "Abra en la roca," "Colección de Poemas," "Cartucho," "Las manos de mamá," and "Apuntes sobre la vida militar de Francisco Villa." Essays: *Apuntes sobre la vida militar de Francisco Villa* (Notes about the Military Life of Francisco Villa) (México: EDIAPSA, 1940). *Ritmos indígenas de México* (Native Rhymes of Mexico), by Nellie and Gloria Campobello (México: SEP, 1940). "Francisco Villa - octavo aniversario de su muerte," in *Revista de Revistas* 4 (July 1931): 5. "Bocetas de Nellie," in *El Universal gráfico* (Jan.-Dec. 1934). "Martín Luis Guzmán, a propósito de *El hombre y sus armas*," in *Ruta* 6 (Nov. 1938): 5. "Apuntes sobre la danza griega y la azteca," in *INBA*, Sept. 3, 1968.

BIBLIOGRAPHY: Ermilo Abreu-Gómez, "*Las manos de mamá* de Nellie Campobello," in *Letras de México* 14 (Feb. 1938): 3-5. Fernando Alegría, *Breve historia de la novela hispanoamericana* (México: Eds. de Andrea, 1959), p. 171. Beatrice Berler, "The Mexican Revolution as Reflected in the Novel," in *Hispania* 47 (1964), 41-47. John S. Brushwood, *Mexico in Its Novel* (Austin: University of Texas Press, 1966). Mario Calleros, "Las mesas de plomo. Nellie Campobello," in *Ovaciones*, suppl. no. 89 (Sep. 8, 1963): 2. Emmanuel Carballo, "Nellie Campobello," in *México en la Cultura* 486 (July 6, 1958): 1-2; *19 protagonistas de la literatura mexicana del siglo XX* (México: Empresas Editoriales, 1965), pp. 327-38. Antonio Castro Leal, *La novela de la Revolución Mexicana*, vol. 1 (México: Aguilar, 1959), pp. 891-93. Helia D'Acosta, *Veinte mujeres* (México: Editores Asociados, 1971), pp. 49-59. Gabriela De Ber, "Nellie Campobello's Vision of the Mexican Revolution," *American Hispanist* (Mar.-Apr. 1979): 14-16. Juan José Domenchina, "En torno a la Revolución que nos contaron y a la novela de la Revolución Mexicana," in *Tiempo* (April 18, 1959): 58. Orlando Gómez-Gil, *Historia crítica de la literatura hispanoamericana* (New York: Holt, Rinehart and Winston, 1968). Manuel Pedro González, *Trayectoria de la novela en México* (México: Botas, 1951), pp. 287-90. Carlos González Peña, "La tragedia de unas manos," in *El Universal* (July 13, 1950). Martín Luis Guzmán, *El hombre y sus armas* (México: Botas, 1938), p. iv. "Nellie Campobello y *Las manos de mamá*," in *El Universal* (Feb. 27, 1938); in *Ruta* 6 (Nov. 15, 1938): 42-43. Sara Hernández Cata, "*Las manos de mamá*," in *Novedades* (May 10, 1950). Gary D. Keller, "El niño en la Revolución mexicana: Nellie Campobello, Andrés Iduarte y César Garizurieta," in *Cuadernos Americanos* 170 (1970): 142-51. Walter M. Langford, *The Mexican Novel Comes of Age* (Notre Dame, Ind.: University of Notre Dame Press, 1971). Luis Leal, *Breve historia del cuento mexicano* (México: Eds. de Andrea, 1956); *Antología del cuento mexicano* (México: Eds. de Andrea, 1957). Doris Antonio Magaña Esquivel, "Cinco novelistas de la Revolución," in *El Nacional* (March 5, 1950): 1, 8. Doris Meyer, "Nellie Campobello's *Las manos de mamá*: A Rereading," in *Hispania* 68 (Dec. 1985) 747-52; "Divided against Herself: The Early Poetry of Nellie Campobello," in *Revista de Estudios Hispánicos* 20, 2 (1986): 51-63. Doris Meyer et al., *Cartucho and My Mother's Hands* (Austin: University of Texas Press, 1988). Francisco Monterde, "*Las manos de mamá* de Nellie Campobello," in *Letras de México* 23 (Jan. 16, 1938): 4. Ernest R. Moore, *Bibliografía de novelistas de la revolución mexicana* (México: n.p. 1941). "Novelists of the Mexican Revolution: Nellie Campobello," in *Mexican Life* 1, 17 (Feb. 1941): 21-22. Rand F. Morton, *Los novelistas de la Revolución mexicana* (México: Cultura, 1949), pp. 161-70. Michèle Muncy, "Nellie Campobello: Anverso y reverso de la historia," in *SECOLAS* 19 (Mar. 1988): 54-61. José Muñoz Orta, "Los libros de Nellie Campobello," in *Impacto* 11 (Nov. 1960): 63. Indiana Nájera, "Nellie Campobello, mujer," in *El Universal Gráfico* (Nov. 28, 1946). Marta Portal, "Nellie Campobello," in *Proceso narrativo de la Revolución mexicana* (Madrid: Espasa Calpe, 1980), pp. 125-27. Dudly Pitts, ed., *Anthology of Contemporary Latin American Poetry* (Norfolk, Conn.: n.p., 1942). Malkah Rabel, "Nellie Campobello y la novela de la Revolución mexicana," in *México en la Cultura* 509 (Dec. 14, 1958): 2, 6. Roberto Ramos, *Bibliografía de la Revolución Mexicana*, vol. 2 (México: n.p., 1935). Alma Reed, "Mexico Honors Founders of the National Ballet," in *The News* (April 14, 1963). Octavio Rivera, "Estampas de la Revolución a través de Nellie Campobello," in *Magisterio* (Durango, Dec. 1961): 40-41; "Nellie Campobello," in *La Voz de Durango* (Sept. 16, 1963). Vito Alexio Robles, "Las memorias dictadas por el General Villa," in *Correo de Parral* (July 28, 1936). Paul Rogers, *Escritores contemporáneos de México* (Cambridge, Mass.: Houghton Mifflin, 1949). John Rutherford, *An Anotated Bibliography of the Novels of the Mexican Revolution of 1910-1917* (Troy, N.Y.: Whitston, 1972). José Juan Tablada, "México de día y de noche--Campobello y *Las manos de mamá*," in *Excelsior* (Dec. 10, 1939). Miguel Tomasina, "*Mis libros*--Una grata sorpresa," in *El Universal* (Nov. 5, 1960). Juan Uribe-Echeverría, "La novela de la Revolución mexicana y la literatura hispanoamericana actual," *in Anales de la Universidad de Chile* (Santiago) 93, 4 (1935): 61-65. Rafael Heliodoro Valle, "Rincón de libros--*Cartucho* de Nellie Campobello," in *Excelsior* (July 6, 1932).

                                                                    MICHELE MUNCY

CAMPOS, Julieta (1932-). Campos was born in Havana, Cuba, on May 8, 1932. She received her doctorate from the School of Philosophy and Letters at the University of Havana. Later she won a scholarship from the Alianza Francesa, which enabled her to study at the Sorbonne (1953-54), where she received a diploma in contemporary French literature. She has been living in Mexico since 1955 and has translated for the Fondo de Cultura Económica and for the publishing house Siglo XXI. In 1966-1967, she was the recipient of a scholarship given by the Centro Mexicano de Escritores.

Julieta Campos is best known for her great knowledge of contemporary literature, especially French and Hispanic. She has been involved with literary criticism for *Novedades, Siempre!, Revista de la Universidad de México* (which she directed from 1981 to 1984), *Revista Mexicana de Literatura, Plural* and *Vuelta*. In 1965 she wrote an essay, *La imagen en el espejo* (The Image in the Mirror), which shows her profound knowledge of contemporary literature. Her first novel, *Muerte por agua* (Death by Water) (1965), situated her as representative of the "nouveau roman" among Hispanic Americans. Her second novel, *Celina o los gatos* (Selina or the Cats, 1968) unites five stories with the common theme of mystery represented by cats. In 1974 she won the Premio Xavier Villaurrutia with her novel *Tiene los cabellos rojizos y se llama Sabina* (She Has Reddish Hair and Her Name Is Sabina).

WORKS: Essays: *La imagen en el espejo* (The Image in the Mirror) (México: UNAM, 1965). *El oficio de leer* (The Job of Reading) (México: FCE, 1971). *Función de la novela* (Purpose of the Novel) (México: Mortiz, 1973). *La herencia obstinada* (The Obstinant Inheritance) (México: FCE, 1982). Novels: *Muerte por agua* (Death by Water) (México: FCE, 1965). *Celina o los gatos* (Selina and the Cats) (México: Siglo XXI, 1968). *Tiene los cabellos rojizos y se llama Sabina* (She Has Reddish Hair and Her Name Is Sabina) (México: Mortiz, 1974). *El miedo de perder a Eurídice* (The Fear of Losing Eurydice) (México: Mortiz, 1979). Monographs: *Las voces de la naturaleza* (Voices of Nature), written in collaboration with Enrique González Pedrero (Villahermosa: Gobierno de Tabasco, 1982).

BIBLIOGRAPHY: Rosario Castellanos, "Tendencias de la novelística mexicana contemporánea," in *Universidad de México* 20, 7 (México, March 1966): 11. Miguel Bustos Cercedo, Review of *Muerte por agua*, in *Letras de ayer y hoy* 7 (México, March 1966): 22-23. Gustavo Esteva, "Julieta Campos: un viento fresco en la literatura mexicana," in *La Cultura en México* 337 (July 31, 1968): xii. Heriberto García Rivas, *Historia de la literatura mexicana*, vol. 4 (México: Porrúa, 1974), p. 363. Natacha González Casanova, Review of *Muerte por agua*, in *El Día* (México, Feb. 26, 1966): 9. Martha Ochnike Loustaunan, "México's Contemporary Women Novelist," thesis, University of New Mexico, Albuquerque, 1973. Beth Miller and Alfonso González, *26 Autoras del México actual* (México: Costa-Amic, 1978), pp. 77-94. Aurora M. Ocampo, *Cuentistas mexicanas* (México: UNAM, 1976), pp. viii, 245. Rinda Rebeca Stowell Young, "Six Representative Women Novelists of Mexico (1960-1969)," thesis, University of Illinois at Urbana, 1975. Ramón Xirau, Review of *Muerte por agua*, in *Diálogos* 4 (Mexico, May-June 1966): 45-46.

MIRTA BARREA-MARLYS

CAMPOS, Marco Antonio (1949-   ). Campos was born in Mexico City on February 23, 1949. He studied law and is presently director of the area of workshops and lectures within the Departamento de Difusión Cultural of the Unversidad Nacional

Autónoma de México. He is also director of the literary review and chapbook series Punto de Partida published by that same university. He coordinates a number of workshops and readings for the Instituto Nacional de Bellas Artes such as Domingos Literarios and writes in the Mexican weekly *Proceso*. It is a well-known fact throughout Mexican literary circles that Campos has singlehandedly published, promoted, and motivated most of those who are now important young Mexican writers through Punto de Partida. Apart from this, he also produces a literature program through Radio UNAM and is a recognized literary translator.

His poetry is often an introspective look; it deals with the act of writing and with his great love for Italian history and culture. A good example of such elements is his "That Voice in Piraeus": It came / from far away like something unexpected. / At Piraeus, the women / sat in a row / 'You are home'--they sang / you opened your eyes wide / That voice, my God, / it was my own.

WORKS: *Muertos y disfraces* (Dead and Costumes) (México: INBA, 1974). *Una seña en la sepultura* (A Sign in the Tomb) (México: UNAM, 1978). *Hojas de los años* (Pages of the Years) (México: Premiá, 1981).

BIBLIOGRAPHY: José Joaquín Blanco, *Crónica de la poesía mexicana* (México: Katún, 1981), pp. 264-70. Sandro Cohen, *Palabra nueva: Dos décadas de poesía en México* (México: Premiá, 1981), pp. 19-20, 175-79. Jorge González de León, *Poetas de una generación (1940-1949)* (México: UNAM, 1981), pp. 15-17. Jaime Moreno Villareal, *La línea y el círculo* (México: Universidad Autónoma Metropolitana, 1981).

RICARDO AGUILAR

CAMPOS, Rubén M. (1876-1945), poet, novelist, musician. Campos contributed to various publications, among them *El Plectro, El Demócrata*, the *Revista Moderna*, the *Gaceta Musical, El Mundo Ilustrado, Nosotros, México, Vida Moderna, El Universal*, and *El Centinela*. In 1919 he was appointed to the Consulate of Mexico in Milano, Italy. He also taught in the Escuela Nacional Preparatoria, the Escuelas Normales de Profesores y Profesoras, the Universidad Nacional, the Escuela Nacional de Bellas Artes, the Conservatorio Nacional, and the National Museum of Archeology, History and Ethnography.

Campos' poetry has been characterized as melodious with a richly worked lexicon. His novel belongs to the psychological genre. He also wrote librettos, short stories, a travel book, and various studies in musical and literary folklore.

WORKS: *Cuentos mexicanos* (Mexican Stories) (México: Aldasoro, 1897). *Zulema* (libretto for Ernesto Elorduy) (México: Aguilar Vera, 1902). *La flauta de Pan* (Pan's Flute) (México: n.p., 1902). *Claudio Oronoz* (México: J. Ballescá, 1906). *Las alas nómadas* (Nomadic Wings) (Barcelona: Araluce, 1922). *Tlahuicole* (Opera) (México: T. Gráficos, 1925). *Quetzolcóatl* (Opera) (México: T. Gráficos, 1928). *El folklore literario de México* (Literary Folklore of Mexico) (México: T. Gráficos, 1929). *El folklore musical de las ciudades* (Musical Folklore of the Cities) (México: SEP, 1930).

La producción literaria de los aztecas (Literary Production of the Aztecs) (México: Gráficos, 1936).

BIBLIOGRAPHY: Salvador Azuela, "El poeta de Guanajuato, Rubén M. Campos," *Novedades* (June 21, 1945). Genaro Estrada, *Poetas nuevos de México* (México: Porrúa, 1916), pp. 19-21. Raymond L. Grismer and Mary B. Macdonald, *Vida y obras de autores mexicanos* (Havana: Alfa, 1945), pp. 31-33. Pedro Henríquez Ureña, "Notas sobre Claudio Oronoz," *Revista Moderna* (June 1906): 239-40. Juan B. Iguíniz, *Bibliografía de novelistas mexicanos* (México: Imp. de la Sría. de Relaciones, 1926), p. 56. Luis Leal, *Breve historia del cuento mexicano* (México: Eds. de Andrea, 1956), pp. 68. Juan de Linza, "Hombres de letras," *Crónica* (Apr. 15, 1907). Francisco Monterde, *Bibliografía del teatro en México* (México: Monografías Bibliográficas Mexicanas, 1933), pp. 93-95. José Juan Tablada, "Máscaras. Rubén M. Campos," *Revista Moderna* (Aug. 1903): 225-26; "Claudio Oronoz, novela por Rubén M. Campos," *Revista Moderna* (Feb. 1906): 376-77. Manuel Ugarte, "Notas de México. Los escritores," *Revista Moderna* (June 1900). Esperanza Velázquez Bringas and Rafael Heliodoro Valle, *Indice de escritores* (México: Herrero Hermanos, 1928), pp. 44-45. Jesús Villalpando, "Claudio Oronoz, novela por Rubén M. Campos," *Savia Moderna* (July 1906): 309-12. Jesús Zavala, "Rubén M. Campos," *El Libro y el Pueblo* 17 (1955): 27-30.

BARBARA P. FULKS

CAMPOS Ramírez, Alejandro (1919-   ), poet, critic, and reporter; pseudonym Alejandro Finisterre. Born in Finisterre, Spain, on May 16, 1919, Campos Ramírez completed most of his education in Spain, then moved on to Paris, Rome, and London, where he received specialized training in graphic arts. He was one of the cofounders of the Spanish journal *Paso a la Juventud* in 1936 and also served as editor-in-chief of the bilingual newspaper *L'Espagne*. After a journey in 1951 that took him throughout all of Spanish America, he settled in Guatemala. When Castillo Armas came into power there a few years later, he moved to Mexico, where he became the director of Ecuador 0º0'0", a concern that initially limited its publications to poetry. Widely traveled, he has contributed to Mexico City's *El Nacional*, as well as to several French and Argentine publications. His most significant literary contributions have undoubtedly been his publications on Spanish-American, Mexican, and Spanish poetry.

WORKS: *Cantos quintos* (Fifth Songs) (Madrid: Unguina, 1936). *Seis danzas catalanas* (Six Catalan Dances) (Barcelona: Monistrol, 1937). *Cantos esclavos* (Slave Songs) (Paris: Combat, 1948). *Historia de la danza española* (History of Spanish Dance) (Paris: Combat, 1948). *Cantos rodados* (Boulders) (Roma: Danesi, 1950). *Poesía de Ecuador* (Ecuadorean Poetry) (Quito: Casa de la Cultura, 1952). *Poesía de Guatemala* (Guatemalan Poetry) (London: Wartelow and Sons, 1953). *18 de julio* (July 18) (México: Ecuador, 1956). *Cumbres borrascosas: antología de adolescencia* (Stormy Heights: An Anthology of Adolescence) (México: Ecuador, 1956). *Café, coña y puro* (Coffee, Joke, and Cigar) (México: Ecuador, 1956). *Poesía en México* (Poetry in Mexico) (México: Ecuador, 1957, 1959), *Con, sin, sobre, tras las poesía* (With, Without, About, Beyond Poetry) (México: Ecuador, 1959). *Poesía gallega contemporánea* (Contemporary Galician Poetry) (México: Ecuador, 1960). *Netsuke, haikai* (México: Ecuador, 1962), *Rail* (Rail) (México: Ecuador, 1964).

BIBLIOGRAPHY: Anon., "Labor editorial de Alejando Finisterre," *Nivel* 1O (Oct. 25, 1963): 4. Andrés Henestrosa, "La nota cultural," *El Nacional* (Oct. 1, 1964): 3. Aurora M. Ocampo de Gómez and Ernesto Prado Velázquez, *Diccionario de escritores eexicanos* (México: UNAM, 1967), pp. 57-58.

JANIS L. KRUGH

CAMPUZANO, Juan R. (1912-), teacher, journalist, prose writer. Campuzano was born February 4, 1912, in Tixtla, Guerrero, Mexico. Since 1931 he has been a teacher specializing in Mexican history and literature. He has traveled the world extensively, founded and directed twelve newspapers, and received various literary prizes. Among his works of fiction are several collections of short stories, for example, *La hija del caporal* (The Foreman's Daughter), *Cuentos para niños y para hombres* (Stories for Men and Children); several novels, *La sombra íntima* (The Intimate Shadow), *La voz de la tierra* (The Voice of the Earth); and several biographical essays, *Semblanza del padre Hidalgo* (Portrait of Father Hidalgo), *Semblanza de Altamirano* (Portrait of Altamirano), and *Hidalgo, padre y maestro de México* (Hidalgo, Father and Teacher of Mexico). His stories show the influence of Arévalo Martínez, and his style is noteworthy for its use of the short sentence, which gives the sensation of quickness to his story pacing.

WORKS: *Un maestro rural* (A Country Teacher) (México: n.p., 1938). *La hija del caporal* (The Foreman's Daughter) (México: n.p., 1944). *Jesusón* (Big Jesus) (México: n.p., 1945). *La sombra íntima* (The Intimate Shadow) (México: n.p., 1946). *Semblanza del padre Hidalgo* (Portrait of Father Hidalgo) (México: Colección Cuauhtémoc, 1953). *Semblanza de Altamirano* (Portrait of Altamirano) (México: n.p., 1955). *Hidalgo, padre y maestro de México* (Hidalgo, Father and Teacher of Mexico) (México: Centro Cultural Guerrerense, 1964). *Cuentos para niños y para hombres* (Stories for Men and Children) (México: Instituto Federal de Capacitación del Magisterio, 1964). *Cuentos de amor y de muerte* (México: SCE., 1964). *La voz de la tierra* (The Voice of the Earth) (México: Ed. Magisterio, 1965). *La voz de la sangre* (The Voice of the Blood) (México: Ed. Magisterio, 1965). *Cuentos de mi barrio* (Short Stories of My Neighborhood) (México: Dept. Cult. del D.F., 1975).

BIBLIOGRAPHY: Antonio Acevedo Escobedo, "Notas de caza menor. Un novelista de Guerrero," *El Nacional* (Feb. 6, 1966): 3, 8. Heriberto García Rivas, *150 biografías de mexicanos ilustres* (México: Ed. Diana, 1964), pp. 500-01. Luis Leal, *Breve historia del cuento mexicano* (México: Eds. de Andrea, 1956), p. 143; *Bibliografía del cuento mexicano* (México: Eds. de Andrea, 1958), p. 32. Aurora M. Ocampo de Gómez and Ernesto Prado Velázquez, *Diccionario de escritores mexicanos* (México: UNAM, 1967), p. 58.

TERESA R. ARRINGTON

CANTON, Wilberto (1923-1979). A native of Mérida, Yucatán, Wilberto Cantón was born on July 15, 1923, and obtained a law degree at the UNAM in 1948, but decided to pursue a career in literature, working on and even founding several student newspapers and contributing to many of the leading Mexican journals, including *Excelsior*, *Cuadernos de Bellas Artes*, and *Cuadernos Americanos*. He also founded and was editor of *Espiga*, a literary magazine. Cantón was granted a scholarship by the Universidad de Chile to study in its summer school and later received a grant from the French government to pursue studies at the Sorbonne. He also traveled throughout South America and Europe in conjunction with his studies.

In 1942, he won first prize in a poetry contest to celebrate the inauguration of the new Universidad de Sonora. He published two volumes of verse, *Segunda estación* (Second Season, 1943) and *Dos poemas* (Two Poems, 1955).

Although he was successful as a poet and essayist and even wrote one children's novel, he is most noted for his achievements in the theater. His last published piece was the inconclusive play, *Retrato de mi padre* (Portrait of My Father, 1978), dealing with the role of journalism in Mexican history, particulary during the Revolution. The play won the Primer Concurso Nacional de Obras de Teatro Social. Apparently, Cantón intended to rework and lengthen the play, but he died shortly thereafter, on March 5, 1979.

His highly acclaimed theatrical works, even though many were controversial and sometimes censored or banned, place him as one of Mexico's outstanding playwrights of the twentieth century. Most of his plays have been performed to critical acclaim.

He was influenced by several well-known dramatists, including Xavier *Villaurrutia, Rudolfo *Usigli, Jacinto Benavente, Henrik Ibsen, Arthur Miller, and Tennessee Williams. His social theater was largely inspired by these men. Some of the existentialist French writers, such as Jean Paul Sartre, also influenced his work. But perhaps his greatest influence was his own observation of Mexican society, especially since his plays tended to reflect what he witnessed and heard.

Recognizing the need for greater social awareness, for more persistent action to benefit the impoverished and for truly confronting the plaguing issues of society, Cantón created characters and episodes that would draw attention to his message and purpose. Some of his plays caused quite an uproar, particularly among the more conservative elements of society.

As a playwright, he began in 1946 with a short work, *Cuando zarpe el barco* (When the Boat Weighs Anchor). His second play, *Saber morir* (To Know How to Die), was performed in 1958. It attempted to illustrate some of the popular existentialist theories in vogue at that time. His play *La escuela de cortesanos* (The Courtiers' School) was performed in 1954 at the Festival Dramático of the Instituto Nacional de Bellas Artes. It was a politicized farce set in the colonial period which, in this case, appears to be a metaphor for the contemporary period.

In 1957 two other of his works were performed: *Nocturno a Rosario* (Nocturn to Rosario) and *Pecado mortal* (Mortal Sin) The first concerns the romantic legend of the poet Manuel Acuña and Rosario de la Peña. *Pecado mortal* was initially censured because of its purportedly sexually explicit and graphic material, but later allowed to make its debut. *Los malditos* (The Damned 1958), his most controversial play, was prohibited in the capital, and was moved to the Teatro Degollado in Guadalajara. The major reason for its censorship was that the play offered no moral. The issue of artistic freedom was hotly debated both in the newspapers and in theatrical circles. When *Los malditos* was permitted to be performed in Mexico City, it met with astounding success, as there were more than 3,000 performances by 1979. A play noted for its realism, it deals with an effort to purify the defects of society.

Another major work for which he won the Juan Ruiz de Alarcón prize is *Nosotros somos Dios* (We Are God, 1962), a very favorably critiqued play, seen as possibly his best. It takes place during the Revolution of 1910, specifically during the regime of Victoriano Huerta. Focusing on the loss of revolutionary ideals caused by the grab for power and its benefits, the play espouses the philosophy that each man is God and should, therefore, act in a manner in accordance with the highest ideals.

In *¿Qué pasa con el teatro en México?* (What's Wrong with the Theater in Mexico), published in 1967, Cantón wrote that the theater ought to be both enjoyable and a work of art. He also felt that a play should give the public a sense of history and society, inspiring theatergoers to enlarge their vision of themselves and the world.

Critics, notes Carl Shirley, generally divide his plays into those that employ a historical setting or use actual historical figures in imaginary situations and those that deal with contemporary social problems. *Nosotros somos Dios* is regarded as his historical play, dealing with individual responsibility set against a backdrop of the Revolution of 1910. It was later made into a movie, *La sangre derramada*. *Malditos* (1958; (revised in 1971), fitting the second category, is a stark portrayal of the problem of juvenile delinquency. He also won first prize in the Festival de Teatro Latino in New York in 1970 and honorable mention in the Concurso Internacional de Teatro "León Felipe" in Paris in 1972.

In *Inolvidable* (Unforgettable)(1961), he created Marcela, a prostitute, and included graphic descriptions of the effects of incest on a family, causing this play to be censured. It made its debut, however, in Buenos Aires to critical acclaim, but was banned from Mexico until 1970, when a revised version with a new title, *Unas migajas de felicidad* (Some Crumbs of Happiness), satisfied the censors. The play, despite its social content, is quite poetic, illustrating Cantón's ability to integrate successfully two genres.

A successful innovator, Cantón caught and held spectator attention by using interesting theatrical devices, such as multilevel or multiscenic stages, temporal changes, etc. He also invited spectators to take part in some of his plays, becoming co- creators, especially of the outcome. He was also interested in theater about theater, an interest that culminated in 1976 with the play *Juegos de amor* (Games of Love), in which he integrated techniques of pure artifice.

With *Inolvidable* and the one-act *El juego sacrado* (The Sacred Game), Cantón began experimenting with role-playing and the presentation of a play within a play. In *Inolvidable*, the author examines five characters' ability to control their lives. Four are hiding a secret: an incestuous relationship between a brother and sister. They all discover that they have been living theatrical lives. As they take off their masks and shed their roles, the real truths are revealed. In *El juego sagrado*, costumes, props, and makeup are the theatrical elements used to create the play for which Cantón was indebted to Calderón de la Barca and his *La vida es sueño*. The "juego sagrado" is only illusory, although it seems real, especially when reality seems illusive.

Wilberto Cantón enjoyed a wide variety of experiences in the theater, as an editor and as a critic. For many years he held important posts with the Instituto Nacional de Bellas Artes, including that of chief of public relations, head of the Theatre Department, director of *Cuadernos de Bellas Artes*, and director of the television series "La Hora de Bellas Artes." He was president of the Asociación de Críticos Teatrales and edited several anthologies of dramatic literature. He was the head of the editorial department of the Universidad Autónoma de México and director of the *Diario del Sureste* of Mérida and of the journal *Cuadernos de Bellas Artes*. Cantón's active involvement in the cultural and literary affairs of Mexico was cut short by his premature death in 1979.

WORKS: Poetry: *Segunda edición* (Second Edition) (México: UNAM, 1943). *Dos poemas* (Two Poems) (Mendoza, Argentina: n.p., 1955). Essay: *La ciudad de México. Aguila y sol de su vida* (Mexico City. Eagle and Sun of Its Life) (México: n.p., 1946). *Posiciones* (Positions) (México: UNAM, 1950). "Respuesta a Carlos Solórzano" (Reply to Carlos Solórzano), in *Siempre* (Aug. 23, 1967): xiii. Theater: *Cuando zarpe el barco* (When the Boat Weighs Anchor), performed in 1946. *Saber morir* (To Know How to Die), performed in 1950; in *Cuadernos americanos* (May-June 1950): 233-88. *La escuela de cortesanos* (The Courtiers' School), performed in 1954; in *Panorama del teatro en México* 1, 3 (Sept. 1954): 35-46; (México: Col. Teatro Mexicano, 1956). *Nocturno a Rosario* (Nocturn to Rosario), performed in 1957 (México: Ed. Los Presentes, 1956). *Pecado mortal* (Mortal Sin), performed in 1957. *Los malditos* (The Damned), performed in 1959 (México: Col. Teatro Mexicano, 1959); in *Teatro mexicano 1958*, edited by Luis G. Basurto (Madrid: Ed. Aguilar, 1959), pp. 240-314. *El jardín de las Gorgonas* (The Garden of the Gorgons), in *Tercera antología de obras en un acto* (México: Col. Teatro Mexicano, 1960), pp. 11-33. *Tan cerca del cielo* (So Close to Heaven), performed in 1961. *Inolvidable* (Unforgettable) (México: Ecuador, 1961). *Nosotros somos Dios* (We Are God), performed in 1962; in *La Palabra y el Hombre* 26 (April-July 1963): 315-76. *Nota roja* (Red Note), performed in 1963 (México: Ecuador, 1964). *Todos somos hermanos* (We Are All Brothers), performed in 1963. *Murió por la patria* (He Died for His Country), performed in 1964. *Pecado mortal/Malditos* (Mortal Sin/The Damned) (México: Ed. Novaro, 1971). *Retrato de mi padre* (Portrait of My Father) (México: Editorial Popular de los Trabajadores, 1978). Prologues: Bernardo Ortiz de Montellano, *Sueño y poesía* (Dream and Poetry), notes (México: UNAM, 1952). *El teatro en México* (The Theater in Mexico), vol. 2, 1958-1964, prol. (México: INBA, 1965).

BIBLIOGRAPHY: Robert M. Assardo, "Temas existencialistas en *Nosotros somos Dios* de Wilberto Cantón," in *Caribe* 2, 1 (1977):33-46. François Baguer, Review of *Nosotros somos Dios*, in *Cuadernos de Bellas Artes* 4, 9 (Sept. 1963): 31-34. Robert L. Bancroft, "The Problem of Marcela's Future in Cantón's *Inolvidable*," in *Romance Notes* 14, 2 (1972): 269-74. Luis G. Basurto, *Teatro mexicano 1958* (México: Ed. Aguilar, 1959), pp. 20, 246-47. José Hugo Cardona, "Teatro de la Semana," review of *Nosotros somos Dios*, in *Revista de la Semana* (Nov. 11, 1962): 6. Fausto Castillo, Review of *Los malditos*, in *México en la Cultura* 501 (Oct. 19, 1958): 9. Juan García Ordoño, "Wilberto Cantón y el INBA," in *Ovaciones* 93, (Oct. 6, 1963): 2. Juan García Ponce and José Luis Ibáñez, "Teatro, *Nocturno a Rosario*," in *Universidad de México* 12, 2 (Oct. 1957): 28. Orlando Gómez-Gil, *Historia crítica de la Literatura Hispanoamericana* (New York: Holt, Rinehart and Winston, 1968), p. 731. Celestino Gorostiza, in *Teatro mexicano del siglo XX*, vol. 3 (México: FCE, 1956), p. xxii. Pedro Guillén, "La noche de los poderosos," review of *Nota roja*, in *Siempre!* 542 (Nov. 13, 1963): 16-17; "Cultura en México," review of *Nota roja*, in *Revista Mexicana de Cultura* 907 (Aug. 16, 1964): 2. Antonio Magaña Esquivel, "Estreno de *Saber morir*," in *El Nacional* (Aug. 1950); "En amor y en política, dos comedias de escándalo," review of *Nota roja*, in *Revista Mexicana de Cultura* 866 (Nov. 3, 1963): 11; *Medio siglo de teatro mexicano, 1900-1961* (México: INBA, Dept. of Lit., 1964), pp. 84, 124, 146-48.

Antonio Magaña Esquivel and Ruth S. Lamb, *Breve historia del teatro mexicano* (México: Eds. de Andrea, 1958), pp. 140-50. María Luisa Mendoza, "El teatro," review of *Nota roja*, in *El gallo ilustrado* 70 (Oct. 27, 1963) 4. Marciano Navarrete, "La nota roja de W. Cantón," in *México en la Cultura* 762 (Oct. 27, 1963): 4. Salvador Novo, ed., *¿Qué pasa con el teatro en México?* (México: Ed. Novaro, 1967), pp. 187-90. Aurora M. Ocampo de Gómez and Ernesto Prado Velázquez, *Diccionario de escritores mexicanos* (México: UNAM, 1967), pp. 58-59. Mara Reyes, "Diorama teatral," review of *Nosotros somos Dios*, in *Diorama de la Cultura* (Nov. 4, 1962): 2. Mauricio de la Selva, Review of *Nota roja*, in *Diorama de la Cultura* (May 16, 1965): 4. Carl R. Shirley, "Reflections on the Career of Wilberto Cantón," in *Latin American Theatre Review* 13, 1 (Fall 1980): 67-69; "A *Curriculum Operum* of Mexico's Wilberto Canton," in *Latin American Theatre Review* 13, 2 (1980): 47-56; "The Metatheatrical World of Wilberto Cantón," in *Latin American Theatre Review* 23, 2 (Spring 1990): 43-53; "The Seamy Side of Mexico City in Wilberto Cantón's Plays," in *Hispanic Literatures*, 9th Annual Conference Proceedings, edited by Juan Cruz Mendizábal (Indiana, Penna.: Indiana University of Pennsylvania, 1983), pp. 309-22; "The Role of Journalism in the Life and Theater of Wilberto Cantón," in *Hispanic Literatures*, 11th Annual Conference Proceedings, edited by Juan Cruz Mendizábal (Indiana, Penna.: Indiana University of Pennsylvania, 1985), pp. 379-91. Rafael Solana, Review of *Nota roja*, in *Siempre!* 540 (Oct. 30, 1963): 50-52; Review of *Murió por la patria*, in *Siempre!* 563 (April 8, 1964): 53. Carlos Solórzano, Review of *Nosotros somos Dios*, in *Ovaciones* 46 (Nov. 11, 1962): 5; *Testimonios teatrales de México* (México: UNAM, 1973), p. 219. S. Samuel Trifilo, "The Theater of Wilberto Cantón," in *Hispania* 54, 4 (1971): 869-75. John F. Tull, Jr., "El mundo teatral de Wilberto Cantón," in *Duquesne Hispanic Review* 6, 2 (1967): 1-7. Joseph F. Vélez, "Entrevista con Wilberto Cantón," in *Latin American Theatre Review* 13, 1 (Fall 1979): 71-75.

JEANNE C. WALLACE

CARBALLIDO, Emilio (1925-). Born in Córdoba, Veracruz, on May 22, 1925, Emilio Carballido, Mexico's premier playwright, as well as an important novelist and teacher, studied literature, theater arts, and English at the Universidad de México. While still an infant, he moved with his family to Mexico City, remaining there until 1939. In a significant move, he joined his father for a year in Córdoba. This experience introduced him to a wide variety of new ideas and new geography. Returning to Mexico City in 1940, he continued his schooling and, in 1946, wrote his first play, *Los dos mundos de Alberta* (The Two Worlds of Alberta). His first published play, *La zona intermedia* (The Intermediate Zone), came two years later, in 1948. Awarded a fellowship by the Rockefeller Foundation in 1950, he spent a year in New York. He also received two scholarships from the Centro Mexicano de Escritores. Many of his theatrical works have won literary prizes both in Mexico and abroad. For instance, in 1955, he was recognized by *El Nacional*, INBA, and UNAM. His play *Un pequeño día de ira* (A Small Day of Wrath) won the Premio Casa de las Américas in 1963.

In 1957, he journeyed throughout Europe and Asia as the public relations advisor for the National Ballet. Long a world traveler, he has given conferences in many universities and served as a visiting professor in such educational institutions as Rutgers University in 1965, the Rutgers Summer Program in Spain in 1969, and the University of Pittsburgh in 1970. He also served as a jury member for the Premio Casa de las Américas de Cuba in 1963. He has contributed stories, theater and articles of literary criticism to the cultural supplements of many magazines, newspapers, and journals in Mexico and to specialized papers in many places. He became a member of the Academia Mexicana de la Lengua in 1976, and he was the director of publications for the Editores Mexicanos Unidos, stimulating the publication of Mexican theatrical works. He worked in Xalapa at the Universidad Veracruzana, as the underdirector of the School of Theatre and as a teacher and member of the Consejo Editorial. He also taught drama at INBA and was director of the School of Theatre. Much in demand as a teacher of theatrical arts (Dramatic Theory, Acting and Directing), Carballido has been steadily engaged by a significant and increasing number of drama schools and universities in general. In 1975, he founded *Tramoya*, a theater journal of original plays which, since 1985, has been a joint venture of the Veracruzana and Rutgers University-Camden, under the editorship of Eladio Cortés and Carballido, himself.

Emilio Carballido is one of the most well-known and respected writers in Mexico and also has been one of the most influential promoters of the theater. A teacher of several generations of theater students, Carballido was discovered in 1950 by Salvador Novo, who encouraged him with his play *Rosalba y los Llaveros* (Rosalba and the Llaveros). The same year, he produced the sacramental play *La zona intermedia* (The Intermediate Zone). These two works illustrate his preference for two distinct types of play, one focusing on the effects of daily reality in Mexican life, and the other dealing with *magical realism as manifested in the sacramental work. *Rosalba y los Llaveros* recreates the traditional provincial middle-class family and the asphyxiating atmosphere in which the characters live. Other works, such as *La danza que sueña la tortuga* (The Dance the Turtle Dreams), *Felicidad* (Felicity), *D.F.* (a collection of one-act plays set in the capital), *Un pequeño día de ira* (A Small Day of Wrath), *Silencio, pollos pelones, ya les van a echar su maíz* (Silence, Featherless Cocks, Your Corn Is Coming Soon), and *Tiempo de Ladrones* (Time of Thieves)--(the story of Chucho el Roto), follow the same patterns. In *Tiempo de ladrones*, Carballido makes the protagonist, a nineteeth-century popular personality of legendary fame, a contemporary figure. *La hebra de oro* (The Golden Thread) is an example of the use of magical realism, as are *El día que se soltaron los leones* (The Day They Let the Lions Loose), *El relojero de Córdoba* (The Watchmaker from Córdoba), *Medusa*, and *Las Cartas de Mozart* (Mozart's Letters). His plays, of contemporary interest, are performed in many countries and in many languages. In 1986, the play *Ceremonia en el templo del tigre* (Ceremony in the Temple of the Tiger), written in 1985, was chosen to celebrate the fortieth anniversary of the Escuela de Arte Teatral of INBA. It is a serious reflection on Mexican and Central American roots. Other themes are sensitive issues of colonial life and struggles and the corrupt political mechanism that allows a rural feudalism to thrive. A recent play, *Rosa de dos aromas* (A Rose of Two Scents), uproariously funny and satirical, has been performed to capacity audiences close to 3,000 times.

Carballido has published five fairly lengthy novels. They are *La veleta oxidada* (The Rusted Weathervane, 1956), *El norte* (The North, 1958), *Las visitaciones del diablo* (The Visits from the Devil, 1965), *El sol* (The Sun, 1970), and *El tren que corría* (The Train That Kept Going, 1984). Based on an actual happening, *El tren que corría* is a hilarious story of several very different people, intent upon going to Monterrey by train. Unfortunately, they miss the train, so they decide to take a taxi to the next train station. When they arrive, the train is just leaving. The taxi driver then takes them to the next station. This repeats itself over and over, with extraordinarily funny happenings, until finally they arrive in Monterrey by taxi. All the characters, except one, the young woman who was supposed to get married in Monterrey, go on their way. The woman cancels her marriage and goes off with the taxi driver. All of the action occurs within a very realistic framework, producing a novel of entertaining value. Carballido also has a short novel, *Los zapatos de hierro* (The Iron Shoes), which could be classified as a story, but Carballido prefers to call it a novel. The first four novels mentioned contain the same elements that characterize his early theater: "costumbrismo" (treatment of customs), life in the capital compared to country living, and class struggles. But, regardless of the topics, Carballido employs humor, especially light humor, in all of his plays, although it is much more apparent in *La veleta oxidada*. Humor serves largely to break the dramatic tension created by the characters' situations.

As can be seen, he excels in all the genres in which he has worked. A most distinguished maestro, Emilio Carballido is one of Mexico's finest.

WORKS: Short Stories: *La caja vacía* (The Empty Box) (México: FCE, 1962). *El poeta que se volvió gusano y otros cuentos* (The Poet Who Turned into a Worm and Other Stories) (México: Extemporáneos, 1978). *Los zapatos de fierro* (The Iron Shoes) (México: Grijalbo, 1983). Stories in Anthologies: "La desterrada" (The Exiled), in Emmanuel Carballo, *El cuento mexicano del siglo XX*, pp. 675-87; in Héctor Gally, *30 cuentos de autores mexicanos*, pp. 99-117. "La paz después del combate" (Peace after Combat), in Gustavo Sainz, *Jaula de palabras*, pp. 116-26. "La caja vacía," in Gustavo Sainz, *Los mejores cuentos mexicanos*, pp. 189-96. Anthologies: *Teatro joven de México* (Young Theater of Mexico), fifteen works selected and presented by Emilio Carballido (México: Novaro, 1973); vol. 2, prologue and selection (México: EDIMUSA, 1979). *Más teatro joven* (More Young Theater), selected and presented (México: EDIMUSA, 1982). *El arca de Noé* (Noah's Ark), anthology, prologue, "Apostillas a un tomo ideal de teatro infantil" (Annotations to an Ideal Volume of Children's Theater) (México: SEP, 1974). *Carpintería dramática* (Dramatic Woodworking), anthology, prologue (México: UNAM, 1979). Luisa Josefina Hernández, *Las fuentes ocultas* (Hidden Sources), note (México: Extemporáneos, 1982), p. 1. *Escándalo en paraíso y 4 obras ganadoras. 1er Concurso de teatro Salvador Novo* (Scandal in Paradise and Four Winning Works. The First Salvador Novo Theater Competition), prologue (México: EDIMUSA, 1984). *Dos crónicas* (Two Chronicles), in *Crónicas de grupo*, pp. 39-44. *Avanzada* (Advanced), selection and introduction (México: EDIMUSA, 1984). *9 obras jóvenes* (Nine Works of the Young), selection and introduction (México: EDIMUSA, 1985). Aristotle, *La poética* (Poetry), presentation (México: EDIMUSA, 1985). *Teatro para adolescentes* (Theater for Adolescents), selection and presentation (México: EDIMUSA, 1985). *Teatro para obreros* (Theater for Workers), anthology and notes (México: EDIMUSA, 1985). *Jardín con animales* (Garden with Animals), anthology, selection and prologue (México: EDIMUSA, 1985). *Teatro Joven de México* (Young Theater of Mexico) (México: EDIMUSA, 1985). *Avanzada, más teatro joven de México* (Advanced, More Young Theater of Mexico) (México: EDIMUSA, 1985). *Teatro para jóvenes* (Theater for Youngsters) (México: EDIMUSA, 1986). Novels: *La veleta oxidada* (The Rusty

Weather-Vane) (México: Los Presentes, 1956). *El Norte* (The North) (Xalapa: Universidad Veracruzana, 1958); in *Dos novelas mexicanas* (Montevideo: Arca, 1967); in *Quince relatos de la América Latina* (La Habana: Casa de las Américas, 1970), pp. 355-92. *La veleta oxidada* and *El Norte* (México: Novaro, 1971; Xalapa: Universidad Veracruzana, 1980). *Las visitaciones del diablo* (Visits from the Devil) (México: Mortiz, 1965). *El sol* (The Sun) (México: Mortiz, 1970); 2nd ed. (México: Grijalbo, 1980). *El tren que corría* (The Train That Kept on Going) (México: FCE, 1984). Theater: *Auto de la triple porfía* (Play about the Triple Importunity), performed in 1948; published with *La zona intermedia* (The Intermediate Zone, 1950) and *Escribir, por ejemplo* (Writing, for Example, 1950) (México: Unión Nacional de Autores, 1951). *El suplicante* (The Supplicant), 1950, in *Antologías de obras en un acto* 1 (México: Col. de Teatro), pp. 63-81. *Rosalba y los Llaveros* (Rosalba and the Llaveros), 1950, in *Panorama del teatro en México* (México: n.p.), pp. 21-67; in *Teatro de Emilio Carballido* (México: FCE, 1960), pp. 151-247; in *Teatro hispanoamericano*, edited by Frank Dauster (New York: Harcourt, Brace and World, 1965); *Rosalba y los Llaveros y otras obras de teatro* (México: FCE/SEP, 1984). *Escribir, por ejemplo* (Writing, for Example), 1950 (México: Unión Nacional de Autores, 1951). "El invisible" (The Invisible), Libretto for ballet, performed in 1952. *El viaje de Nocresida* (Nocresida's Journey), in collaboration with Sergio Magaña, performed in 1953. *La sinfonía doméstica* (The Domestic Symphony), performed in 1953. *El pozo* (The Well), opera in verse, 1953. *La danza que sueña la tortuga* (The Dance the Turtle Dreams), performed in 1955 with the title *Las palabras cruzadas* (Crossed Words), in *Teatro mexicano del siglo XX*, 2, edited by Celestino Gorostiza, pp. 135-206. *Felicidad*, 1955; in *Concurso Nacional de Teatro. Obras premiadas 1954-1955* (México: INBA, 1956), pp. 197-292; (Xalapa: Universidad Veracruzana, 1960); with "Un pequeño día de ira" (A Little Day of Wrath) (México: UNAM, 1972). *La hebra de oro* (The Golden Thread), 1956; and with *El lugar y la hora* (Place and Time) (México: UNAM, 1957). *D.F.* (México: Col. Teatro Mexicano, 1957); 2nd ed., with one less and five new plays (Xalapa: Universidad Veracruzana, 1962); 3rd ed., with two more plays (México: Novaro, 1973); 4th ed., twenty-six plays (México: Grijalbo, 1978); 5th ed. (1979); 6th ed. (1983). *13 veces el D.F.* (D.F. Thirteen Times) (México: EDIMUSA, 1985). *Selaginela*, 1959. *Cinco pasos al cielo*, three-act play for children, in collaboration with Luisa Bauer and Fernando Wagner, 1959. *Las estatuas de marfil* (The Marble Statues), 1960 (Xalapa: Universidad Veracruzana, 1960). *El relojero de Córdoba* (The Watchmaker from Córdoba), 1960; in *Tres piezas teatrales* (New York: Holt, Rinehart and Winston, 1970), pp. 134-83. *Teatro* (Theater), includes *El relojero de Córdoba*, *Medusa*, *Rosalba y los Llaveros*, and *El día que se soltaron los leones* (The Day the Lions Were Set Free), La Habana, 1963, México, 1978 (México: FCE, 1960); 2nd ed. (México: FCE, 1976); 3rd ed. (1979). "La lente maravillosa" (The Marvelous Lens), "Guillermo y el nahual" (Guillermo and the Nahual), and "El jardinero y los pájaros" (The Gardener and the Birds), for children, 1960. "Homenaje a Hidalgo" (Homage to Hidalgo), in Palacio de Bellas Artes, 1960. "Macario," based on story by B. Traven, film by Roberto Gavaldón, 1961. "Misa de seis" (Mass at Six), operatic version of "Primera misa" (First Mass), in Palacio de Bellas Artes, 1962. *Un pequeño día de ira* (A Little Day of Wrath) (La Habana: Casa de las Américas, 1962). *Silencio, pollos pelones...* (Silence, Bald Chickens...), 1963, in *Teatro mexicano 1963*, edited by Antonio Magaña Esquivel (México: Aguilar, 1965); in *Tres obras* (Three Works) (with *Un pequeño día de ira* and *Acapulco, los lunes*) (México: Extemporáneos, 1978); 2nd ed. (México: EDIMUSA, 1985). *Los hijos del Capitán Grant* (The Children of

Captain Grant), for children, adapted from work of Jules Verne, 1964, in *5 obras para teatro escolar* (five Works for School Theater), vol. 2 (México: INBA, 1972), pp. 9-85. *Yo también hablo de la rosa* (I Also Speak about the Rose), 1966; (México: INBA, 1966) in *Teatro mexicano del siglo XX*, vol. 5, edited by Antonio Magaña Esquivel, pp. 234-76. *Te juro Juana, que tengo ganas* (I Swear to You, Juana, That I Feel Like It), 1967; with *Yo también hablo de la rosa* (México: Novaro, 1970); with *Yo también hablo de la rosa* and *Fotografía en la playa* (Photograph on the Beach), 1984 (México: EDIMUSA, 1979). *Las noticias del día* (The Daily News) (México: Gousen Edit., 1968). *Medusa*, 1968 (Englewood Cliffs, N.J.: Prentice-Hall, 1972); in *Teatro mexicano 1968*, edited by Antonio Magaña Esquivel (México: Aguilar, 1974), pp. 30-104. *Almanaque de Juárez* (Almanac of Juarez), 1969 (Monterrey, N.L.: Edit. Sierra Madre, 1972). *Acapulco los lunes* (Acapulco on Mondays), 1970 (Monterrey, N.L.: Edit. Sierra Madre, 1969). *Un vals sin fin sobre el planeta* (An Endless Waltz on the Planet), 1970. "Los novios" (The Sweethearts), comedy for film, 1970. *Las cartas de Mozart* (Mozart's Letters), México, 1975. *La educastradora*, adaptation of play by Robert Althayne, México, 1977. *Un cuento de Navidad* (A Christmas Story), with "El censo" (The Census) (México: SEP/CONASUPO, 1980). *Tres comedias* (Three Plays) (*Un vals sin fin sobre el planeta*, *La danza que sueña la tortuga*, and *Felicidad*) (México: Extemporáneos, 1981). *¿Quién anda ahí?*, Oct. 15, 1982, more than 400 performances, SEP. *Orinoco*, 1982; with *Las cartas de Mozart* and *Felicidad* (México: EDIMUSA, 1985). *A la epopeya, un gajo* (To the Epic, a Broken-Off Branch) (Toluca: UAEM, 1983). *Tiempo de ladrones. La historia de Chucho el Roto* (Time of Thieves. The Story of Pooch the Broken), 1985 (México: Grijalbo, 1983). Plays in Anthologies: "El censo," in *12 obras en un acto*, selection and prologue by Wilberto Cantón (México: Finisterre, 1967), pp. 55-66. "El relojero de Córdoba," in *Literatura hispanoamericana del siglo XX*, edited by Homero Castillo and Audrey G. Castillo. *3 novelas, 3 novelas cortas, 3 piezas teatrales* (New York: Holt, Rinehart and Winston, 1970), pp. 131-83; in *El teatro de Vinohrady* (Prague, Czechoslovakia: Segundo Festival Internacional Cervantino en Guanajuato, 1974). "La lente maravillosa," "Guillermo y el Nahua," and "Las lámparas del cielo y de la tierra," in *El arca de Noé*, prologue and selection 1874, 1979, pp. 99-110, 191-214, 231-72. "Yo también hablo de la rosa," en *9 dramaturgos hispanoamericanos* (Ottawa, Canada: Girol Books, 1979). "Un pequeño día de ira," in *Teatro de la Revolución Mexicana*, pp. 1337-67. "La fonda de las siete cabrillas," "Los dos catrines," and "Sainetes y mojigangas," in *Teatro para adolescentes*, pp. 159-96, 203-10, 235-85. "Apolonio y Bodoconio," "Nahui Ollin," "Nora," in *Teatro para obreros*, pp. 27-40, 137-55, 221-41. "Sucedido de ranas y sapos," in *Jardín con animales*, pp. 65-80. Short Stories in Journals: "La caja vacía," *Revista Mexicana de Literatura* 6 (July-Aug. 1956): 535-42. "La desterrada," *Revista de la UNAM* 2 (Oct. 1956): 7-10; in *Anuario del Cuento Mexicano 1962*, pp. 68-78. "La paz después del combate," *La Palabra y el Hombre* 10 (Apr.-Jun. 1959): 247-55; in *Anuario del Cuento Mexicano 1959*, pp. 40-48. "Los prodigiosos" *El Libro y el Pueblo* 2-3 (Oct. 1959-Mar. 1960): 43-49. "Las conferencias," *México en la Cultura* 592 (July 18, 1960): 3. "Cubilete," *Mexico en la Cultura* 665 (Dec. 10, 1961): 3-4. "Por celebrar del infante...," *Diorama de la Cultura* (Dec. 23, 1979): 4-6. "Christmas Eve in Highland Park," in *Sábado* 321 (Dec. 24, 1983): 4. Essays in Journals: "Olivia Zúñiga, *Retrato de una niña triste*." in *Revista Mexicana de Cultura* 220 (June 17, 1951): 11. "El opus uno de José Giacoman," in *Prometeus* 2, 2 (March 1952): 121-22. "Ricardo Cortés Tamayo, *Sonata María de los Angeles de Teul*," in *Revista Mexicana de Cultura* 291 (Oct. 26, 1952): 10. "Lázaro Meldicú, *Columpio*," in *Revista Mexicana de Cultura*

301 (Jan. 4, 1953): 10. "Raúl Cervantes Ahumada, *Napalá*," in *Revista Mexicana de Cultura* 303 (Jan. 18, 1953): 10. "Enríque Azcoaga, *El poema de los tres carros*," in *Revista Mexicana de Cultura* 306 (Feb. 8, 1953) 12. "Salvador Novo, *Las aves en la poesía castellana*," in *Revista Mexicana de Cultura* 349 (Dec. 6, 1953): 12. "Ficción" (Sergio Galindo, *Polvos de arroz:* L. J. Hernández, *Los huéspedes reales*, in *Revista Mexicana de Literatura* 1 (Jan.-Mar. 1959): 75-77. "La amenaza número uno del teatro mexicano. La estulticia del inefable licenciado Peredo," in *México en la Cultura* 540 (July 20, 1959): 9. "Kiyoshi Takahashi. Su encuentro con lo mexicano," in *México en la Cultura* 555 (Nov. 1, 1959): 7. "La poca digna agonía del teatro mexicano," in *México en la Cultura* 563 (Dec. 27, 1959): 8. "Que trata de gobernantes y escritores," in *Revista de la UNAM* 7 (Mar. 1960): 10. "*Terror y miserias del Tercer Reich*" (Brecht), in *México en la Cultura* 577 (Apr. 3, 1960): 8. "*El Bordo,* la nueva novela de Sergio Galindo," in *México en la Cultura* 601 (Sept. 18, 1960): 4; *Sábado* 321 (Dec. 24, 1983): 4. "Comentario a las leyes de la censura previa mexicana," *Revista Mexicana de Literatura* 5-8 (May-Aug, 1961): 29-36. "El auge de la novela japonesa. Conversación con Saburo Shiroyama," *México en la Cultura* 639 (June 11, 1961): 3-4. "Nuevamente, Sabines" (*Diario semanario y poemas en prosa*), *México en la Cultura* 642 (July 7, 1961): 5. "El teatro de Osvaldo Dragún," *México en la Cultura* 663 (Nov. 26, 1961): 7, 9. "Selec. de fragmentos de *Poética*, de Aristóteles," *Revista de la Escuela de Arte Teatral* 5 (INBA, 1962): 7-22. "Rosario Castellanos," *El Centavo* 58 (Feb. 1964): 23. "Acerca de *Las tentaciones de María Egipciaca*," *La Cultura en México* 284 (July 26, 1967): xv. "Novo, maestro," *Revista Mexicana de Cultura* 1061 (July 30, 1967): 6. "Tenemos abandonados a los jóvenes dramaturgos," *El Gallo Ilustrado* 477 (Aug. 5, 1971): 13. "Griselda Gámbaro o modos de hacernos pensar en la manzana," *Revista Iberoamericana* 73 (Oct.-Dec. 1970): 629-34. "Guillermina Bravo. ¿Quién le quita lo bailado?," *La Cultura en México* 602 (Aug. 22, 1973): ix-x. "También los autores somos pueblo...," *Siempre!* 1059 (Oct. 10, 1973): 2, 69. "Identidad y universalidad en la dramaturgia latinoamericana," *Tramoya* 12 (July-Sept. 1978): 88-90. "Teatro campesino en Nueva York," *Tramoya* 16 (July-Sept. 1979): 53-55. "México en su corazón," *Tramoya* 17 (Oct.-Dec. 1979): 38-43. "Sobre creación colectiva," *Tramoya* 20 (July-Sept. 1980): 34-36. "Entrevista a Marta Palau," *La Semana de Bellas Artes* 173 (Mar. 25, 1981): 10-11. "Guillermina Bravo. Album biográfico," *La Semana de Bellas Artes* 199 (Sept. 23, 1981): 4-6. "Una ílusión..." (Efrén Hernández), *Tramoya* 23, (Jan.-Mar. 1982): 101-2. "Se inauguró muestra de teatro en la UAM," *El Heraldo de México* (Oct. 17, 1982): 2C. "La puesta en escena de *La historia del soldado*," *Proceso* 317 (Nov. 29, 1982): 56-57. "Escuela para escándalo" *Sábado* 277 (Feb. 26, 1983): 9. "Reflexiónes sobre Tina Modotti...," *Sábado* 291 (June 4, 1983): 6. "El saco ajeno de De Ita" *Unomásuno* (Aug. 27, 1983): 2. "Homenaje a Hidalgo," *Sábado* 307 (Sept. 17, 1983): 1-2. "Rafael Elizondo (1930-1984)," *México en el Arte* 9 (Summer 1985): 21-22. Novels in Journals: "Las visitaciones del diablo," frag., *La Palabra y el Hombre* (Apr.-June 26, 1963): 299-307; *Revista Mexicana de Literatura* 9-10 (Sept.-Oct. 1963): 25-30; *El Heraldo Cultural* 1 (Nov. 14, 1965): 8-9. "Cinco maneras de perder el tren," *Diálogos* 117 (May-June 1984): 39-45. Poetry in Journals: "Nocturno iluminado" and "Atrás los siglos," *América* 59 (Feb. 1949): 118-24. "La creación," "Viejo corrido de la muerte y el caballero," and "Valsecito," *América* 60 (May 1949) 207-11. "Nocturno de Córdoba," "Limpio está el aire de la noche," *Fuensanta* 7 (June 31, 1949): 3. "Constelaciones y derrumbes," *Fuensanta* 9-10 (Aug.-Sept. 1949): 4. "Glosa y resolución," *América*, 64, Dec. 1950, pp. 36-37. "La semana," "En que da excusas y explicaciones a una rosa," *El Caracol Marino* 9 (Jan. 1955); in *Anuario de*

la Poesía Mexicana 1955, pp. 39-41. Plays in Journals: "Auto sacramental de la zona intermedia," *América* 58 (Nov.-Dec. 1948): 73-112. "Auto de la triple porfía," *México en el Arte* 8 (1949): n.p. "Medalla al mérito," *América* 61 (Aug. 1949): 201-14. "El triángulo sutil, farsa para *snobs* en un acto," *América* 63 (Feb. 1950): 181-86. "'El lugar y la hora,' pieza en un acto," *América* 65 (Apr. 1951): 123-30. "Rosalba y los Llaveros," *México en la Cultura* 149 (Dec. 9, 1951): 2; 150 (Dec. 16, 1951): 2; 151 (Dec. 23, 1951): 2; 152 (Dec. 30, 1951): 2. "Selaginela," *Prometeus* 1 (Dec. 1951): 61-65; *Revista Mexicana de Cultura* 348 (Nov. 29, 1953): 3. "El lugar y la hora," *Revista Mexicana de Cultura* 257 (Mar. 2, 1952): 8-9; 258 (Mar. 9, 1952): 8-9; 259 (Mar. 16, 1952): 8-9. "Ermesinda," *Prometeus* 4 (July 1952): 42-44 (performed in 1952). "Parásitas," *Revista Mexicana de Cultura* 288 (Oct. 5, 1952): 3, 6. "Misa primera," *Estaciones* 4 (Winter 1956): 570-77. "El censo," *La Palabra y el Hombre* 1 (Jan.-Mar. 1957): 98-110. "El suplicante," in collaboration with Sergio Magaña, *Revista de la UNAM* 4 (Dec. 1958): 8-11. "Las estatuas de marfil. Acto III," *México en la Cultura* 579 (Apr. 17, 1959, 5, 7. "Pastores de la ciudad," in collaboration with Luisa Josefina Hernández, *La Palabra y el Hombre* 12 (Oct.-Dec. 1959): 625-52. "La perfecta casada," *La Palabra y el Hombre* 20 (Oct.-Dec. 1961): 685-91. "Una tarde de ira," *Casa de las Américas* 10 (Jan.-Feb. 1962): 43-86; "Un pequeño día de ira," *Ovaciones* suppl. 180 (June 21, 1965): 1-3. "Medusa," *México en la Cultura* 691 (June 10, 1962): 10. "Teseo," *La Palabra y el Hombre* 24 (Oct.-Dec. 1962): 651-73; *México en la Cultura* 711 (Nov. 4, 1962): 4. "Silencio, pollos pelones, ya les van a echar su máiz," *La Palabra y el Hombre* 31 (July-Sept. 1964): 509-71. "Te juro Juana, que tengo ganas...," *La Palabra y el Hombre* 35 (July-Sept. 1965): 487-530. "Yo también hablo de la rosa," *Revista de Bellas Artes* 6 (Nov.-Dec. 1965): 5-22. "Antes cruzaban los ríos," *Revista de Bellas Artes* 14 (Mar.-Apr. 1967): 4-7. "Las noticias del día," *IPN* (Mar. 1967); also in *El Heraldo de Espectáculos* 127 (Apr. 28, 1968): 11-13. "La adoración de los magos," in collaboration with Rosario Castellanos *Revista de Bellas Artes* 24 (Nov.-Dec. 1968): 17-54. "8 1/2," comedy in one act, in collaboration with Jesús Assaf, *El Heraldo de Espectáculos* 212 (Dec. 7, 1969): 12-14. "Acapulco, los lunes. Algunas escenas en entredicho," *Diorama de la Cultura* (Apr. 26, 1970): 5. "El final de un idilio," *Revista de la UNAM* 6 (Feb. 1971). "Una rosa con otro nombre," *La Palabra y el Hombre* 1 (Jan.-Mar. 1972): 63-70; *Revista de Bellas Artes* 16 (July-Aug. 1974): 40-47. "Delicioso domingo," *Sagitario* 2 (Feb. 1972); 5-25; *La Cultura en México* 546 (July 26, 1972): iii-iv. "La fonda de las siete cabrillas," adaption of *Don Bonifacio* by Manuel Eduardo de Gorostiza, prólogue by Emilio Carballido, *Revista de Bellas Artes* 19 (Jan.-Feb. 1975): 50-64. "Dificultades," obra en un acto, con nota biobibliográfica, *La Semana de Bellas Artes* 4 (Dec. 31, 1977): 10-11. "Dos obras y un modelo," *Tramoya* 10 (Jan.-Mar. 1978): 105-13. "¡Unete, pueblo!," *La Semana de Bellas Artes* 21 (Apr. 1978): 14-15. Nahui Ollin," *Los Universitarios* 139-140 (Mar. 1979): 5-8. "Hoy canta el fénix en nuestro gallinero," *Revista de la UNAM* 10 (June 1980): 18-23. "Los días," obra en un acto, *Casa del Tiempo* 6 (Feb. 1981): 27-31. "Nora," *Diálogos* 99 (May-June 1981): 30-36. "El invisible," *Casa del Tiempo* 11 (July 1981): xlvi-xlvii. "Conmemorantes," *La Palabra y el Hombre* 41 (Jan.-Mar. 1982): 37-41. "Cuento de Navidad," *El Gallo Ilustrado* 1070 (Dec. 26, 1982): 17-18. "5 obras en un acto" ("Estufas," La pandilla maldita," "Una pequeña serenata," "Firmeza del paisaje" and "Se acabó el tiempo del amor"), *Repertorio* 8-9 (Dec. 1982-Jan. 1983): 1-43. "Dos obras inéditas de Emilio Carballido" ("Estufas" and "Conmemorantes"), *El Gallo Ilustrado* 1078 (Feb. 20, 1983): 6-8. "Yo también hablo de la rosa," fragment, *El Gallo Ilustrado* 1094 (June 12, 1983): 17. "¿Quién anda ahí?," *México en el Arte* 4 (Spring 1984): 33-37.

Translation: "Borges. Por primera vez en español uno de sus poemas ingleses," version by J. E. Pacheco and Emilio Carballido, *México en la Cultura* 543 (Aug. 9, 1959): 1.

BIBLIOGRAPHY: Alejandro Acevedo Valenzuela, "El tren que nos llevó" (*El tren que corría*), *La Guía* 172, 11 (Jan. 1985): 4. Marco Antonio Acosta, "Charla con Emilio Carballido," *Revista Mexicana de Cultura* 198 (Nov. 12. 1972): 3; "Foro escénico. *Las cartas de Mozart*," *Revista Mexicana de Cultura* 359 (Dec. 21, 1975): 7; "Emilio Carballido y el teatro político," *Revista Mexicana de Cultura* 397 (Sept. 12, 1976): 6; "Dos novelas de Emilio Carballido," *El Nacional* (Apr. 9, 1981): 21; "Madurez de Emilio Carballido en su nueva obra teatral," *Revista Mexicana de Cultura* 147 (Oct. 3, 1982): 7. Enrique Aguilar, "Las charlas de fantasía" (*Los zapatos de (fierro)*, *La Guía* 152 (Aug. 24, 1984): 11; "Ficción, destreza y buen humor" (*El tren que corría), El Semanario Cultural* 130 (Oct. 14, 1984): 3. Marco Tulio Aguilera Garramuño, "Alegría de la condición humana..." *(Orinoco), Excelsior* (Jan. 16, 1983): 4. Sandra Altamirano, "El teatro mexicano, *Revista Mexicana de Cultura* 98 (Nov. 18, 1979): 4. Antonio Alvear Olea, "La SEP debería cerrar el Centro de Capacitación de Televisa," *El Nacional* (May 2, 1984): 6. Anon., "*La danza que sueña la tortuga*," *Cuadernos de Bellas Artes* 7-8 (July-Aug. 1962): 126; "La caja vacía," *Cuadernos de Bellas Artes* 1 (Jan. 1963): 90; *Tiempo* 1082 (Jan. 1963); "Los libros al día. *Yo también hablo de la rosa*," *La Cultura en México* 249 (Nov. 23, 1966): xix; *Revista de Bellas Artes* 14 (Mar.-Apr. 1967): 95-96; "Teatro" *(Te juro Juana que tengo ganas)*, *Siempre!* 746 (Oct. 11, 1967): 46-48; "La figura de la semana: Emilio Carballido," *El Heraldo de Espectáculos* 112 (Jan. 7, 1968): 2; "*Medusa*," *Acanto* 2 (Feb. 1969): 70; "Diálogo con Emilio Carballido: *Medusa* es un tipo de teatro que ya no hago, no sé si insistiré," *El Nacional* (Apr. 24, 1969): 8; "Víctor Moya consideró inmoral la obra *Acapulco, los lunes*," *Excelsior* (Apr. 18, 1970)): 6D; "Galería de dramaturgos. Emilio Carballido," *Revista de la Semana* (Feb. 20, 1972): 2; "Obra de Emilio Carballido presentada en el Teatro del Este de París" (*Yo también hablo de la rosa), Excelsior* (Nov. 30, 1973): 13B; "Cuatro en una sola pieza," *La Gaceta de Cuba* 157 (June 1977): 23; "Existe corrupción 'hasta sexual': Emilio Carballido," *Unomásuno* 7 (Nov. 21, 1977): 23; "Estudia Cancino obras de Ibargüengoitia, y Magaña para filmarlas en 79," *Unomásuno* 22 (Dec. 1978): 16; "Estrenan hoy" *(El día que se soltaron los leones)*, *Unomásuno* (Nov. 15, 1978): 18; "Emilio Carballido presenta hoy nuevo libro de teatro en Bellas Artes" *(26 obras de teatro*: 4th ed. of *D.F.*), *Unomásuno* (Apr. 10, 1979): 21; "Emilio Carballido: La exclusión de cartelera significa una demolición de autores nacionales. Presentó su nuevo libro: *D.F. 26 obras de teatro*," *Unomásuno* (Apr. 12, 1979): 19; "Presentarán hoy obras de teatro infantil" ("La lente maravillosa"), *Excelsior* (May 20, 1979): 4B; "Es necesario una vida teatral más sólida: Emilio Carballido," *Gaceta UNAM* 43, 25 (June 1979): 28; "Las Más representativas" *(Teatro), El Sol de México en la Cultura* 281 (Feb. 17, 1980): vii; "En España es más importante crear público de teatro que teatro: Emilio Carballido," *Unomásuno* (July 17, 1980): 19; "Participación de México en el II Festival de teatro latinoamericano en Nueva York," *Excelsior* (Aug. 20, 1980): 1C; "El autor y su obra: *El arca de Noé*," *El Correo del Libro* 24 (Nov. 15, 1980): 2; *La Onda* 397 (Jan. 18, 1981): 17; "Emilio Carballido dirige otra obra teatral..." (de Alejandro Licona), *El Día*, (Feb. 8, 1981): 19; "Entre los escolares hay una gran capacidad teatral: Emilio Carballido," *Excelsior* (Nov. 16, 1981): 8; "Homenaje a Emilio Carballido," *Excelsior* (Dec. 4, 1981): 11C, 16C; (Dec. 6, 1981): 10B; "*Orinoco*... se irá a España," *El Sol de México en la Cultura*

(Sept. 5, 1982): 1D; "...Emilio Carballido estrena" *(Orinoco)*, *Proceso* 305 (Sept. 6, 1982): 56; "La obra *D.F. 2 a.m.* llegó a las 200 representaciones," *Excelsior* (Sept. 15, 1982): 19B; "Piden los dramaturgos que otorgue el IMSS sus teatros para obras mexicanas," *Proceso* 329 (Feb. 21, 1983): 58-59; *"Orinoco," Siempre!* 1549 (Mar. 2, 1983): 50; "Sabor a río Papaloapan" *(Los zapatos de fierro)*, *El Sol de México en la Cultura* 456 (July 10, 1983): i, viii; *"Más teatro joven,"* *Nexos* 68 (Aug. 1983): 61; "La crítica, fenómeno de reflexión más a menos profunda: Emilio Carballido," *Excelsior* (Dec. 6, 1983): 6 Cult.; "Aportación original," *El Sol de México en la Cultura* 479 (Dec. 18, 1983): i-ii; "Pastorela de Emilio Carballido, montada por trabajadores del IMSS," *El Sol de México en la Cultura* (Dec. 24, 1983): 2 Cult.; "Ciudad con 'collage' dramático" *(D.F. 26 obras en un acto)*, *El Sol de México en la Cultura* 486 (Feb. 5, 1984): vii; "Obras de Brecht y Emilio Carballido en Costa Rica," *Unomásuno* (Mar. 4, 1984): 15; "Ataque y contra ataque de la provincia" *(Rosalba y los Llaveros)*, *El Sol de México en la Cultura* 493 (Mar. 25, 1984): i, vi; "Estreno teatral con Emilio Carballido," *El Nacional* (June 19, 1984): 6; "No hay meta" *(El tren que corría)*, *El Sol de México en la Cultura* 506 (June 24, 1984): v; "Se inició en Tabasco el rodaje de *Orinoco,"* *El Día* (July 19, 1984): 22; "Emilio Carballido: la muestra, un logro político," *Unomásuno* (July 23, 1984): 17; "Obras de Emilio Carballido..." *(Chucho el Roto),"* *La Jornada* (Sept. 21, 1984): 25; "Producirá la Cía. Nal. de Teatro la obra *Tiempo de ladrones,"* *Excelsior* (Sept. 22, 1984): 10B; *"El tren que corría,* un libro distinto," *Punto* 101 (Oct. 8-14, 1984): 22; "Vuelve...*Tiempo de ladrones,"* *Excelsior* (Jan. 10, 1985): 1B, 3B; "En Villahermosa fue la premiere de *Orinoco,"* *El Nacional* (Apr. 21, 1985): 8, 4th. Sect; "Homenaje a Emilio Carballido por sus 60 años de vida," *El Día* (Apr. 23, 1985): 23 Espectáculos; "Afirma Emilio Carballido: *Fotografía en la playa* me ha dado gran satisfacción," *La Cultura al Día* (June 8, 1985): 2; "Emilio Carballido presentó su antología de teatro infantil: *Jardín con animales,"* *La Cultura al Día* (Sept. 12, 1985): 3. Guadalupe Appendini, "Casa de conciliación del espíritu es la Academia: Yáñez" (Emilio Carballido propuesto para ocupar el sillón que dejó vacante Salvador Novo), *Excelsior* (Sept. 18, 1976): 1B- 3B. Ludovico Arrieta, "Emilio Carballido y la timidez de la subversión," *Diorama de la Cultura* (Aug. 22, 1976): 12-13. Norberto Asenjo, "Hay que eliminar la mentalidad empresarial de los funcionarios relacionados con la cultura: Emilio Carballido," *El Nacional* (Jan. 25, 1984): 7, 3rd. Sect.; "Los dramaturgos mexicanos dispuestos a recuperar espacios...: Emilio Carballido," *El Nacional* (Aug. 21, 1984): 6; *"Jardín con animales...,"* *El Nacional* (Sept. 12, 1985): p. 6, 2nd Sect. Patricia Avila, "Un deleite...*Tiempo de ladrones,"* *Punto* 67 (Feb. 13-19, 1984): 21. Juan Antonio Ayala, *"El tren que corría,"* *El Sol de México en la Cultura* 137 (Dec. 2, 1984): 3. Esther Barbará, "Teatro," *Revista de Literatura Argentina e Iberoamericana* 2 (1960): 141-42. Angel Bárcenas, *"Lazona intermedia,"* *Revista Mexicana de Cultura* 278 (July 27, 1952): 10; *"Teatro* de Emilio Carballido," *Revista Mexicana de Cultura* 996 (May 1, 1966): 10; "La rosa y Emilio Carballido" *(Yo también hablo de la rosa)*, *Revista Mexicana de Cultura* 1027 (Dec. 4, 1966): 15; "Libros. *Te juro Juana...,"* *Revista Mexicana de Cultura* 1072 (Oct. 15, 1967); "Novelas mexicanas en Uruguay" *(El Norte)* *Revista Mexicana de Cultura* 1082 (Dec. 24, 1967): 15; "Apostillas de Emilio Carballido al teatro para niños," *El Nacional* (June 19, 1974): 15; *"Las cartas de Mozart,* ¿nos hallamos ante la mejor obra de Emilio Carballido?," *El Nacional* (July 20, 1974): 15; "Libros de la Universidad Veracruzana" *(La veleta oxidada, El Norte)*, *El Nacional* (Jan. 19, 1981): 17. Cristina Barrera, "Entrevista con Emilio Carballido," *El Libro y la Vida* 27 (July 19, 1970): 8-9. Fernando Belmont, "Emilio Carballido: de más locales depende que el teatro sobreviva," *Unomásuno* (Sept. 13, 1982): 18; "Nuestro teatro depende de múltiples insatisfacciones: Emilio Carballido," *Unomásuno* (Oct. 15, 1983): 17; "Desde el Cervantino, *Tiempo de ladrones*," *Unamásuno* Nov. 10, 1984): 18; "Emilio Carballido, sobre el tema de los luchadores...," *Unomásuno* (July 27, 1985): 19; (July 28, 1985): 18. María Elvira Bermúdez, "Emilio Carballido y Luisa Josefina," *(D.F.)*, *Diorama de la Cultura* (Nov. 18, 1962): 4; "Novelas mexicanas en 1965" *(Las visitaciones...) Diorama de la Cultura* (Jan. 9, 1966): 3, 5; "Un cuento maravilloso" *(Los zapatos de fierro)*, *Revista Mexicana de Cultura* 20 (July 10, 1983): 12; "Novelas en 1984" *(El tren que corría) Revista Mexicana de Cultura* 85 (Dec. 23, 1984): 10. Jacqueline Eyring Bixler, "Freedom and Fantasy: A Structural Approach to the Fantastic in Emilio Carballido's *Las cartas de Mozart*," *Latin American Theater Review* 14, 1 (Fall 1980): 15-23; "Emilio Carballido and the Epic Theatre: *Almanaque de Juárez*," *Crítica Hispánica* 1 (1980): 13-28; "Theory and Technique in Selected Plays of Emilio Carballido (1968-1978)," Ph.D. Diss., University of Kansas, 1982; "Myth and Romance in Emilio Carballido's *Conversación entre las ruinas*," *HJ* 1 (Fall 1984) 21-36; "The Family Portrait: Dramatic Contextuality in Emilio Carballido's *Un vals sin fin sobre el planeta and Fotografía en la playa*," *Chasqui* 1 (Nov. 1984): 66-85; "A Theatre of Contradictions: The Recent Works of Emilio Carballido," *Latin American Theater Review* 18, 2 (Spring 1985): 56-66. "Historical and Artistic Self-Consciousness in Carballido's *José Guadalupe (Las glorias de Posada)*," in *Mester* 17, 1 (Spring 1988): 15-27. Pedro Bravo-Elizondo, "*Una tarde de ira*," in *Teatro hispanoamericano de crítica social* (Madrid: Playor, 1975) John S. Brushwood, "*The Norther*, trad. de Margaret Sayers Peden," *Review 69* New York (1970): 73-74; *México en su novela*, pp. 64, 65, 70, 90, 103-04, 121-22; *La novela hispanoamericana...*, pp. 236-37. Miguel Bustos Cercedo, "Nuevas corrientes," *La creación...* (Xalapa: Editora del Gobierno, 1977): vol. 2, pp. 373-84. Angelina Camargo, "No es mi preocupación buscar la identidad...: Emilio Carballido," *Excelsior* (Oct. 9, 1981): 2-3 Cult.; "La esencia nacional se lleva adentro...: Emilio Carballido," *Excelsior* (Oct.15, 1981): 2 Cult,; "Emilio Carballido alaba la labor de la OSN en Oaxaca," *Excelsior* (Mar. 22, 1983): 1; "Emilio Carballido y la literatura infantil" *(Los zapatos de fierro)*, *Excelsior* (Sept. 6, 1983): 5; "El dramaturgo presenta al popular bandido como un anarquista con ideas socialistas. Chucho el Roto, francotirador...: Emilio Carballido," *Excelsior* (Dec. 20, 1983): 5 Cult.; "Los trenes han sido la sangre de México...: Emilio Carballido" "Nueva novela de Emilio Carballido" *(El tren que corría), Excelsior* (Aug. 4, 1984): 4, 6 Cult.; "Ecos cervantinos" *(Tiempo de ladrones), Excelsior* (Nov. 10, 1984): 6. Antonio Camrgo Ríos, "Resurge el mito de Chucho el Roto," *El Nacional* (Nov. 10, 1984): 6. Federico Campbell, "La multiplicidad de relaciones" *(El sol)*, *La Cultura en México* 465 (Jan. 6, 1971): v. Marco Antonio Campos, "Emilio Carballido y Mario Vargas Llosa" *(Los zapatos de fierro) (Proceso* 351 (July 25, 1983): 59-61. Bernardo Candal, "Dramaturgia Nacional: un caso extraño. Nuevos premios para escritores," *El Día* (Apr. 10, 1984): 22. Wilberto Cantón, "*Un pequeño día de ira*," *Excelsior* (Aug. 3, 1976): 1, 5 Espectáculos; "Teatro, *D.F.*," *Excelsior* (May 23, 1978): 4B; "El autor y la obra" *(Un pequeño día de ira)*, in *Teatro de la Revolución Mexicana*, pp. 1333-36. Manuel Capetillo, "Teatro. De una muerte por coraje" *(Las cartas de Mozart)*, *El Sol de México en la Cultura* 58 (Nov. 9, 1975): 14-15; "*El día que se soltaron los leones*," *El Sol de México en la Cultura* 218 (Dec. 3, 1978): 11; "Homenaje Nacional al dramaturgo Emilio Carballido," *El Sol de México en la Cultura* 376 (Dec. 20, 1981): 6; "*Felicidad*", *El Sol de México en la Cultura* 460 (Aug. 7, 1983): 3; "Teatro. Importancia de *Tiempo de ladrones*," *Unomásuno* (Nov. 28, 1984): 15; (Dec. 5, 1984):

17. Miguel Capistrán, "Carballido, folletinista," *Diorama de la Cultura* (Dec. 12, 1965):
7. Emmanuel Carballo, "Emilio Carballido, narrador," *La Cultura en México* 191 (Oct.
13, 1965): xvii; "Diario público de... Emilio Carballido y Galindo" *(El Norte)*, *Diorama
de la Cultura* (Dec. 31, 1967): 5; "Revaloración antológica. Cuentistas mexicanos de
hoy," *Diorama de la Cultura* (Apr. 6, 1969): 6. Patricia Cardona, "Un buen Gorostiza
es mejor que un plomizo y confuso Shakespeare: Emilio Carballido," *Unomásuno*
(Nov. 16, 1979): 17; "No creo que en nuestro medio existan más de tres personas que
hagan crítica teatral: Emilio Carballido," *Unomásuno* (June 18, 1980): 16; "Existe un
creciente deterioro en la administración de las artes en México, indicó Emilio
Carballido," *Unomásuno* (July 24, 1982): 22. Roberto Cardoso, "Mojiganga de Emilio
Carballido...," *El Nacional* (June 5, 1984): 9. Rosario Castellanos, "Obras de Emilio
Carballido" and "Establecimiento del diálogo," in *Juicios sumarios*, pp. 45-46. Fausto
Castillo, *"Felicidad,"* *México en la Cultura* 627 (Mar. 19, 1961): 7. Ricardo Castillo
Mireles, "Emilio Carballido defiende su período como director de la Escuela de
Teatro del INBA," *El Sol de México*, (July 22, 1976): 9A. Gustavo A. Cervantes,
"Emilio Carballido y su compromiso," *El Nacional* Nov. 21, 1979): 17. Francesca
Colecchia, "Emilio Carballido, *The Golden Thread and Other Plays*, trad. de Margaret
Sayers Peden, Austin, University of Texas Press, 1970," *Revista Iberoamericana* 75
(April-June 1971): 464. José Luis Colín, "Entrevista. En el escenario, Emilio
Carballido," *El Sol de México en la Cultura* 71 (Feb. 8, 1976): 4-5. José Francisco
Conde Ortega, *"Tiempo de ladrones,"* in *Abside* (Oct. 1, 1984): 5. Eladio Cortés, "Dos
antologías" *(Teatro joven* and *El arca de Noé)*, *Tramoya* 14 Jan.-March 1979): 101-2;
"Las novelas cortas de Emilio Carballido: Temática y técnica," in *LA CHISPA '87:
Selected Proceedings*, edited by Gilbert Paolini (New Orleans: Tulane University Press,
1987); "La ironía social en el primer teatro de Emilio Carballido," in *De literatura
hispánica*, edited by Eladio Cortés (México: EDIMUSA, 1989), pp. 45-54; "El aspecto
humorístico en la novelística de Carballido," in *De literatura hispánica* (México:
EDIMUSA, 1989), pp. 55-64. Sandra Messinger Cypess, *"Tres obras,"* *Hispamérica* 23-
24 (Aug.-Dec. 1979): 192-95; "I, too, speak..." *(Yo también hablo de la rosa)*, *Latin
American Theatre Review* 18, 1 (Fall, 1984): 45-52; "Changing Configurations of Power
from the Perspective of Mexican," in *Drama, Ideologies, and Literature: Journal of
Hispanic and Lusophone Discourse Analysis* 2, 2 (Fall 1987): 109-23. Frank Dauster,
"Teatro," *Revista Iberoamericana* 50 (July-Dec. 1960): 347-48; "El teatro de Emilio
Carballido," *La Palabra y el Hombre* 23 (July-Sept. 1962): 369-84; in *Ensayos sobre
teatro hispanoamericano* (Sept. 1975) (SepSetentas, 208): 127-42. *"Tiempo de ladrones,
tiempo de libertad,"* in *Crítica Hispánica* 8, 1 (1986): pp. 19-26; *"Fotografía en la playa*:
Rosalba Thirty Years Later," in *In Retrospect: Essays on Latin American Literature*,
edited by Elizabeth S. Rogers and Timothy J. Rogers (York, S.C.: Sp. Lit. Pubs. Co.,
1987). Juan Duch, "A mitad del Atlántico...," entrevista, *Siempre!* 1112 (Oct. 16,
1974): 44-45. Marta Aurora Espinosa, "Emilio Carballido crítica a 'Teatro de la
Nación' porque cierra sus puertas a autores mexicanos," *Unomásuno* (May 6, 1980):
21. Pablo Espinosa, "No creo tener un estilo personal de hacer teatro: Emilio
Carballido," *La Jornada* (Oct. 20, 1984): 24. Tomás Espinosa, "Telón" *(El relojero de
Córdoba), Su otro yo* (May 4, 1978): 4; "Emilio Carballido, el dramaturgo de
Córdoba," interview, *El Sol de México en la Cultura* 188 (May 7, 1978): 2-5; "Emilio
Carballido y los leones," *Diorama de la Cultura* (Dec. 10, 1978): 6; "El *D.F.* de Emilio
Carballido," *Diorama de la Cultura* (April 29, 1979): 3; *"Fotografía en la playa,"
Diorama de la Cultura* (Nov. 18, 1979): 3; "Medusa en la cueva," *Diorama de la
Cultura* (Nov. 9, 1980): 3; *"Orinoco,"* *El Nacional* (Oct. 2, 1982): 14; *"Tiempo de*

ladrones," *Revista Mexicana de Cultura* 43 (Dec. 18, 1983): 11; "*Te juro Juana que tengo ganas*," *Punto* 84 (June 11-17, 1984): 23; "*Tiempo de ladrones*," *Punto* 117 (Jan.28-Feb. 3, 1985): 20-21. José Estrada, "*Te juro Juana que tengo ganas* la farsa y la picaresca," *La Cultura en México* 300 (Nov. 15, 1967): xiv. Sadot Fabila H., "*Las visitaciones del diablo*, nueva obra de Carballido," *El Día* (Oct. 9, 1965): 9. Héctor Fontanar, "Nombres de México. Emilio Carballido, dramaturgo y novelista," *El Día* (July 17, 1964). Emilio Fuego, "Tenemos hambre de teatro mexicano, dice Emilio Carballido," *Excelsior* (Feb. 15, 1984): 8. José Luis Gallegos, "Representa la película *Orinoco*, el trabajo más trascendente que he desempeñado: Ana Luisa Peluffo," *Excelsior* (Dec. 12, 1984): 11. Héctor Gally, "*El Sol*," *La Cultura en México* 464 (Dec. 30, 1970): xii; "Emilio Carballido," in *30 cuentos de autores mexicanos*, p. 97. Adalberto García, "Hacia una organización de las obras de Emilio Carballido: Una perspectiva cronológica," *DAI* 47, 5 (Nov. 1986): 1738A-39A. Margarita García Flores, "Emilio Carballido: ¿alguien puede ser mexicano dos veces," *La Onda* 125 (Nov. 2, 1975): 6-7; in *Cartas marcadas* (UNAM, 1979): 179-86. Alejandra García Hernández, "Emilio Carballido: A partir de la muerte de Juárez comienza el deterioro político de nuestro país: el robo, la sinvergüenzada," *Unomásuno* (Jan. 31, 1984): 15. Juan García Ponce, "Teatro. *Felicidad, D.F.*," *Revista de la UNAM* (July 11, 1957): 26, 31; "*La hebra de oro*," *Revista de la UNAM* (Jan. 5, 1958): 29; "Dos dramaturgos mexicanos: Usigli y Carballido," *Artis* (Guatemala) 2 (July 1960). Juan García Ponce and José Luis Ibáñez, "Teatro: *Rosalba y los llaveros*," in *Revista de la UNAM* (Sept. 1, 1958): 27-28. Emilio García Riera, *Historia documental del cine mexicano*, vol. 5 (México: Eds. Era, 1974), p. 342; vol. 6, (1975), pp. 214, 215, 290, 321; vol. 8 (1977), pp. 39, 44, 46, 322, 325, 326. Juan Garibay Mora, "Emilio Carballido y su forja como comediógrafo...," *Excelsior* (Dec. 21, 1981): 1; (Dec. 22, 1981): 1. Margo Glantz, "Todos hablamos de la rosa," *La Cultura en México* 229 (July 6, 1966): viii. Alyce Golding Cooper, *Teatro mexicano contemporáneo* (México: UNAM, 1962), pp. 32-33, 48-52, 57-60, 109-18. Lourdes Gómez, "Para leerse en voz alta," *Punto* 119 (Feb. 11-17, 1985): 22-23. Andrés González Pagés, "Palabras con Emilio Carballido," *El Día* (March 30, 1964): 9. Javier González Rubio, "El teatro mexicano, perdido entre la búsquenda y la nostalgia," *Unomásuno* 45 (Dec. 30, 1977): 16-17. Celestino Gorostiza, *Teatro mexicano siglo XX* vol. 3 (México: FCE, 1956), pp. 133-34. Miguel Guardia, "El teatro en México, *Rosalba y los llaveros*," *México en la Cultura* 59 (March 19, 1950): 5; "El teatro en México. *El viaje de Nocresida*," *México en la Cultura* 226 (July 19, 1953): 2; "El teatro en México. *La hebra de oro*," *México en la Cultura* 376 (June 3, 1956): 4; "Obras premiadas... *Felicidad*," *Estaciones* 4 (Winter 1956): 598-600; "*Silencio pollos...*," *Diorama de la Cultura* (Feb. 23, 1964): 7; "*El relojero de Córdoba*," *Diorama de la Cultura* (Feb. 26, 1978): 8; "Homenaje a Emilio Carballido," *Diorama de la Cultura* (Dec. 27, 1981): 14; "*Orinoco...*," *Diorama de la Cultura* (Sept. 12, 1982): 14. Juan Guerrero Zamora, "Dramaturgos mexicanos vistos desde Europa," *México en la Cultura* 757 (Sept. 22, 1963): 4. Dagoberto Guillaumin Fentanes, Introduction a *Silencio pollos...Un pequeño día de ira. Acapulco, los lunes*, in *Tres obras* (Three Works) (with *Un pequeño día de ira* and *Acapulco, los lunes*) (México: Extemporáneos, 1978), pp. 5-9. Arturo Guzmán, "Vals, danza y felicidad" (*Tres comedias*), *Tiempo Libre* 75 (Oct. 16-22, 1981): 34. Olga Harmony, "Emilio Carballido: la escuela de teatro tiene hambre (económica) atrasada," *Diorama de la Cultura* (Sept. 23, 1973): 14; "*Orinoco*," *Unomásuno* (Feb. 16, 1983): 16. Alejandro Hermida, "Teatro mexicano actual...," *Proceso* 225 (Feb. 23, 1981): 39-50; "Emilio Carballido y Santander: censura y comercio...," *Excelsior* (Jan. 2, 1983): 3.

Luisa Josefína Hernández, "Emilio Carballido no duerme," *América* 65 (April 1951): n.p.; "*Felicidad*," *México en la Cultura* 436 (July 25, 1957): 8; "Tres novelas cortas de 1958" (*El Norte*), *Revista de la UNAM*, (June 10, 1959): 36-37; "*Silencio, pollos pelones...*," *Ovaciones* Suppl. 111 (Feb. 9, 1964): 6. Jorge A. Huerta, "The Influence of Latin American Theater on 'Teatro Chicano,'" in *Revista Chicano-Riqueña* 11, 1 (1983): 68-77. Jorge Ibargüengoitia, "Teatro. *Rosalba y los llaveros*," *La Cultura en México* (April 7, 1962): 1. María Idalia, "*Yo también hablo de la rosa*, en toda Francia," *Excelsior* (Oct. 23, 1973): 1-2; "También el español se partió como espejo, afirma Emilio Carballido" (*Orinoco*), *Excelsior* (April 15, 1983): 2B, 6B; "A precios populares *Te juro Juana que tengo ganas*," in *Excelsior* (May 17, 1984) 1B, 3B-4B; "El plaza para los concursos Celestino Gorostiza y Salvador Novo...," *Excelsior* (June 5, 1984): 1B, 3B; "Emilio Carballido comunica su madurez... en la obra *Fotografía en la playa*," *Excelsior* (Sept. 5, 1984): 1B, 7B. Fernando de Ita, "En verdad se soltaron los leones en la puesta en escena de Oceranski," *Unomásuno* (Nov. 23, 1978): 21; "...*Orinoco* Quiere ser un acto de amor a Venezuela y su gente," *Unomásuno* (Sept. 25, 1982): 26; "La Escuela de Arte Teatral...: Emilio Carballido," *Unomásuno* (Jan. 21, 1983): 17. José Agustín, "Reconsiderar su Obra," *Excelsior* (Dec. 11, 1981): 7A. R. A. Kerr, "La función de la intermediaria en *Yo también hablo de la rosa*," *Latin American Theatre Review* 12, 1 (Fall 1978): 51-60. Roberto Lago, "A propósito de *Rosalba y los llaveros*," *México en la Cultura* 61 (April 2, 1950): 5. Ruth S. Lamb, *Bibliografía del teatro mexicano del siglo XX* (México: Eds. de Andrea, 1962), pp. 37-39. Carlos Landeros, "Con los pollos pelones... En México, la censura es como mal de ojo," *El Día* (Feb. 11, 1964): 11. Luis Leal, *Bibliografía del cuento mexicano* (México: Eds. de Andrea, 1958), p. 33; "Notas sueltas sobre el teatro de Emilio Carballido," *Casa de las Américas* (May-June 30, 1965): 96-99; *Breve historia de la literatura hispanoamericana* (New York: Alfred A. Knopf, 1971), pp. 315-16, 361. Vicente Leñero, "Reseña teatral. *Las cartas de Mozart*," *Excelsior* (Nov. 6, 1975): 1C; "*Un pequeño día de ira*," *Excelsior*, (June 10, 1976). Oswaldo Augusto López, "*Un pequeño día de ira:* Crítica a la realidad social en su conjunto," *Latin American Theatre Review* 9, 1 (Fall 1975): 29-35. Malcolm Scott MacKenzie, "Emilio Carballido: An Ideational Evolution of His Theatre," in *DAI* 42, 4 (Oct. 1981): 1654A. Merry MacMasters, "Se estrenó *Fotografía en la playa*," *El Nacional* (July 31, 1984): 6. Enrique Macín Rascón, "Entrevista con Emilio Carballido," *Metamorfosis* (Feb. 12, 1981): 20-25. Mary Madiracca, "Temas clásicos en el teatro de Carballido," *Diorama de la Cultura* (Sept. 18, 1977): 6. Sergio Magaña, "Un triunfo de Emilio Carballido" (*La danza que sueña la tortuga*), *Diorama de la Cultura* (Oct. 23, 1955): 3. Antonio Magaña Esquivel, "Teatro...*Rosalba y los llaveros*," *Revista Mexicana de Cultura* 602 (Oct. 12, 1958): 12; "Los estímulos de Aristófanes en Azar, Emilio Carballido y Novo," *Revista Mexicana de Cultura* 815 (Nov. 11, 1962): 11; *Medio siglo de teatro mexicano 1900-1961* (México: INBA, 1964), pp. 134-35; "Buen momento del teatro mexicano" (*Silencio, pollos pelones...*), *Revista Mexicana de Cultura* 939 (March 28, 1965): 11; "El teatro. *Te juro Juana que tengo ganas*," *Revista Mexicana de Cultura* 1073 (Oct. 22, 1967): 11; "El teatro mexicano en 1967" (*Te juro Juana que tengo ganas*), *Revista Mexicana de Cultura* 1087 (Jan. 28, 1968): 11; "El teatro. Una excelente farsa de Emilio Carballido" (*Silencio pollos...*), *El Nacional*, Suppl. 10 (May 26, 1968): 11; "El mito griego del amor mortal" (*Medusa*), *El Nacional*, Suppl. 28, (Oct. 6, 1968): 11; "Realismo mágico de Emilio Carballido" *Revista Mexicana de Cultura* 68 (May 17, 1970): 7; "*Acapulco los lunes*, muestra a otor Emilio Carballido," *Revista Mexicana de Cultura* 77 (July 19, 1970): 7; "Emilio Carbillido," en *Teatro mexicano siglo XX*, vol. 5, 231-33; "México llegó a París" (*Yo también hablo de la rosa* puesta en Francia), *Revista Mexicana de Cultura* 57 (Nov. 4, 1973): 9; "Teatro. *Un pequeño día de ira*," *Revista Mexicana de Cultura* 383 (June 6, 1976): 7; "Emilio Carballido y su relojero de la Colonia," *Revista Mexicana de Cultura* 12 (March 26, 1978): 7. Antonio Magaña Esquivel and Ruth S. Lamb, *Breve historia del teatro mexicano* (México: Eds. de Andrea, 1958), pp. 143-44, 145-46. Adolfo Martínez Solórzano, "Emilio Carballido fue homenajeado por sus 60 años de vida," *El Nacional* (April 29, 1985): 6. Héctor Martínez Tamez, "El inesperado humor exacerbado," *La Onda* 183 (Dec. 12, 1976): 8. Eduardo Mejía, "Un retrato del *D.F.*," *La Guía* 143 (June 22, 1984): 10. Felipe Mejía, "Las visitaciones a la ciudad y la provincia vacía," *La Cultura en México* 1038 (Feb. 17, 1982): ix-xi. Juan Vicente Melo, "Emilio Carballido, *Las estatuas de marfil*," *Estaciones* 18 (Summer 1960): 120-22. Graciela Mendoza, "Entrevista al alimón. Héctor Azar y Emilio Carballido," *El Nacional* Suppl. (Aug. 23, 1968). María Luisa Mendoza, "*La danza que sueña la tortuga*," *El Gallo Ilustrado* 1 (July 1, 1962): 4; "*Silencio pollos...*," *El Gallo Ilustraado* 66 (Sept. 29, 1963): 4; "El teatro, *El relojero de Córdoba*," *El Gallo Ilustrado* 112 (Aug. 16, 1964): 4; "*Te juro Juana que tengo ganas*," *El Gallo Ilustrado* 300 (Nov. 15, 1967): 4; "Al fin aquella *Medusa*," *El Gallo Ilustrado* 327 (Sept. 29, 1968): 4. Margarita Mendoza López, "*Orinoco...*," *Revista Mexicana de Cultura* 2 (Feb. 27, 1983): 14; "¿Eds. de obras dramáticas mexicanas?," *Revista Mexicana de Cultura* 63 (May 6, 1984): 7. Teresa Miaja, "*Te juro Juana que tengo ganas*," *Revista Mexicana de Cultura* 81 (Sept. 9, 1984): 14. Tununa Mercado, "Cómo escriben los que escriben," *Revista de Revistas* 144 (March 5, 1975): 28. María del Carmen Millán, "La trilogía de Emilio Caballido" (sus tres primeras novelas), *Revista de Bellas Artes* 6 (Nov.-Dec. 1965): 81-82. Carlos Monsiváis, "*La hebra de oro*," *Estaciones* 10 (Summer 1958): 196-98. Francisco Monterde, "Teatro. *La hebra de oro*," *Revista de la UNAM* (June 10, 1956): 27-28. José Antonio Montero, "El premio de Emilio Carballido," *Ovaciones*, Suppl. 56 (Jan. 20, 1963): 5. Matías Montes Huidobro, "Zambullida en el *Orinoco* de Carballido," in *Latin American Theatre Review* 15, 2 (Spring 1982): 13-25. Juan Miguel de Mora, "*Yo también hablo de la rosa*," *El Heraldo Cultural* (April 25-30, 1966): 10-11; "*Te juro Juana que tengo ganas*," *El Heraldo Cultural* 101 (Oct. 15, 1967): 13; "La *Medusa* de Carballido," *El Heraldo Cultural* 152 (Oct. 6, 1968): 4-5. Felipe Morales, *200 personajes mexicanos* (México: Eds. Ateneo, 1952), pp. 69-70. Sonia Morales, "Homenaje mínimo al dramaturgo máximo," *Proceso* 269 (Dec. 28, 1981): 46-47; "Emilio Carballido rechaza el premio teatral 'Francois Baguer,' por cuestiones ideológicas...," *Proceso* 433 (Feb. 18, 1985): 52-53. Eugene L. Moretta, "Spanish American Theatre of the 50's and 60's: Critical Perspectives on Role Playing," *Latin American Theatre Review* 13, 2 (Spring, 1980): 5-30. Miriam Moscona, "La vida secreta de especies singulares," *México en el Arte* 2 (Fall 1983): 84. María Muro, "*Felicidad*. El pequeño mundo de la clase media," *Excelsior* (July 31, 1983): 3 Cult. Rita Murúa, "Una visión fragmentaria de la provincia mexicana" *Revista Mexicana de Literatura* 11-12 (Nov.-Dec. 1962): 78-81. Marciano Navarrete, "Sólo una obra extraordinaria en el teatro mexicano, en 1966" (*Yo también hablo de la rosa*), *Revista Mexicana de Cultura* 1034 (Jan. 22, 1967): 1. Salvador Novo, "Y hablaron lenguas diferentes," *Sábado* 368 (Nov. 3, 1984): 11. Pedro Raúl Ocampo, "El furor optimista" *Sábado* 258 (Oct. 16, 1982): 16. Jorge Olmo, "El teatro de Emilio Carballido," *Revista de la UNAM* (July 11, 1960): 29. Cristina Pacheco, "Emilio Carballido habla sobre la sexualidad explícita y el coyote ¿qué?," *Siempre!* 1291 (March 22, 1978): 30-31, 46-47, 70. José Emilio Pacheco, "Emilio Carballido: *D.F.*," *Estaciones* 6 (Summer 1957): 230;

"Nota sobre los cuentos de Emilio Carballido," *Revista Mexicana de Cultura* 294 (Sept. 15, 1974): 3. Adriana Padilla Avilla, "Emilio Carballido: el lenguaje de ciudad," *El Nacional* (April 14, 1979): 15. Beatriz Pagés Rebollar, "El tren del Huatusquillo, cumbre de la infancia de Emilio Carballido," *El Sol de México en la Cultura* 433 (Jan. 23, 1983):. 8. Armando Partida, "Entrevista con Emilio Carballido," *La Cabra* (May 8, 1978): 5-6; "El teatro. Personajes sin traza" (*Te juro Juana que...*) *El Sol de México en la Cultura* 125 (Sept. 9, 1984): 5; (Sept. 15, 1984): 5; "Familia en claroscuro: *Fotographia en la playa*," *El Sol de México en la Cultura* 129 (Oct. 7, 1984): 5. Federico Patán, "Emilio Carballido, *A la epopeya un gajo*," in *Sábado* 330 (Feb. 25, 1984): 11; "*El tren que corría*," in *Sábado* 362 (Oct. 6, 1984): 12-13. Margaret S. Peden, "Emilio Carballido, autor dramático. Su obra de 1948 a 1966," thesis, Missouri, 1966; "Tres novelas de Emilio Carballido," *La Palabra y el Hombre* 43 (July-Aug. 1967) 563-580; "Emilio Carballido, curriculum operum," *Latin American Theatre Review* 1, 1 (Fall 1967): 38-49; in *Texto Crítico* (Jan.-April 1976): 94-112; "Theory and Practice in Artaud and Emilio Carballido," *Modern Drama* 11 (1968): 132-42; "Emilio Carballido *Fotografía en la playa*," *Texto Crítico* 10 (May-Aug. 1978): 15-22; *Emilio Carballido* (Boston; Twayne, 1980); "Emilio Carballido. Curriculum operum," in *Orinoco. Las cartas de Mozart. Felicidad*, ed. cit., pp. 259-83. Lourdes Penella, "Te juro Emilio, que tengo...," *La Guía* 144 (June 29, 1984): 12; "Revelado en la playa" (*Fotografía en la playa*), *La Guía* 156 21 (Sept. 1984): 12; "Chucho, el reventado," *La Guía* 174 (Jan. 25, 1985): 11. Mauricio Peña, "La maestría de Emilio Ccarballido en el teatro," *El Heraldo de Espectáculos* (Oct. 10, 1982): 4-5. Braulio Peralta, "Emilio Carballido: Poliítica teatral nefasta, omite a autores mexicanos," *Unamásuno* (Dec. 9, 1981): 27; 'Peter Weiss no era un autor dogmático: Emilio Carballido," *Unomásuno* (May 13, 1982): 19. Elda Peralta, "Emilio Carballido: El teatro chicano, la política y la censura," *Plural* 100 (Jan. 1980): 60-64. Fernando Pérez Rincón, "*Tiempo de ladrones, la historia de Chucho el Roto*," *La Semana de Bellas Artes* 116 (Feb. 20, 1980): 14-15. Karen Peterson, "Existential Irony in Three Carballido Plays," *Latin American Theatre Review* 10, 2 (Spring 1977): 29-35. Nadia Piamonte, "En México, el teatro está afectado por las transnacionales de la cultura: Emilio Carballido," *Unamásuno* (June 19, 1979): 18. Margarita Pinto, "El estado del teatro en México," *Sábado* 102 (Oct. 27, 1979): 13. Galvarino Plaza, "*La caja vacía*," *Cuadernos Hispanoamericanos* 334 (Apr. 1978): 173. Ambra Polidori, "Emilio Carballido y el teatro chicano," *Unomásuno* (Feb. 9, 1980): 16. Eduardo Quiles, "Entrevista al dramaturgo Emilio Carballido," *El Heraldo Cultural* 396 (June 10, 1973): 8-9. Malkah Rabell, "La *Medusa* o el secreto de ser héroe," *El Día* (Sept. 25, 1968): 12; "Guillaumin habla de *Acapulco, los lunes*," *El Día* (May 29, 1978): 13; "Semblanza de un autor mexicano: Emilio Carballido," *El Día* (June 19, 1970): 13; "*Acapulco los lunes*," *El Día* (July 22, 1970): 11; "Cartelera. *El relojero de Córdoba*," *Los Universitarios* 115-116 (Mar. 1978): 25; "Optimismo diario. Los dramaturgos mexicanos," *Los Universitarios* 135-136 (Jan. 1979): 9-10. Abel Ramos Nájera, "Quedar solo, a lo que más temo: Emilio Carballido," *Unomásuno* (Jan. 16, 1983): 20. René Rebetez, "Lo fantástico en la literatura mexicana contemporánea," *Espejo*, 2, 20 (1967): 45; *El Heraldo Cultural* 275 (June 4, 1971): 9. Juan José Reyes, "Un bello relato para niños," *El Sol de México en la Cultura* 65 (July 17, 1983): 3; 90 (Jan. 1984): 3; "*Tiempo de ladrones*," *El Sol de México en la Cultura* 108 (May 13, 1984): 3; "*El tren que corría*," *El Sol de México en la Cultura* 134 (Nov. 11, 1984): 3. Mara Reyes, "Diorama teatral," *Diorama de la Cultura* (Nov. 18, 1962): 3; "*Silencio pollos...*," *Diorama de la Cultura* (Sept. 22, 1963): 8; "*Yo también hablo de la rosa*," *Diorama de la Cultura* (Apr. 30, 1966): 4, 5. Luis Reyes de la Masa, "*Yo también hablo de la rosa*," *El Nacional* (Apr. 23 1966): 5; (Apr. 24, 1966): 5; "Obras de Magaña, Ustinov y Carballido," *Revista Mexicana de Cultura* 996 (May 10, 1966): 11; "Deliciosa farsa mexicana," *México en la Cultura* 969 (Oct.15, 1967): 4; "*Medusa* o la oscuridad escénica," *México en la Cultura* 1019 (Sept. 29 1968): 4; "El teatro. Magnífica reposición de *Medusa*," *México en la Cultura* 1053 (May 25, 1969): 4. Salvador Reyes Nevares, "Teatro de Emilio Carballido," *México en la Cultura* 577 (Apr. 4, 1960): 4. Gladys Rodríguez, "Deliciosa obra. Una fábula con realismo mágico," *Excelsior* (July 24, 1983): 2. César Rodríguez Chicharro, "*El Norte*," *Revista Mexicana de Cultura* 608 (Nov. 23, 1958): 11. Eduardo Rodríguez Solís, "¡Qué odiosa es la maestra!," *La Onda* 229 (Oct. 30, 1977): 1, 16; "El relojero atormentado," *La Onda* 246 (Feb. 26, 1978): 3, 20. Víctor Ronquillo, "Chucho, el Roto, según Emilio Carballido," *El Nacional* (Dec. 13, 1983): 1. Jorge Ruffinelli, "*El Norte/Polvos de arroz*, Historias secretas," *Marcha* 1378 (Jan. 19, 1968): 29; "...Invitation au voyage" *Sábado* 373 (Dec. 8, 1984): 8; "Chucho el Roto, un hijo colectivo," *Latin American Theatre Review* 18, 2 (Spring 1985): 67-70. Eusebio Ruvalcaba, "Papeles" *(Teatro joven de México y Más teatro joven)*, *El Gallo Ilustrado* 1133 (Mar. 11, 1984): 15. Concepción Sada, "Una nueva generación de autores de teatro," *Cine Mundial* (Aug. 22, 1954): 13. Gustavo Sáinz, "Escaparate de libros," *México en la Cultura* 864 (Oct. 10, 1965): 7; *Jaula de palabras*, p. 469; *Los mejores cuentos mexicanos*, pp. 7-9, 298. Francisco Sánchez, "El esperado amor desesperado" (film based on *La danza que sueña la tortuga o Palabras cruzadas*), *Revista Mexicana de Cultura* 414 (Jan. 9, 1977): 7. George O. Schanzer, "El teatro hispano americano de post mortem" *(La zona intermedia)*, *Latin American Theatre Review* 7, 2 (Spring 1974): 5-16. Guillermo Schmidhuber de la Mora, "Nueva dramaturgia mexicana," *Latin American Theatre Review* 18, 1 (Fall 1984): 13-16. Esther Seligson, "*El relojero de Córdoba*," *Proceso* 70 (Mar. 6, 1978): 57-58. Eugene R. Skinner, "Emilio Carballido: temática y forma de tres autos," *Latin American Theatre Review* 1 (1969): 37; "Emilio Carballido: *The golden thread and other plays*," *Latin American Theatre Review* 2, (1971): 86. Rafael Solana, "El Concurso de Comedia Mexicana de *El Nacional*" (Prize for *Palabras cruzadas*), *Revista Mexicana de Cultura* 417 (Mar. 27, 1955): 10, 14; "Un joven dramaturgo," *Revista de la Semana* (May 12, 1957): 4; "Emilio Carballido y el teatro de provincia," *El Día* (Feb. 24, 1956): 5; "Eds. de obras teatrales" (pertaining to EDIMUSA), *El Día* (July 27, 1984): 4. Carlos Solórzano, "La crítica de *Los pollos pelones*," *La Cultura en México* 108 (Mar. 11, 1964): xvii; *Testimonios teatrales de México* UNAM (1973): 133. Helena Villacres Stanton, "The Mexican Reality in the Theatre of Emilio Carballido," Ph.D. Diss., University of California, Riverside, 1976; "*El almanaque de Juárez* y México en 1968," *Latin American Theatre Review* 12, 2 (Spring 1979): 3-12. Bruce Swansey, "Retrato de una familia en exteriores" *(Fotografía en la playa)*, *Proceso* 410 (Sept. 10, 1984): 58-59. Cándido Tafoya, "La presencia femenina como enfoque en obras selectas de Emilio Carballido," *DAI* 47, 2 (Aug. 1986): 541A. Diana Taylor, "Mad World, Mad Hope: Carballido's *El día que se soltaron los leones*," in *Latin American Theatre Review* 20, 2 (Spring 1987): 67-76. Humberto Tejera, "*Yo también hablo de la rosa*," *México en la Cultura* 919 (Oct. 30, 1966): 6. Solomon H. Tilles, "La importancia de la 'palabra' en *Rosalba y los llaveros*," *Latin American Theatre Review* 8, 2 (Spring 1975): 39-44. Gerardo de la Torre, "*El sol*," *Revista Mexicana de Cultura* 106 (Feb. 7, 1971): 6. Danubio Torres Fierro, "*Las cartas de Mozart* de Emilio Carballido: Así que pasen 25 años," *Diorama de la Cultura* (Nov. 30, 1975) 10. Juan Tovar, "Los pollos pelones de Emilio Carballido," *Ovaciones*, Suppl. 90 (Sept. 15,

1963): 4; "Juana y su gente," *El Heraldo de México*, Suppl. de Espectáculos, 105 (Nov. 19, 1967): 6-7; "Algún gesto no sabe uno de quién" *La Vida Literaria* (Sept. 27, 1972): 19-20; Presentación a *Emilio Carballido*, dice, UNAM, 1973, *(Voz Viva de México)*, reproduced in *Letras de Veracruz* (Xalapa) 1 (July-Sept. 1973): 5-15. Ignoacio Trejo Fuentes, "*Los Zapatos de fierro,*" *La Guía* 119 (Jan. 6, 1984): 10. James J. Troiano, "Illusory Worlds in Three Stories by Emilio Carballido," in *Hispanic Journal* 10, 2 (Spring 1989): 63-79. Federico Urtaza, "De trenes y tranvías" *(El tren que corría), La Jornada. Libros* 5 (Feb. 16, 1985): 3. Tomás Urtusástegui, "Emilio Carballido, ¿autor o director?," *Revista Mexicana de Cultura* 81 (Sept. 9, 1984): 14. Carlos Valdés, "Balance 1962: el cuento" *(La caja vacía), La Cultura en México* 46 (Jan. 2, 1963): vi. Gonzalo Valdés Medellín, "No prefiero ningún género teatral en especial, pero...: Emilio Carballido," *Unomásuno* (Feb. 11, 1983): 17; "...entrevistas con Emilio Carballdio, Magaña y Zapata," *Revista Mexicana de Cultura* 17 (June 19, 1983): 4; "El sentido del humor de Emilio Carballido," interview, *Sábado* 341 (May 12, 1984): 13. Various, Homenaje, *El Día* (May 31, 1969): 13; *Letras de Veracruz* 1 (July-Sept. 1973): 3-34; Centro de Investigaciones Lingüístico-Literarias, "*El sol,* novela de iniciación," *Texto Crítico* 3 (Jan.-Apr. 1976): 68-93. Jaime Vázquez, "Los mejores autores de 1983...," *Excelsior* (Dec. 31, 1983): 4. Mary Vázquez Amaral, *El teatro de EC 1950-1965* (Costa Amic, 1974). Patricia Vega, "Declara Emilio Carballido: se piensa que todos los clásicos son buenos, menos los mexicanos," *La Jornada* (Jan. 28, 1985): 23; "Emilio Carballido cumple 60 años...," *La Jornada* (May 22, 1985): 25. Arqueles Vela, *Fundamentos de la literatura mexicana* (México: Patria, 1966), p. 163. Joseph F. Vélez, "Una entrevista con Emilio Carballido," *Latin American Theatre Review* 7, 1 (Fall 1973): 17-24. Víctor Villela, "*El sol,* fragmentos de sobremesa," *El Heraldo Cultural* 276 (Feb. 21, 1971): 4-5. Fernando Wagner, "Elige *La Medusa y Los argonautas* como las mejores obras de teatro," *El Día* (May 8, 1965): 10. Raymond L. Williams, "*Yo también hablo de la rosa...,*" *Latin American Theatre Review* 14, 2 (Spring 1981): 97-98. Oscar Wong, "*El tren que corría...,*" *El Nacional* (Sept. 24, 1984): 6. "*Yo también hablo de la rosa,*" *México en la Cultura* 895 (May 15, 1966): 4. Cuauhtémoc Zúñiga, "un mexicano mueve la melena," *La Onda* 285 (Nov. 26, 1978): 1, 16.

MICHELE MUNCY

CARBALLIDO, Reynaldo (1949-   ). Born on May 7, 1949, in Tequisistlán, Oaxaca, Reynaldo Carballido studied theater arts at the Taller de Composición Dramática del Instituo Politécnico Nacional. He also received a teaching degree in Spanish literature from the normal school.

In addition to his work as a teacher, he is also a noted young author of very powerful plays. In his work, he depicts how the established systems often corrupt mankind and are corrupted themselves. The majority of his plays are of one act and have been performed, often to critical acclaim.

WORKS: Theater: *La señora de gris* (The Lady in Gray), performed in Mexico, 1972. *Acto social* (Social Act), performed in Mexico, 1975. *Los mandamientos de la ley del hombre* (The Commandments of the Law of Man), performed in Mexico, 1979. *El periódico* (The Newspaper), performed in Mexico, 1980. *La corriente* (The Current), performed in Mexico, 1980; in Emilio Carballido, *Teatro joven de México*, vol. 2

(México: UAM, 1983): pp. 175-98. "Sombras ajenas" (Detached Shadows), in Emilio Carballido, *Más teatro joven* (México: Editores Mexicanos Unidos, 1982): pp. 43-56. Works in Journals: Five one-act plays ("Moto en Delegación," "La señora de gris," "El periódico," "Acto social," and "Los mandamientos de la ley del hombre"), in *Tramoya* 9 (Oct.-Dec., 1977): 66-110. "Sombras ajenas," in *Tramoya* 18 (Jan.-March 1980): 49-58. "Nosotros los de entonces" (Ourselves, from Way Back When), in *El Gallo Ilustrado* 1050 (Aug. 8, 1982): 15-16. "Cenicienta" (Cinderella), in *Ovaciones* (Sept. 27, 1982). "Compañía" (Company), in *Danza y Teatro* (July-Aug. 1983).

BIBLIOGRAPHY: "Datos biográficos," in *El Gallo Ilustrado* 1050 (Aug. 8, 1982): 2. Marco Antonio Acosta, "Tres valores jóvenes de la nueva literatura dramática," in *Revista Mexicana de Cultura* 17 (March 30, 1980): 7. Emilio Carballido, in *Teatro joven de México*, vol. 2 (México: UAM, 1983), p. 347; *Más teatro joven* (México: EDIMUSA, 1982), pp. 54-55. Antonio Magaña Esquivel, "Surgen nuevos dramaturgos mexicanos," in *Revista Mexicana de Cultura* 77 (May 31, 1981): 7.

MICHELE MUNCY

CARBALLO, Emmanuel (1929-) critic, poet, and short story writer. Carballo was born on July 2, 1929 in Guadalajara, Jalisco. While there, he edited the journals *Ariel* (1949-53) and *Odisea* (1952). He also published a book of poetry, *Amor se llama* (It Is Called Love), in 1951. He moved to Mexico City, where he was affiliated with the Mexican Writers Center from 1953 to 1955. Along with Carlos *Fuentes, he founded *Revista Mexicana de Literatura*. In 1954 he published a collection of short stories, *Gran estorbo la esperanza* (Great Hindrance to Hope). His major contribution, however, has been as a literary critic and literary journalist. He has served on the editorial committee of the journal *Casa de las Américas* and contributed to it a regular column.

In *Amor se llama*, Carballo portrays love as a means of overcoming solitude and giving one's life meaning. He draws on religious and biblical images to reinforce his theme. His collection of short stories, *Gran estorbo la esperanza*, confronts issues such as alienation, meaning, and absurdity. *Eso es todo* (That Is All) is a poem that captures the voice of loved enmeshed in a sado-masochistic love affair. He has also written a number of prologues to books, has edited works, has conducted interviews, and has written numerous reviews. He is a perceptive and thorough critic who has played an important role in formulating and clarifying the literary issues.

WORKS: Poetry: *Amor se llama* (It Is Called Love) (Guadalajara: Et Caetera, 1951). *Eso es todo* (That Is All) (México: Editorial Diógenes, 1972). Stories: *Gran estorbo la esperanza* (Great Hindrance to Hope) (México: Los Presentes, 1954). Scholarly Works: *José López Portillo y Rojas, Cuentos completos* (Complete Short Stories), edition and prologue (Guadalajara: Eds. del Instituto Tecnológico de Guadalajara, 1952). *Emilio Rabasa, La guerra de tres años-seguido de poemas inéditos y desconocidos* (The Three Years' War--Collection of Unpublished and Unknown Poems), edition and prologue (México: Ed. Libro-México, 1955). *Cuentistas mexicanos modernos*, 2 vols. (Modern Mexican Short Story Writers), edition and prologue (México: Libro-México, 1956). *José López Portillo y Rojas, Algunos cuentos* (Some Short Stories), edition and prologue (México: UNAM, 1956). *El cuento mexicano del siglo XX, Antología* (The Mexican Short Story of the Twentieth Century, Anthology), edited with bibliography (México: Empresas Editoriales, 1964). *Del costumbrismo al realismo crítico* (From Manners and Customs to Critical Realism) (Bogotá: Espiral, 1964). *19 protagonistas de la literatura mexicana del siglo XX* (Nineteen Prominent Authors of Twentieth-Century Mexican Literature), edition and prologue (México: Empresas Editoriales, 1965). *Agustín Yáñez* (La Habana: Casa de las Américas, 1966). *Jaime Torres Bodet*, edition (México: Empresas Editoriales, 1968). *Narrativa mexicana de hoy*, edition and prologue (Madrid: Alianza Editorial, 1969). *Las Fiestas patrias en la narrativa nacional* (The Native Festivals in the National Narrative), edition and prologue (México: Diógenes, 1982). *La poesía mexicana del siglo XIX* (Mexican Poetry of the Nineteenth Century), edition and prologue (México: Editorial Diogenes, 1984). *Protagonistas de la literatura hispanoamericana del siglo XX* (Prominent Authors of Twentieth-Century Hispanic American Literature, interviews), edition with prologue (México: UNAM, 1986).

BIBLIOGRAPHY: Federico Alvarez, Review of *El cuento mexicano del siglo XX*, in *La Cultura en México* 148 (Dec. 16, 1964): xvii. Anon., "Poemas de Emmanuel Carballo y una nota sobre su obra," *Nivel* 9 (Sept. 25, 1963): 4. Archibald Burns, Review of *Gran estorbo la esperanza*, in *Revista de la Universidad de México* 9, 5-6 (Jan.-Feb. 1955): 30-31. Heriberto García Rivas, *Historia de la literatura mexicana*, vol. 4 (México: Textos Universitarios, 1971), pp. 519-20. Carlos González Peña, *History of Mexican Literature*, translated by Gusta Barfield Nance and Florence Johnson Dunstan (Dallas: Southern Methodist University Press, 1968), p. 472. Aurora M. Ocampo de Gómez and Ernesto Prado Velázquez, *Diccionario de escritores mexicanos* (México: UNAM, 1967), p. 61. Pedro Shimose, ed., *Diccionario de autores iberoamericanos* (Madrid: Ministerio de Asuntos Exteriores, 1982), p. 92. Carlos Valdés, Review of *Gran estorbo la esperanza*, in *Ideas en México* 9-10 (Jan.-Apr. 1955): 87-88.

MARK FRISCH

CARDENAS, Nancy (1934-). Cardenas was born in Parras, Coahuila, on May 29, 1934. She did her elementary and secondary schooling in her native area, then attended preparatory school in Celaya, Guanajato; and in Mexico City, she took a degree in letters, with a specialization in dramatic art. She studied theory and composition with Luisa Josefina Hernández. From 1960 to 1961 she had a scholarship at Yale University, in the United States, where she studied theater directing. In 1961 she traveled around Europe, and studied in Warsaw, Poland.

Nancy Cárdenas has dedicated herself wholly to the study of theater, whether it be in acting, writing, or giving overview courses on special topics in the areas of theory and practice. She has worked for University Television; she has directed student theatrical groups, and she has done film criticism. She has won several awards for her theatrical productions, including the 1970 prize from the Asociación de Críticos de Teatro and another the "El Heraldo" prize in 1980.

WORKS: Theater: "Ella se estuvo en el tapanco," (She Was Up in the Loft), play in three acts, unpublished, no date given. *El cántaro seco* (The Empty Pitcher), play in one act (México: Imp. Universitaria, UNAM, 1960). *La vida privada del profesor Kabela* (The Private Life of Professor Kebela), play in one act, broadcast on La Serie Nuevo Teatro de Radio Universidad, in Mexico, 1963. Studies: *El cine polaco* (Polish Cinema). Cuadernos de cine, no. 1 (México, 1962). Eds. de la UNAM, "Aproximaciones al teatro de vanguardia" (Drawing Close to the Theater of the Vanguard), thesis, Facultad de Filosofía y Letras, UNAM, México 1965. Poetry: "Ahora un poco de flores para ti" (Now A Few Flowers for You), in *El Gallo Ilustrado* 421 (July 19, 1970): 4. *Amor de verano* (Summer Love) (México: Katún, 1985).

BIBLIOGRAPHY: Ruth S. Lamb, *Bibliografía del teatro mexicano del siglo XX* (México: Eds. de Andrea, 1962), p. 39. Aurora M. Ocampo de Gómez and Ernesto Prado Velázquez, *Diccionario de escritores mexicanos* (México: UNAM, 1967), p. 62.

PETER G. BROAD

CARDENAS PEÑA, José (1918-1963), poet and diplomat. José Cardenas Peña was born in San Diego de la Unión, Guanajuato, on March 17, 1918. In 1947, in Buenos Aires, with the poets León Benarós and J. Rodolfo Wilcock he founded the journal of cultural exchange, *Correspondencia México Argentina*. On various occasions he was commissioned by the Office of International Relations (Affairs) to represent Mexico abroad. In 1952 he was commissioner of the Mexican delegation to the UNESCO in Paris. His poetry deals mostly with love themes, but it also reflects the many crises in life as well as the spirit of the times. *Llanto subterráneo* (Underground Weeping) is a testimony of anguish and desolation. Its only salvation is love. *Conversación amorosa* (Passionate Conversation) laments the passing of time and suggests that only through love is the individual able to forget himself and experience the true meaning of life. *Retama del olvido* (The Bitterness of Oblivion) is a death eulogy in honor of the Italian poet Giacomo Leopardi, for whom, as was the case with Cárdenas, nature was almost always his enemy. *Adonáis o la elegía del amor y Canto de Dionisio* (Adonais or the Elegy of Love and Song to Dionysius) is an optimistic, youthful book in which love is simultaneously a promise and an afirmation.

WORKS: *Sueño de sombras* (Dream of Shadows) (México: Eds. Angel Chapero, 1940). *Llanto subterráneo, Poemas 1940-1941* (Underground Weeping, Poems 1940-1941) (México: Letras de México, 1945). *La ciudad de los pájaros* (City of Birds) (Buenos Aires: Ed. de la Universidad de La Plata, 1947). *Conversación amorosa* (Passionate Conversation) (México: Letras de Mexico, 1950). *Retama del olvido y otros poemas* (The Bitterness of Oblivion and Other Poems) (México: FCE, 1955). *Adonáis o la elegía del amor y Canto de Dionisio* (Adonais or the Elegy of Love and Song to Dionysius) (México: n.p., 1961). *Los contados días* (The Last Days) (México: FCE, 1964).

BIBLIOGRAPHY: Jesús Arellano, Review of *Conversación amorosa* (Passionate Conversation), in *Fuensanta*, 8-9, (Aug. 1950): 6. M.B., "José Cárdenas Peña," *México en la Culture* 759 (Oct. 6, 1963): 8. Antonio Castro Leal, ed., *La poesía mexicana moderna* (México: FCE, 1953), p. 444. Raúl Leiva, *Imagen de la poesía mexicana contemporanea* (México: UNAM, 1959), pp. 183-288, 357-58. José Luis Martínez, *Literatura mexicana: siglo XX. 1910-1949* (México: Ant. Libr. Robredo, 1950), p. 26; "Escaparate de libros," *Mexico en la Cultura* 822 (Dec. 20, 1964): 6. "Introducción a *Poemas de José Cárdenas Peña*," in *La Cultura en México* 90 (Nov. 6, 1963): vi-vii. Aurora M. Ocampo de Gómez and Ernesto Prado Velázquez, *Diccionario de escritores mexicanos* (México: UNAM, 1967), p. 62. Carlos Valdés, Review of *Retama del olvido* (The Bitterness of Oblivion) in *Revista de la UNAM* 9, 3-4 (Nov.-Dec. 1954): 31. Ramón Xirau, Review of *Los contados días* (The Last Days) in *Diálogos* 3 (Mar.-Apr. 1965): 44-45.

MARGARITA VARGAS

CARDOZA y Aragón, Luis (1904-), poet, art critic, short story writer, and essayist. Born in Guatemala city, Cardoza y Aragón lived in the United States in 1920 and in Paris from 1921 to 1929. He has been in Mexico since 1929. He served as juror of the Casa de las Américas literary awards in 1964 and in 1975.

WORKS: Poetry: *Luna Park* (Luna Park) (n.p.: n.p., 1923). *La torre de Babel* (Babel's Tower) (n.p.: n.p., 1930). *El sonámbulo* (The Sleepwalker) (n.p.: n.p., 1937). *Poesía* (Poetry) (México: Letras de México, 1949). *Pequeña sinfonía del Nuevo Mundo* (Small Symphony of the New World) (Guatemala: Libro de Guatemala, 1948; México: UNAM, 1969). *Quinta estación: Obra Poética* (Fifth Season: Poetic Works) (México: n.p.: n.d.). *Poesías completas y algunas prosas* (Complete Poetry with Some Prose Fiction) (México: FCE, 1977). Short Stories: *Maelstrom* (Guatemala: n.p., 1926). *Nuevo Mundo* (New World) (Jalapa: Universidad Veracruzana, 1960). *Los hombres que dispersó la danza, leyendas zapotecas* (The Men Who Were Dispersed by the Dance, Zapotec Legends) (México: Imp. Universitaria, 1945). *Dibujos de ciego* (Drawings of a Blind Man) (México: Siglo XXI, 1969). Essay: *La nube y el reloj* (The Cloud and the Clock) (México: UNAM, 1940). *Apolo y Coatlicue: Ensayos mexicanos de espina y flor* (Apollo and Coatlicue: Mexican Essays of Flower and Thorn) (México: La Serpiente Emplumada, 1944). *Guatemala, las lineas de su mano* (Guatemala, the Lines in Her Hand) (México: FCE, 1955). *La revolución guatemalteca* (The Guatemalan Revolution) (México: Cuadernos Americanos, 1955). *Orozco* (Orozco) (México: UNAM, 1959). *José Guadalupe Posada* (José Guadalupe Posada) (México: UNAM, 1964). *México, Pintura activa* (Mexico, Active Painting) (México: Era, 1961). *Gunther Gerzso* (México: UNAM, 1972). *Antonín Artaud 1896-1948* (México: UNAM, 1962). *Ricardo Martínez* (Ricardo Martínez) (México: Mortiz, 1981). *Guatemala con una piedra adentro* (Guatemala with a Rock Tied to It) (México: Cuadernos Americanos, 1983). *Diego Rivera* (Diego Rivera) (México: Dir. Grl. de Publicaciones y Medios, 1986). *Antología* (Anthology) (México: SEP, 1988).

BIBLIOGRAPHY: "Cardoza y Aragón: Algunas líneas de su mano," *Casa de las Américas* 90 (1975): 71-75, interview. Elisa Davila, "El poema en prosa en Hispanoamérica: A propósito de Luis Cardoza y Aragón," *DAI* 44 (6) (1983): 1806A, University of California, Santa Barbara. Francois Gaudry and Joseph M. Oliveras, "Un Temoin du voyage au Mexique d'Antonin Artaud," *La Quinzaine Litteraire* 465

(1986): 15-16. "El grito y la decepción: Entrevista con Luis Cardoza y Aragón," *Quimera* (Spain) 11 (1986): 54-55, 58-61. José Mejfa, "Los últimos poemas de Luis Cardoza y Aragón," *Cuadernos Americanos* 193 (1974): 185-203.

MIRTA A. GONZALEZ

CARNES, Luisa (1905-1964), novelist, short story writer, biographer, and journalist. Carnes was born in Madrid on January 4, 1905. She was an established novelist and an active contributor to literary journals when she moved to Mexico in 1939 with her husband, writer Juan *Rejano. She continued her articles, primarily for the literary and cultural sections of *El Nacional* and *Novedades*. Her articles were written under the pseudonym Clarita Montes. She died on March 12, 1964, from her injuries in an automobile accident.

Carnés gained her reputation with her second novel, *Natacha*. Her last novel, *Juan Caballero*, deals with the Spanish Civil War. Her protagonist, who is fighting against Franco, is the idealized creation of a novelist removed from the scene in space and time who writes about her native land with nostalgic recall. However, her narrative style is direct and flowing, demonstrating depth of feeling and keen observation.

WORKS: *Peregrinos del Calvario* (Pilgrims of Calvary) (Madrid: Espasa-Calpe, 1929). *Natacha* (Madrid: Companía Ibero-Americana de Publicaciones, 1930). *Tea Rooms* (Madrid: Editorial Juan Pueyo, 1932). *Juan Caballero* (México: Editorial Novelas y Atlante, 1956). *Cumpleaños* (Birthday) (México: Ecuador, 1965). *Los vendedores de miedo* (Merchants of Fear) (México: Ecuador, 1966). *Rosalia de Castro*, 2nd ed. (México: Ecuador, 1964).

BIBLIOGRAPHY: Dolores Castro, Review of *Los vendedores de miedo*, in *Nivel* 40 (April 25, 1966): 4. Heriberto García Rivas, *150 biografías de mexicanos ilustres*, vol. 4 (México: Diana, 1964), p. 230. Antonio Iglesias Laguna, *Treinta años de novela española: 1938-1968*, vol. 1, 2nd ed. (Madrid: Editorial Prensa española, 1970), pp. 29, 87. José R. Marra López, *Narrativa española fuera de España (1939-1961)* (Madrid: Ediciones Guadarrama, 1963), p. 493.

KENNETH M. TAGGART

CARPIO, Manuel (1791-1860), novelist and poet. Carpio was born in Cosamaloapán, Veracruz, on March 1, 1791. As a child, he moved with his family to Puebla. Later, he matriculated in the Conciliate Seminary to study Latin, philosophy, and theology. He decided to enter the medical school of the University of Mexico, graduating in 1832. He was a professor of hygiene and physiology in the medical school. In addition, he served as a representative to the legislature in Veracruz and as a representative in the Federal Chamber. A conservative, he did not actively participate in politics. He was both famous and popular among the intellectuals of his time. He influenced the development of Mexican poetry. Few poets had as many publications as he during the nineteenth century. By the end of the century, however, critics were writing strong contradictory judgments about his work. One important text by José Bernardo Couto was particularly defamatory.

A romantic academician, Manuel Carpio could dramatically interpret nature in his work. A savvy man, he translated Hippocratic aphorisms and predictions. His natural religious inclination, his profound biblical knowledge, and his interest in both oriental and historic topics are reflected in some of his most important works: *La tierra santa* (The Holy Land), "Oda a la Virgen de Guadalupe," "La ausencia," and "Toma de Jerusalem por los Romanos." His great eloquence, attacked by his detractors, caused other critics to consider him one of the best epic poets in Mexico. Even more significant than the differing opinions regarding the quality of his poetic production is his place in the history of Mexican literature.

WORKS: *Aforismos y pronósticos de Hipócrates* (Aphorisms and Predictions of Hippocrates) (México: Oficina de Mariano Ontiveros, 1823). *La tierra santa* (The Holy Land) (México: n.p., 1832). Poesías (Poems), edition and prologue by José Joaquín Pesado (México: Imp. de M. Murguía, 1849); reprinted in 1874, 1875, and 1876. *Poesías del señor don Manuel Carpio con su biografía escrita por el señor don José Bernardo Couto* (Poetry of Manuel Carpio with His Biography Written by José Bernardo Couto), 1st and 2nd eds. (México: Imp. de Andrade y Escalante, 1860); 3rd ed. (Imp. y Libr. de la Enseñanza, 1876); 4th ed. (Dublan y Cía, 1882); 5th ed. (Libr. de la Enseñanza, 1883). *Poesías sagradas del Dr. Manuel Carpio* (Sacred Poems by Dr. Manuel Carpio) (León: Imp. de Francisco Rodríguez, 1875). *Poesía* (Poetry) (Jalapa: Universidad Veracruzana, 1987).

BIBLIOGRAPHY: José Bernardo Couto, "Biografía de D. Manuel Carpio," in *Memorias de la Academia Mexicana*, vol. 1, no. 3 (México: Imp. de F. Díaz de León, 1878), pp. 277-300. Frank Dauster, *Breve historia de la poesía mexicana* (México: Eds. de Andrea, 1956), pp. 90-91. Francisco R. Illescas and Juan Bartolo Hernández, *Escritores veracruzanos* (Veracruz: n.p., 1945), pp. 47-48. Esther Hernández Palacios and Angel José Fernández, *La poesía veracruzana* (Xalapa: Universidad Veracruzana, 1984). María del Carmen Millán, *El paisaje en la poesía mexicana* (México: Imp. Universitaria, 1952), pp. 127-34. Silvestre Moreno Cora, "Estudio literario leído en la vela literaria extraordinaria dedicada por la sociedad Sánchez Oropeza a celebrar el centenario del nacimiento del poeta mexicano D. Manuel Carpio, la noche del 4 de abril de 1891," in *Obras* (México: Imp. de Victoriano Agüeros, 1901), pp. 283-313. Marcelino Menéndez y Pelayo, *Historia de la poesía hispanoamericana* (Madrid: Libr. general de Victoriano Suárez, 1911), pp. 148-50. José Emilio Pacheco, *La poesía mexicana del siglo XIX* (México: Empresas editoriales, 1965), p. 129. Francisco Pimentel, *Historia crítica de la literatura y de las ciencias en México desde la conquista hasta nuestros días* (México: Libr. de la Enseñanza, 1865); *Historia crítica de la poesía en México*, in *Obras*, vol. 5 (México: Tip. Económica, 1904), pp. 7-38. Alfonso Reyes, "El paisaje en la poesía mexicana del siglo XIX," in *Obras completas*, vol. 1 (México: FCE, 1955), pp. 220-29. José María Roa Barcena, "Conferencia acerca de D. Manuel Carpio," in *Obras*, vol. 4 (México: Imp. de B. Agüeros, 1902), pp. 371-91. Francisco Sosa, "El poeta Carpio," in *Revista mensual mexicana* (México: Imp. de Jens y Zapíain, 1877), pp. 107-18; "La poesía de Carpio," in *La juventud literaria*, vol. 2 (México; n.p., 1888), pp. 78-99; *Biografías de mexicanos distinguidos* (México: Ed. de la Sría. de Fomento, 1884), pp. 204-07. Luis G. Urbina, *La vida literaria en México*

(Madrid: n.p., 1917), pp. 148-50. Octaviano Valdez, *Poesía neoclásica y académica* (México: UNAM, 1946), pp. 19-21. José Zorrilla, *México y los mexicanos* (México: Eds. de Andrea, 1955), pp. 109-10.

DELIA GALVAN

CARREÑO, Alberto María (1875-1962), historian, academic, and statesman interests. Business, diplomacy, and law were among the primary interests of Carreño. He was director of the Escuela Superior de Comercio, advisor to diverse industries, secretary to the ambassador of Mexico in Washington, and professor of Spanish, commerce, geography, economics, and history. He taught at the Law School of Fordham University in New York. At the time of his death he was lifetime secretary of the Academia Mexicana de la Lengua, vice president of the Instituto Cultural Hispanoamericano and Director of the Academia de Historia of Mexico.

His published works include books on history, geography, economy, and literature. The Language Academy is indebted to him for the publication of its history, published as part of his memoirs, and the preparation of bibliographies of all its members.

WORKS: *El cronista Luis González Obregón. Cuadros viejos* (The Historian Luis González Obregón. Old Portraits) (México: Imp. France, 1915). *Fray Domingo de Betanzos, fundador en la Nueva España de la Venerable Orden Dominicana* (Brother Domingo de Betanzos, Founder in New Spain of the Venerable Dominican Order) (México: Imp. Victoria, 1924). *La lengua castellana en México* (The Spanish Language in Mexico) (México: Imp. Victoria, 1925). "Consideraciones nuevas sobre un viejo tema," *Divulgación Histórica* (Nov. 15, 1942): 39-56. *La diplomacia extraordinaria entre México y Estados Unidos, 1789-1947* (The Extraordinary Diplomacy between Mexico and the United States, 1789-1947) (México: Ed. Jus, 1951). *Memorias de la Academia Mexicana* (México: UNAM, 1961). *México y los Estados Unidos de América: apuntaciones para la historia del acrecentamiento territorial de los Estados Unidos a costa de México desde la época colonial hasta nuestros días* (Mexico and the United States: Notes for the History of the Territorial Expansion of the United States at the Expense of Mexico from Colonial Times to the Present) (México: Ed. Jus, 1962). *Efemérides de la Real y Pontificia Universidad de México, 1593-1727* (Main events of the Royal and Pontifical University of Mexico, 1593-1727) (México: UNAM, 1963).

BIBLIOGRAPHY: Anon., Obituary in *México en la Cultura* (Sept. 9, 1962): 9; "El soneto revolucionario místico surgió en México," *México en la Cultura* (Oct. 10, 1965): 31; *Memorias de la Academia Mexicana* 7 (México, 1945): 169; 8 (México, 1946): 26-61. Henrique González Casanova, "Alberto María Carreño," *Ovaciones* (Sept. 9, 1962): 5. Carlos González Peña, *Historia de la literatura mexicana* (México: Porrúa, 1966), p. 437. Raymond L. Grismer and Mary B. Macdonald, *Vida y obras de autores mexicanos* (Havana: Ed. Alfa, 1945), pp. 35-41. Andrés Henestrosa, "La Nota Cultural," *El Nacional* (Aug. 27, 1965): 3. José Luis Martínez, *Literatura mexicana, siglo XX. 1910-1949* (México: Ant. Libr. Robredo, 1950), pp. 70, 124, 127. Javier Morente, "Sala de Lectura," *Excelsior* (March 10, 1963): 2. Ernesto de la Torre Villar, "Alberto María Carreño," *Boletín de la Biblioteca Nacional* 14 (1963): 25-38.

BARBARA P. FULKS

CARRILLO y Ancona, Crescencio (1837-1897). Carrillo y Ancona was born in Izmal, Yucatán, on April 19, 1837. His mother, Josefa Florentina Ancona, held a degree in primary instruction, and gave him his early instruction. Upon the death of his father, in 1848, Carrillo y Ancona went to Mérida, where he entered the Seminario Conciliar de San Ildefonso. He received his degree in philosophy and was ordained a priest in 1860.

His academic and literary activities took many forms, including reforms in the seminary pedagogy, the founding of the journals *El Repertorio Pintoresco* and *El Eco de la Fe*, and contributing to numerous others. He was a member of the Sociedad de Geografía y Estadística and other Mexican and foreign learned societies. He founded the Catholic University of Mérida in 1885, and created the Colegio Católico, with the Museo Yucateco, to which he donated his large personal collection. In 1884 he was named associate bishop of Yucatán, and in 1887, bishop of the diocese of Yucatán. He died in the Episcopal Palace of Mérida on March 19, 1897.

Although he wrote fiction with a religious purpose, his most important works are historic, including the *Historia antigua de Yucatán* (The Ancient History of Yucatán) and *El obispado de Yucatán* (The Bishopric of Yucatán). In the legend *Historia de Welina* (History of Welina), he presents the duality of the mestizo soul and the saving power of the Christian missionaries during the Spanish conquest of Mexico. This theme is repeated in *El santuario de la aldea* (The Sanctuary of the Village).

WORKS: *Historia de Welina* (History of Welina) (Mérida: Imp. de José Dolores Espinosa, 1862); other editions 1883, 1919. *Historia antigua de Yucatán* (Ancient History of Yucatán), 2nd ed. (Mérida: Gambóa Guzmán y Hno. Impresores, 1883). "El origen de Belice" (The Origin of Belice), in *Boletín de la Sociedad de Geografía y estadística* 4 (México, 1878): 254-64. Numerous legends were published in journals and in *El santuario de la aldea* (The Sanctuary of the Village) (Mérida: Imp. de Gambóa Guzmán, 1883). *El obispado de Yucatán. Historia de su fundacion y de sus opispos, desde el siglo XVI, hasta el XIX, seguida de las Constituciones sinodales de la Diócesis y otros documentos relativos* (The Bishopric of Yucatan. History of Its Foundation and of Its Bishops, from the Sixteenth Century to the Nineteenth, Followed by the Synodal Constitutions and Other Related Documents) (Mérida: Imp. y Lit. de Recardo B. Caballero, 1892).

BIBLIOGRAPHY: Ignacio Altamirano, *La literatura nacional* (México: Porrúa, 1949), vol. 2, pp. 86-91. Heriberto García Rivas, *Historia de la literatura mexicana* (México: Textos Universitarios, 1972), vol. 2, p. 261. Juan B. Iguiñiz, *Bibliografía de novelistas mexicanos* (México: Imp. de la Sría de Relaciones, 1926), pp. 60-63. María del Carmen Millán, *Diccionario de escritores mexicanos* (México: UNAM, 1967), pp. 65-66.

FILIPPA B. YIN

CARRION, Ulises (1941-). Born in San Andrés Tuxtla, Veracruz, January 28, 1941, Carrión studied first in Xalapa, then got his teaching certificate from the Escuela Normal Veracruzana. Later, he furthered his education at the Universidad Veracruzana. Carrión won the state prize for short stories in 1960, spurring him to publish his work in journals such as *La Palabra y el Hombre* and cultural supplements such as *México en la Cultura*. Despite not having written or published extensively, he has made significant contributions in several literary disciplines, including theater, essay, and the short story. *La muerte de Miss O.* (The Death of Miss O.) (1966), a collection of six stories in which he fluctuates between psychological and realistic prose, is perhaps his most well-known and highly acclaimed work. Skillfully employing the interior monologue (somewhat reminiscent of both Marcel Proust and William Faulkner), Carrión creates vivid and engaging characters whose psychological self-expression is tinged with realism. In 1970, he published another six-story collection, *De Alemania* (From Germany), considered a more mature work. Here, he has perfected the interior monologue, which is the primary manner in which his characters disclose themselves. In some stories, the salient characteristic is alienation, but in others, Carrión employs humor as a catalyst. Since such characteristics are not always mutually exclusive, he does achieve a delicate balance between the two.

WORKS: *"El asalto"* (The Assault), *Revista Mexicana de Literatura* 11-12 (Nov.-Dec. 1962): 17-22. "Fragmentos de una novela" (Fragments of a Novel), in *Revista Mexicana de Literatura* 9-10 (Sept.-Oct. 1963): 16-24. "Tú, sin vino" (You, Without Wine), in *La Palabra y el Hombre* 28 (Oct.-Dec. 1963): 693-736. *García Moreno. El santo del patíublo* (García Moreno. The Saint of the Gallows) (México: FCE, 1965). *La muerte de Miss O.* (The Death of Miss O.) (México: Eds. Era, 1966). *De Alemania* (Of Germany) (México: Mortiz, 1970). "Textos y poemas" (Texts and Poems), in *Plural* 16 (Jan. 1973): 31-33. "Una cosa por otra" (One Thing for Another), play in *Diálogos* 32 (March-April 1970): 32-55.

BIBLIOGRAPHY: Huberto Batis, Review of *La muerte de Miss O.*, in *El Heraldo Cultural* 28 (May 22, 1966): 13. María Elvira Bermúdez, "Cuentos sobresalientes del setenta," *Diorama de la Cultura* (Dec. 27, 1970): 7, 16. Miguel Bustos Cerecedo, *La creación literaria en Veracruz*, vol. 2 (Xalapa: Editora del Gobierno de Veracruz, 1977), pp. 442-46. Marta Aurora Espinosa, "Ulises Carrión, creador del sistema errátil: el libro es una forma anticuada de comunicación," interview, *Unomásuno* (Sept. 5, 1982): 21. Margo Glantz, comp., *Onda y escritura en México. Jóvenes de 20 a 23* (México: Siglo Veintiuno, 1971). Juan Vicente Melo, Review of *La muerte de Miss O.*, in *Revista de Bellas Artes* 9 (May-June 1966): 103-4. Aurora M. Ocampo de Gómez and Ernesto Prado Velázquez, *Diccionario de escritores mexicanos* (México: UNAM, 1967), p. 66. Gustavo Sáinz, "Temática, proyección y técnica en el arte renovado del cuento," in *México en la Cultura* 764 (Nov. 1963): 1.

JEANNE C. WALLACE

CASASUS, Joaquín D. (1858-1916). Born in Frontera, Tabasco, on December 22, 1858, Joaquín D. Casasús became a lawyer, teacher, banker, businessman, and diplomat. Considered a brilliant man and great humanist, he successfully combined his various endeavors, particularly law and business. He served Mexico in international conferences on the sciences and also was part of the diplomatic corps.

A member of several important associations, including the Liceo Hidalgo and the Academia Mexicana, which he chaired for the last four years of his life (he died on February 25, 1916, in New York). He was the founder and major supporter of the Liceo Altamirano, whose associates, all members of the cultural and literary community, met regularly for intellectual stimulation and dissemination of ideas.

The author of numerous books about law and economics, Casasús also was a poet, prosewriter, biographer, and translator. *Musa antigua* (Ancient Muse) and *Versos y cien sonetos* (Poems and One Hundred Sonnets) constitute his poetic contribution. As a prosewriter, he wrote a book of eulogies, *En honor de los muertos* (In Honor of the Dead), focusing especially on Romero Rubio, Ignacio *Altamirano, Justo *Sierra, and Angel de la *Peña. Of his translations, he published elegant editions of such poets as Henry W. Longfellow, Horace, and Virgil, and he included biographical information with some. He occasionally used the pseudonym Efraín M. Lozano.

WORKS: Poetry: *Musa antigua* (Ancient Muse) (México: Escalante, 1904); 2nd ed., enlarged (1911). *Versos* (Poems) (pseudonym Efraín M. Lozano) (Tepic: n.p., 1910). *Cien sonetos* (One Hundred Sonnets) (pseudonym Efraín M. Lozano) (México: Imp. Lacaud, 1912). Prose: *En honor de los muertos* (In Honor of the Dead) (México: Escalante, 1910). *El libro para ti* (The Book for You) (pseudonym Efraín M. Lozano) (Tepic: n.p., n.d.). *Cartas literarias* (Literary Letters) (pseudonym Efraín M. Lozano) (Tepic: n.p., n.d.). Translations and Biographies: *Evangelina*, translation of Longfellow's poem (México: Tip. El Gran Libro de J. F. Parrés, 1885). *Algunas odas de Q. Horacio Flaco* (Some of Q. Horacio Flaco's Odes) (México: Escalante, 1899). *Las bucólicas de Publio Virgilio Marón* (Virgil's Pastorals) (México: Escalante, 1903). *Cayo Valerio Catulo, su vida y sus obras* (Cayo Valerio Catulo, His Life and His Works) (México: Escalante, 1904). *Las elegías de Tibulo, de Ligdamo y de Sulpicia* (The Elegies of Tibulo, Ligdamo, and Sulpicia) (México: Escalante, 1905). *Las poesías de Cayo Valerio Catulo* (The Poetry of Cayo Valerio Catulo) (México: Escalante, 1905). *Tibulo, su vida y sus obras* (Tibulo, His Life and His Works) (México: Escalante, 1905).

BIBLIOGRAPHY: Ignacio M. Altamirano, Prologue to *Evangelina* (México: Tip. El Gran Libro de J. F. Parrés, 1885). Alberto María Carreño, *Notas para una biografía del Lic. Joaquín D. Casasús* (México: Imp. Franco-Mexicana, 1916); *Memorias de la Academia Mexicana* (México: Jus, 1945-1960), vol. 7, pp. 156-57; vol. 8, pp. 62-67; "Elegías de Propercio traducidas por el Dr. Joaquín Casasús con una introducción por Alberto María Carreño," in *Memorias de la Academia Mexicana*, vol. 17, pp. 9-39; "El centenario del Doctor Joaquín D. Casasús," vol. 17, pp. 89-110. Balbino Dávalos, *Ensayos de crítica literaria* (México: Tip. y Lit. La Europea, 1901). Genaro Fernández MacGregor, "El Dr. D. Joaquín Casasús como diplomático," in *Memorias de la Academia Mexicana*, vol. 17, pp. 111-18. Gabriel Méndez Plancarte, *Horacio en México* (México: UNAM, 1937), pp. 149-60. Amado Nervo, "Don Joaquín D. Casasús," in *Obras completas*, vol. 1 (Madrid: Aguilar, 1962), pp. 1318-19. Aurora M. Ocampo de Gómez and Ernesto Prado Velázquez, *Diccionario de escritores mexicanos* (México: UNAM, 1967), pp. 66-67. Manuel Puga y Acal, "Ante los restos del Sr. Licenciado don Joaquín D. Casasús," in *Memorias de la Academia Mexicana*, vol. 9, pp. 274-76. Luis G. Urbina, *Hombres y libros* (México: El Libro Francés, 1923).

JEANNE C. WALLACE

CASO, Antonio (1883-1946), philosopher, critic, and teacher. Antonio Caso was born in Mexico City on December 19, 1883, and died there on March 6, 1946. He studied at the National Preparatory School and then in the School of Jurisprudence. Together with José *Vasconcelos, Alfonso *Reyes and Pedro *Henríquez Ureña, he began to delve deeply into philosophy. This group was the first to attack Positivism and to introduce new philosophical ideas in Mexico. They were joined by others and soon formed the so-called Generation of 1910 (1915 to others). The "generation" had come together as a result of the publication of a literary journal, *Savia Moderna*, founded by Alfonso *Cravioto and Luis *Castillo Ledón in 1906. Besides young Mexican writers, the group included two brothers from the Dominican Republic, Pedro and Max Henríquez Ureña and the Spaniard, José Escofet, who joined them later. A new cultural and literary era was begun by this generation, which included philosophers, critics, novelists and poets. They were joined by other artistic people such as orators, painters (like Diego Rivera) and the composer Manuel M. *Ponce. After *Savia Moderna* was suspended, the Generation of 1910 sought direct contact with the people, and so they founded the Society of Conferences, which became the Ateneo de la Juventud in 1909 (and, later, the Ateneo de México [Mexico's Atheneum]), and the first Popular University in 1913. Foreign cultural influences were no longer limited to the French; young writers studied all major literatures, particularly the Castillian, whose study they introduced in preparatory schools and in the Graduate School of the University. This Generation, which had begun by rebelling against the former's canon, also condemned the usual Bohemian lifestyle of most writers. They became disciplined, serene, and tenacious scholars.

It was Antonio Caso who initiated courses in philosophy at the Graduate School of Mexico's National University in 1910, and soon he was to become known as "el Maestro," *the Teacher*. In 1915 he was named director for a few months of the National Preparatory School, and, years later, he was president of the University from 1920 to 1923. He also traveled throughout Spanish America and lectured in several foreign countries. Caso was to become more than a famous professor and defender of academic freedom, however, for he began to write and to articulate original philosophical theories. He wrote essays and literary criticism, and expressed his own lyricism in two volumes of poetry, *Crisopeya* (1931) and *El políptico de los días del mar* (1935). He was also a noteworthy polemicist and belonged to many national and international professional associations and societies. Caso is considered a high model of spiritual strength, integrity, and purity. He was in essence, a creator and teacher. He was the first Mexican philosopher to preach Henri Bergson's concepts; his own philosophy is summarized in his major book, *La existencia como economía, como desinterés y como caridad* (Existence as Economics, as Non-Profit and as Charity, 1919).

WORKS: *Obras completas* (Complete Works), foreword by Juan Hernández Luna; compiled by Rosa Krauze de Kolteniuk; revised by Carlos Valdes (México: UNAM, 1971); includes bibliographies. *Conferencias del Ateneo de la Juventud* (Conferences at the Youth Atheneum), [by] Antonio Caso et al.; foreword, notes, and appendices by Juan Hernández Luna (México: UNAM, 1962). *La existencia como economía, como desinterés y como caridad* (Existence as Economics, as Non-Profit and as Charity) (México: Eds. México Moderno, 1919); 3rd ed. (México: SEP, 1943). *La persona humana y el estado totalitario* (Human Beings and Totalitarian States) (México: UNAM, 1941). *Poemas* (Poems), foreword by Rubén Bonifaz Nuño

(México: UNAM, 1985), vol. 25 of Complete Works. *Principios de estética* (Aesthetics) (México: Publicaciones de la Secretaría de Educación, 1926). *El problema de México y la ideología nacional* (Mexico and Its National Ideology) (México: Biblioteca Mínima Mexicana, 1923). *Sociología* (Sociology) (México: Publicaciones Cruz O., 1980, c. 1945). *Ensayos críticos y polémicos* (Polemical and Critical Essays), vol. 14, no. 6 (México: Cultura, 1922); foreword by Julio Jiménez Rueda. *Ramos y yo* (Ramos and I [an essay of personal evaluation]) (México: Cultura, 1927). *Positivismo, neopositivismo y fenomenología* (Positivism, Neo-Positivism and Phenomenology) (México: UNAM, 1941). *Crisopeya* (México: Cultura, 1931). *El políptico de los días del mar*, illustrated by Luis Meléndez (Santiago de Chile: Eds. Ercilla, 1935).

BIBLIOGRAPHY: Ermilo Abreu Gómez, "Antonio Caso," *Sala de retratos*, BEP, no. 167 (México: SEP, 1947). Salvador Azuela, "Evocando al maestro Caso," *El Universal* (June 17, 1946). Miguel Angel Cevallos, "Antonio Caso conspirador," *Luminar* 3-4 (1946). Eduardo Colin, *Rasgos* (México: Imp. Manuel L. Sánchez, 1934). Genaro Fernández MacGregor, *Carátulas* (México: Botas, 1935). José Gaos, "El sistema de Caso," *Luminar* 3-4 (1946). Margo Glantz, "La dimensión americana en Antonio Caso," *Filosofía y Letras* 39 (1950). Carlos González Peña, "Nuestros pensadores. Antonio Caso," *Vida Moderna* 21 (Feb. 9, 1916). Pedro Henríquez Ureña, "Mis recuerdos de Antonio Caso," *Luminar* 3-4 (1946). Rosa Krauze de Kolteniuk, *La filosofía de Antonio Caso* (México: UNAM, 1961). José Luis Martínez, *El ensayo mexicano moderno*, vol. 1 (México: FCE, 1958), pp. 159-79. Samuel Ramos, "La filosofía de Antonio Caso," *Cuadernos Americanos* (May-June 1946). Alfonso Reyes, *Pasado inmediato y otros ensayos* (México: El Colegio de México, 1941). Leopoldo Zea, "Antonio Caso y la realidad mexicana," in *Papel Literario*, suppl. of *El Nacional* (Caracas, July 21, 1955).

HERLINDA HERNANDEZ

CASTELLANOS, Rosario (1925-1974), poet, novelist, short story writer, journalist, professor, and diplomat. Born in Mexico City on May 24, 1924, Rosario Castellanos grew up in Comitán, Chiapas. Her family moved to Mexico City, after losing its landholdings to agrarian reform (1942), and Castellanos finished high school in the capital city. In 1950 she received a master's degree in philosophy from the Universidad Nacional Autónoma de México, with a thesis titled "De la cultura femenina" (On Feminine Culture). This work is considered the point of departure for Mexico's contemporary feminist movement. A scholarship allowed her to pursue graduate studies in Spain, at Madrid's Universidad complutense. Upon her return to Mexico she became involved in a variety of jobs. She worked for the Institute of Indian Affairs both in Chiapas (1956-1957) and Mexico City (1958-1961); was appointed professor of comparative literature and public relations officer at the UNAM; and wrote weekly columns for the newspaper *Excelsior* and for the cultural supplements of *Novedades* (The Latest News) and *Siempre!* (Always!). In 1958 she married Ricardo Guerra, a philosophy professor, and gave birth to one son, Gabriel. She resigned from the university in 1966, to protest the government's mishandling of the UNAM's president, and became a visiting professor in the United States at the

Universities of Wisconsin, Indiana, and Colorado. After her divorce, she was appointed Mexico's ambassador to Israel (1971) and moved there with her young son. While serving as a diplomat she also taught classes at the University of Tel-Aviv. She died in Israel in 1974, as a result of an accidental electrocution.

Castellanos' literary career started early and by the time of her death she was the most influential woman writing in Mexico. Her first books of poetry appeared (1948) before she graduated from the UNAM (1948; *Trayectoria del polvo* and *Apuntes para una declaración de fé*). Her parents' deaths (both in 1948) and a bout with tuberculosis (1952) produced many of the dark, despairing poems contained in these two works. *El rescate del mundo* showed a change toward a simpler expression and themes closer to everyday reality. *Poemas* (1952) elaborated a series of feminist concerns that climaxed in *En la tierra de en medio* (In the Land of In-Between) (1972), a painfully ironic collection of autobiographical poems. Two years before her death she prepared a personal anthology, *Poesía no eres tú* (You Are Not Poetry), which contains an excellent overview of her most representative poems.

Through grants received in 1953 and 1954 she carried out research in Chiapas that she incorporated in her first novel, *Balún Canán*. This work, which received the Chiapas Prize in 1958, is a personal childhood account seen through the eyes of a nine-year-old girl narrator. It describes the cultural confrontation between the natural magic world of the Indians and the pragmatic world of white culture. Her second novel, *Oficio de tinieblas*, continued and expanded the same themes. It questioned the structures of power through a panoramic view of racism, sexism, and oppression in the Chiapas of the 1930s. This novel, which won the Sor Juana Inés de la Cruz Prize, has been described as the most artistic and the best of Mexico's *indigenista* novels. Castellanos' third novel, *Ritos de iniciación*, moves the action from the Indian-Ladino mythical world of Chiapas to contemporary Mexico City. It narrates the fictionalized story of an adolescent girl at Mexico's National University in the 1940s. In addition to these novels, Castellanos has written several collections of short stories which present a strong feminist indictment of the chauvinistic world that surrounded her. In overall development they show the same pattern evident in her full-length narrative. That is, they move from the anthropological portrayal of social and racial prejudices in the provinces to the examination of the alienating world of urban life.

Aside from these works of poetry and fiction, Castellanos also published two collections of essays, prior to her death. Not surprisingly, since they deal with the literary and social topics of the day, they present her social and feminist concerns in a straightforward manner.

WORKS: Poetry: *Trayectoria del polvo* (Dust's Trajectory) (México: Costa Amic, 1948). *Apuntes para una declaración de fe* (Notes for a Declaration of Faith) (México: Eds. América, Revista Antológica, 1948). *De la vigilia estéril* (From a Sterile Vigil) (México: Eds. América, Revista Antológica, 1950). *El rescate del mundo* (The World's Ransome) (Tuxtla Gutiérrez: Departamento de Prensa y Turismo, 1952). *Poemas 1953-1955* (Poems 1953-1955) (México: Colección Metáfora, No. 7, 1957). *Al pie de la letra* (Literally) (Xalapa: Editorial Veracruzana, 1959). *Lívida luz* (Livid Light) (México: UNAM, 1960). *Poesía no eres tú. Obra poética (1948-1871)* (You Are Not Poetry. Poetic Works [1948-1971]) (México: FCE, 1972). *Meditación en el umbral* (Poetic Anthology), compiled by Julián Palley; prologue by Elena Poniatowska (México: FCE, 1985). Novels: *Balún Canán* (Nine Guardians [New York, 1959])

(México: FCE, 1957). *Oficio de tinieblas* (Ritual of Darkness) (México: Mortiz, 1962). *Ritos de iniciación* (Rites of Initiation) (México: n.p., 1966). Short Stories: *Ciudad Real* (Royal City) (Xalapa: Editorial Veracruzana, 1960). *Los convidados de agosto* (August Guests) (México, D.F.: Era, 1964). *Album de familia* (Family Album) (México, D.F.: Mortiz, 1971). Essays: *Sobre cultura femenina* (On Feminine Culture) (México: Ed. America, 1950). *Juicios Sumarios* (Summary Judgments) (Xalapa: Universidad Veracruzana, 1966). *Materia memorable* (Memorable Matters) (México: UNAM, 1969). *La novela mexicana contemporánea y su valor testimonial* (The Mexican Contemporary Novel and Its Testimonial Value) (México: Instituto Nacional de la Juventud Mexicana, 1972). *Mujer que sabe latín...* (A Woman Who Knows Latin...) (México: SEP, 1973). *El uso de la palabra* (The Use of Words) (México: Excelsior, 1974). *El mar y sus pescaditos* (The Sea and Its Little Fishes) (México: SEP, 1975). Theater: *El eterno femenino* (The Eternal Feminine) (México: FCE, 1975).

BIBLIOGRAPHY: Maureen Ahern, and Mary Seale Vásquez, eds., *Homenaje a Rosario Castellanos* (Valencia, Spain: Albatros, 1980). Helen M. Anderson, "Rosario Castellanos and the Structures of Power," *Contemporary Women Authors of Latin America. Introductory Essays*, edited by Doris M. Meyer and Margarita Fernández Olmos (Brooklyn: Brooklyn College Press, 1983), pp. 22-32; Germaine Calderón, *El universo poético de Rosario Castellanos* (México: UNAM, 1979). María Rosa Fiscal, *La imagen de la mujer en la narrativa de Rosario Castellanos* (México: UNAM, 1980). Graciela Hierro de Matte, "La filosofía de Rosario Castellanos," *Plural* 10, 120 (Spring 1981): 29-33. Beth Miller, *Rosario Castellanos. Una conciencia feminista en México* (Chiapas: UNACH, 1983). Kirsten F. Nigro, "Rosario Castellanos: Debunking of the Eternal Feminine," *Journal of Spanish Studies: Twentieth Century* 8, 1-2 (Spring-Fall 1980): 89-102. Aurora M. Ocampo, "Debe haber otro modo de ser humano y libre: Rosario Castellanos," *Cuadernos Americanos* 250, 5 (1983): 199-212. Pearl Schwartz, *Rosario Castellanos. Mujer que supo latín* (México, D.F.: Katún, 1984).

MARIA A. SALGADO

CASTELLANOS Quinto, Erasmo (1879-1955), poet and educator. Erasmo Quinto Castellanos was born in Santiago Tuxtla, Veracruz, on August 3, 1879, and he died in Mexico City on December 11, 1955. He studied law but soon abandoned it to take up teaching in his native state. Later, he transferred to Mexico City and eventually came to replace Amado *Nervo in his teaching duties while the latter served as ambassador abroad. Castellanos Quinto was appointed for life Chair of Spanish Language at the National Preparatory School, and he also taught Peninsular literature and world literature at the university's School of Philosophy and Letters. He was elected a member of Mexico's Academy of the Spanish Language, and he published a book of poetry, *Del fondo del Abra*. His inspired poetry is intense, yet delicate, and presents several themes. His work has been compiled and published posthumously by Roberto Oropeza Martinez: *Poesía inédita* (1962). Among his essays are two that merit mention, one on Dante, *Las siete murallas* or *El castillo de la fama* (The Seven Walls or The Castle of Fame), and the other on Cervantes, *El triunfo* *de los encantadores* (The Triumph of the Sorcerers). He received a prize for the second one from the Cervantes Society of Mexico.

WORKS: *Del fondo del abra: Poemas líricos*, introduction by Leonardo Pasquel and foreword by Luis G. Betancourt (Tacubaya, México: Citlaltepetl, 1962, c. 1922). *Poesía inédita* (Unpublished Poetry), foreword by Roberto Oropeza Martínez (México: Porrúa, 1962). "Discurso elogio del academico don Luis G. Urbina," read at the Mexican Academy of the Language, April 4, 1922.

BIBLIOGRAPHY: Alberto María Carreño, Bibliographical note, *Memorias de la Academia Mexicana*, vol. 7 (México, 1945): 170-71. "Bibliografía de Erasmo Castellanos Quinto," *Memorias de la Academia Mexicana de la Lengua*, vol. 8 (México, 1946): 71-72. Ileana Gómez-Llata Andrade, *La poesía del maestro Erasmo Castellanos Quinto*, thesis (México: Universidad Iberoamericana, 1965).

HERLINDA HERNANDEZ

CASTERA, Pedro (1838-1906). Pedro Castera was born in Mexico City on the September 29, 1838. While little is known of his early life and studies, it is known that he fought against the French intervention and the second empire. He was awarded the rank of commandant for his valor in the siege of Querétaro. Castera was also a miner and had a lifelong love of treasure searches.

As a writer Castera can be placed as a pivotal figure between Romanticism and Realism. He wrote articles for journals, short stories, and novels. Castera became editor of *La República* after Ignacio *Altamirano left this position in 1882. Several of his works were published through the journal press. Also in 1882 his novel *Carmen* appeared in serial form. Castera's popularity in later years was due to this novel, inspired by the general reception given Jorge Isaac's novel *María*. Other novels show the life of the miners, a novelty and precursor to the period of Realism. *Los maduros* (Those of Age) is the first novel in México to show the world of the working class.

Castera was a deputy to the Union Congress and a member of the Societies of Mexican Mining and of Geography and Statistics. For reasons unknown, but apparently related to politics, Castera was interned for mental illness in the Hospital of San Hipólito for a period of time. He made a complete recovery and resumed his duties with both *El Universal* and *La República*. He died, alone and poor, in Tacubaya, D.F., on December 5, 1906.

WORKS: *Cuentos mineros. Un combate* (Mining Stories. A Battle) (México: Imp. de E.D. Orozco y Cía., 1881). *Las minas y los mineros* (Mines and Miners), vol. 1 (México, 1882). *Impresiones y recuerdos* (Impressions and Memories) (México: Imp. del Socialista, de S. Lopez, 1882). *Carmen* (México: Ed. de la República, 1882; México: Eufemio Abadiano, 1887; México: Libr. de la Vda. de Bouret, 1920; México: Porrúa, 1986). *Los maduros* (Those of Age) (México: Tip. de la República, 1882). *Ensueños y armonías* (Daydreams and Harmonies) (poetry) (México, 1882). *Querens* (Querens) (novel) (México: Biblioteca de "El Universal," 1890; 2nd ed. (El Paso, Texas: Talleres Linotipográficas de "La Patria," 1923). *Dramas en un corazón* (Dramas in a Heart) (novel) (México: Tip. de E. Dublán y Cía., 1890).

BIBLIOGRAPHY: J. S. Brushwood, *The Romantic Novel* (Columbia, Missouri: n.p., 1954), pp. 48-49, 63-64. Heriberto García Rivas, *Historia de la literatura mexicana* (México: Textos Universitarios, 1972), vol. 2, p. 141. Aurora M. Ocampo de Gómez and Ernesto Prado Velázquez, *Diccionario de escritores mexicanos* (México: UNAM, 1967), pp. 70-71.

FILIPPA B. YIN

CASTILLO, Florencio M. del (1828-1863). Born in Mexico City on November 27, 1828, Florencio M. del Castillo was a journalist and fiction writer. His first essays, of a political nature, were published in *El Monitor Republicano*, of which he later became an editor. A liberal, he vehemently defended the ideas and principles of reform, as he understood them. Active in political affairs, he served in several public capacities, including a short term in a constitutional congress in 1857, where he seized the opportunity to advocate political and social reforms. He was exiled on at least two occasions because of his fiery oratory and vitriolic written attacks against governmental policies.

In addition to fighting with his pen, he took up arms against the French intervention, and was arrested in August 1863 and detained in a place of dismal conditions. His confinement at that time cost him his life. He was gravely ill upon his release, and he died shortly thereafter in a hospital on October 27, 1863.

Besides his political writings and activities, del Castillo was among the first in Mexico to cultivate the short story and short novel. The noted writer and literary critic Ignacio *Altamirano saw him at that time as the foremost writer of sentimental literature, similar to some of the Romantics in Spain and France. Del Castillo experimented with what was called the "social novel," depicting the complexities of society and attempting to do so by combining psychology with the characteristics of the typical Romantic novel. Like the work of many of his contemporaries, however, his writing was overly sentimental, indeed, melodramatic, seeking to extract every bit of emotion from both the characters and the readers. The short novels that comprise *Horas de tristeza* (Hours of Sadness), published in 1850, are, as the title of the collection suggests, filled with sadness, suffering, and the various tragedies that befall human beings.

His most complex novel, *Hermana de los ángeles* (Sister of the Angels), is a study of the plight of women who sacrifice themselves in one way or another. A longer novel than his others, although not well-developed, it is overwhelmingly sad, an atmosphere that characterizes and pervades much of del Castillo's work.

Because his narration in general is quite poor, he is not considered a good novelist. He is overly concerned with the plight of the less fortunate in the middle class, whose suffering and tragedy he repeatedly addresses in his works. Despite the limitations and shortcomings of his Romantic novels, del Castillo did enjoy a certain amount of popularity, primarily because the Romantic novel was still in vogue at the time.

WORKS: *Amor y desgracia u horas de tristeza* (Love and Misfortune or Hours of Sadness) (México: Imp. de V. García Torres, 1849). *La corona de azucenas* (The Crown of White Lilies) (México: Imp. de V. García, Torres, 1849). *¡Hasta el cielo!* (Until Heaven!) (México: Imp. de V. García Torres, 1849). *Dolores ocultos* (Hidden

Pains) (México: Imp. de V. Garcí Torres, 1849). *Horas de tristeza* (Hours of Sadness), contains all of the above (México: Manuel Ituarte, 1850). "Don Manuel Eduardo de Gorostiza," in *Biblioteca Mexicana Popular y Económica*, vol. 1 (México: Tip. de V. García Torres, 1851), pp. 133-36. *Hermana de los ángeles* (Sister of the Angels) (México: Establecimiento Tip. de Andrés Boix, 1854). *Expiación* (Expiation), also called *Culpa* (Blame) (México: n.p., 1854). *Botón de rosa* (Rose Bud) (México: n.p., 1854); in José Mancisdor, *Cuentos mexicanos del siglo XIX*, 2nd ed. (México: Edit. Nueva España, 1946), pp. 161-69. *Dos horas en el hospital de San Andrés* (Two Hours in the Hospital of Saint Andrew). *Obras completas* (Complete Works) (México: n.p., 1872). *Botón de rosa, En un cementerio, Don Manuel E. Gorostiza* (Rose Bud, in a Cemetery, Don Manuel E. Gorostiza) (México: Bibl. de La Orquesta, 1875). *Obras. Novelas cortas* (Works. Short Novels) (México: Imp. de V. Agüeros, 1902).

BIBLIOGRAPHY: Ignacio M. Altamirano, *La literatura nacional* (México: Porrúa, 1949), vol. 1, pp. 46-49; vol. 2, pp. 169-78; in *Boletín Bibliográfico de la Secretaría de Hacienda y Crédito Público* 281 (Oct. 1963): 2-3. John S. Brushwood, *The Romantic Novel in Mexico* (Columbia, Mo.: n.p., 1954), pp. 22, 23-25, 27, 35, 64-65, 68; *Mexico in Its Novel* (Austin: University of Texas Press, 1966), pp. 76-77, 138-39. John S. Brushwood and José Rojas Garcidueñas, *Breve historia de la novela mexicana* (México: Eds. de Andrea, 1959), pp. 25-27. Juan B. Iguíñez, *Bibliografía de novelistas mexicanos* (México: Imp. de la Sría. de Relaciones, 1926), pp. 68-70. Luis Leal, *Breve historia del cuento mexicano* (México: Eds. de Andrea, 1956), pp. 41-42. Ernesto Lemoine V., "Otro centenario luctuoso. Florencio M. del Castillo," in *Boletín Bibliográfico de la Secretaría de Hacienda y Crédito Público* 281 (Oct. 15, 1963): 4-5. Aurora M. Ocampo de Gómez and Ernesto Prado Velázquez *Diccionario de escritores mexicanos* (México: UNAM, 1967), pp. 71-72. Francisco Pimentel, "Novelistas y oradores mexicanos," in *Obras Completas* (México: Tip. Económica, 1903-1904), pp. 324-27. Teresa Rulfo y de Rosenzweig, *Las heroinas de la novela mexicana del siglo XIX* (México: n.p., 1954), p. 68. Carlos J. Sierra, "Ensayo hemerográfico de Florencio María del Castillo Velasco," in *Boletín Bibliográfico de la Secretaría de Hacienda y Crédito Público* 281 (Oct. 15, 1863): 6-12. Francisco Sosa, *Biografías de mexicanos distinguidos* (México: Ed. de la Sría de Fomento, 1884), pp. 233-37. Ralph Warner, *Historia de la novela mexicana en el siglo xix* (México: Ant. Libr. Robredo, 1953), pp. 20-21. José Zorrilla, *México y los mexicanos* (México: Eds. de Andrea, 1955), pp. 133-34.

JEANNE C. WALLACE

CASTILLO LEDON, Amalia. See GONZALEZ CABALLERO DE CASTILLO LEDON, Amalia.

CASTILLO LEDON, Luis (1879-1944), historian, literary critic, and poet. Castillo Ledón was born in Santiago Ixcuintla, Nayarit, on January 17, 1879 and died in Mexico City on October 7, 1944. He attended primary school in his hometown and preparatory school in a boy's school in Guadalajara. He began to write poetry at an early age and worked with several newspapers while in Guadalajara. He later moved to Mexico City to continue working as a journalist. Together with Alfonso *Cravioto, he founded the literary magazine *Savia Moderna* in 1906. In addition to his journalistic work, he served as secretary and director of the National Museum of Archaeology, History and Ethnology; grammar professor at the National Preparatory School; and government representative for his native district. He also belonged to the Academy of History.

His poetry is collected in a single volume: *Lo que miro y lo que siento* (What I See and What I Feel). It is a product of his youth with a note of intimacy and a certain sensuous air that denotes Gabriele D'Annunzio's influence. But even though Castillo Ledón showed an affinity for poetry and fiction, he chose to make history his life's work. Like other members of his generation, he was a serious scholar; he paid attention to details and delved deeply into Mexican history, especially the Independence period. Beginning in 1908, he followed Hidalgo's itinerary from his birth to his martyrdom; he took many photographs and collected documents and data from all the historical places. He dedicated his life to the study of Miguel Hidalgo y Costilla, the "father of the country," the man who first led the Mexican people in their struggle for independence. Castillo Ledón wanted to introduce Mexicans to a great historical figure who was largely unknown, and so he spent more than thirty tenacious years on this task. This monumental work, titled *Hidalgo: la vida del héroe* (Hidalgo: The Hero's Life), was published posthumously in two thick volumes in 1948-1949.

WORKS: "Los mexicanos autores de operas" (Mexican Opera Writers), *Anales del Museo Nacional de Arqueología, Historia y Etnología* 3rd series, vol. 2 (1910): 315-54. *Lo que miro y lo que siento* (What I See and What I Feel) (Madrid: Tip. Artística, 1916). *El chocolate* (Chocolate) (México: Dir. Gen. de Bellas Artes, 1917). *Antigua literatura indigena mexicana* (Pre-Columbian Mexican Literature) (México: Imp. Victoria, 1917). *Origenes de la novela en México* (Origins of the Mexican Novel) (México: Museo Nac. de Arq., Hist. y Etno., 1922). *El Museo Nacional de Arqueología, Historia y Etnografía, 1825-1925* (The National Museum of Archaeology, History and Ethnography) (México: Museo Nacional, 1924). *El Paseo de la Viga y de Santa Anita* (the Boulevard of The Viga and Saint Anne) (México: n.p., 1925). *La fundación de la ciudad de México* (The Founding of Mexico City) (México: Cultura, 1925). *La conquista y colonización española en México, su verdadero carácter* (The Spanish Conquest and Colonization in Mexico, Its True Character) (México: Museo Nacional, 1932). *Estudio preliminar al "Epistolario" de Juan de la Granja* (Preliminary Study to Juan de la Granja's "Epistolario") (México: Museo Nacional, 1937). *Hidalgo: la vida del héroe* (Hidalgo: The Hero's Life) (México; n.p. 1948-1949).

BIBLIOGRAPHY: Genaro Estrada, *Poetas nuevos de México* (México: Porrúa, 1916), pp. 25-27. Isidro Fabela, "El *Hidalgo* de Luis Castillo Ledón," in *Maestros y amigos* (México: INBA, 1962), pp. 43-46. Carlos González Peña, "Los compositores líricos mexicanos," in *El Mundo Ilustrado* (Jan. 8, 1911). Artemio de Valle-Arizpe, *Historia de la ciudad de México según los relatos de sus cronistas*, 4th ed. (México: Ant. Libr. Robredo, 1946), pp. 479-81.

                                                      HERLINDA HERNANDEZ

CASTILLO NAJERA, Francisco (1886-1954). Castillo Nájera was born in Durango November 25, 1886. Early in his life he moved to Mexico City, where he studied medicine. Upon graduation from medical school in 1913, he went abroad for further training in Paris, Berlin, Brussels, and New York. After travel and study in Europe and the United States, Castillo Nájera returned to México and became a professor at the School of Medicine. In 1915 he joined the army as a doctor and fought against the forces of Zapata and later of Villa. In 1918 he was appointed to the board of the Juárez Hospital. During his distinguished medical career he was named president of the National Academy of Medicine (1932).

A well-known diplomat, he served as minister in the Mexican delegation in China, Belgium, Holland, Sweden, France, and the United States off and on between 1922 and 1947. Many of his speeches given in international conferences in European and Latin American countries were later published in México. Known mainly as a poet, Castillo Nájera is also the author of numerous essays on medicine, politics, language, and literature. He published three books of poetry, *Albores* (Dawns, 1906), *El gavilán corrido* (The Sparrow-Hawk) (1934), and *Treguas líricas* (Lyrical Intermissions) (1946). He gained fame and recognition with his famous popular ballad *El gavilán corrido*, in which he re-creates the lyrical romantic story of Jesús de Cienfuegos, the revolutionary Mexican hero.

In 1931 he edited and translated a volume of Belgian poetry, including critical notes, *Un siglo de poesía belga, 1830-1930* (A Century of Belgian Verse, 1830-1930). Five years later he published *Consideraciones sobre el español que se habla en México* (Considerations Relative to Spanish Spoken in Mexico, 1936). His last work was a book of criticism on *Manuel Acuña* (1950). Four years later Castillo Nájera died in Mexico City.

WORKS: Poetry: *Albores* (Durango: Imp. de Alberto de Alvarado, 1906). *El gavilán* (México: Ed. México Nuevo, 1939). *Treguas líricas* (México: Editora Cortés, 1945). Essays: *Consideraciones sobre el español que se habla en México* (New York: Instituto de las Españas en América, 1936). *Voz de México en el extranjero. Discursos y alocuciones* (México: Imp. de la Secretaría de Relaciones Exteriores, 1936). *Manuel Acuña* (México: Imp. Universitaria, 1950).

BIBLIOGRAPHY: Heriberto García Rivas, *Historia de la literatura mexicana* (México: Porrúa, 1972), pp. 60-61. Carlos González Peña, *Historia de la literatura mexicana* (México: Porrúa, 1981), p. 270. Aurora M. Ocampo de Gómez and Ernesto Prado Velázquez, *Diccionario de escritores mexicanos* (México: UNAM, 1967), pp. 72-73.

                                                                NORA ERRO-PERALTA

CASTILLO y Lanzas, Joaquín M. del (1801-1878), poet, politician, and diplomat. Castillo y Lanzas was born in Jalapa, Veracruz, on November 11, 1801. He attended Stong Huest and Oldttald Reen schools in England; then he went to the University of Glasgow, Scotland, and to the Seminary of Vergara in Spain. On his return to Mexico he was appointed chargé d'affaires in the United States (1833-1837) and later plenipotentiary minister in London (1853-1855, 1866). He was the first to translate

Lord Byron's poetry into Spanish. He imitated the Ecuadorian José J. de Olmedo in his ode *A la victoria de Tamaulipas* (To the Victory in Tamaulipas). He was the editor of *Mercurio* and *Diario de Veracruz* (1825) and *La Euterpe* (1826).

WORKS: *A la victoria de Tamaulipas* (To the Victory in Tamaulipas) (México: n.p., n.d.). *Oicios Juveniles* (Youthful Pastimes) (Philadelphia: E. G. Dorsey, 1835). *Elementos de Geografía para uso de los establecimientos de instrucción pública* (Elements of Geography for the Institutions of Public Instruction) (without the author's name (México: n.p., 1835).

BIBLIOGRAPHY: Julio Jiménez Rueda, *Letras mexicanas en el siglo XIX* (México: FCE, 1944), p. 89; *Historia de la literatura mexicana* (México: Botas, 1960), p. 195. Francisco Sosa, *Biografías de mexicanos distinguidos* (México: Tip. de la Secretaría de Fomento, 1884), pp. 226-29.

JOSEPH VELEZ

CASTRO, Dolores (1923-   ). Born in Aguascalientes on April 12, 1923, Dolores Castro studied both law and letters at the Universidad Nacional. She took courses in art at the University of Madrid for the academic year 1950-1951. Between 1974 and 1976 she took further studies in literature and linguistics at the Asociación Nacional de Universidades e Institutos de Enseñanza Superior. In 1983 she studied radio at the Instituo Latinoamericano de Comunicación Educativa. A journalist, poet, and radio producer, she has made a significant contribution to culture and the arts. Her literary and administrative involvement with various journals has helped develop her career. Under the auspices of UNAM and the Palacio de Bellas Artes, she has given conferences on literature. She has published several volumes of poetry and a novel.

Dolores Castro was accorded attention with the publication of her poem *El corazón transfigurado* (The Transfigured Heart), in 1949. Her main volumes since then are *Nocturnos* (Nocturns) (1950), *Siete poemas* (Seven Poems) (1952), *La tierra está sonando* (The Earth Is Ringing) (1959), and *Cantares de vela* (Songs of Vigilance) (1960). Her poetic style is considered mature, clear, sensitive, and distinctive. She also published the novel, *La ciudad y el viento* (The City and the Wind), in 1962, which deals with Mexican provincial life in the post-revolution years.

WORKS: Poetry: *El corazón transfigurado* (The Transfigured Heart) (México: Eds. de "América," 1949). *Dos nocturnos* (Two Nocturns) (México: Icaro, 1952). *Siete poemas* (Seven Poems) (México: Los Epígrafes, 1952). *La tierra está sonando* (The Earth Is Ringing) (México: Imp. Universitaria, 1959). *Cantares de vela* (Songs of Vigilance) (México: Jus, 1960). "Nocturno" (Nocturn) in *Revista de Bellas Artes* 10 (July-Aug. 1966): 48. *Soles* (Suns) (México: Jus, 1977). "¿Qué es lo vivido?" (What Is Having Lived?), in *Sábado* 155 (Oct. 25, 1980): 16. "Poemas" (Poems), in *Revista Mexicana de Cultura* 10 (April 24, 1983): 5. "Xalapa bajo la lluvia" (Xalapa under the Rain), in *Sábado* 326 (Jan. 27, 1984): 7. Novel: *La ciudad y el viento* (The City and the Wind) (Xalapa: Universidad Veracruzana, 1962). Essays: Weekly column: "Los hechos y la cultura," in *Nivel*, from Oct. 25, 1964, to Oct. 25, 1965. "Evocación y poesía," in *Rosario Castellanos, El verso, la palabra y el recuerdo* (México: Instituto

Mexicano Israelita, Costa-Amic, 1984), pp. 38-44. Theater: *Dicha y desdichas de Nicolás Méndez* (Fortune and Misfortunes of Nicolás Méndez), in collaboration with Efrén Hernández, Rosario Castellanos, and Marco Antonio Millán, in *América* 65 (April 1951): 161-310.

BIBLIOGRAPHY: Griselda Alvarez, *Diez mujeres en la poesía mexicana del siglo XX* (México: Sría de Obras y Servicios, 1974). Anon., "Mujeres de México," in *Nivel* 21 (Sept. 25, 1960): 1-2, 6. "Poetisas mexicanas, Dolores Castro," in *Nivel* 232 (April 30, 1982): 12. Jesús Arellano Meléndez, Review of *El corazón transfigurado*, in *Fuensanta* 1, 5 (April 30, 1949): 4. Alfredo Cardona Peña, "Poesías de Dolores Castro," in *Nivel* 1 (Jan. 25, 1963): 1-2. Emilio Carballido, Review of *Dos nocturnos*, in *El Nacional*, Suppl. 182 (Sept. 17, 1950): 11. Emmanuel Carballo, Review of *La ciudad y el viento*, in *La Cultura en México* 28 (Aug. 20, 1962): xvi. Carmen Castellote, "El mundo poético de Dolores Castro; su raíz es la verdad, su hábito, la imaginación," in *Los Universitarios* 197 (Mar. 1982): 31, 32. Antonio Castro Leal, *La poesía mexicana moderna* (México: FCE, 1953), pp. 483-84. Frank Dauster, *Breve historia de la poesía mexicana* (México: Eds. de Andrea, 1956), p. 179. Virginia Durán Campello, "Castro y Azar hablan de Rosario Castellanos," in *Revista Mexicana de Cultura* 84 (Oct. 7, 1984): 4, 5. Heriberto García Rivas, *Historia de la literatura mexicana*, vol. 4 (México: Porrúa, 1974), p. 350. Joaquín Gutiérrez Niño, "Dolores Castro, el valor de la entidad," in *El Nacional* (Feb. 18, 1980): 9. Ignacio Méndez, Review of *La ciudad y el viento*, in *México en la Cultura* 701 (Aug. 19, 1962): 11. Carlos Newman, "Grandes poetisas mexicanas," in *Nivel* 255 (Mar. 31, 1984): 2, 3. Aurora M. Ocampo de Gómez and Ernesto Prado Velázquez, *Diccionario de escritores mexicanos* (México: UNAM, 1967), pp. 74-75. Germán Pardo García, "La poetisa mexicana Dolores Castro," in *Nivel* 193 (Jan. 1979): 5. "Dolores Castro," in *Nivel* 255 (Mar. 31, 1984): 3. Javier Peñalosa, "Esencia de Dolores Castro," in *Nivel* 1 (Jan. 25, 1963): 1-2. Salvador Reyes Nevares, Review of *Cantares de vela*, in *México en la Cultura* 581 (April 30, 1960): 4. Héctor Valdes, *Poetisas mexicanas, siglo XX. Antología* (México: UNAM, 1976), p. 105.

JEANNE C. WALLACE

CASTRO, José Agustín (1730-1814). Castro was born in 1730 in Valladolid, Michoacán. He was a notary in the ecclesiastical tribunal of this region and between 1791 and 1797 was chief notary of the Tribunal of Justice and chief vicar of the bishopric of Puebla. He died in 1814.

Castro is notable for his emphasis on the national and indigenous and thus was a writer of the transitional period between colony and independence. These tendencies are particularly evident in his two plays *Los remendones* (The Cobblers) and *El Charro* (The Charro), which represent the first attempts of the nineteenth century to represent onstage genuinely Mexican features. He published his poetry in three volumes, *Miscelánea de poesías sagradas y humanas,* the first two volumes published in Puebla in 1797 and the third in Mexico in 1809. These volumes contain short poems; religious *loas*; autos; verse lives of St. Augustine, St. Francis of Assisi, and St. Louis Gonzaga; versions of Latin poems; a prose piece, *Exhortación privada a una novicia* (Private Exhortation to a Novice); and the theater pieces previously mentioned. His poetry is noted for complicated and prosaic language, provincialisms, and rich description of local customs.

WORKS: *Miscelánea de poesías sagradas y humanas* (Puebla: n.p., 1797). *Poesías humanas* (México: Arizpe, 1809).

BIBLIOGRAPHY: Gabriel Méndez Plancarte, *Horacio en México* (México: Eds. de la Universidad Nacional, 1937). Luis G. Urbina, *Antología del Centenario* (México: n.p., 1917). Rodolfo Usigli, *México en el teatro* (México: Mundial, 1932).

ANITA K. STOLL

CASTRO LEAL, Antonio (1896-1981). Antonio Castro Leal was born on March 2, 1896, in San Luis Potosí. He received a law degree from the Universidad Nacional de México, but chose journalism as his profession. A member of the Generation of 1915, he went on to become a distinguished critic, essayist, and storywriter. He also wrote a little poetry, sometimes using the pseudonym Miguel Potosí. But Castro Leal is especially known for his prologues and editions of the many works of Mexican authors.

Among his many service positions, he was the director of the Colección de Escritores Mexicanos of the Porrúa publishing company, rector of the Universidad Nacional de México for a short time, head of the Departamento de Bellas Artes (1934), and the first director of the Palacio de Bellas Artes. He also held several diplomatic posts in Europe and America, including Mexico's ambassador for UNESCO in Paris from 1949 to 1952. He founded and directed the *Revista de Literatura Mexicana*. A member of a number of distinguished academies and associations, Castro Leal had a long and active career. He died in Mexico City January 7, 1981.

Antonio Castro Leal was greatly influenced by English literature, copying to an extent some of its salient characteristics in his own writings. A prose writer and critic, he has carefully constructed elegantly written essays, including a substantial work on the life and work of *Ruiz de Alarcón, plus others on some famous modern writers. He has also written impressive analyses of modern Mexican poetry. His prologues, essays, and studies place him as a critic of the first category among contemporary writers.

He received recognition as a story writer, especially for his tales and fantasies. Much of his original work had been initially published in magazines and journals, both in Mexico and elsewhere. Along with other writings, some of the previously published were gathered in one volume, entitled *El laurel de San Lorenzo* (The Laurel Wreath of Saint Lorenzo), and published in 1959. Elements of light comedy, satire, and occasionally mystery characterize several of his stories. He also created psychological profiles of some of his characters.

He is, perhaps, more well known as a prologuist, with introductory biographical sketches, notes, and studies about a number of significant writers. There was criticism, however, notably by Emmanuel *Carballo, that Castro Leal's prologues really weren't this. This published attack generated a sharp rebuttal by Antonio Castro Leal, who defended himself against what he considered to be untruth.

WORKS: Essays: *Juan Ruiz de Alarcón, su vida y su obra* (Juan Ruiz de Alarcón, His Life and His Works) (México: Ed. Cuadernos Americanos, 1943). "Las dos partes del Quijote" (The Two Parts of the Quijote), conference, El Colegio Nacional, México, 1948. "La poesía mexicana moderna" (Modern Mexican Poetry), conference, July 11, 1953, Academia Mexicana de la Lengua, prologue of vol. 12 of the Col. de Letras Mexicanas (México: FCE, 1953). "Un mensaje a la América Latina y Una elegía por España," Mexico, 1960. "Sobre el mexicanismo de Don Juan Ruiz de Alarcón," in *CN/M* 6, 4 (1969): 85-126. *Francisco de la Maza, historiador y crítico de arte* (Francisco de la Maza, Historian and Art Critic) (México: Ed. de la Academia de Artes, 1970). Editions, Translations, Prologues: *Las cien mejores poesías (líricas) mexicanas* (The One Hundred Best Mexican Lyrical Poems), in collaboration with Manuel Toussaint and Alberto Vásquez del Mercado (México: n.p., 1914); 2nd ed. (México: Porrúa, 1935); 3rd ed. (México: n.p., 1939); 4th and 5th eds. (México: Porrúa, 1953, 1962). Bernard Shaw, *Vencidos* (Conquered), translation and comments (México: Cultura, 1917). *Poesías de Leopoldo Lugones,* (Poems by Leopoldo Lugones) selection and study (México: Cultura, 1923). *Antología de poetas muertos en la guerra 1914-1918* (Anthology of Poets Killed in the War 1914-1918), prologue and notes (México: Cultura, 1919). *Poemas en prosa de Pedro Prado* (Pedro Prado's Poems in Prose), selection and prologue (México: Cultura, 1923). Percy B. Shelley, *Adonais,* translated in collaboration with Manuel Altolaguirre (México: n.p., 1938). *Ingenio y sabiduría de don Juan Ruiz de Alarcón* (Ingenuity and Wisdom of Juan Ruiz de Alarcón), selection and prologue (México: Porrúa, 1939). *Las cien mejores poesías mexicanas modernas* (The One Hundred Best Modern Mexican Poems), selection and study (México: Porrúa, 1935); 2nd ed. (1939); 3rd ed. (1953, 1962, and 1970). *Páginas escogidas de José Vasconcelos* (Selected Pages from José Vasconcelos), selection and prologue (México: n.p., 1940). *Poesías completas de Salvador Díaz Mirón* (Complete Poetry of Salvador Díaz Mirón), study, notes, and bibliography (México: Porrúa, 1941); 2nd ed. (1945). *Poesía de Francisco de Terrazas* (Poetry of Francisco de Terrazas), edition, prologue, and notes (México: Porrúa, 1941). *Dos o tres mundos* (Two or Three Worlds), stories and essays by Alfonso Reyes, selection and prologue (México: Letras de México, 1944). *El viento de Bagdad* (The Wind of Bagdad), stories and essays of José Vasconcelos, selection and prologue (México: Letras de México, 1945). Vols. 11-49 of the Colección de Escritores Mexicanos, editions and prologues (México: Porrúa, 1945-1947). *La obra de Enrique González Martínez* (The Works of Enrique González Martínez), prologues of various studies (México: Ed. del Colegio Nacional, 1951). *La poesía mexicana moderna* (Modern Mexican Poetry), anthology, study, and notes (México: UNAM, 1953). *Poesías completas y El minutero* (Complete Poetry and the Minute-Hand) of Ramón López Velarde, edition and prologue (México: Porrúa, 1953). *Al filo del agua* (The Edge of the Storm) by Agustín Yáñez, prologue (México: Porrúa, 1955); 2nd ed. (1965). H. Levin, *James Joyce, Introducción crítica* (James Joyce, Critical Introduction), translation to English and notes (México: FCE, 1959). *La novela de la Revolución Mexicana* (The Novel of the Mexican Revolution), 2 vols., selection, prologue and studies (Madrid-México-Buenos Aires: Aguilar, 1960). Manuel Payno, *Los bandidos de Río Frío* (The Bandits of Cold River), edition and prologue of 2nd ed. (México: Porrúa, 1959). Maurice Dobb, *Introducción a la Economía* (Introduction to Economics), translation from English (México: FCE, 1959); 3rd ed. (1961). *Cuatro comedias de Juan Ruiz de Alarcón* (Four Plays by Juan Ruiz de Alarcón) study, texts, and commentaries (México: Porrúa, 1961); 2nd ed. (1964). Pascual Almazán, *Un hereje y un musulmán* (A Heretic and a Muslim), edition, notes, and prologue (México: Porrúa, 1962). José Rubén Romero, *Obras Completas* (Complete Works), prologue of 2nd ed. (México: Porrúa, 1963). *Luis G. Urbina 1864-1934* (México: Edit. Colegio Nacional, 1964). *La Novela del México Colonial* (The Novel of Colonial Mexico), 2 vols., prologue, selections, and notes (Madrid and México: Aguilar, 1964). Mariano Silva y Aceves, *Cuentos y poemas* (Stories and Poems), prologue (México: UNAM, 1964). *Las tragedias de Shakespeare* (Shakespeare's Tragedies), comments (México: El Colegio Nacional, 1964). *Juana Inés de la Cruz*, poetry, theater, and prose; edition and prologue (México: Porrúa, 1965). Stories: *El laurel de San Lorenzo* (The Laurel Wreath of Saint Lorenzo) (México: FCE, 1959). *El pueblo de México espera* (The People of Mexico Wait) (México: Cuadernos Americanos, 1966). *Thoreau y su discípulo Cassius Clay* (México: El Colegio de México, 1967). Series titled *Los cien mejores poemas de ...* (The Best One Hundred Poems of...), the following authors: *Salvador Díaz Mirón, Rubén Darío, Manuel Gutiérrez Nájera, Luis G. Urbina, Amado Nervo, Enrique González Martínez, Julio Herrera Reissig, José Santon Chocano, Leopoldo Lugones, José Martí* (México: Aguilar, 1969-1974). *Hombres e ideas de nuestro tiempo* (Men and Ideas of Our Time) (México: UNAM, 1969). *Díaz Mirón, su vida y su obra* (Díaz Mirón, His Life and Works) (México: Porrúa, 1970). *Francisco de la Maza, historiador y crítico de arte* (Francisco de la Maza, Historian and Art Critic) (México: Academia de Artes, 1970). *El español, instrumento de una cultura y otros ensayos* (The Spanish Language, Representation of a Culture and other Essays) (México: SEP, 1975).

BIBLIOGRAPHY: Ermilo Abreu Gómez, "Nueva obra sobre Ruiz de Alarcón," in *Letras de México* 5 (May 15, 1943): 1-2; *Sala de retratos* (México: Leyenda, 1946), pp. 66-67; "Del pecado antológico," review of *Las cien mejores poesías mexicanas modernas*, in *Letras de México* 2 (Feb. 15, 1939): 3-4; Review of *¿A dónde va México?*, in *Revista Mexicana de Cultura* 47 (Dec. 21, 1969): 6. Francisco Aguilera, *The Archive of Hispanic Literature on Tape* (Washington, D.C.: Library of Congress, 1974), pp. 117-18. Emmanuel Carballo, "La novela de la Revolución," in *México en la Cultura* 586 (June 1960): 4; Review of "La novela del México Colonial," in *La Cultura en México* 156 (Feb. 10, 1965); "Los prólogos de Castro Leal tienen buenas ideas, lástima que no sean suyas," in *La Cultura en México* 156 (Feb. 10, 1965): xv; "Como polemista, don Antonio es más Castro que Leal," in *La Cultura en México* 163 (March 31, 1965): xv. Alfredo Cardona Peña, "Entrevista con Antonio Castro Leal," in *Las Letras Patrias* 1 (Jan.-March 1954): 127-36. Antonio Castro Leal, "Las opiniones de Carballo son atrevidas, lástima que también sean infundadas," in *La Cultura en México* 161 (March 17, 1965): xiv. Enrique Díez Canedo, Review of *Juana Ruiz de Alarcón*, in *El Hijo Pródigo* 1, 3 (June 1943): 186-87. Héctor Fontanar, "Nombres de México, Antonio Castro Leal, escritor y político," in *El Día* (July 24, 1964): 9. Andrés Henestrosa, "Adiós a Antonio Castro Leal," in *Excelsior* (Jan. 10, 1981): 7A. Alfredo Lacen, "Habla Castro Leal: Las obras clásicas deben traducirse en un lenguaje comprensible para el público," in *El Día* 401 (Aug. 5, 1963): 11. Ross Larson, *Fantasy and Imagination in the Mexican Narrative* (Tempe: Arizona State University, 1977), p. 52. Luis Leal, *Breve historia de la literatura hispanoamericana* (New York: Alfred A. Knopf, 1971), p. 130; *Bibliografía del cuento mexicano* (México: Eds. de Andrea, 1958), pp, 35-36. Raúl Leiva, "Importante selección de Castro Leal. La novela colonial en México," in *México en la Cultura* 831 (Feb. 21, 1965): 8. José Luis Martínez, *El ensayo mexicano moderno* (México: FCE, 1958 and 1971), pp. 399-400. Porfirio Martínez Peñaloza, "Antonio Castro Leal. In memoriam," in *Boletín de la*

Academia Mexicana (Jan.-June 1981): 116-18. Javier Morente, Review of *Un hereje y un musulmán*, in *Diorama de la Cultura* (Dec. 16, 1962): 2. Aurora M. Ocampo de Gómez and Ernesto Prado Velázquez, *Diccionario de escritores mexicanos* (México: UNAM, 1967), pp. 75-76. Jorge Olmo, Review of *El laurel de San Lorenzo*, in *Revista de la Universidad de México* 14, 6 (Feb. 1960): 31. José Emilio Pacheco, Review of *El laurel de San Lorenzo*, in *México en la Cultura* 569 (Feb. 7, 1960): 4. Jesús Silva Herzog, *Biografías de amigos y conocidos* (México: Cuadernos Americanos, 1980), pp. 87-88. Various, "Antonio Castro Leal en la Cultura," in *Nivel* 21 (Sept. 25, 1964): 1-5, 10; "Homenaje conjunto en memoria de Agustín Yañez y Antonio Castro Leal," in *Memoria de El Colegio Nacional* 1 (1982): 29-32. Serge I. Zaitzeff, "Alfonso Reyes y Antonio Castro Leal: Un diálogo literario," (Berlin: Ibero-American Institute, 1986). Francisco Zendejas, "La poesía mexicana moderna," in *México en la Cultura* 246 (Dec. 1953): 2.

JEANNE C. WALLACE

CAVO, Andrés (1739-1803), teacher and historian. After becoming a Jesuit priest in 1758, this native of Guadalajara occupied several teaching positions in Puebla and Nayar before the Society's expulsion from Mexico in 1767. He was an admirer and disciple of Father José Julián Parreño, a Cuban Jesuit and a former rector of the Colegio de San Ildefonso in Mexico City. The two priests traveled to Spain aboard the same ship, and from there they were both sent to Rome. Believing that his resignation from the Society of Jesus would permit him to return to México, Cavo pursued the matter with government officials on a subsequent visit to Spain. Failing to secure the permission he needed, he went back to Rome, where he completed his major works before his death in 1803.

Cavo's principal work, *La historia civil y politica de México* (The Civil and Political History of Mexico), is one of the earliest to recount viceregal history up to the time of the formation of the Army of the Three Guarantees (1521-1766), and it may be considered as a continuation of Francisco Javier *Clavijero's history of the Aztecs, *La historia antigua de México* (The Ancient History of Mexico). The first edition of Cavo's historical account was published in 1836 by Carlos María de *Bustamante under the title *Los tres siglos de México* (Three Centuries of Mexican History), and a subsequent edition, appearing in 1949, was prepared by Ernest J. Burrus. Another important work by Cavo is his *De Vita Josephi Juliani Parrenni Havannensis* (The Life of José Julián Parreño of Havana), the biography of his dear friend and colleague. Correspondence and translations comprise the remaining portion of Cavo's writings.

WORKS: *Los tres siglos de México* (Three Centuries of Mexican History) (México: Imp. de J. R. Navarro, 1852; Xalapa: Tip. Veracruzana de A. Ruiz, 1870). *De Vita Josephi Juliani Parrenni Havannensis* (The Life of José Julián Parreño of Havana) (the manuscript was completed in 1792 and is at the University of Texas at Austin).

BIBLIOGRAPHY: Alfonso Reyes, *Letras de la Nueva España* (México: FCE, 1948), pp. 128-29. Víctor Rico González, *Historiadores mexicanos del siglo XVIII* (México: UNAM, 1949).

JULIE GREER JOHNSON

CEBALLOS Maldonado, José (1919-   ). Ceballos Maldonado was born in Puruándiro, Michoacán, but his early years were spent in Uruapan. He studied at the Universidad Michoacana de San Nicolás de Hidalgo in Morelia and later at the University of Guadalajara, where he attended Medical School and received his medical degree in medicine and surgery. He specialized in pediatrics at the Hospital Infantil de México and worked as a pediatrician in the city of Uruapan. He traveled extensively throughout Europe and the world.

Although he practiced medicine as a career, Maldonado always showed interest in literature. He has written novels and short stories such as *Blas Ojeda* (1964), comprised of twelve stories based on Mexican life in Uruapan and *Bajo la piel* (Under the Skin) (1966), a novel which shows the same Mexican reality as his stories but with greater perception and depth of characters.

WORKS: Short Stories: *Blas Ojeda* (México: Costa-Amic, 1964). *Del amor y otras intoxicaciones* (Of Love and Other Intoxications) (México: Novaro, 1974). "Las botas federicas," in *Nosotros* (July 15, 1963). "La Carta" (The Letter) in *México en la Cultura* 806 (Aug. 30, 1964): 3. "La justicia de don Porfirio," in *Horizontes* 35-36 (Feb. 15-April 15, 1964): 26-28. Novels: *Bajo la piel* (Under the Skin) (México: Costa-Amic, 1966; Morelia: Balsal, 1972). *Después de todo* (After All) (México: Diógenes, 1969). *El demonio apacible* (The Peaceful Devil) (México: Premiá, 1985).

BIBLIOGRAPHY: Carmen Arteaga de Padilla, "Recato y tabú," review of *Blas Ojeda*, in *El Centavo* 60 (México, June 1964): 5-6. John S. Brushwood, *México en su novela* (México: FCE, 1973), p. 118; *La novela mexicana (1967-1982)* (México: Grijalbo, 1985), pp. 52-53, 83. Raúl Arreola Cortés, "*Blas Ojeda*, promesa y realidad," in *El Centavo* 60 (México, June 1964): 2-4. Emmanuel Carballo, "Entre libros. *Blas Ojeda*," in *Nivel* 14 (México, Feb. 25, 1964): 3. José Ceballos Maldonado, Review of his short story, "La justicia de Don Porfirio," in *Horizontes* 35-36 (México, 1964): 26-28. Andrés Henestrosa, "La nota cultural," review of *Blas Ojeda*, in *El Nacional* (México, Feb. 15, 1964): 3. Salvador Molina M., "Todo depende del color del cristal con que se miran las cosas," review of *Blas Ojeda*, in *El Centavo* 60 (México, June 1964): 1. Javier Morente "José Ceballos Maldonado," in *El Centavo* 60 (México, June 1964): 12-13. Gustavo Sáinz, "Escaparate," review of *Blas Ojeda*, in *El Centavo* 60 (México, June 1964): 10-11. Humberto Tejera, Review of *Blas Ojeda*, in *Horizontes*: 35-36 (México, 1964): 34-35. Ignacio Trejo Fuentes, "Nueva novela de José Maldonado Ceballo, un demonio nada apacible," in *La Cultura al Día* (Aug. 25, 1985): 2.

                                                                    MIRTA BARREA-MARLYS

CENICEROS y Villarreal, Rafael (1855-1933), dramatist and novelist. Born in Durango, Durango, on July 11, 1855, Ceniceros y Villarreal studied in his native city and at a young age won a prize at the Seminario Conciliar for a composition entitled "La descripción de la siembra" (Description of Sowing). Not long afterwards, he wrote his first play, the sacred drama *La plenitud de los tiempos* (The Abundance of the Ages). His theatrical piece *Tempestades del alma* (Storms of the Soul) premiered in Durango in 1876. Ceniceros y Villarreal taught Latin in the Escuela de Comercio.

After receiving his law degree he moved to Zacatecas, where he established a legal practice. He contributed to the magazine *La Primavera*, was editor- in-chief of the *Revista Forense*, and founded and edited a religious weekly *La Rosa del Tepeyac* (1891-1895). He taught Spanish language and literature classes and between the years 1892 and 1906, wrote a series of moralistic dramas: *Flores de invierno* (Winter Flowers), *La tapatía* (The Girl from Guadalajara), and *El vengador de su honra* (The Avenger of His Honor). His collection of fables, *Páginas para mis hijas* (Pages for My Daughters), is a standard text in the Catholic schools of Zacatecas. For a few months in 1910 he was interim governor of Zacatecas, a post he was occupying when the Revolution erupted. He died in Mexico City in 1933.

In addition to his work as a dramatist, Ceniceros y Villarreal is also the author of two novels, both of which are concerned with traditional morality, customs, and values. The first and best-known of these, *La siega* (The Harvest), is a regional novel in the romantic vein. It is a love story that portrays customs in a provincial city and ends with Christian morality triumphing over injustice. The second, *El hombre nuevo* (The New Man), tells in an overly sentimental and didactic fashion the story of a young woman's act of redemption. As novelist and dramatist Ceniceros y Villarreal exalts traditionalism and uses literature to teach proper standards of conduct, characteristics which diminish his appeal to many contemporary readers.

WORKS: *La siega* (The Harvest) (Zacatecas: Talls. de Nazario Espinosa, 1905). *Obras*, vol. 1 (novels), Biblioteca de Autores Mexicanos, no. 58 (México: Imp. de Victoriano Agüeros, 1908). *Obras*, vol. 2 (short stories), Biblioteca de Autores Mexicanos, no. 68 (México: Imp. de Victoriano Agüeros, 1909).

BIBLIOGRAPHY: John S. Brushwood, *Mexico in Its Novel* (Austin: University of Texas Press, 1966), pp. 145-46, 160. *Enciclopedia de México*, vol. 3 (México: SEP, 1987), p. 1466. Juan B. Iguíniz, *Bibliografía de novelistas mexicanos* (México: Sría de Relaciones Exteriores, 1926), pp. 76-78. Joaquina Navarro, *La novela realista mexicana* (México; Cía Gral. de Ediciones, 1955), pp. 237-241. Angel M. Ocampo de Gómez and Ernesto Prado Velázquez, *Diccionario de escritores mexicanos* (México: UNAM, 1967), pp. 77-78.

MELVIN S. ARRINGTON, JR.

CERNUDA, Luis (1902-1963), poet, teacher, and essayist. Luis Cernuda was born in Seville, Spain, and died in Mexico City. He studied law and literature at the University of Seville from where he graduated with a law degree in 1925. Cernuda's teaching career began in 1928 at the Ecole Normal of Toulouse, France. He also taught at the universities of Glasgow in Scotland and Cambridge in England, the National University of Mexico, University of California at Los Angeles and San Francisco State College in the United States. Cernuda was forced into exile after the Civil War, and lived in England and the United States before moving to Mexico in 1951. He taught in California from 1960 to 1963. He returned to Mexico City in 1963, where he died in November. Luis Cernuda belongs to the vanguardist movement known as La generación del '27. His major contributions are as poet and as literary critic. He is one of the outstanding poets of our century.

WORKS: Poetry: *Perfil del aire* (The Air's Profile), 4th Supplement to *Litoral* (Malaga: Imp. Sur, 1927). *Los placeres prohibidos* (Forbidden Pleasures) (Madrid: n.p., 1933). *Invitación a la poesía* (An Invitation to Poetry) (Madrid: Ed. "La tentativa poética," 1933). *Donde habite el olvido* (Where Oblivion May Dwell) (Madrid: Signo, 1934). *El joven marino* (The Young Sailor) (Madrid: Héroe, 1936). *La realidad y el deseo* (Reality and Desire) (Madrid: Cruz y Raya, 1936). *Las nubes* (The Clouds) (Buenos Aires: Rama de Oro, 1943). *Como quien espera el alba* (As If Waiting for Dawn) (Buenos Aires: Losada, 1947). *Vivir sin estar viviendo* (Living without Being Alive) (n.p.: n.p., 1949). *Con las horas contadas* (With Time Running Out) (México: n.p., 1956). *Poemas para un cuerpo* (Poems for a Body) (Málaga: Imp. Dardo, 1957). *Desolación de la quimera* (The Disconsolate Chimera) (México: Mortiz, 1962). *Antología poética* (Poetic Anthology), edited by R. Santos Torroella (Barcelona: Plaza y Janis, 1970). *Perfil del aire con otras obras olvidadas e inéditas* (Profile of the Air with Other Forgotten and Unpublished Works) (London: Tamesis, 1971). *Poesie di Luis Cernuda*, translated by Francesco Tentori Montalto (Milano: Lerici Editore, 1962). *The Poetry of Luis Cernuda*, translated by Anthony Edkins and Derek Harris (New York: New York University Press, 1971). *Selected Poems of Luis Cernuda*, edited and translated by Reginald Gibbons (Berkeley: University of California Press, 1977). *Poesía completa* (Complete Poetry) (Barcelona: Barral, 1974). Prose: *Ocnos* (Ocnos) (London: The Dolphin, 1942; 3rd edition augmented (Jalapa: Universidad Veracruzana, 1963). *Tres narraciones* (Three Narrations) (Buenos Aires: Imín, 1948). Essay: *Variaciones sobre tema mexicano* (Variations on a Mexican Theme) (México: Porrúa y Obregón, 1952). *Estudios sobre poesía española contemporánea* (Studies on Contemporary Spanish Poetry) (Madrid: Guadarrama, 1957). *Pensamiento poetico en la lírica inglesa, siglo XIX* (Poets on Poetry in Nineteenth-Century English Verse) (México: Imp. Universidad, 1958). *Poesía y literatura* (Poetry and Literature) (Barcelona: Seix Barral, 1960). *Díptico español 1960-1961* (Bogotá: Mito, 1961). *Cartas a Euqenio de Andrade* (Letters to Eugenio de Andrade) (Zaragoza: Olifante, 1988). *La realidad y el deseo, XI, Desolación de la Quimera*, (Reality and Wish, XI, The Disconsolate Chimera) (México: Mortiz, 1962). *Crítica, ensayos y evocaciones* (Criticism, Essays, and Evocations) (Barcelona: Seix Barral, 1971). *Prosa completa* (Complete Prose), edited by Derek Harris and Luis Maristany (Barcelona: Barral, 1975). Theater: *La familia interrumpida* (The Interrupted Family), introduction by Octavio Paz, in *Vuelta* 108 (1985): 27-43. Translations: *Holderlin, Poemas* (México: Seneca, 1942). *Shakespeare, Troilo y Cresida* (Madrid: Insula, 1953).

BIBLIOGRAPHY: Rupert C. Allen, "Luis Cernuda: Poet of Gay Protest," *Hispanófila* 28 2-83 (1985): 61-78. Jacques Ancet, *Luis Cernuda: une étude* (Paris: Seghers, 1972). Rafael Argullel, "Cernuda romántico," *Quimera* 15 (1982): 29-32. Manuel Ballestero, *Poesía y reflexión: la palabra en el tiempo* (Madrid: Taurus, 1980). Gastón Baquero, *Darfo, Cernuda y otros temas poéticos* (Madrid: Ed. Nacional, 1969). Douglas Barnette, "Luis Cernuda y su generación: La creación de una leyenda," *Revista de Estudios Hispánicos* 181 (1984): 123-32. Esther Bartolomi Pons, "Tiempo, amor y muerte en el lenguaje poético de Luis Cernuda," *Insula* 36, 415 (1981): 1, 12; "Cernuda y Ocnos: Entre el amor y el olvido" *Insula* 36, 420 (1981): 4, 5. C. G. Bellver, "Luis Cernuda and T. S. Eliot: A Kinship of Message and Motifs," *Revista de Estudios Hispánicos* 17, 1 (1983): 107-24. Kevin J. Bruton, "Luis Cernuda's Exile Poetry and Coleridge's Theory of Imagination," *Comparative Literature Studies* 21, 4 (1984): 383-95; "Luis Cernuda's Debt to Holderlin: Symbolical Reference and

Internal Rhythm," *Revue de Litérature Comparée* 58, 229 (1984): 37-49: "The Cemetery Poems of Luis Cernuda," *Anales de la literatura española contemporánea* (Boulder) 13, 3 (1988): 189-208. José L. Cano, "Unamuno y Cernuda en dos poemas," *Cuadernos Hispanoamericanos* 440-41 (1987): 320-22. "Una comedia inacabada y sin titulo," *Revista de Occidente* 70 (1987): 119-37; "Cartas de Luis Cernuda a José Luis Cano," *Insula* 43, 498 (1988): 17-24. José María Capote Benot, *El período sevillano de Luis Cernuda* (Madrid: Gredos, 1971); "El surrealismo en la poesía de Luis Cernuda" (Sevilla: Universidad de Sevilla, 1976). Guillermo Carnero, "Luis Cernuda y el purismo poético," *Vuelta* 12, 144 (1988): 63-65. Alexander Coleman, *Other Voices: A Study of the Late Poetry of Luis Cernuda* (Chapel Hill: University of North Carolina Press, 1969). Richard K. Curry, "En torno a la poesía de Luis Cernuda: Crítica, metacrítica, y crítica," *DAI* 43 (1983): 2360A, Arizona State University. Agustín Delgado, *La poética de Luis Cernuda* (Madrid: Ed. Nacional, 1975). Harris Derek, trans., *Luis Cernuda: A Study of the Poetry* (London: Tamesis, 1973). Anthony Edkins and Harris Derek, *The Poetry of Luis Cernuda* (New York: New York University Press, 1971). Miguel García-Posada, "Cernuda y Garcilaso: Ecos garcilasianos en la elegía 'A un poeta muerto (F.G.L.),'" *Insula* 39, 455 (1984): 1, 3. Christine Garrido-Bassanini, "De eros y poética: itinerarios de José Lezama Lima y Luis Cernuda," *DAI* 49 (1988): 516A-17A, Purdue University. Carmelo Gariano, "Aspectos clásicos de la poesía de Luis Cernuda," *Hispania* 2 (1965): 234-46. Salvador Jiménez Fajardo, "The Yankee winter of Luis Cernuda," *Cincinnati Romance Review* 2 (1983): 40-48; *Luis Cernuda* (New York: Twayne, 1978); *The Word and the Mirror: Critical Essays on the Poetry of Luis Cernuda* (Cranbury, N.J.: Associated Univeristy Presses, 1989). James Mandrell, "Cernuda's 'El indolente': Repetition, Doubling, and the Construction of Poetic Voice," *Bulletin of Hispanic Studies* 65, 4 (1988): 383-95. Luis Martínez Cuitino, "El reflejo del mundo en la obra de Luis Cernuda," *Revista de Literatura* 45, 90 (1983): 127-48. Rafael Martínez Nadal, "Luis Cernuda, Edward Wilson y T. S. Eliot," *Insula* 37, 432 (1982): 1, 10. *Españoles en la Gran Bretaña, Luis Cernuda: el hombre y sus temas* (Madrid: Hiperion, 1983). Enrique Molina Campos, "Cernuda crítico literario," *Insula* 208 (1964): 7. C. B. Morris, *This Loving Darkness: The Cinema and Spanish Writers 1920-1936* (New York: Oxford University Press, 1980). Elisabeth Muller, *Die Dichtung Luis Cernudas* (Geneva: E. Droz, 1962). Jacobo Muñoz and J. L. García Molina, eds., *Homenaje a Luis Cernuda* (Valencia: La caña gris, 1962). José M. Naharro Calderón, "Estudio de las relaciones de la poesía española del interior: Apuntes para una revisión histórico-crítica y documental (1927-1946)," *DAI* 46 (1986): 3734A, University of Pennsylvania; "Ecos cernudianos en la poesía de Gil de Biedma," *Cuadernos Hispanoamericanos* 428 (1986): 157-62. Fernando Ortiz, "Luis Cernuda: Del mito a la elegía," *Nueva Estafeta* 24 (1980): 67-73; "T. S. Eliot en Cernuda," *Cuadernos Hispanoamericanos* 416 (1985): 95-104. Carlos-Pellegrin Otero, "Cernuda y los románticos ingleses," *Quimera* 15 (1982): 33-38. Hilda Pato, "El 'tú' (y el 'otro') en la poesía de Luis Cernuda," *Anales de la Literatura Española Contemporánea* 11, 3 (1986): 225-35; *Los finales poemáticos en la obra de Luis Cernuda* (Boulder: Society of Spanish and Spanish American Studies, 1988). Octavio Paz, "La palabra edificante (Luis Cernuda)," *Cuadrivio* (México: Mortiz, 1965), pp. 165-203; "On Poets and Others," translated by Michael Schmidt (New York: Seaver Books, 1986). Lucie Personneaux Conesa, "La comparaison poetique dans l'oeuvre de Luis Cernuda," *Iris* [Montpellier Cedex] 3 (1982): 91-114. Patricia Pinto, "Lo mítico, una nueva lectura de Ocnos," *Acta Literaria* [Chile] 6 (1981): 119-38. Manuel Ramos Ortega, *La prosa literaria de Luis Cernuda: El libro*

168   CERVANTES DE SALAZAR, Francisco

"*Ocnos*" (Sevilla: Diputación Provincial, 1982). Cisar Real Ramos, *Luis Cernuda y la 'Generación del 27'* (Salamanca: Universidad de Salamanca, 1983). Jorge Rodríguez Padrón, "Juan Ramón Jiménez-Luis Cernuda: Un diálogo crítico," *Cuadernos Hispanoamericanos* 376-78 (1981): 886-910. José Romera Castillo, "Autobiografia de Luis Cernuda: Aspectos literarios," *L'Autobiographie en Espagne* (Aix-en-Provence, 1982). Francisco Romero, "El muro, la ventana: La 'otredad' de Luis Cernuda," *Cuadernos Hispanoamericanos* 396 (1983): 545-75. Carlos Ruiz Silva, *Arte, amor y otras soledades en Luis Cernuda* (Madrid: De la Torre, 1979). Carlos Sáinz de la Maza, "Arcángeles vencidos: Amor o destrucción en la narrativa de Luis Cernuda," *Revista Canadiense de Estudios Hispánicos* 12, 1 (1987): 15-58. Richard A. Seybolt, "*Donde habite el olvido*: Poetry of Nonbeing," INTI: *Revista de Literatura Hispanica* 24-25 (1986-87): 127-36. Bernard Sicot, "Gide et Cernuda: Les jardins de l'Eden retrouvé," *Cahiers du Monde Hispanique et Luso-Bresilien* 43 (1984): 125-49. Philip Silver, "*Et in Arcadia ego*": *A Study of the Poetry of Luis Cernuda* (London: Tamesis, 1965). C. Christopher Soufas, Jr., "'Et in Arcadia ego': Luis Cernuda, Ekphrasis and the Reader," *Anales de la literatura española contemporanea* 7, 1 (1982): 97-107. "Cernuda and Daemonic Power," *Hispania* 66, 2 (1983): 167-75. Galbán Suárez and Eugenio Guerra, "Sobre la biblioteca privada de Luis Cernuda en Mount Holyoke," *Insula* 40, 468 (1985): 13. Jenaro Talins, *El espacio y las máscaras* (Barcelona: Anagrama, 1975). "Birds in the Night. 'Lecturas' de Cernuda desde la generación del 50," *Revista de Occidente* 86-87 (1988): 156-65. Manuel Ulacia, *Luis Cernuda: Escritura, cuerpo y deseo* (Barcelona: Laia, 1984); "Escritura, cuerpo y deseo en la primera parte de la obra poética de Luis Cernuda," *DAI* 46 (1985): 715A, Yale University; "El teatro de Narciso: 'Luis de Baviera escucha Lohengrin'" *Vuelta* 12, 144 (1988): 68-72. Jorge Valdés, "Perfil del aire dos etapas de la evolución poética de Luis Cernuda," *American Hispanist* 4, 32-33 (1979): 8-13; "La aportación de égloga, elegía, oda a la evolución poética de Luis Cernuda," *At Home and Beyond: New Essays on Spanish Poets of the Twenties*, edited by Salvador Jiménez Fajardo and John C. Wilcox (Lincoln: University of Nebraska-Lincoln, 1983). Jamres Valender, *Cernuda y el poema en prosa* (London: Tamesis, 1984); "Aire vacío: Un poema de Luis Cernuda," *Insula* 40, 467 (1985): 4; *La prosa narrative de Luis Cernuda* (Michoacán: Universidad Autónoma de Michoacán, 1984). "Cernuda y Lezama Lima," *Vuelta* 12, 144 (1988) 65-67. Gerardo Velásquez Cueto, "Para una lectura de 'Un río, un amor' de Luis Cernuda," *Insula* 39, 455 (1984): 3, 7. Luis Miguel Vicente, "El tema de México en José Moreno Villa y Luis Cernuda," *Mester* 16, 2 (1987): 25-34. Concha Zardoya, "Luis Cernuda el 'peregrino' sin retorno," *Insula* 35, 400-401 (1980): 14, 36.

                                        MIRTA A. GONZALEZ

CERVANTES DE SALAZAR, Francisco (1513 or 1514-1575). Cervantes de Salazar was born in 1513 or 1514 in Toledo, Spain. He studied humanities and canon law, and served as Latin secretary to Cardinal García Loaysa. In 1550 or 1551 he emigrated to Mexico where he taught Latin grammar in a private school and studied arts and theology at the university, founded in 1553. He began his ecclesiastical career in 1555 and obtained a canonship in the archbishopric of Mexico in 1563. He was named chronicler for the City of Mexico by the City Council in 1559. He became rector of the university in 1567 and apparently continued this position until his death in 1575.

Cervantes de Salazar was one of the principal chroniclers who gathered data on the history and ethnography of Mexico. His most important book is *Crónica de la Nueva España* (Chronicle of New Spain), written at the command of City Council. The manuscript of this work was sent by the author to Spain in 1567 with a request for the post of royal chronicler. This manuscript was uncovered in the early 1900s, catalogued in the National Library of Madrid as an anonymous manuscript. The first volume was published in 1914 and the second and third in 1936. The *Chronicle* is fragmentary since the first part, which was to include the period up to the conquest of Yucatán, either was never written or was lost; and the second part, which was to be a history of the conquest, breaks off with Columbus sending Villafuerte and Sandoval to the Pacific Ocean. Cervantes de Salazar's sources were the *Letters* of Cortés; the memoirs of Alonso de Ojeda and Andrés de Tapia, captains in Cortés' army; the *Memoranda* of Motolinia; the work of López de Gómara; and the information gathered from others who had taken part in the conquest who were still living in Mexico City twenty-five years later from whom he received useful information. The *Chronicle* is valued for its understanding and evaluation of the events it describes.

As a humanist Cervantes de Salazar had dealt with works of Oliva and Vives, and in Mexico he published *Túmulo imperial* (Imperial Tomb), a description of a tomb erected to commemorate the funeral rites of Charles V, including several poems in Latin and Spanish said to be the first expressions of Spanish poetry in America in the Italian manner. His three *Diálogos* (Dialogs), written in Latin and appended to the colloquia of Juan Luis Vives, were translated into Spanish by Joaquín *García Icazbalceta under the title *México en 1554* (Mexico in 1554). They provide precise historical documentation of the early organization of the University of Mexico and the life and customs of the people at that time.

WORKS: *México en 1554*, translated by Joaquín García Icazbalceta (in *Obras* de Joaquín García Icazbalceta, México: UNAM, 1939), *Túmulo imperial*, original edition (México: Antonio de Espinosa, 1560), reproduced by Joaquín García Icazbalceta in *Bibliografía mexicana del siglo XVI* in 1886, new edition by Agustín Millares Carlo (México: FCE, 1954). *Crónica de Nueva España*, vol. 1 (Madrid: Hauser and Menet, 1914); vols. 2-3 (México: Talleres gráficas del Museo Nacional de Arqueología, Historia y Etnografía, 1936).

BIBLIOGRAPHY: See *Bibliografía mexicana del siglo XVI* cited above. Joaquín García Icazbalceta, "Dr. Francisco Cervantes de Salazar." in Manuel Orozco y Berra *Diccionario universal de historia y geografía*, vol. 2 (Mexico: Libr. Andrade, 1855), pp. 305-6. Luis Islas García and Juan de Dios Varela, *Homenaje al doctor Francisco Cervantes de Salazar* (México: Eds. Orión, 1954). Agustín Millares Carlo, *Cartas recibidas de España por Francisco Cervantes de Salazar (1569-1575)* (México: Porrúa, 1946); *Apuntes para un estudio biobibliográfico del humanista Francisco Cervantes de Salazar* (México: Eds. Filosofía y Letras, UNAM, 1958). Margarita Peña, "La ciudad de México en los diálogos de Francisco Cervantes de Salazar" *Escritura: Teoría y crítica literarias* 6 (1981): 125- 51.

ANITA K. STOLL

CETINA, Gutierre de (1520-1554). Cetina was born in Sevilla, Spain, in 1520 into a noble and wealthy family. Being a man both of arms and letters, he represented the ideal of the period. As a soldier he traveled in Italy and Germany, was a friend of the important writers of his time, and traveled to New Spain in 1547 in the company of his uncle, don Gonzalo López, procurator general of New Spain. On a night in 1554 in Puebla de los Angeles he was fatally stabbed while under the window of Leonor de Osma. It is not known which if any of his poems were written in New Spain. There are seventy-eight of his creations in a manuscript found in the National Library of Madrid entitled *Flores de varia poesía* (Garlands of Varied Poetry), which was compiled in Mexico in 1577. It seems likely that he carried with him to the New World the Italianate forms that he employed in his poems. He is best known for the sonnet that begins "Ojos claros, serenos."

WORKS: *Obras de Gutierre de Cetina*, 2 vols., introduction and notes by Joaquín Hazañas y la Rúa (Sevilla: n.p., 1895).

BIBLIOGRAPHY: Joaquín Hazañas y la Rua, introduction and notes to the *Obras de Gutierre de Cetina* (Sevilla: n.p., 1895). Marcelino Menéndez y Pelayo, *Historia de la poesía hispanoamericana* (Madrid: Imp. V. Suárez, 1911), pp. 27-30. José Rojas Garcidueñas, *El teatro de Nueva España en el siglo XVI* (México: n.p., 1935), pp. 70-72. Renato Rosaldo, *Flores de varia poesía*, study and edition (México: Abside, 1952).

ANITA K. STOLL

CHAMPOURCIN, Ernestina de (1905-   ), poet, novelist, and translator. Born in Vitoria, Spain, Champourcin and her husband, poet Juan José *Domenchina, came to Mexico in 1939 and worked for many years as translators for Fondo de Cultura Económica. She founded the journal *Rueca* and has contributed poetry to other journals. She has also written reviews for *Gaceta Social de México* and has taught literature.

Champourcín has been compared to other Latin American poets. Her verse has an erotic tone similar to that found in the poetry of Alfonsina Storni. Also, there are elements of mysticism similar to those in the work of Guadalupe Amor. Her poetry is finely crafted from a technical point of view. Her literary production includes a novel, but her main work has been in translation of works in literary criticism and social and political studies from Portuguese, French, and English for Fondo de Cultura Económica.

In 1972, twelve years following the death of her husband, Champourcín returned to Spain, where she has resided since.

WORKS: *En silencio* (In Silence) (Madrid: Espasa-Calpe, 1925). *La voz del viento* (The Wind's Voice) (Madrid: Compañía Interamericana de Publicaciones, 1931). *El cántico inútil* (Useless Song) (Madrid: Eds. Aguilar, 1936). *La casa de enfrente* (The House across the Street) (Madrid: Edición Signo, 1936). *Presencia a oscuras* (Presence in the Dark) (Madrid: Colección Adonís, Editorial Rialp, 1952). *El nombre que me diste* (The Name You Gave Me) (México: Ecuador, 1964). *Cárcel de los sentidos* (Prison of the Senses) (México: Ecuador, 1964).

BIBLIOGRAPHY: Rafael Espejo-Saavedra, "Sentimiento amoroso y creación poética en Ernestina de Champourcín" in *Revista/Review Interamericana* 12, 1 (Spring 1982): 38-39. Aurora M. Ocampo de Gómez and Ernesto Prado Velázquez, *Diccionario de escritores Mexicanos* (México: UNAM, 1967), pp. 90-91. Mauricio de la Selva, "Asteriscos," in *Diorama de la Cultura* (July 19, 1964): 4. Guillermo de Torre, "Dos Libros de Ernestina de Champourcín," in *El Sol* (June 1936). Angel Valbuena Pratt, *Historia de la literatura española*, vol. 3, 6th ed. (Barcelona: Editorial Gustavo Gili, 1960), p. 690. Arturo del Villar, "Ernestina Champourcin," *La Estafeta Literaria* 556 (Madrid) (Jan. 15, 1975): 10-15.

KENNETH M. TAGGART

CHAVEZ, Gilberto (1908-   ). Chavez, born in Cotija, Michoacán, is an extremely prolific novelist. A great narrator, he draws his characters from humble environments. They usually live hazardous and even antisocial lives. At times, the author is able to create suspense with the use of digressions and dilatory descriptions. The reader is submerged in an atmosphere of probabilities. *Playa paraíso* (Paradise Beach) is a novel with an ironic title that does not correspond at all to anything pleasant. A young tourist falls in love with a waitress whose husband is a drunkard. A lewd policeman is murdered while attempting to rape one of the waitress's daughters. Tension is created between the waitress's modesty and the tourist's timid advances. A sense of guilt finally forces him to flee without further pursuing his erotic interest. It is a realistic novel with romantic touches and the coloring of newspaper serial stories ("folletín"). *Dos noches y un amanecer* (Two Nights and a Dawn) is a short novel and five stories. The first narration, *Dos noches* (Two Nights), is filled with multiple situations. A frustrated musician is constantly at risk because he is a womanizer. The agility and variety of the anecdotes are interesting and almost cinematographic. In the short story *Rancho tras la lomita* (Hut over the Little Hill), the excesses and iniquities of the Revolution are criticized. The peasant protagonist, strong and naive in his essential goodness, is hanged like a bandit by those who were supposed to restore order.

WORKS: *Playa paraíso* (Paradise Beach), Premio Lanz Duret 1956 (México: Porrúa, 1947). *Fruto de tormenta* (Fruit of Storm) (México: Botas, 1950). *Dos noches y un Amanecer* (Two Nights and a Dawn) (México: Botas, 1952). *Batalla sin fin* (Endless Battle) (México: Editorial Olimpo, 1953). *Sendero de milagros* (Miracle Lane) (México: Botas, 1955). *Una sombra en los brazos* (A Shadow in the Arms), Premio Lanz Duret (México: Botas, 1956). *Alguien cambió el final* (Someone Changed the Ending) (México: Costa-Amic, 1966). *Mientras pasa la lluvia* (As the Rain Falls) (México: Costa-Amic, 1968). *Goza del verde camino* (Rejoice on the Green Road) (México: Costa-Amic, 1962). *El batallador* (The Warrior), Premio Nacional de Novela José Rubén Romero, 1980 (México: Mortiz, 1986).

BIBLIOGRAPHY: Luis Leal, *Bibliografía del cuento mexicano* (México: Eds. de Andrea, 1958), pp. 40-41. John S. Brushwood and José Rojas Garciadueñas, *Breve historia de la novela mexicana* (México: Eds. de Andrea, 1959), p. 80.

RICHARD D. WOODS

CHUMACERO, Alí (1918-   ), poet and critic. Alí Chumacero was born in Acaponeta, Nayarit, on July 9, 1918. In 1929 he moved to Guadalajara and in 1937 settled in Mexico City. In 1947, with José Luis *Martínez, Jorge *González Durán, and Leopoldo Zea, he founded and became the editor of the literary journal *Tierra Nueva*. He also played a major role in the edition of the journals *Letras de México* and *El hijo pródigo* and in *Novedades's* literary supplement, *México en la Cultura*. For several years he served as the director of the Fondo de Cultura Económica, one of Mexico's most prestigious publishing houses.

He has written numerous prologues to important texts and while at the Fondo de Cultura Económica, he was in charge of preparing for publication the complete works of Gilberto *Owen, Xavier *Villaurrutia, Mariano *Azuela, and Efren *Hernández. In addition to his work on *Contemporáneos*, he has also written reviews and articles on literary figures whose main topic of concern was the Mexican Revolution. Between 1952 and 1953 he held fellowships at El Colegio de Mexico and at the Centro Mexicano de Escritores.

Throughout his career, he has received numerous awadrs and honors. In 1944, his book *Páramo de sueños* (Wilderness of Dreams) was awarded the Rueca Prize and in 1982, his complete works merited the prestigious Xavier Villaurrutia Prize for poetry.

In *Páramo de sueños* and *Imágenes desterradas* (Exiled Images) the language is more abstract and its tone is reminiscent of Villaurrutia. In *Palabras en reposo* (Words at Rest) the characters are concrete, and each poem narrates a story. Nevertheless, this concreteness is extremely rigorous in its composition and makes the poems much more difficult to read. Part of its difficulty stems from its high erudition, which is based on biblical passages that bring to mind Ramón *López Velarde and T. S. Eliot. Through the themes of solitude, time, and death, he wishes to define a language which best expresses the perennial problems of humanity. His search for that language frequently leads him to a void or a silence, thus reflecting the frustration of the search.

WORKS: Poetry: *Páramo de Sueños* (Wilderness of Dreams) (México: Imp. Universitaria, 1944). *Imagenes desterradas* (Exiled Images) (México: Nueva Floresta, 1948). *Palabras en reposo* (Words at Rest) (México: FCE, 1956); 2nd ed., enlarged (1965). *Responso del peregrino* (The Pilgrim's Response) (México: UNAM, 1980). *Poesía completa* (Complete Poems) (México: Premiá Editora, 1980). Essays: "*Babel*, de Enrique González Martínez," in *La obra de Enrique González Martínez*, pp. 228-29. "Ramón López Velarde, el hombre solo," *El hijo pródigo* 39 (1946): 145-48. "Gregorio López y Fuentes," *Letras de México* 4, 9 (1943): 1-2. "Recinto de Octavio Paz," *Tierra Nueva* 9-10 (1941): 175-77. "José Revueltas." *Letras de México* 4, 24 (1944): 5. "El Pedro Páramo de Juan Rulfo," *Revista de la UNAM* 9, 8 (1966): 24-26. "La poesía de Xavier Villaurrutia," *Humanismo* 9-l0 (1953): 34-44. "Prólogo," in Xavier Villaurrutia's *Poesía y teatro completos* (México: FCE, 1953), pp. vii-xxxiv. "Prólogo," in Xavier Villaurrutia's *Obras*, 2nd ed. (México: FCE, 1966), pp. ix-xxx.

BIBLIOGRAPHY: Jesús Arellano, *Antología de los 50 poetas contemporáneos de México* (México: Eds. Alatorre 1952), p. 51. Marco Antonio Campos, "Responso del peregrino, Alí Chumacero entrevistado por Marco Antonio Campos," *Vuelta* l0, 111 (Feb. 1986): 35-38. José M. Clave, "Entrevista: Alí Chumacero: Defensa con el endecasilabo," *Razones* 20 (Oct.-Nov. 1980): 56. Frank Dauster, *Breve historia de la poesía mexicana* (México: Eds. de Andrea, 1956), pp. 177-78. Raúl Leiva, "Alí Chumacero," in *Imagen de la poesía mexicana contemporánea* (México: UNAM, 1959), pp. 267-68. José Luis Martínez, *Literatura mexicana: siglo XX. (1910-1949)* (México: Ant. Libr. Robredo, 1949), p. 80. María del Carmen Millán, *Literatura mexicana* (México: Ed. Esfinge 1962), p. 305. Javier Molina, "La soledad no es privativa de los poetas; es una riqueza de todos los seres humanos: Alí Cumacero," *Unomásuno* (Oct. 5, 1980): 17. Aurora M. Ocampo de Gómez and Ernesto Prado Velázquez, *Diccionario de escritores mexicanos* (México: UNAM, 1967), p. 146. Eunice Odio, "Nostalgia del paraíso," *Cultura* 19 (Jan.-Mar. 1961): 62-67. Cristina Pacheco, "La poesía no es privilegio del poeta, con Alí Chumacero en sus cuarenta años de escritor," *Siempre!* 31 (Nov. 1980). Octavio Paz, *Poesía en movimiento* (México: Siglo XXI Eds., 1966), pp. 20, 280. Evelyn Picón Garfield, "La poesía de Alí Chumacero," *Revista de la Universidad* 20 (Dec. 1982): 15-19. Alfredo A. Roggiano, "*Páramo de sueños* seguido de *Imágenes desterradas*," *Revista Iberoamericana* 54 (1962): 413-20. Jacobo Sefami, *El destierro apacible y otros ensayos* (México: Premiá, 1987), pp. 33-101. Sara Velasco, *Escritores jaliscienses, Tomo II (1900-1965)* (Guadalajara: University of Guadalajara, 1985), pp. 185-86. Ramón Xirau, "Alí Chumacero," in *Poesía iberoamericana contemporánea* (México: SepSetentas, 1972), pp. 149-54.

MARGARITA VARGAS

CLAVIJERO, Francisco Javier (1731-1787). Clavijero was born in Veracruz in 1731. His father held a series of posts in several small towns, and Clavijero apparently began early on to learn and appreciate the native languages and his native land. He became a Jesuit in 1748 and continued his study of languages: Hebrew, Nahuatl, French, Portuguese, Latin, Greek, German, and English. He was also familiar with many other indigenous Mexican languages. He took advantage of the documents collected by *Sigüenza y Góngora which further enriched his wide background of knowledge. He left New Spain when the Jesuits were expelled in 1767 and, once in Italy, set himself to writing *Historia antigua de México* (Ancient History of Mexico). He followed the history with *Disertaciones* in order to amplify points in the history and to correct imprecisions which he discovered in the works of other authors. He died in Bologna in 1787.

Clavijero's history is a model of clarity and conciseness, wide knowledge and penetrating judgment, precision and exactness. Although first written in Spanish, it was translated into Italian for its first publication and was soon highly regarded. It was translated into German and English. The first Spanish text, which was published in 1826, was a translation from the Italian. The original text was printed in 1945. His *Historia de la Antigua o Baja California* (History of Ancient or Lower California) had as its object to defend the Jesuit order from attacks made on it.

WORKS: *Historia antigua de México*, prologue and notes by Mariano Cuevas (México: Porrúa, 1945). *Historia de la Antigua o Baja California* (México: Juan R. Navarro, 1852). *Capítulos de historia y disertaciones*, prologue and selection of Julio Jiménez Rueda (México: UNAM, 1944).

BIBLIOGRAPHY: Rafael García Granados, "Clavijero, Estudio Bibliográfico," in *Filias y Fobias* (México: Porrúa, 1937). Julio Le Riverend Brusone, "La Historia antigua de México del Padre Francisco Javier Clavijero," in *Estudios de historiografía de la Nueva España* (México: El Colegio de México, 1945). Gabriel Méndez Plancarte, *Humanistas del Siglo XVIII* (México: UNAM, 1941). José Miranda, "Clavijero en la Ilustración mexicana" *Cuadernos Americanos* 28, 4 (1946): 180-96.

ANITA K. STOLL

COLIN, Eduardo (1880-1945), poet and critic. Eduardo Colin was one of the members of the generation of El Ateneo de la Juventud and one of the founders of the journal *Savia Moderna*. He also contributed to the last numbers of *Revista Moderna*. Born in Mexico City on June 19, 1880, he completed law school, then entered the diplomatic service and served abroad in several legations of the Mexican government. He was also the assistant director of the National Library and lectured in several schools and universities. He died in Cuernavaca on March 20, 1945.

Colín began as a poet and ended his literary career with a book of short stories, *Mujeres* (Women). In between, he developed into an important critic. In his first book of poetry, *La vida intacta* (The Untouched Life), he revealed himself as a profound and strong poet with great sensibility. His critical works concern themselves with the main figures of Modernism as well as the writers and poets of his time whom he knew and could advise. *Siete cabezas* (Seven Heads) is a detailed study of several European authors, including Jules Laforgue, Miguel de Unamuno, Ramón del Valle-Inclán, and Eça de Queiroz. He was more concerned with ideas than with form, and he is an important source for understanding the literature of the old continent at the beginning of the twentieth century. Colín's *Verbo selecto* (Select Words) examines Latin American writers in a fashion similar to his work on the European writers.

WORKS: *La vida intacta* (The Untouched Life) (Madrid: Tip. Artística, 1916). *Siete cabezas* (Seven Heads) (Bogotá: Imp. Juan Casís, 1921). *Verbo selecto* (Select Words) (México: Imp. Murgía, 1922). *Rasgos* (Strokes) (México: Imp. Manuel León Sánchez, 1934). *Mujeres* (Women) (México: Fábula, 1934).

BIBLIOGRAPHY: Genaro Estrada, *Poetas nuevos de México* (México: Porrúa, 1916), pp. 34-35. José Luis Martínez, "Las tres patrias," in *México y la cultura* (México: SEP, 1946), p. 435. Francisco Monterde, "Eduardo Colin," in *Biblos* 3, 138 (1921): 145-46. José de Jesús Núñez y Domínguez, "De antaño y hogaño," in *Revista de Revistas* (June 18, 1916).

HERLINDA HERNANDEZ

COLINA, José de la (1934-). De la Colina was born in Santander, Spain, on March 29, 1934. At the end of the Civil War he went with his family first to France, then to Belgium, Santo Domingo, and Cuba, and since 1940 he has been a resident of

Mexico. He has been a reporter, an advertising artist, a proofreader, a translator, a movie critic. He has contributed to *Ideas de México*, "México en la cultura" (supplement of *Novedades*), the literary supplement to *El Nacional*; *Universidad de México*; *Revista Mexicana de Literatura*; *La Palabra y el Hombre*; *Nuevo Cine*; "La Cultura en México" (supplement of *Siempre!*), *Espejo*, and to *Política*. Other literary journals and supplements include *La Gaceta de Cuba*, *Cine Cubano*, *Revista Casa de las Américas*, *Le chateau du verre* in Belgium, and *Contrechamp* and *Positif*, in France. José de la Colina was first published in literary supplements and journals. In his first book, *Cuentos para vencer a la muerte* (Tales to Conquer Death), spontaneity and a personal tone dominate. *Ven, caballo gris* (Come, Gray Horse), consists of tales whose theme is exile, whether real or symbolic and his prose is already that of a mature narrator; his style is dynamic, and he seeks "a solidarity that unites innumerable solitary hearts." *La lucha con la pantera* (Battle with the Panther) gives us de la Colina as a writer who has achieved his own language, in which he successfully combines realist prose with the fantastic. The result is a poetically suggestive fusion.

WORKS: Short Stories: *Cuentos para vencer a la muerte* (Tales to Conquer Death) (México: Los Presentes, 1955). *Ven, caballo gris* (Come, Gray Horse) (Xalapa: Universidad Veracruzana, 1959). *La lucha con la pantera* (Battle with the Panther) (Xalapa: Universidad Veracruzana, 1962). Studies: *El cine italiano* (Italian Cinema) in *Cuadernos de cine 3* (México: UNAM, 1962). "Transparencia de Emilio Prados" (The Transparency of Emilio Prados), in *La Palabra y el Hombre* 19 (1976): 33-35. "In Memoriam: Pier Paolo Pasolini," in *La Palabra y el Hombre* 17 (1976) 3-5. "Ramón mismo ramonismo" (Ramón Ramonism Itself), in *Plural* 29 (1974): 39-46. Translation: G. Sadoul, *Las maravillas del cine*, translated from the French (México: FCE, 1950; 2nd ed., 1960).

BIBLIOGRAPHY: Anon., "La tarea literaria," review of *La lucha con la pantera*, in *La Cultura en México* 43 (Dec. 12, 1962): xvii; Review of *La lucha con la pantera*, in *Cuadernos de Bellas Artes* 4, 1 (Jan. 1963): 90. Huberto Batis, "De la Colina: Relato y poesía," in *La Cultura en México* 51 (Feb. 6, 1962): xvi-xvii. Ma. Elvira Bermúdez, "El caballo y la hierba," in *Excelsior* (Dec. 6, 1959). Emmanuel Carballo, Review of *Cuentos para vencer a la muerte*, in *México en la Cultura* 338 (Sept. 11, 1955): 2; *Cuentistas mexicanos modernos*, vol. 1 (México: Libro-Mex, 1956), pp. xxxi-xxxii; vol. 2, p. 275; *El cuento mexicano del siglo XX* (México: Empresas Editoriales, 1964), pp. 96-97. Carlos Elizondo, Review of *Cuentos para vencer a la muerte*, in *Hoy* (Sept. 10, 1955). Henrique González Casanova, "Un cuento de nunca acabar: los cuentistas," in *La Cultura en México* 74 (July 17, 1963): xviii. Luis Leal, *Breve historia del cuento mexicano* (México: Eds. de Andrea, 1956), p. 146; *Bibliografía del cuento mexicano* (México: Eds. de Andrea, 1958), p. 37. Juan Vicente Melo, Review of *Ven, caballo gris*, in *La semana cultural*, suppl. to *El Dictamen* (Dec. 6, 1959). Manuel Michel, Review of *Cuentos para vencer a la muerte*, in *Ideas de México* 2, 11 (May-June 1955): 146-47. Aurora M. Ocampo de Gómez and Ernesto Prado Velázquez, *Diccionario de escritores mexicanos* (México: UNAM, 1967), p. 82. José Emilio Pacheco, Review of *Ven, caballo gris*, in *La Palabra y el Hombre* 12 (Oct.-Dec. 1959): 709-11. Elena Poniatowska, Interview with José de la Colina, in *México en la Cultura* 393 Sept. 30, 1956): 1, 6. Salvador Reyes Nevares, Review of *Ven, caballo gris*, in *México en la Cultura* 549 (Sept. 20, 1959): 4. Gustavo Sáinz, Review of *La lucha con la pantera*, in *México en la Cultura* 714 (Nov. 25, 1962): 11. Rubén Salazar Mallén, "Letras: Difusión y concentración," review of *Ven, caballo gris*, in *Mañana* (Sept. 19, 1959): "Letras, Dominio del oficio," Review of *La lucha con la pantera*, in *Mañana*, (Dec. 19, 1962). Jacques Thirard, "Le réalisme fantastique de José de la Colina," introduction to two short stories, in *Le chateau du verre* (Belgium, Jan.-Mar. 1963). Carlos Valdés, Review of *Ven, caballo gris*, in *Universidad de México* 14, 2 (Oct. 2, 1959): 30; in *México en la Cultura* 556 (Nov. 8, 1959): 4; Review of *La lucha con la pantera*, in *La Cultura en México* 43 (Dec. 12, 1962): xx; "El cuento." Balance, 1962, in *La Cultura en México* 46 (Jan. 1963): vi-vii. Juan Luis Velázquez, "Elogio adulto de José de la Colina," in *Impacto* (Oct. 24, 1956).

YOLANDA S. BROAD

COLLADO Alva, Casimiro del (1822-1898). Collado Alva was born on March 4, 1822, in Valle de Leendo, Santander, Spain. Between 1833 and 1835, he studied philosophy at the Colegio de Escuelas Pías del Real Valle de Carriedo. He settled in Mexico in 1836, where he was a lucrative businessman. In 1841 he became a member of the Academia de Letrán and the Ateneo de México. That same year he founded, together with José María *Lafragua, the newspaper *El Apuntador*, a literary publication that included theatrical reviews. In addition, he was president of the Sociedad Española de Beneficencia from 1870 to 1871. He was also correspondent for the Real Academia Española and one of the founders of the Academia Mexicana (1875), which nominated him, together with José Ma. *Roa Bárcena, to collect an anthology of Mexican poets for the fourth centennial of America's discovery. He published poetry in the literary magazine *El Domingo* (1871-1873) and *El Nacional* (1880-1884).

His poetry, which in its beginnings reminds us of that of José Zorrilla, is considered among the best in the Romantic tradition of Mexico. He died in Mexico City on March 28, 1898.

WORKS: "El cuento de la vieja" (The Old Woman's Story), in *Liceo Mexicano* (México: J. M. Lara, 1844). "Oriental," in *Liceo Mexicano* (México: J. M. Lara, 1844). *Poesías* (Poetry) (Madrid: Fontaner, 1880). "Jesús," in *El Renacimiento* (The Renaissance) (México: Francisco Díaz de León and Santiago White, 1869). "Oda a México" (Ode to Mexico), in *Memorias de la Academia*, no. 3 (México, 1878), pp. 221-28. "El lago" (The Lake), in *Memorias de la Academia*, no. 1 (México, 1886) pp. 76-78. *Ultimas poesías* (Latest Poems) (México: Sría. de Fomento, 1895). "En memoria del Sr. D. Joaquín García Icazbalceta" (In Memory of Don Joaquín García Icazbalceta), in *Memorias de la Academia*, no. 1 (México, 1895). "Laurus nobilis" (Poem to Guillermo Prieto), in *Memorias de la Academia*, vol. 4 (México, 1910), pp. 129-30.

BIBLIOGRAPHY: Victoriano Agüeros, *Escritores mexicanos contemporáneos* (México: Escalante, 1880). Alberto María Carreño, *Memorias de la Academia Mexicana* (México, 1945), pp. 171-72. Jesús García Gutiérrez, *La poesía religiosa en México (Siglos XVI-XIX)* (México: n.p., 1919), p. 148. Manuel Payno, "El poeta y literato Casimiro Collado," in *El Federalista* 83 (México, April 8, 1871). José Zorilla, *México y los mexicanos* (México: Eds. de Andrea, 1955), pp. 119-23.

MIRTA BARREA-MARLYS

CONTEMPORANEOS. *See* VANGUARDIST Prose Fiction in Mexico.

CORDERO, Salvador (1876-1951), novelist. Salvador Cordero was born in Mexico City on August 10, 1876. There, he attended primary, secondary, and preparatory school. He enrolled in law school, but having to abandon his studies, he soon devoted himself to the study of literature. He also began to teach and, over the years, held positions in several institutions of higher learning. He was secretary of the National Museum of Archaeology, History and Ethnology; librarian of the Department of State; censor for the Bouret Publishing House; mayor of Tlalpan and then of Mixcoac (present suburbs of Mexico City), and he belonged to various national and international literary associations. He was also a correspondent of the Royal Spanish Academy and member of the Mexican Academy of the Spanish Language. He died in Mexico City on February 18, 1951.

Cordero became known through *Memorias de un Juez de Paz* (Memoirs of a Justice of the Peace), which recorded his personal impressions of the happiness, sadness, shortcomings, and social mores of his time. His second book *Semblanzas lugareñas* (Local Sketches), reveals an original writer who does not imitate other novelists, Mexican or foreign; rather, he depicts local events which, though common, are as colorful and rich in detail as paintings by the late nineteenth- century masters.

WORKS: *Memorias de un Juez de Paz* (Memoirs of a Justice of the Peace), 2nd ed. (México: Vda. de Ch. Bouret, 1913). *Semblanzas lugareñas* (Local Sketches) (México: Vda. de Ch. Bouret, 1917). *Barbarismos, galicismos y solecismos de uso más frecuente* (México: Vda. de Ch. Bouret, 1918). *La literatura durante la guerra de Independencia* (Literature during the Independence War) (México: Vda. de Ch. de Bouret, 1920). "Importancia práctica de la lectura y de la recitación en la enseñanza del idioma nacional" (Practical Importance of Reading and Recitation in the Teaching of the National Language), Address to the Mexican Academy of the Spanish Language, in *Discursos en la Academia Mexicana de la Lengua* (México: 1920). *El Brincón* (The Jumpy One) (México: Vda. de Ch. Bouret, 1920). *Memorias de un alcalde* (Memoirs of a Mayor) (México: Vda. de Ch. Bouret, 1921).

BIBLIOGRAPHY: Alberto María Carreño, *Memorias de la Academia Mexicana*, vol. 3 (1945), p. 172; vol. 8 (1946), p. 74. Francisco Monterde, "Escritores mexicanos contemporaneos. D. Salvador Cordero," in *Biblos* 2, 74 (June 19, 1920): 93-94. Joaquina Navarro, *La novela realista mexicana* (México: Cía. Gral. de Ediciones, 1955), pp. 95-99.

HERLINDA HERNANDEZ

CORDOVA, Luis (1908-). Luis Córdova was born in Orizaba, Veracruz. He studied law and graduated from the Universidad Nacional Autónoma de México. He has written for the principal newspapers of Mexico. A fine narrator of short stories, he combines subtle irony with social criticism. A poetic tone coexists with realistic, somber and revealing accounts of the most negative aspects of post-revolutionary Mexican society. A Neorealist, with Mariano *Azuela as his inspirational antecedent, he is able to combine Neorealism with fantasy, imagination, and illusion. In a letter dated October 2O, 1988, the author stated: "Luchamos por la épica moderna que es lo social. Buscamos la verdad causal en la sociedad, para darle Voz estetica" (We fight for a modern epic that is all things social. We seek causal truth in society, to give it an aesthetical voice).

Los alambrados (The Wired Men) is a story that narrates the plights of illegal Mexicans in the United States. The "alambrados" speak in a language burdened with dread, as if about to confront prison or even death. La sirena precisa (The Exact Mermaid) is a collection of short stories with a variety of themes. A social problem is presented and a message, not always obvious, is enunciated. These are stories in which optimism and faith in human destiny prevail.

WORKS: Mr. Parker, Mr. Jenkins y Mr.Hughes (México: 1935). Los negocios de Palacio van despacio (México: n.p., 1944). Los alambrados (The Wired Men) (México: Editorial Coacalco, 1955). Cenzontle y otros cuentos (México: Eds. de Andrea, 1955). Tijeras y listones (Scissors and Ferrets) (México: Eds. de Andrea, 1956). La sirena precisa (The Exact Mermaid) (México: UNAM, 1960). Lupe Lope y otros cuentos (Lupe Lope and Other Stories) (México: Eds. de Andrea, 1959). Gran lago (México: Eds. de Andrea, 1962). "El Tejón." in Emmanuel Carballo El cuento mexicano del siglo XX (México: Empresas Editoriales, 1964), pp. 293-299. Los indios verdes (The Green Indians) (México: FCE, 1969).

BIBLIOGRAPHY: Ruth S. Lamb, Bibliografía del teatro mexicano del siglo XX (México: Eds. de Andrea, 1962), p. 42. Luis Leal, Breve historia del cuento mexicano (México: Eds. de Andrea, 1956), p. 124. Antonio Magaña Esquivel and Ruth S. Lamb, Breve historia del teatro mexicano (México: Eds. de Andrea, 1958), p. 160. María Elvira Bermúdez, Narrativa mexicana revolucionaria (México: Editorial Ecoma, 1975).

ALICIA G. WELDEN AND RICHARD D. WOODS

CORREA Zapata, Dolores (1853-1924), poet, essayist, and educator. Correa Zapata was an important writer of pedagogical articles, as well as an occasional writer of lyric poetry. Born in Teapa, Tabasco, on February 23, 1853, she studied pedagogy in Mexico City, she taught there for ten years before being named subdirector of the grade school connected with the National Normal School for Teachers in Mexico City. In addition to her many articles on the subject of education, she published two books of poetry, Estelas y bosquejos (Wakes and Outlines) (1886) and Mis liras (My Lyres) 1917. Correa Zapata died in Mexico City on May 24, 1924, and is best remembered as a pioneer in education in Mexico.

WORKS: *Estelas y bosquejos* (Wakes and Outlines) (México: Correa Zapata, 1886). *Mis liras* (My Lyres) (México: Correa Zapata, 1917). In addition, she authored numerous educational materials and articles.

BIBLIOGRAPHY: *Biblos* 3, 12 (México, March 12, 1921), pp. 40-42. Aurora M. Ocampo de Gómez and Ernesto Prado Velázquez, *Diccionario de escritores mexicanos* (México: UNAM, 1967), pp. 84-85.

PATRICIA HART

COUTO, José Bernardo (1803-1862), poet, journalist, lawyer, diplomat. Couto was born in Orizaba, Veracruz, on December 29, 1803. He was an outstanding student of philosophy and jurisprudence in the College of San Ildefonso, where he received his law degree on August 9, 1823. He was a member of the Academy, Board of Directors, and later became president of that institution. He served in the diplomatic corps and signed the treaty between Mexico and the United States establishing the boundary between those two countries at the end of the war on February 2, 1847. He died on November 11, 1862.

Couto was interested in geography, history and biography, and in canon law as reflected in his *El Discurso sobre la constitución de la iglesia* (The Discourse on the Constitution of the Church). His encyclopedic inclinations are amply demonstrated in his contribution to the *Diccionario de Historia y Geografía* (Dictionary of History and Geography). His classic taste is best expressed in his translation of Horace's *Arte Poético* (Poetic Art). He began to publish *El Mosaico Mexicano*, a literary journal, in 1836.

WORKS: *La mulata de Córdoba* (The Mulatto Woman from Córdoba), in the early issues of *El Mosaico Mexicano* (Mexican Mosaic) (México: n.p., 1836). *El Discurso sobre la Constitución de la iglesia* (Discourse on the Constitution of the Church) (México: n.p., n.d.). He contributed to the *Diccionario de historia y geografía* (Dictionary of History and Geography) (México: n.p., 1853-1856). *Biografía de Manuel Carpio* (Biography of Manuel Carpio) (México: n.p., 1860). *Poesías de Carpio* (Carpio's Poems) (México: n.p., 1876). *Diálogo sobre la historia y la pintura de México* (Dialogue on the History and Painting of Mexico) (México: FCE, 1947).

BIBLIOGRAPHY: Guillermo Díaz-Plaja and Francisco Monterde, *Historia de la literatura española e historia de la literatura mexicana* (México: Porrúa, 1968), p. 509. Julio Jiménez Rueda, *Historia de la literatura mexicana* (México: Botas, 1960), pp. 235-37. Raimundo Lazo, "Historia de la literatura hispanoamericana, El siglo XIX" (México: Porrúa, 1976), pp. 62-63.

JOSEPH VELEZ

CRAVIOTO, Alfonso (1883-1955), poet, jurist, and politician. He was born in Pachuca, Hidalgo, on January 24, 1883, and he died in Mexico City on September 11, 1955. He studied in Pachuca and then attended law school in Mexico City. He spent some time in prison for his satirical writings against the Díaz government.

Cravioto belonged to a new group of writers that had the journal *Savia Moderna* as its core. He and Luis *Castillo Ledón had founded this literary publication in 1906. This generation of intellectuals would go on to form the group Ateneo de la Juventud, though each member was distinguished by his own strong personality.

Cravioto was very active politically and he held numerous posts, among them director of the Institute Of Fine Arts; representative to the federal government; president of the Senate; ambassador to Cuba, Guatemala, Bolivia, and other countries; and member of the Mexican Academy of the Spanish Language (1939) and of History. Among his first works are two studies of pictorial art, one dedicated to Eugenio Carrière and the other to Germán Gedovius. Cravioto enjoyed art and poetic prose and his own pen has been compared to a painter's brush. During a break from politics, he wrote the only poetry he collected: *El alma nueva de las cosas viejas* (The New Soul of Old Things); it was inspired by the environment of Mexico's colonial period, on a "return to the past," due, perhaps, to the anguish caused by the Revolution. Cravioto's book was one of the first to give rise to the style of "Colonialism," which appeared around 1917. It is a series of sketches of colonial aspects and characters, and it is important more for its value as literary history than as poetry. The author's lyricism is sacrificed at the expense of historical accuracy and variety of themes.

WORKS: *Carranza and Public Instruction in Mexico* (New York: n.p., 1915). "Eugenio Carrière" (Address), 1916. "Germán Gedovius" (Address), 1916. *Aventuras intelectuales a través de los números* (Intellectual Adventures throughout the Numbers) (La Habana: n.p., 1937; México: n.p., 1938). *El alma nueva de las cosas viejas* (The New Soul of Old Things) (México: Eds. México Moderno, 1921). *La labor social de la Sociedad Mexicana de Geografía y Estadística* (Address) (México: n.p., 1938). "Tres personalidades" (Speech), in *Memorias de la Academia Mexicana* 14 (1956): 7-10. "El elogio de Cervantes hecho por Don Quijote," in *Memorias de la Academia Mexicana* 12 (1955): 39-42. "Repertorio metódico del lenguaje" (Unpublished). *Anahuac y otros poemas*, edited by Agustín Velázquez Chávez (México: Nueva Voz, 1969).

BIBLIOGRAPHY: Alberto María Carreño, *Memorias de la Academia Mexicana* 7 (1945): 350-51; 8 (1946): 76. Eduardo Colín, *Verbo selecto* (México: Murgía, 1922), pp. 105-9. Genaro Fernández MacGregor, *Carátulas* (México: Botas, 1935), pp. 151-61. Manuel González Montesinos, "El uso y el abuso del idioma," *Memorias de la Academia Mexicana* 16 (1958): 41-44. Carlos González Peña, "Poesía y acción," *Memorias de la Academia* 14 (1956): 11-18. José Luis Martínez, "Las letras patrias," *México y la cultura* (México: SEP, 1946), p. 439. Porfirio Martínez Peñalosa, "Los poetas de *Revista de Revistas*," *Mexico en la Cultura* 993 (Apr. 13, 1966): 1-2. Diego de Pereda, *Alfonso Cravioto* (La Habana: Imp. Ucar, García y Cía., 1934). José Luis Martínez, *Literatura mexicana del siglo XX (1910- 1949)*, vol. 1 (México: Ant. Lib. Robredo, 1949), pp. 18-20.

                                                          HERLINDA HERNANDEZ

CRUZ, Salvador de la (1922-1979), journalist, poet and essayist. Salvador de la Cruz was born in Parras, Cohauila, on January 1, 1922. He studied humanities in the

United States, and he has taught at the Carlos Septién School of Journalism. His poetry, although very carefully written, lacks true emotion.

WORKS: Poetry: *Carta a un amigo ausente y presente* (Letter to a Present Absent Friend) (México: n.p., 1945). *Imagen de tu voz y otros poemas* (Image of Your Voice and Other Poems) (México: n.p., 1954). *Valle de nada* (Valley of Nothingness) (México: Fuensanta, 1955). *La balada de la ciudad* (The Ballad of the City) (Xalapa: Universidad Veracruzana, 1962). Essay: *Nuevos novelistas iberoamericanos* (New Spanish-American Novelists) (México: Unidad Mexicana de Escritores, 1955). *La novela iberoamericana actual* (The Contemporary Spanish-American Novel) (México: SEP, 1956). "Búsqueda de México: La juventud y los destinos de nuestra América" (Youth and the Destiny of Our America) *Cuadernos* (Paris) 1962: n.p.

BIBLIOGRAPHY: Jesús Arellano, *Antología de los 50 poetas contemporáneos de México* (México: Eds. Alatorre, 1952), pp. 11, 13, 69-72. Rosario Castellanos, "Valle de nada," *Metáfora* 3 (1955): 39.

ALFONSO GONZALEZ

CRUZ, Sor Juana Inés de la (1651-1695). Juana Ramírez de Asuaje (or Asbaje) was born on November 12, 1651, on a farm in San Miguel Nepantla. Sor Juana's father was a military man of Basque origin, and her mother was native to Mexico. Her parents were not married, and it has been speculated that Sor Juana's illegitimate birth contributed to a great deal of anxiety for her. On the other hand, there are those who claim that, as a child, she was oblivious to the truth about her birth. Regardless of her family's circumstances, she was raised in a family structure that provided necessary nurturing for her. She was especially close to her maternal grandfather. A child prodigy, she learned to read when she was three. By the time she was six or seven she wanted to attend the university. She even asked her mother to dress her as a boy so that she could go to Mexico City for an education. When she was eight, she composed a Eucharistic *loa*, no longer extant. Around this time, she did go to live with relatives in the capital, although not as a boy. She learned Latin in a very short time and wrote poetry in it. By 1665, she merited the attention of the wife of the viceroy, Marqués de Mancera. Brought to the court, she astounded those present with her knowledge, her aptitude, and her talent. She was subjected to a public oral examination by forty learned men from various disciplines, from which she emerged triumphant. Following this, she was recognized as a female intellectual, an almost unheard of phenomena in the seventeenth century.

Sor Juana was extremely knowledgeable about many different subjects, including music, mathematics, physics, theology, literature, and painting. In the court, she was solicited to write poetry for special occasions and to demonstrate her brilliance at court events. All this activity came to a halt when she made an irrevocable decision to enter the convent, deciding that she was not interested in marriage. Many have speculated upon her reasons for this, but most critics agree that it was because in the convent she could pursue her studies and be the intellectual that she wanted to be. Others question her lack of interest in men. A few, however, subscribe to the idea that she really did have a religious vocation. Thus, in 1667, she entered the San José

Convent of the Descalced Carmelites. The order was so austere, however, that she became ill and was forced to leave, entering, instead, the less restrictive cloistered Convent of San Jerónimo. She was much happier there, since she was able to combine her religious responsibilities and activities with her studies.

Called the Tenth Muse, Sor Juana acquired an extensive library of more than 4,000 books, an incredible number for anyone at that time. She kept abreast of literary currents throughout the Western world. Her writings embrace virtually every literary style and genre. Spanish writers such as Luis de Góngora, Francisco de Quevedo, Lope de Vega, and others all influenced her. A product of both the Renaissance and the Baroque, she blended classical traditionalism with the newer poetic movements. Her exquisite poem, "Primero sueño" (First Dream), considered her most important single work, is a very complex, intricate, and delicate poem, with metaphorical language and interesting rhythmic and rhyme schemes. It is a baroque masterpiece, which still invites critical examination. She wrote many *villancicos* (Christmas carols), sonnets, love poems, spiritual and religious poems, and others that express a feminist attitude. She has aptly been called the "first feminist of America."

In addition, Sor Juana also published theater, mostly of an allegorical nature. She wrote short interludes as well as full-length religious plays. *El cetro de José* (Joseph's Scepter), *El Mártir del Sacramento, San Hermenegildo* (St. Hermenegildo, the Sacrament's Martyr), and *Divino Narciso* are her *autos sacramentales*, which all follow Spanish theological models. She also wrote *Los empeños de una casa* (The Tasks of a House) and *Amor es más laberinto* (Love Is A Greater Labyrinth), both secular plays, the latter in collaboration with Juan de Guevara.

Sor Juana's prose also is of outstanding quality. When the Marqués de Mancera became the new viceroy, Sor Juana was commissioned to write verses and to plan the allegorical arch. She wrote *Neptuno alegórico* (Allegorical Neptune) to commemorate the event in 1680. Two other pieces of great interest are her *Crisis sobre un sermón* (Crisis about a Sermon) and the very famous *Respuesta a Sor Filotea*. Sor Juana critiqued a sermon that she heard, and her viewpoint was published. In response to her critique, she received a letter from "Sor Filotea de la Cruz," in reality, the bishop of Puebla, who exhorted her to dedicate herself more fully to her religious and sacred duties. It took her three months, but she wrote a response, autobiographical in nature, defending the rights of women, especially the right to an education. She also reaffirmed her abhorrence of the idea of marriage. Defending her choice of entering the convent, for both religious and educational reasons, she indicated that she could see no wrong in writing poetry, since even the Bible contains it. Shortly after sending this letter, Sor Juana gave up her personal library, sold her mathematical and musical instruments, donating profits to the poor. She spent the remaining years of her life caring for her sisters in the convent. These were trying times for Mexico, due to a staggering number of difficulties, including famine, floods, epidemics, and Indian uprisings. All this took its toll on Sor Juana, the major lyric poet of colonial Spanish America, and she died on April 17, 1695.

In the last two decades there has been greatly renewed interest in Sor Juana and her work. An unusually large number of books, articles and other notes about her life and her writings are now available. Most books contain bibliographical information; therefore, for further references, consult any one of them.

WORKS: *Obras completas* (Complete Works), 4 vols. (México and Buenos Aires; FCE, 1951-1957). Individual works are also available.

BIBLIOGRAPHY: Anita Arroyo, *Razón y pasión de Sor Juana* (México: Porrúa y Obregón, 1952). P. Diego Calleja, *Vida de Sor Juana* (México: Ant. Libr. Robredo, 1936). Frank Dauster, *Breve historia de la poesía mexicana* (México: Eds. de Andrea, 1956), pp. 41-46. Enrique Díez-Canedo, in *Letras de América* (México: FCE, 1944), pp. 51-70. Manuel Durán, "Hermetic Traditions in Sor Juana's *Primero Sueño*," in *University of Dayton Review* 16, 2 (1983): 107-15. Sergio Fernández, *Homenajes a Sor Juana, a López Velarde, a José Gorostiza* (México, 1972). Genaro Fernández MacGregor, *La santificación de Sor Juana Inés de la Cruz* (México: Cultura, 1932). Ilse Heckel, "Los sainetes de Sor Juana Inés de la Cruz," in *Revista Iberoamericana* 13, 25 (1947): 135-40. Julio Jiménez Rueda, *Sor Juana Inés de la Cruz en su época* (México: Porrúa, 1952). Alfonso Junco, *El amor de Sor Juana* (México: Jus, 1951). Francisco de la Maza and Elías Trabulse, *Sor Juana Inés de la Cruz ante la historia* (México, 1980). Ludwig Pfandl, *Sor Juana Inés de la Cruz, la Décima Musa de México. Su vida. Su poesía. Su psique*, edition and prologue by Francisco de la Maza, translation by Juan Antonio Ortega y Medina (México: UNAM, 1963). Guillermo Ramírez España, *La familia de Sor Juana Inés de la Cruz* (México: Imp. Universitaria, 1947). Alfredo A. Roggiano, "Conocer y hacer en Sor Juana Inés de la Cruz," in *Revista de Occidente* 15 (1977): 51-54. Georgina Sabat de Rivers, "Sor Juana y su *Sueño*: Antecedentes científicos en la poesía española del siglo de oro," in *Cuadernos Hispanoamericanos* 310 (1976): 186-204; "El *Neptuno* de Sor Juana: Fiesta barroca y programa político," in *University of Dayton Review* 16, 2 (1983): 63-73; "Sor Juana Inés de la Cruz," in *Latin American Writers*, vol. 1, edited by Carlos A. Solé (New York: Charles Scribner's Sons, 1989). Lota M. Spell, *Cuatro documentos relativos a Sor Juana* (México: Imp. Universitaria, 1947). Arturo Torres Ríoseco, "Sor Juana Inés de la Cruz," in *Revista Iberoamericana* 12, 23 (1947): 13-38. Various, *Homenaje del Instituto de Investigaciones Estéticas a Sor Juana Inés de la Cruz, en el tercer centenario de su nacimiento*, with a study by Manual Toussaint (México: Imp. Universitaria, 1952); *Homenaje a Sor Juana Inés de la Cruz en el tercer centenario de su nacimiento* (Madrid: Real Academia Española, 1952).

JEANNE C. WALLACE

CUELLAR, José Tomás de (1830-1894) novelist, costumbristic sketch writer, and dramatist, known by the pseudonym Facundo. José Tomás de Cuellar was born in Mexico City on September 18, 1830. He studied in the Colegio de San Gregorio, the Colegio de San Ildefonso and, later, in the Colegio Militar de Chapultepec where, along with Mexico's famous "boy heroes," he took part in the defense of Chapultepec Castle against the invasion of the United States Army on September 13, 1847. Afterwards, Cuellar went on to study art at the Academia de San Carlos. Throughout his lifetime, he remained an active figure in the art world, achieving some fame as a painter and photographer who specialized in portraits and street scenes. He was also recognized as an important man of letters during the second half of the nineteenth century, particularly for his work in the costumbrista vein.

Cuellar's career as a writer began in 1848, when he wrote a moving piece in honor of those who had died during the war against the United States. He soon began to publish on a regular basis in *La Ilustración Mexicana* (Mexican Enlightenment) and *El Semanario de Señoritas* (The Ladies' Weekly). Like most writers of his age, Cuellar did not limit his efforts to a single genre. He penned novels, sketches, articles, poems and dramas, with impressive speed, if not always with the best literary results. By 1869, Cuellar was fairly well known in the nation's capital. It is unclear why he uprooted himself to move to the provincial town of San Luis Potosi but once there, he continued to pursue his literary career as a costumbristic sketch writer. He also wrote several installment novels, which he published in *La Ilustración Potosina* (Potosian Enlightenment), and he completed work on his historical novel, *El pecado del siglo* (The Sin of the Century). This latter work is set in the late eighteenth-century and portrays the crumbling world of the Spanish aristocracy in Mexico. It combines romantic, costumbristic, and realistic detail. Castro Leal regards it as a novel of some merit, and he postulates that its relative obscurity in the history of Mexican letters may be due to the fact that it was published by a small, provincial press and not widely distributed among readers. Cuellar may have reached the same decision for soon afterward he returned to Mexico City.

In 1871, he published the first volume of *La linterna mágica* (The Magic Lantern), a series of costumbristic sketches which would, by the time of his death, encompass twenty-four volumes. Cuellar also continued to publish costumbristic articles and poems in Mexican and Spanish American newspapers such as *La Ilustración Mexicana*, *El Siglo XIX*, *El Laberinto*, *Las Cosquillas*, *El Eco del Comercio*, *El Correo de México*, *El Eco de Ambos Mundos*, *El Federalista*, and *La Libertad*. Cuellar's achievements in the literary and artistic world brought him recognition by the Mexican government in 1872, when he was given the first of several prestigious diplomatic posts. His work as a diplomat took him to Washington, D.C., where he lived for ten years and, later, to Europe. Only when failing eyesight and poor health forced his retirement did Cuellar return to Mexico. He died in Mexico City on February 11, 1894, and is buried in the Panteón de Dolores among other alumni of the Colegio Militar.

Cuellar is generally recognized as the first to give costumbrismo a place in Mexican letters. He is seen as a follower of *Fernández de Lizardi, and a precursor of Angel de *Campo (Micros). In his costumbristic sketches and novels, the moralizing tone does not predominate over the satirical humor. The didactic element is usually present in the events narrated in the story rather than in the tone of the narrator. Cuellar's work is remarkable for the lively dialogue, accurate reproduction of atmosphere and types and for the dynamic quality of his prose. The target of most of his satirical barbs is Mexico's middle class. Through caricature, he exaggerates the weaknesses and pretensions of society types such as the spoiled child, the rogue, the affected girl, the opportunist, the womanizer, etc., in order to make them objects of ridicule. Cuellar, like many liberals of his generation, blamed the middle class for allowing Mexico to go to ruin. Nevertheless, his works are seldom emotional or political in tone. Instead, he maintained a cool distance from the characters he sought to portray, regarding them with a sardonic smile rather than with open scorn. Cuellar, himself, defined his goal in *La linterna mágica* as that of creating a work in which "everything is Mexican, everything is ours, or that which is important to US." As the name of the collection implies, Cuellar attempted to copy reality in the pages of his text as he might copy reality in a photograph. He saw the three defining elements of his narrative art as the accurate and exact portrayal of real people or types, the incorporation of local color, and the clear distinction between good and evil. Some of his most famous costumbristic novels and sketches include: *Historia de Chucho el Ninfo* (The Story of Chucho, the Fop), *La nochebuena* (Christmas Eve), *Ensalada de* *pollos* (Chicken Salad), *Bailes y Cochino* (The Bailiff and the Pig), *Las jamonas* (The Hefty Women), *Las gentes "son así"* (People Are Like That), *Los mariditos* (The Little Husbands), *Los fuereños* (The Provincial People), *Isolina, la exfigurante* (Isolina, the Ex-theater Extra) and *Gabriel el cerrajero* (Gabriel the Locksmith).

Although Cuellar is best knowm today for his costumbristic prose pieces, he was considered an important dramatist in the second half of the nineteenth century. His play *Deberes y sacrificios* (Duties and Sacrifices) was staged first in Mexico City in 1855 and later, in Madrid, where it featured the renowned Spanish actress Matilde Díaz. The Spanish dramatist Zorrilla wrote glowing praise of the work. In 1866, Cuellar met with another theatrical success in Mexico, when his two-act satirical play, *Natural y figura* (Naturalness and the Outward Image), attracted large audiences and won him the Golden Pen Award of the Asociación Gregoriana. Written and staged at the height of the French Intervention, the play ridiculed those middle-class Mexicans who aped foreign customs. Other dramatic pieces by Cuellar include *El arte de amar* (The Art of Loving), *El viejecito Chacón* (The Old Man Chacon), *¡Qué lástima de muchachos!* (What Pitiful Boys), *Azares de una venganza* (The Hazards of Vengeance), *Redención en el Oriente* (Redemption in the East), and *Cubrir las apariencias* (Covering Up Appearances). Most of these plays were presented in Mexico City and met with at least a mild success. Only *Deberes y sacrificios* (Duties and Sacrifices) was published; the others have been lost.

WORKS: *Deberes y sacrificios* (Duties and Sacrifices) (México: Imp. de Juan R. Navarro, 1855). *Ensalada de pollos y Baile y cochino* (Chicken Salad and The Bailiff and the Pig), edited by Antonio Castro Leal (México: Porrúa, 1946). *Estampas del siglo XIX* (Engravings from the Nineteenth Century), edited by Rubén Salazar (México: SEP, 1944). *Historia de Chucho el ninfo y La Noche Buena* (The Story of Chucho the Fop and Christmas Eve), edited by Antonio Castro Leal (México: Porrúa, 1942). *La linterna mágica* (The Magic Lantern), 24 vols. (México: Imp. de Ignacio Cumplido, 1871-72); 2nd ed. (Barcelona: Espasa y Co. 1889); 3rd ed. (México: UNAM, 1941). *Obras poéticas* (Poetic Works) (México: Imp. de Ignacio Cumplido, 1856); *El pecado del siglo* (The Sin of the Century) (San Luis Potosí: Tip. del Colegio Polimático, 1869); reprinted in *La novela del México colonial*, edited by Antonio Castro Leal (México: Aguilar, 1964), vol. 1, pp. 181-396; *Versos* (Verses) (Santander: Blanchard y cía, 1891). *Vistazos Estudios sociales* (A Look at Social Types) (Santander: Blanchard y cía, 1890).

BIBLIOGRAPHY: Ignacio Altamirano, *La literatura nacional* (México: Porrúa, 1949), vol. 1, pp. 105-7. Carlos González Peña, *Historia de la literatura mexicana* (México: SEP, 1928), pp. 438-40. M. B. Kingsley, *Estudio costumbrista de la obra de Facundo* (México: 1944). Luis Leal, *Breve historia del cuento mexicano* (México: Eds. de Andrea, 1956), pp. 48-49. María del Carmen Millán, *Literatura mexicana* (México: Edit. Esfinge, 1962), p. 160.

CYNTHIA K. DUNCAN

CUENCA, Agustín (1850-1884), poet and dramatist. Born in Mexico City on November 16, 1850, Cuena studied in the Colegio de San Ildefonso along with contemporaries Manuel *Acuña and Justo *Sierra. In 1870 he began to study law but soon decided he preferred journalism and poetry, and his articles appeared in opposition papers, *El Porvenir* and *El Interino*. Some of his poetry was published in *El Parnaso Mexicano*, but he died in Mexico City on June 30, 1884, without seeing any volumes of verse in print. He was survived by his wife, Laura *Mendez, who was also a writer. Although Cuenca left behind only about thirty poems, they stand out for their musicality and ornate refinement. The earlier poems were full of baroque expressions and gongorisms, but the later ones, like *Arbol de mi vida* (Tree of My Life) and *La mañana* (The Morning), develop an elegant personal voice. Together with Justo Sierra, he is considered a Mexican precursor of modernism. Cuenca's one theatrical piece, *La cadena de hierro* (The Iron Chain), was staged on August 20, 1876, in the Gran Teatro Nacional de México. His biography, "Angela Peralta de Castera," was a romantic idealization, circulated among his friends and mentioned in their writings, but never published.

WORKS: "Angela Feralta de Castera" (written 1873, unpublished). *La cadena de hierro* (The Iron Chain) (Orizaba: El Ferrocarril, 1881). *Poemas selectos* (Selected Poems) (México: Biblioteca de Autores Mexicanos Modernos, 1-20). "Magdalena" (unpublished, year of composition uncertain).

BIBLIOGRAPHY: José Joaquín Blanco, *Crónica de la poesía mexicana* (México: Libro de Bolsillo, 1983), p. 26. Frank Dauster, *Breve historia de la poesía mexicana* (México: Eds. de Andrea, 1956), p. 88. Heriberto García Rivas, *Historia de la literatura mexicana*, vol. 2 (México: Porrúa, 1972), pp. 90, 183. Carlos González Peón, *History of Mexican Literature* (Dallas: Southern Methodist University Press, 1943-1968), pp. 276-77, 282, 464. Sergio Howland Bustamante, *Historia de la literatura mexicana* (México: F. Trillas, 1967), pp. 181, 187. Francisco Monterde, *Agustín F. Cuenca. El prosista. El poeta de transición* (México: UNAM, 1942). Aurora M. Ocampo de Gómez and Ernesto Prado Velázquez, *Diccionario de escritores mexicanos* (México: UNAM, 1967), pp. 88-89. Enrique de Olavarría y Ferrari, *Colección de los mejores autores*, vol. 45 of *Poesías líricas mexicanas* (Madrid: Biblioteca Universal, 1878). José Emilio Pacheco, *La poesía mexicana del siglo XIX* (México: Empresas Editoriales, 1965), pp. 305-15. Juan de Dios Peza, *Poetas y escritores modernos mexicanos* (México: Filomena Mata, 1878), pp. 25-27. Agustín del Saz, *Antología general de la poesía mexicana, siglos XVI-XX* (Barcelona: Bruguera, 1972).

PATRICIA HART AND JOSEF HELLEBRANDT

CUESTA, Jorge (1903-1942), poet and essayist. Jorge Cuesta was born in Córdoba, Veracruz, on September 21, 1903. He completed the requirements for a major in chemistry at UNAM, except for the thesis, and worked in that profession during most of his life. He joined the group of poets known as the "Contemporáneos" and became affiliated with literary journals of the period: *Contemporáneos, Examen, Tierra Nueva,* and others. He also wrote political essays. His marriage to Guadalupe Marín, whose vibrant temperament was completely the opposite of Cuesta's, lasted only a short time with their son, Antonio, remaining in his custody. Jorge Cuesta had mental problems throughout much of his life and was committed to a sanatorium twice. He committed suicide August 13, 1942, while recovering from nearly bleeding to death after he emasculated himself.

Cuesta's poetry is limited in production to some twenty-eight poems, but his influence over other poets of the Contemporáneos group and over subsequent Mexican writers is considerable because of his desire to develop new freedom of expression, not only for Mexican poetry but also for national political and social identity. His close personal friend and fellow Contemporáneo poet, Elías *Nandino, published Cuesta's poetry after his death. Predominant themes are time, the conflict of good and evil, and death. The latter, especially, appears as a constant and dark presence in his poetry. His tormented character is manifested in his predominant focus on his inner self. His obsession with sin and guilt is also evident, and the subsequent allusion to self-punishment foreshadows the manner of his suicide.

WORKS: *El plan contra Calles* (The Plan against Calles) (México: n.p., 1934). *Poesía de Jorge Cuesta* (Poetry of Jorge Cuesta) (México: Tierra Nueva, 1942). *Crítica de la reforma del Artículo Tercero* (Criticism of the Reform of Article Three) (México: n.p., 1943). *Poesía de Jorge Cuesta* (Poetry of Jorge Cuesta) (México: Editorial Estaciones, 1958). *Poemas y ensayos* (Poems and Essays), 4 vols. (México: UNAM, 1964). - *Antología* (Anthology), Serie Poesía Moderna, n. 14 (México: UNAM, 1977). *Poemas, ensayos y testimonios* (Poems, Essays, and Testimony), vol. 5 (México: UNAM, 1981).

BIBLIOGRAPHY: Inés Arredondo, "Acercamiento al pensamiento artístico de Jorge Cuesta," thesis, UNAM, 1974. Raúl Leiva, *Imagen de la poesía mexicana contemporánea* (México: UNAM, 1959), pp. 145-50. Carlos Montemayor, "Jorge Cuesta," *Revista de la Universidad de México* 28, 8 (April 1974): 17-24. Aurora M. Ocampo de Gómez and Ernesto Prado Velázquez, *Diccionario de escritores mexicanos* (México: UNAM, 1967), pp. 89-90. Louis Panabire, *Itinerario de una disidencia [1903-1942]*, translated by Adolfo Castañón (México: FCE, 1983). Nigel Grant Sylvester, "The Poetical Works of Jorge Cuesta," Diss., University of California, Berkely, 1975. Xavier Villarrutia, "In Memoriam: Jorge Cuesta," *Letras de México* 21 (Sept. 15, 1942).

KENNETH M. TAGGART

CUEVA, Juan de la (1543-1610). Juan de le Cueva was born in Seville around 1543. He traveled to New Spain with his brother, who later held official positions there. He lived in New Spain from 1574 to 1577 and then returned to Spain. He died in Seville in 1610. Twenty-five of his sonnets, an elegy, a sextina, three madrigals, and two odes appeared in *Flores de varia poesía*, collected in México in 1577. Along with Gutierre de *Cetina and Eugenio *Salazar de Alarcón he represented the arrival of the current literary activity in Spain in the New World. His claim to fame rests mainly on his plays based on traditional Spanish themes, such as *Los siete Infantes de Lara* (The Seven Princes of Lara) and *La libertad de España por Bernardo del Carpio* (The Freeing of Spain by Bernardo del Carpio). He is a precursor of Lope de Vega and is therefore important and influential in the eventual development of Spanish Golden Age drama. It is said that his verse anticipated all later Spanish poetry even more than his theater anticipated theatrical development.

WORKS: *Tragedias y comedias de Juan de la Cueva* (Madrid: Ed. de Bibliófilos Españoles, 1917). *Conquista bélica* (Sevilla: n.p., 1603, reprinted 1795). José Rojas Garcidueñas, *El teatro de Nueva España en el siglo XVI* (México: n.p., 1935). Francisco A. de Icaza, "Gutierre de Cetina y Juan de la Cueva," *Boletín de la Real Academia Española* 3 (1916). Renato Rosaldo, *Flores de varia poesía* (México: Abside, 1952).

ANITA K. STOLL

D

DALLAL, Alberto (1936-). Alberto Dallal was born in Mexico City on June 6, 1936. He studied architecture in the National University and has been a professor in the Escuela Nacional Preparatoria and in private schools. He has done acting and has been the assistant to the director of the Grupo de Teatro of the National School of Architecture (renamed: Studies in Set Design). He has been an editor of the journal *Universidad de México* and contributed to *La Palabra y el Hombre, Cuadernos Americanos*, and to *La Cultura en México*, the literary supplement of the journal *Siempre!*. Alberto Dallal first appeared in the journals *Cuadernos del Viento* and *Revista Mexicana de Literatura*, where he published short stories and poems. He also writes theater, of which he has published two plays: *El capitán queda inmóvil* and *El hombre debajo del agua*. In the first of these, he intermixes lines from Ungaretti with his own writing; in the second, with an original story and plain, direct language, he re-creates an atmosphere where he does not fear to include either humor, poetry, or message, a message that affirms that good deeds lack efficacy when they do not pass from the level of the individual to that of the collective.

In his collection of short stories, *Geminis*, he combines the meticulousness of writing with a pursuit of consciousness through the act of love: his objectives are not so much founded in expression, feeling, thought, or deed as in the search for a manner of being: upon reaching the act of love, to convert it to intelligence, where contact between two or three beings occurs as an intransigent experience, as discovery, as the definitive acquisition of consciousness.

Brushwood finds the novel *El poder de la urraca* to be influenced by such cinematic procedures as the fade-in, present in the absence of transition between chapters, so that while Dallal writes chronologically, the reader is not shown where the shifts take place. Dallal writes about the universality of relationships between people, who could be anywhere.

WORKS: Theater: *El capitán queda inmóvil* (The Captain Stays Still), one-act play, in *La Palabra y el Hombre* 17 (Jan.-Mar. 1961): 149-60. *El hombre debajo del agua* (The Man Under Water), three-act play, Colección Ficción, no. 48 (Xalapa: Universidad Veracruzana, 1962). *Siete Piezas para la escena* (Seven Plays for the Stage). Studies: *Discurso de la danza* (The Discourse of Dance). *La danza moderna* (Modern Dance). *El amor de las ciudades* (The Love of Cities). *Gozosa revolución* (Joyful Revolution). "Treinta años de teatro experimental en México" (Thirty Years of Experimental Theater in Mexico), in *Diálogos* 17 (July-Aug. 1981): 65-73. "Lo inasible y lo docil" (The Ungraspable and the Docile), in *Cuadernos Americanos* 202 (1975): 248-55. Novels: *El poder de la urraca* (The Power of the Magpie) (1969). *Las ínsulas extrañas* (The Strange Isles). Short Stories: *Geminis*, a collection of eight stories (México: Arte y Libros, 1974).

BIBLIOGRAPHY: Anon., Bibliographic note, in *Anuario del cuento mexicano 1962* (México: Depto. de Lit., INBA, 1963), p. 111; Review of his plays, back cover of *El hombre debajo del agua* (Xalapa: Universidad Veracruzana, 1962); Review of *Geminis*, back cover of book (México: Arte y Libros, 1974). John S. Brushwood, *México en su novela* (México: FCE, 1966, 1973), pp. 118-19. Aurora M. Ocampo de Gómez and Ernesto Prado Velázquez, *Diccionario de escritores mexicanos* (México: UNAM, 1967), p. 92. Teresinha Pereira, "A Linguagem nos Contos de Alberto Dallal," in *Belo Horizonte* 20, suppl. to *Minas Gerais*, Minas Gerais, Brazil (May 10, 1978).

YOLANDA S. BROAD

DAUJARE Torres, Félix (1920-   ), poet. Born on July 8, 1920, in San Luis Potosí, Daujare Torres was educated exclusively there, receiving a law degree from the Universidad Potosina. He has contributed to *Cuadrante*, *Letras Potosinas*, and *Estilo*, journals published in the city of his birth. Daujare Torres was initially influenced by the Uruguayan poet, Julio Herrera y Reissig. But his later works exhibit his own unique style, inspired by Mexico's indigenous heritage and the gods that ruled that part of the pre-Columbian world.

WORKS: *De tu mar y de tu sueño, sonetos* (From Your Sea and from Your Dream, Sonnets) (San Luis Potosí, 1952). *Definiciones* (Definitions) (San Luis Potosí, 1960). *Cuarta dimensión* (Fourth Dimension) (San Luis Potosí, 1963). *El que domina en la aurora* (The One Who Rules at Dawn) (México: Pájaro Cascabel, 1964). *La razón de la noche* (Night's Reason) (México: Pájaro Cascabel, 1965). *Xipe Totec* (México: Pájaro Cascabel, 1967). *Color de fuego y de tíempo* (The Color of Fire and Time) (México: Pájaro Cascabel, 1969).

BIBLIOGRAPHY: Huberto Batis, Review of *El que domina en la aurora*, in *La Cultura en México* 118, 20 (May 20, 1964): xviii. Andrés Henestrosa, "La nota cultural," review of *El que domina en la aurora*, in *El Nacional* (May 26, 1964): 3. Jesús Medina Romero, *Antología de poetas contemporáneos (1910-1953)*, Biblioteca de Autores Potosinos, no. 1 (Universidad Autónoma de San Luis Potosí, 1953), p. 17. Aurora M. Ocampo de Gómez and Ernesto Prado Velázquez, *Diccionario de escritores mexicanos* (México: UNAM, 1967), pp. 92-93. Luis Mario Schneider, Review of *La razón de la noche*, in *La Palabra y El Hombre* 35 (July-Sept. 1965): 540-41.

JANIS L. KRUGH

DAVALOS, Balbino (1866-1951), poet, translator, and diplomat. Balbino Dávalos was born in Colima on March 31, 1866. His first original poems, versions and translations of European poets, were published in *Revista Azul*, *El Mundo Ilustrado*, and other magazines and newspapers. After receiving his law degree, he began his career in the Foreign Service (1897), and went to Washington as a secretary of the embassy of México. He served his country as a diplomat in England, Germany, and Portugal. As a professor, his activities included teaching at the Facultad de Filosofía y Letras (School of Philosophy and Letters) of the National University of Mexico, the School of Romance Languages of the University of Minnesota (1917), and Columbia University in New York. He died on October 2, 1951 in Mexico City.

His translations into Spanish of Théophile Gautier (Symphony in White Major), Paul Verlaine, Algernon Charles Swinburne, Edgar Allan Poe, Maurice Maeterlinck (Monna Vanna, drama) and Henry W. Longfellow, made modern European and American literature accessible to Mexican readers. After his original poetry, *Las ofrendas* (The Offerings), he received laudatory criticism from Rubén Darío. Julio *Jiménez Rueda includes Balbino Dávalos among the group of "Poetas modernistas" (Modernismo). According to Francisco *Monterde, Davalos' "Memoirs" remain dispersed in various newspapers and magazines.

WORKS: *Las Ofrendas* (The Offerings) (Madrid: Tip. de la Revista de Archivos, 1909). *Discursos leídos ante la Academia Mexicana* (Speeches Delivered before the Mexican Academy of Language) (México: Imp. Labor, 1930). Translations: *Los grandes poetas norteamericanos* (The Great American Poets) (México: Tip. de la Oficina Impresora del Timbre, 1901). *Monna Vanna of M. Maeterlinck* (México: Bouret, 1902). *Musas de Francia* (Muses of France) (Lisboa: Tip. de la Editora Limitada, 1913). *Musas de Albión* (Muses of Albion) (México: Ed. Cultura, 1930).

BIBLIOGRAPHY: Pedro Henríquez Ureña, *Las corrientes literarias en la América Hispánica* (México: FCE, 1954), pp. 179, 259. Julio Jiménez Rueda, *Historia de la Literatura Mexicana* (México: Botas, 1957), pp. 294, 321. Francisco Monterde, *Historia de la Literatura Mexicana* (México: Porrúa, 1960), p. 578. Amado Nervo, "Musas de Francia," in *Obras completas* (Madrid: Aguilar, 1962), vol. 1, pp. 1327-29.

                                                        BAUDELIO GARZA

DAVALOS, Marcelino (1871-1923), poet, writer of short stories, and dramatist. Marcelino Dávalos was born on April 26, 1871, in Guadalajara. He studied in local schools, including the Liceo de Varones de Guadalajara (prestigious high school for male students). In 1900 he obtained his law degree from the Escuela de Jurisprudencia (School of Jurisprudence) and served in several public offices of the State of Jalisco. He was a congressman until 1913. Marcelino Dávalos participated very actively in the Congreso Constituyente (Assembly of Representatives who wrote the Mexican Constitution) in Querétaro in 1917. For two years, up to 1919, Dávalos was a consultant lawyer in the Secretaría de Comunicaciones y Obras Públicas (Department of Communications). From 1919 he held important positions as an employee of the Mexican government in Mexico City and contributed to *El Universal*, *El Mundo Ilustrado* and, other newspapers and magazines of the capital city. Dávalos died in Mexico City on September 19, 1923.

Among his short stories, the collection *¡Carne de cañón!* (Cannon Flesh!) portrays the drama of Porfirio Diaz' dictatorship. As a poet, Dávalos is considered a delicate romantic in *Mis dramas íntimos* (My Intimate Dramas), *Iras de Bronce* (Angers of Bronze), and *Del Bajío y arribeñas*. As a dramatist, Dávalos shows concern about social and national issues since the beginning of his production. The topic of his drama *Guadalupe* is the problem of alcoholism and its tendencies to be hereditary.

Other dramas written during the years of the Mexican Revolution are *¡Viva el amo!* (Long Live the Master!), *Lo viejo* (Old Things), and *El crimen de Marciano* (Marciano's Crime). Very few dramatists show the mastery of dramatic techniques that Dávalos does.

WORKS: Drama: *El último cuadro* (The Last Scene), 1900. *Guadalupe*, 1903. *Así pasan*, 1908. *¡Viva el amo!* (Long Live the Master!), 1910. *Lo viejo* (Old Things), 1911. *Aguilas y estrellas* (Eagles and Stars), 1916. *Jardines trágicos* (Tragic Gardens) (México: Imp. del Museo Nacional de México, 1916). Poetry: *Iras de bronce* (Angers of Bronze), 1916. *Mis dramas íntimos* (My Intimate dramas), 1917. *Monografía del teatro* (Monograph of the Theater) (México: Ed. de la Dirección Gral. de Educación Publica, 1917).

BIBLIOGRAPHY: Julio Jiménez Rueda, *Historia de la Literatura Mexicana* (México: Botas, 1957), p. 337. Francisco Monterde, *Historia de la Literatura Mexicana* (México: Porrúa, 1960), p. 579. José Rojas Garciadueñas, "Prólogo," in *Así pasan* (México: UNAM, 1945), pp. ix-xxv.

BAUDELIO GARZA

DAVILA, María Amparo (1928-   ), short story writer and poet. Born in Pinos, Zacatecas, on Februrary 21, 1928, Dávila had a lonely and rather unhappy childhood. At age seven, she was taken to San Luis Potosí, where she was educated in a convent. There at the age of eight, she began to write poems, and at ten, short stories. She published several books of poetry, but is better known for her short stories, some of which have been translated.

Her stories are first-rate in quality and intense in impact. The ending is often unexpected. Her earliest books, in particular *Tiempo destrozado* (Squandered Time) and *Música concreta* (Concrete Music), are in the mode of writers such as Franz Kafka, Julio Cortázar, and Adolfo Bioy Casares. The imagination often finds itself enmeshed in a harsh reality as her characters struggle with issues such as death, solitude, the complexity of human relationships, and the control of one's fate.

WORKS: Poetry: *Salmos bajo la luna* (Moonlight Psalms) (San Luis Potosí: n.p., 1950). *Perfil de soledades* (Profile of Lonely Places) (San Luis Potosí: Talls. El Troquel, 1954). *Meditaciones a la orilla del sueño* (Meditations on the Edge of a Dream) (San Luis Potosí: n.p., 1954). Stories: *Tiempo destrozado* (Squandered Time) (México: FCE, 1959). *Música concreta* (Concrete Music) (México: FCE, 1964). *Arboles petrificados* (Petrified Trees) (México: Mortiz, 1977). *Muerte en el bosque* (Death in the Forest) (México: Lecturas Mexicanas, 1985), Compilation of stories from *Música concreta* and *Tiempo destrozado*.

BIBLIOGRAPHY: Anon., Review of *Tiempo destrozado*, in *Perfumes y Modas* 33 (May-June 1959). Huberto Batis, Review of *Música concreta*, in *La Cultura en México* 143 (Nov. 11, 1964): p. xviii. Emmanuel Carballo, "Amparo Dávila entre la realidad y la irrealidad," in *La Cultura en México* 141 (Oct. 28, 1964). Heriberto García Rivas, *Historia de la literatura mexicana*, vol. 4 (México: Textos Universitarios, 1971), pp. 357-58. Carlos González Peña, *History of Mexican Literature*, translated by Gusta

Barfield Nance and Florene Johnson Dunstan (Dallas, Texas: Southern Methodist University Press, 1968), p. 450. Aurora M. Ocampo de Gómez and Ernesto Prado Velázquez, *Diccionario de escritores mexicanos* (México: UNAM, 1967), p. 94. Eunice Odio, "Un verdadero libro de cuentos," in *El Libro y el Pueblo*, Epoca III, no. 1 (July-Sept. 1959): 96-101. Pedro Shimose, ed., *Diccionario de autores iberoamericanos* (Madrid: Ministerio de Asuntos Exteriores, 1982), p. 133. José Vázquez Amaral, Review of *Tiempo destrozado*, in *New York Times Book Review* (Sept. 18, 1960).

MARK FRISCH

DELGADO, Juan B. (1868-1929), poet, diplomat, professor. Delgado was born in Querétaro on August 28, 1868. His education in the Seminario Conciliar de Querétaro (Seminary of Querétaro) was oriented toward classical literature and humanism. Delgado finished his college education in Mexico City and then began his diplomatic career. He served his country in Nicaragua, Spain (1912), Italy (1919), and Costa Rica (1921). During his travels, he wrote several books of bucolic and descriptive poetry and works of criticism. His activities as a professor of literature and language included the Escuela Nacional Preparatoria (National Preparatory School) in Mexico City and the Colegio Civil (Civil College) in Monterrey. *Revista de Revistas* and *Mercurio* of New Orleans were two magazines in which Delgado wrote. He died in Mexico City on March 8, 1929.

With his early works, *Natura, Poemas de los arboles* (Poems of Trees) *Poemas de la naturaleza* (Poems of Nature), Delgado distinguished himself as a poet of nature and received enthusiastic criticism from Rubén Darío and José Juan *Tablada, both poets of modernist orientation (Modernismo).

WORKS: *Juveniles* (Juvenile, poems) (México: Imp. de Luciano Frías y Soto, 1894). *Natura* (México: n.p., 1895). *Canciones surianas* (Songs of the South) (México: Tip de J. Aguilar Vera y Cía., 1900). *Poemas de los arboles* (Monterrey: Imp. de J. Cantu Leal, 1907). *El cancionero nómada* (The Nomadic Song Book) (Managua: 1912; México: 1927). "París y otros poemas descriptivos," in *De mi cosecha* (Guadalajara: Imp. de Ancira y Hno., 1899), pp. 101-6. Octaviano Valdés, "Introducción" *Poesía neoclásica y académica* (México: UNAM, 1946), pp. vii-xiv.

BAUDELIO GARZA

DELGADO, Rafael (1853-1914), novelist and writer of short stories. Born in Córdoba, Veracruz, Rafael Delgado received his first schooling at the Colegio de Nuestra Señora de Guadalupe in Orizaba, and later in the Colegio Nacional de Orizaba, where in 1895 he began as a teacher of geography, history, and literature. The profoundly religious education he received and imparted there is definitely reflected in his work. His quiet life was spent in teaching and writing up until his death in Orizaba on May 20, 1914. Although he produced poetry, drama, criticism, and textbooks, his literary reputation is confined exclusively to his fiction: four novels and a number of short stories. His novels were popular during his lifetime, and their fame increased after his death, even though critic Luis *Leal points out that they sometimes seem like fragments of a longer work. As a novelist, Delgado was considered one of the best of the Mexican end-of-the-century writers, along with Emilio *Rabasa and Jose López *Portillo y Rojas. *La calandria* (The Lark) (1891), his first novel, is reminiscent of Fernán Caballero's *La gaviota* (The Seagull), and tells the story of a poor girl, Calandria, who comes to a tragic end because she chooses to love a no-good man with money over a man of her own class. Critic E. Gómez Bringas sees the depiction of local color and the costumbrist description as the strongest points, while others mention characterization, landscape, and the sense of nationalism. Delgado's other novels, *Angelina* (1895), *Los parientes ricos* (Rich Relatives) (1903), and *Historia vulgar* (Common Story) (1904), are all characterized by a costumbrist romanticism that does address certain social problems, but in a way that is sometimes ingenuous. Some of his stories are simply costumbrist sketches, but others, like *El desertor, La mentira, Mi vecina, Justicia popular, Rigel,* and *El asesinato de Palma Sola,* stand on their own as fully developed stories with rounded characters. Delgado also authored a short novel, *La apostasía del padre Arteaga* (The Apostasy of Father Arteaga) (1902) and several plays. At its best, his fiction pre-figures the strong storytelling that would later emerge from the Mexican Revolution.

WORKS: *La calandria* (The Lark) (México: Revista Nacional de Letras y Ciencias, vol. 3, 1890). *Angelina* (Orizaba: Pablo French, 1891). *Los parientes ricos* (Rich Relatives) (México: Agüeros, 1903). *Historia vulgar* (Common Story) (México: Editora Católica, 1904). *Cuentos y notas* (Stories and Notes) (México: Agüeros, 1902). *La apostasía del padre Arteaga* (The Apostasy of Father Arteaga) (México: Agüeros, 1902). *Sonetos* (Sonnets) (México: Nueva Voz, 1940). *Obras completas* (Complete Works) (Veracruz: Biblioteca de Autores Veracruzanos, 1953), includes his plays, *La caja de dulces* (The Box of Sweets, premiered in 1878) and *Una taza de té* (A Cup of Tea, 1878), along with *El caso de conciencia* (A Case of Conscience, 1880), a theatrical adaptation of a work by Octave Feuillet. In addition, Delgado authored pedagogical materials, textbooks, speeches and editorials.

BIBLIOGRAPHY: Paul F. Allemand, "Rafael Delgado, Costumbrista mexicano," *Anales del Museo Nacional de Arqueología, Historia y Etnología* 7, 1 (México, 1931): 147-236. Julián Amo, "La vida y la obra de don Rafael Delgado a la luz de documentos ineditos," *Excelsior* (Aug. 22, 1953): 6, 17. Salvador Calvillo Madrigal, "Rafael Delgado," *El Nacional* (May 20, 1953). Antonio Castro Leal, Prologue to *Angelina* (Orizaba: Pablo French, 1891). Heriberto García Rivas, *Historia de la literatura mexicana*, vol. 2 (México: Porrúa, 1972), pp. 93-180. Carlos González Peña, *History of Mexican Literature* (Dallas, Texas: Methodist Universitv Press, 1968), pp. 318-20, 464. Sergio Howland Bustamante, *Historia de la literatura mexicana* (México: F. Trillas, 1967), p. 208. Aurora M. Ocampo de Gómez and Ernesto Prado Velázquez, *Diccionario de escritores mexicanos* (México: UNAM, 1967), pp. 96-97. Agustín del Saz, *Antología general de la poesía mexicana* (Barcelona: Bruguera, 1972), pp. 125-32.

PATRICIA HART AND JOSEF HELLEBRANDT

DIAZ BARTLETT, Tomás (1919-1957), physician and poet. Born in Tenosique on February 5, 1919, Díaz Bartlett received his elementary education in his native state of Tabasco. His subsequent educational experiences took place in a variety of Mexican cities. Having specialized in surgery, he obtained his medical degree in Mexico in 1945. He practiced medicine for only two years because he became ill and was bedridden until his death in Mexico City in 1957. It may be said that his poetry was born from the invalid's need to share his suffering and to alleviate his solitude.

WORKS: *Bajamar* (Low Tide), prologue by Carlos Pellicer (México: Ed. Cultura Tall. Graf., 1951). *Con displicencia de árbol* (With the Indifference of a Tree) (México: Libr. Madero, 1955). *Oficio de Cadaver* (Office of Cadaver) (México: Ed. *Revista de Bellas Artes*, 1958). *Poesías completas de Tomás Díaz Bartlett* (Complete Poetry of Tomás Díaz Bartlett) (Tabasco: Consejo Editorial del Gobierno del Estado de Tabasco, 1979).

BIBLIOGRAPHY: María Elvira Bermúdez, "Dos obras póstumas" (one of these deals with *Oficio de cadáver*), in *Diorama de la Cultura* (April 12, 1959): 2. Alí Chumacero, "El dolor creó una de las poesías de mayor hondura humana en las letras mexicanas," *México en la Cultura* 523 (March 22, 1959): 4. Horacio Espinosa Altamirano, "Evocación de Tomás Díaz Bartlett," *Boletín Bibliográfico de la Secretaría de Hacienda y Crédito Público* 271 (May 15, 1963): 18-19. Aurora M. Ocampo de Gómez and Ernesto Prado Velázquez, *Diccionario de escritores mexicanos* (México: UNAM, 1967), pp. 96-97. Eunice Odio, "Tomás Díaz Bartlett, Imagen de la fuga," *México en la Cultura* 290 (Oct. 1, 1954)): 3. Carlos Pellicer, "Un nuevo poeta: Díaz Bartlett," *México en la Cultura* 57 (March 5, 1950): 3; Prologue to *Bajamar* (México: Ed. Cultura Tall. Graf., 1951); "En memoria del poeta mártir: Tomás Diaz Bartlett," *México en la Cultura* 416 (March 10, 1957): 3. Miguel Rubio Candelas, "Pasión y muerte de un poeta," *Nivel* 105 (1971): 1-2, 4-5, 7-8. Fernando Sánchez Mayans, Review of *Con displicencia de arbol*, in *Metáfora* 4 (Sept.-Oct. 1955): 39-40.

JANIS L. KRUGH

DIAZ COVARRUBIAS, Juan (1837-1859). Díaz Covarrubias was born in Jalapa, Veracruz, on December 27, 1837. His father was the poet José de Jesús Díaz, a soldier dedicated to the insurgents' cause and a well-known politician. On the death of José Díaz, the mother removed her family to the capital in search of greater economic stability for her three sons. There, young Juan became one of a group of romantic writers together with Manuel Mateos and Ignacio M. *Altamirano. Together they read their first works and became familiar with the works of Lord George Byron, Victor Hugo, and Alexandre Dumás as well as with other Mexican writers.

Díaz Covarrubias studied medicine and became an intern in the Hospital of San Andrés in 1857. Díaz Covarrubias, Manuel Mateos, and others volunteered their services to the liberal forces under the command of Degollado in Tacubaya. Márquez' conservative forces won the battle, after which Márquez ordered that all prisoners, including civilians and medical personnel, be executed by a firing squad. Díaz Covarrubias thus became one of the "Martyrs of Tacubaya," whose unjust death spurred the liberal forces to greater efforts and final victory in 1867.

Díaz Covarrubias' early writings in periodicals and poetry show his liberal, romantic inclinations. His *Páginas del corazón* (Pages from the Heart), dedicated to José

Zorrilla, give evidence of the writer's gifts which were never fully developed. At the same time, his novel *Gil Gómez el insurgente* (Gil Gómez the Insurgent) is one of the first historic novels of Mexico, certainly first to defend independence. Díaz Covarrubias condemns the pseudoaristocracy in *La clase media* (The Middle Class) and in *El Diablo en México* (The Devil in Mexico). Although his career was tragically foreshortened, his work presents the romantic and historic currents of his day and presaged the directions that future writing would take.

WORKS: *Impresiones y sentimientos* (Impressions and Sentiments) (México: Imp. de Vicente García Torres, 1857). *Páginas del corazón* (Pages from the Heart) (México: Imp. de Vicente García Torres, 1857). *Gil Gómez el insurgente o la hija del médico* (Gil Gómez the Insurgent or The Doctor's Daughter) (México: Imp. de Vicente Segura, 1858; México: Imp. de V. Agüeros, 1902; México: Premiá Editora, 1982). *La clase media* (The Middle Class) (México: Tip. de M. Castro, 1858). *El Diablo en México* (The Devil in Mexico) (México: Imp. de M. Castro, 1858). *Impresiones y sentimientos* (México: Libro-Mex, 1955). *Poesías escogidas de Juan Díaz Covarrubias* (Selected Poems of Juan Díaz Covarrubias) (México: Tip. de Abadiano, 1888). Two editions of his complete works have been done, one shortly after his death and one more recently: *Obras completas de Juan Díaz Covarrubias* (Complete Works of Juan Díaz Covarrubias), 2 vols. (México: Tip. de M. Castro, 1859-1860); and Nueva Biblioteca Mexicana, Instituto de Investigaciones Estéticas (México: UNAM, 1959).

BIBLIOGRAPHY: Ignacio M. Altamirano, "Los Mártires de Tacubaya," in *Paisajes y leyendas* (México: Edicion de R. F. Warner, 1949), pp. 79-87. J. S. Brushwood, *The Romantic Novel* (Columbia, Missouri: n.p., 1949), pp. 23-25, 64-65. Heriberto García Rivas, *Historia de la literatura mexicana* (México: Textos Universitarios, 1972), vol. 2, pp. 131, 160-61. Carlos González Peña, *History of Mexican Literature*, translated by Gusta Barfield Nance and Florene Johnson Dunstan (Dallas, Texas: Southern Methodist University Press, 1968), pp. 236-38. Julio Jiménez Rueda, *Letras mexicanas en el siglo XIX* (México: FCE, 1944), p. 106. Aurora M. Ocampo de Gómez and Ernesto Prado Velázquez, *Diccionario de escritores mexicanos* (México: UNAM, 1967), pp. 97-98. J. Lloyd Read, *The Mexican Historical Novel 1826-1910* (San Marcos, Texas: n.p., 1939), pp. 131-33. Jefferson Rea Spell, "Juan Díaz Covarrubias: a Mexican Romantic," in *Hispania* 15, (Oct. 1932): 327-44.

FILIPPA B. YIN

DIAZ DEL CASTILLO, Bernal (1492?-1584?). One of the most influential chroniclers of the period of discovery and conquest of the New World, Bernal Díaz del Castillo was born in Medina del Campo, Spain, in the 1490s, although the exact date is not known. A man of little formal education, he traveled to the West Indies with Pedro Arias de Avila around 1514, settling in Cuba. He took part in several expeditions to Mexico, including the one with Hernán Cortés in which he served as a soldier. As a reward for his work, he was given territory in New Spain, but chose instead to relocate in Guatemala where he worked in important posts until his death.

Known as the premier chronicler of the conquest, Bernal Díaz del Castillo wrote the highly impassioned *Historia verdadera de la Conquista de la Nueva España* (True

Story of the Conquest of New Spain), considered by some to be the best of its kind and by others to be a distortion of reality. The narrative is detailed and precise, direct and clear. In it, he humanizes Cortés and also points out the important role of the soldiers in the conquest. A member of the masses himself, Díaz del Castillo wrote without any particularly literary style. Instead, he put down on paper what he recalled, embellishing it in such a way that often his readers are simply drawn into the sixteenth century of which he writes. There have been many editions of his *Verdadera historia*, a work that is still being discussed and assessed today.

WORKS: *Historia verdadera de la Conquista de la Nueva España* (True History of the Conquest of New Spain) (Madrid: Imp. del Reyno, 1632). More recent editions include (México: Edit. Porrúa, 1955, 1960, and 1962).

BIBLIOGRAPHY: Enrique Anderson-Imbert, *Spanish American Literature*, vol. 1 (Detroit, Mich.: Wayne State University Press, 1969), pp. 42-44. Anita Arroyo, "Bernal Díaz del Castillo, el veraz," in her *América en su literatura*, 2nd ed. (Puerto Rico: Editorial Universitaria, Universidad de Puerto Rico, 1978), pp. 60-66. Luis González Obregón, *Cronistas e historiadores* (México: Botas, 1936). Ramón Iglesias, various essays in *El hombre Colón y otros ensayos*, ed. (México: El Colegio de México, 1944). José de J. Núñez y Domínguez, *Documentos inéditos acerca de Bernal Díaz del Castillo* (México: Talls. Gráf. del Museo Nacional, 1933). Auror M. Ocampo de Gómez and Ernesto Prado Velázquez, *Diccionario de escritores mexicanos* (México: UNAM, 1967), p. 98.

ELADIO CORTES

DIAZ DUFOO, Carlos (1861-1941). Born in Veracruz on December 4, 1861, Carlos Díaz Dufoo lived largely in Europe as a child. He returned to Mexico in 1884 when he was twenty-three years old, having studied and published, mostly in Spain. Thus, his character formation was basically European, but he never lost his sense of Mexican identity and nationality.

An avid writer, Díaz Dufoo began publishing in various literary journals. In 1887 he became the director of *El Ferrocarril Veracruzano*, and later he served in a similar capacity for *La Bandera Veracruzana*. While in his home state of Veracruz, he was a participant in a duel, which, despite his being victorious, caused him extreme anguish. Finding himself in constant turmoil, he chose to return to the capital, a move which enabled him to join the editorial staff of *El Siglo XIX* and *El Universal*, both distinguished journals of that time. In a comfortable liaison with Manuel *Gutiérrez-Nájera, he founded *Revista Azul* in 1894. Upon Gutiérrez Nájera's death, he became the sole director. With Reyes Spíndola he founded *El Imparcial* in 1896, and he stayed on the staff until 1912. He was also the director of *El Mundo*. He contributed to *El Cómico* with delightful articles signed with the pseudonym Moneguillo. A member of the Mexican delegation to the Exposition of Paris in 1900, he had the opportunity to visit several European capitals and to attend various international congresses. In collaboration with Manuel Zapata, he directed *El Economista Mexicano* until 1911. After Reyes Spindola's paper disappeared, Díaz Dufo had a five-year lapse in journalistic activities. But he took them up again in

1917, with the appearance of *Excelsior*, contributing also to *Revista de Revistas*. In addition to the pseudonym already mentioned, he also used Argos, Pistache, Petit Bleu, Cualquiera, El Implacable, and Gran Eleazar.

His interest in the theater was established as early as 1885 when he wrote *Entre vecinos* (Between Neighbors) and *De gracia* (About Grace), comic one-act plays in verse. The first of these was performed in the Teatro Nacional on May 20, 1885. In 1929, his play *Padre mercader* (Merchant Father) was performed seventy-three times in the old Teatro Ideal. As a story-writer, he had published his *Cuentos nerviosos* (Nervous Stories) in 1901.

A professor of law, business, and commerce, Díaz Dufoo was considered the premier economist of his time. He participated in commissions for creating the government's budget, and he was also a member of advisory boards in various companies.

WORKS: Theater: *Entre vecinos* (Between Neighbors) (México: Tip. de Gonzalo A. Esteva, 1885). *De gracia* (About Grace), performed in Teatro Nacional, May 20, 1885 (México: Tip. de Gonzalo A Esteva, 1885). *Padre mercader* (Merchant Father), performed in Teatro Ideal, Aug. 24, 1929 (México: Imp. de M. León Sánchez, n.d.). *La fuente del Quijote* (The Fountain of the Quijote), performed May 31, 1930, in Teatro Ideal, *La jefa* (The Boss), neither performed nor published. *Sombras de mariposas* (Shadows of Butterflies) (México: Polis, 1937). Prose: *Cuentos nerviosos* (Nervous Stories) (México: J. Ballescá y Cía, Sucs., 1901). Prologue to Manuel Gutiérrez Nájera's *Hojas sueltas* (México: Murguía, 1912). *Ignacio Torres Adalid* (México: n.p., 1912). "De Manuel Gutiérrez Nájera a Luis G. Urbina," in *Memorias de la Academia Mexicana* 11 (1955): 203-14. Economic Papers: *México, 1876-1892*, statistical study. *México, su evolución industrial* (Mexico, Its Industrial Evolution), chapters in *México, su evolución social*, vol. 2. *Limantour* (México: Eusebio Gómez de la Puente, 1910); 2nd ed., enlarged (México: Imp. Victoria, 1922). *Les finances du Mexique* (The Finances of Mexico), translation by M. A. Dupont (Paris: Félix Alcan, n.d.). *México y los capitales extranjeros* (Mexico and Foreign Capitals) (México: Imp. Francesa, 1918). *Lecturas de Economía Política* (Readings in Political Economics), 2nd ed. (México: J. Ballescá y Cía, Sucs., n.d.). *Una victoria financiera* (A Financial Victory) (México: Vda. de Ch. Bouret, 1920). *La cuestion del petróleo* (The Question of Petroleum) (México: Eusebio Gómez de la Puente, 1921). *Robinson mexicano* (Mexican Robinson) (México: Ballescá y Cía, Sucs., n.d.). "El Instituto de Estudios y Reformas Sociales" (The Institute of Studies and Social Reforms), in *Conferencias preliminares*, vol. 1 (México: Imp. Victoria, 1922). *Comunismo contra capitalismo* (Communism versus Capitalism), 2nd ed. (México: Botas, 1941).

BIBLIOGRAPHY: Alberto María Carreño, in *Memorias de la Academia Mexicana*, vol. 8 (México: Edit. Jus, 1946), pp. 101-2. Federico Gamboa, "Viaje del Parnaso," in *Memorias de la Academia Mexicana*, vol. 11 (1955): 215-19. Carlos González Peña, "Un maestro: Díaz Dufoo," in *Gente mía* (México: Edit. Stylo, 1946), pp. 119-25. Francisco R. Illescas and Juan Bartolo Hernández, *Escritores veracruzanos* (Veracruz: n.p., 1945), pp. 220-25. Antonio Magaña Esquivel, *Medio siglo de teatro mexicano, 1900-1961* (México: Dept. de Lit., INBA, 1964), pp. 43-44. Amado Nervo, "Carlos Díaz Dufoo," in *Obras completas*, vol. 2 (Madrid: Aguilar, 1962), pp. 27-29. José de Núñez y Domínguez, "*Limantour*, el libro de D. Carlos Díaz Dufoo," in *Revista Moderna* (Nov. 1910): 157-58. Roberto Núñez y Domínguez, *50 close-ups* (México:

Botas, 1935), pp. 5-8. "Cómo se fundó la *Revista Azul*," in *Revista de Revistas* 26, 1371 (Aug. 30, 1936). Aurora M. Ocampo de Gómez and Ernesto Prado Velázquez, *Diccionario de escritores mexicanos* (México: UNAM, 1967), pp. 98-99. Victoriano Salado Alvarez, "Don Carlos Díaz Dufoo," in *De mi cosecha* (Guadalajara: Imp. de Ancira y Hno., 1899), pp. 87-92; "Máscaras," in *Revista Moderna* 6, 13 (July 1903): 193-94.

JEANNE C. WALLACE

DIAZ MIRON, Salvador (1853-1928), poet, journalist, teacher, and politician. Salvador Díaz Mirón distinguished himself in particular as a poet and orator. The son of Manuel Díaz Mirón, a journalist and public functionary, he was born in Veracruz on December 14, 1853. He became a man of fiery temperament, the object of intense dread and admiration. The violence of his articles forced him to flee to the United States in 1876. After his return two years later, he became a congressman. His belligerent attitude through the years forced him into a number of duels, one of which cost him the use of his right arm. Other duels led to his imprisonment and to the killing of two of his adversaries. Nonetheless, he was generally perceived as a just and honorable man and was very popular among the people. His opposition to Porfirio Díaz forced him to leave Mexico a second time. He first traveled to Spain, and later established himself in Cuba, where he worked as a teacher. After his return to Mexico, he became director of the Veracruz Preparatory School, where he also taught classes in history. Because of a disagreement with his students, he resigned in 1927 and died a year later, on June 12, 1928.

  Despite his active public life, the center of Díaz Mirón's career was his intense preoccupation with the language of poetry. In comparing his life and his works, it may be said that both his personality and his poetry exhibit the same violent contrasts. In his early works he was a Romantic, with the passion and loftiness characteristic of that movement. But he soon began a conscious renovation of the language that made his works revolutionary enough to influence some of the major early Modernists, poets such as Rubén Darío and José Santos Chocano. His courageous, self-assured quest for perfection and for absolute purity of expression resulted in the writing of *Lascas* (Chips of Stone), the only book he would recognize as his own--he disclaimed all his previous works as fraudulent and imperfect. *Lascas*, and the unpublished and more elaborate book that followed it, *Astillas y triunfos* (Splinters and Triumphs), are written in his definitive style. It is a style based in part on the complex baroque tradition of Góngora and Quevedo. In this second poetic phase his poems lost the emotion, spontaneity, and musicality that had made him a popular poet in the early part of his career, but his verses gained in formal control, brilliant plastic imagery, and rhythmic subtleties. In other words, Díaz Mirón's poetic trajectory changed from that of a popular poet to that of a poet's poet.

WORKS: Poetry: *Antología poética* (Poetic Anthology), edited by Antonio Castro Leal (México: UNAM, 1953). *Lascas* (Chips of Stone) (Xalapa: Litografía del Gobierno del Estado, 1901). *Poesías* (Poems) (New York: Casa Hispano-Americana, 1895). *Poesías* (Paris: n.p., 1900). *Poesías completas* (Complete Poems), biography, notes, and bibliography by Antonio Castro Leal (México: Porrúa, 1945). Prose: *Prosas*

(Prose), prologue and commentary by Leonardo Pasquel (México: Biblioteca de Autores Veracruzanos, 1954).

BIBLIOGRAPHY: José Almoina, *Díaz Mirón. Su poética* (México: n.p., 1958). Ricardo Fernández Mira, *Salvador Díaz Mirón el turbulento* (Buenos Aires: Talls. Gráficos Contreras, 1936). Roberto Meza Fuentes, *De Díaz Mirón a Rubén Darío* (Santiago de Chile: Nascimiento, 1940). Francisco Monterde, *Salvador Díaz Mirón, Documentos, Estética* (México: UNAM, 1956).

MARIA A. SALGADO

DIAZ Y DE OVANDO, Clementina (1920-   ), critic, specializing in nineteenth-century Mexican literature. Born in Mexico City on November 7, 1920, Clementina Díaz y de Ovando graduated from the Universidad Nacional Autónoma de México with bachelor's and doctoral degrees in literature. She has been a professor at the National Preparatory School and at the Mexican Writers Center. She has also carried out research under the auspices of the Aesthetic Research Institute of the National University of Mexico. She has collaborated in several of Mexico City's journals, newspapers, and supplements. Her literary essays have frequently appeared in the Anales del Instituto de Investigaciones Estéticas, in the journal *Universidad de México*, and in *El Nacional*. Her publications most often deal with the works of Juan *Díaz Covarrubias and Vicente *Riva Palacio. Other authors about whom she has written include Ignacio *Altamirano, Manuel *Gutiérrez Nájera, Manuel Romero de Terreros, Sor Juana Inés de la *Cruz and Father Luis Felipe Neri de Alfaro.

WORKS: *La poesía del Padre Luis Felipe Neri de Alfaro* (The Poetry of Father Luis Felipe Neri de Alfaro) (México: UNAM, 1947). *El Colegio Máximo de San Pedro y San Pablo* (México: UNAM, 1951, 1985). *Dos novelistas veracruzanos* (Two Novelists from Veracruz) (México: UNAM, 1952). *Juan Díaz Covarrubias. Obras completas* (Juan Díaz Covarrubias. Complete Works), 2 vols., preliminary study, edition, and notes by Clementina Díaz y de Ovando (México: UNAM, 1959). "La incógnita de algunos ceros de Riva palacio" (The Unknown Quantity in Some of Riva Palacio's Zeroes), thesis, UNAM, México, 1965. Vicente Riva Palacio, *Los ceros* (Zeroes), preliminary study, edition, and notes by Clementina Díaz y de Ovando (México: UNAM, 1967). *La escuela nacional preparatoria* (The National Preparatory School) (México: UNAM, 1972). *Antología de Vicente Riva Palacio* (An Anthology of Vicente Riva Palacio) (México: UNAM, 1976). *El cerro de las campanas: memorias de un guerrillero* (The Hill of Bells: Memoirs of a Guerrilla Fighter) (México: Ed. Porrúa, 1976). *Carlos VII: el primer Borbón en México* (Charles VII: The First Bourbon in Mexico) (México: UNAM, 1978). *La Ciudad Universitaria de México* (The University City of Mexico) (México: UNAM, 1980). *Cuentos del general* (The General's Stories) (México: Porrúa, 1986).

BIBLIOGRAPHY: "Bibliografía de Clementina Díaz y de Ovando," *Anales del Instituto de Investigaciones Estéticas* 2, *Bibliografías de los investigadores* (México, 1961), pp. 157-63. Andrés Henestrosa, "Alacena de Minucias," review of her essay on Riva Palacio published in *Anales del Instituto de Investigaciones Estéticas* 32, in *Revista*

Mexicana de la Cultura 837 (April 14, 1963): 4; "La nota cultural," review of her doctoral thesis, in *El Nacional* (Sept. 29, 1965): p. 3. Aurora M. Ocampo de Gómez and Ernesto Prado Velázquez, *Diccionario de escritores mexicanos* (México: UNAM, 1967), p. 101.

JANIS L. KRUGH

DIEZ-CANEDO, Enrique (1879-1944), poet, literary critic, and diplomat. Díez-Canedo was born in Badajoz, Spain, on January 7, 1879, and died in Cuernavaca, Mexico, on June 6, 1944. He was educated in Madrid and Barcelona. In his early years, he was a clear product of the Generation of 1898 as evidenced by his critical point of view; yet his intelligence and understanding of new tendencies that made him a teacher and guide for writers of the next generation.

In 1902 he began to attend conferences at the Ateneo de Madrid and to work as a journalist while he taught at the School of Languages. In 1909 he traveled to France and lived in Paris until 1911. Back in Madrid, he became an instructor at the School of Arts and Crafts and director of programs at the Center of Historical Studies. As a journalist, he wrote for *El Liberal*; as literary critic for *Diario Universal*; as reviewer of plays for *El Globo*, *La Pluma*, and *El Sol*; and as commentator for *La Voz*. He also began what would be a long association with literary journals: *España*, *Indice*, *Tierra Firme*, and *Madrid*.

In 1927, as an employee of the Spanish government under the Second Republic, he traveled and lectured throughout Latin America. In 1931 he was invited by the University of Columbia's Summer School and thus began his second trip through American countries. Then, in 1932 he was named minister of the Spanish Legation in Uruguay. In 1935 he was inducted into the Royal Academy of the Spanish Language and then traveled to the Philippines to lecture at the University of Manila. In 1936, the president of the Spanish Republic, Manuel Azaña, named him ambassador to Argentina.

As a result of the Spanish Civil War and of the subsequent fall of the Republican government, Díez-Canedo went into exile in 1938 and settled in Mexico until his death. In Mexico he collaborated with the literary journals *Revista Moderna*, *Revista Iberoamericana*, *Letras de América*, *El Hijo Prodigo*, *Letras de México*, and *Taller*, and with the newspaper *Excelsior*. Also, he was a professor at El Colegio de México and at UNAM's School of Philosophy and Letters while he lectured at other institutions. The essays on literary criticism written by Díez-Canedo represent the most intelligent and sharp of his period; they focus on foreign writers, Spanish writers, especially his contemporaries, and, above all, Spanish- American writers. He was also a distinguished translator and a poet for minorities; his poetry has delicate shades and subtle concepts and shows a fine imagination. It was reviewed very favorably around 1920 by Miguel de Unamuno and Juan Ramón Jiménez. His first books of poetry, *Versos de las horas* (Poetry in Time) (Madrid, 1906) and *La visita del sol* (The Visit of the Sun) (Madrid, 1907), reflect the Modernist style and the spirit of the Generation of 1898. There is much of Rubén Darío in the "Recreaciones Arqueológicas." Later, in *La sombra del ensueño* (Dream Memories) (1910), one notices the intimist tone of Juan Ramón Jiménez; in *Algunos versos* (Some Verses) (1924), the influence of Valle-Inclán; and finally, with *Epigramas americanos* (American Epigrams) (Madrid, 1928), Díez-Canedo finds his personal voice. He is now in direct contact with objects; his poems are graphic expressions of first impressions, of images that suggest, of quick intuitions as perceived by an authentic poet. *El Desterrado* (In Exile), written ten years later, follows the same line though its dark and harsh tone also reflects the poets's anguish.

Extraordinarily well-versed and with an exquisite taste, Díez-Canedo was an authority on all literary subjects. An intellectual above all, disciplined and well-balanced, he helped, advised, and encouraged many other writers. Because of his association with the Spanish Republicans, Díez-Canedo was largely unknown in Spain during the last decades. On the centenary of his birth, Ediciones Almar of Salamanca published an anthology of his poetry in an attempt to save a writer who has been unjustly forgotten by his countrymen, since his works are not easily found in Spain. (José María Fernández Gutiérrez wrote the foreword and made the selection for the Almar anthology.)

WORKS: Poetry: *Antología poética* (Poetic Anthology), ed. José María Fernández Gutiérrez (Salamanca: Eds. Almar, 1980); includes bibliographical references. *Conversaciones literarias* (Literary Conversations), 1st series: 1915-1920; 2nd series: 1920-1924 (México: Mortiz, 1964); 3rd series: 1924-1930 (México: Mortiz, 1965). *Estudios de poesía española contemporánea* (Contemporary Spanish Poetry Essays) (México: Mortiz, 1965). *Artículos de crítica teatral: el teatro español de 1914 a 1936* (México: Mortiz, 1968). Anthologies: *Las cien mejores poesías españolas* (The Best One Hundred Spanish Poems) (México: Nuestro Pueblo, 1940). *La poesía francesa del romanticismo al superrealismo* (French Poetry from Romanticism to Surrealism) (Buenos Aires: Ed. Losada, 1945). Essays: *Sala de retratos* (Hall of Portraits) (San José, Costa Rica: n.p., 1920). *Los dioses en el Prado* (The [Mythological] Gods in the Prado Museum) (Madrid: Compañía Ibero-americana de Publicaciones, 1931). *Juan Ramón Jiménez en su obra* (Juan Ramón Jímenez in His Works) (México: El Colegio de México, 1944). *Letras de América: estudios sobre las literaturas continentales*, 2nd ed. (México: FCE, 1983). Forewords: León Felipe, *Verso y oraciones de caminante* (Verse and Prayers of a Traveler) (Madrid: Imp. Juan Pérez Torres, 1920). Enrique González Martínez, *El romero alucinado* (The Hallucinated Pilgrim) (Madrid: Ed. Saturnino Calleja, S.A., 1925). Translations: Benedetto Croce, *La historia como hazaña de la libertad* (History as a Feat of Freedom), translated from the English (México: FCE, 1960). Verlaine, *Cordura* (Sagesse), 1923. John Webster, *La duquesa de Malfi: tragedia* (Duchess of Malfi), translated from the English (Madrid: Calpe, 1920). Jean de La Fontaine, *Las fábulas de La Fontaine*, selected and translated in verse by Díez-Canedo; illustrated by T. C. Derrick (Madrid: Calleja, 1918).

BIBLIOGRAPHY: Antonio Acevedo Escobedo, *Díez-Canedo crítico* (México: "El Nacional," Apr. 4, 1965). Dámaso Alonso, *Poetas españoles contemporáneos* (Madrid: Gredos, 1968). Max Aub, *Enrique Díez-Canedo* (México: Boletín de la Corporación de antiguos alumnos de la Institución Libre de Enseñanza de Madrid, Grupo de Mexico, Circular no. 73); It reproduces the speech given by Max Aub on June 5, 1964, at the Ateneo de México on the twentieth anniversary of Díez-Canedo's death; it also includes the speech given by Juan de Dios Bojórquez, "Un hispano mexicano: Enrique Díez-Canedo." Rufino Blanco Fombona, "Un poeta preterido: Enrique Díez-Canedo," *Motivos y Letras de España* (Madrid, 1930). Arturo Cova, "Don Enrique y su lección de crítica," *El Nacional* (México, Aug. 30, 1964). Ricardo Domenech, "Los trasterrados," *Cuadernos para el Diálogo* (Madrid, June 1966). José Mancisidor, "Don Enrique Díez-Canedo," *El Nacional* (México, June 12, 1944). José Monleón, "Reencuentro con Enrique Díez-Canedo," *El Triunfo* 598 (Madrid, Mar. 1974). Demetrio Aguilera-Malta, "La rosa de los vientos," review of *Conversaciones literarias*, in *El Gallo Ilustrado* 117 (Sept. 20, 1964): 4. Margarita García F., "Correo de lecturas," review of *Conversaciones literarias*, in *El Día* (May 21, 1965): 9. Francisco Giner de los Ríos, "Poesía española en México. 1939-1949," in *Literatura mexicana siglo XX*, 2nd part (México: Ant. Libr. Robredo, 1950). Pedro Henríquez Ureña, "Los valores hispanos: Sanín Cano y Enrique Díez-Canedo," *Sur* 23 (n.d.). José Luis Martínez, *Literatura mexicana siglo XX [1910-1949]* (México: Ant. Libr. Robredo, 1950). Javier Peñalosa, "Nombres, títulos y hechos," homage to Díez-Canedo on the twentieth anniversary of his death (June 5, 1964), evening at El Ateneo Español, *México en la Cultura* 795 (June 14, 1964): 3 (cf. entry for Max Aub and Juan de Dios Bojórquez). Xavier Villaurrutia, Review of *Juan Ramón Jiménez en su obra*, in *El Hijo Pródigo*, year II, 5 (Sept. 15, 1944): 185.

HERLINDA HERNANDEZ

DOLUJANOFF, Emma (1922-), short story writer and novelist. Emma Dolujanoff was born in Mexico City. She studied medicine at the National University and received an M.D. degree in 1945. She was awarded a scholarship at the Centro Mexicano de Escritores in 1957 and in 1958. A psychiatrist by training, Dolujanoff explores the mental problems of her fictional characters.

WORKS: Short Stories: *Cuentos del desierto* (Stories of the Desert) (México: Botas, 1959). *El gallo de oro* (The Golden Cock), in *Anuario del cuento mexicano* (México: INBA, 1960). *El venado niño* (The Child Deer), in *Anuario del cuento mexicano* (México: INBA, 1962), pp. 92-93. Novels: *Adiós, Job* (Good-Bye, Job) (México: FCE, 1961). *La calle del fuego* (The Street of Fire) (México: UNAM, 1966).

BIBLIOGRAPHY: Emmanuel Carballo, Review of *Cuentos del desierto*, in *México en la Cultura*, (May 11, 1959): 2. Frances R. Dorward, "The Short Story as a Vehicle for Mexican Literary Indigenismo," *Letras Femeninas* 13, 1-2 (1987): 53-66. Javier Peñalosa, "Entrevista" (Interview), *México en la Cultura* 781 (1964): 3.

ALFONSO GONZALEZ

DOMENCHINA, Juan José (1898-1959), novelist, literary critic, essayist, and poet. Domenchina was born in Madrid on May 18, 1888. He studied in Madrid and began his career as a writer, working intensively in numerous publications such as *Los Lunes*, *La Pluma*, *El Sol*, *El Inparcial*, and *Revista de Occidente*. He was actively involved as secretary to Manuel Azaña, and during the Civil War, he was secretary of the National Institute of the Book. At the beginning of the Spanish Civil War he married Ernestina de *Champourcín, and in 1939 he moved to Mexico, where he resided until his death on October 27, 1959.

He was noted as poet of a *baroque style, and in his works reason dominates over the emotions. The anguish and the nostalgia that he had for his homeland is the predominant characteristic of the poetry produced during his Mexican exile. He is well known for his journalistic works published in Madrid under the name of Gerardo Rivera, in which he demonstrated his psychological attitude as well his knowledge of the new Spanish poetry.

WORKS: *Del poeta eterno* (Of the Eternal Poet) (Madrid: Mateu, 1922). *Poemas escogidos* (Selected Poems) (Madrid: Mateu, 1922). *El hábito* (The Habit) (Madrid: La Novela Mundial, 1926). *La corporeidad de lo abstracto* (Corporeity of the Abstract) (Madrid: Renacimiento, 1929). *La túnica de Neso* (Neso's Tunic) (Madrid: La novela mundial, 1929). *El tacto fervoroso* (Fervent Touch) (Madrid: Renacimiento, 1930). *Dédalo* (Labyrinth) (Madrid: Bib. Nueva, 1932). *Poesías completas 1915-1934* (Complete Poetry) (Madrid: Signo, 1936). *Poesías escogidas* (Selected Poems) (México: Casa de España, 1940). *Destierro* (Exile) (México: Atlante, 1942). *El diván de Abz-ul-Abrib* (Abz-ul-Abrib's Armchair) (México: Centauro, 1945). *Crónicas de Gerardo Rivera* (Chronicles of Gerardo Rivera) (Madrid: Aguilar, 1936). *Nuevas crónicas de Gerardo Rivera* (New Chronicles of Gerardo Rivera) (Barcelona: Juventud, 1938).

BIBLIOGRAPHY: Max Aub, *La poesía española contemporánea* (México: Imp. Universitaria, 1954). Francisco Giner de los Ríos, "Poesía española en México," in *Literatura mexicana siglo XX* (México: Ant. Libr. Robredo, 1950), p. 180. Federico Carlos Sáinz de Robles, *Historia y antología de la poesía española* (Madrid: Aguilar, 1955), pp. 200, 1712-15. Angel Valbuena Pratt, *Historia de la Literatura Española*, vol. 3 (Barcelona: Gustavo Gili, 1960), pp. 610-13. Ramón Xirau, *Poesía hispanoamericana y española* (México: Imp. Universitaria, 1961), pp. 145-47.

SILKA FREIRE

DUCH Colell, Juan (1920-), poet. Duch Colell is an important poet, although his production is scant. His poetry, of a committed orientation, is a precise reflection of the reality and the moment in which it is written.

Juan Duch Colell was born in Mérida, Yucatán, in 1920. The son of Catalán emigrés, he went to Spain with his family, living in Barcelona from 1921 to 1936. Around the time of the outbreak of the Spanish Civil War, he returned to the land of his birth as a journalist. Between 1953 and 1957, he was an editor for the *Diario del Sureste*, and between 1958 and 1961, he was the general director of fine arts for the state of Yucatán. Afterwards, in Mexico, from 1962 to 1967 inclusive and again from 1972 to 1980, he was a contributor to popular and political magazines and journals. For a four-year period (1967-1971), he was a correspondent in Moscow for the weekly papers *La Voz de México* and *Siempre!*.

His experience in Moscow and his Catalán background were instrumental in the formation of his very cautious leftist philosophical and political tendencies. This wary affiliation is also his answer to the socioeconomic conditions of his native region. Nonetheless, he never neglects the cultural values of that region. He has recently been employed as the technical director of the editorial collections of Tierra Nuestra and Yucatán en las Letras. Under his directorship, the first publication of the beautifully presented and titled *Textos y estampas del Mayab* (Texts and Portraits of the Mayab) appeared.

In 1980 the state government of Yucatán ordered the printing as a collection of several previously edited *plaquettes*, under the simple title *Juan Duch. Poemas.* With a number of prologues by different authors, the volume includes thirty-two poems written between 1944 and 1978, with themes as varied as love, the Mayan inheritance, and political and social protest. More than mere influences, there are recollections of León Felipe and Pablo Neruda.

Without a doubt, Juan Duch is a committed poet. But more than he is committed to politics, he is committed to both art and life. Some of the most noteworthy titles in his lyrical works are "Primera salida y retorno al silencio" (First Exit and Return to Silence), "Canto a Gustavo Río" (Song to Gustavo Río), "Por el mar" (By the Sea), and many others in the collection *Abuelo/Taller* (Grandfather/Shop), written in 1978, published two years later.

WORKS: *Abuelo/Taller* (Grandfather/Shop) (Mérida: Eds. del Gobierno de Yucatán, 1980).

BIBLIOGRAPHY: Santiago Burgos Brito, "La poesía de Juan Duch," speech given in Ochil, Yucatán, Sept. 3, 1950. *Enciclopedia Yucatanense*, vol. 5 (México: n.p., 1946). José Esquivel Pren, *Historia de la literatura en Yucatán*, vol. 18 (México: Eds. de la Universidad de Yucatán, 1981).

                                                                              MICHELE MUNCY

DUEÑAS, Guadalupe (1920-   ). Born in Guadalajara, Jalisco, on October 19, 1920, Guadalupe Dueñas is most recognized for her work as a short story writer. Her first publications were actually poems, but she abandoned that field in order to dedicate herself more fully to the short story. In 1954, she published *Las ratas y otros cuentos* (The Rats and Other Stories), which appeared in *Abside*. Much of her work is in anthologies, magazines, journals and literary supplements to major newspapers. In addition, some of her best, most universal stories have been translated into other languages and published in the United States and many of the European nations. She is also widely published in Latin America. She received a scholarship from the Centro Mexicano de Escritores to work on a novel. The best of her early work was gathered in a collection entitled *Tiene la noche un árbol* (The Night Has a Tree), for which she was awarded the José María Vigil Prize in 1959. Her writing is characterized by minute attention to details, even to repugnant ones. Dueñas' work is considered truly original, mixing elements from various narrative schools.

WORKS: *Las ratas y otros cuentos* (The Rats and Other Stories), *Abside* 17, 3 (July-Sept. 1954): 337-49. *Tiene la noche un árbol* (The Night Has a Tree) (México: FCE, 1958).

BIBLIOGRAPHY: Alberto Bonifaz Nuño, Review of *Tiene la noche un árbol*, in *Universidad de México* 13, 1 (Sept. 1958): 30. Emmanuel Carballo, "Las ratas," in *México en la Cultura* 315 (April 3, 1955): 2; *El cuento mexicano del siglo XX* (México:

Empresas Editoriales, 1965), p. 81. Dolores Castro, Review of *Tiene la noche un árbol*, in *La Palabra y el Hombre* 9 (Jan.-March 1959): 131-43. Aurora M. Ocampo de Gómez and Ernesto Prado Velázquez, *Diccionario de escritores mexicanos* (México: UNAM, 1967), p. 104. Carlos Valdés, Review of *Las ratas y otros cuentos*, in *Universidad de México* 9, 8 (April 1955): 27.

MICHELE MUNCY

DURAN, Manuel (1925-   ). Born in Barcelona, Spain, on March 28, 1925, Manuel Durán moved to Mexico in 1942, becoming a Mexican citizen in 1947. He completed his studies in his new home, getting his law degree from UNAM in 1949. He also studied literature at the same university. Durán has been actively involved with organizations dedicated to improving the welfare of all people, such as UNESCO and the United Nations. He has traveled extensively throughout many nations of the world, both as a private citizen and in conjunction with his work. Recognized as an outstanding and distinguished university professor in the United States, Manuel Durán has taught Spanish and Latin American literature to several generations of students.

A poet, translator, essayist, and critic, Manuel Durán has written extensively. *La paloma azul* (The Blue Dove) (1959), a poetic volume about Mexico City, is considered one of his most important works. Much of his poetry has been influenced by the Surrealist school. He has published in many journals in Mexico, Spain, and the United States. He is a frequent contributor to *Cuadernos Americanos*, *Revista Mexicana de Literatura*, *Revista Hispánica Moderna*, *Insula*, and other journals.

WORKS: Poetry: *Puente* (Bridge) (México: n.p., 1946). *Ciudad asediada* (Besieged City) (México: FCE, 1954). *La paloma azul* (The Blue Dove) (México: FCE, 1959). *El lugar del hombre* (The Place of Man) (México: UNAM, 1965). Essays: *El superrealismo en la poesía española contemporánea* (Superrealism in Contemporary Spanish Poetry) (México: n.p., 1952). *Entre magia y cibernética. Las máquinas vivas* (Between Magic and Cybernetics. Living Machines), in collaboration with Ramón Xirau (México: El Unicornio, 1959). *La ambigüedad en "El Quijote"* (Ambiguity in *The Quijote*) (Xalapa: Universidad Veracruzana, 1960). *Genio y figura de Amado Nervo* (Genious and Figure of Amado Nervo) (Buenos Aires: Edit. Universitaria, 1968). "Jaime Sabines and Marco Antonio Montes de Oca: A Study in Contrasts," in *Mundus Artium* 3, 2 (1970): 44-55. "Dos grandes poetas mexicanos de hoy: Sabines y Montes de Oca" (Two Great Mexican Poets of Today: Sabines and Montes de Oca), in *La Cultura en México* 483 (May 12, 1971): vii-x. "In Memoriam: Jaime Torres Bodet, Salvador Novo, Rosario Castellanos," in *Revista Iberoamericana* 41, 90 (Jan.-March 1975): 79-83. Anthologies: *Antología de la poesía italiana* (Anthology of Italian Poetry) (México: UNAM, 1961). On Lorca, *A Critical Anthology* (Englewood Cliffs, N. J.: Prentice-Hall, 1962). *Antología de la revista "Contemporáneos,"* editor (México: FCE, 1973).

BIBLIOGRAPHY: John Coleman, Review of *Entre magia y cibernética*, in *Revista Hispánica Moderna* 2 (April 1961): 165-66. Frank Dauster, *The Double Strand* (Lexington: University Press of Kentucky, 1987), pp. 30, 144. Aurora M. Ocampo de

Gómez and Ernesto Prado Velázquez, *Diccionario de escritores mexicanoa* (México: UNAM, 1967), pp. 104-5. Marcelino C. Peñuelas, Review of *La ambigüedad en el Quijote*, in *Revista Hispánica Moderna* 2 (April 1963): 171-72. Ramón Xirau, Review of *El lugar del hombre*, in *Diálogos* 6 (Sept.-Oct. 1965): 41.

JEANNE C. WALLACE

DURAN Rosado, Esteban (1905-), short story writer and essayist. Duran Rosado was born in Sucilá, Yucatán, on December 25, 1905. He was a teacher in his early years but has dedicated most of his life to the profession of journalism, most recently as proofreader for literary and cultural supplements of the newspaper *El Nacional*.

Durán Rosado has published his short stories and articles in various periodicals for nearly thirty years, but his works published separately are not numerous: three books of short stories and three studies on other topics. Nevertheless, he is considered a short story writer of significance. "La muerte verdadera" won a prize in a literary contest held by *El Universal*. His collection of stories entitled *Marcela* is his most recent and well-known work.

WORKS: *Lo esotérico en la lengua maya* (Esoteric Elements in the Mayan Language) (México). *Una vida al servicio del pueblo* (A Life Of Dedicated Service) (Mérida). *Cárdenas y el gran ejido henequenero de Yucatán* (Cárdenas and the Great Henequin Cooperative of Yucatán) (México: B. Costa-Amic, 1963). *Cuentos de amor y de muerte* (Stories of Love and Death) (Mérida). *Crónicas retrospectivas* (Retrospective Chronicles) (Mérida). *Marcela, cuentos* (Marcela, Short Stories) (México: Editorial Castalia, 1963).

BIBLIOGRAPHY: María Elvira Bermúdez, "El cuento mexicano en 1963," in - *Diorama de la Cultura* (Jan. 5, 1964): 8. Alva Dors, "Una novela y varios cuentos," in *Mexico en la Cultura* 752 (Aug. 18, 1963): 8. Fedro Guillén, "*Marcela*," in *Horizontes* 6, 34 (Dec. 15, 1963): 35-36. Aurora M. Ocampo de Gómez and Ernesto Prado Velázquez, *Diccionario de escritores mexicanos* (México: UNAM, 1967), p. 105.

KENNETH M. TAGGART

E

ECHEVERRIA DEL PRADO, Vicente (1898-   ), poet. Born in Pénjamo, Guanajuato, on April 5, 1898, Echeverría del Prado studied architecture in Guadalajara, Jalisco and taught mathematics at the National Polytechnic Institute for more than thirty-five years. He had traveled to the United States and in his later years concerned himself solely with his literary work. His literary works enbodied a deep interest in the sonneto, which is the author's dominant form and is exemplified throughout his many publications.

WORKS: *Voces múltiples* (Multiple Voices) (México: Cultura, 1927). *Vida Suspensa* (Suspended Life) (México: Mundial, 1933). *Perfiles inviolados* (Inviolate profiles) (México: Fábula, 1947). *Con el silencio en cruz* (With the Silence in Cross) (México: Juan Pablos, 1950). *La dicha lenta* (The Slow Happiness) (México: Los Presentes, l956).

BIBLIOGRAPHY: Arturo Capdevila, "La poesía de Vicente Echeverría del Prado," *México en la Cultura* 762 (1963): 3. Jesús Flores Aguirre, "La poesía de Vicente Echeverría del Prado," *Nivel* 7 (1963): 1. Luis Terán Gómez, "Vicente Echeverría del Prado, un gran poeta mexicano," *Nivel* 7 (1963): 1.

SILKA FREIRE

EGUIARA y Eguren, Juan José de (1696-1763). A bibliographer and theologian, Eguiara y Eguren was born in Mexico City. He studied art, philosophy and theology at the Royal and Pontifical University, from which he obtained the degree of *Bachiller* in 1712, and of *Licenciado* and doctor in 1715. Between 1713 and 1722 he was a substitute teacher at the same university in rhetoric, theology, and bible studies. In 1723 he earned a permanent chair at the university. At the Metropolitan Cathedral Eguiara y Eguren was treasurer, cantor and canon. He was named bishop of Yucatán in 1751, but did not accept the position because of his complete involvement with his famous *Biblioteca Mexicana* (Mexican Library). He died in 1763. While Eguiara y Eguren wrote mainly sermons and eulogies, he is remembered today for his *Biblioteca Mexicana*. It is a biobibliographical dictionary of all writers who were born, wrote, or flourished in Mexico from 1521 to 1763. It includes all works printed or in manuscript up to the time of Eguiara y Eguren's death. The dictionary was conceived as a rebuttal to the dean of Alicante, don Manuel Martí, who had stated in writing that writers born or educated in the Americas were either nonexistent or of a very low caliber.

Though Eguiara y Eguren completed only two volumes of his ambitious dictionary, up to the letter J, his work represents the foundations of modern Mexican bibliography. José Mariano *Beristáin y Souza used Eguiara y Eguren's work as the basis for his own *Biblioteca Hispano Americana Septentrional* in 1883.

WORKS (printed and over fifty pages in length): *Vida del venerable padre don Pedro de Arellano y Sossa* (Life of the Venerable Father Don Pedro de Arellano y Sossa) (México, 1747). *Selectae Dissertationes Mexicanae* (Selected Mexican Dissertations) (México, 1746). *Praelectio Theologica* (Theological Treaties) (México, 1747). *Biblioteca Mexicana* (Mexican Library), vol. 1 (letters A, B, C) (México, 1755); vol. 2 (letters D, E, F, G, H, I, J). This last work may be found, in manuscript, at the University of Texas at Austin. Prologues to the *Biblioteca Mexicana*," edited by Agustín Millares Carlo (México: FCE, 1944). "Sor Juana Inés de la Cruz," *Biblioteca Mexicana*, translated by Demetrio Frangos, edited by Ermilo Abreu Gómez (México: Porrúa, 1936).

BIBLIOGRAPHY: Joaquín García Icazbalceta, "Las 'Bibliotecas' de Eguiara y de Beristáin," *Obras de Joaquín García Icazbalceta* (México: Agüeros, 1896), pp. 119-46. Agustín Millares Carlo, *Don Juan José de Eguiara y Eguren 1696-1763 y su Biblioteca Mexicana* (México: Col. Filosofía y Letras, 1957). José Mariano Beristáin de Souza, *Biblioteca Hispanoamericana Septentrional*, vol. 1. (México: Amecameca, 1883), pp. 447-53. Manuel Toussaint, "Printing in Mexico during the XVI Century," *Mexican Art and Life* 7 (1939): 13.

ALFONSO GONZALEZ

ELGUERO, Francisco (1856-1932), lawyer, writer, and teacher. Francisco Elguero was born on March 24, 1856 in Mochoacán. He was the son of don Manuel Elguero and doña Guadalupe Iturbide. Elguero studied at the Ateneo Mexicano of don Celso Acevedo, where he became the disciple of don Rafael Angel de la Peña. He completed his preparatory and professional studies at the Seminario Conciliar in Michoacán and was received before the Tribunal of Michoacán in 1880 as a lawyer. During this time, he founded the newspaper *El Derecho Cristiano* (Christian Law) in Morelia. Between the years 1881 and 1883, he was a judge in Zamora. He later practiced law in the state capital. Because of political disturbances in 1911, he went to live in Mexico City, where he became a distinguished member of the forum there. He was elected deputy to the Union Congress representing Zamora, Michoacán, in 1912 and served until the legislative body was dissolved in 1913. He participated in many debates and was a professor of forensics at the National School of Law. In 1914 he went to the United States, where he remained until 1916 when he left for Havana. He lived there until 1919, when he returned to Mexico and continued his practice of law. In 1925 he left for his native city of Morelia, where he died on December 17, 1932.

During his residence in the United States, he wrote *Historia de las Leyes de Reforma, hasta la caída del General Díaz* (History of Reform Laws from the Fall of General Díaz) and *Recuerdos de un desterrado* (Memories of an Exile). He founded the magazines *Reliquias de América Español* and *Museo Intelectual*, and he, along with José Elguero, Francisco de *Olaguíbel, and don Antonio de la *Peña y Reyes, founded the magazine *América Española*. In 1906 he published *Algunos versos* (Some Verses) and translated J. M. Heredia, Banville, Malherbe, Victor Hugo, Mad, Coppé, William Shakespeare, Lamartine, Akermann, Virgil, and Horace as well as several fragments from *La Atlántida* by Verdaguer. In 1918 he published, in *Diario de la Marina* in Havana, 330 articles of historic journals and apologues, which were edited in Madrid in 1920.

Elguero arduously studied philosophy, theology, law, sociology, Spanish history and literature, as well as Latin, English, French and Italian. As a young man, using the pseudonym Senior, he published poetry in the magazines *La Revista Literaria* and *La Revista Católica*. He became well known for his work in the press, the courts, the church, and through his treatises.

WORKS: *La Inmaculada* (The Immaculate) (México: n.p., 1905). *Algunos versos* (Some Verses) (Morelia: Francisco Antúnez, 1906). *Recuerdos de viaje* (Memories of a Voyage) (Morelia: n.p., 1909). *Lecciones de elocuencia forense* (Lessons on Forensics) (México: M. León Sánchez, 1914). *Reliquias de América Española* (Relics of Spanish America) (México: Tip. Salesiana, 1922). *La tragedia de Padilla* (The Tragedy of Padilla) (México: Tip. Salesiana, 1924). *La anarquía demagógica y la administración de justicia en Michoacán* (Demogogic Anarchy and Judicial Administration in Michoacán) (n.p., n.d.). *Diálogos eucarísticos* (Eucharistic Dialogues). *Comentarios a pensamientos religiosos de Luis Veulliot* (Commentaries on the Religious Thoughts of Luis Veuillot) (n.p., n.d.). *Vanguardia* (Vanguardism) (n.p., n.d.). *Un gran mexicano: Don Agustín Abarca* (A Great Mexican: Don Agustín Abarca) (n.p., n.d.).

BIBLIOGRAPHY: *Biblos* 2, 101 (Dec. 25, 1920): 201-2. Alberto María Carreño, *Memorias de la Academia Mexicana*, vol. 7 (1945) 179-80; vol. 8, (1945): 103-8. Alfonso Junco, "Don Francisco Elguero," in *Excelsior* (Aug. 6, 1928). Félix F. Palavicini, *Los diputados. Lo que se ve y lo que no se ve de la Cámara*, 2nd ed. (México: Imp. Francesa, 1915-1916). Pedro Serrano, *Hispanistas mexicanos* (México: n.p., 1920). Mariano de Jesús Torres, *Parnaso michoacano o antología de poetas michoacanos* (Morelia: Eds. El Centinela, 1905). Octaviano Valdés, *Poesía neoclásica y académica* (México: n.p., 1946), pp. xli-clii. Emeterio Valverde Téllez, *Bibliografía filosófica mexicana*, 2nd ed. (León: Jesús Rodríguez, 1913).

DENISE GUAGLIARDO BENCIVENGO

ELIZONDO, Salvador (1932-   ). Born on December 19, 1932, in Mexico City, Salvador Elizondo has had an extraordinary education, having attended several universities in different countries. After completing his primary and secondary studies in Mexico, he went to the University of Ottawa for his undergraduate work. From there, he went to school in Italy, France, and England, studying, among other disciplines, film. He returned to Mexico to study at UNAM during the academic year 1952-1953. In 1963, he received a scholarship from the Centro Mexicano de Escritores to pursue further studies. He has published widely in newspapers and journals. A novelist, short story writer, poet, translator, and journalist, Elizondo has become well-known in literary circles and among the general Mexico public for his works. He became an editor for the literary magazine *Estaciones* in 1960, and two years later, he founded *S. Nob*, another journal. He produced his first film, *Apocalipsis 1900*, in 1965.

He received the Xavier Villaurrutia Prize for his novel, *Farabeuf o la crónica de un instante* (Farabeuf or the Chronicle of an Instant) (1965). The pages of *Farabeuf* are filled with situations of violence, sadism, horror, and magic. Not all of his work is so characterized, however. His poetry, with a hint of surrealism, is somewhat more subdued, although it deals with man's inner drama.

WORKS: *Poemas* (México: Author's Edition, 1960). *Luchino Visconti* (México: UNAM, 1963). *Farabeuf o la crónica de un instante* (Farabeuf or the Chronicle of an Instant) (México: Mortiz, 1965). *Salvador Elizondo*, autobiography (México: Empresas Editoriales, 1966). *Narda o el verano* (Narda or the Summer) (México: Eds. Era, 1966).

BIBLIOGRAPHY: Huberto Batis, "Tortura y erotismo," review of *Farabeuf*, in *El Heraldo Cultural* 15 (Feb. 20, 1966): 14. John Bruce-Novoa, "Entrevista con Salvador Elizondo," in *La Palabra y el Hombre* 13 (1972): 57-62. Ricardo Cano Gavería, "Salvador Elizondo o el suplicio como escritura," in *Quimera* 15 (Jan. 1982): 50-52. Juan Carvajal, "Tres entrevistas: Elizondo: Nada se puede instaurar en el mundo sin un rito," in *La Cultura en México* 214 (March 23, 1966): i-iv. José de la Colina, "Salvador Elizondo, de la poesía secreta," in *México en la Cultura* 577 (April 4, 1960): 2. Carol Clark D'Lugo, "Elizondo's *Farabeuf*: A Consideration of the Text as Text," in *Symposium* 39, 3 (Fall 1985): 155-66. Margo Glantz, "*Farabeuf*, escritura barroca y novela mexicana," in *Barroco* 3 (1971): 29-37. Lillian Manzor-Coats, "Problemas en *Farabeuf* mayormente intertextuales," in *Boletín Bibliográfico de Hacienda* 88, 3-4 (1986): 465-74. Aurora M. Ocampo de Gómez and Ernesto Prado Velázquez, *Diccionario de escritores mexicanos* (México: UNAM, 1967), pp. 107-8. Elena Poniatowska, "En el cine mexicano no hay cerebros que funcionen," in *El Día* (Nov. 12, 1963): 14. Ramón Xirau, Review of *Farabeuf*, in *Diálogos* 4 (May-June 1966): 43-44. Gabriel Zaid, "Sobre el realismo de *Farabeuf*," in *Revista de Bellas Artes* 7 (Jan.-Feb.): 103-4.

MICHELE MUNCY

ERRO, Luis Enrique (1897-1955), astrononer, politician, novelist. Born in Mexico City on January 6, 1897, Erro completed his primary school in Morelia, Michigan. His education included civil engineering, law, history, and mathematics. Although his educational pursuits were manifold, he was noted to be an oustanding speaker and eventually engaged in mercantile activities. In 1923, because of his involvement in the rebellion of Adolfo de la Huerta, Erro was exiled fron Mexico, later returning as director of technical education and econonic statistics. He participated in numerous activities of a political nature, including advisor to the presidency (1935-1955). He died in Mexico City on January 18, 1955. Erro was founder of the National Observatory of Astrophysics in Puebla in 1941 and editor of the *Astronomical Journal* in 1947. His narrative technique is denonstrated in his only novel, *Los pies descalzos* (Bare Feet), which reflects his social opinion and embraces his broad and versatile personality. His narrative is a good example of novelistic technique for the strict treatment of the plot.

WORKS: *El pensamiento matemático contemporáneo* (Contemporary Mathematical Thought) (México: Biblioteca Enciclopédica Popular, 1944). *Axioma. El pensamiento matemático contemporáneo* (Axiom, Contemporary Mathematical Thought) (México: Letras de México, 1944). *Los pies descalzos* (Bare Peet) (México: Cía. General de Ediciones, 1951).

BIBLIOGRAPHY: John S. Brushwood and José Rojas Garcidueñas, *Breve historia de la novela mexicana* (México: Eds. de Andrea, 1959), pp. 125-26. Alí Chumacero, "La literatura mexicana en 1951," *México en la cultura* (México: SEP, 1951). Clara Henigsber, "Los pies descalzos," in *Filosofía y Letras* (México: Imp. Universitaria, 1953), pp. 332-36. Julia Hernández, *Novelistas y cuentistas de la revolución* (México: n.p., 1960), pp. 50-51. José Luis Rublúo Islas, "Homenaje al escritor Luis Enrique Erro (1897- 1955)," in *Boletín Bibliográfico de Hacienda* 306 (1964): 7-9.

SILKA FREIRE

ESCOBEDO, Federico (1874-1949), poet and priest. Born in Guanajuato, Escobedo began his studies there, entered seminary in 1887, and was later sent to Spain. Poor health cut short his studies with the Jesuits, and he returned to his homeland to fulfill his ministry and his literary career. He spent the last years of his life in Puebla, where he died November 13, 1949. A humanist, Escobedo belonged to the Arcadia Romana with the name Tamiro Miceneo and was a member of the Academia de la Lengua. He wrote in both Latin and Spanish, and his style has been categorized as neoclassic with modernist and romantic overtones. He is important also as a translator, his most notable translation, with annotations, being that of Rafael *Landívar's *Rusticatio Mexicana*, titled *Geórgicas mexicanas* in Escobedo's translation.

WORKS: *Carmina latina* (Puebla, 1902). *Poesías: odas breves, salmos y trenos, épicas, sonetos, notas del alma* (Poetry: Brief Odes, Psalms and Laments, Epics, Sonnets, Notes of the Soul) (Puebla: Talleres de la Imp. Artística, 1903). *Madrigales marianos* (Marian Madrigals) (Puebla, 1903). *Pro-Patria* (Pro-Country) (Puebla, 1910). *Miscuitutili dulci* (Sweet Miscellany), in honor of D. Marcelino Menéndez y Pelayo) (México, 1912). "Manzoni en México (Manzoni in Mexico), speech to the Mexican Academy, April 1917), in *Memorias de la Academia Mexicana Correspondiente de la Española* 9 (1954): 134-71. *Cauces hondos* (Deep Channels) (México, 1919). "A don Agustín Iturbide, libertador de México" (Ode to Don Agustín Iturbide, Liberator of Mexico), in *América Española* Sept. 28, 1921). *Idilio trágico* (Tragic Idyll) (Teziutlán, 1922). *Rapsodias bíblicas horacianas y soledades canoras* (Horatian Biblical Rhapsodies and Melodious Solitudes) (Teziutlán, 1923). *Siempre antiguo y siempre nuevo* (Always Old and Always New) (Teziutlán, 1927). *La sombra de Virgilio* (Virgil's Shadow), legend in Latin and Spanish (Teziutlán, 1930). "La Virgen de mi patria" (The Virgin of My Country), in *Memoria del Congreso Guadalupano* (México: Tipografía de la Esc. Salesiana, 1932). *Elegía* (Elegy), in honor of the Archbishop Montes de Oca, 1940. *Aromas de leyenda* (Whiffs of Legend) (Puebla: Ed. Journal Sus Ojos, 1941).

Cánticos sagrados (Sacred Canticles) (Puebla, 1946). "Seila o la hija de Jefté" (Seila or Jefte's Daughter), *Bohemia Poblana* (June 1948). Translation: *Geórgicas mexicanas, metered version of Rafael Landívar's Rusticatio mexicana* (Tezuitlán, 1925).

BIBLIOGRAPHY: *Biblos* 3 (1921): 161-62. Alberto María Carreño, *Memorias de la Academia Mexicana* 7 (1945): 180-81; 8 (1946): 109-10. Enrique Cordero y T., "Presencia de ausentes ilustres," *Memorias de la Academia Mexicana* 16 (1958): 149-65. Gustavo Couttolenc Cortés, *Federico Escobedo traductor de Landívar* (México: Ed. Jus, 1973). Enrique Gómez Haro, "Inauguración del monumento a Federico Escobedo" (speech), *Bohemia Poblana* (Jan. 1951). Agustín Haro y Tamariz, "Crítica: *Drama Seila o la hija de Jefté*, de Federico Escobedo," *Bohemia Poblana* (June 1948). Ronald Hilton, *Who's Who in Latin America* (Stanford, Calif.: Stanford University Press, 1946), p. 37. José López Portillo y Rojas, *Contestación* (Answer) to the speech of Federico Escobedo: Manzoni in Mexico (México: Imp. I. Escalante, S.A., 1917). Joaquín Márquez Montiel, *Hombres célebres de Puebla*, vol. 2 (México: Ed. Jus, 1955), pp. 45-53. Alfonso Méndez Plancarte, *San Juan de la Cruz en México* (México: FCE, 1954), pp. 64-67. Gabriel Méndez Plancarte, *Horacio en México* (México: Ed. de la Universidad Nacional, 1937), pp. 271-84. Luis Nava, "Federico Escobedo," *Bohemia Poblana* (May 1953). Rubén Romero, "Laudanza para Federico Escobedo," *Bohemia Poblana* (Jan. 1951). "Homage," *Bohemia Poblana* (Dec. 1949).

BARBARA P. FULKS

ESPEJO, Beatriz (1939-   ). Born September 19, 1936, in Veracruz, Beatriz Espejo received her teaching certification at the Universidad Nacional in Mexico City and has taught literature at several different schools. After she took a course on Latin American literature with Xavier *Icaza, her term paper, a study of Carlos *Fuentes' *Los días enmascarados*, was published in *Revista de Filosofía y Letras*; that was the beginning of her writing career. Well known in the literary world especially for her short stories, Espejo was greatly influenced by her grandmother, an exceptional story teller whose penchance was for ghost stories and other tales of intrigue. Espejo's stories have been published in several important literary magazines and journals, such as *Estaciones, Cuadernos del Viento*, and *Revista de Filosofía y Letras*. Magical elements are integral parts of many of Espejo's stories, bearing resemblance to some of the work of Ramon *López Velarde (who was the subject of her master's thesis). Two of her primary inspirations were Rabindranath and Juan Ramón Jiménez.

Beatriz Espejo was the founder and director of the journal *El Rehilete* (The Barbed Dart), which lasted ten years. Its editorial board and entire staff were made up entirely of women. The journal was discontinued almost the same day she received a scholarship for the Centro Mexicano de Escritores, in 1971, for her projected novel "Los eternos dioses," never finished. Interested in the plastic arts, she was asked to direct a history of Mexican painting by Editorial Ferro, a task which she enthusiastically accepted. After three years, however, the company went bankrupt, although many of the agreed-upon sixty-four installments had been published. She then turned to Emmanuel *Carballo, her husband, to publish the remainder of the installments which she had completed. Afterwards, she entered the Centro de Investigaciones Literarias at the university and continued with her literary career. Her doctoral dissertation was on Julio *Torri and was published in 1986 as *Julio Torri, voyerista desencantado* (Julio Torri, Disenchanted Voyeurist).

Although she attempted to write poetry, she discovered that it was not her area of strength, so she turned more completely to the short story as her major literary genre. Love and death are her two major themes. In general, her stories arise from personal experiences (of which "Florencia: 1569," with its clear autobiographical element, is an example), from dreams, and from her other readings. Her first published book of stories, *La otra hermana* (The Other Sister), appeared in 1958. A 1960 story, "La luna en el charco" (The Moon in the Puddle), is a fable dealing with a secret society of dreamers who attempt to retreat from their daily frustrations.

Espejo has claimed that writing is not a pleasant task for her and, indeed, becomes an illness to which she succumbs in an attempt to conquer death and to derive meaning from life. Some of her later, more mature, work demonstrates her artistic creativity and her increasing skill at narrating. *Muros de azogue* (Walls of Quicksilver), a series of interrelated stories about the demise of a twentieth-century provincial family, is a primary example of her ability as a short story writer.

WORKS: "*[Los días enmascarados]*" (The Masked Days), in *Revista de Filosofía y Letras* 55-56 (1954): 261-73. *La otra hermana* (The Other Sister), in *Cuadernos del Unicornio* 1 (México 1958): "La luna en el charco" (The Moon in the Puddle), in *ES* 19 (1960): 79-88. "El poeta de la luz y del color (entrevista)" (The Poet of Light and Color [Interview]), essay, in *El Rehilete* 9 (1963): 6-9. "Juan José Arreola y la ingenuidad perdida" (Juan José Arreola and Lost Ingenuity), essay, in *La Gaceta* 10, 108 (1963): 6. *Trasfondo biográfico en la obra de Ramón López Velarde* (Biographical Background in the Work of Ramón López Velarde), master's thesis (México: UNAM, 1963). "Confesiones de A." (Confessions of A.), in *Ovaciones* 147 (México 1964): 2-3. "[Fundación del entusiasmo]" (<Foundation of Enthusiasm>), monograph, in *El Rehilete* 10 (1964): 52-53. *Muros de azogue* (Walls of Quicksilver) (México: Editorial Diógenes, 1979). "La modelo," story, in *Narrativa hispanoamericana,* 1816-1981, edited by Angel Flores, vol. 6 (México: Siglo XXI, 1985), pp. 17-26. *Julio Torri, voyerista desencantado* (Julio Torri, Disenchanted Voyeurist) (México: UNAM, 1986).

BIBLIOGRAPHY: Fabienne Bradu, "Crónica de dos crónicas," in *Vuelta* (Nov. 1988): 46-47. Angel Flores, ed. *Narrativa hispanoamericana 1816-1981,* vol. 6: *La generación de 1939 en adelante* (México: Siglo XXI, 1985), pp. 17-26; *Los narradores ante el público* (México: Mortiz, 1966), pp. 211-19. Aurora M. Ocampo de Gómez and Ernesto Prado Velázquez, *Diccionario de escritores mexicanos* (México: UNAM, 1967), p. 109. Gustavo Sáinz, Review of "El retorno," in *México en la Cultura* 764 (Nov. 10, 1963): 1. Serge Zaitzeff, Review of *Julio Torri, voyerista desencantado,* in *Revista Iberoamericana* 53, 141 (Pittsburgh, 1987): 1068-69.

JEANNE C. WALLACE

ESPINOSA Altamirano, Horacio (1931-), poet, essayist, and journalist. Espinosa Altamirano was born in Mexico City on December 3, 1931. He has collaborated in magazines and periodical supplements, particularly in *El Nacional* and the *Boletín Bibliográfico de la Secretaría de Hacienda,* and founded the magazine *Bandera* (Flag) in 1955. He has traveled abroad extensively.

WORKS: Poetry: *Testimonios de América en la sangre* (Blood Testimonials of America) (México: Edit. Linea, 1953). *Playas de sol* (Sunny beaches) (México: Estaciones, 1959). *Los signos del destierro* (Signs of Exile) (México: Eds. de Andrea, 1962). *Oratorio del sur* (Oratory) (México: *Cuadernos Americanos*, reprint, 1965). *El ruiseñor armado* (The Armed Nightingale) (México: Ediciones de la Revista Zarza, 1966). *Toda la furia* (All the Fury), 2nd ed. (México: Ediciones Universo, 1977). *Poemas Próceres* (Exalted Poems) (México: Finisterre [1969?]. *Apocalipsis apócrifo* (Apocryphal Apocalypse) (México: Ediciones Universo, 1975). Essays: *El incomensurable, inaudito, inverosimil e inusitado Diego Rivera* (The Incommensurate, Extraordinary, Unbelievable, and Unusual Diego Rivera) (México: EDAMEX, 1985). *Chile y Allende* (México: B. Costa-Amic, 1972).

BIBLIOGRAPHY: Manuel Durán, Review of *Los signos del destierro*, in *Books Abroad* 38, 2 (Spring 1964): 176. Various authors: "La poesía de Horacio Espinosa Altamirano," in *Nivel* 2 (Feb. 25, 1963): 1-2, 4. Javier Peñalosa, Review of *Oratorio del Sur*, in *Nivel* 25 (Jan. 25, 1965): 4. Salvador Reyes Nevares, Review of *Playas del sol*, in *México en la cultura* 568 (Jan. 31, 1960): 4.

NORA EIDELBERG

ESTEVA, José María (1818-1904), poet. José María Esteva was born in Veracruz. He distinguished himself as a regional poet who depicted the customs of his own state. These can readily be observed in his poem "El jarocho" (nickname for the people from Veracruz). His work includes Mexican legends such as *La mujer blanca* (The White Woman).

WORKS: *Poesías* (Poems) (Veracruz, 1850). *La mujer blanca* (The White Woman) (La Habana, 1868; México, 1883). *Tipos veracruzanos y Composiciones varias* (Types from Veracruz and Various Compositions) (Xalapa, 1894). *La campana de la misión* (The Mission's Bell) (Xalapa, 1894). *Miguel Jifes o el Polígloto* (México: Imp. I. Cumplido, 1873; Xalapa: n.p., 1902).

BIBLIOGRAPHY: Carlos González Peña, *Historia de la literatura mexicana. Desde los origenes hasta nuestros dias* (México: Porrúa, 1981), p. 158. Juan B. Iguíniz, *Bibliografía de novelistas mexicanos* (México: Imp. Sría de Relaciones Exteriores, 1926), p. 111. Francisco R. Illescas and Juan Bartolo Hernández, *Escritores veracruzanos* (Veracruz: n.p., 1945), pp. 84-87. María del Carmen Millán, *Literatura mexicana* (México: Editorial Esfinge, 1962), p. 144. Julio Jiménez Rueda, *Historia de la Literatura Mexicana* (México: Botas, 1960), p. 224. Ralph E. Warner, *Historia de la novela mexicana en el siglo XIX* (México: Ant. Libr. Robredo, 1953), p. 113.

JOSEPH VELEZ

ESTRADA, Genaro (1887-1937). A distinguished diplomat, professor and author, Genaro Estrada was born on June 2, 1887, in Mazatlán, Sinaloa. He died on September 29, 1937, in Mexico City. He began his career as a journalist in his home area, then went to Mexico City around 1912, participating in many of the cultural activities of the city. A professor at the Escuela Nacional Preparatoria, he soon became involved in the affairs of government, serving his country in a variety of posts over the years and especially between 1927 and 1930. He was, for instance, the ambassador to Spain and the minister to Portugal and Turkey during this time period. A professor at UNAM, Estrada was also the founder of the Academia Mexicana de la Historia and of the series Monografías Bibliográficas Mexicanas. Estrada put together the volume on Amado *Nervo for this series. He also contributed to several important newspapers and journals, including *El Diario, Contemporáneos, Revista de Revistas,* and *Hoy.*

A man of many talents, Genaro Estrada authored poems, essays, articles, and books in a number of areas. As a colonialist, he endeavored, along with other members of his generation, to revive interest in Mexico's past. In 1926, he published the novel *Pero Galín,* a pleasant, yet critical colonialist book, which actually marks the end of that type of novel. Enrique Anderson-Imbert notes that Estrada creates a caricature of himself in *Pero Galín,* in the protagoniast, a "man with a mania for the archaic, oblivious of the present, who suddenly marries an ultramodern young girl, breaks into the movie world, and is cured of his anachronism."

As a poet, he created interesting compositions along the lines of the vanguard school. Authoring four books of verse, Estrada was a satirist who used language and literary techniques to express his views poetically.

Besides his original creative work, Genaro Estrada wrote several important prologues for critical editions of various Mexican authors. He was also a translator, although his work was limited, apparently, to Jules Renard and H. I. Priestley. When he died at age fifty, Estrada was still very active in most of his literary and academic endeavors.

WORKS: *Poetas nuevos de México* (New Poets of Mexico), anthology with notes (México: Porrúa, 1916). *La linterna sorda* (The Deaf Lantern), translation of Jules Renard, with study (México: Tip. de Murguía, 1919). *Las municipalidades de la América española* (The Municipalities of Spanish America), translation of H. I. Priestley (México: n.p., 1921). *Visionario de la Nueva España* (Visionary of New Spain) (México: Tip. de Murguía, 1921). *Bibliografía de Amado Nervo* (México: Monografías Bibliográficas Mexicanas, 1925). *Pero Galín* (México: Edit. Cultura, 1926). *Crucero* (Cross-Bearer), poetry (México: Edit. Cultura, 1928). *Escalera* (Staircase), poetry (México: Eds. del Murciélago, 1929). *El tesoro de Monte Albán* (The Treasure of Monte Albán) (Madrid: n.p., 1932). *Ascensión de la poesía* (Ascension of Poetry) (Madrid: Edit. Bécquer, 1934). *Paso a nivel* (Step to Level), poetry (Madrid: Eds. Héroes, 1933). *Senderillos al ras* (Little Footpaths on the Level) (Madrid: n.p., 1934). *200 notas de bibliografía mexicana* (200 Notes about Mexican Bibliography) (México: MBM, 1935). Prologue to Amado Nervo, *Poesías completas* (Madrid: Biblioteca Nueva, 1935). *Genio y figura de Picasso* (Genius and Figure of Picasso) (México: Imp. Mundial, 1936). *El arte mexicano en España* (Mexican Art in Spain) (México: Porrúa, 1937-1942). *Bibliografía de Goya* (México: FCE, 1940).

BIBLIOGRAPHY: Ermilo Abreu Gómez, "Genaro Estrada," in Ernesto Higuera, *Antología sinaloense* (Culiacán: Eds. Culturales del Gobierno del Estado de Sinaloa, 1958), pp. 65-69. Enrique Anderson-Imbert, *Spanish American Literature,* vol. 2 (Detroit: Wayne State University Press, 1969), pp. 467, 512. José Gorostiza, "Motivos.

Escalera," in *Contemporáneos* 14 (July 1929): 341-44. Raymond L. Grismer and Mary B. MacDonald, *Vida y obras de autores mexicanos* (La Habana: Edit. Alfa, 1945), pp. 51-53. Juan B. Iguíniz, "Don Genaro Estrada. Elogio," in *Memorias de la Academia de la Historia Correspondiente de la Real de Madrid* 1, 4 (1942): pp. 336-46. Julio Jiménez Rueda, *Antología de la prosa en México*, 2nd ed. (México: Botas, 1938), pp. 449-500. Mario Mariscal, "Genaro Estrada, escritor, traductor, editor y difusor de libros," in *El Libro y el Pueblo* 12, 5 (May 1934): 244-47. Aurora M. Ocampo de Gómez and Ernesto Prado Velázquez, *Diccionario de escritores mexicanos* (México: UNAM, 1967), pp. 110-11. Alfonso Reyes, *Pasado inmediato y otros ensayos* (El Colegio de México, 1941), pp. 165-78. Artemio de Valle Arispe, *La muy noble y leal ciudad de México, según relatos de antaño y hogaño* (México: Edit. Cultura, 1924), pp. 249-51. Xavier Villaurrutia, *Textos y pretextos* (México: La Casa de España en México, 1940), pp. 71-78. "*Homenaje* to Genaro Estrada," in *Letras de México* 18 (Nov. 1, 1937).

ELADIO CORTES

ESTRADA, Josefina (1957-   ), short story writer. Josefina Estrada was born in Mexico City and studied journalism at the UNAM. In 1980 she received a grant from the Instituto Nacional de Bellas Artes to attend a writing course, and since then she has been publishing her short stories in different anthologies and journals, among them Gustavo Sáinz's *Jaula de palabras*, *La Semana de Bellas Artes*, *El Universal*, *Su otro yo*, and *Letra*. Josefina Estrada works today in the Literature Section of the INBA.

WORKS: *Panegírico*, in *Narrativa Hispanoamericana, 1816-1981*, edited by Angel Flores, vol. 6 (México: Siglo XXI, 1985), pp. 361-69.

ELADIO CORTES

ESTRIDENTISMO. *See* VANGUARDIST PROSE FICTION IN MEXICO.

F

FARIAS de Isassi, Teresa (1878-?), playwright and novelist. Farias de Isassi was born in Saltillo, Coahuila, in 1878, but her family moved to San Luis Potosí when she was still a child. There, she studied under Agustín Guerling, a teacher who had a great influence on her. Manuel José *Othón, the well-known poet, used to spend long periods of time resting at the estate owned by Teresa's wealthy family. His acquaintance no doubt had an influence on her affinity for bucolic poetry. As she grew up, she studied five different languages and was able to read the literary masterpieces of each in the original version. As a result, she was extremely well-versed in literature, and this is evident in her writings. She married General Adolfo M. Isassi, and with him traveled throughout Europe and North America.

Farias de Isassi belonged to a group of women writers who, sometimes successfully and always with enthusiasm, took to the stage their point of view regarding Mexico's problems. Her plays were staged in Mexico at the beginning of the twentieth century and were quite successful. Among others, Amado *Nervo and Enrique *González Martínez were very positive in their reviews of her ability as a playwright and novelist. Her play *Cerebro y corazón* (Heart and Brain) received a prize in an open contest organized by Justo *Sierra.

WORKS: Theater: *Cerebro y corazón* (Heart and Brain) (San Luis Potosí: Imp. y Lit. de M. Esquivel y Cía., 1907). *Como las aves* (Like Birds) (México: Talls. Grafs. del Gobierno Nacional, 1919). *Fuerza creadora* (Creative Force) (México, n.d.). *Religión de amor* (Love's Religion) (México, n.d.). *Nuevos horizontes* (New Horizons) (México, n.d.). *Páginas de la vida* (Pages from Life) (México, 1942). *Sombra y luz* (Light and Shadow) (México: Imp. y Lit. El Escritorio, 1912). *La sentencia de muerte* (Death Sentence), translated by Lillian Saunders (New York: n.p., 1925). Novel: *Nupcial* (Nuptial) (Barcelona: Edit. Maucci Hnos., 1915). Essay: *Ante el gran enigma* (Facing the Great Mystery) (México: Botas, 1938).

BIBLIOGRAPHY: Juan B. Iguiñiz, *Bibliografía de novelistas mexicanos* (México: Imp. Sría Relaciones Exteriores, 1926), p. 114. Francisco Monterde, *Bibliografía del teatro en México* (México: Imp. Sría. Relaciones Exteriores, 1933), p. 135. José Luis Martínez, *Literatura mexicana, siglo XX (1910-1949)*, vol. 1 (México: Ant. Libr. Robredo, 1949), p. 68.

HERLINDA HERNANDEZ

FERNANDEZ, Angel José (1953-   ), poet and essayist. Fernández was born in Jalapa, Veracruz, on May 19, 1953; he studied Spanish literature at both the Universidad Iberoamericana de Mexico and the Universidad Veracruzana. The author of numerous reviews, articles and essays, he has combined his literary studies with editorial work, having served as editor of *La Palabra y el Hombre*. He was also responsible for newsletters like *Papel de Envolver* in the publication department of the same university. Most recently, he has been editor of the Colección Manantial en la Arena of the Literary Linguistic Research Center. In the Veracruzana, he is working on a comprehensive edition of the poetry of Enrique González Llorca. In his own poetry, patterned after the Spanish classics, Fernández uses traditional metrics and techniques. He seeks lyric perfection, often choosing complex forms, disguised with simplicity. In *De un momento a otro* (From One Moment to Another), the best of his production from 1972 to 1984 is gathered. Most of his themes are those found in universal poetry: love, absent figures, loneliness, and death.

WORKS: *Sombras, voces y, presagios* (Shadows, Voices and Omens) (Jalapa: Universidad Veracruzana, 1975). *Sobre la muerte* (About Death) (Jalapa: Ed. of the School of Artes Plásticas, 1976). *Escribir sin para qué* (Writing without a Reason) (México: Ed. Máquina de Escribir, 1979). *Aprender de una sombra* (Learning from a Shadow) (México: El tucán de Virginia, 1981). *Facts* Textos de AJF y dibujos de Pepe Maya (Jalapa: Universidad Veracruzana, 1981). *Algo así* (Something Like That) (Morelia: Universidad Nicolaita, 1982). *Epigramas de mayo* (Epigrams of May) (Jalapa: Universidad Veracruzana, 1982). *Arenas de cristal* (Crystal Sand) (Jalapa: Ed. Papel de Envolver, 1982). *Florilegio de antorchas contra el tiempo* (Anthology of Torches against the Weather) (Jalapa: Universidad Veracruzana, 1983). *Antología de Porfirio Barba-Jacob* (Tuxtla Gutiérrez: UNACH, 1984). *La poesía veracruzana* (Poetry from Veracruz), in collaboration with Esther Hernández Palacios (Jalapa: Universidad Veracruzana, 1984). *Furia en los elementos* (Fury in the Elements), in *Azoro de voces. 18 poetas veracruzanos y un intrépido* (Startling Voices. 18 Poets from Veracruz and One Intrepid) (Cordova: Ed. Nueva Imprenta Trueba, 1986). *De un momento a otro* (From One Moment to Another) (Tuxtla Gutiérrez: UNACH, 1985).

BIBLIOGRAPHY: Sandro Cohen, *Palabra nueva* (México: Premiá, 1981), pp. 239-44. Enrique Jaramillo-Levhi, *La poesía erótica en México* (México: Domes, 1979). *Poesía joven de México* (México: UNAM, 1981), pp. 51-53.

ESTHER HERNANDEZ-PALACIOS

FERNANDEZ, Sergio (1926-). Born in Mexico City on February 26, 1926, Sergio Fernández received his doctorate in Spanish literature at the Universidad Nacional de México. Recipient of a scholarship from the Instituto de Cultura Hispánica in Madrid, he traveled to Europe in 1953, the first of several such journeys. In 1955 he became a full-time professor at UNAM, having taught in various places before this time. He has contributed to some of the most significant literary journals and newspapers, such as *La Palabra y el Hombre*, *Universidad de México*, and *Hispania*, a publication in the United States.

With his master's and his doctoral theses, Sergio Fernández became known as an exceptional essay writer. He later wrote several highly regarded books of essays, including *Cinco escritores hispanoamericanos* (Five Hispanic American Writers), *Ensayos sobre literatura española de los siglos XVI y XVII* (Essays on Spanish Literature of the sixteenth and seventeenth Centuries), and *Las grandes figuras del Renacimiento y el Barroco* (Great Renaissance and Baroque Figures). In the first, he searches for the essence of the Hispanic American. In *Ensayos*, he treats the theme of love as manifested in the works of some of the most representative authors of the period, such as Fernando de Rojas, Garcilaso de la Vega, Lope de Vega, and others. In 1958 he published his first novel, *Los signos perdidos* (The Lost Signs), in which problems of embittered loneliness and solitude emerge as the central theme. His second novel, *En tela de juicio* (In Question), is similar to the first in terms of characterization and context. Fernández' rich and detailed narration of even the smallest facts and happenings gives character to the novel, even though the larger story is told in a minimal way. *Retratos del fuego y la ceniza* (Portraits of Fire and Ash), published in 1968, is a collection of forty-two articles originally published in *El Día*. About famous female literary characters, such as the Celestina, the book provides insightful, and at times philosophical, portraits which seem to bring them to life.

Over the years, Fernández has turned more and more to the essay as his preferred medium of expression. In 1972, he published *Homenajes a Sor Juana, a López Velarde, a José Gorostiza* (Homages to Sor Juana, to López Velarde, to José Gorostiza), a rather lengthy book of three essays dedicated to the lives and works of three of the most prominent Mexican authors. This endeavor was followed in 1973 by another book of essays, entitled *Miscelánea de mártires* (Miscellany of Martyrs), a collection of forty-five short articles, most of which are about the *Quijote*. The remainder discuss the lives and works of such authors as Alejo Carpentier, Horacio Quiroga, and José *Revueltas. *Segundo sueño* (Second Dream), which harks back to Sor Juana's *Primero sueño* (First Dream), is a 420-page exploration of love and sexuality and is similar to its predecessor in form and content. It was published in 1976.

In 1983, Fernández published *Los desfiguros de mi corazón* (The Disfigurements of My Heart), basically a collection of anecdotes, revolving in part around the Mexico City of the 1950s and 1960s and provincial Mexican life. Foreign events and other influences also provide Fernández with anecdotal material. The author employs techniques of most of the literary genres in his work, plus theatrical devices. It is, perhaps, one of his most ambitious efforts for the integration of so many different techniques in this somewhat autobiographical account.

WORKS: Studies: *Ideas sociales y políticas en el "Infierno" de Dante y en "Los sueños" de Quevedo* (Social and Political Ideas in Dante's "Inferno" and in Quevedo's "The Dreams"), master's thesis (México: Imp. Universitaria, 1950). *Ventura y muerte de la picaresca* (Fortune and Death of the Picaresque), doctoral dissertation (México: Imp. Universitaria, 1953). *Cinco escritores hispanoamericanos* (Five Hispanic American Writers) (México: UNAM, 1958). *Ensayos sobre literatura epsañola de los siglos XVI y XVII* (Essays on Spanish Literature of the sixteenth and seventeenth Centuries) (México: UNAM, 1961). *Las grandes figuras españolas del Renacimiento y el Barroco* (Great Renaissance and Baroque Figures) (México: Edit. Pormaca, 1966). Prologues: Miguel de Cervantes, *Novelas Ejemplares*, commentary (México: Porrúa, 1961). *La caricatura de la Revolución Mexicana*, prologues by Manuel González Ramírez and Sergio Fernández (México: FCE, n.d.). Novels: *Los signos perdidos* (The Lost Signs) (México: Gral. de Ediciones, 1958). *En tela de juicio* (In Question) (México: Ed. Mortiz, 1964).

BIBLIOGRAPHY: Jorge Amezcua, Review of *En tela de juicio*, in *Boletín Bibliográfico de la Secretaría de Hacienda y Crédito Público* 320 (June 1, 1965): 20-21. Juan

Antonio Ayala, Review of *Los signos perdidos*, in *Armas y Letras* (1958). Huberto Batis, Review of *Cinco escritores hispanoamericanos*, in *Universidad de México* 13, 1 (Sept. 1958): 29-30. Emmanuel Carballo, "El año de la novela," in *México en la Cultura* 511 (Dec. 28, 1958): 1, 11; Review of *En tela de juicio*, in *La Cultura en México* 142 (Nov. 4, 1964): xvii. Rosario Castellanos, "La novela mexicana contemporánea y su valor testimonial," in *Hispania* 47, 2 (May 1964): 223-24, 229; "Un acontecimiento literario," review of *En tela de juicio*, in *Cuadernos del Viento* 47-48 (Sept.-Dec. 1964): 742. Dolores Castro, "Los hechos y la cultura," review of *En tela de juicio*, in *Nivel* 28 (April 25, 1965): 12. Alí Chumacero, "Novelistas de nuestro continente," in *México en la Cultura* 497 (Sept. 21, 1958): 4. Alberto Dallal, "Sobre dos novelas," review of *En tela de juicio*, in *Diálogos* 5 (July-Aug. 1965): 51-52. Beatriz Espejo, "Sergio Fernández, escritor vitalmente sin objeto preciso," in *Cuadernos del Viento* 47-48 (Sept.-Dec. 1964): 748-50. Aurora M. Ocampo de Gómez and Ernesto Prado Velázquez, *Diccionario de escritores mexicanos* (México: UNAM, 1967), pp. 111-12. Margarita Peña, Review of *En tela de juicio*, in *El Rehilete* 2 (Sept. 1964): 60-61. Salvador Reyes Nevares, Review of *Los signos perdidos*, in *México en la Cultura* 509 (Nov. 4, 1964): 7; "Una conciencia totalmente lúcida y fiel," review of *En tela de juicio*, in *La Cultura en México* 142 (Nov. 4, 1964): xvii. Gustavo Sáinz, Review of *En tela de juicio*, in *México en la Cultura* 806 (Aug. 30, 1964): 7.

                                                      JEANNE C. WALLACE

FERNANDEZ DE CORDOVA, Ignacio (1777-1816), poet and fable writer. Fernández de Cordova's precise date of birth is not known, probably either June 17 or July 31. Born in Valladolid (now Morelia), he completed his secondary education at the School of San Nicolás and later studied medicine in Madrid. He returned to Mexico to obtain his medical degree at the Universidad Real y Pontífica. He practiced medicine in Michoacán and was the director of the Hospital Juan de Dios in Morelia. In support of the cause for independence, he enlisted in the military as a doctor for the Insurgent Column of Hidalgo. He died in Morelia on September 8, 1816.

Although he cultivated lyric poetry, his most noteworthy achievement was his work as a fabulist. He took great pride in creating truly visual, picturesque stories. He published *Fábulas* (Fables) in 1815. His *Fábulas escogidas* (Selected Fables) was published posthumously in 1928.

WORKS: *Fábulas* (Fables) (1815). *Fábulas escogidas* (Selected Fables) (Valladolid: Imp. José M. de Oñate, 1928).

BIBLIOGRAPHY: Cayetano Andrade, *Antología de escritores nicolaitas 1540-1940* (México: n.p., 1941), pp. 55-60; *Antología del centenario* (México: Imp. de Manuel de León Sánchez, 1910), vol. 2, pp. 791-93. Jesús Romero Flores, *Páginas de historia* (México: Imp. de la Escuela 1 de Huérfanos, 1921). Mariano de Jesús Torres, *Parnaso Michoacano, o antología de poetas michoacanos* (Morelia: private printing by author, 1905).

                                                ESTHER HERNANDEZ-PALACIOS

FERNANDEZ DE LIZARDI, José Joaquín (1776-1827), poet, writer of fables, dramatist, novelist, and journalist. Fernández de Lizardi was born in Mexico City, on November 15, 1776. He completed his early studies in Tepozotlán. Later, his parents sent him to Mexico City to study Latin with Professor Manuel Enriquez. After that, he studied in El Colegio de San Ildefonso. When he was sixteen, he graduated from the high school program at the University of Mexico. When he was seventeen, he studied theology. He became a provisional judge in the jurisdiction of Acapulco, Guerrero. In 1812, during the Insurgent Revolution, he became lieutenant of justice in Taxco, Guerrero. When Morelos took over the city, Lizardi surrendered his position and arms. Consequently, he was taken prisoner by the royalists and sent to Mexico City. Also in 1812, taking advantage of the Spanish Constitution's guarantee of freedom of the press, Lizardi founded the newspaper *El Pensador Mexicano* (The Mexican Thinker), which he subsequently used as his pseudonym. In this paper, he criticized Viceroy Venegas, resulting in the suppression of his right to free speech. Lizardi was imprisoned. In 1813, he published articles related to the nationwide plague. During 1815-1816, he published two newspapers: *Alacenas de Friolera* (Cupboards of No Importance) and *Caxoncito de la Alacena* (Little Drawer of the Cupboard). In 1820, he established the Public Society of Reading on De la Cadena Street, which facilitated the distribution of books and newspapers through subscriptions. He also published another newspaper, *El Conductor Eléctrico* (The Electric Conductor). Around 1822, he began to be disappointed in the Emperor Iturbide. He then became a member of the Freemasons, the center of true liberalism. Because he caused his editors difficulties with his articles, he bought his own press and published his work from 1822-1823. In the latter year, he published a paper called *El Hermano del Perico* (The Brother of the Parakeet). In 1824, he felt disappointed with the context of the third article of the constitution. He published a biweekly page called "Conversaciones del Payo y el Sacristán" (Conversations between the Peasant and the Sacristan) in which church-state affairs were discussed. In 1825, he was named editor of *La Gaceta del Gobierno* (The Government Gazette). He received the military rank of retired captain. In 1826, he founded his last newspaper: *Correo Semanario de México* (Weekly Correspondence of Mexico). On April 27, 1827, ill from tuberculosis and in poverty, he drew up his *Testamento y Despedida* (Testament and Farewell). That was the end of his work as a reformer of political and social abuse. He wrote a simple epitaph, which summarized his life and his work: "Aquí yace el pensador mexicano, quién hizo lo que pudo por su patria" (Here lies the Mexican thinker, who did what he could for his country). He died June 21, 1827.

Fernández de Lizardi is one of the most important figures in Mexican literature and he lived during a transitional period. He decided to work in favor of independence and liberalism. There are a moral sense, a didactic intention, and a liberal and reformistic message in all his work. His lively, popular style is rich in expressive forms. His productiveness is incomparable. A creator of fables, specialized calendars, pamphlets, dramatic pieces, and pasteurelles, he was also a poet, novelist, translator, and journalist. As a poet, he cultivated a variety of types ranging from the humorous to the religious and political. He found the fable best suited to his didactic interests. He portrayed contemporary topics with strokes of local color. His dramatic production, nationalistic in theme, dealt with religious, social, and political affairs. Initiating of the novel in Spanish America, Lizardi's four such works are classics of the picaresque, typical regional literature. Pursued and imprisoned for his political and social ideas, he turned to fiction to propagate his beliefs, mixing plot with didactic observations. In *El Periquillo Sarniento* (The Mangy Parakeet), he creates an unusual character, the "mestizo" vagabond, who differs from his counterpart in the Spanish picaresque. In *Vida y hechos del famoso caballero don Catrín de la Fachenda* (Life and Works of the Famous Gentleman don Catrín de la Fachenda), he effectively uses irony, sarcasm, and mockery. He skillfully incorporates proverbs and popular sayings into the text of his works.

WORKS: *Polaca que en honor de nuestro católico monarca, el señor don Fernando VII cantó J.F. de L.* (Pole, Who in Honor of Our Catholic King, Don Fernando VII Sang J.F. of L.) (1808). *Diálogos críticos sobre diferentes asuntos* (Critical Dialogues on Different Matters) (1811). *Canto al glorioso protomártir San Felipe de Jesús* (Song to the Glorious Protomartyr Saint Philip of Jesus), reprinted in *Ratos entretenidos* (Enjoyable Moments) (n.d.). *La muralla de México en la Protección de María Santísima Nuestra Señora* (The Wall of Mexico in the Protection of Mary, Our Most Holy Lady) (n.d.). *Aviso patriótico a los insurgentes a la sordina* (Patriotic Notice to the Secret Insurgents) (n.d.). *La verdad pelada y el perico y la verdad* (The Naked Truth and the Parakeet and the Truth) (n.d.). *Las quejas de los ahorcados* (The Complaints of the Hanged Men) (n.d.). *El sacristán enfermo* (The Ill Sacristan) (n.d.). *Busca usted quién cargue el saco que yo no he de ser el loco* (You Look for Someone to Carry the Bag Because I Will Not Be the Crazy One) (n.d.). *¿De Venus, Baco y Birján a cual le van?* (Of Venus, Baco and Birjain, On Which One Do You Bet?) (n.d.). *Denuncia de los cabellos que faltan que presentar* (Denunciation of the Hair That Fails to Appear) (n.d.). *Aunque la mona se vista de seda, mona se queda* (Even Though the Monkey Wears Silk, It Is Still a Monkey) (1812). *Si la envidia fuera tiña, ¿cuántos tiñosos hubiera?* (If Envy Were a Ringworm, How Many Scabs Would There Be? (1812). *El voto de México en la muerte de la reina Nuestra Señora* (Mexico's Vote in the Death of the Queen Our Lady) (1819). *Diálogo ideal por el pensador mexicano entre Juan Diego y Juan Bernardino* (Ideal Dialogue by the Mexican Thinker between Juan Diego and Juan Bernardino) (1820). *La nueva tonada del trágala, trágala* (The New Tune of the "Trágala, Trágala" [political song against absolutism]) (1822). *Epitalamio* (Epithalamium) (1823). *Diálogos de los muertos* (Dialogues of the Dead) (1825). *Güeritos de los setenta años y muchachos de anteojos* (Seventy-Year-Old Blondes and Boys with Glasses) (1825). *Ratos entretenidos o miscelánea útil, curiosa* (Enjoyable Moments or Useful, Curious Miscellany) (1819). *Fábulas del pensador* (Fables of the Thinker) (1817). *Obras I, Poesía y Fábulas* (Works I, Poetry and Fables) (1963). *Auto Mariano para recordar la milagrosa aparición de Nuestra Señora Madre y Señora de Guadalupe)* (Marian Play to Remember the Miraculous Appearance of Our Holy Mother Lady and Lady of Guadalupe) (n.d.). *Pastorela en dos actos* (Pastourelle in Two Acts) (n.d.). *Todos contra el payo y el payo contra todos)* (Everybody against the Peasant and the Peasant against Everybody) (n.d.). *Unipersonal del arcabuceado* (Unipersonal of the Harquebussed) (1822). *El negro sensible* (The Sensible Black Man) (1825). *La tragedia del P. Arenas* (The Tragedy of P. Arenas) (1827). *El fuego de Prometeo* (The Fire of Prometheus) (n.d.). *Obras, II, Teatro* (Works, II, Theater) (1965). *Pronóstico curioso en el que se miente alegremente acosta de la nubes y de la atmósfera* (Curious Prediction Happily Based on Lies about the Clouds and the Atmosphere) (1816). *Calendario histórico y político para el año bisiesto de 1824)* (Historical and Political Calendar for Leap Year, 1824) (n.d.). *Calendario histórico y pronóstico político para el año del señor de 1825)* (Historical

Calendar and Political Forecast for the Year of the Lord, 1825) (1825). *Calendario para el año de 1825. Dedicado a las señoritas americanas* (Calendar for the Year, 1825. Dedicated to American Girls) (1825). *El periquillo sarniento* (The Mangy Parakeet) (1816). *Noche tristes* (Sad Nights) (1818). *Noches tristes y día alegre* (Sad Nights and Happy Day) (1949). *La Quijotita y su prima* (The Little Quixote and Her Cousin (1818). *Vida y hechos del famoso caballero don Catrín de la Fachenda* (Life and Works of the Famous Gentleman don Catrín de la Fachenda) (1812). *Don Catrín de la Fachenda y fragmentos de otras obras* (Don Catrín de la Fachenda and Fragments of Other Works) (1944). *El pensador mexicano* (The Mexican Thinker) (1812-1814). *Pensamientos extraordinarios* (Extraordinary Thoughts) (1812). *Alacena de frioleras* (Cupboard of No Importance) (1815-1816). *Caxoncito de la alacena* (Little Drawer of the Cupboard) (1815). *Las sombras de Heráclito y Demócrito* (Shadows of Heracles and Democrates) (1815). *El conductor eléctrico* (The Electric Conductor) (1820). *El amigo de la paz y la patria* (Friend of Peace and the Nation) (1822). *El payaso de los periódicos* (The Clown of the Newspapers) (1823). *Las conversaciones del payo y del sacristán* (Conversations of the Peasant and the Sacristan (1824). *El correo semanario de México* (The Weekly Correspondence of Mexico) (1826-1827).

BIBLIOGRAPHY: Ignacio M. Altamirano, *Revistas literarias de México* (México: F. Díaz de León y S. White, 1868), pp. 42-46. Mariano Azuela, *100 años de novela mexicana* (México: Botas, 1947), pp. 35-51. Carlos María de Bustamante, *Diario histórico de México* (Zacatecas: n.p., 1896), pp. 885 and 441; *Historia del emperador Agustín de Iturbide* (México: n.p., 1846), pp. 162, 192, 268. Miguel Capistrán, "Apuntaciones acerca de *Periquillo sarniento*," *Cuadernos de la hemeroteca nacional* 1 (México, 1966). María Teresa Dehesa y Gómez Farias, *Introducción a la obra dramática de José Joaquín Fernández de Lizardi*, thesis (México: UNAM, 1961). Sergio Fernández, "El mensaje del periquillo en el momento de la independencia," *Filosofía y Letras* 47-48 (México, 1952): 275-86. Luis González Obregón, "Don José Joaquín Fernández de Lizardi, apuntes biográficos," in *Liceo Mexicano* (México, 1892):7-12; *Los restos del pensador mexicano* (México: n. p., 1893). Carlos González Peña, "El pensador mexicano y su tiempo," *Conferencias del Ateneo de la Juventud* 5 (México: UNAM, 1962), pp. 69-81.   Lafaye Jacques, "El pensador mexicano de España," in *Vuelta* 107 (México, 1985): 14-17. Luis Leal, *Breve historia del cuento mexicano* (México: Eds. de Andrea, 1956), pp. 28-30. López y López, "Modismos y refranes del *Periquillo sarniento*," *Universidad de Mexico* 1, 6 (1931): 462-82. Lugares Ríos, "El sequincentenario del *Periquillo*" *Revista Mexicana de Cultura* 994 (1966): 7-26. Francisco Monterde, "Fernández de Lizardi, novelista," *Cultura Mexicana* (México: Ed. Intercontinental, 1946), pp. 119-27. Ernest Moore, "Una bibliografía descriptiva, *El periquillo sarniento*," *Revista de Literatura Mexicana* 1, 2 (México, 1940): 307-17. Margarita Palacios Sierra, *Estudios preliminares e índices del periodismo de José Joaquín Fernández de Lizardi* (México: UNAM, 1965), pp. 180-206. Sergio Pitol, "Sobre el *Periquillo sarniento*," *Revista de la UNAM* 421 (1986): 3-7. Paul Radin, *An Annotated Bibliography of the Poems and Pamphets of José Joaquín Fernández de Lizardi* (San Francisco: n.p., 1940). Joaquín Ramírez Cabanas, "El pensador mexicano, periodista," *UNAM* 2, 11 (México, 1931): 387-93. Nicolas Rangel, "El pensador mexicano. Nuevos documentos y noticias biográficas," *El Libro y el Pueblo* 4, 10-12 (México, 1925): 41-50. Alfonso Reyes, "El *Periquillo Sarniento* y la crítica mexicana," *Simpatías y diferencias*, 3rd series (Madrid, 1922). Clementina Rojas de Zúñiga, *Estudios mongráficos acerca de "La Quijotita y su prima,"* thesis (México:

UNAM, 1936). Emma Solís, *Lo picaresco en las novelas de Fernández de Lizardi*, thesis (México: UNAM, 1952). Francisco Sosa, *Biografías de mexicanos distinguidos* (México: Ofna. Tip. de la Sría. de Fomento, 1884), pp. 362-65. Jefferson Spell Real, "Mexican Society as Seen by Fernando de Lizardi," in *Hispania* 8, 3 (1925): 145-65; "The Genesis of the First Mexican Novel," in *Hispania* 14 (1931): 53-58. Luis G Urbina, "Estudio preliminar," in *Antología del Centenario*, pp. 128-45, 157-63; *La vida literaria en Mexico* (Madrid, 1917), pp. 310-99. Ubaldo Vargas Martínez, prologue to *Obras, II Teatro* (ed. cit.). Ralph E. Warner, *Historia de la novela mexicana en el siglo XIX* (México: Col. Clásicos y Modernos, 1953), no. 9, pp. 4-10. Agustin Yáñez, preliminary study to *El pensador mexicano* (México: UNAM, 1954), pp. 5-52.

ESTHER HERNANDEZ-PALACIOS

FERNANDEZ de San Salvador, Agustín Pomposo (1756-1842), public servant and political writer. The apparent descendant of the last king of Texcoco, Ixtlilxóchitl, and European nobility, Fernández de San Salvador staunchly opposed the movement for Mexico's independence. Born in Toluca on September 20, 1756, he was an eminent figure of the viceroyalty and occupied several of its most prestigious posts. During his career, he was the legal advisor of the Royal Audiencia and held the rectorship of the university three times. He was also instrumental in the establishment of a university in Mérida.

As the revolutionary movement gained momentum in Mexico, Fernández de San Salvador wrote a considerable number of politically oriented works in undistinguished prose, some of which appeared in the *Diario de México* (Mexican Daily) under the pseudonym "Mopso." His dedication to Spain's government was unflagging and he continued his support even when family members became totally involved in the military efforts for the cause of independence.

Fernández de San Salvador's poetry, written before the insurgence, is less notable than his prose. Many of his poems, such as *La America llorando por la temprana muerte de su amado, su padre, su bien y sus delicias el Excelentísimo señor don Bernardo de Gálvez conde de Gálvez* (America Grieving Over the Untimely Death of Her Beloved, Her Father, Her Good and Her Delight, the Excellent Gentleman Bernardo de Gálvez, Count of Gálvez), were composed to honor viceregal dignitaries.

WORKS: *La America llorando por la temprana muerte de su amado, su padre, su bien y sus delicias, el Exmo. Sr. don Bernardo de Gálvez, Conde de Gálvez* (America Grieving over the Untimely Death of Her Beloved, Her Father, Her Good and Her Delight, the Excellent Gentleman Bernardo de Gálvez, Count of Gálvez) (México: Imp. de Ontiveros, 1787). *Los dulcísimos amores, poemitas de Mariano de Jesús* (The Sweetest Loves, The Poems of Mariano de Jesús) (México: Imp. Ontiveros, 1802). *La America en el trono español, exclamación . . . que da alguna idea de lo que son los diputados de estos dominios en las Cortes* (America on the Spanish Throne, Exclamation . . . That Gives Some Idea of What the Deputies of These Dominions Are Like in the Courts) (México: Imp. de Ontiveros, 1810). *Memoria cristiano-política sobre lo mucho que la Nueva España debe temer de su desunión en partidos, y las grandes ventajas que puede esperar de su unión y confraternidad* (A Christian Political Memoir about the Great Extent to Which New Spain Should Fear Splintering into Factions, and the Great Advantages That One Can Expect from Unity and

Brotherhood) (México: Imp. de Ontiveros, 1810). *Carta de un padre a sus hijos* (Letter of a Father to His Chiidren) (México: Imp. de Valdés, 1810). *Las hazañas de Hidalgo, Quijote de nuevo cuño, facedor de entuertos* (The Deeds of Hidalgo, a New Type of Quixote, Doer of Wrongs) (México: Imp. de Valdés, 1810). *Convite a los verdaderos amantes de la religión católica y de la patria* (Invitation to the True Lovers of the Catholic Religion and of Our Country) (México: Imp. de Ontiveros, 1812). *Desengaños que a los insurgentes de Nueva España, seducidos por francmasones agentes de Napoleón, dirige la verdad de la religión católica y la experiencia* (Disillusionments by Which the Insurgents of New Spain, Seduced by the Freemasonry Agents of Napoleon, Learned the Truth about the Catholic Religion and Experience) (México: Imp. de Ontiveros, 1812). *Advertencia en favor de la sacratísima dignidad sacerdotal* (Admonition in Favor of the Most Sacred Priestly Dignity) (México: Imp. de Ontiveros, 1813). *El modelo de los cristianos presentado a los insurgentes de América* (The Christian Model Presented to the Insurgents of America) (México: Imp. de Ontiveros, 1814).

BIBLIOGRAPHY: Carlos González Peña, *History of Mexican Literature*, translated by Gusta Barfield Nance and Florene Johnson Dunstan (Dallas: Southern Methodist University Press, 1968), pp. 176-77. Pedro Henríquez Ureña, *Estudios mexicanos* (México: FCE, 1984), pp. 162-66.

JULIE GREER JOHNSON

FERNANDEZ MacGregor, Genaro (1883-1959), lawyer, educator, journalist, and novelist. Fernández MacGregor was born in Mexico City on May 4, 1883. He attended private schools and then studied law at the National School of Jurisprudence, where he obtained his degree in November of 1907. Soon after, he found his true calling in international law. He became director of international matters for the Department of Foreign Relations (State) and, later, its consultant. In that capacity, he represented Mexico at several international meetings. He was also attracted to teaching and thus taught Spanish language and literature at the National Preparatory School, and international law, public and private, at the university. He was one of the founders of the Mexican Academy of International Law and editor of its journal. He also belonged to the Mexican Society of Geography and Statistics and to the Academy of Jurisprudence and Legislation, and he was president of the National University of Mexico (UNAM). He contributed to several literary journals: *Revista Moderna, Savia Moderna, Vida Moderna,* and *Pegaso.* He wrote many articles on different topics for Mexico City's newspapers, especially for *El Universal.* He died in Mexico City, on December 22, 1959.

Fernández MacGregor published his *Novelas triviales* (Trivial Novels) in 1918; these were brief narrations of sharp analysis and juicy style. Best known among them is the story "Un mulus ex-machina," awarded the first prize in a contest organized by the Department of Fine Arts. During the same year, he published the translation of various short stories by Remy de Gourmont, with a foreword in *Cultura,* and he wrote some chronicles of customs of the United States. In 1919, also in *Cultura,* he published some translations of Mark Twain, with a study.

WORKS: *Gabriel D'Annunzio* (México: n.p., 1908). *Jorge Washington* (México: n.p., 1915). *Novelas triviales* (Trivial Novels) (México: Botas, 1918). *Remy de Gourmont,* translation and foreword by Genaro Fernández MacGregor, *Cultura* 6, 1 (México, 1918). *Mark Twain*, translated and foreword by Genaro Fernández MacGregor, *Cultura* 10, 3 (México, 1919). *Artículos publicados en la Revista Mexicana de Derecho Internacional referentes a la investigación hecha por el subcomité senatorial de los Estados Unidos acerca de los daños y perjuicios sufridos por ciudadanos norteamericanos durante la Revolución Mexicana y conclusiones de dicha investigación* (Articles Published in the Mexican Journal of International Law in Reference to the Investigation Carried Out by the Subcommittee of the U.S. Senate Concerning Damages Suffered by North American Citizens during the Mexican Revolution and Conclusions of Such an Investigation), special edition directed by Genaro Fernández MacGregor (México: Ant. Imp. de Murguía, 1921). *D. H. Lawrence* (México: n.p., 1925). *Apunte crítico sobre el arte contemporáneo* (Critical Notes on Contemporary Art) [address] (México: Edit. Cultura, 1931); and in *Memorias de la Academia Mexicana* 10 (1954): 363-79. *La santificación de Sor Juana Inés de la Cruz* (The Sanctification of Sor Juana Inés) (México: Cultura, 1932). *Carátulas* (Masks) (México: Botas, 1935). "Salvador Díaz Mirón," in *Conferencias del Palacio de Bellas Artes* (México: Talleres gráficos de la nación, 1935). José María Luis Mora, *El doctor Mora redivivo* (Dr. Mora Remembered), selection and critical study by Genaro Fernández MacGregor (México: Botas, 1938). *Genaro Estrada* (México: Edit. Fabula, 1938). *Mies tardía* (México: Cultura, 1939). *La inteligencia de México está con México* (Mexico's Intelligentsia Is with Mexico), Cuatro discursos de José Rubén Romero, Enrique González Martínez, Genaro Fernández MacGregor and Manuel Avila Camacho (Four speeches by . . .) (México: Sría. de Gobernación, 1942). *Vasconcelos*, selection and foreword by Genaro Fernández MacGregor. (México: SEP, 1942). *Notas de un viaje extemporáneo* (Notes from an Extemporaneous Trip) (México: Stylo, 1952). *El Istmo de Tehuantepec y los Estados Unidos* (The Isthmus of Tehuantepec and the United States) (México: Editorial "Elede," 1954). "La paz y la guerra según Cervantes," *Memorias de la Academia Mexicana* 12 (1955): 135-43. *En la era de la mala vecindad* (In the Era of Bad Relations [with the United States]) (México: Botas, 1960), posthumous. *El río de mi sangre: memorias* (The Course of My Life: Memoirs) (México: FCE, 1969), posthumous.

BIBLIOGRAPHY: Ermilo Abréu Gómez, *Sala de retratos* (México: Leyenda, 1946), pp. 92-93. Emmanuel Carballo, *19 protagonistas de la literatura mexicana del siglo XX* (México: Empresas Editoriales, 1965), pp. 51-60. Alberto María Carreño, *Memorias de la Academia Mexicana* 7 (1945): 183-84; 8 (1946): 116-17; "Genaro Fernández Mac Gregor," *Memorias de la Academia* 17 (1960): 176-77. Jorge Cuesta, "La enseñanza de Ulises," review of *Carátulas*, in *Poemas y ensayos*, vol. 3, pp. 268-81. Juan B. Iguiñiz, *Bibliografía de novelistas mexicanos* (México: Imp. Sría. Relaciones Exteriores, 1926), pp. 127-30. Rafael López, "Mística o mundana?," *El Libro y el Pueblo* 10, 6 (Aug. 1932): 49-50. José Luis Martínez, *El ensayo mexicano moderno*, vol. 1 (México: FCE, 1958), p. 180. Porfirio Martínez Peñalosa, "¿Un enigma literario? Fernández Mac Gregor," in *Revista Mexicana de Cultura* 916 (Oct. 18, 1964): 1, 4; 918 (Nov. 1, 1964): 5. Alejandro Quijano, Address, *Memorias de la Academia Mexicana* 10 (1954): 380-85. José Rojas Garcidueñas, *Genaro Fernández Mac Gregor, escritor e internacionalista* (Genaro Fernández Mac Gregor, Writer and Internationalist), Induction Address, Academy of the Spanish Language, read on June 22, 1962. Carlos J. Sierra, "Periodistas mexicanos del siglo XX, Bibliohemerografía, Fuentes para el estudio del pensamiento contemporaneo (Genaro Fernández Mac Gregor)" in *Boletín*

Bibliográfico de la Secretaría de Hacienda y Crédito Público 10, 2nd period, suppl. to no. 295 (May 15, 1964): 2-12.

HERLINDA HERNANDEZ

FERRETIS, Jorge (1902-1962), short story writer, novelist, journalist, and politician. Jorge Ferretis was born in Río Verde, San Luis Potosí. He served as congressman for his home state (1952-1957). Ferretis directed two newspapers in San Luis Potosi, *La Voz* and *El Potosí*. He was a socialist who believed that art had to serve as an instrument for bettering the social conditions of humankind. He is known as a novelist of the Mexican Revolution.

WORKS: Novels: *Tierra caliente* (The Fiery Land) (Madrid: Espasa Calpe, 1935). *El sur quema* (The South Burns) (México: Botas, 1937). *Cuando engorda el Quijote* (When the Quijote Gets Fat) (México: México Nuevo, 1937). *San automóvil* (Saint Automobile) (México: Botas, 1938). Short Stories: *Hombres en tempestad* (Men in the Storm) (México: Cima, 1941). *El coronel que asesinó a un palomo y otros cuentos* (The Coronel Who Assassinated a Dove and Other Stories) (México: FCE, 1952). *Libertad obligatoria* (Mandatory Freedom), introduction by Mauricio Magdaleno (México: FCE, 1967), includes previously unpublished work. Essays: *¿Necesitamos inmigración?* (Do We Need Immigration?) (México: El Universal, 1934).

BIBLIOGRAPHY: Paul Howard Holden, "The Creative Writings of Jorge Ferretis: Ideology and Style," *DAI* 27 (1966): 207A-208A, University of Southern California. Enrique Pupo-Walker, "La transposición de valores pictóricos en la narrativa de Ferretis y Rulfo," *Nueva Narrativa Hispanoamericana* (1971): 95-103. R. Salazar Mallín, "El miedo al hombre interior en la novela mexicana," *Letras de México* 18 (1937): 6.

MIRTA A. GONZALEZ

FILM AND LITERATURE. The Mexican film industry has been widely acknowledged as one of the oldest and most prolific in Latin America. From its beginnings in the 1890s to the present day the cinema has played a significant role in shaping Mexican cultural and societal attitudes. Early films were rather limited in scope, often dealing with current events and episodes in the nation's history. Then in the 1930s the silent film gave way to the talking picture, and filmmakers, under the influence of Hollywood, began emphasizing fiction rather than reality. As a consequence of these innovations, the industry experienced a period of rapid growth. Mexican studios, during their heyday in the 1940s, 1950s, and 1960s, produced an average of 100 films per year. Large-scale commercial operations have continued to develop, and Mexico today remains one of the leading film-producing countries in the world.

In Latin America the advent and diffusion of motion pictures coincided with the maturity of the theater. Movies, however, proved to be unfair competition since they were a more popular art form in the sense of being more accessible to the masses. Along with the growing popularity of the cinema, an inevitable bond was emerging between film and literature. Filmmakers found two literary genres, the novel and the drama, to be especially well suited for adaptation to the big screen.

In Mexico motion pictures based on literary works, particularly novels, have been one of the mainstays of the industry. The 1931 remake of the 1918 silent film *Santa*, derived from the Federico Gamboa novel, was a pivotal production in the fledgling mode known as the "talkie." *Santa* injected a new vigor into the cinematic enterprise and paved the way for a host of later adaptations--*Los de abajo* (1939), *La vida inútil de Pito Pérez* (1943), *Los bandidos de Río Frío* (1954), *Pedro Páramo* (1966), and *El apando* (1975) being only a few of the many Mexican novels which have made the transition from the printed page to the screen. A more recent example is *Old Gringo* (1989), adapted from the 1985 Carlos Fuentes novel. This film, which has received considerable attention in the United States, offers a speculative version of what happened to the American writer Ambrose Bierce, who disappeared into revolutionary Mexico in 1913. *Old Gringo* is a major Hollywood production, the result of a pooling of resources by the two countries.

Despite a steady stream of joint projects and other forms of collaboration, Mexican filmmakers, with the sole exception of Luis Buñuel, have failed to achieve name recognition in the United States. Emilio "El Indio" Fernández, who is considered one of Mexico's greatest directors, is a prime example. Fernández, best known for his sympathetic portrayal of the country's indigenous populations, fostered a "Mexican school" of filmmaking in the 1940s and 1950s, a nationalistic cinema which mirrored a phenomenon that was already occurring in literature, painting, and other forms of artistic expression. Two of his early films, *Flor silvestre* and *María Candelaria*, both from 1943, are today considered classics. These pictures, which showcased the talents of Dolores del Río and Pedro Armendáriz, were made from adaptations written by Fernández and novelist Mauricio Magdaleno. Fernández teamed with Magdaleno on various other film projects, and the latter also worked with Buñuel, preparing the screenplay adaptation for *Gran Casino*.

Internationally acclaimed Spanish-born filmmaker Luis Buñuel (b. 1900-d. Mexico City, 1983) spent his most active years in Mexico, where he directed a series of lesser-known films in addition to several masterpieces. Many of his Mexican productions were, admittedly, commercial ventures aimed at a wide audience. It is important to note, however, that it was the financial success of *El gran calavera* (The Great Madcap, 1949) which enabled him to make one of his greatest films, the award-winning *Los olvidados* (The Young and the Damned, 1950). Each of Buñuel's "Mexican" films, to one degree or another, bears the mark of his unique vision, a style characterized by surrealistic imagery and a relentless satirical assault on the authority of church, state, and bourgeois values and institutions, all of which he finds morally bankrupt.

Buñuel directed more than thirty motion pictures during his illustrious career. More than half of these were made during his Mexican period, which one may date from 1947, the year of *Gran Casino*, to 1965, when the short feature *Simón del desierto* (Simon of the Desert) was released. Several of these films were adapted from literary works, such as *Ensayo de un crimen* (The Criminal Life of Archibaldo de la Cruz, 1955), which was based on a Rodolfo Usigli story. Three of these were masterpieces derived from novels penned by non-Mexican authors, namely:

Abismos de pasión (1953), a reworking of Emily Brontë's *Wuthering Heights*; *The Adventures of Robinson Crusoe* (1954), made in English and adapted from the Daniel Defoe classic (this was Buñuel's first color feature and his first Mexican film to be commercially successful on an international scale); and *Nazarín* (1958), taken from the Benito Pérez Galdós novel.

In addition to these Buñuel films, many other Mexican pictures have taken their inspiration from non-Mexican literary works. One of the most famous of these is *Doña Bárbara* (1943), adapted from the novel by Rómulo Gallegos, with María Félix in the title role. Others that deserve mention are the following: *La barraca* (1944), based on the homonymous novel by Vicente Blasco Ibáñez; *Fando y Lis*, a 1967 adaptation of the Fernando Arrabal play; and *En este pueblo no hay ladrones*, a 1965 film version of the Gabriel García Márquez short story. In 1983 Brazilian filmmaker Ruy Guerra directed *Eréndira*, a Mexican production of another García Márquez story.

Collaborative efforts such as *Eréndira* and *Old Gringo* are not just recent phenomena. One of Emilio Fernández's best-known films, *La perla* (The Pearl, 1945), was based on the John Steinbeck novel. American novelist Steinbeck, it should be noted, was involved in two important cinematic endeavors with Mexican connections-- he wrote the story for *The Forgotten Village* (1944), a documentary set in a remote Mexican Indian village, and he authored the screenplay for *¡Viva Zapata!* (1952), with Marlon Brando as the charismatic revolutionary figure. Mexican locales have provided fertile soil for numerous American productions over the years, such as *¡Viva Zapata!* and the film versions of B. Traven's *Treasure of the Sierra Madre* (1948) and the Malcolm Lowry novel *Under the Volcano* (1984), to name just a few examples.

For some critics and directors picturesque locations were insignificant when compared with other more weighty considerations. In Latin America the decade of the sixties witnessed the arrival of a Marxist cinema, one which attacked neocolonialism, cultural imperialism, and a variety of social and political problems. The first significant manifestation of this approach came in the late fifties in Brazil with the appearance of Cinema Novo and social realism. In Mexico, this new movement found expression in the Nuevo Cine group of young leftist writers and filmmakers. In the pages of their magazine of the same name (published 1961-62), they distanced themselves from the producers of "establishment" films and called for a new focus and direction in Mexican cinema. Among their number was film critic Carlos Monsiváis, who served on the editorial board of Nuevo Cine.

In addition to Monsiváis, Magdaleno, and Fuentes, other major literary figures have also maintained close ties to the cinema. Novelist José *Revueltas, for example, worked on the screenplay for the Buñuel film *La ilusión viaja en tranvía* (Illusion Travels by Streetcar, 1953), and Juan *Rulfo, one of the most renowned fiction writers of the twentieth century, was involved to a greater or lesser degree in the production of no less than eleven motion pictures. His participation took various forms--he wrote adaptations and screenplays, saw his own works adapted, and even made a brief screen appearance. In addition, his screenplay for the 1964 film *El gallo de oro* has been published in book form.

Despite the enormous appeal of widely distributed forms of printed material such as comics and magazines, the cinema continues to be the dominant mass entertainment medium in the Hispanic world. Films reflect and, at the same time, help to shape customs and values. Movies have been chiefly responsible for the diffusion of Mexican culture (most noticeably in the areas of language, music, clothing styles, and behavior) among culturally diverse Spanish-speaking peoples. As a consequence of its far-reaching influence on popular culture, Mexican cinema has, in recent decades, become a field worthy of serious academic research. Film studies have intellectual appeal not only to literary scholars concerned with narrative genres and techniques but also to sociologists, anthropologists, and others interested in the interaction of popular culture with national traditions and social mores.

BIBLIOGRAPHY: Virginia Higginbotham, *Luis Buñuel* (Boston: Twayne Publishers, 1979). Carl J. Mora, Mexican Cinema: *Reflections of a Society, 1896-1980* (Berkeley: University of California Press, 1982). Joan Mellen, ed., *The World of Luis Buñuel: Essays in Criticism* (New York: Oxford University Press, 1978). Beatriz Reyes Nevares, *The Mexican Cinema: Interviews with Thirteen Directors* (Albuquerque: University of New Mexico Press, 1976).

MELVIN S. ARRINGTON, JR.

FINISTERRE. See CAMPOS Ramirez, Alejandro.

FLORES, Manuel M. (1840-1885). Manuel Flores was born in San Andrés Chalcicomula in the state of Puebla. He studied in both the Colegio de Minería and the Colegio de San Juan de Letrán in the capital. At the outbreak of the civil war in 1857, Flores took part in the activities which Ignacio *Altamirano organized. His adherence to liberal ideals led to jail and then exile during the period of French intervention. After the republican victory, however, Flores served various times as deputy to the Congress of the Union. He also taught literature and history in the capital. Flores' bohemian lifestyle conferred poverty on him in spite of the general popularity of his poetry. Difficult circumstances, aggravated by illness and blindness, apprently precluded the union of Flores with his love of many years, Rosario de la Peña, muse of many romantic writers. Flores died, alone and blind, in Mexico City in 1885.

Flores' poetry has been judged to be the greatest expression of Mexican romanticism. His themes are nature, love as the fountain of life and justification of man on earth, and earthly passion as the highest endeavor. Flores' erotic temperament and his spiritual exaltation provided an undercurrent of tension in his works. His imitations and translations of Hugo, Goethe, Schiller and others in the third part of *Pasionarias* (Passion Flowers) attest to his admiration of the giants of the romantic period and to his skill in rendering their works into Spanish.

WORKS: *Pasionarias* (Passion Flowers) (Puebla de Zaragoza: Tip. del Hospital General del Estado, 1874). *Páginas locas* (Mad Pages) (Puebla: n.p., 1878). *Poesías inéditas* (México: Bouret, 1910). *Rosas caídas* (Fallen Roses) (México: n.p., 1953).

BIBLIOGRAPHY: Ignacio Altamirano, *La literatura nacional* (México: Porrúa, 1949), vol. 3, pp. 67-92. Carlos González Peña, *History of Mexican Literature*, translated by Gusta Barfield Nance and Florene Johnson Dunstan (Dallas: Southern Methodist University Press, 1968), pp. 211, 279-81. Heriberto García Rivas, *Historia de la literatura mexicana* (México: Textos Universitarios, S.A., 1972), vol. 2, pp. 89, 175.

Joaquín Márquez Montiel, *Hombres célebres de Puebla* (México: Edit. Jus., 1952), vol. 1, pp. 8-14. José Emilio Pacheco, *La poesía mexicana del siglo XIX* (México: Empresas Editoriales, 1965), pp. 275-93.

FILIPPA B. YIN

FRIAS Y SOTO, Hilarión (1831-1905), costumbristic sketch writer, novelist, journalist. Frías y Soto was born in Queretaro, but spent most of his adult life in and around Mexico City, where he studied and later practiced medicine. He played an active role in politics, serving as a congressman and writing political essays that were published in local newspapers. His most lengthy treatise, *Juárez glorificado o la intervención y el imperio ante la verdad histórica* (Juárez Glorified or Intervention and Empire Confronted by Historical Truth), is a defense of the actions of Juárez and the Mexican people in general who, rather than allow foreign powers to rule their country, resorted to civil war. He was editor of the small but extremely popular newspaper *La orquesta* (The Orchestra), which was founded in 1868. This newspaper served as a vehicle for the publication of many of his own costumbristic sketches, known collectively by the title *Album fotográfico* (Photographic Album), and for his two brief, satirical novels, *Volcán* (Vulcano) and *El hijo del estado* (The Son of the State). Vulcano is considered to be the first Mexican realist novel. Frías y Soto's costumbristic sketches portray easily recognizable types of the age; bandits, nuns, priests, widows, traveling salesmen, beggars, and the like. Although they lack detail, they are clearly drawn and accurate representations. Ignacio *Altamirano admired his elegant style, his colorful, charming language, and his bright imagination, stating that as a costumbristic sketch writer, Frías y Soto had few rivals.

WORKS: *Album fotográfico* (Photographic Album) (México: n.p., 1854). *El hijo del estado* (Son of the State) (México: La Orquesta, 1868). *Juárez glorificado o la intervención y el imperio ante la verdad histórica* (Juarez Glorified or Intervention and Empire Confronted by Historical Truth) (México: Imp. Central, 1905). *Volcán* (Vulcano) (México: La Orquesta, 1868).

BIBLIOGRAPHY: Ignacio Manuel Altamirano, *La literatura nacional* (México: Porrúa, 1949), vol. 1, pp. 77-79. Luis González Obregón, *Breve noticia de los novelistas mexicanos del siglo XIX* (México: n.p., 1889), pp. 48-49. Luis Leal, *Breve historia del cuento mexicano* (México: Eds. de Andrea, 1956), pp. 47-48. Malcolm McLean, *El contenido literario del "El siglo XIX"* (Washington, D.C., n.p., 1940), pp. 40-42 and 60. Jefferson R. Spell, "The Costumbrista Movement in Mexico," *PMLA* 50 (1935): p. 311.

CYNTHIA K. DUNCAN

FUENTE, Carmen de la (1923-). Born in Mexico City, Carmen de la Fuente studied to be a literature and linguistics teacher. In addition, she became the chief of education and a professor of Mexican literature at the Instituto Politécnico Nacional. She has contributed poems to several literary supplements in such papers as *El Nacional*, *Vértice* (of which she was the founder), and *Zarza*.

Her poetry represents the fruition of vital experience and her favorite theme is love: love of parents, children, mankind, and life. Although she has not written or published extensively, her work is considered to be of high quality.

WORKS: Poetry: *Anhelos interiores* (Internal Longings) (México: Ed. Vértice, 1944). *De la llama sedienta* (Of the Thirsty Flame) (México: Ed. Stylo, 1952). *Lázaro Cárdenas* (México: n.p., 1953). *Canto al hombre* (Song to Man) (México: S.A.L.M., 1953). *Las ánforas de abril* (The Amphoras of April) (México: Eds. de la Revista Zarza, 1963). *Entre combate y tregua* (Between Battle and Truce) (México: Cuadernos Zarza, 1965).

BIBLIOGRAPHY: Jesús Arellano, "Las ventas de don Quijote," in *Nivel* 32 (Aug. 25, 1965): 5. Ismael Diego Pérez, "Carmen de la Fuente o la poesía," in *Revista de la Semana* (Feb. 9, 1964): 4. Juan Rejano, Review of *Las ánforas de abril*, in *Revista Mexicana de Cultura* 875 (Jan. 5, 1964): 6. Mauricio de la Selva, Review of *Las ánforas de abril* in *Diorama de la Cultura* (Aug. 4, 1963): 4.

JEANNE C. WALLACE

FUENTES, Carlos (1928-). One of the most important writers in Mexican history, Carlos Fuentes was born in Panama City on November 11, 1928, where his father worked for the Mexican government. Biographer F. Javier Ordiz Vázquez highlights many of the interesting aspects of his life, particularly of his rather unusual childhood. Mexico itself was only a remote reality for the young Fuentes, who spent most of his youth in the United States, being educated in Washington D.C., where his father worked. Additional moves to Buenos Aires, Santiago (Chile), and finally to Mexico City (in 1944) provided him with broad educational experiences, although his cosmopolitan liberal background was temporarily squashed in the Mexican school. Influenced by his friend and mentor Alfonso Reyes, whom he had initially met in Buenos Aires, he reluctantly went to law school at the Universidad Nacional de México. Like his father, Fuentes served for some time as secretary to the Mexican delegate of the International Law Commission of the United Nations in Geneva (1950). During his year in Geneva, he wrote his doctoral dissertation, returning to Mexico in 1951. He also was a press secretary of the U.N. Information Center.

Fuentes was totally immersed in his literary career by 1955. Along with Emmanuel Carballo, he founded and edited the *Revista Mexicana de Literatura* in 1956. From 1956 until 1959, Fuentes was director of international cultural relations for Mexico's Ministry of Foreign Affairs. In the early 1960s, Fuentes embraced the cause of the Cuban Revolution, traveling around Latin American, promulgating its ideals. As a consequence of his leftist, militant position, he fell into disfavor with the U.S. government, which denied him entry for six years. In the mid-sixties he went to live in France, and from 1975 to 1977 he also served as México's ambassador there, relinquishing the position because of dissatisfaction with the Mexican government. He was active in the literary vanguard movement, and he had other cultural and political involvements. Following his divorce from his first wife, actress Rita Macedo, Fuentes married Silvia Lemus, a journalist, in 1975. For many years, both in Mexico and France, Fuentes has written and published stories, novels, plays and essays that have attracted international attention. Toward the end of the 1970s, Fuentes began to feel disenchanted with the Cuban regime when his friend, the Cuban poet Padilla, was jailed. Along with a number of other writers and intellectuals, Fuentes signed a letter of protest. In turn, Fuentes was strongly criticized by Mario Benedetti, who accused him of living a very pleasant life in exile, in comparison to what other writers, who chose to stay in their native America, had to endure. Nonetheless, throughout the 1980s, Fuentes continued to live in various European nations as well as in the United States. He has been a visiting professor in a number of important educational institutions, bringing to them his critical and literary expertise. Along with several other prominent writers, such as Octavio *Paz, he has truly brought about a renovation in contemporary Latin American letters.

Fuentes was greatly influenced not only by Alfonso Reyes but by Salvador *Novo in Mexico and Honoré de Balzac in France. Like Charles Dickens and Benito Pérez Galdós, Fuentes spent many days and hours frequenting different social environments that he later used in his narratives. F. Javier Ordiz Vázquez affirms that Fuentes' cosmopolitan background, a primary factor in his career, and his personal identification with the themes and ideas of Alfonso Reyes have been instrumental in his intepretation of the Mexican as a specific manifestation of the essential universality of humankind. A friend of José Donoso, Fuentes has also sustained long-term friendships with Octavio Paz and Luis Buñuel, both of whom influenced his literary endeavors.

Fuentes has been the recipient of a number of important literary prizes throughout his career. His novel *Cambio de piel* (A Change of Skin) won the Biblioteca Breve prize in Barcelona upon its publication in 1967. In 1975 Fuentes received the Javier Villaurrutia prize in Mexico City and in 1977 the Rómulo Gallegos prize in Venezuela for his novel *Terra nostra*. In 1977, he also received the Premio de los Embajadores de París. In 1979 he won the Premio Alfonso Reyes in Mexico. In 1984 he was awarded the National Prize for Literature in Mexico. He also received the prestigious Premio de Literatura en Lengua Castellana "Miguel de Cervantes" in 1987.

Several of his novels, such as *Cambio de piel* (A Change of Skin), *La muerte de Artemio Cruz* (The Death of Artemio Cruz), *El aire más transparente* (Where the Air Is Clear), *Terra Nostra*, and *Gringo viejo* (The Old Gringo) are landmarks of Latin American fiction. *Gringo viejo* has been a best-seller in the United States and was made into a highly acclaimed movie. An author with a global vision and a humanist with a cosmopolitan orientation, Fuentes creates narratives of enduring recognition. He also wrote an important book of literary criticism, *La nueva novela hispanoamericana* (The New Latin American Novel), in which he highlights a number of internationally acclaimed Latin American authors who have spawned a universal renaissance in fiction and have been instrumental in revitalizing Latin American identity. A narrative innovator himself, Fuentes has truly enriched world literature through masterful characterization and linguistic ingenuity, plus adroit handling of such elements as time, space, and point of view. He fuses the real world of social, political, and economic problems with the world of myth and legend, creating panoramic narratives that are both universal and Mexican.

Los días enmascarados (The Masked Days) is Fuentes' first major work. It contains three short stories that form the antecedents for *El aire más transparente*. In three of these stories, Fuentes creates gods who portray both negative and positive forces and who demand an accounting of Mexico's upper classes and a return to moral responsibility.

Despite living many years of his life abroad, Fuentes has long been interested in the theme of Mexican national identity. This quest for origins is a basic theme in *La región más transparente*, a kaleidoscopic narrative of Mexico that fuses ancient and contemporary historical periods. The novel, embracing all social classes and most languages spoken in Mexico, satirizes and scorns those upper-class and socially aspiring groups who have hypocritically betrayed themselves, their countrymen, and their nation especially through unmitigated desire for power and money.

La muerte de Artemio Cruz is another of his most important works. It deals with the failure of post-revolutionary Mexico to implement the goals of the Revolution, the betrayal of its ideals, and the way that one group of power-hungry exploiters is replaced by another. Artemio Cruz, a composite figure, reveals his life through his thoughts during the last twelve hours before his death.

Todos los gatos son pardos (All Cats Are Brown) is one of Fuentes' several plays. An epic drama about the conquest of Mexico, Quetzalcóatl is evoked as the god of life, love, and justice. Alluding to the Tlatelolco massacre in 1968, Fuentes depicts a nation plagued by bloodshed and violence, a nation awaiting its redeemer.

Carlos Fuentes has worked to capture the essence of Mexico in the modern world. His writing reveals influences from different literary schools, ranging from the traditional to the surrealist. His narrative is, in general, highly complex, integrating and balancing various layers of literary elements.

WORKS: *Los días enmascarados* (The Masked Days) (México: Los Presentes, 1954); 2nd ed. (México: Novaro, 1966). *La región más transparente* (Where the Air Is Clear) (México: FCE, 1958). *Las buenas conciencias* (The Good Conscience) (México: FCE, 1959). Carlos Fuentes et al., "Izquierda, subdesarrollo y guerra fría: Un coloquio sobre cuestiones fundamentales," in *Cuadernos Americanos* 19 (May-June 1960): 53-69; *Aura* (México: Era, 1962). *La muerte de Artemio Cruz* (México: FCE, 1962). *Cantar de ciegos* (Song of the Blind) (México: Joaquín Mortiz, 1964). *The Death of Artemio Cruz*, translated by Sam Hileman (New York: Farrar, Straus, 1964). Autobiographical sketch, in *Los narradores ante el público*, 1st series (México: Joaquín Mortiz, 1966), pp. 137-55; *Cambio de piel* (A Change of Skin) (México: Joaquín Mortiz, 1967). *Zona sagrada* (Sacred Zone) (México: Siglo XXI Editores, 1967). *A Change of Skin*, translated by Sam Hileman (New York: Farrar, Straus and Giroux, 1968). *París: La revolución de Mayo* (Paris: The Revolution of May), essay (México: ERA, 1968). *Cumpleaños* (Birthday) (México: Joaquín Mortiz, 1969). *El mundo de José Luis Cuevas* (The World of José Luis Cuevas) (México: Galería de Arte Misrachi, 1969). *La nueva novela hispanoamericana* (The New Hispanic-American Novel) (México: Joaquín Mortiz, 1969). *El tuerto es rey* (The One-Eyed Man Is King), theater (México: Joaquín Mortiz, 1970). *Todos los gatos son pardos* (All the Cats Are Brown), theater (México: Siglo XXI, 1970). *Casa con dos puertas* (House with Two Doors), essay (México: Joaquín Mortiz, 1971). *Los reinos imaginarios. Teatro hispano-mexicano* (The Imaginary Kingdoms. Hispanic-Mexican Theater), contains *Todos los gatos son pardos* (All the Cats Are Brown) and *El tuerto es rey* (The One-Eyed Man Is King) (Barcelona: Barral, 1971). *Los reinos originarios* (The Native Kingdoms), theater (Barcelona: Barral, 1971). *Tiempo mexicano* (Mexican Time), essay (México: Joaquín Mortiz, 1971). *Obras completas* (Complete Works), vol. 1 (México: Aguilar, 1974). *Cervantes o la crítica de la lectura* (Cervantes or Criticism of Reading), essay (México: Joaquín Mortiz, 1976). *Terra Nostra*, translated by Margaret S. Peden (New York: Farrar, Straus, and Giroux, 1976). *La cabeza de la hidra* (The Head of the

Hydra) (México: Joaquín Mortiz, 1978); (Barcelona: Libr. Editorial Argos, 1978). *Terra Nostra* (Our Land) (México: Joaquín Mortiz, 1978). *Una familia lejana* (A Far-Away Family) (México: ERA, 1980). *Agua quemada* (Burned Water), stories (México: FCE, 1981). *Orquídeas a la luz de la luna* (Orchids by the Light of the Moon), theater (Barcelona: Barral, 1982). "On Reading and Writing Myself: How I Wrote *Aura*," in *World Literature Today* 57, 4 (Autumn 1983): 531-39. *Gringo viejo* (Old Gringo) (México: FCE, 1985).

BIBLIOGRAPHY: Bertie Acker, *El cuento mexicano contemporáneo. Rulfo, Arreola y Fuentes* (Madrid: Playor, 1984). Jaime Alazraki, "*Terra Nostra*: Reencuentro con la historia," in *Texto Crítico* 11, 33 (Sept.-Dec. 1985): 32-45. Andrés Amorós, "Carlos Fuentes," in his *Introducción a la novela hispanoamericana actual*, 2nd ed. (Salamanca: Anaya, 1973), pp. 141-54; "Análisis de la novela *Cumpleaños*," in *Vida Literaria* 2 (1970): 4-16. José Anadón, "Entrevista a Carlos Fuentes (1980)," in *Revista Iberoamericana* 49, 123-24 (April-Sept. 1983): 621-30. Andrés O. Avellaneda, "Mito y negación de la historia en *Zona sagrada* de Carlos Fuentes," in *Cuadernos Americanos* 175 (1971): 239-48. David Bary, "Poesía y narración en cuatro novelas mexicanas," in *Cuadernos Americanos* 234, 1 (1981): 198-210. Emilio Bejel and Elizabethann Beaudin, "*Aura* de Fuentes: la liberación de los espacios simultáneos," in *Hispanic Review* 36 (1978): 465-73. José María Bernáldez, "La reconstrucción de México [*Terra nostra*]," in *Cuadernos Hispanoamericanos*, 314-15 (1976): 656-60. Rei Berroa, "La crítica de Fuentes como lectura conflictiva: De Fuentes, a España, a Cervantes," in *Texto Crítico* 13, 36-37 (1987): 44-53. Carlos Blanco Aguinaga, "Sobre la idea de la novela en Carlos Fuentes," in his *De mitólogos y novelistas* (Madrid: Turner, 1975), pp. 73-108. Carole C. Bland, "Carlos Fuentes' *Cambio de piel*: The Quest for Rebirth," in *Journal of Spanish Studies* 4, 11 (Fall 1976): 77-88. Steven Boldy, "*Cambio de piel*: Literature and Evil," in *Bulletin of Hispanic Studies* 66 (Jan. 1989): 55-72; "Fathers and Sons in Fuentes' *La muerte de Artemio Cruz*," in *Bulletin of Hispanic Studies* 6, 1 (Jan. 1984): 31-40. Becky Boling, "Parricide and Revolution: Fuentes's *El día de las madres* and *Gringo viejo*," in *Hispanófila* 32 (Jan. 1989): 73-81. Robert Brody and Charles Rossman, eds., *Carlos Fuentes: A Critical View* (Austin: University of Texas Press, 1982). Gary L. Brower, "Fuentes de Fuentes: Paz y las raíces de *Todos los gatos son pardos*," in *Latin American Theatre Review* 5, 1 (1971): 59-68. John S. Brushwood, "Sobre el referente y la transformación narrativa en la novelas de Carlos Fuentes y Gustavo Sainz," in *Revista Iberoamericana* 116-17 (July-Dec. 1981): 49-54. Emmanuel Carballo, "Carlos Fuentes," in *Diecinueve protagonistas de la literatura mexicana del siglo XX* (México: Empresas Editoriales, 1965), pp. 427-48. Alina Camacho-Gingerich, "La historia como ruptura trágica y fusión erótica en *Una familia lejana* de Carlos Fuentes," in *Inti* 28 (Fall 1988): 59-66. V. Emilio Castaneda, "*The Death of Artemio Cruz*: The False Gods and the Death of Mexico," in *The Centennial Review* 30, 2 (Spring 1986): 139-47. Debra A. Castillo, "Travails with Time: An Interview with Carlos Fuentes," in *Review of Contemporary Fiction* 8, 2 (Summer 1988): 153-65. Debra A. Castillo and Sandra L. Dunn, "Carlos Fuentes," in *Review of Contemporary Fiction* 8, 2 (Summer 1988): 147-291. Raúl Chávarri, "Notas para el descubrimiento de una novela [*Las buenas conciencias*]," in *Cuadernos Hispanoamericanos* 180 (1964): 526-31. Joseph Chrzanowski, "Consideraciones temáticas-estéticas en torno a *Todos los gatos son pardos*," in *Latin American Theatre Review* 9, 1 (1975): 11-17; "The Double in 'Las dos Elenas' by Carlos Fuentes," in *Romance Notes* 18 (1977): 127-39; "The Artistic Depiction of Fantasy-Reality in the

Uncollected Short Stories (1949-1957) of Carlos Fuentes," in *Journal of Spanish Studies: Twentieth Century* 1 (1973): 127-39; "The Artistic Depiction of the Element of Fantasy-Reality in *Aura* (1962) by Carlos Fuentes," in *Kentucky Romance Quarterly* 24 (1977): 47-54; "Patricide and the Double in Carlos Fuentes's *Gringo viejo*," in *International Fiction Review* 16, 1 (Winter 1989): 11-16. Antonio J. Ciccone, "The Supernatural Persistence of the Past in *Los días enmascarados* by Carlos Fuentes," in *Latin American Literary Review* 3, 6 (1975): 37-58. Marcelo Coddou, "Terra Nostra o la crítica de los cielos. Entrevista a Carlos Fuentes," in *American Hispanist* 3, 24 (1978): 8-10. Rafael Cordero Anaya, "La destrucción trinitaria," in *Cuadernos Hispanoamericanos* 253-54 (1971): 319-23. Will H. Corral, "Gringo viejo/ruso joven o la recuperación dialógica en Fuentes," in *Cuadernos Americanos* 1, 6 (1987): 121-37; "Las entrevistas de Carlos Fuentes y las implicaciones críticas de lo dicho," in *Texto Crítico* 10, 28 (Jan.-April 1984); 104-13. Luis F. Costa, "Patterns of Discovery and Conquest in Carlos Fuentes' *Terra Nostra*," in *Exploration* 9 (Dec. 1981): 23-41. Ruth Katz Crispin, "The Artistic Unity of *La región más transparente*," in *Kentucky Romance Quarterly* 16 (1959): 277-87. John T. Cull, "On Reading Fuentes: Plant Lore, Sex, and Death in *Aura*," in *Chasqui* 18, 2 (Nov. 1989): 18-25. Frank Dauster, "La transposición de la realidad en las obras cortas de Carlos Fuentes," in *Kentucky Romance Quarterly* 19 (1972): 301-15. Guy Davenport, "Distant Relations: A Conjunction of Opposites," in *Review of Contemporary Fiction* 8, 2 (Summer 1988): 238-40. Luis Dávila, "Carlos Fuentes y su concepto de la novela," in *Revista Iberoamericana* 47, 116-17 (July-Dec. 1981): 73-78. Mary E. Davis, "The Twins in the Looking Glass: Carlos Fuentes's *Cabeza de hidra*," in *Hispania* 65, 3 (Sept. 1982): 371-76. Alberto Díaz-Lastra, "Carlos Fuentes y la revolución traicionada," in *Cuadernos Hispanoamericanos* 185 (1965): 369-75. Paul B. Dixon, "*La muerte de Artemio Cruz* and Baroque Correlative Poetry," in *Hispanófila* 28 (May 1985): 93-102. Herman P. Doezma, "An Interview with Carlos Fuentes," in *Modern Fiction Studies* 18, 4 (Winter 1972-1973): 491-503. Cynthia Duncan, "Carlos Fuentes' 'Chac Mool' and Todorov's Theory of the Fantastic: A Case for the Twentieth Century," in *Hispanic Journal* 8, 1 (Fall 1986): 125-33; "The Living Past: The Mexican's History Returns to Haunt Him in Two Short Stories by Carlos Fuentes," in *The Fantastic in World Literature and the Arts*, edited by Donald E. Morse (Westport, Conn: Greenwood Press, 1987), pp. 141-47. Gloria Durán, "Carlos Fuentes, *Cumpleaños*: A Mythological Interpretation of an Ambiguous Novel," in *Latin American Literary Review* 2, 4 (Spring-Summer 1974): 75-86; *La magia y las brujas en la obra de Carlos Fuentes* (México: UNAM, 1976); English version, enlarged and revised, *The Archetypes of Carlos Fuentes: From Witch to Androgyne* (Hamden, Conn.: Shoe String Press, 1980). Manuel Durán, "Carlos Fuentes," in *Tríptico mexicano: Juan Rulfo, Carlos Fuentes, Salvador Elizondo* (México: SEP, 1973). John P. Dwyer, "Conversation with a Blue Novelist," in *Review* 12 (1974): 54-58. Claudio Esteva Fabregat, "Transparencia de México," in *Cuadernos Hispanoamericanos* 39 (1959): 210-13. Wendy B. Faris, "*Ulysses* in Mexico: Carlos Fuentes," in *Comparative Literature Studies* 19, 2 (1982): 236-53; *Carlos Fuentes* (New York: Frederick Ungar, 1983); "Desire and Power, Love and Revolution: Carlos Fuentes and Milan Kundera," in *Review of Contemporary Fiction* 8, 2 (Summer 1988): 273-84. María Teresa Fernández Muñoz, "El lenguaje profanado: *Terra Nostra* de Carlos Fuentes," in *Cuadernos Hispanoamericanos* 359 (1980): 419-28. Malva E. Filer, "Los mitos indígenas en la obra de Carlos Fuentes," in *Revista Iberoamericana* 127 (April-June 1984): 475-89. James D. Fogelquist, "Tiempo y mito en *Cambio de piel*," in *Cuadernos Americanos* 231 (1980): 96-107. David W. Foster, "*La región más transparente* and the Limits of Prophetic Art," in *Hispania* 56 (1973): 35-42. Bernard Fouques, "El espacio órfico de la novela en *La muerte de Artemio Cruz*," in *Revista Iberoamericana* 91 (1975): 237-48; "Escritura y diferencia: *Cambio de piel* de Carlos Fuentes," in *Cuadernos Americanos* 262, 5 (1985): 223-31. Martha Paley Francescato, "*Una familia lejana*: Crónica de varias lecturas cercanas," in *Discurso Literario* 3, 2 (Spring 1986): 317-27; "Acción y reflexión en cuentos de Fuentes, Garro, y Pacheco," in *Romance Quarterly* 33, 1 (Feb. 1986): 99-112. Bienvenido de la Fuente, "*La muerte de Artemio Cruz*: observaciones sobre la estructura y sentido de la narrativa en primera persona," in *Explicación de Textos Literarios* 6 (1978): 143-51. Sylvia Fuentes, "Carlos Fuentes: Estos fueron los palacios," in Reina Roffe's *Espejo de escritores* (Hanover, N.H.: Eds. del Norte, 1985), pp. 81-104. Adriana García de Aldridge, "Herejía y portento en 'Carne esferas, ojos grises junto al Sena' de Carlos Fuentes," in *Cuadernos Americanos* 188 (1973): 231-46; "La dialéctica contemporánea: 'tiempo propio-tiempo total' en *Cumpleaños*," in *Revista Iberoamericana* 108-9 (July-Dec. (1979): 513-36. Fernando García Nuñez, "La frontera norte de México en *Gringo viejo* de Carlos Fuentes," in *Plural* 198 (March 1988): 41-44; "Notas sobre la frontera norte en la novela mexicana," in *Cuadernos Americanos* 2, 4 (1988): 159-68; "La imposibilidad del libre albedrío en *La cabeza de la hidra*, de Carlos Fuentes," in *Cuadernos Americanos* 1, 252 (Jan.-Feb. 1984): 227-34. Zunilda Gertel, "Semiótica, historia y ficción en *Terra Nostra*," in *Revista Iberoamericana* 116-17 (July-Dec. 1981): 63-72. Helmy F. Giacoman, ed., *Homenaje a Carlos Fuentes: Variaciones en torno a su obra* (New York: Las Américas, 1971). Isaac Goldenberg, "Perspectivismo y mexicanidad en la obra de Carlos Fuentes," in *Cuadernos Hispanoamericanos* 271 (1973): 15-33. A. González-Arauzo, "No Other Ends Than Possessions," in *New Mexico Quarterly* 31, 4 (1962): 268-70. Luis González-del-Valle and Antolín González-del-Valle, "La humanidad de Artemio Cruz y su proceso de autoconocimiento," in *Chasqui* 3, 2 (1974): 53-55. Roberto González Echeverría, "*La muerte de Artemio Cruz* y Unamuno: una fuente de Fuentes," in *Cuadernos Americanos* 177 (1971): 197-207; "*Terra Nostra*: Teoría y práctica," in *Revista Iberoamericana* 116-17 (July-Dec. 1981): 289-98. Edith Grossman, "Myth and Madness in Carlos Fuentes' *A Change of Skin*," in *Latin American Literary Review* 3, 5 (1974): 97-110. Carl Gutiérrez, "Provisional Historicity: Reading through *Terra Nostra*," in *Review of Contemporary Fiction* 8, 2 (Summer 1988): 257-65. Daniel de Guzmán, *Carlos Fuentes* (New York: Twayne, 1972). Lanin A. Gyurko, "The Artist Manqué in Fuentes' *Cambio de piel*," in *Symposium* 31 (Summer 1977): 126-50; "Individual and National Identity in Fuentes' *La cabeza de la hidra*," in *Latin American Fiction Today*, edited by Rose S. Minc (Montclair, N.J.: Ediciones Hispamérica, 1980), pp. 33-48; "The Myths of Ulysses in Fuentes' *Zona sagrada*," in *Modern Language Review* 69 (1974); "Structure and Theme in Fuentes' *La muerte de Artemio Cruz*," in *Symposium* 34 (Spring 1980): 29-41; "El yo y su imagen en *Cambio de piel* de Carlos Fuentes," in *Revista Iberoamericana* 76-77 (July-Dec. 1971): 689-709; "The Self as Ironic Hero in Fuentes' *Las buenas conciencias*," in *Horizontes* 31-32 (1972-1973): 85-118; "Women in Mexican Society: Fuentes' Portrayal of Oppression," in *Revista* Double in Fuentes' *Orquídeas a la luz de la luna*," in *Horizontes* 30, 59-60 (1986-1987): 57-92; "The Self and the Demonic in Fuentes' *Una familia lejana*," *Revista/Review Interamericana* 12, 4 (Winter 1982-1983): 572-620; "Myth and Mythification in Fuentes' *Aura* and Wilder's *Sunset Boulevard*," in *Hispanic Journal*, 7, 1 (Fall 1984): 91-113; "Novel into Essay: Fuentes' *Terra Nostra* as Generator of Cervantes o la crítica," in *Mester* 11, 12 (1983): 16-35. Linda B. Hall, "The Cipactli Monster: Woman as Destroyer in Carlos Fuentes," in

Southwest Review 60 (1975): 246-55. Karen Jane Hardy, "Freddy Lambert as 'Narrator' of *Cambio de piel*," in *Hispania* 61 (1978): 270-78. Luis Harss and Barbara Dohmann, "Carlos Fuentes, or the New Heresy," in *Into the Mainstream: Conversations with Latin American Writers* (New York: Harper and Row, 1967), pp. 276-309; "Carlos Fuentes, Mexico's Metropolitan Eye," in *New Mexico Quarterly* 36, 1 (1966): 26-55. Patricia Hart, "Nuevas fuentes sobre Carlos Fuentes: Un antepasado sorprendente de *Aura*," in *Chasqui* 16, 2-3 (Nov. 1987): 37-49. M. Kasey Hellerman, "The Coatlicue-Malinche Conflict: A Mother and Son Identity Crisis in the Writings of Carlos Fuentes," in *Hispania* 57 (1974): 868-75. Norma Helsper, "*Terra Nostra*: A Historical Novel for Our Times," in *La Chispa '82*, edited by Harry L. Kirby (Baton Rouge: Louisiana State University Press, 1984), pp. 112-21. Javier Herrero, "Carlos Fuentes y las lecturas modernas del Quijote," in *Revista Iberoamericana* 108-9 (1979): 555-62. Candace K. Holt, "*Terra Nostra*: Indagación de una identitad," in *Revista de Estudios Hispánicos* 17, 3 (Oct. 1983): 395-406. Ivar Ivask, special Carlos Fuentes Issue, *World Literature Today* 57, 4 (Autumn 1983). Regina Janes, "*Terra Nostra*: Charting the Terrain," in *Literary Review* 23, 2 (1974): 261-71. André Jansen, "*Todos los gatos son pardos*, o la defensa de la mexicanidad en la obra de Carlos Fuentes," in *Explicación de Texto Literarios* 11, 2 (1974): 83-94; "Carlos Fuentes y la guerra del petróleo," in *Explicación de Texto Literarios* 9, 2 (1981): 183-91. Djelal Kadir, "Carlos Fuentes: Culpable inocencia y profeta del pasado," in *Revista Iberoamericana* 47, 116-17 (July-Dec. 1981): 55-61. Emma Kafalenos, "The Grace and Disgrace of Literature: Carlos Fuentes' *The Hydra Head*," in *Latin American Literry Review* 15, 29 (Jan.-June 1987): 141-58. Ludmila Kapschutschenko, "*La muerte de Artemio Cruz, Zona sagrada, Cambio de piel*: Expresión literaria del laberinto de la existencia," in *La Chispa '81* (conference proceedings), edited by Gilbert Paolini (New Orleans: Tulane University, 1981), pp. 141-48. William Kennedy, "Carlos Fuentes: Dreaming of History," in *Review of Contemporary Fiction* 8, 2 (Summer 1988): 234-37. Lucille Kerr, "The Paradox of Power and Mystery: Carlos Fuentes' *Terra Nostra*," in *PMLA* 95, 1 (1980): 91-102. Thomas J. Knight, "The Setting of *Cambio de piel*," in *Romance Notes* 24, 3 (Spring 1984): 229-32. Thomas J. Knight and Flora M. Werner, "'Timeliness' in Carlos Fuentes' *Cambio de piel*," in *Latin American Literary Review* 4, 7 (Fall-Winter 1975): 23-30. Phillip Koldewyn, "*La cabeza de la hidra*: Residios del colonialsimo," in *Mester* 11, 1 (1982): 47-56. Enrique Krauze, "La comedia mexicana de Carlos Fuentes," in *Vuelta* 12, 139 (June 1988): 15-27. Ross Larson, "Archetypal Patterns in Carlos Fuentes' 'La muneca reina,'" in *Mester* 11, 1 (1982): 41-46. Luis Leal, "Realism, Myth, and Prophecy in Fuentes' *Where the Air Is Clear*," in *Confluencia* 1, 1 (Fall 1985): 75-81. Monique Lemaître, "Enajenación y revolucion en *Todos los gatos son pardos* de Carlos Fuentes," in *Revista Iberoamericana* 112-23 (July-Dec. 1980): 553-62; "Territorialidad y transgresión en *Gringo viejo* de C. Fuentes," in *Revista Iberoamericana* 53, 141 (Oct.-Dec. 1987): 955-63. Susan F. Levine, "The Pyramid and the Volcano: Carlos Fuentes' *Cambio de piel* and Malcolm Lowry's *Under the Volcano*," in *Mester* 11, 1 (1982): 25-40. H. E. Lewald, "El pensamiento cultural mexicano en *La región más transparente*," in *Revista Hispánica Moderna* 32, 3-4 (July-Oct. 1967): 216-23. Juan Loveluck and Isaac Levy, eds., *Simposio Carlos Fuentes: Actas* (South Carolina: University of South Carolina, Department of Foreign Languages and Literature, 1980). Carmen Lugo-Filippi, "*La muerte de Artemio Cruz y La modificación*," in *Revista de Estudios Hispánicos* 8 (1981): 11-23. Alfred MacAdam and Alexander Coleman, "An Interview with Carlos Fuentes," in *Book Forum* 4 (1978-1979): 672-85. Juan Manuel Marcos, "La tercera orilla de Fuentes," in *Revista Letras* 37 (1988): 177-82. José Luis Martín, "Presencia del simbólico 'dragón verde' en la narrativa de Carlos Fuentes," in *Revista de Estudios Hispánicos* 8 (1981): 41-48. George R. McMurray, "*Cambio de piel*: An Existential Novel of Protest," in *Hispania* 70 (1969): 150-54. Cherie Meacham, "The Process of Dialogue in *Gringo viejo*," in *Hispanic Journal* 10, 2 (Spring 1989): 127-37. Robert G. Mead, Jr., "Carlos Fuentes, Mexico's Angry Novelist," in *Books Abroad* 38, 4 (Autumn 1964): 380-82. Luis Méndez and Esther Hernández Palacios, "*Gringo viejo*: La frontera salvaje," *Nuevo Texto Crítico* 1, 1 (1988): 115-21. Mario Merlino, "Artemio Cruz o la ficción del poder," in *Cuadernos Hispanoamericanos* 325 (1977): 132-42. Floyd Merrell, "Communication and Paradox in Carlos Fuentes' *The Death of Artemio Cruz*: Toward a Semiotics of Character," in *Semiótica* 18 (1976): 339-60. David L. Middleton, "An Interview with Carlos Fuentes," in *Southern Review* 22, 2 (Spring 1986): 342-55. Oscar J. Montero, "The Role of Ixca Cienfuegos in the Thematic Fabric of *La región más transparente*," in *Hispanófila* 58 (1976): 61-83. Michael Moody, "Existentialism, Mexico and Artemio Cruz," in *Romance Notes* 10 (1968): 27-31. Joanna Petry Mroczkowska, "Geografía simbólica en *Terra Nostra*, de Carlos Fuentes," in *Revista Iberoamericana* 51, 130-31 (Jan.-June 1985): 261-71. Marc Nacht, "Carlos Fuentes and Malintzin's Mirror," in *Review of Contemporary Fiction* 8, 2 (Summer 1988): 211-16. Julio Ortega, "Carlos Fuentes: Para recuperar la tradición de La Mancha," in *Revista Iberoamericana* 55, 148-49 (July-Dec. 1989): 637-54; "Estructura e identidad en *Una familia lejana* de Carlos Fuentes," in *Texto Crítico* 13, 36-37 (1987): 36-43. Julio Ortega and Carl Mentley, "Christopher Unborn: Rage and Laughter," in *Review of Contemporary Fiction* 8, 2 (Summer 1988): 285-91. F. Javier Ordiz Vázquez, *Carlos Fuentes* (Barcelona: Editorial Anthropos, 1988). Louis Parkinson Zamora, "Magic Realism and Fantastic History: Carlos Fuentes's *Terra Nostra* and Giambattista Vico's *The New Science*," in *Review of Contemporary Fiction* 8, 2 (Summer 1988): 249-56. Robert A. Parsons, "The Allegorical Dimension of Carlos Fuentes' *Terra Nostra*," in *Hispanic Journal* 7, 2 (Spring 1986): 93-99; "Mirror Symbolism in Carlos Fuentes' *Terra Nostra*," in *College Language Association Journal* 31, 1 (Sept. 1987): 77-86. Octavio Paz, "Mask and Transparency," in *Alternating Current*, translated by Helen Lane (New York: Viking, 1973), pp. 40-45. Octavio Paz and Sandra L. Dunn, "The Question of Carlos Fuentes," in *Review of Contemporary Fiction* 8, 2 (1988): 186-88. Margaret S. Peden, "The World of the Second Reality in Three Novels by Carlos Fuentes," in *Otros mundos, otros fuegos; fantasía y realismo mágico en Iberoamérica*, Yates ed.(East Lansing, Mich.: Michigan State University, 1975), pp. 83-87; "*Terra nostra*: A Translator's Diary," in *Translation* 5 (1978): 10-17; "A Translator's Recollections," in *Review of Contemporary Fiction* 8, 2 (Summer 1988): 182-85; "Translating the Boom: The Apple Theory of Translation," in *Latin American Literary Review* 15, 29 (Jan.-June 1987): 159-72. Luis H. Peña, "Escritura del paisaje y paisaje de la escritura: Fuentes y Rulfo," in *Cuaderos de Aldeeu* 1, 2-3 (May-Oct. 1983): 393-98. Eduardo Peñuela, "Myth and Language in a Play by Carlos Fuentes," in *Latin American Theatre Review* 13, 1 (1979): 15-27. Janet Pérez, "The Triple Lunar Goddess in *Aura* and 'In a Flemish Garden,'" in *Review of Contemporary Fiction* 8, 2 (Summer 1988): 189-98. Lucrezio Pérez Blanco, "*La cabeza de la hidra* de Carlos Fuentes: Novelaensayo de estructura circular," in *Cuadernos Americanos* 221 (1978): 205-22. Gerald W. Petersen, "Punto de vista y tiempo en *La muerte de Artemio Cruz* de Carlos Fuentes," in *Revista de Estudios Hispánicos* 6, 1 (1972): 85-95; "A Literary Parallel: 'La cena' by Alfonso Reyes and *Aura* by Carlos Fuentes," in *Romance Notes* 12 (1970): 41-44. Aida Elsa Ramírez Mattei, *La narrativa de Carlos Fuentes: Afán por la armonía en la multiplicidad antagónica del mundo* (San Juan: University de Puerto Rico, 1983); "*Una familia lejana*: Exorcismo de la herencia y conciencia de culpa: Nostalgia del ser en la naturaleza y el tiempo," in *Revista de Estudios Hispánicos* 8 (1981): 35-40. Richard Reeve, "Los cuentos de Carlos Fuentes: De la fantasía al neorealismo," in *El cuento hispanoamericano ante la crítica*, edited by Enrique Pupo-Walker (Madrid: Castalia, 1973), pp. 249-63; "Carlos Fuentes and the New Short Story in Mexico," in *Studies in Short Fiction* 8 (1971): 169-79; "Octavio Paz and Hiperion in *La región más transparente*: Plagiarism, Caricature, or . . . ?," in *Chasqui* 3, 3 (1974): 13-25; "Carlos Fuentes," in *Narrativa y crítica de nuestra América*, edited by Joaquín Roy (Madrid: Castalia, 1978), pp. 287-316; "Un poco de luz sobre nueve años oscuros: Los cuentos desconocidos de Carlos Fuentes," in *Revista Iberoamericana* 36 (1970): 473-80. Walter Rela, "Medio siglo de la historia política mexicana (1903-1955) explicada en *La muerte de Artemio Cruz*," in *Tropos* (Michigan State University) 13, 1 (Spring 1986): 1-17. Emir Rodríguez Monegal, "El México alucinado de Carlos Fuentes," in *Narradores de esta América*, vol. 2 (Buenos Aires: Alfa, 1974), pp. 247-64. Jorge Rodríguez Padrón, "*Cambio de piel*, una delicada intervención de cirugía ética," in *Cuadernos Hispanoamericanos* 296 (1975): 389-402. Joaquín Rodríguez Suro, "Religión e historia en *Todos los gatos son pardos* de Carlos Fuentes," in *Veritas* 24, 93 (March 1979): 45-51; "La religión y el amor en *La región más transparente* de Carlos Fuentes," in *Veritas* 24, 95 (Sept. 1979): 336-53. Nelson Rojas, "Time and Tense in Carlos Fuentes' *Aura*," in *Hispania* 61 (1978): 859-64. Santiago Rojas, "Modalidad narrativa en *Aura*: Realidad y enajenación," in *Revista Iberoamericana* 113-113 (July-Dec. 1980): 487-98. Harry Rosser, "The Disintegration and Reconstruction of Artemio Cruz," in *Apocalyptic Visions Past and Present*, edited by JoAnn James and William Cloonan (Tallahassee: Florida State University Press, 1988). Joaquín Roy Cabrerizo, "Represión, derecho y narración: de la protesta en Asturias y Fuentes al realismo 'mágico-jurídico' en García Márquez," in *Explicación de Textos Literarios* 2, 2 (1974): 101-8. Jorge Ruffinelli, "Las ciudades perdidas de Carlos Fuentes," in *Texto Crítico* 10, 28 (Jan.-April 1984): 114-21. Gustavo Sáinz, "Carlos Fuentes: Un deslumbramiento permanente," in *Confluencia* 1, 1 (Fall 1985): 69-74. Fernando F. Salcedo, "Técnicas derivadas del cine en la obra de Carlos Fuentes," in *Cuadernos Americanos* 22 (1975): 175-97; "Los 'monjes': Personajes claves en *Cambio de piel* de Carlos Fuentes," in *Hispanófila* 25 (May 1982): 69-82. Carmen Sánchez Reyes, *Carlos Fuentes y "La región más transparente*" (San Juan, Puerto Rico: University of Puerto Rico, 1975). Susan C. Schaffer, "The Development of the Double in Selected Works of Carlos Fuentes," in *Mester* 6, 1 (1977): 81-86. Britt-Marie Schiller, "Memory and Time in *The Death of Artemio Cruz*," in *Latin American Literary Review* 15, 29 (Jan.-June 1987): 93-103. Mary Seale-Vázquez, "Character and its Development in Fuentes' *A Change of Skin*," in *Latin American Literary Review* 6, 12 (1978): 68-85. Mauricio de la Selva, "*La región más transparente*," in *Cuadernos Americanos* 100 (1958): 581-83. William L. Siemens, "Maniqueísmo e inmortalidad en *Cambio de piel*," in *Explicación de Texto Literarios* 1, 2 (1974): 123-30. John H. Sinnigen, "El desarrollo combinado y desigual y *La muerte de Artemio Cruz*," in *Cuadernos Hispanoamericanos* 396 (June 1983): 697-707. John Skirius, "Mexican Introspection in the Theater: Carlos Fuentes," in *Revista de Estudios Hispánicos* 12, 1 (1978): 25-40. Irvin D. Solomon, "A Feminist Perspective of the Latin American Novel: Carlos Fuentes' *The Death of Artemio Cruz*," *Hispanófila* 33 (Sept. 1989): 69-75. Joseph Sommers, "The Field of Choice: Carlos Fuentes," in *After the Storm: Landmarks in the Modern Mexican Novel* (Albuquerque: University of New Mexico

Press, 1968), pp. 133-64. María Stoopen, '*La muerte de Artemio Cruz*': *una novela de denuncia y traición* (México: UNAM, 1982). Catherine Swietlicki, "Doubling, Reincarnation, and Cosmic Order in *Terra Nostra*," in *Hispanófila* 27 (Sept. 1983): 93-104. Santiago Tejerina-Canal, "Point of View in *The Death of Artemio Cruz*: Singularity or Multiplicity?," in *Review of Contemporary Fiction* 8, 2 (Summer 1988): 199-210; "*La muerte de Artemio Cruz* y Ortega: Texto e intertexto," in *La Chispa '85*, edited by Gilbert Paolini (New Orleans: Tulane University, 1985), pp. 349-60. Roger D. Tinnell, "*La muerte de Artemio Cruz*: A Virtuoso Study in Sensualism," in *Modern Language Notes* 93 (1978): 334-38. Jonathan Tittler, "*Gringo viejo/The Old Gringo*' The Rest Is Fiction," in *Review of Contemporary Fiction* 8, 2 (Summer 1988): 241-48. Danubio Torres Fiero, "Carlos Fuentes: Miradas al mundo actual," in *Vuelta* 43 (1980): 41-44. Joseph Tyler, "'Chac-Mool': A Journey into the Fantastic," in *Hispanic Journal* 10, 2 (Spring 1989): 177-83. José-Miguel Ullán, "Carlos Fuentes, salto mortal hacia mañana," in *Insula* 1, 245 (1967): 12-13. M. E. de Valdés, "Fuentes on Mexican Feminophobia," in *Review of Contemporary Fiction* 8, 2 (Summer 1988): 225-33. Víctor M. Valenzuela, "Carlos Fuentes: novelista mexicano," in his *Ensayos sobre literatura hispanoamericana* (Pittsburgh, Penn.: Latin American Literary Review Press, 1978), pp. 20-27. José Vázquez Amaral, "*The Death of Artemio Cruz* by Carlos Fuentes," in his *The Contemporary Latin American Narrative* (New York: Las Américas, 1970), pp. 29-35. Luis M. Villar, "Lenguaje y sociedad de consumo en *La muerte de Artemio Cruz*," in *Plural* 198 (March 1988): 45-50; "Imagen de los sindicatos en *La muerte de Artemio Cruz*," in *Discurso Literario* 1, 1 (Fall 1983): 79-93. Ileana Viqueira, "*Aura*: Estructura mítico-simbólica," in *Revista de Estudios Hispánicos* 8 (1981): 25-33. Richard J. Walter, "Literature and History in Contemporary Latin America," in *Latin American Literary Review* 15, 29 (Jan.-June 1987): 173-82. Shirley A. Williams, "*Cambio de piel*: The Quest for Quetzalcoatl and Total Fiction," in *Hispanic Journal* 8, 1 (Fall 1986): 109-24; "Polo Febo as Quetzacoatl: The Mythic Structuring of *Terra Nostra*," in *Centennial Review* 30, 2 (Spring 1986): 228-37. Jason Wiess, "An Interview with Carlos Fuentes," in *Kenyon Review* 5, 4 (Fall 1983): 105-18. Jerry W. Wilson, "Steinbeck, Fuentes, and the Mexican Revolution," in *Southwest Review* 67, 4 (Autumn 1982): 430-40. George Gordon Wing, "A Gallery of Women in Carlos Fuentes's *Cantar de ciegos*," in *Review of Contemporary Fiction* 8, 2 (Summer 1988): 217-24; "Some Remarks on the Literary Criticism of Carlos Fuentes," in *Carlos Fuentes: A Critical View*, edited by Robert Brody and Charles Rossman (Austin: University of Texas Press, 1982), pp. 200-215. Lauro Zavala, "Forma y mito en *Gringo viejo*," in *Nuevo Texto Crítico* 1, 1 (1988). Eilenn H. Zeitz, "La muerte: Una nueva aproximación a *Aura*," in *Explicación de Texto Literarios* 12, 2 (1983-1984): 79-89.

JEANNE C. WALLACE

G

GALINDO, Sergio (1926-   ). Born in Xalapa, Veracruz, on September 2, 1926, Sergio Galindo studied in his hometown, then in Mexico City, where he attended the UNAM, and then, in France. He was a professor of theatrical arts in Xalapa in 1953. Recipient of a scholarship from the Centro Mexicano de Escritores (1955-1956), he wrote *La justicia de enero* (The Justice of January), a novel inspired by his own experiences as an immigration agent. He has also worked in the editorial department of a number of significant newspapers and journals.

  Galindo is a novelist and dramatist who prefers to focus his work on life in the provincial cities and towns of Mexico. Targeting the upper middle class, in particular, he illuminates their conflicts, their system of values, their aspirations. He has also written a novel about the Revolution, *El Bordo* (1960), a narrative treasure illustrating both devastating and heartening consequences of the external world of the characters' inner life. Characterized by precise, sharp language and heightened by sensory images, *El Bordo* is just one of several successful works by Sergio Galindo.

WORKS: *La máquina vacía* (The Empty Machine) (México: Ediciones Fuensanta, 1951). *Polvos de arroz* (Sands of Rice) (Jalapa-México: Universidad Veracruzana, 1958). *La justicia de enero* (The Justice of January) (México: FCE, 1959). *El Bordo* (México: FCE, 1960). *La comparsa* (The Masquerade) (México: Joaquín Mortiz, 1964).

BIBLIOGRAPHY: Enrique Anderson-Imbert, *Spanish American Literature*, vol. 2 (Detroit: Wayne State University Press, 1969), pp. 119-20. Emilio Carballido, "Sergio Galindo: *Polvos de arroz*," in *Estaciones* 3, 10 (Summer 1958): 192. Rosario Castellanos, "La novela mexicana contemporánea y su valor testimonial," in *Hispania* 47, 2 (May 1964): 223-24, 229. Raúl Chávarri, "La novela moderna mexicana," in *Cuadernos Hispanoamericanos* 58, 173 (May 1964): 376. Manuel Durán, Review of *La justicia de enero*, in *Revista Hispánica Moderna* 26, 3-4 (July-Oct. 1960): 143-45. Aurora M. Ocampo de Gómez and Ernesto Prado Velázquez, *Diccionario de escritores mexicanos* (México: UNAM, 1967), pp. 123-24. Joseph Sommers, "The Mexican Novel of 1964," review of *La comparsa*, in *Books Abroad* 39, 2 (Spring 1965): 144-46; Review of *La comparsa*, in *Hispania* 48, 3 (Sept. 1965): 621-22.

JEANNE C. WALLACE

GALLY C., Héctor. (1942-   ). Born in Mexico City, January 4, 1942, Hector Gally studied philosophy at the Universidad Nacional Autónoma de México. At twenty-one, he began publishing stories. His first major publication was *Diez días y otras narraciones* (Ten Days and Other Narrations), a collection of stories noted for their keen observations, especially of nature. Two short novels, *Víctor* (Victor) (1964), considered a psychoanalytical work, and *Los restos* (The Remains) (1966); three collections of stories, *Diez días y otras narraciones* (Ten Days and Other Narrations) (1963), *Hacia la noche* (Toward Night) (1965), and *El agua de los arroyos* (The Water of the Streams) (1974); and two anthologies, one of stories (1967), for which he wrote a prologue and notes, and the other of the writings of Camilo Torres (1971), comprise most of his literary production.

In *El agua de los arroyos*, considered a more mature work, he aptly combines diversity with thematic unity in this series of stories, several of which deal with interpersonal relationships (children and parents, men and women, etc.). A critical book casting doubt upon certain nineteenth-century institutions, the work appeals to the intellectual and creative reader. His style is characterized primarily by imagination, humor, drama, and the use of contemporary literary techniques such as the insightful short phrase or sentence.

WORKS: *Diez días y otras narraciones* (Ten Days and Other Narrations) (México: Editorial Pax-México, 1963). *Víctor* (Victor) (México: Costa-Amic, 1964). *Hacia la noche* (Toward Night) (México: Costa-Amic, 1965). *Los restos* (The Remains) (México: Edit. Pax-México, 1966). "Carlos Fuentes;" *Ovaciones* (Mexico) 292 (Aug. 27, 1967): 15. *Treinta cuentos de autores mexicanos* (Thirty Stories by Mexican Authors), prologue and notes by Héctor Gally C. (México: Edit. Pax-México, 1967). *El agua de los arroyos* (The Water of the Streams) (México: Joaquín Mortiz, 1974).

BIBLIOGRAPHY: Ermilo Abreu Gómez, "El libro de hoy. Cuentos, novelas, memorias y crónicas," review of *Víctor*, in *Revista Mexicana de Cultura* 901 (July 5, 1964): 7. David William Foster, *A Dictionary of Contemporary Latin American Authors* (Phoenix: Publishers Press, 1975). Héctor Gally, "Héctor Gally dice," in *Ovaciones* 238 (Aug. 14, 1966): 1-4. Carlos González Peña, *Historia de literatura mexicana desde los orígenes hasta nuestros días*, 15th ed. (México: Porrúa, 1984), p. 322. Manuel Lerín, "Narraciones de Héctor Gally," in *Revista Mexicana de Cultura* 872 (Dec. 15, 1963): 15. Aurora M. Ocampo de Gómez and Ernesto Prado Velázquez, *Diccionario de escritores mexicanos* (México: UNAM, 1967), p. 124. Salvador Reyes Nevares, Review of *Los restos*, in *La Cultura en México* 235 (Aug. 17, 1966): xviii. Humberto Tejera, review of *Diez días y otras narrationes*, in *Horizontes* 35-36 (1964): 33.

JEANNE C. WALLACE

GAMBOA, Federico (1864-1939), novelist, playwright, journalist, and diplomat who began his literary career by translating French plays. Gambóa was born in Mexico City on December 22, 1864; His father, General Manuel Gambóa, had become famous in 1847 for his participation in the war against the United States. His father later became governor of Jalisco, and during the French intervention of 1862, he fought against Benito Juárez. Federico's mother died when he was only eleven years old. He traveled extensively through Europe and Central, South, and North America as a diplomat of the Mexican government and as a correspondent of the Spanish Royal Academy. Discredited during his time for his adherence to the Porfirio Díaz regime, he has been admired for some of his writings. Gambóa generally presents his characters within a problematic atmosphere, be it social or personal. His first effort in fiction was in 1889 when he published *Del natural*, a collection of short stories. It is from this beginning that the influence of naturalism is noticed. The characters are trapped and controlled by a predetermined fate which, through factors such as environment and heredity, leaves very few possibilities for individual and social change through personal initiative. But it was not until 1903 with the publication of *Santa* (Saint) that Gambóa became well known. Generally, this novel has been used as the prototype of naturalism in Mexican literature due in large part to the popularity of the novel. This popularity has been such due to the sympathy that the protagonist elicits from the reader, as he tries, through great efforts, to escape her tragic fate. Santa is a young lady from rural Mexico who, once she travels to the big city, is trapped in a cruel environment. She falls so deep that we find her trying to survive as a prostitute. Finally, she is saved by the love of a blind character named Hipólito.

Although naturalism was very attractive as a literary phenomenon, it was very difficult for Mexican writers in general because of the strong religious feeling and the idea of free will, inherent in Christianity. Along these lines, individuals have the capability of changing their fate as long as they decide that they want to better themselves. God gives that option. Gambóa, through most of his works, is very able in his depiction of Mexican society. In *Santa*, he makes very strong social comments on how conservative and closed Mexican society can be to some people, especially to those who come from rural areas in search of better opportunities in the city. His idea of a society that offers very few possibilities for change is also his comment on Mexican traditional values, such as Christianity and social justice, which, in this case, are very selective. Gambóa's characters seem to be surrounded by a romantic spirit; they are very sentimental, but the two naturalistic elements of heredity and environment seem to dominate their lives. Generally, the development of his characters takes place in the city, but he goes further in the sense that he concentrates his characters in the poorest neighborhoods where their integration into the mainstream of Mexican society will be limited. And as is typical of Santa, he creates characters who usually will have a harder time escaping their condition: a blind man, a prostitute, etc.

Gambóa's influences are varied. In content he was influenced by French naturalism and mainly by the work of Emile Zola (1840- 1902). On the other hand, his style resembles more closely the symbolist side of modernism because of his careful selection of beautiful language. This is something new in the sense that there is a combination of careful style with popular elements, poor neighborhoods and characters typical of these neighborhoods. This is a contrast, at least in content, to the the Modernists, who chose to portray ideal and faraway locations with noble characters that corresponded to these situations.

WORKS: *Del natural* (About Natural Things) (México: n.p., 1888). *Apariencias* (Appearances) (Buenos Aires: Casa Editora de Jacobo Peuser, 1892). *Impresiones y recuerdos* (Impressions and Memoirs) (Buenos Aires: Arnaldo Moen, Editor, 1893). *Suprema ley* (Supreme Law) (Pars: n.p., 1896). *Metamórfosis* (Metamorphosis) (México: n.p., 1896). *Santa* (México: n.p., 1903). *Mi diario* (My Diary) (Guadalajara: Imp. de la Gaceta de Guadalajara, 1907). *Reconquista* (Reconquest) (Barcelona: n.p., 1907). *La llaga* (The Wound) (México: n.p., 1910). *La novela mexicana* (The Mexican

Novel) (México: Eusebio Gómez de la Puente, 1914). Dramas: *La última campaña* (The Last Campaign) (México: n.p., 1900). *La venganza de la gleba* (Revenge of the Glebe) (Washington, D.C.: n.p., 1904). *A buena cuenta* (San Salvador: n.p., 1907). *Entre hermanos* (Between Brothers) (México: n.p., 1928). *Mi diario* (My Diary) 5 vols. (1907-1938), memoirs. *Novelas* (Novels) (México: Letras Mexicanas, 1965).

BIBLIOGRAPHY: Ignacio M. Altamirano, *Influence de la Littrature Francaise sur la Littrature Mexicaine* (México: Librería Cosmos, n.d.). Mariano Azuela, *Cien años de novela mexicana* (México: Ediciones Botas, 1947). John S. Brushwood, "The Mexican Understanding of Realism and Naturalism," *Hispania* 43, 4 (Dec. 1960); *Mexico in Its Novel* (Austin: University of Texas Press, 1966). C. Hooker, *La novela de Federico Gambóa* (Madrid: n.p., 1971). Bart L. Lewis, "Myth in Federico Gambóa's *Santa*," *Mester* 6 (1976): 32-37. Francisco Mena, "Federico Gambóa y el Naturalismo, como expresión ideológica y social," *Explicación de Textos Literarios* 1, 2: 207-14. Seymour Menton, "Federico Gambóa: un análisis estilístico," *Humanitas* 4 (1963). Ernest R. Moore, "Federico Gambóa, Diplomat and Novelist," *Books Abroad* 14 (1940): 364-67; "Bibliografía de obras y crítica de Federico Gambóa," in *Revista Iberoamericana* 2, 3 (April 1940): 271-79. A. Millard S. L. Rosenberg, "El naturalismo en México y don Federico Gambóa," *Bulletin Hispanique* 36: 472-87. Silvana Serafín, "La citta in *Santa* di Federico Gambóa," *Studi di Letteratura Ispano-Americana* 15-16 (1983): 159-66.

OSCAR SOMOZA

GAMBOA, José Joaquín (1878-1931), playwright, critic, journalist, and teacher. He was born in Mexico City on January 20, 1878. After prep school, he began to study law, but gave it up to devote himself to journalism and literature. His interest in the history and social development of his country led him to become a world history teacher from 1900 to 1907 at the National Preparatory School. During this time, he wrote short stories and some plays that were staged. Between 1908 and 1923 he was a member of the diplomatic corps, a position most likely taken because of his disenchantment with the state of theater in Mexico. While stationed in Europe, he was able to witness in Paris the success of several playwrights of the day.

Following his diplomatic service, Gamboa returned to Mexico filled with visions of the dramatic forms which had been revolutionizing European theater. In the past, he had translated Gabrielle D'Annunzio's work, *La Gioconda*, as well as works by the French playwrights Robert des Flers, Francis de Croisset, Charles Mere, Henri Bernstein, and Alfred Capus among others. Now, he began to write play reviews for the daily *El Universal*, as he would continue to do until his death on January 30, 1931. As a playwright, Gamboa developed through several periods that saw him move from the writing of opera libretti in the Italian manner, through adaptations of European plays, into a form of realism, and finally into a sort of allegorical symbolism. His early experience with comic opera led him to write a zarzuela entitled *Soledad* (Solitude) in collaboration with Miguel Pereyra in 1899. Belonging, also, to the first period are *La carne* (Flesh), later titled *Teresa* (1903), *La muerte* (Death) (1904), *El hogar* (The Hearth), and *El día del Juicio* (Last Judgement Day) (1905), then *Un día vendrá* (A Day Will Come)(1908). His second period began in 1923 with *El Diablo tiene frio*

(The Devil Is Cold) and continued with *Los Revillagigedo* (The Revillagigedo Family) and *Vía crucis* (The Way of the Cross) (1925) plus several one-act plays, like *Cuento viejo* (The Old Tale), to arrive at his third period with *Espíritus* (Spirits) and *Si la juventud supiera* (If Youth Only Knew!) (1927), *El mismo caso* (The Same Case) (1929), *Ella* (She), later titled *Alucinaciones* (Hallucinations) (1930), and *El caballero, la muerte y el diablo* (The Gentleman, Death and the Devil) (1931).

Gamboa represents, within Mexican theater of the end of the nineteenth and the first third of the twentieth century, the transition from realism to symbolism. (His uncle, Federico *Gamboa, the novelist, had initiated the naturalist movement which was akin to realism.) Elements of the symbolic drama, which José Joaquín must have seen while in France, began to appear, first in *El Diablo tiene frío*, which treated the classic story of the Prodigal Son in an almost allegorical manner. In his third period, Gamboa discarded all attempts at realism for abstract symbolism. Close examination of his plays shows that it is a symbolism more like the allegory of the "auto sacramental" than the dreamlike symbolism of the French symbolists. Upon closer examination, one also discovers that Gamboa's method of developing character has striking similarities with the methods found in many of Lope de Vega's plays. This leads one to believe that Gamboa had turned to Spain's Golden Age for part of his technique. So, while there can be little doubt that Gamboa was influenced by the works of modern European symbolists, it would appear that he finally made a curious compromise between the modern forms (which he and his contemporaries tried to popularize) and the forms from an earlier age that had influenced his early development. W. K. Jones calls *El caballero, la muerte y el diablo* "Gamboa's greatest play, and the most powerful of its kind in the Mexican theatre." As a critic and as a playwright, José Joaquín Gamboa had demonstrated his ample knowledge of theatrical technique and control of language; the latter led him to be inducted into the Mexican Academy of the Spanish Language.

WORKS: *Teatro*, foreword by Carlos González Peña, 3 vols. (México: Botas, 1938). [Vol. 1, 1st period: "La carne [Teresa]" (The Flesh, or Theresa), "El hogar" (The Hearth), "La muerte" (Death), "Un día vendrá" (A Day Will Come); vol. 2, period of transition: "Cuento viejo" (The Old Tale), "El Diablo tiene frio" (The Devil Is Cold), "Los Revillagigedo" (The Revillagigedo Family), "Via crucis" (The Way of the Cross); vol. 3, third period: "Alucinaciones" (Hallucinations), "Espíritus" (Spirits), "Si la juventud supiera" (If Youth Only Knew!), "El mismo caso" (The Same Case), "El caballero, la muerte y el diablo" (The Caballero, Death and the Devil).] *A Translation of José Joaquín Gamboa's Play, The Caballero, Death and the Devil* (With an introductory study of his place in the history of Mexican theater), translated by William Leaird Mayhew (Honolulu: University of Hawaii, 1969). *The Knight, Death and the Devil* (*El caballero, la muerte y el diablo*), translated by Theodore Apstein (Austin: University of Texas Press, n.d.). José Joaquín Gamboa, "La Botella de Champagne," *El Universal Ilustrado* (July 5, 1923): 321-41.

BIBLIOGRAPHY: Theodore Apstein, *A Modern Mexican Playwright: José Joaquín Gamboa* (Austin: University of Texas Press, 1940). Luis G. Basurto, *Teatro mexicano, 1958* (México: n.p., 1959); *Catálogo del teatro mexicano contemporáneo* (México: n.p., 1960). Alyce Golding Cooper, *Teatro mexicano contemporáneo, 1940-1962* (México: n.p., 1962). Carlos González Peña, *Gente mía* (México: Edit. Stylo, 1946); *History of Mexican Literature*, translated by Gustan B. Nance and Florene Dunstan (Dallas:

Southern Methodist University Press, 1968). Willis Knapp Jones, *Breve historia del teatro latinoamericano* (México: Eds. de Andrea, 1956); *Behind Spanish American Footlights* (Austin: University of Texas Press, 1966). Ruth S. Lamb, *Bibliografía del teatro mexicano del siglo XX* (México: Eds. de Andrea, 1962). José María Lozano, "En la muerte del dramaturgo José Joaquín Gamboa, el año de 1931," *Discursos y conferencias* (México: n.p., 1947). Antonio Magaña Esquivel and Ruth S. Lamb, *Breve historia del teatro mexicano* (México: Eds. de Andrea, 1958). Armando de María y Campos, *Informe sobre el teatro social (XIX-XX)* (México: n.p., 1959). José Luis Martínez, *Literatura mexicana, siglo XX*, 2 vols. (México: Ant. Libr. Robredo, 1949-1950). Francisco Monterde, *Bibliografía del teatro en México* (México: n.p., 1934). Agustín del Saz, *Teatro hispanoamericano*, 2 vols. (Barcelona: Vergara, 1964). Carlos Solórzano, *El teatro hispanoamericano contemporaneo*, 2 vols. (México: n.p., 1964). Francisco Monterde ed., *Teatro mexicano del siglo XX (1900-1927)*, (México: FCE, 1956). Antonio Magaña Esquivel ed., *Teatro mexicano del siglo XX (1928-1946)* (México: FCE, 1956). Francisco Monterde, "Autores del teatro mexicano: 1900-1950," *México en el arte* 10-11 (1950): 39-46. Carlos Villegas, "Fichas de literatura mexicana, José Joaquín Gamboa," *Armas y Letras* (University of Nuevo León, 1947).

HERLINDA HERNANDEZ

GAMONEDA, Francisco (1873-1953), librarian and archivist. Gamoneda was born in Spain, of Asturian lineage. Family difficulties caused him to end his studies in architecture. He completed his studies in law in Manila, Philippines, and in Madrid. Gamoneda participated in the occupation of the Philippines by the United States. After arriving in Mexico in 1909, he held posts in various publishing firms, classified and catalogued the municipal archives and organized the archives of the Secretaría de Hacienda and the Library of Congress. As head of the Department of Popular Libraries, he established sixteen libraries in the capital. Gamoneda collaborated on the *Diario de Manila* and *El Comercio* in the Philippines. In Mexico he founded the bibliographic journal *Biblos* in 1912, the Spanish-Mexican Ateneo, and, with others, the *Grupo Ariel*, a renowned agency of cultural dissemination. All of his work was directed toward the creation and diffusion of learning and culture.

WORKS: *Memoria sobre la constitución de una Sociedad Librera en México* (Memoir of the Establishment of a Library Society in Mexico) (México: Tip. El Bufete, 1911). *Catálogo del archivo del Ayuntamiento de México* (Archival Catalogue of the City Government of Mexico) (México: Imp. de J. Aguilar Vera, 1921). *Iconografía de gobernantes de la Nueva España* (Iconography of the Governors of New Spain) (México: E. Gómez de la Puente, 1921). *Las artes gráficas en el periodismo* (Graphic Arts in Journalism) (México, 1922). "La producción literaria de la Nueva España" (Literary Production of New Spain), in *Boletín de la Asociación de Bibliotecarios Mexicanos* (Oct. 15, 1924): 7-16 and (Dec. 15, 1924): 24-26. *San Agustín Acolman* (Saint Augustine Acolman) (México: Talls. Gráficos de la Nación, 1925). *Introducción de la imprenta en México* (Introduction of Printing in Mexico) (México: n.p., 1937). *Bibliografía mexicana* (Mexican Bibliography) (México: Asociación de Libreros de México, 1938-39, 1940). *La industria editorial en México. Su presente, su porvenir* (The

Publishing Industry in Mexico. Its Present, Its Future) (México: Edit. México, 1939). *Clasificación bibliográfica* (Bibliographic Classification) (México: n.p., 1941). "El archivo municipal de la ciudad de México, hoy del Departamento del Distrito Federal" (The Municipal Archives of Mexico City, Presently of the Department of the Federal District), in *Revista de Historia de América* (Dec. 1941): 101-28. *Feria del Libro y Exposición del Periodismo* (Book Fair and Journalism Exposition) (México, 1943).

BIBLIOGRAPHY: Several authors, *Homenaje a don Francisco Gamoneda* (México: Imp. Universitaria, 1946).

BARBARA P. FULKS

GARCIA, Telesforo (1844-1918). García was born in Puentenansa, Santander, Spain. Liberal in spirit, he was a distinguished journalist. With Justo *Sierra he founded *La Libertad*; he also contributed to various publications such as *El Federalista*, *El Bien Público*, and *La Legalidad*. García's works were published widely but have largely disappeared. Some of his longer essays, such as those published in the *Revista Positiva*, which adhered to Auguste Comte's ideas, have been preserved. García died in Mexico in 1918.

WORKS: *Los españoles residentes en México* (The Spanish Residents in Mexico), pamphlet (México, 1857). *¿Garantiza mejor el sistema metafísico que el sistema experimental?* (Does the Metaphysical System Provide a Better Guarantee Than the Experimental System?) (México, 1881). *Por la raza* (For the Race) (México, 1902).

BIBLIOGRAPHY: Luis A. Escandón, *Poetas y escritores mexicanos* (México: n.p., 1889). Heriberto García Rivas, *Historia de la literatura mexicana* (México: Textos Universitarios, 1972), vol. 2, p. 231. Aurora M. Ocampo de Gómez and Ernesto Prado Velázquez, *Diccionario de escritores mexicanos* (México: UNAM, 1967), pp. 126-27. Leopoldo Zea, *Apogeo y decadencia del positivismo en México* (México: n.p., 1944), pp. 90, 118-20.

PATRICIA HART

GARCIA Ascot, Jomi (1929-   ), poet, essayist, and film writer. Jomi García Ascot was born in Túnez, but was exiled with his parents to Mexico in 1939. He studied at the National University, where he has devoted himself to teaching literature and film and has undertaken a diversity of artistic and literary projects. He has written film scripts on the Cuban revolution, has authored an essay on Baudelaire, and has written books on music and on the art of Roger Von Gunten. He has written several books of poetry. His film scripts won awards in 1962 and 1963.

His poetry manifests a directness of style and yet a depth of thought that is engrossing. His themes vary widely from the poetic process to love, to time, and to our everyday lives. There are moments in which he seems to lament the human predicament yet, in general, his poetry is affirmative of life and art. His work *Antología personal* (Personal Anthology) is a recent and representative collection of his poetry throughout his career.

WORKS: Essay: *Baudelaire, poeta existencial* (Baudelaire, Existential Poet) (México: Gráfica Panamericana, 1951). *Roger Von Gunten* (México: UNAM, 1979). *Con la música por dentro* (With the Music Within) (México: Casillas Editores, 1982). Poetry: *Un otoño en el aire* (An Autumn in the Air) (México: Era, 1964). *Estar aquí* (To Be Here) (México: UNAM, 1966). *Haber estado allí* (To Have Been There) (Monterrey: Instituto Tecnológico y de Estudios Superiores de Monterrey, 1970). *Seis poemas al margen* (Six Poems on the Margin) (Monterrey: Ediciones Sierra, 1972). *Un modo de decir* (A Manner of Telling) (México: UNAM, 1975). *Poemas de amor perdido y encontrado y otros poemas* (Poems of Lost and Discovered Love and Other Poems) (Monterrey: Ediciones Sierra Madre, 1977). *Antología personal* (Personal Anthology) (México: Martín Casillas, 1983). *Del tiempo y unas gentes* (Of Time and Some People) (México: Edición del Equilibrista, 1986). *Muerte empieza en Polanco* (Death Begins in Polanco) (México: Diana, 1987). Film Scripts: *Los Novios* (The Bride and Groom), 1960. *Un día de trabajo* (A Day of Work), 1960. *En el balcón vacío* (On the Empty Balcony), 1962. *Remedios Varo*, 1967. *El viaje* (The Voyage), 1967.

BIBLIOGRAPHY: José Fernández Angel, "Decir las cosas o un modo de decir," *La Palabra y el Hombre* 21, Nueva Epoca (Jan.-Mar. 1977): 82-83. Heriberto García Rivas, *Historia de la literatura mexicana*, vol. 4 (México: Textos Universitarios, 1971), pp. 358-59. Manuel Lerín, "Libros," review of *Un otoño en el aire*, *Revista Mexicana de Cultura* 911 (Sept. 13, 1964): 15. Angelina Muñiz, "Entre lineas," review of *Un otoño en el aire*, *Diorama de la Cultura* 20 (Sept. 1964): 8. Aurora M. Ocampo de Gómez and Ernesto Prado Velázquez, *Diccionario de escritores mexicanos* (México: UNAM, 1967), p. 127. Ramón Xirau, review of *Un otoño en el aire*, *Diálogos* 1, 1 (Nov.-Dec. 1964): 33-34.

MARK FRISCH

GARCIA Cantú, Gastón (1917-). Born in the city of Puebla on November 3, 1917, García Cantú studied in his native city until his second year of law school. He then taught at the schools of Flores Magón, Venustiano, and the Universidad Poblana. He has resided in Mexico City since 1953, where he was director of the supplement *Mexico en la Cultura* part of the daily *Novedades*, where, along with the magazine *Universidad de Mexico*, he published his first stories. He has also collaborated on the supplement *Siempre!* and was director of the Department of Culture of UNAM.

With his work *Los falsos rumores* (False Rumors) (1955), Gastón García Cantú collected sixteen stories united by the common environment of the provincial village. He does not depict the tranquil rural environment of folkloric writers, but rather the apparently simple but complex world of prejudice, boredom, and ignorance. It is considered to be a bitter but satirically humorous work.

WORKS: Stories: *Los falsos rumores* (False Rumors) (México: FCE, 1955). Essays: *El Mediterráneo americano* (The American Mediterranean) (México: UNAM, 196O). *Cuadernos de Notas* (Notebook of Notes) (México: n.p., 1961). *Papeles públicos*

(Public Papers) (México: n.p., 1963). *Utopías mexicanas* (Mexican Utopias) (México: Era, 1963). *El pensamiento de la reacción mexicana, historia documental, 1810-1962* (The Thought of the Mexican Reaction, Documented History, 1810-1962) (México: Empresas Editoriales, 1965). Prologues: *Desafíos a la nación* (Challenges to the Nation), a collection of texts from Mexican liberalism of the nineteenth century, prologue and notes by García Cantú (México: n.p., 1959). Alfonso Reyes, *Oración del 9 de febrero* (Prayer of February 9), prologue by García Cantú (México: Era, 1963).

BIBLIOGRAPHY: Vicente Lombardo Toledano, "Pensamiento de la Revolución Mexicana," review of *El pensamiento de la reacción mexicana*, in *Siempre!* 614 (México, March 31, 1965): 13, 17. Antonio Magaña Esquivel, "El pensamiento de la reacción mexicana," in *El Nacional* (México, May 16, 1965): 3. Mauricio de la Selva, Review of *El Pensamiento de la reacción mexicana* in *Cuadernos Americanos* (México, July-Aug. 1965): 265-66.

MIRTA BARREA-MARLYS

GARCIA Icazbalceta, Joaquín (1825-1894). Of Spanish parents, Joaquín García Icazbalceta was born in Mexico City on August 21, 1825, but moved to Cádiz, Spain, with his parents and siblings in 1829, a move made largely because of political turmoil following Mexico's independence. A precocious and talented child, he astounded his family and teachers with his amazing literary abilities. Returning to Mexico with his family in 1836, the young Joaquín was tutored at home and began to help his father with writing tasks. Reasonably fluent in several languages, he was also knowledgeable about the classical languages. Inspired to study history by Lucas Alemán, he translated William Prescott's *History of the Conquest of Peru* into Spanish, adding notes and other chapters. It was published around 1850.

A contributor to the *Diccionario Universal de Historia y Geografía* (1852-1856), he made valuable and well-written biographical sketches and critical assessments. He spent many hours gathering original manuscripts and other materials about colonial Mexico and laboriously copying those he had to borrow. He was especially interested in Spain's cultural, religious, and spiritual impact on Mexico.

García Icazbalceta installed a printing press in his home, thus greatly facilitating his publishing endeavors. Among the many studies that he published was a biography of Fray Juan de Zumárraga, the first bishop and archbishop of Mexico. With a strong interest in sixteenth-century Mexican culture and history, he published a biographical bibliography of distinguished Mexicans from that period and included an introductory note on the origins of the printing press in Mexico.

In addition to his recognition as a distinguished historian and researcher, García Icazbalceta was also lauded for his original prose. He successfully combined some of the literary characteristics of the classics with those typical of his day. He wrote several prologues and important letters that have been published. Religious questions and theological positions are topics he frequently discussed in his writings.

He was a member of several prestigious organizations, including the Academia Mexicana, correspondiente de la Real Española. A philologist and linguist, he compiled a partial *Vocabulario de mexicanismos* (Vocabulary of Mexicanisms), which he was unable to complete because of his sudden death in 1894. Due to his work in the linguistic field, he was made the director of the Academia Mexicana in 1883, serving until he died. The *Vocabulario de mexicanismos* was published by his son, Luis García Pimentel, in 1905.

WORKS: History: "Apéndice" (Appendix) to Prescott's *History of the Conquest of Peru*, translated by García Icazbalceta (México: Ed. Rafael de Rafael, 1849); 2nd ed., corrected (1850). "Historiadores de México" (Historians from Mexico), in *Diccionario universal de historia y geografía* (México: Escalante, 1853). "Reseña histórica de la Academia Mexicana" (History Review of the Academia Mexicana), in *Memorias de la Academia Mexicana* 1 (Mexico, 1876): 11-20. "Representaciones religiosas en México, en el siglo XVI" (Religious Performances in Mexico, in the sixteenth Century), in *Coloquios espirituales y sacramentales*, Fernán González de Eslava (México: Imp. de Díaz de León, 1877). *Descripción del Arzobispado de México hecha en 1570, y otros documentos* (Description of the Archbishopric of Mexico Made in 1570 and Other Documents) (México: Imp. Terrazas, 1897). Biographies: *Don Fr. Juan de Zumárraga, primer Obispo y Arzobispo de México* (Don Fray Juan de Zumárraga, the First Bishop and Archbishop of Mexico) (México: Imp. de Díaz de León, 1881); edited by Rafael Aguayo Spencer and Antonio Castro Leal (México: Porrúa, 1947). "Biografías" (Biographies), in *Diccionario Universal de Historia y Geografía* (México: Escalante, 1853-1856). *Opúsculos y biografías* (Tracts and Biographies) (México: UNAM, 1942). Bibliography: *Bibliografía mexicana del siglo XVI* (Mexican Bibliography of the Sixteenth Century) (México: Imp. de Díaz de León, 1886). "Las 'Bibliotecas' de Eguiara y de Beristáin" (The "Libraries" of Eguiara and Beristáin), in *Memorias de la Academia Mexicana*, vol. 1 (México: Imp. de Díaz de León, 1878). *Bibliografía mexicana del siglo XVI* (Mexican Bibliography of the Sixteenth Century), edited by Agustín Millares Carlo (México: FCE, 1954). Linguistics and Philology: "La Danza General en que entran todos los estados de gentes" (The General Dance Which All Types of People Do), in *El Espectador de México*, vol. 4 (México, 1851). "La Academia Mexicana correspondiente de la Real Española," in *Memorias de la Academia Mexicana*, vol. 1 (México: Imp. Díaz de León, 1878). "Francisco de Terrazas y otros poetas del siglo XVI" (Francisco de Terrazas and Other Poets of the Sixteenth Century), in *Memorias de la Academia Mexicana*, vol. 2 (México: Imp. Díaz de León), pp. 357-425. "El Padre Avendaño. Reyertas más que literarias. Rectificaciones a Beristáin" (Father Avendaño. More Than Literary Brawls. Rectifications to Beristáin), in *Memorias de la Academia Mexicana*, vol. 3 (México: Imp. Díaz de León, 1886), pp. 117-44. "Provincialismos mexicanos" (Mexican Provincialisms), in *Memorias de la Academia Mexicana*, vol. 3 (México: Imp. Díaz de León, 1886), pp. 170-90. *Vocabulario de mexicanismos* (Vocabulary of Mexicanisms), published by Luis García Pimentel, vol. I (México: Tip. "La Europea," 1905). Prologues: *Colección de Documentos para la Historia de México* (Collection of Documents for the History of Mexico), vol. 1 (México: Libr. Andrade, 1858); vol. 2 (1866). *Nueva Colección de Documentos para la Historia de México* (New Collection of Documents for the History of Mexico), vol. 1 (México: Libr. Andrade, 1889); vol. 3 (1891); vol. 4 (1892). *Noticias de México* (News about Mexico), Francisco Sedano. Letters: *Carta acerca del origen de la imagen de Nuestra Señora de Guadalupe de México* (Letter about the Origin of the Image of Our Lady of Guadalupe of Mexico), written to Archbishop Pelagio Antonio de Labastida y Dávalos (México: n.p., 1896). *Carta de don Joaquín García Icazbalceta a don José María Vigil aclarando un proceso de la Inquisición en el siglo XVI* (Letter from Joaquín García Icazbalceta to José

María Vigil Clarifying the Matter of a Trial by the Inquisition in the Sixteenth Century) (México: Ant. Libr. Robredo, 19..). *Cartas de don Joaquín García Icazbalceta a José Fernando Ramírez, José María de Agreda, Manuel Orozco y Berra, Nicolás León, Agustín Fischer, Aquiles Gerste y Francisco del Paso y Troncoso* (Letters from . . . to . . .) (México: Eds. Porrúa, 1937). Translations: *Varios viajes de ingleses a la famosa provincia de México* (Several Journeys by Englishmen to the Famous Province of Mexico), translated from English, in *Boletín* of the Sociedad Mexicana de Geografía y Estadística, vol. 1. *Relación de la conquista del Perú* (Story of the Conquest of Peru), by Pedro Sánchez, translated from Italian (México: n.p., 1849). *Historia de la conquista del Perú* (History of the Conquest of Peru), by William Prescott, translated from English (México: Ed. Rafael de Rafael, 1849); 2nd ed., corrected (1850). *México en 1554. Tres diálogos latinos que Francisco Cervantes de Salazar escribió e imprimió en México en dicho año* (Mexico in 1554. Three Latin Dialogues That Francisco Cervantes de Salazar Wrote and Published in Mexico in That Year) (México: Imp. Díaz de León and S. White, 1875). Editions: *Cartas de Hernán Cortés al Emperador Carlos V* (Letters from Hernán Cortés to the Emperor Charles V) (México: Private Ed., 1855). *Historia eclesiástica indiana* (Indian Ecclesiastical History), by Fr. Jerónimo de Mendieta (México: Díaz de León and S. White, 1870). "Poder otorgado por Hernán Cortés a favor de su padre, y diligencias para que Bernardino Vázquez de Tapia volviese a la Nueva España" (Power Granted by Hernán Cortés with the Help of His Father, and Dispatches So That Bernardino Vázquez de Tapia Could Return to Spain), in *Boletín de la Sociedad Mexicana de Geografía y Estadística*, vol. 3 (1871). *Coloquios espirituales y sacramentales y poesías sagradas* (Spiritual and Sacramental Colloquies and Sacred Poems), by Hernán González de Eslava (México: Díaz de León, 1877). *Arte de la lengua maya* (Art of the Mayan Language), by Gabriel de San Buenaventura (México: n.p., 1888). *Opúsculos inéditos, latinos y castellanos* (Unpublished Tracts in Latin and Spanish), by Francisco Javier Alegre (México: Díaz de León, 1889). "Carta original del Barón de Humboldt" (Original Letter from the Barron de Humboldt), in *El Renacimiento*, 2nd epoch (1894). Complete Works: *Obras de don Joaquín García Icazbalceta* (Works by Joaquín García Icazbalceta), 10 vols. (México: Imp. de don Victoriano Agüeros, 1896-1899).

BIBLIOGRAPHY: Victoriano Agüeros, "Don Joaquín García Icazbalceta," in *Escritores mexicanos contemporáneos* (México: Escalante, 1880), pp. 35-56; "Don Joaquín García Icazbalceta," in *Divulgación histórica* 3, 1 (Mexico, 1941). Alberto María Carreño, "La obra personal de los miembros de la Academia Mexicana," in *Memorias de la Academia Mexicana*, vol. 8 (México: Edit. Jus, 1946), pp. 126-37; "D. Joaquín García Icazbalceta," in *Memorias de la Academia Mexicana*, vol. 13 (México: Edit. Jus, 1955), pp. 250-75; in *Abside* 9, 2 (1945). Antonio Castro Leal, Prologue to *Don Fr. Juan de Zumárraga, Obispo y Arzobispo de México*. Juan Comas, Review of *Bibliografía mexicana del siglo XVI*, in *Revista de la Universidad de México* 9, 3-4 (Nov.-Dec. 1954): 30. Federico Gómez de Orozco, *Catálogo de la colección de manuscritos relativos a la historia de América formada por Joaquín García Icazbalceta* (México: Sría. de Relaciones Exterioes, 1927). Luis González Obregón, *Un tipógrafo ilustre: don Joaquín García Icazbalceta* (México: Talls. Tip. de *El Universal*, 1924). Manuel Guillermo Martínez, *Don Joaquín García Icazbalceta* (México: Porrúa, 1950). Aurora M. Ocampo de Gómez and Ernest Prado Velázquez, *Diccionario de escritores mexicanos* (México: UNAM, 1967), pp. 127-29. Sara Sefchovich, *México: País de ideas, país de novelas* (México: Edit. Grijalbo, 1987), p. 43. *El trato con escritores* (México:

INBA, Dept. de Lit., 1964), p. 13. Artemio de Valle-Arispe, "Don Joaquín García Icazbalceta," in *Historia de la ciudad de México según los relatos de sus cronistas*, 4th ed. (México: Robredo, 1946), pp. 277-80. Emilio Valton, *Homenaje al insigne bibliógrafo mexicano Joaquín García Icazbalceta* (México: Imp. Universitaria, 1954).

JEANNE C. WALLACE AND MIRTA BARREA-MARLYS

GARCIA Iglesias, Sara (1917-). Born in Mexico City on April 29, 1917, Sara García Iglesias studied chemistry, pharmacology, and biology at the Universidad Nacional. For three years she worked at the Hormona Laboratories and later founded and directed the Servet Laboratories of medicinal products. She traveled throughout Europe from 1949 to 1955 and later took trips to the United States. She has resided in Ozuluana, Veracruz, since 1955 and was president of the municipality from 1958 to 1961. Since then, she has been devoted to her ranch, El Bejuco, an inspiration for her novels.

Sara García Iglesias became known with her novel *El jagüey de las ruinas* (The Large Pool of the Ruins) (1944), which received the Miguel Lanz Duret prize in 1943, awarded by *El Universal*. Rich in customs of the region of Huasteca, the novel is about a family of landowners around the middle of the nineteenth century, facing a violent and barbaric world. Sentimental scenes are surrounded by historical events of battles at the time of the Reformation. The language also reflects popular phrases and regionalisms. In her second and last novel, *Exilio* (Exile) (1957), Sara García Iglesias develops the theme of cohabitation of Mexicans with exiled Spaniards and shows the conflicts in adaptation and understanding that arise from the situation in her country.

WORKS: Studies: *Los ácidos grasos del aceite de Tortuga en la tuberculosis experimental del cuy* (The Fatty-Acids of Turtle Oil in the Experimental Tuberculosis of the Guinea-Pig), thesis in chemistry-pharmacology-biology (México: UNAM, 1940). Novels: *El jagüey de las ruinas* (The Large Pool of the Ruins) (México: Porrúa, 1944). *Emilio* (México: FCE, 1957). *Isabel Moctezuma, la última princesa Azteca* (Isabel Moctezuma, the Last Aztec Princess) (México: Xóchitl, 1946).

BIBLIOGRAPHY: Antonio Acevedo Escobedo, Review of *Exilio*, in *El Nacional* (México, Sept. 22, 1957): 3, 8. Efraín Tomás Bo, Review of *El jagüey de las ruinas*, in *Letras de Mexico* 4, 24 (México, Dec. 1, 1944). Elvira Bermúdez, "Discurso sobre la literatura femenina," in *Las Letras Patrias* 3 (México, July-Sept. 1954): 34. Jacobo Chencinsky, Review of *Exilio*, in *Letras Nuevas* 1 (México, Nov.-Dec. 1957): 48. Ma. de la Luz Grovas, "Una impresión sobre *El jagüey de la ruinas*," in *Boletín de la Asociación de Universitarias Mexicanas* 5, 3 (n.d.): 87-97.

MIRTA BARREA-MARLYS

GARCIA NARANJO, Nemesio (1883-1962). García Naranjo was born in Lampazos, Nuevo León, on March 8, 1883. He was educated in his native state, as well as in Mexico City, where he attended the National University, from which he received a law degree. A poet and well-known orator, he became a member of the Atheneum group, where he brilliantly spoke for the expansion of Mexican culture. A volume of his *Discursos* (Addresses) appeared in 1923. García Naranjo was very involved in the politics of the time and was an anti-Madero deputy. He became minister of education in Huerta's cabinet. As minister of education he campaigned against positivism and changed the programs of study, lecturing widely, criticizing the philosophy of Auguste Comte. Upon the fall of Huerta in 1914, he fled to the United States. He was in exile for eighteen years.

A prominent journalist, he founded the newspaper *La Tribuna* and contributed to a number of newspapers and magazines in Mexico as well as abroad. He was a member of the Mexican Academy. He died in Mexico City on December 21, 1962.

García Naranjo wrote essays, poetry, theater, and short stories. Devoted to journalism and history, he published a study of *Porfirio Díaz* (1930), and another of *Simón Bolivar* (1931). His memoirs were gathered in a ten-volume collection. In these volumes he narrates the story of his life and offers his recollections of the rise and fall of Madero, as well as his travels with General Huerta. He wrote, and successfully presented a comedy, "El vendedor de muñecas" (The Doll Salesman), in 1937.

WORKS: Essays: *Venezuela y su gobernante* (New York: Carranza and Co., 1927). *Porfirio Díaz* (San Antonio, Texas: Casa Editorial Lozano, 1930). *Simón Bolivar* (San Antonio, Texas: Casa Editorial Lozano, 1931). *En los nidos de antaño* (Monterrey: Talls. de El Porvenir, 1959). Memoirs: *Bajo el signo de Hidalgo* (Monterrey: Talls. de El Porvenir, 1953). *Elevación y caída de Madero* (Monterrey: Talls. de El Porvenir, 1962). *Mis andanzas con el General Huerta* (Monterrey: Talls. de El Porvenir, 1962). Theater: "El vendedor de muñecas," *Teatro mexicano contemporáneo* (México: Impresora Juan Pablos, n.d.).

BIBLIOGRAPHY: Aurora M. de Ocampo de Gómez and Ernesto Prado Velázquez, *Diccionario de escritores mexicanos* (México: UNAM, 1967), p. 130. John Rutherford, *An Annotated Bibliography of the Novels of the Mexican Revolution of 1910-1917* (Troy, N. Y.: Whitston, 1972), pp. 49-50. Alberto Valenzuela Rodarte, "Mexicanos que han escrito memorias. García Naranjo. Los tres últimos tomos", in *Abside* 4 (Oct.-Dec. 1964): 445-52.

NORA ERRO-PERALTA

GARCIA Ponce, Juan (1932-). Born in Mérida, Yucatán, on September 22, 1932, García Ponce began his studies in Mérida and later studied dramatic arts at the Facultad de Filosofía y Letras in Mexico City. He received scholarships fom the Centro Mexicano de Escritores (1957-1958) and from the Rockefeller Foundation (1960-1961). He was a literary critic, using both his name and the pen name Jorge Olmo, for the magazines *Universidad de México*, of which he was chief editor, and *Revista Mexicana de Literatura*, which he directed.

Juan García Ponce became known as a critic of art, theater, and literature in general. In 1956 he received the award Premio Ciudad de México for his novel *El Canto de los grillos* (The Song of the Crickets), in which the author confronts conflicting worlds such as the capital versus the province and old age against youth. Through his short stories *Imagen primera* (First Image) (1963) and *La Noche* (The Night) (1963) he obtained immediate recognition as one of the best short story writers of his generation. His career as a novelist began with *Figura de paja* (Straw

Figure) (1964), in which he constructs a simple yet cruel world. The world according to García Ponce is viewed as a web of human relationships in an absurd world where the novelist tells but does not judge. In *La casa en la playa* (The House at the Beach) (1966), his second novel, García Ponce presents two couples in Mérida and concentrates on the psychological makeup of the protagonist, as she deals with the struggle between her interior world and the world that surrounds her.

In 1977 García Ponce won the Elías Souraski Award of the Arts and was decorated with the Cruz de Honor de Primera Clase para Ciencias y Artes given by the Austrian government in 1982.

WORKS: Theater: *Alrededor de las anémonas* (Around the Wind-Flowers), comedy in three acts, manuscript held by UNAM. *La noche transfigurada* (The Transformed Night), unpublished. *El día más feliz* (The Most Joyful Day), monologue, three-act play, unpublished. *El canto de los grillos* (The Song of the Crickets) (México: UNAM, 1958). *La feria distante* (The Distant Fair) in *CV* 51-52 (Mar.-Apr. 1965): 821-3O. *El otoño y las hojas* (Autumn and the Leaves), three-act play, unpublished. *Doce y una trece* (Twelve Plus One Equals Thirteen), staged 1964. *Sombras* (Shadows), in *Revista Mexicana de Literatura* 2 (Apr.-June 1959): 136-49. *Catálogo razonado* (The Itemized Catalogue) (México: Premiá Editora, 1982). Short Stories: "Cariátides" (Caryatids), in *Anuario del cuento mexicano 196O* (México: INBA, 1961), pp. 111-18. "Reunión de familia" (Family Reunion), in *Anuario de cuento mexicano 191O* (México: INBA, 1962), pp. 1O6-25. *Imagen primera* (First Image), six short stories (Jalapa: Universidad Veracruzana, 1963). *La noche* (The Night), three stories ("Amelia," "Tajmara," and "La noche") (México: Era, 1963). *Cuentos y relatos* (Stories and Tales) (México: FCE, 1972). *Antología personal* (A Personal Anthology) (México: Liberta Sumaria, 198O). *Figuraciones* (Imaginations) (México: FCE, 1982). *El gato y otros cuentos* (The Cat and Other Stories) (México: FCE, 1984). Autobiographies: *Juan García Ponce* (México: Empresas Editoriales, 1966). Essays: *Cruce de caminos* (Crossroads) in *Cuadernos de la Facultad de Filosofía, Letras y Ciencias* 29 (Jalapa: Universidad Veracruzana, 1965). *Nueva visión de Klee* (New Vision of Klee) (México: Madero, 1966). *Rufino Tamayo* (México: Galería Misrachi, 1967). *Entrada en materia* (Entrance into Matter) (México: Imp. Universitaria, 1968). *La aparición invisible* (The Invisible Apparition), 1968. *Nueve pintores mexicanos* (Nine Mexican Painters) (México: Era, 1968). *El reino milenario* (The Millennial Kingdom) (Uruguay: Arca Montevideo, 1969). *Cinco ensayos* (Five Essays) (Guanajuato: Universidad de Guanujuato, 1969). *Thomas Mann vivo* (Thomas Mann Live) (México: Era, 197O). *Vicente Rojo* (México: Imp. Universitaria, 1971). *Joaquín Claussell*, (México: Fondo Plástica Mexicana, 1973). *Trazos* (Outlines) (México: Imp. Universitaria, 1974). *Antología y pornografía. Pier Clossowsky, teología en su obra: una descripción* (Anthology and Pornography. Pier Clossowsky, Theology and His Works: A Description) (México: Era, 1975). *Errancia sin fin: Musil, Borges, Clossowsky* (Endless Wandering: Musil, Borges, Clossowsky) (Madrid: Anagrama, 1981). *Las huellas de la voz* (The Sound of the Voice) (México, 1982). *Una lectura pseudognóstica de la pintura de Bathus* (A Pseudoagnostic Reading of the Painting of Bathus) (México: n.p., 1986). *Apariciones* (Apparitions), an anthology of essays (México: Letras Mexicanas, *FCE*, 1987). Novels: *La presencia lejana* (The Distant Presence) (Montevideo, Uruguay: Arca, 1968). *La cabaña* (The Cabin) (México: Mortiz, 1969). *La vida perdurable* (The Everlasting Life) (México: Mortiz, 197O). *El nombre ovidado* (The Forgotten Name) (México: Era, 197O). *El Libro* (The Book) (México: n.p.,

1970). *La invitación* (The Invitation) (México: Mortiz, 1972). *Unión* (The Union) (México: Mortiz, 1974). *El gato* (The Cat) (Buenos Aires: Ed. Sudamericana, 1974). *Crónica de la intervención* (Chronicle of Intervention) (Barcelona, Spain: Bruguera, 1982). *De ánimo* (Of Spirit) (México: Los Abriles, 1984). Translations: Arthur Kopit, *¡Ay, papá, pobre papá, estoy muy triste porque en el clóset te colgó mamá!* (Oh Dad, Poor Dad, I Am Very Sad Because Mom Hung You in the Closet), play staged in 1964. William Styron, *La larga marcha* (The Long March) (México: Mortiz, 1965). Prologue: Cuevas, *Cuevas por Cuevas* (México: Era, 1965).

BIBLIOGRAPHY: Anon., Bibliographical note in *Anuario del cuento mexicano 1961* (México: INBA, 1962), p. 1O6; "Juan José Gurrola filmará una historia de García Ponce" ("Tajimara"), in *El Día* (Dec. 4, 1964): 11. Federico Campbell, "Cesare Pavese y Juan García Ponce," a comparison between "Viaje de bodads" and "Amelia," in *Cuadernos del Viento* 52-53 (May-June 1965): 846-47. Miguel Donoso Pareja, "Dos libros de Juan García Ponce," in *El Día* (Oct. 1, 1964): 11. J.A.G., "Espejo de libros. Juan García Ponce," Review of *La Noche*, in *Boletín Bibliográfico de la Secretaría de Hacienda y Crédito Público* 285 (Dec. 15, 1963): 26. Margarita García Flores, "La verdad sospechosa de Juan García Ponce," in *El Día* (Nov. 14, 1965): 4. Carlos González Peña, *History of Mexican Literature*, translated by Gusta Barfield Nance and Florene Johnson Dunstan (Dallas, Texas: Southern Methodist University Press, 1969), p. 451. María Luisa Mendoza, "La trayectoria de un escritor mexicano," in *El Día* (Nov. 3, 1963): 4; "Desde la barricada de la minoría. Habla Juan García Ponce de su voto, de su postura y de su verdad," in *El Día* (Feb. 4, 1965): 9. José Antonio Montero, "La vida de los libros. Dos novelas afines" (*En tela de juicio* y *Figura de paja*), in *Nivel* 23 (Nov. 25, 1964): 3. José Pacheco, Review of *El canto de los grillos*, in *Letras Nuevas* 4 (July-Aug. 1958): 45-47. Javier Peñalosa, Review of *Imagen primera*, in *Nivel* 11 (Nov. 25, 1963): 4, 12. José Pubén, Review of *Figura de paja*, in *Eco* 62 (June 1965): 229-31. Damián Trueba, Review of *Imagen primera*, in *Boletín Bibliográfico de la Secretaría de Hacienda y Crédito Público* 286 (Jan. 1, 1964): 2O. Ramón Xirau, Review of *Figura de paja*, in *Diálogos* 1 (Nov.-Dec. 1964): 32; Review of *Cruce de caminos*, in *Diálogos* 2, 3 (Mar.-Apr. 1966): 43.

                                                                MIRTA BARREA-MARLYS

GARCIA Terrés, Jaime (1924-   ). Born in Mexico City on May 24, 1924, García Terrés first became a lawyer. He then studied other disci-plines in France, a move that enabled him to become more fully aware of international trends in literature, aesthetics, and philosophy. Upon his return to Mexico, he became involved in some of the most important cultural institutions of the twentieth century, such as the Instituto Nacional de Bellas Artes and the Universidad Nacional Autónoma de México. He has supervised the highly respected publication *Universidad de México* and has been a regular contributor to many newspapers and literary journals both in Mexico and elsewhere. He is also considered one of the best translators in Latin America, if not the prèmiere translator. He has written and published essays as well. But primarily he is a poet, a member of the Generation of 1954, most of whose members were born around 1925.

García Terrés expects that a conscientious writer would assume a highly developed sense of responsibility toward his readers and the public in general and so noted in a stern essay in 1949. A literary critic of considerable renown, he compiled *La feria de los días* (The Fair of the Days), a volume of the articles that he had previously published in *Universidad de México*. As a poet, he is known for the simplicity of his verse, the clear manner in which his poetry is presented, and the easy, yet sober style of writing. In 1956 he published *Las provincias del aire* (The Provinces of the Air), and in 1961, *Los reinos combatientes* (The Warfaring Realms), the latter a more mature, more lyrical expression of verse. Nostalgia is one of the keynotes or dominant characteristics of his poetry. He seeks a structural and thematic balance in his verse, consequently producing generally well-polished poetry that combines reason with emotion.

Corre la voz (The Voice Flows) is a much later work (1980), a more mature poetry, simple yet profound, with a marked accent of nostalgia in some of the poems. Concerned with the flight of time, one of the poems in the volume, "Figuras al atardecer," a beautiful short lyric, is reminiscent in tone, theme, and style to some of the poetry of both Antonio Machado and Jorge Manrique. Yet there is a significant difference in that "Figuras al atardecer" focuses on the timelessness of the eternal present, conquering death and reflecting more on what is, simply savoring, but not dwelling on, what was.

WORKS: Essays: *Panorama de la crítica literaria en México* (Panorama of Literary Criticism in Mexico) (México: García Terrés, 1941). *Sobre la responsabilidad del escritor* (On the Writer's Responsibility) (México: n.p., 1949). *La feria de los días* (The Fair of the Days) (México: UNAM, 1961). Poetry: *El hermano menor* (The Younger Brother) (México: n.p., 1953). *Correo nocturno* (Nocturnal Mail) (México: Talls. Tip. REM, 1954). *Las provincias del aire* (The Provinces of the Air) (México: FCE, 1956). *La fuente oscura* (The Dark Fountain) (Bogotá: Ed. de la revista Mito, 1961). *Los reinos combatientes* (The Warfaring Realms) (México: FCE, 1961). *Grecia 60. Poesía y verdad* (Greece 60. Poetry and Truth) (México: Eds. Era, 1962). *Corre la voz* (The Voice Flows) (México: Mortiz, 1980). Anthology: *100 imágenes del mar* (100 Images of the Sea), selection, notes, and versions (México: UNAM, 1962).

BIBLIOGRAPHY: Enrique Anderson Imbert, *Historia de la literatura hispanoamericana*, vol. 2 (México: FCE, 1954), p. 281. Emmanuel Carballo, "El libro de la semana: *Las provincias del aire*," in *México en la Cultura* 400 (Nov. 18, 1965): 2. Frank Dauster, *The Double Strand* (Lexington: University of Kentucky Press, 1987), p. 29. Manuel Durán, "Música en sordina: Tres poetas mexicanos: Bonifaz Nuño, García Terrés, Aridjis," in *Plural* 8 (1972): 29-31. Raúl Leiva, *Imagen de la poesía mexicana contemporánea* (México: UNAM, 1959), pp. 329-31. José Lorenzo, "Jaime García Terrés: La búsqueda de la iluminación," in *Vida Literaria* 24 (1972): 25-27. Sara Moirón, "Latinoamérica se salvará como un todo, ya que ningún país se salva solo" (Interview), in *México en la Cultura* 574 (March 14, 1960): 1, 10. Carlos Monsiváis, *La poesía mexicana del siglo xx* (México: Empresas Editoriales, 1966), pp. 65, 703. *New Poetry of Mexico*, selection with notes, by Octavio Paz et al. (New York: E. P. Dutton, 1970), pp. 90-91. Aurora M. Ocampo de Gómez and Ernesto Prado Velázquez, *Diccionario de escritores mexicanos* (México: UNAM, 1967), p. 132.

JEANNE C. WALLACE

GARDEA, Jesús (1939-), novelist, short story writer, poet. Gardea received the 1980 Xavier Villaurrutia Award for his collection of short stories *Septiembre y los otros días* (September and the Other Days). Born in Ciudad Delicias, Chihuahua, on July 2, 1939, he studied odontology at the Universidad Autónoma de Guadalajara, from where he graduated in 1966. After practicing this profession for several years, he abandoned it in favor of teaching and is currently a professor at the Universidad Autónoma de Ciudad Juárez, Chihuahua. He has contributed to various Mexican journals and newpapers.

Although Gardea did not publish his first book until age forty, he was one of the most prolific Mexican writers of the 1980s. In little over a decade he has published seven novels, four collections of short stories, and a book of poetry. In his books he creates or re-creates, in concise and direct language, free of artifice, a hot, sun-drenched world that could be the Chihuahuan desert where he grew up.

Like William Faulkner, Juan *Rulfo, Gabriel García Márquez, or Juan Carlos Onetti, Gardea offers us an imaginary geographical space, Placeres, reminiscent of his native Delicias. In *Los viernos de Lautaro* (Lautaro's Fridays) the stories take place in a small, arid town inhabited by solitary, resigned characters, whose actions and beliefs are often fatalistic and where time seems to remain still. In his novel *El sol que estás mirando* (The Sun You Look At), Gardea tells the story, through the eyes of a young boy, of the town Placeres, somewhere in the northern Mexican desert. Here, as in pre-Columbian mythologies, the sun is a powerful force to contend with. The omnipresent sun burns with blinding light and suffocating heat, devouring the lives of the people it touches: "The sun eats the woman's legs, uncovered up to her thighs, and her face," "The heat in the patio buzzed like bees," "The daily heat was killing me. I was walking like in a dream and spinning around in an oven," the narrator tells us. In *Los músicos y el fuego* (The Musicians and the Fire), Gardea takes the reader once again to the heat and aridity of Placeres, where the air "tasted like dried mud," and to the marginal lives of several of its inhabitants: Bistrain, Amezcua, Montes, Valdivia. In his prose, Gardea skillfully captures images, feelings, memories, geographic details, and patterns of behavior. He is more interested in creating a particular ambiance than in patterns of action or plot.

WORKS: Novel: *El sol que estás mirando* (The Sun You Look At) (México: FCE, 1981). *La canción de las mulas muertas* (The Dead Mules' Song) (México: Oasis, 1981). *El tornavoz* (The Sounding Board) (México: Mortiz, 1983). *Soñar la guerra* (Dreaming the War) (México: Oasis, 1984). *Los músicos y el fuego* (The Musicians and the Fire) (México: Océano, 1985). *Sóbol* (México: Grijalbo, 1985). *El diablo en el ojo* (The Devil in the Eye) Not published. Poetry: *Canciones para una sola cuerda* (Songs for a Single String) (México: UAEM, 1982). Short Story: *Los viernes de Lautaro* (Lautaro's Fridays) (México: Siglo XXCI, 1979). *Septiembre y los otros días* (México: Mortiz, 1980). *De alba sombría* (Of Somber Dawn) (New Hampshire: Ed. del Norte, 1984). *Las luces del mundo* (The Lights of the World) (México: Universidad Veracruzana, 1986).

BIBLIOGRAPHY: Margo Glantz, "Los nombres que matan: Jesús Gardea," in *Literatures in Transition: The Many Voices of the Caribbean Area*, edited by Rose S. Minc (Upper Montclair, N.J.: Hispamerica, 1982), pp. 53-58. Rose S. Minc, "'Diálogo' con Jesús Gardea," in *Literatures in Transition: The Many Voices of the Caribbean Area* (Upper Montclair, N.J.: Hispamerica, 1982), pp. 59-62.

ALINA CAMACHO-GINGERICH AND ELADIO CORTES

GARFIAS, Pedro (1901-1967), poet. Garfias was born in Salamanca, Spain. He founded the journal *Tableros* and directed *Horizontes*, both Spanish Ultraísta periodicals. After 1939 he lived in Mexico, where he published most of his work. He is regarded as one of the first Ultraísta poets.

WORKS: *El ala del sur* (The Wing of the South) (Seville: n.p., 1926). *Primavera en Eaton Hastings* (Spring in Eaton Hastings) (México: FCE, 1939). *Poesías de la guerra española* (Poems of the Spanish War) (México: Minerva, 1941). *Elegía a la presa Dnieprostoi* (Elegy to the Dnieprostoi Dam) (México: Diálogo, 1943). *De soledad y otros pesares* (Of Solitude and Other Sorrows) (Nuevo León: Universidad de Nuevo León, 1948). *Viejos y nuevos poemas* (Old and New Poems) (México: Eds. Internacionales, 1951). *Río de aguas amargas* (River of Bitter Waters) (Guadalajara, Jalisco: n.p., 1953). *Antología Poética*, edited by Juan Rejano (México: Finisterre, 1970). *De soledad y otros pesares, antología* (Of Solitude and Other Sorrows, Anthology) (Madrid: Helios, 1971).

BIBLIOGRAPHY: Max Aub, *La poesía española contemporanea* (México: Imp. Universitaria, 1954), pp. 219-22. Trinidad Barrera López, "Un poeta olvidado: Pedro Garfias. Notas sobre *El ala del sur (1926)* y *Primavera en Eaton Hasting (1939)*." *Andalucía en la generación del 27* (Sevilla: Universidad de Sevilla, 1978): 25-60. Alfredo Cardona Peña, "Pedro Garfias, serafín de la sombra," in *Pablo Neruda y otros ensayos* (México: Eds. de Andrea, 1955), pp. 141-45. Enrique García Ruiz, Introduction, *Lo que Pedro nos decía* (Guadalajara, Jalisco: Ed. Colegio Internacional, 1971). Alfredo García Vicente, *Pedro Garfias (1901-1967): Antología homenaje* (Monterrey, Nuevo León: Ed. Sierra Madre, 1972). Luis Jiménez Martos, "Valdivieso, Laffon, Oliver y algunos otros poetas de los años veinte," *La estafeta literaria* 618-19 (1977): 16-19. Claude Le Bigot, "*El ala del sur* de Pedro Garfias y la visualización del texto político," *Insula* 364 (1977): 1, 5. Emilio Miro, "Poesía: Rafael Morales, Pedro Garfias," *Insula* 27 (1972): 6. Federico Carlos Sainz de Robles, *Historia y antología de la poesía española del siglo XII al XX* (Madrid: Aguilar, 1955), pp. 209, 1634. Angel Sánchez Pascual, *Pedro Garfias, vida y obra* (Barcelona: U. Pozanco, 1980). "Hacía la recuperación de Pedro Garfias," *Cuadernos Hispanoamericanos* 412 (1984): 168-78. Gloria Videla, *El Ultraísmo* (Madrid: Gredos, 1963).

MIRTA A. GONZALEZ

GARIBAY, Ricardo (1923-   ). Ricardo Garibay was born into a well-educated, intellectually stimulating family on January 18, 1923, in Tulancingo, Hidalgo. In his youth Garibay's maternal grandfather was his first teacher. From him he learned a love of literature, especially of the classics, and a sense of dedication and persistence to create truly polished verse. Garibay's parents also instilled in him similar values and objectives.

Friends with Rubén *Bonifaz Nuño, Henrique González Casanova, Fausto Vega, and others of the same generation, Garibay partook of the usual discussions of the day, revolving around existential issues. Reading, writing, talking, and walking were among his favorite activities in the later years of his adolescence.

Following secondary school studies, Garibay studied both law and literature at UNAM and became involved with experimental theater. He abandoned the pursuit of a career in law, being more interested in his literary endeavors. He read the Bible, the *Iliad*, and the *Odyssey* and was also inspired by a number of internationally well-known authors, among whom are included San Juan de la Cruz, William Faulkner, Earl Wasermann, José *Vasconcelos, Marcel Proust, and James Joyce.

He returned to law school and got married in 1948. In 1952, while a literature professor, he received a fellowship from the Centro Mexicano de Escritores. During the period from 1948 to 1955, he wrote and contributed articles to literary journals and newspaper supplements, such as *Universidad de México* and *Novedades*, participated in conferences and published a number of stories and the work *Mazamitla* (1955), considered either a long story or a short novel, dealing with the assassination of a humble peasant. In 1955 he turned to the film industry as his means of livelihood. Although he was not particularly successful in this endeavor, which he abandoned after several years, Garibay had traveled widely throughout Mexico and had developed much of the raw material for his literary production which would come later.

Among his later works are *Beber un cáliz* (To Drink a Chalice) (1965), a somewhat emotional work dealing with the death of his father. In 1970, he published *Lo que es del César* (That Which Belongs to Caesar), followed by *La casa que arde de noche* (The House That Burns at Night) in 1971, a novel considered one of his best works. Two recent works are *Par de reyes* (Pair of Kings) in 1983 and *Taíb* in 1988. Also, in 1984, he published *Confrontaciones* (Confrontations).

WORKS: Stories and Tales: *La nueva amante* (The New Lover) (México: Costa-Amic, 1946). *Cuadernos* (Notebooks) (México: Costa-Amic, 1950). *Cuentos* (Stories) (México: n.p., 1952). *Mazamitla* (México: n.p., 1955). *Beber un cáliz* (To Drink a Chalice) (México: Mortiz, 1965). *Lo que es del César* (What Belongs to Caesar) (México: Mortiz, 1970). *La casa que arde de noche* (The House That Burns at Night) (México: Mortiz, 1971). *Par de reyes* (Pair of Kings) (México: Eds. Océano, 1983). *Confrontaciones* (Azcapotzalco, D.F.: UAM, 1984). *Taíb* (México: Edit. Grijalbo, 1988). Essay: *Nuestra Señora de Soledad en Coyoacán* (Our Lady of Solitude in Coyoacán) (México: n.p., 1955). Biography, in *Los narradores ante del público* (México: Mortiz, 1966), pp. 61-65.

BIBLIOGRAPHY: Carmen Andrade, "Ricardo Garibay y sus mejores novelas *Bellísima bahía* y *La casa que arde de noche*," in *Vida Literaria* 24 (1972): 17-18. Jesús Arellano, Review of *Mazamitla*, in *Metáfora* 2 (May-June 1955): 38-39. Emmanuel Carballo, *Cuentistas mexicanos modernos*, vol. 1 (México: Eds. Libro-Mex, 1956), pp. xxiv, 93-94. Gabriel Careaga, "La novela," review of *Beber un cáliz*, in *México en la Cultura* 876 (Jan. 2, 1966): 3. Lourdes de la Garza, Review of *Beber un cáliz*, in *El Rehilete* 14-15 (July-Oct. 1965): 103-4. José Luis González, Review of *Mazamitla*, in *Ideas de México* 2, 11 (May-June 1955): 143-44. Aurora M. Ocampo de Gómez and Ernesto Prado Velázquez, *Diccionario de escritores mexicanos* (México: UNAM, 1967), p. 133. Margarita Peña, "Aparta de mi este cáliz," in *Ovaciones* 180 (June 21, 1965): 7. Manuel Scorza, Review of *Mazamitla*, in *México en la Cultura* 330 (July 17, 1955): 2.

JEANNE C. WALLACE

GARIBAY K., Angel María (1892-?). Born in Toluca, June 18, 1892, Garibay attended the Seminario de México (Seminary of Mexico) and was ordained a priest in 1917. A very scholarly member of the priesthood, he possessed an excellent knowledge of biblical Greek, Latin, Aramaic, and Hebrew, and even prepared a Hebrew dictionary. Above all, he was an acclaimed student of Nahautl, one of the most important indigenous languages of Mexico. He also had an admirable command of English, German, Italian, and French. Garibay worked with many indigenous and rural communities for more than twenty years following his ordination. With an intense desire to truly understand indigenous peoples, he spent most of his spare time studying their customs, traditions, and language. In 1941, Garibay was named a lectorate canon of the Basílica de Guadalupe and left the indigenous communities. At his new post, he studied and explicated the Bible, using its original languages as his point of departure. A distinguished member of the Academia Mexicana de la Lengua, he wrote for both Mexican and foreign newspapers, magazines, and journals, such as *El Lábaro, El Estudiante, Anales del Museo Nacional de Arqueología, Filosofía y Letras, México en el Arte, América Indígena,* and *Cuadernos Americanos.* In 1952 he was named "professor extraordinaire" at the Universidad Nacional de México. Beginning in 1956, he served as their director of the Seminario de Cultura Náhautl. Throughout his distinguished life, he received many accolades, diplomas, and honors. An eminent and learned humanist, he also taught and guided a new generation of students to appreciate and understand pre-Hispanic culture. This outstanding priest has often being considered the most competent expert and greatest authority on pre-Conquest literature, culture, and language. He was awarded the Premio Nacional de Literatura 1965 for his outstanding achievements. His studies (resulting in the *Historia de la literatura náhautl* [History of Nahautl Literature], 1954) have transformed the appraisal of ancient Mexico. Along with others in this field of literary endeavor, Garibay has shown the need to consider the indigenous antecedents in order to study Mexican literature. Although his work with indigenous cultures was his most significant achievement, Garibay was also an authority of Hebrew, Latin, and Greek language and culture, completing a variety of studies in the field.

WORKS: *El arte de la dirección* (The Art of Direction) (México: Asilo Patricio Sauz, 1922). *La poesía lírica azteca. Esbozo de síntesis crítica* (Aztec Lyrical Poetry. Sketch of a Critical Synthesis) (México: Asbide, 1937). *Esquilo, Trilogía de Orestes* (Esquilo, Trilogy of Orestes) (México: Asbide, 1939). *Llave del Náhuatl* (Key to Nahuatl) (México: Otumba, 1940); 3rd ed. (México: Porrúa, 1970). *Poesía indígena de la Altiplanicie* (Indigenous Poetry of the Tableland) (México: UNAM, 1940). *Epica náhuatl* (Nahuatl Epic) (México: UNAM, 1945). *Historia de la literatura náhuatl* (History of Nahuatl Literature), 2 vols. (México: Porrúa, 1953, 1954). *Verdad de la ficción. Acotaciones a un triálogo* (The Truth of Fiction. Notes of a Trialogue) (México: Academia Mexicana de la Lengua, 1954). *Fray Bernardino Sahagún Historia general de las cosas de Nueva España* (Fray Bernardino Sahagun "General History of the Things of New Spain"), 4 vols. (México: Porrúa, 1956). *Supervivencias de cultural intelectual precolombina entre los otomíes de Huitzquilucán* (Survival of Pre-Columbian Intellectual Culture among the Otomís of Huitzquilucán), special edition, no. 33 (México: Instituto Indigenista Interamericano, 1957). *La palabra humana* (The Human Word), in collaboration with J. G. Azevedo (México: UNAM, 1958). Natalicio González' *Ideología guaraní* (Guaraní Ideology), prologue (México: Instituto Indigenista Interamericano, 1958). *Veinte himnos sacros de los nahoas* (Twenty Sacred

Hymns of the Nahoas) version, introduction, notes (México: UNAM, 1958). Fray Diego de Landa's *Relación de las cosas de Yucatán* (Account of the Affairs of Yucatán), introduction, 8th ed. (México: Porrúa, 1959). Miguel León Portilla's *La filosofía náhuatl estudiada en sus fuentes* (Nahuatl Philosophy Studied in Its Sources), prologue (México: Instituto Indigenista Interamericano, 1956); 2nd ed. (México: UNAM, 1959). Fernando Díaz Infante's *Quetzalcóatl. Xochimapictli, Colección de poemas nahuas* (Xochimapictli, Collection of Nahautl Poems), version, introduction and notes (México: Eds. Culturales Mexicanas, 1959). *Visión de los vencidos. Relaciones indígenas de la Conquista* (Vision of the Conquered. Indigenous Accounts of the Conquest), version of Nahuatl texts (México: UNAM, 1959). *Vida económica de Tenochtitlan. I. Pochtecáyotl* (Economic Life of Tenochtitlan. Art of Trading), version, introduction, appendices (México: UNAM, 1961). *Esquilo. Las siete tragedias*) (Esquilo. The Seven Tragedies), translation from Greek with an introduction (México: Porrúa, 1962). *Sófocles. Las siete tragedias* (Sophocles. The Seven tragedies), translation from Greek with an introduction (México: Porrúa, 1962). Fernando Díaz Infante's *Quetzalcóatl. Ensayo psicoanalítico del mito nahua* (Quetzalcoatl. Psychoanalytical Essay of the Nahuatl Myth) (Jalapa: Cuadernos de la Universidad Veracruzana, 1963). *Los maestros prehispánicos de la palabra* (The Pre-Hispanic Masters of the Word) (México: Ediciones Cuadernos Americanos, 1963). *Panorama literario de los pueblos nahuas* (Literary Panorama of the Nahuatl Peoples) (México: Porrúa, 1963. "Los historiadores del México Antiguo" (The Historians of Ancient Mexico), *Ovaciones* (Dec. 8, 1963): 2-5. *Diccionario Porrúa de Historia, Biografía y Geografía de México* (Porrúa's Dictionary of Mexican History, Biography, and Geography), prologue (México: Porrúa, 1964). *Historiadores de la época colonial* (Historians of the Colonial Period) (México: Ediciones Cuadernos Americanos, 1964). *Mitología griega. Dioses y héroes* (Greek Mythology. Gods and Heroes) (México: Porrúa, 1964). *Libellus de Medicina libus indorum interbis*, introduction to Spanish version of Aztec manuscript (México: Editions of IMSS, 1964). *Eurípides, Las diecinueve tragedias* (Eurípides, The Nineteen Tragedies), introduction, notes, and translation (México: Porrúa, 1964). *Voces de Oriente* (Eastern Voices), anthology of literary texts from the Near East (México: Porrúa, 1964). *La literatura de los aztecas* (The Literature of the Aztecs), anthology (México: Joaquín Mortiz, 1964). *Poesía náhuatl* (Nahuatl Poetry), vol. 1 (México: UNAM, 1964); vol. 2 (México: UNAM, 1966). *Teogonía e historia de los mexicanos* (Theogony and History of the Mexicans), edition, notes and prologue (México: Porrúa, 1965). *Teatro helénico* (Hellenic Theater) (México: INBA, 1965). *Proverbios de Salomón y sabiduría de Jesús Ben Sirak* (Proverbs of Solomon and Wisdom of Jesús Ben Sirak), translation from Hebrew, notes, and prologue (México: Porrúa, 1966). *Cantares mexicanos* (Mexican Songs), vol. 3, part 2 (México: UNAM, 1968).

BIBLIOGRAPHY: Arturo Arnáiz y Freg, "El sabio Angel María Garibay," in *Ovaciones* 102 (1963): 1; *Cuadernos Americanos* 23 (1968): 148-52. Alberto Bonifaz Nuño, Review of *Poesía náhuatl*, in *Anuario de Letras* (1964): 356-57. Alí Chumacero, "Las letras mexicanas en 1953," Review of *Historia de la literatura náhuatl*, in *Las Letras Patrias* (1954): 122; "Dos lustros de ensayo literario (1953-1963)," in *La Cultura en México* (1963): xiii. Frank Dauster, *The Double Strand* (Lexington: University of Kentucky Press, 1987), pp. 103, 123. Héctor Fontanar, "Nombres de México, Angel María Garibay K., humanista," in *El Día* (Sept. 7, 1964): 9. Felipe García Beraza, "Los hechos y la cultura," in *Nivel* (Dec. 1963): 12. Raúl Leiva, Review of *Poesía indígena*, in *Nivel* 2 (Feb. 1963): 3. Miguel León Portilla, "El presbítero y doctor Angel María Garibay K.," in *Diorama de la Cultura* (Oct. 27, 1963): 3-4. Antonio Magaña Esquivel, Review of *Las diecinueve tragedias de Eurípides*, in *El Nacional* (March 15, 1964): 5. Javier Morente, Review of *Poesía náhuatl*, vol. 1, in *Diorama de la Cultura* (April 5, 1964): 4; Review of *Voces de Oriente*, in *Diorama de la Cultura* (May 24, 1964): 2. Angelina Muñiz, Review of *Poesía náhuatl*, vol. 1, in *Diorama de la Cultura* (April 19, 1964): 8. José Muñoz Cota, "Poesía náhuatl," in *Revista Mexicana de Cultura* (May 3, 1964): 3. Salvador Novo, "Cartas a un amigo," in *Hoy* (March 12, 1960): 19-22. Aurora M. Ocampo de Gómez and Ernesto Prado Velázquez, *Diccionario de escritores mexicanos* (México: UNAM, 1967), pp. 133-35. José Emilio Pacheco, Review of *Estudios de cultura náhuatl*, in *La Cultura en México* (Nov. 6, 1963): 137-38. Salvador Reyes Nevares, "Las antiguas culturas prehispánicas," in *La Cultura en México* (Oct. 28, 1964): xviii-xix. Mauricio de la Selva, Review of *Poesía indígena*, in *Cuadernos Americanos* (March-April 1963): 259. Rafael Solana, "El año del padre Garibay," in *El Libro y el Pueblo* (Oct. 1963): 1-2. Carlos Valdés, Review of *Historia de la literatura náhuatl*, in *Revista de la Universidad de México* 9 (Aug. 1954): 28. Various, *Estudios de cultura náhuatl*, volume published in honor of Dr. Angel María Garibay K., vol. 4 (México: UNAM, 1963).

JEANNE C. WALLACE

GARIZURIETA, César (1904-1961), short story writer, novelist, essayist, and critic. Garizurieta was born in TuxpAn, Veracuz, and died in Mexico City. His professional training was in law, and he became a magistrate on the Supreme Court. He was also a member of Congress and served in the diplomatic service, holding posts in Europe as well as in this hemisphere.

Although Garizurieta wrote in many genres, he is probably best known for his narrative works in which the primary vehicle for his themes are rural characters and traditions of his home state of Veracruz. Perhaps his most accessible work today is *Isagoge sobre lo mexicano*. In the four essays of this volume, he treats the development of Mexican character and identity, literature and art, asserting that the latter genres have not reached their maturity and singling out humor and reserve as the dual facets of Mexican character. The latter idea is reflected in his fiction.

WORKS: *Política agraria* (Agrarian Policies) (México: n.p., 1931). *Singladura* (A Day's Navigation) (México: A. Chápero, 1937). *Realidad del éjido* (Reality of the Cooperative) (México: Ed. Dialéctica, 1938). *Resaca* (Undertow) (México: Ed. Dialéctica, 1939). *El apóstol del ocio* (Apostle of Leisure) (México: Ed. Mundo Nuevo, 1940). *Un trompo baila en el cielo* (A Top Spins in Heaven) (México: Botas, 1942). *El diablo, el cura y otros engaños* (The Devil, the Priest, and Other Deceits) (México: Stylo, 1947). *Realidades mexicanas* (Mexican Realities) (México: SEP, 1949). *Isagoge sobre lo mexicano* (Exordium on Things Mexican) (México: Porrúa, 1952). *Memorias de un niño de pantalón largo; páginas autobiográficas* (Memories of a Child in Long Pants, Autobiographical Notes) (México: Ed. Ruta, 1959).

BIBLIOGRAPHY: Carlos González Peña, *Historia de la literatura mexicana, desde los orígenes hasta nuestros días* (México: Porrúa, 1966), p. 308. Luis Leal, *Breve historia del cuento mexicano* (México: Eds. de Andrea, 1959), p. 137. José Luis Martínez, *Literatura mexicana: siglo XX, 1910-1949, Segunda parte* (México, Ant. Libr. Robredo, 1950), p. 49. Aurora M. Ocampo de Gómez and Ernesto Prado Velázquez, *Diccionario de escritores mexicanos* (México: UNAM, 1967), p. 135. Elvira Vargas, "Recuerdo de César Garizurieta," in *México en la Cultura* 630 (April 9, 1961): 3.

                                                                       KENNETH M. TAGGART

GARRO, Elena (1920-) novelist, short story writer, playwright. Garro was born in Puebla, Mexico, on December 15, 1920, to a Mexican and a Spanish father. She spent much of her childhood in Iguala, Guerrero, the setting, she indicates, for her novel *Los recuerdos del porvenir* (*Recollections of Things to Come*). Her parents spent a great deal of time reading to themselves and to the children. According to Garro, she acquired her love of literature from them and her fascination with the interplay of fantasy and reality from the writers of the Spanish Golden Age, such as Miguel de Cervantes, Lope de Vega, and Pedro Calderón de la Barca.

She also was very interested in dance. At seventeen Garro was choreographer of the University Theater. She attended the National University (UNAM), where she was enrolled in the College of Philosophy and Letters.

She married Octavio *Paz in 1937 and only then took an interest in writing. She became a reporter and champion of the downtrodden, even to the point of spending time as an inmate in a women's jail in order to expose the poor living conditions. The family lived in many places as a result of Paz' studies and diplomatic appointments. While in Paris, Garro knew many writers of the surrealist group such as Benjamin Péret and André Breton. Her first novel and best-known work, *Los recuerdos del porvenir*, was written in Switzerland during a long convalescence.

Garro had many problems regarding her citizenship and passport since she had failed to choose Mexican citizenship at twenty-one. A notable detail regarding the writing and publication of Garro's works is the fact that many of them were written long before their appearance in print. She describes writing *Recuerdos* in the 1950s and then storing the manuscript in a trunk for several years. It was almost destroyed before finally appearing in 1963, winning the prestigious Villarrutia Prize for 1964. It was translated into English in 1969. Another early work, the play *Felipe Angeles*, written in 1954, appeared in an obscure journal, *Coatl*, in 1967, but was only performed at the National University in 1979 when it was finally published as a separate volume. Her excellent short story collection, *La semana de colores* (The Week of Colors), was also written in the fifties and published in 1964, and another novel, *Y Matarazo no llamó* . . . (And Matarazo Did Not Call . . .), was published in 1991 but written in 1957.

The break in the Garro-Paz marriage had become definitive by 1959. She lived in Paris until 1963 and then returned to Mexico, where she continued her work as a writer and reporter, still championing the powerless. When the attack on the gathering in Tlatelolco in 1968 took place, she was named as one of the intellectual instigators of the unrest and was jailed for nine days. Although nothing was proved, she fled to the United States and then to Spain, where she lived in obscurity for several years. Since 1980, she has lived as a near-recluse in Paris with her daughter. With the help of her friend Emilio *Carballido, she has seen the publication of four new books: *Andamos huyendo Lola* (We Are Fleeing Lola) (1980), a collection of short stories, and three novels, *Testimonios sobre Mariana* (Testimonies about Mariana) (1981), *Reencuentro de personajes* (Reencounter of Characters) (1982), and *La casa junto al río* (The House by the River) (1983). A collection of one-act plays published in 1957 with the title *Un hogar sólido y otras piezas en un acto* (A Solid Home and Other One-Act Plays) was amplified to contain the three-act play *La dama boba* (The Lady Simpleton) and all of her other one-act plays except *La señora en su balcón* (The Lady on Her Balcony), which was republished in 1983 under the title of *Un hogar sólido*.

Women and the plight of those on the periphery are constant concerns in Garro's work and these figures are often the narrators and/or protagonists. Their persecution and exploitation are related through violent images, language, and atmosphere, creating a world of alienation and loneliness and providing implicitly a criticism of the oppressing forces. Other recurring themes are time and memory. Her conception of time coincides with that of the pre-Columbian culture of Mexico: chronological or linear time represents the everyday world of strife and struggle while cyclical or eternal time is a mythic state of happiness and perfection. She understands memory as related to both past and future and emphasizes the repetitive nature of human action.

A kind of magical reality, present in many of her works, may be described as the occurrence of events not realistically possible yet presented matter-of-factly by the author. (*See* Magical Realism.) This mixture of fantasy and reality in her works is obviously an influence of the surrealists who took very seriously the beliefs of the pre-Columbian cultures.

Garro wrote *Recuerdos del porvenir* as homage to memories of her childhood home, Iguala. This poetic novel is divided into two parts, each centering on a woman. The beautiful Julia is the mistress of General Rosas, the commanding officer of the force occupying the town of Ixtepec during the Cristero Revolt. The tragedy and violence of the situation is described by the town as a collective narrator. At the end of the first part, Julia flees with a foreigner, Felipe Hurtado, who has been presented in magical-mythical terms, leaving the reader to decide what happened to them. Isabel becomes Rosas' mistress in the second part, which shows the death and destruction of the town and its people. At the end of the novel, Isabel has turned to stone because of her love for Rosas and abandonment of her family. *Testimonios sobre Mariana*, the first of three novels to be published nearly twenty years after the now-classic *Recuerdos del porvenir*, also deals with the themes of time, memory, and violence found in *Recuerdos*. As in her other novels, much of the violence is manifested as persecution. It concerns the memories of three different people of Mariana, the wife of a well-known Latin American archaeologist living in Paris. The first account presented is that of Vicente, Mariana's lover, who believes that they have found the perfect love. However, a divorce from his wife is not possible, and Mariana cannot leave her husband, Augusto, because of their daughter, Natalie. The second, and quite different, account, is presented by Mariana's friend, Gabrielle, who describes her as victimized by Augusto and his circle of friends. However, Gabrielle fails to give her support to Mariana because of Augusto's money. The third point of view is that of André, who befriends Mariana and falls in love with her. He discovers that Mariana and Natalie have apparently been driven to suicide by Augusto but have nevertheless appeared several times to André, who through his profession of undying love spares them the constant repetition of their suicidal leap from a balcony. The second of the recently published works was written in the 1960s, according to Garro's own recollection in an interview with this writer. *Reencuentro de personajes* is the story of an unhealthy, sadomasochistic relationship between the heroine and her lover, Frank. Garro recalls that some of the characters in this novel were inspired by the very characters who appeared in Francis Scott Fitzgerald's work *Tender Is the Night*. She met this author while living in Switzerland. The themes of *Testimonios sobre Mariana* and *Recuerdos del porvenir*, time, memory, and violence, are again prominent, and as in *Testimonios*, much of the violence takes the form of the persecution of the female protagonist.

La casa junto al río, a short novel in detective style with an underlying mythic structure, recounts the search of the heroine Consuelo for the truth about her vanished relatives. The tale of mystery regarding the past is again the setting for her preoccu- pation with the same themes already described. The story ends with Consuelo's murder, which is presented again in a magic realist fashion reminiscent of the end of *Testimonios sobre Mariana* and the first half of *Recuerdos del porvenir*. With her death she passes to another, happier dimension where she is reunited with the sought-after family members. The same themes are also present in her two collections of short stories. The early *La semana de colores* is a poetic collection of stories illustrating the whole gamut of Garro's concerns.

All of Garro's theatrical work dates from the fifties and sixties. The three-act play *Felipe Angeles* was her first theatrical work. It is a tragedy based on the life of a heroic general of the Mexican Revolution. Using the structure of classical Greek theater, she dramatizes her criticism of the Revolution through this "docudrama" form which has become popular among Spanish American playwrights.

Her other three-act work, *La dama boba*, is a clear demonstration of her interest in the Spanish classics and her concern for the downtrodden rural Mexicans.

WORKS: *Un hogar sólido y otras piezas en un acto* (Xalapa: Universidad Veracruzana, 1958); 2nd ed. (1983), amplified to contain all of her dramatic work except the one-act *La señora en su balcón* and the three-act *Felipe Angeles*. *La señora en su balcón. Tercera antología de obras en un acto* (México: Colección Teatro Mexicano, 1960). *Los recuerdos del porvenir* (México: Mortiz, 1963); 2nd ed. (Mortiz, 1980). *La semana de colores* (Xalapa: Universidad Veracruzana, 1964). *Felipe Angeles* (México: UNAM, 1979). *Andamos huyendo Lola* (México: Mortiz, 1980). *Testimonios sobre Mariana* (México: Grijalbo, 1981). *Reencuentro de personajes* (México: Grijalbo, 1982). *La casa junto al río* (México: Grijalbo, 1983). Translations of Elena Garro: *Recollections of Things to Come*, translated by Ruth L. C. Simms (Austin: University of Texas Press, 1969, reprinted 1986). *Un hogar sólido (A Solid Home)*, translated by Francesca Colecchia and Julio Matas, *selected Latin American One-Act Plays* (Pittsburgh, Penn.: University of Pittsburgh Press, 1973). *The Lady on Her Balcony*, translated by Beth Miller, in *Shantih* 3, 3 (Fall-Winter 1976): 36-44, also in Anita Stoll, *A Different Reality* (Lewisburg: Bucknell University Press 1990), pp. 59-68. *Los Perros [The Dogs]*, translated by Beth Miller, in *Latin American Literary Review* 8, 15 (1979): 68-85; also in Stoll, *A Different Reality*, pp. 68-79. *El Rastro*, in *Tramoya* 21-22 (First Epoch), (Sept.-Dec. 1981): 55-67; also in *Antología*, vol. 1, in *Tramoya* (15 Aniversary, 1990): 7-19.

BIBLIOGRAPHY: Robert K. Anderson, "La cuentística mágico-realista de Elena Garro," in *Selecta: Journal of the Pacific Northwest Council on Foreign Languages* 3

(1982): 117-21; "Myth and Archetype in *Recollections of Things to Come*," in *Studies in Twentieth Century Literature* 9, 2 (Spring 1985): 213-27; "The Poetic Mode in Elena Garro's *Los recuerdos del porvenir*," in *Proceedings of the Indiana University of Pennsylvania's Fifth Annual Conference on Hispanic Literatures* (Indiana: Indiana University of Pennsylvania, 1979), pp. 257-66; "La realidad temporal en *Los recuerdos del porvenir*," in *Explicación de textos literarios* 9, 1 (1981): 25-29. Daniel Balderston, "The New Historical Novel: History and Fantasy in *Los recuerdos del porvenir*," in *Bulletin of Hispanic Studies* 66, 1 (Jan. 1989): 41-46. Angel Bárcenas, Review of *La dama boba*, in *Revista Mexicana de Cultura* 889 (Apr. 12, 1964): 15. María Elvira Bermúdez, "Dramaturgas," in *Diorama de la Cultura* (Apr. 5, 1959): 4; "La novela mexicana en 1963," in *Diorama de la Cultura* (Jan. 19, 1964): 8. Francisco Beverido Duhalt, "Los perros de Elena Garro: La ceremonia estéril," in *Texto Crítico* 12, 34-35 (1986): 118-35. María Dolores Bolívar, "Ascensión Tun en la tradición del discurso de la mujer en América Latina," *Nuevo Texto Crítico* 2, 4 (1989): 137-43. Sandra Boschetto, "Romancing the Stone in Elena Garro's *Los recuerdos del porvenir*," in *Journal of the Midwest Modern Language Association* 22, 2 (Fall 1989): 1-11. Richard Callan, "El misterio femenino en *Los perros* de Elena Garro," in *Revista Iberoamericana* 46, 100-101 (1980): 231-35; "Analytical Psychology and Garro's 'Los pilares de doña Blanca'," in *Latin American Theatre Review* 16, 2 (Spring 1983): 31-35. Wilberto Cantón, "El teatro de Elena Garro: La poesía contra el absurdo," in *La Cultura en México* 191 (Oct. 13, 1965): xv. Emmanuel Carballo, "Todo es presente," in *La Cultura en México* 109 (Mar. 18, 1964): xix; "La novela y el cuento," in *La Cultura en México* 151 (Jan. 6, 1965): v; "El mundo mágico de Elena Garro," in *La Cultura en México* 158 (Feb. 24, 1965): xv-xvi; "Elena Garro," in *Protagonistas de la literatura mexicana* (México: Consejo Nacional de Fomento Educativo, 1986), pp. 490-518. Dolores Castro, "Los hechos y la cultura," in *Nivel* 22 (Oct. 25, 1964): 12. Eladio Cortés, "*Memorias de España*: obra inédita de Elena Garro." in E. C. *De literatura hispánica* (México: Editores Mexicanos Unidos, 1989), pp. 65-77; "*Felipe Angeles*, Theater of Heroes," in Stoll, *A Different Reality*, pp. 80-89. Sandra Messinger Cypess, "Titles as Signs in the Translation of Dramatic Texts," in *Translation Perspectives II: Selected Papers, 1984-1985*, edited by Marilyn Gaddis Rose (Binghamton: State University of New York at Binghamton, 1985), pp. 95-104; "Visual and Verbal Distances in the Mexican Theater: The Plays of Elena Garro," in *Woman as Myth and Metaphor in Latin American Literature*, edited by Carmelo Virgilio and Naomi Lindstrom (Columbia: University of Missouri Press, 1985), pp. 44-62; "The Figure of La Malinche in the Texts of Elena Garro," in Stoll, *A Different Reality*, pp. 117-35. Peter G. Earle, "*Los recuerdos del porvenir* y la fuerza de las palabras," in *Homenaje a Luis Alberto Sánchez* (Madrid: Insula, 1983), pp. 235-42. Frank Dauster, "El teatro de Elena Garro: Evasión e ilusión," in *Revista Iberoamericana* 57 (1964): 84-89; "El teatro de Elena Garro: Evasión e ilusión," *Ensayos sobre teatro hispanoamericano* (México: SeptSetentas, 1975): pp. 66-77; "Elena Garro y sus *Recuerdos del porvenir*," in *Journal of Spanish Studies* 8, 1-2 (1980): 57-65; "Success and the Latin American Writer," in *Contemporary Women Authors of Latin America: Introductory Essays* (Brooklyn: Brooklyn College Press, 1983), pp. 16-21. Cynthia Duncan, "La culpa es de los tlaxcaltecas': A Reevaluation of Mexico's Past Through Myth," in *Crítica hispánica* 7 (1985): 105-20. Manuel Durán, "El premio Villaurrutia y la novela mexicana contemporánea" in *La Torre* 49 (Jan.-Apr. 1965): 233-38. "The Theme of the Avenging Dead in 'Perfecto Luna': A Magical Realist Approach," in Stoll, *A Different Reality*, pp. 90-101. María Inés Fernández de Ciocca, "*Los recuerdos del porvenir* o la novela del tiempo," in *Revista Interamericana de Bibliografía/Inter-American Review of Bibliography* 36 (1986): 39-51. Martha Paley Francescato, "Acción y reflexión en cuentos de Fuentes, Garro, y Pacheco," in *Romance Quarterly* 33 (Feb. 1986): 99-112. Mark Frisch, "Absurdity, Death and the Search for Meaning in Two of Elena Garro's Novels," in Stoll, *A Different Reality*, pp. 183-93. Delia V. Galvan, "The Recent Writings of Elena Garro, 1979-83," *DAI* 47, 6 (Dec. 1986): 2173A-74A; "*Felipe Angeles*: Sacrificio heroico," *Latin American Theatre Review* 20 (Spring 1987): 29-35; "Las heroínas de Elena Garro," in *La Palabra y el Hombre* 65 (Jan.-Mar. 1988): 145-53; *Las obras recientes de Elena Garro* (Querétaro: Universidad Autónoma de Querétaro, 1989); "Feminism in Elena Garro's Recent Works," in Stoll, *A Different Reality*, pp. 136-46. Kay Sauer García, "Woman and Her Signs in the Novels of Elena Garro: A Feminist and Semiotic Analysis," in *DAI* 48, 3 (Sept. 1987): 660A. Alyce Golding Cooper, *Teatro mexicano contemporáneo, 1940-1962* (México: UNAM, 1962), p. 130. Harvey L. Johnson, "Elena Garro's Attitudes toward Mexican Society," in *South Central Bulletin* 40, 4 (Winter 1980): 150-52. Ruth S. Lamb, *Bibliografía del teatro mexicano del siglo XX* (México: Eds. de Andrea, 1962), pp. 57-58. Carlos Landeros, "Papel de la mujer en la obra teatral de seis escritoras mexicanas," in *Actas del Sexto Congreso Internacional de Hispanistas* (Toronto: University of Toronto Press, 1980), pp. 443-45. Catherine Larson, "Recollection of Plays to Come: Time in the Theater of Elena Garro." in *Latin American Theatre Review* 22, 2 (Spring 1989): 5-17; "The Dynamics of Conflict in '¿Qué hora es?' and 'El Duende,'" in Stoll, *A Different Reality*, pp. 102-16. Manuel Lerín, "Relatos desquiciantes," in *Revista mexicana de cultura* 926 (Dec. 27, 1964): 15. Monique J. Lemaitre, "El deseo de la muerte y la muerte del deseo en la obra de Elena Garro: Hacia una definición de la escritura femenina en su obra," in *Revista Iberoamericana* 55, 148-49 (July-Dec. 1989): 1005-17. Antonio Magaña Esquivel, *Medio siglo de teatro mexicano, 1900-1961* (México: INBA, 1964), pp. 159-60. Antonio Magaña Esquivel and Ruth S. Lamb, *Breve historia del teatro mexicano* (México: Eds. de Andrea, 1958), p. 161. Magdalena Maiz, "Una aproximación al paisaje cotidiano: Narrativa femenina mexicana," in *Cuadernos de Aldeeu* 1, 2-3 (May-Oct. 1983): 347-54. Joan Frances Marx, "Aztec Imagery in the Narrative Works of Elena Garro: A Thematic Approach," in *DAI* 47, 1 (July 1986): 193A; "The Parsifal Motif in *Testimonios sobre Mariana*: Development of a Mythological Novel," in Stoll, *A Different Reality*, pp. 170-82. Adriana Mendez Rodenas, "Tiempo femenino, tiempo ficticio: *Los recuerdos del porvenir*, de Elena Garro," in *Revista Iberoamericana* 51, 132-33 (July-Dec. 1985): 843-51. Doris Meyer, "Alienation and Escape in Elena Garro's *La semana de colores*," in *Hispanic Review* 55, 2 (Spring 1987): 153-64. Patricia G. Montenegro, "Structures of Power and Their Representations in Three Fictional Works by Elena Garro" *DAI* 47, 9 (Mar. 1987): 3441A. Gabriela Mora, "Rebeldes fracasadas: una lectura feminista de *Andarse por las ramas* y *La señora en su balcón*," in *Plaza* (Harvard University) 5-6 (1981-1982): 115-31; "*La dama boba* de Elena Garro: Verdad y ficción, teatro y metateatro," in *Latin American Theater Review* 16, 2 (1983): 15-22; "*Los perros* y *La mudanza* de Elena Garro: designio social y virtualidad feminista," in *Latin American Theater Review* 8, 2 (1975): 5-14. Patricia M. Mosier, "Protagonista y lector como detectives: Punto de vista en *La casa junto al río* de Elena Garro," in *Texto Crítico* 13, 36-37 (1987): 92-105. Michéle Muncy, "Encuentro con Elena Garro," in *Hispanic Journal* 7, 2 (Spring 1986): 69-76, also in *Deslinde* (University of Nuevo León) 5, 14 (1987): 39-44; "Perseguidos y perseguidores: El juego de la violencia en la obra de Elena Garro," in *Proceedings of the Indiana University of Pennsylvania's Tenth Annual*

272 GARRO, Elena

Conference on Hispanic Literatures (Indiana: Indiana University of Pennsylvania, 1985), pp. 308-18; Review of *Recollections of Things to Come*. Elena Garro," in *Hispanic Journal* 9, 2 (Spring 1988): 152-53; "The Author Speaks . . . ," in Stoll, *A Different Reality*, pp. 23-37; "Elena Garro and the Narrative of Cruelty," in Stoll, *A Different Reality*, pp. 147-58. Gloria Feman Orenstein, *The Theater of the Marvelous*: *Surrealism and the Contemporary Stage* (New York: New York University Press, 1975), pp. 110-17. Ane-Grethe Ostergaard, "El realismo de los signos escénicos en el teatro de Elena Garro," in *Latin American Theatre Review* 16, 1 (Fall 1982): 53-65. Luis Guillermo Piazza, "México y el tiempo en tres novels muy recientes," in *Cuadernos* 84 (May 1964): 107. Laura Radchik, "Las memorias de Cronos en las manecillas de Dios," in *Plural* 204 (Sept. 1988): 82-85. Mara Reyes, "Diorama teatral," in *Diorama de la cultura* (Apr. 28, 1963): 7. Salvador Reyes Nevares, Review of *Un hogar sólido*, in *México en la cultura* 517 (Feb. 8, 1959): 2. Martha Robles, "Tres mujeres en la literatura mexicana: Rosario Castellanos, Elena Garro, Inís Arredondo," in *Cuadernos Americanos* 246, 1 (1983): 223-35. Lady Rojas-Trempe, "Teatralización en la memoria de Elena Garro," in *Crítica de Teatro Latinoamericano* 1 (1989): 135-41; "Elena Garro dialoga sobre su teatro con Guillermo Schmidhuber: Entrevista," in *Revista Iberoamericana* 55, 148-49 (July-Dec. 1989): 685-90; "El brujo en '*La semana de colores*' de Elena Garro," in *Mitos en Hispanoamérica: Interpretación y literatura*, edited by Lucia Fox Lockert (East Lansing: Nueva Crónica, 1989). Lorraine Roses, "La expresión dramatica de la inconformidad social en cuatro dramaturgas hispanoamericanas," in *Plaza: Revista de Literatura* 5-6 (Fall-Spring 1981-1982): 97-114. Harry Enrique Rosser, "Form and Content in Elena Garro's *Los recuerdos del porvenir*," in *Revista de Estudios Canadienses* 2 (1978): 282-95. Patricia Rubio de Lertora, "Funciones del nivel descriptivo en *Los recuerdos del porvenir*," in *Cahiers du Monde Hispanique et Luso-Bresilien/Caravelle* 49 (1987): 129-38. Carmen Salazar, "In *illo tempore*: Elena Garro's *La semana de colores*," in *In Retrospect: Essays on Latin American Literature*, edited by Elizabeth S. Rogers and Timothy J. Rogers (York, S. C.: Spanish Literature Publications Co., 1987), pp. 121-27. Teresa Anta San Pedro, "La héroe de mil caras: Una caracterización de los personajes femeninos en la narrativa de Elena Garro," in *DAI* 48, 3 (Sept. 1987): 664A-65A. "La caida de los 'dioses' en el cuento de Elena Garro 'El día que fuimos perros'," in *Monographic Review/Revista Monográfica* 4 (1988): 116-26. Susan Spagna, "The Fantastic in the Works of Elena Garro: Questioning the Limits of Reality," thesis, University of California, Riverside, 1989. Emma Susana Speratti, el teatro breve de Elena Garro," in *Revista de la Facultad de Humanidades* (San Luis Potosí, July-Dec. 1960): 333-42. Anita Stoll, ed., *A Different Reality: Essays on the Works of Elena Garro* (Lewisburg, Penn.: Bucknell University Press, 1990); "Elena Garro's/Lope de Vega's *La dama boba*: Seventeenth Century Inspiration for a Twentieth-Century Dramatist," in *Latin American Theater Review* 23, 2 (Spring 1990): 21-31. Carlos Solórzano, "El teatro de Elena Garro: Una nueva frescura literaria," in *La Cultura en México* 167 (Apr. 28, 1965): xviii-xix. Joseph Sommers, Review of *Los recuerdos del porvenir*, in *Books Abroad* 39, 1 (Winter 1965): 68-69. Margarita Tavera Rivera, "Strategies for Dismantling Power Relations: The Dramatic Texts of Elena Garro," in *DAI* 47, 6 (Dec. 1986): 2175A. Kathleen D. Wilson Taylor, "La nueva narrativa mexicana: Revisiones y subversiones de la historia," in *DAI* 50, 4 (Oct. 1989): 959A. Vicky Unruh, "Free-Plays of Difference: Language and Eccentricity in Elena Garro' Theater," in Stoll, *A Different Reality*, pp. 38-58. Antonieta Eva Verwey, *Mito y palabra poética en Elena Garro* (México: U.A. de Querétaro, 1982). Raúl Villaseñor,

"Libros. Rev. of *Los recuerdos del porvenir*," in *Vida Universitaria* (Jan. 26, 1964): 7.
Francisco Zendejas, "El premio Villaurrutia de literatura," in *Diorama de la Cultura*
(Mar. 1, 1964): 7.

MICHELE MUNCY

GENIN, Augusto (1862-1931). The son of a French father and a Belgian mother,
Augusto Genin was born in Mexico City on June 18, 1862, and he died there on
December 3, 1931, but considering himself French, he chose to retain that nationality.
As a boy, he studied in France for many years, returning to Mexico in 1879. Travels
throughout Mexico and parts of the United States offered him materials for essays
he would write on a variety of subjects. During his lifetime, Genin had a number of
business ventures, serving at one time, for instance, as an agent for the French
government in the sale of Mexican tobacco. He also wrote several articles on that
subject. An astute businessman, he was able to combine his commercial interests with
his literary proclivities. He even converted his home into a center for Mexican and
French poets. Some of the most important literary figures of the day, such as the
esteemed Manuel *Gutiérrez-Nájera, frequented the meetings in his home.

Actually, most of his works, including his poetry and his essays, are in French, while
only a few are in Spanish. Almost single-handedly, Augusto Genin became the main
cultural link between France and Mexico in the early twentieth century. Because of
his commercial ventures also connecting the two countries, he found himself in an
unusual and enviable situation. A poet, translator, and dramatist, he also wrote
historical studies of Mexico and France; researched the dance, music, and song of
ancient Mexico; and drew attention to some of the ancient Indian legends.

WORKS: *Estudios sobre las razas mexicanas* (Studies about the Mexican Races)
(México: n.p., 1885); in French (1886). *Cuadro sinóptico de historia de México*
(Synoptic Picture of the History of Mexico) (México: Montauriol y Cía., 1887). *La
Fédération*, scène en vers (México: n.p., 1889). *Poèmes Aztèques* (Aztec Poems) (Paris:
n.p., 1890); 2nd ed. (México: n.p., 1908); text titled *Légendes et Récits du Mexique
Ancien* (Paris: n.p., 1923). *México, las capitales del mundo* (Mexico, The Capitals of
the World), in French (n.p.: n.p., 1892); in Spanish (Barcelona: n.p., 1893). *Le
Mexique en 1897* (Mexico in 1897), in *Le Nouveau Monde*, Paris, 1897. *Les Etats-Unis
Mexicains*, French translation of the work of R. de Zayas Enríquez (México: Imp. du
Ministère de Fomento, 1889). *Teotihuacán*, French translation of the work of Antonio
Peñafiel (México: Imp. du Ministère de Fomento, 1900). *La Révolution Française*,
poem (México: n.p., 1907). *La Marseillaise et la Mort de Rouget de Lisle*, poem
(México: n.p., 1909). *Pour Paris*, poem (México: n.p., 1910. *France-Mexique*, poem
(México: n.p., 1910). *Notes sur le Mexique* (Notes about Mexico) (México: Lacaud,
1910). *Vers pour Elle* (París: n.p., 1913). *Poèmes d'Amour* (París: n.p., 1913). *Notes sur
les Danses, la Musique et les Chants des Mexicains anciens et modernes* (Notes about
Ancient and Modern Mexican Dance, Music, and Song) (París: n.p., 1913). *Vers pour
la France* (México: n.p., 1918). *Sacrifice*, drama (París: n.p., 1925). *El Robinson
español* (The Spanish Robinson) (Madrid: Espasa-Calpe, 1927). *Rose Pompon*, drama

(París: n.p., 1927). *Les français au Mexique, du XVIècle a nos jours* (The French in Mexico, from the sixteenth Century until Our Day) (París: Nouvelles Editions Argo, 1933). *Poémes Choisis* (Selected Poems) (París: Editions de la France Universelle, n.d.).

BIBLIOGRAPHY: Luis A. Escandón, *Poetas y escritores mexicanos* (México: Imp. Ireneo Paz, 1889). Aurora M. Ocampo de Gómez and Ernesto Prado Velázquez, *Diccionario de escritores mexicanos* (México: UNAM, 1967), p. 137. Esperanza Velázquez Bringas and Rafael Heliodoro Valle, *Indice de escritores* (Talls. Gráf. de Herrero Hermanos Sucs., 1928), pp. 110-14.

JEANNE C. WALLACE

GERVITZ, Gloria (1943-). Gervitz was born in Mexico City on March 29, 1943. She studies history of art at the Universidad Iberoamericana in Mexico City. She is an avid arts and film collector. She has recently been traveling throughout Mexico and the United States holding readings of her work at universities and community centers. She regularly teaches a workshop on Don Quijote in Mexico City.

In both her books, *Shajarit* and *Yiskor*, Gervitz reaches into childhood memory and uses these elements to construct a syncretic vision of various generations that are spanned through the voices and faces of grandmotherly/fatherly Russian-Jewish immigrants, present-day women faced with the dichotomy of Judaism and Christianity and powerful erotic passages. Sandro Cohen suggests that the imagery in this poetry is heavily laden with a sense of pain yet vaporizes into a state of intimate frenzy dyed in red and other strong colors. Objects, dates, and persons fly around the poetic first person as planets around a star. "Her diaspora is perfect, complete and total."

WORKS: *Shajarit* (México: Imp. Madero, 1979). *Yiskor* (México: Esnard Editores, 1987).

BIBLIOGRAPHY: Sandro Cohen, *Palabra nueva: Dos décadas de poesía en México* (México: Premiá 1981), pp. 16-17, 68-73. José Joaquín Blanco, *Crónica de la poesía mexicana* (México: Katún, 1981), pp. 264-70. Jaime Moreno Villareal, *La línea y el círculo* (México: Universidad Autónoma Metropolitana, 1981). Sergio Mondragón, *República de poetas* (México: Martín Casillas, 1985), pp. 123-35.

RICARDO AGUILAR

GINER DE LOS RIOS, Francisco (1917-). Born in Madrid, Spain, on December 30, 1917, Francisco Giner de los Ríos, a noted poet, studied both at the University of Madrid and at Washington University in Washington, D.C., before the outbreak of the Spanish Civil War. Following its conclusion in 1939, he went to live in Mexico, continuing his studies at UNAM. He worked both for the FCE and for the Colegio de México, the latter under Alfonso *Reyes. He has continued to be of service at a variety of positions in Mexico City, including working as an agent for the university bookstore and as an editor.

Initiating his literary career with the publication of a few poems in the Spanish journal *Floresta, de prosa y verso*, Francisco Giner de los Ríos published his first book of poems, *La rama viva* (The Living Branch), in Mexico in 1940. His friend and mentor, Juan Ramón Jiménez (editor of *Floresta*) wrote the prologue for *La rama viva*. He has written several other volumes of poetry, a major study on Spanish poetry, and an essay on Antonio Machado, which has merited good reviews.

WORKS: Poetry: *La rama viva* (The Living Branch), prologue by Juan Ramón Jiménez (México: FCE, 1940). *Pasión primera* (First Passion) (México: Tierra Nueva, 1941). *Romancerillo de la fe* (Little Poem of Faith) (Guadalajara: Tiempo Literario, 1941). *Los laureles de Oaxaca. Notas y poemas de un viaje* (The Laurels of Oaxaca. Notes and Poems about a Journey) (México: Tierra Nueva, 1948). *Jornada hecha* (Day's Journey Done) (México: FCE, 1953). *Poemas mexicanos* (Mexican Poems) (México: UNAM, 1958). Anthology: *Tesoro de romances españoles* (Treasury of Spanish Poems) (México-Paris-New York: Bibl. de Cultura Técnica, 1939). *Las cien mejores poesías españolas del destierro* (The 100 Best Spanish Poems Written in Exile), notes (México: Ed. Signo, 1945). Essay: "Poesía española en México. 1939-1949," in José Luis Martínez, *Literatura mexicana siglo XX*, vol. 2 (México: Ant. Libr. Robredo, 1950), pp. 175-85. "Invitación a la poesía de Alfonso Reyes," in *Cuadernos Americanos* 7, 6 (1948). *A Don Antonio Machado al cumplir los 20 años de su muerte* (To Don Antonio Machado on the Twentieth Anniversary of His Death), prologue (1961). Translations: F. C. Bartlett, *La propaganda política* (Political Propaganda) (México: FCE, 1941). Augusto Comte, *Primeros ensayos* (First Essays) (México: FCE, 1942). R. H. Tawney, *La igualdad* (Equality) (México: FCE, 1945). N. H. Baynes, *El imperiod bizantino* (México: FCE, 1949).

BIBLIOGRAPHY: Anita Arroyo, *América en su literatura*, 2nd ed. (Puerto Rico: Editorial Universitaria, Universidad de Puerto Rico, 1978), pp. 299, 354. Max Aub, *La poesía española contemporánea* (México: Imp. Universitaria, 1954), pp. 186-87. Benjamín Jarnés, "De nuevo, el corazón," review of *La rama viva*, in *Hoy* 179 (July 27, 1940). Juan Ramón Jiménez, "Ardoroso y constante," in *Letras de México* 2, 13 (Jan. 15, 1940). Aurora M. Ocampo de Gómez and Ernesto Prado Velázquez, *Diccionario de escritores mexicanos* (México: UNAM, 1967), pp. 137-38.

ELADIO CORTES

GLANTZ, Margo (1930-), novelist, essayist, critic, and translator. Born in Mexico City on January 28, 1930, Margo Glantz studied in Mexico, Italy, and England and obtained a doctorate at the University of Paris in art history. She has taught at the UNAM (National University of Mexico) and has adapted theater works. She directs the magazine *Punto de partida* and contributes to cultural publications. She has directed the Literary Department at the INBA (National Institute of Fine Arts) (1982-1986) and has written essays on literature of the absurd. In both her novels and critical essays, Glantz shows an iconoclastic attitude toward the mores and myths of the human condition. In *El día de tu boda* (Your Wedding Day), she portrays Mexican life of the twenties and thirties, its European influences, and the adaptation of these European influences by Mexico. The book is handsomely illustrated with postcards of the era, whose significance and importance, as a means of communication, she discusses in detail.

WORKS: Essays: *Tennesse [sic] Williams y el teatro norteamericano* (Tennessee Williams and North American Theater) (México: UNAM, 1964). *Onda y escritura en México* (New Wave Writing in Mexico) (México: Siglo Veintiuno Editores, 1971). *Viajes en México* (Travels in Mexico) (México: FCE, 1982). *Repeticiones* (Repetitions) (Xalapa: Universidad Veracruzana, 1979). *Intervención y pretexto* (Intervention and Pretext) (México: UNAM, 1980). *Las Genealogías* (Geneologies) (México: Casillas, Editores, 1981), *El día de tu boda* (Your Wedding Day) (México: Cultura/SEP, 1982). Novels: *Las mil y una calorías* (A Thousand and One Calories) (México: Premiá, 1978). Translations: W. C. Wright, *Para comprender el teatro actual* (Understanding Today's Theater-Cinema, Stage, Television) (México: FCE, 1962). Tennessee Williams, *Baby Doll*, translation and adaptation for television drama, presented by Teatro Terrasola, México, 1964. Jerzy Grotowski, *Hacia un teatro pobre* (Toward a Poor Theater), (México: Siglo XXI, 1983). Thomas Kyd, *La tragedia española* (Spanish Tragedy) (México: UNAM, 1976).

BIBLIOGRAPHY: Fausto Castillo, "Entre Moby Dick y Blanche Dubois," review of Tennesse Williams, in *El Día* (Aug. 31, 1964): 11. Graciela Mendoza, "Mujeres de hoy," in *Diario de la Tarde* (Nov. 26, 1964): 5. Salvador Novo, "De Otli a la autopista," review of *Viajes en México*, in *Novedades* (Nov. 23, 1964).

NORA EIDELBERG

GODOY, Emma (1918-), poet, essayist, novelist, and dramatist. Born March 25, 1918, in Guanajuato, Guanajuato, Emma Godoy attended the Universidad Nacional Autónoma de México where she received a bachelor's degree in psychology and education and a master's and doctoral degree in philosophy. She did postgraduate work in philosophy at the Sorbonne and in art history at the Louvre. She held teaching positions at the Escuela Nacional de Maestros from 1947 and at the Escuela Normal Superior from 1949. In 1973 she retired from teaching. Her novel *Erase un hombre pentafácico* (There Once Was a Pentaphasic Man) was well received in the United States, and in 1961 or 1962, it won the William Faulkner Prize. This work deals with the philosophical problem of free will and was inspired by José Clemente Orozco's painting *Hombre pentafásico*. She has written biographies on Mahatma Gandhi and Gabriela Mistral and essays on women, the aged, abortion, euthanasia, art, and Hindu doctrine. She writes mainly love poems and religious poetry that is reminiscent of the mystics. Her poems refer to the relationships of the individual with divinity. Solitude, eroticism, and religion are her prevalent topics. Her theatrical piece, *Cain, el hombre* (Cain, the Man), has obvious religious overtones, but according to Godoy, it is also about the problem of unfulfillment, the artist who knows she will never reach perfect beauty or total truth.

WORKS: Poetry: *Pausas y arena* (Pauses and Sand) (México: Abside, 1948); 2nd ed. (Guanajuato: Universidad of Guanajuato, 1964). *Del torrente* (From/Of the Torrent) (México: Edit. Jus, 1975). Biographies: *Mahatma Gandhi* (México: Edit. Diana, 1982). *Gabriela Mistral.* Essays: *Doctrinas hindúes* (Hindu Doctrine) (1967). *Sombras de magia: poesía y plástica* (Magical Shadows: Poetry and Art) (México: FCE, 1968). *La mujer en su año y en sus siglos* (Woman in Her Year and Her Centuries) (México: Edit. Jus, 1975). *Que mis palabras te acompañen* (May My Words Accompany You) (México: Edit. Jus, 1976). *Antes del alba y al atardecer* (Before Dawn and At Dusk) (México: Edit. Jus, 1979). Novel: *Erase un hombre pentafácico: novel y algo más.* (There Once Was a Pentaphasic Man: A Novel and Something More) (México: Edit. Jus, 1973). Short Story: *Palomas sobre el mundo* (Doves above the World) (México: Edit. Diana, 1987). Theater: *Cain, el hombre* (Cain, the Man) (México: Edit. Jus, 1967).

BIBLIOGRAPHY: John S. Brushwood, *Mexico in Its Novel* (Austin: University of Texas Press, 1966), p. 49. Antonio Castro Leal, ed., *La poesía mexicana moderna* (México: FCE, 1953), p. 453. José Luis Martínez, *Literatura mexicana: siglo XX. 1910-1949: Primera Parte* (México: Ant. Libr. Robredo, 1949), p. 84. Beth Miller and Alfonso González, *26 autoras del México actual* (México: Costa-Amic, 1978), pp. 221-36. Hector Valdés, *Poetisas mexicanas Siglo XX* (México: UNAM, 1976), pp. 57-67.

MARGARITA VARGAS

GOMEZ de la Cortina, José (1799-1860), novelist, better known as El Conde de la Cortina. Although he was born and died in Mexico City, Gómez de la Cortina was of Spanish nationality. At age fifteen, he was sent to Madrid where he studied at the court and at the Academy of Alcalá de Henares. He became part of the Spanish Diplomatic Service. In 1829, he became a member of the Royal Academy of History. He left unpublished a biographical dictionary of renowned Spaniards. In 1832, he moved to Mexico, and shortly thereafter, in 1833, he founded the Institute of Geography and Statistics. That same year, he was sent away, the victim of a proscription law. In 1834, invited by Santa Anna, he returned to Mexico. He served as governor of Mexico City in 1836 and as minister of finance during 1838-1839. He contributed to the publication of *El Registro Trimestral* (The Quarterly Record), *La Revista Mexicana* (The Mexican Magazine), *El Imparcial* (The Impartial), *El Seminario* (The Seminar), *El Mosaico* (The Mosaic), *El Ateneo Mexicano* (The Mexican Cultural Club), and *El Apuntador* (The Prompter), and he directed the famous literary newspaper, *El Zurriago* (The Lash).

A scholar, grammarian, historian, and philologist, he wrote and published many books, among the most outstanding of which are dictionaries and biographies. Most of his work is unpublished, and some of his published books are lost, such as his two novels, *Leona y Euclea* (Leona and Euclea) and *La ciega de Trieste* (The Blind

Woman from Trieste). His short novel, *La Calle de don Juan Manuel* (Don Juan Manuel Street), is considered the first short story of Mexican literature based on legend.

WORKS: None of the following are dated. *Origen histórico de la Ciudad de Puebla* (Historic Origin of the City of Puebla). *La fundación de Puebla* (The Founding of Puebla). *Puebla, cuna de la independencia de México* (Puebla, Cradle of Mexican Independence). *Puebla y la bella literatura* (Puebla and Beautiful Literature). *El episcopado y la civilización en Puebla* (The Episcopate and Civilization in Puebla). *El clero y la independencia mexicana* (The Clergy and Mexican Independence). *Galería de obispos angelopolinos* (Gallery of "Angelopolinos" Bishops). *Contingente de Puebla al caudal de la literatura patria* (Puebla's Share of the Abundance of Patriotic Literature). *Biografía del Venerable don Juan de Palafox y Mendoza, bienhechor de Puebla y de los Indios* (Biography of the Venerable don Juan de Palafox y Mendoza, Benefactor of Puebla and of the Indians). *El pleito entre los Jesuitas de Puebla y el venerable Palafox y Mendoza* (The Litigation between the Jesuits of Puebla and the Venerable Palafox y Mendoza). *Apuntes para un diccionario biográfico de poblanos ilustres* (Notes for a Biographical Dictionary of Illustrious Poblanos). *Lo que Puebla debe a los españoles* (What Puebla Owes to the Spaniards). *Episodios históricos desconocidos* (Unknown Historic Episodes). *Tradiciones y leyendas de Puebla y otros poemas* (Traditions and Legends of Puebla and Other Poems). *La música de Puebla* (Music of Puebla). *Las calles hablan* (The Streets Talk). *Primera parte de la numeración cronológica de governantes del territorio poblano* (First Part of the Chronological Enumeration of Governors of Puebla Territory). *Versos* (Verses). *Algunos versos* (Some Verses). *Por España* (Through Spain).

BIBLIOGRAPHY: Enrique Fernández Ledesma, "El Conde de la Cortina y el Baile de su alteza," in *Galería*, (n.d.): 115. Luis González Obregón, *Breve noticia de los novelistas mexicanos en el siglo XIX* (México: Tip. de O.R. Spindola y Cía, 1889), pp. 16-17. Marcelino Menéndez y Pelayo, *Historia de la poesía hispanoamericana* (Madrid: Libr. Gral. de Victoriano Suárez, 1911), pp. 171-72. Francisco Pimentel, *Obra completas de Francisco Pimentel* (México: Tip. Económica, 1903-1904), vol. 5, p. 296. Lloyd J. Read, *The Mexican Historical Novel 1826-1910* (New York: Instituto de las Españas, 1939), p. 72. José Guadalupe Romero and J. M. Pereda, "Biografía del Exmo. Sr. D. José María Justo Gómez de la Cortina," in *Boletín de la Sociedad Mexicana de Geografía y Estadística* 8 (1860): 249-66. Francisco Sosa, *Biografías de mexicanos distinguidos* (México: Ed. de la Sría. de Fomento, 1884), pp. 274-85. José Zorrilla, *México y los mexicanos (1855-1857)* (México: Eds. de Andrea, 1955), pp. 101-7.

DELIA GALVAN

GOMEZ Haro, Enrique (1877-1956), poet, scholar, and orator. He was born in the city of Puebla on July 14, 1877. He studied law at the Seminario Palafoxiano (Catholic University) of Puebla. There, too, he taught international, constitutional, and administrative law. He also taught logic and history at other Catholic schools in the city, and he served as a judge in Puebla and Cholula. He was a member of the

Mexican Academy of the Spanish Language, of the Society of Geography and Statistics, and of the International Academy of History in Paris. He died in his native city on February 9, 1956.

Among his important works are three collections of poetry: *Versos* (Verses), *Algunos versos* (Some verses), and *Por España* (For Spain). Most of his writings, however, are a product of his research into the important historical and social events of his native city and state.

WORKS: *Origen histórico de la ciudad de Puebla* (Historical Origin of Puebla). *La fundación de Puebla* (The Founding of Puebla). *Galería de obispos angelopolitanos* (Gallery of Bishops from Puebla de los Angeles), 1899. *Poblanos ilustres: Apuntes para un Diccionario* (Illustrious Citizens of Puebla: Notes for a Dictionary) (Puebla, 1910). *Puebla y la bella literatura* (Puebla and Her Fine Literature). *Puebla, cuna de la Independencia mexicana* (Puebla, Keystone of Mexican Independence). *Lo que Puebla debe a los españoles* (What Puebla Owes to the Spaniards). *El clero y la Independencia mexicana* (The Clergy and Mexican Independence). *Biografía del venerable don Juan de Palafox y Mendoza* [Bishop], *bienhechor de Puebla y de los indios, 1640-1740* (Biography of the Venerable don Juan de Palafox y Mendoza, Benefactor of Puebla and of the Indians, 1640-1740) (Puebla: Ambrosio Nieto, 1940?). *El pleito entre los jesuitas de Puebla y el venerable Palafox y Mendoza* (The Dispute between the Jesuits and the Venerable Palafox y Mendoza). *Tradiciones y leyendas de Puebla y otros poemas* (Traditions and Legends of Puebla and Other Poems). *Existencia legal de los seminarios: Lo que han sido para México* (The Legal Existence of Seminaries: What They Have Meant to Mexico) (México: Publicaciones de la Academia Mexicana de Jurisprudencia y Legislación, 1944). *La música de Puebla* (Puebla's Music).

BIBLIOGRAPHY: Alberto María Carreño, *Memorias de la Academia Mexicana* 7 (1945): 187: 8 (1946): 140-41. Enrique Cordero y T., "Exaltación a don Enrique Gómez Haro," *Bohemia Poblana* 104 (Jan. 1952); "Duelo: fallecimiento de don Enrique Gómez Haro," *Bohemia Poblana* 150 (Mar. 1956); *Exlibris de autores poblanos* (Puebla: Imp. Estrada, 1960), pp. 33-34. Domingo Couoh Vázquez, "Un ciudadano ejemplar: E. Gómez Haro," *Bohemia Poblana* 104 (Jan. 1962); "El licenciado Gómez Haro, su fallecimiento," *Bohemia Poblana* 150 (Mar. 1956).

HERLINDA HERNANDEZ

GOMEZ Mayorga, Mauricio (1913-), architect and poet. Born August 5, 1913, in Mexico City, Gómez Mayorga received his degree in architecture in 1938 from the Universidad Nacional Autonoma de México. He has worked as an active architect and architectural critic as well as, internationally, as a poet. Gómez Mayorga has also served on several international architectural commissions and tribunals and he belonged to the literary *Grupo Taller*, along with other writers such as Octavio *Paz, Efrain *Huerta, Alberto Quintero Alvarez, and Neftalí *Beltrán.

Gómez Mayorga began writing creatively in his student days and has since developed a body of work in poetry and prose along with his professional writing as an architect. His poetry includes *Vírgenes muertas* (Dead Virgins), *Palabra perdida* (The Lost Word), and *Muerte en el bosque* (Death in the Forest). His prose works include *¿Qué hacer por la ciudad de México?* (What to Do for Mexico City?), *Genio y figura de nuestro idioma* (Form and Character of Our Language), *Ensayos críticos de arquitectura* (Critical Essays on Architecture), and *9 sátiras políticas* (nine Political Satires). He was still actively writing in 1987.

WORKS: *Vírgenes muertas* (Dead Virgins) (México: Edit. Fábula, 1934). *Palabra perdida* (The Lost Word) (México: Taller Poético, 1937). *Muerte en el bosque* (Death in the Forest) (México: Edit. Estaciones, 1957). *¿Qué hacer por la ciudad de México?* (What to Do for Mexico City?) (México: Costa-Amic, 1957). *Genio y figura de nuestro idioma* (Form and Character of Our Language) (México: SEP, 1966). *9 sátiras políticas* (nine Political Satires) (1971). *Ensayos críticos de arquitectura* (Critical Essays on Architecture) (1977).

BIBLIOGRAPHY: Aurora Ocampo de Gómez and Ernesto Prado Velázquez, *Diccionario de escritores mexicanos* (México: UNAM, 1967), p. 140. *Enciclopedia de México*, directed by José Rogelio Alvarez, vol. 6 (México: SEP, 1987), pp. 3410-11.

TERESA R. ARRINGTON

GOMEZ PALACIO, Martín (1893-?). Born in Durango on September 7, 1893, Gómez Palacio embarked upon a career in law, with an advocation in literature. A member of the short-lived literary association Nuevo Ateneo de la Juventud, founded in 1919, he was active in the cultural community, along with Carlos *Pellicer, Jaime *Torres Bodet, and José *Gorostiza, and he participated in many of the literary events of the day. Gómez Palacio's literary production is comprised of poetry, novels, and short stories.

A flor de la vida (To the Flower of Life) (1921) is considered one of his finest poetic works. Artistically lauding the rustic life of the provinces, he strives to show man's harmony with his natural surroundings. His novels, however, are quite different thematically, dealing mostly with revolutionary topics, as in *El mejor de los mundos posibles* (The Best of All Possible Worlds) (1927). A highly skilled and competent writer, Gómez Palacio peppers his narratives with irony and satire. As a social commentator of the revolutionary and post-revolutionary scene, he creates vignettes that truly illustrate the human cost of societal problems. In later works, he focuses less on the Revolution, although never quite abandoning it as a theme. Rather, he integrates it with more modern, and often didactic, themes.

WORKS: *La vida humilde* (The Humble Life), poetry (México: n.p., 1918). *A flor de la vida* (To the Flower of Life), poetry (México: Libr. Española, 1921). *Poesías* (Poems) (México: Colección Cultura, n.d.). *La loca imaginación* (The Crazy Imagination) (México: Botas, 1915). "A la una, a las dos, y a las . . .," (A One and a Two and a . . .), story (México: Edit. Cultura, 1923). "El santo horror" (The Holy Horror), story (San Luis Potosí: Imp. Beramen, 1925). *El mejor de los mundos posibles* (The Best of All Possible Worlds) (México: Imp. Politécnica, 1927). *Entre riscos y entre ventisqueros* (Between Cliffs and Between Snow-Drifts) (México: Eds. La Razón, 1931). *La venda, la balanza y ejpá* (The Blindfold, the Balance, and Ejpá) (México: Botas, 1935). *Viaje maduro* (Mature Journey) (México: Ed. Polis, 1939).

GOMEZ Robelo, Ricardo

281

El potro (The Colt) (México: Botas, 1940). *Cuando la paloma vence al cuervo* (When the Dove Conquers the Crow) (México: Botas, 1953). *La ambición del diablo* (The Devil's Ambition) (México: Botas, 1962).

BIBLIOGRAPHY: Ermilo Abreu Gómez, *Sala de retratos* (México: Edit. Leyenda, 1946), pp. 108-10; "Fantasmas y ladrones. Los viajes de Martín Gómez Palacios," *Revista Mexicana de Cultura* 855 (Aug. 18, 1963): 5; "Páginas de ayer," review of *Entre riscos y entre ventisqueros*, *Revista Mexicana de Cultura* 882 (Feb. 23, 1964): 4. Lanin A. Gyurko, *Mountaineering and Mythmaking in Gómez Palacio's "Entre riscos y entre ventisqueros"* (Morgantown: West Virginia University Press, 1982). Aurora M. Ocampo de Gómez and Ernesto Prado Velázquez, *Diccionario de escritores mexicanos* (México: UNAM, 1967), p. 140.

JEANNE C. WALLACE

GOMEZ Robelo, Ricardo (1884-1924). A brilliant orator, Gómez Robelo belonged to the Atheneum of Youth, a group of writers, with whom he shared the same philosophical concerns. Opposed to the materialistic philosophy of the positivist, Gómez Robelo initiated the campaign against positivism early in his career. From 1901 to 1914 he contributed to the most important magazines in Mexico. He published his poems, prose, and translations in *El Mundo Ilustrado*, *Revista Moderna*, and *Savia Moderna*.

A lawyer by profession, he held many government posts. During the government of Huerta, he served as attorney general. When Huerta fell in 1914, Gómez Robelo was forced to live in exile. Between 1915 and 1920 he lived in San Antonio, Texas, and Los Angeles, California. There he resumed his journalistic career and joined the staff of *Revista Mexicana*, where he wrote mostly political articles.

Upon his return to Mexico in 1920, he continued to publish in magazines such as *México Moderno*, *Azulejos*, and *El Maestro*. After 1921 he stopped writing to pursue other cultural activities as inspector of libraries, and in the Department of Fine Arts. He died in Mexico City, after a long and painful illness, on August 6, 1924, when he was only forty years old.

Gómez Robelo wrote poetry and prose. His first poem, "Nupcial," appeared in *El Mundo Ilustrado* on September 28, 1905. In 1906 he published a brief volume of poems and translations entitled *En el camino* (On the Road). The theme of this book is love. In these poems he delves into the feelings provoked by the presence or absence of women. While in exile, he wrote another book of poems, *Sátiros y amores* (Satyrs and Loves), published posthumously in 1984 by Fernando Tola de Habich.

During his brief career he participated in many journals with a variety of articles on literary criticism, politics and history, chronicles and translations. He composed a biography of Porfirio Díaz named *Album de Díaz* (Díaz' Album) that was published by *Revista Mexicana* in 1916. His last work was an analysis and study of symbols in pre-Columbian cultures entitled *El significado esotérico de algunos símbolos nahoas* (The Esoteric Meaning of Some Symbols in Nahuatl), published in 1924 by the National Museum of Anthropology, History and Ethnography.

WORKS: Poetry: *En el camino* (México: n.p., 1906). *Sátiros y amores* (México: Premiá Editores, 1984). Essays: *Album de Díaz* (San Antonio: Revista Mexicana, 1916).

BIBLIOGRAPHY: Aurora M. Ocampo de Gómez and Ernesto Prado Velázquez, *Diccionario de escritores mexicanos* (México: UNAM, 1967), pp. 140-41. Fernando Tola de Habich, "Ricardo Gómez Robelo: olvidos y precisiones," *Texto crítico* 10, 29 (May-Aug. 1984): 206-18. Serge I. Zaitzeff, "La obra de Ricardo Gómez Robelo," *Abside* 39, 2 (Apr.-June 1975): 224-39.

NORA ERRO-PERALTA

GOMIS Soler, José (1900-), jurist, philologist, novelist, and essayist was born in Argelia, educated in Spain, and exiled in Mexico City after 1940. He served as public prosecutor of the Supreme Court, and as professor of Arab law and Arab grammar at the Escuela de Altos Estudios Marroquíes in Tetuán before being exiled from Spain. In Mexico he has worked as a journalist and editor of the weekly *Tiempo*.

WORKS: Essays: *Derecho civil musulmán* (Moslem Civil Law) (Tetuán: n.p., 1926). *Elementos de derecho civil mexicano* (Elements of Mexican Civil Law), co-author (México: Excelsior, 1942, 1943). *Teoría qeneral de las obligaciones* (General Theory of Obligations) (México: Excelsior, 1944). Short Stories: *Leyendas del Mogreb: cuentos y leyendas marroquíes* (Legends of the Mogreb: Moroccan Stories and Legends) (Melilla: n.p., 1920). Novels: *Cruces sin Cristo* (Crosses without a Christ) (México: Cía. Grl. de Ediciones, 1952). *Andanzas y aventuras de Berruguín* (Adventures and Misadventures of Berruguin) (México: Ed. EDAL, 1960).

BIBLIOGRAPHY: José R. Marra López, *Narrativa española fuera de España* (Madrid: Guadarrama, 1963), p. 518.

MIRTA A. GONZALEZ

GONGORISM. See BAROQUE.

GONZALEZ, José Luis (1926-), short story writer, novelist, and essayist. González was born in the Dominican Republic on March 8, 1926, of a Dominican mother and a Puerto Rican father. His family moved to Puerto Rico when he was four years old. González completed his bachelor's degree in political science in 1946 and moved to New York to do graduate work and lived in that city four years. Because of his strong advocacy of independence for Puerto Rico, he lived in exile in Europe, principally in Czechoslovakia, from 1950 to 1952. He then moved to Mexico and became a Mexican citizen in 1955. He completed a doctorate at the University of Mexico, where he presently holds a post as professor of Latin American literature and sociology of literature. He also has been a visiting professor in various universities in Europe, Puerto Rico, and the United States.

When González was an undergraduate at the University of Puerto Rico, he received his first literary inspiration from the Dominican writer Juan Bosch, during the latter's period of exile in Puerto Rico. Life in New York provided the background for many of González' short stories: "Paisa," "En Nueva York," "Paisaje," and "La noche en que volvimos a ser gente." In his fiction and essays he deals primary with the theme of the Puerto Rican Diaspora and the political future of the island. He has also written a historical novel dealing with the invasion of the island by the Americans in 1898, entitled *La llegada*. His style is unadorned, yet manifests highly poetic imagery and extensive use of dialogue. Action is reminiscent of Ernest Hemingway, especially in the World War II battle scenes of the first two parts of *Mambrú se fue a la guerra*. He is one of the first Puerto Rican novelists to utilize humor to enhance the presentation of his themes. In his essays he demonstrates a great degree of freedom and objectivity regarding the history, present status, and future of his homeland, remaining an ardent advocate for Puerto Rican independence, but taking a broader worldview of the entire political-cultural-sociological phenomenon. He is a very prolific writer and an active professor and lecturer at a number of universities. The quality of his work was recognized by his contemporaries in Mexico when he was awarded the prestigious Premio Xavier Villarrutia for *Balada de otro tiempo*.

WORKS: *En la sombra* (In the Shadow) (San Juan: Imp. "Venezuela," 1943). *Cinco cuentos de sangre* (Five Stories of Blood)(San Juan: Imp. "Venezuela," 1945). *El hombre en la calle* (The Man on the Street) (San Juan: Ed. Bohique, 1948). *Paisa* (Paisa) (México: FCE, 1950). *En este lado* (On This Side) (México: Eds. Los Presentes, 1954). "La tercera llamada" (The Third Call), in *Sin Nombre* 1, 2 (Oct.-Dec. 1970): 28-40. "La noche que volvimos a ser gente" (The Night We Became People Again), in *Revista del Instituto de Cultura Puertorriqueña* 14, 52 (July-Sept. 1971): 3-10. *Mambrú se fue a la guerra y otros relatos* (Mambrú Went Off to War and Other Tales) (México: Mortiz, 1972). "Liberación" (Liberation), in *Caravelle* 18 (1972): 117-27. *Cuento de cuentos y once más* (Story of Stories and Eleven More) (México: Extemporáneos, 1973). *En Nueva York y Otras Desgracias* (In New York and Other Misfortunes) (México: Siglo Veintiuno Editores, 1973). "Te tragó la ballena" (The Whale Swallowed You Up), in *Sin Nombre* 1 (July-Sept. 1973): 16-19. "Historia de vecinos" (Neighbor's Tale), in *Sin Nombre* 5, 4 (April-June 1975): 21-28. *La galería y otros cuentos* (The Gallery and Other Stories) (México: Era, 1977). "Un nuevo narrador mexicano" (A New Mexican Narrator), in *Plural* 71 (Aug. 1977): 24-25. *Balada de Otro Tiempo* (Ballad of Another Time) (Río Piedras: Ediciones Huracán, 1978). "Puerto Rico en la hora cero" (Puerto Rico at Zero Hour), in *Revista de la Universidad de México* 34, 3 (Nov. 1979): 29-31. "Puerto Rico: el país de cuatro pisos" (Puerto Rico: The Country of Four Stories), in *Plural* 9, 2 *Epoca*, no. 99 (Dec. 1979): 14-25. "Delito de opinión: la lección de un holocausto" (Crime of Opinión: The Lesson of a Holocaust) in *Revista de la Universidad de México* 34, 6-7 (Feb.-March 1980): 100-2. *La llegada* (Crónica con "Ficción") [The Arrival (Chronicle with "Fiction")] (México: Mortiz, 1980). *El país de cuatro pisos y otros ensayos* (The Country of Four Stories and Other Essays) (Río Piedras: Ediciones Huracán, 1980). *Las caricias del tigre* (The Tiger's Caresses) (México: Mortiz, 1984). *El oído de Dios* (The Ear of God) (México: Era, 1984). *Nueva visita al país del cuarto piso* (New Visit to the Country of the Fourth Story)(Santurce: Libros del Flamboyán, 1986). *Ballad of Another Time*, translated by Asa Zatz (Tulsa: Council Oak Books, 1987).

BIBLIOGRAPHY: Arcadio Díaz Quiñones, *Conversación con José Luis González* (Río Piedras: Ediciones Huracán, 1976); "José Luis González, premio Villarrutia," in

Plural 8, 90 (March 1979): 62-63. Juan Escalera Ortíz, "Estilo, técnica y temática en *'La noche que volvimos a ser gente'* de José Luis González," in *Revista/Review Interamericana* 10, 3 (Fall 1980): 320-25. "La emigración puertorriqueña a Nueva York en los cuentos de José Luis González, Pedro Juan Soto y José Luis Vivas Maldonado," Ph.D., University of Iowa, Iowa City, 1981. Juan Flores, "The Puerto Rico That José González Built: Comments on Cultural History," in *Latin American Perspectives* 11, 3 (Summer 1984): 173, 184. Nora G. Orthmann and Caridad L. Silva de Velázquez, "José Luis González: observaciones sobre su obra y su generacion," in *Sin Nombre* 10, 2 (July-Sept. 1979): 29-38. Hector M. Otero, "José Luis González and National Mass Consciousness in Puerto Rico," Ph.D., Florida State University, Tallahasse, 1987. Raúl Alberto Román-Riefkhl, "Crónica de una llegada anunciada: *La llegada* de José Luis Gonzlez," in *Caravelle* 43 (1984): 69-80. Isabel Ruscalleda Bercedóniz, "Bibliogragía de José Luis González," in *Texto Crítico* 5, 12 (Jan.-March 1979): 115-27. Universidad Veracruzana, "Aproximación a *Balada de otro tiempo* de José Luis González," in *Texto Crítico* 5, 12 (Jan.-March 1979): 92-114.

KENNETH M. TAGGART

GONZALEZ Bocanegra, Francisco (1824-1861). González Bocanegra was born on January 8, 1824, in San Luis Potosí to a Spanish father and a Mexican mother. His family went to Spain in 1829, following the expulsion of the Spaniards, and remained there until Spain recognized Mexico's independence in 1836. Once again in Mexico, González Bocanegra continued his studies and became a businessman. He went on to hold several government positions, including general administrator of highways, theater censor, and editor of the *Diario Oficial del Supremo Gobierno.* He belonged to several important associations and was one of the founders of the Liceo Hidalgo. A distinguished figure, he wrote poetry, an autobiography, essays, a play, and the lyrics to the Mexican national anthem, for which he has won a place in Mexican history. He died on April 11, 1861, struck down by typhoid fever.

He drew inspiration for his poetry from Quintana, Cienfuegos, Gallego, and Zorrilla. Most of his poems were published in the literary newspapers of the day. González Bocanegra authored one play, *Vasco Núñez de Balboa,* a historical drama which depicts the violent fight between Vasco Núñez de Balboa and Pedrarias Dávila. He began another, *Faltas y expiación* (Faults and Expiation), but never finished it. As the official government censor, he left a legacy of ninety-seven critical judgments on plays performed in Mexico. They are contained in the manuscript *Censura de Teatros* (Censure of Theaters).

WORKS: *Francisco González Bocanegra, su vida y su obra* (Francisco González Bocanegra, His Life and His Works), contains *Vida del corazón* (Life of the Heart), several poems, *Vasco Núñez de Balboa, Faltas y expiación* (Faults and Expiation), *Censura de Teatros, México, 1859* (Censure of Theaters, Mexico, 1859) and two speeches (México: Imp. Universitaria, 1954).

BIBLIOGRAPHY: Bernardino Beltrán, *Historia del Himno Nacional Mexicano y narraciones históricas de sus autores, don Francisco González Bocanegra y don Jaime Nunó* (México: Talls. Tip. de la Nación, 1939). Rafael Díaz de León, *Los autores del*

Himno Nacional (San Luis Potosí: Edit. Valores Humanos, 1937). Heriberto García Rivas, *150 biografías de mexicanos ilustres* (México: Edit. Diana, 1964), pp. 187-88. Aurora M. Ocampo de Gómez and Ernesto Prado Veláquez, *Diccionario de escritores mexicanos* (México: UNAM, 1967), pp. 142-43. Joaquín Antonio Peñalosa, *Entraña poética del Himno Nacional* (México: Imp. Unversitaria, 1955). Jesús Zavala, "Semblanza del autor del Himno Nacional Mexicano," in *El Heraldo*, (San Luis Potosí, Feb. 17, 1948); "Para la biografía de Francisco González Bocanegra," in *El Heraldo* (San Luis Potosí, Oct.-Dec. 1952).

JEANNE C. WALLACE AND MIRTA BARREA-MARLYS

GONZALEZ Caballero, Antonio (1931-), painter, playwright, poet, and short-story writer. He was born in San Luis Potosí on June 20, 1931. He exhibited his paintings in México and abroad before becoming a playwright. He wrote his first play in 1958, *Señoritas a disgusto* (Ladies at Displeasure), staged in 1960 and restaged in 1980, which received the prize *El Heraldo* as best play of the year. His plays fit into the costumbrista (comedies of manners) line of Mexican theater and show a keen observation of life through a freshness and spontaneity in the dialogue. In 1964 his *Comedias a medio pelo* received the prize Juan Ruiz de Alarcón.

WORKS: Theater: *Señoritas a disgusto* (Ladies at Displeasure), (1958). *Una pura ... y dos con sal* (One Plain ... and Two with Salt), three acts (1964). *El medio pelo* (1964), made into a movie. *Los jóvenes asoleados* (The Suntanned Youths) (1967). *Nilo, mi hijo* (Nilo, My Son) (1967), filmed under the title *La casa del pelícano* (The House of the Pelican). One-act plays: *Asesinado imperfecto* (Imperfect Murder), *El mago* (The Magician), *Los dos amigos* (The Two Friends).

BIBLIOGRAPHY: Luisa Josefina Hernández, Review of *El medio pelo, Ovaciones* 142 (Sept. 13, 1964): 6. Antonio Magaña Esquivel, "Teatro. Homenaje a González Caballero," *El Nacional* (Sept. 22, 1964): 5.

NORA EIDELBERG

GONZALEZ Caballero de Castillo Ledón, Amalia (1902-1974), journalist, playwright, and essayist. González Caballero de Castillo Ledón was born in San Jerónimo, Tamaulipas; she died in Mexico City. An early feminist, she founded and collaborated with the Ateneo Mexicano de Mujeres (The Mexican Atheneum for Women) (1937-1949), an association which grouped together the women writers of that time. She wrote a weekly column entitled *Siluetas en fuga* (Fugacious Silhouettes) for the daily *Excelsior* (1946-1952).

WORKS: *Cubos de noria* (Hubs in the Chain Pump) (México: n.p., 1934). *Coqueta* (Coquette) (México: n.p., 1937). *Cuando las hojas caen* (When The Leaves Fall) (México: Stylo, 1945). *Bajo el mismo techo* (Under the Same Roof) (México: n.p,

1955). *Peligro, Deshielos* (Danger, Thawing Ice), first staged as *La verdad escondida* (The Hidden Truth) in 1963. Essays: *El movimiento intelectual femenino en México* (The Mexican Intellectual Movement) (México: SEP, 1937). *Cuatro estancias poéticas: Alfonso Reyes, Manuel Gutiérrez Nájera, Luis G. Urbina y Victor Hugo* (Four Poetic Sojourns: Alfonso Reyes, Manuel Gutiérrez Nájera, Luis G. Urbina, and Victor Hugo) (México: Eds. del Seminario de Cultura Mexicana, 1964).

BIBLIOGRAPHY: Ruth Lamb, ed., "Papel de la mujer en la obra teatral de seis escritoras mexicanas," Actas del Sexto Congreso Internacional de Hispanistas celebrado en Toronto del 22 al 26 de agosto de 1977 (Toronto: Dept. of Spanish and Portuguese, University of Toronto, 1980). Roberto Nuñez y Domínguez, *Descorriendo el telón: Cuarenta años de teatro en México* (Madrid: Ed. Rollin, 1956), pp. 363-65. Beth Miller and Alfonso González, *26 autoras del México actual* (México: Costa-Amic, 1978), pp. 139-52.

MIRTA A. GONZALEZ

GONZALEZ CALZADA, Manuel (1915-), journalist, essayist, novelist, critic, and biographer. González Calzada was born in Villahermosa, Tabasco, on July 7, 1915. He completed his elementary studies in his native city and later studied independently. He has traveled throughout Mexico. As a journalist, he has been a contributor to the supplement of *El Nacional*, and to *Novedades, Todo, Impacto, Nadie, Hoy*, etc.

   González Calzada is noted for his historical biography, *Las Casas: procurador de los Indios* (Las Casas, Proctor of the Indians), which won a prize given by the Talleres Gráficos de la Nación in 1948. His novel, *42 grados a la sombra* (42 Degrees in the Shade), is a series of stories that center upon one main character and one topos, the Tabascan countryside.

WORKS: *Ensayo, criticismo y biografía de la juventud izquierdista de México* (Leftist Youth of Mexico) (México: Congreso Constituyente de la CESUM, 1938). *Tomás Garrido (al derecho y al revés)* (Thomas Garrido [Forward and Backward]) (Pubs. y Eds. Españolas, R. en P., 1940). *Tabasco en dos conferencias* (Tabasco in Two Lectures) (México: Ed. by the writer, 1950). *Las Casas: procurador de los indios* (Las Casas, Proctor of the Indians) (México: Ed. Talls. Graf:. de la Nación, 1951; Consejo Ed. del Gob. del Estado de Tabasco, 1981). *José Martí*, introduction, collection of letters (México: Ed. by the writer, 1953; Consejo Ed. del Gob. del Est. de Tabasco, 1981). *Hombres y libros* (Men and Books) (México: Robredo, 1984). *Historia de la revolucion en Tabasco* (History of the Revolution in Tabasco) (México: 1972); (Consejo Ed. del Gob. del Est. de Tabasco, 1981). *Vascos en México* (Basque in Mexico) (México: Costa-Amic, 1975). *Los caciques y la tierra: dos ensayos* (Political Bosses and the Land: Two Essays) (México: Ed. Regina de los Angeles, 1976). *Documentos para la historia de Tabasco* (Documents for the History of Tabasco) (México: Comisión del Grijalvo, 1976). *El agrarismo en Tabasco* (Agrarianism in Tabasco) (Consejo Ed. del Gob. del Est. de Tabasco, 1980). *La Revolución Mexicana ante el pensamiento de José Carlos Mariátegui* (The Mexican Revolution and the Thoughts of José Carlos Mariátegui) (Consejo Ed. del Gob. del Est. de Tabasco,

1980). *Tabasco: hombres y nombres: historia y cultura* (Tabasco, Men and Names: History and Culture) (Consejo Ed. del Gob. del Est. de Tabasco, 1981). *Tabasco, 27 de febrero de 1864* (Tabasco, February 27, 1864) (Consejo Ed. del Gob. del Est. de Tabasco, 1981). *De como vieron y contaron los cronistas de Indias el Descubrimiento y Conquista de Tabasco* (How the Chroniclers of the New World Saw and Told the Conquest of Tabasco) (México: Consejo Ed. del Gob. del Est. de Tabasco, 1981). *Los vascos en México* (The Basques in Mexico) (Consejo Ed. del Gob. del Est. de Tabasco, 1981). Narrative Fiction: *42 grados a la sombra* (42 Degrees in the Shade) (México: Eds. Humanismo, 1954). *A esas horas y . . .* (At These Times and . . .) (México: Ed. Regina de los Angeles, 1976). *Entre puntos y comas* (Between Semicolons) (México: Consejo Ed. del Gob. del Est. de Tabasco, 1980). Theater: *Cafe París Expreso: Tragicomedia en dieciséis años* (Cafe Paris Expreso: Tragicomedy in Sixteen Years) (México: Federación Ed. Mexicana, 1973; México: Consejo Ed. del Gob. del Est. de Tabasco, 1980).

BIBLIOGRAPHY: Henrique González Casanova, Review of *42 grados a la sombra*, in *México en la Cultura* 270 (May 23, 1954): 2. Aurora M. Ocampo and Ernesto Prado Velázquez, *Diccionario de escritores mexicanos* (México: UNAM, 1967), p. 144.

JOAN SALTZ

GONZALEZ DE ESLAVA, Fernán (?-?). González de Eslava was born in Spain but exactly where is not known. He arrived in Mexico in 1558 and became a priest. He appears to have spent his life in clerical duties and literary pursuits. Several of his poems appear in *Flores de varia poesía*, collected in 1577, and in 1588 he was commissioned to write a play for the Corpus Cristi celebrations. Although the date of his death is not known, he was still alive in 1596.

His theatrical creations, sixteen colloquies, belong to the type of theater written before the influence of Lope de Vega. Many of these works are really staged stories rather than full theater pieces, with little action or development of conflict. His four *entremeses* (interludes) are especially interesting for the characterization and representation of local customs. His works are particularly important for the material they provide for the linguist and the historian, since they are rich with information on customs and manner of thought and speech of the colony. His poetry, which is particularly good when he treats popular themes, belongs to the tradition of Juan López de Ubeda and José de Valdivieso.

WORKS: *Coloquios espirituales y sacramentales*, edition, prologue, and notes by José Rojas Garciadueñas (México: Porrúa, 1958).

BIBLIOGRAPHY: Amado Alonso, "Biografía de Fernán González de Eslava" *Revista de Filología Hispánica* 2, 3 (n.d.): 213-321. Frida Weber von Kurlat, "Lo cómico en el teatro de Fernán González de Eslava" (Buenos Aires: University of Buenos Aires, 1963); "El teatro anterior a Lope de Vega y la novela picaresca (A propósito de los Coloquios espirituales y sacramentales de Hernán González de Eslava)," *Filología* 6 (1960): 1-27.

ANITA K. STOLL

GONZALEZ de Mendoza, José María (1893-1967). A naturalized Mexican, José María González de Mendoza was born in Sevilla, Spain, on June 23, 1893. He received his basic elementary instruction in Andalucía, his secondary studies in Sevilla and Mahón, then studied mathematics for several years while still in Spain. By this time, however, his family had already moved to Mexico, so he joined them in 1910, finding employment as an accountant in a commercial firm for about ten years. In 1923, he went to France to study at the Sorbonne and other schools, remaining there for five years. These were years in which the young González de Mendoza met some of the most influential people in his life, people who encouraged his literary endeavors and befriended him. In addition to his studies, he worked for *El Universal Ilustrado de México* as a foreign correspondent. Consequently, his literary vocation was truly awakened during this period. He was especially influenced by the philosophies of Arthur Schopenhauer and Friedrich Wilhelm Nietzsche, whose works he studied and absorbed. He also established a close friendship with Alfonso *Reyes, with whose assistance he secured a position as a member of the Mexican Diplomatic Service. González de Mendoza remained for many years in that capacity, serving at various times in Paris, Madrid, Brussels, Lisbon, and Havana, retiring from public administration in 1960. At home in Mexico, he also worked in various government departments, such as agriculture and external relations. During the 1930s, he was named to a number of special commissions, serving as a delegate to international conferences. One such conference, held in Brussels in 1938, was the Fourth International Conference on the Utilization of Wood. He was given membership in the Academia Mexicana de la Lengua in 1950, the Real Academia Española in 1952, and the Academia Nacional de Historia y Geografía in 1956. He died of a heart attack in Mexico City on April 10, 1967.

González de Mendoza preferred to be called by his chosen pseudonym, the Abate de Mendoza (Abbé de Mendoza). He occasionally used other pseudonyms as well, including Alvaro de Alhamar, Melchor de Navamuel, Clitandro, and Gonzalo Deza Méndez. His literary career-side by side with his diplomatic career-was impressive. He initiated it by publishing in the journal *Alma Bohemia* in 1917. Then, in 1919, he published a book of stories, *La emoción dispersa* (Scattered Emotion). Later, in 1925, he followed it with *El hombre que andaba y otros cuentos verosímiles* (The Man Who Was Walking and Other Likely Stories). His one novel was *La luna en el agua* (The Moon in the Water), also published in 1925. Here and there he published a few scattered poems during the early part of his career. He was awarded first prize in a contest of the Fourth Centennial of the Birth of Miguel de Cervantes, sponsored by the Academia Mexicana in 1947. From 1948 to 1953, he was the director of the journal *México de hoy*.

Although he wrote only a few stories, some poetry (hai kai style), and a novel, he was most well known for his essays and prologues. He wrote, for instance, more than 2,500 articles and essays on a wide range of subjects, including travel journals, biographical sketches, studies of works by other authors, and ethical, moral, and philosophical questions. A highly erudite thinker and writer, he was considered one of the leading intellectuals of the first half of the twentieth century. He studied and wrote about the works of José Juan *Tablada, Mariano *Azuela, Alfonso Reyes, Francisco *Monterde, Francisco *Urquizo, Miguel de Cervantes, and many others. Through his intensive studies, he recognized and made known the predilection of Sor Juana Inés de la *Cruz for science. Considered a creative and inventive man, González de Mendoza kept himself well-informed of the latest literary news and trends, enabling him to make critical assessments based on the latest information. In collaboration with Miguel Angel Asturias, González de Mendoza translated into Spanish many of Georges Raynaud's French versions of the *Popol Vuh* and the annals of *Xahil*, containing the indigenous literary myths, stories, and legends. He also wrote critical essays about Mayan literature.

José María González de Mendoza's greatest recognition and fame clearly came from his essays. But, as can be discerned from his business and diplomatic career, he was a well-rounded man, known also for his innate capabilities, his compatibility, personality and sense of justice.

WORKS: Stories and Novel: *La emoción dispersa* (Scattered Emotion) (México: Libr. Española, 1919). *El hombre que andaba y otros cuentos verosímiles* (The Man Who Was Walking and Other Likely Stories), "La novela semanal" (México: *El Universal Ilustrado*, 1925). *La luna en el agua* (The Moon in the Water), novel (México: *El Universal Ilustrado*, 1925). Essays: More than 2,500 articles in various journals, magazines, and newspapers. *La pintura de Angel Zárraga, Arquitectura* (The Painting of Angel Zárraga, Architecture) (México: n.p., 1941). *Algunos pintores del Salón de Otoño* (Some Painters of the Salón de Otoño) (México: SEP, 1942). *Los temas mexicanos en la obra de Alfonso Reyes* (Mexican Themes in the Work of Alfonso Reyes) (México: PEN Club, 1945). *Las etapas del Nómade* (The Stages of the Nomad) (México: Academia Nacional de Historia y Geografía, 1946). *Biógrafos de Cervantes y Críticos del "Quijote"* (Biographers of Cervantes and Critics of the "Quijote"), in *Memorias de la Academia Mexicana*, vol. 12 (México: Jus, 1955), pp. 220-26. *Carlos Noriega Hope y 'El Universal Ilustrado'* (México: INBA, 1959). *Carlos Luquín, escritor y crítico* (Carlos Luquín, Writer and Critic) (México: Editorial Periodística e Impresora, 1963). Prologues: Mariano Azuela, *Mala yerba* (México: Botas, 1937). *Amado Nervo y la crítica literaria* (Amado Nervo and Literary Criticism) (México: Botas, n.d.). José Juan Tablada, *Los mejores poemas de José Juan Tablada* (México: Porrúa, 1943). Cliserio R. Aranda, *Sueños fugaces* (México: Talls. Gráf. de la Nación, 1949). Alfonso Reyes, *Verdad y mentira* (Madrid: Aguilar, 1950). Rafael Carrasco Puente, *Hemerografía de Zacatecas* (México: Sría. de Relaciones Exteriores, 1951). Agustín Loera y Chávez, *Viñetas ilustres* (México: Cultura, 1951). Marte R. Gómez, *Las Comisiones Agrarias del Sur* (México: Porrúa, 1961). Francisco Monterde, *Netsuke* (México: Finisterre, 1962). Enrique Cordero y Torres, *Historia compendiada del Estado de Puebla 1531-1963*, 3 vols. (Puebla: Eds. del Grupo Poético "Bohemia Poblana," 1964). Pascual Ortiz Rubio, *Memorias* (México: Academia Nacional de Historia y Geografía, 1963). *Relaciones diplomáticas entre México y el Brasil, 1822-1923* (Diplomatic Relations between Mexico and Brazil, 1822-1923) (México: Sría. de Relaciones Exteriores, 1964). Translations: *El Libro del Consejo* (The Book of Advice), from French, Georges Raynaud, in collaboration with Miguel Angel Asturias (Paris: Edit. Paris-America, 1927); 2nd ed. (México: UNAM, 1939). *Anales de los Xahil*, from French, Georges Raynaud, in collaboration with Miguel Angel Asturias (Paris: Edit. Paris-America, 1928); 2nd ed., revised (Guatemala: n.p., 1937); 3rd ed. (México: UNAM, 1946).

BIBLIOGRAPHY: Luis Leal, *Bibliografía del cuento mexicano* (México: Eds. de Andrea, 1958), p. 60. José Luis Martínez, *Literatura mexicana del siglo XX, 1910-1949*, vol. 1 (México: Ant. Libr. Robredo, 1949), pp. 54, 70, 138, 327; vol. 2 (1950), p. 54. León Pacheco, "Mexicanos en París. El Abate de Mendoza," in *México en la Cultura*

726 (Feb. 17, 1963): 8. Ramón Xirau, Prologue to *Ensayos selectos de José María González de Mendoza* (México: FCE, 1970), pp. 7-21. *El trato con escritores* (México: INBA, 1961), pp. 127, 152.

JEANNE C. WALLACE

GONZALEZ DURAN, Jorge (1918-), poet and essayist. González Durán was born in Guadalajara, Jalisco, on July 7, 1918. In 1940, along with José Luis *Martínez, Alí *Chumacero, and Leopoldo Zea, he helped found the journal *Tierra Nueva*. He received the 1944 Premio Nacional de Literatura (National Literary Award) for his collection of poetry, *Ante el polvo y la muerte* (Before Dust and Death). This, his only book, shows a strong influence by Gustavo Adolfo Becquer and Juan Ramón Jiménez. The main themes in his book are solitude and death; hope is given only through contact with love. He studied law and literature. He was head of the Departamento de Bibliotecas and Jaime *Torres Bodet's secretary at the Office of International Affairs (Secretaría de Relaciones Exteriores).

WORKS: Poetry: "Seis asonancias y un epilogo" (Six Assonances and an Epilogue), *Tierra Nueva* 1 (Jan.-Feb. 1940). *Ante el polvo y la muerte* (Before Dust and Death) (México: Imp. Universitaria, 1945). Essays: *La superación cultural de Mexico en seis años de actividad nacional* (The Cultural Improvement of Mexico in Six Years of National Activity) (México: Secretaría de Gobernación, Capítulo V, 1946).

BIBLIOGRAPHY: Jesús Arellano, *Antología de los poetas contemporáneos de Mexico* (México: Eds. "Alatorre," 1952), p. 51. Frank Dauster, *Breve historia de la poesía mexicana* (México: Eds. de Andrea, 1956), pp. 177-78. Raúl Leiva, *Imagen de la poesía mexicana contemporánea* (México: UNAM, 1959), pp. 271-76, 359. José Luis Martínez, *Literatura mexicana: siglo xx. 1910-1949* (México: Ant. Librería Robr., 1950), p. 54. Aurora M. Ocampo de Gómez and Ernesto Prado Velázquez, *Diccionario de escritores mexicanos* (México: UNAM, 1967), p. 146. Sara Velasco, *Escritores jalicienses*, vol. 2: 1900-1965 (Guadalajara: Universidad of Guadalajara, 1985), pp. 182-84.

MARGARITA VARGAS

GONZALEZ-GERTH, Miguel (1926-). An educator, a bilingual poet, short story writer, translator, and even a farmer, González-Gerth was born on August 15, 1926, in Mexico City, the son of an army officer of Spanish descent and a musician mother of German descent. He has had a distinguished and productive career, with many noteworthy achievements. He lived in Spain with his parents between 1934 and 1935, an experience that influenced his career greatly. In 1940, he left Mexico for Texas, making the United States his permanent home. He is completely bilingual and writes in both English and Spanish.

González-Gerth finished high school in Texas, then went to the university and completed an undergraduate major in chemical engineering, but then switched to Spanish, French, and English literature for a second major, receiving his B.A. from the University of Texas in 1950. He completed his M.A. at the same place in 1955, then went to Princeton University, where he got another M.A. in 1960 and a Ph.D. in 1973.

He began his teaching career at the Lawrenceville School in 1956. He has been at the University of Texas in Austin since 1965, becoming a full professor in 1987. He defines his fields of specialization as Hispanic literature of the nineteenth and twentieth centuries, Mexican and Spanish peninsular history of the sixteenth and twentieth centuries, comparative literature, and English and American literature.

In addition to his university position, González-Gerth writes poetry, does translations, and is, by vocation, a naturalist, a "self-employed weekend farmer," who owns a 600-acre working farm, complete with wildlife reserves. He has also served for quite a few years as the co-editor of the *Texas Quarterly* and as general editor of The *University of Texas Iberian Series*. He has published extensively in anthologies and magazines, such as the *New York Times Book Review* and the *Texas Quarterly*. In some of his work, he integrates poetry with photography, producing interesting results. He has translated some of the works of Jorge Guillén, Luis *Cernuda, and Federico García Lorca, among others. He was honored when his 1964 edition of *The Infinite Absence* won a place among the fifty books of the year, chosen by the American Institute of Graphic Arts.

Regarding his own, often philosophical, poetic expression and viewpoint, González-Gerth remarks: "For me, poetry is putting words together in a way that makes both sense and music. But the finished poem must be more than that; it must be a revelation that points to yet another mystery."

His critical studies on Ramón Gómez de la Serna and the vanguard, Hernán Cortés and other Latin Americans, to name a few, are important works with excellent analysis and documentation. He has written several books of poetry, *Desert Sequence* (1956), *The Musicians* (1977), both in English and *En vísperas del olvido* (On the Eve of Oblivion) (1967) and *Palabras inútiles* (Useless Words) (1988).

WORKS: Books and Articles: "Bécquer, su concepto de la poesía" (Bécquer, His Concept of Poetry), in *Insula* (Spain) 15, 166 (1960): 3, 12. "Pastores y cabreros en el *Quijote*" (Shepherds and Goatherds in the *Quijote*), in *La Torre* (Puerto Rico) 9, 34 (1961): 1-2. "El mundo extravagante de Ramón Gómez de la Serna" (The Extravagant World of Ramón Gómez de la Serna), in *Insula* 92, 183 (1962): 1-2. "The Image of Spain in American Literatura, 1815-1865," in *Journal of Inter-American Studies* IVZ, 2 (1962): 257-72. "Spanish American Novels in Translation," in *Southwest Review* 54, 3 (1964): 293-95. "The Poetics of Gustavo Adolfo Bécquer," in *Modern Language Notes* 80, 2 (1965): 185-201. "La tertulia de Ramón" (Ramón's Gathering), in *Hispania* 50, 2 (1967). "The Tragic Symbolism of Federico García Lorca," in *Texas Quarterly* 13, 2 (1970): 56-63. "A Probable Source of Julio Herrera y Reissig's *Ciles alucinada*," in *Romance Notes* 11, 1 (1970): 1-3. "El simbolismo trágico de Federico García Lorca," in *La Torre* 19, 73-74 (1971): 265-76. "*Libro de bueno y Libro de Alexndre*: A Study of Two Parallel Passages," in *Studia hispánica in honorem R. Lapesa* (Madrid-Zaragoza, 1972). "Hermetismo y utopismo en Vicente Aleixandre" (Hermeticism and Utopia in Vicente Aleixandre), in *Peña Labra* (Santander, Spain) 28 (1978): 3-18. "Themes and Images of the Indian in Spanish American Literature," in *Perspectives on Contemporary Literature* 3, 2 (Nov. 1977): 12-20. "A Note on Franz Marc," in *Texas Quarterly* 20, 3 (Summer 1978): 125-29. "Nature and Society in the Poetry of Vicente Aleixandre," in *Texas Quarterly* 20, 4 (Winter 1978): 206-14. "Hernando Cortés, Captain-General of New Spain," in *Library Chronicle of the University of Texas at Austin*, new series, 13 (1980): 83-89, reprinted in Institute of Latin American Studies Reprint Series no. 236 (1983). "The Road, the Eye, by

Michael Anderson," in the *Pawn Review* 4 (1981): 155-59. "Ramón Gómez de la Serna's Faded Image," in *Essays on Hispanic Literature in Honor of Edmund L. King*, edited by Sylvia Molloy and Luis Fernández-Cifuentes (London: Támesis Books Limited, 1983), pp. 91-92. Book chapter in Gustavo Adolfo Bécquer, *El escritor ante la crítica*, edited by Russell P. Sebold (Madrid: Ediciones Taurus, 1984). "León Felipe Comes to Texas," in *Library Chronicle of the University of Texas at Austin*, new series, 27 (1984): 105-13. "Borges and Texas: Farewell to a Friend," in *Vortex* (San Antonio, Texas) 1, 2 (Fall 1986), reprinted in Institute of Latin American Studies Reprint Series no. (1988). Essays: "A Daughter of the Land: A Character Sketch of Betty González-Gerth, 1925-1982," printed together with "The Worship of God" by John Frederick Jansen (Austin, 1982). Translations: "Rainer Maria Rilke's 'The Eleventh Dream'" (with a critical introduction), in *Trace* 57 (1975): 133-34. "Thirteen Poems and Some Drawings by Angel González" (with a critical introduction), in *Texas Quarterly* 20, 1 (1977): 7-35. "7 Poems by José Hierro" (with a critical introduction), in *Concept*, also published as issues 2-4 of *Texas Arts Journal* (1978): 119-33. "Twenty-one Poems by Vicente Aleixandre," in the *Texas Quarterly* 20, 4 (Winter 1978): 174-214. *Being and Death*, by José Ferrater-Mora (Berkeley and Los Angeles, 1965). *Violence in Colombia*, by Germán Guzmán Campos, Orlando Fals Borda, and Eduardo Umaña Luna (University of Texas Press). *Valle-Inclán Centennial Series*, edited by Ricardo Gullón et al. (Austin, 1968). *Image of Mexico*, with Sheila Ohlendorf, 2 vols. (Austin, 1969). *Views across the Border: Cultural Conflict and Accommodation*, edited by Stanley R. Ross et al. (Albuquerque, 1976). Poetry and Prose: *A Labyrinth of Imagery: Ramón Gómez de la Serna's "Novelas de la Nebulosa"* (London: Támesis Books Limited, 1986). *Image of Spain*, edited with R. Martínez López and M. Enguídanos (Austin, 1961). *Rubén Darío Centennial Studies*, edited with G. D. Schade (Austin, 1970). *An Hispanic Miscellany*, edited by Miguel González-Gerth (with a critical introduction and original translations), a special issue of *Texas Quarterly* 28, 1 (Spring 1975). *Essay on Waiting* (1950). *Desert Sequence and Other Poems* (Austin: Nonpareil Press, 1956). *The Infinite Absence* (Iowa City: Stonewall Press, 1964). *En vísperas del olvido* (On the Eve of Oblivion) (México: Editorial Cultura, 1967). "The Musicians and Other Poems," in *Texas Quarterly*, suppl. to 20, 3 (1977). *La ausencia infinita/The Infinite Absence*, introduction by James Boyer May (Austin, 1986). *Palabras inútiles* (Useless Words) (Madrid: Taller de Fernández Ciudad, 1988). Ramón Gómez de la Serna, *Aphorisms*, selected and translated into English from *Greguerías*, with a critical introduction. *Retórica del viento* (Rhetoric of the Wind) (Madrid: Editorial Hiperión, 1989).

BIBLIOGRAPHY: LaVerne Harrell Clarke, *Focus 101* (Chico, Calif.: Heidelberg Graphics, 1979). *Contemporary Authors* (Detroit: Gale Research Company, n.d.), pp. 280-81. Aurelio García Cantalapiedra, "Miguel González-Gerth," in *Peña Labra* (Santander, Spain) 15 (Spring 1975): 13. Ernest Kay, ed., *International Who's Who in Poetry* (Cambridge, England: International Biographical Centre, 1978).

ELADIO CORTES

GONZALEZ León, Francisco (1862-1945). Born in Lagos de Moreno, Jalisco, on September 10, 1862, Francisco González León became a pharmacist and a man of letters. He used his pharmacy as a meeting place for both aspiring and established writers of the area. Antonio Moreno y Oviedo, Mariano *Azuela and José Becerra were among those often present at the meetings. González León also taught classes at the local secondary school.

He first became known as a poet when he won an award in 1903 at the Juegos Florales de Lagos for his poem "Pleito homenaje" (Homage Litigation). But in general he was not well received for his early poetic work, partly because the themes he chose to develop were not the popular ones of his time. Later, he turned to others that would prove more acceptable to the critics, such as those revolving around life in the provinces. A selection of his best poems, published in 1922 under the title of *Campanas de la tarde* (Bells of the Afternoon), was made by Pedro de Alba and Ramón *López Velarde. This collection was critically acclaimed as a pleasant and praiseworthy contribution to Mexican poetry. A number of years later, in 1937, the national university published González León's *De mi libro de horas* (From My Book of Hours), another book of poems, but much to the author's dismay, it was scarcely recognized. Stunned by this negative experience, reminiscent of the reception of his earlier poetry, he refused to publish anything else. However, in 1943, ten of his poems were published in *Antología de poetas laguenses* (Anthology of Poetry from Lagos). Also, in 1946, the year after his death, *Agenda* appeared, a compilation of the book that he had planned to publish by himself, despite his earlier refusal.

Aspects of provincial life and nostalgic reflections of former times provide most of the thematic material for González León's poetry. Indeed, he introduced the theme of provincial life as a poetic element in Mexican poetry, elevating it from a level of simple rusticity to one of grace, candor, and charm. Many comparisons have been made between González León and Ramón *López Velarde. It has been said, for instance, that González León, as the immediate precursor of López Velarde, may have stimulated the latter's use of such literary recourses as the "esdrújula" (where the accent falls on the antepenultimate syllable) and lyrical reiteration for the sake of cadence, movement, or rhythm. A number of critics wrote articles attempting to determine whether it was a matter of influence or coincidence that López Velarde's poetry resembles González León's. However, many poets at that time were inspired by and copied the techniques particularly of foreign writers, and as a consequence, their poetry shared a common soil. Nonetheless, some of the similarities between López Velarde and González León are striking.

WORKS: *Megalomanías* (Lagos: n.p., 1908). *Maquetas* (Scale Models) (Lagos: n.p., 1908). *Campanas de la tarde* (Bells of the Afternoon) (México: n.p., 1922); 2nd ed. (México: Edit. Cultura, 1948). *De mi libro de horas* (From My Book of Hours) (México: Imp. Universitaria, 1937). *Agenda* (México: Nueva Voz, 1946). *Poesías completas* (Complete Poetry) (México: Cía. Edit. y Librera Ars, n.d.). *Las cuatro rosas* (The Four Roses), collected by Andrés Henestrosa (México: n.p., 1963).

BIBLIOGRAPHY: Salvador Azuela, "El poeta de Lagos," in *Novedades* (March 22, 1945); "López Velarde y González León," in *El Universal* (Aug. 21, 1954). John S. Brushwood, *Mexico in Its Novel* (Austin: University of Texas Press, 1966), p. 196. Antonio Castro Leal, *La poesía mexicana moderna* (México: FCE, 1953), pp. 54-55. Eduardo Colín, *Rasgos* (México: Imp. Manuel León Sánchez, 1934), pp. 87-94. Frank Dauster, *The Double Strand* (Lexington: University Press of Kentucky, 1987), pp. 9, 10. Luis Leal, *Panorama de la literatura mexicana actual* (Washington, D.C.: Unión Panamericana, Sría. General de la OEA, 1968), p. 31. Alfredo Maillefert, notes to

De mi libro de horas (México: UNAM, 1937). María del Carmen Millán, "Ramón López Velarde y Francisco González León ¿Influencia o coincidencia?," in *Literatura Iberoamericana, Influjos Locales*, Memorias del X Congreso del Instituto Iberoamericano de Literatura Iberoamericana (México: n.p., 1965), pp. 221-23. Carlos Monsiváis, *La poesía mexicana del siglo XX* (México: Empresas Editoriales, 1966), pp. 13-15, 155. Aurora M. Ocampo de Gómez and Ernesto Prado Velázquez, *Diccionario de escritores mexicanos* (México: UNAM, 1967), pp. 147-48. Allen W. Phillips, *Francisco González León, el poeta de Lagos* (México: INBA, 1964); "Ramón López Velarde y Francisco González León, ¿Influencia o coincidencia?," in *Literatura Iberoamericana, Influjos locales*, Memorias del X Congreso del Instituto Interamericano de Literatura Iberoamericana (México: n.p., 1965), pp. 35-49.

JEANNE C. WALLACE

GONZALEZ Martínez, Enrique (1871-1952). Born in Guadalajara, Jalisco, on April 13, 1871, González Martinez was a medical doctor, professor, and diplomat. For a time he was the undersecretary of education (1913). He started to publish when he was very young. His first poems appeared in *Savia Moderna*, a journal founded in 1906 by the poets Alfonso *Cravioto and Eduardo *Colín. He himself founded several ephemeraljournals, among them *Argos* (1907-1908) and *Arte* (1911). In 1911 he moved to Mexico City, where he joined the Ateneo de la Juventud (Atheneum of Youth), a group made up of young, promising, and very prominent intellectals of the time. This group included people like Alfonso *Reyes, Antonio *Caso, José *Vasconcelos, Pedro *Henríquez Ureña, and Luis G. Urbina. In 1917, together with Ramón *López Velarde and Efrén *Rebolledo, he published the journal *Pegaso*. For a while, he also translated into Spanish the works of several French poets. He was the father of Enrique *González Rojo, a poet who did not attain much fame and who died in 1939. The Mexican ambassador to Chile (1920-1922), Argentina (1922-1924), and Spain and Portugal (1924-1931), he returned to Mexico in 1931. In 1944 he was awarded the literature prize Manuel Avila Camacho, while receiving the nomination in 1949 for the Nobel Prize for Literature. Influenced by Lamartine, Poe, Verlaine, and Baudelaire, he was one of the few whose poetry had already matured when he arrived in Mexico City for the first time. González Martínez is the best representative of the closing of the Modernist period with his poem "Tórcele el cuello al cisne" (Wring the Swan's Neck) (1911), which is an aesthetic statement in reaction against the frivolity and emphasis on external beauty of Modernism. He represents the culmination of the metaphysical tendency during this period. He wants to replace the swan, which was the ultimate symbol of the Modernists, with the owl, which to him becomes a new symbol. It represents Minerva in mythology and also knowledge and sensitivity. The debate is still prevalent today as to González Martínez' intent with the poem. Some feel that it marked the "swan song" of Modernism while others feel that González Martínez was not so much trying to end the movement but merely criticizing those servile imitators who did not look for any reflective and serious meanings in poetry. Throughout his poetry, González Martínez wants to delve more into the meaning of life rather than to observe and admire external beauty. This emphasis on a combination of ideas and beauty is what González Martínez calls "interior landscape." As a result of having lived and practiced the Modernist influence in his first period, and also because of his effort in trying to get away from that influence, González Martínez is known today as the first of the post-Modernists.

WORKS: Poetry: Names of publishing companies were not available. *Preludios* (Preludes) (Mazatlán: 1903). *Lirismos* (Lyricisms) (Mocorito: 1907). *Silnter* (Mocorito: 1909). *Los senderos ocultos* (Hidden Paths) (México: 1911). *La muerte del cisne* (The Swan's Death) (México: 1915). *Jardines de Francia* (Gardens of France) (México: 1915). *La hora inútil* (The Useless Hour), selections from his first two books (México: 1916). *El libro de la fuerza, de la bondad y del ensueño* (The Book of Strength, of Kindness, and of Illusion) (México: 1917). *Parábolas y otros poemas* (Parables and Other Poems) (México: 1918). *La palabra del viento* (The Word of the Wind) (México: 1921). *El romero alucinado* (The Hallucinated Pilgrim) (Buenos Aires: 1923). *Las señales furtivas* (The Furtive Signals) (Madrid: 1925). *Poemas de ayer y de hoy* (Poems from Yesterday and Today) (México: 1926). *Poemas truncos* (Unfinished Poems) (México: 1935). *Ausencia y canto* (Absence and Song) (México: 1937). *El diluvio de fuego* (The Deluge of Fire) (México: 1938). *Tres rosas en el ánfora* (The Roses in the Amphora) (México: 1939). Poemas (Poems) (México: 1940). *Bajo el signo mortal* (Under the Mortal Sign) (México: 1942). *Poesías completas* (Complete Poetry Works) (México: 1944). *Segundo despertar y otros poemas* (Second Awakening and Other Poems) (México: 1945). *Vilano al viento* (Thistle Flower to the Wind) (México: 1948). *Babel* (México: 1949). *El nuevo Narciso y otros poemas* (The New Narcissus and Other Poems) (México: 1952; pub. posthumously). *Obras completas* (Complete Works) (México: 1971). Memoirs: *El hombre del buho* (The Man of the Owl) (México: 1944). *La apacible locura* (Gentle Madness) (México: 1951).

BIBLIOGRAPHY: Robert K. Anderson, *Spanish American Modernism: A Selected Bibliography* (Tucson: University of Arizona Press, 1970). John S. Brushwood, *Enrique González Martínez* (New York: Twayne, 1969). Donald Charles Milne, "Mysticism in the Poetry of Enrique González Martínez," *Dissertation Abstracts International* 39: 4298A. Pedro Gringoire, "González Martínez o la búsqueda de autenticidad," *Cuadernos Americanos* 197 (1974): 681-87. Harry L. Rosser, "Enrique González Martínez: 'Matacisnes' y concepción estética," *Cuadernos Americanos* 243, 4 (1982): 181-88. José Luis Martínez, ed., *La obra de Enrique González Martínez* (México: Edición del Colegio Nacional, 1951). Porrata and Santana, eds., *Antología comentada del Modernismo* (Sacramento: California State University, 1974). Homero Castillo, *Antología de poetas modernistas hispanoamericanos* (Toronto and London: Blaisdell, 1966). Eugenio Florit and José Olivio Jiménez, *La poesía hispanoamericana desde el modernismo* (New York: Appleton Century Crofts, 1968), p. 687.

OSCAR SOMOZA

GONZALEZ OBREGON, Luis (1865-1938). Luis González Obregón, a beloved and popular historian and writer, was born on August 25, 1865, in Guanajuato, moving to Mexico City when he was two years old. A student of Ignacio *Altamirano, he went to the Escuela Nacional Preparatoria. In 1885, along with some school friends, he founded the Liceo Mexicano Científico y Literario (Mexican Scientific and Literary Lyceum). By 1890 he was publishing articles in *El Nacional* about the city's past. He gathered them together, and in 1891, he published *México viejo* (Old Mexico), which was later amplified. These anecdotal stories, plus a work called *Las calles de México* (The Streets of Mexico, 1922), are his most famous literary pieces.

González Obregón worked for the Museo Nacional de Antrolpología e Historia (National Museum of Anthropology and History). He later had responsibility for the archives of the nation. He was a member of the Academia Mexicana and the Academa de la Historia. A prolific writer, he published many articles of historical interest in the newspapers and journals. To honor his work as the premier historian of Mexico City, his name was given to the street where his house was located. Blindness overcame him in his old age, and he died of stomach cancer on June 19, 1938, in Mexico City.

WORKS: *Acta de la inauguración de las obras del desagüe del Valle de México* (Record of the Inauguration of the Drainage Works of the Valley of Mexico) (México: I. Escalante, 1900). *Breve reseña de las obras del desagüe del Valle de México* (Brief Review of the Drainage Works of the Valley of Mexico) (México: Tip. de Francisco Díaz de León, 1901). *La limpia y desagüe de la ciudad de México al través de los tiempos* (Cleanliness and Drainage of the City of Mexico across Time) (México: J. S. Guerrero y Cía., 1903). *Los precursores de la Independencia mexicana en el siglo XVI* (The Precursors of Mexican Independence in the sixteenth Century) (Paris and México: Bouret, 1906). *Las sublevaciones de indios en el siglo XVII* (The Indian Uprisings in the seventeenth Century) (México: Imp. del Museo Nacional, 1907). *Don Guillén de Lampart, La Inquisición y la Independencia en el siglo XVII* (Don Guillén de Lampart, the Inquisition and Independence in the seventeenth Century) (Paris and México: Bouret, 1908). *Las lenguas indígenas en al conquista espiritual de la Nueva España* (The Indigenous Languages in the Spiritual Conquest of New Spain) (México: M. León Sánchez, 1917). *Cuauhtémoc* (México: Sría. de Relaciones Exteriores, 1922). *Epoca colonial. México viejo* (Colonial Period. Old Mexico) (México: Tip. de la Escuela Correccional de Artes y Oficios, 1891); 2nd series (México: Tip. Sría. de Fomento, 1895); two series (Paris: Bouret, 1900); new series enlarged, *México viejo 1521-1581* (México: Edit. Patria, 1966). *La vida en México en 1810* (Life in Mexico in 1810) (México: Bouret, 1911); 2nd ed. (México: Stylo, 1943). *Vetusteces* (Antiquities) (México: Bouret, 1911); 2nd ed. (México: Stylo, 1943). *Croniquillas de la Nueva España* (Little Chronicles of New Spain) (México: Botas, 1936). Biography: *Don Joaquín Fernández de Lizardi "El Pensador Mexicano"* (México: Sría. de Fomento, 1888). *Breve noticia de los novelistas mexicanos en el siglo XIX* (A Little Information about the Mexican Novelists in the nineteenth Century) (México: Spíndola y Cía., 1889). *Los restos del Pensador Mexicano* (The Remains of the Mexican Thinker) (México: Sría. de Fomento, 1893). *El capitán Bernal Díaz del Castillo, conquistador y cronista de la Nueva España* (Captain Bernal Díaz del Castillo, Conqueror and Chronicler of New Spain) (México: Sría. de Fomento, 1894). *Don Justo Sierra, historiador* (Justo Sierra, Historian) (México: Museo Nacional, 1907). *Cronistas e historiadores* (Chroniclers and Historians) (México: Botas, 1936). *Ensayos históricos y biográficos* (Historical and Biographical Essays) (México: Botas, 1937). Plus many prologues to old works and to more modern ones.

BIBLIOGRAPHY: Alberto María Carreño, *El cronista Luis González Obregón, Cuadros vivos* (México: Botas, 1938). José Castillo y Piña, "In memoriam. Don Luis González Obregón," in *Mis recuerdos* (México: Imp. Rebollar, 1941), pp. 321-25.

Antonio Castro Leal, *La novela del México colonial*, vol. 2 (México and Buenos Aires: Aguilar, 1964), pp. 979-1098. Nemesio García Naranjo, "Don Luis González Obregón," in *Memorias de la Academia Mexicana* 13 (1955): 46-59. Carlos González Peña, *Gente mía* (México: Stylo, 1946), pp. 27-33, 67-74. José Luis Martínez, *Literatura mexicana siglo XX, 1910-1949*, vol. 2 (México: Ant. Libr. Robredo, 1950), pp. 57-58. Aurora M. Ocampo de Gómez and Ernesto Prado Velázquez, *Diccionario de escritores mexicanos* (México: UNAM, 1967), pp. 151-53. Artemio de Valle-Arizpe, "Luis González Obregón," in *Historia de la ciudad de México según los relatos de sus cronistas*, 4th ed. (México: Ant. Libr. Robredo, 1946), pp. 287-89.

MICHELE MUNCY

GONZALEZ Peña, Carlos (1885-1955). González Peña was born in Lagos de Moreno, Jalisco, on July 7, 1885. He completed his primary education in his native town and his secondary education in Guadalajara. In 1902 he moved to Mexico City, where he supported himself with a bureaucratic post. In Mexico City he founded and directed the magazines *México* (1914), *Vida Moderna* (1915), and *El Universal Ilustrado* (1917). He was a contributor to *La Patria, El Mundo Ilustrado, Artes y Letras*, and *El Universal*. While pursuing a career in journalism, González Peña wrote poetry, plays and novels. He published four novels: *De noche* (At Night) (1905), *La chiquilla* (The Little Girl) (1907), *La musa bohemia* (The Bohemian Muse) (1909), and *La fuga de la quimera* (The Chimera's Flight) (1919).

Invited by President Wilson in 1918, he spent several weeks in the United States. He collected his impressions of this trip in *La vida tumultuosa* (The Tumultuous Life) (1920). His interest in teaching led him to write many books for classroom use. He wrote *Manual de literatura castellana* (Manual of Spanish Literature) (1921) and in 1928 *Historia de la literatura mexicana* (History of Mexican Literature). This book was revised by the author several times, and it is widely used today as a textbook in Mexico and other countries.

A member of the prestigious group the Atheneum of Youth (El Ateneo de la Juventud), González Peña is better known as an essayist. Between 1945 and 1950 he published a series of books that reflect an interest in many fields: *Flores de pasión y de melancolía* (Flowers of Passion and Melancholia) (1945), essays written between 1927-1944 about emperors, singers, dancers, and romantic individuals; *El hechizo musical* (Musical Enchantment) (1946), essays on various musicians; *Claridad en la lejanía* (Clearness in the Distance) (1947), essays on the major literary figures of Mexico's Colonial period and nineteenth century, especially Ignacio Manuel *Altamirano; and *El alma y la máscara* (The Soul and the Mask) (1948), reviews of plays and essays on the Mexican theater.

An active participant in the intellectual life of his time and a member of the Mexican Academy, he was awarded the Manuel Avila Camacho Prize in 1947. He died in Mexico City on August 2, 1955, leaving a rich legacy to the Mexican people.

WORKS: Novels: *La chiquilla* (México: n.p. 1907). *La musa bohemia* (Valencia: F. Sampere y Cía., 1908). *La fuga de la quimera* (México: México Moderno, 1919). Essays: *Historia de la literatura mexicana* (México: Cultura, 1928). *Flores de pasión*

GONZALEZ PINEDA, Francisco

y melancolía (México: n.p., 1945). *El alma y la mascara* (México: Stylo, 1948). *Claridad en la lejanía* (México: Stylo, 1947).

BIBLIOGRAPHY: John S. Brushwood and José Rojas Garcidueñas, *Breve historia de la novela mexicana* (México: Eds. de Andrea, 1959), pp. 75-76. Aurora M. Ocampo de Gómez and Ernesto Prado Velázquez, *Diccionario de escritores mexicanos* (México: UNAM, 1967), pp. 153-54. Carlos González Peña, *Historia de la literatura mexicana* (México: Porrúa, 1981), p. 260.

NORA ERRO-PERALTA

GONZALEZ PINEDA, Francisco (1918-), essayist and novelist. Born in Huetamo, Michoacdn, on July 3, 1918, González Pineda went to school in Toluca and in Mexico City. He studied medicine at the Universidad Nacional Autónoma de Mexico and later received his doctorate from the University of Paris. He contributed to *Cuadernos del viento* and in *Humanitas*. From 1942 to 1952 he had a scholarship in Washington to specialize in psychiatry. His stories are crude, real, full of fantasy and superstition. They portray a Mexican people who live in a fantasy world from which they cannot escape. His novel *Todo el tiempo es mañana* (All the Time Is Tomorrow) is concerned with the disintegration of the Mexican family, the members which have lost their frame of reference and no longer accept the old value system.

WORKS: Essays: *El mexicano: su dinámica psicosocial* (The Mexican: His Psychosocial Dynamics) (México: Editorial Pax, 1959); 2nd ed. (Asociación Psicoanalítica Mexicana, A.C., 1961). *El mexicano: psicología de su destructividad* (The Mexican: The Psychology of His Destruction), 2nd ed. (México: Asociación Psicoanalítica Mexicana, A.C., 1963). Narrative: *Solimán y otros relatos* (Solimán and Other Stories) (México: Cuadernos del Viento, 1961). *Todo el tiempo es mañana* (All the Time Is Tomorrow) (1963).

BIBLIOGRAPHY: Ross Larson, *Fantasy and Imagination in the Mexican Narrative* (Tempe: Arizona State University Press, 1977), p. 93.

MARGARITA VARGAS

GONZALEZ ROJO, Enrique (1899-1939) poet. Born in Sinaloa, in the state of Sinaloa, on August 25, 1899, González Rojo and died in México City on May 9, 1939. He is the son of the poet Enrique González Martínez. As a young man, he collaborated in the publication of the literary journal *San-Ev-Ank* (1918). He studied in México City and was in charge of the literary section of *El Heraldo de México* and was part of the literary group Contemporáneos. (*See* Vanguardist Prose Fiction in Mexico.) While José *Vasconcelos was minister of education (1923-1924), González Rojo was in charge of the Departamento de Bellas Artes.

González Rojo's death at an early age did not allow him to reach his highest potential in his poetry, but he did write some admirable works.

WORKS: Poetry: *El puerto y otros poemas* (The Port and Other Poems) (México: Cultura, 1923; Colofón: 1924). *Espacio* (Space) (Madrid: Mundo Latino, 1927).

Viviendas en el mar (Dwellings in the Sea) (México: n.p., 1927). *Romance de José Conde* (Romance of José Conde) (México: Letras de México, 1939). *Elegías romanas y otros poemas* (Roman Eulogies and Other Poems) (México: n.p., 1941). *Estudios de cristal* (Crystal Studies) unfinished. Short Story: "La inocente aventura del Trópico, Relato del segundo oficial Charlie Raeburn, de la Marina Mercante Americana y al servicio de la United Fruit Co." (The Innocent Adventure of the Tropics), *Contemporánoes* 1, 1 (June 1928): 20-27. "El día más feliz de Charlot" (Charlot's Happiest Day), *Contemporáneos* 1, 5 (Oct. 1928): 113-30. Essays: "Picaresca mexicana" (Mexican Picaresque), *Excelsior* (July 1938).

BIBLIOGRAPHY: Antonio Castro Leal, *La poesía mexicana moderna* (México: FCE, 1953), p. 25. Jorge Cuesta, *Antología de la poesía mexicana moderna* (México: Contemporáneos, 1936), p. 163. Frank Dauster, *Breve historia de la poesía mexicana* (México: Eds. de Andrea, 1956), pp. 163-64. Merlin H. Foster, *Los Contemporáneos, 1920-1912, perfil de un experimento vanguardista mexicano* (México: Eds. de Andrea, 1964), pp. 76-82. Carlos González Peña, *Historia de la literatura mexicana*, 1928 (México: Porrúa, 1966), p. 273. Manuel Lerín, "Enrique González Rojo," in *Antología sinaloense*, edited by Ernesto Higuera, vol. 1 (Culiacán, Sinaloa: Ediciónes Culturales del Gobierno del Estado de Sinaloa, 1958), pp. 127-31. José Luis Martínez, *Literatura mexicana del siglo xx, 1910-1949* (México: Ant. Libr. Robredo, 1949), pp. 30, 37; vol. 2 (1950), pp. 58-59. Aurora M. Ocampo de Gómez and Ernesto Prado Velázquez, *Diccionario de escritores mexicanos* (México: UNAM, 1967), p. 154. Guillermo Sheridan, *Los contemporáneos ayer* (México: FCE, 1985). Luis G. Urbina, "Libros de México bajo árboles de Castilla: cuatro poetas. Comentarios líricos," review of *Espacio*, *El Universal*, (Oct. 3, 1926). Esperanza Velázquez Bringas and Rafael Heliodoro Valle, *Indice de Escritores* (México: Talls. Gráficos de Herrero, 1928), p. 123. Xavier Villaurrutia, "Enrique González Rojo, *El Puerto y otros poemas mas*," *Atenas* 1, (July 1924): p. 8.

EDNA A. REHBEIN

GONZALEZ ROJO, Enrique, Jr. (1928-), critic, poet, essayist. González Rojo was born in Mexico City in October of 1928. Both his father and his grandfather were poets of some renown. He traveled extensively to the Far East and to Europe. He studied philosophy at the National University; his philosophical orientation is evident in many of his poems. He has also written a number of essays on Marxist issues.

   González Rojo's poetry plays out the conflict between philoso- phical and universal themes and contemporary issues. After defining himself in his early works, he finds a voice and a philosophical vision in his more recent works. His work *El quíntuple balar de mis sentidos (o el monstruo y otras mariposas)* (The Quintuple Bleating of My Senses, or the Monster and Other Butterflies) has as a central theme the inner conflicts of man's soul. His later works *Para deletrear el infinito* 1970 and 1985 (To Decipher Infinity) deal with this motif as well as others relating to art, life, death, the void, God, materialism, and the nature of existence. They represent a continuing effort to define the infinite with a style that is at times direct and at times experimental.

WORKS: Poetry: *Luz y silencio* (Light and Silence) (Sonora: Hermosillo, 1947). *Dimensión imaginaria* (Imaginary Dimension), poetry, essay combined (México:

Cuadernos Americanos, 1953). *La tierra de Caín: 3 poemas de González Rojo, Raúl Leiva y Eduardo Lizalde* (The Land of Cain, three poems by Gonzalez Rojo, Raul Leiva, and Eduardo Lizalde) (México: Ideas de México, 1956). *El cuaderno de buen amor* (The Notebook of Good Love) (México: Cuadernos del Unicornio, 1959). *Para deletrear el infinito* (To Decipher Infinity) (México: Cuadernos Americanos, 1972). *El antiguo relato del principio* (The Former Story of the Beginning) (México: Diógenes, 1974). *El quíntuple balar de mis sentidos* (The Quintuple Bleating of My Senses) (México: Mortiz, 1976). *A solas con mis ojos* (Alone with My Eyes) (México: Edit. Liberta Sumaria, 1980). *Por los siglos de los siglos* (Through the Centuries of the Centuries) (México: Edit. Papeles Privados, 1981). *El tercer Ulises* (The Third Ulysses) (México: Signos, 1982). *La larga marcha* (The Long March) (México: Oasis, 1982). *Una gramática iracunda: antología poética* (An Angry Grammar: Poetic Anthology) (México: Katún, 1985). Essays: *Anarquismo y materialismo histórico* (Anarchism and Historical Materialism) (México: UNAM, 1959). *Para leer a Althusser* (Reading Althusser) (Méxicoy: Diógenes, 1974). *Hacia una teoría marxista del trabajo intelectual y trabajo manual* (Toward a Marxist Theory of Intellectual Labor and Manual Labor) (México: Grijalbo, 1977). *Teoría científica de la historia* (Scientific Theory of History) (México: Diógenes, 1979). *La revolución proletario-intelectual* (The Intellectual-Proletariat Revolution) (México: Diógenes, 1981). *Con la matriz en alto* (With a High Matrix) (México: TEA, 1982). *Epistomología y socialismo* (México: Diógenes, 1985). *La naturaleza de los llamados países socialistas* (The Nature of the So-Called Socialist Countries) (México: Domes, 1986). *Los trabajadores manuales y el partido* (The Manual Laborers and the Party) (México: Domes, 1986). *Génesis y estructura de la revolución cultural* (Genesis and Structure of Cultural Revolution) (México: Domes, 1987). *Los grilletes de eros* (The Shackles of Eros) (México: Domes, 1988). *José Revueltas* (México: Domes, 1988).

BIBLIOGRAPHY: Emmanuel Carballo, "Dos libros recientes de poesía," Review of *Dimensión imaginaria*, in *México en la Cultura* 238 (Oct. 11, 1953). Heriberto García Rivas, *Historia de la literatura mexicana*, vol. 4 (México: Textos Universitarios, 1971), p. 358. Sonja Karsen, Review of *El quíntuple balar de mis sentidos (o el monstruo y otras mariposas*, in *World Literature Today* 52, 1 (Winter 1978): 87. Aurora M. Ocampo de Gómez and Ernesto Prado Velázquez, *Diccionario de escritores mexicanos* (México: UNAM, 1967), p. 155. Federico Patón, "González Rojo y Carlos Oliva: poetas en contraste," *Diálogos* 19, 111 (May-June 1983): 79-81. Mauricio de la Selva, "Cuatro libros de poesía," *Cuadernos Americanos* 185 (1972): 255-62. Nigel Grant Sylvester and Mark Cramer, Review of *El quíntuple balar de mis sentidos (o el monstruo y otras mariposas* by Enrique González Rojo and *Asamblea plenaria* by Alfredo Cardona Peña, in *Chasqui* 8, 2 (Feb. 1979): 118-19.

MARK FRISCH

GOROSTIZA, Celestino (1904-1967). Born in Villahermosa, Tabasco, on January 31, 1904, Celestino Gorostiza, a distinguished playwright and theatrical director, pursued his education in Aguascalientes and in Mexico City. Throughout his lifetime, he held a number of important positions of public service. He was, for example, on the staff of the secretary of public education, working at a variety of tasks. He became the head of the theater department in the Instituto Nacional de Bellas Artes. A professor of dramatic arts and acting of INBA, he also became its general director. Gorostiza received distinctions and honors from a very young age. A writer of literary and theatrical criticism, he also wrote plays, directed them, and, on occasion, acted in them. Along with other distinguished Mexican playwrights, including Xavier *Villaurrutia, Salvador *Novo, and others, he participated in the creation of the Teatro Ulises (1927-1928), which sought to revitalize the theater. He also founded in 1932 the Teatro de Orientación, becoming closely involved in all of its activities. An excellent translator, he produced Spanish versions of the plays of such esteemed writers as Eugene O'Neill and Marcel Achard. Founder also of the Academia Cinematográfica, he influenced many other promising playwrights of younger generations. He died on January 11, 1967, in Mexico City.

At first, Gorostiza remained intimately involved with his own studies and his dedication to the theater as a director. He then became deeply interested in the societal problems of Mexico. His play *El color de nuestra piel* (The Color of Our Skin) (1952), which confronts racial isssues in Mexico, was a resounding success. A gripping, sorrowful, and moving story, the play won the prestigious Premio Juan Ruiz de Alarcón in 1956.

Gorostiza was among those who changed the director of the national theater in Mexico, renewing and affirming it as a vital cultural part of today's society. Among other things, he set up theater competitions and festivals, and he helped younger authors get their start in the field. Gorostiza also wrote a highly regarded and valuable essay on the theater for the third volume of *Teatro mexicano del siglo XX*.

WORKS: *El nuevo paraíso* (The New Paradise) (México: Eds. Contemporáneos, 1930). *La escuela del amor* (The School of Love), 1933 (México: Eds. Artes, Gráficas 1935). *Ser o no ser* (To Be or Not To Be), 1934 (México: Eds. Artes Gráficas, 1935). *Escombros del sueño* (Dream Debris) (México: Letras de México, 1939). *La reina de nieve* (The Snow Queen) (México: n.p., 1942). *La mujer ideal* (The Ideal Woman) (México: n.p., 1943). *El color de nuestra piel* (The Color of Our Skin) (México: Eds. de Andrea, 1953). *Columna social* (Social Column) (México: Costa-Amic, n.d.). *La leña está verde* (The Wood Is Green), in *Teatro Mexicano 1958* (México: Aguilar, 1958), pp. 321-77. *Teatro mexicano del siglo XX*, vol. 3, study (México: FCE, 1956).

BIBLIOGRAPHY: Juan García Ponce, Review of *La leña está verde*, in *Universidad de México* 13, 3 (Nov. 1958): 28-29. Miguel Guardia, "The Mexican Theater: Celestino Gorostiza," in *Mexican Cultural Bulletin* 15 (July 1935). Willis Knapp Jones, *Breve historia del teatro latinoamericano* (México: Eds. de Andrea), pp. 163-65, 169-70, 194. Ruth S. Lamb, "Celestino Gorostiza y el teatro experimental en México," in *Revista Iberoamericana* 23, 45 (Jan.-June 1958): 141-45. Antonio Magaña Esquivel, "Celestino Gorostiza, director y comediógrafo," in *Letras de México* 2, 16 (April 15, 1940): 6; *Medio siglo de teatro mexicano, 1900-1961* (México: INBA, 1964), pp. 67-72. Aurora M. Ocampo de Gómez and Ernesto Prado Velázquez, *Diccionario de escritores mexicanos* (México: UNAM, 1967), pp. 155-56). "La obra de Celestino Gorostiza y la crítica," in *Nivel* 17 (May 25, 1964): 1-2. Xavier Villaurrutia, "Un nuevo autor dramático," in *Texto y pretextos* (México: FCE, 1940), pp. 177-82.

JEANNE C. WALLACE

GOROSTIZA, José (1901-1973), poet, diplomat, and teacher. José Gorostiza was born in villahermosa, Tabasco. He taught at the National University and at the Escuela Nacional de Maestros (1929, 1932). He belonged to the Vanguardist group, los Contemporáneos (1928-1931), and he was a member of the Academia Mexicana de la Lengua. His most important poetic work is *Muerte sin fin* (Endless Death), a metaphysical poem reminiscent of Gongora's *Soledades* and Sor Juana's *Primero sueño*. Small in quantity when compared to that of other poets of his generation, the poetry of José Gorostiza is among the best.

WORKS: *Canciones para cantar en las barcas* (Songs to Sing on Boats) (México: Cultura, 1925). *Muerte sin fin* (Endless Death) (México: Cultura, 1939). *Poesía* (Poetry) (México: FCE, 1964), contains previous and unpublished work. *Death without End*, translated by Laura Villaseñor (Austin: University of Texas Press, 1969). *Prosa* (Prose) (Guanajuato: Universidad de Guanajuato, 1969).

BIBLIOGRAPHY: Emmanuel Carballo, "José Gorostiza, poet para toda la vida," *La Cultura en México* 140 (Oct. 21, 1964): xiii; "José Gorostiza (1901-1973)," *19 Protagonistas de la literatura mexicana* (México: FCE, 1986), pp. 250-65. Francisco J. Cevallos, "Presencia y fuga de José Gorostiza: Lectura, praxis y hermeniutica," in *Hispania* 69, 4 (1986): 837-44. Andrew P. Debicki, *La poesía de José Gorostiza* (México: Eds. de Andrea, 1962). Elsa Dehennin, *Antithèse, oxymore et paradoxisme: Approches rhétoriques de la poèsie de José Gorostiza* (Paris: Didier, 1973). Sergio Fernández, *Homenajes a José Gorostiza* (México: SEP, 1972). Juan Gelpí, *Enunciación y dependencia en José Gorostiza: estudio de una máscara poética* (México: UNAM, 1984). Emma Godoy, "De '*Muerte sin fin*,' sólo la vida," *Abside* 37 (1973): 32-47. Manuel Mejía Valera, "Acerca de la elaboración teorítica de la poesía," *Cuadernos Americanos* 243, 4 (1982): 103-11. Mordecai S. Rubín, *Una poética moderna: "Muerte sin fin" de José Gorostiza* (University: University of Alabama Press, 1966). Miguel Vihuela, "Un aspecto de la poesía de José Gorostiza," *Mester* 5, 1 (1974): 3-9. Ramón Xirau, *Tres Poetas de la soledad* (México: Ant. Libr. Robredo, 1955), pp. 13-20.

MIRTA A. GONZALEZ

GOROSTIZA, Manuel Eduardo (1789-1851), dramaturgist. Gorostiza was born in Veracruz, Veracruz, on October 13, 1789. Even though, his life was situated in his two countries, Mexico and Spain, his work was of Spanish essence. At age six, after the death of his father, he moved with his mother and brothers to Madrid. At age seven, he entered the House of Pages of the king, and grew up in the court. In 1808, he joined the Spanish Army, with the rank of captain, to fight against the French invasion. In 1811, he married Juana Castillo de Portugal and moved to France. Three years later, in 1814, he retired from the military service with the rank of colonel, and in 1816, he moved to Madrid. In 1818, he presented the premier of his first original comedy, *Indulgencia para todos* (Indulgencefor Everybody). From that moment he kept writing and presenting his plays. Gorostiza became very successful in his two countries. He stood put as a liberal speaker supporting the constitution and the Cadiz movement, and he founded the political seminary El Cetro Constitucional (The constitutional scepter). In 1822, he moved to Paris to translate and adapt French plays, but after the royal decree of expulsion and confiscation of his possessions, he left Paris in 1823 and moved to England, which was safer for liberals. Soon, he was publishing in several newspapers.

He established relations with several Mexican diplomats who were negotiating the British acknowledgment of Mexican independence. Gorostiza offered his services to his native country and he was immediately commissioned to initiate relations with the Lower Countries, being named general consul in Brussels. Later, he was the Mexican ambassador in London. In 1831 he published *Cartilla política* (Political Booklet), addressed to the Congress of the Free and Sovereign State of Veracruz. The intention was to explain to the citizens of the new free states the political truth in which these were composed. In the same year, Gorostiza moved back to Mexico, where he was in charge of the reorganization of the educational system, the supervision of the general Theater, and the direction of the national library. From 1838 to 1848, he was the manager of the principal theater of Mexico.

In 1836, because of the threat of a revolution in Texas, he had to accept the charge of plenipotentiary of Mexico in the United States. In 1837, he was named state counselor, and in 1838, he was placed in charge of the Ministry of Finance, of Internal Affairs, and all Foreign Relations. In 1841, he was named director of the monopoly of tobacco, which permitted him to buy a house in Tacubaya and make "one of his dreams come true," to establish a correctional house for young delinquents. In 1836, he formed a military corps, called Batallion of Braves, which he offered to Santa Anna to defend Mexico against the North American invasion. He thought Texas should be defended as part of the Mexican territory. On August 30, Mexico was defeated and Gorostiza was imprisoned. He lost most of his fortune, and, later, his daughter Luisa died. Alone, in misery, he died in Mexico City on October 22, 1851.

His works are of Neoclassical style, but the last ones are Romantic. He continued the comedy of characters and customs, which had been initiated by Juan *Ruiz de Alarcón. His work contains moral teaching, the dialogue has ingenuity and grace, and the characters are ably drawn. *Las costumbres de antaño* (Long Ago Customs) and *Contigo pan y cebolla* (Bread and Onion with You) have the touch of nationalism, and compare the Mexican scene with fashionable Europe. Gorostiza translated and adated many foreign plays, especially French. His most famous play, *Indulgencias para todos* (Indulgence for Everybody), was adapted and sent to the theaters of Berlin and Vienna from 1858 to 1874.

WORKS: *Indulgencias para todos* (Indulgence for Everybody) (Madrid: n.p., 1918); (México: UNAM, 1942). *Las costumbres de antaño* (Long Ago Customs) (Madrid: n.p., 1819). *Tal para cual o las mujeres y los hombres* (Made for Each Other, or the Women and the Men) (Madrid: n.p., 1820). *Don Dieguito* (Madrid: n.p., 1820). *Eljugador* (The Player) (Madrid: n.p., 1820). *Virtud y Patriotismo o el primero de enero de 1820* (Virtue and Patriotism, or June the 1st of 1820) (Madrid: n.p., 1921). *Galería en miniatura de los más célebres periodistas, folletistas, y articulistas de Madrid* (Miniature Gallery of the Most Distinguished Journalists, Pamphleteers, and Writers of Madrid) (Madrid: n.p., 1822). *El amigo íntimo* (The Intimate Friend), vol. 11 (Brussels: n.p., 1828). *Tambien hay secreto en mujer* (There Is a Secret in Women Also) (Brussels: n.p., 1926). *Lo que son mujeres* (What Women Are Like), vol. 1 (Brussels: n.p., 1921). *Contigo pan y cebolla* (Bread and Onion with You) (London: n.p., 1833). *Las costumbres de antaño o la pesadilla* (Long Ago Customs or the

Nightmare) (México: n.p., 1933). *El cocinero y el secretario* (The Cook and the Secretary) (Madrid: n.p., 1940).

BIBLIOGRAPHY: Maria Esperanza Aguilar M., *Estudio bibliográficode D. Manuel Eduardo de Gorostiza* (México: n.p., 1932). Ignacio Manuel Altamirano, "Manuel Eduardo de Gorostiza, Dramaturgo," in *Obras completas de Altamirano* (México: SEP, 1949), pp. 184-89. Florencio M. Del Castillo, *Don Manuel Eduardo de Gorostiza* (México: Imp. de V. Agueros, 1902), pp. 495-508. Manuel García Díaz, *Cinco comedias originales de Don Manuel Eduardo de Gorostiza* (México: n.p., 1951). Mariano José de Larra, "Representacion de la comedia nueva de D. Manuel Eduardo de Gorostiza titulada *Contigo pan y cebolla*," in *Revista Española* (1883), reproduced in *Artículos de crítica literaria y artística* (Madrid: Espasa-Calpe, 1960), pp. 85-93, and in *Artículos completos de Larra* (Madrid: Aguilar, 1961), pp. 500-7. Antonio Magaña Esquivel, "El teatro en el centenario de Manuel Eduardo de Gorostiza. Su obra dramatica," in *Revista Mexicana de Cultura* 13 (1952): p. 13. Armando de María y Campos, "El teatro en la conmemoración centurial de Gorostiza. Nuevas noticias sobre sus producciones y probable nomina completa de sus obras," in *Novedades* (Feb. 5, 1952): 1, 10. *Manuel Eduardo de Gorostiza, su tiempo, su vida y su obra* (México: Tall. Gráficos de la Nación, 1959). Alfonso Mendez Plancarte, "San Juan de la Cruz en México," in *Letras Mexicanas* 54 (1959): 58-59. Francisco Monterde, *Bibliografía del teatro en México* (México: Monografías Bibliográficas Mexicanas, 1933), pp. 69-73. Felipe Reyes, edition and note of Manuel Eduardo de Gorostiza: *Tal para cual*, in *Tramoya* 21-22 (1981): 5-44. José María Roa Barcena, *Datos y Apuntes para la biografía de D. Manuel Eduardo de Gorostiza* (México: Imp. de F. Díaz de León, 1877); also in *Memorias de la Academia mexicana correspondiente de la Real Española* 1 (1876): 90-204; *Obras de D. José M. Roa Barcenas* (México: Imp. de Agüeros, 1902), vol. 1, no. 41, pp. 207-369. Francisco Sosa, *Biografías de mexicanos distinguidos* (México: Ed. de la Sría. de Fomento, 1884, pp. 242-48. Emma Susana Sperati Piñero, "El teatro Neoclasico en la literatura mexicana: *Indulgencia para todos* de Manuel Eduardo de Gorostiza," in *Revista Iberoamericana* 19, 38 (1954): 326-32. Manuel Torres, "La luz en el vértice. Presencia cultural de Manuel Eduardo de Gorostiza," in *El Nacional*, 1st part (Dec. 30, 1951); 2nd part (Jan. 6, 1952); 3rd part, (Jan 13, 1952).

ESTHER HERNANDEZ-PALACIOS

GOYTORTUA, Jesús or Claudio Vardel or Fidel (1910-?), novelist and short story writer. Born in San Luis Potosí, Goytortúa went to school in Tampico and Monterrey; he moved to Mexico City in 1923 and went to UNAM for a year of law school and then took courses in literature. While working at the Ministry of Agriculture he founded and directed the journal *Las Democracias*. He received the Lanz Duret Prize in 1944 for his *cristero* novel *Pensativa* and the Mexico City Prize in 1947 for *Lluvia roja*, in which he combines fact and imagination to narrate the end of the Obregon administration. The carefully planned *Pensativa*, according to Walter M. Langford, has a "compelling plot and a swift-moving narrative."

WORKS: Short Story: "Mi hermano Rosendo" (My Brother Rosendo), in *Revista de Revistas* (April 6, 1931). *El jardín de lo imposible* (The Garden of the Impossible)

(México: Stylo, 1938). Novel: *Pensativa* (Pensive), 2nd. ed. (México: Porrúa, 1947), filmed by Filmex and translated into English, Italian, and French, and published by chapters in *El Universal* starting in April 1945, *Lluvia roja* (Red Rain) (México: Porrúa, 1947), also filmed by Filmex. *Cuando se desvanece el arco iris* (When the Rainbow Vanishes) (México: Stylo, 1949). *Gemma* was filmed.

BIBLIOGRAPHY: John S. Brushwood, *Mexico in Its Novel* (Austin: University of Texas Press, 1966), pp. 12-13, 229. John S. Brushwood and José Rojas Garcidueñas, *Breve historia de la novela mexicana* (México: Eds. de Andrea, 1959), pp. 112-13. Alí Chumacero, Review of *Pensativa*, in *El Hijo Pródigo* 29 (Aug. 15, 1945): 121. Jacobo Dalevuelta, "¿Quién es el autor?" (on *Pensativa*), in *El Universal* (April 3, 1945). Manuel Pedro González, *Trayectoria de la novela en México* (México: Botas, 1951), pp. 310-11, 374-76. Enrique F. Gual, Review of *Lluvia roja*, in *El Nacional* (April 27, 1947). Benjamín Jarnés, "Libros. Mundo novelesco," review of *Pensativa*, in *Manana* (July 28, 1945). Walter M. Langford, *The Mexican Novel Comes of Age* (Notre Dame: University of Notre Dame Press, 1972), pp. 38-46. Luis Leal, *Bibliografía del cuento mexicano* (México: Eds. de Andrea, 1958), p. 62. Mauricio Magdaleno, Review of *Pensativa*, in *El Universal* (April 17, 1945). José Luis Martínez, *Literatura mexicana del siglo XX, 1910-1949*, vol. 1 (México: Ant. Lib. Robredo, 1949), pp. 67, 68, 245, 254, 256; vol. 2 (1950), p. 59. Helen F. Yeats, *A Study of the Lanz Duret Prize Novels* (México: n.p., 1948), pp. 63-77.

DELIA GALVAN

GUADALAJARA, José Rafael (1863-?). José Rafael Guadalajara was born on July 10, 1863, in Mexico City. A precocious child, he later studied law but abandoned his potential career after two years, turning instead to business, and family concerns. He successfully combined family, business and literary interests.

Guadalajara's first publications were poems that appeared in the weekly journal *La Familia*. Involved in a variety of significant literary publications during his lifetime, Guadalajara founded and directed both *El Fígaro Mexicano* and *El Mexicano*. In 1891, he published one novel, originally called *Sara. Páginas del primer amor*, which, in subsequent editions, he changed to *Amalia. Páginas del primer amor*. Actually written several years before its publication, when both Romanticism and Realism were in vogue, the novel is within the tradition of Romantic sentimentality, dealing with immense suffering of a young woman who goes insane when she is separated from her beloved. Containing a series of extremely sensitive juvenile love letters, the novel enjoyed considerable popularity, especially because of its theme which captured the imagination of the public at that time. John Brushwood notes that the novel, set in Mexico City in 1883 during Holy Week, is written as an autobiography and, to a large extent, may very well be, true.

For a time, Guadalajara was a French professor at the Escuela Nacional Preparatoria. But his main employment was in accounting, and he held several important government posts.

WORKS: *Sara. Páginas del primer amor* (Sara. Pages of First Love) (México: Imp. de las Escalerillas, 1891). *Amalia. Páginas del primer amor* (México: n.p., 1899).

BIBLIOGRAPHY: John S. Brushwood, *Mexico in Its Novel* (Austin: London: University of Texas Press, 1966), p. 127; *The Romantic Novel in Mexico* (Columbia: The University of Missouri Press, 1954), pp. 51, 71. Juan B. Iguíniz, *Bibliografía de novelistas mexicanos* (México: Imp. de la Sría. de Relaciones, 1926), pp. 161-63. Aurora M. Ocampo de Gómez and Ernesto Prado Velázquez, *Diccionario de escritores mexicanos* (México: UNAM, 1967), p. 160. Sara Sefchovich, *México: país de ideas, país de novelas* (México: Editorial Grijalbo, 1987), p. 58.

JEANNE C. WALLACE

GUARDIA, Miguel (1924-   ). Born in Mexico City on August 17, 1924, Miguel Guardia first pursued a career in law, but then became more interested in the theater, particularly as a critic, and in poetry. He was one of the founders of the Agrupación de Críticos de Teatro and vigorously worked for the educational and critical aims of the group. Guardia received a fellowship from the Centro Mexicano de Escritores in 1953 to research and study Mexican theater, one of his major interests. He has been an active member of the Academia de Ciencias y Artes Cinematográficas, participating in many of its functions. A frequent contributor to many important literary magazines and supplements, such as *México en el arte*, *Revista de América*, *Prometeus*, *Metáfora*, and *El Nacional*, Miguel Guardia, in addition to being a theater critic, has written several volumes of original poetry and plays. *Tema y variaciones* (Theme and Variations), a collection of his poetry written between 1948 and 1951, is a tender expression of reality as experienced sensually. The sonnets, "romances," and other poems of this three-sectioned volume blend traditional poetic structures with contemporary nuances. In *El retorno y otros poemas* (The Return and Other Poems) (1956) and *Palabra de amor* (Word of Love) (1965), his major themes are love, solitude, and man's place in society.

WORKS: Poetry: *Ella nació en la Tierra* (She Was Born on the Earth) (México: n.p., 1951). *Tema y variaciones (1948-1951)* (Theme and Variations [1948-1951]) (México: n.p., 1952). *El retorno y otros poemas* (The Return and Other Poems) (México: Revista Bellas Artes, 1956). *Palabra de amor* (Word of Love) (México: n.p., 1965). Theater: *¡Ay Dios mío!* (Oh My God!), one-act play, in *América* 61 (1949): 287-320. *El niño de jabón* (The Child Made of Soap), performed 1958 (México: Impresora Económica, 1952). Essay: "Instituto Nacional de Bellas Artes, seis años de teatro" (National Institute of Fine Arts, Six Years of Theater), in *El teatro en México*, vol. 2: (1958-1964 (México: INBA 1965).

BIBLIOGRAPHY: Jesús Arellano, *Poetas jóvenes de México* (México: Eds. Libro-Mex, 1955), pp. 7, 92; "Poesía mexicana en 1956," review of *El retorno y otros poemas*, in *Metáfora* 14 (May-June 1957): 10-16. Antonio Castro Leal, *La poesía mexicana moderna* (México: FCE, 1953), pp. 488-89. Frank Dauster, *Breve historia de la poesía mexicana* (México: Eds. de Andrea, 1956), p. 181.   Ruth S. Lamb, *Bibliografía del teatro mexicano del siglo XX* (México: Eds. de Andrea, 1962), p. 61. Raúl Leiva, *Imagen de la poesía mexicana contemporánea* (México: UNAM, 1959), pp. 321-28, 359.   Aurora M. Ocampo de Gómez and Ernesto Prado Velázquez, *Diccionario de escritores mexicanos* (México: UNAM, 1967), p. 160.
JEANNE C. WALLACE

GUERRERO, Jesús R. (1911-   ). Guerrero was born in Michoacan. Raised in a modest environment of peasants, he has the knowledge to create characters filled with life who are capable of stirring the reader's emotions with their struggle against adversity. The author's prose is unadorned, dynamic, and interesting. José Revueltas stated in the foreword to *Los olvidados* (The Forgotten): "Las rudas páginas de Jesús Guerrero, sus hermosas páginas de piedra, laten y respiran una expresion fidedigna, directa y pura" (The hard pages of Jesús Guerrero, his beautiful pages of stone, pulsate and breathe a faithful, direct and pure expression). According to Mónico Neck in the foreword to *Oro blanco* (White Gold), Guerrero liked to write close to Juárez's tomb: "Escribía con lápiz sobre cuaderno escolar" (He wrote with a pencil on a school copybook).

Los olvidados (The Forgotten) is a complex work with elements of prostitution, alcohol, sex, and the vortex of the Revolution. It is a novel of sorrow and violence. *Oro blanco* (White Gold) depicts life in a workers camp in the cotton fields at the turn of the century. The exploitation of entire families is described; the style is Naturalistic.

WORKS: *Oro blanco* (White Gold) (México: Fuente Cultural, 1941). *Los olvidados* (The Forgotten) (México: Edit. Estampa, 1944). *Los días apagados* (Faded Days) (México: Botas, 1946). *Reflejos de luz humana* (Reflections of Human Light) (México: Botas, 1948). *El punto final* (The Final Point) (México: Botas, 1953). *El corral pintado* (The Painted Corral) (México: Botas, 1953).

BIBLIOGRAPHY: John S. Brushwood and José Rojas Garciadueñas, *Breve historia de la novela mexicana* (México: Eds. de Andrea, 1959), pp. 80-81. Luis Leal, *Bibliografía del cuento mexicano* (México: Eds. de Andrea, 1958), pp. 62-63.

ALICIA G. WELDEN

GUEVARA, Fray Miguel de (1585-1646?), poet and philologist. Guevara was born in Mexico City. He was ordained a priest in the Augustine Order in 1611 and was a "Consultor" in Tiripitío, Michoacán, in 1621. He held various positions of importance in several dioceses of the Michoacin area, the last of which was that of "visitador" in the province of San Nicolás Tolentino (1643-1646). After this date there are no records of his whereabouts, and it is assumed that he died during that year.

Guevara's known writings are a grammar text of the Matlaltzinga language and a handfull of sonnets found in manuscript form in 1913. The theme of most of them is an exploration of man's relationship to Christ. Though there is still some controversy about its authorship, "No me mueve mi Dios para quererte" (I Am Not Moved, My Lord, To Love You) is one of the most beautiful sonnets to Christ written in Spanish. A sincere and moving monologue, the poem has been attributed to Guevara because it was found with several other sonnets signed by him and because it has stylistic and thematic similarities to Guevara's poetry.

WORKS: *Arte doctrinal y modo general para aprender la lengua matlaltzinga* (Doctrinal Art and General Method for Learning the Matlatzinga Language) (México: n.p., 1634-38). "No me mueve mi Dios para quererte" (I Am Not Moved, My Lord, To

Love You), "Levántamente Señor que estoy caído" (Pick Me Up, My God, For I Have Fallen), "Poner al hijo en la Cruz" (To Place Your Child on the Cross), and other undated sonnets found by Alberto María Carreño in 1913 in México City.

BIBLIOGRAPHY: Marcel Bataillon, "El anónimo del soneto 'No me mueve mi Dios . . ., '" in *Nueva Revista de Filología Hispánica* 4 (1950): 254-69. Alberto María Carreño, *Joyas literarias del siglo XVII encontradas en México: Fray Miguel de Guevara y el célebre soneto castellano "No me mueve, mi Dios, para quererte"* (México: Imp. Francomexicana, 1915). Alfonso Reyes, *Letras de la Nueva España* (México: FCE, 1948), pp. 100-101, 122.

ALFONSO GONZALEZ

GUILLEN, Fedro (1920-   ), journalist, essayist, poet, and author of short stories. Fedro Guillén was born on May 16, 1920, in Mexico City. After receiving his law degree from the Universidad Nacional Autónoma de México (1949), he entered the diplomatic service and served in Guatemala City (1951-1954). He later worked on the Commission of Interamerican Studies under the leadership of Isidro Fabela. In 1956 he became a journalism professor and chair of the Journalism Department in the School of Social and Political Sciences at UNAM. His travels have taken him through much of Spanish America, including Quito, Ecuador, where he taught journalism in 1962. As a journalist, he has contributed to in several newspapers and magazines both in Mexico and abroad: Mexico City's *Excelsior, El Nacional,* and *Siempre!;* Guatemala City's *El Imparcial;* and Caracas's *El Nacional.* He also has served as the editor of the magazine *El Libro y el Pueblo.*

Guillén was first introduced to the literary world in the magazine *Espiga* (1944-1945). His literary works are comprised mostly of essays, and short stories-*Atrás está la bruma* and *Rodeada por el sueño*-and one poetic work, *El laurel y la sombra,* inspired by his mother.

WORKS: *Vida y pasión de dos ciudades: Guatemala y México* (Life and Passion of Two Cities: Guatemala and Mexico) (México: Espiga, 1945). *Atrás está la bruma* (The Haze Is behind Us) (México: Ed. del Cristal Fugitivo, 1948). *Guatemala, genio y figura* (Guatemala, Spirit and Character) (Guatemala: Eds. del Ministerio de Educación, 1954). *La semilla en el viento* (Seed on the Wind) (México: Ed. Ecuador, 1959). *La aurora es inmortal* (Dawn Is Immortal) (México: Ed. Ecuador, 1961); 2nd ed. (Quito: Casa de la Cultura Ecuatoriana, 1963). *El laurel y la sombra* (The Laurel and the Shadow) (México: Ed. Ecuador, 1963). *Guatemala, prólogo y epílogo de una revolución* (Guatemala, Prologue and Epilogue of a Revolution) (México: Cuadernos Americanos, 1964). *Rodeada por el sueño* (Surrounded by the Dream) (México: Rafael Campos Ramírez, 1966). *Romain Rolland y la Paz* (Romain Rolland and Peace) (México: SEP, 1966). *Belisario Domínguez, un hombre en el senado* (Belisario Dominguez, A Man in the Senate) (México: SEP, 1967). *Antología de Martin Luther King* (Anthology of Martin Luther King) (México: Costa-Amic, 1968). *Jesús Silva Herzog* (México: Empresas Editoriales, 1969). *Isidro Fabela, defensor de España . . .* (Isidro Fabela, Defender of Spain . . .) (México: Finisterre, 1970?). *Vladimir Ilich-Lenin: un hombre entre los hombres* (Vladimir Ilich-Lenin: A Man among Men)

(México: SEP, 1970). *El ensayo actual latinoamericano, antología* (The Present-Day Latin American Essay, Anthology) (México: Eds. de Andrea, 1971). *Nuestro Belén* (Our Bethlehem) (México: Finisterre, 1973?). *Homenaje póstumo a Miguel Angel Asturias* (Posthumous Tribute to Miguel Angel Asturias) (Guatemala: Congreso de la Unión, XLIX Lesgislatura, 1974). *Vasconcelos, "apresurado de Dios"* (Vasconcelos. "Spurred On by God") (México: Novaro, 1975). *Jesús Silva Herzog, Isidro Fabela, José Vasconcelos* (México: UNAM, 1980). *Fabela y su tiempo: España, Cárdenas, Roosevelt* (Fabela and His Time: Spain, Cárdenas, Roosevelt) (México: SRA-CEHAM, 1981). *Simbad y Ulises* (Sinbad and Ulysses) (Domés, 1984; Guatemala: Ed. Universitaria, Universidad de San Carlos de Guatemala, 1985).

BIBLIOGRAPHY: María Elvira Bermúdez, "Tres modalidades de la ficcion," review of *El laurel y la sombra*, in *Diorama de la Cultura* (Dec. 15, 1963): 8. Diego Córdoba, "Los Guillén y El laurel y la Sombra," in *Diorama de la Cultura* (Oct. 13, 1963): 3. Esteban Durán Rosado, Review of *El laurel y la sombra*, in *Revista Mexicana de la Cultura* 858 (Sept. 8, 1963): 15; "Libros. Guatemala revolucionaria," review of *Guatemala, prólogo y epílogo de una revolución*, in *Revista Mexicana de la Cultura* 911 (Sept. 13, 1964): 15. Andrés Henestrosa, "La nota cultural," review of *Guatemala prólogo...*, in *El Nacional* (Sept. 4, 1964): 3. Aurora M. Ocampo de Gómez and Ernesto Prado Velázquez, *Diccionario de escritores mexicanos* (México: UNAM, 1967), pp. 161-62. José Emilio Pacheco, Review of *El laurel y la sombra*, in *La Cultura en México* 88 (Oct. 23, 1963): p. xix. Javier Peñalosa, "El laurel de Fedro," *México en la Cultura* 759 (Oct. 6, 1963): 3. Antoniorrobles, "Respuesta abierta a Fedro Guillén," in *Revista Mexicanade la Cultura* 865 (Oct. 27, 1963): 6. Gustavo Sáinz, "Escaparate de libros," review of *Guatemala, prólogo...*, in *México en la Cultura* 811 (Oct. 4, 1964): 7. Mauricio de la Selva, "Asteriscos," review of *El laurel y la sombra*, in *Diorama de la Cultura* (Sept. 8, 1963): 4; "Asteriscos," review of *Guatemala, prólogo . . .*, in *Diorama de la Cultura* (Sept. 27, 1964): 8; in *Cuadernos de la Cultura* (Sept. 27, 1964): 8; in *Cuadernos Americanos* 6 (Nov.-Dec. 1964): 283-85.

JANIS L. KRUGH

GURIDI y Alcocer, José Miguel (1763-1828), writer and orator. Born in San Felipe Ixtacuiztla, Tlaxcala, on December 26, 1763, he achieved much success both as a member of the legal profession and as an ecclesiastic. After obtaining degrees in theology and canon law from the Palafox Seminary in Puebla and the University of Mexico, respectively, he was sent to Spain in 1810 as an elected official from Tlaxcala to the high Spanish court. Distinguishing himself both as a member of this body and as its president, he returned home after two years, and there he assumed high-ranking positions in the Church. He supported the revolutionary movement in Mexico and signed the Act of Independence as a member of the Provisional Congress.

Guridi y Alcocer was well known for his oratory on both political and religious themes, and his speeches in support of independence were some of the most effective of the revolutionary period. He wrote on such diverse topics as Latin grammar, modern philosophy, and the evils of gambling, and he also exercized his literary talents as a poet. His most notable work contains an autobiographical profile, which he compiled in 1801 and 1802, and it describes as well, in neoclassical style, the dramatic backdrop of an era of upheaval in Mexican history.

WORKS: *Sermón que en las honras del señor don Baltasar Ladrón de Guevara, del Conseio de S. M, Regente que fue de esta Real Audiencia y honorario en el Supremo de Indias* (Sermon in Honor of Sir Baltasar Ladran de Guevara, of His Majesty's Council, Regent of the Royal Audiencia and Honorary of the Supreme Council of the Indies) (México: Imp. Jiuregui, 1804). *Arte de la lengua latina* (The Art of the Latin Language) (México: Imp. Ontiveros, 1805). *Sermón de gracias por la jura de Fernando VII* (Sermon of Thanksgiving for the Oath of Fernando VII) (México: Imp. de Arizpe, 1808). *Sermón de Nuestra Señora de Guadalupe predicado en la función del Ilustre y Real Colegio de Abogados en San Francisco de México* (Sermon of Our Lady of Guadalupe Delivered at the Public Ceremony of the Illustrious and Royal College of Lawyers at San Francisco of Mexico) (México: Imp. de Arizpe, 1810). *Censor extraordinario* (Extraordinary Censor) (Cádiz: Imprenta de don Agapito Fernández, 1812). *Representación de la Diputacion Americana a las Cortes de España* (Representation of American Deputation in the Courts of Spain) (London: Schulze and Dean, 1812). *Exortación que para el juramento de la Constitución en la parroquia del Sagrario* (Exhortation for the Swearing in of the Constitution in the Parish of Sagrario) (México: Imp. de Alejandro Valdés, 1820). *Apología de la Aparición de Nuestra Señora de Guadalupe de México* (Defense of the Appearance of Our Lady of Guadalupe of Mexico) (México: Imp. de Alejandro Valdés, 1820). *Discurso sobre los daños del juego* (Discourse Regarding the Evils of Gambling) (México: Imp. de Valdés, 1832). *Apuntes de la vida de don José Miguel Guridi y Alcocer formados por él mismo en fines de 1801 y principios del siguiente de 1802* (Notes on the Life of Don Jose Miguel Guridi y Alcocer Taken by Him at the End of 1801 and the Beginning of 1802) (México: Moderna Librería Religiosa de José L. Vallejo, 1906).

BIBLIOGRAPHY: Carlos González Peña, *History of Mexican Literature*, translated by Gusta Barfield Nance and Florene Johnson Dunstan (Dallas: Southern Methodist University Press, 1968), pp. 183-84. Pedro Henríquez Ureña, *Estudios mexicanos* (México: FCE, 1984), pp. 182-86. Luis G. Urbina, *La vida literaria de Mexico* (México: Porrúa, 1965), pp. 354-57.

                                                                JULIE GREER JOHNSON

GUTIERREZ Hermosillo, Alfonso (1905-1935). Gutierrez Hermosillo was born in Guadalajara on August 15, 1905. He was reared in a privileged environment. As a child, he showed great interest in poetry, composing verses and excelling in the recitation of poems.

In his native city he joined a group of individuals affiliated with the *Bandera de Provincias* (1929-1930) and *Campo* (1930) magazines. In 1931, one year after earning his law degree, he moved to Mexico City in search of more opportunities to exercise his literary vocation. There he practiced law and supplemented his income by writing newspaper articles. He also worked for the Ministry of Foreign Affairs and the Public Ministry. On June 28, 1935, he died tragically in a streetcar accident.

Although the theater was his greatest obsession, he is best known for his lyric poetry. Agustín *Yáñez has characterized his poetics as a will toward affectation. Opposed to simplicity, he composed poems that reveal a deep commitment to "selection, purity and spiritual aristocracy" (Yáñez) and to the mastery of thoughts, emotions, and techniques. His limited repertoire of poems, many of extreme delicacy, was compiled and published in a posthumous volume entitled *Itinerario* (Itinerary). Among his friends and mentors were Xavier *Villaurrutia, Alfredo Gómez de la Vega, Celestino *Gorostiza and Agustín *Yáñez.

WORKS: Poetry: *Cuento de abuela* (Grandmother's Story) (México: n.p., 1927). *Cauce* (Riverbed) (Guadalajara: Eds. Campo, 1931). *Itinerario* (Itinerary) (México: Abside, 1937). *Tratados de un bien difícil* (Treatises on a Difficult Good) (Santiago, Chile: Eds. Ercilla, 1937). *Coros de presencias* (Choruses of Appearances) (México: n.p., 1938). Plays: *Teatro* (Theater: Complete Works) (México: UNAM, 1945). *La sombra de Lázaro*; *La escala de Jacob*; *La justicia, señores*; *El día de su muerte* (Lázaro's Shadow; Jacob's Ladder; Justice, Gentlemen; The Day of His Death) (México: UNAM, 1945). Short Stories: *Mi tío don Jesús y otros relatos* (My Uncle Don Jesús and Other Stories) (México: Eds. Occidente, 1945).

BIBLIOGRAPHY: Efraín González Luna, Prologue to *Itinerario*, by Alfonso Gutiérrez Hermosillo (México: Abside, 1937), pp. 5-15. Octavio Paz, "Imagen de A. Gutiérrez Hermosillo," *Letras de México* 11, 16 (July 16, 1937): 1-2. José Revueltas, "La carta a un amigo difunto," *Taller* 1, 4 (July 1939): 51-52. Agustín Yáñez, *Alfonso Gutiérrez Hermosillo y algunos amigos* (México: Eds. Occidente, 1945), pp. 7-19.

ROBERT K. ANDERSON

GUTIERREZ-NAJERA, Manuel (1859-1895), poet and journalist. Born in Mexico City on December 22, 1859, of a middle-class family, Gutiérrez-Najera was educated at home, first by his mother and later by private tutors. His mother wanted him to have an ecclesiastical career and initiated him early in the reading of the Spanish mystics: San Juan de la Cruz, Santa Teresa de Jesús, Fray Luis de Leon, and Fray Luis de Granada. Later he studied classical and French literatures. He was a prolific and precocious writer who did not stop publishing after his first article appeared in the journal *La Iberia* when he was thirteen years old. In fact, his entire short life was spent working for the daily press, either in the editorial rooms or in his capacity as a writer. Together with his friend Carlos *Díaz Dufoo he founded *Revista Azul* (1892-1893), a review that became the rallying point for Modernism in Spanish America. His many contributions to Mexico's newspapers and magazines appeared sometimes under his own name and sometimes under one of his several pseudonyms: M. Can Can, Junius, Puck, Recamier, El Cura de Jalatlaco, Perico el de los Palotes, and, of course, the most famous of all, El Duque Job. Following surgery in Mexico City, Gutiérez-Nájera died on February 3, 1895, at the height of his career at the age of thirty-five.

Gutiérrez-Nájera belongs to an outstanding generation of Spanish American Modernist poets. He made notable contributions in three different areas: poetry, short fiction, and journalism. In poetry, he is known not for his innovations in metrics, but for the changes he wrought in the mood of the poetic image. He began these long-lasting innovations by infusing the stilted expression of his time with borrowings from the major modern French poets, from the Romantic Musset to the Symbolists. Although his verses do show traces of Romanticism (sadness, unrequited love, mystery, death), he was, in essence, a Modernist, known for the musicality of his verse, his refined and elegant expression, and his exquisite sensibility. His aestheticism turned ordinary objects into figures of pure beauty. Following Parnassian tenets, he gloried in creating plastic imagery, drawn with the brilliant colors of his Modernist palette, but he could also be a suggestive poet, presenting ineffable visions in the vague musical language prescribed by the Symbolists. The poems that best show his control of form and his original treatment of theme are those he wrote under the title "Odas breves."

Narrative prose is the second area in which Gutiérez-Nájera became an innovator. In fact, for some critics prose and not poetry is the genre in which he made his most important contributions. He was obviously conscious of the need to change Spanish letters and spoke of his ability to cross (cruzar) French and Spanish by fusing French concepts with Spanish expression. He accomplished this feat both in his verse and in his prose, but it is in the latter, in his masterful chronicles and short stories, where a careful reader becomes aware of the extent to which he transformed Spanish narrative. *Cuentos frágiles* and *Cuentos color de humo* are in reality a kind of poetry in which he presents frivolous, and sometimes humorous, lyric caprices of French inspiration. This does not preclude his rising at times to the plane of metaphysical concerns or mournful meditations.

Gutiérez-Nájera's third area of innovation is journalistic prose. He is best known for his *crónicas* (chronicles), a genre he created, which became a popular way of writing not only among other Modernists, but also, and especially, among the writers of the next generations.

WORKS: Poetry: *Poesías de Manuel Gutiérrez Nájera* (Poems by Manuel Gutiérrez Nájera). Prologue by Justo Sierra (México: Ofna. Impresora de Estampillas, 1896). *Poesías* (Poems) (Paris and México: Bouret, 1897). *Poesías completas* (Complete Poems), edited and prologue by Francisco González Guerrero (México: Porrúa, 1958) Prose: *Cuentos frágiles* (Fragile Stories) (México: Imp. del Comercio de E. Dublín, 1883). *Cuentos color de humo y cuentos frágiles* (Stories the Color of Smoke and Fragile Stories). (Madrid: América, 1920). *Obras de Manuel Gutiérrez Nájera* (prose) (Works by Manuel Gutiérrez Nájera [prose]), 2 vols. (México: Ofna. Impresora de Estampillas, 1898). *Obras inéditas de Manuel Gutiérrez Nájera (Crónicas de Puck)* (Unpublished Works by Manuel Gutiérrez Nájera [Puck's Chronicles]), edited by E. K. Mapes (New York: Instituto de las Españas, 1939). *Prosa (cuentos y crónicas)* (Prose [short stories and chronicles]) (San José de Costa Rica: Alsina, 1912).

BIBLIOGRAPHY: Antonio Acevedo Escobedo, *Los cuatro poetas. Gutiérrez Nájera, Urbina, Icaza, Tablada* (México: SEP, 1944). *En torno a Gutiérrez Nájera y las letras mexicanas del siglo XIX* (México: Botas, 1960). Carlos Gómez del Prado, *Manuel Gutiérrez Nájera* (México: Eds. de Andrea, 1964). Roberto Meza Fuentes, *De Díaz Mirón a Rubén Darío.* (Santiago de Chile: Nascimiento, 1940). Iván Schulman, "El color en la poesía de Gutiérrez Nájera," *Revista Hispánica Moderna* 23, 1 (Enero 1957): 1-13. Nell Walker, *The Life and Works of Manuel Gutiérrez Nájera* (Columbia: University of Missouri Press, 1927).

MARIA A. SALGADO

GUZMAN, Franciso de Paula (1843-1884). Guzmán was born in Mexico City on February 8. 1843. Little is known of his studies beyond his receiving the professional title of lawyer. He practiced this profession and then, as his interest in the classics deepened, he became professor of Latin in the National Preparatory School. He published essays in the literary edition of *El Tiempo* and in the *Memorias* of the Academia Mexicana de la Lengua. Guzmán's poetry is deeply humanistic and mystic, influenced by Fray Luis de León, among others.

WORKS: Guzmán's works were found in numerous daily publications and literary magazines but have not been collected in a single volume. The few compositions of his that are known were published in *El Tiempo*, literary edition (México, 1883); and in various of the *Memorias de la Academica Mexicana de la Lengua* of the same period.

BIBLIOGRAPHY: Alberto María Carreño, *Memorias de la academia Mexicana* 6 (1945): 191-92; 8 (1946): 171. Carlos González Peña, *History of Mexican Literature*, translated by Gusta Barfield Nance and Florene Johnson Dunstan (Dallas, Texas: Southern Methodist University Press, 1968), p. 214. Aurora M. Ocampo de Gómez and Ernesto Prado Velázquez, *Diccionario de escritores mexicanos* (México: UNAM, 1967), p. 166. José María Vigil, "Necrología," in *Memorias de la Academia Mexicana Correspondiente de la Real Española* 2, 4 (1884): 460-73.

FILIPPA B. YIN

GUZMAN, Martín Luis (1887-1976). Martín Luis Guzmán, a noted novelist, essayist, and journalist, was born in Chihuahua on October 6, 1887. He died in Mexico City on December 22, 1976, after a long and fulfilling career. Guzmán revealed his journalistic talents at an early age, when he published a journal, *La Juventud* (Youth), in Veracruz, beginning in 1900. In 1913, he received his law degree in Mexico City. While still a student, he edited *El Imparcial* and taught classes at the high school level. His political views began to take shape in earnest following the death of his father at the hands of revolutionaries in 1910. In 1911, he became part of the famous literary group El Ateneo de México.

During the early years of the Mexican Revolution, he was linked for varying amounts of time to Francisco Madero, Venustiano Carranza, and Pancho Villa. Carranza had him imprisoned for a short while, and upon his release, he went into exile in Spain and the United States, from 1915 to 1920. When he returned to Mexico, he joined the staff of *El Heraldo de México* as chief editor and became politically involved with the new government. He founded *El Mundo* in 1922, but in 1925 he went into exile again in Spain for eleven years. At the outbreak of the Spanish Civil War, he returned to Mexico, where he secured a position as a correspondent for *El Universal*. In 1942, he founded the well-known periodical *El Tiempo*. He was accepted as a member of the Academia Mexicana de la Lengua in 1954. The recipient of the Manuel Avila Camacho Prize and the National Prize for Literature in 1958, Guzmán, was rewarded for his significant literary contributions, especially those involving novels and essays reflecting the Mexican Revolution.

Guzmán's journalist career really began in 1915 with the publication of *La querella de México* (The Dispute of Mexico), a pessimistic essay about Mexican morality. This essay was followed by *A orillas del Hudson* (On the Banks of the Hudson, 1920), a group of poems in prose, plus critical essays on politics and literature. This was written in New York, where he spent part of his exile.

The second phase of Guzmán's literary career began with *El águila y la serpiente* (The Eagle and the Serpent) (1928), which is generally considered to be his masterpiece and the major literary event of the year. A gripping eye-witness account of the people, circumstances, and events of the Mexican Revolution, the work, although categorized by Guzmán as a novel, is more an autobiographical chronicle and essay. The political and military leaders are exposed in all their human dimensions. It is a fascinating, chilling, and powerful documentary of the goals of the revolution and the betrayal of those same goals. It is about power: the acquisition, the use, and the abuse of power. What is most convincing about the work is that Guzmán himself lived many of the experiences he narrates and accurately transmits what he saw, felt, and heard during those turbulent days. Critic Lanin Gyurko calls his style "lucid, direct, eloquent, and incisive." The portrait Guzmán creates of Pancho Villa, in particular, is perhaps the most compelling aspect of *El águila y la serpiente*.

Another of his most famous works is the novel of espionage and intrigue, *La sombra del caudillo* (The Shadow of the Tyrant) (1929), a work focused on the political turmoil and general instability of the 1920s. Filled with suspense, violence, and mass murder, *La sombra del caudillo* deals with all the shadowy figures who dominate the Mexican scene.

Guzmán also wrote biographical portraits, the most noted being a four-volume set, *Memorias de Pancho Villa* (Memories of Pancho Villa) (1938-1940). It is not considered to be of the same high artistic and literary quality as his other works. Nonetheless, the work paints an extraordinary picture of a man viewed as the incarnation of evil by some and as a folk hero by others.

WORKS: Fiction: *El águila y la serpiente* (The Eagle and the Serpent), in *El Universal* (1926); (Madrid: Aguilar, 1928); many subsequent editions. *La sombra del caudillo* (The Shadow of the Tyrant), in *El Universal* (1929); (Madrid: Espasa-Calpe, 1929); many subsequent editions. *Memorias de Pancho Villa* (Memories of Pancho Villa), 4 vols. (México: Botas, 1938-1940). *Filadelfia, paraíso de conspiradores* (Philadelphia, Paradise of Conspirators) (Madrid: n.p., 1938); *Filadelfia, paraíso de conspiradores y otras historias noveladas* (Philadelphia, Paradise of Conspirators and Other Novelized Stories) (México: Cía. General de Ediciones, 1960). *Kinchil* (México: n.p., 1946). *Islas Marías* (México: Cía. General de Ediciones, 1959). Biography: *Mina el mozo: héroe de Navarra* (Mina the Youth: Hero of Navarra) (Madrid: Espasa-Calpe, 1932); retitled *Javier Mina: Héroe de España y México* (Javier Mina, Hero of Spain and Mexico) (México: Cía. General de Ediciones, 1951). Essays: *La querella de México* (The Dispute of Mexico) (Madrid: Imp. Clásica Española, 1915); with *A orillas del Hudson y otras páginas* (On the Banks of the Hudson and Other Pages) (México: Cía. General de Ediciones, 1959). *A orillas del Hudson*, in *Revista Universal* (New York, 1917); (México: Botas, 1920). *Aventuras democráticas* (Democratic Adventures) (Madrid: Cía. Iberoamericana de Publicaciones, 1931); in *Letras de México*, 1932. *Apunte sobre una personalidad* (Notes on a Personality), in *Academia* (México: Cía. General de Ediciones, 1959). *Academia. Tradición. Independencia. Libertad* (Academics. Tradition. Independence. Freedom), collected speeches (México: Cía.

General de Ediciones, 1959). *Necesidad de cumplir las leyes de Reforma* (Necessity to Comply with the Reform Laws) (México: Empresas Editoriales, 1963). *Pábulo para la historia* (Pabulum for History) (México: Cía. General de Ediciones, 1960). "Francisco Villa," transcript of a speech, in *El Día* (Sept. 27, 1964): 2. Chronicles: *Muertes históricas* (Historical Deaths) (México: Cía. General de Ediciones, 1958). *Febrero de 1913* (February of 1913) (México: Empresas Editoriales, 1963). *Crónicas de mi destierro* (Chronicles of My Exile) (México: Empresas Editoriales, 1963). "Un texto desconocido de Martín Luis Guzmán (Cómo acabó la guerra en 1917)" (An Unknown Text of Martín Luis Guzmán-How the War Ended in 1917), in *Ovaciones* 127 (May 24, 1964): 4-5. Translations: "Traducciones de poemas de Amy Lowell y otros poetas de lengua inglesa" (Translations of Poems by Amy Lowell and Other Poets of the English Language), in *Revista Universal* (New York, 1917). John Masefield, *Los fieles* (The Faithful), tragedy, in collaboration with Enrique Díez Canedo, in *Contemporáneos* 18-19 (Nov.-Dec. 1929): 245-92, 354-421. Complete Works: *Obras completas*, 2 vols. (México: Cía. General de Ediciones, 1961-1963).

BIBLIOGRAPHY: Ermilo Abreu Gómez, "Martín Luis Guzmán, crítica y bibliografía," in *Hispania* 35, 1 (Feb., 1952): 70-73; "Martín Luis Guzmán," in *Revista Interamericana de Bibliografía* 2 (April-June 1959: 119-35; *Martín Luis Guzmán* (México: Leyenda, 1968). Fernando Alegría, *Nueva historia de la novela hispanoamericana* (Hanover, N.H.: Ediciones del Norte, 1986), pp. 138-40. Sophie L. Bidault, "Aspectos estéticos en *La sombra del caudillo*," in *Neophilologue* 73, 4 (Oct. 1989): 548-59. Juan Bruce-Novoa, "*El aguila y la serpiente* en las versiones estadunidenses," in *Plural* 17 (Oct. 1987): 16-21; "Martín Luis Guzmán's Necessary Overtures," in *Discurso Literario* 4, 1 (Autumn 1986): 63-83. John S. Brushwood, *Mexico in Its Novel* (Austin: University of Texas Press, 1966): 200-203. Nellie Campobello, "Martín Luis Guzmán," in *Ruta* (Nov. 15, 1938): 42-43. Emmanuel Carballo, "Las obras completas de Martín Luis Guzmán," in *Nivel* 16 (April 25, 1964): 3, 12; *El cuento mexicano del siglo xx* (México: Empresas Editoriales, 1964), 24-27, 29; *Diecinueve protagonistas de la literatura mexicana del siglo veinte* (México: Empresas Editoriales, 1965), pp. 61-99. Arturo Castellanos, "La novela de la Revolución Mexicana," in *Cuadernos Hispanoamericanos* 184 (April 1965): 123-46. Antonio Castro Leal, *La novela de la Revolución* (México and Buenos Aires: Aguilar, 1958), pp. 159-61. "Capítulos del Aguila en *La sombra del caudillo*," in *La Palabra y el Hombre* 69 (Jan.-March 1989): 41-52. Carlos Cortínez, "Simetría y sutileza en la narrativa de Martín Luis Guzmán," in *Revista Canadiense de Estudios Hispánicos* 12, 2 (Winter 1988) 221-34. Fernando Curiel, "La querella de Martín Luis Guzmán," in *Americas Review* 17, 3-4 (Fall-Winter 1989): 179-84. James Seay Dean, "Extreme Unction for Past Power and Glory: Four Fictions on the Mexican Revolution," in *Revista de Estudios Hispánicos* 17, 1 (Jan. 1983): 89-106. Enrique Díez Canedo, *Letras de México* (México: FCE, 1944), pp. 376-79. Christopher Domínguez, "Martín Luis Guzmán: El teatro de la política," in *Vuelta* 11, 131 (Oct. 1987): 23-31. Margo Glantz, "La novela de la Revolución Mexicana y *La sombra del caudillo*," in *Revista Iberoamericana* 55, 148-49 (July-Dec. 1989): 869, 878. Manuel Pedro González, *Trayectoria de la novela en México* (México: Botas, 1951), pp. 200-214. Lanin A. Gyurko, "Martín Luis Guzmán," in *Latin American Writers*, vol. 2, Carlos A. Solé, editor-in-chief (New York: Charles Scribner's Sons, 1989), pp. 655-662. "Homenaje a Martín Luis Guzmán," in *Nivel* 23 (Nov. 25, 1964): 1-3, 6-8. Helen Phipps Houck, "Las obras novelescas de Martín Luis Guzmán," in *Revista Iberoamericana* 3, 5 (1941):

139-58. Luis Leal, "*La sombra del caudillo*, Roman à Clef," in *Modern Language Journal* 36, 1 (1952): 16-21. José Luis Martínez, *Literatura mexicana siglo xx*, vol. 1 (México: Ant. Libr. Robredo, 1949), pp. 193-98. F. Rand Morton, *Los novelistas de la Revolución Mexicana* (México: Cultura, 1949), pp. 115-140. Aurora M. Ocampo de Gómez and Ernesto Prado Velázquez, *Diccionario de escritores mexicanos* (México: UNAM, 1967), pp. 166-68. Carlos Ramos Gutiérrez, Review of *El águila y la serpiente*, in *Metáfora* 14 (May-June 1957): pp. 38-39. Mauricio de la Selva, Review of *Crónicas de mi destierro*, in *Cuadernos Americanos* 5 (Sept.-Oct. 1964): 280. Ruth Stanton, "Martín Luis Guzmán's Place in Modern Literature," in *Hispania* 26 (1943): 136-38.

JEANNE C. WALLACE

H

HELGUERA, Ignacio (1899- ?), short story writer and novelist. Born in Peñoles, Durango, Helguera became a businessman and later taught at Rider College in Trenton, New Jersey.

His work consists of both short stories and novels. His first book, *El hallazgo engañoso y otros cuentos* (The Deceitful Discovery and Other Stories) (1955), is a collection of eighteen stories. Though these works have some flaws with respect to the creation of character, they are well written and the plots are carefully developed. Written with these strengths and weaknesses are his first novel, *Las mancuernillas* (The Cuff Links) (1955), and the collections *El monstruo y otros cuentos* (The Monster and Other Stories) (1955), and *La hija de Bolívar y otros cuentos* (Bolivar's Daughter and Other Stories) (1963).

WORKS: Short Stories: *El hallazgo engañoso y otros cuentos* (The Deceitful Discovery and Other Stories) (México: Editorial Muñoz, 1955). *El monstruo y otros cuentos* (The Monster and Other Stories) (México: Editorial Tezontle, FCE, 1955). *Narraciones norteñas* (Northern Narratives) (México: Col. México Lee, 1960). *La hija de Bolívar y otros cuentos* (Bolivar's Daughter and Other Stories) (México: Editorial del autor, 1963). Novel: *Pancho Rizos* (México: Editorial del autor, 1955). *Las mancuernillas* (The Cuff Links) (México: Editorial del autor. Imprenta Muñoz, 1955). *Caín cabalga* (Cain Rides) (México: Col. México Lee, 1960). *Huellas de redencíon* (Tracks of Redemption) (México: Libro-México, 1960).

BIBLIOGRAPHY: Anon., "Nuevo libro de relatos del excelente Ignacio Helguera," in *El Universal* (México, Jan. 26,1964): 3; Review of *La hija de Bolívar y otros cuentos*, in *Cuadernos de Buenos Aires* 2 (Feb. 1964): 96. Jesús Arellano, Review of *El hallazgo engañoso y otros cuentos*, in *Metáfora* 4 (Sept.-Oct. 1955): 41-42. María Elvira Bermúdez, "Otros cuentos," review of *La hija de Bolívar y otros cuentos*, in *Diorama de la Cultura* (April 19, 1964): 7. Henrique González Casanova, "Autores y libros," *México en la Cultura* 262 (March 28, 1954): 2. Andrés Henestrosa, "La Nota Cultural," review of *La hija de Bolívar y otros cuentos*, in *El Nacional* (March 20, 1964): 3. Luis Leal, *Bibliografía del cuento mexicano*, Colección Manuales Studium, 21 (México: Ediciones de Andrea, 1958), p. 67. Aurora M. Ocampo de Gómez and Ernesto Prado Velázquez, *Diccionario de escritores mexicanos* (México: Universidad Nacional Autónoma de México, 1967), p. 168. Carlos Ramos Gutiérrez, Review of *Las mancuernillas*, in *Metáfora* 9 (July-Aug. 1956): 33-34. Gustavo Sainz, "Escaparate," review of *La hija de Bolívar y otros cuentos*, in *México en la Cultura*, 774 (Jan. 19, 1964): 5.

EDNA A. REHBEIN

HENESTROSA, Andrés (1906-). Henestrosa was born in Ixhuatán, Oaxaca, on November 30, 1906. He attended preparatory school in Mexico City and studied law for a time at the National University. He also worked for the Minister of Education's José *Vasconcelos' educational reform program, taught Mexican and Spanish American literature at the secondary and university levels, and was publisher of the magazines *El Libro y el Pueblo* and *Letras Patrias*. Furthermore, he served as director of literature for the National Institute of Fine Arts, deputy to the National Congress, and since 1964 has belonged to the Mexican Academy of the Spanish Language.

Henestrosa's most celebrated works are his *Los hombres que dispersó la danza* (The Men That the Dance Dispersed) and *Retrato de mi madre* (Portrait of My Mother). The former established him as an important "indigenista" author. In it he presents an imaginative reconstruction and re-elaboration of twenty-six stories and legends from his Zapotec homeland. Using a simple and refreshing style, he endeavors to decipher the meaning of the Zapotec theogonies. The publication of his *Retrato de mi madre*, a brief but impressive memoir of his mother during his youth, provides additional testimony to his superior literary skills. His nonfictional books cover a gamut of topics. His many essays, articles, and short narratives have appeared in a myriad of magazines, journals, and newspapers and as prologues and contributions to numerous books.

WORKS: Stories and Narratives: *Los hombres que dispersó la danza* (The Men That the Dance Dispersed) (México: Imprenta Universitaria, 1945). *Retrato de mi madre* (Portrait of My Mother) (México: Publicaciones Alcaraván, 1940). *Los cuatro abuelos* (The Four Grandparents) (México: Ed. del Autor, 1961). *Sobre el mí* (About Me) (México: Ecuador, 1966). Other: *Fray Alonso Ponce: Viaje a la Nueva España* (Fra Alonso Ponce: A Journey to New Spain) (México: SEP, 1947). *Periodismo y periodistas de Hispanoamérica* (Journalism and Journalists from Spanish America), written in collaboration with José Antonio Fernández de Castro (México: SEP, 1947). *Los hispanismos en el idioma zapoteco* (Hispanicisms in the Zapotec Language) (México: Academia Mexicana, 1965). *La batalla de Juchitán* (The Battle of Juchitán) (México: Taller Técnica Gráfica, 1966). *Desde México y España* (From México and Spain) (México: A. Finisterre, 1967). *Tres cartas autobiográficas* (Three Autobiographical Letters) (México: SEP, 1967). *Una alacena de alacenas* (A Closet of Closets) (México: INBA, 1970). *Espuma y flor de corridos mexicanos* (Froth and Flowers of Mexican Ballads) (México: Ed. Porrúa, 1977). *El remoto y cercano ayer* (Yesterday, Close Yet Remote) (México: Ed. Porrúa, 1979). *Caminos de Juárez* (The Ways of Juárez) (México: FCE, 1985).

BIBLIOGRAPHY: Francisco Aguilera and Georgette Magassy Dorn, eds., *The Archive of Hispanic Literature on Tape* (Washington, D.C.: Library of Congress, 1974), pp. 220-21. Alfredo Cardona Peña, *La entrevista literaria y cultural* (México: UNAM, 1978), pp. 172-79; *Semblanzas mexicanas* (México: B. Costa-Amic, 1955), pp. 99-102. Henrique González Casanova, Introduction to *Una alacena de alacenas*, by Andrés Henestrosa (México: Eds. de Bellas Artes, 1970), pp. 11-15. Ernesto Mejía Sánchez, Introduction to *Andrés Henestrosa* (collected works), by Andrés Henestrosa (México: Ed. Novara, 1969), pp. 9-14. Octaviano Valdés, "Una bella prosa singular de Andrés Henestrosa," in *Abside* 41, 1 (Jan-Mar. 1977), 30-34.

ROBERT K. ANDERSON

HENRIQUEZ Ureña, Pedro (1884-1946). Henríquez Ureña was born in Santo Domingo, Dominican Republic, on June 29, 1884, the son of Francisco Henríquez Carvajal, an outstanding man of letters and a lawyer who became president of his country, and Salomé Ureña, a distinguished poet and educator. He studied in the Dominican Republic through high school, but was forced to leave because of the unstable political situation. Most of his adult life was spent in voluntary exile in other countries.

While pursuing his high school diploma he published theater chronicles, and literary essays in magazines and newspapers. In 1901 he went to New York and there he wrote some of his best poems. But it was in 1904, after he moved to Havana, that the prose writer emerged. In this city he published chronicles, essays, critical articles and more poetry. His brother Max founded and directed the magazine *Cuba Literaria* in Santiago de Cuba, to which Pedro contributed frequently.

In 1906 Pedro Henríquez Ureña moved to Mexico City and joined a group of writers in *Revista Moderna de Mexico*, directed by the poet Jesús E. *Valenzuela. Three years later a group of writers -- Antonio *Caso, Jesús T. *Acevedo, Alfonso *Reyes, Rafael *López and Pedro *Henríquez Ureña -- founded the influential El Ateneo de la Juventud. This group of young writers and intellectuals was responsible for the rebirth of humanism and the break with positivist thought in early twentieth-century Mexican literature. During his first years in Mexico he wrote numerous articles and essays that were published in Mexico, Cuba, and Santo Domingo.

In 1915 Pedro Henríquez Ureña accepted a position in the Romance Language Department at the University of Minnesota to teach Spanish and Latin American literature, and began to study for his doctoral degree. His doctoral dissertation, *La versificación irregular en la poesía española* (Irregular Versification in Spanish Poetry), was later published in Spain with a prologue by don Ramón Menéndez Pidal. This book is considered essential in the study of Spanish poetry. Between 1917 and 1920 he and Alfonso Reyes, later dean of Mexican letters, studied in Madrid at the Center of Historical Studies.

Shortly afterwards José *Vasconcelos, then minister of education in his country, asked him to return to Mexico to help reorganize the educational system. There he occupied many posts in the government and at the university. In Mexico he contributed to *Savia Moderna* and organized the series American Library for Fondo de Cultura Económica. When the political situation in Mexico worsened, he decided to move to Argentina. He taught at the University of Buenos Aires, where he held the Chair of Latin American literature from 1925 until his death. In Argentina his writing matured and he published his best works. On April 5, 1934, he was elected to the Argentinian Academy of Letters. Between 1938 and 1942 he wrote numerous prologues for the collection One Hundred Master Works published by Editorial Losada.

The Dominican writer was invited by Harvard to occupy the prestigious Charles Eliot Norton Chair for the 1940-1941 academic year. The eight conferences that he presented in his course were later published by Harvard with the title *Literary Currents in Hispanic America*. The translation of this work, *Las corrientes literarias en la América Hispánica*, appeared in Mexico in 1949. He died suddenly on May 11, 1946, while on his way to the university to teach his classes.

Although Henríquez Ureña began his literary career writing poetry, he distinguished himself with the literary essay. His first book, *Ensayos críticos* (Critical Essays, 1905), includes essays on Rubén Darío, José Enrique Rodó, Oscar Wilde, Bernard Shaw,

Modernism in Cuban poetry, etc. This volume by the young writer was very well received by the critics and merited an enthusiastic comment by José Enrique Rodó. His next publication, *Horas de estudio* (Hours of Study, 1910), was a series of essays on philosophy and Spanish and Latin American literature.

In 1928 Pedro Henríquez Ureña selected his best articles written in Argentina for a volume called *Seis ensayos en busca de nuestra expresión* (Six Essays in Search of Our Literary Expression). In this book he presents the history of the trends that formed our literary culture in a clear and precise language. The author traces the literary history in Spanish America to emphasize the creation and development of its authentic expression. He continues to clarify the relationship between literature and culture in Latin America in his next book, *Las corrientes literarias en la América Hispana* (Literary Currents in Hispanic America). In this volume Henríquez Ureña studies and analyzes the literary history of Spanish America. He divides the work into different periods -- the discovery, the creation of a new society, the flowering of the colonial world, the declaration of intellectual independence, romanticism and anarchy -- and concludes with two chapters on pure literature and contemporary problems. The first six chapters present a sociohistorical point of view while the last two are literary. The critic treats the features of each aesthetic period and characterizes the tendencies and works of each writer. In his discussions he blends the literary and social aspects, and makes references to music, art, philosophy, and science. *Las corrientes literarias en la América Hispana* is a clear, precise history of literary and cultural development in Latin America. His last work, published posthumously, *La historia de la cultura en la América Hispana* (History of Culture in Hispanic America, 1947), is a synthesis of the cultural development in Spanish America in its historical evolution.

As a philologist he wrote many essays on linguistics. In 1921 he wrote the essay "Observaciones sobre el español en América" (Observations of the Spanish in America). His pursuit of these studies led to the famous and well-known article, "El supuesto andalucismo de América" (The Supposed Andalucian Quality of the Spanish Language in America). In this article he stated that the Spanish language in Spanish America presents great variety and diversity. He further stated that it is too simplistic to identify the linguistic phenomena in Spanish America with those of Andalucia. To prove his point, he studied and investigated the origin of the Spanish language in America. His interest in linguistics and the study of languages persisted, leading to important articles on the Spanish of Mexico and of Santo Domingo.

Pedro Henríquez Ureña, an outstanding writer and critic, well-known for his literary and philosophical essays, trained and shaped a new generation of essayists in Latin America.

WORKS: Essays: *Horas de estudio* (París: Ollendorf, 1910). *La versificación irregular en la poesía castellana* (Madrid: Publicaciones de la Revista de Filología Española, 1920). *Seis ensayos en busca de nuestra expresión* (Buenos Aires: Babel, 1928). *La cultura y las letras en Santo Domingo* (Buenos Aires: Biblioteca de Dialectología Hispanoamericana, 1936). *El español en México, los Estados Unidos y la América Central* (Buenos Aires: Biblioteca de Dialectología Hispanoamericana, 1938). *Literary Currents in Hispanic America* (Cambridge, Mass.: Harvard University Press, 1945). *Historia de la cultura en la América hispánica* (México: FCE, 1947). *Las corrientes literarias en la América Hispana*, translated by Joaquín Díez Canedo (México: FCE, 1949).

BIBLIOGRAPHY: Emilio Carilla, "Pedro Henríquez Ureña: biografía comentada," *Revista Interamericana de Bibliografía* 27, (1966); 227-39. Julio Jaime Julia, *El libro jubilar de Pedro Henríquez Ureña* (Santo Domingo: Universidad Nacional Pedro Henríquez Ureña, 1984). Juan Jacobo de Lara, *Pedro Henríquez Ureña: su vida y su obra* (Santo Domingo: Universidad Nacional Pedro Henríquez Ureña, 1975). Luis Leal, "Pedro Henríquez Ureña, crítico de la literatura hispanoamericana," in *Revista Interamericana de Bibliografía* 27 (1966), 241-53. "Homenaje a Pedro Henríquez Ureña," in *Revista Iberoamericana* 21, 41-42 (Jan.-Dec. 1956).

NORA ERRO-PERALTA

HEREDIA y Heredia, José María (1803-1839), poet, critic, and lawyer. Heredia was born in Santiago, Cuba, in 1803. His father, Francisco Heredia y Mieses, was a member of the Spanish judiciary and occupied minor posts in Cuba until he became oidor-regente (inspector-regent) of the Audience in Caracas (1812-1817). José M. Heredia began his law studies in the universities of Caracas. His father was transferred in 1818 to Mexico, where he died in 1820. José M. Heredia returned to La Habana to continue his studies, and there he received his Law degree. He left Cuba for political reasons and lived, for a time, in Boston and then in New York. He moved to Mexico at the invitation of President Guadalupe Victoria. He was appointed to various posts. He died in Mexico in 1839.

While Heredia lived in New York, he visited Niagara Falls, and based on that experience he wrote his famous poem "Niágara." As he traveled by ship to Mexico, he composed other poems such as "Himno del desterrado" (Hymn of the Exiled). In Mexico he wrote critiques, short stories, and a translation of Sir Walter Scott's Waverly, in three volumes. Amado Alonso and Julio Caillet-Bois considered Heredia "the most important critic in the Spanish language in the nineteenth century, until the appearance of Marcelino Menéndez y Pelayo." Most of his works of criticism appeared in *El Iris* (The Iris) and in *La Miscelánea* (Miscellany).

WORKS: "En el Teocally de Cholula" (On the Teocally of Cholula) (1820). "Niágara" (1824). *Poemas* (Poems) (New York, 1825; Toluca, 1832). "Himno del desterrado" (Hymn of the Exiled) (1825). "Misantropía" (Misanthropy) (n.d.). "En mi cumpleaños" (On My Birthday) (n.d.). "Desengaños" (Disillusions) (n.d.). "Historia de un salteador Italiano" (History of an Italian Highway Robber), short story (1841). A translation of Scott's Waverly, in three volumes (1833). "Ensayo sobre la novela" (Essay on the Novel), in *La Miscelánea* (Miscellany) (1832). *Poetas ingleses contemporáneos* (contemporary English Poets) (n.d.), an adaptation of the play Eduardo IV o el usurpador (Edward IV or the Usurper) (n.d.).

BIBLIOGRAPHY: Enrique Anderson-Imbert and Eugenio Florit, *Literatura Hispanoamericana. Antología e Introducción Histórica* (New York: Holt, Rinehart and Winston, 1960), 218-19). Orlando Gómez-Gil, *Historia Crítica de la Literatura Hispanoamericana* (New York: Holt, Rinehart and Winston, 1968), 201-05. Julio Jiménez Rueda, *Historia de la Literatura Mexicana* (México: Ediciones Botas, 1960), 223, 282, 286. Raimundo Lazo, *Historia de la Literatura Hispanoamericana. El siglo XIX (1780-1914)* (México: Editorial Porrúa, 1967), 270-74, 276, 279. Francisco S.

Stimson and Ricardo Navas-Ruiz, *Literatura de la América hispánica. Antología e historia*, vol. 1 (New York: Dodd, Mead, 1971), 241-43.

JOSEPH VELEZ

HERNANDEZ, Efrén (1904-1958), poet, short story writer, and novelist. Efrén Hernández was born in León, Guanajuato, December on 1, 1904. With his friend, Rubén Salazar Mallén, he founded the journal *América* in 1942, to which he contributed many humorous articles under the pseudonym Till Ealling, which recalls the German practical joker Till Eulenspiegel. An active participant in literary groups of his time, he is credited with discovering Juan *Rulfo. Also, he influenced other younger writers such as Rosario *Castellanos and Luisa Josefina *Hernández. A small, humble man, sickly throughout his life, he died in Tacubaya, Federal District, on January 28, 1958.

Hernández felt that literature and philosophy were inextricably linked. His work is characterized by simple wisdom and deep tenderness and sympathy for his fellow man. He was influenced heavily by the Spanish mystic poets, especially Fray Luis de León from whom he developed a concern for the passing of time and the role of memory as a key to the past and indicator of the future. Possibly derived from Unamuno is his idea that life and death are different modes of reality. The influence of Cervantes may be seen in his psychological novel *La paloma, el sótano y la torre* (The Dove, the Basement, and the Tower), which treats the conflict of reason and emotion and in his short story "Tachas" which deals with the conflict between reason and imagination. *Cerrazón sobre Nicomaco* is considered his masterpiece because of its spontaneity and profundity. His style is highly polished; his prose is chacterized by elegant simplicity, use of anonymous protagonists, and extensive use of Mexicanisms, expecially diminutives. An atmosphere of solitude pervades his poetry. The humor and simplicity of his stories permit appreciation on a superficial plane that belies the profound psychological and philsophical nature of his work.

WORKS: *El señor de palo* (Man of Wood)(México: Edición de Estudiantes, 1932). *Hora de horas* (Hour of Hours) (México: 1936. *Cuentos* (Stories) (México: UNAM, 1941). *Tachas* (Objections) (México: SEP, 1943). *Entre apagados muros* (Between Dark Walls) (México: Imprenta Universitaria, 1943). *Cuentos* (Stories) (México: SEP, 1947). *Cerrazón sobre Nicomaco. Ficción harto doliente* (Cloudy Day Over Nicomaco. Very Mournful Fiction) (México: 1946). *La paloma, el sótano y la torre* (The Dove, the Cellar, and the Tower) (México: SEP, 1949). *Sus mejores cuentos* (His Best Stories) (México: Novaro, 1956). *Obras: poesía, novela, cuentos* (Works: Poetry, Novel, Short Stories) (México: FCE, 1965).

BIBLIOGRAPHY: María Teresa Bosque Lastra, "La obra de Efrén Hernández," thesis, Universidad Iberoamericana, 1963. John S. Brushwood, *Mexico in Its Novel: A Nation's Search for Identity* (Austin: University of Texas Press, 1966), 232-33. Frank Dauster, *Breve historia de la poesía mexicana* (México: de Andrea, 1956), 170. Esteban Durán Rosado, "La naturalidad de lo absurdo en la cuentística de Efrén Hernández," in *Revista Mexicana de la Cultura* 977 (Dec. 19, 1965): 1. Mary M. Harmon, *Efrén Hernández: A Poet Discovered* (Hattiesburg: University of Mississippi Press, 1972). Luis Leal, *Breve historia del cuento mexicano* (México: de Andrea, 1956),

130-31. Eduardo Valadés, "Efrén Hernández o de la inocencia," in *México en el Arte* 11 (Winter 1985-1986): 8-11.

KENNETH M. TAGGART

HERNANDEZ, Francisco (1946-). Hernández was born in San Andrés Tuxtla, Veracruz, on June 20, 1946. He works as an adman for a Mexico City public relations firm, and apart from writing some of the most important poetic work of his generation, he is responsible for writing some of the catchiest Tide and Coke commercials aired on Mexican radio and television.

Hernández writes very personal, tortured poetry. Poetry serves him to put aside the guilt of writing ads, to forget his daily comings and goings along Mexico's Madison Avenue. Sandro Cohen writes that if it weren't for his poetry, he would have died long ago. His early *Gritar es cosa de mudos* (Mute People Shout) is written is biting verse kicking its way to survival. He develops into a black humorist using the character traits of classic film characters, famous painters, musicians, and writers as metaphors for his torment. He is also a memorable, descriptive poet. There are poems in *Mar de fondo* that describe feverish glimpses of a childhood illness cured through witchcraft. Lush descriptions of jungles, seas, rivers, and the fauna that dwell within them flow abundantly throughout. His use of seafaring language is also a unique element of his verse as are dramatically erotic passages. He describes his last work, *De cómo Robert Schuman fue vencido por los demonios* (Of How Robert Schuman Was Defeated by the Devils), as a dual autobiography, that is, Schuman's and his mirror-like own. This is a wonderful book in which the score of Schuman's *Nachtstücke* appears side by side with his poem.

WORKS: *Gritar es cosa de mudos* (Mute People Shout) (México: Libros escogidos, 1974). *Cuerpo disperso* (Disperse Body) (México: UNAM, 1982). *Mar de fondo* (Heavy Seas) (México: Joaquín Mortiz, 1982). *De cómo Robert Schuman fue vencido por los demonios* (Of How Robert Schuman Was Defeated by Devils) (México: Ediciones del Equilibrista, 1988).

BIBLIOGRAPHY: Sandro Cohen, *Palabra nueva: Dos décadas de poesía en México* (México: Premiá, 1981), 15, 108-14. José Joaquín Blanco, *Crónica de la poesía mexicana* (México: Katún, 1981), 264-70. Jorge González de León, *Poetas de una generación (1940-1949)* (México: UNAM, 1981), 65-69. Enrique R. Lamadrid and Mario Del Valle, *Un ojo en el muro/An Eye Through the Wall: Mexican Poetry: 1970-1985* (Santa Fe, N.M.: Tooth of Time Books, 1986), 115-23. Jaime Moreno Villareal, *La línea y el círculo* (México: Universidad Autónoma Metropolitana, 1981). Alejandro Sandoval, *Veinte años de poesía en México: El premio de poesía de Aquascalientes, 1968-1988* (México: Joaquín Mortiz, 1988), 179-87.

RICARDO AGUILAR

HERNANDEZ, Luisa Josefina (1928-). The noted drama professor, playwright, and novelist, Luisa Josefina Hernández was born on November 2, 1928, in Mexico City.

As a child in Mexico, she learned German, French, and English. She attended the preparatory school Colegio Luis G. León. She entered law school in 1946, but abandoned her legal studies in order to major in English literature and theater at UNAM. In 1955, she graduated as a teacher in her chosen field. Later, she pursued drama at Columbia University. She has been teaching play writing, composition, and dramatic theory at UNAM for more than twenty-five years. When her former professor, Rodolfo *Usigli, the noted dramatist, vacated the position of chair of dramatic composition, she replaced him. She received a scholarship twice from the Centro Mexicano de Escritores and once from the Rockefeller Foundation.

She has been a contributor to such journals as *México en la Cultura* (1958-1961), *La Cultura en México* (beginning in 1962), and *Ovaciones*. In addition to being a playwright and teacher, she is also a television commentator and a translator of Brecht, Zweig, Miller, and Shakespeare. She has continued to write for magazines and newspapers, and she gives theater workshops, especially to students.

Luisa Josefina Hernández has taken several important trips, the first of which was to New York, in 1955, to spend a year studying theater. In 1956, she went to Europe and in 1963, she went to Cuba to teach play writing. Another trip to Spain in 1969 provided her with the inspiration for a series of writings on famous paintings. Since then, she has made numerous trips, both to various parts of the United States and to Spain. She was a major participant in a theater symposium at the University of Kansas in 1983. She taught at the University of Colorado in the late 1980s.

Hernández was only twenty-three when she wrote her first play, *Aguardiente de caña* (Sugarcane Hard Liquor), in 1951, for which was awarded a prize in the literary competition Festival de la Primavera. She also won the prize given by *El Nacional* for her comedy, *Botica modelo* (Model Pharmacy) in 1954. Three years later, she received the award given by INBA for the play *Los frutos caídos* (The Fallen Fruits), which was her master's thesis. *Nostalgia de Troya* (Nostalgia of Troy), from 1970, won the Magda Donato Prize for literature.

At the beginning of her career, she wrote following the dictates of the school of realism, which characterized both *Los frutos caídos* and *Los huéspedes reales* (The Royal Guests). Bearing the influence of the works of such writers as Henrik Ibsen and Eugene O'Neill, her characters are often victims of society whose behavior is frequently irrational, their spiritual lives crushed.

In 1960, however, her style changed as she began to experiment with the newest dramatic tendencies. *La fiesta del mulato* (The Mulatto's Orgy), a work that is both entertaining and didactic, is structurally complex and finely balanced.

One of the main themes in her theater is the changing role of women in society (which also characterizes her novels). Victims of a moral code that isolates and condemns most women to an inferior social status, the female protagonists react either with resignation to their circumstances or with renewed struggle to overcome the injustices they experience. Unfortunately, most of the women wage fruitless battles against the established order.

Indigenous themes are also found in Hernández' work. She treats the Indians with dignity and respect, seeking to illuminate the problems they face by creating scenes and situations that focus on social disorder.

Very much concerned with the younger generation, one of her latest plays, *El orden de los factores*, deals ironically with the problems of the middleclass who are struggling to come to terms with their own hypocrisy. She transmits to the stage and in her pages an awareness of the toxic environment in which most people live. Rather than try to solve problems, she presents them in all their facets, giving the audience/reader the option of dealing with them.

It has already been mentioned that Luisa Josefina Hernández has written novels. As excellent as she is in theater arts, she is equally so in the novel, having already published seventeen. While it is difficult to select just one as being considered "the best," *La cabalgata* (The Cavalcade), written in 1969 but not published until 1988, is a shining example of her work. The novel takes us to the fascinating world of characters who travel through the slow road of their daily lives. The two protagonists, Gregoria and Hortensia, create magical worlds that emanate from the materialization and visualization of their unconscious desires. The two keynotes of the novel are nostalgia and melancholy. It is a work in which magical realism (unlike strict realism of her earlier works) guides the reader through interesting and occasionally brutal aspects of life. Her excellent and captivating writing, both in the theater and in the novel as well as her involvement in the cultural community, through her teaching, attendance at literary symposiums and conferences, etc., ensure Luisa Josefina Hernández a dominant place in Mexican literature.

WORKS: Novels: *El lugar donde crece la hierba* (Xalapa: Universidad Veracruzana, 1959). *La Plaza de Puerto Santo* (México: FCE, 1961). *Los palacios desiertos* (México: Mortiz, 1963). *La cólera secreta* (Xalapa: Universidad Veracruzana, 1964). *La primera batalla* (México: Era, 1965). *La noche exquisita* (Xalapa: Unversidad Veracruzana, 1965). *El valle que elegimos* (México: Mortiz, 1965). *La memoria de Amadís* (México: Mortiz, 1967). *Nostalgia de Troya* (México: Siglo XXI, 1970). *Los trovadores* (México: Mortiz, 1973). *Apostasía* (México: UNAM, 1978). *Las fuentes ocultas* (México: Extemporáneos, 1980). *Apocalipsis cum figuris* (Xalapa: Universidad Veracruzana, 1982). *Carta de navegaciones submarinas* (México: FCE, 1987). *La Cabalgata* (México: Océano, 1988). *Almeida* (México: FCE, 1989).   Theater: *Aguardiente de caña*, performed in 1950. *La corona del ángel*, performed in 1951. *La llave del cielo*, performed in 1954. *Los frutos caídos*, performed in 1955. *Teatro mexicano del siglo XX*, in *Teatro mexicano contemporáneo* (Madrid: Aguilar, 1962), 435-510. *Los huéspedes reales* (Xalapa: Universidad Veracruzana, 1958). *La calle de la gran ocasión* (Xalapa: Universidad Veracruzana, 1962). *Escándalo en Puerto Santo*, performed in 1962. *Los duendes*, in *Teatro mexicano 1963* (México: Aguilar, 1965), 239-305. *La hija del Rey*, in *Cuarta Antología de obras en un acto* (México: Col. de Teatro mexicano, vol. 24 1965), 7-15. *Quetzalcóatl*, in *Cuadernos de Lectura Popular*, vol. 172 (México: SEP, 1968). *Danza del Urogallo múltiple*, in *Teatro mexicano 1971* (México: Aguilar, 1974), 233-63. *Popol Vuh y La paz ficticia* (México; Novaro, 1974). *Auto del divino preso* (Guanajuato, 1976). "Jerusalén-Damasco," staged in Caracas, Spring 1980. "Apócrifa," staged in México, 1980. "El orden de los factores," staged in México, 1983. *El orden de los factores, Oriflama, En una noche como esta*, three plays, in *Tramoya* 12-13 (Oct.-Dec. 1987): 6-39, 43-96, 98-148. *El amigo secreto* in *Tramoya* 25, (Oct.-Dec 1990): 5-48. *Antología*, vol. 1, in *Tramoya*, 25th Aniversary, with the following plays: *Pavana de Aranzazu, Hécuba, La fiesta del mulato, Ciertas cosas, Jerusalem/Damasco*, and *El Amigo Secreto*. Short Stories and Prose: "Tierra adentro," in *Barcos de Papel* 1 (Jan.-Feb. 1948): 25-26. "Indecisión," in *América* 60 (1949): 46-49. "Dos cuentos de Luisa Josefina Hernández: 'Girando bajo el sol' y 'Tú y yo nos parecemos," in *América* 61 (Aug. 1949): 143-48. "Fragmento biográfico dedicado a las arañas," in *América* 63 (June 1950): 100-16. Essays: "Carballido no duerme," in *América* 65 (April 1951). "*Los signos . . .* de Sergio" (Magaña), in *America* 65 (April

1951). "Promesa para el cuento" (*La máquina vacía* by Sergio Galindo), in *América* 66 (Aug. 1951). "D.F. de Carballido," in *La Palabra y el Hombre* (April-June 1957): 101-2. "O'Neill en Broadway y en México" (*Viaje de un largo día hacia la noche*), in *México en la Cultura* 432 (June 30, 1957): 8. "*Felicidad* de Carballido," in *México en la Cultura* 436 (July 25, 1957): 8. "Bertolt Brecht, Su teatro," in *México en la Cultura* 439 (Aug. 18, 1957): 1, 8. "Carta a Juan García Ponce," in *México en la Cultura* 446 (Oct. 6, 1957): 8. "Sobre María Luisa Algarra," in *México en la Cultura* 447 (Oct. 13, 1957): 8. "*Volpone,*" in *México en la Cultura* 450 (Nov. 3, 1957): 7. "Una luna para el bastardo," in *México en la Cultura* 465 (Feb. 9, 1958): 8. "Teatro. Mesas separadas," in *México en la Cultura* 467 (March 30, 1958): 8. "Osborne sólo siente amor por sus personajes cuando los ve caídos," in *México en la Cultura* 475 (April 20, 1958): 8. "Carta a Rafael Solana" in *México en la Cultura,* vol. 484 (June 22, 1958): 8. "Teatro. Arthur Miller descendiente de Esquilo," in *México en la Cultura* 486 (July 6, 1958): 9. "Sobre el teatro de Bertolt Brecht," in *Revista UNAM* (Aug. 12, 1958): 15. "El asesinato en la Catedral," in *México en la Cultura* 520 (March 1, 1959): 8. "Trayectoria de Arthur Miller," in *México en la Cultura* 530 (May 10, 1959): 8. "La religión de T. S. Elliot se parece demasiado al psicoanálisis," in *México en la Cultura* 532 (May 24, 1959): 8. "Tres novelas cortas de 1958," in *Revista UNAM* (June 10, 1959): 36-37. "*Dulce ave de juventud.* Un nuevo camino para Tennessee Williams," in *México en la Cultura* 536 (June 21, 1959): 9. "Cinco pasos al cielo," in *México en la Cultura* 544 (Aug. 16, 1959): 8. "*La cantante calva,* de Ionesco," in *México en la Cultura* 545 (Aug. 23, 1959): 9. "*Sangre verde,*" in *México en la Cultura* 549 (Sept. 20, 1959): 9. "*Despertar de primavera,*" in *México en la Cultura* 569 (Feb. 7, 1960): 8. "Bertold Brecht en México," in *México en la Cultura* 575 (March 30, 1960): 8. "*Hamlet* dirigido por Raúl Cardona," in *México en la Cultura* 578 (April 10, 1960): 8. "*Electra*" (de Sófocles, paráfrasis de Diego de Meza, representada por el grupo de poesía en Voz Alta), in *México en la Cultura* 580 (April 24, 1960): 10. "Las piezas de Yukio Mishima," in *México en la Cultura* 582 (May 8, 1960): 8. "*Amadeo,*" in *México en la Cultura* 584 (May 22, 1960): 8. "Teatro. Los autores nacionales al margen de los teatros de su país," in *México en la Cultura* 591 (July 10, 1960): 10. "La interpretación mexicana de Samuel Beckett," in *México en la Cultura* 597 (Aug. 22, 1960): 7. "En el teatro Xola. *Beckett or el honor de Dios* de Jean Anouilh," in *México en la Cultura* 627 (March 19, 1961): 7. "50 años después, la obra de Strindberg levanta en México los espectros de la censura y de la estulticia," in *México en la Cultura* 630 (April 9, 1961): 1, 8. "*La ronda*, de Schnitzner a través de Alexandro," in *México en la Cultura* 638 (June 4, 1961): 8. "El gesticulador en O'Neill y en Usigli," in *México en la Cultura* 639 (June 11, 1961): 7. "El teatro estudiantil de la UNAM presenta dos comedias irlandesas," in *México en la Cultura* 644 (July 16, 1961): 8. "La censura y el teatro," in *Revista Mexicana de Literatura* (May 5 - Aug. 8, 1961): 37-38. "Rinocerontes: dos actitudes frente a la obra de Ionesco," in *México en la Cultura* 648 (Aug. 13, 1961): 8. "La obsesión de México," in *México en la Cultura* 653 (Sept. 17, 1961): 7, 9. "Ibsen, vía Arthur Miller, Una obra didáctica," in *México en la Cultura* 655 (Oct. 1, 1961): 8. "Apunte sobre el teatro del Siglo de Oro," in *Revista de la Escuela de Arte Teatral del INBA* 5 (1962): 45-50; also in *Tramoya* 4 (July-Sept. 1976): 88-91. "Shakespeare en Bellas Artes," in *Ovaciones*, suppl. 109 (Jan. 26, 1964): 7. "Obra complaciente y confusa," in *Ovaciones*, suppl. 110, February 2, 1964, 7. "*Silencio pollos...* de Emilio Carballido," in *Ovaciones*, suppl. 111 (Feb. 9, 1964): 6. "*Los secuestradores de Altona* de Sartre," in *Ovaciones*, suppl. 112 (Feb. 16, 1964): 7. "*Feliz como Larry* de Donagh Mac Donagh," in *Ovaciones*, suppl. 113 (Feb. 23, 1964): 6. "Reyes y los veintes," in

Ovaciones, suppl. 114 (March 1, 1964): 8. *"El gesticulador* de Rodolfo Usigli," in *Ovaciones*, suppl. 115 March 8, 1964): 7. *"Pérez Jolote* en teatro," in *Ovaciones*, suppl. 116 (March 15, 1964): 8. *"El sueño de una noche de verano* en inglés," in *Ovaciones*, suppl. 117 (March 22, 1964): 7. "Melodrama en el Xola," in *Ovaciones*, suppl. 118 (March 29, 1964): 6. *"Hasta que la suerte nos separe,"* in *Ovaciones*, suppl. 119 (April 5, 1964): 6. "Frisch en el Teatro Milán," in *Ovaciones*, suppl. 121 (April 19, 1964): 4. "Con Casanova," in *Ovaciones*, suppl. 122 (April 26, 1964): 7. "Otra vez Shakespeare," in *Ovaciones*, suppl. 124 (May 10, 1964): 6. *"El diario de un loco,"* in *Ovaciones*, suppl. 125 (May 17, 1964): 7. "Otro monólogo en el Teatro Urueta," in *Ovaciones*, suppl. 126 (May 24, 1964): 2. "Otro panorama," in *Ovaciones*, suppl. 127 (May 31, 1964): 7. "Obras en un acto," in *Ovaciones*, suppl. 131 (June 28, 1964): 2. *"El amor médico,"* in *Ovaciones*, suppl. 132 (July 5, 1964): 7. "No escarmientran," in *Ovaciones*, suppl. 134 (July 10, 1964): 6. "Usigli," in *Ovaciones*, suppl. 135 (July 26, 1964): 7. *"El inmenso mar* de Terence Ratting," in *Ovaciones*, suppl. 136 (Aug. 2, 1964): 6. "Todavía *Divinas palabras,"* in *Ovaciones*, suppl. 137 (Aug. 9, 1964): 6. *"El juglarón.* Teatro didáctico," in *Ovaciones*, suppl. 138 (Aug. 16, 1964): 8. "Dolores del Río en el Insurgentes," in *Ovaciones*, suppl. 139 (Aug. 23, 1964): 7. "Otra vez teatro clásico," in *Ovaciones*, suppl. 140 (Aug. 30, 1964): 3. *"El bosque petrificado* de Robert Sherwood," in *Ovaciones*, suppl. 141 (Sept. 6, 1964): 6. *"El medio pelo* de Antonio González Caballero," in *Ovaciones*, suppl. 142 (Sept. 13, 1964): 6. "Novedades en la Sala Chopin," in *Ovaciones*, suppl. 143 (Sept. 20, 1964): 6. *"Agonía de la rosa* de William Inge," in *Ovaciones*, suppl. 144 (Sept. 27, 1964): 7. "Teatro en Tepozotlán," in *Ovaciones*, suppl. 145 (Oct. 4, 1964): 6. "Ha muerto Sean O'Casey," in *Ovaciones*, suppl. 146 (Oct. 11, 1964): 6. "O'Neill en la UNAM," in *Ovaciones*, suppl. 147 (Oct. 18, 1964): 6. *"Rebelde* de Alfonso Paso," in *Ovaciones*, suppl. 148 (Oct. 25, 1964): 6. *"Después de la caída* de Arthur Miller," in *Ovaciones*, suppl. 150 (Nov. 8, 1964): 6. "Arthur Miller y Fellini," in *Ovaciones*, suppl. 152 (Nov. 22, 1964): 6. *"La pérgola de las flores,"* in *Ovaciones*, suppl. 154 (Dec. 6, 1964): 6. *"Locuras felices* de Arau y Alexandro," in *Ovaciones*, suppl. 155 (Dec. 13, 1964): 7. "Diáspora," in *Ovaciones*, suppl. 156 (Dec. 20, 1964): 7. "Homenaje a Emilio Carballido," in *Letras de Veracruz* 1 (July-Sept. 1973): 17-23. *Caprichos y disparates de Francisco de Goya* (México: UNAM, 1979.) "La pasión del poder. La tragedia del rey Macbeth," in *Thesis* 2 (July 1979): 41-47. "Obituario. Rodolfo Usigli," in *Tramoya* 16 (July-Sept. 1979): 56-57. "Apuntes para una adaptación de 'La Celestina,'" in *Tramoya* 24-25 (April- Sept. 1982): 4-11. Novel Summaries: "El lugar donde crece la hierba," in *México en la Cultura* 540 (July 20, 1959): 3, 5. "La calle de la gran ocasión," in *Revista UNAM* (May 9, 1960): 9. "La Plaza de Puerto Santo," in *México en la Cultura* 589 (June 26, 1960): 4. "La cólera secreta," in *Ovaciones*, suppl. 151 (Nov. 15, 1964): 8. "Carta de navegaciones submarinas," in *Espejo* 5 (1968): 17-24. "Apocalípsis cum figuris," in *La Palabra y el Hombre* 13 (Jan.-March 1975): 29-37. *Sábado* 254 (Sept. 18, 1982): 6-7. "La cabalgata," in *La Semana de Bellas Artes* 190 (July 22, 1981): 4-5. Theater: "El ambiente jurídico," in *América* 64 (Dec. 1950): 209-24. "Agonía," in *América* 65 (April 1951): 95-110. "Afuera llueve," in *Prometeus* 4 (July, 1952): 45-68. "Botica modelo," in *El Nacional* (1953). "Los sordomudos," in *América* 69 (March, 1954): 133-50. "Los huéspedes reales," in *La Palabra y el Hombre* 2 (April-June 1957): 91-95. "La hija del Rey," in *México en la Cultura* 518 (Feb.13, 1959): 12. "Dos diálogos de 'La calle de la gran ocasión,'" in *México en la Cultura* 567 (Jan. 24, 1960): 3. "Los duendes," in *La Palabra y el Hombre* 14 (April-June 1960): 153-204. "La paz ficticia," in *México en la Cultura* 598 (Aug.28, 1960): 3, 10; 599 (Sept. 4, 1960): 5. "Historia de un anillo," in

La Palabra y el Hombre 20 (Oct.-Dec. 1961): 693-723. "Arpas blancas . . . conejos dorados," in *La Palabra y el Hombre* 28 (Oct.-Dec. 1963): 637-91. "Clemencia," in *Cuadernos de Bellas Artes* 3 (March 1963): 61-80; 4 (April 1963): 65-92. "Popol Vuh," in *La Palabra y el Hombre* 40 (Oct.-Dec. 1966): 699-734. "Quetzalcóatl," in *Revista de Bellas Artes* 17 (Sept.-Oct.1974): 48-64. "Pavana de Aranzazu," in *Tramoya* 1 (Oct.-Dec. 1975): 14-37. "Hécuba," in *Tramoya* 5 (Oct.-Dec. 1979): 4-29. "Ciertas cosas," in *Tramoya* 18 (Jan.-March 1980): 4-10. Poetry: "Las canciones de Puck," in *América* 66 (Aug. 1951): 98-101. Translations: David Flasterstein, *El haz de luz*, translation of Luisa Josefina Hernández, in *America* 66 (Aug. 1951): 110-20. Jean Anouilh, *Medea*, translation of Luisa Josefina Hernández, in *Prometeus* 5 (Sept. 1952): 121-52.

BIBLIOGRAPHY: Leonardo Acosta, "Luisa Josefina Hernández, novelista," in *Casa de las Américas* 40 (Jan.-Feb. 1967): 139-41. José Amezcua, "Luisa Josefina Hernández: el amor como arma," in *Boletin Bibliográfico de Hacienda* 290 (March 1, 1964): 22. Enrique Anderson Imbert, in *Historia* de la literatura . . . II, 323-24. Anon., "El lugar donde crece la hierba," in *México en la Cultura* 541 (July 26, 1959): 4; "La Plaza de Puerto Santo," in *Cuadernos de Bellas Artes* (July 7, 1961): 78; (Jan.1, 1962): 76; "La calle de la gran ocasión," in *Cuadernos de Bellas Artes* (Sept. 9, 1962): 50; "Dos nuevas novelas mexicanas," in *México en la Cultura* 768 (Dec. 8, 1963): 3; "Su mesa de redacción," in *Diorama de la Cultura* (Feb. 2, 1964): 4; "'La cólera secreta,' es una novela de la mayor calidad," in *Revista de la Semana* (March 13, 1966): 3; "Triunfa Luisa Josefina Hernández en el género de la dolce vita," in *Revista de la Semana* (March 13, 1966): 3, 5; "Una buena traducción," in *Revista de la Semana* (Feb. 5, 1967): 3; "El concurso de Protea. Entrevista con Luisa Josefina Hernández," in *Tramoya* 6 (Jan.-Narch 1977): 121-23; "Karl Sternheim 'Los calzones . . .' Introducción y traducción de Luisa Josefina Hernández," in *Filosofía y Letras* 3 (July-Aug. 1978): 17-18; "La obra *Los duendes* se escenificará en Canal 11," in *Excélsion* (March 21, 1980): 11C; "Nuestros colaboradores," in *Tramoya* 17 (Oct.-Dec. 1979: 112. Jesús Arellano, "Las Ventas de don Quijote," in *Nivel* 36 (Dec. 25, 1965): 3. Francois Baguer, "Críticas," in *Teatro mexicano 1963*, ed.cit., 236-37. Huberto Batis, "La Plaza de Puerto Santo," in *Cuadernos del Viento* (July 12, 1961): 190; "Los palacios desiertos," in *La Cultura en México* 104 (Feb. 12, 1964): xviii; "La cólera secreta," in *La Cultura en México* 170 (May 19, 1965): xvi; in *Vida Nicolaíta* 13 (June 1965): 9, 14; "La primera batalla," in *El Heraldo Cultural* 3 (May 28, 1965): 12; in *La Cultura en México* 197 (Nov. 24, 1965): 15; "Los libros. Luisa Josefina Hernández," in *La Cultura en México* 260 (Feb. 8, 1967): 14; in *El Heraldo Cultural* 66 (Feb. 12, 1967): 15. Diana Belessi, "Críticas," in *Teatro mexicano 1971*, ed. cit., 229-31. Ma. Elvira Bermúdez, "Dramaturgas," in *Diorama de la Cultura* (April 5, 1959): 4; "Luisa Josefina Hernández y . . .," in *Diorama de la Cultura* (Nov. 18, 1962): 4; "La novela mexicana en 1963," in *Diorama de la Cultura* (Jan. 19, 1965): 8; "Novelas mexicanas en 1965," in *Diorama de la Cultura* (Jan. 2, 1966): 6; (Jan. 9, 1966): 3, 5; "Otra novela de Luisa Josefina Hernández," in *México en la Cultura* 1080 (Dec. 10, 1967): 15; "Novelas de 1967," in *Diorama de la Cultura* (Jan. 7, 1968): 3. Ginette Blanche, "Los huéspedes reales," in *Revista de la Semana* (May 19, 1968): 5. Fabienne Bradu, "Apocalipsis cum figuris," in *Vuelta* (July 30, 1983): 41-42. Sylvia J. Brann, "El arte literario de Luisa Josefina Hernández," master's thesis, University of Illinois, 1967; "El teatro y las novelas de Luisa Josefina Hernández," Ph.D. diss., University of Illinois, 1969; "Una lucha por sobrevivir: *Los Palacios desiertos*," in *Explicación de Textos Literarios* 1, 1 (1972): 64-71. "El fracaso de la voluntad en las comedias de

Luisa Josefina Hernández," in *Latin American Theatre Review* 7, 1 (Fall 1973): 25-31. John S. Brushwood, in *México en su novela*, 90-91, 121. Wilberto Cantón, "Los frutos caídos," in *Diorama de la Cultura* (May 26, 1957): 2. Emilio Carballido, "Los huéspedes reales," in *La Palabra y el Hombre* 8 (Oct.-Dec. 1958): 478-79; in *Revista Mexicana de Literatura* 1 (Jan.-March 1959): 76-77; "Las fuentes ocultas," ed. cit.: 1. "Un mundo de más de cuatro dimensiones," in *El Sol de México en la Cultura* 334 (Feb. 22, 1981): 1-11. Emmauel Carballo, "De cómo Puerto Santo no era un Santo Puerto," in *México en la Cultura* 640 (June 18, 1961): 4; "Entre libros," in *Nivel* 15 (March 25, 1964). 3; "Novelas y cuentos," in *La Cultura en México* 203 (Jan. 5, 1966): vi. Gabriel Careaga, "La novela," in *México en la Cultura* 876 (Jan. 2, 1966): 3. Lucila Carmona Lozano, "Estudio de la obra novelística de Luisa Josefina Hernández," master's thesis, Guanajuato, Gto. Ed. de la autora, 1970. Jaime Casillas Rábago, "Teatro. 'El Popol Vuh,'" in *El Nacional* (July 15, 1967): 5, 8. Rosario Castellanos, "La novela mexicana contemporánea y su valor testimonial," in *Hispania* (May 2, 1964): 223-24, 229-30. Fausto Castillo, "Arpas doradas y conejos blancos," in *México en la Cultura* 525 (April 5, 1959): 8, 10; "Invitación a leer," in *El Gallo Ilustrado* 94 (April 12, 1964): 4; "Breve historia de un desencanto," in *El Gallo Ilustrado* 176 (Nov. 7, 1965): 4; "¡Autor, autor!," in *El Gallo Ilustrado* 184 (Jan. 2, 1966): 4. Caty, "Historia de un anillo," in *El Gallo Ilustrado* 6 (Aug. 5, 1962): 4; "Escándalo en Puerto Santo," in *El Gallo Ilustrado* 22 (Nov. 25, 1962): 4. José de la Colina, "El lugar donde crece la hierba," in *México en la Cultura* 542 (Aug. 2, 1959): 4. Mary Lou Dadadoub, "El cautivo mundo de Luisa Josefina Hernández," in *Diorama de la Cultura* (May 28, 1978): 6-7. Alberto Dallal, "La cólera secreta," in *Revista de Bellas Artes* 1 (Jan.-Feb. 1965): 94-95. Frank N. Dauster, "Historia del teatro hispanoamericano. Siglos XIX-XX," in Kentucky Romance Quarterly 2, (1967): 82-83; "Social Awareness in Contemporary Spanish American Theater," in *Kentucky Romance Quarterly* 2 (1967): 120-125; "La forma ritual en *Los huéspedes reales*," in *Sepsetentas* 208 (1975): 60-65. "The Ritual Feast: Study in Dramatic Form," in *Latin American Theater Review* 9, 1 (1975): 5-9. "Success and the Latin American Writer," in *Contemporary Women Authors of Latin America*, edited by Doris Meyer and Margarite Fernández Olmos (Brooklyn: Brooklyn College Press, 1983), 16-21. Socorro Díaz, "La danza del Urogallo múltiple," in *El Gallo Ilustrado* 464 (May 16, 971): 4. Luis Adolfo Domínguez, "Reseña a *La memoria de Amadís*," in *La Palabra y el Hombre* (Apr.-June 1968): 338-39. José Donoso, "Una pálida y desfalleciente novela de Luisa Josefina Hernández," in *La Cultura de México* 157 (Feb. 17, 1965); xvi. Esteban Durán Rosado, "Reencuentro con Luisa Josefina Hernández," in *El Nacional*, suppl. 880 (Feb. 9, 1964): 4; "Cada quien tiene derecho de elegir su valle," in *Revista México en la Cultura* 985 (Feb. 13, 1966): 6; "Otra novela de Luisa Josefina Hernández," in *Revista México en la Cultura* 1080 (Dec. 10, 1967): 15. Till Ealling (Efrén Hernández), "Luisa Josefina Herández," review of *Agonía*, in *América* 65 (April 1965): 96. "Luisa Josefina Hernández," in *Enciclopedia de México* 6 (1977): 403. Tomás Espinosa, "El teatro múltiple de Luisa Josefina Hernández," in *La Semana de Bellas Artes* 24 (May 17, 1978): 12-15; "Crítica de libros. 'Apostasía,'" in *Revista México en la Cultura* 45 (Nov. 12, 1978): 13; "Dramatis personae" (interview), in *La Semana de Bellas Artes* 72 (April 18, 1979): 8-11; "Caprichos y disparates" in *Diorama de la Cultura* (Sept. 15, 1979): 6. RAF, "Con *Los duendes* sólo quiero divertir a la gente," in *México en la Cultura* 722 (Jan. 20, 1963): 4. Sergio Fernández, "La novela en 1959," in *México en la Cultura* 536 (Dec. 27, 1959): 11. Mario Enrique Figueroa, "Los trovadores," in *Revista México en la Cultura* 237 (Aug. 12, 1973): 6.

Héctor Gally, "Nostalgia de Troya," in *La Cultura en México* 458 (Nov. 18, 1970): xii. Margarita García Flores, "Luisa Josefina Hernández: mi compromiso es la verdad," in *La Onda* 265 (July 9, 1978): 4. Agustín García Gil, "Una criatura mítica, entrevista con Luisa Josefina Hernández," in *Escénica* 4-5 (Sept. 1983): 46-48. Juan García Ponce, "Luisa Josefina Hernández," in *México en la Cultura* 510 (Dec. 21, 1958): 8; "Teatro. 'Arpas blancas . . .,'" in *Revista UNAM* (April 8, 1959): 29-30; "El lugar donde crece la hierba," in *Revista México en la Cultura* 8-9 (Feb.-March, 1960): 51. Lourdes de la Garza, "Los palacios desiertos," in *El Rehilete* 10 (Feb. 1964): 53-54. Sergio Gómez Montero, "Tiempo de alegoría," in *Sábado* 314 (Nov. 5, 1983): 11. Anamari Gomiz, "Ensayo. Las narradoras de un país desconocido," in *Los Universitarios* 129-130 (Oct. 1978): 7-12. José Luis González, "Revolución sin épica," in *Revista UNAM* (Nov. 3, 1965): 30. Luis F. González Cruz, "Sobre *Apocrypha*, de Luisa Josefina Hernández," in *Consenso* 2-3 (May 1978): 21-24. "Luisa Josefina Hernández: El eterno femenino," in *Tramoya* 24-25 (April-Sept. 1982): 93-99. Mauricio González de la Garza, "Un largo día hacia la nada," in *Diorama de la Cultura* (March 31, 1968): 4. Enrique González Rojo, "La noche exquisita," in *Boletín Bibliográfico de Hacienda* 339 (March 15, 1966): 20-21. Celestino Gorostiza, in *Teatro mexicano del siglo XX*, 402. Miguel Guardia, "El teatro en México. *Los sordomudos*," in *México en la Cultura* 600 (Sept. 11, 1960): 8; "La nueva Malinche," in *Diorama de la Cultura* (April 26, 1964): 4. José Luis Ibáñez, "Teatro. 'Los frutos caídos,' in *Revista UNAM* 10 (June 1957): 29-30. John Kenneth Knowles, "Luisa Josefina Hernández: A Study of her Dramatic Theory and Practice," master's thesis, Salisbury State College, Naryland, 1966; "Luisa Josefina Hernández: Teoría y práctica del drama," translated by Antonio Argudín, revision and presentation of Tomás Espinoza, in *Revista UNAM* (1980); "Luisa Josefina Hernández. El laberinto de la forma," in *Dramatists in Revolt. The New Latin American Theater* (Austin: University of Texas Press, 1976). Ruth S. Lamb, *Bibliografía del teatro . . .,*" 64; "Papel de la mujer en la obra de seis escritoras mexicanas," in *Actas del sexto Congreso Internacional de Hispanistas*, edited by Alan M. Gordon and Evelyn Rugg (Toronto: University of Toronto Press, 1980), 443-45. Janis Lynne Krugh, "Solitude and Solidarity: Major Themes and Techniques in the Theater of Luisa Josefina Hernández," in *DAI* 47, 6 (Dec. 1986): 2174A. Georgina Landa, "El Urogallo. Vanguardia en la regresión," in *Diorama de la Cultura* (April 25, 1971): 11. Hernán Lara Zavala, "Apocalipsis Cum Laude," in *Plural* 143 (Aug. 1983): 55-56. Hernán Lara Zavala and Severino Salazar, "La literatura como elección y la elección en la literatura, diálogo con Luisa Josefina Hernández," in *Revista México en la Cultura* 129 (July 18, 1971): 3. Luis Leal, *Breve historia de la literatura hispanoamericana*, 315, 316. Leon F. Lyday and Jorge W. Woodyard, *A Bibliography of Latin American Theater Criticism: 1940-1974* (Austin: University of Texas Press, 1976). Antonio Magaña Esquivel, "Estreno de *Los frutos caídos*," in *El Nacional* (May 4, 1957); "Teatro. El segundo estreno mexicano de 1958," in *Revista México en la Cultura* 572 (March 16, 1958): 12; "Teatro. La convocatoria para los festivales del INBA en 1958," in *Revista México en la Cultura* 570 (March 2, 1958): 12; *Breve historia . . .* 147; *Medio siglo de teatro mexicano*, 137-38; *Teatro mexicano 1963*, ed. cit., 235, 237-38; "Hernández-Mendoza: estreno Urogallo," in *Revista México en la Cultura* 123 (June 6, 1971): 7; "Luisa Josefina Hernández," in *Teatro mexicano (1971)*: 227. Armando de María y Campos, "Teatro. *Los frutos caídos*," in *Novedades* (May 15, 1957): 1, 6; "Críticas" (*Los duendes*), in *Teatro mexicano 1963*, edited by Antonio Magaña Esquival, 237. Helen Marston, Review of *La noche exquisita*," in *Books Abroad* 41 (l967): 75. Ellú Martí, "Libros. *Los trovadores*," in *El Heraldo Cultural* 406

(Aug. 26, 1973): 11. Jorge R. McMurray, Review of *La memoria de Amadís*, in *Books Abroad* 43 (1969): 84. Felipe Mejía, "Mundo de juguete," in *La Cultura en México* 998 (April 15, 1981): xii-xiii. María Luisa Mendoza, "5 jóvenes del joven teatro," in *Diorama de la Cultura* (June 9, 1957): 4; (July 21, 1957): 3; "New Directions for Mexican Theatre," in *Américas* (April 10, 1958): 13-17; "El teatro. 'Clemencia,'" in *El Gallo Ilustrado* 72 (Nov. 10, 1963): 4; "Luisa Josefina Hernández sin anteojos," in *El Día* (Jan. 26, 1964): 2. Ignacio Merino, "*Danza del Urogallo múltiple*, tradición y vanguardia teatral," in *Revista Sábado* (May 30, 1971): 16. Beth Miller, "Entrevista con Luisa Josefina Hernández," in *Los Universitarios* 44-45 (March 15-31, 1975): 20; "Seis escritoras mexicanas frente al feminismo," in *Mujeres en la literatura* (México: Fleischer, 1978), 83-86. Sara Moirón, "¿Por qué no se escriben novelas policíacas en México?," in *Revista de Revistas* 114 (Aug. 7, 1974): 41. Javier Molina, "Luisa Josefina Hernandez: Una obra prodiga," in *Tramoya: Cuaderno de Teatro* (Universidad Veracruzana/Rutgers University-Camden) 12-13 (Oct.-Dec. 1987): 40-42. Agustín Monsreal, "Del trato interior del alm con su Dios," in *El Heraldo Cultural* 365 (Nov. 5, 1972): 5. Michèle Muncy, "Entrevista con Luisa Josefina Hernández," in *Latin American Theater Review* 9, 2 (Spring 1976): 69-77. Angelina Muñiz, "La Serie del Volador," in *Diorama de la Cultura* (Feb. 2, 1964): 7. Eduardo Naval, "Una novela ninguneada, *Los Palacios desiertos,*" in *Ovaciones*, suppl. 292 (Aug. 27, 1967): 2. Kirsten F. Nigro, "*La fiesta del mulato*," in *Latin American Theater Review* 13, 2 suppl. (Summer 1980): 81-86; "Entrevista a Luisa Josefina Hernández," in *Latin American Theater Review* 18, 2 (Spring 1985): 101-4. Salvador Novo, "Cartas a un amigo," in *Hoy* 1232 (Oct. 1, 1960): 20. Christine Pacheco, "Con Luisa Josefina Hernández. La misoginia no existe," in *Siempre!* 1321 (Oct. 18, 1978): 41-43. José Emilio Pacheco, "Luisa Josefina Hernández, *El lugar donde crece . . .,*" in *Estaciones* 16 (Winter 1959): 499-500. Terry Palls, "Enajenación brechtiana en cuatro dramas de Luisa Josefina Hernández," in *El Urogallo* 7 (Jan.-Feb. 1979): 84-87. Clara Passafari, "Los secretos senderos de Luisa Josefina Hernández," in *Los cambios . . .*, 250-63. Javier Peñalosa, "Nombres, títulos y hechos," in *México en la Cultura* 786 (April 12, 1964): 3. Fernando Pérez Rincón, "Oriflama de Luisa Josefina Hernández," in *La Semana de Bellas Artes* 116 (Feb. 20, 1980): 10. Luis Guillermo Piazza, "México y el tiempo en tres vovelas muy recientes," in *Cuadernos* 84 (May, 1964): 107-8. Margarita Pinto, "El estado del teatro en México," in *Sábado* 102 (Oct. 27, 1979): 13. L. H. Quackenbush, "The **Auto** in Contemporary Mexican Drama," in *Kentucky Romance Quaterly* 21 (1974): 15-30. Malkah Rabell, "*Los huéspedes reales*," in *El Día* (March 6, 1968): 9. Mara Reyes, "Diorama teatral," in *Diorama de la Cultura* (April 5, 1959): 4; (Jan. 27, 1963): 7; (Nov. 10, 1963): 3. Salvador Reyes Nevares, "*El lugar donde crece la hierba*," in *México en la Cultura* 99 (Jan. 8, 1964): iii. Teresa Rodríguez, "Entrevista con Luisa Josefina Hernández," in *Chasqui* 16, 1 (Feb. 1987): 77-82. César Rodríguez Chicharro, "*Los palacios desiertos*," in *La Palabra y el Hombre* 31 (July-Sept. 1964): 573-76. Rodolfo Rojas Zea, "Luisa Josefina Hernández revoluciona el teatro en busca de respuestas para el espíritu humano," in *Excelsior* (Nov. 2, 1971): 4-D. Juan Rulfo, "*Los palacios desiertos*," in *Books Abroad* 3 (Summer 1964): 294. Miguel Sabido, "Luisa Josefina Hernández, escritora sin publicista," in *El Heraldo Cultural* 18 (March 13, 1966): 6. Concepción Sada, "Una nueva generación de autores teatrales," in *Cine Mundial* (Aug. 22, 1954): 13. Mauricio de la Selva, "Asteriscos," in *Diorama de la Cultura* (Feb. 16, 1964): 4, 8; *Cuadernos Americanos* 2 (March-April 1964): 281-82; "Asteriscos," in *Diorama de la Cultura* (March 20, 1965): 4; "*La Primera batalla*," in *Cuadernos Americanos* 2 (March-April 1966): 264-67; in *Diorama de la Cultura* (May 22, 1966):

4; "Con Luisa Josefina Hernández," in *Diorama de la Cultura* (Nov. 15, 1970): 2; "Luisa Josefina Hernández y el amor al oficio," in *Diorama de la Cultura* (July 8, 1973): 6, 14. Carlos Solórzano, "*Escándalo en Puerto Santo*," in *Ovaciones*, suppl. 48 (Nov. 25, 1962): 5; *La Cultura en México* 43 (Dec. 12, 1962): xviii; "Balance 1962," in *La Cultura en México* 46 (Jan. 2, 1963): xvii; *Teatro latinoamericano en el siglo XX* (México: Pormaca, 1964), 178; "Luisa Josefina Hernández adapta con maestría el *Popol Vuh*," in *La Cultura en México* 273 (May 10, 1967): xiv; "Teatro en Filosofía y Letras. Una experiencia universitaria," (Luisa Josefina Hernández, directora de la obra de O'Neill, *El gran dios Brown*), in *La Cultura en México* 291 (Sept. 13, 1967): xiv. Margarita Suzán, "La memoria de Amadís," in *Gaceta UNAM* 3 (Feb. 1, 1968): 14. Juan Tovar, "Críticas," in *Teatro mexicano (1971)*, ed. cit., 228-29. Fernando de Toro, *Brecht en el teatro hispanoamericano contemporáneo: Acercamiento semiótico al teatro épico en Hispanoamérica* (Ottawa: Girol Books, 1984). Damián Trueba, "Publicaciones de la Universidad Veracruzana," in *Boletín Bibliográfico de Hacienda* 316 (April 1, 1965): 23. José Vázquez Amaral, "La novela de Luisa Josefina, Fuentes y Elena Garro," in *El Gallo Ilustrado* 191 (Feb. 20, 1966): 2-3. Eduardo de la Vega Alfaro, "La Plaza de Puerto Santo," in *Unomásuno* 172 (May 8, 1978): 16. Gloria Feiman Waldman, "Three Female Playwrights Explore Contemporary Latin American Reality: Myrna Casas, Griselda Gambaro and Luisa Josefina Hernández," in *Latin American Women Writers: Yesterday and Today*, edited by Yvette E. Miller and Charles M. Tatum (Pittsburgh: Carnegie-Mellon University, 1977), 75-84. Francisco Zendejas, "Yet . . .," " in *Excélsior* (Dec. 5, 1967): 2-B, 8-B; "Multilibros," in *Excélsior* (Oct. 28, 1978): 15-B; "Gótica y surrealista," in *Excélsior* (Aug. 21, 1982): 2.

MICHELE MUNCY

HERNANDEZ Campos, Jorge (1921-), poet, translator, novelist, and author of short stories. Hernández Campos was born on July 19, 1921, in Guadalajara, where he first studied and worked as a bookkeeper. In Mexico City he studied at the Preparatory School, took courses in the humanities and received a scholarship to the Colegio de México. From 1950 to 1964 he worked for the FAO, and for part of that time at the headquarters in Rome. He has also worked for the National Institute of Fine Arts (INBA). Widely traveled, he has visited the United States and, in connection with his work for the FAO, several European countries, Africa and South America.

Hernández Campos first became known as a poet with the publication of his first book, *Parábola del terrón y otros poemas* (Parable of the Clod and Other Poems). His second collection of poems, *A quien corresponda* (To Whom It May Concern), a nostalgic reminiscence of Mexico, was written in Italy. He is also known for his translations from English to Spanish and from Nahuatl to Italian. A number of his short stories have been published in magazines and supplements both in Mexico and abroad.

WORKS: *Parábola del terrón y otros poemas* (Parable of the Clod and Other Poems) (México: Ed. Firmamento, 1945). *G. Conger, W. Chan, S. Sakamapi, D. T. Suzuki and J. Takakusu, Filosofía del Oriente, translated from English by Jorge Hernández Campos and Jorge Portilla (México: FCE, 1950, 1964)*. David George Hogarth, *El antiguo oriente* (The Old Orient), translated from English by Jorge Hernández Campos

(México: FCE, 1951, 1957). W. H. Hadow, *Ricardo Wagner* (Richard Wagner), translated from English by Jorge Hernández Campos (México: FCE, 1951, 1964). J. M. Murray, *El estilo literario* (The Literary Style), translated from English by Jorge Hernández Campos (México: FCE, 1951, 1956). Tomás Bledsoe, *Lluvia y fuego* (Rain and Fire), translated from English by Jorge Hernández Campos (México: Eds. Cuadernos Americanos, 1952). H. R. Patch, *El otro mundo en la literatura medieval*, translated from English by JHC (México: FCE, 1954). *El vals* (The Waltz) (Madrid: Eds. de la Novela del sábado, 81, 1954). G. R. Crone, *Historia de los mapas* (History of Maps), translated from English by Jorge Hernández Campos and Luis Alaminos (México: FCE, 1956). T. S. Eliot, *Asesinato en la catedral* (Murder in the Cathedral), translated from English by Jorge Hernández Campos (México: UNAM, 1960). *A quien corresponda: poemas de Jorge Hernández Campos* (To Whom It May Concern: Poems by Jorge Hernández Campos) (México: Imprenta Universitaria, 1961). Angel María Garibay, *Poesía indígena*, translated to Italian by Jorge Hernández Campos under the title *Canti aztequi* (Parma, Italy: Ed. Guanda, 1961). N. Abbagnado and A. Bisaberghi, Historia de la pedagogía (History of Pedagogy), translated from Italian by Jorge Hernández Campos (México: FCE, 1964). *Dr. Atl, 1875-1964* (México: UNAM, 1985). *La experiencia* (Experience) (México: FCE, 1986).

BIBLIOGRAPHY: Anon., Review of *A quien corresponda*, in *México en la Cultura* 632 (April 23, 1961): 2; Review of *A quien corresponda*, in *Cuadernos de Bellas Artes* 3; 1 (Jan. 1962): 75. Jesús Arellano, Review of *El vals*, in *Metafora* 5 (Nov.-Dec. 1955): 38-39. Gastón García Cantú, "Las vueltas," review of *El Vals*, in *México en la Cultura* 330 (July 17, 1955): 2. Aurora M. Ocampo de Gómez and Ernesto Prado Velázquez, *Diccionario de Escritores Mexicanos* (México: UNAM, 1967), 175-76.

JANIS L. KRUGH

HIDALGO, María Luisa (1918--), poet and novelist. Hidalgo was born in Guadalajara, Jalisco, on May 5, 1918. She contributed to literary journals such as *Prisma, Papel de Poesía, Letras de México, Abside, Xalixtlico, Summa, Et Caetera, Revista de Educación,* and *Tierra Nueva*. In 1949 she received first place in a contest for children's theater and in 1955 the Premio Jalisco for *Lo cordial de la mentira* (The Cordiality of Lying). She has taught at the Escuela Normal since 1934 and studied literature at the University of Guadalajara. With her husband, Adalberto *Navarro Sánchez, she has participated in numerous cultural enterprises and in the promotion of literature.

Her poems deal with the anguishes of the world and shows a true love for the powerful visions poetry can create.

WORKS: Poetry: *Prisión distante* (Distant Prison) (Guadalajara, n.p., 1937). *Retorno amargo* (Bitter Return) (Guadalajara: n.p., 1937-1938). *Presagio a la muerte* (Premonition of Death) (Guadalajara, n.p., 1938). *Angel angustioso* (Anguished Angel) (Guadalajara, n.p., 1940). *Cuentas de cuentos* (Story Beads) (Guadalajara: Ed. Et Caetera, 1951). *Lo cordial de la mentira* (The Cordiality of Lying) (Guadalajara: n.p., 1955). *Renato Camaleón y otros* (Renato Chameleon and Others) in *Estaciones*

1, 3 (Fall 1956); *Et Caetera* 6, 21-22 (Jan.-June 1957); (Guadalajara: Casa de Cultura Jalisciense, 1960).

BIBLIOGRAPHY: Antonio Castro Leal, ed., *La poesía mexicana moderna* (México: FCE, 1953), 455-57. José Luis Martínez, *Literatura mexicana: siglo XX. 1910-1949* (México: Antigua Librería Robredo, 1950), 63. Ross Larson, *Fantasy and Imagination in the Mexican Narrative* (Tempe: Arizona State University Press, 1977), 37. Sara Velasco, *Escritores jalicienses, vol. 2: (1900-1965)* (Guadalajara: University of Guadalajara, 1985), 202-4.

MARGARITA VARGAS

HUERTA, David (1949-). Huerta was born in Mexico City on October 8, 1949. He studied philosophy and letters at the Universidad Nacional Autónoma de México. He has traveled widely throughout Europe, the United States, and South America where he has read from his work at colleges and universities. He has taught at the University of Maryland as distinguished visiting professor. He is a long-time translator and editor of the FCE, where he has been editor of *La Gaceta.* He writes a weekly column for the Mexican weekly *Proceso.*

One of Mexico's leading young poets, his work has been hailed as the intelligent conversation of language with itself. Sergio Mondragón suggests that Huerta's poems constitute a process of meditation around the idea of being ("ser" and "estar"), about the intrinsic nature of writing, style and form themselves. A wellspring of ideas and voices, Huerta's poetry tends toward development of free and blank verse imbued with the author's exuberant knowledge of language and structure. His last published work, *Incurable,* was reviewed as one of the great works of contemporary Mexican poetry. Several important writers and critics were very disappointed when Huerta did not receive that year's prestigious Premio Nacional de Letras.

WORKS: *El jardín de la luz* (The Garden of Light) (México: UNAM, 1972). *Cuaderno de noviembre* (Notebook of November) (México: Era, 1976). *Huellas del civilizado* (Footsteps of the Civilized One) (México: La Máquina de Escribir, 1977). *Versión* (Version) (México: FCE, 1978). *El espejo del cuerpo* (The Body's Mirror) (México: UNAM, 1980). *Incurable* (Incurable) (México: Era, 1987).

BIBLIOGRAPHY: José Joaquín Blanco, *Crónica de la poesía mexicana* (México: Katún, 1981), 264-70. Sandro Cohen, *Palabra nueva: Dos décadas de poesía en México* (México: Premiá, 1981), 18, 21, 186-91. Jorge González de León, *Poetas de una generación (1940-1949)* (México: UNAM, 1981), 73-78. Enrique R. Lamadrid and Mario Del Valle, *Un ojo en el muro/An Eye Through the Wall: Mexican Poetry: 1970-1985* (Sante Fe, N.M.: Tooth of Time Books, 1986), 125-31. Sergio Mondragón, *República de poetas* (México: Martin Casillas, 1985), 147-62. Jaime Moreno Villareal, *La línea y el circulo* (México: Universidad Autónoma Metroplitana, 1981).

RICARDO AGUILAR

HUERTA, Efraín (1914-1982), poet. Eraín Huerta was born in Silao, Guanajuato, on June 18, 1914. He began his schooling in León and Querétaro, and he prepared for the university and began law studies in Mexico City. He became a professional journalist in 1936, working on many of the leading newspapers of both the capital and other states. He was also been a film critic. He belonged to the Grupo *Taller* (1938-1941), a literary journal which brought together, among others, Neftalí *Beltrán, Octavio *Paz, and Rafael *Solana. He traveled extensively in the United States and Europe. The French government awarded him the Academic Palms in 1945. In 1952 he visited Poland and the Soviet Union.

Huerta stands out in the *Grupo Taller* generation by virtue of his strong lyrical consciousness and his passionate interest in the redemption of man and the destiny of nations that seek in their organization new norms of life and justice. *Los hombres del alba* (Men of the Dawn) (1944) includes his two earlier books, *Absoluto amor* (Absolute Love) (1933) and *Línea del alba* (Line of Dawn) (1936), along with other poems published in magazines up to 1944. His two main themes are love and solitude-love seen with desolate tenderness, filled alternately with death and life, together with the constant theme of rebellion against injustice. In *Poemas de viaje, 1949-1953* (Travel Poems, 1949-1953) (1956) his themes are messages of peace, struggle against racial discrimination, the music of the Blacks, their customs, etc. The second part of *Estrella en alto* (Star on High) (1956) also has a combative, political theme. Mexico City has inspired beautiful and desperate poems that show both Huerta's love and his hate for the city while attacking its defects. Huerta was awarded the National Poetry Prize in 1976.

WORKS: Poetry: *Absoluto amor* (Absolute Love) (México: Fábula, 1935). *Línea del alba* (Line of Dawn) (México: Fábula, Taller Poético, 1936). *Poemas de guerra y esperanza* (Poems of War and Hope) (México: Ediciones Tenochtitlán, 1943). *Los hombres del alba* (Men of the Dawn), prologue by Rafael Solana (México: Géminis, 1944), contains most of the poems of *Absoluto amor* and *Línea del alba*. *La rosa primitiva* (The Primitive Rose) (México: Nueva Voz, 1950). *Poesía* (Poetry) (México: Canek, 1951). *Los poemas de viaje, 1949-1953* (Travel Poems, 1949-1953 [United States, Soviet Union, Czechoslovakia, Hungary], illustrated by Alberto Beltrán (México: Litoral, 1956). *Estrella en alto y nuevos poemas* (Star on High and New Poems), Col. Metáfora, 4 (México: 1956). *Para gozar tu paz* (To Enjoy Your Peace), Cuadernos del Cocodrilo, 3 (México: 1957). *¡Mi país, oh mi país!* (My Country, Oh My Country!) (México: 1959). *Elegía de la policía montada* (Elegy of the Mounted Police) (México: 1959). *Farsa trágica del presidente que quería una isla* (Tragic Farce of the President Who Wanted an Island) (México: 1961). *La raíz amarga* (The Bitter Root) (México: 1962). *El Tajín* (México: Cuadernos de Pájaro Cascabel, 1963). "Responso por un poeta descuartizado" (Prayer for a Dismembered Poet), in *Revista de la Universidad de México* 21, 71 (March 1967): 14-15. "El morro" (The Snout) and "Permiso para el amor" (Permission to Love), in *Casa de las Américas* 10, 55 (July-August 1969): 72. "A cuatro poemínimos" (To Four Poeminimums), in *Comunidad* 4, 22 (Dec. 1969): 801-7. "¿Quién es que no ama a Virginia Woolf?" (Who Doesn't Love Virginia Woolf?), in *Revista de la Universidad de México* 29, 6 (Feb.-Mar. 1975): 21. "Seis poemas" (Six Poems), in *La palabra y el hombre* 12 (Oct.-Dec. 1974): 46. "Sonetos inolvidables" (Unforgettable Sonnets), in *Revista de la Universidad de México* 30,1 (Sept. 1975): 1-6. *Poesía, 1935-1968. Poemas prohibidos y de amor* (Prhohibited and Love Poems) (1973). *Los eróticos y otros poemas* (The Erotic Ones and Other Poems) (1974). *Circuito interior* (Interior Circuit) (1977). *Transa poética* (1980). Essay: *Maiakovski, poeta del futuro* (Mayakovski, Poet of the Future) (México: Col.

Cultura, 1956). "La poesía actual de México" (Current Mexican Poetry), in *Espejo* 1, 2 (2d trimester, 1967): 13-22. "Luminaria de Guanajuato" (*Luminaria* of Guanajuato), in *Revista de la Universidad de México* 23, 4 (Dec. 1968): 17-19. "Un deporte, unos escritores" (A Sport, Some Writers), in *Espejo* 3, 9 (Oct.-Dec. 1969): 141-51. *Textos profanos* (1979).

BIBLIOGRAPHY: Ricardo D. Aguilar, "La poesía de Efraín Huerta," in *DAI* 37: (1976): 2910A; "Efraín Huerta and the New School of Mexican Poets," *Latin American Literary Review* 11, 22 (Spring-Summer 1983): 41-45. Anon., Biobibliographical note in *Anuario de la poesía mexicana 1962* (Mexican Poetry Annual 1962) (México: Dept. of Literature, INBA, 1963), 66; "Recital poético de Efraín Huerta" (Poetry Recital by Efraín Huerta) *El Día* 9 (June 1965): 9. Jesús Arellano, "Poesía mexicana en 1956" (Mexican Poetry in 1956), review of *Estrella en alto* (Star on High) in *Metáfora* 14, (May-June 1957): 10-16; "Efraín Huerta, el poeta proscrito" (Efraín Huerta, Proscribed Poet), *Nivel* 63 (July 1962): 5. Emmanuel Carballo, "El libro de la semana: *Los poemas de viaje*" (The Book of the Week: *Travel Poems*), in *México en la Cultura* 388, (Aug. 26, 1956): 2. Antonio Castro Leal, *La poesía mexicana moderna* (México: FCE, 1953), xviii-xxix, 410. Alí Chumacero, "La poesía, 1963" (Poetry, 1963), in *La Cultura en México* 99 (Jan. 8, 1964): vii. Frank Dauster, *Breve historia de la poesía mexicana* (México: de Andrea, 1956), 175; *The Double Strand: Five Contemporary Mexican Poets* (Lexington: University Press of Kentucky, 1987). David William Foster, *Mexican Literature: A Bibliography of Secondary Sources* (Metuchen, N.J.: Scarecrow Press, 1981). Aquiles Fuentes, "Nombres de México: Efraín Huerta, poeta y periodista" (Names of Mexico: Efraín Huerta, Poet and Journalist), *El Día* (May 11, 1964): 9. Andrés González Pages, "Efraín Huerta: Perfil del poeta vivo," in *Plural* 67 (1977): 56-57. Francisco Hernández and Pedro Orgambide, "Efraín Huerta, el poeta en el ojo del ciclón," *Casa de las Américas* 24, 139 (1983): 21-26. Raúl Leiva, *Imagen de la poesía mexicana contemporánea* (México: UNAM, 1959), 227-38, 359. José Luis Martínez, *Literatura mexicana siglo XX*, vol. 1, 77-78, 181; vol. 2, 63. Juana Meléndez, "Tres plaquetas de Pájaro Cascabel" (Three Plaquettes from Pájaro Cascabel), review of *El Tajín*, in *Letras Potosinas* 21, 14-15 (July-Dec. 1963): 52-53. María del Carmen Millán, Review of *Los hombres del alba* (Men of the Dawn), in *Rueca* 4, 14 (Spring 1945): 61-62. Carlos Monsiváis, *La poesía mexicana del siglo XX* (México: Empresas Editoriales, 1966), 55-56, 58-59, 557. Aurora M. Ocampo de Gómez and Ernesto Prado Velázquez, *Diccionario de Escritores Mexicanos* (México: UNAM, 1967), 176-77. Julio Ortega, "La poesía de Efraín Huerta," *Revista de la Universidad de México* 23, 11, (Supplement, 1979). Javier Peñalosa, "*El Tajín* de Huerta" (Huerta's *El Tajín*), in *México en la Cultura* 759 (Oct 6, 1963): 3. Robert E. Rhodes, "Poems in Spanish and English of Alejandro Aura, Margarita Michelena and Efraín Huerta: Poets of the Dreamed Reality," in *DAI* 34 (1974): 6604A (N.M.). Mauricio de la Selva, "Asteriscos" (Asterisks), review of *El Tajín* in *Diograma de la Cultura*, Oct. 27, 1963: 8. A. Silva Villalobos, Review of *Los poemas de viaje*, in *Metáfora* 11 (Nov.-Dec. 1956): 36-37. Pedro Shimose, ed., *Diccionario de Autores Iberoamericanos* (Madrid: Ministerio de Asuntos Exteriores, 1982), 219-20. Rafael Solana, "Efraín Huerta," in *Nivel* 26 (Feb. 25 1961): 1-4. Roberto Venegas, "Poetas mexicanos, Efraín Huerta," in *Diograma de la Cultura* (Aug. 16, 1964): 7. Guadalupe Guillermo Villarreal Salgado, "Amor, poesía y revolución en la obra de Efraín Huerta," in *DAI* 41 (1980): 1072A.

PETER G. BROAD

I

IBARGÜENGOITIA, Jorge (1928-1983). A noted dramatist, novelist, chronicler, and esteemed journalist, Jorge Ibargüengoitia was born in Guanajuato on January 22, 1928. He studied civil engineering in Mexico City. In 1949, he left the field of engineering to study dramatic art at the Universidad Nacional (1951-1954), under the tutelage of Rodolfo *Usigli. A frequent traveler, he spent time in Europe, the United States, and Cuba. In 1955 he was awarded a fellowship from the Rockefeller Foundation to study theater in New York. He also received a two-year fellowship from the Centro Mexicano de Escritores, from 1954 to 1956. He wrote theatrical works, did translations, and critiqued and reviewed plays for different magazines and literary supplements, such as *Siempre!* and the *Revista Mexicana de Literatura*.

Ibargüengoitia wrote two articles per week for the daily *Excélsior*, from 1969 to 1976, totaling more than 800 articles on a wide range of topics. He was fascinated by airplanes and often wrote about them in his columns. Two other frequent themes were the negative effects of urban growth on man and tasteless architectural extravagances in the city and its environs. In an ironic twist of fate, Jorge Ibargüengoitia was killed in an airplane accident near Madrid on November 27, 1983.

Greatly influenced by Rodolfo *Usigli and Vicente *Leñero, Ibargüengoitia got his start in the theater in 1954 with *Susana y los jóvenes* (Susanna and the Young People), performed during the season of the Unión Nacional de Autores. *Clotilde en su casa* (Clotilde in Her Home) was performed in 1955 with the title *Un adulterio exquisito* (An Exquisite Act of Adultery). A wry mocking commentary on human morality, the play reveals the essence of characters when they are stripped of pretense. He received a prize and mention at Concursos de Teatro Latinoamericano de Buenos Aires in 1956 for *La lucha con el ángel* (The Fight with the Angel), an unpublished play, written in 1955.

About halfway into his career, Ibargüengoitia shifted from theater to prose. Like Leñero and perhaps because of him, Ibargüengoitia began writing novels and stories in the 1960s. Prose gave him the opportunity for greater character development as well as for expanded spatial and temporal dimensions. Federico Campbell, in an article about Ibargüengoitia, relates the genesis of the writer's transition from plays to novels. He had finished *Ante varias esfinges* (In Front of Various Sphinxes) and sent a copy of it to Usigli, who considered him his best student. Usigli was not impressed and wrote a scathing reply, criticizing in particular the use of Anglicisms in the work. Nonetheless, the play was broadcast on Radio Universidad. But Ibargüengoitia, stunned by the letter from Usigli, began to veer away from writing plays. At first, he tried his hand at historical plays, focusing, for instance, on the assassination of Alvaro Obregón, in the award-winning *El atentado* (The Assassination Attempt), a bitterly funny, delightful farce, attacking everyone connected with the murder. The play actually planted the seed for his later novel, *Los relámpagos de agosto* (Lightning Flashes of August), based on the memories of a revolutionary general toward the end of the Mexican Revolution. In 1960, he also wrote *La conspiración vendida* (Conspiracy Sold), a play that freely reconstructs the precipitating episode of the Mexican war for independence in 1810. He was awarded the Premio Ciudad de Mexico for the play, although it is somewhat lacking in spark and vitality. His last novel, *Los pasos de López* (López' Steps), stems from this play.

In general, the performances of his plays were not well received by the critics, which made the transition to the novel more rapid and intense. Ibargüengoitia himself was a theater critic for the *Revista de la Universidad de México*, a position which he continued to hold for several years following his abandonment of the theater as his literary genre.

Most of his narrative material comes from police reports, interviews and his own imagination. *Dos crímenes* (Two Crimes) is a novel of intrigue. Inspired partially by the historical figure of Periandro, tyrant of Corinth, it is a tale about the assassination of Queen Melissa by her husband the king. In revenge, the townspeople then murder the king's son, his chosen successor.

Jorge Ibargüengoitia's untimely death cut short the career of a truly gifted writer. He will be remembered as an emminent and distinguished author of critically important works.

WORKS: *Susana y los jóvenes* (Susan and the Young People, 1953), performed in 1954: in *Teatro mexicano contemporáneo* (México: Aguilar, 1958). *El rey tiene cuernos* (The King Has Horns) (México: n.p. 1954). *Clotilde en su casa* (Clotilde in Her Home), performed in 1955 with the title *Un adulterio exquisito* (An Exquisite Act of Adultery); in *Teatro mexicano del siglo XX*, vol. 3 (México: FCE, 1956), 680-741; (Xalapa: Universidad Veracruzana, 1964). "Mi vida con Josefina" (My Life with Josephine), in *Anuario del cuento mexicano 1954* (México: INBA, 1955). *La lucha con el ángel* (The Fight with the Angel), 1955, unpublished, mention at Concursos de Teatro Latinoamericano de Buenos Aires, 1956. *El peluquero del rey* (The King's Hairdresser), performed by Teatro Popular, since 1956. *Tres obras en un acto* (Three One Act Plays) ("El loco amor viene" [Crazy Love Comes], "El tesoro perdido" [Lost Treasure], and "Dos crímenes" [Two Crimes]), written in 1956. *Ante varias esfinges* (Before Various Sphinxes), on Radio Universidad; in *La Palabra y el Hombre* 15 (July-Sept. 1960): 131-71. *Pájaro en mano* (Bird in Hand), 1959, with *El viaje superficial* (The Superficial Journey) (Xalapa: Universidad Veracruzana, 1964). *El viaje superficial*, in *Revista Mexicana de Literatura* (June-Sept. 1960). "Amor de Sarita y el profesor Rocafuerte" (The Love of Sarita and Professor Rocafuerte), in *Anuario del cuento mexicano 1961* (México: INBA, 1962), 126-29. "La ley de Herodes," in *S. NOB* 4 (July 11, 1962): 2-4. "La mujer que no," in *Revista Mexicana de Literatura*, 1962. "What became of Pampa Hash?," in *S. NOB* 1 (June 20, 1962): 2-4. *Los buenos manejos* (Good Handling), 1960. *La fuga de Nicanor* (Nicanor's Flight), in *Teatro del Recreo Infantil del Bosque* (Mexico, 1960):15-25. *El tesoro perdido* (Lost Treasure), in *Universidad de México* (Aug. 1960): B3-4. *El atentado* (The Attempted), 1961, in *Revista Mexicana de Literatura* 11-12 (Nov.-Dec. 1964): 2-4. *Milagro en el mercado viejo* (Miracle in the Old Market), *El atentado* (The Assassination Attempt), with Osvaldo Dragún (La Habana: Casa de las Américas, 1963), 143 *Tres piezas en un acto* (Three One-Act Plays) (México: UNAM, 1963). *Clotilde, El viaje y El pájaro* (Clotilde, The Journey, and The Bird) (Xalapa: Universidad Veracruzana, 1964). *La conspiración vendida* (The Conspiracy Sold), in *Revista de Bellas Artes* 3 (May-June

1965): 29-60. *Los relámpagos de agosto* (Lightning Flashes of August) (Havana: Casa de las Américas, 1964); 2nd ed. (México: Joaquín Mortiz, 1965). *La ley de Herodes y otros cuentos* (The Law of Herod and Other Stories) (México: Joaquín Mortiz, 1967). *Maten al león* (Kill the Lion), novel (México: Joaquín Mortiz, 1969). *Viajes en la América ignota* (Journeys in Unknown America) (México: Joaquín Mortiz, 1972). *Estas ruinas que ves* (These Ruins That You See), novel (México: Organización Editorial Novaro, 1975). *Los pasos de López* (López' Footsteps) (México: Ediciones Océano, 1982). *Las muertas* (The Dead) (Madrid: Mondadori España, 1987). *Autopsias rápidas* (Fast Autopsies) (México: Vuelta, 1988). *Dos crímenes* (Two Crimes) (Madrid: Mondadori, 1988). *Muertas* (The Dead) translated to Italian as *Il caso delle donne morte* (Torino: Einaudi, 1989).

BIBLIOGRAPHY: Demetrio Aguilera Malta, review of *Los relámpagos de agosto*, in *El Gallo Ilustrado* 165 (Aug. 22, 1965): 4. Arturo Azuela, "Jorge Ibargüengoitia: Múltiples espejos de utopias gastadas," in *Cuadernos Americanos* 4, 255 (July-Aug. 1984): 75-79. Angel Bárcenas, Review of *Tres piezas en un acto*, in *Revista Mexicana de Cultura* 858 (Sept. 8, 1963): 15. Juan José Barrientos, "El grito de Ajetreo: Anotaciones a la novela de Ibargüengoitia sobre Hidalgo," in *Revista de la Universidad de México* (Aug. 1983): 15-23. Huberto Batis, Review of *Clotilde, El viaje y El pájaro*, in *La Cultura en México* 123 (June 24, 1964): xix; Review of *Los relámpagos de agosto*, in *La Cultura en México* 142 (Nov. 4, 1964): xviii; Review of *El Atentado*, in *La Cultura en México* 165 (April 14, 1965): xvi. Juan D. Bruce-Novoa and David Valentín, "Violating the Image of Violence: Ibargüengoitia's *El atentado*," in *Latin American Theatre Review*, 12, 2 (1979): 13-21. Federico Campbell, "Ibargüengoitia: La sátira histórico-política," in *Revista Iberoamericana* 55, 148-149 (July-Dec. 1989): 1047-55. Emmanuel Carballo, "La novela reaccionaria por dentro y por fuera," Review of *Los relámpagos de agosto*, in *La Cultura en México* 130 (Aug. 12, 1964): xvi. Irene del Corral, "Humor: When Do We Lose It?," in *Translation Review* 27 (1988): 25-27. René Delgado, Interview, *Los escritores* (México: Editorial Proceso, 1982). Edmundo Desnoes, Review of *Los relámpagos de agosto*, in *Casa de las Américas* 4, 25 (July-Aug. 1964): 96-98. Verónica Sylvia González de León, "La narrativa de Jorge Ibargüengoitia," *DAI* 43, 7 (Jan. 1983). Miguel Guardia, Review of *Los relámpagos de agosto*, in *Diograma de la Cultura* (Aug. 29, 1965): 7. Fidel de León Sánchez, "Moralidades de la literatura popular en la narrativa de Jorge Ibargüengoitia," *DAI* 47, 2 (1986). Adelia Lupi, "Carcajadas de calaveras en Jorge Ibargüengoitia y en José Guadalupe Posada," Paper read at the Ibero-American Institute, Berlin, Aug. 18-23, 1986; and in *Actas del IX Congreso de la Asociación Internacional de Hispanistas*, 2 vols. (Frankfurt am Main: Vervuert, 1989). Rita Murúa, Review of *Los relámpagos de agosto*, in *Revista de Bellas Artes* 3 (May-June 1965): 98-99. Jorge Olmo, Review of *Los relámpagos de agosto*, in *Universidad de México* 19, 2 (Oct. 1964): 30. Aurora M. Ocampo de Gómez and Ernesto Prado Velázquez, *Diccionario de Escritores Mexicanos* (México: UNAM, 1967), 177-78. Octavio Paz, Comments on *Las muertas*, in *México en la obra de Octavio Paz. II. Generaciones y semblanzas* (México: FCE, 1988). Javier Peñalosa, Review of *Los relámpagos de agosto*, in *Nivel* 32 (Aug. 25, 1965): 4. David Jon Schuster, "A Critical Introduction to Three Plays of the Mexican Revolution: Rodolfo Usigli, *El gesticulador*; Vicente Leñero, *El juicio*; Jorge Ibargüengoitia, *El atentado*," *DAI* 48, 5 (Nov. 1987). "Suplemento: Jorge Ibargüengoitia," in *Vuelta* 100 (March 1985): 43-57. Sharon Keefe Ugalde, "Beyond Satire: Ibargüengoitia's *Maten al león*," in *Discurso Literario* (Spring 1984): 217-229.

Mario Trejo, Review of *El atentado*, in *Casa de las Américas* 3, 20-21 (Sept.-Dec. 1963): 74-75.

JEANNE C. WALLACE

ICAZA, Francisco de Asís de (1863-1925), critic, historian, poet, and diplomat. Born in Mexico City on February 2, 1863, Icaza grew up in the capital, where he studied at the Mexican Liceo and later graduated from the National University with a law degree. At the Liceo he had occasion to meet the popular novelist and military man, General Vicente *Riva Palacio. When Riva Palacio was appointed minister plenipotentiary to Mexico's joint legation to a number of European countries (1886), he invited the young man to accompany him as second secretary, and thus launched Icaza's successful diplomatic career. Except for an extended assignment in Germany (1904-1912), Icaza lived the rest of his life in Madrid, where he married, where his children were born, and where he died on May 24, 1925.

Icaza is best known as a critic and literary historian. As such, he became very influential in Spain's intellectual circles. He was twice named vicepresident of the Ateneo de Madrid, and became a corresponding member of Spain's Royal Academies of the Language, History, and Fine Arts. In his own country, he was a member of the Mexican Academy of the Language and was awarded a *doctor honoris causa* by the University of Mexico in 1920.

As a poet, Icaza was a delicate and melancholic poet whose poems evidence his impeccable good taste. He was a conscientious artist who was concerned with attaining formal perfection and kept himself aloof from literary schools and passing fads. Typical of this attitude are his collections *Efímeras* and *Lejanías*. In his *Cancionero de la vida honda y de la emoción fugitiva*, he succeeded in assimilating the brief and direct expression of the traditional Peninsular *cancioneros* (Song-Books).

As a critic and historian, Icaza was best known as a rigorous researcher. He was a learned critic of acute insights, who used his classical Spanish prose in his many journalistic essays and intellectually challenging studies. Aside from the many books he wrote, Icaza contributed to several journals and newspapers. In Spain, his articles appeared in *Revista de Libros* (Review of Books) and *Revista de Archivos* (Review of Archives), and in Mexico, in *El Universal* (The Universal), *El Universal Ilustrado* (The Illustrated Universal), and *El Libro del Pueblo* (The Book of the People). Icaza was a foremost expert on Cervantes. His books of criticism won a number of prestigious awards. Three of them were awarded prizes by the Royal Spanish Academy of the Language. Additionally, *Lope de Vega, sus amores y sus odios* won Spain's National Prize of Literature, and his study of Miguel de Cervantes' *Novelas ejemplares* (Exemplary Novels) won the Ateneo de Madrid competition. His thorough and insightful investigations of literary and historical figures made him one of the undisputed authorities on literary history in his day.

WORKS: Poetry: *Lejanías* (Distances) (Madrid: Rivadeneyra, 1889). *Efímeras* (Ephemerals) (Madrid: Rivadeneyra, 1892). *La canción del camino* (Song of the Road) (Madrid: Rivadeneyra, 1905). *Cancionero de la vida profunda y de la emoción furtiva* (Song-Book of the Deep Life and the Fleeting Emotion) (Madrid: Tall. Poligráficos San Lorenzo, 1922). Essays and Criticism: *Examen de críticos* (Investigation of Critics) (Madrid: Rivadeneyra, 1894). *Las "Novelas Ejemplares" de*

Cervantes (Madrid: Rivadeneyra, 1901). *La universidad alemana* (The German University) (Madrid: Rivadeneyra, 1915). *De cómo y por qué "La tía fingida" no es de Cervantes* (How and Why "The Pretended Aunt" Is Not by Cervantes) (Madrid: Imp. Clásica Española, 1916). *Supercherías y errores cervantinos puestos en claro* (Cervantian Frauds and Errors Clarified) (Madrid: Renacimiento, 1918). *El "Quijote" durante tres siglos* (The "Quijote" Through Three Centuries) (Madrid: Renacimiento, 1918). History: *Sucesos reales que parecen imaginados, de Gutierre de Cetina, Juan de la Cueva y Mateo Alemán* (Real Happenings That Seem to Be Imaginary in ...) (Madrid: Imp. Fortanet, 1919). *Conquistadores y pobladores de la Nueva España* (Conquistadors and Settlers of Mexico) 2 vols. (Madrid: El Adelantado de Segovia, 1923). *Lope de Vega, sus amores y sus odios* (Lope de Vega, His Loves and His Hatreds), edition, prologue, notes by Ermilo Abreu Gómez (México: Porrúa, 1962). *Páginas escogidas* (Selected Writings), prologue and selection by Luis Garrido (México: UNAM, 1958). OTHER WORKS: *Antología crítica de poetas extranjeros* (Critical Anthology of Foreign Poets) (Madrid: Juan Pueyo, 1919).

BIBLIOGRAPHY: Ermilo Abreu Gómez, "Notas sobre Francisco A. de Icaza." *Letras de México* 5, 117 (Nov. 1945), 2-3. Genaro Estrada, *Poetas nuevos* (México: Porrúa, 1916), 141-48. Carlos González Peña, "Icaza: el poeta y el crítico," *Claridad en la lejanía* (México: Stylo, 1946): 229-36. Max Henríquez Ureña, *Breve historia del modernismo* (México: FCE, 1954), 282-83; José Martínez Ruiz, *Obras completas* (Madrid: Aguilar, 1947), vol. 1, 182-222. Alejandro Quijano, "Francisco A. de Icaza." *Memorias de la Academia Mexicana* 10 (1954): 191-204.

MARIA A. SALGADO

ICAZA, Xavier (1892-?), poet, dramatist, novelist, and short story writer. Born in Durango, Xavier Icaza studied law at the Universidad de México and worked in a number of areas including law, public relations, the diplomatic field, teaching, and writing. He taught literature at the Universidad Nacional Autónoma de México and wrote for the magazine *Novedades*.

Icaza's experimentation with the blending of the various forms of prose fiction and poetry makes his works difficult to place into traditional categories. He wrotes about a wide range of themes, including politics, the Mexican Revolution, and the world of psychology. One of his most outstanding works is *Panchito Chapopote, retablo tropical o relación de un extraordinario sucedido de la heróica Veracruz* (Panchito Chapopote, Tropical Sketch or Retelling of an Extraordinary Event in the Heroic Veracruz) (1928). In this work, Icaza experiments with the traditional form of the narrative by incorporating techniques from different genres, particularly from theater and cinema, and the fragmentation of sentences and settings. The result is a series of fast-paced sketches or anecdotes that suggest the rapid development of the Mexican Revolution. Besides the technical experiments of interest, the unifying thread is the idea of foreign interest in the Mexican petroleum industry and the outbreak of the Mexican Revolution of 1910. This same interest in cinematic technique was already apparent in his earlier play, a farce entitled *Magnavoz* (Magnavox) (1926), for which the author received an award in the same year.

WORKS: Poetry: *Marea encendida* (Inflamed Sea) (México, 1937). *Tríptico* (Trilogy) (México, 1937). *Tríptico de amor y desamor* (Trilogy of Love and Unlove) (México,

1940). *Ráfaga de los soles* (Flash of the Suns) (México: Colección Cuadernos de Herminio Ahumada, 1955). Theater: *Magnavoz* (Magnavox) (Xalapa: Talleres Gráficos del Gobierno de Veracruz, 1926); 2nd ed. (México 1962). *Discurso mexicano* (Mexican Discourse) (México 1926). *Tamales y libros* (Tamales and Books) (México: Coloquios, 1929). *Coloquio guadalupano* (Guadaloupean Colloquy) (México: Retablo, 1931). *Retablo de Nuestra Señora de Guadalupe* (Sketch of Our Lady of Guadalupe) (México: Editorial Cultura, Maderas de Leal, 1931); 2nd ed. (1955). *Trayectoria* (Trajectory) (México: Universidad Obrera de México, 1936). *Saeta en llamas* (Arrow in Flames) (México: *Novedades*, 1952). *De Chalma y los Remedios*, Los Presentes, no. 94 (México: Ed. de Andrea, 1963). Novel Sketch and Short Story: *Dilema* (Dilemma) (México: Ed. Andrés Botas e hijo, 1921). *La hacienda, novela mexicana* (The Hacienda, a Mexican Novel) (México: El Universal Ilustrado, 1921). *Gente mexicana* (Mexican People) (Xalapa: n.p., 1924). *Panchito Chapopote, retablo tropical o relación de un extraordinario sucedido de la heróica Veracruz* (Panchito Chapopote, a Tropical Sketch or Retelling of an Extraordinary Event in the Heroic Veracruz) (México: Editorial Cultura, 1928); 2nd ed. (México: Aloma, Centro Mexicano de Escritores, 1961). *Mitote de la Toloacha* (Festivities of the Toloacha) (México: n.p.,1955). *Coloquio de Juan Lucero* (Colloquium of Juan Lucero) (México: Aloma, Centro Mexicano de Escritores, 1962). *La Patrona* (The Patron) (México: Aloma, Centro Mexicano de Escritores. 1962). *El cantar de Chaneque* (The Chant of Chaneque) (México: n.p., 1962). *Caracol mexicano* (The Mexican Sea Shell) (México: n.p., 1962). *Corona de las tres divinas niñas* (The Crown of the Three Divine Girls) (México: n.p., 1963). Essay and Prose: *Nietzche*, selection and notes by Icaza (México: 1919). *Acerca de Carlyle* (About Carlyle) (México: n.p., 1921). *Nuestros héroes y nuestra juventud* (Our Heroes and Our Youth) (México: n.p., 1923). *Magnavoz, discurso* (Discussion of Magnavox) (México: n.p., 1926). *Marxism y antimarxismo* (Marxism and Anti-Marxism) (México: n.p., 1934). *La Revolución Mexicana y la literatura* (The Mexican Revolution and Literature) (México: Imprenta del Palacio de Bellas Artes, 1934). *La tragedia del régimen actual* (The Tragedy of the Current Regime) (México: n.p., 1935). *El nuevo Derecho Obrero* (The New Workers' Rights) (México: n.p., 1935). *Cuadernos de Derecho Obrero* (Notebook of Workers' Rights) (México: n.p., 1935). *El conflicto del petróleo en México* (The Petroleum Conflict in México) (México: n.p., 1938). *Interpretación de la Revolución Mexicana* (Interpretation of the Mexican Revolution) (México: n.p., 1947). *Viaje a la leyenda* (Trip to the Legend) (México: Talleres de Lito Offset Torres, 1963).

BIBLIOGRAPHY: F. de A., "Biobibliografía de Xavier Icaza," *De Chalma y los Remedios*, Los Presentes, no. 94 (México: Ed. de Andrea, 1963), 119-22. Gabriela Becerra, ed., *Estridentismo: Memoria y valoración* (México: FCE, 1983). José María Benítez, "El Estridentismo, El Argorismo, Crisol," *Las revistas literarias de México* (México: INBA, 1963), 145-64. John S. Brushwood, "Las bases del vanguardismo en Xavier Icaza," *Texto Crítico* 24-25 (1984): 161-70; *Mexico in Its Novel* (1st ed., 1966) (Austin: University of Texas Press, 1975), 200. John S. Brushwood and José Rojas Garcidueñas, *Breve historia de la novela mexicana*, Manuales Studium, no. 9 (México: Ed. de Andrea, 1959), 106. Miguel Bustos Cerecedo, "Estridentistas en la sombra," in *Estridentismo: Memoria y valoración*, edited by Gabriela Becerra (México: FCE, 1983), 260-86. Merlin H. Forster and K. David Jackson, *An Annotated Guide to Vanguardism in Latin American Literature* (Westport, Conn.: Greenwood Press, to be published in 1990). Carlos González Peña, *Historia de la literatura mexicana* (1928;

México: Porrúa, 1966), 263. Ruth S. Lamb, *Bibliografía del teatro mexicano del siglo xx*, Col. Studium, no. 33 (México: Ed. de Andrea, 1956), 66. Luis Leal, *Bibliografía de cuento mexicano*, Col. Studium, no. 21 (México: Ed. de Andrea, 1958), 71-72. Germán List Azurbide, *El movimiento estridentista* (Xalapa, Veracruz: Ediciones de Horizonte, 1926). Leonor Llach, *El Libro y el Pueblo* 5 (Sept. 1963): 2. Antonio Magaña Esquivel and Ruth S. Lamb, *Breve historia del teatro mexicano*, Manuales Studium, no. 8 (México: Eds. de Andrea, 1958), 158. José Luis Martínez, *Literatura mexicana siglo XX, 1910-1949*, Clásicos y Modernos, vol. 1, no. 3 (México: Libr. Robredo, 1949), 50; vol. 2, no. 4 (1950), 64. F. Rand Morton, *Los novelistas de la Revolución Mexicana* (México: Edit., 1941), 233-34. Aurora M. Ocampo de Gómez and Ernesto Prado Velázquez, *Diccionario de escritores Mexicanos* (México: UNAM, 1967), 179. Helen Louise Rapp, *La novela del petróleo en México*, M.A. Thesis, Universidad Autónoma de México (México: Cursos Temporales, 1957). Edna Aguirre Rehbein, "Vanguardist Techniques in Mexican Prose Fiction, 1923-1964," Ph.D. Diss., University of Texas, 1988, 144-63. Adolfo Reyes, "Cómo nació, creció y qué hizo Juan Lucero y quién escribió su coloquio," *México en la Cultura* 713 (Nov. 18, 1962): 11. Luis Mario Schneider, *El Estridentismo. México 1921-1927*, (México: UNAM, 1985); and *El Estridentismo o una literatura de la estrategia* (México: Ediciones de Bellas Artes, 1970). Ruth Stanton, "Development of Xavier Icaza as Leader in the 'Estridentista' School of Mexican Literature," *Hispania* 21, 4 (Dec. 1938): 271-80.

EDNA A. REHBEIN

IDUARTE Foucher, Andrés (1907-1984). Born in Villahermosa, Tabasco, Iduarte Foucher is a classical prototype of the Latin American man of letters for his versatility and achievement in several fields. Educated in Mexico, France, Spain, and the United States, he received his Ph.D. from Columbia University, where he taught Spanish American literature from 1939 to 1972. Lawyer and journalist, he contributed to the periodicals *Universidad de México*, *Cuadernos americanos*, and *Excelsior*. Iduarte also served his government in the departments of the Treasury, Labor, and Foreign Relations. From 1952 to 1954 he was head of the National Institute of Bellas Artes. Three subjects dominated Iduarte's writings---his own life, Mexico, and literature, be it of his own country or of Spanish America. Intertwined with these ample topics are the themes of Spain, the United States, Latin America, and Hispanism developed in the genres of autobiography, biography, the essay, editorial, or news article. His writings reflect his career as a journalist and professor. Perhaps more then any other Mexican outside of José *Vasconcelos, Iduarte has focused on his own life, and *Un niño en la Revolución mexicana* is the best of his four autobiographies.

WORKS: *Un niño en la Revolución mexicana* (A Young Boy in the Mexican Revolution) (México: Editorial Ruta, 1951). *Sarmiento, Martí, Rodó* (Habana: Impr. El siglo XX, 1955). *Don Pedro de Alba y su tiempo* (Don Pedro de Alba and His Time) (México: Editorial Cultura, 1963). *Tres escritores mexicanos* (Three Mexican Writers) (México: Editorial Cultura, 1967). *El mundo sonriente* (México: FCE, 1968). *Familia y patria* (Family and Country) (México: Secretaría de Comunicaciones y Transportes, 1975). *En el fuego de España* (In the Fire of Spain) (México: J. Mortiz, 1982). *México en la nostalgia* (Nostalgic México) (México: Joaquín Mortiz, 1984).

BIBLIOGRAPHY: Demetrio Aguilera Malta, "Homenaje a Andres Iduarte," in *Cuadernos americanos* 228, 1 (1980): 58-87. Carlos González Peña, *History of Mexican Literature* (Dallas: Southern Methodist University Press, 1968), 465-66; *Enciclopedia de México* (México: Instituto de la Enciclopedia de México, 1973), vol. 7, 114. José Luis Martínez, *The Modern Mexican Essay* (Toronto: University of Toronto Press, 1965), 395. Aurora Ocampo de Gómez and Ernesto Prado Velázquez, *Diccionario de escritores mexicanos* (México: UNAM, 1967), 179-80.

RICHARD D. WOODS

IGUINIZ, Juan Bautista (1881-?), bibliographer, teacher and scholar. Iguíniz was born in Guadalajara, Jalisco, on August 29, 1881. He attended private primary and secondary schools; his preparatory school was the Seminary of Guadalajara. Later, he moved to Mexico City and attended classes at the National Museum of Archaeology, History, and Ethnology. Starting in 1910, he held positions at the National Museum and the National School of Library Science, in several libraries within the city, and at the Department of State, where he became chief historian from 1928 to 1933. From 1951 to 1956 he was director of the National Library, and after 1956, he was a full-time researcher at the History Institute of the National University (UNAM). From 1916 on (for more than fifty years), he lectured on bibliography and library science at several educational institutions like the National School of Library Science, the National School of Graduate Studies (1922-1923), and other schools and institutes in Mexico City. From 1953 on, he was professor of bibliology and the history of libraries in the School of Philosophy and Letters, UNAM, and of bibliography at the Central Library of the same university. He belonged to several cultural associations, among them the Mexican Academy of History (which corresponds to the Royal Academy of Madrid) and the Mexican Society of Geography and Statistics.

Iguíniz's bibliography is vast and covers many areas, for he was interested in graphic arts, bibliology and bibliography, libraries in general, library science, biography, history, criticism and bibliographic history, descriptions of travel, genealogy, and heraldry. He published a great number of articles in newspapers, proceedings, and bulletins. He contributed to specialized Mexican and foreign journals. He conducted research into the press and journalism of his native city, Guadalajara. He also published several bibliographic studies that have been very useful tools for critics and scholars in general. His most important works are *Bibliografía de novelistas mexicanos* (Bibliography of Mexican Novelists), 1926, *Bibliografía biográfica mexicana* (Biographical Mexican Bibliography), 1930, *Disquisiciones bibliográficas* (Bibliographical Disquisitions), 1943, *Bibliografía de los escritores de la Compañía de Jesús* (Bibliography of Jesuit Writers), 1945, and *México bibliográfico* (Bibliographical Mexico), 1959. Another study, not bibliographical, is *El libro. Epítome de bibliología* (A Book. Epitome of Bibliology), 1946, in which he offers a model research paper, useful for all who wish to know books better.

WORKS: *El Colegio de San Juan Bautista de Guadalajara* (St. John the Baptist's College in Guadalajara) (México: A. García Cubas, 1912). *Catálogo de seudónimos, anagramas e iniciales de escritores mexicanos* (Catalog of Pseudonyms, Anagrams, and Initials of Mexican Writers) (París: Vda. de Ch. Bouret, 1913). *Exlibris de bibliófilos mexicanos* (Exlibris of Mexican Bibliophiles), continuation and illustration of the collection formed by Dr. Nicolás León (México: Imp. del Museo Nacional de Arqueología, Historia y Etnología, 1913). *Los historiadores de Jalisco* (The Historians of Jalisco), awarded a prize (México: Sría. de Hacienda, Depto. de Comunicaciones, 1918). *El escudo de armas nacionales* (The National Coat of Arms) (París: Imp. FrancoMexicana, 1920). *Las bibliotecas de México* (Mexico's Libraries) (México: El Universal, 1924). *Bibliografía de novelistas mexicanos*, Introduction to the Mexican Novel by Francsco Monterde (México: Monografías Bibliográficas Mexicanas, no. 3, 1926; reprint, New York: B. [Burt] Franklin, 1970). *Bibliografía biográfica mexicana* (México: Sría. de Relaciones Exteriores, 1930). *El periodismo en Guadalajara [1890-1915]* (Journalism in Guadalajara) (México: Anales del Museo Nacional de Arqueología, Historia y Etnografía, 1932; reprint, Guadalajara: Universidad de Guadalajara, 1955). *La imprenta en la Nueva España* (The Press in New Spain [Mexico]) (México: Porrúa Hnos., 1938). *Hay que leer* (One Must Read) (México: Edit. Helios,1940). *Disquisiciones bibliográficas* (México: Gráfica Panamericana, 1943); 2nd series (México: UNAM, 1965). *Bibliografía de los escritores de la Provincia Mexicana de la Compañía de Jesús desde su restauración en 1816 hasta nuestros días* (México: Edit. Colonial, 1945). *El libro. Epítome de bibliología* (México: Edit. Porrúa, 1946). *Léxico bibliográfico* (Bibliographic Lexicon) (México: UNAM, 1959). Introduction to *Memorias tapatías* by José Ignacio Dávila Garibi (Guadalajara: n.p., 1920 and 1953).

BIBLIOGRAPHY: Domingo Buonocore, Review of *Léxico bibliográfico*, in *Universidad* 51 (Argentina: Univ. Nacional del Litoral, Jan.-Mar. 1962): 337-38. Carlos González Peña, *Historia de la literatura mexicana*, 9th ed. (México: Porrúa, 1966). Luz Margarita Iguíniz, "Bibliografías mexicanas contemporáneas, Juan B. Iguíniz," *BBN* (2nd period) 10, 4 (Oct.-Dec. 1959): 45-60. José Luis Martínez, *Literatura mexicana siglo XX* (México: Antigua Librería Robredo, 1950). Agustín Millares Carlo, Review of *Disquisiciones bibliográficas* in *Letras de México* 1, 7 (July 15, 1943): 6. Salvador Reyes Nevares, Review of *Léxico bibliográfico*, in *México en la Cultura* 573 (Mar. 6, 1960): 4.

HERLINDA HERNANDEZ

ILLESCAS, Carlos (1919? or 1918?-), poet, essayist, and fictionwriter. Born in Guatemala, Guatemala, in 1918 or 1919, Carlos Illescas arrived in Mexico in 1944 as a diplomat. The year 1954 marked the fall of Jacobo Arbenz democratic government and Illescas' last year as a diplomat. He requested and was granted political asylum in Mexico. He has been a university professor and published his poetry, essays, and short stories in numerous literary supplements and journals, including *El Nacional*, *Revista de la Universidad de El Salvador*, *Lanzas y Letras*, and *Muro y Viento of Guatemala*. He has written scripts for movies, radio, and televison. In Guatemala he founded the *Grupo Acento* with Augusto *Monterroso, Raúl *Leiva, Enrique Juárez Toledo, and Otto Raúl González. He formed part of the Editorial Board in the Revista de Guatemala.

WORKS: *Friso de Otoño* (Autumn Frieze) (México: de Andréa, 1959). *Ejercicios de Poesía* (Exercises in Poetry) (México: El gallo de oro, 1960). *Requiem del obsceno* (Requiem of the Obscene) (México: Ediciones el Unicornio, 1963; Premiá Editora,

1982). *Los cuadernos de Marsias* (Marsias Notebooks) (México: Trazo, 1973). *Manual de simios y otros poemas* (Manual of Monkeys and Other Poems) (México: UNAM, 1977). *El mar es una llaga* (The Sea Is a Wound) (México: Ed. Liberta-Sumaria, 1979). *Fragmentos reunidos* (Reunited Fragments) (México: n.p., 1981). *Usted es la culpable* (You're the Guilty One) (México: Ed. Katún, 1983).

BIBLIOGRAPHY: María Elvira Bermúdez, "Letanía y Requiem," review of *Requiem del obsceno*, in *Diograma de la Cultura* (Aug. 4, 1963): 4. Evodio Escalante, ed., *Antología del Segundo Festival Internacional de Poesía: Morelia, 1983* (México: Joaquín Mortiz, 1984), 143. Aurora M. Ocampo de Gómez and Ernesto Prado Velázquez, *Diccionario de escritores mexicanos* (México: UNAM, 1967), 182.

MARGARITA VARGAS

INCLAN, Federico Schroeder (1910-1981), playwright. Born in Mexico City, Inclán was a student of the humanities and a graduate of mechanical and electrical engineering. He attended the University of California, and he has been a miner, salesman, streetcar worker, merchant, and farmer. He wrote thirty-four works, including tragedies, dramas, comedies, and detective comedies. His concerns, both heavy and lighthearted, are historical, social, psychological and moral. An author in contact with reality, Inclán received awards from INBA and CREA. In addition, he won the Fiestas de Primavera Award, and twice won the Juan Ruiz de Alarcón Award. He is an intelligent, keen, direct observer of life; his dramatic techniques include those of the Greek tragedy.

He was first known for *Luces de carburo* (Carbide Lights), which represents the hardships and problems of miners. The critics considered *Hoy invita la Güera* (Blondie Invites Today), a comedy, the best play of 1955.

WORKS: Plays: *Luces de carburo* (México: n. p., 1951). *Y aun hay flores* (And There Are Still Some Flowers) (México: n. p., 1951). *El duelo* (The Duel) (México: n. p., 1951). *Espaldas mojadas cruzan el Bravo* (Wetbacks Crossing the Rio Grande) (México: n. p., 1951). *Hidalgo* (México: Teatro Mexicano, 1953). *Cuartelazo* (Military Uprising) (México: n. p., 1954). *Hoy invita la Güera*, in *Teatro mexicano del Siglo XX*, vol. 3 (México: FCE, 1956). *Una mujer para los sabados* (A Woman for Saturdays) (México: n. p., 1956). *El deseo llega al anochecer* (Desire Arises at Dusk) (México: n. p., 1956). *La última noche con Laura* (The Last Night with Laura) (México: n. p., 1956). *Pueblo sin hombres* (Town without Men) (México: n. p., 1957). *Trágico amanecer* (Tragic Dawn) (México: n. p., 1957). *El seminarista de los ojos negros* (The Black-eyed Seminarist) (México: n.p., 1958). *Una esfinge llamada Cordelia* (A Sphinx Named Cordelia), in *Teatro mexicano 1958* (México: Aguilar, 1959). *El caso de Pedro Ventura* (The Case of Pedro Ventura) (México: n. p., 1959). *Detrás de esa puerta* (Behind That Door) (1959). *Cada noche muere Julieta* (Julieta Dies Every Night) (1960). *El enemigo* (The Enemy), in *Cuadernos de Bellas Artes* 1 (Aug. 1960). *Deborah* (1960). "Doroteo Arango" (1960). *La ventana* (The Window), in *Antología de obras en un acto*, vol. 2, 36-47. *Malintzín* (1961). *Una noche con Casanova* (A Night with Casanova) (1964). *Turco para señoras* (Turkish Bath for Ladies) (1965). *Derecho de Asilo* (Right of Asylum) (1966). *Cuando mueren los dioses* (When the Gods Die)

INCLAN, Luis G.   347

(1980). *Los dos Juárez* (The Two Juarezes). *Frida Kahlo*. *Don Quijote murió del corazón* (Don Quixote Died of a Heart Condition). Unpublished, "Dos mujeres y un cadáver" (Two Women and a Corpse), "Un caso para la policía" (A Case for the Police), "La vida oculta de Jesús" (The Secret Life of Jesus), and "Moctezuma, Cuauhtémoc y Malinal." For television he wrote a historical series, "Hombres de México" (Mexican Men).

BIBLIOGRAPHY: Anon., "Teatro. Dos opiniones de Federico S. Inclán," in *Ideas de México* (July-Aug. 1953): 41-42. Review of *Hoy invita la Güera*, in *Cuadernos de Bellas Artes* 11, (Nov.- 1962): 74. Review of *Una noche con Casanova* in *Cuadernos de Bellas Artes* 5 (May 1964): 102. Luis G. Basurto, *Teatro Mexicano, 1958* (México: Aguilar, 1959), 103-60. Lucile C. Charlebois, "El teatro de la generacion de 1898: Una síntesis," *DAI* 43, 8 (1982): 2691A (University of Massachusetts). Carlos González Peña, *Historia de la literatura mexicana* (México: Porrúa, 1966), 324. Celestino Gorostiza, Prologue in *Teatro mexicano del siglo XX* (México: FCE, 1956), xvi. Miguel Guardia, "El teatro en México, *Hoy invita la Güera*," in *México en la Cultura* 367 (April 10, 1956): 4. "Teatro en México, *El deseo llega al anochecer*, in *México en la Cultura* 329 (Sept. 23, 1956): 5. Luisa Josefina Hernández, "Con Casanova," in *Ovaciones* 122 (April 26, 1964): 7. Ruth S. Lamb, *Bibliografía del teatro mexicano del siglo XX* (México: de Andrea, 1962), 144-45. Antonio Magaña Esquivel, Review of *Una noche con Casanova*, in *El Nacional* (April 8, 1964): 11; *Medio siglo de teatro mexicano, 1900-1961* (México: INBA, 1964), 121, 122, 124, 136-37, 162; "La última comedia del año 1964 es de autor mexicano," review of *Una mujer para los sábados* (January 2, 1965): 7; Review of *Deborah*, in *Revista Mexicana de Cultura* 951 (June 20, 1965): 11; "Bikinis y chistes en dos comedias mexicanas," review of *Turco para señoras*, in *Revista Mexicana de Cultura* 959 (Aug. 15, 1965): 11. Marcela del Río, "Hidalgo y el teatro histórico," in *BBH* 256 (Oct. 1, 1962): 18. Concepción Sada, "Una nueva generación de autores teatrales," in *Cine Mundial* (Aug. 22, 1954): 15. Rafael Solana, Review of *Una noche con Casanova*, in *Siempre!* 566 (April 29, 1964): 50. Carlos Solórzano, Review of *Hoy invita la Güera*, in *Ovaciones* 45 (Nov. 4, 1962): 5. Mario Martín Ugarte, "La posición de Federico Schroeder Inclán en el teatro mexicano contemporáneo," *DAI* 32, 8 (1971): 4764A (University of Southern California, 1 971).

DELIA GALVAN

INCLAN, Luis G.   (1816-1875), novelist, journalist, publisher. Inclán was born in Rancho Carrasco, Hacienda de Tlalpan, on June 21, 1816. He studied for three years in the Seminario Conciliar, and then returned to work in the Hacienda. He seemed to prefer working in the fields to attending school. He became manager of Boia Hacienda, and later moved to Pócaro, Michoacán, to gain knowledge of the hot zone agriculture. In 1847 he bought one of the first lithography shops in Mexico, and later he bought a press in which he published songs, prayers, and religious pictures. He died on October 23, 1875. He edited *El Jarabe* (Syrup) (1860), written by Niceto Zamacois, and a seventh edition of *El Periquillo Sarniento* (The Itching Parrot) (1865), by *Fernández de Lizardi. He also wrote two volumes of the first edition of his novel *Astucia* (Astuteness), dealing with the Mexican riders who made a living by smuggling tobacco. He describes life and customs of the second third of nineteenth century Mexico. All of Inclán's production is about themes of rural life.

WORKS: *Reglas con que un colegial puede colear y lazar* (Rules by Which a Student Can Throw a Bull by Pulling Its Tail and Rope) (1860). *Astucia. El Jefe de los Hermanos de la Hoja o los charros contrabandistas de la Rama* (Astuteness, the Chief of the Hoja Brothers or the Smuggler Horse Riders of Rama), 2 vol. (1865, 1866). *Ley de Gallos* (Rules for Cock Fights) (n.d.). *Recuerdos del Chamberín o sea, Breve relación de los hechos más públicos y memorables de este noble caballo* (Remembrances about Chamberin or a Brief Relation of the Most Public and Memorable Deeds of This Noble Horse) (1867). *Regalo delicioso para el que fuere asqueroso* (Gift for Him Who May Be Queasy) (1867). *El capadero de la hacienda de Ayala* (The Tobacco Shop of the Ayala Hacienda) (1872). He left unpublished two novels: *Los Tres Pepes* (The Three Pepes), and *Pepita la planchadora* (Pepita the Ironer).

BIBLIOGRAPHY: Guillermo Díaz-Plaja and Francisco Monterde, *Historia de la Literatura Española e Historia de la Literatura Mexicana* (México: Editorial Porrúa, S.A., 1968), 527-28. Carlos González Peña, *Historia de la literatura mexicana. Desde los origenes hasta nuestros días* (México: Editorial Porrúa, S.A., 1981), 168-69. Julio Jiménez Rueda, *Antología de la Prosa en México* (México: Ediciones Botas, 1946), 257. María del Carmen Millán, *Literatura Mexicana* (México: Editorial Esfinge, 1962), 181-82.

JOSEPH VELEZ

IZQUIERDO de Albiñana, Asunción (1914-), novelist. Izquierdo has published under the pseudonymns Ana Mairena, Alba Sandoiz, and Pablo María Fonsalba as, well as under her own name. Born in San Luis Potosí, she made her first appearance on the literary scene in 1938 with her novel *Andréida*, for which she used her own name. Her second novel, *Caos* (Chaos), was also published under her name, but for her third book, issued in 1945, she used the pseudonym Alba Sandoiz. This semi-autobiographical work presents an excellent analysis of psychological development. *Taetzani* was published one year later under the same penname. This was an evocation of the original inhabitants of Nayarit and their conquest by the Spaniards. For her fifth novel, *La ciudad sobre el lago* (The City on the Lake), published in 1949, she adopted the surname of Pablo María Fonsalba. She then published nothing until 1961, when *Los extraordinarios* (The Extraordinary Ones) was published under yet another pseudonym, Ana Mairena. This is the novel of a murder, or more exactly, of a murderer, in which the entire action takes place while the murderer is waiting for his victim. In 1964 she published a transcription of the oral traditions of the Cora Indians of western Mexico concerning the Creation of the universe. This was issued in a bilingual edition with an English version by Elinor Randall.

WORKS: *Andréida, El tercer sexo* (Andréida, The Third Sex) (México: Ediciones Botas, 1938). *Caos* (Chaos) (México: Ediciones Botas, 1940). *La selva encantada* (The Enchanted Jungle) (México: Ediciones Botas, 1945). *Taetzani*, illustrated by Emilia Ortiz (México: Editorial Ideas, 1946). *La ciudad sobre el lago* (The City on the Lake) (México: n.p., 1949). *Los extraordinarios* (The Extraordinary Ones) (Barcelona: Seix-

Barral, 1961). *El gran nayar* (The Great Nayar). *Majakuagymoukeia*, bilingual ed., English by Elinor Randall, Colección Acuario, no. 1 (México: El Corno Emplumado, 1964).

BIBLIOGRAPHY: John S. Brushwood, *México en su novela* (México: FCE, 1973), 81-82. Emmanuel Carballo, "La última novela de una escritora enmascarada: *Los extraordinarios*," in *México en la Cultura* 650 (Aug. 27, 1969): 2-9. Víctor Fuentes, Review of *Los extraordinarios*, in *Rev. H. M.* 2-4 (April-Oct. 1962): 344-45. Manuel Pedro González, *Trayectoria de la novela en México* (México: Ediciones Botas, 1951), 339-50. Luis Leal, *Bibliografía del cuento mexicano* (México: de Andrea, 1958), 134. Aurora M. Ocampo de Gómez and Ernesto Prado Velázquez, *Diccionario de Escritores Mexicanos* (México: UNAM, 1967), 14. Lynn Ellen Rice Cortina, *Spanish-American Women Writers* (New York: Garland, 1983), 179.

PETER G. BROAD

J

JIMENEZ-RUEDA, Julio (1896-1960). Born April 10, 1896, in Mexico City, Julio Jiménez Rueda was schooled there, receiving his law degree in 1919 and his doctorate in literature in 1935. An educator, playwright, essayist, novelist and story writer, journalist, and diplomat, he had a varied and distinguished career. For more than forty years, Jiménez served in a number of important educational capacities, reaching the highest level in his profession, professor emeritus and dean of the Facultad de Filosofía y Letras at the Universidad Nacional Autónoma de México. In addition, he represented the university in several congresses in various places. As a result of his literary and educational work, he received honors and distinctions from both national and foreign institutions. In addition to his university teaching duties in Mexico, which included Mexican and Spanish literature and history of art, he also taught Spanish, Mexican, and Latin American literature as a visiting professor at the Universities of Missouri, Texas, and Illinois. For a while, he was the director of a number of journals, including *El Estudiante* and *La Revista Iberoamericana*. He also made signifcant literary contributions to such journals as *Excelsior, El Universal*, and *El Heraldo*. His essays, such as "El afeminamiento en la literatura mexicana" (Effeminacy in Mexican Literature), were sometimes controversial, inspiring rebuttals from other writers. He was also a member of several important associations, including the Academia Mexicana correspondiente a la Española and the Academia Hispanoamericana de la Historia de Buenos Aires.

In addition to his literary and educational endeavors, Jiménez Rueda also served his country as a diplomatic secretary for a year and a half in both Montevideo and Buenos Aires, shortly after completing his education. An outstanding citizen, he helped to foster greater cultural ties between Mexico, Uruguay and Argentina.

In the field of letters, Jiménez Rueda was especially noted for both his research and his creativity. When he first started publishing, he focused on the events and social life of the colonial period. He was therefore considered part of the group known as the "colonialists," writers dedicated to re-creating that part of the past in their work. His first book, *Cuentos y diálogos* (Stories and Dialogues), was published in 1918. He also wrote the play *Sor Adoración del Divino Verbo* (Sister Adoration of the Divine Verb), plus *Moisén* and *Novelas coloniales* (Colonial Novels).

Perhaps the most valuable part of his work is his research, both in literature and in history. His *Historia de la literatura mexicana* (History of Mexican Literature), published in 1928 and amplified in successive editions, was a signifcant contribution to literary history. This study is complemented by his *Antología de la prosa en México* (Anthology of Prose in Mexico), *Letras mexicanas en el siglo XIX* (Mexican Letters in the nineteenth Century), *Juan Ruiz de Alarcón y su tiempo* (Juan Ruiz de Alarcón and His Era), and many other studies, appearing either as prologues or as independent works.

In the field of history he wrote several fundamental works, including *Herejías y superticiones en la Nueva España* (Heresies and Superstitions in New Spain), and two volumes of his incomplete *Historia de la cultura en México* (History of Culture in Mexico), a work interrupted by his death in Mexico City on June 25, 1960.

He was also highly interested in the theater, with his first theatrical work, *Balada de Navidad* (Christmas Ballad), performed in 1918. This was followed by many more plays written and performed in the 1920s. His play *La silueta de humo* (The Smoke Silhouette) received critical acclaim. Although he wrote relatively few original plays, he was very actively involved in the Mexican theater. A major theater in Mexico has been named for Jiménez Rueda, who so inspired several generations of aspiring authors.

WORKS: Stories and Chronicles: *Cuentos y diálogos* (Stories and Dialogues) (Paris: Bouret, 1918). *Bajo la cruz del sur* (Under the Cross of the South) (México: Libr. of Manuel Mañón, 1922). "Cuento romántico (a la manera de 1850)" (Romantic Story [in the manner of 1850]), in *Tres cuentos inéditos mexicanos* (México: n.p., 1923); also in *Cuatro siglos de literatura mexicana* (México: Ed. Leyenda, 1946), 987-90. *Moisén* (México: Ed. Cultura, 1924). *La desventura del Conde Kadski* (The Misfortune of Count Kadski) (México: Botas, 1935). *Don Pedro Moya de Contreras, primer inquisidor de México* (Pedro Moya de Contreras, First Inquisitor in Mexico) (México: Eds. Xóchitl, 1944). *Vidas reales que parecen imaginarias* (Real Lives That Appear Imaginary) (México: Nueva Cultura, 1947). *Novelas coloniales* (Colonial Novels) (México: n.p., 1947). Theater: *Balada de Navidad* (Christmas Ballad), performed in 1918. *Camino de perfección* (Road to Perfection) (México: Imp. Bouret, 1918). *Como en la vida* (As in Life) (México: Talls. Gráfs. de la Nación, 1919). *Sor Adoración del Divino Verbo* (Sister Adoration of the Divine Verb) (México: Gómez de la Puente, 1923). *Tempestad sobre las cumbres* (Storm over the Heights) (México: Gómez de la Puente, 1923). *Lo que ella no pudo prever* (What She Could Not Foresee) (México: Ed. Cultura, 1923). *La caída de las flores* (The Fall of the Flowers) (México: Gerardo Sisniega, 1923; also México: Edit. Cultura, 1923). *Cándido Cordero, empleado público* (Simple Lamb, Public Employee), farce (México: n.p., 1925); 2nd ed. (Madrid: Espasa-Calpe, 1927). *Toque de Diana* (Diana's Touch), in *Contemporáneos* 1, 4 (Sept. 1928): 55-83. *La silueta de humo* (The Smoke Silhouette) (Madrid: Espasa-Calpe, 1928) and in *Teatro mexicano del siglo XX* (Mexican Theater of the Twentieth Century) (México: FCE, 1956), 489-547. *Miramar* (México: Imp. Universitaria, 1943). *El rival de su mujer* (His Wife's Rival) (México: Imp. Universitaria, 1943). Essays: *Resúmenes de literatura mexicana* (Summaries of Mexican Literature) (México: n.p., 1918). "El afeminamiento en la literatura mexicana" (Effeminacy in Mexican Literature), in *El Universal* 20 (Dec. 1924). *Historia de la literatura mexicana* (History of Mexican Literature) (México: n.p., 1928): 5th ed., corrected and enlarged (México: n.p., 1953): 6th ed., enlarged (México: Botas, 1957). "Juan Ruiz de Alarcón," address presented to the Palacio de Bellas Artes (México: IBA, 1934). "Lope de Vega," article (México: n.p., 1936), and in *Memorias de la Academia Mexicana* 11 (1955): 220-28. *Juan Ruiz de Alarcón y su tiempo* (Juan Ruiz de Alarcón and His Era) (México: Porrúa, 1939). *Letras mexicanas en el siglo XIX* (Mexican Letters in the Nineteenth Century) (México: FCE, 1944). *Herejías y superticiones en la Nueva España* (Heresies and Superstitions in New Spain) (México: Imp. Universitaria, 1946). *Historia de la cultura en México. El virreinato* (History of Culture in Mexico. The Viceroyalty) (México: Edit. Cultura, 1950). *El humanismo, el barroco y la contrarreforma en el México virreinal* (Humanism, the Baroque and the Counter-reformation in the Mexico of the Viceroyalty) (México: Edit. Cultura, 1951), and in *Memorias de la Academia Mexicana*, XIV, 1956, 260-271. *Sor Juana Inés de la Cruz en su época* (Sor Juana Inés de la Cruz During Her Times) (México: Porrúa, 1951). *Las constituciones de la antigua Universidad* (Constitutions of the Old University) (México: Universidad de México, 1952). *Lengua y literatura españolas* (Spanish Language and Literature), with R. Cordero Amador (México: Edit. Paideia, 1952). "Santa Teresa y Sor Juana, un paralelo imposible" (Saint Teresa and Sor Juana, an Impossible Parallel), in *Memorias de la Academia Mexicana* 13 (1955): 223-241. "El habla de los conquistadores" (The Speech of the Conquerors), offprint of in *Memorias de la Academia Mexicana de la Historia* 16, 3 (1955). *Historia jurídica de la Universidad de México* (Judicial History of the University of Mexico) (México: Imp. Universitaria, 1955). "Realidad y fantasía en la obra de Cervantes" (Reality and Fantasy in the Works of Cervantes), in *Memorias de la Academia Mexicana* 12 (1955): 60-71. "La imprenta en la época virreinal" (The Press in the Period of the Viceroyalty), in *Memorias de la Academia Mexicana* 13 (1955): 19-21. "Don Francisco de Quevedo y Villegas," in *Memorias de la Academia Mexicana* 13 (1955): 289-96. "Don Jacinto Benavente," in *Memorias de la Academia Mexicana* 15 (1956): 95-97. "El doctor Francisco Castillo Nájera," in *Memorias de la Academia Mexicana* 15 (1956): 268-69. *Estampas de los siglos de oro* (Pictures of the Golden Ages) (México: UNAM, 1957). *Historia de la cultura en México. El mundo prehispánico* (History of Culture in Mexico. The Prehispanic World) (México: Edit. Cultura, 1957). Anthology: *Antología de la prosa en México* (Anthology of Mexican Prose) (México: UNAM, 1931); 3rd ed. (México: Botas, 1946). Translations: Jules Romains, *Amadeo y los caballeros en fila* (Amadeus and the Noblemen in a Row), in *Contemporáneos* 2, 13 (June 1929): 215-239. Prologues: Juan Ruiz de Alarcón, *La verdad sospechosa*, preliminary notes, in *Cultura* 4, 2 (1917): iii-xi, 3-5. Juan Ruiz de Alarcón, *Los pechos privilegiados*, introduction, in *BEU* 5 (Mexico, 1939).

BIBLIOGRAPHY: Ermilo Abreu Gómez, *Sala de retratos* (México: Edit. Leyenda, 1946), 147-48. John S. Brushwood and José Rojas Garcidueñas, *Breve historia de la novela mexicana* (México: Eds. de Andrea, 1959), 86-87. María Canales Chávez, *Jiménez y su obra*, thesis (México: UNAM, 1959). Emmanuel Carballo, *19 protagonistas de la literatura mexicana del siglo XX* (México: Empresas Editoriales, 1965), 169-79. Alberto María Carreño, *Memorias de la Academia Mexicana*, vol. 7 (México: Edit. Jus, 1945), 358-59; vol. 8 (1946), 177-79. Genaro Fernández MacGregor, *Memorias de la Academia Mexicana*, vol. 13 (1955), 242-49. Raymond L. Grismer and Mary B. MacDonald, *Vida y obras de autores mexicanos* (Havana: Editorial "Alfa," 1945), 85-86. Walter M. Langford, *The Mexican Novel Comes of Age* (Notre Dame, Ind.: University of Notre Dame Press, 1971), 30. Luis Leal, *Breve historia del cuento mexicano* (México: Eds. de Andrea, 1956), 98; *Bibliografía del cuento mexicano* (México: Eds. de Andrea, 1958), 73-74; *Panorama de la literatura mexicana actual* (Washington, D.C.: Unión Panamericana, 1968), 24, 26, 33, 112. Antonio Magaña Esquivel, *Medio siglo de teatro mexicano, 1900-1961* (México: INBA, 1964), 26, 28, 30, 31-32, 40, 56, 59, 65, 69, 85; "Homenaje a Jiménez Rueda," in *El Nacional* (June 11, 1965): 5. José Luis Martínez, *Literatura mexicana siglo XX, 1910-1949*, vol. 1 (México: Ant. Libr. Robredo, 1949), 15-18, 88, 118, 140; vol. II (1950), 66; *El ensayo mexicano moderno*, vol. 1 (México: FCE, 1958), 380. Ernesto Mejía Sánchez, review of *Historia de la cultura en México* (El mundo prehispánico), in *Universidad de México* 13, 1

(Sept. 1957): 4. María Luisa Mendoza, Review of the inauguration of the "Teatro Jiménez Rueda," in *El Día* (Nov. 26, 1965): 2. Margarita Mendoza López, Review of Jiménez Rueda's life and work, in *Teatro, Boletín de información e historia* 7 (July 1955): 2-3. Francisco Monterde, *Teatro mexicano del siglo XX*, vol. 1 (México: FCE, 1956), 486-88; "Julio Jiménez Rueda," in *Revista Iberamericana* 25, 50 (July-Dec. 1960): 303-8. Aurora M. Ocampo de Gómez and Ernesto Prado Velázquez, *Diccionario de Escritores Mexicanos* (México: UNAM, 1967), 183-85. Bernardo Ortiz de Montellano, *Antología de cuentos mexicanos* (Madrid: n.p., 1926), 277. Sara Sefchovich, *México: país de ideas, país de novelas* (México: Editorial Grijalbo, 1987), 84, 85, 86. Rodolfo Usigli, *México en su teatro* (México: Imprenta Mundial, 1932), 24, 27, 28.

JEANNE C. WALLACE

JUAREZ, Jorge Ramón (1907). Juárez was born in Veracruz. From early childhood he was interested in poetry, music, and the arts. A precocious talent, he published *Hojeando el pasado* (Turning to the Past) when he was only twelve years old. In 1942 he relocated with his family to Spain, after the tragic death of his brother.

Pancho Villa y otros poemas (Pancho Villa and Other Poems) is a compilation of his works written between 1930 and 1935. The first poem, which lends its title to the book, praises the leader of the Revolution. Modernist influence is obvious, especially in metric liberties, topic, and style. Ruben Dario's presence is visible: the text "Canto a la Revolución" (Song to the Revolution) closely follows "Marcha triunfal" (Triumphant March). Modernist style is interrupted only when Romanticism is emphasized: the poem "Cráneos" (Skulls) details the macabre, death, and decomposition. There are also suggestive contrasts between life and death. In other poems Gustavo Adolfo Becquer's melancholy and sorrow predominate. *Luna en las manos* (Moon in the Hands) consists of seventeen romances and three lullabies. The romances have a Modernist ring resembling that of Federico García Lorca. *Romancero Jarocho* has the inspiration of Lorca's *Romancero gitano*. Noteworthy are "Romance de la noche jarocha," the autobiographical "Romance de Perfecto Muñoz," which refers to a goldsmith of Veracruz who lived 100 years and was a soldier and the author's grandfather, and "Romance de Odilón Romero," which deals with the topic of "caciquismo." *Sonetos para la geografía romántica de Veracruz* (Sonnets to the Romantic Geography of Veracruz) is dedicated to exalt the author's homeland and Orizaba, where he was raised. Orizaba, Xalapa, Valle de Pluviosilla, Cocolapán, El Yute, and Los Cerritos are evoked in perfectly constructed sonnets. *Urna verbal* (Word Shrine) addresses patriotic and military topics. *Arpa de sotavento* (Leeward Harp) is an excellent edition of the poems that appeared in *Romancero jarocho*.

WORKS: *Pancho Villa y otros poemas* (Pancho Villa and Other Poems) (México: n.p., 1935). *Luna en las manos* (Moon in the Hands) (México: Imprenta Excelsior, 1945). *Romancero jarocho* (México: SEP, 1946). *Urna verbal* (Word Shrine) (México: Eds. Lascas, 1948). *Como tajo de hielo* (As a Piece of Ice) (México: Eds. Lascas, 1950). *Arpa de sotavento* (Leeward Harp) (México: Col. Suma Veracruzana, 1969). *Meridiano de sombra* (Meridian of Shadow) (México: Col. Suma Veracruzana, 1970).

BIBLIOGRAPHY: Anon., "La poesía de Jorge Ramón Juárez." in *Nivel* 3 (Mar. 25, 1963): 4. Neftalí Beltran, Review of *Como Tajo de Hielo*, in *México en la Cultura* 91 (Oct. 29, 1950): 7. Antonio Castro Leal, *La poesía mexicana moderna* (México: FCE, 1953), 398.

ALICIA G. WELDEN

JUNCO, Alfonso (1896-1975). Alfonso Junco was born on February 25, 1896, in Monterrey, where he completed his studies, later going to Mexico City. An accountant until 1954, he retired and dedicated himself mostly to research, writing, and literature. From 1926, he contributed to several important literary journals and wrote for various publications in Spain and the United States.

In 1955 he became the director of *Abside*, a journal dedicated to Mexican culture. Influential in the cultural affairs of the nation, he was also an active member of the Academia de la Lengua during his distinguished career.

A devout Catholic, he represented all Mexican Catholics at a special eucaristic congress in Budapest in 1937. His travels also took him to other European nations, the United States, and several Latin American countries.

Aside from his work at *Abside*, Alfonso Junco published many volumes, including poetry, various types of essays, literary criticsm, etc. As a young poet, he tended to follow in the footsteps of Enrique *González Martínez for a while. As he matured, however, he constructed his own path, with quite original verse. Much of his later poetry deals with religious themes. The central purpose of most of his writing was to disseminate his views on Catholicism and the political, social, and philosophical ideas that he considered important. A review of some of the titles of his works will indicate the extent of the religious theme in his writing. In his essays, especially, he expressed himself clearly, with concision and classical style. He died in 1975, a much admired and respected man. An edition of *Abside* was dedicated to him, with many articles about the positive impact he had on so many people both in Mexico and abroad.

WORKS: Poetry: *Por la senda suave* (By the Soft Path) (Monterrey: n.p., 1917). *El alma estrella* (The Star Soul) (México: n.p., 1920). *Posesión* (Possession) (México: n.p., 1923). *Florilegio eucarístico* (Eucharistic Anthology) (México: n.p., 1926). *La divina aventura* (The Divine Adventure) (México: n.p., 1938). *Antología* (Anthology) (México: n.p., 1960). Essays and Prose: *Fisonomías* (Facial Expressions) (Buenos Aires: n.p., 1927). *La traición de Querétero* (The Treachery of Querétero) (México: n.p., 1930). *Cristo* (Christ) (México: n.p., 1931). *Un radical problema guadalupano* (A Radical Problem of Guadalupe) (México: n.p. 1932). *Motivos mexicanos* (Mexican Motives) (Madrid: n.p., 1933). *La carta atenagórica de Sor Juana* (The Athenagoric Letter of Sor Juana) (Lisbon: n.p., 1933). *Inquisición sobre la Inquisición* (Inquisition about the Inquisition) (México: n.p., 1933); 2nd ed., augmented (1949). *Un siglo de México* (A Century of Mexico) (México: n.p., 1934); 5th ed., enlarged (México: Editorial Jus, 1963). *Casas que arden* (Houses That Burn) (México: n.p., 1934). *Carranza y los orígenes de su rebelión* (Carranza and the Origins of His Rebellion) (México: n.p., 1935). *Lope, ecuménico* (Lope, Ecumenical) (México: n.p., 1935). *Gente de México* (People of Mexico) (México: n.p., 1937). *Lumbre de México* (Light of

Mexico) (México: n.p., 1938). *Savia* (Vital Fluid) (México: n.p., 1939). *La vida sencilla* (The Simple Life) (México: n.p., 1939). *El difícil paraíso* (The Difficult Paradise) (México: n.p., 1940). *Sangre de Hispania* (Spanish Blood) (México: n.p., 1940). *Tres lugares comunes* (Three Common Places) (México: n.p., 1943). *Egregios* (Illustriousness) (México: n..p., 1944). *El milagro de las rosas* (The Miracle of the Roses) (México: n.p., 1945). *España en carne viva* (Wounded Spain) (México: n.p., 1946). *El gran teatro del mundo* (The Great Theater of the World) (Madrid: n.p., 1947). *El amor de Sor Juana* (The Love of Sor Juana) (México: Editorial Jus, 1951). *Tras la huella de Sor Juana* (On the Trail of Sor Juana) (México: n.p., 1951). *¡Novedad en la Academia!* (News in the Academy!) (México: n.p., 1953). *Los ojos viajeros* (The Traveling Eyes) (México: Editorial Jus, 1955). *Controversia con Don Antonio Caso* (Controversy with Antonio Caso) (México: n.p., 1955). *Sotana de México* (Cassock of Mexico) (México: n.p., 1955). *El libro de la invitación* (The Book about the Invitation) (México: n.p., 1958). *El increíble Fray Servando* (The Incredible Friar Servando) (México: n.p., 1959). *Othón en mi recuerdo* (Othon in My Recollection) (México: n.p., 1959). *México y los refugiados* (Mexico and the Exiled) (México: n.p., 1959). *Ejemplaridad de Rubén Darío* (The Example of Rubén Darío), in *Abside* 31, 1 (Jan.-March 1967): 36-46. *La jota de México y otras danzas* (The "Jota" of Mexico and Other Dances) (México: Jus, 1967). *De los primeros dineros a los setenta febreros* (From the First Monies to the Seventy Februaries) (México: Jus, 1970). "El amor humano y el amor divino en Sor Juana Inéz" (Human Love and Divine Love in Sor Juana Inés), *Abside* 37, 2 (1973): 166-89. *Poesía completa* (Complete Poetry) (México: Jus, 1975). Prologue: Alfonso Méndez Plancarte, *Cuestiúnculas gongorinas* (México: de Andrea, 1955).

BIBLIOGRAPHY: Anon., in *Anuario de la poesía mexicana 1960* (México: INBA, 1961), 84. Aurora M. Ocampo de Gómez and Ernesto Prado Velázquez, *Diccionario de Escritores Mexicanos* (México: UNAM, 1967), 185-86. Various, in *Abside* 39 (1975), includes "Duelo de las letras: Murió Alfonso Junco," author not cited, 3-8; Eduardo Alcalá, "Morir de su propia muerte," 47-53; Carlos Alvear Acevedo, "Ausencia de Junco, literato, filósofo, historiador," 27-30; Alejandro Avilés, "Alfonso Junco: Diáfano como hombre y escritor," 31-34; Luis G. Basurto, "Hombre de México: Alfonso Junco," 67-70; Luis Beltranena Sinibaldi, "En la muerte de un egregio," 137-39; Antonio Brambila, "Alfonso Junco," 36-41; Emilio de la Cruz Hermosilla, "Alfonso Junco," 59-62; Sergio Delmar Junco, "Mi abuelo," 95-96; Guillermo Díaz-Plaja, "Alfonso Junco con su Dios," 63-66; José H. Estrada Morales, "El mejicanismo de Alfonso Junco," 112-14; María de la Luz García Alonso, "Nos falta un poeta," 97-100; Emma Godoy, "Caballero sin mancha," 41-46; Josefina Gómez, "Un poeta en casa," 127-33; Humberto Junco, "En México," 80-84; Samuel B. Lemus, "Alfonso Junco," 73-75; Ricardo Margáin Zozaya, "Junco ante la crítica," 85-94; Emilio Marín Pérez, "Luto en las letras hispánicas," 355-58; Rubén Marín, "Don Alfonso Junco, gran señor de las letras castellanas," 116-23; Joaquín A. Peñalosa, "Semblanza de Alfonso Junco," 14-23; Eduardo E. Ríos, "Genio y figura . . . de Alfonso Junco," 9-13; Antonio Ríus Facius, "Cómo conocí a Alfonso Junco," 24-26; Rafael Solana, "Muertos ilustres," 71-72; Juan I. Tena Ybarra, "En la muerte de Alfonso Junco," 57-58; Octaviano Valdés, "Alfonso Junco," 413-20; José Vasconcelos, "Bienvenida a Alfonso Junco," 101-11.

JEANNE C. WALLACE

L

LABASTIDA, Jaime (1939-). Born in Los Mochis, Sinaloa, on June 13, 1939, Labastida, educated at the Universidad Nacional de México, became a noted philosophy professor at the Escuela Nacional Preparatoria. He began his literary career by publishing poems and essays in several local periodicals and newspaper supplements. In collaboration with Antonio Rodríguez, he compiled the *Antología del cuento mexicano moderno* (Anthology of the Modern Mexican Story), an important collection of stories. With four other poets of his generation, he published in two anthologies of socially committed poetry, *La espiga amotinada* (The Rebellious Spike) (1960) and *Ocupación de la palabra* (Occupation of the Word) (1965). In the prologue to *La espiga amotinada*, expressing his concerns for the needs of mankind, he remarks that "we live in an age of crisis and a poet who is merely a passive reflection of our times is a poet in crisis." Thus, his approach to literature is a socially committed one, similar to that of other members of his generation.

Labastida also penned the prologue for a selection of the writings of Aníbal Ponce, *Humanismo y revolución* (Humanism and Revolution), in which he appears sympathetic to Ponce and his Marxist leanings. Interested in the work of José *Revueltas, he published an article about him in 1973. A year later, he wrote the prologue for *El amor, el sueño y la muerte en la poesía mexicana* (Love, Dream and Death in Mexican Poetry), followed two years later by a critical article about the state of Mexican poetry. With continued interest in the life of José Revueltas, Labastida wrote an essay entitled "Para desmitificar a Revueltas," in which he portrays Revueltas as a very human man caught in the contradictions between his leftist leanings and his intellectual elitism. Although controversial, the essay is considered quite informative and stimulating.

In his poetry, Labastida often uses striking and vivid images of urban life. With vehement passion, he confronts the problems of contemporary society. He celebrates life, yet tempers that joyous celebration by acknowledging that there are problems which must be resolved.

A highly acknowledged writer, he won the 1981 Premio International de Poesía de la Paz (International Poetry Prize for Peace) in Baja California for his poetic work *De las cuatro estaciones.*

WORKS: "En descenso," in *La espiga amotinada* (México: FCE, 1960), 197-240. *Ocupación de la palabra*, anthology (México: FCE, 1965). Prólogo, in his *El amor, el sueño y la muerte en la poesía mexicana* (México: Instituto Politécnico Nacional, 1969), 15-131. Prologue to *Humanismo y revolución* by Aníbal Ponce (Lima: Ediciones Populares Los Andes, 1970). "José Revueltas. Literatura realidad y política," *Revista de Bellas Artes* 9 (1973): 31-40. *El amor, el sueño y la muerte* (México: Organización Editorial Novaro, 1974; also México: Novaro, 1974), 7-82. "La

poesía mexicana, 1965-1976," in *Revista de la Universidad de México* 30, 12 (1976): 2-9.
"Para desmitificar a Revueltas," *Plural Excelsior* (Mexico) 20, 3, III (Dec. 1980): 26-31.
"La poesía mexicana (1965-1976)," in *Revista de la Universidad de México* (August 1983).

BIBLIOGRAPHY: Ricardo Aguilar Melantzón, "Efraín Huerta and the New School of Mexican Poets," in *Latin American Literary Review* 11, 22 (1983): 41-56. Federico Alvarez, Review of *Ocupación de la palabra*, in *Revista de Bellas Artes* 3 (May-June 1965): 91-95. Eduardo César, "Sobre *La espiga amotinada*," in *Lugar de encuentro*, edited by Norma Klahn and Jesse Fernández (México: Editorial Katún, 1987), 191-204. Merlin H. Forster, ed., *La muerte en la poesía mexicana* (México: Editorial Diógenes, 1970), 161, 187-88. David William Foster, *A Dictionary of Contemporary Latin American Authors* (Phoenix, Arizona: Publishers Press, Inc., 1975), 57. Isabel Frayre, "Cinco poetas," in *Revista de la Universidad de Mexico* 20, 2 (Oct. 1965): 28. Carlos González Peña, *Historia de la literatura mexicana*, 15th ed. (México: Porrúa, 1984), 300-302. Porfirio Martínez Peñaloza, *Los cinco poetas de la espiga amotinada* (México: Instituto Cultural Mexicano Israelí II, 1966). "Nuevos poetas," *Revista mexicana de literatura* 6-7 (Dec. 1959-Jan. 1960): 30-32. Aurora M. Ocampo de Gómez and Ernesto Prado Velázquez, *Diccionario de Escritores Mexicanos* (México: UNAM, 1967), 186. Ramón Xirau, Review of *Ocupación de la palabra*, in *Diálogos* 6 (Sept-Oct. 1965): 43.

JEANNE C. WALLACE

LAFRAGUA, José M. (1813-1875), journalist, lawyer, diplomat, novelist. Lafragua was born in Puebla on April 2, 1813. On October 21, 1835, he received his law degree and taught civil law. He devoted much of his time to literature and politics. He was appointed ambassador to Spain (1857-1860); he became temporary justice of the Supreme Court on August 3, 1867. He also served as the first director of the National Library. In 1872 he was appointed secretary of relations and was, at the same time, the fifth justice of the Supreme Court. He died in Mexico City on November 15, 1875.

Lafragua was very active in journalism, contributing to *El ensayo literario* and *El Ateneo Mexicano*, among others. He and the Spaniard Casimiro del Collado founded *El Apuntador* (The Recorder) in 1841, a publication devoted to literary and theatrical critique. He wrote only a historical-romantic novel dealing with the last years of Montezuma, although he translated numerous plays from the French.

WORK: *Netzula* (México: n.p., 1832), also included in Biblioteca de Autores Mexicanos, no. 33 (México: Agüeros, 1901), 265-306.

BIBLIOGRAPHY: Fernando Alegría, *Breve historia de la novela hispano-americana*, Manuales Studium, no. 10 (México: Ediciones de Andrea, 1959), 83. Carlos González Peña, *Historia de la literatura mexicana. Desde sus origenes hasta nuestros dias.* (México: Editorial Porrúa, 1981), 141. Francisco Sosa, chapter in *Biografías de mexicanos distinguidos* (México: Oficina Tipográfica de la Secretaría de Fomento, 1884), 560-63.

JOSEPH VELEZ

LANDIVAR, Rafael (1731-1793), poet and scholar. Landívar was born in Santiago de los Caballeros, Guatemala. Before traveling to the capital of New Spain in 1749, he completed a degree as "Maestro en Artes" from the University of San Carlos. While in Mexico he became a Jesuit in 1755 and taught rhetoric and poetics at Puebla and Tepotztlán. Landívar returned to his native Guatemala in 1761, and became chancellor of the Colegio de San Francisco de Borja in 1767, the year Jesuits were expelled from all Spanish territories. He lived in exile in Bolonia, Italy, where he continued to teach and wrote his acclaimed *Rusticatio Mexicana*. He died while in exile, on September 27, 1793.

Rafael Landívar's *Rusticatio Mexicana*, written in Italy and in Latin, stands as one of Spanish America's greatest descriptive poems. According to many critics, the Spanish translation of this poem surpasses in scope and objectivity such classics as Bernardo de *Balbuena's *Grandeza Mexicana* or Andrés Bello's *Oda a la agricultura de la zona tórrida*. First published in Modena, Italy, in 1781, *Rusticatio Mexicana* is a grandiose hymn to America. It describes in detail the flora and fauna, the industries, the mining, the agriculture, cattle raising, and the pastimes of eighteenth-century New Spain. Its initial claim to objectivity notwithstanding, the poem exudes a nostalgic love for the lost fatherland. Its classical model is Virgil, and the didactic mode is ever present.

WORKS: *Rusticatio mexicana* (Rustic Mexico) (Modena, Italy, 1781). Translations in prose: (1) Ignacio Loureda, *Rusticatio mexicana* (México: Franco Americana, 1942), and 2) Octaviano Valdés, *Por los campos de México* 1941 (México: UNAM, 1942). Translation in verse, Federico Escobedo, *Georgicas Mexicanas* (México: SEP, 1924).

BIBLIOGRAPHY: Antonio Batres Jauregui, "Rafael Landívar," *Literatos guatemaltecos* (Guatemala, n.p., 1896), 43-107. Marcelino Menéndez y Pelayo. *Antología de poetas hispanoamericanos* (Madrid, 1893), clxiv, clxix.

ALFONSO GONZALEZ AND JOSEPH VELEZ

LAZO, Agustín (1898-?), artist, art critic, translator, playwright. Born in México City, Agustín Lazo completed his bachelor's degree at the Escuela Nacional Preparatoria and studied art at the Academia de Bellas Artes. His first art exhibit was in 1926. He worked in Paris from 1928 through 1930, where he began his career specializing in making scenery. Upon his return to Mexico, he took charge of scenery in a number of major theaters and presented adaptations of works by writers such as Giraudoux, Pirandello, San Secondo, Bontempelli, and Shakespeare. He collaborated with Xavier *Villaurrutia, a member of the Contemporáneos group, on some of these adaptations. (*See* Vanguardist Prose Fiction in Mexico.) He was professor of art at the Instituto Nacional de Bellas Artes for a number of years.

Lazo became involved in the theater in 1946 as a translator. It was then that he published his first dramatic work, *Segundo Imperio* (Second Empire), which is about the trials of Carlota and Maximilian in Mexico. In 1947, his work *La huella* (The Footprint), a comedy about the Mexican Revolution, was first performed. *El caso de don Juan Manuel* (The Case of Don Juan Manuel), written in 1948, is a well-written work about the psychological problems of Juan Manuel Solórzano, who played a key role in Mexican colonial history.

WORKS: Theater: *Segundo imperio* (Second Empire), Libros del Hijo Pródigo (México: Eds. Letras de México, 1946); 2nd ed. (1957). *La huella* (The Footprint), first performed in 1947, Col. Teatro Mexicano Contemporáneo, no.1 (México: Sociedad Gral. de Autores de México, 1947); 2nd ed. (México: Editor Atenea, 1947). *La mulata de Córdoba* (The Mulatto of Córdoba), in collaboration with Xavier Villaurrutia, music by Pablo Moncayo; first performed in 1948 (México: Eds. de México en el Arte, 1948). *El caso de don Juan Manuel* (The Case of Don Juan Manuel), first performed in 1948, (México: Editor Atenea, 1948); in *Teatro mexicano del siglo XX*, vol. 3, Prologue and notes by Celestino Gorostiza, Letras Mexicanas, no. 27 (México: FCE, 1956), 66-132. *El don de la palabra* (The Gift of the Word), first performed in 1950.

BIBLIOGRAPHY: Anon., *Catálogo del teatro mexicano contemporáneo* (México: INBA, 1956), 27-29. Alyce Golding Cooper, *Teatro mexicano contemporáneo, 1940-1962*, Ph.D. Diss., Facultad de Filosofía y Letras (México: UNAM, 1962), 27-28, 30, 50, 60, 66. Celestino Gorostiza, *Teatro mexicano del siglo XX*, vol. 3, foreword by Gorostiza, Letras Mexicanas, no. 27 (México: FCE, 1956), 65. Ruth S. Lamb, *Bibliografía del teatro mexicano del siglo XX*, Col. Studium, no. 33 (México: Ed. de Andrea, 1962), 70. Antonio Magaña Esquivel and Ruth S. Lamb, *Breve historia del teatro mexicano*, Manuales Studium, no 8 (México: Ediciónes de Andrea, 1958), 125, 141-42. Antonio Magaña Esquivel, "Escenógrafos," *Imágenes del teatro*, 103-8; "Agustín Lazo, dramaturgo," *Sueño y realida del teatro*, 143-47; *Medio siglo de teatro mexicano, 1900-1961* (México: INBA, 1964), 60, 65, 69, 70, 78, 80, 105, 119, 120, 134, 146. José Luis Martínez, *Literatura mexicana del siglo xx, 1910-1949*, Clásicos y Modernos (México: Antigua Librería, Robrero, 1949), vol 1, no. 3, 30, 37; vol. 2, no. 4 (1950), 68. Aurora M. Ocampo de Gómez and Ernesto Prado Velázquez, *Diccionario de escritores Mexicanos* (México: UNAM, 1967), 188.

EDNA A. REHBEIN

LEAL, Luis (1907-). Born on September 17, 1907, Luis Leal completed his high school studies in the United States. He got his B.S. from Northwestern University and his M.A. and Ph.D. from the University of Chicago, graduating in 1950. He taught in quite a number of universities in the United States, including Northwestern, Chicago, and Emory. He also served terms as a visiting professor at UNAM and at Guadalajara. Very actively involved in scholarship and teaching, Luis Leal has distinguished himself as a literary historian, particularly of Spanish American literature and the Mexican short story. In 1956, he published a *Breve historia del cuento mexicano* (Short History of the Mexican Story), a very valuable tool for students of literature. Interested particularly in the stories revolving around the Mexican Revolution, Leal published an essay, in collaboration with Edmundo *Valadés, entitled *La Revolución y la letras*. Luis Leal is well-known both in Mexico and in the United States for his careful research and meticulously presented portraits. In 1961, he published *Mariano Azuela. Vida y obra* (Mariano Azuela. Life and

Works), a thorough and investigative portrait of the famous Mexican. Ten years later, in 1971, he broadened his perspective, publishing *Breve historia de la literatura hispanoamericana* (Short History of Spanish American Literature), another excellent history of literature.

WORKS: *México, civilizaciones y culturas* (Mexico, Civilizations and Cultures) (Boston: Houghton Mifflin, 1955). *Pedro Henríquez Ureña en México*, offprint of *Revista Iberoamericana* 21, 41-42 (1956): 229-33. *Breve historia del cuento mexicano* (Short History of the Mexican Story) (México: Eds. Andrea, 1956). "Jicoténcal, primera novela histórica en castellano" (Jicoténca, First Historical Novel in Spanish), in *Revista Iberoamericana* 25, No. 49 (1960): 9-31. *La Revolución y las letras* (The Revolution and Literature), in collaboration with Edmundo Valadés (México: INBA, 1960). *Mariano Azuela. Vida y obra* (Mariano Azuela. Life and Works) (México: Eds. de Andrea, 1961). "Literatura mexicana 1940-1963," in *Panorama das Literaturas das Americas* 4 (Angola: Municipio de Nova Lisboa, 1965), 1997-2050. *Historia del cuento hispanoamericano* (History of the Spanish American Story) (México: Eds. de Andrea, 1966). *Breve historia de la literatura hispanoamericana* (Brief History of Spanish American Literature) (New York: Alfred A. Knopf, 1971). Anthologies: Amado Nervo, ed., *Sus mejores cuentos* (His Best Stories) (Boston: Houghton Mifflin, 1951). *Antología del cuento mexicano* (Anthology of the Mexican Story) (México: Eds. de Andrea, 1957). *El cuento veracruzano* (Stories from Veracruz) (Xalapa: Edit. Universidad Veracruzana, 1966). *El cuento mexicano de los orígenes al modernismo* (The Mexican Story from its Origins until Modernism) (Buenos Aires: Edit. Universitaria de Buenos Aires, 1966). Other: *Bibliografía del cuento mexicano* (Bibliography of the Mexican Story) (México: Eds. de Andrea, 1958). *Anuario del cuento mexicano 1960* (Annual Report of the Mexican Story 1960), prologue (México: INBA, 1961).

BIBLIOGRAPHY: Demetrio Aguila Malta, Review of *Historia del cuento hispanoamericano*, in *El Gallo Ilustrado* 192 (Feb. 27, 1966): 4. Fernando Alegría, *Nueva historia de la novela hispanoamericana* (Hanover, N.H.: Ediciones del Norte, 1986), 3, 7, 8. Jesús Arellano, review of *Breve historia del cuento mexicano*, in *Metáfora*, 9 (July-Aug. 1956): 34-35. Vicente T. Mendoza, Review of *México, civilizaciones y culturas*, in *Boletín Bibliográfico de Antropología Americana*, Part 2, vol. 18 (Mexico, 1956), 226-27. Aurora M. Ocampo de Gómez and Ernesto Prado Velázquez, *Diccionario de Escritores Mexicanos* (México: UNAM, 1967), 188-89. Carlos Valdés, Review of *Breve historia del cuento mexicano*, in *Universidad de México* 10, 12 (Aug. 1956): 30-31.

LINO GARCIA

LEAL Cortés, Alfredo (1931-). Leal Cortés was born on February 25, 1931, in Guadalajara, Jalisco where he later was involved with the magazines *Ariel* and *Ex Caetera*. In Mexico City he contributed to the *Universidad de México*, a yearly directory published by the National Institute of Fine Arts and the Sunday supplement of the daily *Ovaciones*, which he directs together with Emmanuel *Carballo. Besides being a novelist and short story writer, Alfredo Leal Cortés has also been interested in sociological studies.

WORKS: Novel: *Desde el río* (From the River) (México: Joaquín Mortiz, 1965).

BIBLIOGRAPHY Jesús Arellano, "Las ventas de don Quijote," review of *Desde el río*, in *Nivel* 35 (Nov. 25, 1965): 3. Emmanuel Carballo, *Cuentistas mexicanos modernos*, vol. 2 (México: Libro-Mex, 1956), 245. Gabriel Careaga, "La novela," in *México en la Cultura* 876 (Jan. 2, 1966): 3. Luis Leal, *Bibliografía del cuento mexicano* (México: Ed. de Andrea, 1958), 75. José Muñoz Cota, "Por los caminos de la novela," in *Rev. Méxicana de Cultura* 983 (Jan. 30, 1966): 4. Aurora M. Ocampo de Gómez and Ernesto Prado Velázquez, *Diccionario de Escritores Mexicanos* (México: UNAM, 1967), 189.

MIRTA BARREA-MARLYS

LEDUC, Renato (1897-   ), journalist, poet, humanist. Born in Tlalpan in 1897, Leduc completed his studies at the law school and later served in the   Mexican consulate in Paris (1995), in England (1841), and in other countries.
    Although he has written for the magazines *Siempre!* and *Política*, he is recognized for his column "Banqueta" which appeared in *Excelsior*. Leduc's writings defend the common people, reflecting a sense of humor for which he is famous. He is considered one of the most inportant critics of Mexican life.

WORKS: *Los banquetes* (The Banquets) (México: n.p., 1932). *Sonetos* (Sonnets) (México: Alcancía, 1933). *Prometeo* (Prometheus) (México: Alcancía, 1933). *Prometeo mal encadenado* (Prometheus Badly Chained) (México: Alcancía, 1934). *Versos y Poemas* (Verses and Poems) (México: Alcancía, 1940). *El corsario beige* (The Beige Corsair) (México: Alcancía, 1940). *Banqueta* (México: Margen, 1961). *Apuntes de una vida singular* (Notes of a Singular Life) (México: Océano, 1989).

BIBLIOGRAPHY: Rafael Aguayo Spencer, *Flor de moderna poesía mexicana* (México: Libro-Mex, 1955), 76, 137. Alí Chumacero, "La poesía de Renato Leduc;" in *Ovaciones* 71 (May. 5, 1963): 2; "La poesía. 1963," in *La Cultura en México* 99 (Jan. 8, 1964): xvi. Arturo Sotomayor, "Renato Leduc, poeta involuntario," in *Letras de México* 4, 18 (June. 1, 1944): 1-2, 10.

SILKA FREIRE

LEIVA, Raúl (1916- ?), poet and critic. Leiva was born in Guatemala City, Guatemala, on Septembar 24, 1916. In 1941 he won the Primer Premio de Poesía Centroamericana. He lived in Mexico at different periods of his life; during his first stay, from 1942 to 1943, he published his first book of poetry, *Angustia* (Anguish), and became friends with writers who were contributors to *Tierra Nueva*. In 1945, together with Luis *Cardoza y Aragón, Leiva founded the *Revista de Guatemala*. As the result of the military takeover by Castillo Armas, Leiva left Guatemala, and after 1945 he lived in Mexico City, where his poetry, essays, and literary criticism appeared in numerous Mexican magazines and literary supplements. In 1967 he became editor of the Dirección General de Publicaciones at UNAM.

In 1940, Leiva was one of a group of poets whose work was published in the magazine *Acento*, which paid tribute to young writers of moment in Guatemala. Later in México, he collected a series of essays about Mexican poets from the period of the Vanguard movement to the generation born in the early l920s which appears in *Imagen de la poesía mexicana contemporánea* (1929). Leiva's critical articles appeared in a column in *Nivel* entitled Bibliográfica por Raúl Leiva, and in *Diorama de la Cultura*, in *Excelsior*. In 1965 he began writing a regular column of literary criticism in *México en la Cultura*, the supplement of *Novedades*. Leiva won first prize in the 1963 Concurso Internacional de Crítica Literaria, organized by Fondo de Cultura Económica in México.

WORKS: Poetry: *Angustia* (Anguish) (México: Letras de México, 1941). *En el pecado* (In Sin) (Guatemala: *Acento*, 1943). *Sonetos de amor y muerte* (Sonnets of Love and Death) (Guatemala: *Acento*, 1944). *Batres Montufar y la poesía* (Batres Montufar and Poetry) (Guatemala: *Acento*, 1944). *Norah o el ángel* (Norah, or the Angel) (Guatemala: *Acento*, 1946). *El deseo* (Desire) (México: Letras de México, 1947). *Mundo indígena* (Indigenous World) (Guatemala: Saker-Ti, 1949). *Sueño de la muerte* (Dream of Death) (Guatemala: pub. by the author, 1950). *Poemas* (Poems) (Guatemala: Ministerio de Educación Pública, 1952). *Oda a Guatemala y otros poemas* (Ode to Guatemala and Other Poems) (Guatemala: Saker-Ti, 1953). *Danza para Cuauhtémoc* (Dance for Cuauhtémoc) (México: Los Presentes, 1955). *La tierra de Caín* (The Land ff Cain), with Enrique González Rojo and Eduardo Lizalde (México: Eds. Ideas de México, 1956). *Nunca el olvido* (Never Oblivion) sonnets (México: Eds. Ideas de México, 1957). *Aguila oscura* (Dark Eagle), poem to Benito Juárez (México: Ed. Ecuador, 1959). *Eternidad tu nombre* (Eternity Your Name) (México: Ed. Ecuador, 1962; México: Gráficas Menhir, 1962). *Memorie du Temps* (Memory of Time) trad. of Henri de Lescoit (Nice: Profils Poetiques des Pays Latins, 1962). *Palenque*, adapted by Henri de Lescoit (Nice: Profils Poetiques des Pays Latins, 1962). *La serpiente emplumada* (The Plumed Serpent) Intro. by Carlos Pellicer (México: Ed. Ecuador, 1965). *Transfiguraciones* (Transfigurations) (México: UNAM, 1969). *Poesía* (Poetry) (México: División de Educación y Cultura, 1974). *Palabra en el tiempo: obra Poética* (Word in Time: Poetic Work) (Guatemala: Universidad de San Carlos de Guatemala, 1975). Essays: *Muerte y poesía* (Death and Poetry), addendum to *Revista de Guatemala* (Guatemala: 1946). *Los sentidos y el mundo* (The Senses and the World) (Guatemala: Eds. del Min. de Ed. Pub., 1952). *Imagen de la poesía mexicana* (Image of Contemporary Mexican Poetry) (México: Imp. Universitaria, 1959). Introductions and Anthologies: *La Poesía de Federico García Lorca* (The Poetry of Federico García Lorca), edition and introduction (Guatemala: Biblioteca de Cultura Popular, Oct. 29, 1952). *La poésie contemporaine au Guatemala* (Contemporary Poetry in Guatemala) (Belgium: Courrier du Centro International d'Etudes Poétiques, 1963). "La poesía de Miguel Angel Asturias," (The Poetry of Miguel Angel Asturias), *Revista Iberoamericana* 35, 87-100. "La poesía de José Gorostiza" (The Poetry of José Gorostiza) *Cuadernos Americanos* 163, 220-37. "La poesía de Marco Antonio Montes de Oca" (The Poetry of Marco Antonio Montes de Oca) 167, 174-93. "Cuatro calas desmitificadoras sobre Rubén Darío" (Four Demythifying Probes of Rubén Darío) *Universidad de la Habana* 184-85 (May-June 1967): 141-51. "La poesía de Rubén Bonifaz Nuño: Desde *Fuego de pobres* hasta *El ala del tigre"* (The poetry of Rubén Bonifaz Nuño: From Fire of the Poor to The Wing of the Tiger), *Cuadernos Americanos* 175, 167-83. "La poesía de Rubén Bonifaz Nuño: Desde *Imagen* hasta *El manto y la corona*," (The Poetry of Rubén Bonifaz Nuño: From Image to The Cloak and the Crown), *Cuadernos Americanos* 174, 165-86. "Elías Nandino," *Nivel* 96 (1970): 1-2. "Charles Baudelaire, nuestro contemporáneo" (Charles Baudelaire, Our Contemporary) *Cuadernos Americanos* 156, 201-16; also (México: Finisterre, 1967). *Aproximación a la poesía* (Approximation to Poetry) (México: Finisterre, 1968). "Aproximación a la 'Suave patria'" (Approximation of the "Gentle Fatherland"), *Vida Literária* 21, 11-14. "Blas de Otero, conciencia poética de España" (Blas de Otero, Poetic Conscience of Spain), *Cuadernos Americanos* 184 (1972): 209-24. *La prosa de López Velarde* (The Prose of López Velarde) (México: UNAM, 1971). *Iluminaciones: crítica literaria* (Illuminations: Literary Criticism) (México: Ed. Letras, 1973). "La revolución francesa y sus hombres de letras" (The French Revolution and Its Men of Letters), *Cuadernos Americanos* 196, 63-90. *Introducción a Sor Juana: Sueño y realidad* (México: UNAM, 1975).

BIBLIOGRAPHY: Demetrio Aguilera Malta, "La rosa de los vientos," review of *La serpiente emplumada* in *El Gallo Ilustrado* 182 (Dec. 19, 1965): 4. José Alvarado, "Correo Menor. Un libro de Raúl Leiva," review of *Imagen de la poesía mexicana contemporánea*, in *Diorama de la Cultura* (Mar. 15, 1959): 2. Anon., Review of *Eternidad tu nombre*, in *Ideas, Artes y Letras* (Lima) 13, 52 (Sept. 1962). Review of first prize of Crítica Bibliográfica del FCE, in *México en la Cultura* 771 (Dec. 29, 1963): 6; "Papel y tinta," review of first prize won by Raúl Leiva for critical note on *Antología de Alfonso Reyes*, in *México en la Cultura* 103 (Feb, 5, 1964): xix; "Premio internacional de crítica," in *El Gallo Ilustrado* 85 (Feb. 9, 1964): 3; "Síntesis bibliobiográfica de Raúl Leiva," in *México en la Cultura* 874 (Dec. 19, 1965): 3. Jesús Arellano, "Raúl Leiva exalta la poesía mexicana," in *El Nacional* (Mar. 1, 1959); "Las ventas de don Quijote," in *Nivel* 37 (Jan 25, 1966): 3. Juan Antonio Ayala, review of *Imagen de la poesía mexicana contemporánea*, in *Revista Universitaria* (April 1, 1959). Huberto Batis, Review of *La serpiente emplumada*, in *México en la Cultura* 202 (Dec. 29, 1965): xvi. Alberto Bonifaz Nuño, Review of *Danza para Cuauhtémoc*, in *Universidad de México* 10, 5 (Jan., 1965): 30-31. Alí Chumacero, "La poesía de Raúl Leiva," in *El Nacional* (May, 1947): 2-3. "Raúl Leiva y la lírica mexicana de hoy," in *México en la Cultura* 519 (Feb. 22, 1959): 5. Frank Dauster, Review of *Imagen de la Poesía mexicana contemporánea*, in *Revista Iberoamericana* 35, 49 (Jan.-June 1960): 173-77. Eduardo González Lanuza, Review of *Imagen de la poesía mexicana contemporánea*, in *Sur* (Buenos Aires) 264 (May-June 1960). Fedro Guillén, "La antología de Raúl Leiva," in *El Nacional* (Mar. 7, 1959): 2. Andrés Henestrosa, "Raúl Leiva," in *El Nacional* (Mar. 27, 1959): 4. Consuelo Howtt, "Leiva, One of Guatemala's Outstanding Young Poets," in *Books Abroad*, 1949. Aurora M. Ocampo de Gómez and Ernesto Prado Velázquez, *Diccionario de escritores mexicanos* (México: UNAM, 1967), 191-92. José Emilio Pacheco, Review of *Imagen de la poesía mexicana contemporánea*, in *Universidad de México* 8, 8 (April, 1959); 26. Carlos Pellicer, Review of *Danza para Cuauhtémoc*, in *Universidad de México* 10, 7 (Mar 1956): 29. Rafael del Río, "Un nuevo libro de Raúl Leiva," review of *En el pecado*, in *Letras de México* 1, 7 (July 15, 1943): 3. Rubén Salazar Millán, "La poesía en México. Raúl Leiva," in *Mañana* 810 (Mar. 7, 1959). "La poesía de Raúl Leiva," in *Nivel* 4 (April 25, 1963): 1-2.

JOAN SALTZ

LEÑERO, Vicente (1933-   ). Vicente Leñero, a noted journalist, playwright, and novelist, was born in Guadalajara, Jalisco, on June 9, 1933. A student at UNAM and at the Escuela de Periodismo, he studied engineering and journalism. The recipient of a scholarship from the Instituto de Cultura Hispánica de Madrid, he went to Spain in 1956 to continue his studies. Many of his works have been highly acclaimed, thus Leñero has received a number of awards, including the international Biblioteca Breve Prize in 1963 and a fellowship from the Centro de Escritores Mexicanos where he studied with Juan José *Arreola. Some of his most important works are highlighted below.

His first published work, a collection of stories entitled *La polvareda y otros cuentos* (The Cloud of Dust and Other Stories) (1959), focuses on the inherent conflicts between city and country life. Two years later, in 1961, he published his first novel, *La voz adolorida* (The Afflicted Voz), a monologue of a mentally ill man whose moments of lucidity are vividly contrasted with his periods of insanity.

In another novel, *Los albañiles* (The Bricklayers, 1964), Leñero tackles the ethics of the Mexican judicial system and focuses on such matters as guilt, using both traditional and experimental narrative techniques. The novel, posing questions of the working man's environment, deals with the assassination of a guard of a building undergoing construction. The later stage version of *Los albañiles* was even more highly acclaimed than the novel.

A few years later, Leñero published *A fuerza de palabras* (By Dint of Words) (1967), a continuation of *La voz adolorida*. Structured without paragraphs, the novel does have many realistic characteristics. Time, like a lightning flash, disappears, leaving only space filled with memories and minute details.

Estudio Q (Studio Q, 1965), another novel, looks at the differences between truth and illusion. A television actor is unable to separate his real life from his role, therefore confusing his two "realities," losing his sense of authenticity. Leñero demonstrates many technical advances in this work. The stage version of *Estudio Q*, called *La carpa*, also won critical applause.

In *El garabato* (The Scrawl, 1967) he also displays great narrative and technical versatility. Using the genre of the detective story, Leñero writes a book in which there are several narrative levels that do not merge and only the inner novel is completed, the other elements ironically and purposefully unfinished. The text of a manuscript called "El garabato" is contained within the larger novel. Through the use of a fictitious writer, Leñero ingeniously frames a novelistic structure in which what matters most is how what happens is told. The novel raises questions about truth, fiction, and responsibility.

Many of Leñero's works exhibit a decidedly Christian attitude. The author challenges the Church to act responsably in dealing with moral and ethical issues. When Father Lemercier introduced psychoanalysis into a Benedictine monastery in Cuernavaca, the event caused quite a stir. Studies determined that often candidates for the priesthood had ulterior motives. Inspired by and as a reaction to the controversy created by this situation, in 1969 Leñero published a play, *Pueblo rechazado* (A Rejected People), in which he examines the conflicting attitudes (particularly liberal versus traditional) prevalent at the time.

Pueblo rechazado was followed almost immediately by *Compañeros* (Companions) in 1970, a play focusing on an attempt to understand what took the protagonist (purportedly Che Guevara) to Bolivia and to his death. Dramatic tension is heightened by the interplay of Guevara's conflicting personality characteristics, effectively created by the use of two Guevaras.

His play *El juicio* (The Trial) (1972) deals with the trial of José de León Toral and Concepción Acevedo, accused of the assassination of President-elect Alvaro Obregón in 1928. He has also written a dramatic version of Oscar Lewis's *Los hijos de Sánchez* (The Children of Sánchez).

Leñero published two other significant works in the 1970s: *Redil de ovejas* (Flock of Sheep) (1973) and *El evangelio de Lucas Gavilán* (The Gospel According to Lucas Gavilán (1979). Reflecting the dogmatic viewpoint of the Roman Catholic Church in Mexico, *Redil de ovejas* centers on a conflict between Mexican Catholics and Mexican communists. Somewhat similar in theme, *El evangelio de Lucas Gavilán* parodies the Gospel of Luke, set in contemporary Mexico. A caustic satire of society, Leñero deals with the pain and conflicts of the working class poor.

Leñero published a prize-winning, suspense-filled play, *La mudanza* (The Move) (1980), about the problems and tribulations of a couple when they move to a mysterious colonial house. Although the action is simple, the couple snipe at each other constantly. The play has been described as a gripping and chilling work of sociopolicial importance. An unexpected twist occurs when the "miserables" take over the house.

Cajón del sastre (The Tailor's Drawer) (1981) is an anthology of Leñero's first short stories and periodical articles. Some of his stories would later be incorporated in his novels. In the same year, he also published *Martirio de Morelos* (Morelos' Martyrdom), which captures the final days of the Mexican patriot. The historical account of judicial and religious sanctions against Morelos is re-created in the work. To reflect the narrative voice, Leñero uses a "lector" (reader). In 1982, the author published *Vivir del teatro* (Living Off the Theater), a sometimes humorous, sometimes distancing compendium of memories about his plays and novels, plus information about his journalistic activities. The book also includes a kaleidoscopic view of contemporary Mexican literary life.

La gota de agua (The Drop of Water, 1984) is a novel about water shortages in Mexico City and the problems that the situation creates, a problem experienced by Leñero himself. The work is very detailed and sometimes tedious because of the numerous explanations regarding plumbing and hydraulic engineering.

A pioneer of both the "nonfiction" novel and of documentary theater, Leñero, through his works, has been able to successfully integrate several pressing societal concerns. Among these are the contrast between official versions of current events and of history and actual fact, questions of morality and social justice, and the relationship between reality and illusion. His novels deal more with contemporary issues and events, while his dramatic works tend more toward expository treatment of historical matters.

WORKS: *La polvareda y otros cuentos* (The Cloud of Dust and Other Stories) (México: Edit. Jus, 1959). *Los albañiles* (The Bricklayers), novel (Barcelona: Editorial Seix Barral, 1964). *Estudio Q* (Studio Q), novel (México: Joaquín Mortiz, 1965). *El garabato* (The Scrawl) (México: Joaquín Mortiz, 1967). *A fuerza de palabras* (By Dint of Words), novel (Buenos Aires: Centro Editor de América Latina, 1967). *El derecho de llorar y otros reportajes* (The Right to Cry and Other Articles) (México: Instituto Nacional de la Juventud Mexicana, 1968). *La zona rosa y otros reportajes* (The Red-Light District and Other Articles) (México: Instituto Nacional de la Juventud

Mexicana, 1968). *Pueblo rechazado* (Rejected Town), theater (México: Joaquín
Mortiz, 1969). *Compañeros* (Companions), theater, in *Diálogos* (Mexico) 6, 2 (March-
April 1970): 14-27. "¿Por qué un teatro documental?," in *La Vida Literaria* (Mexico)
1, 4 (May 1970): 8-9. *El juicio, el jurado de León Toral y la madre Conchita* (The
Trial, the Jury of León Toral and Mother Conchita) theater (México: Joaquín Mortiz,
1972). *Redil de ovejas* (Flock of Sheep) (México: Joaquín Mortiz, 1973). *El evangelio
de Lucas Gavilán* (The Gospel According to Lucas Gavilán) (Barcelona: Seix Barral,
1979). *La mudanza* (The Move), photos by Rogelio Cuéllar, theater (México: Joaquín
Mortiz, 1980). *Cajón de sastre* (Tailor's Drawer), stories (México: Editorial Univ.
Autómona de Puebla, 1981). *Martirio de Morelos* (Martyrdom of Morelos),
documentary-drama (México: Editorial Ariel y Seix Barral, 1981). *Vivir del teatro*
(Living Off the Theater) (México: Joaquín Mortiz, 1982). *La gota de agua* (The
Drop of Water), novel (México: Plaza & Janés, 1984).

BIBLIOGRAPHY: Danny J. Anderson, "Genre and Subgenre in the Novels of
Vicente Leñero," *DAI* 47, 2 (Aug. 1986): 540A; *The Novelist as Critic* (n.p.: Peter
Lang, 1989). Huberto Batis, Review of *Los albañiles*, in *La Cultura en México* 154
(Jan. 27, 1965): xvii; Review of *Estudio Q*, in *La Cultura en México* 177 (July 7, 1976)
xiv. Mario Benedetti, "México en el pantógrafo de Vicente Leñero," in his *Letras del
continente mestizo*, 2nd ed. (Montevideo: Arca, 1969), 232-36. María Elvira
Bermúdez, review of *Estudio Q*, in *Diograma de la Cultura* (Jan. 9, 1966): 3. Francisco
Beverido Duhalt, "Mantener su verdad entre nosotros [*El juicio*]," in *Conjunto* 19
(1974): 105-8. Judith I. Bissett, "Constructing the Alternative Version: Vicente
Leñero's Documentary and Historical Drama," in *Latin American Theatre Review* 18,
2 (Spring 1985): 71-78. Jacqueline Eyring Bixler, "Historical (Dis)Authority in
Leñero's *Martirio de Morelos*," in *Gestos* 2 (Nov. 1986): 87-97. Teresa Bolet
Rodríguez, "Modalidades del caso y del proceso jurídico en el drama hispano-
americano," *DAI* 47, 12:(June 1987): 4405A-46A. Jorge Campos, "Letras de América.
Colombia y México: dos novelas [*Los albañiles*]," in *Insula* 219 (1965): 11. Emmanuel
Carballo, "La novela y el cuento," review of *Los albañiles*, in *La Cultura en México*
151 (Jan. 6, 1965): 11. Gabriel Careaga, "La novela," review of *Estudio Q*, in *México
en la Cultura* 876 (Jan. 2, 1966): 3. Fred M. Clark and María A. Salgado,
"Documentary Theatre in Mexico: Vicente Leñero's *Pueblo rechazado*," in *Romance
Notes* 13 (1971): 54-60. Lucie Clark, "[*Los albañiles*]," in *Cuadernos Americanos* 162
(1969): 219-23. Fernando Cruz, "The Documentary Theater of Vicente Leñero," *DAI*
46, 12 June, 1986): 3731A. José Donoso, "Vicente Leñero, un enriquecimiento de la
novela mexicana," in *La Cultura en México* 155 (Feb. 3, 1965): xii-xiv. Beatriz Espejo,
"Entrevista con Vicente Leñero," in *Ovaciones* 176 (May 23, 1965): 4-5. Luciana
Figuerola, "Los códigos de veridicción en *El garabato* de Vicente Leñero," in *Semiosis*
4 (Jan.-June 1980): 31-59. David Williamm. Foster, comp., *A Dictionary of
Contemporary Latin American Authors* (Tempe: Center for Latin American Studies,
Arizona State University, 1975), 59; *Handbook of Latin American Literature* (New
York: Garland, 1987), 394-95. Lucía Garavito, "La narración y la focalización como
base para un análisis de la novelística de Vicente Leñero," in *Semiosis* 4 (Jan.-June
1980): 61-82. Lois S. Grossman, "*Los albañiles*, novel and play: A Two-Time
Winner," in *Latin American Theatre Review* 9, 2 (1976): 5-12; "*Redil de ovejas*: A
New Novel from Leñero," in *Romance Notes* 17 (1976): 127-30. Joel Hancock,
"Vicente Leñero's Recent Drama: *La mudanza* as 'Theatre of Cruelty,'" in *From Pen
to Performance: Drama as Conceived and Performed*, edited by Karelisa V. Hartigan

(Lanham, Md.: University Press of America, 1983), 43-50. Blanca Haro, "Vicente Leñero: mi soledad es mi libertad," in *La Cultura en México* 194 (Nov. 3, 1965): xiii. Tamara Holzapfel, "Leñero: el teatro como institución moral," in *Texto Crítico* 10 (1978): 23-31; "*Pueblo rechazado*: Educating the Public through Reportage," in *Latin American Theatre Review* 10, 1 (1976): 15-21. Owen L. Kellerman, "*Los albañiles* de Vicente Leñero: Estudio de la víctima," in *Hispanófila* 70 (Sept. 1980): 45-55. Walter M. Langford, "Vicente Leñero: A Mexican Graham Greene?," in his *The Mexican Novel Comes of Age* (Notre Dame: University of Notre Dame Press, 1971), 151-67. John M. Lipski, "Vicente Leñero: Narrative Evolution as Religious Search," in *Hispanic Journal* 3, 2 (Spring 1982): 41-59. Iris Josefina Ludmer, "Vicente Leñero, *Los albañiles*. Lector y actor," in *Nueva novela latinoamericana*, edited by Jorge Lafforgue (Buenos Aires: Paidós, 1969-1972), vol 1, 194-208. Sharon Magnarelli, "Una entrevista con Vicente Leñero," in *Gestos: Teoría y práctica del Teatro Hispánico* 3, 6 (Nov. 1988): 140-47. José Luis Martínez Morales, "Leñero: Ficción de la realidad, realidad de la ficción," in *Texto Crítico* 10, 29 (May-Aug. 1984): 173-87; "Asesinato, la novela del lector," in *Texto Crítico* 13, 36-37 (1987): 54-67. María Luisa Mendoza, "*Los albañiles* construyeron una casota sólida para la novelística mexicana," in *El Día* (Jan. 17, 1965): 4. Eugene Moretta, "Sergio Magaña and Vicente Leñero: Prophets of an Unredeemed Society," in *Hispanic Journal* 2, 2 (Spring 1981): 51-70. Kirsten F. Nigro, "Entrevista a Vicente Leñero," in *Latin American Theatre Review* 18, 2 (Spring 1985): 79-82; "La mudanza de *La mudanza* de Vicente Leñero," in *Revista Canadiense de Estudios Hispánicos* 12, 1 (Autumn 1987): 57-69. Julio Ortega, "Un ejercicio narrativo de Leñero," in his *La contemplación y la fiesta*, 2nd ed. (Caracas: Monte Avila, 1969), 183-88. José Emilio Pacheco, "Dos novelas de Vicente Leñero," in *Diálogos* 6 (1965): 38-40. Elena Poniatowska, "La seriedad del escritor Vicente Leñero," in *El Día* (Nov. 1, 1965): 4. Angelica Prieto Inzunza, "Componente discursiva y estructuras profundas en *Los albañiles*," in *Semiosis* 16 (Jan.-June 1986): 73-98. Malkah Rabell, "*El juicio* y el caso de Aarón Hernán," in *Revista de la Universidad de México* 26, 9 (1972): 39-40. Salvador Reyes Nevares, "Leñero: la internacionalización de nuestra novela," in *La Cultura en México* 165 (April 14, 1965): xvi. Humberto Robles, "Aproximaciones a *Los albañiles* de Vicente Leñero," in *Revista Iberoamericana* 73 (1970): 579-99. Darío Ruiz Gómez, "*Los albañiles*," in *Eco* 63 (1965): 321-324. Gustavo Sainz, "Temática, proyección y técnica en el arte renovado del cuento," in *México en la Cultura* 764 (Nov. 10, 1963): 3, 5. George O. Schanzer, "El medio tiene un mensaje, en Vicente Leñero," in *Actas del VIII Congreso de la asociación internacional de hispanistas*, edited by A. David Kossoff et al. (Madrid: Istmo, 1986). David Jon Schuster, "A Critical Introduction to Three Plays of the Mexican Revolution: Rodolfo Usigli, *El gesticulador*; Vicente Leñero, *El juicio*; Jorge Ibargüengoitia, *El atentado*," *DAI* 48, 5 (Nov. 1987): 1060A. Mary L. Seale, "Two Views of Contemporary Mexico," in *SAB* 41, 4 (1976): 48-55. Andrés Sorel, Review of *Los albañiles*, in *Cuadernos Hispanoamericanos* 195 (March 1966): 579-82. Charles M. Tatum, "*El juicio*," in *Chasqui* 2, 1 (1972): 55-57. "Vicente Leñero," in *Los narradores ange el público* (México: Joaquín Mortiz, 1966-1967), vol 1, 175-88. Ramón Xirau, "*La voz adolorida*," in *La Palabra y el Hombre* 22 (1962): 311-13.

JEANNE C. WALLACE

LEON FELIPE. See CAMINO Galicia, León Felipe.

LIRA Alvarez, Miguel Nicolás — 369

LERIN, Manuel (1915-), poet and critic. Lerín was born in Atlixco, State of Puebla, where he began his university studies. He later received a degree in law at the Universidad Nacional Autónoma de México in Mexico City. Lerin's literary works were first published in the magazines *Taller Poetico* and *Cuadernos de Valle de México*. He was a member of the editorial board of the magazine *América* and has written critical articles for *El Nacional*.

WORKS: Anthologies: *29 cuentistas mexicanos actuales* (29 Mexican Short Story Writers), edited and notes by Marco Antonio Millán (México: Ed. de la *Revista America*, 1945). *Juan M. Mateo: polígrafo liberal* (Juan M. Mateos: Liberal Poligrapher) (México: Sec. de Ed. Pub., 1967). *Neruda y México* (Neruda and Mexico) (México: B. Costa-Amic, 1973). Poetry: *Canto a la Revolución Mexicana* (Song to the Mexican Revolution) (México, 1949). *Proclama a Juárez* (Civil Words to Juárez) (México, 1957). *Palabras civiles* (Civil Words) (México: D. de B., 1953). *Glosa Política* (Political Gloss) (México, 1958). *Contra reloj* (Against the Clock) (México: B. Costa-Amic, 1978).

BIBLIOGRAPHY: Antonio Castro Leal, *La poesía mexicana moderna*, Letras Mexicanas, no 12 (México: FCE, 1953), 417. Aurora M. Ocampo de Gómez and Ernesto Prado Velázquez, *Diccionario de escritores mexicanos* (México: UNAM, 1967), 193.

JOAN SALTZ

LIRA Alvarez, Miguel Nicolás (1905-1961). Miguel N. Lira was born in Tlaxcala, Tlaxcala, on October 14, 1905. A lawyer by profession, he also became a professor of literature, a printer, an editor and a writer. He served his government as director of publishing for the Ministry of Public Education, Supreme Court secretary, and district judge in Chiapas and Tlaxcala. He also founded the National University Press and the Fábula Publishing Company, and edited *Huytlale*, a literary review.

   Lira was a poet, playwright, and novelist who found inspiration in "popular" themes, legends, and ballads. With the publication of *Tú* (You) at the age of twenty, he established himself as a fine lyric poet. His career in the theater began in 1938 with the debut of his *Vuelta a la tierra* (Return to the Soil). The initial novel of this already established poet and playwright, *Donde crecen los tepozanes* (Where the "Tepozanes" Grow), is perhaps his best-known work. A legendary story of an Indian in a Tlaxcalan village, with scenes of witchcraft and local customs, a work that presents the partial synthesis of European and Indian cultures, this novel testifies to Lira's ability to express the "popular" through dialogue, dramatic expression and lyric sensitivity. Lira established himself as a novelist of the Mexican Revolution with the publication of his prize-winning *La escondida* (The Hidden One) and *Mientras la muerte llega* (While Death Arrives).

WORKS: Poetry: *Tú* (You) (Tlaxcala: Imprenta de Tlaxcala, 1925). *La guayaba* (The Guava) (Tlaxcala: El Gobierno de Tlaxcala, 1927). *Corrido de Domingo Arenas* (Ballad of Domingo Arenas) (México: Ed. Alcancía, 1932). *Segunda soledad* (Second Solitude) (México: Ed. Fábula, 1933). *México-pregón* (Mexican Announcement) (México: Ed. Fábula, 1933). *Coloquio de Linda y Domingo Arenas* (Linda and

Domingo Arena's Colloquy) (México: Ed. Fábula, 1934). *Tlaxcala, ida y vuelta* (Round Trip to Tlaxcala) (Tlaxcala: Talleres Gráficos del Estado, 1935). *Retablo del indio recién nacido* (Altarpiece of the Recently Born Child) (Tlaxcala: Talleres Gráficos del Estado, 1935). *Música para baile* (Music for Dancing) (México: Ed. Fábula, 1936). *Corrido-són* (Sound of the Ballad) (México: Ed. Fábula, 1937). *En el aire de olvido* (In the Air of Oblivion) (México: Ed. Fábula, 1937). *Corrido de Alfonso Reyes* (Ballad of Alfonso Reyes) (México: Ed. Fábula, 1938). *Si con los ojos* (If with Your Eyes) (México: Ed. Fábula, 1938). *Carta de amor* (Love Letter) (México: Ed. Fábula, 1938). *Corrido del marinerito* (Ballad of the Little Sailor) (México: Ed. Fábula, 1941). *Canción para dormir a Pastillita* (Song to Put Pastillita to Sleep) (México: SEP, 1943). *Romance de la noche maya* (Ballad of the Mayan Evening) (México: Ed. Fábula, 1944). *Soneto a la niña pensativa* (Sonnet for the Pensive Girl) (México: Imp. Cervantina, 1956). *Corrido de amor a Tapachula* (Love Ballad for Tapachula) (Tlaxcala: Huytlale, 1958). *Viva el Obispo Munive* (Long Live Bishop Munive) (Tlaxcala: Estrada, 1959). *Catarino Maravillas* (Tlaxcala: Talleres Gráficos del Gobierno, 1959). *Acto de Gracias* (Act of Thanksgiving) (Tlaxcala: Estrada, 1960). *Carta abierta a la Revolución* (Open Letter to the Revolution) (México: Estaciones, 1961). *La guayaba y otros documentos* (The Guava and Other Documents) (México: Nueva Voz, 1968). Plays: *Vuelta a la tierra* (Return to the Soil) (México: Ed. Fábula, 1940). *Linda* (México: Ed. Fábula, 1942). *Carlota de México)* (Carlota of México) (México: Ed. Fábula, 1943). *El diablo volvió al infierno* (The Devil Returned to Hell) (México: Ed. Fábula, 1946). Novels: *Donde crecen los tepozanes* (Where the "Tepozanes" Grow) (México: EDIAPSA, 1948). *La escondida* (The Hidden One) (México: EDIAPSA, 1948). *Una mujer en soledad* (A Woman Alone) (México: FCE, 1956). *Mientras la muerte llega* (While Death Arrives) (México: Libro-Mex., 1958). Other Works: *Andrés Quintana Roo* (México: Eds. de la Universidad Nacional, 1936). *Mi caballito blanco* (My Little White Horse) (México: SEP, 1943). *Itinerario hasta el Tacaná* (Itinerary to Tacaná) (México: Eds. de Andrea, 1958).

BIBLIOGRAPHY: Raúl Arreola Cortés, "La influencia lorquiana en Miguel N. Lira," *Revista Hispánica Moderna* 8, 4 (Oct. 1942): 304-20; *Miguel N. Lira: el poeta y el hombre* (México: Ed. Jus, 1977); "Notas sobre la obra poética de Miguel N. Lira," *Humanitas* 4 (1963): 257-68. John S. Brushwood, *México in Its Novel* (Austin: University of Texas Press, 1966), 14-16, 25. Manuel Pedro González, *Trayectoria de la novela en México* (México: Eds. Botas, 1951), 367-73. Raymond L. Grismer and Mary B. MacDonald, *Vida y obras de autores mexicanos* (Havana: Ed. Alfa O'Reilly, 1945), 93-95. Antonio Magaña Esquivel, *La novela de la revolución mexicana* (México: Ed. Porrúa, 1974), 168-74. Alfredo Ortiz Morales, "Miguel N. Lira: vida y obra," Ph.D. Diss., University of Southern California, 1966.

ROBERT K. ANDERSON

LITERATURE OF THE BAROQUE IN MEXICO. The European Baroque spread to all the Latin American territories, especially where there had been major indigenous civilizations, as was the case of the territory of New Spain. But, as studies have indicated, America had been baroque much before the arrival of the Europeans: the essential features and characteristics of pre-Hispanic art and literature coincided with the Western concept of the baroque. The European Baroque arrived in seventeenth-century America and encountered an indigenous baroque which it struggled against, rejected, or incorporated into a new form that remained long after Spain had abandoned its Baroque in favor of Neoclassicism. America's vision of life and literature continues to be classified as neo-baroque; it is present in the works of many of its contemporary authors.

In literature the Baroque probably had its greatest positive evaluation in the *Apologético* (1662), by the Peruvian Luis de Espinosa Medrano, el Lunarejo. In this important work Espinosa Medrano defends and praises Luis de Góngora's "culterano" style, less than forty years after the death of the author of the *Soledades*, against the attacks of the Portuguese Manuel de Faria y Sousa. Twentieth-century re-evaluation commences with Pedro *Henríquez Ureña who considers Bernardo de Balbuena the true initiator of this new Baroque style. This style incorporates Góngora, Lope , and Quevedo in a synthesis different from the Spanish "conceptismo" and "culteranismo." Emilio Carilla believes that the characteristics found in the European Baroque (contention, opposition and antithesis, embellishment, individualization of that which is ugly and grotesque, disillusionment, transcendence of religious ideals) are also present in the American Baroque, although to a lesser degree. Mariano Picón-Salas, in *De la conquista a la independencia* (From the Conquest to Independence), takes into consideration the historial and social differences between Spain and America when he describes what he terms "El barroco de Indias" (The Baroque of the Indies). Paul Westheim in his *Ideas fundamentales del arte prehispánico en México* (1957) (Fundamental Ideas of Pre-Hispanic Art in Mexico) offered a thesis, influenced by Worringer and Ernst Cassirer, of a mythic conception of pre-Hispanic reality. Based on Westheim's theory, Alfredo Roggiano has offered his own conclusions about the American Baroque. Among the characteristics of the indigenous baroque, which makes it unique and different from its European counterpart, Roggiano enumerates the following: it stems from myth, that is, reality is myth; immanence of reality: the magical does not know causal contradiction, the deformed tragic is not an allusion but a presence; the invisible becomes visible by the use, among other elements, of animal idols and symbols, grotesque forms of sculpture and of the identification of meaning; more than doing, it is a being, presence captured according to a specific mythic sense or meaning, incarnation of deities or metaphysical concepts. Contemporary authors like José Lezama Lima and Severo Sarduy, who have explained the American Baroque in important essays, have incorporated it into their work, and it is an essential element of their vision of the world and of literature.

Irving A. Leonard in his book *Baroque Times in Mexico* (1959) indicates that the Baroque enters the New World for the first time with the arrival in Mexico of the archbishop and viceroy of New Spain, Fray García Guerra. It coincides also with the arrival in the colonies at the beginning of the sixteenth century of the *cancioneros* (collections of lyrical poems) and *romanceros* (collection of Spanish Romances), where Góngora's poetry appears, and with Pedro de Espinosa's *Las flores de poetas ilustres* (1605) (Flowers of Illustrious Poets). Mexican colonial life was very propitious for the development of Baroque literature. The capital of New Spain, built upon the ruins of the Aztec capital, Tenochtitlán, had become the center of New World civilization. Education had reached new heights, new schools were opened, and the university had been founded. The history, language, and culture of pre-Columbian civilizations were carefully studied, thus creating new branches in philology and history. Seventeenth-century New Spain was a more civilized, stronger, and more prosperous society than that of New England. Only a minority of its inhabitants, however, had access to the two great institutions of learning of the time: the Church and the university. Next to those two, the court was the other cultural center whose main preoccupation was aesthetic and social. Octavio *Paz describes the society of New Spain as minoritary, masculine, learned, indigenous, clerical, "conceptista," and affected, where the cultural exchange would be divided between the Church in the form of a sermon, the classroom in the form of a lesson, and at the court in the form of a "tertulia." The writers coming from Spain brought with them the Italianate and humanistic tradition of Garcilaso and the Spanish Renaissance. These writers exerted their influence and opened new avenues of expression. Some of those who came stayed. One of the first peninsular writers to visit New Spain was the novelist Mateo Alemán, the author of *El pícaro Guzmán de Alfarache* (The Rascal Guzmán de Alfarache), who arrived with Fray García Guerra's entourage in 1608. One year later, he published his *Ortografía castellana* (Castillian Orthography), and in 1613, his *Sucesos de D. Fray García Guerra, Arzobispo de México* (Events in the Life of Fray García Guerra, Archbishop of Mexico) and *Oración fúnebre* (Funeral Chant). Other peninsular literary figures made their presence felt, among them Luis de Belmonte Bermúdez, who in 1609 published in Mexico his poem *Vida del Padre Maestro Ignacio de Loyola* (Life of Father Ignacio de Loyola); Diego Mejía, who translated Ovidio's *Heroidas*; and the poets Juan de la *Cueva and Gutierre de *Cetina. The first Mexican-born poet who distinguished himself was Francisco de *Terrazas (1525?-1600?); three of his sonnets survive in the manuscript anthology entitled *Flores de varia poesía* (Flowers of Varied Verse) (1577).

Bernardo de *Balbuena (1561?-1627) is recognized as the poet who marks in Mexico the transition from the Renaissance to the Baroque. The author of a bucolic novel written in verse, *Siglo de Oro en las selvas de Erifile* (Golden Age in the Jungles of Erifile) (1608) and of an an epic poem entitled *El Bernardo, o victoria de Roncesvalles* (Bernardo, or Victory at Roncesvalles) (1624), he is best known for his poem *Grandeza mejicana* (Mexican Grandeur) (1604), in which he lavishly praises the city of Mexico. The qualities and virtues of the capital of New Spain are greatly exaggerated; we find here a certain baroqueness which has been attributed to the Mexican landscape itself but which obviously has also to do with literary modes and traditions. Mexicans continued reading the peninsular Baroque writers, especially Góngora, but also Quevedo and Calderón. Poetry flourished in seventeenth-century New Spain. There were many imitators, most of them clerics and some of them, certainly, lacking in imagination. Some opponents of the Baroque considered the poetry of this period, with a few exceptions, mediocre and lacking in good taste. They criticized the Gongorists' dependence on Latin and their use of "empty words." What made the poetry of the period sometimes frustrating, however, was not so much lack of quality but of originality in its themes. Whatever their deficiencies, these writers were as a group generally superior to both their Neoclassic and Romantic counterparts. The poets of the seventeenth-century displayed their talent and virtuosity in poetic jousts and triumphant arches, such as the one celebrated at the Universidad de México in 1682, in honor of the Immaculate Conception. Over 500 entries were received; 68 were given awards. Carlos de Sigüenza y Góngora talks about them in his work entitled *Triumpho Parthénico*. These poets were the maximum respresentatives of Gongorism in New Spain. Among the poets who participated in the Triunfo Parthénico, as the event was called, were Luis de Sandoval y Zapata, Juan de Guevara, José López Avila, Pedro Muñoz de Castro, Francisco Ayerra y

Santa María, and don Carlos de Sigüenza y Góngora. In addition to the abovementioned Triunfo Parthénico, some of the most prominent poetic jousts of the period were the Festivo aparato con que la Compañía de Jesús celebró a San Francisco de Borja (Festive Pomp by the Company of Jesus in Honor of St. Francis of Borja); the Funerales pompas de D. Felipe IV y plausible aclamación de D. Carlos II (The Funeral Pomp of Philip IV and Plausible Acclaim of Charles II); the Neptuno alegórico en honor del Conde de la Laguna (Allegorical Neptune in Honor of the Count of Lagunas); and the Marte católico, dedicado al Duque de Albuquerque (Catholic Tuesday, Dedicated to the Duke of Albuquerque). Among the best writers of this period, the following should be mentioned: Luis de Sandoval y Zapata, member of an illustrious Mexican family, author of several interesting sonnets to the Virgin of Guadalupe and of a historic "romance" to the Avila brothers, decapitated in Mexico City for conspiring for Mexican independence; the poet and playwright Agustín de Salazar y Torres, whose work published in two volumes in *Cítara de Apolo* (Apollo's Zither) (Madrid; 1681, 1689) shows the influences of Calderón and Góngora, was praised by Calderón himself, and he, in turn, influenced other important Mexican writers of his time; Matías de *Bocanegra, the Jesuit author of the popular *Canción a la vista de un desengaño* (Allegorical Song of Disillusion), a parable about the excellences and advantages of the religious life; Juan de Guevara, chaplain of the monastery of St. Inés, a fine Gongorist poet, collaborated with Sor Juana Inés de la *Cruz in the play, *Amor es más laberinto* (Love Is a Labyrinth); Juan de Palafox y Mendoza, viceroy of New Spain and bishop of Puebla, and author of *Varón de deseos* (Man of Desires), *Cartas pastorales* (Pastoral Letters), *Año espiritual* (Spiritual Year), and *El Pastor de Nochebuena* (The Christmas-Eve Shepherd), who, in spite of his expressed wish to write with clarity and precision, gave us some fine pieces of Baroque prose. But clearly the two most important figures of the colonial Mexican Baroque are Carlos de Sigüenza y Góngora (1645-1700) and Sor Juana Inés de la Cruz (1648-1695).

Carlos de Sigüenza y Góngora, Baroque poet in the "culterano" style, historian, scientist, professor of astrology and mathematics, was a Jesuit priest with a profound knowledge of indigenous cultures. We detect in his work the beginnings of a Mexican national identity: in his *Teatro de virtudes políticas* (Theater of Political Virtues), he juxtaposes biblical and classical figures with legendary Aztec leaders as models that should be followed by all wise leaders, and his *Primavera indiana* (Indian Spring) is a hymn to the Virgin of Guadalupe, the patron saint of Mexico. Sigüenza's rational mind and scientific knowledge makes him a precursor of Mexican Neoclassicism. His *Manifiesto filosófico contra los cometas* (Philosophical Manifiesto against Comets) was written to combat the superstitions of his time. Sigüenza's *Los infortunios de Alonso Ramírez* (The Misfortunes of Alonso Ramírez) is considered the Mexican precursor to *Fernández de Lizardi's picaresque novel, *El Periquillo Sarniento*.

Sor Juana Inés de la Cruz is the most outstanding literary figure not just of seventeenth-century Mexico but of all colonial America, and one of the most important in the history of Spanish American literature. Born Juana Inés Ramírez de Asbaje, in 1651, she rejected life at the court to became a nun, embracing the religious life at the Convent of San Jerónimo. Endowed with a great mind, she participated in the intellectual life of the times. Her well-known work, *Respuesta a Sor Filotea de la Cruz* (Answer to Sor Filotea), is an autobiographical document in which she feigned humility in order to defend her thirst for knowledge in all areas, including secular matters. She defends the rights of women to study and to acquire knowledge. Cultivating all the literary genres of her times, Sor Juana epitomizes the height of the Baroque in Mexico.

BIBLIOGRAPHY: Juan José Arróm, *Esquema generacional de la letras hispano-americanas. Ensayo de un método* (Bogotá, 1963). Steven Bell, "México," in *Handbook of Latin American Literature*, edited by William Foster (New York: Garland, 1987), 329-403. Emilio Carilla, *El barroco literario hispánico* (Buenos Aires: Nova, 1969); *La literatura barroca en Hispanoamérica* (Anaya: 1973). Juan Durán Duzio, "Reflexión en torno al llamado *barroco americano*," in *El barroco en América, XVII Congreso del IILT* (Madrid: Ediciones Cultura Hispánica del Centro Iberoamericano de Cooperación, 1978). Carlos González Peña, *Historia de la literatura mexicana* (México: Porrúa, 1949). Helmut Hatzfeld, *Estudios sobre le barroco* (Madrid, 1964). Pedro Henríquez Ureña, *Las corrientes literarias en la América española* (México: FCE, 1949). Raimuno Lazo, *Historia de la literatura hispanoamericana. El período colonial (1492-1780)* (México: Porrúa, 1965). Irving Leonard, *Baroque Times in Old Mexico* (Ann Arbor: University of Michigan Press, 1959). José Lezama Lima, *La expresión americana* (La Habana: Instituto Nacional de Cultura, 1957). José Luis Martínez, *De la naturaleza y carácter de la literatura mexicana* (México: FCE, 1960). Alfonso Méndez Plancarte, *Poetas novohispanos. Segundo Siglo (1621-1721)* (México: UNAM, 1944). Aurora M. Ocampo de Gómez and Ernesto Prado Velázquez, *Diccionario de escritores mexicanos* (México: UNAM, 1967). Edmundo O'Gorman, *La invención de América* (México: FCE, 1958); *Meditaciones sobre el criollismo* (México, 1970). José Pascual Buxó, *Góngora en la poesía novohispana* (México: UNAM, 1960). Octavio Paz, *Las peras del olmo*, 2nd ed. (México: UNAM, 1965); *Sor Juana Inés de la Cruz o Las Trampas de la Fe* (México: FCE, 1982). Mariano Picón Salas, *De la Conquista a la Independencia* (México: FCE, 1944). Alfredo A. Roggiano, "Acerca de dos barrocos: el de España y el de América," in *El Barroco en América. XVII Congreso del IILT* (Madrid: Ed. Cultura Hispánica del Centro Iberoamericano de Cooperación, 1978), 39-48. Luis Alberto Sánchez, *Góngora en América* (Quito: Imp. Nacional, 1927). Severo Sarduy, "El barroco y el neobarroco," in *América Latina en su literatura* (México: Siglo XXI--UNESCO, 1972), 167-84; *Barroco* (Buenos Aires: Editorial Sudamericana, 1974). Karl Vossler, *Escritores y poetas de España*, translated by Carlos Clavería (Buenos Aires, 1947). Paul Westheim, *Ideas fundamentales del arte prehispánico en México* (México: FCE, 1957).

                                              ALINA CAMACHO-GINGERICH

LIZALDE, Eduardo (1929-), poet, short-story writer and critic. Lizalde was born on July 14, 1929 in Mexico City and studied philosophy at the National University. He has traveled widely through Europe, the Soviet Union, Cuba and China. From 1954 to 1957, he contributed articles, essays, and poems regularly to the journal *Universidad de México,* and he has contributed work to a number of other prominent Mexican journals. He has directed and written film scripts in collaboration with Julio Pliego and also has been a film critic for television and radio. He has worked as editor of publishing for the National University and has also served as secretary of its summer schools.

Lizalde has written mostly poetry, but he has also published a collection of short stories and a study of Luis Buñuel. His poetry has an imaginative vitality that is captivating. His themes move from the political, social, and humorous to questions such as the nature of love and of the creative process. *Cada cosa es Babel* (Everything Is Babel) is a work that deals extensively with creativity. Animal imagery appears frequently in some of his later poetry. The tiger and other animals are powerful Darwinian and Hobbesian symbols not only for mankind's beastial and self interested nature, but also for his universal tendencies. The work *Memoria del tigre* (Memory of the Tiger) is a collection of several different works and offers a varied and representative selection of his work.

WORKS: Poetry: *La furia blanca* (The White Fury) (México: 1956). *La mala hora* (The Wicked Hour) (México: Los Presentes, 1956). *La tierra de Caín* (The Land of Cain), three poems by Lizalde, González Rojo, and Raúl Leiva) (México: Ideas de México, 1956). *Odesa y Cananea* (México: Libreria de M. Porrúa, 1958). *La sangre en general* (Blood in General) (México: 1959). *Cada cosa es Babel* (Everything is Babel) (México: Editorial Diana, 1969). *El tigre en la casa* (The Tiger in the House) (Guanajuato: Universidad de Guanajuato, 1970). *La zorra enferma* (The Sick Fox) (México: 1974). *Caza Mayor* (Major Hunt) (México: UNAM, 1979). *Autobiografía de un fracaso* (Autobiography of a Failure) (México: 1981). *Tercera Tenochtitlán* (Third Tenochtitlan) (México: Katun, 1982). *Memoria del tigre* (Memory of the Tiger) (México: Katun, 1983). *Tigre, tigre* (Tiger, Tiger) (México: Biblioteca joven, 1985). Stories: *La cámara* (The Chamber) (México: Imprenta Universitaria, 1960). Essays: *Luis Buñuel* (México: UNAM, 1962).

BIBLIOGRAPHY: Marco Antonio Campos, "Doce Preguntas a Eduardo Lizalde" *Revista de Bellas Artes* 24, new series (Nov.-Dec. 1975): 24-27. Marco Antonio Campos, "La garra y el corazón del tigre: Eduardo Lizalde entrevistado," *Vuelta* 10, 14 (May 1986): 46-50. Adolfo Castañón, "Una palabra visionaria," Review of *La zorra enferma*, in *Plural* 5, 3 (Dec. 1975): 64-5. Erika Domínguez Cervantes, "Enrique Lizalde: Actores y sindicalismo," *Plural* 12, 136 (Jan. 1983): 56-59. Heriberto García Rivas, *Historia de la literatura mexicana*, vol. 1 (México: Textos Universitarias, 1971), 359. Victor Manuel Mendiola, "Review of Memoria del tigre," *Vuelta* 7, 84 (Nov. 1983): 50-51. Josué Morales Caballero, "El arquetipo y sus predicados," *La Palabra y el Hombre* 36, new series (Oct.-Dec. 1980): 103-05. Jaime Moreno Villarreal "Más le queda al tigre cuando envejece," *Universidad de México* 34, 5 (Jan. 1980): 41-42. Aurora M. Ocampo de Gómez and Ernesto Prado Velázquez, *Diccionario de escritores mexicanos* (México: UNAM, 1967), 194-95. Guillermo Sheridan, Review of Caza mayor by Eduardo Lizalde," *Vuelta* 4, 38 (Jan. 1980): 35-37. Ramón Xirau, "Eduardo Lizalde en su Caza mayor," *Diálogos* 16, 92 (Mar-Apr. 1980): 47-48.

MARK FRISCH

LOBILLO, Jorge (1943-   ). Born in Jalapa, Veracruz, Lobillo never went beyond junior high school. When he was quite young, he began to publish in magazines and newspapers. He moved to Paris, where he lived for several years, then spent a short while in Barcelona.

His most important work, *Mutilación del agua* (Mutilation of Water) reflects his essential preoccupation -love- which he describes as passionate, erotic, sometimes frustrated, and occasionally given to tenderness and mercy.

During his first highly creative period, Lobillo's poetry reached its most climactic point. With a sensuality reminiscent of Arabic poetry, he sings to the human body and to nature, expressing the profound truth of essential solitude.

WORKS: *Provisión en fuga* (Provision in Escape) (Jalapa: Ed. Juglar, 1971). *Semana marítima y otros poemas* (Maritime Week and Other Poems) (Jalapa, Ed. El Gato, 1973). *Memoria: Integridad del sueño* (Memory: Integrity of the Dream) (Jalapa: Universidad Veracruzana, 1974). *Mutilación del agua* (Mutilation of Water) (México: El Milenio, 1981).

BIBLIOGRAPHY: Esther Hernández-Palacios and Angel José Fernández, *La poesía veracruzana* (Jalapa: Universidad Veracruzana, 1984).

ESTHER HERNANDEZ-PALACIOS

LOMBARDO de Caso, María (1905-1964). Lombando de Caso was born in Teziutlán, Puebla, on December 6, 1905. She studied philosophy and archaeology. After marrying Alfonso Caso, the renowned Mexican archaeologist, she collaborated with him in his professional endeavors.

Lombardo de Caso's literary output was not extensive. She published one volume of short stories and two novels. The former, *Muñecas de niebla* (Dolls of Fog), contains ten well-organized short narratives replete with rich and suggestive images. In this collection she continually evokes types and scenes, both real and invented, which were inspired by her childhood in her native town. Her first novel, *Una luz en la otra orilla* (A Light on the Other Shore), exhibits this same "realista-costumbrista" propensity. This adventure book alludes to the spiritual liberation of women and confirms the author's ability to say things simply, in everyday speech. In her short novel, *La culebra tapó el río* (The Snake Covered the River), Lombardo penetrates and depicts the Indian soul that remains hidden from and largely untouched by the mainstream of México.

WORKS: Short Stories: *Muñecas de niebla* (Dolls of Fog) (México: Imprenta Nuevo Mundo, 1955). Novels: *Una luz en la otra orilla* (A Light on the Other Shore) (México: FCE, 1959). *La culebra tapó el río* (The Snake Covered the River) (Xalapa: Universidad Veracruzana, 1962).

BIBLIOGRAPHY: I. Bar-Lewaw, Review of *La culebra tapó el rio*, by María Lombardo de Caso, *Hispania* 46, 4 (Dec. 1963): 858. Review of *Muñecas de niebla*, by María Lombardo de Caso, *Hispania* 46, 4 (Dec. 1963): 857-58. Luis Cardoza y Aragón, "María Lombardo de Caso," *Cuadernos Americanos* 136, 5 (Sept.-Oct. 1964): 216-23. "Homenaje a María Lombardo de Caso en el primer aniversario de su muerte," *La Cultura en México* 178 (July 14, 1965): i-vi. Luis Leal, Review of *Una luz en la otra orilla*, by María Lombardo de Caso, *Revista Hispánica Moderna* 27, 2 (April 1961): 161-62. Elena Poniatowska, "María Lombardo de Caso," *México en la Cultura*

541 (July 26, 1959): 1-2. Joseph Sommers, "El ciclo de Chiapas: nueva corriente literaria," *Cuadernos Americanos* 133, 2 (Mar.-April 1964): 246-61.

ROBERT K. ANDERSON

LOPEZ, Rafael (1873-1943), poet and journalist. Educated by private instructors and his own reading, López had become an outstanding new poet by the time he was thirty years old. His closest associates were Ramón *López Velarde, Enrique *González Martínez, Amado *Nervo, José Juan *Tablada, Jesús E. *Valenzuela, and Urbina, the latter of whom secured for López a career as public functionary. He taught Spanish literature, was director of the National General Archives, and was the first director of the Instituto de Investigaciones Estéticas of the Universidad Nacional.

A lifelong journalist, he was published in numerous newspapers and journals, among them *Mundo Ilustrado, Savia Moderna, Argos, Revista de Revistas, Nosotros, Revista Moderna, El Imparcial, El Independiente,* and *El Universal.* His column, Prosas transeúntes (Transient Prose), pseudonymously signed Lázaro Feel, became a famous section of *El Universal.* Only a small part of his journalistic production has been collected and published in a volume appropriately titled *Prosas transeúntes.* He published only one book of poetry, *Con los ojos abiertos* (With Open Eyes), which has appeared in a number of editions. His plastic imagery has been compared to that of Rubén Darío and José María Heredia, while his intonation resembles that of Salvador *Díaz Mirón and Santos Chocano. At times his expression rises above the Modernist sensibility and displays an intimate tone and lyric grace. The topics of his heroic poetry include economics, national heroes, evocations of historical episodes, descriptive re-creations of cities and countrysides, and expressions of the ideals of liberty and rebellion.

WORKS: POETRY: *Con los ojos abiertos* (With Open Eyes) (México: Biblioteca del Ateneo, 1912). *Poemas* (Poems) (México: Edic. Cultura, 1941). *La bestia de oro y otros poemas* (The Golden Beast and Other Poems) (México: Ed. Orientaciones, 1941). *Obra poética* (Poetic Work) (México: Ed. Universidad de Guanajuato, 1957). *La Venus de la Alameda* (The Venus of the Alameda), anthology (México: SEP, 1973). Prose: *Prosas transeúntes* (Transient Prose) (México: Aztlán, 1925); 2nd ed. (México: Ed. Bellas Artes, Dept. of Literature, 1966). *Crónicas escogidas* (Selected Chronicles) (México: FCE, 1970).

BIBLIOGRAPHY: Salvador Azuela, "Rafael López," *Novedades* 30 (July 1943): 3; "Un homenaje a Rafael López," *El Universal* (Jan. 3, 1953): 10; "El poeta de los volcanes," *El Universal* (Oct. 3, 1953). Huberto Batis, "Rafael López: *Prosas transeúntes,*" *El Heraldo Cultural*, Sunday Supplement of *El Heraldo de México* (Feb. 20, 1966): 15. Djed Bórquez, "Hombres de México. Rafael López," *Excelsior* (Jan. 11, 1963): 6, 8. Antonio Castro Leal, "Las correcciones en Rafael López," *El Hijo Pródigo,* 3 (1944): 71-77. Eduardo Colín, "Rafael López," *Novedades* (April 1912); *Verbo selecto* (México: Ed. México Moderno, 1922), 75-83. Salvador Cordero, "Con los ojos abiertos," *Nosotros* 1 (1912). Jorge Cuesta, *Antología de la poesía mexicana moderna* (México: Contemporáneos, 1928), 52. Alberto Dallal, Review of *Prosas transeúntes,* *Universidad de México* 20 (1966): 38. Genaro Estrada, *Poetas nuevos de México*

(México: Eds. Porrúa, 1916), 149-51. Genaro Fernández MacGregor, "Rafael López," *El Universal* (Nov. 21, 1920): 25-34; "Rafael López y la música," *El Universal* (Dec. 20, 1943); "El poeta Rafael López y la Academia," *El Universal* (Aug. 2, 1948). Jesús Flores Aguirre, "La sombra de Píndaro," *Papel de Poesía* (Sept. 1943). Carlos González Peña, "Rafael López," *El Mundo Ilustrado* (Nov. 1912). Raymond L. Grismer and Mary B. MacDonald, *Vida y obras de autores mexicanos* (La Habana: Ed. Alfa, 1945), 99-100. Daniel Gurrúa Urgell, "Rafael López," *Letras de México* (Aug. 15, 1943): 1-2. Max Henríquez Ureña, "Rafael López," *Revista Moderna* (Jan. 1908): 277-78. "Los de la nueva hora," *Crónica* (Guadalajara) Dec. 1907 (signed René d'Orange). Manuel Horta, "El banquete a Rafael López," *Antena* (Sept. 1924). José Luis Martínez, *Literatura mexicana siglo xx, 1910-1949* (México: Robredo, 1950), vol. 1, 9-10; vol. 2, 69. Miguel D. Martínez Rendón, "Evocación de Rafael López," *Elocuencia nuevo-leonesa*, edited by Genaro Salinas Quiroga (Monterrey: University of Nuevo León, 1956) 177-80. María del Carmen Millán, "De un poeta muerto," *Rueca 2* (1943): 35-37. Carlos Monsiváis, *La poesía mexicana del siglo XX* (México: Empresas Editoriales, S.A., 1966). Luis Noyola Vázquez, "Rafael López, transeúnte," in *Revista Mexicana de Cultura*," Sunday supplement of *El Nacional* (March 27, 1966). Roberto Núñez y Domínguez ("Roberto el Diablo"), *50 Close-ups* (México: Ed. Botas, 1935), 231-37. Gregorio Ortega, *Hombres, mujeres* (México: Aztlán, 1926); 2nd ed. (México: Ed. Bellas Artes, 1966), 31-36. Alfonso Reyes, "De re bibliográfica. *Con los ojos abiertos*," *Biblos 1* (1920): 81-84. José Juan Tablada, Review of *Con los ojos abiertos*, in *El Mundo Ilustrado* (Dec. 8, 1912). R.N.D., "Homenaje a Rafael López," *Revista de Revistas* (Aug. 1, 1943). Manuel Torres, "Rafael López, hierofante del arte," *El Nacional* (Aug. 9, 1953): 3, 7; (Aug. 16, 1953): 3, 5. Rafael Heliodoro Valle, "El libro de Rafael López (*Con los ojos abiertos*)," *Nosotros* (March 1914): 228-30. Various, "Homenaje al poeta Rafael López," *Revista Mexicana de Cultura*, Sunday supplement of *El Nacional* (Apr. 18, 1954). Xavier Villaurrutia, "A la memoria de Rafael López," *El Hijo Pródigo* (Aug. 1943): 321. Jesús Zavala, "El alma lírica de Rafael López," *El Universal* (July 18, 1943).

BARBARA P. FULKS

LOPEZ Chiñas, Gabriel (1911-) was born in Juchitán, Oaxaca. López Chiñas graduated as a lawyer from the Universidad Nacional Autónoma de México. He was the director of Radio Universidad and a teacher of Spanish and world literature in elementary and secondary schools. His poetry and stories appear in many reviews and anthologies. In 1937, he edited *Neza*, a review dedicated to divulge Zapotecan culture. He has also worked with *Profils Poetiques*, a bilingual Spanish-French review. His work expresses the culture of the Zapotecan people. His bilingual publications (Zapotec-Spanish) denote his interest in promoting the culture and the language. *Juchitán. Canto segundo* (Juchitán. Second Song), poems about his homeland and childhood, is a book with heart-rending images of ancestral sorrow accumulated throughout the centuries. *Guendaxheela. El casamiento* (Guendaxheela. The Wedding) is narrative poetry detailing in simple language the life and customs of the Zapotecans. *Mentiras y chistes* (Lies and Jokes), a compilation from oral tradition, is an important contribution to Mexican culture.

WORKS: *Vinnigulasa. Cuentos de Juchitán* (Vinnigulasa. Stories from Juchitán) (México: Editorial Neza, 1940). *Conejo y coyote* (Rabbit and Coyote), Spanish, Zapotec, and English edition (México: Ed. Vinnigulasa, 1943). *Toloache* (México: Firmamento, 1947). *Canto del hombre a la tierra* (Song of Man to Earth) (México: Firmamento, 1951). *Los telares ilusos* (The Beguiled Looms) (México: Pliegos Gear, 1953). *Mar* (Sea) (México: Ed. del Autor, 1960). *Juárez* (México: Author's Edition, 1965). *Xhtlldxa Guendananna. Palabras de sabiduria* (Xhtlldxa Guendananna. Words of Wisdom), (Spanish-Zapotec ed.) (n.p.: n.p., 1969). *Mentiras y chistes* (Lies and Jokes), Zapotec-Spanish ed. (México: Pájaro Cascabel, 1967). *El concepto de la muerte entre los Zapotecas* (The Concept of Death among the Zapotecas) (México: Ed. Vinnigulasa, 1969). *Juchitán. Canto segundo* (Juchitán. Second Song) (México: Ed. Vinnigulasa, 1971). *Guendaxheela. El casamiento* (Guendaxheela. The Wedding), Zapotec-Spanish ed. (México: Complejo Editorial Mexicano, 1975). *El zapoteco y la literatura zapoteca del Istmo de Tehuantepec* (Zapotec and Zapotecan Literature of the Isthmus of Tehuantepec), Zapotec-Spanish ed. (n.p.: n.p., 1982).

BIBLIOGRAPHY: Anon., Bibliographical note in *Anuario del cuento mexicano 1960* (México: INBA, 1961), 146. Alberto Bonifaz Nuño, Review of *Vinnigulasa*, in *Estaciones* 4, 13 (1959): 115. Luis Leal, *Breve historia del cuento mexicano* (México: Ed. de Andrea, 1958), 118.

ALICIA G. WELDEN

LOPEZ Páez, Jorge (1922-), fiction writer and playwright. López Páez was born in Huatusco, Veracruz. He earned a law degree and studied literature at the National University. His most memorable works tend to focus on the world of children.

WORKS: Short Story: *El que espera* (He Who Waits) (México: Icaro, 1950). *Los mástiles* (The Masts) (México: Los presentes, 1955). *Los invitados de piedra* (The Stone-like Guests) (Jalapa: Universidad of Veracruzana, 1962). *Pepe Prida* (Pepe Prida) (México: Mortiz, 1965). *Mi hermano Carlos* (My Brother Carlos) (México: FCE, 1965). Novels: *El solitario atlántico* (The Solitary Atlantic) (México: FCE, 1958). *Hacia el amargo mar* (Toward the Bitter Sea) (Jalapa: Universidad of Veracruzana, 1964). *In Memoriam Tia Lude* (México: UNAM, 1974). *La costa* (The Coast) (México: Mortiz, 1980). Theater: *La última visita* (The Last visit) (México: Los Epigrafes, 1951).

BIBLIOGRAPHY: Huberto Batis, "La Cultura en México," supplement of *¡Siempre!* (April 21, 1965): 16; Review of *Hacia el amarqo mar*, in "La Cultura en México," supplement *¡Siempre!* (Aug. 11, 1965): 16. Emmanuel Carballo, "El pecado por exceso," *La Cultura en México* (Aug. 22, 1962): 15; Review of *Los invitados de piedra*, in "La cultura en México," supplement of *¡Siempre!* (Nov. 24, 1965): 17. Alfonso González, interview, California State University, Los Angeles, Oct. 2, 1989. Beatriz Reyes Nevares, "Con López Páez," in "La Cultura en México," supplement of *¡Siempre!* (Aug. 18, 1965): 16.

ALFONSO GONZALEZ

LOPEZ PORTILLO y Rojas, José (1850-1923), novelist, playwright, poet, critic, historian, travel writer. Born in Guadalajara on May 26, 1850, José López Portillo y Rojas was the son of a prominent Jalisco family. He studied law in Guadalajara, and after receiving his degree in 1871 he took a long trip, first to the United States, and then over the next three years through Europe, Egypt, and Palestine. On returning home to begin his law practice, he wrote and published his first book, a travelogue titled *Eqipto y Palestina, apuntes de viaje* (Egypt and Palestine, Notes of a Voyage) (1874). Once again in Guadalajara he married and began teaching law at the School of Jurisprudence. In addition to his practice and teaching he continued to write and also held a variety of public offices in the judiciary, in Congress, as governor of Jalisco and, finally, as secretary of foreign relations. In 1886 he founded *La República Literaria* along with Manuel Alvarez del Castillo and Esther *Tapia de Castellanos. He edited the journal for four years, including articles on science, art, and letters. He was named perpetual secretary of the Mexican Academy of the Lanquage in 1908 and director in 1916, a post in which he served until his death in Mexico City on (May 22, 1923).

López Portillo wrote on a wide variety of topics, including judicial concerns, philosophy, history, and religion. He authored poetry, short stories, legends, and theatrical pieces, but there is no doubt that he is best known as a writer of fiction. In his short fiction he shows himself to be a talented regionalist writer with naturalist influences. These works consist of *Seis leyendas* (Six Legends) (1883), *Novelas cortas* (Short Novels) (1900), *Sucesos y novelas cortas* (Incidents and Short Novels) (1903), and *Historias, historietas y cuentecillos* (Histories, Short Stories and Little Tales) (1918). Of these stories, Enrique Anderson Imbert singles out "En diligencia" (The Stagecoach) as a deft representation of the problem of the literary struggle between naturalism and romanticism. López Portillo is bestknown, nevertheless, for his full-length novels: *La parcela* (The Plot of Ground) (1895), *Los Precursores* (The Precursors) (1909), and *Fuertes y debiles* (The Strong and the Weak) (1919). The most famous of these, *The Plot of Ground*, tells the story of a dispute between two despotic landowners, Pedro Ruiz and Miguel Diza, who fight over a piece of land with little value, using all the dirty arms at their disposal while their children, Gonzalo and Ramona, fall in love and ultimately overcome the parental feud and marry, during a brief truce. J. Sapiña notes that the regional atmosphere is painted with a vigorous hand, and González Pego sees in the work the marked influence of Spanish contemporary, José María de Pereda. Salado Alvarez points out that love is revealed in the book through "warm humanity, affection for people and things, faith in life, progress and the fulfillment of all the great and good that inspires and pervades the author." In general, Emmanuel *Carballo, who re-edited and commented on López Portillo's important works in 1945, sees the author as one who, "like the majority of the members of his generation, lived in a world in which soars of a school in decline -- Romanticism -- concur with the foundations of another school that is being initiated -- Realism."

WORKS: Short Stories: *Seis leyendas* (Six Legends) (Guadalajara: Francisco Arroyo de Anda, 1883). *Novelas cortas* (Short Novels) (México: Agüeros, 1900). *Sucesos y novelas cortas* (Incidents and Short Novels) (México: Agüeros, 1903). *Historias, historietas y cuentecillos* (Histories, Short Stories and Small Tales) (Paris and México: Charles Bouret, 1918). *Cuentos completos* (Complete Stories), edited and with prologue by Emmanuel Carballo (Guada- lajara: Carballo, 1952). Novels: *La parcela*

(The Plot of Ground) (México: Agüeros, 1898). *Los Precursores* (The Precursors) (México: Agüeros, 1909). *Fuertes y debiles* (The Strong and the Weak) (México: Librería Española, 1919). Travel: *Egipto y Palestina, apuntes de viaje* (Egypt and Palestine, Notes of a Voyage) (México: Díaz de León and S. White, 1874). Poetry: *Armonías fugitivas* (Fugitive Harmonies) (Guadalajara: La República Literaria, 1892). Drama: *La Corregidora* (The Magistrate's Wife), unpublished, but premiered in Guadalajara in 1899. Criticism: *Rosario, la de Acuña* (Acuña's Rosario) (México: Librería Española, 1920).

BIBLIOGRAPHY: Carlos G. Amezaga, *Poetas mexicanos* (Buenos Aires: Pablo E. Coni and Sons, 1896), 342-47. Mariano Azuela, *Cien años de la novela mexicana* (México: Fondo de Cultura Economica, 1958). Emmanuel Carballo, prologue and editor of *Cuentos completos* (Complete Stories). Antonio Castro Leal, Prologue to *La parcela* (México; Porrúa, 1945). Heriberto García Rivas, *Historia de la literatura mexicana*, vol. 2 (México: Porrúa, 1972), 217. Carlos González Peña, *History of Mexican Literature* (Dallas: Southern Methodist University Press, 1943-1968), 317-18, 472. Sergio Howland Bustamante, *Historia de la literatura mexicana* (México: F. Trillas, 1967), 207. Roberto Núñez y Domínquez, *Centenarios cincuentenarios* (México: Talleres Gráficos de La Nación, 1951). Aurora M. Ocampo de Gómez and Ernesto Prado Velázquez, *Diccionario de escritores mexicanos* (México: UNAM, 1967), 198-200.

PATRICIA HART AND JOSEF HELLEBRANDT

LOPEZ VELARDE, Ramón (1888-1921), poet and essayist. López Velarde was one of the most important and authentic poetic voices in Spanish American literature in the period of transition from Modernism to the movements of the vanguard. Born on June 15, 1888, in Jérez (now Ciudad García) in the state of Zacatecas, the oldest son of nine children, he studied in the Seminario Conciliar de Zacatecas, and in Aguascalientes at the Seminario Conciliar de Santa María de Guadalupe and the Instituto Científico y Literario. In 1911 he received a law degree in San Luis Potosí. A year before that he had met and befriended the revolutionary leader Francisco I. Madero. López Velarde began writing and publishing poetry as a young man; in 1906, while still a student in Aguascalientes, he founded with a few friends a journal, *Bohemio* (Bohemian), and soon after that, he became a frequent contributor to such regional publications as *El Eco de San Luis* (The Echo of San Luis) and *El Regional* (The Regional). His name became well known in the provinces. He also published frequently in the Catholic newspaper, *La Nación* (The Nation). In 1914 he established permanent residency in Mexico City, where he held, in addition to several bureaucratic posts, the position of professor of literature at the Escuela Nacional Preparatoria and the Escuela de Altos Estudios. While living in the capital he wrote for several magazines and newspapers, including *Revista de Revistas* (Review of Reviews), *Vida Moderna* (Modern Life), *El Universal Ilustrado* (The Illustrated World), and *México Moderno* (Modern Mexico). He also directed with several poet friends the weekly *Pegaso* (Pegasus), and worked for the publishing house Cultura (Editorial México Moderno, S.A.). He died of bronchial pneumonia at age thirty-three in Mexico City on June 19, 1921.

López Velarde's work has three thematic phases: the Mexican province, a nationalistic period, and a phase of personal anguish. In his lifetime he published only two books of poetry: *La sangre devota* (Consecrated Blood) (1916) and *Zozobra* (Anguish) (1919). Posthumously, four volumes of his work have been edited: one of poetry, *El son del corazón* (The Sound of the Heart) (1932), which includes his wellknown poem, "La suave patria" (The Gentle Fatherland); and three of prose, *El minutero* (The Minute Hand) (1933), *El don de febrero* (February's Gift) (1952), and *Prosa política* (Political Prose) (1953).

In spite of a very sparse literary production, López Velarde occupies a prominent place in Mexican letters. Octavio *Paz places him, together with Juan José *Tablada, at the beginning stages of contemporary Mexican poetry; they initiate what Paz calls the "tradición de la ruptura" (tradition of rupture). López Velarde, in effect, makes his impact during the dying stages of Modernism. He was influenced by the poetry of Lugones, Laforgue, Herrera y Reissig, Baudelaire, and González Blanco, among others, out of which he created an original voice: personal and intimate, genuinely Mexican but also universal. He cultivated provincial themes in his work, and the province, real and imagined, is a magnetic presence. Although López Velarde was regarded by some as the most Mexican of the Mexican poets because of his desire to discover the essence of his fatherland, his greatest achievement was the creation of a poetic language. Xavier *Villaurrutia, who together with Paz and Allen W. Phillips, is his best critic, has pointed to the complexity of López Velarde's work: "In the eyes of everyone, the poetry of Ramón López Velarde is set in a provincial, Catholic, orthodox atmosphere. The Bible and the catechism are indisputably the ever-handy books of the poet; his love is romantic love; his only loved one, Fuensanta. But these are the general characteristics, the visible links of his poetry, not the more special lines or the more secret frontiers."

López Velarde developed an art that used common objects in our daily lives and found ways to transcend the ordinary. The prosaic tone of his poetry is derived from the everyday language spoken in the cities, which he combines with literary tradition to create a new lyric voice. He strove for a correspondence between word and emotion since he believed language should not be separate or distinct from either life or the poet. As Allen Phillips has stated: "The prose and poetry of López Velarde have a central point from which all themes emerge: the discovery and definition of a personality. His best poems are not descriptive in the ordinary sense but convey with dramatic intensity the spiritual conflict within his conscience and, by extension, humanity's conscience. López Velarde in his best moments strips the soul bare, with all modesty, and writes about the disillusionments, the doubts and indecisions, the joys and sorrows inherent in life itself."

WORKS: Poetry: *La sangre devota* (Consecrated Blood) (México: Ed. Revista de Revistas, 1916); 2nd ed. (México: Eds. R. Loera y Chávez, 1941). *Zozobra* (México: Eds. México Moderno, 1919). *El son del corazón* (The Sound of the Heart), prologues by Djed Bórquez and Genaro Fernández MacGregor, epilogue by Rafael Cuevas (México: Bloque de Obreros Intelectuales, 1932). *Poemas escogidos* (Selected Poems), selection and prologue by Xavier Villaurrutia (México: Ed. Cultura, 1935); 2nd ed., enlarged (México: Nueva Cultura, 1940). *El león y la virgin* (The Lion and the Virgin), prologue and selection by Xavier Villaurrutia, *Biblioteca del Estudiante Universitario*, no. 40 (México: UNAM, 1942). Prose: *El minutero* (The Minute Hand), preceded by poems by José Juan Tablada and Rafael López (México: Imp. Murguía,

1933). *El don de febrero y otras prosas* (February's Gift and Other Prose), prologue by Elena Molina Ortega, Serie Letras, no. 8 (México: Imp. Universitaria, 1952). *Prosa política* (Political Prose), prologue by Elena Molina Ortega, Serie Letras, no. 10 (México: Imp. Universitaria, 1952). Poetry and Prose: *Obras completas* (Complete Works), Col. Atenea, no. 11 (México: Ed. Nueva España, 1944). *Poesías, cartas, documentos e iconografía* (Poems, Letters, Documents, and Iconography), prologue by Elena Molina Ortega, Serie Letras, no. 9 (México: Imp. Universitaria, 1952). *Poesías completas y el minutero* (Complete Poetry and the Minute Hand), edited and prologue by Antonio Castro Leal, *Colección de Escritores Mexicanos*, no. 68 (México: Porrúa, 1953). Prologue: Francisco González León, *Campanas en la tarde* (Bells in the Afternoon), prologue by López Velarde (México: n.p., 1922); 2nd ed., prologue by López Velarde and Alonso de Alba (México: Edit. Cultura, TGSA 1948).

BIBLIOGRAPHY: Ermilo Abreu Gómez, "Ramón López Velarde," in his *Sala de retratos* (México: Leyenda, 1946), 166-68. Antonio Acevedo Escobedo, *López Velarde en su mediodía* (México: UNAM, 1962). Pedro de Alba, *Ramón López Velarde* (México: UNAM, 1958); "Aniversario de Ramón López Velarde," in *El hijo pródigo* 39 (México, 1946): 125-64. David N. Arce, "Bibliografías mexicanas contemporáneas, 14: obra y glosario de Ramón López Velarde," in *Boletín de la Biblioteca Nacional* vol 2, 3-4 (México, 1963): 85-103; "Obra y glosario de Ramón López Velarde," in *Boletín de la Biblioteca Nacional* 14, 3-4 (México, 1963): 85-101. Federico Berrueto, *Entraña y voz de López Velarde* (México: AEPS, 1958). *Calendario Ramón López Velarde* (México: SEP, 1971). Bernardo Calzada, *Amado Nervo y Ramón López Velarde* (México: Osasis, 1957). Jorge Campos, "López Velarde, el provinciano," in *Insula* 198 (1963): 11. Emmanuel Carballo, "Ramón López Velarde, político de campanario," in *Revista de la Universidad de México* 8, 9 (1954): 27-28. Alberto J. Carlos, "El vaivén sentimental en un poema de Ramón López Velarde: La bizarra capital de mi estado," in *Duquesne Hispanic Review* 8, 2 (Pittsburgh, 1969): 33-45. Benjamín Carrión, "Sé igual y fiel," in *Cuadernos Americanos* 177 (México, 1971): 113-46. Antonio Castro Leal, "Prólogue," in *Poesías completas y el minutero*, by Ramón López Velarde (México: Porrúa, 1963): vii-xxii. Ali Chumacero, "Ramón López Velarde, el hombre solo," in *El hijo pródigo* 39 (1946): 145-148, and in "*El hijo pródigo*" *antología* (México: Siglo XXI, 1979): 149-158. Eduardo Colin, "Ramón López Velarde," in his *Rasgos* (México: Manuel León Sánchez, 1934): 35-46. Juan María Corominas, "Valor semántico de la poesía de Ramón López Velarde," in *DAI* 38 (1971): 1376A-77A. Rafael Cuevas, *Panorámica de las letras. I. Ramón López Velarde* (México: Ediciones de la Revista de Bellas Artes, 1956). Jorge Cuesta, "La provincia de López Velarde," in his *Poemas y ensayos* (México: UNAM, 1964), Vol. 2, 246-50. Guillermo Díaz Plaja, "El tratamiento de la realidad en la poesía de Ramón López Velarde," in *Alcance* (June 1952): 3-4. Baltasar Dromundo, *Vida y pasión de Ramón López Velarde* (México: Guaranía, 1954). Horacio Espinosa Altamirano, "Meditaciones en torno a Ramón López Velarde," in *Boletín Bibliográfico de la Secretaría de Hacienda y Crédito Público* 296 (México, 1964): 8-9. Fernando Esquivel, "La mujer en la poesía de López Velarde," in *Abside* 24 (1960): 206-32. Enrique Fernández Ledesma, "Ramón López Velarde," in *México Moderno* 2, 11-12 (1921): 262-271. Genaro Fernández MacGregor, "Ramón López Velarde," in his *Carátulas* (México: Botas, 1935), 77-87. Genaro Fernández MacGregor and José Luis Martínez, *El ensayo mexicano moderno* (México: FCE, 1958), vol. 1, 180-85. David William Foster, *Mexican Literature: A Bibliography of Secondary Sources* (Metuchen,

N.J.: Scarecrow Press, 1981), 222-33. Carmen de la Fuente, "El simbolismo y Ramón López Velarde," in *Cuadernos Americanos* 170 (1970): 175-90. Concepción Gálvez de Tovar, *Ramón López Velarde en tres tiempos y un apéndice sobre el ritmo velardeano* (México: Porrúa, 1971). Patricia García, "Claves estéticas de Ramón López Velarde," in *Cuadernos Americanos* 189 (1975): 211-17. Manuel González Calzada, "Investigación sobre López Velarde," in his *Hombre y libros* (México: Antigua Librería Robredo, 1954), 83-86. Carlos González Peña, "López Velarde: el poeta de la provincia," in his *Gente mía* (México: Stylo, 1946), 127-33. Nicolás Guillén, "López Velarde, el poeta de *La suave patria*," in *Bohemia* 51 (1960): 56-57, 95-96. María Ibargüengoitia, *La poesía de López Velarde* (México: Cultural, 1936). Fortino Ibarra de Anda, "López Velarde y su *Suave patria*," in *Vida Universitaria* 271 (Monterrey, 1956): 7-10 and in his *20 años de libros; ensayos de crítica* (México: Juventa, 1956), 29-43. Bernardo Jiménez Montellano, "Baudelaire y Ramón López Velarde," in *Revista Iberoamericana* 22 (1946): 295-309. Thomas Kooreman, "The Creation of an Intimate Country in Two Works by Ramón López Velarde, *Novedad de la patria* and *Suave patria*," in *Romance Notes* 10 (Chapel Hill, N.C., 1968): 37-40. Daniel Kuri Brena, "Notas en torno a la poesía de López Velarde," in *Abside* 11 (1947): 393-413. Raúl Leiva, "Ramón López Velarde (1888-1921)," in his *Imagen de la poesía mexicana contemporánea* (México: UNAM, 1959), 33-47; "Sobre la poesía y la estética de López Velarde," *Revista de la Universidad de México* 25, 10 (1971): 9-18. Raúl Leiva and Jorge Ruedas, *La prosa de López Velarde* (México: UNAM, 1971). Jesús Medina Romero, *Lectura de Ramón López Velarde* (Monterrey: Sierra Madre, 1957). Antonio Magaña-Esquivel, "La mujer en la poesía. Ramón López Velarde," in *Revista de la Universidad de Yucatán* 16 (1961): 65-72. José Luis Martínez, "Examen de Ramón López Velarde," in Ramón López Velarde, *Obras* (México: FCE, 1971), 7-57. Juana Meléndez de Espinosa, *La suave patria de Ramón López Velarde* (San Luis Potosí, México: Universidad Potosina, 1971). Elena Molina Ortega, *Ramón López Velarde: estudio biográfico* (México: Ed. Universitaria, 1952). Frederic W. Murray, *La imagen arquetípica en la poesía de Ramón López Velarde* (Chapel Hill: University of North Carolina Press, 1972). Francisco Monterde García Icazbalceta, "Ramón López Velarde y la provincia," in *Cuadernos Americanos* 194 (1974): 245-53; "*La suave patria* de López Velarde," in his *Cultura mexicana: aspectos literarios* (México: Internacional, 1946), 293-300. Amado Nervo, "*Sangre patricia*," in his *Semblanzas y crítica literaria* (México: Ed. Universitaria, 1952), 145-48. Luis Noyola Vázquez, *Fuentes de Fuensanta. La ascención de López Velarde* (México: La Impresora, 1947); *Fuentes de Fuensanta: tensión y oscilación de López Velarde* (Zacatecas, México: Gobierno Constitucional del Estado, 1971). José Emilio Pacheco, "Nota sobre una enemistad literaria: Reyes y López Velarde," in *Texto Crítico* 2 (1975): 153-59. Margarita Paz Paredes, *Ramón López Velarde* (México: UNAM, 1953). Octavio Paz, "Introducción a la historia de la poesía mexicana," in *Las peras del olmo* (México, 1957), 3-31; "El lenguaje de López Velarde," in *Las peras del olmo* (México: Ed. Universitaria, 1957), 86-94; "El camino de la pasión (Ramón López Velarde)," in *Cuadrivio*, 3rd ed. (México: Joaquín Mortiz, 1969), 67-130; also as "The Road of Passion," in *The Siren and the Seashell and Other Essays on Poets and Poetry* (Austin: University of Texas Press, 1967), 67-111. Allen W. Phillips, *Ramón López Velarde: el poeta y el prosista* (México: INBA, 1962); "Una amistad literaria: Tablada y López Velarde," in *Nueva Revista de Filología Hispánica* 15 (Mexico, 1961), 605-16; "Dos prosas no coleccionadas de Ramón López Velarde," in *Cuadernos de Bellas Artes* 5, 7 (Mexico, 1964): 17-21; "González León y López Velarde," in *Francisco González León, el poeta de Lagos* (México: 1964), 58-71; "Notas sobre un poema de Ramón López Velarde," in *Revista Hispánica Moderna* 27 (New York, 1961): 113-19; "Nuevos estudios sobre López Velarde," in *Revista Hispánica Moderna* 19 (New York, 1953): 94-99; "Otra vez *Fuensanta*: despedida y reencuentro," in *Revista Iberoamericana* 79 (1972): 199-214; "Otra vez López Velarde," in *Cuaderno de Bellas Artes* 4, 10 (1963): 25-42.; "Ramón López Velarde en la poesía hispanoamericana del postmodernismo," in *Cinco estudios sobre literatura mexicana contemporánea* (México: SepSetentas, 1974), 123-43; "Reproducción y comentario de algunas prosas olvidades de Ramón López Velarde," in *Revista Iberoamericana* 51 (1961): 155-80; "El tema de la provincia en la obra de López Velarde," in *Cuadernos de Bellas Artes*, 3, 7-8 (Mexico, 1962): 25-36. Arturo Rivas Sainz, *El concepto de la zozobra* (Guadalajara, México: Eos, 1944); *La redondez de la creación. Ensayo sobre Ramón López Velarde* (México: Jus, 1951). Manuel A. Serna-Maytorena, "De lo poético y su exactitud en la lírica de López Velarde," *DAI* 28 (1968): 2697A. Bernardo Suárez, "La prosa de Ramón López Velarde," *DAI* 31 (1970): 1297A; "Facetas en la estética de Ramón López Velarde," in *Cuadernos Hispanoamericanos* 309 (Madrid, 1976): 414-22; "El impresionismo en la prosa de Ramón López Velarde," in *Cuadernos Americanos* 195 (México, 1974): 206-19. Jaime Torres Bodet, "Cercanía de López Velarde," in *Contemporáneos* 28-29 (1930): 111-35; also in *Atenea* 71 (1931): 63-79. Xavier Villaurrutia, "Arabe sin hurí," in *Fábula: hojas de México* 3 (1934): 50-54; "Encuentro con Ramón López Velarde," in *El Libro y el Pueblo* 12 (1934): 321-25; "Prólogo," in Ramón López Velarde, *El león y la virgen* (México: UNAM, 1942), vii-xxxiii; "Prólogo," in Ramón López Velarde, *Poesías escogidas* (México: Cultura, 1935), 9-32, also reprinted as "La poesía de Ramón López Velarde," in José Luis Martínez's, *El ensayo mexicano moderno* (México: FCE, 1958), vol. 2, 43-62, also translated as "The Poetry of Ramón López Velarde," in José Luis Martínez's, *The Modern Mexican Essay* (Toronto: University of Toronto Press, 1965), 310-25.

JEANNE C. WALLACE

LOPEZ y Fuentes, Gregorio (1897-1966). López y Fuentes was born in the Hacienda El Mamey in the Huasteca region in the state of Veracruz. He went to Mexico City to become a teacher, but his studies were suddenly interrupted by the Victoriano Huerta coup. By necessity he became a journalist, writing for several Mexico City newspapers. An admirer of Rubén Darío, he wrote poetry imitating the Nicaraguan in 1914. From 1937 to 1945 he edited the newspaper *El Universal*. He was a member of the group of writers who received their inspiration from the Mexican Revolution of 1910. This literary movement was initiated by Mariano *Azuela (1873-1952) with his novel *Los de abajo* (1915).

Tierra (Land) (1932), one of López y Fuentes better-known novels, traces the Emiliano Zapata agrarian reform movement from 1910 to 1920. Although Zapata and his agrarian principles are showcased in the novel, there is no one character who becomes the protagonist. López y Fuentes wants to showcase the whole struggle for land. There is one character, Antonio Hernández, who participates more like a symbol for this struggle. He represents the Indian in his ineptness at gaining freedom through land. *Tierra* has often been described as a pessimistic novel because it offers few and limited possibilities for the Indian in his efforts to obtain what is rightfully his. The side of the landowner is also seen as something very real. Once they realize that the side represented by Porfirio Díaz is about to fall, they change sides and give their support to the new government. This allows them to keep their property and to receive the favor of the new administration. This is how the novel seems to resolve the conflict at the end, which is basically a continuation of the status quo.

El indio (1935) won the National Literature Prize. Here López y Fuentes again ignores the individual character for the sake of focusing on the whole problem as it affects the masses as a collective entity, rather than looking for individual solutions. There is a strong critical perspective against the power structures for not doing anything meaningful to improve the Indians' lot. López y Fuentes has said that "the writer nourishes himself on the historical time that he lives in." That seems to be an accurate statement. He has admitted to the influence of direct events in his own life and his experiences with peasants in the small farm that his father owned in the state of Veracruz. And it is from these direct experiences that he created many of his characters.

Campamento (Military Camp) (1931) is a novel in which he recounts the experiences that a group of Mexican Soldiers go through as they prepare to battle the invading American troops in 1914. He personally participated in that battle. *Arrieros* (Mule Drivers) (1937) is a folkloric account of mule drivers, of their customs, traditions, and way of life in general.

WORKS: Novels: *Campamento* (Military Camp) (México: 1931). *Tierra* (Land) (México: 1932). *Mi general* (My General) (México: 1934). *El indio* (México: 1935); *They That Reap*, translated by Anita Brenner, llustrations by Diego Rivera (New York: Frederick Ungar, 1937). *Arrieros* (Mule Drivers) (México: 1937). *Huasteca* (México: 1939). *Cuentos campesinos de México* (Peasant Short Stories of Mexico) (México: 1940). *Acomodaticio* (Opportunistic) (México: 1943). *Los peregrinos inmóviles* (The Immobile Pilgrims) (México: 1944). *Entresuelo* (Entresol) (México: 1948). *Milpa, potrero y monte* (Corn Field, Pasture Ground, and Mount) (México: 1951).

BIBLIOGRAPHY: Mariano Azuela, *Cien años de novela mexicana* (México: Eds. Botas, 1947). John S. Brushwood, *Mexico in Its Novel* (Austin: University of Texas Press, 1966), 215-17, 231-32. Emmanuel Carballo, *Diecinueve protagonistas de la literatura mexicana del siglo XX* (México: Empresas Editoriales, S.A., 1965). Walter M. Langford, *The Mexican Novel Comes of Age* (Notre Dame: University of Notre Dame Press, 1971). Rogelio Rodríguez Coronel, ed., *Recopilación de textos sobre la novela de la Revolución mexicana* (Habana: Casa de las Américas, 1975). Cynthia Steele, "Literature and National Formation: Indigenista Fiction in the United States (1820-1860) and in Mexico (1920- 1960)," *DAI* 41, 7 (Jan. 1981): 3127A.

OSCAR SOMOZA

LUQUIN, Eduardo (1896-). Born in Sayula, Jalisco, Luquín did his early schooling at the Liceo de Varones in Guadalajara. He then prepared for a diplomatic career in Mexico City. He was an officer in the revolutionary army of Venustiano Carranza. In 1925 he entered the diplomatic service and held various posts in Antwerp,

Switzerland, Barcelona, Valencia, San Salvador, Ecuador, Chile, etc. His activity during the Spanish Civil War earned him the Cross for Military Merit, awarded him by the Mexican government. He was a member of the Mexican Academies of Language, Geography, and History.

Luquín was a prolific writer. His bibliography includes five novels, three volumes of stories, ten volumes of essays and travel impressions, four volumes of memoirs, one volume of history, and two volumes of sociology. He also wrote numerous articles for both Mexican and foreign periodicals. An elegant stylist, he was at his best when developing the psychology of his characters.

WORKS: Stories, Memoirs, and Novels: *El indio* (The Indian) (México: n.p., 1923). *Agosto y otros cuentos* (August and Other Stories) (México: Ed. El Universal Ilustrado, 1924). *La mecanógrafa* (The Typist) (México: n.p., 1925). *Intermedio. Divagaciones* (Intermission. Wanderings) (México: n.p., 1925). *Telones de fondo* (Backdrops) (Madrid: Cuentos, 1928). *Figuras de papel (miscelánea)* (Paper Figures) (México: Imp. Mundial, 1936). *Tumulto: Memorias de un oficial del Ejército Constitucionalista* (Tumult: Memoirs of an Officer in the Constitutionalist Army) (México: Ed. Imp. Quintero, 1936). *Agua de sombra, relatos* (Shadow Water, Stories) (México: Edit. B. Costa-Amic, 1937). *Espejismo* (Mirage) (Barcelona: n.p., 1938). *Los embozados* (The Muffled) novel (México: n.p., 1942). *Los perros fantasmas* (The Ghost Dogs), novel (México: Edit. Costa-Amic, 1943). *Extranjeros en la tierra* (Strangers in the Land) (Quito: 1944). *Los hermanos Gabriel* (The Gabriel Brothers), novel (México: Edit. Costa-Amic, 1945). *Espigas de infancia y adolescencia* (Grains of Childhood and Adolescence), autobiography (México: Edit. Costa-Amic, 1948). *Aguila de oro (espejo del pistolero)* (Golden Eagle: Mirror of the Gunfighter) (México: Edit. Costa-Amic, 1950). *El temor a Dios* (The Fear of God) (México: SEP, 1951). *Rosas de sangre y otros relatos* (Blood Roses and Other Stories) (México: n.p., 1956). *La cruz de mis vientos* (The Cross of My Winds) (Havana: Casa de las Américas, 195?). *La virgen y la diosa* (The Virgin and the Goddess) (México: Costa-Amic, 1962). *Serpiente de dos cabezas* (Two-Headed Snake), novel (México: Costa-Amic, 1963). *Entre el ángel y el demonio* (Between the Angel and the Devil [A new version of *The Muffled*]) (México: Costa-Amic, 1964). *Seis novelas* (Six Novels) (México: n.p., 1965). Chronicles and Essays: *Diagrama* (Diagram), travel (México: Imp. Mundial, 1930). *Ecuador: Impresiones de viaje* (Ecuador: Travel Impressions) (Quito: 1933). *Verde y azul* (Green and Blue) (The Hague: H. Stols Mastricht, 1939). *Ondas cortas* (Short Waves), essay, 1st series (México: 1940). *Ondas cortas* (Short Waves), essay, 2nd series (México: 1943). *Confidencias* (Confidences), essay (México: Costa-Amic, 1947). *El matrimonio del cielo y el infierno* (The Marriage of Heaven and Hell) (México: n.p., 1953). *Ondas cortas* (Short Waves), essay, 3rd series (México: Imp. Artística, 1954). *México en el extranjero* (Mexico Abroad) (México: n.p., 1961). *El escritor y la crítica* (The Writer and Criticism), induction speech for the Mexican Academy of Language, response by José María González de Mendoza (México: MAL, 1963). *Entre guiones* (Between Hyphens). *La profesión del hombre* (The Profession of Man). *Análisis espectral del mexicano* (Spectral Analysis of the Mexican).

BIBLIOGRAPHY: Anon., Review of *El escritor y la crítica*, in *Bulletin of the Centro Mexicano de Escritores* 11, 2 (Jan. 6, 1964). Huberto Batis, Review of *El escritor y la crítica*, in *La Cultura en México* 104, 12 (Feb. 1964): xviii. John S. Brushwood and

José Rojas Garcidueñas, *Breve historia de la novela mexicana* (México: Ed. de Andrea, 1959), 135-36. Salvador Calvillo Madrigal, Review of *El temor a Dios*, in *Revista Mexicana de Cultura* 210 (April 8, 1951): 11; Review of *El matrimonio del cielo y el infierno*, in *Revista Mexicana de Cultura* 341 (Oct. 11, 1953): 12. Esteban Durán Rosado, Review of *Entre el ángel y el demonio*, in *Revista Mexicana de Cultura* 886 (March 22, 1964): 15. José María González de Mendoza, Review of *Los perros fantasmas*, in *Letras de México* 9, 5 (June 1, 1945): 112; Review of the novels, *El escritor y la crítica*, in ed. cit. Celestino Gorostiza, "*Tumulto* de E. Luquín," *Letras de México* 10 (July 1, 1937). Luis Leal, *Bibliografía del cuento mexicano* (México: Ed. de Andrea, 1958), 82-83. C.M., Review of *Aguila de oro*, in *Revista Mexicana de Cultura* 151 (Feb. 12, 1950): 11. José Luis Martínez, *Literatura Mexicana. Siglo XX*, vol. 1, 38, 133; vol. 2, 72. Rufino Martínez, Review of *Ondas cortas, segunda serie*, in *Letras de México* 6 (June 15, 1943): 7. Mario Martini, "Muestrario de letras: Tres académicos ante el caso E. Luquín," *México en la Cultura* 723 (Jan. 27, 1963): 3. Javier Morente, "Sala de lectura," Review of *Entre el ángel y el demonio*, in *Diorama de la Cultura* (April 5, 1964): 4. Angelina Muñiz, "Entre líneas," Review of *Entre el ángel y el demonio* in *Diorama de la Cultura* (May 10, 1964): 8. Aurora M. Ocampo de Gómez and Ernesto Prado Velázquez, *Diccionario de Escritores Mexicanos* (México: UNAM, 1967), 264. Javier Peñalosa, Review of *Entre el ángel y el demonio*, in *México en la Cultura* 779 (Feb. 23, 1964): 3. Salvador Reyes Nevares, Review of *La virgen y la diosa*, in *La Cultura en México* 6 (March 28, 1962), xvi. Gustavo Sainz, "Escaparate," Review of *El escritor y la crítica*, in *México en la Cultura* 776 (Feb. 2, 1964): 5. Rodolfo Veloz B., "Muestrario de las letras: Eduardo Luquín dice su verdad literaria," in *México en la Cultura* 724 (Feb. 3 Feb, 1963): 3. Carlos Zalcedo, "La actualidad literaria: *Agua de sombra*, de Luquín," *Letras de México* 15, (Sept. 16, 1937).

PETER G. BROAD

M

MADERO, Luis Octavio (1908-1964), was born in Morelia on August 24, and he died in Mexico City on August 15, 1964. Talented journalist and playwright, Madero's plays deal mainly with social concerns. *Los alzados* (The Rebels) is the story of a group of peasants who rise in revolt against landowners and town potentates. They represent a disorganized and spontaneous movement driven by a desire for revenge and justice. The play introduces some humorous elements and authentically portrays small-town characters, the military official, the emotional and compassionate innkeeper, the meticulous and bureaucratic clerk of the court. It is a theater of social intention and critical realism. *Sindicato* (Syndicate) is the story of workers at a printing press fighting for a union. The leader is killed in an attack against the strikers. The play has a minimal stage decor with changes being indicated by quick curtain draws. Both plays received excellent critical reviews.

WORKS: *Claustro* (Cloister) (México: n.p., 1933). *Los alzados y Sindicato* (The Rebels and Syndicate), plays (México: Ed. México Nuevo, 1937). *El octubre español* (Spanish October) (México: Talleres Gráficos de La Nación, 1938). *Con música al sureste* (With Music to the South East) (México: n.p., 1938. *El momento social mexicano desde el punto de vista del arte* (Mexico's Social Actuality from the Point of View of Art) (México: Ed. México Nuevo, 1939).

BIBLIOGRAPHY: Anon., "El escritor y diplomático Luis Octavio Madero, falleció ayer." in *El Día* (Aug. 16, 1964):3. Ruth S. Lamb, *Bibliografía del teatro mexicano del siglo xx* (México: Ed. de Andrea, 1962), p. 74. Luis Leal, *Bibliografía del cuento mexicano* (México: Ed. de Andrea, 1956), p. 83. Jesús Romero Flores, *Leyendas y cuentos michoacanos* (México: Ed. Botas, 1938), vol. 2, pp. 84-120.

ALICIA G. WELDEN

MAGALONI, Honorato Ignacio (1898-), poet. Magaloni was born on January 25, 1898, in Mérida, Yucatán, where he did studies through high school. He later did additional studies in the United States. He served as director of *El Faro* in 1920, and editor-in-chief of *El Diario del Sureste* in Mérida in 1921. He was also director of the journal *Poesía en América*, which began publication in 1952. His first work was a collection of poetry, produced jointly by his brother, Humberto Magaloni, and him, in 1939. Later he wrote and published on his own.

Magaloni's interest in understanding and exploring indigenous culture and traditions is apparent in his choice of themes, which include his descriptions of his ancestors' beliefs in spiritualism and magic.

WORKS: Poetry: *Polvo tropical* (Tropical Dust) (México: Editorial Stylo, 1947). *Oído en la tierra* (Ear to the Ground) (México: Editorial Stylo, 1950). *Signo* (Sign) (México: Cuadernos Americanos, 1952). *Ocho poetas mexicanos* (Eight Mexican Poets) (México: Abside, 1955).

BIBLIOGRAPHY: Jesús Arellano, *Antología de los 50* (México: Ediciones Alatorre, 1952), pp. 167, 457. Antonio Castro Leal, *La poesía mexicana moderna*, Letras mexicanas, no. 12 (México: FCE, 1953), p. 252. Frank Dauster, *Breve historia de la poesía mexicana*, Manuales Studium, no. 4 (México: Eds. de Andrea, 1956), p. 181. Aurora M. Ocampo de Gómez and Ernesto Prado Velázquez, *Diccionario de escritores mexicanos* (México: UNAM, 1967), p. 205.

EDNA A. REHBEIN

MAGAÑA, Sergio (1924-1990). Born on September 24, 1924, in Tepalcatepec, Michoacán, Magaña died in Mexico in September 1990. Sergio Magaña received degrees in sciences and related subjects at UNAM before embarking on a career in literature. His first book, a novel, *Los suplicantes* (The Supplicants), was published in 1942. He subsequently published a book of stories, *El ángel roto* (The Broken Angel) in 1946. With *El molino del aire* (The Air-Mill), a novel, he won the prize for literature from the newspaper, *El Nacional*. He is most known, however, for his plays and his contributions to various publications as a theater critic.

His first dramatic attempt was a 1947 scene, "La noche transfigurada" (The Transfigured Night), which was performed in the Facultad de Filosofía y Letras at the Universidad Nacional. Sergio Magaña then produced *Los signos del zodíaco* (The Signs of the Zodiac) in 1951, assessed as one of the premier works of the contemporary Mexican theater. Capturing the imagination of the public, Magaña proved to have all the attributes of an outstanding playwright. With *Moctezuma II*, performed in 1954, Magaña turned to the tragedy, but largely ignored the classical methods. In the play, he presents Moctezuma as a refined, clairvoyant figure whom the gods destroy because he is ahead of his time.

In *El pequeño caso de Jorge Lívido* (The Little Case of Jorge Lívido), performed in 1958, Magaña presents another facet of his creative capacity. Tackling the problem of justice and the psychological methods by which modern man obtains criminal confession, it is a gripping story of realistically presented police intrigue.

Medea (1965) uses the historical theme of Cortés and La Malinche, fused with Greek roots. Combining myth and history, Magaña demonstrates that present reality is structured by permanent and symbolic values that span the centuries.

Los motivos del lobo (The Wolf's Motives) (1966) is an urban drama in which the author, using stories of psychological horror taken from the newspapers of the day, treats the theme of solitude in contemporary society. Focusing on a family kept from discovering the real world outside the confines of the home, he even shows a scene of incest in a state of unconsciousness, presenting it is an unbiased manner. He creates almost an idyllic internal climate, based on innocence and candor, which is suddenly and devastatingly interrupted by the sense of morality of the outside world.

WORKS: Story: *El ángel roto* (The Broken Angel) (México: n.p., 1946). *El padre nuestro* (Our Father) (México: n.p., 1947). Novel: *Los suplicantes* (The Supplicants) (México: n.p., 1942. *El molino de aire* (The Air-Mill) (México: Eds. de la Revista

Mexicana de Cultura, 1954). Theater: *La noche transfigurada* (The Transfigured Night), performed in 1947, Mexico. *El suplicante* (The Supplicant), performed in 1950; in *Antología de obras en un acto*, vol. 1, pp. 63-81. *Los signos del zodíaco* (The Signs of the Zodiac), performed in Mexico City in 1951 (México: Ed. Colección Teatro Mexicano, 1953); in *Teatro mexicano del siglo XX*, edited by Celestino Gorostiza, vol. 3 (México: FCE, 1956), pp. 208-325. *El reloj y la cuna* (The Watch and the Cradle), performed in Mexico City in 1952. *El viaje de Nocresida* (Nocresida's Journey), in collaboration with Emilio Carballido, performed in Mexico City in 1953. *Moctezuma II*, performed in Veracruz in 1953, in 1954 in Mexico city; in *Panorama del Teatro en México* 1, 1 (July, 1954): 35-82; Act I, in *Cuadernos de Bellas Artes* 4, 9 (Sept. 1963): 69-108; Act II, in *Cuadernos de Bellas Artes* 4, 10 (Oct. 1963): 73-112; Act III, in *Cuadernos de Bellas Artes* 4, 11 (Nov. 1963): 57-104. *Moctezuma II* in *Panorama del Teatro en México* 1 (July, 1954): 35-82. *Meneando el bote* (Shaking the Boat), in *Cine mundial* (Aug. 22, 1954): 15. *El pequeño caso de Jorge Lívido* (The Little Case of Jorge Lívido), performed in 1958; in *Teatro mexicano 1958,* edited by Luis G. Basurto (México: Edit. Aguilar, 1959), pp. 167-240. *El anillo de oro* (The Golden Ring), performed in Mexico City in 1960. *Rentas congeladas* (Frozen Incomes), performed in Mexico City in 1960. *Los motivos del lobo* (The Wolf's Motives), performed in Mexico City in 1966. *Medea 1965*, unpublished. *Los argonautas* (The Argonauts), Act I, in *Ovaciones* 189 (Aug. 22, 1965): 4-5. *Ensayando a Moliere* (Rehearsing Moliere), performed in different cities in 1966 by Teatro Trashumante, INBA. Prologue: André Moreau, *Entre bastidores* (Behind the Scenes) (México: n.p., 1965).

BIBLIOGRAPHY: Jorge Carlos Barberi, "Comentario fílmicos," review of the film *Los signos del zodíaco*, in *Revista Mexicana de Cultura* 884 (March 8, 1964): 12. Mario Beauregard, "Habla Sergio Magaña," in *México en la Cultura* 855 (Aug. 8, 1965): 4. Wilberto Cantón, Review of *El pequeño caso de Jorge Lívido*, in *Diorama de la Cultura* (Aug. 10, 1958): 2. Emmanuel Carballo, *Cuentistas mexicanos modernos*, vol. 2 (México: Eds. Libro-Mex, 1956), p. 135. Juan García Ponce, "Teatro. *El pequeño caso de Jorge Lívido*," in *Universidad de México* 12, 12 (Aug. 1958): 28-29; "La ambición, rasgo predominante en la poesía dramática de Sergio Magaña," in *México en la Cultura* 507 (Nov. 30, 1958): 10. *Teatro mexicano del siglo XX*, edited by Celestino Gorostiza, vol. 3 (México: FCE, 1956), pp. cci-xxii, 207. Joaquín S. Gregorio, "Teatro," in *Universidad de México* 8, 7 (March, 1954): 21-22. Miguel Guardia, "El teatro en México. *Los signos del zodíaco*," in *México en la Cultura* 110 (March 11, 1951): 5, 6; "Sergio Magaña se enfrenta con honesta valentía a una terrible diosa: La Justicia," in *México en la Cultura* 490 (Aug. 3, 1958): 9; "*Los signos del zodíaco*," in *El Libro y el Pueblo* 3, 1 (July-Sept. 1959): 110-14. Juan Guerrero Zamora, "Dramaturgos mexicanos vistos desde Europa," in *México en la Cultura* 757 (Sept. 22, 1963): 4. Ruth S. Lamb, *Bibliografía del teatro mexicano del siglo XX* (México: Eds. de Andrea, 1962), pp. 74-75. Luis Leal, *Breve historia del cuento mexicano* (México: Eds. de Andrea, 1958), p. 146; *Bibliografía del cuento mexicano* (México: Eds. de Andrea, 1958): 83. Antonio Magaña Esquivel, *Medio siglo de teatro mexicano, 1900-1961* (México: INBA, Dept. de Lit., 1964), pp. 107, 121, 122, 131, 135-36, 155. Antonio Magaña Esquivel and Ruth S. Lamb, *Breve historia del teatro mexicano* (México: Eds. de Andrea, 1958), pp. 145-47. Aurora M. Ocampo de Gómez and Ernesto Prado Velázquez, *Diccionario de Escritores Mexicanos* (México: UNAM, 1967), pp. 205-6. Malkah Rabel, "Sergio Magaña habla de *Los signos del zodíaco*, in

MAGAÑA Esquivel, Antonio

México en la Cultura 538 (July 5, 1958): 9. Mara Reyes, Review of *Moctezuma II*, in *Diorama de la Cultura* (July 11, 1965): 5. Carlos Solórzano, Review of *Los motivos del lobo* and *Medea 1965*, "Lo criminal y lo histórico nutren la reaparición de Magaña," in *La Cultura en México* 155 (Feb. 3, 1965): xviii-xix. Luis Suárez, "El escritor mexicano ante una dolorosa alternativa. O se agacha o se muere de hambre. El gobierno lo ignora y las camarillas lo aíslan, dice Magaña," in *Siempre!* 636 (Sept. 1, 1965): 44-45. Juan Tovar, Review of the film on *Los signos del zodíaco*, in *Ovaciones* 77 (June 16, 1963): 4. Carlos Valdés, Review of *Moctezuma II*, in *Universidad de México* 9, 8 (April 1955): 28. Fernando Wagner, "Fernando Wagner elige *La Medusa* y *Los argonautas* como las mejores obras de teatro," in *El Día* (May 8, 1965): 10.

JEANNE C. WALLACE

MAGAÑA Esquivel, Antonio (1909-   ), essayist, novelist, playwright, theater historian. Born in Mérida, Magaña Esquivel is a lawyer from UNAM. He studied theater and literature, has theater columns in *El Nacional* and *Tiempo* and teaches Spanish and Mexican literature in high schools. He has held positions in government ministries. He was founder and president of Agrupación de Críticos de Teatro en México, a member of the Film Arts and Sciences Academy, and he was in charge of Teatro Foraneo of INBA.

Magaña Esquivel won the Mexico City National Literature Prize for his second novel, *La tierra enrojecida* (The Ground Turned Red) (1951). His works on theater are widely consulted; Salvador *Novo praised *Sueño y realidad del teatro* (Dream and Reality of Theater). He has organized regional drama festivals and the National Theater Contest, and as a playwright, he is best known for *Semilla del aire* (Seeds in the Air), staged in 1956 and awarded the *El Nacional* prize.

WORKS: Essay and Criticism: *Imagen del teatro* (Image of the Theater) (México: Letras de México, 1940) *Arte y litertura de la Revolucion* (Art and Literature of the Revolution) (Editora del Sureste, 1948). *Sueño y realidad del teatro* (Dream and Reality of Theater) (México: INBA, 1949). *Teatro mexicano del Siglo XX* (Mexican Theater of the Twentieth Century), vol. 2, edited by Antonio Magaña Esquivel (México: FCE, 1956). *Breve historia del teatro mexicano* (Brief History of the Mexican Theater), coauthored with Ruth Lamb (México: Ediciones de Andrea, 1958). *Tres conceptos de la crítica teatral* (Three Concepts of Theater Criticism), coauthored with María Luisa Mendoza and Marcela del Río (México: UNAM, 1962). "El teatro y el cine," by Magaña Esquivel in *México. 50 años de Revolución*, n.e. (México: FCE, 1962). *Medio siglo de teatro mexicano 1900-1961* (Half a Century of Mexican Theater) (México: INBA, 1964). "Las publicaciones teatrales," by Magaña Esquivel in *El teatro en México*, n.e. (México: INBA, 1965), vol. 2 pp. 1958-64. Novel: *El ventrilocuo* (The Ventriloquist) (México: Letras de Mexico, 1944). *La tierra enrojecida* (The Ground Turned Red) (México: Porrúa, 1951). Biography: *Vicente Guerrero, el héroe del sur* (Vicente Guerrero, The Southern Hero) (México: Xochitl, 1946). Theater: *Semilla del aire* (1956). *El sitio y la hora* (Place and Time) (1961). *La undécima musa* (The Eleventh Muse) (1968). *Contrapunto* (Counterpoint) (1970). *El que vino a hacer la guerra o Western navideño en un solo tiro* (The One Who Came to Make War or Christmas Western in One Shot) (1980). Prologues in Anthologies: *Tres conceptos de la crítica teatral* (Three Concepts of Theater Criticism), with María

Luisa Mendoza and Marcela del Río (México: UNAM, 1962). *Teatro mexicano 1963* (Mexican Theater), edited by Antonio Magaña Esquivel, plays by Salvador Novo, Luisa Josefina Hernández, Emilio Carballido, and Solana (Madrid and México: Aguilar, 1965). *La novela de la Revolucion* (The Novel of the Revolution) (México: Instituto Nacional de Estudios Históricos de la Revolución Mexicano, 1965). *El espectador* (The Spectator) (1969). *Teatro mexicano 1964* (Mexican Theater 1964) , edited by Antonio Magaña Esquivel (Madrid: Aguilar, 1967). *Don Alvaro o la fuerza del sino y romances históricos del Duque de Rivas* (1971). *Salvador Novo* (1971). *Teatro mexicano 1969* (1972). *Obras de Alejandro Casona* (Works of Alejandro Casona) (1972). *Teatro mexicano del Siglo XIX* (Mexican Theater of the Nineteenth Century) (1972). *Teatro Mexicano 1971* (Mexican Theater 1971) (1974).

BIBLIOGRAPHY: Anon., "El teatro y el cine," in *Tiempo* 53, 1109 (1963): 53. "Nuevo libro sobre teatro de Antonio Magaña Esquivel," in *Revista de la Semana* (Dec. 27, 1964): 3. "Notable libro sobre la novela de la Revolucion," in *Revista de la Semana* (June 27, 1965): 3. Anita Arroyo, "Los dos Juanes de México" *Razón y pasión de Sor Juana* (México: Porrúa, 1952), pp. 272-74. Luis G. Basurto, Review of *Semilla del aire*, in *Excelsior* (Oct. 24, 1956): 3C. Huberto Batis, Review of *Medio siglo de teatro mexicano*, in *La Cultura en México* 150 (Dec. 30, 1964): xix; Review of *La novela de la Revolución* in *La Cultura en México* n. 18 (August 11, 1965), xvii. Antonio Castro Leal, Review of *Imagen del teatro*, in *Revista de Literatura Mexicana* 1 (July-Sept., 1940): 182-83. Hugo Cervantes, "Breve historia del teatro y el cine mexicanos," in *Mexico y la Cultura* 717 (Dec. 16, 1962). Ali Chumacero, "Panorama de los últimos libros. *Teatro mexicano del Siglo XX*," in *México en la Cultura* 386 (Aug. 1956): 2. Guillermo Duque Gómez, Review of *El ventrilocuo*, in *Revista de las Indias* 75 (Bogota, 1945): 15. Arturo Gamboa Garibaldi, "Antonio Magaña Esquivel" in *Enciclopedia Yucatanense*, vol. 5 (Gobierno de Yucatan: 1946), pp. 682, 776. Ruth S. Lamb, *Bibliografía del teatro mexicano del siglo xx* (México: Eds. de Andrea, 1962), pp. 75, 135-136; "La edición de *Teatro mexicano 1963*," in *El Nacional* (June 23, 1964): 5. Luis Leal, *Bibliografía del cuento mexicano* (México: Ed. de Andrea, 1958), p. 84. Antonio Magaña Esquivel y Ruth S. Lamb, *Breve historia del cuento mexicano* (México: Ed. de Andrea, 1956), p. 109, 155-6. María Luisa Mendoza "Medio siglo carretela con Magaña Esquivel," in *El Gallo Ilustrado* 138 (Feb. 1965): 4. Margarita Mendoza López, Review of life and works in *Teatro: Boletín de Información e Historia* (March 1955): 1-2. Marcela Michelin, Review of *La tierra enrojecida*, in *Books Abroad* (Autumn 1952). Cipriano R. Xerif, "Medio siglo de teatro mexicano y yo," in *México en la Cultura* 825 (Jan.10, 1965): 4. Isaac Rojas Rosillo, Review of *Sueño y realidad del teatro*, in *México en la Cultura* 32 (Sept. 11, 1949): 7 Rafael Sánchez Ocana, Review of *Semilla del aire*, in *El Nacional* (Oct. 22, 1956).

DELIA GALVAN

MAGDALENO, Mauricio (1906-   ). Magdaleno was born on May 13, 1906. He attended both primary and secondary schools in Aguascalientes. He continued his education in México City, attending the National Preparatory School and studying letters at the National Autonomous University. His professional vita includes work as a journalist, teacher of history and Spanish literature, and film writer. He also held a number of government positions such as legislator, director of cultural affairs and director of fine arts and of libraries for the Ministry of Public Education.

With regard to his literary vocation, Magdaleno first manifested great interest in the theater, founding the *Teatro de Ahora* in 1932. He later turned toward fiction and the essay. The primary focus of his most celebrated works is the Mexican Revolution and its failure to improve the lot of the people.

Much of Magdaleno's fame has been attributed to his novelistic production. For example, his *El resplandor* (Sunburst) is considered by some critics to be an "indigenista" masterpiece and the best Mexican novel of the thirties. This work depicts one of the most backward and impoverished regions of México. The collective protagonist is a poor Otomí Indian community segregated from and continually exploited by generations of wealthy landowners. Deviating from a traditional straightforward style, Magdaleno ruptures linear time. Through dream and stream-of-consciousness sequences, he confers some thought-provoking psychological and aesthetic dimensions upon the novel.

WORKS: Novels: *Mapamí* (México: Talleres de Revista de Revistas, 1927). *El compadre Mendoza* (México: Ed. México, 1934). *Campo Celis* (Celis Field) (México: Eds. MAM, 1935). *Concha Bretón* (México: Eds. Botas, 1936). *El resplandor* (Sunburst) (México: Eds. Botas, 1937). *Sonata* (México: Eds. Botas, 1941). *Sunburst*, translation of *El resplandor* by Anita Brenner (New York: The Viking Press, 1944). *Cabello de elote* (Corn Silk) (México: Ed. Stylo, 1949). *La tierra grande* (The Extensive Land) (México: Austral, 1949). Stories: *El ardiente verano* (The Burning Summer) (México: FCE, 1954). Plays: *Teatro revolucionario mexicano* (Mexican Revolutionary Theater) (Madrid: Ed. Cenit, 1933). Other Works: *Vida y poesía* (Life and Poetry) (Santiago, Chile: Ed. Ercilla, 1936). *José María Luis Mora, el civilizador* (Pachuco: Instituto Científico y Literario de Pachuca, 1935). *Polonia* (Poland) (México: Eds. de Amigos de Polonia, 1939). *Fulgor de Martí* (The Brilliance of Martí) (México: Eds. Quetzal, 1940). *Rango* (Rank) (Buenos Aires: Ed. Americalee, 1941). *Tierra y viento* (Land and Wind) (México: Ed. Stylo, 1948). *Ritual del año* (Ritual of the Year) (México: Los Presentes, 1955). *Las palabras perdidas: viñetas de Alberto Beltrán* (Lost Words: Vignettes of Alberto Beltrán) (México: FCE, 1956). *Panuco 137* in Antonio Magaña Esquivel, *Teatro mexicano del siglo xx* (Mexico: FCE, 1956), pp. 98-150. *La idea liberal de Mora* (Mora's Liberal Concept) (México: Seminario de Cultura Mexicana, 1962). *La aventura del norte* (The Northern Adventure) (México: Seminario de Cultura Mexicana, 1963). *Ricardo Flores Magón, el gran calumniado* (Ricardo Flores Magón, The Great Slandered One) (México: Eds. de la Chinaca, 1964). *La voz y el eco* (The Voice and the Echo) (México: Seminario de Cultura Mexicana, 1964). *Hacia un reencuentro americano* (Toward an American Clash) (Acapulco: Ed. Americana, 1966). *Agua bajo el puente* (Water under the Bridge) (México: FCE, 1968). *Retórica de la Revolución* (Rhetoric of the Revolution) (México: Instituto de Estudios Históricos de la Revolución Mexicana, 1978). *Hombres e ideas de la Revolución* (Men and Ideas of the Revolution) (México: Instituto Nacional de Estudios Históricos de la Revolución Mexicana, 1980).

BIBLIOGRAPHY: John S. Brushwood, *Mexico in Its Novel* (Austin: University of Texas Press, 1966), pp. 19-21, 217-18. Leonard S. Klein, ed., *Latin American Literature in the Twentieth Century* (New York: Ungar, 1986), pp. 172-74. Walter M. Langford, *The Mexican Novel Comes of Age* (Notre Dame: University of Notre Dame Press,

1971), pp. 38, 42, 43, 46, and 72. Dennis J. Parle, "Las funciones del tiempo en la estructura de *El resplandor* de Magdaleno," *Hispania* 63, 1 (March 1980): 58-68; "El tiempo y la historicidad como factores estructurales en la obra de Mauricio Magdaleno," Ph.D. diss. University of Kansas 1976. Joanne Causey Ratchford, "Recurring Themes and Views in the Major Works of Mauricio Magdaleno," Diss. University of Virginia, 1967. Harry L. Rosser, *Conflict and Transition in Rural México: The Fiction of Social Realism* (Waltham, Mass.: African Studies Association of Brandeis University, 1980), pp. 57-63, and 120-29. Donald Schmidt, "Changing Techniques in the Mexican Indigenist Novel," Ph.D. diss. University of Kansas, 1972, pp. 63-99. Joseph Sommers, *After the Storm* (Albuquerque: University of New Mexico Press, 1968), pp. 23-33. Ruth Stanten, "The Realism of Mauricio Magdaleno," *Hispania* 22, 4 (Dec. 1939): 345-53.

ROBERT K. ANDERSON

MAGDALENO, Vicente (1908-   ). Magdaleno was born in Tabasco, Villa del Refugio. As a child he indirectly experienced some of the events of the Revolution. He and his brother Mauricio, also a writer, recall a happy childhood. Their father allowed them many liberties: "Nosotros nos hicimos en bibliotecas públicas, más que en las aulas" (We were educated in public libraries rather than in classrooms) (Interview by Beatriz Popes Rebollar, *El Sol de México*, 12-5-83). He occupied the directorship of Spanish and literature courses at the Escuela Nacional Preparatoria and also was the director of the Miguel de Cervantes Library. A poet and essayist, he displays in his works a creative faculty and original thought. He is a Panamericanist and a humanist. When writing essays the poet discovers facets hidden to intellectual analysis. When writing poetry, the essayist reveals philosophical and metaphysical depths. His style is contemporary without following a particular school. He writes with the sobriety of the classicists and the flair of the Modernists and "Creacionistas."

Floresta plena (Full Forest) is a compilation of forty-six years of his poetry. In order to follow the poet's trajectory this book is essential, and it should become the reference book for the study of his poetry. *Hombres como antorchas* (Men Like Torches) is a collection of essays of great humanistic value. The author's impressive erudition becomes evident. He upholds, as is his invariable tendency, the defense of Hispanic spiritual and humanistic values. *Juárez en la poesía* (Juárez in Poetry) is an anthology in homage to Benito Juárez on the centennial of his death. *Banderas contra el huracán* (Flags against the Hurricane) is a collection of essays on Mexico's heroes of Independence. The author states that Mexico's idiosyncrasy is similar to that of all Spanish America. He cites similar feelings for social justice, constitutionality, and a nationalism free of expansionist interests.

WORKS: Poetry: *La soledad de Piedra* (Solitude of Stone) (México: Imprenta Mundial, 1934). *Atardecer sin lirios* (Sunset without Lilies) (México: n.p., 1938). *Sueños como obsidiana* (Dreams Like Obsidian) (México: Amatista, 1952). *Ascensión a la tierra* (Ascent to Earth) (México: Ed. Cuadernos Americanos, 1956). *Arboles juntos* (Trees Together) (México: Xochipilli, 1963). *Juárez en la poesía* (Juárez in Poetry) (México: Comisión Nacional para la Conmemoración del Centenario del fallecimiento de Don Benito Juárez, 1972). *Floresta plena* (Full Forest) (México:

Colección Xochipilli, 1981). Essays and Prose: *Paisaje y celaje de México* (Landscape and Skyscape of Mexico) (México: Stylo, 1952). *Hombres como antorchas* (Men like Torches) (México: Porrúa, 1968). *La flecha de cactus* (Cactus Arrow) (México: Ed. Oasis, 1969). *Banderas contra el huracán* (Flags against the Hurricane) (México: Porrúa, 1976). *Oropéndola* (The Golden Oriole) (México: Costa-Amic Editor, 1977). *Humaniora* (Humaniora) (México: Editorial Porrúa, 1987). Theater: *Sacramento* (Sacrament) (México: Costa-Amic Editor, 1980).

BIBLIOGRAPHY: Antonio Castro Leal, *La poesía mexicana moderna* (México: FCE, 1953), p. 389. Frank Dauster, *Breve historia de la poesía mexicana* (México: Ed. de Andrea, 1956), p. 176. Porfirio Martínez Peñalosa, *Anuario de la poesía mexicana 1961* (México: INBA, 1962), p. 63.

ALICIA G. WELDEN

MAGICAL REALISM, a narrative mode that is fundamentally Third World in its orientation and is commonly associated with certain types of novels and short stories written in developing nations such as Mexico. Thematically, magical realist works in Latin American explore facets of folk culture, mythology, religion, history, and geography that are unique to the New World experience.

The magical realist writer believes that New World reality is more extraordinary and marvelous than anything the imagination of man can create. As its name implies, magical realism is a combination of two concepts that, in fully developed nations, normally stand in opposition to one another. In Third World countries, magic and reality can coexist on the same plane, and are not necessarily in conflict. The magical realist text does not challenge the reader to enter into a "game" in the same sense that the fantastic one does. Instead, it attempts to re-create convincingly a world in which magic and reality exist simultaneously and are equally powerful in the formation of a people's worldview. One system of reference or one set of beliefs does not attempt to explain the other and to dominate. Instead, a balance is established between them, which gives the characters of magical realist fiction a unique point of view. Unlike the fantastic, magical realism does not negate reality: it simply portrays it from an expanded perspective, which sometimes carries it beyond the realm of logic and reason. Magical realism, as a term, was coined in 1925 by the German art critic, Franz Roh, who used it to describe postexpressionist painting in northern Europe. It is unclear how the term later became associated with Latin American fiction. Roh's book, *Nach-Expressionismus: Magischer Realismus*, was translated into Spanish in 1927 in a *Revista de Occidente* edition, and by the 1930s, magical realism had become a well-known term throughout western Europe, although its original connotation was not always maintained and its meaning was not always clear. Many Latin Americans, including Alejo Carpentier, Miguel Angel Asturias, and Arturo Uslar Pietri were, in Europe during the 1920s and 1930s; it is possible that they may have simply picked up the term and later transferred it to their own shores. Juan Ramón Jiménez was probably the first to link magical realism to Latin American when, in 1942, he used the term to describe Pablo Neruda's poetry. Jiménez's use of the term was gratuitous, however, for it showed no relationship to Roh's original conception of it.

Furthermore, Jiménez's association of magical realism to poetry did not have any lasting consequences. By 1948, the term had become almost exclusively attached to prose fiction. Uslar Pietri was the first Latin American to use the term with reference to his own native literature. Almost simultaneously, however, Alejo Carpentier invented another label for this "new" type of literature emerging in Latin America. He called it **lo real maravilloso**, which contributed to the confusion since, for many years, critics were unsure if magical realism and **lo real maravilloso** were one in the same thing. Today, Carpentier's definition of **lo real maravilloso** is generally regarded as one of the best definitions of magical realism, although he calls it by another name. Throughout the 1950s, 1960s, and 1970s, critics struggled with the need to define the concept of magical realism. Some, in desperation, declared the term null and void because its meaning was so elusive. Others continued to insist on the need to untangle the confusion and some, like Jaime Alazraki and Lorraine Elena Ben-Ur, succeeded in doing so.

Despite the confusion that has surrounded the term since its introduction to Latin American literary criticism in the late 1940s, it continues to be valuable because it sets apart a particular kind of narrative that does not fit comfortably into any other mode. Magical realism is not pure fantasy because it contains a substantial amount of realistic detail and is based on popular folk beliefs, historical fact, religious traditions, or legends that many people hold to be true. Unlike the fantastic, magical realism does not cause the reader to feel that his or her own world is being torn apart by supernatural forces. The attitude and approach in magical realist fiction is quite different. While the fantastic or fantasy writer sets out to create a world, the magical realist observes and penetrates one that already exists. The latter kind of literature is not a mimetic type, however, for the magical realist writer does not stop at superficial documentation. His goal is not that of the fantastic writer; he does not want the reader to feel fear, doubt, or hesitation but, rather, to come to believe, as he does, in the marvelous nature of the New World experience. The degree to which the magical element in the text surprises, startles, or unsettles the reader may vary to a large extent, depending on how greatly it differs from the reader's owm perception of what is "normal," "logical," or "real." Some magical realist fiction may seem to border on the fantastic, since events described in the narrative strike the reader as impossible; but, when seen from within the worldview of the characters, these "impossible" occurrences are accepted as ordinary happenings because they are firmly grounded in religion, myth, legend, or historical tradition.

As some critics have observed, the fantastic tends to be cultivated today in societies where people no longer believe in magic. In Mexico, belief in magic does exist, not only among so-called primitive peoples, but also among all those who are aware of the magical qualities inherent in Latin America's unique culture, geography, and history. As Latin Americans have discovered more about themselves and about their heritage, they have experienced a reawakened interest in the myths and legends that have shaped their nations' growth. They use Latin America's bicultural folklore, in which European beliefs have merged with indigenous or African ones, to explore the possibility that reality may be more complex and more mysterious than what is traditionally portrayed in literature. They attempt to use uncharted zones of myth and legend in the same way that others have portrayed everyday life in Latin America, without surprise, fear, or doubt. The reader, who may not always share the same worldview as the characters of magical realist texts, may initially react to the situations described as if they were flights of fantasy. However, because these magical elements are presented in a cultural context that gives them deeper meaning, the reader must ultimately see that the texts contain some essential truths. In the hands of some of Latin America's most talented writers, like Miguel Angel Asturias, Alejo Carpentier, Arturo Uslar Pietri, and Gabriel García Márquez, magical realism has become a highly effective, artistic tool with which one may explore regional, national, or continental identity.

In Mexico, magical realism is an important trend in letters, but it has not yet been cultivated by a wide circle of writers. Probably the most outstanding example of a magical realist text in Mexico is Juan *Rulfo's classic novel, *Pedro Páramo*. Magical realist elements can also be found in some of the works of Elena *Garro, Rosario *Castellanos, Guadalupe *Dueñas, José *Revueltas, Eraclio *Zepeda, and Alberto *Bonifaz Nuño, among others.

BIBLIOGRAPHY: Jaime Alazraki, "Para una revalidación del concepto realismo mágico en la literatura hispanoamericana," in *Homenaje a Andrés Iduarte*, edited by Jaime Alazraki et al. (Clear Creek, Ind.:   American Hispanist, 1976), pp. 9-21. Lorraine Elena Ben-Ur, "El realismo mágico en la crítica hispanoamericana," *Journal of Spanish Studies. Twentieth Century* 4, 3 (1976): 149-63. Alejo Carpentier, "De lo real maravilloso americano," in *Tientos y diferencias* (México: UNAM, 1964), pp. 115-35 (originally published as the prologue to *El reino de este mundo*, 1949). James Irish, "Magical Realism: A Search for Caribbean and Latin American Roots," *Literary Half Yearly* (University of Mysore) 2, 2 (1970): 127-39. Luis Leal, "El realismo mágico en la literatura hispanoamericana," *Cuadernos americanos* 152 (1967): 230-35. Donald Yates, ed., *Otros mundos, otros fuegos: Fantasía y realismo mágico en Iberoamérica*, Memorias del XVI Congreso Internacional de Literatura Iberoamericana, 1973 (Pittsburgh, IILI, 1975).

CYNTHIA K. DUNCAN

MAILLEFERT, Alfredo (1889-1941). Maillefert was born in Taretan, Michoacán. When he was ten years old, he went to Morelia, where he took private classes and learned French, the language of his ancestors, and English. He had no particular career. His permanent avocation was literature, especially the essay and the theater. He was a member of the Liceo Michoacano (Michoacán Lyceum). In 1919 he went to Mexico City, where he contributed to *La Antorcha* and *La República*. He also got a job in the Oficina de Monumentos Artísticos de la Secretaria de Educación Pública (Office of Artistic Monuments of the Secretary of Public Education), by the side of Jorge Enciso, who named him secretary of the Exposición de Arte Popular (Exposition of Popular Art), organized for the 1921 Centennial. Around that time, Maillefert returned to Morelia with the hope of recovering his land, and he secured a position as a French teacher in the Colegio de San Nicolás de Hidalgo (School of San Nicolás de Hidalgo) and as a Spanish teacher in the Escuela Normal (Normal School). He returned to Mexico City in 1926. He took the post of subdirector of the Oficina de Extensión Educativa (Office of Educational Extension) by radio, of the secretary of education (1933) and participated in several dramatic works. He began to publish in newspapers and magazines. In 1934, he began work as a French and Hispanic American literature teacher at the Escuela Nacional Preparatoria (National

Preparatory School). He was employed by the Departamento del Distrito Federal (Department of the Federal District) and also worked as a translator and proofreader for the Imprenta Universitaria (University Press). He died in Mexico City on August 12, 1941.

Related to *Gutiérrez Nájera, of whose prose he compiled an anthology, Maillefert also exhibited with El Duque Job certain spiritual affinities. His hearty fondness for French literature is noted by José Luis *Martínez, who adds: "But his sensitiveness only knew two territories: the things of his native land, to which he dedicated poetic and moving evocations, and the liking for books. His literary criticism, which cut down to the softness of his spirit all his readings, was typically impressionistic, and his constant model, Azorín."

WORKS: "Apuntes sobre González León" (Notes on González León), in *El Libro y el Pueblo* 12, 9 (Sept. 1934): 455-57. "El diabolismo de Valle-Inclán" (Diabolism of Valle-Inclán), in *El Libro y el Pueblo* 12, 12 (Dec. 1934): 607-10. *Laudanza de Michoacán* (Praiseworthiness of Michoacán) (México: UNAM, 1937). "Estampas de Morelia: las montañas" (Images of Morelia: the Mountains), in *Leyendas y cuentos michoacanos*, edited by Jesús Romero Flores (México: Botas, 1938), vol. 1, pp. 325-28. "Micrós," in *Revista de la Universidad de México* vol. 25 (Feb. 1938): 20. *Ancla en el tiempo* (Anchor in Time), Gentes y paisajes, (Morelia: Universidad Michoacana, 1940). Prologue to Manuel Gutiérrez Nájera, *Cuentos, crónicas y ensayos* (Stories, Chronicles and Essays), Biblioteca del Estudiante Universitario, 20 (México: UNAM, 1940). *Los libros que leí* (The Books I Read), prologue by Agustín Yáñez (México: UNAM, 1942). "Mi abuelo paterno" (My Paternal Grandfather), in *Cuatro siglos de literatura mexicana* (México: Edit. Leyenda, 1946), pp. 850-52. *Una historia que contar* (A Story to Tell), Papeles de un provinciano (México: Ed. Jus, 1946) contains "La soledad" (Solitude), "El amor" (Love), "La amistad" (Friendship), "La ciudad" (The City), "Lecturas" (Readings), "Motivos de viaje" (Reasons for a Journey), "Epílogo en 1938" (Epilogue in 1938).

BIBLIOGRAPHY: Ermilo Abreu Gómez, Sala de retratos (México: Edit. Leyenda, 1946), pp. 174-76. Cayetano Andrade, *Antología de escritores nicolaitas (1540-1940)* (México: n.p., 1941), pp. 773-75. David N. Arce, *Presencia y prosa de Alfredo Maillefert* (México: INBA, 1950). Salvador Azuela, "Un libro póstumo de Maillefert," in *El Universal* (April 22, 1946): 5C. Miguel Bustos Cerecedo, "Los olvidados, Alfredo Maillefert Vidales," in *Nivel* (2nd epoch), 38 (Feb. 25, 1966): 5. Luis Leal, *Bibliografía del cuento mexicano* (México: Eds. de Andrea, 1958), p. 84. José Luis Martínez, *Literatura mexicana siglo XX, 1910-1949*, vol. 1 (México: Ant. Libr. Robredo), pp. 60, 100, 117, 118, 127, 137, 138; vol. 2 (1950), p. 74; *El ensayo mexicano moderno*, vol. 1 (México: FCE, 1958), p. 264. Octaviano Valdés, "Laudanza de Michoacán. Alfredo Maillefert," in *Abside* (Nov. 1937): 55-57. Esperanza Velázquez Bringas and Rafael Heliodoro Valle, *Indice de escritores* (México: Studio of the Herrero Brothers, 1928). Agustín Yáñez, Prologue to *Los libros que leí* (México: UNAM, 1942).

MICHELE MUNCY

MANCISIDOR, José (1894-1956). Born in Veracruz on April 20, 1894, José Mancisidor was both a lifelong revolutionary and a man of letters, whose professions were teaching and journalism. A contributor to many of the important journals in his area, such as *El Dictamen, El Gladiador,* and others, Mancisidor was also a director of the Mexican Russian Institute and the founder of the Liga de Escritores y Artistas Revolucionarios. He died suddenly September 2, 1956, while still active in his profession.

A commentator on social issues, Mancisidor was recognized as a noteworthy novelist and also a story-writer. Considered one of his most significant works, the novel *Frontera junto al mar* (Frontier by the Sea) (1925), which was awarded a national prize, depicts the heroic battle of resistance by the people of Veracruz against the invasion by U.S. marines in 1914. Another novel, *El alba en las simas* (Dawn in the Chasms), traces and describes in gripping detail the national takeover of Mexican petroleum from foreign companies and the consequent redevelopment of the industry in Mexican hands.

His revolutionary political views can be found especially in his essays on such well-known historical figures as Zolá, Marx, Lenin, Juárez, Hidalgo, and others. Most of his writings, both fiction and nonfiction, are supportive of his views. Not only his political commitment to such figures and their views, but the tenor of his life in keeping with a strongly communistic political belief system, constitute Mancisidor's essential legacy.

WORKS: Essays: *Carranza y su política internacional* (Carranza and His International Politics) (Veracruz: n.p. 1929). "Romero," in *Homenaje a Rubén Romero* (México: Imp. Mundial, 1937). "José Rubén Romero," in *El Nacional* (July 10, 1937). *Zola, soñador y hombre* (Zola, Dreamer and Man) (México: Ed. Dialéctica, 1940). *Henri Barbusse, ingeniero de almas* (Henri Barbusse, Engineer of Souls) (México: Edit. Botas, 1945). *Literatura contemporánea* (Contemporary Literature), appendix to *Historia de la literatura rusa,* by K. Waliszevski (México: n.p., 1945). *Balzac, el sentido humano de su obra* (Balzac, Human Meaning in His Work) (México: UNAM, 1952). *Sobre literatura y filosofía* (On Literature and Philosophy) (México: Eds. Litoral, 1956). *Máximo Gorki: su filosofía y su religión* (Máximo Gorki: His Philosophy and His Religion) (México: Col. Cultura, 1956). Stories and Tales: *Cómo cayeron los héroes* (How the Heroes Fell) (México: n.p., 1930). "El sargento" (The Sergeant) (México: n.p., 1932). *Ciento veinte días* (One Hundred and Twenty Days) (México: Edit. México Nuevo, 1937). *La primera piedra* (The First Stone) (México: Edit. Stylo, 1950). *El juramento* (The Oath) (México: n.p., 1947). *El destino* (The Destiny) (Cuba: n.p., 1947). *Me lo dijo María Kaimlova* (María Kaimlova Told Me It) Los Presentes, no. 35 (México: n.p., 1955). Novels: *La asonada* (The One in Accord) (Veracruz: Eds. Integrales, 1931). *La ciudad roja* (The Red City) (Veracruz: Eds. Integrales, 1932). *Nueva York revolucionario* (Revolutionary New York) (Veracruz: Eds. Integrales, 1935). *De una madre española* (From a Spanish Mother) (México: Edit. México Nuevo, 1938). *En la rosa de los vientos* (In the Rose of the Winds) (México: EDIAPSA, 1940). *Frontera junto al mar* (Frontier by the Sea) (México: FCE, 1953). *El alba de las simas* (The Dawn of the Chasms) (México: n.p., 1953); 2nd ed. (México: Edit. América Nueva, 1955); re-edited in Buenos Aires, with title *Nuestro petróleo* (Our Petroleum). *Se llamaba Catalina* (Her Name Was Catalina) (Veracruz: Universidad Veracruzana, 1958). *Otra vez aquellos días* (Those Days Again), unfinished novel. *La semilla del hombre* (The Seed of Man), unfinished novel. *Imágenes de mi tiempo* (Images of My Time), unfinished novel. Anthologies: *Angulos de México* (Angles of Mexico), selection of stories (México: n.p., 1940). *Cuentos mexicanos del siglo XIX* (Mexican Stories of the Nineteenth Century), selection, prologue, and notes, 2nd ed. (México: Edit. Nueva España, [1946]). *Cuentos mexicanos de autores contemporáneos* (Mexican Stories of Contemporary Authors), selection, prologue, and notes (México: Edit. Nueva España, n.d., [1946]). Theater: *Frontera junto al mar* (Frontier by the Sea) (Mexico, 1954). *El joven Juárez* (The Young Juárez), film, 1955.   A variety of movie plots, including   "¡Arriba Madero!" (Up with Madero!), "El mundo de la infancia y adolescencia de Juárez" (Juárez' World of Infancy and Adolescence), among others. Biography and History: "Síntesis histórica del movimiento social en México" (Historical Synthesis of the Social Movement in Mexico), appendix to *Historia general del socialismo y de las luchas sociales* (General History of Socialism and of Social Fights), by Max Beer (México: n.p., 1940). *Hidalgo, Morelos, Guerrero* (México: Edit. Grijalvo, 1956). *Historia de las luchas sociales en Mexico* (History of the Social Wars in Mexico) (México: n.p., n.d.). *Historia de la Revolución Mexicana* (History of the Mexican Revolution) (México: n.p., 1958); 4th ed. (México: Libro-Mex, 1964). *Obras completas de José Mancisidor* (Complete Works of José Mancisidor), 4 vols. (Xalapa: Gobierno del Estado de Veracruz, 1979/1980).

BIBLIOGRAPHY: Ermilo Abreu Gómez, *Sala de retratos* (México: Edit. Leyenda, 1946), pp. 177-78. Federico Alvarez, Review of *Historia de la Revolución Mexicana*, in *La Cultura en México* 116, 6 (1964): xviii. John S. Brushwood and José Rojas Garcidueñas, *Breve historia de la novela mexicana* (México: Eds. de Andrea, 1959), pp. 101-2. Miguel Bustos Cerecedo, Review of *El alba de las simas*, in *Metáfora* 2 (May-June, 1955): 39. Antonio Castro Leal, *La novela de la Revolución*, vol. 2 (México and Buenos Aires: Edit. Aguilar, 1958), pp. 455-56. Alí Chumacero, "Las letras mexicanas en 1953," review of *Frontera junto al mar*, in *Las Letras Patrias* 1 (Jan.-March, 1954), pp. 118-20; "Panorama de los últimos libros, José Mancisidor, *Máximo Gorki: su filosofía y su religión*," in *México en la Cultura* 383 (July 22, 1956): 2. Gastón García Cantú, "Siete ensayos de José Mancisidor," review of *Sobre literatura y filosofía*, in *México en la Cultura* 391 (Sept. 16, 1956): 2. Efraín Huerta, "El maestro Mancisidor," in *El Libro y el Pueblo* 18, 25 (Sept.-Oct., 1956): 119-20.   Francisco R. Illescas and Juan Bartolo Hernández, *Escritores Veracruzanos*, review of his life and work (Veracruz: n.p., 1945), pp. 516-19. Luis Leal, *Breve historia del cuento mexicano* (México: Eds. de Andrea, 1962), pp. 122-23; *Bibliografía del cuento mexicano* (México: Eds. de Andrea, 1958), p. 85. José Mancisidor, "Mi deuda con Azuela," in *El Nacional* (Aug. 2, 1956): 3. Ernest Moore, *Bibliografía de novelistas de la Revolución Mexicana* (México: n.p., 1941), pp. 51-52, 102-4. F. Rand Morton, *Los novelistas de la Revolución Mexicana* (México: Edit. Cultura, 1949), pp. 172-83, 191-92. Camerino Navarro, "Mancisidor y la Revolución," in *Crisol* 77 (May, 1935): 305-8. Aurora M. Ocampo de Gómez and Ernesto Prado Velázquez, *Diccionario de escritores mexicanos* (México: UNAM, 1967), pp. 210-11. Rafael L. de los Ríos, "La última novela de José Mancisidor," in *Letras de México* 25 (May 15, 1938): 12. César Rodríguez Chicharro, Review of *Frontera junto al mar*, in *Ideas de México* 4 (March-April, 1954): 184-86. Jesús Romero Flores, *Maestros y amigos: recuerdos y semblanzas de algunos escritores* (México: Costa-Amic, 1971). Various, "Homenaje a José Mancisidor, in *México en la Cultura* 389 (Sept. 2, 1956): 14-20 . "Homenaje a Mancisidor," in *El Centavo* 4, 50 (July, 1962): 7-14. Calvert J. Winter, Review of *Asonada*, in *Books Abroad* 8 (1934): 229.

JEANNE C. WALLACE

MAPLES Arce, Manuel (1898-1981), poet and critic. Maples Arce was born in Papantla, Veracruz, on May 1, 1898. He did his early studies in Veracruz and then went to México City, where he received his law degree from the Universidad Nacional in 1925. He later studied French literature and art history at the Sorbonne in Paris. He became involved in state government at twenty-seven years of age and had a great deal of impact encouraging the publication of literary and educational writings. He continued serving in a number of political positions and diplomatic posts in Europe and Latin America, including his ambassadorship to Japan and to Lebanon.

In the early 1920s, Maples Arce initiated a poetic revolution that led to the formation of the Estridentista literary group. (*See* Vanguardist Prose Fiction in Mexico.) His collections of poetry, *Andamios interiores* (Interior Platforms) (1922) and *Urbe* (Metropolis) (1924), were products of this period, during which he tried to break with the old poetic tradition and create new ways of expression.

Maples Arce also wrote a number of collections of literary essays, including *Peregrinación por el arte de México* (Pilgrimage Through Mexican Art) (1952), and *Ensayos japoneses* (Japanese Essays) (1959), which is a result of his travels in Japan. He has contributed to a number of journals and newspapers both in México and in other countries.

WORKS: Poetry: *Andamios interiores* (Interior Platform) (México: Editorial Cultura, 1922). *Urbe* (Metropolis) (México: Andrés Botas e hijos, 1924). *Metropolis*, English translation by John Dos Passos (New York: T. S. Book Company, 1929). *Poemas interdictos* (Interdict Poems) (Xalapa: Horizonte, 1927); *Poemes interdits*, translated to French by Edmond Vandercammen, (Bruxelles: Cahiers du journal des poétes, 1936). *Memorial de la sangre* (Blood Memorial) (México: Talleres Gráficos de la Nación, 1947). *Las semillas del tiempo: obra poética 1919-1980* (México: FCE, 1981), preliminary study by Rubén Bonifaz Nuño. Anthology: *Antología de la poesía mexicana moderna* (Anthology of Modern Mexican Poetry) (Rome: Poligráfica Tiberina, 1940). Essay: *Paisaje en la literatura mexicana* (Landscape in Mexican Literature) (México: Editores Porrúa, 1944). *El arte mexicano moderno* (México: n.p., 1945); *Modern Mexican Art* (London: A. Zwemmer, n.d.); *Peregrinación por el arte de México* (Pilgrimage through Mexican Art) (Buenos Aires, n.p., 1952). *Incitaciones y valoraciones* (Incitations and Appraisals) (México: Cuadernos Mexicanos, 1957). *Ensayos japoneses* (Japanese Essays) (México: Editorial Cultura, 1959). Sketch: *A la orilla de este río* (At the Edge of This River), illustrated by Leopoldo Méndez (México: Edición Plenitud, 1964). Prologue: Germán List Arzubide, *Esquina* (Corner), poetry (México, n.p., 1924). *Siete cuentos mexicanos* (Seven Mexican Short Stories), selection and foreword by Maples Arce (Panamá: Bibl. Selecta, 1946).

BIBLIOGRAPHY: Emilio Abreu Gómez, "Maples Arce y la poesía," *Revista Mexicana de Cultura* (Jan. 13, 1952); "Los libros y otros engaños, Manuel Maples Arce," *Revista Mexicana de Cultura* 858 (Sept. 8, 1963): 4; "El libro de hoy, cuentos, novelas, memorias y crónicas," review of *La orilla de este río*, in *Revista Mexicana de Cultura* 901 (July 5, 1964): 7. Anon., Review of *A la orilla de este río*, in *México en la Cultura* 789 (Mayo 3, 1964): 3; "Memorias de un poeta," *Revista de la Semana* (Jan. 31, 1965): 3. Jesús Arellano, *Antología de los 50 poetas contemporáneos de México* (México: Edición Alatorre, 1952), pp. 51-59, 455-56; "Las ventas de don Quijote. Revisión de algunos nombres de la literatura mexicana. Manuel Maples

Arce," *Nivel* 46 (Oct. 25, 1962): 5. Rubén Bonifaz Nuño, Preliminary study to *Las semillas del tiempo: obra poética 1919-1980* (México: FCE, 1981). John S. Brushwood, "Contemporáneos and the Limits of Art," *Romance Notes* 2 (Spring 1964): 128-32. Antonio Castro Leal, "Antología de la poesía mexicana moderna," *Revista de Literatura Mexicana* 1, 2 (Dec.-Oct., 1940): 379-81; *La poesía mexicana moderna*, Letras Mexicanas 12 (México: FCE, 1953), pp. 24-25, 255. Jorge J. Crespo de la Serna, "El río en el recuerdo de Maples Arce," *El Día* (March 5, 1965): 5. Jorge Cuesta, *Antología de la poesía mexicana moderna* (México: Contemporáneos, 1928), pp. 130-40. Alí Chumacero, "Panorama de los últimos libros, *Incitaciones y valoraciones*," *México en la Cultura* 420 (April 7, 1957): 2. Frank Dauster, *Breve historia de la poesía mexicana*, Manuales Studium, no. 4 (México: Ediciónes de Andrea, 1956), pp. 167-68. Gonzálo Deza Méndez [J. M. González de Mendoza], "Bibliografía," in *Nuevo Mundo* (April 15, 1952). Enrique Díez-Canedo, *Letras de América* (México: FCE, 1944), pp. 251-57. Esteban Durán Rosado, "La historia de si mismo," review of *A la orilla de este río*, in *Revista Mexicana de Cultura* 902 (June 12, 1964): 10. Merlin H. Forster, *Historia de la poesía hispanoamericana* (Clear Creek, Ind.: American Hispanist, 1981), pp. 136, 138. Merlin H. Forster and K. David Jackson, *An Annotated Guide to the Vanguard in Latin American Literature* (Westport, Conn.: Greenwood Press, to be published in 1990). Mauricio Fresco, "Hablando de Maples Arce," in *Hoy* (Jan. 24, 1942): 52, 82. Francisco González Guerrero, *Los libros de los otros* (México: Recensiones, 1947). Carlos González Peña, *Historia de la literatura mexicana* (1928; México: Porrúa, 1966), p. 274. Andrés Henestrosa, "La nota cultural" and "Estridentismo," *El Nacional* (July 3, 1964): 3, 7; "La nota cultural," review of *A la orilla de este río*, in *El Nacional* (July 21, 1954): 3. Francisco R. Illesca and Juan Bartolo Hernández, *Escritores veracruzanos* (Veracruz, Veracruz, 1945), pp. 572-73. Luis Leal, "El movimiento estridentista," in *Los vanguardismos en la América Latina*, edited by Oscar Collazos (Barcelona: Ediciones Península, 1977), pp. 105-16. Raúl Leiva, *Imagen de la poesía mexicana contemporánea* (México: UNAM, 1959), pp. 67-73. Germán List Arzubide, *El movimiento estridentista* (Xalapa, Veracruz: Eds. Horizonte, 1927). José Luis Martínez, *Literatura mexicana del siglo xx, 1910-1949*, Clásicos y Modernos (México: Ant. Libr. Robredo, 1949), vol. 1, no. 3, pp. 29, 96; vol. 2, no. 4 (1950), pp. 74-75. Kenneth Charles Monahan, "Maples Arce y el Estridentismo," Thesis, Northwestern University, 1973. Carlos Monsiváis, *La poesía mexicana del siglo XX* (México: Empresas Editoriales, 1966), pp. 48-53, 335; and "Los estridentistas y los agoristas," in *Los vanguardismos en la América Latina* (Barcelona: Ediciones Península, 1977), pp. 117-22. José Muñoz Cota, Review of *La orilla de este río*, in *Revista Mexicana de Cultura* 895 (May 24, 1964): 1-2. Oliver T. Myers, review of *Ensayos Japoneses*, in *Revista Hispánica Moderna* 27, 2 (April, 1961,): 165. Elías Nandino, Review of *Ensayos japoneses*, *Estaciones* 4, 14 (Summer 1959): 243. Aurora M. Ocampo de Gómez and Ernesto Prado Velázquez, *Diccionario de escritores Mexicanos* (México: UNAM, 1967), pp. 211-12. Gregorio Ortega, *Hombres, mujeres* (México: Aztlán, 1926), pp. 105-8; 2nd ed. (México: Bellas Artes, 1966). Octavio Paz, ed., *Poesía en movimiento, 1966* (México: Siglo Veintinuno, Ed., 1980), pp. 358-64. Emiliano Quiroz, "Manuel Maples Arce y sus recuerdos del estridentismo," *Cultura en México*, supplement of *Siempre!* 438 (May 12, 1971): ii-v. Salvador Reyes Nevares, Review of *Ensayos japoneses*, *México en la Cultura* 543 (Aug. 9, 1959): 4. José Rojas Garcidueñas, "Estridentismo y Contemporáneos," *Revista de la Universidad de México* 6, 7 (Dec. 2, 1952): 11. Gustavo Sainz, Review of *A la orilla de este río*, *México en la Cultura* 800 (July 19, 1964): 7. Mauricio de la Selva, "Asteriscos," review of *A la orilla de este río,* in *Diorama de la Cultura* (Sep. 20, 1964): 4. Guillermo Sheridan, *Los Contemporáneos ayer* (México: FCE, 1985). Rogelio Sinán, *Los valores humanos en la lírica de   Maples Arce* (México, n.p., 1959). Rafael Solana, "El paisaje de la literatura mexicana (capítulos que olvidó Maples Arce)," *Mañana* (Jan. 6, 1945): 5-6. Philip Ward, ed., *The Oxford Companion to Spanish Literature* (Oxford: Clarendon Press, 1978), p. 358.

EDNA A. REHBEIN

MAR, María del. See MOLT, Angela.

MARIA y Campos, Arnando de (1897-   ), journalist, prose writer. Born in Mexico City on May 23, 1887, Arnando de María y Campos received his degree fron the Scientific Institute of Mexico in 1914. He had traveled to Europe and the Middle East upon several occasions and is credited not only as a writer but also as technical advisor of theater and movies, editor, reporter, and chronicler. He functioned as a political advisor and private secretary of Juan Sánchez Azcona, a performer and director of radio (1899-1940), and head of the Theatre of Fine Arts. He was associated with several national organizations and was the first president of the Journalism Club of Mexico.

His literary contributions emphasize his knowledge of subject matter and refined narrative style. He had written for most of the newspapers and magazines of Mexico.

WORKS: *Poemas de Primavera* (Spring's Poems) (México: Victoria, 1816). *Mis triviales pecados* (My Trivial Sins) (México: Victoria, 1916). *Frivolerias* (Frivolities) (México: Imp. Nacional, 1919). *El Primer amor* (The First Love) (México: Don Quijote, 1820). *Un par de ojos azules* (A Pair of Blue Eyes) (México: Don Quijote, 1920). *Visiones urbanas* (Urban Visions) (México: Botas, 1921). *Fifí* (México: Hesperia, 1925). *Voces de madres sobre el Océano* (Voices of Mothers over the Ocean) (México: Teatro del Aire, 1938). *Crónicas de teatro de hoy* (Chronicles of Today's Theater) (México: Botas, 1941). *Ponciano, el torero con bigotes* (Ponciano, the Mustached Bullfighter (México: Xóchitl, 1943). *Carlota de Bélgica* (Carlota of Belgiun) (México: Rex, 1944). *Seis comedias para oírse* (Six comedies to be heard) (México: Eds. Populares, 1945).

BIBLIOGRAPHY: Ruth S. Lamb, *Bibliografía del teatro mexicano del siglo xx* (México: Ed. de Andrea, 1962), pp. 76, 136. José Luis Martínez, *Literatura mexicana siglo xx, 1910-1949* (México: Ant. Libr. Robredo, 1949, 1950), vol 1, pp. 71, 138, vol 2, pp. 75-6.

SILKA FREIRE

MARTINEZ, José Luis (1918-   ), critic and poet. Born in Atoyac, Jalisco, Martínez attended elementary school at the Colegio Renacimiento in Ciudad Guzmán and high school in Guadalajara. He enrolled in medical school for two years at the UNAM but switched to literature in 1938 and completed his studies in 1943. He taught Spanish and Mexican literature, the Spanish language, and literary criticism from 1940 to 1965. His main interest has been to analyze and study Mexican literature. He is considered one of Mexico's best critics and historians. He became a member of the Academia Mexicana de la Lengua (Mexican Language Academy) in 1958 and its president in 1985. The Real Academia Española (Spanish Language Academy) invited him to form part of its association in 1960.

In addition to his academic duties, Martínez has held many political positions: he was Mexico's ambassador to Lima from 1961 to 1962, to the UNESCO in Paris from 1963 to 1964, and to Athens in 1971. He was the general director of the Instituto Nacional de Bellas Artes (National Institute of the Arts) from 1965 to 1970. He served in the Comisión Nacional de los Libros de Texto Gratuito (National Commission of Free Textbooks) from 1967 to 1971. In 1967 he was elected a member of the board of trustees of the Colegio de México. In 1968 he served as president of the Mexican delegations to UNESCO's Fifteenth General Conference, held in Paris. He was president of Mexico's PEN Club from 1968 to 1969. With Alí *Chumacero, Jorge *González Durán, and Leopoldo Zea he founded the journal *Tierra Nueva* in 1940. In 1943 he edited *Letras de México*, and from 1943 to 1946 he collaborated in *El Hijo Pródigo* and *Nueva Revista Mexicana de Literatura*. He co-edited *Estaciones* in 1956.

WORKS: Poetry: *Elegía por Melibea y otros poemas* (Elegy for Melibea and Other Poems) (México: Tierra Nueva, 1940). Prologue to *Poesía romántica* (Romantic Poetry), edited by Alí Chumacero. (México: UNAM, 1941), pp. ix-xxvi. Essays: *El concepto de la muerte en la poesía española del siglo XV* (The Concept of Death in Fifteenth-Century Spanish Poetry) (México: El Colegio de México, 1942). Selection and Introduction, *Literatura indígena moderna* (Modern Indian Literature) (México: Ediciones Mensaje, 1942). *La técnica en literatura. Introducción* (Introduction to Literary Technique) (México: Letras de México, 1943). "Las letras patrias. De la epoca de la Independencia a nuestros días" (Our Country's Letters. From the Independence to the Present), in *México y la cultura* (México: SEP, 1946), pp. 385-72. *Situación de la literatura mexicana contemporánea* (The Situation of Contemporary Mexican Literature) (México: Cultura, 1948). *Literatura mexicana: siglo XX. 1910-1949* (Twentieth-Century Mexican Literature [1910-1949] (México: Antigua Librería Robredo, 1949-50). *Literatura mexicana: siglo XX. 1910-1949: Guías bibliográficas* (Twentieth-Century Mexican Literature. 1910-1949: Bibliographic Guide) (México: Antigua Librería Robredo, 1950). *Los problemas de nuestra cultura literaria* (The Problems of Our Literary Culture) (Guadalajara: Ediciones Et Caetera, 1953). *Problemas literarios* (Literary Problems) (México: Obregón, 1955). *La emancipación literaria de México* (The Literary Emancipation of Mexico) (México: Robredo, 1955). *La expresión nacional. Letras mexicanas del siglo XIX* (México: UNAM, 1955). *El ensayo mexicano moderno* (The Mexican Modern Essay) (México: FCE, 1958); 2nd ed. (1971). *De la naturaleza y carácter de la literatura mexicana* (About the Nature and Character of Mexican Literature) (México: FCE, 1960). *Nezahualcóyotl* (México: SEP, 1972). *Unidad y diversidad de la literatura latinoamericana. Seguido de la emancipación de Hispanoamérica* (Unity and Diversity of Latin American Literature, Followed by the Emancipation of Hispanic America) (México: Joaquín Mortiz, 1972). Prologue to *Agustín Yáñez: Obras escogidas* (México: Aguilar, 1973). Edition and prologue to *Manuel Acuña. Obras: poesías, teatro, artículos y cartas* (México: Porrúa, 1975). Edited and annotated Justo Sierra's *Crítica y artículos literarios* (México:

UNAM, 1977). Annotated and indexed Justo Sierra's *Viajes (En tierra yankee, en la europa latina)* (México: UNAM, 1977. Selection of texts for *Zapata, Iconografía* (Iconography of Zapata) (México: FCE, 1979). *El códice florentino y la historia general de Sahagún* (The Florentine Codice and Sahagún's General History) (México: Dirección de Difusión y Publicaciones del Archivo General de la Nación, 1982). Edited Pedro Henríquez Ureña's *Estudios mexicanos* (México: FCE-SEP, 1984). *Nezahualcóyotl: vida y obra* (Nezahualcóyotl: Life and Works) (México: FCE, 1972; SEP, 1984). *El ensayo: Siglos XIX y XX de Justo Sierra a Carlos Monsiváis* (The Essay: Nineteenth and Twentieth Centuries, from Justo Sierra to Carlos Monsiváis) (México: PROMEXA, 1985). *El libro en Hispanoamérica: origen y desarrollo* (Books in Spanish America: Origin and Development), 2nd ed. (Madrid: Fundación Germán Sánchez Ruipérez, 1986).

BIBLIOGRAPHY: Ermilo Abreu Gómez, Review of *Literatura mexicana. Siglo XX*, in *Revista Interamericana de Bibliografía* 1, 1 (Jan.-Mar. 1951): 29-31; *The Modern Mexican Essay*, translated by H. W. Hilborn (Toronto: University of Toronto Press, 1965). María Luisa Mendoza, "El Teatro. La tercera ventana de José Luis Martínez," in *El Día* 133 (Jan. 10, 1965): 4. Sara Velasco, *Escritores jalicienses Tomo II (1900-1965)* (Guadalajara: Universidad of Guadalajara, 1982),pp. 222-29.

MARGARITA VARGAS

MARTINEZ de Navarrete, José Manuel (1768-1809), poet and teacher of Latin. A native of Zamora, Michoacán, and a devoted student of Latin, Martínez de Navarrete followed a religious calling even as a youth and entered Querétaro's Franciscan monastery of San Pedro and San Pablo at the age of nineteen. After continuing his study of Latin as well as theology at Pueblito and Celaya, he became a professor of Latin.   As an ordained priest, Martínez de Navarrete taught and preached in Valladolid (Morelia), Rioverde, Silao, and San Antonio Tula; he ended his career in the post of guardian at the monastery of Tlalpujahua, where he died on July 19, 1809.

Although Martínez de Navarrete never attained the fame of Sor Juana Inés de la *Cruz, his lyric poetry is often regarded as second only to that of the renowned Tenth Muse. Influenced by the Spanish poet Juan Meléndez Valdés and educated in the Latin tradition, he demonstrated an unusual clarity and sensitivity in his poetic works that represent the height of neoclassical expression in Mexico. His odes describing nature constitute the best examples of the eloquent simplicity that characterizes his poetry. His amorous verse, which closely follows the rhetorical conventions of his time, is his least original contribution to Mexico's literary history. His earliest poems were published in the *Diario de México* (Mexican Daily) beginning in 1806, and his *Entretenimientos poéticos* (Poetic Diversions) was published in 1823 in a two-volume set.

WORKS: *Panegírico de la Purísima Concepción de María* (Panegyric of the Purist Conception of Mary) (México: Diario de México, 1806). *Divina Providencia* (Divine Providence) (México: Diario de México, 1808). *Entretenimientos poéticos* (Poetic Diversions) (México: Imprenta de Valdes, 1823; París: Librería de Lecointe, 1835).

Poesías (Poems) (México: Tipografía de Victoriano Agüeros, 1904). *Poemas inéditos* (Unpublished Poems) (México: Sociedad de Bibliófilos Mexicanos, 1929).

BIBLIOGRAPHY: Anon., *Fray Manuel Martínez de Navarrete: Homenaje en el bicentenario de su nacimiento, 1768-1968* (Morelia: Cuadernos de Cultura Popular Biblioteca Michoacana, no. 48, 1968). Carlos González Peña, *History of Mexican Literature*, translated by Gusta Barfield Nance and Florene Johnson Dunstan (Dallas: Southern Methodist University Press, 1968), pp. 121-23. Pedro Henríquez Ureña, *Estudios mexicanos* (México: FCE, 1984), pp. 149-52. Francisco Monterde, "Prólogo" in *Poesías profanas* by Martínez de Navarrete (México: UNAM, 1939).

JULIE GREER JOHNSON

MARTINEZ Ortega, Judith (1908-). Martínez Ortega was born in Mexico on February 17, 1908. A world traveler and a member of the diplomatic corps, she is not a prolific writer. However, her brief *La isla* (The Island), for its honest portrayal, may well be one of Mexico's better autobiographies written by a woman. *La isla y tres cuentos* (The Island and Three Stories) is mainly Martínez Ortega's memoir of 1931, the year she spent as the secretary of General Francisco J. Mújica on the Islas Marías, a penal colony on the Pacific coast near Nayarit. Impressions of the enervating and depressing environment both inside and outside the prison are maintained throughout in one of the most realistic memoirs ever written in México. She treats themes rarely broached in Mexican autobiography: rape, homosexuality, and prostitution. The titles of Martínez Ortega's short stories, "Cristina," "Julieta," and "Eva" betray her interest in women. In a realism-naturalism more characteristic of the Porfiriato, the author perceives women as involved with men unworthy of them.

WORKS: *La isla y tres cuentos* (México: Imprenta Universitaria, 1959).

BIBLIOGRAPHY: Aurora M. Ocampo de Gómez and Ernesto Prado Velázquez, *Diccionario de escritores mexicanos* (México: UNAM, 1967), p. 217.

RICHARD D. WOODS

MARTINEZ Peñaloza, Porfirio (1916-). Martínez Peñaloza was born on May 24, 1916, in Morelia, Michoacán. He completed his baccalaureate at the Escuela Libre in Michoacán and went on to further studies in the Faculties of Medicine and Philosophy and Letters at the UNAM. He has traveled to Spain and the United States and has given lectures at the Miguel Cervantes Institute in Madrid and at the Universities of Valencia and Malaga (1947-48). In the United States he has lectured on literature as well as the popular arts of Mexico at the Universities of Kansas, Missouri, and Washington. He was professor of literature at the Instituto Tecnológico of Monterrey (1948-49), a fellow at the Colegio de México (1950), vice president of the Department of Artesans of the Banco Nacional de Fomento (1961-63), and an assistant in the Department of Literature of the INBA (1960-63). He more recently lent his services to the Banco Nacional de Comercio Exterior.

Martínez Peñaloza has written poetry, essays, narrations, and literary criticism; his criticism has been published in magazines and literary supplements of Mexico and abroad, especially in *Revista Mexicana de Cultura*, the supplement of the newspaper *El Nacional*. He began his work in journalism in 1937 at the magazine *México al Día* using the pseudonym Dr. Theofrastro Amiba. He later contributed to *Arbor, Proa*, and *Estilo*, of San Potosí; on *Papel de poesía*, of Saltillo, Coahuila; on magazines and newspapers of Michoacán, such as *Viñetas de Literatura Michoacana*, which he co-founded and co-directed. He has also used the pseudonym Gabriel de López in the magazine *Viñetas*, and Pepito Grillo in *Logos*. He founded and directed, in collaboration with others, the magazine *Trivium* (1949-50) in Monterrey, Nuevo León. His works encompass literary investigation and the popular arts of Mexico. He is well known for his valuable contributions to the clarification of certain aesthetic and linguistic problems as seen in Mexican literature of the nineteenth century, especially in works of Modernism.

WORKS: Stories: *Dos motivos de navidad* (Two Christmas Motives) (Morelia: n.p., 1941). *Tres relatos de amor* (Three Stories of Love) (Monterrey: Col. Camelina, 1949). Essay: *La nacionalidad mexicana* (The Mexican Nationality) (México: n.p., 1945). *Franciso Manuel Sánchez de Tagle*, selection and prologue, Cuadernos de Literatura Michoacana (Morelia, Michoacán 1951). Prologues, *Anuarios de la poesía mexicana 1959, 1960 y 1961* (Annuals of Mexican Poetry, 1959, 1960, and 1961) (México: Department of Literature, INBA, 1960, 1961, 1962). Prologues, *Anuarios del cuento mexicano 1959, 1961, 1962* (Annuals of the Mexican Story, 1959, 1961, 1962) (México: INBA, 1960, 1962, 1963). Manuel Gutiérrez Nájera, *Obras* (Works); vol. 1, compiled by E. K. Mapes, introduction by Porfirio Martínez Peñaloza, Nueva Biblioteca Mexicana, no. 4 (México: UNAM, 1959). *Los cinco poetas de la espiga amotinada* (Five Poets of the Rebellious School) (México: Publs. of the Instituto Cultural Mexicano Israelí, 1966). *La poesía de Alberto Herrera* (The Poetry of Alberto Herrera) (Morelia: Ed. Camelina, 1966). *Algunos epígonos del modernismo y otras notas* (Some Members of the School of Modernism and Other Notations), with a letter by don Jaime Torres Bodet (Morelia: Ed. Camelina, 1966).

BIBLIOGRAPHY: Anon., "Mexicanos en España," in *Dígame* (Madrid, Dec. 9, 1947): 17-18; "Un periodista azteca," in *Jornada* (Valencia, March 10, 1948): 18. Boyd G. Carter, "*La Revista Azul*" (in *Las revistas literarias de México*, no editor (México: INBA, 1963), 1st series, pp. 50, 59; *En torno a Gutiérrez Nájera* (México: Botas, 1960), pp. 11, 23 and ss. Horacio Espinosa Altamirano, "Martínez Peñaloza, rastreador de Herrera," in *Revista Mexicana de Cultura* 1022 (Oct. 30, 1966): p. 15. Andrés Henestrosa, "La nota cultural," in *El Nacional* (July 16, 1966): 3. Aurora M. Ocampo de Gómez and Ernesto Prado Velázquez, *Diccionario de Escritores Mexicanos* (México: UNAM, 1967), pp. 217-18. Delio J. Ponjoán, "El personaje del mes. Porfirio Martínez Peñaloza," in *Revista Mexicana de Cultura* (Nov. 1965), 7 and 28. Jesús Romero Flores, *Diccionario michoacano de historia y geografía* (Morelia: Ed. Gobierno del Estado, 1960), p. 258.

DENISE GUAGLIARDO BENCIVENGO

MARTINEZ Sotomayor, José (1895-1980). Born in Guadalajara on January 25, 1895, José Martínez Sotomayor studied law in Jalisco and then at the Universidad Nacional de México. He served his country in a variety of legal capacities and participated in the activities celebrating the twentieth-fifth anniversary of the Mexican Revolution. In addition to his law career, Martínez Sotomayor was distinguished as a short story writer, having published in various anthologies and magazines, as well as producing several volumes of stories.

WORKS: *La rueca del aire* (The Twisting of the Wind) (México: Imp. Mundial, 1930). *Lentitud* (Slowness) (México: Imp. Mundial, 1933). *Discurso pronunciado por el señor Lic. José Martínez Sotomayor con motivo del XXVI aniversario de la Revolución* (Speech Given by José Martínez Sotomayor, Esquire, for the Twenty-Sixth Anniversary of the Revolution) (México: Agrupación Pro-Madero, 1937). *Locura* (Craziness) (México: Letras de México, 1939). *El reino azul* (The Blue Reign) (México: Ediciones "América," 1952). *El puente* (The Bridge) (México: Revista Antológica, 1957). *El semáforo* (The Traffic Light) (México: Ed. Latino Americana, 1963). *La mina* (The Mine) (México: Oasis, 1968). *Doña Perfecta Longines* (México: Costa-Amic, 1970). *Perfil y acento de Guadalajara* (Silhouette and Accent of Guadalajara) (México: FCE, 1970). *Obra completa (poesía y teatro)* (Complete Works [Poetry and Theater]) (Cuevas de Almanzora, Almería: Librería Mary-Reyes, 1973). *Trama de vientos* (Plot of Winds) (Xochimilco, D.F.: Edit. Offset, 1987).

BIBLIOGRAPHY: José Alvarado, "El cuento mexicano," in *Romance* 3 (March 1, 1940): 18. Jesús Arellano, Review of *El puente*, in *Metáfora* 17 (Nov.-Dec. 1957): 42-43. María Elvira Bermúdez, "El cuento mexicano en 1963," in *Diorama de la Cultura* (Jan. 5, 1964): 8. John S. Brushwood and José Rojas Garcidueñas, *Breve historia de la novela mexicana* (México: de Andrea, 1959), pp. 133-34. Mario Calleros, "Las mesas de Plomo," review of *El semáforo*, in *Ovaciones* 114 (March 1, 1964): 8. Emmanuel Carballo, "El cuento," in *Ovaciones* 65 (March 24, 1963): 2; *El cuento mexicano del siglo XX* (México: Empresas Editoriales, 1964), pp. 56-57. Ramón Gálvez, "Meridiano crítico. I. Martínez Sotomayor reafirma su señorío literario," in *El Libro y el Pueblo* 6 (Oct. 1963): 13-15. Luis Leal, *Breve historia del cuento mexicano* (México: de Andrea, 1956), pp. 129-30; *Bibliografía del cuento mexicano* (México: Eds. de Andrea, 1966), pp. 87-88. Manuel Lerín, Review of *El semáforo*, in *Revista mexicana de Cultura* 868 (Nov. 17, 1963): 14. Daniel Moreno, "Hombres y letras," review of *El semáforo*, in *Revista Mexicana de Cultura* 866 (Nov. 3, 1963): 2. Javier Morente, Review of *El semáforo*, in *Diorama de la Cultura* (Dec. 22, 1963): 2, 4. Aurora M. Ocampo de Gómez and Ernesto Prado Velázquez, *Diccionario de escritores mexicanos* (México: UNAM, 1967), p. 218. José Emilio Pacheco, Review of *El semáforo*, in *La Cultura en México* 761 (Oct. 20, 1963): 3. Juan José Prado, "Martínez Sotomayor, cuentista," in *Letras* 1 (Guadalajara, 1940): 7. Gustavo Sainz, "Escaparate," review of *El semáforo*, in *México en la Cultura* 970 (Oct. 13, 1963): 11. Mauricio de la Selva, Review of *El semáforo*, in *Diorama de la Cultura* (Nov. 24, 1963): 3. Xavier Villaurrutia, Review of *Locura*, in *Letras de México* 2, 10 (Oct. 15, 1939): 25-6.

JEANNE C. WALLACE

MASIP, Paulino (1899-1963), poet, dramatist, and fiction writer. Paulino Masip was born on May 11, 1899 in La Granadella, Lérida, Spain, and died on September 11, 1963, in Cholula, México. He studied in Spain and became a journalist, and directed

La Voz and *El Sol*. He worked for *La Rioja*, the daily paper, and *Estampa*. He also served as theater critic for *El Heraldo* and editor-in-chief for *Ahora*. The Spanish Civil War began while he was working with *La Voz*, so he moved to Barcelona, where he became technical director of *La Vanguardia*. He traveled to Paris, working for the embassy, and went to México in 1939 as a political refugee, later becoming a Mexican national. There he worked with the theater and later with cinema, working for Grovas and Diana Films. He did several cinematic adaptations, but he also worked on his own writing.

His first literary work, which was not very well done, was a collection of poetry, *Remansos líricos (Lyrical Ponds)* (1918). He is best known for his plays, which he wrote while in both Spain and México, and for his novels, which were written while Masip was in México. One of his most outstanding novels is *El Diario de Hamlet García* (The Diary of Hamlet García) (1944), which is somewhat autobiographical. It is about the life of a philosophy professor in Madrid during the Spanish Civil War.

WORKS: Poetry: *Remansos líricos* (Lyrical Ponds) (Madrid: Séneca, 1918). Theater: *El collar* (The Necklace), comedy, written in 1927, unpublished. *Dúo* (Duo), comedy performed in Madrid in 1928, published with *El abolengo* (The Ancestry) by Manuel Linares Rivas in *La Farsa* 3, 102 (Madrid, Aug. 31, 1929). *La frontera* (The Border) (Madrid: Séneca, 1934). *El báculo y el paraguas* (The Staff and the Umbrella), comedy in *La Farsa* 10, 443 (Madrid, March 14, 1936). *El hombre que hizo un milagro* (The Man Who Performed a Miracle), farce (México: Ed. Atlante, 1944), later filmed under the title *El barbero prodigioso* (The Prodigious Barber) in Mexico and in Argentina. *El escándalo* (The Scandal), an adaptation of Alarcón's novel, performed in México in 1948. *El emplazado* (The Summoned), farce, Teatro Mexicano Contemporáneo, no. 19 (México: Sociedad General de Autores, 1950). Essay: *Cartas a un español emigrado* (Letters to an Immigrant Spaniard) (México: Junta de Cultura Española, 1939). Short Story and Novel: *Historias de amor* (Love Stories) (México: Empresas Editoriales, 1943). *El diario de Hamlet García* (The Diary of Hamlet García), written in 1941 (México: Imp. M. L. Sánchez, 1944). *De quince llevo una . . .* (One Out of Fifteen), short stories (México: Séneca, 1949). *La trampa* (The Trap), short novels, foreword by Max Aub (México: Ardeval, 1953). *La aventura de Marta Abril* (The Adventure of Marta Abril) (México: Stylo, 1953).

BIBLIOGRAPHY: M. Fernández Almagro, Review of *El báculo y el paraguas*, in *La Voz* (México: Jan. 8, 1936) 3c. Anon., "Crónica literaria," review of *El diario de Hamlet García*, in *El Mercurio* (Argentina: Nov. 24, 1944): 19. Max Aub, Foreword to *La trampa* (México: Ardeval, 1953). Angel de las Bárcenas, Review of *El escándalo*, in *Claridades* (Dec. 7, 1947): 14. Antonio Espina, Review of *El báculo y el paraguas*, in *El Sol* (Madrid: Jan. 7, 1936): 5. G.A.G., "Libros y autores," review of *Cartas a un emigrado español*, in *Nosotros* 3, 25 (Feb. 1940): 12. Aurora M. Ocampo de Gómez and Ernesto Prado Velázquez, *Diccionario de escritores Mexicanos* (México: UNAM, 1967), pp. 218-19. Rafael del Río, Review of *Historias de amor*, in *Letras de México* 1, 7 (Oct. 15, 1943): 6. Luis Santullano, "Los libros. Cuentos casi morales," review of *De quince llevo una*, in *El Nacional*, 1949, 3C. Florentino M. Torner, Review of *El diario de Hamlet García*, in *El Nacional* (July 11, 1944): 2C. Gonzalo Torrente Ballester, *Panorama de la literatura española contemporánea* (Madrid: Eds. Guadarrama, 1961), vol. 1, pp. ii, 366. Angel Valbuena Prat, *Historia de la literatura española*, vol. 3 (Barcelona: Gustavo Gili, 1960), p. 726. Mariano Viñuales, "La vida y los libros. Los personajes de Paulino Masip," *Cenit* (Toulouse, France) 4, 45 (Sept., 1954): 1344-48.

EDNA A. REHBEIN

MASTRETA, Angeles (María de) (1949-). Angeles Mastreta was born in Puebla, on October 9, 1949. She completed her primary and secondary education in Puebla and then moved to Mexico City. She graduated from the National University of Mexico with a degree in communications and journalism. In 1974 she was awarded a scholarship by the Center of Mexican Writers, and she subsequently published *Pájara pinta*, a book of erotic poetry.

A well-known journalist, she writes daily columns for *Excélsior* and *Ovaciones*. She contributes articles to *Uno más Uno*, *La Jornada*, and *Proceso*. She was the director of culture for ENEP-Acatlán from 1975 to 1977 and of the Chopo Museum from 1979 to 1982.

In 1985 Mastreta's first novel, *Arráncame la vida* (Snatch My Life), won the Mazatlán Literary Prize, and became enormously popular. The story, set in the 1930s and 1940s, narrates the life of a woman, Catalina Guzmán, married to a Mexican politician, General Andrés Ascencio. Mastreta begins the narrative with the marriage of Catalina to Andres when she is fourteen years old and ends with his death. Narrated from the point of view of the protagonist, the novel portrays Ascencio as a womanizing, overbearing man engaged in conquering women and assassinating his rivals. In spite of his corruption and cruelty, she supports him and fulfills her duties. However, when he dies she rejoices as she sees her opportunity to lead her own life. The novel demythifies the traditional concept of the hero and presents the liberation of women.

WORKS: Poetry: *La pájara pinta* (México: Altiplano, 1975). Novel: *Arráncame la vida* (México: Océano, 1985).

BIBLIOGRAPHY: Jean Franco, *Plotting Women* (New York: Columbia University Press, 1989), p. 184. Josefina Lara, *Diccionario de escritores contemporáneos de México* (México: INBA, 1988), p. 135.

NORA ERRO-PERALTA

MATEOS, Juan (1831-1913), novelist, dramatist, journalist, and poet. Mateos stands out today for his work in the historical novel, but during his lifetime he was also recognized for his theatrical pieces. He was born in Mexico City in 1831. He studied first at the Colegio de San Gregorio and, later, in 1847, at the Instituto Científico y Literario de Toluca, where he became a disciple of Ignacio Ramírez (El Nigromante). Mateos soon adopted the liberal views of his teacher and became interested in politics. He continued his education at the Colegio de Letrán, but the Revolution of Ayutla and the French intervention interrupted his studies. Mateos was profoundly affected by the death of his brother in 1859, who was, along with the poet Juan *Díaz Covarrubias, executed in Tacubaya for his revolutionary activities. Mateos himself then became actively embroiled in Mexico's struggle against the French, and he turned to journalism as an outlet for his liberal views. He published in *El Monitor*

Republicano (The Republican Monitor), *El Siglo XIX* (The Nineteenth Century), *El Imparcial* (The Impartial One), and *La Orquesta* (The Orchestra). He was eventually arrested and imprisoned in San Juan de Ulva for his verbal attacks against the Emperor Maximilian. Mateos managed to escape from prison, however: he then joined the republican forces of Benito Juárez. After the fall of the Empire and the restoration of the Juárez government, Mateos was named secretary of the Supreme Court of Justice. He also became a deputy in Congress, where he gained a reputation as a fiery orator due to his staunch defense of the liberal cause. Motivated by an unbending patriotism in all that he undertook, Mateos was regarded as one of Mexico's great mean during his lifetime. He died in Mexico City in 1913 and was buried in the Rotunda of Illustrous Men.

Mateos was a prolific and enormously popular writer in the second half of the nineteenth century. One of his contemporaries, Vicente *Riva Palacio, wrote in 1882, "There is scarcely a corner of our country where one of his [Mateos'] works has not penetrated." Mateos had few, if any, literary pretensions. He wrote quickly, without concern for form. Although he had a natural gift for storytelling, his novels are sometimes marred by abrupt shifts in plot, superficial treatment of the subject matter, a lack of depth in the characters, and an overabundance of melodrama. However, as both Riva Palacio and Ignacio *Altamirano note, Mateos gave his reading public what they wanted, a better understanding of their nation's struggle for identity and perhaps more importantly, a sense of national pride. Mateos' first novel, *El Cerro de las Campanas* (The Hill of the Bells), was published in 1868. It was followed by *El sol de mayo* (The May Sun) in the same year. Both novels deal with the French intervention and Maximilian's ill-fated empire. They obviously reflect the author's own political views, but they are, nonetheless, a fairly accurate picture of the times. In them, the full tragedy of the situation emerges due to the incorporation of many historical details. Mateos' position in the National Congress Library gave him access to the private correspondence of the French and English ambassadors, which was his primary source of inspiration for these novels. *Sacerdote y caudillo* (Priest and Military Leader) was published in 1869. It portrays the life and times of Padre Hidalgo, the village priest who led México in her war of independence against Spain. *Los insurgentes* (The Insurgents), also published in 1869, is a continuation of *Sacerdote y caudillo*. Together, these two works are generally regarded as Mateos' best efforts in prose fiction. One of their most interesting features is the incorporation of a legend that links Mexico's independence from Spain to the intervention of supernatural forces. *Memorias de un guerrillero* (Memoirs of a Warrior), published in 1897, is the story of Mexico's flamboyant dictator Santa Anna and the attempts of the Mexican people to restore democracy to their country. *La majestad caída* (Fallen Majesty), written between 1911 and 1913 and published posthumously, deals with the overthrow of another of Mexico's strongmen, Porfirio Díaz. Other novels written by Mateos include *Sor Angélica, memorias de una hermana de la caridad* (Sister Angelica, Memoirs of a Sister of Mercy) (1875); *Los dramas de México* (Dramas in Mexico) (1887); *Las olas altas* (The High Waves) (1899); *La baja marea* (The Low Tide) (1899); *El vendedor de periódicos* (The Newspaper Vendor) (1899); *Las olas muertas* (The Dead Waves) (1899); *Sangre de niños, primer año del siglo XX* (Children's Blood, the First Year of the Twentieth Century) (1901) and *Sepulcros blanqueados* (White Tombs) (1902). Most of these novels are in the historical vein. While they cannot be considered "great literature" by modern standards, they are, nevertheless, of some importance in Mexican letters because of their lofty aim: their single goal is to instill patriotism and to create a sense of national pride in the Mexican people.

Mateos may be the most prolific Mexican dramatist of his age if contemporary biographers are to be believed. About fifty plays are attributed to him, although most of them have been lost. Mateos coauthored a number of plays with Riva Palacio, and it is sometimes difficult to determine from the comments of contemporaries which plays were published and which were merely presented on the stage. Most of Mateos' plays were considered "scathing" and some, "notorious." He wrote about an equal number of comedies and serious dramas. Before 1867, he wrote *Odio hereditario* (Hereditary Hate), *La político manía* (Political Mania), *La hija del cantero* (The Stonecutter's Daughter), *Borrascas de un sobretodo* (Dangers of an Overcoat), *La catarata del Niágara* (Niagara Falls), and *Martín el demente* (Martin the Demented). In 1867, he wrote a factual drama entitled *La muerte de Lincoln* (The Death of Lincoln). Between 1867 and 1881, he wrote *El novio oficial* (The Official Bridegroom), *El plagio* (Plagiaism), *El otro* (The Other Man), *Los grandes tahures* (The Great Gamblers), *La monja alferez* (The Ensign Nun), *La rubia y la morena* (The Blond and the Brunette), *El ave negra* (The Black Bird), and *El incendio del portal de Mercaderes* (The Fire in the Merchants' Arcade). Mateos' poetry merits little attention since, for the most part, it was written in his youth and is a rather obvious imitation of the Spanish romantic, José Zorrilla.

WORKS: *El cerro de las campanas* (The Hill of the Bells) (México: Imprenta de I. Cumplido, 1868). *Los insurgentes* (The Insurgents) (México: Hermanos Maucci, 1902). *La majestad caída* (Fallen Majesty) (México: Hermanos Maucci, n.d.). *Memorias de un guerrillero* (Memoirs of a Warrior), 2 vols. (México: El mundo, 1897). *Sacerdote y caudlillo* (Priest and Military Leader) (México: Hermanos Maucci, n.d.).

BIBLIOGRAPHY: Ignacio Altamirano, *La literatura nacional* (México: Porrúa, 1949), pp. 61-64; Carlos González Peña, *Historia de la literatura mexicana* (México: Secretaria de Educación pública, 1928), pp. 465-66; María del Carmen Millán, *Literatura mexicana* (México: Edit. Esfinge, 1962), pp. 163-64. John Lloyd Read, *The Mexican Historical Novel* (New York: Instituto de las Españas en los Estados Unidos, 1939), pp. 213-28. Vicente Riva Palacio, *Los ceros, galería de contemporáneos* (México: Imprenta de F. Díaz de León, 1982), pp. 223-39.

CYNTHIA K. DUNCAN

MEDINA Romero, Jesús (1921-   ), critic, poet, and author of short stories. Medina Romero was born in Ibarra, Guanajuato, on January 8, 1921. His education was entirely completed in San Luis Potosí. Although he was trained as an attorney, his love of literature led him into a teaching career at the Universidad Potosina, where he offered courses in Spanish and Spanish American literature.

His contributions to the university have been significant: he founded and edited two cultural journals there (*Aula* and *Cuadrante*), he established the Biblioteca de Autores Potosinos series, and he has served as editor of the Potosí University Press. He has also assumed an active role in government, having held office at the state level and having been elected a Representative to Congress at the national level. His literary work consists primarily of poetry.

WORKS: *El día sonoro* (The Sonorous Day) (San Luis Potosí, n.p., 1943). *Poemas terrenales* (Worldly Poems) (San Luis Potosí, n.p., 1946). *Cuatro elegías para llorar tu amor* (Four Elegies to Mourn Your Love), illustrated by Luis Chessal (San Luis Potosí, n.p., 1950). *Sonetos de amor integral* (Sonnets of Integral Love) (San Luis Potosí: n.p., 1951). *Antología de poetas contemporáneos, 1910-1953* (Anthology of Contemporary Poets, 1910-1953), study, selection and notes by Jesús Medina Romero (San Luis Potosí: Biblioteca de Autores Potosinos, Universidad Autónoma de San Luis Potosí, 1953). *Poemas* (Poems) (San Luis Potosí: Instituto Potosíno de Bellas Artes, 1961). *Recuerdos de Quintín Paredes* (Recollections of Quintín Paredes) (San Luis Potosí: n.p., 1961). *Los bienaventurados* (The Blessed) (San Luis Potosí: 1967). *Lectura de Ramón López Velarde* (Reading Ramón López Velarde) (México: Ediciones Sierra Madre, 1972). *Orfeo 71* (Orpheus 71) (México: Ed. Cuadernos Americanos, 1973).

BIBLIOGRAPHY: Aurora M. Ocampo de Gómez and Ernesto Prado Velázquez, *Diccionario de Escritores Mexicanos* (México: UNAM, 1967), p. 221.

JANIS L. KRUGH

MEDIZ Bolio, Antonio (1884-1957). Mediz Bolio was born on October 13, 1884, in Mérida, Yucatán, where he spent most of his early childhood on his father's hemp plantations. He studied in his native city of Mérida, where he graduated from law school in 1907. He became involved in politics and was a strong supporter of Madero. This involvement with Madero caused him to be persecuted by Victoriano Huerta and eventually he was forced to leave Mexico. He lived in exile in La Havana, Cuba.

Upon his return he occupied many government posts in his own state of Yucatán. He was a representative of the Congress of Yucatán from 1929 to 1930. A well-known lawyer and politician, he joined the diplomatic corps. As a career diplomat, with the rank of minister, he traveled widely, representing his country before the governments of Europe and Central and South America between 1919 and 1932.

While he was busy pursuing a career in politics and foreign diplomacy, Mediz Bolio was also writing and producing a series of plays and studying the Mayan language and culture extensively. He achieved international renown with his studies of Mayan history and language. He translated, arranged, and published *El libro de Chilam Balam de Chumayel* (The Book of Chilam Balam de Chumayel) and wrote a book of Mayan legends, *La tierra del faisán y el venado* (The Land of the Pheasant and the Deer). In 1946, he became a member of the Mexican Academy of Language. During the presidency of Ruiz Cortines, the Mexican writer was senator of the republic representing Yucatán. On December 15, 1957, he died in Mexico City after a serious illness.

Mediz Bolio won praise as a poet, a playwright, and a journalist. In his youth he cultivated romantic poetry. He was a good poet, as his book *En el medio del camino* (In the Middle of the Road) attests. In the first decade of the century, he composed dramas, comedies, operettas, and musical comedies, and even a comedy of social thesis, *La ola* (The Wave). In addition he conceived a dramatic poem of indigenous matter, *La flecha del sol* (The Arrow of the Sun). In his theater he follows Spanish tradition, and his works show the influence of Manuel Linares Rivas and Jacinto Benavente. His works include comedies, dramas, and historical dramas: *Mirza* (Mirza), *El marquesito enamorado* (The Marquis in Love), *Vientos de montaña* (Winds from the Mountain), *La ola* (The Wave), *El sueño de Iturbide* (Iturbide's Dream), *La suerte musical* (Musical Destiny), and *Cenizas que arden* (Ashes That Burn). Beginning with his play *La ola* (The Wave), he was the first author to introduce a social thesis. He also wrote scripts for the movies.

Mediz Bolio delved into the roots of the Mayan people and studied the ancient books and manuscripts to produce a series of works: *El libro de Chilam Balam de Chumayel* (The Book of Chilam Balam de Chumayel) and *La tierra del faisán y del venado* (The Land of the Pheasant and the Deer); the former is one of the most valuable Mayan codices from the eighteenth century. Chilam Balam is the name of an ancient priest, author of the prophecies included in the last part of the book. Chumayel refers to the town where the manuscript was found about the middle of the nineteenth century. The book contains religious texts, historical accounts, chronologies and magic formulas for religious initiation, and the prophecies already mentioned. His *Tierra del faisán y del venado*, written in Spanish, and acclaimed by many as his greatest work, is a re-creation of ancient Mayan legends. In this book Mediz Bolio elaborates themes from old traditions, fragments in ancient books, ritual dances and present day superstitions to create a work of art. He presents this account in a poetic language similar to that of a Mayan poet. This volume has been translated into many European languages.

WORKS: Poetry: *Evocaciones* (Mérida: Impresora Gambóa Guzmán, 1903). *En medio del camino* (México: Librería de Bouret, 1919). Narrative and Legends: *La tierra del faisán y del venado* (Buenos Aires: Contreras y Sanz, 1922). *The Land of the Pheasant and the Deer*, translated by Enid E. Perkins (México: Editorial Cultura, 1935). Translations: *El libro de Chilam Balam de Chumayel* (Costa Rica: Impresora Lehmann, 1930). Theater: *La ola* (México: Ateneo Peninsular, 1918).

BIBLIOGRAPHY: Carlos González Peña, *History of Mexican Literature* (Dallas: Southern Methodist University Press, 1968), p. 398. Aurora M. Ocampo de Gómez and Ernesto Prado Velázquez, *Diccionario de escritores mexicanos* (México: UNAM, 1967), pp. 221-22. Leopoldo Peniche Vallado, "Antonio Mediz Bolio: personalidad y obra," *Cuadernos Americanos* 5, 256 (Sept.-Oct. 1984): 122-43.

NORA ERRO-PERALTA

MEJIA Sánchez, Ernesto (1923-). Born in Nicaragua on July 6, 1923, Ernesto Mejía Sánchez studied science, philosophy, literature, and law at the Universidad de Oriente y Mediodía. He moved to Mexico in 1944, making it his adopted land. He got a master's degree in Spanish literature in 1951 from UNAM, then pursued doctoral studies in Spanish philology at the Universidad Central de Madrid. A professor of morphology, syntax, stylistics, and Spanish and Latin American literature, he has received many distinctions and invitations to other countries to give courses, conferences, and to take part in literary congresses. In 1950 he won "Rubén Darío" poetry prize in Nicaragua for his collection of poems, *La impureza* (Impurity). He is a member of several important literary and cultural associations in Nicaragua. In 1955 he received another prize for poetry in El Salvador for his book *Contemplaciones europeas* (European Contemplations) (1957). He has worked as a literary critic for such journals as *Revista Iberoamericana* and *Nueva Revista de Filología Hispánica*. He was the editor of *Cuadernos del Taller de San Lucas* in Nicaragua and had a similar position for *Los Presentes* in Mexico and *La Tertulia* in Madrid. He was responsible for the publication of the complete works of Alfonso *Reyes.

Ernesto Mejía Sánchez has distinguished himself as an essaywriter and critic of Spanish American letters and as a poet of great expressive quality. His poetry, finely worked, achieves the union of purity in expression and good technique in its execution. As an essaywriter and researcher, he studied Rubén Darío's narrative work and his evolution as a Modernist poet, writing essays that constitute a major contribution to the field. Indeed, he has produced volumes such as *Cuentos completos de Rubén Darío* (Complete Stories of Rubén Darío) (1950) and *Poesía de Rubén Darío. Libros poéticos completos y antología de la obra dispersa* (Poetry of Rubén Darío. Complete Poetic Books and Anthology of the Scattered Work) (1952). In addition to his massive work on Darío, he also wrote exceptional essays on Manuel *Gutiérrez Nájera, José Martí, and poetry from Nicaragua.

WORKS: Poetry: *Ensalmos y conjuros* (Spells and Incantations) (México: Cuadernos Americanos, 1947). *La carne contigua* (Contiguous Flesh) (Buenos Aires: Ed. Sur, 1948). *El retorno* (The Return) (México: Los Presentes, 1950). *Antología (1946-1952)* (Anthology [1946-1952]) (Madrid: n.p., 1953). *Contemplaciones europeas* (European Contemplations) (El Salvador: Dept. Edit. San Salvador, 1957). *Poemas* (Poems) (Buenos Aires: Ed. Sur, 1963). Studies and Essays: *La mujer nicaragüence en los cronistas y viajeros* (The Nicaraguan Woman in the Chroniclers and Travelers), in collaboration with José Coronel Urtrecho, in *Cuadernos del Taller de San Lucas* 1 (Nicaragua, 1942). *Darío y Montalvo* (Darío and Montalvo), offprint of the *Nueva Revista de Filología Hispánica* (El Colegio de México) 2, 2 (1948): 360-72. *Cuentos completos de Rubén Darío* (Complete Stories of Rubén Darío), edition and notes (México: FCE, 1950). *Los primeros cuentos de Rubén Darío* (The First Stories of Rubén Darío), edited (México: Eds. de Andrea, 1951); 2nd ed. (México: UNAM, 1961). *Poesía de Rubén Darío. Libros poéticos completos y antología de la obra dispersa* (Poetry of Rubén Darío. Complete Poetic Books and Anthology of Scattered Work) (México: FCE, 1952). *Poesías inéditas del Príncipe de Esquilache* (Unpublished Poems by the Prince of Esquilache), in collaboration with Luis Alberto Ratto, offprint of the *Nueva Revista de Filología Hispánica*, homage to Amado Alonso, 7, 3-4 (1953): 352-63. "Las humanidades de Rubén Darío. Años de aprendizaje" (Humanities of Rubén Darío. Years of Learning), in *Libro jubilar de Alfonso Reyes* (México: UNAM, 1956), pp. 243-63. *Cartas del jueves, de Manuel Gutiérrez Nájera* (Thursday's Letters of Manuel Gutiérrez Nájera), edition and prologue, offprint of *Las Letras Patrias* 5, (1957). *Montalvo y Menéndez Pelayo* (Montalvo and Menéndez Pelayo), *Nueva Revista de Filología Hispánica*, 1958. *Más sobre Montalvo y Menéndez Pelayo* (More about Montalvo and Menéndez Pelayo), offprint of *Nueva Revista de Filología Hispánica* 12, 3-4 (Madrid, 1959): 394-96. *Exposición documental de Manuel Gutiérrez Nájera* (Documentary Exposition of Manuel Gutiérrez Nájera) (México: Imp. Universitaria, 1959). *Los "Pastiches" huguescos de Gutiérrez Nájera* (The Hugoesque "Pastiches" of Gutiérrez Nájera), offprint of *Revista Iberoamericana* 25, 49 (1959): 149-52. *La vida en la obra de Alfonso Reyes* (Life in Alfonso Reyes' Works), offprint of *Humanidades* (Universidad de Nuevo León) 2, 2 (1960): 355-69. "El pensamiento literario de Rousseau" (Rousseau's Literary Thought," in *Presencia de Rousseau* (México: UNAM, 1962), pp. 127-52. *Los últimos días de José Martí* (The Final Days of José Martí), offprint of *Humanitas*, Nuevo León, 1963. *Del primer Santayana* (About the First Santayana), offprint of *Anuario de Letras*, vol. 3 (México: UNAM, 1964). *Mier, defensor de Las Casas* (Mier, Defender of Las Casas), offprint of *Boletín de la Biblioteca Nacional* (México: UNAM, 1964). *Hércules y Onfalia* (Hercules and Onphalia) (México: Ed. by author, 1964). *Más sobre Unamuno y Reyes* (More about Unamuno and Reyes), offprint of *Boletín de la Biblioteca Nacional* 15, 3-4 (July-Dec. 1964). *De Unamuno y Nervo* (About Unamuno and Nervo), offprint of *Anuario de Letras* 4 (1964): 203-35. *Urbina y la biblioteca nacional* (Urbina and the National Library), edited, offprint of *Boletín de la Biblioteca Nacional* 15, 1-2 (Jan.-June 1964). *Rubén Darío en Oxford* (Rubén Darío in Oxford) (Managua: Academia Nicaragüense de la Lengua, 1966). *Las relaciones literarias* (Literary Reports), *Revista Iberoamericana*, 1966, n.p. "Opiniones" (Opinions), in *Vida Literaria* 5, 6 (1970): 26-31. "Una carta de Alfonso Reyes" (A Letter from Alfonso Reyes), in *Vida Literaria* 5, 6 (1970): 41-42. "Anversos y reversos de Julio Torri," in *Revista de Letras* 4 (1972): 234-40. Anthologies: *Romances y corridos nicaragüenses* (Romances and corridos of Nicaragua) (México: Imp. Universitaria, 1946). *Nueva poesía nicaragüense* (The New Poetry of Nicaragua) (Madrid: n.p., 1949). *Cinco poetas hispanoamericanos en España* (Five Spanish American Poets in Spain) (Madrid: n.p., 1953).

BIBLIOGRAPHY: Víctor Adib, "Los libros. La pluma en la mano," review of *Cuentos completos de Rubén Darío*, in *México en la Cultura* 80 (Aug. 13, 1950): 7. Federico Alvarez, Review of *Los últimos días de José Martí*, in *La Cultura en México* 81 (Sept. 4, 1963): xviii; Review of *Del primer Santayana*, in *La Cultura en México* 133 (Sept. 2, 1964): xviii; Review of *Mier, defensor de Las Casas*, in *La Cultura en México* 139 (Oct. 14, 1964): xviii. Enrique Anderson Imbert, *Historia de la literatura hispanoamericana*, vol. 2 (México: FCE, 1954), pp. 282-83. Frank Dauster, *The Double Strand* (Lexington: University of Kentucky Press, 1987), p. 112. Clementina Díaz de Ovando, Review of *Romances y corridos nicaragüenses*, in *Revista de Historia de América* (México, June 27, 1949): 189-91. Margarita García Flores, "Entrevista con Ernesto Mejía Sánchez," in *El Día* (Aug. 30, 1965): 9. Andrés Henestrosa, Review of *De Unamuno y Nervo*, in *El Nacional* (Dec. 7, 1965): 3; "La Nota Cultural" (March 17, 1966): 3; (Oct. 5, 1966): 3. Raúl Leiva, Review of *Contemplaciones europeas*, in *Letras Nuevas* 2-3 (Jan.-April 1958): 81-82. Ricardo Llopesa, "El constante reto a la palabra en la poesía de Ernesto Mejía Sánchez: Del poema al prosema," in *Nueva Estafeta* 40 (1982): 67-70; "Reto a la palabra en la poesía de Ernesto Mejía Sánchez," in *Cuadernos Americanos* 246, 1 (1983): 207-13. Aurora M. Ocampo de Gómez and Ernesto Prado Velázquez, *Diccionario de Escritores Mexicanos* (México: UNAM, 1967), pp. 223-24. José Emilio Pacheco, review of *Poemas*, in *La Cultura en México* 85 (Oct. 2, 1963): 9. Various, homage to Ernesto Mejía Sánchez, in *La Prensa Literaria* (Managua, Nicaragua, Jan. 16, 1966): 25; "La poesía de Ernesto Mejía Sánchez," in *Nivel* 39 (March 25, 1966): 1-3, 8-9.

JEANNE C. WALLACE

MEJIA Valera, Manuel (1928-), short story writer, poet, essayist, and critic. Born in Lima, Peru, in 1928, Mejía Valera studied at the Universidad de San Marcos in Lima. He took up residence in Mexico in 1953. He has contributed to newspaper articles, literary reviews, and supplements and worked as a research fellow at the Colegio de México. He also has worked for the Organization of American States.

Mejía Valera has written stories, essays, and poetry. His early stories are carefully written and unify the poetic and fantastic. In his recent work *El testamento del Rey*

Midas (The Testament of King Midas), he achieves a synthesis of style and voice. The prose in the work is complex and poetically charged and draws on various myths and legends of Western civilization in dealing with issues such as religious affirmation and despair.

WORKS: Stories: *La evasión* (The Evasion) (México: Los Presentes, 1954). *Lienzos de sueño* (Canvases of Dream) (México: Cuadernos de Unicornio, 1959). *Un cuarto de conversión* (A Conversion Room) (México: Mortiz, 1966). *En otras palabras* (In Other Words) (México: n.p., 1973). *El testamento del Rey Midas* (The Testament of King Midas) (México: Premia Editora, S.A., 1982). Studies and Editions: *Fuentes para la historia de la filosofía en el Peru* (Sources for the History of Philosophy in Peru) (Lima: Universidad de San Marcos, 1963). *El cuento actual latinoamericano* (The Contemporary Latin American Short Story) (México: Ediciones de Andrea, 1973). *Antología de José María Eguén* (Anthology of José María Eguén) (México: Comunidad Latinoamericana de Escritores, 1974). *El pensamiento filosófico de Octavio Paz* (The Philosophic Thought of Octavio Paz) (México: n.p., 1980).

BIBLIOGRAPHY: Anon., Review of *La evasión*, in *México en la Cultura* 305 (Jan 23, 1955): 2; Review of *Lienzos de sueño*, in *Estaciones* 4, 14 (Summer 1959): 244. Huberto Batis, Review of *Un cuarto de conversión*, in *La Cultura en México* 244 (Oct. 19, 1966): xvii. Emmanuel Carballo, Review of *La evasión*, in *México en la Cultura* 306 (Jan. 30, 1955): 2. Aurora M. Ocampo de Gómez and Ernesto Prado Velázquez, *Diccionario de escritores mexicanos* (México: UNAM, 1967), p. 224. Carlos Valdés, Review of *La evasión*, in *Revista de la Universidad de México* 9, 7 (March 1955): 30.

MARK FRISCH

MELENDEZ de Espinosa, Juana (1914-), poet. Born in San Luis Potosí, Meléndez de Espinosa has spent her entire career in her native city. She first studied at the Instituto Científico y Literario, but then in 1956 she re-enrolled in the university to study letters. She has contributed to literary magazines from around the country, such as *Hierba*, from Torreón, Coahuila; *Armas y Letras*, published in Monterrey, Nuevo León; *Metáfora* and *Nivel*, from Mexico City; and *Estilo*, *Letras Potosinas* and *Cuadrante*, all from San Luis Potosí. She was one of the founders of and teachers in the Taller de Literatura in Difusión Cultural of the Universidad de San Luis Potosí.

   The poetry of Meléndez de Espinosa is that of a nonconforming, rebel spirit which seeks a justification for human existence. She is at her best when she sings of death or of human destiny. She has also practiced literary criticism.

WORKS: Poetry: *Río sin orillas* (River without Banks) (San Luis Potosí: Perfil de estilo, 1954). *En el cauce del sueño* (In the Riverbed of Sleep) (San Luis Potosí: Perfil de estilo, 1957). *Poemas* (Poems) (San Luis Potosí: Instituto Potosino de Bellas Artes, 1959). *Voces del hombre* (Voices of Man) (San Luis Potosí: Universidad Autónoma de San Luis Potosí, 1961). *Por el tiempo y un pájaro* (By Time and a Bird), prologue by Antonio Castro Leal (San Luis Potosí: Universidad Autónoma de San Luis Potosí, 1965). *Esta dura nostalgia* (This Hard Nostalgia) (San Luis Potosí: Academia Potosina de Ciencias y Artes, 1970). *Mirando bajo el árbol donde los pájaros cantan* (Looking under the Tree Where the Birds Sing), commentary by Jorge

Ruedas (San Luis Potosí: Universidad Autónoma de San Luis Potosí, 1972). *Acto que afirma* (Affirming Act) (San Luis Potosí: Universidad Autónoma de San Luis Potosí, 1976). Essay: *Hora de ensayo: asomo a la poesía de Jesús Arellano* (A Look at the Poetry of Jesús Arellano) (San Luis Potosí: Cuadernos de Plata, Letras Potosinas, 1967).   *La suave patria* (The Gentle Homeland) (Guadalajara: Departamento de Bellas Artes, 1971). *Transformación de la literatura contemporánea* (Transformation of Contemporary Literature) (San Luis Potosí: Universidad Autónama de San Luis Potosí, 1977).

BIBLIOGRAPHY: Anon., Review of *Voces del hombre*, in *Cuadernos de Bellas Artes* 10 (Oct. 1961): 60; Biobliographical note in *Anuario de la poesía mexicana 1962* (México: Depto. de Literatura, INBA, 1963), p. 83; "Escaparate de libros," review of *Por el tiempo y un pájaro*, in *México en la Cultura* 831 (Feb 21, 1965): 8; "La poesía de Juana Meléndez de Espinosa," *Nivel* 46 (1966): 1-2, 11. Jesús Arellano, "Las Ventas de Don Quijote, revisión de algunos nombres de la literatura mexicana: poetisa potosina," *Nivel* 2, 6 (June 25, 1963): 5. Antonio Castro Leal, Prologue to *Por el tiempo y un pájaro* (San Luis Potosí: Universidad Autónoma de San Luis Potosí, 1965). Galván Corona, Review of *En el cauce del sueño*, in *Metáfora* 17 (Nov.-Dec. 1957): 42-43. José Antonio Montero, "Poesía femenina," review of *Por el tiempo y un pájaro*, in *Ovaciones*, supplement no. 108 (Nov. 14, 1965): 7. Thelma Nava, "Notas de poesía," review of *Por el tiempo y un pájaro*, in *El Día* 4 (March 1965): 9. Aurora M. Ocampo de Gómez and Ernesto Prado Velázquez, *Diccionario de Escritores Mexicanos* (México: UNAM, 1967), pp. 224-25. J.P., Review of *Río sin orillas*, in *Poesía en América* 3, 4 (Jan.-March 1955): 60. Lynn Ellen Rice Cortina, *Spanish-American Women Writers* (New York: Garland, 1983), p. 182. Mauricio de la Selva, "Asteriscos," review of *Por el tiempo y un pájaro*, in *Diorama de la Cultura* (March 14, 1965): 4. Various authors, "La poesía de Juana Meléndez de Espinosa," *Nivel* 46 (Oct. 25, 1966): 17-23.

PETER G. BROAD

MELO, Juan Vicente (1932-), novelist. Melo was born in Veracruz, Veracruz, on March 1, 1932. At a very young age, he dedicated himself to studying music, his second vocation. When he was fifteen years old, he was employed as a music critic. However, he was a son, grandson, great-grandson, and brother of a medical doctor; thus, he also became a doctor. In 1956, he graduated with academic honors from UNAM, where he received a scholarship to specialize in dermatology in the Saint-Louis Hospital of Paris. While in Paris, he took courses in French literature. He got close to Louis-Ferdinand Celine and Albert Camus who, along with William Faulkner and Joseph Conrad, were his strongest influences. After his return to Mexico in 1958, he established a medical practice in his native city, where he also edited the supplement *La Semana Cultural* with José Emilio *Pacheco. In 1960, he decided to abandon his medical practice, to dedicate himself entirely to literature. He moved to Mexico City and published in the most important magazines and cultural supplements. A contemporary of Sergio *Pitol, Inés *Arredondo, Juan *García Ponce, Juan José Gurrola, Salvador *Elizondo, Tomás *Segovia, and José Emilio *Pacheco, Melo found himself immersed in the artistic environment of Mexico City, earning his living by cultural promotion. He has been the director of La Casa del

Lago in Mexico City and El Museo de la Ciudad in Veracruz. In 1969, he left Mexico City, living alternately between Jalapa and Veracruz.

Much like Holderlin, dreams represent for Melo the most worthy life of man. As a writer of dreams, Melo has described with brilliant clarity life's realities and frustrations. His novel *La Obediencia Nocturna* (The Nocturnal Obedience) deals with the absurdities of life. The language he uses is sometimes very simple, but quite often complex and strange. The words he chooses reflect his own inner turmoil. *La Obediencia Nocturna* (The Nocturnal Obedience) is an existentialist work, where love is sought through the escapes offered by alcohol, a return to infantile behavior, oneiric delirium, Phythagorean magic, music, and death.

WORKS: *La Noche Alucinada* (Hallucinated Night) (México: Ed. Prensa Médica Mexicana, 1956). *Los Muros Enemigos* (Enemy Walls) (Jalapa: Universidad Veracruzana, 1962). *Fin de Semana* (Weekend) (México: ERA, 1964). *Autobiografía* (Autobiography) (México: Empresas Editoriales, 1966). *La Obediencia Nocturna* (The Nocturnal Obedience) (México: ERA, 1969). *El agua cae en otra fuente* (The Water Flows in Another Fountain) (Jalapa: Universidad Veracruzana, 1985).

BIBLIOGRAPHY: Federico Alvarez, Review of *Los Muros Enemigos*, in *Revista de la Universidad* (Mexico) 17, 7 (1963): 31. José Amezcua, "Juan Vincente Melo. La Mímesis de la personalidad," in *Boletín Bibliográfico de la Sría de Hacienda y Crédito Público* 10, 295 (1964): 19. Anon., "Nota Bibliográfica," *Anuario del cuento mexicano* (Mexico, 1962): 236. Review of *Los Muros Enemigos*, in *Cuadernos de Bellas Artes* 1, 1 (1963): 90; Review of *A Fin de Semana* in *Cuadernos de Bellas Artes* 5, 3 (1964): 75-76. Huberto Batis, review of *Fin de Semana*, in *La Cultura en México* 107 (1964): xvii; "Conversación con Juan Vicente Melo Ripoll," in *Cuadernos del Viento* 45-46 (1964): 725-27. Emmanuel Carballo, "La Realidad y el Deseo," Review of *Los Muros Enemigos*, in *La Cultura en México* 35 (1962): 14; "Entre el Pesimismo y la Realidad," review of *Fin de Semana*" in *La Cultura en Mexico*, 111 (1964): 18-19. Armando Castro Mejía, "Entrevista con Juan V. Melo. En La Casa de Lago se alienta a los jovenes compositores . . .," in *La Cultura en Mexico* 139 (1964): 15. Juan Vicente Melo, "La Maffia son los otros, o la autobiografía precoz de Juan Vicente Melo," in *La Cultura en México* 191 (1965): 1-4. Luis Méndez and Esther Hernández-Palacios, "*La Obediencia Nocturna*," un desafío de lo intangible," in *Texto Crítico* 10, 29 (1984): 29-34. Javier Pealosa, "Los Cuentos de Melo," in *México en la Cultura* 759, 1963, p. 3. Elena Poniatowska, "La voluntad de escribir. Entrevista con Juan Vicente Melo," in *La Cultura en México* 35 (1962): 13-14. Jorge Ruffinelli, "Melo: Entre la elegía y el arcano," in *Texto Crítico* 10, 29 (1984): 20-28. Margaret Shedd, Revview of *Fin de Semana* in *Books Abroad* 38, 3 (Summer 1964): 294. Carlos Valdez, "Balance 1962: El Cuento," in *La Cultura en México* 46 (1963): 7. Ramón Xirau, "Los hechos y la cultura," review of *Fin de Semana*, in *Nivel* 15 (1964): 12.

ESTHER HERNANDEZ-PALACIOS

MENDEZ, Concha (1898-   ), poet and dramatist. Concepción Méndez Cuesta was born in Madrid, Spain, on July 27, 1898, but moved to México in 1943. She was from a well-to-do family, and was able to study French, music, and art and to travel extensively. At age twenty-one, she began to travel throughout the world, including England, France, Belgium, Argentina, Uruguay, Brazil, the Canary Islands, and Haiti.

Shortly after her return to Spain, in 1932, she married the poet Manuel *Altolaguirre, and together they edited a number of magazines that were produced by their own publishing company in Madrid, London, and Habana, Cuba.

Concha Mendez published her first collection of poetry, *Inquietudes* (Concerns) (1926), in Spain. She wrote eight others, which were all published after 1943 in Mexico. Her poetry has a warm, musical quality and is rich in imagery. Her works have been translated into a number of languages, including French, English, Italian, and Greek. Most of her plays are directed to a young audience. Her best plays are *El carbón y la rosa* (The Coal and the Rose) (1936) and *El ángel cartero* (The Mailman Angel) (1929). Both were performed for the first time at the Lyceum Club in Madrid.

WORKS: Poetry: *Inquietudes* (Concerns) (Madrid: n.p., 1926). *Surtidor* (Assortment) (Madrid: n.p., 1928). *Canciones de mar y tierra* (Songs of Sea and Land) (Buenos Aires: n.p., 1930). *Vida a vida* (From Life to Life), prologue by Juan Ramón Jiménez (Madrid: La Tentativa Poética, 1932). *Niño y sombras* (Child and Shadows) (Madrid: Héroe, 1936). *Lluvias enlazadas* (Interlocking Rains), poetry, Literary portrait by Juan Ramón Jiménez (La Habana: Col. El Ciervo Herido, 1939). *Poemas, sombras y sueños* (Poems, Shadows, and Dreams) (México: Rueca, 1944). *Villancicos* (Christmas Carols) (México: Rueca, 1945). Theater: *El personaje presentido* (The Foreseen Character), published with *El ángel cartero* (The Mailman Angel) (Madrid: Compañía Iberoamericana de Publicaciones, 1931). *El ángel cartero*, first performed in Madrid in 1929, (Madrid: Companía Iberoamericana de Publicaciones, 1931). *El carbón y la rosa* (The Coal and the Rose), read by Luis Cernuda at the Lyceum Club of Madrid, 1936. *El solitario (tríptico)* (The Loner, In Three Parts), *Hora de España*, 1936 (Valencia). Essays: *Memorias de una loca* (Memories of a Crazy Lady) (Segovia: Barquisimeto, Editorial Nueva, 1955).

BIBLIOGRAPHY: Guadalupe Dueñas, "Sección poética. Concha Méndez Cuesta," *La Mujer de Hoy* 1, 11 (Mexico, July 1961): 76-77. Carlos González Peña, *Historia de la literatura mexicana* (1928; México: Porrúa, 1966), p. 232, 293. Aurora M. Ocampo de Gómez and Ernesto Prado Velázquez, *Diccionario de escritores Mexicanos* (México: UNAM, 1967), p. 226. Juan Ramón Jiménez, Prologue to *Vida a vida* (Madrid: La Tentativa Poética, 1932). Lyrical portrait of Concha Méndez, *Españoles de tres mundos* (Buenos Aires: Losada, 1942), pp. 159-60; *Lluvias enlazadas* (La Habana: Col. El Ciervo Herido, 1939).

EDNA A. REHBEIN

MENDEZ de Cuenca, Laura (1853-1928), poet, novelist, and short story writer, wife of the poet Agustín F. *Cuenca. Méndez de Cuenca was born near Amecameca in the state of Mexico on August 18, 1853. Her most outstanding contributions were in the field of education. She belonged to various scientific and literary associations and served in several important teaching and administrative capacities, among them as a professor at the Escuela de Artes y Oficios para Mujeres (Art and Trade School for Women) and as director of the Escuela Normal para Profesoras (Women's Teachers College) in Toluca. She represented the Mexican government at a number of international conferences on education held in Europe. Her reports on these meetings appeared in official publications dealing with education. Méndez de Cuenca contributed to such Mexico City newspapers as *El Universal*, *El Imparcial*, and *El Correo Español*; she also wrote for the Guadalajara paper *El Mercurio*. During her stay in San Francisco, California, she founded the *Revista Hispano Americana*. She died in Tacubaya, Distrito Federal, in 1928.

As a poet, Méndez de Cuenca is clearly a minor figure. Her poetry is pessimistic in tone and cast in the romantic mold. She published two volumes of prose fiction. The first of these, *El espejo de Amarilis* (Amaryllis's Mirror), is a novel of Mexican customs. The other work, *Simplezas* (Simplicity), contains her short stories. She had numerous admirers and inspired other writers, including the poet Manuel *Acuña.

WORKS: *El espejo de Amarilis* (Amaryllis's Mirror) (México: Linotip. de El Mundo y El Imparcial, 1902). *Tratado de economía doméstica* (Treatise on Domestic Economy) (México: n. p., 1903). *Alvaro Obregón* (Alvaro Obregon) (México: n.p., 1903. *Impresiones de viaje* (Travel Impressions) (México: n.p., 1905). *Vacaciones* (Vacation), a children's book (México: n.p., 1907). *Simplezas* (Simplicity) (Paris: Libr. Paul Ollendorff, 1910).

BIBLIOGRAPHY: Carlos G. Amézaga, *Poetas mexicanos* (Buenos Aires: Pablo E. Coni, 1896), pp. 318-25. Ricardo Dominguez, *Los poetas mexicanos* (México: Pedro J. García, 1888). Juan B. Iguíniz, *Bibliografía de novelistas mexicanos* (México: Sría. de Relaciones Exteriores, 1926), pp. 218-19. Aurora M. Ocampo de Gómez and Ernesto Prado Velázquez, *Diccionario de escritores mexicanos* (México: UNAM, 1967), p. 226. *Enciclopedia de México*, vol. 9 (México: Secretaria de Educación Pública, 1988), p. 5175.

MELVIN S. ARRINGTON, JR.

MENDEZ Plancarte, Alfonso (1909-1955), critic and humorist. Born in Zamora, Michoacán, Méndez Plancarte lived a life similar to that of his brother Gabriel. He studied with the Marists of Zamora and at the Conciliar Seminary in Mexico. In Rome he lived at the Colegio Pío Latino Americano and attended the Gregorian University, receiving his doctorate in philosophy in 1927. Returning to Mexico, he received his doctorate in theology in 1931, was ordained in 1932 and taught at the seminary in Zamora and Mexico. He was director of *Abside*, contributed to *El Universal*, and was a member of the Academy of Language. He and his brother are credited with renewing a humanist tradition in written research.

WORKS: *Mañana del poeta: Prosa y versos ineditos de Amado Nervo* (The Poet's Morning: Amado Nervo's Unpublished Prose and Poetry) (México: Botas, 1938). *Poetas novohispanos: (1521-1721)* (New Hispanic Poets), Biblioteca del Estudiante Universitario, vols. 33, 43, and 54 (México: UNAM, 1942). *El codice "Gómez de Orozco"* (The "Gómez de Orozco" Codex) (México: UNAM, 1945). "León Marchante, Jilguerillo del niño Dios" (León Marchante, Baby Jesus' Singer), in *Abside*, 1945, n.p.. "Díaz Mirón, poeta y artifice" (Díaz Mirón, poet and artist), in *Abside*, 1954, n.p. *Obras completas de Rubén Darío* (Complete Works of Ruben Dario), 4 vols. (Madrid: Aguilar, 1952). *Obras completas de Sor Juana Inés de la Cruz* (Complete Works of Sor Juana Ines de la Cruz), 4 vols. (1951-1957). *Obras completas de Amado Nervo*

(Complete Works of Amado Nervo), coauthored with Francisco Gonzalez Guerrero, 3 vol. (Madrid: 1951-1952). *Díaz Mirón, poeta y artífice* (México: Ant. Libr. Robredo, 1954). *Cuestiúnculas gongorinas* (México: Ed. de Andrea, 1955). *San Juan de la Cruz en México* (México: FCE, 1959).

BIBLIOGRAPHY: Alfredo Cardona Peña, *Semblanzas mexicanas* (Mexican Portraits) (1955). María del Carmen Millán, "Alfonso Méndez Plancarte," in *Revista de Historia de América* (1955). José Luis Martínez, *Literatura mexicana del siglo xx, 1910-1949* (México: Ant. Libr. Robredo, 1949), p. 79.   Various, Homage issue in *Abside*, 1955.

DELIA GALVAN

MENDEZ Plancarte, Gabriel (1905-1949). Gabriel Méndez Plancarte was born in Zamora, Michoacán on January 24, 1905. He studied theology in Zamora, México City, and Rome, receiving doctorates in philosophy and theology, and being ordained to the Catholic priesthood. After returning to México from Europe, he taught Latin, literature, philosophy and theology in a number of institutions within his homeland, the United States, and Canada. He also founded the journal *Abside*, which he directed until his death on December 16, 1949. Furthermore, he was a member of the National Academy of Language.

Méndez Plancarte was known primarily as a poet, humanist and researcher. His poetry, cultivated in beautiful and original strophes, earned the praise of highly respected writers such as Gabriela Mistral, the Nobel-Prize winning poet from Chile. His establishment of *Abside* (1947) and his publication of numerous humanistic studies gained him a reputation as a masterful exponent of Christianity and humanism. Of particular interest is his *Horacio en México* (Horace in México), a study of the influence of this Latin poet upon sixteenth and seventeenth century Mexican literature.

WORKS: Poetry: *Primicias* (First Fruits) (México: Ed. Cultura, 1927). *Oda secular guadalupana* (Secular Ode of Guadalupe) (México: Escuela Tipográfica Salesiana, 1932). *Salmos* (Psalms) (México: Abside, 1942). *Nuevos salmos y odas* (New Psalms and Odes) (México: Abside, 1947). Other Works: *Horacio en México* (Horace in México) (México: UNAM, 1937). *Hidalgo, reformador intelectual* (Hidalgo, an Intellectual Reformer) (México: Eds. Letras de México, 1945). *Los fundadores del humanismo mexicano* (The Founders of Mexican Humanism) (Bogotá: Instituto Caro y Cuervo, 1945).

BIBLIOGRAPHY: Carlos González Peña, *History of Mexican Literature*, translated by Gusta Barfield Nance and Florence Johnson Dunston (Dallas: Southern Methodist University Press, 1968), pp. 374 and 422; "Homage to Gabriel Méndez Plancarte," *Abside*, issue dedicated to Mendez Plancarte, 19, 3 (1950). José Luis Martínez, *El ensayo mexicano moderno*, vol. 2, Letras Mexicanas, 40 (México: Fondo de Cultura Mexicana, 1958), pp. 159-60. "Méndez Plancarte," *Enciclopedia de México*, 1974. Hermann von Bertrab, "Un humanista moderno, Gabriel Méndez Plancarte," *Abside* 19, 4 (Oct.-Dec. 1955): 493-95.

ROBERT K. ANDERSON

MENDOZA, Héctor (1932-1987). Born on July 10, 1932, in Apaseo, Guanajuato, Héctor Mendoza distinguished himself in the theatrical world both as a dramatist and as a director. He received his early schooling in Mexico City. As a university student, he organized and directed theatrical groups, plus some poetry programs. In 1952 he won the Manuel Eduardo de Gorostiza prize for his theatrical piece *Ahogados* (Drowned), and in 1953, he was awarded the Juan Ruiz de Alarcón theater prize for his play *Las cosas simples* (Simple Things). Mendoza studied theater at Yale University from 1957 to 1959, thanks to a Rockefeller Foundation Fellowship. In both 1953 and 1963, he was given a scholarship by the Centro Mexicano de Escritores. He directed his own group and remained very active in the theater. His plays are characterized by realism and social awareness.

WORKS: *Ahogados* (Drowned), staged in 1952. *Las cosas simples* (Simple Things), 1953; in Col. Studium (México: Eds. de Andrea, 1954); in *Teatro mexicano del siglo XX*, edited by Celestino Gorostiza, vol. 3 (México: FCE, 1956), pp. 544-610. *La camelia* (The Poppy), in *Universidad de México*, vol. 13, 10 (June 1959): 13-15. *Salpícame del amor* (Sprinkle Me with Love), in *Ovaciones* 163 (Feb. 7, 1965): 1-5.

BIBLIOGRAPHY: Frank Dauster, "Contemporary Mexican Theater," in *Hispania* 38, 1 (March 1955): 31-34. José Luis Ibáñez, Review of *Las cosas simples*, in *Universidad de México* 13, 4, (Dec. 1958): 27-28. Raúl López Malo, "El teatro experimental en México. Una entrevista con Héctor Mendoza," in *El Día* (Nov. 25, 1964): 9. Héctor Mendoza, "3 directores teatrales relatan su experiencia," in *La Cultura en México* 100 (Jan. 15, 1964): iv-xv. María Luisa Mendoza, Review of *Salpícame de amor*, in *El Gallo Ilustrado* 136 (Jan. 31, 1965): 4. Aurora M. Ocampo de Gómez and Ernesto Prado Velázquez, *Diccionario de Escritores Mexicanos* (México: UNAM, 1967), pp. 228-29. Carlos Solórzano, "Héctor Mendoza resucita a Tirso en un vibrante juego teatral," in *Cultura en México* 217 (April 13, 1966): xvii. Carlos Valdés, Review of *Las cosas simples*, in *Universidad de México* 9, 7 (May, 1954): 31.

ELADIO CORTES

MENDOZA, Vicente T. (1894-1964). A composer and folklorist, Mendoza was born in Cholula, Puebla. Encouraged by his parents to study music, he enrolled in the National Conservatory in 1914. It was up through 1927, while working with the National Forest Service, that he began collecting regional expressions of song, music, and dance and began documenting popular festivals. This job took him to faraway places within Mexico where many of these popular manifestations are still very prevalent. Among other places, he went to Sonora, Chihuahua, and Michoacán.

In 1929 Mendoza was named professor of music theory and voice at the Conservatorio Nacional de Música (National Music Conservatory). Later he was named music inspector for elementary schools. Here he confirmed his suspicions on the lack of scientific documentation within Mexico of its own national music. Greatly admired by folklorists around the world, he became in 1938 the founder and first president of the Folklore Society of Mexico. He and his wife also established the first Mexican School for Folkloric Study. Mendoza continued the tradition of preserving popular culture (folklore) as established by Nicolás León from 1906-1910, and continued by the Mexican musicologist Manuel M. *Ponce in the 1920s. But the efforts to establish scientific bases for the study of folklore still remained at a basic level: the emphasis was still at the descriptive stage. Other well- known researchers before Mendoza were Manuel Gamio, Pablo González Casanova (Sr.), and María Luisa de la Torre Otero, who published *El Folklore en México* in 1933. The difference between Mendoza and these researchers was that he encouraged the study of folklore with strict and scientific principles of research. He brought the field of Mexican folkloric studies to a level equivalent to that of any scientific endeavor, and contributed greatly to the discovery of different historical roots for Mexican traditions. It should be pointed out that he collaborated with his wife, Virginia Rodríguez Rivera (1894-1968), who was an expert folklorist in her own right. From 1936 until his death in 1964, Mendoza had his base of operations at the Instituto de Investigaciones Estéticas (The Institute of Aesthetic Research) of the (UNAM). His musical background helped him concentrate his research on the musical traditions of Mexico dating back to medieval Spain and pre-Hispanic Mexico. At the time of his wife's death in 1968, all their manuscripts were donated to the National Library of UNAM.

Vicente T. Mendoza produced an enormous number of works from 1920 to 1965, most of them dealing with research on popular folklore and in particular with the roots of these popular manifestations. In 1939 he published the work *El Romance español y el corrido mexicano*, where, through a comparative study, he proposes to uncover the detailed relationships between the Mexican *corrido* and the medieval Spanish epic poems, otherwise known as ballads, and with their narrative-epic-lyric makeup. This is a key work by Mendoza, because it is here where he sets the basic pattern and tone of his future research: the relationship between poetry and music. The purpose here was also to determine which influences were Spanish and which ones were autochthonous. In 1954 he published *El corrido mexicano*. Here again he traces the history of the *corrido* all the way back to the Spanish medieval ballads. Although most of the **corridos** that he lists belong chronologically to the twentieth century, there are some samples from the nineteenth century and a few from before that time. His concentration in this book is on the *corrido* of the Mexican Revolution. Listing them by topic, he goes through *corridos* that are historical or revolutionary, those that belong to the agrarian reform movement or the Cristero revolution, political **corridos**, lyrical **corridos**, those about execution by shooting, and **corridos** of valiant men, bandits, famous jails, kidnappings, persecutions, treachery, assassinations, etc.

WORKS: Among many books, short articles, and reviews, the following are generally considered to be outstanding: *El romance español y el corrido mexicano. Estudio comparativo* (México: UNAM, 1939), 400 music samples, prints, and pictures. "Música indígena. Cantos místicos y cosmoénicos," in *Orientación Musical* (Mexico City) 1, 4 (Oct. 1941): 8. "Supervivencia de la cultura azteca.   La canción baile del Xochipitzahua," in *Revista Mexicana de Sociología* (Mexico City) (1943) 4, 4, 87-98. "El grupo musical llamado 'Mariachi,'" in *Revista Universitaria de Guadalajara* (Guadalajara, Jalisco) (1945) 1, 2, 87-89. "La música hispano-mexicana en Nuevo México," in *Universidad de México* (Mexico City) 1, 2 (Nov. 1946): 21, two photos, one drawing. *Lírica infantil de México*, prologue by Luis Santillano, illustrationes by Julio Prieto (México: El Colegio de México, 1951), 193 examples. "El romance tradicional de Delgadina en México," in *Universidad de México* (Mexico City) 6, 69 (Sept. 1952): 8, 17. *El corrido mexicano. Antología introducción y notas de* (México:

FCE, 1954), *70 music examples, 172 literary examples, El corrido de la Revolución Mexicana,* prologue by Jesús Romero Flores. (México: Biblioteca del Instituto Nacional de Estudios Históricos de la Revolución Mexicana, Secretaría de Gobernación, 1956). *Lírica narrativa de México. El Corrido,* Serie de Estudios de Folklore, no. 2 (México: Instituto de Investigaciones Estéticas de la UNAM, 1964).

BIBLIOGRAPHY: Anon., *25 estudios de folklore,* prologue by Justino Fernández (México: UNAM, 1971). Samuel Martí, *Canto, danza y música precortesianos,* prologue by Alfredo Barrera Vázquez (México and Buenos Aires: FCE, 1961). Miguel León Portilla, *La Filosofía Náhuatl estudiada en sus fuentes,* prologue by Angel Ma. Garibay. (México: Instituto Indigenista Interamericano, 1956; Instituto de Investigaciones Estéticas de la UNAM, 1964).

OSCAR SOMOZA

MENENDEZ, Miguel Angel (1905-), also known as Miguel Brisuño. Menéndez was born in Izamal, Yucatán. Raised in that state, he moved to México City as a very young man and became a newspaper reporter. He also gained recognition as a poet, novelist, and essayist.

He first earned public acclaim with his book of interviews, *Hollywood sin pijamas* (Hollywood without Pajamas, 1928), a work followed by some widely praised volumes of poetry. However, the literary work that brought him the greatest recognition was the "indigenist" novel *Nayar* (Nayar), winner of the National Prize for Literature. By sending a "mestizo" protagonist into the most remote mountains of the state of Nayarit, he is able to focus upon the environment and lifestyles of the fatalistic Cora Indians, to interpret their magical world, and, on a symbolical level, to articulate the drama of the mixed-breed as he gropes through the wilderness of his own existence in search of his destiny. His many highly descriptive passages, replete with poetic imagery, have led some critics to conclude that in this narrative the stylist surpasses the novelist. It has been asserted that the interest and recognition fomented by this novel signified the emergence of a new, highly original, and vigorous voice in native letters.

WORKS: Poetry: *Otro libro* (Another Book) (México: n.p., 1932). *Canto a la Revolución* (Song to the Revolution) (México: n.p., 1933). *El rumbo de los versos* (The Way of the Verses) (México: S. Turanzas del Valle, 1936). Novel: *Nayar* (México: Ed. Zamna, 1941); translated by Angel Flores (New York: Farrar and Rinehart, 1942). Other Works: *Hollywood sin pijamas* (Hollywood without Pajamas) (Mérida: Cía. Tipográfica Yucateca, 1928). *Respuesta a Luis Cabrera* (Response to Luis Cabrera) (México: México Nuevo, 1938). *Ideas y direcciones políticas* (Ideas and Political Directions) (México: Ed. Al Servicio del Pueblo, 1940). *La industria de la esclavitud* (The Industry of Slavery) (México: Ed. Zamna, 1947). *Malintzín* (México: La Prensa, 1964). *Vida y muerte de Kennedy* (The Life and Death of Kennedy) (México: Populibros La Prensa, 1964). *Yucatán, problema de patria* (Yucatán, a National Problem) (México: n.p., 1965).

BIBLIOGRAPHY: Adalbert Dessau, *La novela de la Revolución Mexicana* (México: FCE, 1972), pp. 376-80. Arturo Gambóa Garibaldi, "Miguel Angel Menéndez,"

Enciclopedia Yucatanense (Mérida: Ed. Oficial del Gobierno de Yucatán, 1946). Manuel Pedro González, *Tractoria de la novela en México* (México: Eds. Botas, 1951), pp. 377-81. Carlos González Peña, *History of Mexican Literature*, 3rd ed., translated by Gusta Barfield Nance and Florence Johnson Dunston (Dallas: Southern Methodist University Press, 1968), pp. 374, 434. Howard S. Phillips, Review of *Nayar*, in *Books Abroad* 15, 3 (July 1941): 276-79. Donald Schmidt, "Changing Techniques in the Mexican Indigenist Novel," Ph.D. diss., University of Kansas, 1972, pp. 105-28.

ROBERT K. ANDERSON

MEXICAN AUTOBIOGRAPHY. In 450 years of Mexican civilization there have appeared over 300 autobiographies, a number unremarkable when compared to the novel, the short story, or other favorite forms. Although undercounted, life-writing lends itself both to a profile of its status in Mexico and to a selected chronological list of its best examples:

PRE-TWENTIETH CENTURY:
Hernán Cortés, *Cartas de relación* (1519-1526). Bernal Díaz del Castillo, *Verdadera historia de la conquista de la Nueva España* (1623). Fr. Servando Teresa de *Mier, *Memorias* (published in 1946). José *Guridi y Alcocer, *Apuntes de la vida* (published in 1906). Federico *Gamboa, *Impresiones y recuerdos* (1893).

TWENTIETH CENTURY:
Ricardo Flores Magón, *Epistolario revolucionario e íntimo* (1925). Martín Luis *Guzmán, *El águila y la serpiente* (1928). Nellie *Campobello, *Cartucho* (1931). José Rubén Romero, *Apuntes de un lugareño* (1932); *Desbandada* (1934); *Un pueblo inocente* (1934). José *Vasconcelos, *Ulises criollo* (1936). *Martín Luis Guzmán, Memorias de Pancho Villa* (1938). Enrique *González Martínez, *El hombre del buho* (1944). Victoriano Salado Alvarez, *Memorias* (1946). Concha Urquiza, *Obras* (1946). Ricardo *Pozas A, *Juan Pérez Jolote* (1952). Andres *Iduarte, *Un niño en la revolución mexicana* (1954). Alfonso *Reyes, *Parentalia* (1954). Jaime *Torres Bodet, *Tiempo de arena* (1955). Oscar Lewis, *Los hijos de Sánchez* (1965). Ramón *Beteta, *Jarano* (1966). José Clemente Orozco, *El artista en Nueva York* (1971). Margo *Glantz, *Las genealogías* (1981).

This highly selective bibliography indicates the trajectory of Mexican autobiography through almost four centuries: the early years of the conquest and the creation of two classics, Cortés's letters and Bernal *Díaz del Castillo's True History. As in other genres, the seventeenth and eighteenth centuries produce nothing identified as autobiography with the exception of the remarkable *Apuntes de la vida* by D. José Miguel Guridi y Alcocer and the *Memorias* of his contemporary, Fray Servando Teresa de Mier. The fertile period for autobiography in Mexico comes in the twentieth century with the Revolution as catalyst. Each following decade, incremental in the production of this genre, has excellent examples but the years 1928 to 1938, more prolific in canonized texts, can be labeled the golden age of autobiography in Mexico.

Regardless of period, life-writing has subcategories: autobiography proper, memoirs, letters, diaries, oral autobiography, interviews, and the autobiographical novel as well as the autobiographical essay. Briefly, autobiography proper refers to an effort by the subject to present his entire life usually from the perspective of a mature age; memoirs, simply a recording of a fragment of years from a life, present the writer as participant/observer to a major historical event. This form incidentally is by far the most popular in Mexico. All of the other terms are self explanatory except oral autobiography. Also labeled "as-told-to" another, "case history," or "life story," it is the collaborative effort of anthropologist and subject. The narrator, possibly from a pre-literate culture, recounts his life to an amanuensis who acts as prompter, organizer, and editor of the memories of another. The symbiotic relationship prohibits distinguishing the contributions of either. With the presence of all these types, a merited question is the reception of autobiography within the system of literature of Mexico. To paraphrase, how is autobiography treated in reference books, anthologies, and journals, and what is its status among publishers? Bibliographies, dictionaries/encyclopedias, and literary histories comprise the first group. Here autobiography -- often labeled "relato," "crónica," "narración, " and "memorias" -- comes off badly. It has no separate category, and furthermore, those who indulge in life-writing are often noted mainly for other types of work. Historians of literature never accord a chapter to autobiography, rarely mention the word, and often vacillate as to the genre of "novels of the Revolution." Cognizance of autobiography might allow Mexican scholars to recategorize some of the more troublesome examples always incompatible with the term "novel."

Anthologists, or those who create taste among a new generation, privilege autobiography little better than their colleagues. Sixteen anthologies published between 1910 and 1975 do the following: five totally exclude autobiography; four note its presence but with no selection, while seven include one or two examples of life-writing. A perusal of a total of thirty-five journals covering 100 years of Mexican literature yields little: no articles on autobiography, an occasional installment from a larger famous work, and finally, some reviews of current life-writing from this field. These journals rendered a total of ninety-five reviews of Mexican autobiography, but their content calls into question the entire reviewing process in Mexico. Description usually usurps analysis, and autobiographies, judged by a single standard, have one function. As a handmaiden to history, life-writing illuminates a certain period and is valued for information. The highly flawed reviewing process suggests the absence of literary criticism that would note the contribution of life-writing and its relation to the established genres, novel, drama, short story, poetry, and essay.

Finally, a perusal of 295 autobiographies indicates that eleven percent have no publisher listed, so they must be the result of a vanity enterprise. Yet, perhaps the most optimistic note on autobiography in Mexico is that the major publishers -- Botas, Porrúa, FCE, Jus and Empresas Editoriales -- do include autobiographies among their publications.

The genre of autobiography in Mexico occupies an ambiguous position. Although the Mexicans may have produced some of the best life-writing in the Western world, they seem to be oblivious to this genre. Under whimsical nomenclature, autobiography is neglected in reference books, anthologies, and periodicals. Most symptomatic of the genre's precarious status is the descriptive nature of reviews, the product of a system without a serious commitment to literary criticism. However, further research with autobiography may well illuminate more in regard to its status; surely it will uncover more works worthy of the label "autobiography."

Ultimately, the published results of this research might alert Mexicans to an entire corpus of writing in need of analysis. Also, autobiography separated as a genre may well signal a new generation as to its presence and act as a stimulant to further contributions. An ideal for autobiography in Mexico would be to achieve the status accorded to national life-writings in the United States, England, France, and Germany.

BIBLIOGRAPHY: Richard D. Woods, *Mexican Autobiography: An Annotated Bibliography* (Westport, Conn.: Greenwood Press, 1988);   "The Substratum Of Mexican Autobiography," paper read at the Fifteenth International Congress of Latin American Studies, Sept. 21-23, 1988, at San Juan, Puerto Rico; "Mexican Autobiography," *Auto/Biography Studies* 3 (Summer 1988): 1-64.

RICHARD D. WOODS

MICHELENA, Margarita (1917-   ), poet, critic, journalist.   Michelena was born in Pachuca, Estado de Hidalgo, on July 21, 1917. She took a few literature courses at the UNAM and began her literary career in the journal *América*, under the guidance of Efrén *Hernández. In 1943 she founded and coedited the prestigious journal, *Tiras de Colores*. She served as president of the board of directors of the literary journal *El Libro y el Pueblo* from 1960 to 1962; of the political review *Respuesta* from 1961 to 1962; and of the feminine magazine *Kena* in 1963. In 1962 she prepared, for the Centro de Acción Latina of Roma, the study on the Mexican novel and short story for the book *Messico*. In 1975 she became the editor of the magazine *Casa*. She has contributed to the following literary journals and newspapers: *Abside, Examen, Mexico en la Cultura, America, Casa de la Cultura* (Ecuador), *Excelsior, Novedades,* and *El sol de Mexico*. Even though she is known as a poet, critic, teacher, and scriptwriter, she lives off her career as a journalist. Michelena's poetry is intimate and reflects the consciousness of someone who has experienced exile or imprisonment. The events seem to occur between an air of reality and an atmosphere of death. Her poems convey nostalgia and a permanent search. The feeling of solitude predominates her latest poems, which persevere in their need to provide a valid explanation for existence.

WORKS: Poetry: *Paraíso y nostalgia* (Paradise and Nostalgia) (México: Edit. Tiras de Colores, 1945). *Laurel del angel* (Angel's Laurel) (México: Edit. Stylo, 1948). *3 poemas y una nota autobiográfica* (Three Poems and an Autobiographical Note) (México: Edit. de la Sociedad de Amigos del Libro Mexicano, 1953). *La tristeza terrestre* (The Terrestrial Sadness) (México: Eds. de la Revista Antológica América, 1954). *El país más allá de la niebla* (The Country beyond the Fog) (México, FCE, 1969). *Reunión de imágenes* (Reunion of Images) (México: FCE, 1969). Essays: "Las mujeres poetas." Notas en torno a la poesía contemporánea (Women Poets. Notes on Contemporary Poetry) (México: Asociación Mexicana por la Libertad de la Cultura, 1959), pp. 48-54. "Prologue" to Guadalupe Amor, *Poesías completas*, 2nd ed. (México: Ed. Aguilar, 1960).

BIBLIOGRAPHY: Antonio Castro Leal, ed., *La poesía mexicana moderna* (México: FCE, 1953), p. 438. Cynthia Gold, "Margarita Michelena," thesis, University of California, Berkeley, Calif. Marco Antonio Millán, "Los verdaderos grandes poetas nunca han sido populares" (entrevista con Margarita Michelena), in *México en la Cultura* 683 (April 15, 1962): 8. Beth Miller and Alfonso González, *26 autoras del México actual* (México: B. Costa-Amic Ed., 1978), pp. 269-84. Carlos Monsiváis, *La poesía mexicana del siglo XX* (México: Empresas Eds. S.A, 1966), pp. 62-63, 625. Aurora M. Ocampo de Gómez and Ernesto Prado Velázquez, *Diccionario de escritores mexicanos* (México: UNAM, 1967), p. 230. Héctor Valdés, *Poetisas mexicanas, siglo XX* (México: UNAM, 1976), pp. 43-56.

MARGARITA VARGAS

"MICROS." See CAMPO, Angel de.

MIER Noriega y Guerra, José Servando Teresa de (1765-1827), propagandist and literary figure. Mier is one of the few political writers of the independence period to write works of genuine literary merit. Born in Monterrey on October 18, 1765, he entered the religious community of the Dominicans in Mexico City when he was only sixteen years of age. Continuing his training within the Church, he was later ordained as a priest, and at age twentyseven he completed his doctorate in theology. Mier was renowned for his pulpit oratory, and on December 12, 1794, he delivered a controversial sermon on the Virgin of Guadalupe before a distinguished audience. Outraged by the boldness of some of Mier's statements, the archbishop ordered that he be punished for his outspokenness. After being imprisoned in Mexico, Mier was finally sentenced to exile in Spain, where he was confined in a convent near Santander. He was also barred from teaching and from performing some religious duties and had his degree in theology revoked.

In 1795 Mier began his exile in Spain, but his resistance to confinement compelled him to seek freedom continually. He escaped from every convent in which he was placed, his flight taking him to various parts of Spain as well as to France, Italy, Portugal, and finally England. In London he worked for a press supporting Mexico's independence, and there, also, he became involved in an ill-fated mission to return to Mexico. Captured by the royalists, he again became a prisoner in Mexico City, and after being ordered to resume his exile in Spain, he jumped ship in Havana during the return voyage. Following a brief stay in the United States, he was captured again in Mexico. Although he was released for a short time and became a deputy of the Constituent Congress, he was returned to prison by Iturbide and remained incarcerated until 1823, after the Republican revolt.

Mier's major work, his *Memorias* (Memoirs), is a novelesque account of his experiences beginning with his sermon on the Virgin of Guadalupe and continuing with his travels throughout Europe. This lively autobiography, which borders in some passages on the picaresque, contains the portrait of a dedicated revolutionary and a description of the political climate that influenced him. He also wrote the *Historia de la Revolución de Nueva España* (History of the Revolution of New Spain), which appeared in London in 1813 under the pseudonym Don José Guerra. In addition to these two principal works, Mier penned a number of letters and articles on both politics and religion, but their value cannot compare to that of his personal reflections on Mexico's turbulent era of independence.

WORKS: *Historia de la Revolución de Nueva España* (History of the Revolution of New Spain) (Londres: Imprenta de Guillermo Glindon, 1813). *Memorias* (Memoirs) (México: Editorial Porrúa, 1946).

BIBLIOGRAPHY: René Jara, "El Criollismo de Fray Servando Teresa de Mier," *Cuadernos Americanos* 221, 1 (Jan.-Feb. 1979): 141-62. John V. Lombardi, *The Political Ideology of Fray Servando Teresa de Mier, Propagandist for Independence* (Cuernavaca: Centro Intercultural de Documentación, 1968). Marco Antonio Millán, *La fantástica realidad de Fray Servando* (México: Secretaría de Educación pública, 1965). Edmundo O'Gorman, "Prólogo" in *Ideario político* (Caracas: Biblioteca Ayacucho, 1978). Alfonso Reyes, *Fray Servando Teresa de Mier* (México: PRI, Comisión Nac. Editorial, 1976).

JULIE GREER JOHNSON

MILLAN, María del Carmen (1914-   ). Millán was born December 3, 1914, in Teziutlán, Puebla. She completed her studies at the Nacional Preparatory School and in the Faculty of Philosophy and Letters at the UNAM where she obtained her master's and doctoral degrees in Spanish language and literature. She has been professor of Spanish and of literature in several universities of the province and of the United States and Europe. Since 1954 she has been a professor of the Faculty of Philosophy and Letters at the UNAM. She was secretary of the Faculty of Philosophy and Letters from 1960 through 1965 and was director of the Centro de Estudios Literarios, director of the Seminario de Letras Mexicanas and director of its summer courses. As director of the Centro de Estudios Literarios, she has directed many works of research: *Indices de "El Domingo"* (1959), *Indices de "El Nacional"* (1961), *Indices de "El Renacimiento,"* *Obras de Joaquín Fernández de Lizardi, Diccionario de Escritores Mexicanos, Indices de la "Revista Moderna," Indices de la "Revista Azul,"* and *Biobibliografía crítica de la literatura mexicana,* among others. Her work is also dedicated to the essay, to teaching, and to research published in books and in various literary reviews such as *Rueca, Tierra Nueva, Letras de México,* Humanidades, Revista Interamericana de Bibliografía, *Cuadrante, Historia Mexicana, La Palabra y el Hombre,* and *Revista de Bellas Artes.*

  Prologues, essays, studies, and anthologies all refer to Mexican literature on which she is an authority. Her solid information, her sensibility, and her critical responsibility are well known not only in Mexico but in academic circles in Hispanic America, Europe, and the United States. Her valiant and objective work has opened new roads to future researchers in Mexican literature. Her first book, *El paisaje en la poesía mexicana* (1952) (Landscape in Mexican Poetry), won critical acclaim from Alfonso *Reyes and Salvador *Novo. In this book, she presents seven sublime chapters which are comparable to the work of the most representative Mexican poets from Francisco de *Terrazas to Sor Juana Inés de la *Cruz, Bernardo de *Balbuena and Fray Manuel *Martínez de Navarrete through the "symphonic landscape" of Manuel José *Othón. Millán has been concerned with the problems of Mexico, which

432 MOJARRO, Tomás

have always been connected to its literature. In 1956 she published *Ideas de la Reforma en las letras patrias* (Ideas of the Reform in Patriotic Literature). In her 1962 book, *Literatura mexicana* (Mexican Literature), she expounds upon her theories of Mexican literature from pre-Columbian times to the present.

WORKS: Essays: *El paisaje sinfónico* (The Symphonic Landscape) introduction to the poetry of Manuel José Othón (San Luis Potosí, n.p., 1951). *El paisaje en la poesía mexicana* (Landscape in Mexican Poetry) (México: Imp. Universitaria, 1952). *Ideas de la Reforma en letras patrias* (Ideas of the Reform in National Literature) (México: Cuadernos de Orientación Política, 1956). *El Modernismo de Othón* (The Modernismo of Othón), in *Revista Iberoamericana* 29, 47 (1959): 17-23. *Literatura mexicana* (Mexican Literature) (México: Edit. Esfinge, S.A., 1962); 2nd ed. (1963). *La generación del Ateneo y el ensayo mexicano* (The Generation of Ateneo and the Mexican Essay), Homage to Alfonso Reyes, in *Nueva Revista de Filología Hispánica* 2, 3-4 (1961): 30-69, (México: El Colegio de México, 1962). *En torno a "Oficio de tinieblas"* (About "The Ministry of Darkness"), in *Anuario de Letras* 3 (México: UNAM, 1963), pp. 287-99. Prologues and Anthologies: *Cuentos americanos* (American Stories) (México: SEP, 1946). *Poesía romántica* (Romantic Poetry) (México: Libro-Mex, 1957). Angel de Campo, *Ocios y apuntes y la rumba* (Leisure, Notes, and the Rumba), Edition and prologue by María del Carmen Millán (México: Porrúa, 1958). Angel de Campo, *Cosas vistas y cartones* (Things Seen and Cartoons), edition and prologue by María del Carmen Millán (México: Porrúa, 1958). *Doce cuentistas potosinos contemporáneos* (Twelve Contemporary Potosian Story Writers), edited by María del Carmen Millán (San Luis Potosí: San Luis Potosí, 1959). *Poesía de México* (Poetry of Mexico), edited by María del Carmen Millán (Buenos Aires: Edit. Univ. of Buenos Aires, 1966). Ignacio M. Altamirano, *El Zarco, La Navidad en las montañas* (The Clear Waters, Christmas in the Mountains), edited by Maríia del Carmen Millán (México: Porrúa, 1966).

DENISE GUAGLIARDO BENCIVENGO

MOJARRO, Tomás (1932-). Mojarro was born in Jalpa, Zacatecas, on September 21, 1932 and completed his studies there. He went to Guadalajara as a young man and spent several years there establishing himself as a writer. There he collaborated on the magazines *Summa* (Summa) and *Et caetera* (Et caetera), where he published his first poems and stories. He won second prize for the short story in the Second Annual Fair of Jalisco. He began to publish his short stories in several magazines and literary supplements in Mexico City. His story "El arpa" (The Harp) was awarded a prize in the literary competition of *Life en Español* (Life in Spanish) in 1960. Mojarro was a fellow in the Mexican Center for Writers in 1958-1959 and in 1959-1960. His book of short stories, *Cañón de Juchipila* (Cannon of Juchipila), was published in 1960 and his novels *Bramadero* (The Corral) in 1963 and *Malafortuna* (Bad Fortune) in 1966. He is also a contributor to Fondo de Cultura Económica.

Cañón de Juchipila is composed of eight stories marked by an intense and rather petty atmosphere of the southern provinces of Zacatecas. His style is quite elaborate and his characters are bounded by misery and fanatisicism. The same qualities characterize *Bramadero* and *Malafortuna*. The scenes also take place in the provinces, the first in the town of Margil de Minas, which becomes transformed when a highway connects it to the rest of the country. The second novel takes place on a military air base in the southern part of the country, lost in a dry, desolate vast land. Mojarro's writing style and technique are similar to those of Juan *Rulfo. Mojarro's well structured plots with their synthetical style and with well developed and verisimilar characters have enriched the Mexican novel.

WORKS: Short Story: *Cañón de Juchipila* (Cannon of Juchipila) (México: FCE, 1960). Novel: *Bramadero* (The Corral) (México: FCE, 1966). *Malafortuna* (Bad Fortune) (México: Mortiz, 1966). *Tomás Mojarro*, prologue by Emmanuel Carballo (México: Empressas Editoriales, 1966).

BIBLIOGRAPHY: Demetrio Aguilera Malta, Review of *Malafortuna*, in *El Gallo Ilustrado* 217 (Aug. 21, 1966): 4. Federico Alvarez, Review of *Bramadero*, in *La Cultura en México* 59 (Apr. 3, 1963): xx. Manuel Andújar, Emmanuel Carballo and José Agustín, "Tres opiniones sobre *Malafortuna*," in *Ovaciones* 249 (Oct. 30, 1966): 3. Anon., Review of *Bramadero*, in *Cuadernos de Bellas Artes* 4, 5 (May 5, 1963): 87-88. Héctor Gally, "Tomás Mojarro. Interview and Review of *Malafortuna*, in *Ovaciones* 249 (Oct. 30, 1966): 1-3. Luis Leal, *Bibliografía del cuento mexicano* (México: de Andrea, 1958), p. 92. Javier Morente, "Sala de lectura," review of *Bramadero*, in *Diorama de la Cultura* (March 31, 1963): 8. Aurora M. Ocampo de Gómez and Ernesto Prado Velázquez, *Diccionario de escritores mexicanos* (México: UNAM, 1967), pp. 233-34. Gustavo Sainz, "Escaparate," review of *Bramadero* in *México en la Cultura* 729 (March 10, 1963): 9; 733 (Apr. 7, 1963): 3. Joseph Sommers, Review of *Bramadero*, in *Hispania*, 46, 4 (Dec. 4, 1963): 857.

DENISE GUAGLIARDO BENCIVENGO

MOLT, Angela or María del Mar (1913-), a poet and prose writer born in Mexico City. Molt has performed extensively in piano concerts; she was a member of the short-lived Agorismo Movement. Molt has travel extensively through America and Europe. Her first poems apeared in *El Universal*.

WORKS: Poetry: *El alma desnuda* (The Bare Soul) (México: n.p, 1925). *Luna en zozobra* (Anxiety Moon) (México: n.p., 1934). *En ti, sólo distante* (In You, Only Distant) (México: n.p., 1937). *Sombra de flor en el agua* (Flower Shadow on Water) (México: Prisma, 1943). *Canto panorámico de la Revolución* (Song of the Revolution) (México: n.p., 1952). *Perfiles de gloria* (Profiles of Glory) (México: n.p., 1957). *Horizonte de sueños* (Dreams Horizon) (México: Metáfora, 1957). *Vida de mi muerte* (Life of My Death) (México: Ed. Estaciones, 1960). *Fiel trayectoria* (Loyal Trajectory) (México: Ed. Estaciones, 1961). *Atmósfera sellada* (Sealed Atmosphere) (México: Ed. Estaciones, 1961) Prose: *La corola invertida* (The Inverted Corolla) (México: L. Méndez, 1930). *Tres cartas de Hans Gastorp* (Three Letters by Hans Gastorp) (México: Talls. Graf. de la Nación, 1939). *Cántico del amor que perdura* (Song of the Lasting Love) (México: Talls. Graf. de la Nación, 1939). *Luz en la muerte* (Light in Death) (México: n.p., 1945)..

BIBLIOGRAPHY: Rafael Aguayo Spencer, *Flor de Moderna Poesía Mexicana*, (México: Libro-Mex, 1955) pp. 106, 137. Anon., *Anuario de la poesía mexicana 1962*

(México: INBA, 1963), p. 79. Antonio Castro Leal, *La poesía mexicana moderna* (México: FCE, 1953), p. 368. Luis Leal, *Bibliografía del cuento mexicano* (México: de Andrea, 1958), p. 86. José Luis Martínez, *Literatura mexicana siglo XX, 1910-1949*, vol. 1 (México: Robredo, 1949), p. 64; vol. 2, p. 75. R.R., Review of *Sombra de flor en el agua*, in *Letras de Mexico* 14 (Feb. 1944): 4.

DELIA GALVAN

MONDRAGON Aguirre, Magdalena (1913-), journalist, poet, novelist, and dramatist; pseudonym: Vera Seminoreff. Born in Torreón, Coahuila, on July 14, 1913, Mondragón Aguirre went to school in San Antonio, Texas, but returned to Mexico for her higher education studies. She has worked as a journalist for several newspapers in the United States and Mexico, such as *La Opinión, La Prensa, El Universal*, and *Excelsior*. She was the first woman editor of a daily newspaper in Mexico: *Prensa Gráfica* in 1950. In addition, she has directed *Boletín Cultural Mexicano* (1946-1964) and *Solo para ellas* (1952-1958), held administrative posts in various professional organizations of writers and journalists, and has had a museum and a university prize named in her honor.

Mondragón has produced a wide variety of plays and novels, as well as several volumes of poetry. Her best known novels are *Yo, como pobre* . . . (whose English translation, *Someday the Dream*, won the Book of the Month Award in 1947) and *Más allá existe la tierra* (The Land Still Lives). *Yo, como pobre* . . . is set in Mexico City's garbage dumps, and Mondragón realistically re-creates the dehumanizing environment and lifestyle of her characters in a plea for correction of the conditions which lead to their plight. In *Más allá existe la tierra*, a schoolteacher recalls the bloody days of the Cristero uprisings and their effects on the people of her native state. Mondragón uses a traditional style to explore the sociopolitical realities of contemporary Mexico. Her career in journalism has provided her with the background information which so realistically informs her creative works.

WORKS: *Puede que'l otro año* (Maybe Next Year) (México: Editorial Alrededor de América, 1937). *Cuando Eva se vuelve Adán* (When Eve Becomes Adam), staged in 1938; in *Dos obras de teatro*, published with *Torbellino* (México: Enciclopedia Popular de la SEP, 1947). *Souvenir* (Souvenir), staged in 1938. *Torbellino* (Whirlwind) (original title, *La Tarántula*), staged in 1942; in *Dos obras de teatro* (México: Enciclopedia Popular de la SEP, 1947). *Norte bárbaro* (Barbarian North) (Baja California: Imprenta de Marco J. Lara, 1944). *Yo, como pobre* . . . (Someday the Dream) (México: Editorial Ariel, 1944). *La sirena que llevaba el mar* (The Mermaid Who Carried the Sea) (México: Colección México, Grupo América, 1946). *Más allá existe la tierra* (The Land Still Lives) (México: Editorial Cortés, 1947). *Someday the Dream*, translated by Samuel Putnam (New York: Dial Press, 1947). *La tarántula* (The Tarantula), published as *Torbellino* (Whirlwind) in *Dos obras de teatro* (México: Enciclopedia Popular de la SEP, 1947). *El mundo perdido*, a play in three acts (The Lost World), written in 1945 (México: SEP, 1948). *El día no llega* (The Day Won't Come) (México: Editorial Juan Pablos, 1950). *¡Porque me da la gana!* (Because I Feel Like It!) (México: Imp. Universitaria, 1953). *Tenemos sed* (We're Thirsty) (México: Edic. de la Revista Mexicana de Cultura, 1954). *Si mis alas nacieran* (If I Grew wings) (México, 1960). *Habla un espía* (A Spy Talks) (México: Eds. de la Prensa, 1962). *El choque de los justos* (The Problems of the Just) (1962). *Mi corazón es la tierra* (The Land Is My Heart) (1968). *México pelado . . ., pero sabroso!* (Mexico Peeled, But Tasty!) (1973).

BIBLIOGRAPHY: John S. Brushwood, *Mexico in Its Novel* (Austin: University of Texas Press, 1966), pp. 13, 16, 22-23, 221, 230-31. *Enciclopedia de México* (México: SEP, 1988), vol. 9, pp. 5502-3. Manuel Pedro González, *Trayectoria de la novela en México* (México: Ediciones Botas, 1951), pp. 351-55; 400-401. Diane Martínez, ed., *Women Writers of Spanish America: An Annotated Bio-Bibliographical Guide* (Westport, Conn.: Greenwood Press, 1987), pp. 259-60. Aurora M. Ocampo de Gómez and Ernesto Prado Velázquez, *Diccionario de escritores mexicanos* (México: UNAM, 1967), pp. 234-35. Harry L. Rosser, *Conflict and Transition in Rural Mexico: The Fiction of Social Realism* (Waltham, Mass.: Crossroads Press, 1980), pp. 12, 17, 18, 19, 21, 47, 48-57, 162.

TERESA R. ARRINGTON

MONSIVAIS, Carlos (1938-). Carlos Monsiváis, a noted essayist, journalist, translator, and critic, was born in Mexico City on May 4, 1938. He is viewed as one of the most influential writers of the contemporary Mexican narrative, having studied at the Universidad Nacional de México. He has made major contributions to many of the major literary journals and periodicals in Mexico, especially *La Cultura en México*. Recipient of a one-year fellowship from the Centro Mexicano de Escritores in 1962, Monsiváis has dedicated himself to literature, art, radio (at Radio Universidad), and film. At one time he was the director of Voz Viva de México (The Living Voice of Mexico). A keen observer and critic of the contemporary era, he has often been solicited to give conferences at major universities both at home and abroad, such as Monterrey and Harvard. His many valuable translations, adaptations, and original pieces, especially in poetry, give him a place in the literary history of Mexico.

A sharp critic of the contemporary era, Monsiváis is especially known for his humor and sarcasm. He also is exceptionally knowledgeable about twentieth century Mexican poetry, having published an annotated anthology, *La poesía mexicana del siglo XX* (Twentieth Century Mexican Poetry, 1966). His prologue to this very comprehensive and well-arranged anthology is considered an excellent study of contemporary writers and their verse.

Monsiváis is considered one of the finest prose writers in Mexico. Much of his work focuses on and explores varying facets of daily life in Mexico. He particularly targets for criticism false middle-class values that ultimately lead to emptiness and despair.

Días de guardar (Days of Keeping) (1970) studies the calendar of national life, divided into recurrent happenings (the national holidays) and specifically dated happenings. The starting point is the student movement of 1968, with October 2 of that year, the date of the massacre of Tlatelolco, as the catalyst.

Amor perdido (Lost Love) (1977), a diachronical study, focuses on what happened after Tlatelolco. Monsiváis studies a number of Mexican myths from a historical perspective, illustrating how the passage of time affects, differentiates, and modifies them, especially with regard to other myths.

In 1982, Monsiváis published *Nuevo catecismo para indios remisos* (New Catechism for Reluctant Indians), an ironic view of Christian ethics and practices during colonial times. While didactic, the narrative is spiced with subtle irony and humor and is considered one of the joys of Mexican prose. It is made up of hagiographic fragments and catechistic texts which fit it into the Christian tradition, but at the same time, it questions that tradition.

María Eugenia Cossío, in an article, "El diálogo sin fin de Monsiváis," explores the many facets and dimensions of the author's life and literary production. In particular, she focuses on Monsiváis' chronicles, illustrating how they portray Mexican social life through examining legend, myth, history, and the character of the people, especially the middleclass. The author captures and communicates how people really speak and how they really are.

Thematically organized around episodes, each chronicle is both independent and interdependent. Monsiváis often uses selections from political speeches and other official rhetoric to give authenticity and relevancy to the work. The use of drawings, pictures, and newspaper-style titles give the appearance of a news journal, making the chronicles seem more pertinent. The narrative point of view is that of an observer who continually questions various aspects of life and allows readers to participate in the work, by assessing the situations and historical circumstances leading up to those situations. In large measure, Monsiváis' literature is considered pleasurable reading.

WORKS: *Carlos Monsiváis*, prologue by Emmanuel Carballo (México: Empresas Editoriales, 1966). *La poesía mexicana del siglo XX. Antología* (Mexican Poetry of the Twentieth Century. Anthology), editor (México: Empresas Editoriales, 1966). "La brevedad como don de lucidez" (Brevity as a Gift of Lucidity), in *El Gallo Ilustrado* (March 30, 1969): 4. *Días de guardar* (Days of Keeping) (México: Era, 1970). *Amor perdido* (Lost Love) (México: Empresas Editoriales, 1977). *A ustedes les consta. Antología de la crónica en México* (For Your Record. Anthology of the Chronicle in Mexico) (México: Empresas Editoriales, 1979); 2nd ed. (1980). *Nuevo catecismo para indios remisos* (New Catechism for Reluctant Indians) (México: Siglo XXI, 1982). *Carlos Monsiváis* (Azcapotzalco, D.F.: Universidad Autónoma Metropolitana, 1984). Carlos Monsivais, Julianne Burton, and Manuel Rivas, trans., "Landscape, I've Got the Drop on You!' on the 50th Anniversary of Sound Film in Mexico," in *Studies in Latin American Popular Culture* 4 (1985): 236-46. "De la Santa Doctrina al Espíritu Público: sobre las funciones de la crónica en México" (From the Holy Doctrine to the Public Spirit: About the Functions of the Chronicle in Mexico), in *Nueva Revista de Filología Hispánica* 34, 2 (1987): 753. "No con un sollozo, sino entre disparos (notas sobre cultura mexicana 1910-1968)" (Not with a Sob, but Amid Gunshots, [notes about Mexican culture 1910-1968]), in *Revista Iberoamericana* 55, 148-49 (July-Dec., 1989): 715-31.

BIBLIOGRAPHY: Huberto Batis, Review of Monsiváis' *La poesía mexicana del siglo XX. Antología*, in *El Heraldo Cultural* 39 (Aug. 7, 1966): 14. Miguel Capistrán, "La antología de Carlos Monsiváis. Una nueva visión de la poesía mexicana," in *La Cultura en México* 234 (Aug. 10, 1966): vi-viii. Emmanuel Carballo, "Diario público de Carlos Monsiváis, del 4 al 10 de julio," in *Diorama de la Cultura* (July 17, 1966): 3, 6; Prologue to *Carlos Monsiváis* (México: Empresas Editoriales, 1966). Fausto Castillo, "Monsiváis: ¿Autorretrato involuntario?," review of *La poesía mexicana del siglo XX. Antología*, in *El Gallo Ilustrado* 213 (July 24, 1966): 4. María Eugenia

Cossío, "El diálogo sin fin de Monsivais," in *Hispanic Journal* 5, 2 (Spring 1984): 137-43. J. Ann Duncan, *Voices, Visions, and a New Reality: Mexican Fiction since 1970* (Pittsburgh: University of Pittsburgh Press, 1986), pp. 31-33, 56, 200, 220. Margarita García Flores, "Con Carlos Monsiváis," in *El Día* (March 2, 1966): 9. Ignacio Méndez, "Entrevista con Carlos Monsiváis," in *México en la Cultura* 716 (Dec. 9, 1962): 10, 11. María Luisa Mendoza, "Entrevista en contrapunto con Carlos Monsiváis, o el sí y el no de los niños," in *El Día* (Oct. 6, 1963): 4; "Habla un hugonote azteca. Carlos Monsiváis entre vampiros se vio," in *El Día* (Nov. 8, 1965): 2. Aurora M. Ocampo de Gómez and Ernesto Prado Velázquez, *Diccionario de Escritores Mexicanos* (México: UNAM, 1967), pp. 235-36. Luis Guillermo Piazza, "Poesía mexicana del siglo XX," in *Diorama de la Cultura* (July 17, 1966): 5. Sara Sefchovich, *México: país de ideas, país de novelas* (México: Grijalbo, 1987), pp. 43-45, 245-47, 251-53. Gabriel Zaid, "De la antología como infierno de la exclusión," in *La Cultura en México* 238 (Sept. 7, 1966): xv-xvi.

JEANNE C. WALLACE

MONTEFORTE Toledo, Mario (1911-). For political reasons, Monteforte Toledo has lived most of his life in Guatemala. He is a subtle narrator with a great knowledge of childhood. In his prose he narrates realities of Guatemala: its people, nature, and especially and with unforgettable form, its Indians. *La cueva sin quietud* (The Cave without Quiet) is a collection of highly elaborated short stories, preceded by the author's foreword where he states the importance of the genre as an essential expression of a stage of life: "El cuento es una frase de la lengua, una rama de su pensamiento, un compacto haz de figuraciones y de conceptos, no por fragmentario, menos completo en sí," (The short story is a phrase of language, a branch of its thought, a compact beam of figures and concepts, and regardless of how fragmentary, complete in itself.) His entire work never abandons realism. There is a balance between fantasy and reality. The novel *Anaité* obtained the National Award. The title is the name of a tributary to the Usumacinta River that separates Mexico from Guatemala. The book belongs to the cycle of jungle novels. The jungle may well be the protagonist. *Entre la piedra y la cruz* (Between the Stone and the Cross) is a novel conceptualized as critical realism. It is a work in defense of the Indians. The theme is the life of a native family that fights discrimination and misfortune. The author presents the natives governed by cosmic forces and united with Nature as their alma mater. In this link with the earth, the woman-mother has an almost sacred presence. *Cabagüil* is a poem inspired by the Maya-Quiche cosmovision, as it appears in the *Popol-Vuh*. It was written as the basis for a ballet script.

WORKS: Prose: Cabagüil (Guatemala: Imprenta Hispania, 1946). *Anaité* (Guatemala: Editorial El Libro de Guatemala, Fondo de Cultura de la Municipalidad, 1948). *Entre la piedra y la cruz* (Between the Stone and the Cross), Colección Contemporáneos, no. 5 (Guatemala: Editorial El Libro de Guatemala, 1948). *La cueva sin quietud* (The Cave Without Quiet) (Guatemala: Editorial del Ministerio de Educación pública, Contemporáneos # 11, 1949). *Una democracia a prueba de fuego: Homenaje a los que cayeron defendiendo la democracia guatemalteca los días 18 y 19 de julio de 1949* (A Fireproof Democracy: Homage to Those Who Fell in Defense of Gatemala's Democracy on July 18 and 19, 1949) (Guatemala: Dept. de Publicidad de la Presidencia de la República, 1949). *Donde acaban los caminos* (Where the Paths

End) (Guatemala: Tipografía Nacional, 1953). *Una manera de morir* (A Way of Dying) (México: FCE, 1957). *Cuentos de derrota y esperanza* (Short Stories of Defeat and Hope) (Jalapa: Universidad Veracruzana, 1962).

BIBLIOGRAPHY: Fernando Alegría, *Historia de la novela hispanoamericana* (México: De Andrea, 1965), pp. 225-27. Enrique Anderson Imbert, *Historia de la literatura hispanoamericana*, vol. 2 (México: FCE, 1957), p. 227. Ruth S. Lamb, *Antología del cuento guatemalteco* (México: De Andrea, 1959), pp. 13, 125. Salomón Lipp, "Mario Monforte Toledo, Contemporary Guatemalan Novelist," in *Hispania* 4 (Dec. 1961): 420-27. Seymour Menton, *Historia crítica de la novela guatemalteca* (Guatemala: n.p., 1960), pp. 243-76.

ALICIA G. WELDEN AND ELADIO CORTES

MONTERDE, Alberto (1923-). Born in Mexico City, Alberto Monterde pursued his university studies in the United States at Northwestern University in Chicago, then returned to Mexico for his master's degree in Spanish language and literature, which he received in 1953. He taught at the University of California for a year, then received a one-year fellowship to write, given by the Centro Mexicano de Escritores. During this time, he wrote his second book of stories, *Calavera y Jueves Santo* (Skull and Holy Thursday), and a theatrical piece, *Bajo un capelo de silencio* (Under the Dues of Silence). He has written stories, poetry, and essays and has contributed to such journals as *Letras de México*, *América*, and *Universidad de México*.

Before turning to the story for which he is much more wellknown, Monterde dabbled with poetry, publishing *Adiós a la tierra* (Good-Bye to the Land) in 1949. His first prose publication was a story, "Ninguno lo vio llegar" (No One Saw Him Arrive), which appeared in a literary journal in 1950. Later, in 1957, he produced a series of eleven temporally integrated stories, published as *Calavera y Jueves Santo*. The large city, the towns, and the countryside constitute the three scenarios of the work, peopled with representatives of the different classes of society prominent in contemporary Mexico. The structural design of the stories permits the author to present various aspects and kinds of Mexican life, in a stratified kaleidoscopic manner.

He also wrote an important essay, "La poesía pura en la lírica española" (Pure Poetry in the Spanish Lyric), published in 1953. Its significance is that it fills a gap in Mexican letters by dealing with poetic theory, a little-studied literary area.

WORKS: Poetry: *Adiós a la tierra* (Good-Bye to the Earth) (México: private, 1949). Story: "Ninguno lo vio llegar" (Nobody Saw Him Arrive) in *América. Revista Antológica* (México: Eds. de América, 1950). *Calavera y Jueves Santo* (Skull and Holy Thursday), Letras Mexicanas, 37 (México: FCE, 1957). Essay: *La poesía pura en la lírica española* (Pure Poetry in the Spanish Lyric) (México: UNAM, 1953). Theater: *Bajo un capelo de silencio* (Under the Dues of Silence), unpublished.

BIBLIOGRAPHY: Emmanuel Carballo, "Realidad sin mensaje," review of *Calavera y Jueves Santo*, in *México en la Cultura* 455 (Dec. 8, 1957): 2. Raúl González García, Review of *La poesía pura en la lírica española*, in *Revista Mexicana de Cultura* 339

(Sept. 27, 1953): 12. José Luis Martínez, *Literatura mexicana siglo xx, 1910-1949*, vol. 1 (México: Ant. Libr. Robredo, 1949), pp. 84, 341; vol. 2 (1950), p. 82. Aurora M. Ocampo de Gómez and Ernesto Prado Velázquez, *Diccionario de escritores mexicanos* (México: UNAM, 1967), pp. 236-7. Carlos Valdés, Review of *La poesía pura en la lírica española*, in *Universidad de México* 9, 1-2 (Sept.-Oct. 1954): 29-30.

JEANNE C. WALLACE

MONTERDE, Francisco (1894-). Born in Mexico City, August 9, 1894, Francisco Monterde was a well-educated man, receiving his doctorate in letters from the Universidad Nacional de México in 1942. A member of many prestigious scientific and literary associations, including the Academia Mexicana de la Lengua and the Sociedad Mexicana de Geografía y Estadística, Monterde also traveled widely and spoke at many international conferences. His literary work includes virtually every genre. Besides contributing to many of the most well-known literary journals, he produced many fine translations, prologues, and anthologies. Much of his work has been translated to other languages.

A member of the Group of Seven Authors, he was also instrumental in fostering the resurgence of a group, the Unión Nacional de Autores, to create a new theater of comedy and drama. In 1925, the company La Comedia Mexicana was formed. With great enthusiasm he encouraged new authors to participate actively in the Sociedad de Amigos del Teatro Mexicano.

In 1950, with Antonio *Magaña Esquivel, he founded the Agrupación de Críticos de Teatro de México, of which he was honorary president. A literature professor at the university level for almost fifty years, Monterde dedicated his entire life to teaching, studying, and writing. Devoted especially to Mexican literature, he was a prominent poet, dramatist, and novelist. Monterde was particularly interested in Mexican writers of transitional periods and those of modernism, with a myriad of studies reflecting these interests, as his published works attest.

He bore major responsibility for the respected Biblioteca del Estudiante Universitario of the Universidad Nacional de México. A major task he undertook was to correct obscure points of literary history, thus providing a more accurate picture of Mexican literature. He also engaged in intensive research projects to develop bibliographical materials on writers and themes in Mexican literature. Among the first to call attention to Mexico's treasury of colonial literature, he inspired its revitalization. His *El Madrigal de Cetina y el secreto de la escala* (Cetina's Madrigal and the Secret of the Ladder) and *Moctezuma, el de la silla de oro* (Montezuma, He of the Golden Chair) are two of his narrations that reflect such a revitalization. In the second, he combines historical facts, tempered emotion, and poetic quality to produce a penetrating interpretation of the conquered hero, Montezuma. Likewise, realizing the importance of the Revolution to Mexican history and literature, he awakened the literary public to Mariano *Azuela's *Los de abajo*, a hitherto unknown work.

Among his critical studies is an article, "Juárez, Maximiliano y Carlota en las obras de los dramaturgos mexicanos," in which he surveys the various works that deal with the Maximilian theme. One result of the survey is that he recognizes the inherent difficulties Mexican dramatists have experienced in separating the historical events from a Romanticized rendering of them.

Thus, Francisco Monterde, a highly respected and prominent writer, professor, and critic occupies a position of importance in Mexican letters.

WORKS: Poetry: *Itinerario contemplativo* (Contemplative Itinerary), eulogy of José Juan Tablada (México: Ed. Cultura, 1923). *Chapultepec* (México: n.p., 1947). *Netsuke* (México: Ed. Finisterre, 1962). *Sakura* (México: de Andrea, 1963). Novel and Short Story: *El madrigal de Cetina y El secreto de la escala* (Cetina's Madrigal and the Secret of the Ladder) (México: Imp. Victoria, 1918). *Dantón* (México: El Universal Ilustrado, 1922). *Alma de niño* (The Soul of a Child) (Méxxico: El Universal Ilustrado, 1923). *La hermana pobreza* (Sister Poverty) (México: El Universal Ilustrado, 1925). *Un autor novel* (A Novel Author) (Buenos Aires: Virtus, 1925). *Kid*, short novel (México: n.p., 1925). *Cuentos mexicanos* (Mexican Stories) (Santiago de Chile: Ercilla, 1936). *Galería de espejos* (Gallery of Mirrors) (México: Botas, 1937). *Fábulas sin moraleja y finales de cuentos* (Fables without a Moral and Ends of Stories) (México: Imp. Universitaria, 1942). *El temor de Hernán Cortés y otras narraciones de la Nueva España* (Hernán Cortés' Fear and Other Narrations about New Spain)(México: Imp. Universitaria, 1943). *Aventuras de Gynt* (Gynt's Adventures) [of Ibsen], arrangement in story form (México: Eds. Mensaje, 1943). *Moctezuma, el de la silla de oro* (Montezuma, He of the Golden Chair) (México: Imp. Universitaria, 1945; México: Cultura Mexicana, 1946). *El mayor Fidel García* (The Older Fidel García) (México: Col. Lunes, 1946). *Moctezuma II, señor de Anáhuac* (Montezuma II, Lord of Anáhuac) (México: Imp. Universitaria, 1947). *Cuaderno de estampas* (Notebook of Sketches) (México: Ed. de El Unicornio, 1962). *Una moneda de oro y otros cuentos* (A Gold Coin and Other Stories) (México: Seminario de Cultura Mexicana, 1965). Theatrical Works: *Fuera de concurso* (Hors Concours), performed in 1923. *En el remolino* (In the Whirlpool), performed in 1923 (México: Ed. Ateneas, 1924). *Viviré para ti* (I Will Live for You), 1925. *En la esquina* (On the Corner), performed in 1925. *La que volvió a la vida* (The One Who Returned to Life), performed in 1923; translated into English (México: Talls. Gráf. de la Nación, 1926). *Oro negro* (Black Gold), performed in 1930 (México: Talls. Gráf. de la Nación, 1927). *Proteo* (Fickle Person) (México: Ed. "Contemporáneos," 1931); 2nd ed. (México: Ed. Intercontinental, 1944); in *Teatro mexicano del siglo XX*, vol. 2, edited by Antonio Magaña Esquivel (México: FCE, 1956), pp. 5-22. *El terrible Gynt* (The Terrible Gynt), México, performed in 1944. *La careta de cristal* (The Crystal Mask), performed in 1932, in *Teatro Mexicano Contemporáneo 9*, no editor (México: Sociedad General de Autores de México, 1948; México: UNAM, 1954). *Dos comedias mexicanas [La que volvió a la vida y la careta de cristal]* (Two Mexican Plays (The One Who Returned to Life and The Crystal Mask), edited by Louis G. Zenson (Lafayette, Ind.: Haywood, 1953). *Presente involuntario* (Involuntary Present), in *América, Revista Antológica* (México, Eds. de América, 1957). *La careta de cristal* (The Crystal Mask) (México: SGAM, 1958). *Rabinal Achí*, Act I, in *Cuadernos de Bellas Artes* 4, 12 (Dec. 1963): 73-92; Act II, 5, 1 (Jan. 1964): 69-84. Essays, Anthologies, Prologues and Studies: *Los virreyes de la Nueva España* (The Viceroys of New Spain) (n.p.: n.p., 1922). *Manuel Gutiérrez Nájera* (n.p.: n.p., 1925). *Perfiles de Taxco* (Profiles of Taxco) (n.p.: n.p., 1928). *Amado Nervo* (n.p.: n.p., 1929). *Amado Nervo* (México: Talls. Gráf. de la Nación, 1933). *Antología de poetas y prosistas hispanoamericanos modernos* (Anthology of Modern Spanish American Poets and Prose Writers) (México: UNAM, 1931). *Bibliografía del teatro en México* (Bibliography of the Theater in Mexico) (México: Imp. de la Sría. de Relaciones Exteriores, 1933). *En defensa de una obra y de una generación* (In Defense of a Work and of a Generation) (México: n.p., 1935). Fr. Manuel Navarrete, *Poesías profanas* (Secular Poetry), selection and prologue (México: UNAM, 1940). Bernardo de Balbuena, *Grandeza mexicana* (Mexican Grandeur), edition and prologue (México: UNAM, 1941). Rafael Delgado, *Cuentos* (Stories), selection and prologue (México: UNAM, 1942). *Bolívar*, selection and prologue (México: SEP, 1943). Enrique Cordero y Torres, *Poetas y escritores poblanos* (Poets and Writers of Puebla), prologue (Puebla: n.p., 1943). Fernando Calderón, *A ninguna de las tres* (None of the Three), study (México: UNAM, 1944). Manuel Payno, *Artículos y narraciones* (Articles and Narrations), selection and prologue (México: UNAM, 1945). *Anales de los Xahil* (Annals of the Xahil), prollogue (México: UNAM, 1946). *Agustín F. Cuenca. El prosista, el poeta de transición* (Agustín F. Cuenca. The Prose-Writer, the Poet of Transition), Ph.D. diss. (México: UNAM, 1942). Manuel Gutiérrez Nájera, *Cuentos color de humo, Cuentos frágiles, Cuaresma del Duque Job, Dominicales, Fantasías y viajes* (Stories the Color of Smoke, Fragile Stories, Lenten Collection of Duke Job, Of Sundays, Fantasies and Journeys), prologue (México: Edit. Stylo, 1942). *Novelistas hispanoamericanos* (Spanish American Novelists), prologue and selection (México: Eds. Mensaje, 1943). *Cultura mexicana. Aspectos literarios* (Mexican Culture. Literary Aspects) (México: Edit. Intercontinental, 1946). *Goethe y el Fausto* (Goethe and Faust) (México: UNAM, 1949). Autobiographical sketch, in *El trato con escritores* (México: INBA, Dept. de Lit., 1961), pp. 145-60. "Una evasión romántica de Fernando Caballero" (A Fernando Calderón Romantic Evasion), speech, Academia Mexicana de la Lengua, México, 1952. Anita Arroyo, *Razón y pasión de Sor Juana* (Sor Juana's Reason and Passion), prologue (México: Porrúa y Obregón, 1952). *Historia de la literatura mexicana* (History of Mexican Literature) (México: Porrúa, 1955). *Teatro indígena prehispánico (Rabinal Achí)* (Pre-Hispanic Indigenous Theater [Rabinal Achí]) (México: UNAM, 1955). *Salvador Díaz Mirón. Documentos, Estética* (Salvador Díaz Mirón. Documents. Aesthetics) (México: UNAM, 1956). *Díaz Mirón, El hombre, La obra* (Díaz Mirón, the Man, the Work) (México: Eds. de Andrea, 1956). *Teatro mexicano del siglo XX* (Mexican Theater of the Twentieth Century), vol. 1, selection and prologue (México: FCE, 1956). *La literatura mexicana en la obra de Menéndez y Pelayo* (Mexican Literature in the Works of Menéndez y Pelayo) (México: UNAM, 1958). *Obras completas de Mariano Azuela* (Complete Works of Mariano Azuela), vol. 1, prologue (México: FCE, 1958). *La dignidad en Don Quijote, Estudios* (Dignity in Don Quijote, Studies) (México: Imp. Universisataria, 1959). *Carlos Noriega Hope y su obra literaria* (Carlos Noriega Hope and His Literary Work) (México: n.p., 1959). *La tragedia de Fernando Calderón* (The Tragedy of Fernando Calderón) (México: n.p., 1960). Fernando Calderón, *Muerte de Virginia por la libertad de Roma* (Virginia's Death Because of Rome's Liberty) (México: UNAM, 1960). *Ramón López Velarde, el poeta y el prosista* (Ramón López Velarde, the Poet and the Prose-Writer), prologue (México: INBA, 1962). Manuel Gutiérrez Nájera, *Cuentos y cuaresma del Duque Job* (Stories and Lenten Collection of Duke Job), edited and introduction (México: Porrúa, 1963). Federico Gamboa, *Novelas* (Novels), prologue (México: FCE, 1965). *La pajarita de papel* (The Paper Kite) (PEN Club of Mexico), 1924-1925, prologue (México: INBA, 1965). "Amado Nervo en su centenario" (Amado Nervo on His Centennial), in *Revista Interamericana de Bibliografía* 21, 1 (Washington, D.C. (Jan.-March 1971): 3-15. Antonio Raluy Poudevida, *Diccionario Porrúa de la lengua española*, prepared by Francisco Monterde (México: Porrúa, 1976).

BIBLIOGRAPHY: Ermilo Abreu Gómez, Review of *El temor de Hernán Cortés*, in *Revista Iberoamericana*, 7, 14 (Feb. 1944): 423-24; 1921; *Sala de retratos* (México: Editorial Leyenda, 1946), pp. 188-90. Antonio Alatorre, Review of *La literatura mexicana en la obra de Menéndez Pelayo*, in *Nueva Revista de Filogoía Hispánica* 14, 3-4 (July-Dec. 1960): 369-73. Fernando Alegría, *Breve historia de la novela hispanoamericana*, Manuales Studium, (México: Ed. de Andrea, 1959), p. 146. Dors Alva, "Francisco Monterde y el verdadero Hai'Kai," review of *Netsuke* and *Sakura*, in *México en la Cultura* 735 (April 21, 1963): 9. Jesús Arellano, Review of *Salvador Díaz Mirón. Documentos. Estética*, in *Metáfora* 10 (Sept.-Oct. 1956): 35-36. Arturo Arnaiz y Freg, "Francisco Monterde y sus cincuenta años de escritor," in *El Libro y el Pueblo* 4, 3 (July 1963): 1-2. Emmanuel Carballo, "El libro de la semana: *Díaz Mirón. Vida y obra*," in *México en la Cultura* 385 (Aug. 5, 1956): 2; "Teatro y ficción," in *México en la Cultura* 450 (Nov. 3, 1957): 2; Review of *Cuentos y cuaresmas del Duque Job*, in *Nivel* 8 (Aug. 25, 1963): 3. Alfredo Cardona Peña, *Semblanzas mexicanas* (México: Eds. Libro-Mex, 1955), pp. 115-19. Alí Chumacero, Review of *Teatro mexicano siglo XX*, in *México en la Cultura* 380 (July 1, 1956): 2. María Teresa Gómez Gleason, "Francisco Monterde y la Academia Mexicana de la Lengua," in *Revista Mexicana de Cultura* 957 (Aug. 1, 1965): 6-7. Francisco González Guerrero, *En torno a la literatura mexicana* (México: SEP, 1976), pp. 185-88. Carlos González Peña, *Historia de la literatura mexicana*, 8th ed., (México: Porrúa, 1963), pp. 301, 409-40, 431-32. Julio Jiménez Rueda, "Francisco Monterde," in *México en la Cultura* 150 (Dec. 16, 1951): 3. Ruth S. Lamb, *Bibliografía del teatro mexicano del siglo XX* (México: Eds. de Andrea, 1962), pp. 83-84. Ross Larson, *Fantasy and Imagination in the Mexican Narrative* (Tempe: Center for Latin American Studies, Arizona State University, 1977), pp. 26, 33, 43, 103. Luis Leal, *Panorama de la literatura mexicana actual* (Washington, D.C.: Unión Panamericana, 1968), pp. 7, 24, 25, 26, 82, 112. Antonio Magaña Esquivel, *Teatro mexicano del siglo XX*, vol. 2 (México: FCE, 1956), pp. 3-4; *Medio siglo de teatro mexicano, 1900-1961* (México: INBA, 1964), pp. 23, 28, 30, 32-33, 34-36, 39, 62, 63, 65, 79, 119, 155. Armando de María y Campo, *El teatro de género dramático en la Revolución Mexicana* (México: Talls. Gráf. de la Nación, 1957), pp. 196-99. José Luis Martínez, *Literatura mexicana siglo XX, 1910-1949*, vol. 1, (México: Libr. Rodredo, 1949), pp. 15, 18, 40, 213-17; vol. 2 (1950), pp. 82-83; *El ensayo mexicano moderno* (México: FCE, 1958), p. 364. Salvador Novo, "Palabras de Salvador Novo al ofrecer la comida en honor del cincuentenario como escritor del Dr. Francisco Monterde," in *México en la Cultura* 736 (April 28, 1963): 3. Aurora M. Ocampo de Gómez y Ernesto Prado Velázquez, *Diccionario de Escritores Mexicanos* (México: UNAM, 1967), pp. 237-39. Moisés Ochoa Campos, *La oratoria en México* (México: Edit. F. Trillas, 1969), p. 128. Gregorio Ortega, *Hombres, mujeres* (México: Eds. de Bellas Artes, 1966), pp. 99-104. José Emilio Pacheco, Review of *La dignidad de Don Quijote*, in *Estaciones* 4, 14 (Summer 1959): Review of *Sakura*, in *La Cultura en México* 81 (Sept. 4, 1963): xviii-xix Guadalupe Rubens, "El papel de la mujer en las letras contemporáneas. Entrevista con Francisco Monterde," in *México en la Cultura* 41 (Nov. 13, 1949): 7. Sara Sefchovich, *México: País de ideas, país de novelas* (México: Edit. Grijalba, 1987), pp. 84, 86, 118, 137. Rodolfo Usigli, *México en el teatro* (México: Imp. Mundial, 1932), pp. 128-29. Various, "Francisco Monterde y sus cincuenta años de escritor," in *La Cultura en México* 80 (Aug. 28, 1963): ii-vii.

JEANNE C. WALLACE

MONTERROSO, Augusto (1921-), essayist, translator, and author of short stories; often referred to as "Tito" Monterroso. Born in Guatemala City on December 21, 1921, Monterroso lived in his native country until 1944. Openly opposed to Ubico's dictatorship, he was later persecuted by Ponce's government, which led him to seek temporary political asylum in Mexico (1944). From 1945 to 1954 he served in Mexico's diplomatic corps in Bolivia and in his native Guatemala. With the military coup that overthrew Arbenz, he resigned his diplomatic post and found exile in Chile (1954-1956), where he worked as Pablo Neruda's secretary on *La Gaceta de Chile*. He took up permanent residence in Mexico in 1956. He was involved in the founding of a political newspaper in Guatemala, *El Espectador*, and of the *Revista de Guatemala* and *Acento*. He has contributed to a large number of Spanish American and Mexican journals including *Plural, Revista de Bellas Artes, Diálogos, Summa Bibliográfica, Espiga, Revista de la Universidad de México, Cuadernos del Viento, México en la Cultura, La Cultura en México, La Palabra y el Hombre, Revista Mexicana de Literatura, Gaceta del FCE, El Gallo Ilustrado, Diorama de la Cultura*, and *Suplemento Literario de El Heraldo*. He has been employed by UNAM in a variety of positions, with the University Press, and as a professor of literature. He has won several significant literary awards: first prize in Guatemala's National Saker Ti Short Story Contest (1952), Mexico's Magda Donato Literature Prize in 1970 for *La oveja negra y demás fábulas*, and the prestigious Xavier Villaurrutia Prize (1975), which is awarded each year to the best Mexican literary creation.

Although Monterroso has written essays and translated three works, he is best known for his short, often fable-like, stories. These are not nationalistic, but usually are rather ironically descriptive of the immediate reality that most Latin American nations face. His fiction has come to be associated with the dark, skeptical sense of humor so evident in "First Lady" and with the bitter satire with which the theme of imperialistic explotation is treated in "Mr. Taylor." His works have been translated into English, German, Italian and Polish.

WORKS: Prose: *El concierto y el Eclipse* (The Concert and the Eclipse) (México: Ed. Los Epígrafes, 1947). *Uno de cada tres y El centenario* (One out of Three and The Centenary) (México: Ed. Lospresentes, 1952). *Obras completas y otros cuentos* (Complete Works and other Stories) (México: Imprenta Universitaria, 1959, 1960; México: Ed. Joaquín Mortiz, 1971, 1973, 1977, 1980, 1981). *La oveja negra y demás fábulas* (The Black Sheep and Other Fables) (México: Ed. Joaquín Mortiz, 1969, 1971, 1973, 1975, 1977, 1979; Ed. Seix Barral, 1981, 1983; Ed. Nueva Nicaragua, 1982; La Habana: Casa de las Américas, 1985; Ediciones Alfaguera, 1986). *The Black Sheep and Other Fables*, translated by Walter I. Bradbury (Garden City, N.Y.: Doubleday, 1971). *Das gesamte Werk und andere Fabeln* (The Black Sheep and Other Fables), German translation (Zurich: Ed. Diógenes Verlag, 1973). *La oveja negra y obras completas y otros cuentos* (The Black Sheep and Complete Works and Other Stories) (México: SEP, 1986). *Animales y hombres* (Animals and Men) (San José, Costa Rica: Editorial Universitaria Centroamericana, 1971, 1972). *Movimiento perpetuo* (Perpetual Movement) (México: Ed. Joaquín Mortiz, 1972, 1975; Ed. Seix Barral, 1981, 1983). *Wyber proxy na podstawic tomow* (Krakow, Poland: Wydawnictwo Literackie, 1975). *Las ilusiones perdidas: antología personal* (Lost Illusions: A Personal Anthology) (México: FCE, 1975, 1985). *Lo demás es silencio: la vida y obra de Eduardo Torres* (The Rest Is Silence: The Life and Work of Eduardo Torres) (México: Ed. Joaquín Mortiz, 1978; 1979; Ed. Seix Barral, 1982; Cátedra, 1986). *Diez cuentos búlgaros* (Ten Bulgarian Stories) (México: UNAM, 1978). *Viaje al centro de la fábula* (Journey to the Center of the Fable) (México: UNAM, 1981; Martín Casillas Editores, 1982). *Mr. Taylor & Co.* (La Habana: Casa de las Américas, 1982). *La palabra mágica* (The Magic Word) (México: Ediciones Era, 1983; Muchnik Editores, 1985). *Cuentos* (Stories) (Madrid: Alianza, 1986). *La letra e: fragmentos de un diario* (The Letter E: Excerpts of a Diary) (Madrid: Alianza, 1987; México: Ediciones Era, 1987).

BIBLIOGRAPHY: M. D. Arana, "Notas de lectura. Augusto Monterroso," *Novedades* (Oct. 29, 1971): 5c; "Notas de lectura. Premio al escritor Monterroso." *Novedades* (Jan. 17, 1971): 2C. Jesús Arellano, "Augusto Monterroso y otros cuentos," *Revista Mexicana de La Cultura* (Nov. 29, 1959): n.p. Noemí Atamoros, "Tito Monterroso escribe en el cine, la Opera o mientras maneja su auto," *Excelsior* (Nov. 23, 1972): 15. María Elvira Bermúdez, Review of *Obras completas*, in *Diorama de la Cultura* (Dec. 27, 1959): 12. Miguel Capistrán, "Novísimo Tito ilustrado," *Excelsior* (Aug. 2, 1970): n.p. Emmanuel Carballo, "En Guatemala, lo mejor de las letras ha estado siempre dirigido a combatir algo," Interview, *México en la Cultura* (March 22, 1959): 12. Catay, "El Premio Magda Donato a la Oveja Blanca: Tito Monterroso," *El Día* (Feb. 9, 1971): 3. Wilfrido H. Corral, "¿Qué es releer la historia por la alusión, leer el texto cultural y consumir lo leído en la ficcionalización?," *Escritura: Revista de Teoría y Crítica Literaria* 8, 16 (July-Dec. 1983): 191-206; "Genre Displacement and the Reader: The works of Augusto Monterroso," Ph.D. diss., Columbia University, 1984. Fernando Curiel, "La ballena o la mosca. Monterroso: broma en serio," *Diorama de la Cultura* (Dec. 24, 1972): 14. Alí Chumacero, "Augusto Monterroso contra el lugar común," review of *Obras completas*, in *México en la Cultura* 560 (Dec. 7, 1959): 4. José Durand, "Cuentos de Augusto Monterroso," *México en la Cultura* (Aug. 14, 1960); "La realidad copia un cuento fantástico de Augusto Monterroso," *Cuadernos del Viento* 41-42 (March-April 1964): 674. Beatriz Espejo, "Entrevista con Augusto Monterroso," *Revista Kena* (April 16, 1971): 45-52. Edmundo Flores, "Fuga de cerebros," Interview with Monterroso on the subject of the "brain drain," *Visión* (May 5, 1973). Juan García Ponce, "Obras completas y otro cuentos," *Revista de la Universidad de México* 4 (1959): 13. Carmen Galindo, "Monterroso y la crítica de las debilidades del hombre," *Novedades* (Aug. 24, 1972): 5C. Carlos González Salas, "Premio Magda Donato 1970. La oveja negra y demás fábulas," *El Día* (Jan. 17, 1971): 7 . Humberto Guzmán, "Augusto Monterroso deja las pequeñeces y hace *Movimiento perpetuo*," *El Heraldo de México* (Jan. 21, 1973): 12. Blanca Haro, "Cómo no hacer una entrevista con Augusto Monterroso Bonilla o Asalto a cuatro rounds," *Revista Mexicana de Cultura* (March 18, 1973): 34-39. Andrés Henestrosa, Review of *Obras Completas*, in *El Nacional* (Dec. 15, 1959): 3 . Jaime Labastida, "Informe sobre Monterroso," *Plural: Crítica, Arte, Literatura* 11, 4 (1981): 16-18. Hernán Lara Zavala, "El cuento mexicano 1970," *Revista Mexicana de Cultura* (Dec. 27, 1970): 23-31. Raúl López Malo, "Entrevista a Tito Monterroso," *El Día* (Feb. 26, 1965): 9. Norberto Martínez Fernández, "Tras riguroso interrogatorio de cinco horas, Tito Monterroso no logró entrar a EU, donde fue invitado por Universidades," *Excelsior* (April 13, 1972): 6C. Juan A. Masoliver, "Augusto Monterroso o la tradición subversiva," *Cuadernos Hispanoamericanos* 408 (June 1984): 146-54. Ernesto Mejía Sánchez, "The Black Sheep and Other Fables," *Novedades* (June 28, 1971): 11. *Monterroso*, prologue by Jorge Ruffinelli (Xalapa: Universidad Veracruzana, 1976). Rafael Humberto Moreno-Durán, "El lector como animal de presa: entrevista con Augusto

Monterroso," *Quimera: Revista de Literatura* 26 (Dec. 1982): 66-71. Humberto Musacchio, "*Movimiento perpetuo*," *El Nacional* (May 28, 1973): 12. Mariano A. Ortega González, "*Movimiento perpetuo*," *Chasqui* 3, 2 (Feb. 1974): 96-98. José Emilio Pacheco, "Prosa en movimiento" (on *Movimiento perpetuo*), in *La Cultura en México* (Jan. 3, 1973): 16; "*Obras completas y otros cuentos*," *Revista Mexicana de Literatura* (Nov. 1959). Luis Guillermo Piazza, "El arte de escribir en serio con una sonrisa," *Diorama de la Cultura* (March 13, 1960): 6. Elena Poniatowska, "Ser tonto da más popularidad que ser inteligente," Interview, *La Cultura en México* (Feb. 7, 1971): 13. Salvador Reyes Nevares, "*Obras completas y otros cuentos*," *La Vida Literaria* (August 1971): 14. Luis Mario Schneider, "Monterroso: humor y verdad," *Revista de la Universidad de México* (May 1960). Peter Schultze-Kraft, "Homenaje a Augusto Monterroso," *Revista Mexicana de Cultura* (Oct. 3, 1971): 7-14. Rafael Solana, "*Obras completas y otros cuentos*," *La Vida Literaria* (Aug. 1971). Josefina Solares and Ignacio Solares, "La literatura según Tito Monterroso," *Diorama de la Cultura* (Feb. 13, 1972): 7. Ray Verzasconi, "El humorismo en las *Obras completas* de Augusto Monterroso," *Proceedings of the Pacific Northwest Conference of Foreign Languages* 28,1 (1977): 138-41. Federico Zendejas, "Multilibros," *Excelsior* (Nov. 10, 1972); "*Obras completas (y otros cuentos)*," *Excelsior* (June 13, 1971): n.p.

JANIS L. KRUGH

MONTES DE OCA, Marco Antonio (1932-), poet. Montes de Oca was born in Mexico City on August 3, 1932. He studied law for several years at the University of Mexico and took various courses in the School of Philosophy and Letters of the same university. He has undertaken quite diverse projects while devoting himself entirely to poetry. He published his first poem at the age of twenty-one. He was awarded the Xavier Villaurrutia Prize in 1959 and the Mazatlán Prize in 1966. He was a fellow at the Centro Mexicano de Escritores fron 1955 to 1956 and from 1960 to 1961, and also, in 1965, at the Colegio de México. He has edited the *Revista Mexicana de Literatura*. He has published seventeen books, aside from the many poems scattered among journals, annuals, and literary supplements, principally in *Universidad de México, La Palabra y el Hombre, Revista Mexicana de Literatura, Pájaro Cascabel,* and *Cuadernos del Viento*.

In 1953, with the publication of his first book, *Ruina de la infame Babilonia* (Ruin Infamous Babylonia), Marco Antonio Montes de Oca became known as one of the best young poets of Mexico, a judgment that continues to be confirmed with each succeeding book. In *Contrapunto de la fe (Counterpoint of Faith)*, he celebrates the victory of living beauty over death. Here, he has surpassed the aesthetic content of his previous volume, and revealed a poet who seeks personal expression in the profusion of his metaphors, in the resoluteness with which he composes his poems, and in the youthful impetuousness with which he feeds them. Here, his tone of Christian affirmation has become muted. The book marks a clear transition in his career.

Pliego de testimonios gives us a rebellious poet who is already the master of his own peculiar ways of tackling artistic forms. *Delante de la luz cantan los pájaros* brings together his former works and includes a new book, *Ofrendas y epitafios* (Offerings and Epitaths), where vigor and immoderation, plasticity and violence can all be found. *Cantos al sol que no se alcanza* (Songs to the Sun Which Cannot Suffice Itself) is a work where his passion for images overflows once again, although subordinated to his faculty for admiration, and to his force and sensitivity. Much like the work of Carlos *Pellicer, the early verse of Montes de Oca celebrates the luxuriant beauties of nature and the act of poetic creation.

More recent collections, such as *Fundación del entusiasmo* (The Foundation of Enthusiasm) (1963), *La parcela en el Edén* (The Parcel of Land in Eden) (1964), and *Vendimia del juglar* (The Juggler's Vintage Harvest) (1965) have been interpreted by critics as an attempt to return to and relocate his earlier "luminous country." A poet of bold imagination, Montes de Oca is very close to the surrealists in technique: his poems are loosely structured and abound in lexical dislocations and unnatural juxtapositions. Although he has been a rather prolific writer to date, his work has been of generally high quality. He can certainly be counted among Mexico's most important poets of the mid-twentieth century.

WORKS: Poetry: *Ruina de la infame Babilonia* (Ruin of Infamous Babylon) poem, in suppl. to *Medio Siglo* (México, Oct.-Dec. 1953); 2nd ed. (México: Edit. Stylo, 1954); English translation: *On the Ruins of Babylon* (Newnham, Australia: Wattle Grove Press, 1964). *Contrapunto de la fe* (Counterpoint of Faith), prologue by José Enrique Moreno, Los Presentes, no. 25 (Mexico, FCE, 1955). *Pliego de testimonios* (Sheet of Testimonies) (Mexico, Col. Metáfora, 1956). *Delante de la luz cantan los pájaros* (In Front of the Light, Sing the Birds), including previous work and another new book, "Ofrendas y epitafios," Col. Letras Mexicanas, no. 50 (México: FCE, 1959). *Cantos al sol que no se alcanza* (Songs to the Sun Which Cannot Suffice Itself), Col. Tezontle (México: FCE, 1961). *Fundación del entusiasmo* (The Foundation of Enthusiasm), Col. Poemas y Ensayos (México: UNAM, 1963). *La parcela en el Edén* (The Parcel of Land in Eden) (México: Eds. Pájaro Cascabel, 1964). *Vendimia del juglar* (The Juggler's Vintage Harvest) (México: Ed. Joaquín Mortiz, 1965). *Las fuentes legendarias* (The Legendary Springs) (México: Ed. Joaquín Mortiz, 1966). *Pedir el fuego* (Requesting Fire) (México: Ed. Joaquín Mortiz, 1968). *Poesía reunida* (Collected Poetry) (México: FCE, 1971). Editor, *El surco y la brasa* (The Furrow and the Ember), an anthology of poetry in translation, Traductores Mexicanos (México: FCE, 1974). *Las constelaciones secretas* (The Secret Constellations) (México: FCE, 1978). *En honor de las palabras* (In Honor of Words) (México: FCE, 1979). *Comparecencias (1968-1980)* (Court Appearances) (México: n.p., 1980). *Tablero de orientaciones*, (Directional Board) (México: Premia Editora e INBA, 1984). Autobiography: *Autobiografía* (México: Empresas Editoriales, 1967).

BIBLIOGRAPHY: Federico Alvarez, Review of *Fundación del entusiasmo*, in *La Cultura en México* 104 (Feb. 12, 1964): xviii; Review of *La parcela en el Edén*, in *La Cultura en México* 147 (Dec. 9, 1964): xviii; Review of *Vendimia del juglar*, in *Revista de Bellas Artes* 4 (July-Aug. 1965): 89-91. Anon., Biobibliographic note, in *Anuario de la poesía mexicana* (México: Depto. de Lit., INBA, 1963), p. 91; Review of *Cantos al sol que no se alcanza*, in *Cuadernos de Bellas Artes* 3, 1 (Jan. 1962): 75-76; "Su mesa de redacción," review of *Fundación del entusiasmo*, in *Bulletin. . .*, 11, 2 (Jan. 1964): 4. "Su mesa de redacción," review of *On the Ruins of Babylon*, in *Diorama de la Cultura* (Apr. 12, 1964): 4. Review of *La parcela en el Edén*, in *Revista de la Semana* (Sep. 27, 1964): 3; Mention in "Alliances-Alianzas," *Cahiers du Monde Hispanique et Luso-Brésilien*, no. 49 (Toulouse, France: 1987), pp. 43-61; "¿Es moderna la literatura latinoamericana?," in *Plural: Crítica, Arte, Literatura* (Mexico) 1 (1971): 25-

30. María Dolores Arana, "El torrencial lirismo de Marco Antonio Montes de Oca," in *Papeles de Son Armadans* 245-46 (1976): 263-270. Jesús Arellano, "Poesía mexicana en 1956," review of *Pliego de testimonios*, in *Metáfora* 14 (May-June 1957): 10-16; "Las ventas de Don Quijote," in *Nivel* 19 (July 25, 1964): 3. Homero Aridjis, Review of *Vendimia del juglar*, in *Diálogos* 6 (Sep.-Oct. 1965): 41. Octavio Armand, *Towards a Possible Image of Latin American Poetry* (New York: Review, 1977), pp. 7-117. Huberto Batis, Review of *Vendimia del juglar*, in *La Cultura en México* 179 (July 21, 1965): xvii. Gordon Brotherston, "Marco Antonio Montes de Oca and 'The Splendor of This World,'" in *Books Abroad* 45 (1971): 36-41; "Montes de Oca in the light of the revised versions of *Pliego de testimonios*," in Bulletin of Hispanic Studies 44 (1967): 28-40. Peter Bush, "Montes de Oca: Galdos' Critique of 1898 Quijotismo," in *Bulletin of Hispanic Studies* (Liverpool, England) 61, 4 (Oct. 1984): 472-82. Emmanuel Carballo, "El libro de la semana, *Pliego de testimonios*," in *México en la Cultura* 399 (Nov. 11, 1956): 2. Adolfo Castañón, "Sacrificio e inocencia, [*Lugares donde el espacio cicatriza* and *Se llama como quieras*]," in *Plural* 11 (1975): 63-65. Rosario Castellanos, Review of *Pliego de Testimonios*, in *Metáfora* 13 (Mar.-Apr. 1957): 40. Antonio Castro Leal, Salvador Elizondo, and Salvador Reyes Nevares, "Análisis de poesía reunida," in *Vida Literaria* (México) 15-16 (1971): 22-5. María Belén Castro Morales, "La poesía de Marco Antonio Montes de Oca: La 'inteligencia del lenguaje,'" in *Revista de Filología de la Universidad de La Laguna* (La Laguna, Tenerife, Spain, 1981), pp. 75-80. Alí Chumacero, "Panorama de los últimos libros. *Pliego de testimonios*," in *Mexico en la Cultura* 396 (Oct. 21, 1956): 2; "Montes de Oca, enemigo del reposo o el canto solitario del poeta," in *México en la Cultura* 555 (Nov., 1959): 4; "La poesía, 1963," in *La Cultura en México* 99 (Jan. 8, 1964): xvii. J. M. Cohen, "The Eagle and the Serpent," in *Southern Review* 2, 2 (Spring 1965): 361-74. José de la Colina, Review of *Vendimia del juglar*, in *Universidad de México* 20, 1 (Sept. 1965): 32. Fernando Diez de Urdanivia, Jr., Interview with Marco Antonio Montes de Oca, in *México en la Cultura* 684 (Apr. 22, 1962): 5. Manuel Durán, "Jaime Sabines and Marco Antonio Montes de Oca: A Study in Contrast," in *Mundus Artium: A Journal of International Literature and the Arts* (Richardson, Texas), n.d., 3, 2: pp. 44-55. "Montes de Oca: la traducción como creación, no como tradición [*El surco y la brasa*]," *Revista de la Universidad de México* 29, 12 (1975): 43-44. Salvador Elizondo, "Traducciones: la poesía transformada [Aridjis y Montes de Oca]," in *Plural* 4, 8 (1975): 75-76. Beatriz Espejo, Review of *Fundación del entusiasmo*, in *El Rehilete* 10 (Feb. 1964): 52-53; "Montes de Oca. La poesía no tiene institutos pero a veces nos deja a oscuras," in *El Heraldo Cultural* 13 (Feb. 6, 1966): 11-12. David William Foster, *Mexican Literature: A Bibliography of Secondary Sources* (Metuchen, N.J.: Scarecrow Press, 1981), pp. 237-39. Juan García Ponce, "1965. La poesía," in *La Cultura en México* 203 (Jan. 5, 1966): xiv. Ernesto González Zamora, Review of *Ruina de la infame Babilonia*, in *Ideas de México* 5 (May-June 1954): 224-25. Miguel Guardia, Review of *Contrapunto de la fe*, in *Metáfora* 5 (Nov.-Dec. 1955): 34-36. Alfredo Junco, "Monseñor Montes de Oca," in *Abside* (San Luis Potosí) 35 (1971): 435-48. Jan Lechner, "Hacia una poética de Marco Antonio Montes de Oca," in *Actas del VIII Congreso de la Asociación Internacional de Hispanistas*, edited by David A. Kossoff et al., vol. 2 (Madrid: Istmo, 1986). Raúl Leiva, Review of *Cantos al sol que no se alcanza*, in *Nivel* 38 (Feb. 25, 1962): 3; "La poesía de Marco Antonio Montes de Oca," in *Diorama de la Cultura* (Mar. 17, 1963): 3; "El cacto y el laurel. Montes de Oca y la metáfora," review of *Fundación del entusiasmo*, in *México en la Cultura* 770 (Dec. 1962): 3; "Un poeta mexicano en Australia," in *México en la*

Cultura 785 (Apr. 5, 1964): 3. "Raíces de futuro en la poesía de Marco Antonio Montes de Oca," review of *Vendimia del juglar*, in *México en la Cultura* 855 (Aug. 11, 1965); 6; "La poesía de Marco Antonio Montes de Oca," in *Cuadernos Americanos* (Mexico) 167 (1969): 174-93; "La poesía de Marco Antonio Montes de Oca," in *Cuadernos del Congreso por la libertad de la cultura* 73 (1963): 45-47. Manuel Lerín, Review of *La parcela en el Edén*, in *Revista Mexicana de Cultura* 918 (Nov. 1, 1964): 15. Francisco Lisuori, "Ipandro Acaico a medio siglo de su muerte," in *Abside* (San Luis Potosí) 35 (1971): 468-83. Eduardo Lizalde, "Un poeta, Eduardo Lizalde habla a otro poeta, Marco Antonio Montes de Oca," in *La Cultura en México* 185 (Sept. 1, 1965): xv. Raúl López Malo, Interview of Marco Antonio Montes de Oca, in *El día* (Mar. 5, 1965): 9. Mónica Mansour, "Otra dimensión de nuestra poesía," in *La Palabra y el Hombre* 2 (1972): 33-39. José Antonio Montero, "La poesía de Marco Antonio Montes de Oca," in *El día* (July 28, 1964): 9; Review of *La parcela en el Edén*, in *Nivel* 23 (Nov. 25, 1964): 3. Carlos Monsiváis, *La poesía mexicana del siglo XX* (México: Empresas Editoriales, 1966), pp. 68-70, 769. Marco Antonio Montes de Oca, "Montes de Oca a través de su poesía," in *La Cultura en México* 107 (Mar. 4, 1964): xiii. José Antonio Montero, Review of *La parcela en el Edén* , in *Nivel*, n. 23, 1964, p. 3. Elías Nandino, review of *Pliego de testimonios*, in *Estaciones* 2, 5 (Spring 1955): 94. Aurora M. Ocampo de Gómez and Ernesto Prado Velázquez, *Diccionario de Escritores Mexicanos*, (México: UNAM, 1967), pp. 239-41. Octavio Paz, *Puertas al campo*, Col. Poemas y Ensayos (México: UNAM, 1966); Preface, in Marco Antonio Montes de Oca, *The Heart of the Flute* (Athens: Ohio University Press, 1979), pp. vii-viii; also (Pittsburgh: International Poetry Forum, 1978). Javier Peñalosa, "5 noticias literarias importantes del mes, en México," in *Nivel* 13 (Jan. 25, 1964): 4; "Vendimia y vino del juglar," in *Nivel* 32 (Aug. 25, 1965): 4. Teresinha Alves Pereira, "A poesía de Montes de Oca," in *Minas Gerais Suplemento Literario* (Minas Gerais, Brazil: May 13, 1972): 10. Elena Poniatowska, "Montes de Oca y Juan Rulfo," in *México en la Cultura* 509 (Dec. 14, 1958): 2, 10. Luis Alberto Sánchez, "Sobre la nueva poesía mexicana," review of *Delante de la luz cantan los pájaros*, in *El Libro y el Pueblo* 3, 304 (Oct. 1959) (Mar. 1960): 109-12. Luis Alberto Sánchez, Mauricio de la Selva, Alí Chumacero, "Tres opiniones sobre Montes de Oca," in *Nivel*, n. 29, May 25, 1961, pp. 1, 4, 6. Mauricio de la Selva, Review of *Delante de la luz cantan los pájaros*, in *Revista Iberoamericana* 25, 50 (July-Dec., 1960): 364-68. "Asteriscos," review of *Fundación del entusiasmo*, in *Diorama de la Cultura* (Jan. 12, 1964): 4; "Asteriscos," review of *La parcela en el Edén*, in *Diorama de la Cultura* (Jan. 24, 1965); 4. "Asteriscos," review of *Vendimia del juglar*, in *Diorama de la Cultura* (Sep. 5, 1965): 7; "Novela y poesía. III. Marco Antonio Montes de Oca," in *Cuadernos Americanos* 109 (1960): 287-90. Roberto Venegas, "Poetas mexicanos: Marco Antonio Montes de Oca," in *Diorama de la Cultura* (Sept. 27, 1964): 7, 8. Laura Villaseñor and Octavio Paz, *Heart of the Flute* (Athens: Ohio University Press, 1979). Javier Weimer, "Lectura de Montes de Oca," in *El Gallo Ilustrado* 166 (Aug. 29, 1965): 4. Celia Elaine Richmond Weller, "The Poetry of Marco Antonio Montes de Oca" *DAI* 37 (1977): 5163A-64A. Ramón Xirau, Review of "Las constelaciones secretas," in *Vuelta* 3 (1977): 37-38; "The new poetry of Mexico--Marco Antonio Montes de Oca," in *RB Mex* 10, 4 (1963): 1-2. Gabriel Zaid, "*Las fuentes legendarias*," in his *Leer poesía* (México: Joaquín Mortiz, 1972), pp. 63-64. Armando Zárate, "Los poetas que he conocido: Marco Antonio Montes de Oca," in *Diorama de la Cultura* (May 31, 1964): 1.

YOLANDA S. BROAD

MONTES DE OCA y Obregón, Ignacio (1840-1921), also known as Ipandro Acaico. Montes de Oca y Obregón was born in the city of Guanajuato, on June 26, 1840. Brought up in a well-to-do family, at the age of twelve he was sent to England, where he distinguished himself for his ability to translate and interpret the classical poets. From 1860 to 1863 he studied theology in the Gregorian University of Rome, and was ordained. Here he also pursued studies leading to doctoral degrees in both civil and canonical law. And in Rome he became a member of the Arcadian Academy, where he was known as Ipandro Acaico. Returning to Mexico, in 1865 he was honorary chaplain to Maximilian. In 1871, he was consecrated bishop in Rome. He presided over the diocese of Tamaulipas, then Linares; in 1885 he was appointed to the diocese of San Luis Potosí, which he occupied for thirty-six years. He received numerous honors and titles for his good works, both religious and literary. The Royal Academy of Spain solicited his membership and also asked him to deliver the eulogy of Miguel de Cervantes at the ceremonies held on the tercentenary of *Don Quijote*. A man of keen intellect and prestige, he enjoyed travels both in Mexico and Europe. Returning to his native Mexico from a trip to Europe, he died in New York, where a solemn mass was held in Saint Patrick's Cathedral.

As Ipandro Acaico, Montes de Oca y Obregón translated many of the Greek poets, among them Pindar, Theocritus, and Apolonius of Rhodes. His original poetic works, comprised of hymns, elegies, sonnets, and odes, are considered rather academic and lacking in expression. His obvious love of the classic poets may have constrained him from giving voice to his own inner feelings. His work in prose is also abundant, consisting of eight volumes of *Obras pastorales y oratorias* (Pastoral and Oratorical Works), which contain literary discourses, religious works, and eulogies, which the author also edited in a separate edition.

WORKS: *Poetas bucólicos griegos* (Greek Bucolic Poets), verse translations into Spanish (México: Imp. de Ignacio Escalante, 1877). *Ocios poéticos* (Poetic Pastimes) (México: Imp. de I. Escalante, 1878). *Odas de Píndaro* (Odes of Pindar), verse translations into Spanish (México: Imp. de I. Escalante, 1882). *Oraciones fúnebres* (Funerary Discourses) (Madrid, n.p., 1901). "*Don José María Roa Bárcena y sus obras*" (Don José María Roa Bárcena and His Works), introduction to the *Obras poéticas de Roa Bárcena* (México, n.p., 1913), pp. 5-169. *Obras pastorales y oratorias* (Pastoral and Oratorical Works), 8 vols. (México: Imp. de I. Escalante, 1883-1913). *El rapto de Helena* (The Rape of Helen), verse translation of the Greek poem by Coluto of Licopolis (Madrid, Ed. del Autor, 1917). *A orillas de los ríos, Cien sonetos* (By the River's Banks: One Hundred Sonnets) (Barcelona, Madrid, Valencia: Eds. de Rosas y espinas, 1917). *La argonáutica* (The Argonautica), 2 vols., Spanish verse translation of the Greek poem of Apolonius of Rhodes, 2 vols. (Madrid: Tip. de la Revista de Archivos, Bibliotecas y Museos, 1919-1920). *Nuevo centenar de sonetos* (A New Hundred Sonnets) (Madrid: Tip. de la Revista de Archivos, 1921). *Sonetos póstumos* (Posthumous Sonnets) (México: Bajo el signo de Abside, 1941). *Epistolario de Ipandro Acaico* (Letters of Ipandro Acaico) (San Luis Potosí, 1952).

BIBLIOGRAPHY: Victoriano Agüeros, *Escritores mexicanos contemporáneos* (México, 1880), pp. 9-23. Heriberto García Rivas, *Historia de la literatura mexicana* (México: Textos Universitarios, S.A., 1972), vol. 2, p. 59. Carlos González Peña, *History of Mexican Literature*, translated by Gusta Barfield Nance and Florene Johnson Dunstan (Dallas, Texas: Southern Methodist University Press, 1968), pp.

205, 261, 282-84, 285.   Julio Jiménez Rueda, *Letras mexicanas en el siglo XIX* (México: FCE, 1944), p. 112, 137, 144, 152. Aurora M. Ocampo de Gómez and Ernesto Prado Velázquez, *Diccionario de escritores mexicanos* (México: UNAM, 1967), pp. 241-42. José Franco Ponce, *Ipandro Acaico o Monseñor Montes de Oca y Obregón* (Tlalpam, México: Imp. del Asilo Patricio Sanzz, 1921). Frederick Starr, *Readings from Modern Mexican Authors* (Chicago: Open Court Publishing Company, 1904), pp. 189-203.

FILIPPA B. YIN

MORA, José María Luis (1794-1850), writer, politician, leader and ideologist of the liberals. He promoted liberal reform in 1833. His political influence was notorious in the first half of the 19th century. He was born in Chamacuero, Guanajuato. He studied his first years in Querétaro, in the Escuela Real. Later, he moved to Mexico City to attend the Colegio de San Ildefonso. He graduated in 1818. He received a college degree in 1819 and a doctorate in theology in 1820. At that time, he was ordained as a priest. Several years later, in 1927, he obtained a law degree. In 1821, he was a staff member of *El Seminario Político y Literario* (*The Political and Literary Weekly*), in which he began to espouse his liberal ideas. He became active in politics as a very young age. He was a member of the Provincial Legislation of Mexico. He was a legislator of the State of Mexico and a member of the Yorkina Lodge. He was an opponent of the Itrubide Empire.   In 1833, as counsellor to President Valentín Gómez Farias, he was involved with the proclamation and promulgation of the law considered to be the first liberal reform ever achieved by the party of the same name. The clerical and military opposition to such reform brought about the downfall of the federal government, resulting in Mora's exile in Paris. In 1847, he was named plenipotentiary minister to Great Britain. He died in Paris on July 14, 1850.

Mora stood out as a speaker, political writer and, in particular, as the ideologist of the first liberal reform. The most outstanding of his extensive production are the political writings, which were deemed the best way for the ideological fight that was waged to transform national reality. Consequently, at a very young age, he started out as a journalist, trying to influence public opinion. Most of his articles were published in the *Seminario Político y Literario de México* and in *El Indicador de la Federación Mexicana*. He wrote about the social, political, and economic life of various groups, with their opposing tendencies, their different ways of conceiving the country's organization, which he saw as endangering national stability. He was influenced by European liberalism. He sought out a set of guidelines for the liberal doctrine that would lead to the building of a modern nation.

WORKS: *Papeles inéditos y obras selectas del doctor Mora* (Unpublished Writings and Selected Works of Dr. Mora) (México: Libr. de la Vda. Bouret, 1906). *Ensayos, ideas, y retratos* (Essays, Ideas, and Portraits: (México: UNAM, 1941). *México y sus revoluciones* (Mexico and Its Revolutions) (México: Ed. Porrúa, 1950). *Obras completas* (Complete Works) (México: SEP, Instituto Dr. José María Luis Mora, 1986).

BIBLIOGRAPHY: Luis Chávez Orozco, *La gestión diplomática del Doctor Mora* (México: Publicación de la Sría. de Relaciones Exteriores, 1931). Fernando

Fernández MacGregor, *Mora revivido* (México: Cámara de Senadores, 1963). Jorge Flores D., *José María Luis Mora. Un constructor de México* (México: Sría. de Relaciones Exteriores, 1963). Charles A. Hale, *El liberalismo mexicano en la época de* Mora. 1821-1835 (México: Siglo XXI, 1972). Joaquín Ramírez Cabañas, *El Doctor Mora* (México, UNAM, 1934).

CARMEN BLAZQUEZ DOMINGUEZ AND ELADIO CORTES

MORENO Villa, José (1887-1955). A poet, critic, art historian and painter, José Moreno Villa was born in Málaga, Spain, on February 16, 1887. After studying with the Jesuits in his home city, he went to Germany in 1904 and spent four years learning chemistry and hoping to embark upon a business career. However, when he was in Madrid in 1910, his life took a different turn and he decided to study history, eventually receiving his degree from the University of Madrid.

While in Madrid, he took part in many cultural activities and was a member of various boards and associations. He also taught the history of painting at the university level. His journeys took him all over Europe and to the United States. Like many other intellectuals, he fled Spain in 1939, seeking exile in Mexico, where he lived until his death on April 24, 1955. Quickly embracing his new home, Moreno Villa received a professorship at the Colegio de México and published in a number of well-known journals both in Mexico and elsewhere. Very active in the cultural life of the city, he made his greatest number of contributions to *México en la Cultura*. Moreno Villa's two basic tools were his pen and his paintbrush. His literary work, for which he received early recognition, possessed traditional and lyrical qualities. As an artist, he expressed himself largely as an impressionist. The artist-author wrote excellent essays on such topics as colonial sculpture in Mexico, the plastic arts, and things of interest to children.

WORKS: *Poetry: Garba*, poem (Madrid: Imp. Zavala, 1913). *El pasajero* (The Passenger), poems (Madrid: Imp. Clásica, 1914). *Luchas de "Penas" y "Alegrías" y su transfiguración* (Struggles of "Griefs" and "Happiness" and Their Transfiguration) (Madrid: Alegoría, 1915). *Evoluciones* (Evolutions) (Madrid: Calleja, 1918). *Florilegio* (San José de Costa Rica: El Convivio, 1920). *Colección* (Collection) (Madrid: n.p., 1924). *Jacinta, la pelirroja* (Jacinta, with the Red Hair), in *Litoral* (Málaga, Mar.- Apr., 1929). *Carambas*, 1st, 2nd, and 3rd series (Madrid: n.p., 1931). *Puentes que no acaban* (Unending Bridges) (Madrid: n.p., 1933). *Salón sin muros* (Room without Walls) (Madrid: n.p., 1936). *Puerta severa* (Severe Door) (México: Tierra Nueva, 1941). *La noche del Verbo* (The Night of the Verb) (México: n.p., 1942). *La música que llevaba (1913-1947)* (The Music That Was Going On) (Buenos Aires: Edit. Losada, 1950). *Voz en vuelo a su cuna* (Voice in Flight to Its Cradle) (México: Edit. Ecuador, 1961). Theater: *La comedia de un tímido* (The Play of a Timid One), in *Cuadernos Literarios* (Madrid, 1924). Prose: *Velázquez* (Madrid: Calleja, 1920). *Patrañas* (Cock and Bull Stories) (Madrid: Caro Raggio, 1921; México: n.p., 1941). *Dibujos del Instituto de Gijón* (Drawings from the Instituto de Gijón) (Madrid: Catálogo, 1926). *Pruebas de Nueva York* (Proofs of New York) (Málaga: n.p., 1927; Madrid: Espasa-Calpe, 1928). *Locos, enanos, negros y niños palaciegos de los siglos XVI y XVII* (Crazy People, Dwarfs, Blacks and Palace Children in the Sixteenth and Seventh Centuries) (Madrid: n.p., 1930; México: n.p., 1939). *Cornucopia de México* (México: n.p., 1940; México: Edit. Porrúa y Obregón, 1952). *Doce manos mexicanos* (Twelve Mexican Hands) (México: n.p., 1941). *La escultura colonial mexicana* (Mexican Colonial Sculpture) (México: n.p., 1942). *Leyendo a . . . (Reading . . .)* (México: El Colegio de México, 1944). *Vida en claro* (Clarifying Life), autobiography (México: El Colegio de México, 1944). *Pobretería y locura* (Beggars and Craziness) (México: El Colegio de México, 1945). *Lo que sabía mi loro* (What My Parrot Knew) (México: El Colegio de México, 1945). *Lo mexicano en las artes plásticas* (Mexicanism in the Plastic Arts) (México: n.p., 1948). *Los autores como actores y otros intereses literarios de acá y allá* (Authors as Actors and Other Literary Interests from Here and There) (México: FCE, 1951). Editions and Prologues: Juan de Valdés, *Diálogo de la lengua*, edition and prologue (Madrid: Calleja, 1919). Espronceda, *Poesías*, edition and prologue (Madrid: La Lectura, 1923). Lope de Rueda, *Entremeses*, edition and prologue (Madrid: Clásicos Castellanos, 1924). Translations: E. Wolfflin, *Conceptos fundamentales en la historia del arte* (Fundamental Concepts in the History of Art) (Madrid: n.p., 1919). A. Schnitzler, *Señorita Elisa* (México: n.p., 1945).

BIBLIOGRAPHY: Ermilo Abreu Gómez, *Sala de retratos* (México: Edit. Leyenda, 1946), pp. 191-93. Max Aub, *La poesía española contemporánea* (México: Imp. Universitaria, 1954), pp. 107-9. José Luis Cano, "Reencuentro con Moreno Villa," in *Insula* 37, 428-29 (July-Aug. 1982): 12, 13. Alfredo Cardona Peña, "José Moreno Villa y su poesía," in *Pablo Neruda y otros ensayos* (México: Eds. de Andrea, 1955): 125-34. Luis Cernuda, *Estudios sobre la poesía española contemporánea* (Madrid: Eds. Guadarrama, 1957), pp. 151-64. Birute Ciplijauskaite, "Los 'cuadros cubistas' de José Moreno Villa," in *Studies in Honor of Gustavo Correa*, edited by Charles B. Faulhaber et al (Potomac, Md: Scripta Humanistica, 1986), pp. 47-57. José Francisco Cirre, *La poesía de José Moreno Villa* (Madrid: Edit. Insula, 1963). Gabriel García Maroto, Review of *Pruebas de Nueva York*, in *Contemporáneos* 7 (Dec. 1928): 397-402. Juan Ramón Jiménez, *Españoles de tres mundos* (Buenos Aires: Edit. Losada, 1942), pp. 83-84. Antonio Machado, "El libro *Colección*, del poeta andaluz José Moreno Villa," in *Revista de Occidente* (Madrid) 8, (1925): 359-77. José R. Marra-López, *Narrativa española fuera de España* (Madrid: Eds. Guadarrama, 1963), pp. 60, 117-20, 446. José Moreno Villa, "Autocrítica," in *Revista de Occidente* (Madrid) 6 (1924): 435-40. Octavio Paz, "Vivacidad de José Moreno Villa," in *Las peras del olmo* (México: Imp. Universitaria, UNAM, 1957), pp. 212-14. Juan Pérez de Ayala, "Estudios superficiales," in *Boletín de la Fundación Federico García Lorca* 1, 1 (June 1987): 29-37. Carlos Sainz de Robles, *Historia y antología de la poesía española* (Madrid: Aguilar, 1955), pp. 221-22, 1395-1400. Gonzalo Torrente Ballester, *Panorama de la literatura española contemporánea*, vol. 1 (Madrid: Eds. Guadarrama, 1961), pp. 203, 283-84, 288, 351. Luis Miguel Vicente, "El tema de México en José Moreno Villa y Luis Cernuda," in *Mester* 16, 2 (Fall 1987): 25-34. Howard T. Young, Review of Francisco Cirre's book, in *Hispania* 48, 1 (March 1965): 182.

JEANNE C. WALLACE

"MOTOLINIA." See BENAVENTE, Fray Toribio de.

MUÑOZ, Rafael Felipe (1899-1972). A novelist and short story writer, Muñoz was born in Chihuahua, Chihuahua, where he started his career as a journalist. At the age of sixteen, he personally met Pancho Villa, who was to become a recurrent character in his works. Villa was a very attractive and daring figure to Muñoz because of his opposition to the strong military forces of the Mexican government and also because of his very strong and direct opposition to the meddling of the government of the United States in Mexican internal affairs. Pancho Villa was, and still is, very much admired for his incursion in 1916 into United States territory in Columbus, New Mexico. This event marked the first time that U.S. territory had been invaded by a foreign force. For this reason, Villa held a very strong influence on all the people around him. The subject matter in Muñoz' novels and short stories is based on his own experiences during the years of the Mexican Revolution. These were events in which he participated directly, or even stories and characters which resulted as a consequence of an observed or heard event. This is particularly true of most of the novelists and short story writers of the Mexican Revolution, whose preoccupations were mainly with observation and comment on exterior Mexican reality - nature, the land, the countryside - than preoccupation with the characters' psychology. *Memorias de Pancho Villa* (1923), was written in the year of Villa's assassination. Here, Villa himself tells his own life story, going through some of the most interesting episodes in his life. Villa is shown as a heroic and dominant revolutionary force. There is a great deal of sympathy on the part of the author for Villa's revolutionary ideals. *¡Vámonos con Pancho Villa!* (Let's Go With Pancho Villa) (1931) has been criticized for its technical defects in structure, style, characterization, and ideology, but as a recounting of events during the Mexican Revolution it makes for very pleasant reading. Here we have six very loosely tied short stories dealing with six characters of the town of San Pablo, Chihuahua, and their accounts and deaths in the Villa armed forces. Tiburcio Maya, one of the six, is especially emphasized for his incursion with Villa into Columbus, New Mexico. As an experienced journalist, Muñoz was very able in his depiction of events, and his narrative style is very clear. What is important in this novel is that the people themselves participate in a social movement that will, supposedly, benefit them directly. *Se llevaron el cañón para Bachimba* (They Took the Cannon to Bachimba) (1941) is generally considered to be Munoz' best novel. The focus here is on development of one main character, Alvaro, a thirteen-year-old boy, and his anxiety about the resolution of his own personal situation, but still in the middle of events related to the Revolution. The events within the novel take place around the year 1912. It is right after the fall of Porfirio Díaz and deals directly with Pascual Orozco's revolt against Francisco I. Madero. The novel deals with the years of the Revolution and Alvaro's maturing during these years to realize what is going on. It is through the experiences of Alvaro that Muñoz wants to trace the Mexican Revolution and its own maturity. The descriptions within the novel vary from violent revolutionary scenes to descriptions of rural life, all done very ably with rich imagery. The title for his short story collection, *El feroz cabecilla* (The Fierce Leader) (1928), which, some say, refers to Pancho Villa, comes from the short story of the same title published originally in *El Universal Gráfico*, a Mexico City-based newspaper for which Muñoz also worked. Muñoz confessed that some of these stories are based on real events, while others are not. He uses a combination of reality and imagination. The first few stories of *Si me han de matar mañana* (If I Am to Die Tomorrow) (1934) also appeared in the newspaper *El Universal*. Muñoz admitted that his stories were not very elaborated. He published them as originally written for the reader to judge the effectiveness of his first writing.

WORKS: Novels: *¡Vámonos con Pancho Villa!* (Let's Go with Pancho Villa) (Madrid: Espasa Calpe, 1931). *Se llevaron el cañón para Bachimba* (They Took the Cannon to Bachimba) (Buenos Aires: Espasa Calpe, 1941, written in 1934). Short stories: *El hombre malo* (The Bad Man) (México: Ed. del Autor, 1913). *El feroz cabecilla y otros cuentos de la Revolución en el Norte* (The Fierce Leader and Other Short Stories of the Revolution in the North) (México: Imp de la Cámara de Diputados, 1928). *Si me han de matar mañana* (If I Am to Die Tomorrow) (México: Ed. Botas, 1934). Other Works: *Memorias de Pancho Villa* (Memoirs of Pancho Villa)(México: El Universal Gráfico, 1923). *Santa Anna* (Madrid: Espasa Calpe, 1936), biography. *Obras incompletas, dispersas o rechazadas* (Incomplete, Scattered, or Rejected Works) (México: Ed. Botas, 1967). *Relatos de la Revolución* (México: Utopía Compañía Editorial, 1976).

BIBLIOGRAPHY: John S. Brushwood, *Mexico in Its Novel* (Austin: University of Texas Press, 1966). Emmanuel Carballo, *Diecinueve protagonistas de la literatura mexicana del siglo XX* (México: Empresas Editoriales, 1965). Antonio Castro Leal, *La novela de la Revolución Mexicana*. 2 vols. (México: Aguilar, 1960). Walter M. Langford, *The Mexican Novel Comes of Age* (Notre Dame: University of Notre Dame Press, 1971). María del Carmen Millán, *Antología de cuentos mexicanos*, vol. 2 (México: Editorial Nueva Imagen, 1977).

OSCAR SOMOZA

MURILLO, Gerardo (Dr. Atl) (1875-1964), painter and art critic.   Born in Guadalajara, Murillo decided to go abroad to study painting. During the voyage he changed his name to Atl; in Paris, Leopoldo Lugones completed the pseudonym by adding Doctor to it. Dr. Atl was an active participant in revolutionary politics. He was also known for his explorations of the volcanos of Mexico, particularly Popocatépetl and Paricutín. As a painter he introduced various technical innovations in Mexican painting. Mexican landscapes were his specialty. He was also a critic and head of the Department of Fine Arts at the University of México.

His literary work includes essays, scientific works, criticism, and short stories. Many of his stories are based on themes of the Revolution, and their popular appeal is due in part to his colorful use of the language of the common people. One of his stories, "La perla" (The Pearl), was the inspiration for John Steinbeck's novel of the same name.

WORKS: Studies: *Las sinfonías del Popocatépetl* (The Symphonies of Popocatépetl) (México: n.p., 1921). *Las artes populares en México* (Popular Art in Mexico) (México: n.p., 1921). *Iglesias de México* (Churches of Mexico) (México: n.p., 1926). *Los volcanes* (The Volcanos) (México: n.p., 1930). *Italia, su defensa en México* (Italy, Her Defense in Mexico) (México: n.p., 1936). *Ante la carroza de Ginebra* (Before the Carrion of Geneva) (México: n.p., 1939). *La actividad en el Popocatépetl* (Activity in Popocatépetl) (México: n.p., 1941). *La victoria de Alemania y la situación de la América Latina* (German Victory and the Latin American Situation) (México: n.p., 1941). *A los pueblos de América. Se impone la defensa del Continente contra la política de Roosevelt* (To the Nations of America. The Defense of the Continent Against the Politics of Roosevelt) (México: Acción Mundial, 1941). *Cómo nace y crece un volcán. El Paricutín* (How a Volcano Is Born and Grows. Paricutín) (México: INBA, 1950). Essays: *El paisaje, un ensayo* (The Countryside, an Essay) (México, 1933). *Oro, más oro* (Gold, More Gold) (México: n.p., 1936). *Un grito en la Atlántida* (A Cry in Atlántida) (México: n.p., 1947). Short Stories: *¡Arriba, arriba!* (Victory! Victory!) (México: n.p., 1927). *Cuentos bárbaros* (Barbaric Tales) (México: Ed. Libros Mexicanos, 1930). *Cuentos de todos colores I* (Many-Colored Stories I) (México: Ed. Botas, 1933). *Cuentos de todos colores II* (Many-Colored Stories II) (México: Ed. Botas, 1936). *Cuentos de todos colores III* (Many-Colored Stories III) (México: Ed. Botas, 1941). *Un hombre más allá del universo* (A Man above the Universe) (México: n.p., 1935). "El hombre y la perla" (The Man and the Pearl), in *Cuentos criollos* (Boston: Walsh, 1941). *El Padre Eterno, Satanás y Juanito García* (The Eternal Father, Satán and Juanito García) (México: n.p., 1941). *Gentes profanas en el convento* (Laymen in the Convent) (México, 1950). Memoirs: "Ocho páginas únicas de la autobiografía inconclusa del Dr. Atl". (Eight Unique Pages in the Unfinished Autobiography of Dr. Atl, *Novedades* (Feb 7, 1965): 1, 5.

BIBLIOGRAPHY: Anon., "Escritores mexicanos contemporáneos: Doctor Atl," *Biblos* 4 (1922): 5-6; "El Dr. Atl visionario," *Excelsior* (Sept. 6, 1964): 5-6. "Primer aniversario del Dr. Atl," *El Día* (Sept. 28, 1965): 9. Fernando Arizmendi Cornadó, "Semblanza del Dr. Atl," *El Día* (Jan. 5, 1965): 9. Fernando Benítez, "Dr. Atl, pintor de los volcanes, de las hondas barrancas, de los valles solares," *¡Siempre!* (Dec. 2, 1964): 13. Alfredo Cardona Peña, "Anécdota y concepto del Doctor Atl," *El Día* (Aug. 17, 1964): 9. Ricardo Cortés Tamayo, "El Dr. Atl, maestro de maestros," *El Día* (Aug. 16, 1964): 3. Jorge Crespo de la Serna, "El arte del Dr. Atl," *El Día* (Aug. 20, 1964): 9. P. Fernández Marquéz, "En memoria del Dr. Atl" *El Nacional* (Aug. 30, 1964): 14. Carlos González Peña, *Historia de la literatura mexicana* (México: Ed. Porrúa, 1963), pp. 402, 412. Andrés Henestrosa, "La nota cultural," *El Nacional* (Aug. 7, 1964): 3, 8. Ronald Hilton, *Who's Who in Latin America* (Stanford: Stanford University Press, 1946), p. 82. Luis Leal, *Breve historia del cuento mexicano* (México: Ed. Andrea, 1956), pp. 108-9. Rubén Levin, "Pellicer. Homenaje político al Dr. Atl," *El Universal* (Jan. 31, 1965): 5. Pedro Lozano, "El Dr. Atl, varón del Renacimiento mexicano," *El Día* (Aug. 17, 1964): 3. Antonio Luna Arroyo, "El Dr. Atl, hombre del Renacimiento," *Cuadernos de Bellas Artes* (Oct. 1964): 41-46. Jacobo Mabludovsky, "En la última entrevista de su vida, el Dr. Atl se confesó a *¡Siempre!*," *¡Siempre!* (Sept. 16, 1964): 22-23. Antonio Magaña Esquivel, "El prodigioso Dr. Atl," *El Nacional* (Aug. 27, 1964): 3. M. Maldonado Koerdell, "Vulcanología y vulcanofilia en la pintura del Dr. Atl," *El Nacional* (June 27, 1965): 8-9, 10. José Luis Martínez, *Literatura mexicana siglo XX* (México: Robredo, 1949), vol. 1, p. 48; vol. 2, p. 85. Indiana Nájera, *Barbas y melenas célebres y uno de otro rasurado* (México: Libro-Mex, 1960), pp. 23-28. Margarita Nelken, "El pintor más joven de México," *Excelsior* (Aug. 23, 1964): 3, 8. Raúl Noriega, "Imaginación y realismo en la extraordinaria existencia del gran pintor," *Novedades* (Aug. 16, 1964): 1, 8. Abelardo Ojeda, "El Dr. Atl, precursor del muralismo mexicano," *El Universal* (Aug. 23, 1964): 5. Gregorio Ortega, *Hombres, mujeres* (Mèxico: Ed. Bellas Artes, 1966), pp. 81-84. Gabriel Pereyra, "Genio y figura del Dr. Atl en el recuerdo de cinco personajes," *El Día* (Aug. 22, 1964): 9. Raúl Pérez Mendoza, "Murió el gran pintor y vulcanólogo Doctor Atl," *El Día* (Aug. 16, 1964): 1. Beatriz Reyes Nevares, "El Doctor Atl," *¡Siempre!* (Dec. 2, 1964): 14. Marcela del

Río "Cuando hablé con el Dr. Atl," *Excelsior*, 30 Aug. 1964: 7. Antonio Rodríguez, "Dos fotos que denuncian el carácter divino del Dr. Atl," *El Día* (June 14, 1963): 9. "El Doctor Atl," *El Día* (Aug. 17, 1964): 9. "El Doctor Atl, uno de los grandes mexicanos del siglo," *¡Siempre!* (Aug. 19, 1964): 26, 70. Carlos Rojas Juanco, "El Dr. Atl, vagabundo iluminado," *El Día* (Aug. 23, 1964): 1-3. Arturo Torres Rioseco, *Bibliografía de la novela mexicana* (Cambridge: Harvard University Press, l933), p. 9. Luis G. Urbina, "Libros de México bajo árboles de Castilla: Cuatro poetas," *El Universal* (Sept. 26, 1926): 3, 4; (Oct. 3, 1926): 3, 4. Various, "Homenaje al Doctor Atl," *Novedades* (Jan. 28, 1951): 2-3. "El Dr. Atl en el arte y en la vida de México. Valorización de su obra y su influencia en la plástica mexicana," *Novedades* (Aug. 16, 1964): 1, 4; "Homenaje al Dr. Atl," *Revista de la Universidad de Yucatán* 6 (1964): 109-16; "Juicios sobre el Dr. Atl," *Cuadernos de Bellas Artes* (Oct. 1964): 47-52.

                                                                    BARBARA P. FULKS

MURILLO, Josefa (1860-1898). Born on February 28, 1860, in Tlacotálpam, Veracruz, Josefa Murillo lived in that area her entire life, greatly shortened by broken health. Unable to pursue advanced studies and racked by violent asthma attacks, she was, however, a successful poet, publishing in several journals and other papers. She occasionally used the pseudonyms Xóchitl and Totoloche. Her poetry, much of which was unpublished, revolved mainly around the themes of love and nostalgia. Apparently, her parents intercepted her attempts to acquire a greater education than she could otherwise achieve (or was permitted to achieve) in her home area. It has been documented that she wrote a letter to President Benito Juárez, asking his help in pursuing her academic dreams. It was this letter that was intercepted, thus putting an end to her formal education.

Josefa Murillo never married, although she did have a suitor. Her suitor died, leaving her a bundle of love letters which she asked to have put in her coffin upon her own death. The "alondra de Papaloapán" (lark from Papaloapan), as she was affectionately known, died on September 1, 1898, and her request for the love letters was granted.

WORKS: Various poems appeared in the papers *El Dictamen*, *El correo de Sotavento*, *La Voz de Sotavento,* and *La Voz de Tlacotálpam.*

BIBLIOGRAPHY: Francisco R. Illescas and Juan Bartolo Hernández, *Escritores veracruzanos* (Veracruz: n.p., 1945), pp. 216-17. Margarite Olivo Lara, *Biografías de veracruzanos distinguidos* (México: Imp. del Museo Nacional de Arquología, Historia y Etnografía, 1931), pp. 194-96. Roberto Núñez y Domínguez, "Al margen de un centenario: La alondra del Papaloapán," in *Excelsior* (March 14, 1946): 3C. Aurora M. Ocampo de Gómez and Ernesto Prado Velázquez, *Diccionario de Escritores Mexicanos* (México: UNAM, 1967), p. 247. Leonardo Pasquel, *Josefa Murillo. La alondra de Sotavento* (México: Edit. Citlaltépetl, 1961). Cayetano Rodríguez Beltrán, *Homenaje a la inspirada poetisa Tlacotalpeña Josefa Murillo* (Tlacotálpam: Imp. de la Reforma, 1899). Jesús Romero Flores, "Mil biografías en la historia de México," in *El Nacional* (Oct. 23, 1946): 2.

                                                                    JEANNE C. WALLACE

N

NAJERA, María Esther (1906-), also known as Indiana Nájera. Nájera was born in Teloloápam, Guerrero, on February 5, 1906. She studied at the Institute of Toluca and the National Preparatory School. She also studied in the capital with private teachers and attended the National Conservatory of Music, where she cultivated a life-long love for musical composition.

She began her career as a journalist at the age of twenty-two. In addition to writing newspaper columns and articles, she also honed her talents as a poet, novelist, and short story writer. Her initial works were published in journals and newspapers such as *Excelsior, El Universal*, and *Revista de Revistas*. Later she published many of her own literary creations and sold them herself. Her more than 100 published short stories have been categorized as "narratives of customs and environment." One of her most celebrated works is *Páginas íntimas* (Intimate Pages), a moving and candid autobiography of her life of pain and conflict. Nájera has also achieved recognition in the film industry as a scriptwriter.

WORKS: Poetry: *La señal del amor* (The Sign of Love) (México: Ed. de la Autora, 1946). *A media voz* (In a Low Voice) (México: B. Costa-Amic, 1966). Novels: *Carne viva* (Live Flesh) (México: Imp. Cima, 1943). *Tierra seca* (Dry Land) (México: Eds. Botas, 1945). *Poza Negra* (Black Puddle) (México: Libro Mexicano, 1960). *Cruz Roja* (Red Cross) (México: B. Costa-Amic, 1963). *Amores en tierra de sangre y sol* (Romances in a Land of Blood and Sun) (México: Ed. Divulgación, 1964). Stories: *Pasajeros de segunda* (Second Class Passengers) (México: José C. Torres, 1950). Other Works: *Barbas y melenas célebres, y uno que otro rasurado* (Famous Beards and Mops of Hair, and a Few Shaved People) (México: Ed. Libro Mexicano, 1960). *El cielo eres tú* (You Are the Sky) (México: B. Costa-Amic, 1962). *Y... ¿Quién educa a los padres?* (And Who Educates the Parents?) (México: B. Costa-Amic, 1970). *Escuela práctica de novios* (The Practical School of Fiancées) (México: B. Costa-Amic, 1967). *Páginas íntimas* (Intimate Pages) (México: B. Costa-Amic, 1970).

BIBLIOGRAPHY: John S. Brushwood and José Rojas Garciadueñas, *Breve historia de la novela mexicana*, Manuales Studium, 9 (México: Eds. de Andrea, 1959), p. 81. Gabriela Chazaro Pous, Introduction to *Páginas íntimas* by María Esther Nájera (México: B. Costa-Amic, 1970), pp. 7-9. Helia D'Acosta, *Veinte mujeres* (México: Editores Asociados, 1971), pp. 159-69. Aurora M. Ocampo de Gómez and Ernesto Prado Velázquez, *Diccionario de escritores mexicanos* (México: UNAM, 1967), p. 247. Isabel Schon, *México and Its Literature for Children and Adolescents* (Tempe: Center for Latin American Studies, Arizona State University, 1977), pp. 23-24.

ROBERT K. ANDERSON

NANDINO, Elías (1903-   ), poet. Elías Mandino was born in Cocula, Jalisco, on April 19, 1903. A physician by profession, he has also been a very prolific poet. One the Contemporáneos, he was a close friend and the personal physician of Jorge *Cuesta, another member of the group. (See Vanguardist Prose Fiction in Mexico.) Nandino has also taught literature and was the director of two journals: *Estaciones* (1956-1960) and *Cuadernos de Bellas Artes* (1960-1964).

Nandino has written literally hundreds of poems, primarily sonnets. His place among the Contemporáneos is assured not only because of the quantity and quality of his own production but also because he had published for the first time the poetry of Jorge Cuesta after his death in 1942. Nandino recognizes Xavier *Villaurrutia as his most important poetic influence. Primary themes in Nandino's poetry are love, solitude, and death. The latter is portrayed as a hopeful end within a pantheistic perception of reality.

WORKS: *Canciones* (Songs) (1924) in *Poesía I (1924-1945)* (México: Nueva Voz, 1947). *Espiral* (Spiral) (México: Ed. Norte, 1928). *Color de ausencia* (The Color of Absence) (México: Ed. Norte, 1932). *Eco* (Echo) (México: Imprenta Mundial, 1934). *Río de sombra* (Shadow River) (México: Imprenta Mundial, 1935). *Sonetos* (Sonnets) (México: Editorial Angel Chapero, 1937). *Suicidio lento* (Slow Suicide) (México: Editorial Angel Chapero, 1937). *Poemas árboles* (Tree Poems) (México: Editorial Norte, 1938). *Nuevos sonetos* (New Sonnets) (México: Cuadernos México Nuevo, 1939). *Espejo de mi muerte* (Mirror of My Death) (México: Editorial Isla, 1945). *Poesía I (1924-1945)* (Poetry) (México: Nueva Voz, 1947). *Poesía (II)* (Poetry) (México: Nueva Voz, 1948). *Naufragio de la duda* (Shipwreck of Doubt) (México: Nueva Voz, 1950). *Triángulo de silencios* (Triangle of Silences) (México: Edición Guaranía, 1953). *Nocturna summa* (Nocturnal Summa) (México: FCE, 1955). *Nocturno amor* (Nocturnal Love) (México: Cuadernos del Unicornio, 1958). "Retrato de Jorge Cuesta" (Portrait of Jorge Cuesta), in *Poesía de Jorge Cuesta* (Poetry of Jorge Cuesta) (México: Editorial Estaciones, 1958), pp. 7-13. *Sonetos* (Sonnets) (México: Porrúa, 1959). *Nocturno día* (Nocturnal Day) (México: Estaciones, 1959). *Nocturna palabra* (Night Word) (México: FCE, 1960). *Eternidad del polvo* (Eternity of Dust) (México: Joaquín Mortíz, 1970).

BIBLIOGRAPHY: Rosario Castellanos, "Cartas a Elías Nandino," in *Revista de Bellas Artes* 18, 2nd series (Nov.-Dec. 1974): 20-23. Antonio Castro Leal, *La poesía mexicana moderna*, Letras Mexicanas, no. 12 (México: FCE, 1953), pp. 312-13. Octavio Corvalán, "La poesía de Elías Nandino," in *Nivel* 6 (June 25, 1963): 1. Frank Dauster, *Breve historia de la poesía mexicana*, Manuales Studium, no. 4 (México: Ed. de Andrea, 1956) pp. 165-66. Raúl Leiva, *Imagen de la poesía mexicana contemporanea* (México: UNAM, 1959) pp. 137-44. Carlos Monsiváis, *La poesía mexicana del siglo XX* (México: Empresas Editoriales, 1966), pp. 47, 451. Roberto Venegas, "Poetas mexicanos. Elías Nandino," in *Diorama de la Cultura* (Aug. 9, 1964): 7-8.

KENNETH M. TAGGART

NAVA, Thelma (1931-   ) poet. Nava was born on November 25, 1931 in Mexico City. She studied at the French Institute of Latin America, the Centro Mexicano de Escritores (Mexican School of Writers), and the Casa del Lago (Lake House). She has written poetry and literary criticism for various newspapers and magazines in Mexico City. She, along Beatriz *Espejo and other women writers, founded the magazine *El Rehilete* (The Arrow) and codirected *Pájaro cascabel* (Hawksbell), a collection of poetry.

Thelma Nava is a poet in search of her own language. Her themes are varied although she been most successful in writing about love. In 1962 she received the López Velarde Poetry Award, which was established by the newspaper *Ovaciones* (Ovations).

WORKS: Poetry: *Aquí te guardo yo* (Here I Keep You) (México: Cuadernos del Cocodrilo, 1957). *La orfandad del sueño* (The Dream Orphanage) (México: Eds. Pájaro Cascabel, 1964). *Poemes choisis* (Select Poems) (Niza, France: Profils Poétiques des pays Latins, 1965). *Colibrí 50* (Hummingbird 50) (México: Eds. Pájaro Cascabel, 1966).

BIBLIOGRAPHY: *Anuario de la poesía mexicana 1962* (bibliographical note) (México: INBA, 1963), p. 94. Andrés Henestrosa, "La nota cultural", in *El Nacional* (Oct. 7, 1966): 3. Jesús Arellano, "Thelma Nava y la búsqueda de un lenguaje poético singular," in *México en la Cultura* 792 (May 24, 1964): 7. Salvador Reyes Nevares, Review of *Colibrí 50*, in *La Cultura en México* 240 (Sept. 21, 1966): xvi. M.B.C., "Letras Mexicanas, Thelma Nava," in *Letras de Ayer y de Hoy* 2, 13 (Sept. 1966): 12.

DENISE GUAGLIARDO BENCIVENGO

NAVARRETE, MANUEL DE. See: MARTINEZ DE NAVARRETE, Fr. José Manuel.

NAVARRO Sánchez, José Adalberto (1918-   ), poet. Navarro Sánchez was born in Lagos de Moreno, Jalisco on April 23, 1918. In 1936 he published, with José Cornejo Franco, the cultural notebooks *Indice*. In 1939, he coedited the journal *Prisma* with his wife, María Luisa *Hidalgo. In 1950 he became the editor of *Et Caetera*. He also contributed to journals such as *Prisma*, *Papel de poesía*, *Letras de México*, and *Abside*. His academic contributions have been equally commendable: he has taught at the University of Guadalajara and the Escuela Normal Superior (School for Teachers) and has chaired the Department of Letters in the School of Philosophy at the University of Guadalajara. From 1959 to 1963 he acted as secretary of the Casa de la Cultura Jalisciense (Cultural House of Jalisco), codirected with Ramiro Villaseñorde the Jalisco Library, coordinated the commemorative series of the First Century of the Mexican Reform, served as editor of the series Biblioteca de Autores Jaliscienses Modernos (Library of Modern Jaliscan Authors), and directed various literary supplements.

Navarro Sánchez is highly noted for his immeasurable contribution to Mexican letters through the literary journals he founded and the articles he has written on painting, theater, narrative, poetry, and philosophical ideas.

WORKS: Poetry: *Humana residencia* [Humana resistencia?] (Human Residence/
Resistance) (Guadalajara: Ed. Navegación, 1937). *Voz de ave: Homenaje a González
Martínez* (Bird's Voice: In Honor of González Martínez) (Guadalajara: Ed.
Navegación, 1937). *Nocturno de la esposa* (Wife's Nocturne) (México: Ed. Prisma,
1939). *Pasión de la tierra* (Earth Passion) (Guadalajara: Ed. Tiempo Lit., 1942). *Liras
y palabras dentro del mar* (Verses and Words in the Sea) (Guadalajara: Ed. Teseo,
1944). *Primavera en invierno* (Spring in Winter) (Guadalajara: Eds. Et Caetera, 1951).
Espejo del Gólgota (Golgotha's Mirror) (Guadalajara: Eds. Et Caetera, 1952). *El
sueño herido* (The Wounded Dream) (Guadalajara: Eds. Et Caetera, 1953).

BIBLIOGRAPHY: Antonio Castro Leal, *La poesía mexicana moderna* (México: FCE,
1953), p. 457. José Luis Martínez, *Literatura mexicana, siglo XX. 1910-1949* (México:
Antigua Librería Robredo, 1950), pp. 80-86. Aurora Ocampo de Gómez and Ernesto
Prado Velázquez, *Diccionario de escritores mexicanos* (México: UNAM, 1967), p. 249.
Sara Velasco, *Escritores jaliscienses, Tomo II (1900-1965)* (Guadalajara: Universidad
of Guadalajara, 1985), pp. 193- 201.

MARGARITA VARGAS

NEGRETE, José (1855-1883), novelist and journalist. The son of a foreign diplomat,
Negrete was born in Brussels on January 29, 1855. He spent his early years in
Belgium, France, and Italy, and at age eleven went to Mexico. He studied at the
Colegio de San Ildefonso and the Escuela Nacional de Jurisprudencia, receiving from
the latter his law degree in 1876. He was one of the editors of *La Revista*, and in his
political writings he was a strong supporter of President Lerdo. He enlisted in the
army, which, under the command of General Alatorre, was routed at Tecoac by
forces loyal to Porfirio Díaz. Afterwards, he continued his political journalism, writing
pieces in opposition to the revolution of Tuxtepec (which ushered in the Díaz regime)
until the old Lerdista party eventually became reconciled with the Porfiristas. In 1881
he was given a post as military advisor and the following year was elected to
represent the state of Sinaloa as a deputy in the Congress. He traveled to San
Francisco, California, as a member of a government commission. Shortly after his
return to Mexico, he died in Tepic, Nayarit, on August 24, 1883.

   Well-versed in French literature, Negrete prepared and published a translation of
the younger Alexandre Dumas's *La hija adoptiva* (The Adopted Daughter). Among
his own works are a series of novels, the first of which was *Memorias de Paulina*
(Pauline's Memoirs). This was followed by *Historias color de fuego* (Flame-Colored
Stories). Others include *La niña mártir* (The Child Martyr), a novel dealing with
perversions of various sorts; its sequel, *La mujer verdugo* (The Female Executioner);
and *Memorias de Merolico* (Merolico's Memoirs), ostensibly a novel but in essence
little more than a series of sketches critical of Mexican social customs. As a novelist,
Negrete often lashed out at hypocrisy and other ills of society.

   Despite possessing considerable narrative skills and sharp powers of observation,
he failed to distinguish himself as a writer of quality prose fiction, composing instead
inferior works of a sensationalist nature, the literary by-product of his pessimistic
outlook on life.

WORKS: *Memorias de Paulina* (Pauline's Memoirs) (México: Imp. Poliglota, 1874). *Historias color de fuego* (Flame-Colored Stores) (México: Imp. del Comercio, 1875). *La niña mártir* (The Child Martyr) (México: Imp. y Lit. de I. Paz, 1878). *La mujer verdugo* (The Female Executioner) (México: Imp. y Lit. de I. Paz, 1878). *Memorias de Merolico* (Merolico's Memoirs) (México: Tip. Lit. de F. Mata, 1880).

BIBLIOGRAPHY: John S. Brushwood, *Mexico in Its Novel* (Austin: University of Texas Press, 1966), pp. 109-10; *The Romantic Novel in Mexico* vol. 26, no. 4 (Columbia: University of Missouri Studies, 1954), pp. 47, 75-76. *Diccionario de escritores mexicanos*, no editor (México: SEP, 1988), p. 5770.

MELVIN S. ARRINGTON, JR.

NERVO, Amado (1870-1919). Born in Tepic, Nayarit, Nervo, along with Manuel *Acuña, is still considered one of the most popular poets in México. He started publishing in Mazatlán at a very young age and as a consequence wrote over thirty volumes, including poetry, novel, short story, journalistic articles, prose poems, essays, and one drama. Over three quarters of his complete work is in prose. From Mazatlán he moved to Mexico City, where he occupied several posts in the government of Porfirio Díaz. At first Nervo wanted to become a priest, but he had to abandon the seminary for economic reasons. He studied theology, the physical sciences, and philosophy. As a result of all these endeavors, Nervo passed through stages filled with spiritual doubts. He asked very basic questions and experimented with several "isms," such as Buddhism, and even spiritualism toward the end of his life. But finally he returned to Catholicism. His provincial, Catholic, and conservative education clashed with his inquisitive spirit. He considered himself a universal person who saw the limitations of his education.

He aspired for more. Nervo was a typical Modernist in the sense that he wished very deeply to visit Europe, and especially France, where he lived for fourteen years. He shared an apartment with Rubén Darío for a while. As a result of this experience Darío called him the "Friar of Sighs." He also married a French woman, Ana Cecilia Luisa Daillez, to whom he dedicated a book of poetry *La amada inmóvil* (The Immobile Beloved) (1920), published posthumously in 1929. This is a sentimental and emotional book that contains autobiographical poetry. In it he refers to his wife as Ana or Damiana. He tells the story of his love for her, at the moment when she is dead. This seems to be an important stage in his life, as he tries in vain to communicate with her. When his efforts prove futile, he renounces spiritualism. Another important poem is "Gratia plena," (1920), in which he compares his life to that of the Virgin Mary. He also compares his love, in religious terms, to Mary, describing her as a perfect woman.

Intellectually Nervo is eclectic, combining several influences ranging from the Oriental to those of the European philosophers of the nineteenth century. Amado Nervo founded, with Jesús *Valenzuela, the *Revista Moderna* (1898-1911), which corresponded to the Symbolist period in Spanish American Modernism. As a narrator in the Modernist style, he is considered one of the best in Mexico. In his prose writings he is almost always trying to shock the reader through his presentation of events. This is different from his poetry where, within the Modernist tendency, he is always very gentle, sweet, and pleasant. When Rubén Darío died in 1916, Nervo was the one left to carry the Modernist banner. But it was already too late. Most of the writers, and poets in particular, were already creating poetry in other ways, specifically Vicente Huidobro and César Vallejo. These new ways of looking at and interpreting the world were made even more acute by the events of World War I. He died at the age of forty-nine in Montevideo, Uruguay.

Nervo, along with Manuel *Gutiérrez-Nájera, is considered to be one of the two most important Modernists in Mexico. As a critic he published *Juana de Asbaje* (1910), in which he analyzes the work of Sor Juana Inés de la *Cruz. An interesting anecdote is the mock interview that Amado Nervo had with Sor Juana, even though they lived in different historical periods. He had the reputation of knowing her so well that he could anticipate her answers to his questions.

WORKS: *Perlas negras* (Black Pearls) (México: Imp. de I. Escalante, 1898). *Poemas* (Poems) (Paris: Lib. de la Vda. de Ch. Bouret, 1901). *La hermana agua* (Sister Water) (Madrid: Imp. de los hijos de M. G. Hernández, 1901). *El éxodo y las flores del camino* (The Exodus and the Flowers of the Road) (México: Ofna. Impresora de Estampillas, 1902). *Jardines interiores* (Interior Gardens) (México: Imp. Sucs. de F. Díaz de León, 1905). The former collections follow a purely Modernist tendency. *En voz baja* (In a Low Voice) (París: Ollendorff, 1909). *Serenidad* (Serenity) (Madrid: Renacimiento, 1914). *Elevación* (Elevation) (Madrid: Tip. Artística Cervantes, 1917). *Plenitud* (Plenitude) (Madrid: Tip. Artística Cervantes, 1918). These last collections contain a more personal poetic and lyrical expression. Other works of poetry include: *El arquero divino* (The Divine Archer) (Buenos Aires: 1915-1918), published posthumously in *Obras completas*, edited by Alfonso Reyes, 27 vols. (Madrid: Biblioteca Nueva, 1920). *El estanque de los lotos* (The Lotus Pool) (Buenos Aires: Jesús Menéndez, 1919). *La amada inmóvil* (The Immobile Beloved) (Buenos Aires: 1920). The following are some of his better known novels: *El bachiller* (The Bachelor) (México: El Mundo, 1895). *Pascual Aguilera* (1896) in *Otras vidas* (Barcelona: Ballescá, n.d.). *El donador de almas* (The Donor of Souls) (México: Novelas del Cómico, 1899). *Consuelo*, a **Zarzuela** that was first performed in 1899. *Almas que pasan* (Souls that Pass By) (Madrid: Revista de Archivos, 1906). *Juana de Asbaje* (Madrid: Hernández, 1910) (Essay about Sor Juana Inés de la Cruz).

BIBLIOGRAPHY: Robert R. Anderson, *Spanish American Modernism: A Selected Bibliography* (Tucson: University of Arizona Press, 1970). Homero Castillo, *Antología de poetas modernistas hispanoamericanos* (Toronto and London: Blaisdell, 1966). Manuel Durán, prologue, *Cuentos y crónicas de Amado Nervo* (México: UNAM, Biblioteca del Estudiante Universitario, 1971). Eugenio Florit and José Olivio Jiménez, *La poesía hispanoamericana desde el modernismo* (New York: Appleton Century Crofts, 1968). María Guadalupe García Barragán, "*El bachiller* de Amado Nervo, ¿genes de *Al filo del agua* o teatro de una misma realidad?," *Cuadernos Americanos* 227 (México, 1979): 198-204. Ana María Hernández de López, "Amor, dolor y muerte en cuatro poemas de Amado Nervo," *Cuadernos Americanos* 237, 4 (México, 1981): 135-48. Theodore W. Jensen, "Christian-Pythagorean Dualism in Nervo's *El domador de almas*," *Kentucky Romance Quarterly* 28, 4 (1981): 391-401. José Olivio Jiménez, ed., *Estudios críticos sobre la poesía modernista hispano-americana* (New York: Eliseo Torres, 1975).

OSCAR SOMOZA

NETZAHUALCOYOTL (1402-1472). An important historical and legendary figure in the ancient history of Mexico, Netzahualcóyotl (a name meaning "hungry coyote") was the son of Ixtlixóchitl, a king and lord of Texcoco. He witnessed the assassination of his father by soldiers of Tezozómoc, also a king. Thereafter, for the next several years, Netzahualcóyotl's life was filled with drama and persecution. Eventually, in 1431, or perhaps a year or two later, he became the ruler of Texcoco and spread his dominion through conquests of surrounding areas.

In addition to his importance as a historical figure, Netzalualcóyotl stands out for his magnificent literary contribution. Angel María *Garibay K. and Miguel León-Portilla, both noted students of Indian languages and culture, discerned, through careful research, that the Indian poet was probably responsible for about a dozen poems. What characterizes this poetry is, in essence, an existential theme: anguish and the brevity of life.

Netzalhualcóyotl was much more than a poet and a warrior. He was also a brilliant politician and a skillful leader. Under his direction, Texcoco became a center for the arts and sciences. Among his personal achievements, he counted studies in engineering, astronomy, and related fields. One of the most knowledgeable men of the pre-Columbian period in Mexico, the Aztec leader ruled over a large and prosperous area.

BIBLIOGRAPHY: Carlos María de Bustamante, *Galería de antiguos príncipes mexicanos* (Puebla: Ofna. del Gobierno Imperial, 1821). Alfred Coester, *Historia literaria de la América española* (Madrid: Libr. y Casa Edit. Hernando, 1929), pp. 393-402. Crisanto Cuéllar Abaroa, "Netzahualcóyotl amplía el territorio de Tlaxcalla," in *El Nacional* (May 24, 1956): 10. Rafael García Granados, *Diccionario biográfico de historia antigua de México* (México: Edit. Jus, 1952-1953), vol. 2, pp. 17-51. Angel María Garibay K., *Historia de la literatura náhuatl* (México: Porrúa, 1953-1954), vol. 1, pp. 32, 37, 103, 162, 180, 248, 251, 266, 488-93; vol. 2, p. 381. Frances Gillmore, *Flute of the Smoking Mirror, a Portrait of Netzahualcóyotl, Poet-King of the Aztecs* (Alburquerque: University of New Mexico Press, 1949). Andrés Henestrosa, "El otro gran indio," in *Comunidad Latinoamericana de Escritores Boletín* 12 (1972): 5-9. Miguel León-Portilla, "Netzahualcóyotl de Texcoco. Introducción a su poesía y su pensamiento," in *Universidad de México* 21, 3 (Nov. 1966): i-viii. Aurora M. Ocampo de Gómez and Ernesto Prado Velázquez, *Diccionario de Escritores Mexicanos* (México: UNAM, 1967), pp. 252-53. Francisco de P. Urgell, *Apuntes sobre mitología azteca. Historia de los grandes hombres de Anáhuac* (México: Tip. Literaria, 1878). José María Vigil, *Netzahualcóyotl, el rey poeta* (México: Eds. de Andrea, 1957).

ELADIO CORTES

NORIEGA Hope, Carlos (1896-1934), journalist, essayist, novelist, short story writer, and playwright. He was born in Tacubaya, D.F., on November 6, 1896 and died in Mexico City on November 15, 1934, having lived part of the time in the United States. He studied at the National Preparatory School and at the Law School. He was a technical assistant at the Anthropology Faculty in 1918 and contributed the chapter "Apuntes etnográficos" (Ethnographic Notes) to *La población del Valle de Teotihuacán* (The Population of the Valley of Teotihuacán) (1921). In 1919 he was sent by the newspaper *El Universal* to Los Angeles, where he wrote a dozen articles on what he called "The movie capital," subtitled "Apuntes de viaje de un repórter curioso" (Travel Notes of a Curious Reporter). These were later collected with other works in *El mundo de las sombras* (The Shadow World). For his writings on the cinema he used the pseudonym Silvestre Bonnard. From 1920 until 1934 he was editor of the weekly *El Universal Ilustrado*, which he made the voice of Mexican culture. He was also editor of *La Novela Semanal* from 1922 to 1925. In 1923 he wrote and directed the film *La gran noticia* (The Great News). He also wrote plays, short stories, and short novels. He belonged to the Group of the Seven Dramatic Authors (Los Pirandellos), formed along with Francisco *Monterde, Ricardo Parada León, José Joaquín *Gamboa, Víctor Manuel Díez Barroso, and Lázaro García. The Comedia Mexicana was born out of the remains of this group in 1929.

Some of his stories, such as those collected in *La inútil curiosidad* (Useless Curiosity), deal with love, but have a pessimistic ending. From short fiction he turned his attention to the theater, for which he wrote with skill and a concern for renovation.

WORKS: Essay: *El mundo de las sombras: El cine por dentro y por fuera* (The Shadow World: Inside and Outside the Movies) (México: n.p., 1920). *Apuntes etnográficos del Valle de Teotihuacácan* (Ethnographic Notes on the Valley of Teotihuacácan) (México: Publicaciones de la Dirección de Antropología, 1921). Novel and Short Story: *La inútil curiosidad* (Useless Curiosity), with a lyrical colophon by Francisco Monterde (México: Talleres de *El Universal Ilustrado*, 1923). *"Che" Ferrati, inventor: La novela de los estudios cinematográficos* ("Che" Ferrati, Inventor: The Novel of Cinematographic Studies) (México: Publicaciones Literarias de *El Universal Ilustrado*, April 19, 1923). *El honor del ridículo* (The Honor of the Ridiculous), with a prologue by Salvador Novo (México: Talleres Gráficos de *El Universal Ilustrado*, 1924): contains "El honor del ridículo" (The Honor of the Ridiculous), "Abril" (April), "Las experiencias de Miss Patsy" (The Experiences of Miss Patsy), "El viejo amigo" (The Old Friend), and "Che Ferrati, inventor" (Che Ferrati, Inventor). *Abril* (April) (México: La Novela Corta, 1927). *El chivo encantado* (The Enchanted Goat) (México: La Novela Corta, 1927). *La grande ilusión* (The Grand Illusion) (México: El Universal Ilustrado, n.d.). Theater: *La Señorita Voluntad* (Miss Will), comedy in three acts (México: Talleres Gráficos de la Nación, 1925). *Una flapper* (A Flapper), comedy in three acts (México: n.p., 1925). *Che Ferrati*, comedy, staged in Mexico City in 1926. *Margarita de Arizona*, comedy in three acts, staged in Mexico City in 1929. *Las Experiencias de Miss Patsy y otros cuentos* (The Experiences of Miss Patsy and Other Stories) (México: Premia Editora e INBA, 1986).

BIBLIOGRAPHY: Ermilo Abreu Gómez and Carlos G. Villenave, *Antología de prosistas modernos de México* (Anthology of Modern Mexican Prose Writers) (México: Carlos Rivadeneyra, 1925). Anon., *Biblos* (2d epoch) 1, 4-5, (Aug.-Sept. 1925). P.G.C., "Carlos Noriega Hope: El honor del ridículo," *Antena* 4 (Oct. 1924): 8-9. J. M. González de Mendoza, "Carlos Noriega Hope y *El Universal Ilustrado*" (Lecture), in *Carlos Noriega Hope*, no editor (México: Literature Department, INBA, 1959). Carlos González Peña, *Historia de la literatura mexicana* (History of Mexican Literature) (México: Porrúa, 1928), p. 529. Juan B. Iguíniz, *Bibliografía de novelistas mexicanos* (New York: Burt Franklin, 1970 [reprint of 1926 ed.]), p. 240. Luis Leal, *Bibliografía del cuento mexicano* (México: Ed. de Andrea, 1958), pp. 101-2. Carlos Lozano García and Lázaro Lozano García, "Carlos Noriega Hope . . .," in *Teatro* 11-

12 (Oct. 1956): 12-13, 19. Antonio Magaña Esquivel and Ruth S. Lamb, *Breve historia del teatro mexicano* (México: Eds. de Andrea, 1958), p. 114. Francisco Monterde, *Bibliografía del teatro en México* (México: Monografías Bibliográficas Mexicanas, 1933), p. 234; "Carlos Noriega Hope," *Teatro mexicano del siglo xx*, edited by Francisco Monterde (México: FCE, 1956), pp. 241-42; "Carlos Noriega Hope," in *Carlos Noriega Hope*. Salvador Novo, Prologue to *El honor del ridículo*, pp. 7-10. A. Torres-Ríoseco, *Bibliografía de la novela mejicana* (Cambridge, Mass.: Harvard University Press, 1933), p. 37. Aurora M. Ocampo de Gómez and Ernesto Prado Velázquez, *Diccionario de Escritores Mexicanos* (México: UNAM, 1967), p. 253.

PETER G. BROAD

NOVARO, Octavio (1910-   ), poet and journalist. Born in Guadalajara, Octavio Novar is a graduate of the law school at UNAM. Calling himself a transhuman poet, Novaro as a student directed literary publications and participated in the *El Universal* rhetoric contests. He has taught literature, history, and social sciences at high schools and at Universidad Obrera, and he has been principal at high schools for workers' children. He was press correspondent during the 1947 Interamerican Conference of Foreign Ministers in Brazil; he has also been director of *La Prensa* and *Prensa Gráfica*. Invited by the British Council, he was a World War II correspondent; he has interviewed internationally known personalities, travelled extensively and attended numerous congresses on education and journalism. Novaro was an ambassador to Switzerland during the Lopez Mateos administration, then a representative of an editorial commission for the Secretaría de Educación Pública and was director of Editorial Nuevo Mundo. He was a cofounder and since 1967 has been director of Editorial Novaro. He founded the newspaper *El Popular* and has contributed to *El Universal*, *La Prensa*, *Novedades*, *El Día*, and *México en la Cultura*. He directed *Prensa Gráfica* and *Clarín*, and promoted new literary values in poetry and short the story by supporting *Acento*, *Simbad*, and *Nuevo Mundo* editions. His works are in *Ocho poetas mexicanos* (Eight Mexican Poets) (México: Jus, 1957). His *Inventario de Cenizas* is illustrated by Moreno Capdevilla. An effusive love poet, he was a member of Barandal and also contributed to *Taller*. His poetry describes a realistic society that includes love and revolution; it also has a satirical vein.

WORKS: Poetry: *Sorda la sombra* (The Deaf Shadow) (México: Fabula, 1935). *Canciones para mujeres* (Songs for Women) (México: Simbad, 1936). *Palomas al oído* (Pidgeon Whispers) (México: Simbad, 1937). *Ocho poemas mexicanos* (Eight Mexican Poems) (México: Jus, 1955). *Inventario de Cenizas* (Ashes Inventory) (México: n.p., 1964). *Pliegos de poesía* (Poetry Papers) (México: Castellanova, n.d.), *Vigilias* (Vigils) (México: n.p., 1970). *La niña de Rang Bang* (The Rang Bang Girl) (México: n.p., 1972). *Cantar de Cantares a María* (The Song of Songs to Mary) (México: n.p., 1979). Theater: *Judas o el amor a Dios* (Judas or God's Love), in *México en la Cultura* 684 (April 22, 1962): 1, 6. Fables and Short Stories: *Las jornadas del escriba* (The Writer's Journeys) (México: n.p., 1974).

BIBLIOGRAPHY: Anon., *Ocho poetas mexicanos* (México: Jus, 1957); Biobibliographic entry in *Anuario de la poesía mexicana 1961* (México: INBA, 1962), p. 89; Biobibliographic entry in *Anuario del cuento mexicano 1961* (México: INBA, 1962),

p. 173; "Muestrario de las letras," Review of *Inventario de cenizas*, in *México en la Cultura* 797 (June 28, 1964): 3; "Un gran poeta recuperado: Octavio Novaro, " review of *Inventario de cenizas*, in *Revista de la Semana* (June 28, 1964): 3. Jesús Arellano, *Antología de los 50 poetas contemporáneos de México* (México: Eds. Alatorre, 1952), pp. 13, 185, 457; "Las ventas de Don Quijote," *Nivel* 48 (Dec. 25, 1962): 5. Antonio Castro Leal, *La poesía mexicana moderna* (México: FCE, 1953), p. 375. Frank Dauster, *Breve historia de la poesía mexicana* (México: Eds. de Andrea, 1956), p. 172-76. José Luis Martínez, *Literatura mexicana del siglo XX, 1910-1949*, vol. 1 (México: Ant. Libr. Robredo, 1949), pp. 78, 181; vol. 2 (1950), p. 87. Javier Penalosa, "Nombres, titulos y hechos," review of *Inventario de cenizas*, in *Mexico en la Cultura* 794 (June 7, 1964): 3; "5 noticias literarias importantes del mes en México," *Nivel* 17 (May 25, 1965): 4.

DELIA GALVAN

NOVELO, José Inés (1868-1956), poet and educator. José Inés Novelo was born in Valladolid in the State of Yucatán on April 20, 1868. He studied in Mérida at the Normal School and at the School of Jurisprudence. Later he became a teacher of rhetoric and poetics in the Normal School. In 1902, he was president of the Public Education Council of the State of Yucatan. During his office, Novelo was very enthusiastic in establishing rural schools in Mexico (1909). Novelo occupied several positions during the government of Francisco I. Madero. Mexico's political inestability after 1912 and Novelo's political convictions and ideas were the cause of his long exile in New York and Havana. After his return from exile, he continued to be active in official positions related to education in the State of Yucatan and in Mexico City. In 1937, he was director of *El Diario Oficial de la Federación* (Official Journal of the Federation). Novelo died in Mexico City on September 30, 1956.

Novelo's first book of poetry, *Versos* (Verses) (1893), shows his knowledge of classical poetic techniques and the romantic approach of his poem. The publication of *De mi musa* (From My Muse) (1896) was well received by Modernist poets like Amado *Nervo who emphasized the authentic Hispanic-American virtues of Novelo's inspiration as well as his concern with Mexican traditions. Modern criticism includes Novelo in the group of poets of *Revista Moderna*: Enrique Fernández Granados, Balbino *Dávalos, José Juan *Tablada, and others.

WORKS: *Versos* (Verses) (Mérida: Author's Edition, 1893). *De mi musa* (From My Muse) (Mérida: Author's Edition, 1896). *Gérmenes* (Seeds) (Mérida: Author's Edition, 1905). *Abril* (April) (México: Botas, 1937). *El hombre y otros poemas* (The Man and Other Poems) (México: Botas, 1938). *Mieses de otoño* (Harvests of Autumn) (México: Botas, 1939). *Rezagos líricos* (Lyrical Remnants) (México: Author's Edition, 1949). *Ultimos rezagos líricos* (Last Lyrical Remnants) (México: Author's Edition, 1954).

BIBLIOGRAPHY: Manuel Gutiérrez Nájera, *Obras. Crítica literaria*, vol. 1 (México: UNAM, 1959), pp. 499-501. Julio Jiménez Rueda, *Historia de la Literatura Mexicana* (México: Botas, 1957), p. 249. Amado Nervo, "De mi musa" in *Obras Completas*, vol. 2 (México: Aguilar, 1962), pp. 331-32.

BAUDELIO GARZA

NOVO, Salvador (1904-1974), poet, playwright and journalist. Salvador Novo was born in México City on July 30, 1904. Soon afterwards, his parents moved north to Torreón, where Novo started his education, which was interrupted by the Revolution. Tragedy befell his family when some of its members were killed by Pancho Villa. His father's life was spared, despite his being a Spaniard, because a soldier mistakenly had shot his uncle Francisco, a rich and properous merchant. Novo remained until 1916 in Torreón, where he wrote his first verses. Back in Mexico City, he attended the Escuela Preparatoria (Secondary School) and started what would be his intensive literary life. At school Novo met Xavier *Villaurrutia, Jaime *Torres Bodet, José *Gorostiza, and Jorge *Cuesta, whose friendships would have a lasting and deep influence on him. Together they formed the group known as the Contemporáneos (1928-1931), which was very influential in the cultural life of Mexico. The group founded the magazine *Contemporáneos*, which was short-lived but tremendously significant because it exposed many of the most avant-garde tendencies. (*See* Vanguardist Prose Fiction in Mexico.)

Novo was only eighteen when his first translation, that of the work of Francis James, appeared in *Cultura*, and some of his early poems were published in *El Universal Ilustrado* and in *El Heraldo de México*. In 1924 his first two short plays, *Divorcio* (Divorce) and *La señorita Remington* (Miss Remington) were published in *El Universal Ilustrado*. The following year *Ensayos* (Essays) and *XX Poemas* (Twenty Poems) as well as *Lecturas hispanoamericanas (Spanish American Readings)* appeared. For eight years, from 1924 to 1932, he was director of the Editorial Department of the Education Ministry. From May 1927 to February 1928, he also directed the literary magazine *Ulises*, that he had founded with Villaurrutia. A highlight of this paper was a special section which Novo wrote called "El curioso impertinente," imitating *Don Quijote*. Together with Villaurrutia he took part in the founding of *El teatro Ulises* (The Ulysses Theater), where he translated and directed plays and in which he also acted. From 1930 to 1933 he taught history of theater at the National Conservatory and literature to foreigners at the summer school of the National University, at the same time dedicating himself to writing poetry and to traveling. In 1933 he published *Espejo* (Mirror), an autobiography in verse of his childhood, and *Nuevo amor*, his favorite collection of poems. Also in that year, he published a book of travels, *Jalisco-Michoacán*.

As a reporter at the Panamerican Conference in Buenos Aires, Novo met the Spanish poet Federico García Lorca. Lorca collaborated with Novo by illustrating with drawings the first edition of *Seamen Rhymes*, printed in 1934. His friendship with the Spanish poet resulted in Novo's publishing *El romance de Angelillo y Adela* (The Romance of Angelillo and Adela), inspired by Lorca's *Romancero Gitano*. Following his trip to Argentina, he produced in 1935 another travel book, *Continente vacío, viaje a Sudamérica* (Empty Continent, Journey to South America).

In 1936 he wrote in French *Le Troisiéme Faust*. The book had to be published in Paris since, because of its homosexual overtones, it was considered by the prospective publishers too daring for its time.

He started contributing to *Hoy* with a weekly chronicle about life in the capital. These were later the basis for several books. He dedicated a great deal of his talent to journalism and to essays, some collected and published in 1938 in one of his most important works, *En defensa de lo usado* (In Defense of What Has Been Used). This book was written at the insistance of Gabriela Mistral. Novo also produced many movie scripts. From 1946 to 1952 he headed the Theater Department of INBA, and in 1953 he inaugurated his own theater, La Capilla, an old colonial chapel in which, for four years, he staged and directed a number of plays in addition to directing in other theaters. In 1952 he was elected member of the Academia Mexicana de la Lengua.

As to Novo's literary production, in 1944 he came out with a collection of four sonnets, *Dueño mío* (My Owner) and soon after he published *Florido laude* (Elegant Praise) with drawings by Mary Helen Morgan. He then started to write his memoirs but interrupted his project to publish his *Invitación a la música* (Invitation to Music) and the first edition of one of his major works, *Nueva grandeza mexicana* (New Mexican Greatness), a book inspired by Bernardo de *Balbuena's *Grandeza mexicana*. His serious playwriting really started in 1947 when he made children's adaptations of such works as Cervantes' *Don Quijote* and Luis G. *Inclán's *Astucia*. He also produced an original three-act play, *La culta dama (The Educated Lady)*, in which he demonstrated his mastery, not only as a dramatist but also as a judge of characters, in this case that of high-society Mexicans from the capital. Following this first play, he staged and directed another satirical comedy, *A ocho columnas* (In Eight Columns), in which he criticizes and denounces corrupt journalism. His last three major plays were staged between 1961 and 1963, *Yocasta, o casi* (Yocasta, or Almost), *Ha vuelto Ulises (Ulysses Has Returned)*, and *La guerra de las gordas* (The War of the Fat Ladies).

Novo's work as a stage director and his experience as an actor and an all-around theater man helped him produce an important didactic book, *Diez Lecciones de Actuación Teatral* (Ten Lessons on Theatrical Behavior) (1951). In this work, he demonstrated his extensive mastery of theatrical resources, and like his predecessor Lope de Vega, he established the bases for how an actor must perform and work.

One of Novo's most popular genres was that of the chronicles about the capital. Most of this work was scattered in newspapers and magazines and later collected in several books that gave a very truthful view of Mexican life and history. Because of his extraordinary productivity, he was named by the government as Cronista Oficial de la Ciudad de México in 1965, a position he held until his death on January 13, 1974.

After almost a half century of literary production that included all genres, the impact of Salvador Novo's work is enormous. His poetry is regarded as among the finest in the country. While in some poems he recalls his lost childhood, in others he captures his intimate feelings of love and sadness with a passionate and sharp sensibility, tempered by acid irony. His theater followed a transformation that changed its national character. It is transformed from a classical theater as established by Rodolfo *Usigli, into a forum for social criticism that exalts its pre-Hispanic roots, with works like *Cuauhtémoc* or *El espejo encantado* (The Enchanted Mirror). As an essay writer and journalist, Novo has no equal, for he is credited with changing the ways of the genre. His *A ocho columnas* sharply criticized paid journalism and almost caused a revolution in the press, since many reporters saw thenselves pictured in the play. His three books on presidential periods are an extraordinary exposé of city life. His humorous way of depicting life and the casual manner in which he represented people made Novo an admired journalist.

His last years were embittered by both physical and emotional isolation when his colleagues abandoned him. In a very unpopular move, Novo supported the government in the Tlatelolco massacre. Despite this, he has left an indelible imprint on Mexican life and literature.

WORKS: Theater: "Divorcio," in *El universal ilustrado* (April 30, 1924): 3, 5-6, 47-48. "La señorita Remington," in *El universal ilustrado* 6, 366 (May 15, 1924): 27, 61. *Don Quijote* (México: INBA, 1948). *El coronel Astucia* (México: INBA, 1948). *La culta dama* (México: Imp. Veracruz, 1951); 2nd ed. in *Teatro mexicano del siglo XX* (Néxico: FCE, 1956). *El Joven II* (México: Imp. Muñoz, 1951); 2nd ed. in *Diálogos* (Textos de la Capilla, 1956). *Diálogos* (México: Los Textos de la Capilla, 1956). *A ocho columnas* (México: Textos de la Capilla, 1956). *Don Quijote en la escena* (Monterrey: Universidad of Nuevo León, 1961). *Yocasta, o casi* (México: Textos de la Capilla, 1961). *Ha vuelto Ulises* (México: Ed. Era, 1962). *Cuauhtémoc* (México: Lib. Madero, 1962). *In Pipiltzintzin o la guerra de las gordas* (México: FCE, 1963); 2nd ed. in *Teatro mexicano 1963*, no editor (Madrid: Aguilar, 1965). *El sofá*, in *Cuadernos de Bellas Artes* 4, 8 (Aug. 1963): 53-70; 2nd ed. in *In ticitezcatl o El espejo encantado* (Xalapa: Universidad Veracruzana, 1965). *Antología* (México: Purrúa, 1966). *Diálogo de ilustres en la rotonda*, in *In ticitezcatl . . .*, pp. 164-83. Poetry: *Ensayos* (México: Talls. Graf. de la Nación, 1925). *XX Poemas* (México: Talls. Graf. de la Nación, 1925). *Espejo* (México: Talls. de la Mundial, 1933). *Nuevo amor* (México: La Mundial, 1933); 2nd ed. (México: ARS, 1948). *Canto a Teresa* (Song to Theresa) (México: Fábula, 1934). *Seamen Rhymes*, with drawings by García Lorca (Buenos Aires: F.A. Colombo, 1934). *Romance de Angelillo y Adela* (México: Imp. Mundial, 1934). *Décimas en el mar* (Poems to the Sea) (México: Imp. Mundial, 1934). *Un poema* (One Poem) (México: PLYCSA, 1937). *Poesías escogidas* (Selected Poems) (México: Ed. Cuadernos, 1938). *Dueño mío* (My Owner) (México: A. Chapero, 1944). *Florido Laude* (Elegant Praise) (México: Cultura, 1945). *Poesía (1915-1955)* (Poetry [1915-1955] (México: Impresiones Modernas, 1955). *Sátira* (Satire) (México: Imps. Modernas, 1955). *Antología poética* (Anthology of Poetry) (México: UNAM, 1961). *Poesía* (Poetry) (México: FCE, 1961). *14 Sonetos de Navidad y Año Nuevo* (Fourteen Christmas and New Year Sonnets) (México: Author's Ed., 1968). *Adán desnudo* (Naked Adam) (México: Author's Ed., 1969). *Mea Culpa* (México: EPSA, 1969). Essays: *Ensayos* (Essays) (México: Talls. Graf. de la Nación, 1925). *La educación literaria de los adolescentes* (The Literary Education of the Adolescents) (México: Talls. Graf. de la Nación, 1928). *En defensa de lo usado y otros ensayos* (In Defense of Used Things and Other Essays) (México: Polis, 1938). *Continente vacío* (Empty Continent) (Madrid: Espasa-Calpe, 1935). *Return Ticket* (México: Cultura, 19?8). *Discurso* (Lecture) (México: SEP, 1927). *Jalisco-Michoacán* (México: Imp. Mundial, 1933). *Nueva grandeza Mexicana* (The New Mexican Grandeur) (México: Hermes, 1946). *La televisión* (The Television) (México: INBA, 1948). *Las aves en la poesía castellana* (The Birds in Castillian Poetry) (México: FCE, 1953). *Este y otros viajes* (This One and Other Trips) (México: Stylo, 1951). *Letras vencidas* (Conquered Letters) (Jalapa, Veracruz: Universidad Veracruzana, 1962). *Visión de México* (Vision of Mexico) (México: Madero, 1962). *Toda la prosa* (All the Prose) (México: Empresas Editoriales, 1964). Juárez, Símbolo de la Soberanía Nacional (Juárez, Symbol of National Sovereignty) (México: Sría de Hacienda y Crédito Público, 1966). *México, Imagen de una Ciudad* (Mexico, Image of a City) (México: FCE, 1967). Prologue to *Carta de Villaurrutia a Novo* (Letter of Villaurrutia to Novo) (México: INBA, 1966). History: *El trato con escritores* (Friendship with Writers), 2 vols. (México: INBA, 1961; 2nd vol., 1964). *Breve historia de Coyoacán* (Brief History of Coyoacan) (México: ERA, 1962). *La vida en México en el período presidencial . . .* (Life in México during the Presidential Period of . . .), series of three books, with the same title, for the presidential periods of Lázaro Cárdenas, Manuel Avila Camacho, and

Miguel Alemán (México: Empresas Editoriales, 1964, 1965, 1967). *Cocina mexicana o Historia Gastronómica de la Ciudad de México* (Mexican Cooking or Gastronomic History of the City of México) (México: Purrúa, 1967). *La culta dama*, and Federico S. Inclán, *Hoy invita la güera* (México: Cultura-SEP, 1984).

BIBLIOGRAPHY: Ermilo Abreu Gómez, "El libro de hoy. *Joyas de la amistad*," in *Revista Mexicana de Cultura* 884 (Mar. 8, 1964): 4; Review of *La vida en México en el periodo presidencial de Lázaro Cárdenas*, in *Política* 5, 113 (Jan. 1, 1965): 48. Alfred Adler, review of *La guerra de las gordas*, in *Books Abroad* 38, 3 (Summer 1964):, 294-95. Demetrio Aguilera Malta, "Novo, señor de la palabra," in *El Gallo Ilustrado* 114 (Aug. 30, 1964): 4. Rodolfo Alcaraz, "Un juicio sobre las gordas," in *Ovaciones*, suppl. 70 (Apr. 28, 1963): 4. Federico Alvarez, Review of *Breve historia de la fiebre amarilla*, in *La Cultura en México* 136 (Sep. 23, 1964): xvi. Enrique Anderson Imbert, *Historia de la literatura hispanoamericana*, vol. 2 (México: FCE: 1964), pp. 51, 74, 155, 162. Anon., Review of *Poesía* in *Cuaderno de Bellas Artes* 2, 10 (Oct. 1961): 58-59; Bibliographical note in *Anuario de la poesía mexicana 1962* (México: INBA, 1963), pp. 96-97; Review of *Ha vuelto Ulises*, in *Cuaderno de Bellas Artes* 3, 9 (Sept. 1962): 49; Review of *Breve historia de Coyoacán*, in *Cuaderno de Bellas Artes* 4, 2 (Feb. 1963): 2; Review of *Mil y un sonetos mexicanos*, in *Tiempo* 43, 1102 (Jul. 17, 1963): 47-48; Review of *La guerra de las gordas*, in *Revista de la Semana* (Feb. 2, 1964): 3. "Releamos la prosa del maestro Novo," in *Revista de la Semana* (Sept. 13, 1964): 3; "Novo periodista," in *Revista de la Semana* (Dec. 20, 1954): 3; "Salvador Novo escribió un libreto de ópera," in *Revista de la Semana* (Jan. 23, 1966): 3; "Antología de prosa y verso de Salvador Novo," in *Revista de la Semana* (Sept. 18, 1966): 3. David N. Arce, "Bibliografías mexicanas contemporáneas, XIII, Nómina Bibliográfica de Salvador Novo," in *Boletín de la Biblioteca Nacional* 13, 4 (Oct.-Dec. 1962): 61-89; *Nómina Bibliográfica de Salvador Novo* (México: Biblioteca Nacional, 1963). Jesús Arellano, "Salvador Novo," in *Nivel* 45 (Sept. 25, 1962): 5. Antonio Balmori, Review of *Letras vencidas*, in *México en la Cultura* 706 (Sept. 23, 1962): 9. Mario Bauregard, Review of *La guerra de las gordas*, in *México en la Cultura* 736 (Apr. 28, 1963): 4. Miguel Bautista, Review of *Cuauhtémoc*, in *El Gallo Ilustrado* 31 (Jan. 27, 1963): 1. Salvador Calvillo Madrigal, "Un hilo de Adriadna en el laberinto de Salvador Novo," in *México en la Cultura* 744 (June 23, 1963): 3. Mario Calleros, "Las mesas de plomo de Salvador Novo," in *Ovaciones*, suppl. no. 90 (Sept. 15, 1963): 2. Miguel Capistrán, "Carta de Miguel Capistrán a Salvador Novo, a propósito de su último libro: *La vida en México en el periodo presidencial de Avila Camacho*," in *México en la Cultura* 863 (Nov. 7, 1965): 1-2; "Antología personal de Salvador Novo," in *Diorama de la Cultura* (Sept. 11, 1966): 4. Emilio Carballido, Review of *A ocho columnas*, in *México en la Cultura* 588 (Jun. 19, 1960): 8. Emmanuel Carballo, "La ciudad de México: *Nueva grandeza mexicana*." in *México en la Cultura* 411 (Feb. 3, 1957); Review of *Diálogos*, in *México en la Cultura* 417 (Mar. 17, 1957): 2. "Salvador Novo," in *México en la Cultura* 490 (Aug. 3, 1958): 1, 10; 491 (Aug. 10, 1958): 1, 10. "Salvador Novo, ¿nuevo cronista de la ciudad de México?," in *La Cultura en México* 50 (Jan. 30, 1963): xvi. ¿Quién es Salvador Novo?, in *La Cultura en México* 186 (Sept. 8, 1968): xiv; in *19 protagonistas de la literatura mexicana del siglo XX (México: Empresas Editoriales, 1965)*, pp. 231-62. Antonio Castro Leal, *La poesía mexicana moderna (México: FCE, 1953)*, pp. xxviii, 330-31; Prologue to *Antología de Salvador Novo*, ed. cit. Alí Chumacero, Review of *Letras vencidas*, in *La Cultura en México* 29 (Sept. 5, 1962): xii. Eduardo Colín, *Rasgos* (México: Imp. Manuel León Sánchez, 1934), pp. 111-18.

José de la Colina, Rev. of *Ha vuelto Ulises*, in *Revista Mexicana de Letras* 7-8 (July-Aug. 1962): 54-55. Eladio Cortés, "Salvador Novo y su obra," in *De literatura hispánica*, edited by Eladio Cortés (México: EDIMUSA, 1989), pp. 1-14; "Salvador Novo y el arte del ensayo," in *De literatura*, pp. 15-22; " Novo: La vida en México bajo tres presidentes: Historia o Literatura," in *De literarura*, pp. 23-34; "Elementos míticos en el teatro de Salvador Novo," in *De literatura*, pp. 35-44. Arturo Cova, Review of *La guerra de las Gordas*, in *Revista Mexicana de Cultura* 861 (Sept. 29, 1963): 16. K. B. Crabbe, "An Alternate Interpretation of the Poetry of Salvador Novo," in *Reflexion* 3-4 (1974-1975): 81-99. Frank Dauster, *Breve historia de la poesía mexicana (México: Eds. de Andrea, 1956)*, pp.156-57; "La poesía de Salvador Novo," in *Cuadernos Americanos* 12 (May-June 1961); *Ensayos sobre poesía mexicana (México: Eds. de Andrea, 1963)*, pp. 74-94; "La poesía de Salvador Novo," in *Nivel* 14 (Feb. 25, 1964): 1, 4, 6; "Lo prehispánico en el teatro de Salvador Novo," in *Reflexion* 3-4 (1974-1975): 17-23. Edmundo Domínguez Aragonés, "Crónica novoniana de México," in *El Gallo Ilustrado* 175 (Oct. 13, 1965): 3. Esteban Durán Rosado, Review of *Toda la prosa*, in *Ovaciones* 139 (Aug. 23, 1964): 8. Merlin H. Forster, Review of *Poesía* and *Yocasta, o casi*, in *Revista Iberoamericana* xxviii, 54 (July-Dec. 1962): 386-87; *Los contemporáneos (México: Eds. de Andrea, 1964)*, pp. 83-101, 118-21, 131-33; "Salvador Novo como prosista," in *Acta Neophilológica* 2 (1979): 129-43. Henrique González Casanova, Review of *Cuauhtémoc*, in *La Cultura en México* 44 (Dec. 19, 1962): xv. Enrique González Rojo, Review of *In ticitézcatl*, in *Boletín Bbibliográfico de la Secretaría de Hacienda y Crédito Público* 339 (Mar. 15, 1966): 22. Celestino Gorostiza, *Teatro mexicano del siglo XX* (México: FCE: 1956), pp. iv-xv, 3-4. Raymond L. Grismer and Mary B. Macdonald, *Vida y obra de autores mexicanos (La Habana: Edit. Alfa, 1945)*, pp. 123-25. Miguel Guardia, "El teatro en México. *La culta dama*," in *México en la Cultura* 36 (Sept. 9. 1951): 4-5. Alyce de Kuene, "La realidad existencial y la realidad creada en Pirandello y Salvador Novo," in *Latin American Theater Review* 2, 1 (Fall 1966): 5-14. Ruth S. Lamb, *Bibliografía del teatro mexicano del siglo XX* (México: Eds. de Andrea, 1962), p. 91. Carlos Landeros, "Tan feliz como Novo," in *El Día* (Mar. 6, 1964): 9; "Novo, el poeta," in *Diorama de la Cultura* (April 3, 1966): 3, 6. Luis Leal, *Bibliografía del cuento mexicano (México: Eds. de Andrea, 1958)*, p. 102. Raul Leiva, Imágen de la poesía mexicana contemporánea (México: UNAM, 1959), pp. 165-78. Angel López Fernández, "En torno a un poema de Salvador Novo," in *Reflexion* 3-4 (1974-1975): 100-108. Antonio Magaña Esquivel, *Imagen del teatro* (México, 1940), pp. 83-101; *Sueño y realidad del teatro* (México: INBA, 1949), pp.35-45; "Víspera del teatro mexicano," in *Humanismo* (July 1952): 62.; Review of *El joven II*, in *3 conceptos de la crítica teatral* (México: Libr. Madero, 1962); Review of *La guerra de las gordas*, in *Revista Mexicana de Cultura* 843 (May, 26, 1963): 11; *Medio siglo de teatro mexicano* (México: INBA, 1964), pp. 55-57, 132-34; *Salvador Novo* (México: Empresas Editoriales, 1971). Antonio Magaña Esquivel and Ruth S. Lamb, *Breve historia del teatro mexicano* (México: Eds. de Andrea, 1958), pp. 138-40. José Luis Martínez, *Literatura mexicana siglo XX, 1910-1949*, vol. 1 (México: Ant. Libr. Robredo, 1949), pp. 36-37, 296-98; vol. 2 (1950), p. 88; *El ensayo mexicano moderno* (México: FCE, 1958), pp. 99-100. Carlos Monsiváis, *La poesía mexicana del siglo XX* (México: Empresas Editoriales, 1966), pp. 31-34, 37-39, 489-90. Michele Muncy, *Salvador Novo y su teatro* (Madrid: Atlas, 1970); *Teatro de Salvador Novo* (México: INBA, 1975); "Novo, periodismo y literatura: puntos de contacto," in *XI Annual Hispanic Literaures Conference*, edited by J. C. Mendizábal (Indiana: Indiana University of Pennsylvania, 1985), pp. 217-30; José Emilio Pacheco, Review of *La guerra de las gordas*, in *La Cultura en México* 85 (Oct. 2, 1963): 3; "Notas sobre la vanguardia," in *Casa de las Americas* 20, 18 (Jan.-Feb. 1980): 105-107. Elena Poniatowska, "Salvador Novo," in *México en la Cultura* 438 (Aug. 31, 1957): 5; "Sopa de letras," in *México en la Cultura* 655 (Oct. 1, 1961): 10; "Nota sobre la otra vanguardia," in *Casa de las Américas* 21, 18 (Jan.- Feb. 1981): 103-107. Malkah Rabell, "Salvador Novo," in *México en la Cultura* 590 (July 3, 1960): 12. Luis Reyes de la Maza, "La ópera de Salvador Novo," in *Revista Mexicana de Cultura* 982 (Jan. 23, 1966): 11. Beatriz Reyes Nevares, "De charla con Salvador Novo," in *Siempre!* 585, Sept. 9, 1964, pp. 40-41, 70. Salvador Reyes Nevares, "El ensayo," in *La Cultura en México* 151 (Jan. 6, 1965): vi. José Romano, Review of *Mil y un sonetos mexicanos*, in *México en la Cultura* 750 (Aug. 4, 1963): 9-10. Peter G. Roster, "Bibliografía selecta de Salvador Novo," in *Reflexion* 3-4 (1974-1975): 109-113; "Técnicas irónicas en la poesía de Salvador Novo," in *Reflexion* 3-4 (1974-1975): 24-80; *La ironía como método de análisis: La Poesía de Salvador Novo* (Madrid: Gredos, 1978). Gustavo Sainz, "Escaparate," Review of *La guerra de las gordas*, in *México en la Cultura* 755 (Sept. 8, 1963): 9. Rafael Solana, "Novo el maestro," in *El Libro y el Pueblo* 15 (July 30, 1964): 1-14. Arturo Torres-Rioseco, "Tres poetas mexicanos," in *Revista Iberoamericana* 1 (May 1939): 83-89; *Ensayos sobre literatura latinoamericana* (México: FCE, 1958), pp. 103-104, 177. Rodolfo Usigli, *México en el teatro* (México: Imp Mundial, 1932), pp. 130-31. Carlos Valdés, Review of *Las aves en la poesía castellana*, in *Universidad de México* 3, 10 (June 1954): 31. Esperanza Velázquez Bringas and Rafael Heliodoro Valle, *Indice de escritores* (México: Herrero Hnos., 1928) pp. 198-200. Joseph F. Velez, "Humor en *La guerra de las gordas*, un drama precortesiano de Salvador Novo," in *Explicación de Textos Literarios* 8 (1979-1980): 67-74. Xavier Villaurrutia, *Textos y pretextos* (México: FCE, 1940), pp. 83-88. Ramón Xirau, "Los hechos y la cultura," Review of *Letras vencidas*, in *Nivel* 45 (Sept. 25, 1962): 12. Francisco Zendejas, "Multilibros," Review of *La vida en México en el periodo presidencial de Lázaro Cárdenas*, in *Excelsior* (Dec. 4, 1964): 1B-3B.

MICHELE MUNCY

O

OCAMPO, María Luisa (1905-1974). María Luisa Ocampo was born in Chilpancingo, Guerrero. She studied letters and commerce and had an active career in journalism and business. She also directed a number of public agencies, among them the Ministry of Education's Department of Libraries and School of Librarianship.

Best known as an award-winning playwright and novelist, Ocampo reveals in her literary creations a profound interest in social issues, particularly in the status of women, their problems and contributions to society. Shortly after staging her first play, *Cosas de la vida* (Things of Life), she joined the Group of Seven Authors in an attempt to help the Mexican theater acquire national characteristics as well as to expose the Mexican public to the outstanding European playwrights. Essentially, not only did she excel as a truly Mexican playwright, but she also gained recognition as a translator and adapter of works by Dostoyevsky, O'Neill, and others. Her novelette *La maestrita* (The Little Teacher), considered by some to be her best work, narrates the life of a woman dedicated to the service of her community during the Revolution. Written in first person, it is, at times, markedly subjective and moralizing.

WORKS: Novels: *Bajo el fuego* (Under Fire) (México: Eds. Botas, 1947). *La maestrita* (The Little Teacher) (México: Talleres Gráficos Guanajuato, 1949). *Ha muerto el doctor Benavides* (Doctor Benavides Has Died) (México: Talleres Tipográficos Mercantil, 1954). *Atitlayapán* (México: Unidad Mexicana de Escritores, 1955). *Sombras en la arena* (Shadows in the Sand) (México: Libro-Mex Editores, 1957). *El señor de Altamira* (The Man from Altamira) (México: B. Costa-Amic, 1963). *Una tarde de agosto* (An August Afternoon) (México: B. Costa-Amic, 1966). Plays: *Cosas de la vida* (Things of Life) (México: Talleres Gráficos de la Nación, 1926). *El corrido de Juan Saavedra* (The Ballad of Juan Saavedra) (México: Imp. Mundial, 1934). *La virgen fuerte* (The Strong Virgin) (México: Sociedad General de Autores de México, 1943). *Máscaras* (Masks) (México: Ed. Humanismo, 1953). Other: *Diez días en Yucatán* (Ten Days in the Yucatán) (México: Eds. Botas, 1941).

BIBLIOGRAPHY: John S. Brushwood, *México in Its Novel* (Austin: University of Texas Press, 1966), p. 12. Edna Coll, *Injerto de temas* (San Juan, Puerto Rico: Eds. Juan Ponce de León, 1964), pp. 197-211. Carlos González Peña, *History of Mexican Literature*, translated by Gusta Barfield Nance and Florene Johnson Dunston (Dallas: Southern Methodist University Press, 1968), p. 452. Willis Knapp Jones, *Behind Spanish American Footlights* (Austin: University of Texas Press, 1966), pp. 488-89 and 496. Diane E. Marting, ed., *Women Writers of Spanish America: An Annotated Bio-Bibliographical Guide* (Westport, Conn.: Greenwood Press, 1987), p. 280.

ROBERT K. ANDERSON

OCHOA, Enriqueta (1928-), poet. Ochoa was born in Torreon, Coahuila, on May 2, 1928. At age nine she started writing poetry without being aware of what she was doing. She studied in her native city for her first letters, junior high school, and school of education for elementary schools. She received private lessons in journalism and literature. For several years, she shared her studies with her work of engraved metal in her family jewelry shop. At age nineteen, she published her first book, *Las Urgencias de un Dios* (The Urgencies of a God). After a short period of time in a convent she moved to San Luis Potosí in 1953, searching for new horizons. In the same year, Antonio *Castro Leal included her in his famous anthology, *Poesía Mexicana* (Mexican Poetry). In 1957, she married Francois Toussaint, of French nationality. She lived with him in France and Morocco. In 1964, she returned to Mexico. During 1965-1966, she was professor of Hispanoamerican Literature at UNAM. From 1966 to 1969, she taught classes in the School of Philosophy and Literature at the University of Veracruz in Jalapa. In 1969, she moved to Toluca, where she was professor in the School of Philosophy and Literature at the Escuela Normal Superior. In 1972, she moved to Mexico City, where she worked until 1985 as professor in the College of Sciences and Humanities of UNAM. Since 1985, she has been a researcher at the Secretaría de Educación Pública and director of a literary shop. She is introverted, dedicated to education, not very fond of frequenting with literary colleagues or of promoting herself.

Ochoa's work has been written in loneliness, and for many years she did not reach a big public. It is during the last years that she has been acknowledged; after her publication of *Retorno de Electra* (Return of Electra) in *Lecturas Mexicanas*. She was honored in a great homage in the National Museum of Mexico to celebrate her sixtieth birthday and her nomination for the National Award of Literature in 1988. She is contemporaneous with Jaime Sabines, and Rosario *Castellanos.

The poetry of Enriqueta Ochoa, showing the influence of Milocz, Rilke, and Saint John Perse, is one of the most personal renderings that has been written in Mexico in the last years. In a colloquial tone but carrying biblical echoes, she deals with the most transcendental poetic topics: love and death, Eros and Thanatos. Occasionally, her work resembles that of the mystics. With a language full of musicality, Ochoa writes with exact images and overflowing sincerity, precisely written for her daughter, sister, or some friend. Her poems are painfully personal revelations. Rich in pictorial description, the lyrics of her most important book, *El Retorno de Electra* (Return of Electra) deals with nature as well as inside landscaping, where the elements, full of symbolism, send us to two constants: eroticism and religion.

WORKS: *Las Urgencias de un Dios* (The Urgencies of a God) (México: Ediciones Papel de Poesía, Imp. Miguel N. Lira, 1950). *Los himnos del ciego* (The Hymns of the Blind) (Jalapa: Eds. Caracol Marino, 1968). *Las vígenes terrestres* (The Terrestrial Virgins) (México: Porrúa, 1969). *Cantos para el hermano* (Songs for the Brother) (Jalapa: Universidad Veracruzana, 1973). *Retorno de Electra* (Return of Electra) (México: Diógenes, 1978; México: FCE-SEP, 1987). *Canción de Moises* (Song of Moises) (Jalapa: Universidad Veracruzana, 1984). *Bajo el oro pequeño de los trigos* (Under the Little Gold of the Wheats) (Chapingo: Universidad Autónoma de Chapingo, 1984).

BIBLIOGRAPHY: Jesús Arellano, *Poetas jóvenes de México* (México: Libro-Mex, 1955). Antonio Castro Leal, *Poesía mexicana moderna* (México: FCE, 1953). Rafael

Contreras, *Las miradas de Enriqueta Ochoa a las criptas de la Mística contemporánea* (México: Zacaltepetl, 1984). Carlos Gonzáles Salas, *Antología mexicana de la poesía religiosa, siglo XX* (México: n.p., 1960). Simón Latino, *Antología de la poesía sexual* (Buenos Aires: n.p., 1959). Agustín Velázquez, *Jardín de la poesía mexicana* (México, n.p., 1966).

ESTHER HERNANDEZ-PALACIOS

OCHOA y Acuña, Anastasio María de (1783-1833), poet and novelist. Ochoa y Acuña was born in Huichapán, Hidalgo, on April 27, 1783. He studied philosophy at the college of San Idelfonso, and theology at La Real y Pontifícia Universidad de México. In 1813, he entered the Concilliar Seminary of Mexico and was ordained in 1816. From 1817 to 1827, he occupied different curacies in Querétaro. In 1828, he moved to Mexico City, where he died five years later during a cholera epidemic. His formation was during the transition period between Neoclassicism and Romanticism. Ochoa y Acuña was distinguished by his work as a translator. His translations into Spanish include *Las Herodias* (The Herodias) by Ovidio and *El Bayaceto* (The Bayaceto) by Jean Baptiste Racine. He also assisted in the translation of *La Biblia de Vence* (The Bible of Vence), which was published by Galván. As a poet, he preferred the festive genre. His models were José Iglesias, Lope de Vega, Baltazar de Alcázar, Luis de Góngora, and Francisco Quevedo. Like *Fernández de Lizardi, he was interested in writing about Mexican social life of his time. In *Poesías de un Mexicano* (Poems from a Mexican), he wrote with a picturesque flair about subjects of national interest. He used the pseudonyms Anastasio De Achoso y Ucana and El Tuerto. His novel *Cartas de Odalmira y Elisandro* (Letters to Odalmira and Elisandro) and his comedy *La Huerfana de Tlalnepantla* (The Orphan from Tlalnepantla) are known only by references, because they were never published. It is said thet he developed the narrative and the dramatic genres, respectively. And his poetic interest was in reflecting the customs of the society that surrounded him.

WORKS: *Don Alfonso* (Don Alfonso), tragedy performed in 1811. *Las Herodias* (The Herodias) by Ovidio (México: Imp. de Galván, 1928). *Poesías de un Mexicano* (Poems by a Mexican) (New York: Casa de Lunaza, 1928). *El Amor por Apoderado* (Love by an Agent) (Ms., comedy, s.f.). *La Huérfana de Tlalnepantla* (The Orphan from Tlalnepantla), comedy, known by references. *Cartas de Odalmira y Elisandro* (Letters to Odalmira and Elisandro), novel, known by references.

BIBLIOGRAPHY: Ramón I. Alcaraz, "Ochoa y Acuna," in *Diccionario universal de historia y de geografía*, edited by Manuel Orozco y Berra, 10 vols. (México: Andrade, 1853-1856), wol. 3, pp. 68-75; *El Liceo Mexicano*, vol. 1 (México, n.p., 1844), pp. 152-70. Marcos Arroniz, "Ochoa y Anastasio Acuña," in *Manual de Biografía Mexicana o Galería de Hombres Celebres de México* (Paris: Libr. de Rosa Bouret y Cía., 1857), pp. 252-54. Salvador Cordero, *La literatura durante la guerra de independencia* (París and México: Libr. de la Vda, de Ch. Bouret, 1920), pp. 18-20. Frank Dauster, *Breve Historia de la Poesía Mexicana* (México: Eds. de Andrea, 1956), p. 63. Pedro Henríquez Ureña, "Anastasio de Ochoa," *Antología del Centenario* (México: Imp. de Manuel León Sánchez, 1910), vol. 1, pp. 67-69. Roberto Heredia, *Anastasio de*

Ochoa y Acuña in *Boletín Bibliográfico de la Secretaría de Hacienda y Crédito Público* (México, 1960): 2, 4. Francisco de A. Lerdo, "Ochoa," in *Hombres ilustres Mexicanos*, edited by Eduardo L. Gallo, vol. 3 (México: Imp. de Ignacio Cumplido, 1873-1874). Antonio Magaña Esquivel and Ruth S. Lamb, *Breve historia del teatro Mexicano* (México: Ediciones de Andrea, 1958), p. 51. Gabriel Méndez Plancarte, *Horacio en México* (México: UNAM, 1937), pp. 87-90. Marcelino Menéndez y Pelayo, *Historia de la Poesía Hispano-Americana* (Madrid: Libr. Gral. Victoriano Suárez, 1911), vol. 1, pp. 112-13. Francisco Monterde, *Bibliografía del Teatro en México* in *Monografías Bibliográficas Mexicanas* 28 (México, 1933): 236, 463. Aurelio María Oviedo y Romero, *Biografías de Mexicanos Célebres* (París amd México: Libr. de Ch. Bouret, 1889). Francisco Pimentel, *Obras completas de D. Francisco Pimentel*, 5 vols. (México: Tip. Económica, 1903-1904), vol. 4, pp. 395-426. Francisco Sosa, *Biografías de Mexicanos Distinguidos*: (México: Ed. de la Sría, de Fomento, 1884), pp. 735-37. Arturo Torres-Rioseco and Ralph E. Warner, *Bibliografía de la Poesía Mexicana* (Cambridge, Mass.: Harvard University Press, 1934), pp. 37, 57, 63. Luis G. Urbina, *La vida literaria de México* (Madrid, Hnos. Sáez 1917), pp. 66-67; 250-54. Emeterio Valverde Tellez, *Bio-bibliografía eclesiástica Mexicana* (México: Edit. Jus., 1949), vol. 3, pp. 307-9.

ESTHER HERNANDEZ-PALACIOS

OLAGUIBEL, Francisco M. de (1874-1924), novelist, poet, statesman. Born in Mexico City, Olaguíbel later moved to Toluca with his family. He received his law degree in 1900, then practiced law and taught in several institutions of higher learning in Toluca. He also served in the local Congress before moving back to Mexico City, where he occupied various legislative and administrative posts including that of undersecretary of Foreign Relations.

An active journalist, Olaguíbel wrote for *El Clarín*, *La Tribuna*, and *La Gaceta del Gobierno* in Toluca. In Mexico City he published poems in *Revista Azul* and in *Revista Moderna*. He published *El Imparcial*, contributed to *El Universal* and to various newspapers in Havana, Cuba. In 1894 his novel, *¡Pobre bebé!*, received a literary award from *El Universal*. His poetry is characterized by its musicality, its subtle and recondite technique and its romantic sensibility.

WORKS: Novel: *¡Pobre bebé!* (Poor Baby!) (México: Imp. de El Universal, 1894); 2nd ed. (1901). Poetry: *Oro y negro* (Gold and Black) (Toluca: Patrimonio Cultural y Artístico del Estado de México, 1998). *Canciones de bohemia* (Bohemian Songs) (París: Libr. de Ch. Bouret, 1905). *El poema de Juárez* (Juárez's Poem) (Toluca: n.p., 1906). *Discursos* (Speeches in Honor of Juárez) (Toluca, n.p., 1906). *Rosas de amor y de dolor* (Roses of Love and Sadness) (México: Botas, 1922).

BIBLIOGRAPHY: Alberto María Carreño, *Memorias de la Academia Mexicana* 7 (1945): 201-2; 8 (1946): 218. Francisco Javier Gaxiola, *Gobernantes del Estado de México: Mázquiz, Zavala, Olaguíbel* (México: [s.n.], 1975). Juan B. Iguíniz, *Bibliografía de novelistas mexicanos* (México: Imp. de la Secretaría de Relaciones, 1926), pp. 242-43. Leopoldo Lugones, "Máscaras. Francisco M. de Olaguíbel," *Revista Moderna* (May 6 May,): 145- 47. Amado Nervo, *Semblanzas y crítica literaria* (México: Imp. Universitaria, Serie Letras, 1952), pp. 54-55. Félix F. Palavicini, *Los diputados, lo que*

se ve y lo que no se ve de la Cámara (México: Imp. Francesa, 1916), pp. 53-54.
Victoriano Salado Alvarez, "Carta a don Francisco M. de Olaguíbel," *De mi cosecha*
(Guadalajara: Imp. de Ancira, y Hno., 1899), pp. 1-11.

BARBARA P. FULKS

OLAVARRIA Y FERRARI, Enrique de (1844-1918), novelist, playwright, critic,
historian. Born in Madrid on July 13, 1844, Olavarría y Ferrari moved to Mexico in
1865, was naturalized a Mexican citizen, joined the Liberal party, and began a variety
of political and literary activities. His first novel, *El tálamo y la horca* (The Bridal Bed
and the Scaffold), published in 1868, was a historical novel with typical romantic
intrigue, but his fame rests on his thirty-six volume novel series, *Episodios historicos
mexicanos* (Historical Episodes), written in imitation of Benito Pérez Galdós'
Episodios nacionales (National Episodes).

His literary criticism includes *El arte literario en México* (Literary Art in
Mexico), *Poesías líricas mexicanas* (Mexican Lyric Poetry), and *Reseña histórica del
teatro en México* (A Historical Review of Theater in Mexico). As a historian he
contributed volume 4 to *México a través de los siglos* (Mexico through the Ages), a
multivolume, multiauthor work, and he also published on the subject of pedagogy and
grammar. He died in Mexico City on August 19, 1918.

WORKS: Drama: *El jorobado* (The Hunchback) (México: Díaz de León y White,
1868). *Los misioneros de amor* (Missionaries of Love) (México: Díaz de León y
White, 1868). *La Venus negra* (Black Venus) (México: Ireneo Paz, 1880). Novels: *El
tálamo y la horca* (The Bridal Bed and the Scaffold) (México: Francisco Díaz de
León y White, 1868). *Lágrimas y sonrisas* (Tears and Smiles) (México: Tomas
Francisco Neve, 1870). *Episodios históricos mexicanos* (Mexican Historical Episodes),
36 vols. (México: Francisco Díaz de León y White, 1880-1887). *Venganza y
remordimiento* (Vengeance and Remorse) (México: Francisco Díaz de León y White,
1869). Criticism and History: *El arte literario en México* (Literary Art in Mexico)
(Málaga: Imp. de la Revista de Andalucía, 1877). *Reseña histórica del teatro en México*
(Historical Review of Theater in Mexico) (México: Papelería La Europea, 1895). *El
colegio de San Ignacio de Loyola, vulgarmente Colegio de las Vizcainas, en la actualidad
Colegio de la Paz* (The School of Saint Ignatius Loyola, Commonly Called the School
of the Vizcain Sisters, Presently the School of La Paz) (México: Francisco Díaz de
León, 1889). *Congreso Internacional de Americanistas, primero reunido en México, en
octubre de 1895* (International Congress of Americanists, First Meeting Held in
Mexico, in October of 1895) (México: F. Camacho, 1896). *La sociedad mexicana de
geografía y estadística* (The Mexican Geographic and Statistical Society) (México:
Secretaría de Fomento, 1901).

BIBLIOGRAPHY: Carlos G. Amezaga, *Poetas mexicanos* (Buenos Aires: Pablo E.
Coni and Sons, 1896), p. 368. José F. Godoy, *Enciclopedia biográfica de
contemporáneos* (Washington, D.C.: Thomas W. Cadick, 1898). Carlos González
Peña, *History of Mexican Literature* (Dallas: Southern Methodist University Press,
1968), pp. 318, 326, 333, 351, 355-56. Roberto Núñez y Domínguez, *Centenarios y
cincuentenarios* (México: Talleres Gráficos de La Nación, 1951). Aurora M. Ocampo
de Gómez and Ernesto Prado Velázquez, *Diccionario de escritores mexicanos* (México:

UNAM, 1967), p. 261. Justo Sierra, Prologue to *Lagrimas y sonrisas* (México: Tomas Francisco Neve, 1870). Rodolfo Usiqli, *México en el teatro* (México: Imp. Mundial, 1932), p. 84.

PATRICIA HART AND JOSEF HELLEBRANDT

OLIVA, Oscar (1937-   ).   Oscar Oliva was born on January 5, 1937, in Tuxtla Gutiérrez, Chiapas. A student of various disciplines, including science, engineering, and literature, he has worked as a proofreader and as a teacher in private schools and at the Universidad Veracruzana. He also worked at the Instituto Nacional de Bellas Artes.

As a poet and essayist, Oliva has contributed original work to such literary supplements as *Novedades, El día* and *Ovaciones*. Along with Jaime Augusto *Shelley, Eraclio *Zepeda, Jaime *Labastida, and Juan *Bañuelos, Oliva published some poetry in a controversial anthology, *La espiga amotinada* (1960). The same group also published *Ocupación de la palabra* five years later. Both anthologies have been widely critiqued and somewhat acclaimed.

A man of solitude in his poetry, Oliva faces the shadow of death and examines his own poetic voice in light of the ultimate journey. He received the Premio Nacional de Poesía in 1971 for his book *Estado de sitio* (State of Siege). As its title suggests, the work has a political orientation, focusing on the disturbing aspects of contemporary life and political reality. Not all the poems are, however, of a controversial or protest nature. Furthermore, the poet experiments with a number of different poetic forms, thus indicating a desire to create aesthetically pleasing verse, well structured and balanced.

Oliva believes that it is incumbent upon the poet to deal with social realities, a position he asserts in the prologue to his portion of *Ocupación de la palabra*. In the poem "El artista," he affirms that his intention is to "make the poem break free from the limitations of its paper confines." Although the didactic intent of his poetry is to decry social injustice and political corruption, Oliva does not lose sight of his artistic mission.

In 1984, Oliva published a volume entitled *Trabajo ilegal: poesía, 1960-1982* (Illegal Work: Poetry, 1960-1982). In an interview, Oliva says that this work "is the process of the collapse of a reality like ours, in the middle of class struggles, love, hope and despair." A recurrent poetic theme in these poems is what Oliva sees as the necessity to destroy in order to rebuild.

WORKS: "La voz desbocada" (The Foulmouthed Voice), in *La espiga amotinada* (México: FCE, 1960). *Ocupación de la palabra*, includes *Estado de sitio* (State of Siege) (México: FCE, 1965). *Trabajo ilegal: poesía, 1960-1982* (Illegal Work: Poetry, 1960-1982) (México: Katún, 1984).

BIBLIOGRAPHY: Ricardo Aguilar Melantzón, "Efraín Huerta and the New School of Mexican Poets," *Latin American Literary Review* 11, 22 (Spring-Summer 1983): 41-56. Paula de Allende, "Tres poetas hablan," in *Revista de la Semana* (March 6, 1966): 6. Federico Alvarez, Review of *Ocupación de la palabra*, in *Revista de Bellas Artes* 3 (May-June, 1965): 91-95. Jesús Arellano, "Las ventas de don Quijote," Review of *Ocupación de la palabra*, in *Nivel* 33 (Sept. 25, 1965): 5. Angel Bárcenas,

"Degeneración de la poesía," review of *Ocupación de la palabra*, in *Revista Mexicana de Cultura* 968 (Oct. 17, 1965): 15. Eduardo César, "Sobre *La espiga amotinada*," in *Lugar de encuentro*, edited by Norma Klahn and Jesse Fernández (México: Katún, 1987), pp. 191-204. Merlin H. Forster, ed., *La muerte en la poesía mexicana* (México: Editorial Drógenes, 1970), pp. 159-60. David William Foster, *A Dictionary of Contemporary Latin American Authors* (Phoenix, Ariz.: Publishers Press, 1975), p. 73. Isabel Frayre, "Cinco poetas," in *Revista de la Universidad de México* 20, 2 (Oct. 1965): 28. Carlos González Peña, *Historia de la literatura mexicana*, 15th ed. (México: Editorial Porrúa, 1984), pp. 300-302. Thelma Nava and Miguel Donoso Pareja, "Otra vez la espiga amotinada," in *El Gallo Ilustrado* 162 (Aug. 1, 1965): 1-3. Aurora M. Ocampo de Gómez and Ernesto Prado Velázquez, *Diccionario de Escritores Mexicanos* (México: UNAM, 1967), pp. 261-62. Octavio Paz, Alí Chumacero, José Emilio Pacheco and Homero Aridjis, eds., *New Poetry of Mexico*, bilingual ed. by Mark Strand (New York: Dutton, 1970), pp. 38-39. Alejandro Sandoval, sel., *Veinte años de poesía en México* (México: Joaquín Mortiz, 1988), pp. 43-56. Mauricio de la Selva, Review of *Ocupación de la palabra*, in *Cuadernos Americanos* 5 (Sept-Oct. 1965): 295-300. Ramón Xirau, Review of *Ocupación de la palabra*, in *Diálogos* 6 (Sept-Oct. 1965): 43.

JEANNE C. WALLACE

OLIVARES Carrillo, Armando (1910-1962), poet, essayist, short story writer, and playwright. Born in Guanajuato, Olivares Carrillo obtained his law degree from his state university. He held public positions in the judiciary and legislature in Guanajuato and Veracruz; he taught philosophy and history at Guanajuato University, and then he became its rector. He was an actor in the *entremeses cervantinos*. A founding member of *Garabato*, he also published in *Umbral, Garabato, Novedades*, and *El Nacional*.

Olivares is best known for *Ejemplario de muertes* (Death Exemplary) (1957), stories that explore everyday realism, the fantastic, humor, and the themes of pain, frustration, solitude, anguish, and death. In general, his short stories deal with the physical, metaphysical and ontological.

WORKS: Poetry: *Estatuas de penumbra* (Chiaroscuro Statues) (Guanajuato: Llave, 1940). *Navidad en el mar* (Christmas at Sea) (Guanajuato: Lave, 1954). Essay: *El indio ante el espejo* (The Indian in Front of the Mirror) (Guanajuato: Lave, 1945). *Sinópsis filosófica* (Philosophical Synopsis) (Guanajuato: Llave, 1946). *Alabanza de México* (Praise of Mexico) (Guanajuato: Llave, 1962). Short Stories: *La profecía, juguetes a la manera de Tagore* (The Prophecy, Playthings Tagore Style) (Guanajuato: Llave, 1954). *Ejemplario de muertes* (Death Exemplary), Los Presentes, no. 59 (Mexico, FCE, 1957). *La seca* (The Dry One) (Guanajuato: Llave, 1960). Novel: *Juan Rayas*, not published. Theater: *El integerrimo Madraza* (Madrazo) (Guanajuato: Universidad de Guanajuato, 1960).

BIBLIOGRAPHY: Anon., Review of *El integerrimo Madrazo*, in *México en la Cultura* 632 (April 23, 1961): 4. Juan José Arreola, Note in *El Nacional* (Aug., 1961): 7C. María Elvira Bermúdez, Review of *Ejemplario de muertes*, in *Excelsior* (Feb., 1958):

5C. Emmanuel Carballo, *Cuentistas mexicanos modernos*, vol. 1 (México: Libro-Mex, 1956), pp. 37-39; Review of *Ejemplario de muertes* in *México en la Cultura* 442 (Sept. 8, 1957): 4. Fausto Castillo, Review of *Ejemplario de muertes*, in *Novedades* (Feb. 1957): 2. Alí Chumacero, Note in *Novedades* (Aug. 1960): 7C. Luis Garrido, Note in *Noticias* (Irapuato, Jan. 1960): 5. Luis Leal, *Bibliografía del cuento mexicano* (México: Eds. de Andrea, 1958), pp. 103-4; *Breve historia historia del cuento mexicano* (México: Eds. de Andrea, 1956), pp. 145-46.

DELIA GALVAN

OROPEZA Martínez, Roberto (1927-), poet and critic. Roberto Oropeza Martínez was born in the city of Queretaro on October 16, 1927. During his childhood he accompanied his father, who was an elementary school teacher, in his travels throughout Mexico. At the age of ten he moved to Mexico City, finished his elementary and secondary education there, and began to study medicine. He abandoned that in order to study teaching. He has taught literature, Spanish, and oratory in preparatory schools. He considers himself a disciple of Erasmo *Castellanos Quinto and has edited a book of his poems.

Oropeza Martínez has written poetry since he was very young. His poems are generally clear and simple, although he does experiment to some extent with structure. In *Agua en el cántaro* (Water in the Jug), his love for others and his sensitivity to the beauty of existence, even in difficult moments, come through. The joy and pain of love is a recurring theme in that work. The work contains some striking illustrations as well.

WORKS: Poetry: *Agua en el cántaro* (Water in the Jug) (México: Eds. Ateneo, 1959). *Serenata a la Revolución* (Serenade to the Revolution) (México: Imp. Trejo, 1960). Short Stories: (collaboration) *Cuentos para adolescentes* (Stories for Adolescents) (México: Grupo Ocelotl, 1966). Editions: *Erasmo Castellanos Quinto, Poesía inédita* (Unpublished Poetry), edition and prologue (México: Porrúa, 1962). *Adela Varela de Curto, Cien sonetos* (One Hundred Sonnets), edition and prologue (México: Eds. Ateneo, 1963). *Sor Juana Inés de la Cruz, Los empeños de una casa* (The Obligations of a House) (México: Eds. Ateneo, n.d.). Oratory: *Señores y señoras: he dicho* (Ladies and Gentlemen: I Have Said) (México: Ed. Palenque, 1967).

BIBLIOGRAPHY: Anón, "Poesías no coleccionadas de D. Roberto Oropeza Martínez," *Revista de la Semana* (Jan 30, 1966): 30. Heriberto García Rivas, *Historia de la literatura mexicana*, vol. 4 (México: Textos Universitarios, 1971), p. 356. Aurora M. Ocampo de Gómez and Ernesto Prado Velázquez, *Diccionario de escritores mexicanos* (México: UNAM, 1967), pp. 262-63. R.L. "Review of *Agua en el cántaro*," in *Boletín bibliográfico de la Secretaría de Hacienda y Crédito Público* 325 (Aug. 15, 1965): 20-21.

MARK FRISCH

OROZCO MUÑOZ, Francisco (1884-1950). Orozco Muñoz was born in San Francisco del Rincón, Guanajuato, on October 3, 1884. He spent part of his life in Liege,

Belgium, where he studied medicine. Orozco Muñoz served in the diplomatic corps in Belgium, Spain, and Switzerland. Upon his return to Mexico, he was the director of publications of the National Museum and of the School of Librarians; he worked for the Department of Libraries and was a member of the Seminar in Mexican Culture. On March 8, 1950, he died in Mexico City.

Orozco Muñoz wrote poetry and prose. Two of his books were dedicated to Belgium: *Invasión y conquista de la Bélgica mártir* (The Invasion and Conquest of Martyred Belgium) and *Bélgica en la paz* (Belgium at Peace). He wrote two volumes of poetry: *¡Oh, tú que comienzas a tener un pasado!* (Oh, Thou who Are Beginning to Have a Past!) and *Renglones de Sevilla* (Lines from Seville).

WORKS: Essays: *¡Invasión y conquista de la Bélgica Mártir!* (Madrid: n.p., 1915). *Bélgica en la paz* (México: Librería Cultura, 1919). Poetry: *¡Oh, tú que comienzas a tener un pasado!* (Bruselas: n.p., 1932). *Renglones de Sevilla* (México: La Cigarra, 1947).

BIBLIOGRAPHY: Carlos González Peña, *Historia de la literatura mexicana* (México: Porrúa, 1981), p. 265. Aurora M. Ocampo de Gómez and Ernesto Prado Velázquez, *Diccionario de escritores mexicanos* (México: UNAM, 1967), p. 263.

NORA ERRO-PERALTA

OROZCO y Berra, Fernando (1822-1851). Born on June 3, 1822, in San Felipe del Obraje, Fernando Orozco y Berra studied Latin, philosophy, and medicine, but he chose journalism as his profession. In 1845, he published the theatrical journal *El Entreacto* and later contributed to several politically oriented papers, including *Monitor Republicano*. At the time of his death in 1851, he was the editor of *El Siglo XIX*.

Orozco y Berra wrote some poetry, a few plays, and essays and an autobiographical novel, *La guerra de treinta años* (The Thirty-Year War) (1850). Except for his novel and a few poems, most of his work has never been published. But his novel, even though it has many defects, distinguishes him in a significant way. Carlos *González Peña considers it the first Mexican Romantic novel. It has all of the essential characteristics of a Romantic novel, including the disillusionment of love as the main theme. And a complex, episodic treatment of characters and situations places *La guerra de treinta años* clearly within the framework of the genre. Although it is a novel, it is really about the author's love affairs, somewhat fictionalized and set in Spain rather than Mexico. The title refers to the protagonist's (i.e., author's) thirty-year attempt to find contentment in life without sacrificing his principles and values.

WORKS: *La guerra de treinta años* (The Thirty-Year War) (México: Imp. de Vicente García Torres, 1850).

BIBLIOGRAPHY: Ignacio M. Altamirano, *La literatura nacional* I (México: Edit. Porrúa, 1949), vol. 1, pp. 45-46; vol. 2, pp. 155-65. John S. Brushwood, *The Romantic Novel in Mexico* (Columbia: University of Missouri Press, 1954), pp. 22-26, 29, 42, 76, 83; *Mexico in Its Novel* (Austin and London: University of Texas Press, 1966), pp. 77-78. John S. Brushwood and José Rojas Garciadueñas, *Breve historia de la novela mexicana* (México: Eds. de Andrea, 1959), p. 25. Carlos González Peña, *History of Mexican Literature*, translated by Gusta Barfield Nance and FFlorence Johnson Dunstan (Dallas: Southern Methodist University Press, 1968), p. 228. Juan B. Iguíniz, *Bibliografía de novelistas mexicanos* (México: Imp. de la Sría. de Relaciones, 1926), pp. 245-47. Francisco Monterde, *Bibliografía del teatro en México*, Monografías Bibliográficas Mexicanas (México: Imp. de la Sría de Relaciones, 1933), p. 247. Francisco Pimentel, *Obras completas*, vol. 5 (México: Tip. Económica, 1904), pp. 116-18, 297-302. Francisco Sosa, *Biografías de mexicanos distinguidos* (México: Ed. de la Sría. de Fomento, Ofna. Tip de la Sría de Fomento, 1884), pp. 744-46. Ralph E. Warner, *Historia de la novela mexicana en el siglo xix* (México: Ant. Libr. Robredo, 1953).

JEANNE C. WALLACE

OROZCO y Berra, Manuel (1816-1881). Born on June 8, 1816, in Mexico City, Manuel Orozco y Berra was the son of an insurgent captain, Juan N. Orozco. He studied at the Lancasteriano de Octaviano Chausal School and later enrolled in the School of Mining in 1830 to obtain a degree in topography, which he received in 1834; that same year he moved to Puebla. He also studied law, receiving his degree in 1847. He served as counselor at the court of Tlaxcala. He returned to Mexico City as government counsel, and in September of 1852, he was named archivist then director of the National Archives. In 1856 he received the following commissions: to edit the *Carta General de la Republica*, to create the *Diccionario geográfico*, and to write the *Carta geográfica del Valle de México*. In September of 1857 he was appointed secretary of public works. Orozco went on to hold various other governmental positions which included minister of the Supreme Court (1863); member of the Comisión Científica de México; named by Maximilian as under secretary of the Ministry of Public Works (1864); state counselor (1865); and director of the National Museum (1866). In 1866 he advised Maximilian to leave Mexico and evade a bloody fight. His advice was not taken, however, and upon the death of Maxmilian and the installation of the new government, Orozco y Berra was incarcerated and condemned to four years in prison. Because of poor health, he was allowed to return home in that same year. He never returned to political or public office. He dedicated himself to research and teaching, and also belonged to several academic and scientific societies.

Orozco y Berra collaborated on several newspapers of Puebla and Mexico City, including *El Porvenir* and *El Sainete*, and literary publications such as *La Ilustración Mexicana* and *El Museo*. He wrote poetry and was a translator and producer of theatrical works. He also dedicated himself to write about geography, history, and ethnography. Between 1853 and 1856 he wrote *Geografía de las lenguas y carta ethnográfica de México* (Geography of Languages and Ethnographic Map of Mexico), which was the first work of this type done in the country. Among his other works on geography are *Diccionario universal de historia* (Dictionary of Universal History) and its *Apéndice* (Appendix); *Memoria para la carta hidrográfica del Valle de México* (Codicil to the Hydrographic Map of the Mexican Valley) (1864), and *Memoria para el plano de la ciudad de México* (Codicil to the City Plan of Mexico) (1867), which in spite of their modest titles have a great deal of historic and geographic importance; *Materiales para una cartografía mexicana* (Materials for Mexican Cartography) (1871), which includes some of the first maps of America since the sixteenth century; *Apuntes para la historia de la geografía de México* (Notes on the History of Mexican Geography), which studies the evolution and organization of the territorial divisions. Among his best known historical works are *Historia antigua de México* (Ancient History of Mexico) and *Historia de la dominación española en México* (History of Spanish Domination in Mexico), the latter work not published until 1938 since the author died living it unfinished. It seems, however, that it was a revision of and complement to *Historia de México* by Father Andrés Cavo. Orozco y Berra was one of the first to employ the anthropological sciences in historical investigation and was the first to use, in an integrated and organized manner, the bibliographical archive, giving his historical works fresh interpretations.

WORKS: *A mi madre* (To My Mother), monologue in verse (México: Libr. Teatral de Juan Lechuga, n.d.). *Noticia histórica de la conjuración del Marqués del Valle* (Historical Notice of the Conspiracy of the Marquis del Valle) (México: R. Rafael, 1853). *Diccionario universal de historia y de geografía* (Universal Dictionary of History and Geography), 7 vols. (México: Libr. de Andrade, 1853-1855). *Apéndice al diccionario universal de historia y de geografía* (Appendix to the Universal Dictionary of History and Geography), 3 vols. (México: J.M. Andrade and F. Escalante, 1855-1856). *Geografía de las lenguas y carta etnogrráfica de México* (Geography of Languages and Ethnographic Map of Mexico) (México: J.M. Andrade and F. Escalante, 1864). *Historia de la geografía en México* (History of Mexican Geography) (México: Sría. de Fomento, 1880). *Historia antigua y de la conquista de México* (Ancient History of the Conquest of Mexico) 4 vols. and atlas (México: Gonzalo A. Esteva, 1880); other ed. in 2 vols., *Historia antigua y de las culturas aborígenes de México* (México: Fuente Cultural, 1954); in 4 vols., with a study by Angel Ma. Garibay K., biography of the author, and three bibliographies by Manuel León Portilla (México: Ed. Porrúa, S.A., 1955). *Apuntes para la historia de la geografía en México* (México: F. Díaz de León, 1881). "Conquistadores de México" (Conquerors of Mexico), in the appendix of *Sumaria relación de las cosas de la Nueva España*, by Baltasar Dorantes de Carranza (México: Museo Nacional, 1902). *Historia de la dominación española en México* (History of Spanish Domination in Mexico), 4 vols., Col. Bibl. histórica mexicana de obras inéditas, no. 8 (México: Ant. Libr. Robredo, by J. Porrúa e Hijos, 1938).

BIBLIOGRAPHY: Guillermo Díaz Paja and Francisco Monterde, *Historia de la Literatura Española e Historia de la Literatura Mexicana* (México: Editorial Porrúa, S.A., 1968), pp. 532-33. Carlos González Peña, *Historia de la literatura mexicana. Desde los orígenes hasta nuestros días* (México: Editorial Porrúa, S.A., 1981), pp. 235-37. Francisco Monterde, *Bibliografía del Teatro en México* (New York: Burt Franklin, 1970), p. 247. Aurora M. Ocampo de Gómez and Ernesto Prado Velázquez, *Diccionario de escritores mexicanos* (México: UNAM, 1967), pp. 263-65.

JOSEPH VELEZ

ORTIZ, Luis Gonzaga (1825-1894). Born in Mexico City on April 14, 1825, Luis Gonzaga Ortiz, a noted poet and journalist, was especially interested in the fine arts. Educated in Mexico, he was an experienced traveler who incorporated into his work

484 ORTIZ, Luis Gonzaga

scenes and sensations from his trips, particularly focusing on his time spent in Italy in 1865. Installed as editor of *Diario Oficial* upon his return from this journey, Ortiz excelled in editorial management and was considered an average writer.

Among his literary pursuits was his interest in and cultivation of erotic poetry, a genre with which he achieved considerable success and fame. He also translated several French and Italian works into Spanish. Like most of his contemporaries, he contributed to journals, such as *El Nacional* and others, which reflected the cultural climate of the time. The poem "La boda pastoril" (The Pastoral Wedding) is claimed to be the best of his traditional literary work, written within the framework of the Romantic school. Nostalgia, tenderness, and poetic charm characterize some of his work. Also in the same school is his novel *Angélica*, inspired by his experiences in Italy. Like many of the Romantic works of the time, it is considered overly sentimental and verbose.

He is also credited with introducing the genre of the chronicle in Mexico, a literary field which would occupy a permanant place in the annals of Mexican literature. He died on May 28, 1894, a successful editor and journalist.

WORKS: *Poesías* (Poetry Pieces) (México: Imp. de I. Cumplido, 1856). *Algunas poesías líricas* (Some Lyrical Poems) (México: Ofna. Tip. de la Sría. de Fomento, 1895). *Angélica: Recuerdos de un viaje a Italia* (Angelica: Memories of a Trip to Italy) (México: n.p., 1871). *El vizconde de Muhldorf* (The Viscount of Muhldorf) (México: n.p., 1871). *Ayes del alma* (Sighs of the Soul) (México: n.p., 1872). "Florencio M. del Castillo: algunos rasgos biográficos, su carácter, sus obras" (Florencio M. del Castillo, Some Biographical Traits, His Character, His Works), in Florencio M. del Castillo, *Obras completas* (México: n.p., 1872. *Francesca de Rimini*, translation of the tragedy by Silvio Pellico (México: José María Sandoval, 1882). *Detrás de la nube un ángel* (An Angel Behind the Cloud), 1887, not published.

BIBLIOGRAPHY: Carlos G. Amézaga, *Poetas mexicanos* (Buenos Aires: Imp. de Pablo E. Coni e hijos, 1896), p. 137. John S. Brushwood, *The Romantic Novel in Mexico* (Columbia: University of Missouri Press, 1954), pp. 40, 76; *Mexico in Its Novel* (Austin: University of Texas Press, 1966), p. 109. Luis Gonzaga Obregón, *Breve noticia de los novelistas mexicanos en el siglo XIX* (México: Tip. de O. R. Spíndola y Cía, 1889), p. 32. Manuel Gutiérrez Nájera, *Obras. Crítica literaria*, vol. 1 (México: UNAM, 1959), pp. 529-32. Andrés Henestrosa, "La nota cultural," in *El Nacional* (Dec. 9, 1965): 3. Juan B. Iguíniz, *Bibliografía de novelistas mexicanos* (México: Imp. de la Sría. de Relaciones, 1926), pp. 247-49. Francisco Monterde, *Bibliografía del teatro en México* (México: Monografías Bibliográficas Mexicanas, 1933), pp. 464-65. Aurora M. Ocampo de Gómez and Ernesto Prado Velázquez, *Diccionario de Escritores Mexicanos* (México: UNAM, 1967), pp. 265-66. Enrique Olavarría y Ferrari, *El arte literario en México*, 2nd ed. (Madrid: Espinosa y Bautista, [1878]), pp. 59-62; *Poesías líricas mexicanas*, 3rd ed. (Madrid: Perlado, Páez y Cía, 1910), pp. 168-69. Francisco Sosa, *Los contemporáneos* (México: Imp. de Gonzalo A. Esteva, 1884), pp. 7-11. Arturo Torres-Rioseco, *Bibliografía de la novela mexicana* (Cambridge, Mass.: Harvard University Press, 1933), p. 39. Arturo Torres-Rioseco and Ralph E. Warner, *Bibliografía de la poesía mexicana* (Cambridge, Mass.: Harvard University Press, 1934), p. 63. José Zorrilla, *México y los mexicanos* (México: Eds. de Andrea, 1955), pp. 124, 126, 129.

JEANNE C. WALLACE

ORTIZ DE MONTELLANO, Bernardo (1899-1949), poet and critic. Ortiz de Montellano was born in Mexico City on January 3, 1899 where he died on April 13, 1949. He began writing at a very young age. He was a student at the Escuela Nacional Preparatoria, where he met and began collaborating with the writers who would become part of the literary group the Contemporáneos. (*See* Vanguard Prose Fiction in Mexico). In 1918, together with Jaime *Torres Bodet, José *Gorostiza, Enrique *González Rojo, and Luis Garrido, he formed the Ateneo de la Juventud. The group was called this in honor of the group by the same name formed ten years earlier by *Henríquez Ureña, Alfonso *Reyes, José *Vasconcelos, and Antonio *Caso. He worked for the SEP, where he was in charge of textbook revisions, and taught at a number of universities. In 1928, he, Bernardo J. Gastélum, and the other Contemporáneos, started the literary magazine *Contemporáneos*, from which the group gets its name. Ortiz de Montellano served as editor for three years, from 1929 to 1931. He also directed the magazine *Letras de México* in 1941, and collaborated in the formation of *Cuadernos Americanos* in the same year.

Ortiz de Montellano was a very well-educated and cultured person who kept up with international literary trends and movements and was inspired by Paul Valéry. His themes include the mysterious and fantastic, the pre-Columbian Indian world, and surrealist and Freudian references. In his well-known poem *Primer sueño* (First Dream) (1931), the author tells of the premonition in which he meets the Spanish poet Federico García Lorca, whom he never actually met, and reveals the Spaniard's untimely death, which was to occur five years later.

He perfected the translations that Mariano Rojas had done of the nahuatl poetry and published them in *Contemporáneos*. Even more useful was his *La poesía indígena de México* (Indigenous Poetry of México) (1935), which is an interpretation of the spiritual significance of the poetry rather than of its historical importance. His plays *El sombrerón* (The Big Hat) (1931) and *La cabeza de Salomé* (Salome's Head) (1943) are based on themes in the Nahuatl poetry of the *Popol-Vuh* and of the *Chilam Balam de Chumayel*. In these works, he is able to blend the ancient themes with the new language and rhythm that was popular during his time. His best-known work, published posthumously by the University of México, is *Sueño y poesía* (Dream and Poetry) (1952).

WORKS: Poetry: *Avidez* (Greediness) (México: Ediciones del Ateneo de la Juventud, Librería Cultura, 1921). *El trompo de siete colores* (The Top of Seven Colors) (México: Cultura, 1925). *Red* (Net) (México: Contemporáneos, 1928). *Primer sueño* (First Dream) (México: Contemporáneos, 1931). *Sueños* (Dreams) (México: Contemporáneos, 1933). *Muerte de cielo azul* (Death of Blue Sky) (México: Cultura, 1937). *Sueño y poesía* (Dream and Poetry), preliminary note by Wilberto Cantón, Letras Series, no. 13 (México: UNAM, 1952). Theater: *Pantomima* (Pantomime), for marionets, in *El Espectador* 1, 9 (May 29, 1930): 3. *El sombrerón* (The Big Hat), puppet theater performed by the puppets of the Casa del Estudiante Indígena, in *Contemporáneos* 9, 32 (Jan. 1931): 71-96; also with *La cabeza de Salomé* (Salome's Head) (México: La Estampa Mexicana, 1946). *La cabeza de Salomé*, dramatic poem, in *El Hijo Pródigo* 1, 3 (June 1943): 165-67; also with *El sombrerón*, (México: La Estampa Mexicana, 1946). Short Story: *Cinco horas sin corazón* (Five Hours without a Heart) (México: Letras de México, 1940). *El caso de mi amigo Alfazeta* (The Case of My Friend Alfazeta), prologue by Henrique González Casanova, vignettes by Luis García Robledo (México: Col. "Lunes," no 21, 1946). Anthology: *Antología de cuentos mexicanos* (Anthology of Mexican Stories), prologue and notes by Ortiz de Montellano (Madrid: Calleja, 1926). Essay: *Esquema de la literatura mexicana moderna* (Outline of Modern Mexican Literature) (México: Contemporáneos, 1931). *La poesía indígena de México* (Indigenous Poetry of México) (México: Talleres Gráficos de la Nación, 1935). *Figura, amor y muerte de Amado Nervo* (Figure, Love and Death of Amado Nervo), Colección Vidas Mexicanas (México: Xóchitl, 1943). "Literatura indígena y colonial mexicana" (Indigenous and Colonial Mexican Literature), in *Biblioteca Enciclopédica Popular*, no. 113, (México: SEP, 1946). "Del diario de mis sueños" (From the Diary of My Dreams), unpublished, fragments in *Cuadernos Americanos* (Jan.-Feb., 1949): 217-29. Translation: T.S. Eliot, *Miércoles de ceniza* (Ash Wednesday), translation by Ortiz de Montellano (México: Espiga, 1946).

BIBLIOGRAPHY: Jesús Arellano, *Antología de los 50 poetas contemporáneos de México* (México: Alatorre, 1952), pp. 33-40, 455. John S. Brushwood, "*Contemporáneos* and the Limits of Art," *Romance Notes* 2 (Spring 1964): 128-32; and *Mexico in Its Novel*, 1st ed., 1966 (Austin: University of Texas Press, 1975), pp. 119, 191. Wilberto Cantón, Preliminary notes to *Sueño y poesía* (México: UNAM, 1952). Alfredo Cardona Peña, "Carta de Montellano," *El Nacional* (Nov.10, 1950): 5C; and in *Semblanzas Mexicanas*, Biblioteca Mínima Mexicana, no. 10 (México: Ediciones Libro-Mex., 1955), pp. 120-26. Antonio Castro Leal, "La poesía mexicana moderna," *Letras Mexicanas*, no. 12 (México: FCE, 1953), pp. xxviii, 263. Jorge Cuesta, *Antología de la poesía mexicana moderna* (México: Contemporáneos, 1928), p. 154. Frank Dauster, *Breve historia de la poesía mexicana*, Manuales Studium, no. 4 (México: Ediciones de Andrea, 1956) pp. 160-62; and *Ensayos sobre poesía mexicana*, Colleción Studium, no. 41 (México: Ediciones de Andrea, 1963), pp. 95-107. Jesús Flores Aguirre, "La voz de un poeta mexicano en Perú," *México en la Cultura* 42 (Nov. 20, 1949): 3. Merlin H. Forster, *Los Contemporáneos, 1920-1932, perfil de un experimento vanguardista mexicano*, Colección Studium, no. 46 (México: Ediciones de Andrea, 1964), pp. 56-67, 124, 133-136; and *Historia de la poesía hispanoamericana* (Clear Creek, Ind.: American Hispanist, 1981), p. 141. Merlin H. Forster and K. David Jackson, *An Annotated Guide to Vanguardism in Latin American Literature* (Westport, Conn.: Greenwood Press, 1989). Jean Franco, *An Introductuion to Spanish-American Literature* (Cambridge: Cambridge University Press, 1966), pp. 263-64. José María González de Mendoza, "La obra de Bernardo Ortiz de Montellano," *Cuadernos Americanos* 4 (Aug.-Sept., 1949): 262-74. Carlos González Peña, *Historia de la literatura mexicana*, 1928 (México: Porrúa, 1966), p. 273. Ruth S. Lamb, *Bibliografía del teatro mexicano del siglo XX* (México: Eds. de Andrea, 1962), p. 95. Luis Leal, *Breve historia del cuento mexicano* (México: Eds. de Andrea, 1956), pp. 100-102; *Bibliografía del cuento mexicano* (México: Eds. de Andrea, 1958), p. 105. Raúl Leiva, "La poesía de Bernardo Ortíz de Montellano," in *Cuadernos Americanos* (March-April, 1959): 201-13; and in *Imagen de la poesía mexicana contemporánea* (México: UNAM, 1959), pp. 77-89, 361. José Luís Martínez, *Literatura mexicana siglo XX, 1910-1949* (México: Ant. Libr. Robredo, 1949), vol. 1, pp. 30, 32-33, 98, 149-53, 342; vol. 2 (1950), p. 91. Alfonso Mendez Plancarte, "Simpatías y diferencias," review of *Figura, amor y muerte* by Amado Nervo, in *El Universal*, in 4 installments (Dec.13, 20, 27, 1943 and Jan. 17, 1944). Carlos Monsiváis, *La poesía mexicana del siglo XX*, (México: Empresas Editoriales, 1966), pp. 31-34, 43-44, 347. Aurora M. Ocampo de Gómez and Ernesto Prado Velázquez, *Diccionario de escritores Mexicanos* (México: UNAM, 1967), pp. 266-67. Octavío Paz, *Poesía en movimiento* 1966 (México: Siglo Veintiuno Ed., 1980), pp. 385-95. Guillermo Sheridan, *Los Contemporáneos Ayer* (México: FCE, 1985). Ana Ortiz de Montellano Taylor, "Surrealist Perspective on Bernardo Ortiz de Montellano's *Sueños*," Ph.D. Diss., Yale University, 1979. Various, *Una botella al mar*, letters by Jorge Cuesta, José Gorostiza, Jaime Torres Bodet, Xavier Villaurrutia, about Ortiz de Montellano's *Sueños* (México: Rueca, 1946). Philip Ward, ed., *The Oxford Companion to Spanish Literature* (Oxford: Clarendon Press, 1978), p. 432.

EDNA A. REHBEIN

OTHON, Manuel José (1858-1906). A poet and a lawyer, Manuel José Othón is best known for his sensitive interpretations of the Mexican landscape. He was born to a middle-class family in San Luis Potosí on June 14, 1858, and died in this same city forty-eight years later, on November 28, 1906. Despite Othón's love for poetry, he became a lawyer, and spent most of his life serving as a judge in the tranquil surroundings of the small towns of northern Mexico. He started writing and publishing poems in the local papers from the time he was an adolescent. Most of these early poems were collected in *Poesías*, a book he eventually rejected as too simple and immature. Othón's fame soon spread to the capital, where his works began to appear in Mexico's most prestigious journals, *Revista Azul*, *Revista Moderna*, *El Mundo Literario*, and *El Mundo Ilustrado*. By education and taste, Othón was a classicist, an admirer of Horace, Virgil, Garcilaso de la Vega, and Fray Luis de León. By temperament, however, he was a romanticist, whose descriptions of nature were imbued with his individualistic spirit. But he was also a man of his time, a fact that allowed him to write works that appealed to a more modern sensibility. Despite his modern sensibility, however, he did not like Modernism and wrote his long poem, *El himno de los bosques* (The Hymn of the Forests) to counterpose it to Gutiérrez Nájera's* *Tristissima Vox* (Sad voice). This poem proved conclusively that the classical style of his verse was in no way inferior to the more contemporary expression of the Modernists. His best-known book, *Poemas rústicos*, portrays the beauty of the Mexican landscape by blending a mastery of form with a controlled expression of his feelings. The timeless quality of his poetry earned him an admiration that went beyond the narrow limits of literary schools. In addition to his poetry, Othón wrote narrative fiction and plays. In his tales and short novels the elaboration of his feelings for nature and for the peasants prevails. His theatrical pieces have strong affinities with the melodramatic, sentimental late-Romantic style of the Spaniard José de Echegaray.

WORKS: POETRY: *Poesías* (Poems) (San Luis Potosí: n.p., 1880). *Nuevas poesías* (New Poems) (San Luis Potosí: n.p., 1883). *Ultimas poesías* (San Luis Potosí: n.p., 1888). *Poemas rústicos (1890-1902)* (Rustic Poems) (México: Aguilar y Vera, 1902). *Noche rústica de Walpurgis* (Rustic Walpurgis Night) (México: Imp. Escalante, 1907). *El himno de los bosques* (Hymn of the Forests) (México: Ed. Capullo, 1908). Theater: *Después de la muerte* (After Death) (México: Ed. Dávalos, 1884). *Lo que hay detrás de la dicha* (What Lies behind Good Fortune) (México: Ed. Dávalos, 1886). *El último capítulo* (The Last Chapter) (México: Kaiser, 1906). Other Works: *Obras completas* (Complete Works), edition and prologue by Jesús Zavala (México: Edit. Nueva España, 1945). *Epistolario* (Letters), edited by Jesús Zavala (México: UNAM,

1946). *Poesías y cuentos* (Poems and Short Stories), selection, study, and notes by Antonio Castro Leal (México: Porrúa, 1963).

BIBLIOGRAPHY: Baltazar Dromundo, *Manuel José Othón, su vida y su obra* (México: n.p., 1959). Genaro Estrada, *Poetas nuevos* (México: n.p., 1916). J. López Portillo, *Elogio de Manuel José Othón* (México: 1907). Alfonso Reyes, *Los "Poemas rústicos" de Manuel José Othón* (México: Ateneo de la juventud, 1910; 2nd ed. UNAM, 1962). P. C. Rivera, *Manuel José Othón. Clásico y estóico* (México: n.p., 1939).

MARIA A. SALGADO

OWEN, Gilberto (1905-1952). Of Irish ancestry, Gilberto Owen was born in El Rosario, Sinaloa, on February 4, 1905. As a youth, he studied in Toluca and Mexico City. Jorge *Cuesta, a classmate and close friend at the National Preparatory School, greatly influenced his intellectual development. At the invitation of Xavier *Villaurrutia, both of these cultured young men became affiliated with the Ulises and Contemporáneos groups. (*See* Vanguardist Prose Fiction in Mexico.) Owen later became a diplomat, serving his country in Ecuador, Perú, Colombia, and the United States. While working as vice-consul in Philadelphia, he died on March 9, 1952.

Owen penned some essays and two short novels, but he was known primarily as a poet who referred to himself as the "theological conscience of the Contemporáneos." His verses, influenced by Rubén Darío, Stephane Mallarmé, T. S. Eliot, Juan Ramón Jiménez, and others, emphasize the themes of solitude, desolation, and the antagonism of time in the face of an unintelligible world. Although his originality and spiritualism helped bring new values to the Mexican letters of his time, he has never achieved the full measure of reputation to which his work entitles him. This has been attributed to the fact that he spent so much time in foreign lands as a diplomat and that his writings were not readily available until the posthumous publication of his complete works, *Poesía y prosa* (Poetry and Prose), in 1953.

WORKS: Poetry: *Desvelo* (Insomnia) (México: Ed. del autor, 1925). *Línea* (Line) (Buenos Aires: Ed. Proa, 1930). *Libro de Ruth* (The Book of Ruth) (México: Eds. Firmamento, 1944). *Perseo vencido* (Perseus Conquered) (Lima: Universidad Nacional Mayor de San Marcos, 1948). *Poesía y prosa* (Poetry and Prose) (México: UNAM, 1953). *Primeros versos* (First Verses) (Toluca: Escuela de Artes y Oficios, 1957). Novels: *La llama fría* (The Cold Flame) (México: El Universal Ilustrado, 1925). *Novela como nube* (México: Eds. de Ulises, 1928). Other: *Obras* (Complete Works), edited by Josefina Procopio (México: FCE, 1953).

BIBLIOGRAPHY: Effie Boldridge, "The Poetic Process in Gilberto Owen," *Romance Notes* 14, 3 (Spring 1973): 476-83; "The Poetry of Gilberto Owen," Ph.D. diss., University of Missouri 1970. John S. Brushwood, *México in its Novel* (Austin: University of Texas Press, 1966), pp. 196-99. José Sergio Cuervo, "El mundo poético de Gilberto Owen," Ph.D. diss., University of New York at Buffalo, 1974. Frank Dauster, "El recinto inviolable," in his *Ensayos sobre poesía mexicana* (México: Eds. de Andrea, 1963), pp. 108-19. Merlin H. Forster, "Jorge Cuesta y Gilberto Owen," in his *Los contemporáneos, 1920-1932* (México: Eds. de Andrea, 1964), pp. 102-16. Jaime García Terrés, *Poesía y alquimia. Los tres mundos de Gilberto Owen* (México: Eds. Era, 1980). Tomás Segovia, "Owen: el símbolo y el mito," *Nueva Revista de Filología Hispánica* 29, 2 (1980): 556-73.

ROBERT K. ANDERSON

P

PACHECO, Cristina (1941-), journalist, short story writer. Cristina Pacheco was born in San Felipe, Guanajuato, on September 13, 1941. Her family moved to San Luis Potosí and soon after to Mexico City, where young Cristina began her studies at a preparatory school and later took Spanish literature at the UNAM. In 1960, she started writing for *Novedades* and *El Popular*. She married the writer Emilio *Pacheco in 1962, and by 1964 she was a contributor to the magazine *Sucesos*. Her articles for this journal were signed with the pseudonym of Juan Angel Real, and the columns lasted three years under the name Ayer y hoy (Yesterday and Today). Pacheco used an interesting technique of writing imaginary interviews in which any topic could be discussed, so that two points of view could be read in each article. While she was writing for *Sucesos,* she was also directing women's magazines, *La Familia* (The Family), *La mujer de hoy* (Today's Woman), and *Crinolina*.

In 1966 she was hired as an editorial writer by *El Universal*, and again she wrote in a dialogue form. A few months later, she went to *El Sol*, at first doing the same kind of work as before, but soon she started interviewing people, in many cases from the lowest stratum of society. Her first interview, a talk with José Pagés Llergo, was very important; he is a renowned newspaperman who had never being interviewed before. As a result of that meeting, Pacheco's fame as a successful journalist grew. In 1976, Pagés Llergo lured her to work for *Siempre!*, giving her the job of interviewing writers, politicians, and even common people. Although she still writes for that paper, she has long written a column for *El Día* called "Para vivir aquí." She also writes for *Unomasuno* and has a weekly section, "Mar de historia," in *La jornada*.

Cristina Pacheco's debut as a TV commentator on Channel 13, and later on Channel 11, came about as the result of an interview with Juan de la *Cabada. The two agreed to work together, thus initiating a popular talk show, "De todos modos, Juan te llamas" (Anyway, Your Name Is Juan), which lasted two years. For the past thirteen years, she has been anchoring another popular program, "Aquí nos tocó vivir."

Her first book, *Para vivir aquí* (To Live Here), was published in 1982. A selection of the chronicles that appeared in *El Día* from 1977 to 1980, it covers a wide rage of subjects and people. Pacheco describes what Victor Hugo would call "the misérables," or the forgotten, the characters and colors never seen by the tourist. The most abject poverty and the people who live in it are what Pacheco brings to the book. Perhaps her predecessor could be Angel de *Campo, who already saw at the beginning of the twentieth century what separated the beleaguered proletariat from those members of society who could enjoy the pleasures of life. The sociopsychological value of this first book is incalculable because of the sheer number of "marginados" living today in the Mexico City metropolis.

Her subsequent books also follow the same line of exposing the problems, the filth, the desperation, the lack of communication, and the margination of the poor segment of society. Her short stories reflect the life of the people of the city, the homeless, the abandoned. Treating her subjects with understanding, love, and imagination, she tries to capture their plight and their struggles.

Cristina Pacheco has the ability to transmit in her pages the aims and wishes of the lowest class of people. Through her writing, she gives them dignity. Her characters are realistically portrayed, as is the society in which they circulate.

A recurrent theme in her essays and stories deals with people who abandon the countryside in search of a better life in the city. Since her own parents were farmers, she identifies easily with those who leave their rural homes. Her work speaks largely of the tragedy which befalls many of those who, seeking this renewed lease of life, find only despair and increased hardship.

Her book *La Luz de México* (The Light of Mexico) (1988) is a collage of interviews with painters and photographers. This book differs from her previous work in that many of those whom she interviews are successful and productive members of society. Nonetheless, she exposes their struggles to climb up the social ladder. *La Luz de México* constitutes, like the previous books, a very realistic exposition of a certain segment of the population. It is based in her work in *Unomasuno* and *Siempre!* and is already considered one of the best chronicles of life in Mexico today.

WORKS: *Para vivir aquí* ((To Live Here) (México: Grijalbo, 1982). *Sopita de fideo* (Vermicelli Soup) (México: Océano, 1984). *Cuarto de Azotea* (Room in the Terrace) (México: SEP, 1986). *Zona de desastre* (Disaster Zone) (México: Océano, 1986). *La voz de la tierra* (The Voice of the Earth) (México: SARH, 1986). *La última noche del "Tigre"* (Tigre's Last Night) (México: Océano, 1987). *Luz de México* (Light of Mexico) (Guanajuato: Gobierno del Estado de Guanajuato, 1988). *El corazón de la noche* (The Night's Heart) (México: Eds. El Caballito, 1990).

BIBLIOGRAPHY: Anon., Review of *La voz de la tierra*, in *Casa de las Américas* 26, 64, (Sept.-Oct. 1987): 71-74. Manuel Blanco, Review of *Sopita de fideo*, in *El Nacional* (July 27, 1983): 5. Fausto Castillo, Review of *La última noche del "Tigre"*, in *El Día* (July 1987): 7. Mercedes Charles, "Navegando por el 'Mar de historias.' in *FEM* 11, 56 (México, Aug. 1987): 38-39. Miguel Angel Flores, Review of *Sopita de fideo* in *Proceso* (July 1983): n.p. Manuel Mejía Valera, Review of *Sopita de fideo* in *Excelsior* (July 10, 1983): n.p. Arturo Molina, Review of *La última noche . . .*, in *El Sol de Morelia* (June 1987). Carlos Monsivais, Prologue to *La Luz de México* (Guanajuato: Gobierno del Estado de Guanajuato, 1988), pp. 9-17. Juan José Reyes, Review of Sopita de fideo in *El Nacional* (July 27, 1983): 7. Rafael Solana, Review of *Sopita de fideo* in *El Día* (June 24, 1983): n.p.; Review of *La última noche del "Tigre"* in *Siempre!*, (June 1987): n.p.

MICHELE MUNCY

PACHECO, José Emilio (1939-). Pacheco was born in Mexico City, on June 30, 1939. He studied in the School of Law and the School of Philosophy and Literature of the Universidad Nacional Autónoma de México. He started his writing career with the book of short stories *La sangre de Medusa* (The Blood of Medusa) and with a series of poems published in literary magazines that were collected in a volume entitled *Los elementos de la noche* (The Elements of Night). In 1969 he was awarded the National Prize of Poetry of Aguascalientes for his book *No me preguntes cómo pasa el tiempo* (Don't Ask Me How Time Passes), and in 1973 he won the Prize Villaurrutia for his narrative.

Pacheco's international reputation is based mainly on his poetry, but he is also the author of two novels and several volumes of short stories. In addition, Pacheco is highly regarded as a literary critic, essayist, and translator. He has served on the editorial board of several literary journals, edited several important anthologies of Mexican poetry, collaborated on an anthology of poetry with Octavio *Paz, and translated numerous French and American poets into Spanish.

One of the prominent Mexican poets of the generation after Octavio Paz, Pacheco has written eight books of poetry. In *Los elementos de la noche* he gathers all the poetry he produced between 1958 and 1962. This first volume unveils a powerful poetic personality, delicate, yet striking in imagery. *El reposo del fuego* (Repose of Fire), published in 1966, is a long poem, divided in three sections of fifteen poems each. In this collection Pacheco reveals himself as an accomplished artist sure of his task. *Para matar el tiempo* (To Kill Time) shows even greater maturity. Pacheco's three volumes of poetry (*Elementos de la noche, Reposo del fuego* and *No me preguntes cómo pasa el tiempo*) (Don't Ask Me How the Time Goes By), form a unique parallel with the evolving disillusionment, anxiety, and protest that mark the post- World War II poetry of Mexico and much of Latin America. The progression within these three books brings to light not only an important stage in a poet's growth and maturity, but also embodies the persistent struggle in contemporary Latin American poetry to express social preoccupations without suppressing a lyrical impulse and aesthetic ideals. In his two recent books of poetry, *Irás y no volverás* (You Will Go and You Will Not Return) and *Islas a la deriva* (Drifting Islands), Pacheco enriches and refines his art, confirming his preeminence in contemporary Mexican poetry.

Pacheco's poetry tends toward brevity and economy of language, and it is introspective and metaphysical. The Mexican author is troubled by the cyclic flow of time and the impossibility of recapturing prior experience. He probes deep beneath the surface, often in unconventional forms and with brilliant images, in order to reach the essential meanings of life and experience. His work shows a continuity of poetic worldview characterized by his concern with the incessantly changing elements of time. Man, in the center of the flux, has no fixed perspective as he watches his world continually disintegrating about him. Contemporary man is both agent of destruction in his historical moment and victim of the timeless cosmic process. Pacheco presents man's disharmony with contemporary circumstance, his alienation and nostalgia for a lost past.

Pacheco has written several volumes of haunting and poignant short stories: La sangre de Medusa (Medusa's Blood); *El viento distante* (The Distant Wind), which he substantially revised and augmented in the edition of 1969; and *El principio del placer* (The Pleasure Principle), probably his best-known volume of short stories. In these stories fantasy and reality, past and present fuse constantly to create an unusual atmosphere where a bizarre and unpredictable world coexists with the familiar. These qualities are emphasized by the use of a lyrical language that resembles prose poems rather than narrative.

Throughout the works, rich in variety of ideas and approaches to writing, certain principles remain constant. Pacheco's attention focuses on the condition of mankind and the forces that make life unbearable. To him, history, or life, is the repetition of the same events and feelings. Perhaps the most important characteristic of his short stories is a preoccupation with social and political matters. Pacheco, however, conveys his political ideas in a seemingly objective fashion. Pacheco's narrative techniques are versatile. His style, narrative point of view, and form are constantly varied to suit each subject and the angle from which it is portrayed. A story typical of his style is "Fiesta brava" in *El principio del placer*.

Morirás lejos (You Will Die Far Away), Pacheco's first novel, originally published in 1967 and then revised and amplified in 1977, is experimental. It combines prose with poetry, fiction with document, alluding to other forms such as painting or the cinema, as well as discussing the functions of literature through nonliterary forms of writing such as official documents, records, or newspapers. The novel discusses the role of fiction and the problems of perspective in both art and reality. *Morirás lejos* is divided into five major sections that are interwoven throughout the text. The first and principal part takes place in contemporary Mexico City where an ex-Nazi is being constantly watched by another man, perhaps a Jew. Alternating with these passages are various narratives relating to the persecutions of the Jews. They are divided into four main sections: the siege of Jerusalem by Titus's Roman legionnaires, the destruction of the Warsaw ghetto in 1943, life in the Nazi concentration camps, and Hitler's death. The juxtaposition of these narratives forces the reader to participate in the creation of the work of art by bringing together the two lines of narrative.

The parallel development of document and fiction, which continually intertwine, tends to dissolve the barriers between the different events. History is cyclical and repetitive; the problems are eternal and universal. Pacheco succeeds in creating a unique work of art by using an innovative structure, highly imaginative stylistic devices, and distinctive narrative techniques that place special demands on the reader to convey his image of humanity.

His most recent novel, *La batalla en el desierto* (The Battle in the Desert), is a short *Bildungsroman*. In a bourgeois voice, nostalgically recalling the Mexico City of the 1940s, Pacheco tells of a boy falling in love with his friend's mother, who later commits suicide. This novel is more sociallyoriented than experimental. Its subject reflects a dominant theme in Pacheco: the invasion of Mexico by North American capital and values, which destroy the city and the family, both financially and culturally. This is mirrored in the adolescent protagonist's first love, loss of innocence, capitulation to materialism based on U.S. models, and the destruction of everything he loved in both his personal and collective past.

José Emilio Pacheco, one of Mexico's most versatile and prolific young writers, has enriched and developed contemporary Mexican literature with his innovative narrative and poetry.

WORKS: Poetry: *Los elementos de la noche* (México: UNAM, 1963). *Arbol entre dos muros* (México: UNAM, 1963). *Tree between Two Walls*, translated by E. Doon and G. Brotherston (Los Angeles: Black Sparrow Press, 1969). *El reposo del fuego* (México: FCE, 1966). *No me preguntes cómo pasa el tiempo* (México: Joaquín Mortiz, 1969); *Don't Ask Me How the Time Goes By*, translated by Alastair Reid (New York: Columbia University Press, 1978). *Irás y no volverás* (México: FCE, 1973). *Isla a la deriva* (México: Siglo XXI, 1976). Story: *La sangre de Medusa* (México: Cuadernos del Unicornio, 1958; México: La máquina de escribir, 1978). *El viento distante* (México: Era, 1963); rev. and enl., 1969) (México: Era, 1977). *El principio del placer* (México: Joaquín Mortiz, 1972). Novel: *Morirás lejos* (México: Joaquín Mortiz, 1967): rev. and enl., 1977 (México: Montesinos, 1980). *La batalla en el desierto* (México: Era, 1981).

BIBLIOGRAPHY: Barbara A. Bockus, "José Emilio Pacheco cuentista," *Journal of Spanish Studies* 7 (1969): 5-21. J. A. Duncan, "The Themes of Isolation and Persecution in José Emilio Pacheco's Short Stories," *Ibero-Amerikanisches Archiv* 4 (1978): 243-51; J. A. Duncan, *Voices, Visions and a New Reality* (Pittsburgh: University of Pittsburgh Press, 1986), pp. 35-62. Agnes M. Gullón, "Dreams and Distance in Recent Poetry by José Emilio Pacheco," *Latin American Literary Review* 6, 11 (Fall-Winter 1977): 36-42. Thomas Hoeksema, "José Emilio Pacheco: Signals from the Flames," *Latin American Literary Review* 3, 5 (Fall-Winter 1974): 143-56. Y. Jiménez de Baéz, D. Morán, and E. Negrín, *La narrativa de José Emilio Pacheco* (México: Colegio de México, 1979). Hugo J. Verani, "Disonancia y desmitificación en *Las batallas en el desierto* de José Emilio Pacheco," *Hispamérica* 45 (1985): 29-40.

NORA ERRO-PERALTA

PAGAZA, Arcadio (1839-1918), also known as Clearco Meonio. Arcadio Pagaza was born in Valle de Bravo, México, on January 6, 1830. On finishing his preparatory studies in Valle de Bravo, he enrolled at the Conciliary Seminary in México in 1858, and in 1862 received his priestly orders. As priest he served the cities of Taxco, Cuernavaca, and Tenango del Valle, and in 1895 he was named bishop of Veracruz, which position he occupied until his death on September 11, 1918.

A well-educated humanist, Pagaza enjoyed a lifelong study of the classic poets, which endeavor showed itself in both his translations and in his original works. He was accepted in the Arcadian Academy of Rome with the name Clearco Meonio. Pagaza's first book of verse, *Murmurios de la selva* (Murmurs of the Forest), was greeted with admiration. Marcelino Menéndez y Pelayo speaks of Pagaza as "one of the most polished classical poets who today adorn Spanish literature." He completed a unique work, translating into Spanish the complete lyric works of Horace. In addition, Pagaza translated some of Virgil's epilogues and several books of the *Aeneid*. His love of the classic poets found its way into his own poetry, best known in his descriptive sonnets such as those of the *Sitios poéticos del estado de Veracruz* (Poetic Sites of the State of Veracruz).

WORKS: *María* (México: Tip. de La Voz de México, 1890). *Horacio, Version parafrástica de sus Odas* (Horace, Paraphrastic Version of His Odes) (Jalapa, Veracruz: Imp. El Progreso, 1905). *Virgilio, Trad. parafrástica de las Geórgicas, cuatro libros de la Eneida y dos Eglogas* (Virgil, Paraphrastic Translation of the Georgics, Four Books of the *Aeneid* and Two Eclogues) (Jalapa, Veracruz: Tip. de Luis Junco, 1907). *Obras completas de Publio Virgilio Maron* (Complete Works of Publius Virgilius Maron), translated into Spanish, vol. 1 (Jalapa, Veracruz: Imp. Católica, 1913). *Selva y mármoles* (Forest and Marble), 19 (México: UNAM, 1940); 2nd ed. (1955). *Epistolario de Joaquín Arcadio Pagaza* (Letters of Joaquín Arcadio Pagaza) (San Luis

Potosí: Estilo, 1960). *Poesía* (Poetry) (Jalapa, Veracruz: Universidad Veracruzana, 1985).

BIBLIOGRAPHY: Leopoldo Ayala, *El Virgilio mexicano* (México: Imp. Manuel León Sánchez, 1930). Aurora M. Ocampo de Gómez and Ernesto Prado Velázquez, *Diccionario de escritores mexicanos* (México, 1967), pp. 271-72. Carlos González Peña, *History of Mexican Literature*, translated by Gusta Barfield Nance and Florene Johnson Dunstan (Dallas, Texas: Southern Methodist University Press, 1968), pp. 126, 128, 282, 284-85. Julio Jiménez Rueda, *Letras mexicanas en el siglo XIX* (México: FCE, 1944), pp. 97, 112, 152-53.

FILIPPA B. YIN

PALACIOS, Adela, (1908-), novelist, poet, essayist, short story and textbook writer. Born in Mexico City, Adela Palacios is the widow of Samuel *Ramos. She attended teachers college and typesetting school and took courses of literature at UNAM; she has been teacher and principal, with interests in pedagogy, a writer with the Popular Commission on Public Education, assistant to the president of the Association for Free Textbooks, and a member of the Education Academy.

Winner of over twenty literary prizes, she was a member of Grupo Barandal. A surrealist writer, she prefers the novel. Her poetry has a classical trait with modern development.

WORKS: Short Stories: *Cuadernos escolares* (School Motebooks) (México: Talleres Gráficos del Norte, 1935). *El angelito: Tres cuentos humorísticos* (The Little Angel: Three Humorous Short Stories) (México: Talleres Gráficos del Norte, 1949). *Mi amado Pablo* (My Beloved Pablo) (México: Del Bosque, 1953). *La isla de las mariposas* (The Butterfly Island) (México: n.p., 1964). *Colo Tuit-Tuit* (México: n.p., 1969). Narrative: *Normalista* (México: Olimpo, 1953). *El viaje de los niños del libro en la mano* (The Book in Hand Children's Trip) (México: n.p., 1964). Novel: *Muchachos* (Boys) (México: Talleres Gráficos del Norte, 1945). *Adrian Rubi* (México: Talleres Gráficos del Norte, 1950). *Nacidos para pelear* (Born to Fight), in *Ultimas noticias de Excelsior* (México: Tip. Excelsior, 1951). *El hombre* (The Man) (México: Olimpo, 1955). *Tangente* (Tangent) (México: n.p., 1974). Poetry: *Yo soy tus alas* (México: Escritores y periodistas, 1960). *Viaje* (Málaga, Spain: Dardo, 1961). *Lustros de Eva* (México: n.p., 1968). Essay: *Nuestro Samuel Ramos: Homenaje* (México: Del Bosque, 1960). *Autorretrato de cincuenta años* (México: Ed. del Club de Mujeres, 1964) Other works not published: *La perla Pan* (The Pan Pearl). *El perro de la luna* (The Moon Dog). *Ilde Azar* (1981). *Zaguán cerrado* (Closed Vestibule) (1981). *Como caña de azucar* (Like Sugar Cane). *Ferrani Chaquira* (1985). *Mirta Lemus* (1986). *Los palacios de Adela* (Adela's Palaces) (1986). *Normalista* (School Teacher). *Muchachos* (Boys and Girls). *Ancla del trino* (Trill's anchor).

BIBLIOGRAPHY: Anon., "Poetisa quincuagenaria . . .," *Revista de la Semana* (March 1, 1964): 3. Jesús Arellano, Review of *El hombre* in *Metáfora* 9 (July-Aug. 1956): 38. Emmanuel Carballo, Review of *El hombre*, in *México en la Cultura* 371 (April 1956): 2. Esteban Duran Rosado, "Un poema a la paz y a los recuerdos" review of *Autorretrato de cincuenta años* in *Revista de la Cultura* 888 (April 5, 1964):

15. R.L., Review of *El viaje de los niños del libro en la mano* in *México en la Cultura* 817 (Nov. 15, 1964): 15. Luis Leal, *Bibliografía del cuento mexicano* (México: Eds. de Andrea, 1958), p. 107.

DELIA GALVAN

PALACIOS, Emmanuel (1906-   ). Born in Tolimán, Jalisco, on June 12, 1906, Emmanuel Palacios was a doctor by profession and also held important positions in government. He cultivated his talents as a poet, literary critic, and essayist and was greatly influenced by the intellectuals associated with the *Bandera de provincias* (1929-1930) and *Contemporáneos* (1928-1931), literary reviews of Guadalajara and Mexico City, respectively. (*See* Vanguardist Prose Fiction in Mexico.)

Many of Palacios' writings are found scattered in a variety of magazines and literary supplements published in these two cities. His only published collection of verses, *Vida a muerte* (Life to Death), reveals him to be a refined poet who endeavors to express the world of the sensations in a totally original fashion. His propensity for totally original images or metaphors, as well as his use of "popular" meters, has led some critics to identify Federico García Lorca as a major source of inspiration. His poems are also recognized for their terseness, steady rhythms, and unique balance. His essay *Mariano Azuela: un testimonio literario* (Mariano Azuela: A Literary Testimony) reveals him to be a capable literary critic.

WORKS: Poetry: *Vida a muerte* (Life to Death) (México: Simbad, 1937). Other Works: *Mariano Azuela: un testimonio literario* (Mariano Azuela: A Literary Testimony) (Guadalajara: Universidad de Guadalajara, 1952). *Mariano Azuela y su obra* (Mariano Azuela and His Work) (Los Altos, Jalisco: n.p., 1954).

BIBLIOGRAPHY: Frank Dauster, *Breve historia de la poesía mexicana* (México: Eds. de Andrea, 1956), p. 165. Andrés Henestrosa, *Aguinaldo poético* (México: INBA, 1956), p. 83. Aurora M. Ocampo de Gómez and Ernesto Prado Velázquez, *Diccionario de escritores mexicanos* (México: UNAM, 1967), p. 273.

ROBERT K. ANDERSON

PARDO García, Germán (1902-   ), poet, editor, and journalist. Born in Ibagui, Colombia, Pardo García He had a bitter and painful childhood. As an infant, he was completely paralyzed, and his mother died when he was four. Pardo García was raised by a superstitious and resentful stepmother, and by the Jesuits. He published his first poems in 1918, and has lived in Mexico since 1931. Here he founded the Gaceta de Cultura and directed *Nivel*. A prolific writer, Pardo García is known as an important poet. His poetry portrays a resentful, solitary man.

WORKS: Poetry: *Voluntad* (Will) (Bogotá: n.p., 1930). *Los júbilos ilesos* (The Unscathed Joys) (n.p.: n.p., 1933). *Los cánticos* (The Canticles) (n.p.: n.p., 1935). *Los sonetos del convite* (The Sonnets of the Feast) (n.p: n.p., 1935). *Poderíos* (Power) (n.p.: n.p., 1937). *Presencia* (Presence) (n.p.: n.p., 1938). *Claro abismo* (Clear Abyss) (n.p.: n.p., 1940). *Sacrificio* (Sacrifice) (n.p.: n.p., 1943). *Poemas contemporáneos* (Contemporary Poems) (México: n.p., 1949). *Lucero sin orillas* (Star without Limits) (México: Cuadernos Americanos, 1952). *Acto poético* (Poetic Act) (México: Cuadernos Americanos, 1953). *Poemi contemporanei* (Contemporary Poems) (Torino: Quaderni Iberoamericani, 1953). *U.Z. llama al espacio* (U.Z. Calling Space) (México: Cuadernos Americanos, 1954). *Eternidad del ruiseñor* (Eternity of the Nightingale) (México: Cuadernos Americanos, 1956). *Hay piedras como lágrimas* (There Are Stones Like Tears) (México: Ed. Cultura, 1957). *Centauro al sol* (Centaur under the Sun) (México: Ed. Cultura, 1959). *Osiris preludial* (Preludial Osiris) (México: Ed. Cultura, 1960). *La cruz del sur* (The Southern Cross) (México: Ed. Cultura, 1960). *30 años de labor del poeta colombiano Germán Pardo García: 1930-1960)* (Thirty Years Work of the Colombian Poet Germán Pardo García) (México: Ed. Libros de México, 1961). *Los angeles de vidrio* (The Crystal Angels) (México: Ed. Cultura, 1962). *El defensor* (The Defender) (México: Ed. Cultura, 1964). *Los relámpagos* (Lightnings) (México: Ed. Cultura, 1965). *Mural de España* (Mural of Spain) (Guatemala: Ed. Cultura, 1966). *Elegía italiana* (Italian Elegy) (México: Ecuador, 1966). *Himnos del Hierofante* (Hymns of the Hierophant) (México: FCE, 1969). *Apolo Thermidor* (Apollo Thermidor) (México: Libros de México, 1971). *Escándalo* (Scandal) (México: Libros de México, 1972). *Desnudez* (Nakedness) (México: Libros de México, 1973). *Mi perro y las estrellas* (My Dog and the Stars) (México: Libros de México, 1974). *El héroe* (The Hero) (México: Libros de México, 1975). *Apolo Pankrátor 1917-1975* (Apollo Pankrator 1917-1975) (México: Ed. Libros de México, 1977), anthology which includes an autobiography.

BIBLIOGRAPHY: Mary E. Arenas, "La obra poética de Germán Pardo García," *DAI* 32 (1971): 2670A; George Washington University. Carlos Arturo Caparroso, *Glosa sobre Germán Pardo García* (México: Finisterre, 1969). Boyd G. Carter, "Rodeando a Germán Pardo García y su obra: Enfoques y juicios," *Thesaurus* (Instituto Caro y Cuervo, Colombia) 33 (1978): 495-507. David L. Dickson, "Unity and Development in the Poetry of Germán Pardo García," *DAI* 35 (1974): 3733A, University of Southern California. Carlos García Prada, *Estudios hispanoamericanos* (México: El Colegio de México, 1945), pp. 205-18. Estella Irizarri, "El poeta Germán Pardo García: Clásico, cósmico y americano," in *Cuadernos Americanos* 192 (1974): 243-49. Raúl Leiva, "Summa poética de Germán Pardo García," in *Novedades* 765 (1961): 5. Rafael M. Lucena, Germán Pardo García y su obra poética," in *Novedades* 1011 (1966): 6. James Willis Robb, "Los ángeles y astronautas de Germán Pardo García," in *Explicación de Textos Literarios* 9, 2 (1981): 177-82.

ALFONSO GONZALEZ

PARRA, Porfirio (1856-1912), author of philosophical, scientific, and historical works. Novelist and poet, Porfirio Parra was the leading writer of the second generation of positivists and a major disseminator of positivist doctrines in Mexico. Parra was born in Chihuahua, on February 26, 1856. He began his preparatory studies at the local Instituo Científico y Literario and received a scholarship from his home state, which allowed him to continue his studies at the Escuela de Medicina in Mexico City. As a medical student he became interested in positivism, the prevailing philosophical orientation of that epoch. He was a disciple of Gabino Barreda, whom he replaced as professor of logic at the Escuela Nacional Preparatoria in 1878, the year that he received his medical degree. Parra held various teaching posts in Mexico City. He was director of the Escuela Nacional Preparatoria and the Escuela de Altos Estudios and taught physiology and pathology at the Escuela de Medicina and mathematics at the Escuela de Agricultura. He was a member of the Academia Nacional de Medicina and a corresponding member of the Real Academia Española, and he maintained affiliation with numerous other scientific and literary organizations. He founded the newspapers *El Método* and *El Positivismo*, and contributed to publications such as *La Libertad, Revista de la Instrucción Pública Mexicana, Revista de Chihuahua, Revista Positiva, Gaceta Médica,* and *El Universal.* Elected several times as a deputy to the national congress from Chihuahua and Hidalgo, Parra also served in the Senate, where he represented Aguascalientes. He died in Mexico City on July 5, 1912.

Parra wrote on a variety of academic subjects ranging from science and medicine to history and philosophy. In the latter field he authored a textbook, *Nuevo sistema de lógica inductiva y deductiva* (New System of Inductive and Deductive Logic), which was used at the Escuela Preparatoria. As a historian, he produced several volumes including *Estudio histórico-sociológico sobre la Reforma de México* (Sociohistorical Study of the Reform in Mexico) and *Plan de una historia de Chihuahua* (Outline for a History of Chihuahua). His poetry and speeches were also collected in book form. Other works worthy of mention include his dramatic sketch *Lutero* (Luther) and *Oda a las matemáticas* (Ode to Mathematics). Parra's only novel, *Pacotillas*, is a satirical work that takes aim at society's excesses. Containing elements of *costumbrismo* and employing a narrative technique reminiscent of that of Manuel *Payno, the novel tells the story of an idealistic albeit lazy medical student, Pacotillas, who leaves school, goes to live with his lover, and takes up journalism. The protagonist's major interests are literature and his own personal independence. Unwilling to renounce his social and political opinions, he becomes a victim of his own illusions.

WORKS: *Lutero* (Luther) (México: Tip. de Antonio Mena, 1886). *Oda a las matemáticas* (Ode to Mathematics) (México: Oficina. Tip. de la Sría de Fomento, 1887). *Pacotillas* (Barcelona: Tip. de Salvat e hijo, 1900). *Nuevo sistema de lógica inductiva y deductiva* (New System of Inductive and Deductive Logic) (México: Tip. Económica, 1903). *Estudio histórico-sociológico sobre la Reforma en México* (Sociohistorical Study of the Reform in Mexico) (Guadalajara: Imp. de La Gaceta de Guadalajara, 1906). *Discursos* (Speeches) (México: Tip. Económica, 1907). *Discursos y poesías* (Speeches and Poetry) (México: Guerrero Hnos. y Cía., 1908). *Plan de una historia de Chihuahua* (Outline for a History of Chihuahua) (México: Tip. de Francisco Díaz de León, 1911). *Poesías* (Poetry) (Ciudad Juárez: Escobar Hnos., n.d.).

BIBLIOGRAPHY: John S. Brushwood, *Mexico in Its Novel* (Austin: University of Texas Press, 1966), pp. 157-58. Aurora M. Ocampo de Gómez and Ernesto Prado Velázquez, *Diccionario de escritores mexicanos* (México: UNAM, 1967), p. 274. *Enciclopedia de México*, no editor, vol. 11 (México: SEP, 1988), pp. 6214-15. Ralph E. Warner, *Historia de la novela mexicana en el siglo XIX* (México: Ant. Libr. Robredo, 1953), p. 115.

MELVIN S. ARRINGTON, JR.

PASCUAL Buxó, José (1931-). Born in San Feliú de Guixols, Cataluña, Spain, on February 12, 1931, José Pascual Buxó was exiled from his country because of the Civil War of 1936-1939. He arrived in Mexico in July of 1939. He studied Spanish language and literature at the UNAM and was named professor of Spanish and Mexican literature at that University from 1953 to 1959. He also taught at the University of Guanajuato from 1954 to 2955, and in 1957 at the Universidad Veracruzana. He moved to Venezuela in 1959 and has held several positions at different universities in that country.

While Pascual Buxó was in México he contributed to *México en la Cultura* in the magazine *Novedades*; to the literary supplement of the newspaper *El Nacional*; to the magazine *Ideas,* of which he was director from 1953 to 1956; to *La Palabra y el Hombre*, review of the Universidad Veracruzana; and to the magazine *Bellas Artes*, among others. He has also contributed to the *Anuario de Filología* of the Faculty of Humanities and Education at the University of Zulia since 1962.

Pascual Buxó first became known with the publication of his book of poems entitled *Tiempo de soledad* (A Time of Loneliness) in 1954. *Elegías* (Elegies), published in Mexico in 1955, was his second book. His prose -- esssays, criticism, and anthologies -- have appeared in books as well as in magazines and newspapers. His first book of essays, entitled *Góngora en la poesía novohispana* (Góngora in Novohispanic Poetry) and published in 1960, is an extraordinary study dealing with Gongorist influence in Mexican poetry of the seventeenth century. He discovered excellent examples to show Luis de Góngora's influence.

WORKS: Poetry: *Tiempo de soledad* (A Time of Loneliness) (Guanajuato: Universidad de Guanajuato, 1954). *Elegías* (Elegies) (México: Los Presentes, 1955). *Memoria y deseo* (Memory and Desire) (Maracaibo, Venezuela: University of Zulia, 1963). *Boca del solitario* (Mouth of the Lonely Man) (Maracaibo: University of Zulia, 1964). *Materia de la muerte* (Material of Death) (Maracaibo: University of Zulia, 1966). Essay: *Góngora en la poesía novohispana* (Góngora in Novohispanic Poetry) (México: UNAM, 1960). *En torno a la muerte y al desengaño en la poesía novohispana* (About Death and Deceit in Novohispanic Poetry) (Maracibo: University of Zulia, 1962). *Las jarchyas. Primitiva lírica hispánica* (The "jarchas." Primitive Hispanic Lyric Poetry) (Maracaibo: University of Zulia, 1962). Prologue to César Rodríguez Chicharro, *Aventura del miedo* (Adventure of Fear) (Maracaibo: University of Zulia, 1962). Anthology: *La generación del 98* (The Generation of '98)(México: UNAM, 1956), 2nd ed. (1964). *Arco y certamen de la poesía mexicana colonial (siglo XVII)* (Arc and Controversy of Colonial Mexican Poetry of the Seventeenth Century), edition and prologue (Xalapa: Universidad Veracruzana, 1959). *Vida de Santa María Egipcíaca, Libro de los Tres Reyes de Oriente* (Life of St. Mary, Book of the Three Wise Men), introduction, selection, and notes (Maracaibo: University of Zulia, 1961).

BIBLIOGRAPHY: Ermilo Abreu Gómez, "Con Machado y Góngora," review of *Góngora en la poesía novohispana,* in *México en la Cultura* 635 (May 14, 1961): 4. María Rosa Alonso, "Góngora en la poesía novohispana," in *Humanidades* (Univeristy of the Andes, Mérida, Venez.), 10 (1961): 256-57; "Poesía de José Pascual Buxó," in *Indice Literariio*, suppl. of *El Universal* (Caracas, Venezuela, July 9, 1963): 16. Manuel Andújar, Review of *Tiempo de soledad*, in *Ideas de México.* 6 (July-Aug. 1954,): 260-63. Héctor Azar, "Unos poemas," in *Revista Mexicana de Cultura* (May 26, 1955): 25-6. Emmanuel Carballo, Review of *Tiempo de soledad*, in *México en la*

Cultura (Feb. 13, 1955): 9. Berthy Ríos, "Un libro por España," review of *Memoria y deseo*, in *La Universidad del Zulia* (Maracaibo, Apr. 30, 1963): 36. Juan Abad de la Torre, Review of *Tiempo de soledad*, in *Las Españas* (July 1956): n.p. Arturo Souto Alabarce, "Nueva poesía española en México." in *Ideas de México* 7-8 (Sep.-Dec. 1954): pp.31-37.

DENISE GUAGLIARDO BENCIVENGO

PASO, Fernando del (1935-). A novelist, Fernando del Paso is also known as a poet, and an artist who does paintings, drawings, and publicity artwork. He was born in Mexico City on April 19, 1935. At the National University of Mexico, he earned *bachilleratos* in biological and economic sciences, and pursued two further years of studies in economics. He has traveled in both Central America and the United States. He was a fellow of the Mexican Center for Writers from 1964 to 1965, and a Guggenheim fellow in 1970. He contributes to the BBC Spanish language programs and has done editorial and publicity work. Although not widely recognized until the publication of his novel, *José Trigo*, he had published a book of poetry as early as 1958, and shortly thereafter a short story (in the journal *La Palabra y el Hombre*) written at the same time as he began his famous novel, which was published eight years later, and for which he was awarded the coveted Xavier Villaurrutia Prize. This novel is a great literary-linguistic-sociological achievement; the plot is situated in what would have been the Nonoalco-Tlaltelolco region, and ranges from prehistoric times to the present. The story covers a multiformed and chaotic world that lies between hope and disappointment, where all events are deep-down the paradigms of a greater history. It portrays an "underground" and multifaceted Mexico, popular and mysterious, tied together by unalienable humaneness.

WORKS: Poetry: *Sonetos de lo diario* (Everyday Sonnets) (México: Cuadernos del Unicornio, 1958). Novels: *José Trigo* (México: Siglo XXI Editores, 1966). "Fragmento muy breve de una novela larga," in *Revista de la Universidad de Mexico* 2, 8 (Apr. 1968): 19-20. *Palinuro de México* (Palinurus of Mexico) (México: Ed. Joaquín Mortiz, 1979). *Noticias del Imperio* (News from the Empire) (Madrid: Mondadori, 1987). Short Story: "Camarón, Camarón" (Tip Me, Tip Me), in *Novísimos narradores hispanoamericanos en* marcha, 1964-1980, edited by Angel Rama (México: Marcha Editores, 1981).

BIBLIOGRAPHY: Juan José Barrientos, "La locura de Carlota: Novela e Historia," in *Vuelta* 10, 113 (Apr. 1986): 30-34. David Bary, "Poesía y narración en cuatro novelas mexicanas," in *Cuadernos Americanos* 234, 1 (1981): 198-210. Huberto Batis, Review of *José Trigo*, in *El Heraldo Cultural* 53 (Nov. 13, 1966): 14. Esperanza Z. de Brauldt, "Fernando del Paso y *José Trigo*," in *El Sol* (Oct. 14, 1966). John S. Brushwood, *México en su novela* (México: FCE, 1966), pp. 100-102, 105, 110, 112. Emmanuel Carballo, "Del 13 al 19 de junio. Diario público de . . .," in *Diorama de la Cultura* (June 16, 1966): 3. Juan Carvajal, "*José Trigo* de Fernando del Paso," interview in *La Cultura en México* 225 (June 8, 1966): i-vi. Fausto Castillo, "La magia de la palabra," in *El Día* (Oct. 23, 1966). Raúl Chávarri, "El personaje en la moderna novela mejicana. A propósito de *José Trigo*, de Fernando del Paso," in *Cuadernos*

502 PAYNO y Flores, Manuel

Hispanoamericanos 215 (1967): 395-400. Eduardo Deschamps, "Primeros diez títulos de una Editorial," in *Excelsior* (Sept. 29, 1966): 7C. Adalbert Dessau, *"José Trigo*: Notas acerca de un acontecimiento literario in la novela mexicana," *Bulletin Hispanique* (Bordeaux), 70 (1968): 510-19. *"José Trigo*. Betrachtungen zu einem literarischen Ereignis," in *Lateinamerika*, Herbstsemester 1967, pp. 69-79. Neil J. Devereaux, "Tres escritores representativos de la novelística mexicana reciente," *DAI* 34(1973): 2617A (University of Texas, Austin). Nora Docttori, *"José Trigo*: el terror a la historia," in *Nueva Novela latinoamericana*, vol. 1, edited by Jorge Lafforgue (Buenos Aires: Paídos, 1969), pp. 262-99. Robin W. Fiddian, "James Joyce y Fernando del Paso," in *Insula* (Madrid) 39, 455 (Oct. 1984): 10; *"Palinuro de México*: A World of Words," in *Bulletin of Hispanic Studies* 58 (Apr.2, 1981): 121-33. Jesús Flores Sevilla, *"José Trigo*: un mito sobre Nonoalco-Tlatelolco," in *Revista de la Universidad de México* 24, 5-6 (1970): 16. David William Foster, *Mexican Literature: A Bibliography of Secondary Sources* (Metuchen, N.J.: Scarecrow Press, 1981), pp. 265-66. Blanca Haro, "Fernando del Paso, primogénito del siglo XXI," in *Diorama de la Cultura* (Oct. 9, 1966): 6. Raúl Leiva, Review of *José Trigo*, in *México en la Cultura* 919 (Oct. 30, 1966): 6. Artur Lundkvist, "Tva mexikaner: Carlos Fuentes och Fernando del Paso," in *Utflykter med utlandska forfattare* (Stockholm: Bonniers, 1969), pp. 199-212. María Luisa Mendoza, "No hemos soñado en vano a *José Trigo*," in *El día* (Oct. 9, 1966). Aurora M. Ocampo de Gómez and Ernesto Prado Velázquez, *Diccionario de Escritores Mexicanos* (México: UNAM, 1967), p. 275. Dagoberto Orrantia, "The Function of Myth in Fernando del Paso's *José Trigo*," in *Tradition and Renewal* (Urbana: University of Illinois Press, 1975), pp. 129-38; "The Situation of the Narrator as a Formal Principle in Four Representative Works of the Spanish-American New Novel," in *DAI* 38 (1977): 3535A. (Paso's *José Trigo* inter alia). Luis Guillermo Piazza, "Ambigüedad, lenguaje, desafio," in *La Cultura en México* 245 (Oct. 26, 1966): xviii-xix. María Portal, "Fernando de Paso," in her *Proceso narrativo de la revolución mexicana* (Madrid: Cultura Hispánica, 1977), pp. 237-47. Salvador Reyes Nevares, Review of *Sonetos de lo diario*, in *México en la Cultura* 517 (Feb. 8, 1959): 2. Kjell Risvik, trans., "Fernando del Paso i 'vitenskapens navn': Fra *Palinuro de México*," in *Vinduet* (Oslo) 39, 2 (1985): 45-50. Jorge Ruffinelli, "Notes on *Palinuro de México*," and Jo Anne Englebert, and Edith Grossman, translators of excerpts, in *Latin American Literature and Arts* 28 (Jan.-Apr. 1981): 31-37. Gustavo Sainz, "Fernando del Paso o el arte de imitar," in *El Día* (Oct. 12, 1966). Esther Seligson, *"José Trigo*: una memoria que se inventa," in *TC* 5 (1976): 162-69. Pedro Shimose, *Diccionario de autores iberoamericanos* (Madrid: Ministerio de Asuntos Exteriores, 1982), pp. 326-27. Lilvia Soto, "Tres aproximaciones a *José Trigo*," in *Revista Chilena de Literatura* (Santiago, Chile) 30 (Nov. 1987): 125-54. Elvira Vargas, "Multicosas," in *Novedades* (Oct. 14, 1966). Ramón Xirau, "Lecturas: José Agustín, Navarrete, Del Paso," in *Diálogos* 14 (1967): 24-26. Francisco Zendejas, "Multilibros," in *Excelsior* (Oct. 27, 28, and 29, 1966).

YOLANDA S. BROAD

PAYNO y Flores, Manuel (1810-1894), journalist, novelist, and diplomat. Manuel Payno y Flores was born in Mexico City on June 21, 1810. He began his bureaucratic career in the Custom House. In 1842 he was appointed secretary of the Mexican

Delegation for South America. Because of his political ideas he was persecuted by Santa Anna and was forced to immigrate to the United States. At Santa Anna's fall, he returned to Mexico. He was jailed during the French intervention. Once the Republic was re-established, he was representative and senator as well as professor. He was appointed consul in Santander, and later in Barcelona. He died in San Angel, D.F., on November 4, 1894.

Payno was a very active journalist who wrote on every possible subject. Between 1839 and 1845 he wrote his first romantic narratives, short novels, and short stories. He has been credited with initiating the serial novel in Mexico. His best-known novels of this type are *El fistol del diablo* (The Devil's Tie Pin) and *Los bandidos de Rio Frio* (The Highway Robbers of Rio Frio). He, together with Ignacio *Altamirano, founded *El Federalista* (The Federalist).

WORKS: *El fistol del diablo* (The Devil's Tie Pin), in the *Revista Científica y Literaria* (Scientific and Literary Magazine), 1845- 1846, plus other editions in 1859 and 1887. *El hombre de la situación* (The Man of Circumstances) (1861). *Los Bandidos de Río Frío* (The Highway Robbers of Rio Frio) (México: Ediciones México Moderno, 1919). *Las dos novias, Capricho dramático* (The Two Girl Friends, Dramatic Caprice), in two acts. *Museo Mexicano* (Mexican Museum) (México: lgnacio Cumplido, 1884).

BIBLIOGRAPHY: Enrique Anderson lmbert and Eugenio Florit, *Literatura Hispanoamericana*, Antología e Introducción Histórica (New York: Holt, Rinehart and Winston, 1960), p. 274. Guillermo Diaz-Plaja and Francisco Monterde, *Historia de la Literatura Española e Historia de la Literatura Mexicana* (México: Editorial Porrúa, S.A., 1968), p. 531. Carlos González Peña, *Historia de la Literatura Mexicana. Desde los orígenes hasta nuestros días* (México: Editorial Porrúa, S.A., 1981), pp. 215-16. Raimundo Lazo, *Historia de la literatura hispanoamericana. El siglo XIX* (México: Editorial Porrúa, S.A., 1976), pp. 55-56. Francisco Monterde, *Bibliografía del Teatro en México* (New York: Burt Franklin, 1970), p. 262. Julio Jiménez Rueda, *Antología de la Prosa en México* (México: Ediciones Sotas, 1946), p. 159.

JOSEPH VELEZ

PAZ, Ireneo (1836-1924), novelist, journalist. Paz was born in Guadalajara on July 3, 1836. He received his law degree from the state university in 1861, but he quickly became embroiled in politics and joined the liberal cause to fight against French Intervention and the Empire. His memoirs, *Algunas campañas* (Some Campaigns), deal with his life as a revolutionary and journalist during the years 1863-1876. Later in life, Paz became a staunch supporter of Porfirio Díaz. During the Díaz regime, he served as an alderman in Mexico City, a member of Congress, and president of the Associated Press. During his lifetime, he was the editor of various newspapers, most notably *La Prensa* (The Press) in the nation's capital. He died on October 4, 1924, in Mixcoac.

Paz produced a copious amount of historical fiction, beginning with the publication of *La piedra del sacrificio* (The Sacrificial Stone) in 1871. The work was so popular that it went through three editions in a ten-year period. It was followed by *Amor y suplicio* (Love and Anguish), which had at least seven editions by 1900, *Amor de viejo*

(An Old Man's Love), *Guadalupe, Doña Marina*, and thirteen historical novels grouped under the title *Leyendas históricas* (Historical Legends), with a total of more than 6100 pages. *Amor y Suplicio* first appeared in serial form in the newspaper *Ensayo Literario* (Literary Essay). It is set in the Aztec city of Tenochtitlán and deals with the conquest of Mexico. *Doña Marina* is a sequel to *Amor y suplicio*, and focuses on the period immediately following the conquest.

Leyendas históricas presents famous historical characters, such as Hidalgo, Morelos, Guerrero, Santa Anna, Maximilian, Juárez, Díaz, and Madero, in slightly fictionalized situations. A large part of the material Paz used in his novels was taken directly from histories and popular accounts of the times. In general, Paz's novels lack artistic merit, but they contain valuable historical detail. Most critics find his style undistinguished, at times dull and monotonous. *Manuel Lozada*, one of the *Leyendas históricas*, is an exception. It is considered to be Paz's best work. Similar in many ways to Ignacio *Altamirano's *El Zarco* (The Blue-Eyed Bandit), it deals with banditry in the Mexican countryside, and is a faithful portrayal of Mexican types and customs.

Paz is the author of a volume of sentimental and satirical verse entitled *Cardos y Violetas* (Thistles and Violets). He is also reputed to have written numerous plays, although their titles were not recorded for posterity, and no information about them is available today. His *Album de Hidalgo* (Album of Hidalgo) is a collection of sentiments inscribed by visitors in the register of Hidalgo's residence in Dolores from 1863 to 1874. Paz also wrote a travel guide for foreign businessmen in Mexico, called *Nueva guía de México* (New Guide to Mexico). In addition, he was the owner of a successful publishing house in Mexico City in the last decades of the nineteenth century.

WORKS: *La Piedra del Sacrificio* (The Sacrificial Stone) (México: J. S. Ponce de León, 1871). *Amor y Suplicio* (Love and Anguish) (México: I. Paz, 1873). *Nueva guía de México* (New Guide to Mexico) (México: I. Paz, 1882). *Album de Hidalgo* (México: I. Paz, 1883). *Doña Marina* (México: I. Paz, 1883). *Amor de viejo* (An Old Man's Love) (México: Imp. del Padre Cobos, 1874). *Guadalupe* (México: Imp. del Padre Cobos, 1874). *Leyendas históricas* (Historical Legends) (México: I. Paz, 1885-1886). *Algunas campañas* (Some Campaigns), memoirs (México: n. p., 1863-1876), edited by Salvador Ortiz Vidales (México: SEP, 1944).

BIBLIOGRAPHY: Salvador Ortiz Vidales, Prologue, *Algunas Campañas* (México: SEP, 1944), pp. ix-xiii. John Lloyd Read, *The Mexican Historical Novel* (New York: Instituto de Las Españas, 1939), pp. 234-51.

CYNTHIA K. DUNCAN

PAZ, Octavio (1914-). Octavio Paz was born in Mixcoac in Mexico City on March 31, 1914. His father, Octavio Paz Solórzano, a lawyer who took part in the Mexican Revolution, represented Zapata in México when he went into exile in the United States and was one of the initiatiors of agrarian reform in México. His mother's family were emigrants from Andalucía, Spain. From his childhood, and thanks to his grandfather's well-stocked library, Paz was an avid reader. He studied in Mexico, and had as teachers Carlos *Pellicer, José *Gorostiza, and Samuel Ramos, then went on a scholarship to the United States to study Hispanic poetry. In 1937 he also traveled to Spain with his young wife, Elena *Garro to attend a meeting in Valencia of the "Escritores Antifascistas." This trip gave him the oportunity to meet a great number of important writers, such as Pablo Neruda, Louis Aragón, César Vallejo, André Malraux, Jorge Guillén, Vicente Huidobro, Miguel Hernández, Luis Cernuda, and others who convinced him that there were causes in the world to fight for. In 1938 he returned to Mexico to write a daily column on politics for *El Popular*, a socialist newspaper, and also to found another magazine, *Taller*, which became an important gathering for new poets. He and his generation became known through the magazines Paz founded, *Barandal* (1931-1932), *Cuadernos del Valle de México* (1933-1934) and *Taller Poético* (1936-1938) which later became *Taller* (1938-1941). Many critics name this generation as Grupo *Taller*, and among its members are Rafael *Solana, Alberto Quintero Alvarez, Efraín *Huerta, and Neftalí *Beltrán. In 1944, under the auspices of a Guggenheim Fellowship, Paz studied Spanish American poetry in the United States (New York and San Francisco), discovering North American poetry and reflecting on the differences between the two countries. This work was the seed for *El laberinto de la soledad* (The Labyrinth of Solitude). In 1945 after a trip to Paris where he met several French writers, among them André Breton, he entered the diplomatic service. He has held various posts to France, Japan, Switzerland, and India, among others. In the early 1950s Paz prepared an anthology of Mexican poetry for UNESCO, a book that was translated into English by Samuel Beckett. Those years were very prolific for Paz. Besides *The Labyrinth of Solitude* he finished another major book of poetry, *El arco y la lira* (The Bow and the Lyre). As a consequence of such a distinguished production, he was awarded the Main Prize of the Sixth International Congress of International Poetry in 1963. He has continued directing the magazine *Taller*, and has contributed to many publications, including *El hijo pródigo*, which he helped to found, *Letras de México*, *Hoy*, *México en la Cultura*, *La Cultura en México*, and *Universidad de México*. In 1965 he was named a member of El Colegio Nacional. In 1968 he resigned his post as Mexican ambassador to India to protest the government massacre of student demonstrators in Tlatelolco Square (Plaza de las tres culturas). In 1969 he taught at Cambridge University in England and in Texas. He also held the Charles Eliot Norton Chair of Poetry at Harvard University during the academic year 1971-1972. Upon his return to his native country he founded one of the most influential literary journals, *Plural*, a supplement to the newspaper *Excelsior*. In 1976, after taking over that paper, he founded another monthly, *Vuelta*. It is one of the leading literary and cultural magazines of Latin America today.

Paz published his first poems at age nineteen in *Luna silvestre* (Wild Moon) a collection of adolescent poems characterized by its lyric simplicity. His second work, *Raíz del hombre* (Origin of Man) (1937), displays an erotic lyricism and ardor which he brings back to Mexican poetry. Also in 1937, *Bajo tu clara sombra* (Beneath Your Bright Shadow), thematically similar to *Raíz del hombre*, was published. Both works are considered important volumes that show the development of Paz's writing. Deeply influenced by the surrealists in their emphasis on unusual juxtapositions and the abundant use of metaphors, the rejection of and the lack of communication with the world are the main themes in these two early books. Other constant themes of Paz are sensuality and beauty. In *A la orilla del mundo* (At the Edge of the World) (1942) his poetry departs somewhat from the intimate and he questions the world about his existence. In his later poetry, there are contradictory intuitions: the objective versus the subjective world, singularity and totality, interior conflict and societal conflict. The key to the lyricism in the poetry of Paz is his enthusiasm to resolve thesis and antithesis in order to reestablish man's lost unity. His will to delve into other lives assumes erotic intensities. His thoughts are always looking for new paths which are also apparent in his essays. His first book of essays, *El laberinto de la soledad* (The Labyrinth of Solitude) (1950), purports to explain the Mexican, his way of life, his beliefs, his feelings about death, loneliness, and other elements within Mexican culture which make Mexicans a unique people. The book is actually divided into two parts: the first four chapters comprise an analysis of the Mexican character and the last four are an interpretation of Mexican history and its effect on the Mexican personality. These two themes converge in the Appendix entitled "La dialéctica de la soledad" (The Dialectic of Solitude). The book has influenced many Mexican writers such as Carlos *Fuentes and Vicente *Leñero. Paz's other works include *El arco y la lira* (The Bow and the Lyre) (1956), which is a study of literary theory; *Las peras del olmo* (The Pears of the Elm) (1957); *Cuadrivio* (Quadrivium) (1965), and *Puertas al campo* (1966).

In *Libertad bajo palabra. Obra poética 1935-1958* (Liberty by Word. Poems 1935-1958), Paz put together his most liked books. He studies the mere existence of man and plays with the concepts of conscience, existence, time, and death. With *Posdata* (P.S.) Paz attempts to probe more deeply into the enigma of México's national consciousness and identity, linking it with the broader question of the results of the technological revolution in Latin America.

His works are universally known and have been translated into many languages. He has received honorary doctorates From Boston University (1973), the University of Mexico (1978), Harvard University (1980), and New York University (1984). He also has received numerous awards, among them the Jerusalem Literature Prize (1977); Premio Nacional de Letras in Mexico also (1977); the Cervantes Prize (1981), the most prestigious of Spain, the German booksellers' Peace Prize (1984); the Oslo Poetry Prize (1985); and the Menéndez Pelayo Prize, in Spain (1987). His life's work received worldwide recognition in October, 1990, when he received the Nobel Prize for Literature.

WORKS: Poetry: *Luna silvestre* (Savage Moon) (México: Ed. Fábula, 1933). *¡No pasarán!* (They Will Mot Pass!) (México: Simbad, 1936). *Raíz del hombre* (The Root of Man) (México: Simbad, 1937). *Bajo tu clara sombra y otros poemas sobre España* (Beneath Your Bright Shadow and Other Poems about Spain) (Valencia, Spain: Héroe, 1937); notes by Manuel Altolaguirre; 2nd ed. (Mexico, 1941). *Entre la piedra y la flor* (Between the Rock and the Flower) (México: Nueva Voz, 1941). *A la orilla del mundo* (At the Edge of the World (México: Poesía Hispanoamericana, 1942). *Libertad bajo palabra* (Liberty by Word) (México: FCE, 1949). *¿Aguila o sol?* (Heads or Tails?), poems in prose (México: FCE, 1951); English trans., *Eagle or Sun* by Eliot Weinberger (New York: New Directions, 1976). *Semillas para un himno* (Seeds for a Hymn) (México: FCE, 1954). *Piedra del sol* (The Sun Stone) (México: FCE, 1957); English trans., *Sun Stone*, by Muriel Rukeyser (New York and London: New Directions, 1962). *La estación violenta* (The Violent Season) (México: FCE, 1958). *Agua y viento* (Water and Wind) (Bogotá: Eds. Mito, 1959). *Libertad bajo palabra: obra poética (1935-1957)* (México: FCE, 1960); 2nd ed. (1968). *Dos y uno tres* (Two and One Are Three) (Palma de Mallorca: Eds. Papeles de Son Armadans, 1961).

Salamandra (Salamander) (México: Ed. Joaquín Mortiz, 1962). *El día de Udaipur* (The Day of Udaipur) (Palma de Mallorca, Spain, 1963). *Viento entero* (Pure Wind) (New Delhi: n.p., 1966). *Blanco* (White) (México: Mortiz, 1967); English translation by Eliot Weinberger (New York: The Press, 1974). *Ladera este (1962-1968)* (East Hill) (México: Mortiz, 1969). *La centena (Poemas: 1935-1968)* (The Hundredth) (Barcelona: Barral, 1969). *Topoemas* (México: n.p., 1971). *Configurations* (New York: New Directions, 1971). *Renga* (México: Mortiz, 1972); English translation by Charles Tomlinson (New York: George Braziller, 1972). *El mono gramático* (The Monkey Grammarian) (Barcelona: Seix-Barral, 1974); Englist translation by Helen Lane (New York: Seaver Books, 1981). *Early Poems: 1935-1955* (New York: New Directions, 1973; Bloomington: Indiana University Press, 1974). *3 Notations/Rotations* (Cambridge, Mass.: Harvard University Press, 1974). *Pasado en claro* (The Past Illuminated) (México: FCE, 1975); English trans. *A Draft of Shadows and Other Poems*, trans. by Charles Tomlinson (New York: New Directions, 1979). *Vuelta* (Barcelona: Seix-Barral, 1976). *Poemas (1935-1975)* (Barcelona: Seix-Barral, 1979); Engish translation, *Selected Poems*, by Charles Tomlinson (Middlesex, Eng.: Penguin Books, 1979). *Airborn/Hijos del Aire*, with Charles Tomlinson (México: 1979); 2nd ed (London: Anvil Press, 1981). *Prueba del nueve* (México: 1985). *The Four Poplars* (New York: Red Ozier Press, 1985). *Homage and Desecrations* (New York: Red Ozier Press, 1987). *Arbol adentro (1976-1987)* (Barcelona: Seix-Barral,1987). *A Tree Within* (New York: O. Paz, 1988). Essays: *El Laberinto de la Soledad* (The Labyrinth of Solitude) (México: Cuadernos Americanos, 1950); 2nd ed. (México: FCE, 1959); 3rd ed. (1963); 4th ed. (1964); translated to French, Italian, and English; English translation by Lysander Kemp (New York: Grove Press, 1961). *El arco y la lira; El poema; La revelación poética; Poesía e historia* (The Bow and the Lyre; The Poem; The Poetic Revelation; Poetry and History) (México: FCE, 1956). "¿No hay salida?" (Is There No Exit?), in *Libro jubilar de Alfonso Reyes* (México: UNAM, 1956), pp. 327-29. *Las peras del olmo* (The Pears of the Elm) (México: UNAM, 1965). *Rufino Tamayo* (Rufino Tamayo) (México: n.p., 1959). *Magia de la risa* (The Magic of Laughter), in collaboration with Alfonso Medellín Zenil (Xalapa: Universidad Veracruzana, 1962). *Cuadrivio* (Quadrivium) (México: Joaquín Mortiz, 1965). *Los signos en rotación* (The Signs in Rotation) (Buenos Aires: Ed. Sur, 1965). "Horas situadas de Jorge Guillén," (The Situated Hours of Jorge Guillén) in *Papeles de Son Armadans* 119 (Feb. 1966). *Puertas al campo* (The Field Doors) (México: UNAM, 1966). *Claude Lèvi-Straus, o el nuevo festín de Esopo* (México: Mortiz, 1967); English translation, *Claude Lévi-Strauss: An Introduction*, by J. S. Bernstein and Maxine Bernstein (Ithaca: Cornell University Press, 1970). *Corriente alterna* (México: Siglo XXI, 1967); Engish transation, *Alternating Current*, by Helen Lane (New York: Viking Press, 1973). *Marcel Duchamp o el castillo de la pureza* (México: Era, 1968); English translation, *Marcel Duchamp, or the Castle of Purity*, by Donald Gardner (New York: Grossman, 1970). *Conjunciones o Disyunciones* (México: Mortiz, 1969); English translation, *Conjunctions and Disjunctions*, by Helen Lane (New York: Viking Press, 1974). *Posdata* (P.S.) (México: Siglo XXI, 1970). *El arco y la lira*, 3rd ed. (México: FCE, 1972); English translation, *The Bow and the Lyre* by Ruth L. C. Simms (Austin: University of Texas Press, 1973). *Apariencia desnuda. La obra de Marcel Duchamp* (México: Era, 1973); Englist translation, *Marcel Duchamp: Appearance Stripped Bare* by Rachel Phillips and Donal Gardner (New York: Viking Press, 1978). *El signo y el garabato* (México: Mortiz, 1973). *Los hijos del limo: del romanticismo a la vanguardia* (Barcelona: Seix-Barral, 1974), English translated, *Children of the Mire: Modern Poetry from Romanticism to the Avangard* by Rachel Phillips (Cambridge, Mass.: Harvard University Press, 1974). *The Siren and the Seashell, and Other Essays on Poets and Poetry*, translated by Lysander Kemp and Margaret Seyers Peden (Austin: University of Texas Press, 1976). *Xavier Villaurrutia en persona y en obra* (México: FCE, 1978). *El ogro filantrópico: historia y política (1971-1978)* (México: Mortiz, 1979). *In/mediaciones* (Barcelona: Seix-Barral, 1979). *Sor Juana Inés de la Cruz o las trampas de la fe* (México: FCE, 1982). *Sombras de obra: Arte y literatura* (Barcelona: Seix-Barral, 1983). *Tiempo nublado* (Barcelona, Seix-Barral, 1983); English translation, *One Earth, Four or Five Worlds: Reflexions on Contemporary History*, by Helen Lane (New York: Harcourt Brace Jovanovich, 1985). *Hombres en su siglo y otros ensayos* (Barcelona: Seix-Barral, 1984). "Itinerario poético: Antología comentada," in *La Nacion* (May 5, 1985, Suppl.): 1-2. *Pasión crítica*, edited by H. Verani (Barcelona: Seix-Barral, 1985). *On Poets and Others*, translated by Michael Schmidt (New York: Seaver Books, 1986). *Convergences: Selected Essays on Art and Literature*, translated by Helen Lane (N.Y.: Harcourt Brace Jovanovich, 1987). Theater: *La hija de Rapaccini* (Rapaccini's Daughter) (México: 1956, represented in one of the programs of Poesía en voz Alta). Translations: Matsúo Basho, *Sendas de Oku* (Paths of Oku), poetry; direct version of the Japanese in collaboration with Eikichi Hayashiya (México: UNAM, 1957). *An Anthology of Mexican Poetry*, edited by Octavio Paz, trans. by Samuel Beckett (Bloomington: Indiana University Press, 1958). *New Poetry of Mexico*, selected by Paz, et al., edited by Mark Strand (New York: E. P. Dutton, 1970).

BIBLIOGRAPHY: Ermilo Abreu Gómez, *Sala de retratos* (México: Ed. Leyenda, 1946), pp. 215-16. Demetrio Aguilera Malta, "Evocación de cuatro poetas," review of *Cuadrivio*, in *El gallo ilustrado* 177 (Nov. 14, 1965): 4. Jaime Alazraki, "Para una poética del silencio," in *Cuadernos hispanoamericanos* 343-45 (Jan.-Mar. 1979): 157-84. "Tres formas del ensayo contemporáneo: Borges, Paz, Cortázar," in *Revista Iberoamericana* 48, 118-19 (Jan.-June 1982): 9-20; "The Monkey Grammarian or Poetry as Reconciliation," in *World Literature Today* 56, 4 (Autumn 1982): 607-12; "Octavio Paz's Sor Juana Inés de la Cruz: An Intellectual Feast," in *World Literature Today* 58, 2 (Spring 1984): 225-27. Pedro de Alba, "Trayectoria y horizonte de Octavio Paz," in *Papeles de Poesía* 15 (Nov. 1943): 2. Enrique Anderson Imbert, *Historia de la Literatura Hispanoamericana*, vol. 2 (México: FCE, 1954), pp. 299-300. Enrique Anderson Imbert and Eugenio Florit, *Literatura hispanoamericana* (New York: Holt, Rinehart and Wiston, 1960), pp. 666-67. Anon., Biographical note in *Anuario de la poesía mexicana, 1962* (México: INBA, 1963), p. 102; Anon., "La flecha en el tiempo. Octavio Paz," in *Insula* 230 (Jan. 1966): 2. Frances R. Aparicio, "Epistemología y traducción en la obra de Octavio Paz," in *Hispanic Journal* 8, 1 (1986): 157-67. María Dolores Arana, *Carta de México*, offprint of *Papeles de Son Armadans* 73 (April 1962): n.p.. Jesús Juana Mary Arcelus Ulibarrena, "Metáfora y sinestesia en *Ladera este* de Octavio Paz, in *Thesaurus* (Instituto Caro y Cuervo) 37, 2 (May-Aug. 1982): 299-377. Jesús Arellano, *Poetas jóvenes de México* (México: Ed. Libro-Mex, 1955), p. 21; "Las ventas de Don Quijote," in *Nivel* 1 (Jan. 25, 1963): 5. Inés Arredondo, Review of *Cuadrivio*, in *Revista de Bellas Artes* 5 (Sept.-Oct., 1965): 95-96. Huberto Batis, Review of *Cuadrivio*, in *La Cultura en México* 193 (Oct. 1965): xvi;; Review of Claire Céa's book, *Octavio Paz*, in *La Cultura en México*, No. 196, Nov., 1965, p. XV; "El ensayo literario en 1965," in *La Cultura en México* 203 (Jan. 5, 1966): 2; Review of *Puertas al campo*, in *El Heraldo Cultural* 50 (Oct. 23, 1966): 15.

Manuel Benavides, "Claves filosóficas de Octavio Paz," in *Cuadernos hispanoamericanos* 343-45 (Jan.-Mar. 1979): 11-42. Judith Bernard, "Myth and Structure in Octavio Paz's *Piedra de sol*." in *Symposium* 21, 1 (Spring 1967): 5-13. Gordon Brotherston, "The Traditions of Octavio Paz," in *Latin American Poetry: Origins and Presence* (Cambridge: Cambridge University Press, 1975), chapter 7. Juan Bruce-Novoa, "El hilo de Ariadne: Sor Juana y Octavio Paz," in *Tinta* 1, 5 (Spring 1987): 15-22. John S. Brushwood, "Pésima traducción de Octavio Paz," in *México en la Cultura* 769 (Dec. 15, 1963): 5; Review of *Selected Poems*, in *Hispania* 47, 3 (Sept. 1964): 652-53. Linda Burk, "Cyclical Time in Octavio Paz's *Piedra de sol*," in *Cincinnati Romance Review* 2 (1983): 18-25. Gabriel Caballero and Helen Lane, "Octavio Paz, Iniquitous Symmetries: An Interview," in *American Poetry Review* 16, 5 (Sept.-Oct. 1987): 9-13. Emmanuel Carballo, Review of *Las peras del olmo*, in *México en la Cultura* 420 (April 7, 1957): 2; "Octavio Paz. Su poesía convierte en poetas a sus lectores," in *México en la Cultura* 493 (Aug. 25, 1958): 3; Review of *El laberinto en su soledad*, in *México en la Cultura* 552 (Oct. 18, 1959): 4; "Octavio Paz, in *La Cultura en México* 48 (Jan. 16, 1963): xix; "La presencia de Paz en el ensayo," in *La Cultura en México* 236 (Aug. 24, 1966): viii. Rosa Castro, "La libertad del escritor. Una entrevista con Octavio Paz," in *México en la Cultura* 252 (Jan. 17, 1954): 3. Antonio Castro Leal, *La poesía mexicana moderna* (México: FCE, 1953), pp. xxviii-xxix, 415. Claire Céa, *Octavio Paz* (Paris: Ed. Pièrre Seghers, 1965). Diógenes Cespedes, "Teoría de lo político, teoría de la traducción en Octavio Paz," in *Cuadernos de Poética* 3, 7 (Sept.-Dec. 1985): 58-91. Fernando Charry Lara, "Tres poetas mexicanos. III, Octavio Paz," in *Universidad de México* 11, 5 (Jan. 1957): 14-17; "*Cuadrivio* y *Los signos de rotación* de Octavio Paz," in *Eco* 71 (March 1966): 585-88. France Chiles, "The Bildungsreise of Octavio Paz," in *World Literature Today* 56, 4 (Autumn 1982): 626-31; *Octavio Paz: The Mythic Dimension* (New York: Peter Lang, 1986). Alí Chumacero, "Panorama de los últimos libros. *Entre la piedra y la flor*," in *México en la Cultura* 399 (Nov. 11, 1956): 2; Review of *Piedra de sol*, in *México en la Cultura* 399 (Nov. 1956): 2; Review of *Piedra de sol*, in *México en la Cultura* 459 (Dec. 29, 1957): 2; Review of *La estación violenta*, in *México en la Cultura* 492 (Aug. 17, 1958): 1; "Balance 1962," in *La Cultura en México* 46 (Jan. 2, 1963): iv-v. J. G. Cobo Borda, "Paz's Workshop," in *World Literature Today* 56, 4 (Autumn 1982): 619-25. Daisy Cocco de Filippis, "Octavio Paz: Aguila o sol o el fracaso del surrealismo como camino a la trascendencia," in *Alcance* 6 (June 1987): 2-6. John M. Cohen, *Poesía de nuestro tiempo* (México: FCE, 1964); "The Eagle and the Serpent," in *Southern Review* 2 (Spring 1965): 361-74. Hugo Covantes, "Octavio Paz y la poesía francesa contemporánea," in *México en la Cultura* 875 (Dec. 26, 1965): 4. Jorge J. Crespo de la Serna, "Octavio Paz y Michel Charpentier," in *El Día* (Dec. 3, 1965): 9. John Crispin, "Octavio Paz y Manuel Altolaguirre: Dos visiones de México," in *Insula* 38, 442 (Sept. 1983): 1, 12. Jorge Cruz, "Octavio Paz," in *La Nacion* (Apr. 21, 1985): 1. Jorge Cuesta, Review of *Raíz del hombre*, in *Letras de México* (Feb. 1, 1937): 3, 9; in *Poemas y ensayos*, vol. 3 (México: UNAM, 1964), pp. 282-84. Alberto Dallal, "Octavio Paz y la poesía en Suecia," in *La Cultura en México* 66 (May 22, 1963): xviii. Frank Dauster, *Breve historia de la poesía mexicana* (México: Eds. de Andrea, 1956), pp. 173-75. Xavier Domingo, "Octavio Paz," in *Revista de la Semana* (July 26, 1964): 4; "Exito de Octavio Paz. La crítica literaria francesa acoge favorablemente *El arco y la iris*, in *El Día* (Dec. 11, 1965): 9. Manuel Durán, "Octavio Paz en su libertad," in *México en la Cultura* 408 (Jan. 13, 1957): 2; Review of *Sun Stone*, in *Revista Interamericana de Bibliografía* 26 (April-June 1964): 202-3; "Octavio Paz: The Poet as Philosopher," in *World Literature Today* 56, 4 (Autumn 1982): 591-94. Peter G. Earle, "Octavio Paz y España," in *Revista Iberoamericana* 53, 141 (Oct.-Dec. 1987): 945-53. Joracio Espinosa Altamirano, "Paralelos y discrepancias," (between Octavio Paz and Joaquín Passos), in *Bolletín bibliográfico de la Secretaría de Hacienda y Crédito Público* 269 (April 15, 1963): 14-15; "Octavio Paz o la inteligencia literaria," in *Revista Mexicana de Cultura* 971 (Nov. 7, 1965): 1-2. Mary Farakos, "Octavio Paz y Marcel Duchamp: Crítica moderna para un artista moderno," in *Cuadernos Hispanoamericanos* 410 (Aug. 1984): 79-96. John M. Fein, "The Mirror as Image and Theme in the Poetry of Octavio Paz," in *Symposium* 10, 2 (Fall 1956): 251-70. "El espejo como imagen en la poesía de Octavio Paz," in *Universidad de México* 12, 3 (Nov., 1965): 8-13. *Toward Octavio Paz: A Reading of His Major Poems 1957-1976* (Lexington: University Press of Kentucky, 1986). Antonio A. Fernández-Vázquez, "The Ekphrastic Principle and Transubstantiation in Paz's *Custodia*," in *Crítica Hispánica* 5, 1 (1983): 1-11. Angel Flores, ed., *Aproximaciones a Octavio Paz* (México: Mortiz, 1974). Enrique Florescano, Review of *Magia de la risa*, in *La Palabra y el Hombre* 27 (July-Sept. 1963): 511-16. Isabel Fraire, Review of *Salamandra*, in *Revista Mexicana de Literatura* 7-8 (July-Aug. 1963): 56-57. Peter Frohlicher, "Figuras espaciales y estructuras narrativas en un poema de Octavio Paz ('Trowbridge Street')," in *Crítica semiológica de textos literarios hispánicos,* edited by Miguel Angel Garrido Gallardo (Madrid: Consejo Superior de Investigaciones Científicas, 1986), pp. 761-67. Carlos Fuentes, "Con Octavio Paz en Roma," in *La Cultura en México* 216 (April 6, 1966): 11. Ramón Gálvez, "Octavio Paz, el poeta," in *México en la Cultura* 51 (Jan. 22, 1950): 7. Nestor García Canclini, "La poesía de Octavio Paz: de la palabra a la escritura," in *Caravelle* 21 (1973): 89-103. Juan García Ponce, Review of *Cuatro poetas . . .*, in *Universidad de México* 17, 12 (Aug. 1963): 29-30; "El poder de la poesía," in *La Cultura en México* 88 (Oct. 23, 1963): xvi-xvii; "Pensamiento de poeta," review of *Cuadrivio* and *Los signos en rotación*, in *Universidad de México* 20, 3 (Nov. 1965): 32; "1965. La poesía," in *La Cultura en México* 203 (Jan. 5, 1966): xiii. Jaime García Terrés, Review of *Libertad bajo palabra*, in *Universidad de México* 16, 1 (Sept. 1961): 31. Juan Gil-Albert, "América en el recuerdo y la poesía de Octavio Paz," in *Letras de México* 1 (Jan. 15, 1943): 5, 11. Pere Gimferrer, *Lecturas de Octavio Paz* (Barcelona: Anagrama, 1980); *Octavio Paz* (Madrid: Taurus, 1982). Willard Gingerich, "The Poetics of History: A Defense of the Washington Address of Octavio Paz," in *New Scholar* 9, 1-2 (1984): 13-37. Henrique González Casanova, "Verdad llena de vida," in *El Gallo Ilustrado* 6 (Aug. 5, 1962): 2. Miguel Guardia, "Teatro en México, Segundo programa de Poesía en Voz Alta, *La hija de Rapaccini*, de Octavio Paz," in *México en la Cultura* 386 (Aug. 12, 1956): 5. Jorge Guillén, "In Homage to Octavio Paz, Neustadt Laureate," in *World Literature Today* 56, 4 (Autumn 1982): 607. Ricardo Gullón, "Reverberacion de la piedra," in *Insula* 35, 400-401 (March-April 1980): 3, 26-27. Edwin Honig, "Entrevista con Octavio Paz: Poesía y traducción: Arte de sombras y ecos," in *La Gaceta* 228 (Dec. 1989): 28-33. Roberto Hozven, "Octavio Paz: 'La escritura de la ausencia'," in *Revista Chilena de Literatura* 19, 1 (April 1982): 39-48. Andrés Iduarte, Review of *El laberinto de la soledad*, in *Revista Hispánica Moderna* 27, 1 (Jan. 1951): 53-54; "Octavio Paz y el mundo de don Pedro de Alba," in *México en la Cultura* 759 (Oct. 6, 1963): 1, 9. Ivar Ivask, ed., *The Perpetual Present: The Poetry and Prose of Octavio Paz* (Norman: University of Oklahoma Press, 1973); "Shared Laurel Leaves: From Jorge Guillen to Octavio Paz," in *World Literature Today* 56, 4 (Autumn 1982): 589-90. Olga Juzyn, "Bibliografía actualizada sobre Octavio Paz," in *Inti 15 (Spring* 1982): 98-144. William H. Katra,

"Ideology and Society in *El laberinto de la soledad*, by Octavio Paz." in *Chasqui*, 1986, vol. 15(2-3), pp. 3-13. Lloyd King, "Surrealism and the Sacred in the Aesthetic Credo of Octavio Paz." in *Hispanic Review* 37, July 1969, pp. 382-393. Enrique Krauze, et al., "Octavio Paz: Facing the Century: A Reading of *Tiempo nublado*." in *Salmagundi* 70-71 (Spring-Summer 1986): 129-57. Julia A. Kushigian, "'Ríos en la noche: Fluyen los jardines': Orientalism in the Work of Octavio Paz," in *Hispania* 70, 4 (Dec. 1987): 776-86. Jaime Labastida, "Un artículo crítico sobre Octavio Paz," in *El Gallo Ilustrado* 11 (Sept. 9, 1962): 3; Conference, in *Vida Nicolaita* (Universidad de San Nicolás de Hidalgo) 5 (Oct. 15, 1964): 13. Fernando R. Lafuente, "Octavio Paz: Poesía e historia," in *Revista de Occidente* 6 (July-Aug. 1988): 240-55. Jean Clarence Lambert, "La obra de Octavio Paz juzgada en Francia," in *México en la Cultura* 483 (June 15, 1958) 3. Elba M. Larrea, "Octavio Paz, poeta de América," in *Revista Nacional de Cultura* 26, 162-163 (Jan.-April 1964): 78-88; in *Atenea* 405 (July-Sept. 1964): 159-68. Luis Leal, Review of *El laberinto de la soledad*, in *Revista Iberoamericana* 49 (Jan.-July 1960): 184-86; "Una poesía de Octavio Paz," in *Hispania* 4)Dec. 1965): 841-42. Raúl Leiva, "La poesía de Octavio Paz," in *México en la Cultura* 133 (Aug. 19, 1951): 7; "Un nuevo libro de Octavio Paz: *Semillas para un himno*," in *México en la Cultura* 298 (Dec. 5, 1954): 2; Review of *El arco y la iris*, in *México en la Cultura* 368 (April 8, 1956): 3; Review of *El arco y la iris*, in *Universidad de México* 10, 7 (April 1956): 4; *Imagen de la poesía mexicana contemporánea* (México: UNAM, 1959), pp. 205-26; Review of *Cuatro poetas contemporáneos de Suecia*, in *Nivel* 5 (May 25, 1963): 3; "El libre hombre de soledad," in *El Gallo Ilustrado* 55 (July 14, 1963): 4; Review of *Cuadrivio*, in *México en la Cultura* 863 (Oct. 3, 1965): 6; Review of *Puertas al campo*, in *México en la Cultura* 311 (March 6, 1955): 2. Tonia León, "Structures, Traps and Snares: A Critique of Octavio Paz's Interpretation of *El primero sueno*," in *Confluencia* 2, 1 (Fall 1986): 28-32. José Edil de Lima Alves, "'El prisionero,' de Octavio Paz: Proposta de Analise a Partir do '*Pensamento Radical*,' in *Revista Letras* 29 (1980): 89-108. Frederick Luciani, "Octavio Paz on Sor Juana Inés de la Cruz: The Metaphor Incarnate," in *Latin American Literary Review* (July–Dec. 1987): 6-25. Augusto Lunel, Review of *Semillas para un himno*, in *México en la Cultura* 311 (March 6, 1955): 2. Lelia Madrid, "Octavio Paz o la problemática del origen,." in *Revista de Literatura Hispánica* 28 (Fall 1988): 39-57. Antonio Magaña Esquivel, *Medio siglo de teatro mexicano* (México: FCE, 1956), pp. 158-59. Carlos Magis, *La poesía hermética de Octavio Paz* (México: El Colegio de México, 1978). Juan Malpartida, "El cuerpo y la historia: Dos aproximaciones a Octavio Paz," in *Cuadernos Hispanoamericanos* 468 (June 1989): 45-56. María Martín, "Octavio Paz y la literatura en Francia," in *Diorama de la Cultura* (Aug. 2, 1964): 8. Emma Martinell Gifre, "Estilística de la adjectivación en *El mono gramático* de Octavio Paz," in *Estudios ofrecidos a Emilio Alarcos Llorach*, vol. 4 (Oviedo: Univ. de Oviedo, 1979), pp. 455-78. José Luis Martínez, *Literatura mexicana siglo XX, 1910-1949*, vol. 1 (México: Libr. Robredo, 1949), pp. 25, 77, 79, 95, 111, 125, 130-31, 142, 143, 181-83, 185; vol. 2 (1950), pp. 93-94; *El ensayo mexicano moderno*, vol. 2 (México: FCE, 1958), pp. 302-3; *El trato con escritores* (México: INBA, Dept. de Lit., 1961), pp. 134-35. Diego Martínez Torrón, *Variables poéticas de Octavio Paz* (Madrid: Hiperion, 1979). Blas Matamoro, "Octavio Paz: Del arquetipo a la historia," in *Cuadernos Hispanoamericanos* 367-68 (Jan.-Feb. 1981): 273-87; "El peregrino en su patria." in *Vuelta* 13, 146 (Jan. 1989): 36-38. María Luisa Mendoza, "Algunas preguntas a Octavio Paz," in *El Gallo Ilustrado* 6 (Aug. 5, 1962): 1; "La O por lo redondo," review of *Cuadrivio*, in *El Día* (Sept. 29, 1965): 2. Carl R. Mentley, "The Hermeneutic

Project of Octavio Paz," in *Centennial Review*, 1986, Spring, vol. 30(2), pp. 148-159. Thomas Mermall, "Octavio Paz: *El Laberinto de la Soledad* y el sicoanálisis de la historia," in *Cuadernos Americanos* 27, 1 (Jan.-Feb. 1968): 97-114. María del Carmen Millán, "La inteligencia mexicana," in *México en la Cultura* 728 (March 3, 1963): 7. Cesar Antonio Molina, "Una poesía de convergencias," in *Vuelta* 12, 141 (Aug. 1988): 54-56. Carlos Monsiváis, *La poesía mexicana del siglo XX* (México: Empresas Editoriales, 1966), pp. 550-75. Dolores de la Mora, "¿Cómo nace un poeta?," in *El Gallo Ilustrado* 68 (Oct. 13, 1963): 1. Alberto Moreiras, "Alternancia México/mundo en la posición crítica de Octavio Paz," in *Nueva Revista de Filología Hispánica* 35, 1 (1987): 251-64. Thelma Nava, "Notas de poesía," review of *Viento entero*, in *El Día* (Jan. 22, 1966): 11. Robert Nugent, "Structure and Meaning in Octavio Paz's *Piedra de sol*," in *Kentucky Foreign Language Quarterly* 13, 3 (1966): 138-46. Manuel Nuñez, "Octavio Paz: La construcción de una retórica," in *Cuadernos de Poética* 1, 1 (Sept.-Dec. 1983): 5-11. Julio Ortega, "Aleixandre y Paz: El espacio textual," in *Diálogos* 16, 3 (May-June 1980): 35-37. "Notas sobre Paz," in *Zona Franca* 3, 24 (May-June 198o,): 25-27. "Una hipótesis de lectura," in *Revista de la Universidad de México* 37, 8 (Dec. 1981): 41-44. José Emilio Osses, "La comprensión del texto poético de Octavio Paz," in *Revista Chilena de Literatura* 20 (Nov. 1982): 27-40. José Miguel Oviedo, "Los pasos de la memoria. lectura de un poema de Octavio Paz," in *Revista de Occidente* 14 (Dec. 1976): 42-51. "Return to the Beginning: Paz in His Recent Poetry," in *World Literature Today* 56, 4 (Autumn 1982): 612-18. Tim Padget, "Labyrinth for a Laureate," in *Newsweek* (Oct. 22, 1990): 48. Maria Joan Panico, "Separación entre 'lo mismo' y 'lo otro' en Octavio Paz," *Actas del Sexto Congreso Internacional de Hispanistas* (Toronto: University of Toronto Press, 1980), pp. 558-61. Manuel Pastor, "Concomitancias intelectuales y políticas: Ortega y Octavio Paz," in *Revista de Occidente* 72 (May 1987): 133-54. Javier Peñalosa, Review of *Cuadrivio*, in *Nivel* 35 (Nov. 25, 1965): 4. Rachel Phillips, *The Poetic Modes of Octavio Paz* (Oxford: Oxford University Press, 1972). Alejandro Pizarnik, "El Premio Internacional de Poesía y *Salamandra*," in *México en la Cultura* 767 (Dec. 1, 1963): 5. Elena Poniatowska, "Octavio Paz, roca solar de la poesía," in *México en la Cultura* 450 (Nov. 3, 1957): 3. Camber Melinda Porter, "An Interview with Octavio Paz," in *Partisan Review* 53, 1 (1986): 76-87. Salvador Reyes Nevares, Review of *La estación violenta*, in *México en la Cultura* 495 (Sept. 7, 1958): 4. Luis Rius, Review of Fernando Pessoa's anthology, in *Anuario de Letras*, vol. 2 (México: UNAM, 1962). Arturo Rivas Sainz, "La poesía de Octavio Paz," in *Letras de México* 6 (June 15, 1943): 1-2, 5, 8. Emir Rodríguez Monegal, "Relectura de *El arco y la lira*." in *Revista Iberoamericana* 74, (Jan-Feb. 1971): 35-46. Jorge Rodríguez Padrón, *Octavio Paz* (Madrid: Jucar, 1975). "El tiempo hecho cuerpo repartido (Un análisis de 'Nocturno de San Ildefonso'," in *Cuadernos Hispanoamericanos* 343-345 (Jan.-Mar. 1979): 591-614. Alfredo Roggiano, ed., *Octavio Paz* (Madrid: Ed. Fundamentos, 1979). Isaac Rojas Rosillo, "Los libros. Vigilias de un soñador," in *México en la Cultura* 40 (Nov. 6, 1949): 7. Claudia Rousseau, "Mythic Transcendence: Octavio Paz, Mallarme and Marcel Duchamp Mosaic," in *Journal for the Interdisciplinary Study of Literature* 20, 3 (Summer 1987): 113-27. Carmen Ruiz Barrionuevo, "La incesante búsqueda del lenguaje en la poesía de Octavio Paz," in *Revista de Filología de la Universidad de La Laguna* 3 (1984): 61-81. Georgina Sabat de Rivers, "Octavio Paz ante Sor Juana Inés de la Cruz," in *Modern Language Notes* 100, 2 (March 1985): 417-23; "Biografías: Sor Juana vista por Dorothy Schons y Octavio Paz," in *Revista Iberoamericana* 51, 132-133 (July-Dec. 1985): 927-37. Antonio Sacoto, "El ensayo hispanoamericano contemporáneo," in *Cuadernos Americanos* 2, 3 (1988): 107-20. César Salgado, "Octavio Paz: Poesía de circunstancias," in *Vuelta* 12, 138 (May 1988): 13-21. Enrico Mario Santi, "'Conversar es humano': Entrevista con Octavio Paz," in *La Torre* 3, 9 (Jan.-Mar. 1989): 105-21. Maya Scharer-Nussberger, "Le Centre et la faille," in *World Literature Today* 56, 4 (Autumn 1982): 638-43. Michael Schmidt, "Octavio Paz: The Dream Set Free," in *PN Review* 14, 1 (1987): 37-40. Tomás Segovia, "Entre la gratuidad y el compromiso," in *Revista Mexicana de Literatura* 8 (Nov.-Dec. 1956): 102-13; Review of *Sendas de Oku*, in *Universidad de México* 11, 9 (May 1957): 30; "Una obra maestra de Octavio Paz: *Piedra de sol*," in *La Cultura en México* 189 (Sept. 29, 1965): xiii. Mauricio de la Selva, "Asteriscos," review of *Magia de la risa*, in *Diorama de la Cultura* (March 24, 1963): 3; "Octavio Paz, búsquedas infructuosas," in *Cuadernos de Bellas Artes* 4, 7 (July, 1963): 17-25; Review of *Cuatro poetas . . .*, in *Cuadernos Americanos* 4 (July-Aug. 1963): 279-80. A. Silva Villalobos, Review of *Semillas para un himno*, in *Metáfora* 2 (May-June 1955): 37-38; Review of *Las peras del olmo*, in *Metáfora* 15 (July-Aug. 1957): 40-41. Gyorgy Somlyó, "Octavio Paz y *Piedra de sol*," in *Diálogos* 5 (July-Aug. 1966): 8-12. Emilio Sosa López, "Octavio Paz o el tiempo de la razón ardiente," in *Revista Sur* 349 (July-Dec.1981): 137-46. Lilvia Soto-Duggan, "La palabra-sendero o la escritura analógica: La poesía última de Octavio Paz," In *Inti* 9 (Spring 1979): 79-89. Raymond D. Souza, "The World Symbol and Synthesis in Octavio Paz," in *Hispania* 47, 1 (1964): 60-65. Anthony Stanton, "Genealogía de un libro: *Libertad bajo palabra*," in *Vuelta* 12, 145 (Dec. 1988): 15-21. Luis Suárez, "Octavio Paz habla desde París," in *México en la Cultura* 560 (Dec. 7, 1959): 2. Guillermo Sucre, "Lo que se piensa en el extranjero de la poesía de Octavio Paz," in *Universidad de México* 13, 3 (Nov. 3, 1959): 28-29; "*La máscara, la transparencia: Ensayos sobre poesía hispanoamericana*" (Caracas: Monte Avila, 1975). Christiane Tarroux-Follin, "*Primer día*: Les Premieres Realisations textuelles des structures metaphoriques de *Libertad bajo palabra*, in *Co-textes* 17 (Jan. 1989): 5-42; "Quelques points de repere," in *Co-textes* 17 (Jan. 1989): 43-51; "'Himno entre ruinas': La Reconciliation avec le monde," in *Co-textes* 17 (Jan. 1989): 53-73; "Le Surrealisme d'Octavio Paz en question," in *Co-textes* 17 (Jan. 1989): 75-99. Paul Teodorescu, "Una nueva sensibilidad: La plasmación de una profecía orteguiana en las obras de Octavio Paz y Ernesto Sábato," in *Cuadernos Hispanoamericanos* 403-405 (Jan.-Mar. 1984): 391-423. Manuel Ulacia, "Octavio Paz: Poesía, pintura, música, etcetera: Conversacion con Octavio Paz," in *Revista Iberoamericana* 55, 148-149 (July-Dec. 1989): 615-36. Rodolfo Usigli, "Poeta en libertad," in *Cuadernos Americanos* 49, 1 (Jan.-Feb. 1950): 293-300. Mario J. Valdés, "Comentario hermeneutico sobre la coda de *Piedra de sol*," in *Actas del VIII Congreso de la Asociacion Internacional de Hispanistas*, vol. 2 (Madrid: Istmo, 1986), pp. 681-86. Rima de Vallbona, "Octavio Paz: Prosa en movimiento," in *Kanina* (Universidad de Costa Rica), 6, 1-2 (Jan.-Dec. 1982): 60-66. Graciela Vaserman De Samuels, "The Dialectic of Solitude in the Work of Octavio Paz," in *DAI* 42, 12 (June 1982): 5136A-37A. Roberto Venegas, "Poetas mexicanos. Octavio Paz," in *Diorama de la Cultura* (Aug. 30, 1964): 3, 7. Hugo J. Verani, "Selected Bibliography (1933-1982)," in *World Literature Today* 56, 4 (Autumn 1982): 602-05; "Octavio Paz and the Language of Space," in *World Literature Today* 56, 4 (Autumn 1982): 631-35; *Octavio Paz: Bibliografía crítica* (México: UNAM, 1983); "El acorde y la disonancia: De Jorge Guillén a Octavio Paz," in *Cuadernos Americanos* 1, 6 (1987): 111-20; "Octavio Paz: Primeras letras, 1931-1943," in *Revista Iberoamericana* 55, 148-149 (July-Dec. 1989): 1191-93. Roberto Vernegro, "Una entrevista con Octavio Paz," in *Universidad de México* 8, 6 (Feb. 1954): 24. Víctor

Villela, "Octavio Paz. Rubén Bonifaz Nuño," in *El Heraldo Cultural* 34 (July 3, 1966): 2. James W. Wilkie, "The Historical View of Octavio Paz: A Critique of the Washington Address," in *New Scholar* 9, 1-2 (1984): 1-11. Jason Wilson, "Abrir/cerrar los ojos: a Recurrent Theme in the Poetry of Octavio Paz," in *Bulletin of Hispanic Studies* 48, 1 (Jan. 1971): 44-56; *Octavio Paz: A Study of His Poetics* (Cambridge: Cambridge University Press, 1979). Michael Wood, "The Poet as Critic: Wallace Stevens and Octavio Paz," in *Reinventing the Americas: Comparative Studies of Literature of the United States and Spanish America*, edited by Bell Gale Chevigny et al (New York: Cambridge University Press, 1986), pp. 325-32. Frederick R. Worth, "'Boca que habla y oreja que oye': Consciousness and the Poem in Octavio Paz," in *La Chispa '87: Selected Proceedings*, edited by Gilbert Paolini (New Orleans: Tulane University, 1987), pp. 327-34. Ramón Xirau, "La poesía de Octavio Paz," in *Cuadernos Americanos* (July-Aug. 1951): 288-98; *Tres poetas de la soledad* (México: Ant. Libr. Robredo, 1955), pp. 39-70; Review of *Semillas para un himno*, in *Universidad de México* 9, 5-6 (Jan.-Feb. 1955): 28; "Notas a *Piedra de sol*," in *Universidad de México* 12, 6 (Feb. 1957): 15-16; "Tres calas en la reflexión poética," in *La Palabra y el Hombre* 17 (Jan.-March 1961): 69-85; *Poesía hispanoamericana y española* (México: Imp. Universitaria, 1961), pp. 45-55; Review of *Salamandra*, in *Nivel* 2 (Feb. 25, 1963): 12; "Dos libros de Octavio Paz" (*Cuadrivio* and *Los signos en rotación*), in *Diálogos* 2 (Nov.-Dec. 1965): 39-40; Review of *Viento entero*, in *Diálogos* 2 (Jan.-Feb. 1966): 42. *Octavio Paz: el sentido de la palabra* (México: Mortiz, 1970). Saul Yurkievich, *Fundadores de la nueva poesía latinoamericana: Vallejo, Huidobro, Borges, Girondo, Neruda, Paz.* (Barcelona: Barral, 1973). Jacobo Zabludovsky, "La hora de Octavio Paz," in *Siempre!* 535 (Sept. 25, 1963): 12, 69.

ELADIO CORTES

PAZ Paredes, Margarita (1922-), poet and journalist. Born Margarita Camacho Baquedano in San Felipe Torres Mochas, Guanajuato, Paz Paredes studied at the Universidad Obrera de México and at the National University. Her poetry focuses on the plight of children, the less fortunate, and the victims of political repression.

WORKS: *Sonaja* (Rattle) (México: n.p., 1942). *Oda a Constantino Oumanski* (Ode to Constantino Oumanski) (México: n.p., 1945. *Voz de la tierra* (Voice of the Earth) (México: Firmamento, 1946). *El anhelo plural* (The Plural Wish) (México: Tiras de colores, 1948). *Retorno* (Return) (México: Talleres gráficos, 1948). *Génesis transida* (Fatigued Genesis) (Monterrey: Camelina, 1949). *Elegía a Gabriel Ramos Millín* (Elegy to Gabriel Ramos Millin) (México: Nueva Voz, 1949). *Andamios de sombra* (Scaffolds of Shadow) (México: Stylo, 1950). *Canto a México* (Song to Mexico) (México: Ed. Gear, 1952). *Dimensión del silencio* (The Dimension of Silence) (México: Cuadernos Americanos, 1953). *Presagio en el viento* (Presage in the Wind) (San Salvador: Ministerio de Cultura, 1955). *Casa en la niebla* (House in the Fog) (México: n.p., 1956). *Coloquio de amor* (Colloquium about Love) (México: Ed. Yolotepec, 1957). *Cristal adentro* (Inside Crystal) (México: n.p., 1957). *Los amantes y el sueño* (The Lovers and the Dream) (San Salvador: Ministerio de Cultura, 1960). *Rebelión de ceniza* (Ash Rebellion) (México: Imp. Roall, 1960). *La imagen y su espejo* (The Image and Its Mirror) (México: Costa-Amic, 1962). *El rostro imposible* (The Impossible Face) (México: Ed. Castalia, 1963). *Adán en sombra y noche final y siete oraciones* (Adam in the Shadow, Last Night, and Seven Prayers) (México: Pájaro Cascabel, 1964). Essays: *Viaje a la China popular* (Trip to Popular China) (México: Costa-Amic, 1966).

BIBLIOGRAPHY: Jesús Arellano, *Antología de los 50 poetas contemporáneos de México* (México: Eds. Alatorre, 1952), p. 73. Salvador Calvillo Madrigal, "Poesisas mexicanas: Margarita Paz Paredes," *Nivel* 195 (1979): 6. Antonio Castro Leal, *La poesía mexicana moderna* (México: FCE, 1953), p. 473. Arturo Cova, "La madurez política de Margarita Paz Paredes," Revista Mexicana de Cultura 872 (1963): 16. Raúl Leiva, *Imagen de la poesía mexicana contemporánea* (México: UNAM, 1959), pp. 293-99. Germáb Pardo García, "Memorias de hospital: Poemas de Margarita Paz Paredes," *Nivel* 200 (1979): 6.

ALFONSO GONZALEZ

PELAEZ, Francisco (1911-), short story and prose writer. Born in Mexico City, Francisco Peláez is the brother of the painter Antonio Peláez. The writer uses the pseudonym Francisco Tario. He has contributed to reviews such as *Letras de México*, *Vidas y Cuentos*, and *Revista Mexicana de Literatura*. His writing career began in 1943 with the publication of both his first collection of stories, *La noche* (The Night), and his first and only novel, *Aquí abajo* (Here Below). Since then he has published many more collections of stories, as well as a book of aphorisms, *Equinoccio* (Equinox). Peláez' style has been compared to that of Jorge Luis Borges and that of other writers of the school of *magical realism. His stories involve ghosts, the transmigration of souls, travel to other dimensions, dreams becoming reality, etc., often treated humorously. In later life, Peláez moved to Spain.

WORKS: *Aquí abajo* (Here Below) (México: Ant. Libr. Robredo, 1943). *La noche* (The Night) (México: Ant. Libr. Robredo, 1943). *Equinoccio* (Equinox) (México: Ant. Libr. Robredo, 1946). *La puerta en el muro* (The Door in the Wall) (México: Editorial Costa-Amic, 1946). *Yo de amores que sabía* (What Did I Know of Love) (México, FCE, 1950). *Tapioca Inn: mansión para fantasmas* (Tapioca Inn: Ghost House) (México: Tezontle, 1952). *Una violeta de más: cuentos fantásticos* (One More Violet: Fantastic Stories) (México: Joaquín Mortiz, 1968).

BIBLIOGRAPHY: Ross Larson, *Fantasy and Imagination in the Mexican Narrative* (Tempe: Center for Latin American Studies, Arizona State University, 1977), pp. 6, 8, 14-18, 36, 72-75, 78, 91, 103. Luis Leal, *Breve historia del cuento mexicano* (México: Ediciones de Andrea, 1956), pp. 132-33. Aurora M. Ocampo de Gómez and Ernesto Prado Velázquez, *Diccionario de escritores mexicanos* (México: UNAM, 1967), p. 281.

TERESA R. ARRINGTON

PELLICER, Carlos (1899-1977), poet. Born November 4, 1899, in Villahermosa, Tabasco, Carlos Pellicer studied in Mexico City. He continued his studies in Bogotá, Colombia, where he was sent by the Carranza government, and traveled throughout South America in 1922 while José *Vasconelos served as minister of education. He also traveled and studied in Europe and the Near East between 1926 and 1929. He taught at the high school and the university level. He is best known for his poetry, but he also wrote essays and articles that were published in a number of magazines. He served as director of the Departamento de Bellas Artes for four years, where he worked as museum curator and put together a number of displays.

Carlos Pellicer is known as one of the best contemporary Mexican poets. His lyrical contribution varies greatly. He began participating in literary circles as early as 1914 and is recognized as one of the initiators of the Mexican new poetry. His poetry is musical, rhythmic, and rich in imagery.

Though Pellicer is considered part of the literary group known as the Contemporáneos, there was a great deal of diversity among its members and in the works they produced. (*See* Vanguardist Prose Fiction in Mexico.) Pellicer, like Jaime *Torres Bodet, Bernardo *Ortiz de Montellano, José *Goroztiza, Octavio G. Barreda, and Enrique *González Rojo, became part of the group after its members had already collaborated on a number of works. In 1918, they had published the magazine *San-Ev-Ank*; in 1919, they formed the new Ateneo de la Juventud in honor of the writers who had formed the first Ateneo ten years earlier; from 1922 to 1923, they worked on the magazine *Falange*; and from 1927 through 1928, they finally came together with Xavier *Villaurrutia and Salvador *Novo, who had formed the original group, to write *Ulises*. This work revealed some of the literary concerns that would become most apparent in the magazine *Contemporáneos*, which was published from 1928 through 1931 and from which the group got its name. Pellicer, however, is not as contemporary as the group's title would suggest, because he preferred the tradition and techniques of the earlier descriptive poets rather than the highly intellectual, somewhat elitist poetry of the rest of the group.

Pellicer's complete works were published in 1962, by the Universidad Nacional Autónoma de México and he was awarded the Premio Nacional de Literatura by his government in 1964.

WORKS: Poetry: "Sonetos romanos" (Roman Sonnets) in *Gladios* (México) 1, 1 (Jan. 1916). *Colores en el mar y otros poemas* (Colors in the Sea and Others Poems), illustrated by Roberto Montenegro, dedicated to Ramón López Velarde; poems written in 1915 and 1920 (México: Cultura, 1921). *Piedra de sacrificios* (Sacrificial Stone), Iberoamerican poems, prologue by José Vasconcelos (México: Nayarit, 1924). *Seis, siete poemas* (Six, Seven Poems) (México: Azatlán Editors, 1924). *Oda de junio* (Ode of June) (México: La Pajarita de Papel, 1924). *Hora y 20* (Hour and 20) (Paris: Edit. París-América, 1927). *Camino* (Road) (París: Eds. Estrella, 1929). *5 poemas* (5 poems), Supplement of *Barrandal* (México, 1931). *Esquema para una oda tropical* (Outline for a Tropical Ode) (México: Secretaría de Relaciones Exteriores, 1933). *Estrofas al mar latino* (Stanzas to the Latin Sea) (México: Imp. Mundial, 1934). *Hora de junio* (An Hour in June) (1936), (México: Eds. Hipocampo, 1937). *Ara virginum* (Altar of the Virgin) (México: Revistas de Literatura Mexicana, 1940). *Recinto y otras imágenes* (Place and Other Images), in memory of Genaro Estrada (México: FCE, 1941). *Exágonos* (México: Nueva Voz, 1941). *Discurso por las flores* (Speech for the Flowers) (México: n.p., 1946). *Subordinaciones* (Subordinations) (México: Edit. Jus, 1948). *Sonetos* (Sonnets) (México: Los Presentes, 1950). *Exágonos* (México: Nueva Voz, 1954). *Práctica de vuelo* (Flight Practice), dedicated to Alfonso Reyes, Col. Tezontle (México: FCE, 1956). *Material poético* (Poetic Material [1918-1961]) (México: UNAM, 1962); includes a drawing of the author's picture by Diego Rivera and contains "Colores en el mar y otros poemas," "Piedra de sacrificio," "Hora y 20," "Camino," "Hora de Junio," "Exágonos," "Recinto y otras imagenes," "Subordinaciones," "Práctica de vuelo," and "Poemas no colleccionados." *Con palabras y fuego* (With Words and Fire) (México: FCE, 1962). "Fuego nuevo en honor a José Clemente Orozco" (New Fire in Honor of José Clemente Orozco), in *Los sesenta*, no. 1 (México: Robredo, 1964), pp. 33-38. *Teotihuacán, y 13 de agosto: ruina de Tenochtitlán* (Teotihuacán and August the 13th: Ruins of Tenochtitlán) (México: Eds. Ecuador, 1966). *Primera antología poética: poemas líricos, heroícos, en el paisaje y religiosos* (First Poetic Anthology: Lyric, Heroic, Landscape, and Religious Poems), selection by Guillermo Fernández (México: FCE, l969). *Noticias sobre Nezahualcóyotl y algunos sentimientos* (News about Nezahualcóyotl and Some Thoughts) (México: Gobierno del Estado de México, l972). *Esquemas para una oda tropical* (Sketch for a Tropical Ode) (México: FCE, l976). *Cosilla para el nacimiento* (Things for Birth) (México: Editorial Latitudes, l978). *Antología breve* (Brief Anthology), collection of some poetry previously published in other collections, and some new poems (México: FCE, l986). Biography: *Bolívar, ensayo de biografía popular* (Bolivar, Essay of Popular Biography) (México: n.p., 1922). *Simón Bolivar*, Colección "La Honda del Espiritu" (México: SEP, 1965). Essay, *El trato con escritores* (The Pact with Writers) in collaboration with others (México: INBA, 1961), pp. 187-205. Prologue: *Poemas de Antonio y Manuel Machado* (Poems of Antonio and Miguel Machado), vol. 3 (México: Cultura, 1917). *José María Velasco, pinturas, dibujos, acuarelas* (José María Velasco, Paintings, Sketches, Watercolors), prologue and three sonnets by Carlos Pellicer (México: FCE, l970). *Cartas desde Italia* (Letters from Italy), presentation by Clara Bargellini (México: FCE, l985).

BIBLIOGRAPHY: Ermilio Abreu Gómez, *Sala de retratos intelectuales y artistas de mi época* (México: Editorial Leyenda, S.A., 1946), pp. 217-18. Dors Alva, Sketch to *Con palabras y fuego* (With Words and Fire), in *México en la Cultura* 721 (Jan. 13, 1963): Enrique Anderson Imbert, *Historia de la literatura hispanoamericana* (México: FCE, 1964), vol. 2, p. 51, 74, 155, 156-157. Enrique Anderson Imbert and Eugenio Florit, *Literatura hispanoamericana* (New York: Holt, Rinehart and Winston, 1960), p. 662. Anon., *Album fotográfico* (México: FCE, l982); Bibliographic note in *Anuario de la poesía mexicana 1962*; Literature Department (México: INBA, 1963), p. 108; "Carlos Pellicer escribe acerca de los museos de Tabasco," *Revista de la Semana* (Nov. 18, 1962): 2. *Forjadores de América Latina* (México: Partido Revolucionario Industrial, Comité Ejecutivo Nacional, l976); "Preside Pellicer la Asociación Latinoamericana de Escritores," *El día* (Jan. 27, 1965): 1; "Escaparate de libros," sketch to *Teotihuacán y 13 de agosto: ruina de Tenochtitlan* in *México en la Cultura* 829 (Feb. 29, 1965): 8. Jesús Arellano, "Las ventas de Don Quijote," *Nivel* 44 (Aug. 25, l962): 5. Juan José Arreola, Prologue to *Carlos Pellicer, Voz viva de México*, (México: UNAM, 1960); "Carlos Pellicer," *México en la Cultura* 586 (June 5, 1960): 5; Review on Pellicer in *La Cultura en México* 16 (June 6, 1962): iii. Carolyn Brandt Schlack, "Poetry of Carlos Pellicer," thesis, University of Colorado, l967, p. 7. Mario Calleros, "Las mesas de plomo. Carlos Pellicer," *Ovaciones* 94 (Oct. 13, 1963): 2. Emmanuel Carballo, "El libro de la semana, *Práctica de vuelo*," *México en la Cultura* 391 (Sept. 16, 1956): 2; "Carlos Pellicer o la poesía por la exageración," *Nivel* 37 (Jan. 25, 1962): 6-8; "Conversación con Carlos Pellicer," *La Cultura en México* 16 (June 6, 1962): iii-vii; *Diecinueve protagonistas de la literatura mexicana del siglo XX* (México: Empresas Editoriales, l965), pp. 191-200. Alfredo Cardona Peña, *Semblanzas mexicanas, artistas y escritores del México actual* (México: Eds, Libro-Mex., 1955), pp. 127-30. Rosario Castellanos, "Carlos Pellicer, retratista," *La Cultura en México* 16 (June 6, 1962): vii-viii. Antonio Castro Leal, *La Poesía Mexicana moderna* (México: FCE, 1953), pp. xxii-xxiii, pp. 271-72. Alí Chumacero, "Un poeta juzga a otro poeta," *La Cultura en México* 16 (June 6, 1962): iv-v; "Balance 1962; la poesía," *La Cultura en México* 46 (Jan. 2, 1963): iv; Review of *Con palabras y fuego*, in *La Gaceta* 10, 101 (Jan. 1963): 7. J. M. Cohen, "The Eagle and the Serpent," *Southern Review* 1, 2 (Spring 1965): 361-74. Eduardo Colín, *Rasgos* (México: Imp. Manuel León Sánchez, 1937), pp. 95-103. Jorge Cuesta, *Antología de la poesía mexicana moderna* (México: Contemporáneos, 1928). Frank Dauster, *Breve historia de la poesía mexicana* (México: Eds. de Andrea, 1956), pp. 150-53; *Ensayos sobre poesía mexicana* (México: Eds. de Andrea, 1963), pp. 45-51. Pedro F. De Andrea and George Melnykovich, "Carlos Pellicer: Aportación bibliográfica," *Boletín de la Comunidad Latinoamericana de Escritores* 4 (June 1969): 8-26. Beatriz Espejo, "El poeta de la luz y del color," *El rehilete* 9 (Nov. 1963): 6-9. Horacio Espinosa Altamirano, "Tempestad para un poema de Carlos Pellicer," *Nivel* 37 (Jan. 25, 1962): 9; "La experiencia del viaje en Carlos Pellicer," *Boletín bibliográfico de la Secretaría de Hacienda y Crédito Público* (México) 9, 274 (July 1, 1963): 16-17. Dudley Fitts, *An Anthology of Contemporary Latin American Poetry*, 2nd ed. (Norfolk, Conn.: New Directions, 1947). Merlin H. Forster, "El concepto de la creación poética en la obra de Carlos Pellicer," *Comunidad* 4 (Oct., 1969): 684-88; *Historia de la poesía Hispanoamericana* (Clear Creek, Ind.: American Hispanist, 1981), pp. 136-38, 312-14. Merlin H. Forster and K. David Jackson, *An Annotated Guide to Vanguardism in Latin American Literature* (Westport, Conn.: Greenwood Press, 1990). Rubén Antonio Gamboa, "Poesía de Carlos Pellicer: Búsqueda de la consubstancialidad," thesis, Tulane University, 1967. Ricardo Garibay, "Imágenes de Carlos Pellicer," *La Cultura en México* 38 (Nov. 7, 1962): xiii. Emma Godoy, "La naturaleza, el hombre y Dios en la poesía de Carlos Pellicer," *El Libro y el Pueblo* 4, 3 (July 1963): 7-11, 31. Enrique Gonzáles Casanova, "Carlos Pellicer," *Nivel* 37 (Jan. 25, 1962): 6, 8; "Obra póetica de Pellicer," *La Cultura en México* 16 (Jan. 6,1962): xvii. Carlos González Peña, *Historia de la literatura mexicana*, 1928 (México: Porrúa, 1966), pp. 273, 289, 290, 291, 298. Pedro Guillén, "Posición de Rulfo y Pellicer," (about U.S. intervention in the Dominican Republic), *¡Siempre!* 621 (May 19, 1965): 56-57. Sonja Karsen, Rev. of *Con palabras y fuego*, in *Books Abroad* 38, 2 (Spring 1964): 176-77. Jaime Labastida, "Los sentidos solares de Carlos Pellicer," *El Gallo Ilustrado* 41 (April 7, 1963): 3; *Vida Nicolaíta* 10 (March 1965): 8-9, 10. Othón Lara Barba, "Carlos Pellicer: Testimonios (Ensayo Biblio-iconográfico)," *Boletín del Instituto de Investigaciones Bibliográficas* 5 (Jan.-June 1971): 9-117. Raúl Leiva, *Imagen de la poesía mexicana contemporánea* (México: UNAM, 1959), pp. 91-108; "Bibliografía por Raúl Leiva," review of *Material Poético*, in *Nivel* 39 (March 25, 1962): 2-3. José María Lugo, "Esquemas para una religión del paisaje," *Armas y letras* 8, 3 (Sept. 1965): 63-80. Lloyd Mallan, Mary Vicke, C. V. Vicke, and Joseph Leonard Grucci, *Three Spanish American Poets: Pellicer, Neruda, and Andrade* (Albuquerque: Swallow and Critchlow, 1942). José Luis Martínez, *Literatura mexicana siglo XX, 1910-1949*, Clásicos y Modernos (México: Ant. Libr., Robredo, 1949) 1, no. 3, pp. 14-15, 22, 30-32, 35, 82, 95, 110, 113, 126, 142, 186, 341; vol. 2, no. 4 (1950), p. 94. George O. Melnykovich, "Carlos Pellicer and Creationism," *Latin American Literary Review* 2 (Spring-Summer 1974): 95-111; "Reality and Expression in the Poetry of Carlos Pellicer," thesis, University of Pittsburgh, 1973. Luis Monguió, "Poetas postmodernistas mexicanos," *Revista Hispánica Moderna* 12, 3-4 (July-Oct. 1946):

239-66. Carlos Monsiváis, *La poesía mexicana del siglo XX* (México: Empresas Editoriales, 1966), pp. 31-36, 361. Edward Mullen, *Carlos Pellicer* (Boston: Twayne, 1977); *La poesía de Carlos Pellicer: Interpretaciones críticas* (México: UNAM, 1979). Leonardo Nierman, *Texto de Carlos Pellicer* (México: Artes de México, 1967). Aurora M. Ocampo de Gómez and Ernesto Prado Velázquez, *Diccionario de escritores Mexicanos* (México: UNAM, 1967), pp. 281-83. Francisco Pabón, "Gravitación de lo indígena en la poesía de Carlos Pellicer," thesis, Rutgers University, 1969. José Emilio Pacheco, "El que ama la vida y las palabras," *La Cultura en México* 16 (June 6, 1962): vi. Octavio Paz, "La poesía de Carlos Pellicer," *Las peras del olmo* (México: Imprenta Universitaria, 1957), pp. 95-104; "La poesía de Carlos Pellicer," *Revista Mexicana de Literatura* 5 (May-June 1965): 486-93. Octavío Paz, ed., *Poesía en movimiento*, 1966 (México: Siglo Veintiuno, 1980), pp. 365-84. Javier Peñalosa, "Nombres, títulos y hechos," interviews, in *México en la Cultura* 780 (March 1, 1964): 5. Gabriel Pereyra, "El Premio Nacional de Artes y Ciencias," *El Día* (Dec. 9, 1964): 9; "Colección de Carlos Pellicer, donada por el poeta al pueblo de Teopoztlán," *El Día* (June 16, 1965): 9. María Teresa Ponce de Hurtado, *El ruiseñor lleno de muerte: aproximación a Carlos Pellicer* (México: Editorial Meridiano, 1970). Elena Poniatowska, *Palabras cruzadas* (México: Ediciónes Era, 1961), pp. 101-4, 301-2. Mario Puga, "Carlos Pellicer," *Universidad de México* 10, 6 (Feb. 6, 1956): 16-19. Luis Rius, "El material poético de Carlos Pellicer," *Cuadernos Americanos* 24, 5 (Sept.-Oct. 1962): 239-70. Antonio Rodríguez, "¿Cuándo los millonarios seguirán el ejemplo de Diego Rivera y Pellicer? Ellos donaron a México sus tesoros artísticos," *¡Siempre!* 633 (Aug. 11, 1965): 44-45. Alfredo A. Roggiano, Review of *Material Poético*, in *Revista Iberoamericana* 28, 54 (July-Dec. 1962): 407-12; *México en la Cultura* 914 (Sept. 25, 1966): 3. Francisco J. Santamaría, *La poesía tabasqueña* (México: Ediciónes Santamaría, 1940), pp. 212-13. Mauricio de la Selva, *Astericos*, review of *Teotihuacán y . . .*, in *Diorama de la Cultura* (May 16, 1965): 4. Mark Strand, *New Poetry of México* (New York: E. P. Dutton, 1970). Luis Suárez, "Pellicer," *México en la Cultura* 546 (Aug. 30, 1959): 1, 4. Esther Teitelbaum, "América en la poesía de Carlos Pellicer," thesis, Columbia University, 1975. Jaime Torres Bodet, *Contemporanéos*, Notas de crítica (México: Herrero, Hnos., 1928), pp. 43-44. Various authors, "Edición homenaje por la aparición de *Material Poético*," *El Gallo Ilustrado* 1 (July 1, 1962); "Homenaje a tres poetas: Pellicer, Chumacero, Cernuda," *La Cultura en México* 150 (Dec. 30, 1964): i-iii. Arqueles Vela, "Inmemorial a Carlos Pellicer," poem, in *México en la Cultura* 874 (Dec. 19, 1965): 3. Roberto Venegas, "Poetas mexicanos. Carlos Pellicer," *Diorama de la Cultura* (July 26, 1964): 3. Recaredo Vilches Alcazar, *Carlos Pellicer, su vida y su obra* (México: Editorial La Muralla, 1979). Gabriel Zaid, "Homenaje a la Alegría," *La Cultura en México* 248 (Nov. 16, 1966): xx.

EDNA A. REHBEIN

PEÑA, Carlos Hector de la (1920-   ), biographer, critic, translator, novelist, and author of short stories. Born in Saltillo in 1920, Peña studied literature at UNAM and belonged to the Order of the Company of Jesus. He has contributed to several literary journals. Most of his published work consists of novels, biographies of religious figures, or essays on literature.

WORKS: *Flor de martirio: María de la Luz Camacho, primer martir de la Acción Católica* (Flower of Martyrdom: María de la Luz Camacho, The First Martyr of the "Catholic Action") (México: Buena Prensa, 1940). *Diez y seis años* (Sixteen Years) (México: Buena Prensa; Col. Cía. de Jesús, 1944). *Hernando Santaren, el domador de indios* (Hernando Santaren, Tamer of Indians) (México: Buena Prensa, Col. cía. de Jesús, 1944). *La novela moderna: su sentido y su mensaje (Ensayo de interpretación literario-filosófica)* (The Modern Novel: Its Meaning and Its Message [A Literary Phiiosophical Interpretation) (México: Ed. Jus, 1944). *Historia de la literatura universal* (History of World Literature) (México: E. Ampelec, 1945; México: Ed. Jus, 1950, 1952, 1955, 1959, 1963, 1967, 1971). *Nosotros los muertos, novela* (We the Dead, Novel) (México: Ed. Jus, 1951; 1971; México: Ed. Rep-Mex, 1959). *El hipócrita* (The Hypocrite) (México: Ed. Jus, 1959). *El estanque de los lotos, cuento histórico para niños de ocho a cien años* (The Lotus Pond, Historical Tale for Children from Eight to One Hundred Years Old) (México: Ed. Rep-Mex, 1959). *Antología de la literatura universal* (Anthology of World Literature) (México: Ed. Jus, 1960). *Piel de matar, novela* (México: Ed. Jus, 1975). *Apuntes sobre el teatro francés contemporáneo* (Notes on the Contemporary French Theater) (México: Ed. Jus, 1977). *Don Francisco Monterde* (México: UNAM, 1979).

BIBLIOGRAPHY: Aurora M. Ocampo de Gómez and Ernesto Prado Velázquez, *Diccionario de Escritores Mexicanos* (México: UNAM, 1967), p. 283. Salvador Reyes Nevares, Review of *El hipócrita*, in *México en la Cultura* 518 (Feb. 15, 1979): 4.

JANIS L. KRUGH

PEÑA, Rafael Angel de la (1836-1906). Born in Mexico City on the December 23, 1836, Peña entered the Seminario Conciliar in 1852, where he studied both civil and canonical law. His interest in Latin and Greek and classical literature led him to philological studies. Peña was a teacher at the Colegio de Letras and in the National Preparatory School. In 1875 he was named to the Academia Mexicana Correspondiente de la Real Española and in 1883 was named perpetual secretary of this society. Particularly concerned with conserving the Spanish language in its highest form, his *Gramática teórica y práctica de la lengua castellana* (Theoretical and Practical Grammar of the Spanish Language) earned high praise from Marcelino Menéndez y Pelayo and Rufino José Cuervo. Peña died in Mexico City on May 21, 1906.

WORKS: Numerous presentations are collected in the *Memorias* of the Mexican Academy, 1876-1896. *Gramática teórica y práctica de la lengua castellana* (Theoretical and Practical Grammar of the Spanish Language) (México: n.p., 1898). *Obras de don Rafael Angel de la Peña* (Works of don Rafael Angel de la Peña) (México: V. Agüeros, 1900), includes presentations, literary articles, critical essays, etc.

BIBLIOGRAPHY: Victoriano Agüeros, *Escritores mexicanos contemporáneos* (México, 1880). Carlos González Peña, *History of Mexican Literature*, translated by Gusta Barfield Nance and Florene Johnson Dunstan, (Dallas, Texas: Southern Methodist University Press, 1968), p. 356. Aurora M. Ocampo de Gómez and Ernesto Prado Velázquez, *Diccionario de escritores mexicanos* (México, 1967), pp. 283-84.

FILIPPA B. YIN

PEÑA y Reyes, Antonio de la (1869-1928), diplomat, historian, and critic. Born in Mexico City on May 30, 1869, Antonio de la Peña y Reyes completed preparatory studies in the Liceo Mexicano and received his law degree from the University of Mexico. In 1886 he began his career as a diplomat and served in different capacities. He was a secretary to several Foreign Service ministers. De la Peña y Reyes, besides being a teacher and diplomat, was very active in politics and was a representative to the Congreso de la Unión (Congress of the Union) for fourteen years. Several newspapers and magazines (*La República, El Nacional, El Siglo XIX, Revista Azul*) published his essays, biographies, and articles. He was also a member of the Academia Mexicana de la Lengua (Mexican Academy of Language) and other literary societies. He died in Mexico City on June 24, 1928.

De la Peña y Reyes' works are oriented toward the history of Mexico, as well as to criticism and biography. One of his most valuable contributions was the prologue to part of *Archivo histórico-diplomático mexicano* (Mexican Historical-Diplomatic Archives).

WORKS: *Algunos poetas* (Critical Essays about Some Poets) (México: Imp. de Francisco Flores y Gardea, 1889). *Muertos y vivos, Homenajes* (The Dead and the Living, Homages) (México: Imp. de la Calle de Jesús, 1896). *Artículos y discursos* (Articles and Speeches), prologue by Victoriano Salado Alvarez (México: Tip. La Europea, 1903). *Antología moral* (Moral Anthology), prologue by Luis González Obregón (México: Vda. de Bouret, 1920). *La diplomacia mexicana* (Mexican Diplomacy) (México: Sría. de Relaciones Exteriores, 1923).

BIBLIOGRAPHY: Emiliano Díez Echarri and José María Roca Franquesa, *Historia de la Literatura Española e Hispanoamericana* (Madrid: Aguilar, 1960), p. 1213. Amado Nervo, "Antonio de la Peña y Reyes," Obras Completas, vol. 2 (México: Aguilar, 1962), p. 14. Victoriano Salado Alvarez, "Don Antonio de la Peña y Reyes, a propósito de su libro Muertos y vivos," *Estudios de crítica* (Guadalajara: Imp. de Ancira y Hno., 1899), pp. 75-78.

                                                                    BAUDELIO GARZA

PEÑALOSA, Javier (1921-   ), poet and journalist. Javier Peñalosa was born in Mexico City. He has written for cultural journals and supplements such as *México en la Cultura* and *Nivel*.

WORKS: *Preludio en sombra* (Prelude in the Shadow) (México: Ed. América, 1946). *Poemas* (Poems). *8 poetas mexicanos* (México: Abside, 1955). *La noche nueva* (The New Night) (México: Ed. Jus, 1960). *Paso de la memoria* (The Trail of Memory) (México: Ecuador, 1965).

BIBLIOGRAPHY: Antonio Castro Leal, *La poesía mexicana moderna* (México: FCE, 1953), p. 471; "La poesía de Javier Peñalosa," *Nivel* 37 (1966): 1, 2, 8. Salvador Reyes Nevares, "Los libros al día," Review of *El paso de la memoria* in *La Cultura en México* (Nov. 17, 1965): 15.

                                                                    ALFONSO GONZALEZ

PEÑALOSA, Joaquín Antonio (1822-   ), poet and writer. Joaquín Antonio Peñalosa was born in 1822 in San Luis Potosí, where he completed his studies and received Holy Orders in 1848. He received his degree as a doctor of letters fron the Iberoamerican University in Mexico City, and he taught languages and Latin literature at the University of Potosí.

Peñalosa's literary activities include founding and directing the magazine *Estilo* and membership in several groups such as the Mexican Academy of Language and the Seminary of Mexican Culture. His greatest literary contribution is his renewal of Mexican religious poetry that expresses a simplistic freshness and piety. His essays demonstrate his knowledge of Mexican literature as seen in his critical publication of *Ensayos poéticos inéditos de Manuel José Othón* (Unpublished Poetic Essays of Manuel José Othón).

WORKS: *Ejercicios para los bestezuelos de Dios* (Exercises for the Beasts of God) (México: Abside, 1951). *Sonetos desde la esperanza* (Sonnets from Hope) (México: Abside, 1882). *Francisco González Bocanegra, Su vida y su obra* (Francisco Gonzalez Bocanegra, His Life and Works) (México: Imp. Universitaria, 1884). *Vocabulario y refranero religioso de México* (Vocabulary and Religious Collection of Proverbs of Mexico) (México: Jus, l885).

BIBLIOGRAPHY: Alí Chumacero, "Panorama de los últimos libros,   Luis de Mendizábal," *México en la Cultura* 386 (1956):2. Rafael Montejano Aguinaga, "Vocabulario y refranero religioso de México," *Abside* 1 (l888): 1l6-17. Benjamín Orozco, Francisco González Bocanegra," *Ideas de México* 6 (1954): 264-65.

                                                                        SILKA FREIRE

PEON y Contreras, José (1843-1907). Born in Merida, Yucatán, on January 12, 1843, Peón y Contreras was a respected statesman, doctor, administrator, and writer. He began his studies in his native Yucatán. Influenced by a vigorous family culture, he began to write verses while still an adolescent. His studies, nevertheless, led him to a medical career. In 1863 he moved to the capital, Mexico City, where he established his practice, specializing in psychiatry. After only a few years he was designated director of the Hospital of San Hipólito. Peón y Contreras also served his country well as representative to Congress, first from Yucatán and then from Nuevo León. He became secretary of the houses of deputies and of senators, in succession. En route to Europe in 1906, he suffered an attack that left him paralyzed. He immediately returned to Mexico City, where he died on January 18, 1907.

A late romantic, Peón y Contreras wrote verses, drama, and novels. True to his Mexican heritage, he drew many themes and characters from pre-Hispanic and local history, as well as from the events of the Spanish conquest and succeeding period. Between 1861 and his death in 1907 no fewer than twenty-seven of his plays were presented, in Mérida at first, and then principally in the capital city. In 1876 the Sociedad Dramática Peón Contreras was founded in his honor. Plays were also presented in the Teatro Peón Contreras, named in his honor in his birthplace, Mérida. *La hija del rey* (The King's Daughter), which debuted in Mexico City in 1876, was acclaimed for its high quality, and Peón y Contreras was praised as a worthy heir to the tradition of *Ruiz de Alarcón and * Manuel Eduardo de Gorostiza. Many plays followed in quick succession, including *Un amor de Hernán Cortés* (A Love Affair of Hernán Cortés); *El conde de Peñalva* (The Count of Peñalva); *Impulsos del corazón* (Impulses of the Heart); and *Laureana*. In his poetry Peón y Contreras preferred the romance, giving free reign to exalted patriotism, loyalty and honor, love, sacrifice, and disillusion. Peón y Contreras also wrote two novels, *Taide* and *Veleidosa* (Fickle Woman). In this latter novel he continued to work with the themes that were familiar to his readers and presented characters full of life within a well-structured argument.

WORKS: Theater: Although many of the plays of Peón y Contreras were published individually upon production, they are more accessible in *Obras de José Peón y Contreras* (Works of José Peón y Contreras), Biblioteca de Autores Mexicanos (BAM), no. 4 (México: Imp. de V. Agüeros, editor, 1896); no. 5 (1897). The complete list of individual plays follows. Many of these were not published; they are listed with only the date of presentation: *El castigo de Dios* (God's Punishment) (1861 or 1862?). *El conde de Santiesteban* (The Count of Santiesteban) (1861-1862?). *María la loca* (Mary the Lunatic) (1861-1862?). *¡Hasta el cielo!* (As High as the Sky!) (1876) (México: Dublán y Cía., 1879; México: Agüeros, 1897). *El sacrificio de la vida* (The Sacrifice of Life) (1876) (México: Dublán y Cía., 1879; México: Agüeros, 1897). *Gil González de Avila* (Gil González of Avila) (1876) (México: Dublán y Cía., 1879; Mérida: Gambóa Guzmán, 1883; México: Agüeros, 1896). *La hija del rey* (The King's Daughter) (1876) (México: Dublán y Cía., 1879; México: Agüeros, 1896); (México: UNAM, 1941). *Un amor de Hernán Cortés* (A Love Affair of Hernán Cortés) (1876); (Mérida: Gambóa Guzmán, 1883). *Luchas de honra y de amor* (Struggles of Honor and Love) (1876) (México: Agüeros, 1896). *Juan de Vallalpando* (1876) (Mérida: Gambóa Guzmán, 1883). *Antón de Alaminos* (1876) (México: A. Llanos, 1876; Mérida: Gambóa Guzmán, 1883). *Esperanza* (Hope) (1876) (Mérida: Gambóa Guzmán, 1883; México: Agüeros, 1897). *El conde de Peñalva* (The Count of Peñalva) (1877) (Mérida: Gambóa Guzmán, 1883; México: Cumplido, 1883). *La ermita de Santa Fe* (The Hermitage of Santa Fe), in collaboration with Alfredo Chavero (1877) (México: J. M. Sandoval, 1877). *Entre mi tío y mi tía* (Between My Uncle and My Aunt) (1878). *Doña Leonor de Sarabia* (1878) (Mérida: Gambóa Guzmán, 1883). *Por el joyel del sombrero* (For the Jewel on the Hat) (1878) (Mérida: Gambóa Guzmán, 1883; México: Agüeros, 1896). *El capitán Pedreñales* (Captain Pedreñales) (1879) (Mérida: Gambóa Guzmán, 1883). *Vivo o muerto* (Dead or Alive) (1879) (México: Agüeros, 1896). *Impulsos del corazón* (Impulses of the Heart) (date unknown) (Mérida: Gambóa Guzmán, 1883). *En el umbral de la dicha* (On the Threshold of Happiness) (1885) (México: Tip. de J. Barbier, 1885; La ilustración, 1886; México: Agüeros, 1897). *El bardo* (The Bard) (1886) (México: Imp. José V. Castillo, 1890). *Gabriela* (1888) (México: *Revista Nacional de Letras y Ciencias*, 1889, vol. 2, pp. 1-49; México: Ofna. Tip. de la Sría de Fomento, 1889; México: Leopoldo Burón, 1890; México: Agüeros, 1897). *La cabeza de Ucanor* (The Head of Ucanor) (1890) (Mérida: Gambóa Guzmán, 1890). *Soledad* (Solitude) (1892) (México: Agüeros, 1897). *Laureana* (1893). *Una tormenta en el mar* (A Storm at Sea) (1893). *¡Por la Patria!* (For the Fatherland!) (1894) (México: Ofna. Tip. de la Sría de Fomento, 1896). *Poetry and Prose: Obras en verso y prosa* (Works in Verse and Prose) (México: Dublán y Cía., 1879). *Poesías* (Poetry) (México: Imp. de Ancona y Peniche, 1868). *Romances históricos mexicanos* (Mexican Historical Ballads) (México: Imp. Díaz de León, 1873). *Trovas colombinas* (Columbian Ballads) (México: n.p., 1871). *Romances históricos y*

524 PEREDO, Manuel

dramáticos (Historical and Dramatic Ballads) (México: n.p., 1888). *Obras poéticas de José Peón y Contreras* (Poetic Works of José Peón y Contreras) (Veracruz and México: Biblioteca de Autores Mexicanos, Ramón Laine, editor, 1889). *Obras de don José Peón y Contreras* (Works of José Peón y Contreras), Biblioteca de Autores Mexicanos (BAM), no. 46 (México: V. Agüeros, editor, 1902). *Taide* (México: 1885). *Veleidosa* (Fickle Woman) (México: Imp. de F. Díaz de León, 1891).

BIBLIOGRAPHY: Ermilo Abreu Gómez, "Teatro romántico de Peón y Contreras," in *Clásicos, románticos, modernos* (México: Eds. Botas, 1934). Frank Dauster, *Breve historia de la poesía mexicana* (México: Eds. de Andrea), pp. 86-87. Heriberto García Rivas, *Historia de la literatura mexicana* (México: Textos Universitarios, 1972), vol. 2, pp. 92, 101, 109. Carlos González Peña, *History of Mexican Literature*, translated by Gusta Barfield Nance and Florene Johnson Dunstan (Dallas, Texas: Southern Methodist University Press, 1968), pp. 330-32. Julio Jiménez Rueda, *Letras mexicanas en el siglo XIX* (México: FCE, 1944), pp. 168-69. Aurora M. Ocampo de Gómez and Ernesto Prado González, *Diccionario de escritores mexicanos* (México: UNAM, 1967), pp. 286-87.

FILIPPA B. YIN

PEREDO, Manuel (1830-1890), drama critic. A medical doctor by profession but a poet at heart, Peredo applied his analytical skills to art in countless reviews of theatrical productions in Mexico City. Peredo's comments on theater were regular features in *El Semanario Ilustrado* (The Weekly Illustrated), *El Renacimiento* (Renaissance), and *El Correo de México* (The Mexican Post), as well as in other newspapers. Ignacio Manuel *Altamirano praised Peredo's beautiful use of language, his sound judgment, his manner of criticizing without offending, and his dedication to theater as an art form. Peredo is thought to have exerted a major influence on the growth and development of Mexican theater in the second half of the nine-teenth century. He is also credited with the authorship of at least one play, *El que todo lo quiere* (He Who Wants It All), which was performed in Mexico City in 1868, but was never published. Peredo wrote numerous poems that won him high praise from his contemporaries because of the elegance and purity of their form. His verses were published in local newspapers and recited in literary salons in the capital city, where he played an active role in intellectual and artistic circles. Despite his activity and prominence as a writer during his lifetime, little of Peredo's work is available for study today, since it has not been collected and published in book form, and much of it has been lost.

WORKS: *El que todo lo quiere*, play, staged in Mexico City in 1869. "Edipo, tragedia de don Francisco Martínez de la Rosa. Ensayo Crítico," in *El Artista* 1 (México, 1874): 145-55. *Curso elemental de arte métrica y poética* (México: Aguilar, 1883).

BIBLIOGRAPHY: Ignacio Manuel Altamirano, *La literatura nacional* (México: Porrúa, 1949), vol. 1, pp. 101-4. Carlos González Peña, *Historia de la Literatura Mexicana* (México: Pub. de la SEP, 1928), p. 466.

CYNTHIA K. DUNCAN

PEREZ Moreno, José (1900-   ), fiction writer, journalist, and diplomat. Born in Lagos de Moreno, Jalisco, José Pérez Moreno studied accounting at the National University. Pérez Moreno was elected representative for the State of Jalisco in 1959. He was appointed consul general to Italy in 1966. Several of his stories were published in *El Universal Ilustrado*, and one of them, "La mulata de Córdova," was made into a movie. His novel *El tercer canto del gallo* (The Third Cockcrow) won the "Premio de Novela ciudad de México" in 1958.

WORKS: Short Stories: "La mulata de Córdova (The Mulatta of Córdova), in *Imaginación de México*, edited by Rafael H. Valle (Buenos Aires: Espasa-Calpe, 1945), pp. 204-5. "Y seguía cantando el arroyo" (And the Creek Kept On Singing), in *Anuario del Cuento Mexicano 1954* (México: INBA, 1955), pp. 393-410. Novel: *El tercer canto del Gallo* (The Third Cockcrow) (México: Aguilar, 1957).

BIBLIOGRAPHY: Luis Leal, *Bibliografía del cuento mexicano* (México: De Andrea, 1958), p. 112. Salvador Reyes Nevares, "Autores y libros," *México en la Cultura*. (April 6, 1958): 4.

MIRTA A. GONZALEZ

PESADO, José Joaquín (1801-1861), poet and journalist, a classicist among romantics. José Joaquín Pesado was born in San Agustín del Palmar, Puebla, on February 9, 1801. He was versed in Spanish, Latin, and French. He could read Greek, had a sound knowledge of theology, and was familiar with the Summa of Saint Thomas. He was a corresponding member of the Spanish Academy. He died in Mexico City on March 3, 1861. Pesado cultivated several genres but excelled as a descriptive poet, as evidenced in his work *Sitios y Escenas de Orizaba y Córdoba* (Places and Scenes of Orizaba and Córdoba). He introduced the indigenous genre into Mexican poetry with his collection *Los Aztecas* (The Aztecs), in which *La Princesa de Culhuachn* (The Princess of Culhuachn) appears.

WORKS: *Poesías originales y traducidas* (Original and Translated Poems) (México: Cumplido, 1839). *Escenas del campo y de la aldea de México* (Scenes of Mexican Countrysides and Towns) (México: n.p., n.d.). *Consejos del padre a la hija o la vanidad de la gloria humana* (A Father's Advice to His Daughter or the Vanity of Human Glory), based on the songs attributed to Netzahualcoyátl (México: n.p., n.d.). An adaptation of *Cantar de los Cantares* (Song of Songs) (México: n.p., n.d.). *La Revelación* (The Revelation) (México: Vicente Segura Argüelles, 1856). A translation of Tasso's *Jerusalem Libertada* (Jerusalem Liberated) (México: Vicente Segura Argüelles, 1860). *El libertador de México don Agustín de Iturbide* (México: La Voz de México, 1872). *El pescador negro* (México: Tip. Aguilar Ortiz, 1874).

BIBLIOGRAPHY: María Edmi Alvarez, *Literatura mexicana e hispanoamericana* (México: Editorial Porrúa, 1971), p. 129. Julio Jiménez Rueda, *Historia de la literatura mexicana* (México: Ed. Botas, 1960), pp. 215, 224-28, 235, 266, 267; *Letras mexicanas en el siglo XIX* (México: FCE, 1944), p. 96. José M. Roa Bárcena, Obras, vol. 4:

Biografías, Biblioteca de Autores Mexicanos (México: Imp. de V. Agüero, Ed., 1902). Francisco Sosa, *Biografías de Mexicanos Distinguidos* (México: Oficina Topográfica de la Secretaría de Fomento, 1884), pp. 818-22.

JOSEPH VELEZ

PEZA, Juan de Dios (1852-1910), poet, playwright. Born in Mexico City June 29, 1852, Peza was the son of an important conservative politician, and received a good education in the capital. He began the study of medicine, but soon abandoned it to work as a journalist, and later wrote plays and poetry. In 1878 he went to Spain as a diplomat, and there was exposed to Spanish Romanticism. In Madrid he published in *La Ilustración Española* (The Spanish Enlightenment) and in *Americana*. He received high praise from Ramón de Campoamor, who became his model and teacher. When he returned to Mexico, his wife abandoned him and his two small children, an event that became central to his poetry. His most famous poem, *Fusiles y muñecas* (Toy Guns and Dolls), is a sentimental description of the children playing alone with their toys. Peza was a popular conversationalist, and a frequent figure in literary soirees and gatherings reciting his works, especially in 1876 and 1877. He became known as the official "poeta del hogar" (Poet of the Hearth), and he was the best-known of his generation outside of Mexico.

The sheer volume of poetry that Peza produced caused many to judge him harshly, and in 1888, when Manuel *Puga y Acal, in *Los poetas mexicanos contemporáneos*, dismissed Peza as over-prolific and unimportant, subsequent generations of critics ignored him. Aurora Ocampo de Gómez feels nevertheless that the "narrative value of some of his legendary and traditional poems" deserves further study. Writes J. Sapina, further, "who can say that his exceptional poems did not require an abundant leaf storm in order to be achieved?" After Puga y Acal's harsh criticism, Peza's reputation all but disappeared in his lifetime, and he died in obscurity in Mexico City on March 16, 1910.

WORKS: Poetry: *Poesías* (Poetry) (México: El Siglo XIX, I. Cumplido, 1873). *Horas de pasión* (Hours of Passion) (México: El Porvenir, 1876). *Cantos del hogar* (Songs of the Hearth) (México: Gallegos Hermanos, 1884-1889). *Dos reales de versos festivos* (Two Bits' Worth of Festive Verses) (México: Gallegos, 1888). *Versos del alma* (Verses of the Soul) (Curazao: Bethencourt e Hijos, 1888). *La musa de viaje* (The Muse of Travel) (México: Gallegos, 1889). *Honor y patria* (Honor and Fatherland) (Paris: Garnier, 1891). *Recuerdos y esperanzas* (Memories and Hopes) (Paris: Garnier, 1892). *Flores del alma y versos festivos* (Flowers of the Soul and Festive Verses) (Paris: Earnier, 1893). *Poesías escogidas* (Barcelona: Maucci, 1897). *Leyendas históricas, tradicionales y fantásticas* (Historical, Traditional, and Fantastic Legends) (Paris: Garnier, 1898). *Poesías completas* (Complete Poems) (Paris: Garnier, 1891), contains all the verse dramas. Theater: *La ciencia del hogar* (The Science of the Home) (México: Imp. y Librería de la Enseñanza, 1876). *Tirar la llave* (Throw the Key), *Recuerdos de un veterano* (Memories of a Veteran), and *En vísperas de la boda* (The Night before the Wedding), all included in *Poesías completas*, ed. cit. *Escribiendo un drama* (Writing a Drama), and *Yo Sola* (I Alone) included in *Recuerdos y esperanzas*, ed. cit. *El grito de Dolores* (The Cry of Dolores) (Méxic: J. R. Garrido, 1909). *Granaditas* (Little Pomegranates) (México: Garrido, 1910). *Las dos muñecas* (The Two Dolls) (México: P. Rodríguez, 1899). *Un duelo en el mar* (A Duel on the Sea) (México: Librería Central, 1899). *Hojas de margarita* (Daisy Petals) (México: Ballesch, 1910). In addition, Peza published translations and numerous prologues. He was widely anthologized in his lifetime and later.

BIBLIOGRAPHY: Carlos G. Amezaga, *Poetas mexicanos* (Buenos Aires: Pablo E. Coni and Sons, 1896), pp. 231-50. José Joaquín Blanco, *Crónica de la poesía mexicana* (México: Libro de Bolsillo, 1983), pp. 26, 32, 34. Domingo Couoh Vázquez, "Juan de Dios Peza. Centenario de su nacimiento," *Bohemia Poblana*. 110 (Puebla, July 1952): 15-16. Frank Dauster, *Breve historia de la poesía mexicana* (México: Andrea, 1956), pp. 85-86. Genaro Fernández MacGregor, "El cantor del hogar," *El Universal* (México, June 1952): 7. Heriberto García Rivas, *Historia de la literatura mexicana*, vol. 2 (México: Porrúa, 1972), pp. 189, 217. Carlos González Peña, *History of Mexican Literature* (Dallas: Southern Methodist University Press, 1943-1968), pp. 274-76, 354. Villa Belle Hodd, "Juan de Dios Peza, poeta mexicano," thesis (México: UNAM/Escuela de Verano, 1949). Sergio Howland Bustamante, *Historia de la literatura mexicana* (México: F. Trillas, 1967), pp. 181, 183, 232. Enrique de Olavarría y Ferrari, *El arte literario en México* (Málaga: Imp. de la *Revista de Andalucía*, 1877). Manuel Puga y Acal, *Los poetas mexicanos contemporáneos* (México: Ireneo Paz, 1888). José Emilio Pacheco, *La poesía mexicana del siglo XIX* (Empresas Editoriales, 1965), pp. 333-39. Aurora M. Ocampo de Gómez and Ernesto Prado Velázquez, *Diccionario de escritores mexicanos* (México: UNAM, 1967), pp. 289-91. Agustín del Saz, *Antología general de la poesía mexicana* (Barcelona: Bruguera, 1972).

PATRICIA HART AND JOSEF HELLEBRANDT

PIAZZA, Luis Guillermo (1922-), professor, essayist, novelist. Born in Córdoba, Argentina, on February 10, 1922, Piazza received his doctoral degrees in law and social science and as a teacher of English from the National University of Cordoba. As an expert on Latin American law, Piazza traveled throughout the Americas as advisor and lecturer, also making trips to Europe at the invitation of different countries. His works in the Organization of American States (1949-1950) eventually took him in 1962 to Mexico, where he was assigned as secretary of the Committee of Cultural Action.

His literary contributions, all published in Mexico, included the play *La siesta* (The Nap) (956) and the novel *Los hombres y las cosas sólo querían jugar* (Men and Things Only Wanted to Play) (1953), as well as essays and poems.

WORKS: *La siesta* (The Nap) (México: Obregón, 1956). *Los hombres y las cosas sólo querían jugar* (Men and Things Only Wanted to Play) (México: Ecuador, l953). *El tuerto de oro* (One-Eyed Man of Gold) (México: Era, 1983).

BIBLIOGRAPHY: Emmanuel Carballo, "La siesta," in *México en la Cultura* 972 (1956): 2. Salvador Elizondo, "La aptitud literaria de Luis Guillerno Piazza nos da una nueva e interesante visión de América," in *México en la Cultura* 757 (1963): 9. Luis Guillerno Piazza, "Una nueva visión del país más viejo del mundo," in *México en la Cultura* 177 (1965): 12.

SILKA FREIRE

PIMENTEL, Francisco, Conde de Heras (1832-1893), linguist, literary critic. Pimentel was a great scholar and erudite, although his taste in literature was sometimes questionable. He was familiar with classical and modern letters, and was a tireless reader and researcher. Much of his adult life was devoted to the study of language and literature in Mexico. Nevertheless, he did not seem to feel any real enthusiasm or appreciation for the works produced by his countrymen. He often showed a negative opinion of Mexican literature, relentlessly searching for defects in form, content, and composition, and judging the merits of literary works by their grammatical correctness and moral tone, rather than their artistic sensibility. Beginning in 1868, Pimentel began to publish articles in *La constitución social* (The Social Constitution) and other Mexico City newspapers under the general title *Biografía y crítica de los principales escritores mexicanos* (Biography and Criticism of Major Mexican Writers). Fifteen years later, these articles formed the backbone of a 736-page volume called *Historia crítica de la literatura y de las ciencias en México* (Critical History of Mexican Literature and Erudition). Despite the promise of the title, Pimentel limited his study to poetry, including drama in verse form. Because the book received so much negative commentary, Pimentel revised it and nine years later published a corrected and augmented version entitled *Historia crítica de la poesía en México* (Critical History of Mexican Poetry). Only one-third of the book deals with Mexico's three centuries of colonial literary production. The remainder deals with nineteenth-century poets.

Pimentel considers *Navarrete to be the best poet of the colonial period, and judges him to be far superior to Sor Juana Inés de la *Cruz, whom Pimentel attacks for her adherence to Gongorism. It is principally for his harsh treatment of Sor Juana, and his unjustifiable preference for nineteenth-century writers, that his work is discredited by modern critics. Pimentel's literary histories are primarily catalogs of names and works. Although they contain a great deal of factual information, they show no sensitivity to literature. His prose is correct and clear, but excessively dry and pedantic. Pimentel apparently met with more success as a linguist. His *Cuadro descriptivo de las lenguas indígenas en México* (Descriptive Sketch of Indigenous Languages in Mexico) won prizes both at home and in Europe for its valuable contribution to the study of American linguistics.

WORKS: *Biografía y crítica de los principales poetas mexicanos* (Biography and Criticism of Major Mexican Writers) (México: Imp. Díaz de León, 1869). *Cuadro descriptivo de las lenguas indígenas de México* (Descriptive Sketch of Indigenous Languages in Mexico) (México: Tip. Epstein, 1874-1875). *Historia crítica de la literatura y de las ciencias en México* (Critical History of Mexican Literature and Erudition) (México: Libr. de la Enseñanza, 1883). *Historia crítica de la poesía en México* (Critical History of Mexican Poetry) (México: Tip. de la Secretaría de Fomento, 1892). *Obras completas* (Complete Works) (México: Tip. Económica, 1904). *Antología de Francisco Pimentel* (Anthology of Francisco Pimentel), edited by Eduardo Michelena and J.L. Salcedo Bastardo (Caracas: Ministerio de Educación Nacional, 1950).

BIBLIOGRAPHY: José Luis Martínez, *La expresión nacional* (México: Oasis, 1984), pp. 417-30. Francisco Sosa, prologue, *Obras completas de Francisco Pimentel* (México: Tip. Económica, 1903-1904), pp. v-cx.

CYNTHIA K. DUNCAN

PITOL, Sergio (1933-). Born on March 18, 1933, in Puebla, Sergio Pitol studied in Córdoba and Veracruz. In Mexico, he worked for several publishing firms, including Novaro and Oasis, wrote for various periodicals, and also taught at the University of Veracruz. With a dual career of diplomat, world traveler and writer, Pitol has lived in Rome and Beijing and Warsaw. While in Warsaw, he also worked as a translator. He published two important translations, one of Jerzy Andrzejewski's *Las puertas del paraíso* (The Doors of Paradise) (1965), and one of Kazimierz Brandys' *Cartas a la señora Z* (Letters to Mrs. Z) (1966). Around this same time, he published a short autobiography, with a prologue by Emmanuel *Carballo.

Pitol is primarily recognized as a short story writer. Many of his tales are studies of decadence and corruption in the provincial societies of Córdoba and San Rafael. Quite a few encompass the historical period from the early twentieth century to the era of the Calles regime. Despite the negative thematic material, Pitol maintains an undercurrent of hopefulness in his work.

Pitol began publishing stories in 1958, when "Victorio Ferri cuenta un cuento" (Victorio Ferri Tells a Story) came out. It was included the following year with a group of other stories in *Tiempo cercado* (Enclosed Time). Some of these stories were later rewritten and published again in *Infierno de todos* (Everyone's Hell), along with four others. Because of his diplomatic career, Pitol has written and lived a great part of his life outside Mexico. The collection of stories *Cementerio de tordos* (Cemetery of Thrushes) presents the attitudes of the Mexican abroad, mainly in Europe. Pitol's writing appears neither patriotic nor nostalgic; it is, rather, analytic, examining from different perspectives the essence of being Mexican. His frequent diplomatic junctures have provided him with exceptional raw material for his stories. *Los climas* is one of the literary results of Pitol's travels to China, Poland, and Italy. In these grave, well-constructed stories, he examines such issues as cowardice, jealousy, and impaired hope for change as the characters search for an ideal "climate" in which to live and express themselves. The stories represent Pitol's search for his own identity, his reason for being, and they also focus on the quest for happiness and fulfillment for mankind in general. His residence in other geographical and ethnic climates enables him to view Mexico and its reality with greater objectivity and depth than would otherwise happen.

Sergio Pitol is considered a vigorous writer, but one who distances and isolates himself from others. His first publication, *Tiempo cercado*, was received with indifference, but his book *Infierno de todos* warrented more attention. *Infierno de todos* is a book of stories that evaluate the conflicts of life and intimate relationships, especially the battles between parents and their children. In 1972, he published the novel *El tañido de una flauta* (The Sound of a Flute), a work which is more experimental in style and texture than his previous writings. He uses techniques from the world of the cinema which he imposes on the narrative as a backdrop. A novel whose action takes place mainly in Europe and New York, *El tañido de una flauta* shows aspects of reality splitting between the narrative and the cinema.

In 1981, Pitol published *Nocturno de Bujara* (Bujara's Nocturnal), a group of four sophisticated, intellectual stories by an author at the pinnacle of his creative expression. The tales are both exotic in setting and precise in detail. But Pitol deceives the reader by the dissolution of whatever reality appeared to be into mere words, fragments of speech. The following year, Pitol experimented with techniques reminiscent of Unamuno. *Juegos florales* (Floral Games) represents Pitol's unending task of writing a novel that ends only when a ficticious author ends his own novel.

WORKS: *Victorio Ferri cuenta un cuento* (México: Cuadernos del Unicornio, 1958). *Tiempo cercado* (Enclosed Time) (México: Edit. Estaciones, 1959). *Infierno de todos* (Everyone's Hell) (Xalapa: Universidad Veracruzana, 1964). *Los climas* (Climates) (México: Joaquín Mortiz, 1966). *Sergio Pitol*, prologue by Emmmanuel Carballo (México: Empresas Editoriales, 1966). *El tañido de una flauta* (The Sound of a Flute) (México: Ediciones Era, 1972). *Nocturno de Bujara* (Bujara's Nocturne) (México: Siglo XXI Editores, 1981). *Cementerio de tordos* (Cemetery of Thrushes) (México: Ediciones Océano, 1982). *Juegos florales* (Floral Games) (México: Siglo Veintiuno Editores, 1982). Translations: Jerzy Andrzejewski, *Las puertas del paraíso* (The Doors of Paradise), translated from Polish (México: Joaquín Mortiz, 1965). Kazimierz Brandys, *Cartas a la señora Z* (Letters to Mrs. Z), translated from Polish (Xalapa: Universidad Veracruzana, 1966).

BIBLIOGRAPHY: Lucy Bonilla, Review of *Los climas*, in *Revista de Bellas Artes* 9 (May-June 1966): 104-5. Emmmanuel Carballo, "Entrevista con Sergio Pitol," in *México en la Cultura* 517 (Feb. 8, 1959): 2; "Casi una entrevista con Sergio Pitol," in *La Cultura en México* 164 (April 7, 1965): xvi. Noé Chávez-Magaña, "La generación cuentística mexicana del 1958," *DAI* 43, 9 (March 1983): 3003A. Russell M. Cluff, "Los climas o el cosmopolitismo en los cuentos de Sergio Pitol," in *Texto Crítico* 7, 21 (Apr.-June 1981): 35-50; "Sergio Pitol: Proceso y mensaje en Juegos Florales," in *La Palabra y el Hombre* 58 (Apr.-June 1986): 50-57. Roberto Echavarren, "Sobre *Del encuentro nupcial*," in *Texto Crítico* 7, 21 (Apr.-June 1981): 31-34. David William Foster, comp., *A Dictionary of Contemporary Latin American Authors* (Tempe: Center for Latin American Studies, Arizona State University, 1975), pp. 82-83. Juan García Ponce, "Sergio Pitol: La escritura oblicua," in *Texto Crítico* 7, 21 (Apr.-June 1981): 11-15. Blanca Haro, "Un mexicano en Varsovia. Entrediálogo con Sergio Pitol," in *Diorama de la Cultura* (Sept. 11, 1966): 6. Efraín Kristal, "El rostro y la máscara: Entrevista con Sergio Pitol," in *Revista Iberoamericana* 53, 141) (Oct.-Dec. 1987): 981-94. Manuel Lerín, "Las narraciones de Sergio Pitol," in *Revista Mexicana de Cultura* 938 (March 21, 1965): 15. María Luisa Mendoza, "De Varsovia a Jerusalén. La ventana de Sergio Pitol," in *El Día* (Oct. 24, 1965): 2. Carlos Monsiváis, "Los círculos concéntricos de Sergio Pitol," in *Texto Crítico* 7, 21 (Apr-June 1981): 3-10. Lazlo Javier Moussing, Review of *Tiempo cercado*, in *Estaciones* 4, 14 (Summer 1959): 245-48. Mario Muñoz, "*Infierno de todos*: Formación de un sistema," in *Texto Crítico* 7, 21 (Apr.-June 1981): 18-30. Aurora M. Ocampo, "Bibliografía de Sergio Pitol," in *Texto Crítico* 7, 21 (Apr.-June 1981): 63-67. Margarita Peña, "México y el infierno," in *Ovaciones* 169 (March 28, 1965): 7. Elena Poniatowska, "Elena Poniatowska redescubre en Varsovia a un escritor mexicano: Sergio Pitol," in *La Cultura en México* 185 (Sept. 1, 1965): xiii-xiv. Miguel Riera, "Sergio Pitol, inmune a las odas," in *Quimera* 80 (Aug. 1988): 46-51. César Rodríguez Chicharro, Review of *Infierno de todos*, in *La Palabra y el Hombre* 34 (Apr.-June 1954): 326-28. Publio O. Romero, "Conversación con Sergio Pitol," in *Texto Crítico* 7, 21 (Apr.-June 1981): 51-62. Roberto Vallarino, ed., "Sergio Pitol: veinte años después," in *Semana de Bellas Artes* (México, Aug. 1981): 1-16.

JEANNE C. WALLACE

PIZARRO, Nicolás (1830-1895), novelist. An ardent liberal and supporter of the Juárez government, Pizarro was among the first writers in Mexico to use literature as a vehicle for the expression of the political and social ideology of the Reform. In his first novel, *El monedero* (The Money Purse), he attempts to show how a systematic application of the Laws of Reform would effect Mexican society. He examines the Church and the army, the role of women and of Indians, and the need for a collective effort on the part of the Mexican people to bring stability to the country. The novel is considered by some to be the precursor to Ignacio *Altamirano's *La Navidad en las montañas* (Christmas in the Mountains) because of its emphasis on the importance of social solidarity among the common people of Mexico. Pizarro's second novel, *La coqueta* (The Coquette), is a sentimental work that combines many of the standard conventions of Romanticism with costumbristic scenes of mid-nineteenth century Mexico. Its most interesting feature is the fact that Pizarro uses one of his contemporaries, the writer Juan *Díaz Covarrubias, as a character in the novel.

WORKS: *El monedero* (The Money Purse) (México: Imprenta N. Pizarro, 1861). *La coqueta* (The Coquette) (México: Imprenta N. Pizarro, 1861).

BIBLIOGRAPHY: María del Carmen Millán, *Literatura mexicana* (México: Editorial Esfinge, 1962), p. 167.

CYNTHIA K. DUNCAN

PLACENCIA, Alfredo R. (1873-1930), poet and priest. Having attended seminary in Guadalajara, during which time he suffered privation and poverty, Placencia offered his first mass in Jalisco in 1899. He ministered in small, rural towns. Because of difficulties with his superiors he was exiled in the United States in 1923 and the following year sent from California to El Salvador. In 1929 he returned to Guadalajara, where he died on May 20, 1930.

His greatest literary influences derived from classic Greek and Latin literature and from the Bible. He wrote mystic poetry from 1890 to 1920. His poetic force is rooted in its constant state of mystic communion, its moral integrity, and its tenderness of spirit inspired by the poet's own experiences.

WORKS: *El paso del dolor* (The Passage of Grief) (Barcelona: n.p., 1924). *Del cuartel y del claustro* (Of the Barracks and the Cloister) (Barcelona: n.p., 1924). *El libro de Dios* (The Book of God) (Barcelona: n.p., 1924). "Tres poemas inéditos del Padre Placencia" (Three Unpublished Poems of Father Placencia), in *Abside* 5 (1941): 686-97. *Antología poética* (Poetic Anthology) (México: UNAM, 1946). *Poesías* (Poetry) (Guadalajara: Universidad de Guadalajara, 1959).

BIBLIOGRAPHY: Frank Dauster, *Breve historia de la poesía mexicana* (México: Eds. de Andrea, 1956), p. 133. Raymond L. Grismer, *A Bibliogra-phy of Articles and Essays on the Literatures of Spain and Spanish America* (Minneapolis: Perine, 1935), p. 168. Alfonso Gutiérrez Hermosillo, "Glosa de un poeta desconocido (Alfredo R. Placencia)," El Libro y el Pueblo 11 (1933): 275-85. Carlos Monsiváis, *La poesía mexicana del siglo XX* (México: Empresas Editoriales, S.A., 1966). Arturo Torres-

Rioseco and Ralph E. Warner, *Bibliografía de la poesía mexicana* (Cambridge: Harvard University Press, l934), p. 68.

BARBARA P. FULKS

POETRY IN THE COLONIAL PERIOD. The first poetry in New Spain was written by the followers of Cortés in order to vent their resentment of his division of the spoils of the conquest. This popular and anonymous poetry was followed soon by *villancicos* (Christmas songs), which appear in the religious play *Adán y Eva* (Adam and Eve). There were also poems written in Latin in these early years. Some of these appear in the first book of poetry produced in New Spain: *Manual para adultos* (Manual for Adults), dating from 1540. *Cervantes de Salazar's book describing the occasion of the funeral of Carlos V, *Tumba imperial* . . . (Imperial Tomb . . .), indicates that on the tomb were inscribed many compositions in prose and poetry, Latin and Spanish. A poet and dramatist, Fernán *González de Eslava, is widely cited for evidence of the proliferation of poetry and poets toward the end of this century: "Hay más poetas que estiércol" (There are more poets than dung).

Although there was a general dearth of books brought from Spain to the New World at this time, the influence of the flowering of poetry in Spain arrived in New Spain chiefly through the visits of three Spanish poets. Guiterre de *Cetina traveled to the New World and, true to his courtly behavior, received a mortal wound under the window of a lady. Juan de la *Cueva, who was precursor of the major poetic developments of the generation following him, lived in the New World from 1574 to 1577. Although a minor poet, Eugenio de Salazar spent the longest time, perhaps twenty years, in various parts of New Spain and thus had the greatest effect on the poetry of the New World at the end of the sixteenth century.

The birth of a truly American poetry began with the work of Bernardo de *Balbuena. His epic poem, "La grandeza de México" (The greatness of Mexico), describes the capital of New Spain at the end of the century. His eulogizing tone was continued by *Terrazas in his poem "El nuevo mundo y conquista" (The New World and Conquest), of which only fragments remain. Antonio de Saavedra Guzmán and Gaspar de Villagrá both took up the same subject in their poem-chronicles entitled "El peregrino Indiano" (The Indian Pilgrim) and "Historia de la Nueva México" (History of the New Mexico). One preoccupation receiving increased expression toward the end of this century was the fact that native Spaniards newly arrived in the colonies were given preference for positions by the Spanish crown over native-born Americans (creoles).

As in Spain, Mexican poetry in the seventeenth century was greatly affected by the inventions of Luis de Góngora and *cultismo* (euphuism). Much of the poetry of this period is unremarkable because of this feature, which became more extreme in its preoccupation with obscure and complicated form than in Spain. The genius of Sor Juana Inés de la *Cruz, called the Tenth Muse, the most important writer of the colonial period, spared her from total immersion in the intricately obscure emptiness of the poetry of many followers of Góngora. Alongside some compositions showing this influence, such as *Sueño* (A Dream), are many uncomplicated pieces that are among the best lyrics written in the language. She also excelled in her theatrical works, which include two three-act secular plays and several religious plays. Her essay replying to criticism of her literary endeavors, "Respuesta a Sor Filotea" (Reply to

Sor Filotea), illustrates an outstanding ability to write in prose also, which she did very infrequently.

The reaction to the extremes of Gongorism was brought about by the classical taste of the Jesuits and by the influence of the Spanish neoclassic writers José Cadalso, Tomás de Iriarte, and Juan Meléndez Valdés. Once again the colony surpassed the tendency in the mother country by carrying the new style to extremes. From the excessively decorous, flowery, and obscure *culteranismo* colonial writers passed to another extreme, this time to one of prosaic dullness.

The first poet to return lyricism to poetry after the influence of neoclassicism takes us into the nineteenth century: Manuel de *Navarrete. This poet-priest united the influence of Garcilaso de la Vega and Lope de Vega, as well as the neoclassicist Meléndez Valdés, to his own personal gift for harmony and balance. Along with Sor Juana, Navarrete represents the best poetic flowering of the entire colonial period in Mexico. Following him, in the period preceding the outbreak of the War of Independence, there was a flowering of the early seeds planted in the sixteenth century with the eulogists' praise of New Spain in the form of nationalistic expression through the employment of typically Mexican types and customs. Anastasio María de *Ochoa y Acuña, José Agustín *Castro, Don Andrés *Quintana Roo, Francisco Ortega, and Francisco Manuel Sánchez de Tagle are representative of this nationalism, prophetic of the coming struggle.

ANITA K. STOLL

PONCE, Manuel (1913-), priest, teacher, and poet. Born in Morelia, Michoacan, he went to seminary there and was ordained in 1936. He has been a teacher of history and literature as well as a poet of religious verse, and has worked on several literary reviews, such as *El Hijo Pródigo* (The Prodigal Son), *Letras de México* (Letters of Mexico), and *Viñetas de Literatura Michoacana* (Vignettes of Literature from Michoacán). Although his literary production has been intermittent, Ponce is one of the poets responsible for revitalizing religious lyric poetry in Mexico during the twentieth century.

WORKS: *Ciclo de Vírgenes* (Cycle of Virgins) (México: Abside, 1940). *Cuadragenario y segunda pasión* (Forty Year Old and Second Passion) (México: Abside, 1947). *El jardín increíble* (The Incredible Garden) (México: Editorial Jus, 1950). *Cristo y María* (Christ and Mary) (México: Editorial Jus, 1962).

BIBLIOGRAPHY: Aurora M. Ocampo de Gómez and Ernesto Prado Velázquez, *Diccionario de escritores mexicanos* (México: UNAM, 1967), p. 294.

TERESA R. ARRINGTON

PONIATOWSKA, Elena (1933-), novelist, journalist, shortstory writer, critic, playwright, scriptwriter for television and film. One of Mexico's most important contemporary narrators, Poniatowska has distinguished herself in many areas of Mexican cultural life. She was born in Paris on May 19, 1933, of aristocratic Polish and Mexican ancestry; the family returned to Mexico in 1942. Poniatowska began her career as a journalist interviewing prominent Mexican artists and intellectuals; she honed to perfection the skill of interviewing, and has incorporated this and other journalistic devices into her fiction. A journalist since 1954, and a 1957 scholarhsip recipient from the Centro Mexicano de Escritores, Poniatowska has contributed to *Excelsior, Novedades, El Día, Siempre!, Mañana, Artes de México,* among others, as well as to other foreign journals and newspapers. She began publishing her fiction in journals like *Revista de Literatura Mexicana, La Palabra y el Hombre, Universidad de México,* and *La Cultura en México.*

Los cuentos de Lilus Kikus (Lilus Kikus' Stories), first published in 1954, was Poniatowska's first book. The central character is an isolated but intellectually curious child, Lilus, separated from the others by her aristocratic European background and her intense personality. Lilus wonders, questions, and comments on various facets of Mexican life, from politics to her own interpretation of Catholicism. *Hasta no verte Jesús mío* (Until We Meet Again), a documentary novel or collaborative autobiography, is the story, told in first person, of Jesusa Palancares, a poor, uneducated, but strong Mexican woman, from age five until her old age. The author repeatedly visited Jesusa at her home and faithfully recorded their conversations. In the book she skillfully reproduces Jesusa's speech, thoughts, and life anecdotes: about her marriage and men, participation in the Mexican Revolution, her life as a maid in the capital, her dealings with the supernatural and the occult. Through this story of a woman of the lower class fighting to survive in a male dominated society, Poniatowska sheds light on various aspects of Mexican culture. *La noche de Tlatelolco, testimonios de historia oral* (Massacre in Mexico) is one of the most widely read accounts of the October 2, 1968, student massacre by government forces in Mexico City's "Plaza de las tres culturas," where the author's brother died. In this work she successfully combines journalistic and fictional techniques by intermixing the narration of imaginary characters with the testimonies of real-life witnesses. In *Querido Diego, te abraza Quiela* (Dear Diego) Poniatowska recreates, with poignancy, and from the woman's point of view, the love affair between the Mexican painter Diego Rivera and his Polish mistress through a series of imaginary love letters from her to him. In the collection of short stories *De noche vienes* (You Come at Night) Poniatowska uses a variety of narrative techniques to offer us the lives and thoughts of women from different social backgrounds. Her autobiographical novel, *La "Flor de Lis"* (The "Fleur de Lys"), offers us the life story of Mariana, the narrator and a duchess of mixed parentage, French father and Mexican mother, from her infancy in France until World War II forces her mother, sister, and herself to flee, first to Spain, then Cuba, and finally to Mexico, where the family is eventually reunited in the place that also becomes Mariana's fatherland. In *Nada, nadie* (Nothing, No One) she documents with clarity and skill, through the voices of hundreds of witnesses and victims, the horrors, casualties, and heroic acts of solidarity of the Mexico City earthquake of September 19 and 20, 1985.

WORKS: Novels: *Hasta no verte Jesús mío* (Until We Meet Again) (México: Era, 1969); 23rd ed. (México: Era, 1984). *La noche de Tlatelolco, testimonios de historia oral* (Massacre in Mexico), translated by Helen Lane (New York: Viking, 1975; México: Era, 1971); 42nd ed. (México: Era, 1983). *Querido Diego, te abraza Quiela* (Dear Diego), translated by Katherine Silver (New York: Pantheon Books, 1986; México: Era, 1978; 7th ed. (México: Era, 1984). *La "Flor de Lis"* (The "Fleur de

Lys") (México: Era, 1988). Short Stories: *Los cuentos de Lilus Kikus* (Lilus Kikus'
Short Stories) (Veracruz: Universidad Veracruzana, 1967). *De noche vienes* (You
Come at Night) (México: Grijalbo, 1979). "La borrega," in *Cuentistas mexicanas siglo
XX*, edited by Aurora M. Ocampo (México: UNAM, 1976), pp. 283-84. "Love Story,"
in *Latin American Literary Review* 3, 26 (July-Dec. 1985): 63-73. "La procesión," in
Cuentistas mexicana siglo XX, edited by Aurora M. Ocampo (México: UNAM, 1976),
pp. 81-282. "El recado," in *Cuentistas mexicanas siglo XX*, edited by Aurora M.
Ocampo (México: UNAM, 1976), pp. 285-86. Essays: *Palabras cruzadas* (Crossed
Words) (México: Era, 1961). *Todo empezó el domingo* (It All Started on Sunday)
(México: FCE, 1963). "Alusiones críticas al libro *Hasta no verte Jesús mío*," in *Vida
Literaria* (Mexico) 3 (1970): 3-4. "Las escritoras mexicanas calzan zapatos que les
aprietan," in *Los Universitarios* (Oct. 1975): 4. *El primer primero de mayo* (The First
May First) (México: Centro de Estudios Históricos del Movimiento Obrero
Mexicano, 1976). *Gaby Brimmer* (México: Grijalbo, 1979). *Fuerte es el silencio*
(Silence Is Strong) (México: Era, 1980); 5th ed. (México: Era, 1983). "La literatura
de las mujeres de América Latina," in *Revista de la Educación Superior Asociación
Nacional de Universidades e Institutos de Enseñanza Superior* (Mexico) 10 (April-June
1981): 23-25. *Domingo 7* (Sunday 7) (México: Ed. Océano, 1982); 2nd ed. (México:
Ed. Océano, 1983). *El último guajolote* (The Last Turkey) (México: Cultura, 1982).
Pablo O'Higgins (México: FCE, 1985). *¡Ay vida, no me mereces!* (Life, You Don't
Deserve Me!) (México: Joaquín Mortiz, 1985). *Nada, nadie* (Nothing, No One)
(México: Era, 1988). Theater: *Melés y Teléo*, in *Panoramas* (México) 2 (Summer
1956): 135-299). Photography: *Las mujeres de Juchitau, Las flores de Huamantla,
Moletiques y Pasiones* (forthcoming). Interviews: 5 vols. (forthcoming in *Novedades*
(México).

BIBLIOGRAPHY: Anon., "Alusiones críticas al libro *Hasta no verte, Jesús mío*," in
Vida Literaria 3 (1970): 22-24. Gabriela de Beer, "La revolución en la narrativa de
Campobello, Castellanos y Poniatowska," in *Semana de Bellas Artes* (Mexico) 165
(Jan. 28, 1981): 2-5. Miguel Capistrán, "La transmutación literaria," in *Vida Literaria*
3 (1970): 12-14. Bell Gale Chevigny, "The Transformation of Privilege in the Work
of Elena Poniatowska," in *Latin American Literary Review* 13, 26 (July-Dec. 1985): 49-
62. Ronald Christ, "The Author as Editor," in *Review* 15 (1975): 78-79. "Los cuentos
de Lilus Kikus," in *Recent Books in Mexico* 14, 5 (1967): 5. Miguel Donoso Pareja,
"La caducidad del realismo," in *Vida Literaria* 3 (1970): 10-11. Lucía Fox-Lockert,
"The Magical Way of Self-Transcendence in *Hasta no verte Jesús mío*, paper read at
the Northeastern Modern Language Association conference, University of Pittsburgh
(1977); "Novelística femenina," in *Memorias de la Asociación Internacional de
Hispanistas* (Toronto: A.I.H., 1978); *Women Novelists in Spain and Spanish America*
(Metuchen, N.J.: Scarecrow Press, 1979), pp. 260-77. Carmen Galindo, "Vivir del
milagro," in *Vida Literaria* 3 (1970): 8-9. Margarita García Flores, "Entrevista a Elena
Poniatowska," in *Revista de la Universidad de México* 30, 7 (1976): 25-30. Joel
Hancock, "Elena Poniatowska's *Hasta no verte, Jesús mío*: The Remaking of the
Image of Woman," in *Hispania* 66, 3 (Sept. 1983): 353-59. Harold Hinds, "Massacre
in Mexico," in *Latin American Review* 4, 9 (Fall 1976). Cecilia López Negrete, "Con
Elena Poniatowska," in *Vida Literaria* 3 (1970): 16-20. Martha Oehmke Loustaunau,
"Mexico's Contemporary Women Novelists," Ph.D. diss., University of New Mexico,
1973. Teresa Méndez-Faith, "Entrevista con Elena Poniatowska," in *INTI: Revista de
Literatura Hispánica* 15 (Spring 1982): 54-60. Marís Luisa Mendoza, *Oiga usted*

(México: Ed. Soma, 1973). Beth Miller, "Elena Poniatowska," in *Mujeres en la literatura* (México: Fleischer Editora, 1978), pp. 89-91; "Interview with Elena Poniatowska," in *Latin American Literary Review* 4, 7 (1975): 73-78; "Personajes y personas: Castellanos, Fuentes, Poniatowska y Sainz," in *Mujeres en la literatura* (México: Fleischer, 1978), pp. 65-75. Beth Miller and Alfonso González, "Elena Poniatowska," in *26 autoras del México actual* (México: Costa-Amic, 1978), pp. 299-321. Carlos Monsiváis, "Las palabras cruzadas de Elena Poniatowska: 'Mira, para que no comas olvido . . .'; "Las Precisiones de Elena Poniatowska," in *La Cultura en México* 100 (July 15, 1985): 2-5. Francisco Monteverde, "Cuadro vivo del pueblo," in *Vida Literaria* 3 (1970): 3-4. Aurora M. Ocampo de Gómez and Ernesto Prado Velázquez, *Diccionario de Escritores Mexicanos* (México: UNAM, 1967). Xiuhnel Pérez-Robles, "La noche de Tlatelolco," in *Cuadernos Americanos* 177 (1971): 79-82. Caridad Silva-Velázquez and Nora Erro-Orthman, "Elena Poniatowska," in *Puerta abierta: La nueva escritora latinoamericana* (México: Joaquín Mortiz, 1986), pp. 199-203, 329-32. Elizabeth O. Starcevic, "Breaking the Silence: Elena Poniatowska, A Writer in Transition," in *Literatures in Transition: The Many Voices of the Caribbean Area: A Symposium*, edited by Rose S. Minc (Gaithersburg, Md: *Hispamérica*, 1982), pp. 63-68; "Elena Poniatowska: Witness for the People," in *Contemporary Women Authors of Latin America: Introductory Essays*, edited by Doris Meyer and Margarite Fernández Olmos (Brooklyn: Brooklyn College Press, 1983), pp. 72-77. Cynthia Steele, "La creatividad y el deseo en *Querido Diego, te abraza Quiela*, de Elena Poniatowska," in *Hispamérica* 14, 41 (1985): 17-28. Charles M. Tatum, "Elena Poniatowska's *Hasta no verte Jesús mío*," in *Latin American Women Writers: Yesterday and Today* (Pittsburgh: *Latin American Literary Review*, 1975), pp. 48-58. Juan Manuel Torres, "Hasta el fin de la esperanza," in *Vida Literaria* 3 (1970): 15. Marianne Yampolsky, *La casa en la tierra* (México: Fonapas, 1980). Linda R. Stowell Young, "Six Representative Women Novelists of Mexico 1960-1969," *DAI* 36 (1970): 6092-93.

ALINA CAMACHO-GINGERICH

PORTILLA, Anselmo de la (1816-1879), poet, novelist, historian, literary critic, journalist. Portilla was born in Sobremazas, Spain on February 3, 1816, and died in Mexico City on March 3, 1879. After founding several newpapers, he moved to New York in 1858, because of the political situation in México, and founded *El Occidente* to help the Spanish-speaking population in the American city. After four years, in 1862 he went back to México to live in Veracruz for a while. This Spaniard is best remembered for his continuous efforts to bring Spain and Mexico closer together. With that idea in mind he founded the newspaper *La Iberia* in 1867 and in the supplement of his newspaper he published his celebrated *Biblioteca Histórica* (Historical Library), in which appeared ancient works, unpublished or very rare works of great importance for the national history.

WORKS: *La Revolución de Ayutla* (The Ayutla Revolution) (México: n.p., n.d.). *México en 1856-57* (New York: Imp. S. Hallet, 1858). *De Miramar a México* (From Miramar to Mexico) (México: n.p., n.d.). *Virginia Steward*. (A novel, n.d.). *Cartilla de geografía para niños* (Geography Books for Children) (Orizaba, Ver.: Aburto, 1865). *España en México* (Spain in México) (México: Ignacio Escalante, 1871).

BIBLIOGRAPHY: Carlos González Peña, *Historia de la literatura mexicana. Desde los origenes hasta nuestros dias* (México: Editorial Porrúa, 1981), pp. 178-79. Raimundo Lazo, *Historia de la literatura hispano-americana* (México: Editorial Porrúa, 1976), p. 65. Enrique Olavarría y Ferrari, *Reseña del Teatro de México. 1538-1911* (México: Editorial Porrúa, 1961), vol. 1, pp. 720-27.

JOSEPH VELEZ

POST-REVOLUTIONARY THEATER. The end of the Mexican Revolution found the Mexican theater dominated by inferior farces, operettas, and musical reviews, many of them mediocre imitations of those of Spain. Sensitive to a new emphasis on nationalism, a major concern of post-revolutionary dramatists was to develop a truly Mexican theater, universal in appeal yet national in inspiration.

The first major response to this concern began with the Unión de Siete Autores (The Union of Seven Authors, 1925-1927), which pointed to the low level of Mexican drama and sought to revitalize México's theater by providing models from the best foreign plays. Subsequently, a second and more successful group of experimentalists emerged: the Teatro Ulises (Ulysses Theater, 1928-1929), directed by Salvador *Novo and Xavier *Villaurrutia. This group similarly emphasized the importance of the universality of the theater and turned toward European and American playwrights in order to find new directions in writing, acting, and play production. As a result, they laid the groundwork for a theater with broader universal perspectives, deeper psychological penetration, and expanded poetic dimensions.

In 1932, under the auspices of the Ministry of Public Education, Celestino *Gorostiza, originally a member of the Ulysses Theater, founded the Teatro de Orientación (Orientation Theater), which also brought to México City some of the world's great plays. From this venture emerged a new theatrical public, more capable actors, directors, and playwrights, and many new small theaters. It proved that a a theater relevant to the contemporary national scene could be successful.

Meanwhile, other groups in the capital, such as the Comedia Mexicana (Mexican Comedy) and the Teatro de Ahora (Now Theater), were acting on an opposite theory, namely, that a truly Mexican drama could be developed best by treating the social realities of México, not by emphasizing new theatrical techniques. Thus, the prime stylistic mode embraced by most Mexican dramatists during the 1930s-1950s was realistic; and the model for this type of drama was Rodolfo *Usigli.

In the 1940s, encouraged by the earlier successes of the Unión de Siete Autores, the Teatro Ulises, the Teatro de Ahora, and other "associations," additional experimentalist groups with similar aspirations were established. One of these was Grupo Proa (Proa Group), founded in 1942 under the direction of José Aceves. Another was the Instituto Nacional de Bellas Artes (National Institute of Fine Arts), created in 1946 under the auspices of the Ministry of Public Education. Such groups were instrumental in launching the careers of many promising young playwrights (e.g., Wilberto *Cantón, Emilio *Carballido, Luisa Josefina *Hernández, Sergio *Magaña, and Carlos *Solórzano, to name a few) who were genuinely interested in creating a truly national theater. These dramatists employed themes, primarily realistic, reflecting the basic problems of Mexican society. Another important factor during this period was the immigration of many distinguished foreign directors and actors who enriched the country's dramatic community.

During the 1950s there was a progressive trend from realistic drama to nonrealistic styles fomented, in part, by the activities of the National Institute of Fine Arts and the National Autonomous University. The emergence of absurd drama and the rediscovery of Brecht's political theater likewise had a profound effect upon Mexican theater. Sociopolitical issues became fused with universal concerns and experimental forms. Many plays were imbued with fantasy and with existentialist ideas inspired by Jean-Paul Sartre, Albert Camus, and others. This decade also witnessed the formation of university theatrical groups throughout the country and the debut of the Poesía en Voz Alta (Poetry Aloud) group. Another important factor during this period was the establishment of the Teatro Español en México (Spanish Theater in México), a private enterprise headed by Alvaro Custodio, a native Spaniard. His aim was to improve public taste and all other facets of the theater by producing quality Spanish classical plays in México. The result of these efforts was a veritable theatrical renaissance during the 1950s. With the growing popularity of the stage came more theater halls and theater groups, as well as an increased amount of dramatic criticism, the latter of which was evidenced by the formation of the Agrupación de Críticos de Teatro de México (Association of Mexican Theater Critics).

In the 1960s there was no lack of diversity or of activity in México's theater. Two prime reasons for this increased activity were continued governmental support by the National Insitute of Fine Arts and the establishment in 1960 of the Instituto Nacional de Seguridad Socials (National Institute of Social Security) and its sponsorship of national theater. The former lent most of its support to contemporary Mexican playwrights, providing instruction, publication facilities for critics and dramatists, seasonal fares, competitions and theaters. The latter institute provided free drama courses and theater halls throughout the capital and the provinces where student groups and private producers could provide the public with training on the writing, producing and staging of plays. Both organizations are still extremely active in the 1980s.

During the 1960s plays from all periods and countries could be seen although a majority were of Mexican authorship and in one of the avant-garde styles (e.g., José *Agustín, Emilio *Carballido, Carlos *Fuentes, Elena *Garro, Carlos *Solórzano, Maruxa *Vilalta, and others). The theater, however, entered into a period of crisis. The new Mexican plays failed to equal the success of the fifties. One of the underlying factors was that Mexican dramatists had stopped writing about the "provincia".

The commercial theater of the 1960s and 1970s, which was oriented to middle- and upper-class tastes, took over a number of the larger theaters in México City. Many of the younger Mexican playwrights who began to write during this period alienated this public by attacking traditional social values in their plays. As a result, said dramatists failed to acquire a following. However, the renewed promotion of plays with a provincial setting through the auspices of the National Institute of Fine Arts in conjunction with the La Moderna Company fomented added interest in the national theater.

The 1970s also witnessed an enormous labor by university groups to give native dramatists an opportunity to stage their plays, many of them avant-garde. Furthermore, this decade saw the development of a fringe theater movement sponsored by CLETA (Free Center of Theater and Arts Experimentation), which promoted collective creation and guerrilla theater.

In the 1980s there was considerable interest in the theater in México. The Compañía Nacional de Teatro (National Theater Company), for example, provided encouragement, instruction, and staging opportunities for Mexican dramatists. Currently, however, the Mexican stage can be best characterized by its eclecticism. It would seem that there is something for every age group, taste, and philosophical bias. Unfortunately for those who promote a truly national theater per se, there is an underappreciation of Mexico's native theater talent. Essentially, the paying public seems to still prefer foreign to domestic fare, with U.S. and British imports being the most popular; and even dramatists as renowned as Emilio Carballido and Vicente Leñero are encountering difficulty in staging their works with professional groups. Thus, in order to be a successful dramatist in Mexico today, it is necessary to have great desire and perseverance.

ROBERT K. ANDERSON

POZAS Arciniega, Ricardo (1912-), anthropologist and prose writer. Born May 4, 1912, in Amealco, Querétaro, Pozas Arciniega worked as a teacher from 1929 until he began studies in anthropology in 1939. Since then Pozas has carried out several anthropological studies among various Indian groups, most notably the tzotziles, who were the subject of his novel *Juan Pérez Jolote* (Juan Pérez the Chamula). He has also published nearly 100 studies in journals devoted to sociology and anthropology. His book *Juan Pérez Jolote* has been classified as a documentary novel, as a purely ethnographic/scientific account, and as pure fiction. It recounts the sometimes humorous, sometimes tragic effects of the encounter between members of an Indian comnunity and the outside world, represented by the anthropologist.

WORKS: *Juan Pérez Jolote, biografía de un tzotzil* (Juan Pérez, the Chamula, Biography of a Tzotzil Indian) (México: Acta Antropológica, 1948). *Zis Ma Isa, Libro para ensenar a leer y a escribir la lengua cabecar* (Zis Ma Isa, A Book for Teaching Reading and Writing the Cabecar Language) (San Jose, Costa Rica: n.p., 1948). *Los mazatecos* (The Mazatecos) (México: Editorial de la Revista de Estudios Antropológicos, 1957). *Chamula, un pueblo indio de los altos de Chiapas* (Chamula, An Indian Town in the High Plains of Chiapas) (México: Ediciones del Instituto Nacional Indigenista, 1959). *Juan the Chamula: An Ethnological Re-creation of the Life of a Mexican Indian*, translated by Lysander Kemp (Berkeley: University of California Press, 1969).

BIBLIOGRAPHY: Aurora M. Ocampo de Gómez and Ernesto Prado Velázquez, *Diccionario de escritores mexicanos*. (México: UNAM, 1967), p. 296. *Enciclopedia de México*, vol. 11 (México: SEP, 1988), pp. 6564-65. Kessel Schwartz, *A New History of Spanish American Fiction*, vol. 2 (Miami: University of Miami Press, 1971), p. 298.

TERESA R. ARRINGTON

PRADOS, Emilio (1899-1962), poet. Emilio Prados was born in Málaga, Spain, on March 4, 1899, and died in Mexico City on April 24, 1962. Prados completed his bachelor of arts in Madrid and did two more years of advanced study in natural science at the University of Madrid and at the University of Sevilla. In 1914, together with Manuel *Altolaguirre, he directed the magazine *Litoral*, and between 1924 and 1930, he owned and operated the Imprenta Azul in Málaga, Spain. Prados traveled extensively while working with public relations during the Spanish Republic. He became a political exile in 1938 and moved to Mexico, where he worked for the publishing company Séneca and taught school. While in Mexico, he published in a number of magazines, including *Poesía, Universidad de México, Cuadernos Americanos, Litoral, Presencia,* and *Independencia.* He also published in *Texas Quarterly.*

His literary contribution consists of some fifteen collections of poetry. His poetry is deep and philosophical, oftentimes reflecting on itself. The poetry he wrote after leaving Spain includes a great many complex metaphors, with magical and religious imagery.

WORKS: Poetry: *Tiempo* (Time), (Málaga: Imp. Sur, 1925). *Canciones de farero* (Málaga: Editores Litoral, 1926). *Vuelta* (Turning) (Málaga: Imprenta Sur, 1927). *Llanto subterráneo* (Subterranean Cry) (Madrid: Editor Héroe, 1936); 2nd ed. (México, 1938). *Llanto en la sangre* (Cry in the Blood) (Valencia: Ediciónes Españolas, 1937). *Cancionero menor para combatientes* (Small Songbook for Combatants) (Barcelona: Ediciónes Literarias del Comisariado del Ejército del Este, 1938). *Memoria del olvidado* (Memory of the Forgotten One), Col. Lucero (México: Séneca, 1940). *Mínima muerte* (Minimal Death) (México: Tezontle, FCE, 1942). *Jardín cerrado* (Closed Garden), prologue by Juan Larrea, no. 10 (México: Cuadernos Americanos, 1946). *Antología 1923-1953* (Anthology 1923-1953) (Buenos Aires: Losada, 1954). *Río Natural* (Natural River) (Buenos Aires: Losada, 1957). *Circuncisión del sueño* (Cicumcision of the Dream) Tezontle (México: FCE, 1957). *Sonoro enigma,* no. 24 (Sonorous Enigma) (Palma de Mallorca, España: Eds. de San Armadans, 1958). "Textos y Documentos" (Texts and Documents), Anthology of Emilio Prados, in *Revista Hispánica Moderna* 26, 3-4 (July-Oct. 1960): 179-201. *Aceptación de la palabra* (Acceptance of the Word) (Palma de Mallorca, España: Eds. de Son Armadans, 1961). *La piedra escrita* (The Written Rock), Col. Poemas y Ensayos, no. 1 (México: UNAM, 1961). *Signos del ser* (Signs of Being) (Palma de Mallorca, España: Eds. de Son Armadans, 1962). *Transparencias* (Transparencies) (Málaga: Cuadernos de María Cristina, 1962). *Cuerpo perseguido* (Pursued Body), prologue by Carlos Blanco Aguinaga (Barcelona: Editorial Labor, 1971). *Antología poética, Madrid 1975* (Poetic Anthology, Madrid 1975), foreward by José Sanchís Banus (Frankfurt: Alianza Editorial, 1975). *La piedra escrita* (The Written Rock) 1st ed. (México: Universidad Autónoma Nacional de México, 1961); 2nd ed. (Madrid: Editorial Castalia, 1979), foreword by José Sanchís-Banus. Anthology: *Laurel* (Laurel), anthology of the modern poetry in Spanish language, in collaboration with Juan Gil Albert, Octavio Paz, and Xavier Villaurrutia (México: Séneca, 1941).

BIBLIOGRAPHY: Max Aub, *La poesía española contemporánea* (México: Imprenta Universaria, 1954), pp. 180-82. Carlos Blanco Aguinaga, *Emilio Prados. Vida y obra. Bibliografía. Antología,* Hispanic Institute in the United States (New York: Columbia University, 1960); previously in *Revista Hispánica Moderna* 26, 3-4 (July-Oct. 1960): 1-107; *Lista de los papeles de Emilio Prado en la Biblioteca del Congreso de los Estados Unidos de América* (Baltimore: Johns Hopkins University Press, 1967). Salvador Calvillo Madrigal, Review of *Jardín cerrado,* in *Letras de México* 6, 130 (Jan. 1947):14-15. José Luis Cano, "Un diario íntimo de Emilio Prados," *Diálogos* 6 (Sept.-Oct. 1965): 23-24. P. J. Ellis, *The Poetry of Emilio Prados: A Progression Toward Fertility*

(Cardiff: University of Wales Press, 1981). Eugenio Florit, Review of *Jardín cerrado*, in *Revista Hispánica Moderna* 12, 3-4 (July-Oct. 1946): 274-75. Carlos González Peña, *Historia de la literatura mexicana*, 1928 (México: Porrúa, 1966), pp. 289, 293. Sue Harris Dennis, "The Symbol of the Tree in the Poetic World of Jardín Cerrado," thesis: Tulane University, 1974. Rafael María Lucena, "Emilio Prados, póstumo," *Revista Mexicana de Cultura* 1022 (Oct. 30, 1966): 4. Aurora M. Ocampo de Gómez and Ernesto Prado Velázquez, *Diccionario de escritores Mexicanos* (México: UNAM, 1967), pp. 296-97. Juan Rejano, "Cuadernillo de señales," *Revista Mexicana Cultural* 924 (Dec. 1964): 4. Juan Manuel Ruiz Esparza, Review, of *Llanto subterráneo*, in *Letras de México* 31 (Sept. 1, 1938): 6. José Sanchís-Banus, Foreward, *Antología poética, Madrid 1975* (Frankfurt: Alianza Editorial, 1975); *La piedra escrita* (Madrid, 1979); 2nd ed. (Madrid: Editorial Castalia, 1979); *Seis Lecciones: Emilio Prado, su vida, su obra, su mundo* (Valencia, España: Artes Gráficos Soler, 1987). Gonzalo Torrente Ballester, *Panorama de la literatura española contemporánea*, vol. 1 (Madrid: Ediciónes Guadarrama, 1961), p. 331. Ramón Xirau, *Poetas de México y España* (Madrid: José Porruá Turanzas, Bibliotecas Tenantitlan, 1962), pp. 97-102. Armando Zárate, "Emilio Prados," *Cuadernos de Bellas Artes* 3 (March 1964): 25-36.

EDNA A. REHBEIN

PRIETO, Carlos (1922-), dramatist. Born in Mexico City on August 6, 1922, Prieto completed his studies in Mexico City and Los Angeles, California, then continued his education in law and in philosophy at the UNAM. He also attended the University of Notre Dame, in South Bend, Indiana. From 1961 to 1962, he served in the United Nations, elucidating the social, economic, and cultural concerns of the Hispanic countries.

Although he has written for magazines and has produced several movie documentaries, Prieto's success lies in his theatrical works: *Atentado al pudor* (Indecent Assault); *A medio camino* (In the Middle of the Road), his most famous piece with a revolutionary theme; *Por el ojo de la aguja* (Through the Eye of the Needle); and *El jugo de la tierra* (Substance of the Land). His works, which demonstrated special skill for dramatic narration, have attracted attention for their powerful social criticism, their wit, their simple but ingenious plots, and their themes, which emphasize the Revolution and the social problems of Mexico.

WORKS: *Ashes of Bread* written in English to be staged in USA (1957) and *El jugo de la tierra* (Substance of the Land), in *Teatro mexicano 1959* (México: Aguilar, 1862). *El lépero* (The Rogue) (México: Teatro Mexicano, 1857).

BIBLIOGRAPHY: Luis Basurto, *Teatro mexicano 1959* (México: Aguilar, 1962). Antonio Magaña Esquivel, "Dos dramaturgos mexicanos regresan," in *Revista Mexicana de Cultura* (Aug. 2, 1958). Carlos Mora, "A medio camino," in *Novedades* (June 1958): 9-10.

SILKA FREIRE

PRIETO, Guillermo (1818-1897), poet, educator, historian, politician. Guillermo Prieto was born in Mexico City on February 10, 1818. Because of his poverty and the political turbulence of the time, his education was minimal. However, he was industrious and made his living by working in modest jobs. Soon he became an active politician and revolutionary. He embraced the Ayutla Plan (Treaty), and he was a representative to the Constitutional Congress; he became minister of finance in the Juárez government; he suffered persecution and exile until the triumph of the Republic in 1867. He died in Tacubaya on March 2, 1897.

Guillermo Prieto taught political economy and national history. He and José María Lacunza founded the Academia de Letrán, where the romantic poets met. His first poem, according to himself, was the religious "A Cristo crucificado" (To the Crucified Christ), but this poem is lost. In his old age he became somewhat of an eccentric in his manners and in his general appearance. Nevertheless, he was considered the national poet, for his characters are taken from the common people, adding local color to his poetry. He wrote narratives of local color under the pseudonym of Don Benedeno. His pseudonym "Fidel" became famous, together with his verses of Musa Callejera.

WORKS: *Viajes de orden supremo* (Superb Travels), left unfinished (1857). *Viajes a los Estados Unidos* (Travels to the United States), 3 vols. (México: Imp. de Dublán y Chávez, 1877-1878). *Poesías escogidas* (Selected Poems) (México: Tip. de la Offna. Impresora de Estampillas, 1879, and another edition in 1897). *Musa Callejera* (Muse of the Streets) (México: Filomeno Mata, 1883). *Romancero Nacional* (National Romancer) (México: Tip de la Secretaría de Fomento, 1885). *Economía Política* (Political Economy) (México: Tip. de la Secretaría de Fomento, 1888). *Lecciones de Historia Patria* (Lessons on National History) (México: Tip. de la Secretaría de Fomento, 1890). *Memorias de mis tiempos de 1828 a 1840* (Memoirs) (París: Libr. de la Vda. de Ch. Bouret, 1906). *Memorias de mis tiempos de 1840 a 1853* (París: Libr. de la Vda. de Ch. Bouret, 1906) *Los San Lunes de Fidel* (Fidel's Holy Mondays) (México: León Sánchez, 1923, 2nd. ed. SEP, 1948). Theater: *Patria y honor* (Fatherland and Honor) (México: n.p., n.d.). *Alonso de Avila* (Teatro Principal de Mexico, May 1, 1842). *El Alférez* (The Ensign) (n.d.). *Los tres boticarios* (The Three Pharmacists) (n.d.). *La novia del erario* (The Exchequer's Sweetheart) (n.d.). *El Susto de Pinganillas* (Pinganillas' Scare), dramatic caprice in one act, in verse (México: Colegio de San Ildefonso, March 19, 1843). *A mi Padre* (To My Father), monologue in verse (México: Juan Lechuga, n.d.)

BIBLIOGRAPHY: María Admée Alvarez, *Literatura mexicana e hisoanoamericana* (México: Editorial Porrúa, 1971), pp. 238-39. Guillermo Díaz-Plaja and Francisco Monterde, *Historia de la Literatura Española e Historia de la Literatura Mexicana* (México: Editorial Porrúa, 1968), pp. 520-21. Orlando Gómez-Gil, *Historia Crítica de la Literatura Hispanoamericana* (New York: Holt, Rinehart and Winston, 1968), pp. 62, 297. Carlos González Peña, *Historia de la literatura mexicana, desde los origenes hasta nuestros dias* (México: Editorial Porrúa, 1968), pp. 153-55. Raimundo Lazo, *Historia de la literatura hispanoamericana. El siglo XIX* (México: Editorial Porrúa, 1976), pp. 49-50. Antonio Magaña Esquivel and Ruth S. Lamb, *Breve historia del teatro mexicano* (México: de Andrea, 1958), p. 68. Francisco Monterde, *Bibliografía del Teatro en México* (New York: Burt Franklin, 1970), pp. 284-85. Julio Jiménez Rueda, *Antología de la prosa en México* (México: Eds. Botas, 1946), p. 183; *Historia de la literatura mexicana* (México: Eds. Botas, 1960), pp. 273-75.

JOSEPH VELEZ

PRIETO de Landázuri, Isabel (1833-1876), poet and dramatist. Isabel Prieto was born on March 1, 1833, in Alcázar de San Juan, Spain, but at the age of four or five, she moved with her family to Guadalajara, where she spent most of her life. She professed a great love for her adopted country and considered herself to be completely Mexican in thought and temperament. In 1865, she married her cousin, Pedro de Landázuri, a distinguished soldier. Four years later, when Landázuri was elected to Congress, Prieto accompanied him to Mexico City, where they lived with their two children until 1874. Landázuri was then appointed Mexican consul in Hamburg, and the family moved to Germany, where Prieto died on March 28, 1876.

Prieto fully embraced Romanticism and is generally recognized as Mexico's first Romantic poet, although her work is devoid of many of the excesses associated with that movement. Her style tends to be simple, clear, and straightforward but, at the same time, delicate and graceful. Although her verses are highly subjective and emotional, often tinged with a gentle melancholy, they are restrained and controlled. Contemporary critics praised her for the naturalness and sincerity with which she wrote of everyday life. Her poetry treats themes related to motherhood, the family and home, and childhood, as well as the more standard conventions of Romanticism, such as the torments of unrequited love, and the struggle between violent passion and inescapable duty.

Isabel Prieto began her literary career in 1851, when six of her poems appeared in an anthology entitled *Aurora poética de Jalisco* (Jalisco's Poetic Dawning). She continued to write poetry throughout her lifetime, although it was not until seven years after her death that her verses were finally collected and published. This collection contains Prieto's last work, a "leyenda," or story in verse, entitled "Bertha de Sonnenberg" (Bertha of Sonnenberg), which was written in Germany shortly before her death. It is based loosely on a Rhineland legend, and contains impressively written descriptions of the countryside. The dilemma of the main character, Bertha, is presented with a surprising degree of psychological depth.

Prieto is also credited with the authorship of fifteen original dramas. Her dramatic work is divided almost evenly between comedy and serious pieces, and all but two of the plays, *En el pecado la penitencia* (Penitence in Sin) and *Una noche de carnaval* (A Night during Carnival), are written in verse form. *Las dos son peores* (The Two Are Worse), *Oro y oropel* (Gold and Tinsel), *La escuela de las cuñadas* (The Sister-in-Laws' School), and *¿Duende o Serafín?* (Elf or Angel?) were staged in Guadalajara in the 1860s. *Un lirio entre zarzas* (A Lily among the Brambles) was performed at the Teatro Nacional in Mexico City. According to José María Vigel, all five plays were well received by the public and won excellent notices in the press. *Las dos son peores* and *Las dos flores* (The Two Flowers) were published and circulated widely at home and abroad. They came to the attention of the Spanish dramatist Juan Eugenio Hartzenbusch, who wrote admiringly about both pieces. He praised them for their outstanding versification, their engaging dialogue, and their good development of characters. Despite the limitations normally imposed on her sex, Prieto was a highly educated and literate woman. She had considerable knowledge of Spanish Golden Age literature, as well as the literature of France, Germany, Italy, and England. She was a skilled translator and a noted scholar. In recognition of her contributions to Mexican letters, she was named a member of the Alianza Literaria de Guadalajara (The Literary Society of Guadalajara) a year before her death. While modern critics do not go as far as her contemporaries, who called her "the twin sister

544 PUGA, María Luisa

of Sor Juana," she is still regarded as a figure of considerable importance in the development of Mexican Romanticism.

WORKS: *Las dos flores* (The Two Flowers) (México: Imp. de I. Cumplido, 1861). *Las dos son peores* (The Two Are Worse) (México: Imp. de I. Cumplido, 1861). *Obras Poéticas* (Poetic Works) (México: Impl de I. Paz, 1883).

BIBLIOGRAPHY: Carlos González Peña, *Historia de la literatura mexicana* (México: SEP, 1928), pp. 316-18, 330. José María Vigel, prologue, *Obras poéticas* (México: Imp. de I. Paz, 1883), pp. iii- cxxiii.

CYNTHIA K. DUNCAN

PUGA, María Luisa (1944-). Puga was born in Mexico City on February 3, 1944. She completed her primary education in Acapulco and her secondary studies in Mazatlán, Sinaloa, where her family lived at the time. In 1968 she traveled to Europe and lived in London, Paris, Rome, Madrid, and Paris. While in Europe she visited Nairobi, Kenya, where she remained for a year and a half. Upon her return to Mexico, she published her first novel, *Las posibilidades del odio* (The Forms That Hate Can Take) (1978). Set in Kenya, it deals with the political and social issues of the African people, presented from multiple points of view. It is a highly original and perceptive work.

Throughout her career, Puga has published articles and short stories in *Revista de la Universidad de México, Revista de Bellas Artes, Nexos, La Jornada, Uno más uno,* and *El Universal.* In *Accidentes* (Accidents) (1981), a volume of experimental and creative short stories, Puga introduces a number of characters that confront chaotic and absurd situations. The phantasmagoric and disturbing atmosphere of these stories links this work with the trend of fantastic literature. In her novels *Cuando el aire es azul* (When the Air Is Blue) (1980), *Pánico o peligro* (Panic or Danger) (1983), and *La forma del silencio* (The Form of Silence) (1987), Puga depicts the dilemma of men and women who are searching for new alternatives in their society. These narratives combine aesthetic innovations with political awareness to create a new vision of humanity.

WORKS: Novels: *Las posibilidades del odio* (México: Siglo XXI, 1978). *Cuando el aire es azul* (México: Siglo XXI, 1980). *Pánico o peligro* (México: Siglo XXI, 1983). *La forma del silencio* (México: Siglo Veintiuno, 1987). Short Stories: *Accidentes* (México: Martin Casillas, 1981). *Intentos* (México: Grijalbo, 1987).

BIBLIOGRAPHY: Fabienne Bradu, *Señas particulares: escritora* (México: FCE, 1987), pp. 118-35. J. Ann Duncan, *Voices, Visions and a New Reality* (Pittsburgh: University of Pittsburgh Press, 1986), pp. 198-200. Jean Franco, *Plotting Women* (New York: Columbia University Press, 1989), pp. 182-83. Margaret Sayers Peden, *The Latin American Short Story* (Boston: Twayne, 1983), pp. 133-34.

NORA ERRO-PERALTA

PUGA y Acal, Manuel (1860-1930). Born in Guadalajara on October 8, 1860, Manuel Puga y Acal received most of his formal education in France and Belgium, returning to Mexico upon its completion. A poet and critic, he wrote much of his work, in particular the earlier pieces, in French. Throughout his lifetime, he worked diligently to bring French literature and culture to Mexico, even though most of what he introduced was largely out of vogue in France by the time it got to Mexico.

As a professional journalist, Puga y Acal used his position to foster appreciation of the French symbolists, parnassians, and romantics. He translated or paraphrased in Spanish some of the works of such French notables as Arthur Rimbaud, Charles Baudelaire and Alfred de Musset, little known in Mexico at that time.

He was especially noted for voicing controversial opinions about the work of several Mexican writers, especially *Díaz Mirón, *Gutiérrez Nájera, and Juan de Dios Peza. Taking them to task for what he perceived as their literary deficiencies, he engaged in a polemic that brought a surprising amount of notoriety. The articles he wrote, their replies, and his counterreplies are all contained in the much-debated book *Los poetas mexicanos contemporáneos* (The Contemporary Mexican Poets), a work for which he used the pseudonym Brummel. Actually, he was considered neither conservative nor radical in his criticisms, but rather middle-of-the-road. From the contemporary perspective, he has received a favorable assessment, especially since he had the courage to confront the most notable and public literary figures of his time and to stimulate a healthy literary debate.

Not only a journalist, Puga y Acal also taught both French and Spanish at local schools. A researcher for the Archivo General de la Nación, he produced scholarly and well-documented essays on matters of national historical importance. He was also a member of several distinguished associations, including the Academia Mexicana de la Lengua. He dabbled in poetry to a small extent, producing a few original pieces and also translating some poems by several noted French authors. Manuel Puga y Acal died in Mexico City on September 13, 1930.

WORKS: *Después del beneficio* (After the Benefit) (Guadalajara: Tip. de Luis Pérez Verdía, 1884). *Los poetas mexicanos contemporáneos* (The Contemporary Mexican Poets) (México: Edit. Ireneo Paz, 1888; and México: Imp. Victoria, 1923). *90 documentos para la historia patria* (90 Documents for the Nation's History), editor (Guadalajara: Esc. de Artes y Oficios, 1898). "*Poemas rústicos*, por Manuel José Othón, *Rustic Poems*, by Manuel José Othón), in *Revista Ilustrada* (Guadalajara, Sept. 1902): 15-23. *La intervención francesa y el Imperio de Maximiliano en México* (French Intervention and Maximilian's Empire in Mexico), Emile Ollivier, trans. and notes by Puga y Acal (Guadalajara: Tip. de la Escuela de Artes del Estado, 1906). *Verdad y Talmantes, primeros mártires de la Independencia Mexicana* (Truth and "Talmantes," First Martyrs of Mexican Independence) (México: Tip. de El Progreso Latino, 1908). *Fray Gregorio de la Concepción y su proceso de infidencia* (Friar Gregorio de la Concepción and His Trial for Infidelity), compiled and prologue by Puga y Acal (México: Tip. Guerrero Hnos., 1911). *La Constitución de 1812 en la Nueva España* (The Constitution of 1812 in New Spain), annotations by Puga y Acal (México: Tip. Guerrero Hnos, 1912-1913). *Fundamento de sus opiniones* (Foundations of His Opinions) (México: Imp. Francesa, 1916). *La fase diplomática de nuestra guerra de Independencia* (The Diplomatic Phase of Our War for Independence) (México: Imp. Victoria, 1919). *Lirismos de antaño* (Lyricisms of Yesteryear) (México: Imp. Victoria, 1923). "Ante los restos del Sr. Licenciado don Joaquín D. Casasús" (Before the Remains of Joaquín D. Casasús), in *Memorias de la Academia Mexicana* 9 (1954): 274-76.

546 PUIG Casauranc, José Manuel

BIBLIOGRAPHY: Ermilo Abreu Gómez, "Manuel Puga y Acal," in *Contemporáneos* 26-27 (July-Aug. 1930): 95-96. Alberto María Carreño, *Memorias de la Academia Mexicana*, vol. 7 (México: Edit. Jus, 1945), pp. 213-14; vol. 8 (1946), pp. 259-61. Ezequiel A. Chávez, *Memorias de la Academia Mexicana* vol. 10 (1954), pp. 281-302. Ricardo Domínquez, *Los poetas mexicanos* (México: Imp. de Pedro J. García, 1888). Luis A. Escandón, *Poetas y escritores mexicanos* (México: Ireneo Paz, 1889). Genaro Fernández MacGregor, *Carátulas* (México: Botas, 1935), pp. 107-14. Carlos González Peña, *Gente mía* (México: Edit. Stylo, 1946), pp. 43-49. Raymond L. Grismer, *A Bibliography of Articles and Essays on the Literatures of Spain and Spanish America* (Minneapolis: Perine Book Co., 1935), p. 369. Max Henríquez Ureña, *Breve historia del modernismo* (México and Buenos Aires: FCE, 1954), p. 484. Aurora M. Ocampo de Gómez and Ernesto Prado Velázquez, *Diccionario de Escritores Mexicanos* (México: UNAM, 1967), pp. 300-301. Moisés Ochoa Campos, *La oratoria en México*, anthology (México: Edit. F. Trillas, 1969), p. 346. Victoriano Salado Alvarez, *Memorias*, vol. 1 (México: EDIAPSA, 1946), pp. 219-26. Arturo Torres-Rioseco and Ralph E. Warner, *Bibliografía de la poesía mexicana* (Cambridge, Mass.: Harvard University Press, 1934), p. 70. No editor, *El trato con escritores* (México: INBA, Dept. de Lit., 1961), pp. 49, 50, 51, 102, 156, 167, 170.

JEANNE C. WALLACE

PUIG Casauranc, José Manuel (1888-1939). A doctor, politician, and writer, José Manuel Puig Casauranc was born in Ciudad del Carmen, Campeche, on January 31, 1888. He died in Havana, Cuba, on May 9, 1939. In 1911, he received his license to practice medicine, specifically, surgery. He practiced his profession in Veracruz, Alburquerque (United States), and later, Mexico City. In addition to his work as a doctor, he was actively involved in the political affairs of the nation, serving in several different capacities. At one time, he was an ambassador to the United States and several years later, to Argentina. As a writer, he was quite prolific, serving as an editor, a director, and a contributor to different journals. He wrote more than thirty works, including novels, poems, and stories. In 1931, he founded *La Razón* and *Resumen*. From 1934 until his death, he was a member of the Academia Mexicana.

As a journalist and prose writer, Puig Casauranc supported and furthered many of the social ideas brought about by the Revolution. In his fiction, he tended to combine Realism with Romanticism, both still in vogue at the time. Since he was the secretary of the Department of Public Education from 1924 to 1928, his essays often dealt with pedagogy. His early death at the age of fifty-one cut short a full and active life in three different, yet interrelated professions.

WORKS: *De la vida* (About Life), stories (México: Imp. Nacional, 1922). *Páginas viejas con ideas actuales* (Old Pages with Current Ideas) (México: Talls. Gráfs. de la Nación, 1925). *Poemas de espíritu y de carne* (Spirit and Flesh Poems) (México: Edit. Cultura, 1925). *Para las madres* (For Mothers) (México: Talls. Gráfs. de la Nación, 1925). *La educación pública en México a través de los mensajes presidenciales desde la consumación de la Independencia hasta nuestros días* (Public Education in Mexico via the Presidential Messages from the Beginnings of Independence until Our Times), prologue by Puig Casauranc (México: SEP, 1926). *De otros días* (Of Other Days), stories (México: Ed. Cultura, 1926). *La hermana impura* (The Impure Sister), novel

(México: Ed. Cultura, 1927). *Juárez, una interpretación humana* (Juárez, a Human Interpretation) (México: n.p., 1928). *La cuestión religiosa en relación con la educación primaria en México* (The Religious Question in Relation to Primary Education in Mexico) (México: Talls. Gráfs. de la Nación, 1928). *La obra integral de la Revolución Mexicana* (The Integral Work of the Mexican Revolution) (México: Talls. Gráfs. de la Nación, 1929). *Atlas general de Distrito Federal* (General Atlas of the Federal District) (México: Talls. Gráfs. de la Nación, 1930). *Su venganza* (Revenge), stories (México: Eds. de "La Razón," 1931). *La aspiración suprema de la Revolución Mexicana* (The Supreme Aspiration of the Mexican Revolution) (México: Imp. de la Sría. de Relaciones Exteriores, 1933). *Una política social-económica de preparación socialista* (A Social-Economic Politic of Socialist Preparation) (México: Imp. de la Sría. de Relaciones Exteriores, 1933). *El sentido social del proceso histórico de México* (The Social Sense of the Mexican Historical Process) (México: Botas, 1936). *Los errores de Satanás* (The Mistakes of Satan), farce (Brazil: Edit. Alba, 1937).

BIBLIOGRAPHY: Genardo Fernández MacGregor, *Carátulas* (México: Botas, 1935), pp. 167-8. Jesús Guzmán and Raz Guzmán, *Bibliografía de la Reforma, la Intervención y el Imperio* (México: Imp. de la Sría. de Relaciones Exteriores, 1926), vol. 2, pp. 80-81. Aurora M. Ocampo de Gómez and Ernesto Prado Velázquez, *Diccionario de Escritores Mexicanos* (México: UNAM, 1967), pp. 301-2. Gregorio Ortega Hernández, *Hombres, mujeres* (México: Eds. de Bellas Artes, 1966), pp. 199-213. Félix F. Palavicini, *Los diputados, lo que se ve y lo que no se ve de la Cámara*, 2nd ed. (México: Imp. Francesa, 1915), vol. 1, pp. 283-87.

JEANNE C. WALLACE

Q

QUEVEDO y Zubieta, Salvador (1859-1935). Born on November 20, 1859, in Guadalajara, Salvador Quevedo y Zubieta lived in Mexico until 1882, when he was forced into exile because of his outspoken opposition to the governmental policies of the president of the republic. He had already received his law degree in 1880 and was actively involved in journalistic activity in Mexico City, publishing in a variety of magazines and newspapers, and he had founded a weekly journal, *El Lunes*, violently opposed to the government.

During his brief period of exile, Quevedo y Zubieta, by this time a teacher, lawyer, and writer, went first to Madrid, then to London. In both cities, he took an active part in the cultural community, publishing in journals and newspapers. *El Imparcial*, in Madrid, for example, published his articles about Mexico, noted for their patriotic fervor. In London, he was a correspondent for several Spanish and American newspapers. Returning briefly to Mexico in 1884, he published *Manuel González y su gobierno en México* (Manuel González and His Government in Mexico), a vehement attack on what he felt was González' mishandling of his position. Although the government of González was coming to an end, Quevedo y Zubieta's book effectively destroyed the chances of the followers of González to reestablish or prolong his government.

Taking up residence in Paris in 1885, he went to medical school, becoming a doctor in 1894. He also continued writing, both in Spanish and in French, his adopted language. He worked as a correspondent for the Mexican journals *La Patria* and *El Partido Liberal*. He also founded *La Revue Exotique*, a journal that attracted the attention of some of the most noted French writers of the time who eagerly contributed to it.

In 1895 he returned to Mexico, practicing medicine in the army medical corps, serving in various diplomatic posts, and writing. He occupied the Mexican consulate in Santander in 1897 and held the same position in Saint Nazaire in 1908. Upon his return to Mexico, he became even more actively involved in journalistic pursuits. As a contributor to *El Universal*, he wrote about a wide variety of themes, in response to his mulitple interests. He died on July 6, 1935.

With respect to his literary production, aside from his political essays and papers, he also wrote novels, drama, and stories. Reflecting the school of social realism, his novels, in particular, depict in vivid and sometimes violent and bitter detail the shortcomings and vices of Mexican society. His realism borders on naturalism, with its narrow focus on even the most minute details. Several of his novels and plays are accounts of political figures, such as Porfirio Díaz and Victoriano Huerta, and of the historical periods they represent. Such titles as *México manicomio* (Mexico the Insane Asylum) and *México marimacho* (Mexico a Mannish Woman) are suggestive of works of forceful language and powerful verbal dynamics. He also wrote *Las ensabanadas*

(The Girls Covered with Sheets) and its continuation, *La ley de la sábana* (The Law of the Sheet), psychological historical novels for adults only, whose basic theme revolves around sex education, a little-discussed topic at that time, but as a physician, he was able to promote it. Because he did not see his first plays performed, he was extremely hesitant to attempt to get the later ones published. There is little critical material on the literary production of Quevedo y Zubieta. He is barely mentioned in the histories of literature and seldom reviewed. He left his legacy more as a public servant and physician than as a man of letters; nonetheless, his literary contribution is especially valuable for gaining a clearer understanding of the social customs and practices of the time.

WORKS: *El carnaval de México en 1879* (The Carnival of Mexico in 1879) (México: Tip. de F. Mata, 1879). *Recuerdos de un emigrado* (Memories of an Emmigrant) (Madrid: Rivadeneyra, 1883). *El General González y su gobierno en México* (General González and His Government in Mexico), 2 vols. (México: Est. Tip. de Patoni, 1884-1885); 3rd ed. (Madrid: Espasa-Calpe, 1928). *Un año en Londres* (A Year in London) (Paris: Imp. de Ch. Bouter, 1885). *Récits mexicains, suivi de Dialogues Parisiens* (Paris: Novelle Librairies Parisienne, Albert Savine, Editeur, 1888). *L'étudiante, Notes d'un carabín* (The Student, Notes of a "Carabín") (Paris: C. Marpon and E. Flammarion, 1888); transl. to Spanish, by José P. Rivera, *La estudiante, notas de un "carabín"* (México: Lit. de Filomeno Mata, 1889). "De l'hallaux valgus," thesis for the doctorate in medicine, Paris, 1894. *El lépero* (The Leper) (n.p.: Imp. Eduardo Dublán, 1898), pp. 183-88. *Porfirio Díaz* (Paris and México: Vda. de C. Bouret, 1906). *El caudillo* (The Chief), continuation of *Porfirio Díaz* (Paris and México: Vda. de Ch. Bouret, 1909). *La camada* (The Litter), novel (México: Ch. Bouret, 1912); and in Col. Económica, nos. 572-73 (México: Editora Nacional, 1956). *Campañas de prensa. Los consulados mexicanos. Socialismo* (Campaigns of the Press. The Mexican Consulates. Socialism (Paris and México: Vda. de Ch. Bouret, 1913). *Huerta*, historic drama (México: Botas, 1916); 2nd ed. (Morelia: Roberts, 1932). *Doña Pía o el contrachoque* (Doña Pía or the Countercrash), comedy (México: Talls. Gráfs. de la Escuela Industrial de Huérfanos, 1919). *En tierra de sangre y broma* (In the Land of Blood and Practical Jokes), novel (México: G. Sisniega y Hno., 1921); and in Col. Económica, nos. 576-77 (México: Editora Nacional, 1956). *México manicomio* (Mexico the Insane Asylum), novel (Madrid: Espasa-Calpe, 1927); and in Col. Económica, no. 580 (México: Editora Nacional, 1956). *México marimacho* (México the Mannish Woman), novel (México: Talls. de El Nacional Revolucionario, 1933); 2nd ed. (México: Botas, 1933); and in Col. Económica, nos. 578-79 (México: Editora Nacional, 1956). *Las ensabanadas* (The Girls Covered with Sheets), novel (México: Botas, 1934); and in Col. Económica, no. 574 (México: Editora Nacional, 1956). *La ley de la sábana* (The Law of the Sheet), novel, continuation of *Las ensabanadas* (México: Botas, 1935); and in Col. Económica, no. 575 (México: Editora Nacional, 1956).

BIBLIOGRAPHY: John S. Brushwood, *Mexico in Its Novel* (Austin and London: University of Texas Press, 1966), pp. 165-66. John S. Brushwood and José Rojas Garcidueñas, *Breve historia de la novela mexicana* (México: Eds. de Andrea, 1959), p. 85. Emilio Castelar, prologue to *Recuerdos de un emigrado* (Madrid: Rivadeneyra, 1883). Juan B. Iguíniz, *Bibliografía de novelistas mexicanos* (México: Imp. de la Sría. de Relaciones, 1926), pp. 282-84. Armando de María y Campo, *El teatro de género*

dramático en la Revolución Mexicana (México: Tall. Gráf. de la Nación, 1957), pp.
93-121. José Luis Martínez, *Literatura mexicana del siglo XX, 1910-1949*, vol. 2
(México: Ant. Libr. Robredo, 1949), p. 97. Ernest Moore, *Bibliografía de novelistas
de la Revolución Mexicana* (México: n.p., 1941), pp. 60-63. Joaquina Navarro, *La
novela realista mexicana* (México: Cía. General de Ediciones, 1955), pp. 312-16.
Aurora M. Ocampo de Gómez and Ernesto Prado Velázquez, *Diccionario de
Escritores Mexicanos* (México: UNAM, 1967), pp. 302-3. Manuel Prado González,
Trayectoria de la novela en México (México: Botas, 1951), pp. 290-91. Sara
Sefchovich, *México: País de Ideas, país de novelas* (México: Edit. Grijalbo, 1987), p.
64. Arturo Torres-Rioseco, *Bibliografía de la novela mexicana* (Cambridge, Mass.:
Harvard University Press, 1933), p. 44.

JEANNE C. WALLACE

QUIJANO, Alejandro (1883-1957). Alejandro Quijano was born in Mazatlán,
Sinaloa, on January 5, 1883. He studied in Mexico City, where he graduated with a
law degree from the National University of Mexico in 1907. He taught law and was
the director at the School of Jurisprudence from 1920 to 1922. Like so many of his
contemporaries he was interested in culture and literature, and devoted much of his
time to teaching, lecturing, and writing. He taught literature at the Preparatory
School, was president of the Anglo-Mexican Institute of Culture, and director of the
newspaper *Novedades* after 1946. In 1939 he was elected director of the Mexican
Academy of Language.

 During his career Quijano wrote many books on linguistics, history, and literary
criticism: *Las letras en la educación* (The Letters in Education) (1915); *En la tribuna*
(On the Rostrum) (1919); *La poesía castellana en sus cuatro primeros siglos* (The First
Four Centuries of Spanish Poetry) (1921); *Cervantes y el Quijote en la Academia*
(Cervantes and the *Quixote* in the Academy) (1935); *Los diccionarios académicos*
(Academic Dictionaries); (1940). He also wrote a travel book, *En casa de nuestros
primos* (In Our Cousin's Home) (1918). Quijano's essays have been praised for their
diverse topics, insightful approach, and polished prose.

WORKS: Essays: *Las letras en la educacion* (México: Ant. Imprenta de Murquía,
1915). *En casa de nuestros primos* (México: Ant. Imprenta de Murquía, 1918).
Amado Nervo, el hombre (México: Ant. Imprenta de Murquía, 1919). *En la tribuna*
(México: Eds. Botas, 1937).

BIBLIOGRAPHY: Carlos González Peña, *Historia de la literatura mexicana* (México:
Porrúa, 1981), p. 258. Aurora M. Ocampo de Gómez and Ernesto Prado Velázquez,
Diccionario de escritores mexicanos (México: UNAM, 1967), p. 263.

NORA ERRO-PERALTA

QUIJANO, Margarita (1914-?), literary critic. Quijano was born on October 10, 1914
in Mexico City, where she received a master's and a doctoral degree in humanities
from the Facultad de Filosofía y Letras at the University of Mexico. In 1946 she

received a grant from the British Council to study in London, and in 1947 she attended summer classes at the Universidad de Zaragoza, Spain. In 1948 Quijano completed classes in comparative literature at the Sorbonne in Paris and studied further in Florence, Italy. In 1951 she received a grant from the Institute of Education at Radcliffe, and in 1956 she was the recipient of the Rockefeller grant, with which she made a second trip to Europe in order to continue her studies of the work of William Shakespeare. In the years after 1944, she had posts at the Universidad Femenina, Escuela de Verano, Escuela Nacional Preparatoria, and the Facultad de Filosofía y Letras at the Universidad Nacional de México. In 1954 she was named to full-time professorship in the Facultad de Filosofía y Letras of the aforementioned university.

Quijano dedicated her life to the mastery and research of English literature, especially the works of William Shakespeare. Her works *La Celestina y Otelo* (The *Celestina* and *Othello*) (1957) and *Hamlet y sus críticos* (Hamlet and His Critics) (1962) are the results of that research.

WORKS: Essays: *Manuel M. Flores su vida y su obra* (Manuel M. Flores, His Life and Work) (México: Porrúa, 1946). *La Celestina y Otelo* (The *Celestina* and *Othello*), no. 15 (México: UNAM, 1957). *Hamlet y sus críticos* (México: UNAM, 1962). *Macbeth, Otelo y el Rey Lear: un análisis de sus temas* (*Macbeth, Othello,* and *King Lear*: An Analysis of Their Themes) (México: 1970). Introduction to *Rosas caídas* (Fallen Roses), by Manuel M. Flores (México: UNAM, 1951).

BIBLIOGRAPHY: José Amezcua, Review of *Hamlet y sus críticos*, in *Boletín Bibliográfico de la Secretaría de Hacienda y Crédito Público* 293 (April 15, 1964): 23. Anon., Review of *Hamlet y sus críticos*, in *Cuadernos de Bellas Artes* 4, 1, (Jan. 1963): 92; Review of *Hamlet y sus críticos*, in *Bulletín del Centro Mexicano de Escritores* (May 15, 1962): 3. Jesús Arellano, Review of *La Celestina y Otelo*, in *Metáfora* 16 (Sept-Oct. 1957): 44-45. Raúl Leiva, "Bibliográfica por . . .," review of *Hamlet y sus críticos* in *Nivel* 41 (May, 25 1962): 3; Review of *Hamlet y sus críticos*, in *Anuario de Letras* 2 (1962): 324-26. Aurora M. Ocampo, Review of *La Celestina y Otelo*, in *Letras Nuevas* 1 (Nov.-Dec. 1957): 46-48. Aurora M. Ocampo de Gómez and Ernesto Prado Velázquez, *Diccionario de escritores mexicanos* (México: UNAM, 1967), p. 304.

                                                                      JOAN SALTZ

QUINTANA Roo, Andrés (1787-1851), writer and politician. Quintana Roo was born in Mérida, Yucatán. He spent his first years in La Casa de Chante or Cantor de la Catedral, where he began his studies under the tutelage of the rationalist Pablo Moreno. In the Conciliate Seminary of the Colegio de San Ildefonso, where he was a schoolmate of the liberal federalist Lorenzo de Zavala, he studied philosophy, metaphysics, and art. In 1808, he moved to Mexico City to continue his studies at the Real y Pontífica Universidad. For a while, he worked in a lawyer's office until he took charge of the independence cause. He fought in the army of Ignacio López Rayón and, under his command, collaborated on the publication and edition of *El ilustrador americano* and *El Seminario Patriótico*. Like some of his contemporaries, he started in politics while very young, developing his work as a journalist and speaker. He was a legislator from Puebla at the Congress of Chilpancingo, and he signed the Acta de Independencia (The Independence Affidavit), and El Manifiesto of 1813 (The Manifest of 1813), in which the above-named Congress gave the people a general explanation of events. It was his work, as was the Constitution of Apatzingán in 1814, the latter a collaborative effort with Carlos María *Bustamante. After independence was won, he held several public offices, where his liberal convictions were openly apparent. In 1822, he was the Minister of Foreign Affairs; in 1824 and 1826 he served as magistrate of the Supreme Court of Justice; in 1827 he was plenipotentiary minister of Mexico in London; in 1833 he was secretary of justice; and in 1836 he was elected president of the Academy of San Juan de Letrán. He died in Mexico City in 1851.

Quintana Roo was a productive writer, but a good part of his writings were published anonymously. Even though he wrote some poems, his most well-known work was political. His work was published in *El Ilustrador Americano* (The American Illustrator), *Seminario Patriótico* (Patriotic Weekly), *El Federalista* (The Federalist), *Diario de México* (The Daily of Mexico), and *El Correo de la Federación* (The Mail of the Federation). In his opinion, this was the best way to propagate his republican ideas. In poetry, one of his best known and most often recited poems is "Dieciséis de Septiembre" (September 16), a patriotic and romantic poem, in which freedom is exalted and tyranny is condemned.

WORKS: *Discurso pronunciado por el ciudadano Andrés Quintana Roo en el glorioso aniversario del día 16 de septiembre de 1845* (Speech Given by the Citizen Andrés Quintana Roo on the Glorious Anniversary of September 16, 1845) (México: Imprenta del Aguila, 1845). *Justa memoria del heroismo que en el sitio de Gerona manifestó el Capitán Don Felipe Peón Maldonado, hijo de la ciudad de Mérida de Yucatán* (Fair Memory of Heroism Which Captain Don Felipe Peón Maldonado, Son of the City of Mérida of Yucatán, Manifested at the Site of Gerona) (México: n.p., n.d.).

BIBLIOGRAPHY: *Enciclopedia de México* (México: Impresora y Editora Mexicana, 1977).

CARMEN BLAZQUEZ DOMINGUEZ

QUIRARTE, Vicente (1954-). Quirarte was born in Mexico City on July 19, 1954. He studied Spanish language and literature at the Universidad Nacional Autónoma de México and is presently professor of literature and creative writing at the Universidad Autónoma Metropolitana in Mexico City. He has repeatedly been invited as distinguished visiting professor to Austin College in Sherman, Texas. He is well respected as a Mexican literary critic.

Quirarte's work ranks among the very best in Mexican contemporary poetry. He is a serious, mature young writer who is concerned with producing quality. As in very few other cases in recent Mexican poetry, the scope of his literary production runs a wide gamut. He is equally comfortable writing an entire book of carefully crafted sonnets -- *Fra Filippo Lippi: Cancionero de Lucrecia Buti* -- as he is writing long free-verse poems or prose-poems. His *Puerta de verano* (Summer Door) and his *Vencer a la blancura* (To Conquer Whiteness) are the work of a brilliant imagination. In his seven part "Venice" he is at his best: "I still sleep / with barges beating at my ear / and I can't believe that as I wake / light will not rise through the canals."

WORKS: *Lejos de las naves* (Far from the boats) (México: Punto de partida, 1979). *Fra Filipp Lippi: Cancionero de Lucrecia Buti* (Br. Filipp Lippi: Lucrecia Buti's songbook) (México: UNAM, 1981). *Vencer a la blancura* (To Conquer Whiteness) (México: Premiá, 1982). *Puerta de verano* (Summer's door)(Guadalajara, Jalisco: Cuarto Menguante Editores, 1982). *Plenilunio de la muñeca* (The Doll's Full Moon) (México: Oasis, Libros del Fakir, 1984). *Bahía Magdalena* (Magdalena's Bay) (Xalapa: Ediciones Papel de Envolver, Universidad Veracruzana, 1984). *La luz no muere sola* ((The Light does not die alone) (México: SEP, 1987).

BIBLIOGRAPHY: José Joaquín Blanco, *Crónica de la poesía mexicana* (México: Katún, 1981), pp. 264-70. Sandro Cohen, *Palabra nueva: Dos décadas de poesía en México* (México: Premiá, 1981), pp. 27 and 297. Jorge González de León, *Poetas de una genración* (México: UNAM, 1981), pp. 7-11. Jaime Moreno Villareal, *La línea y el círculo* (México: Universidad Autónoma Metropolitana, 1981).

RICARDO AGUILAR

QUIROZZ Hernández, Alberto (1907-). Born in León, Guanajuato, on November 29, 1907, Quirozz Hernández spent his first two adolescent years at the Seminario Conciliar of León. He studied at the Escuela Nacional Preparatoria but did not graduate, although he was about to conclude his studies. Later, he studied at the Instituto Federal de Capacitación Magisterial. He worked as a librarian and a teacher of Spanish and literature. He considers that being a novelist is and has been his most stable profession. He is a prolific prose writer, poet, playwright, and journalist. He has written on a variety of topics: aesthetics of cinematography, Mexican and American history, the American Civil War, American annexation of the Panama Canal, the Mexican Revolution, and literary celebrities of both countries. He expresses admiration for Walt Whitman, Ernest Hemingway, Carl Sandburg, and others American writers. His style is Impressionist, laced with irony and even skepticism, invariably exhibiting a Mexican point of view.

La situación de la literatura mexicana (The State of Mexican Literature) is an analysis of Mexico's letters and society of the times (1934). *Diario mágico* (Magic Diary) is a work of exalted thought, lyrical in some passages, about life and man. Original in its ideas, it is a beautifully written book. *Cristo Rey o la persecución* (Christ the King or The Persecution) is the inside story of the bloody events of 1926 when Catholic youths conspired and rebelled against the government. in *Historias para Oscar Lewis. El reverso de los hijos de Sánchez* (Stories for Oscar Lewis. The Other Side of The Sons of Sánchez), Herbert Lewis's family members tell their stories as blacks subjected to discrimination. Sex, alcohol, and crime are prevalent. The spontaneity of the testimonial narrative lends realism and credibility to the accounts.

WORKS: *Zigzag novelesco* (Novelistic Zigzag) (México: Editorial Indice, 1929). *La situación de la literatura mexicana* (The State of Mexican Literature) (México: Ediciones Guanajuato, 1934). *Nociones de estética cinematográfica* (Ideas on

Aesthetics of Cinematography) (México: Imprenta J. J. Nava, 1942). *Poesía y teatro infantiles* (Children's Poetry and Plays) (México: Ediciones Educación, 1944). *Chifladuras de Sostenes Trucha* (Whims of Sostenes Trucha) (México: n.p., 1944). *Cristo Rey o la persecución* (Christ the King or The Persecution) (México: Editorial Yucatenense, 1948). *El Profesor Mentoláthum* (Professor Mentholatum) (México: Editora Iberoamericana, 1948). *Los ladrones* (The Thieves) (México: Editorial Iberoamericana, 1950). *Magia silvestre* (Country Magic) (México: Unidad Mexicana de Escritores, 1954). *Paraíso Wesston* (Wesston Paradise) (México: Unidad Mexicana de Escritores, 1956). *Lupe Fusiles* (Lupe Muskets) (México: Libro-Mex Editores, 1957). *El rey Falfifurrias* (King Falfifurrias) (México: Unidad de Escritores, 1958). *Serpiente* (Serpent) (México: Unidad de Escritores, 1959). *Pregones de Navidad* (Christmas Carols) (México: Unidad Mexicana de Escritores, 1960). *Odisea de la Virgen Morena* (Odyssey of the Dark Virgin) (México: Ediciones Unidad Mexicana de Escritores, 1961). *Biografía de Norteamerica* (Biography of North America) (México: Costa-Amic Editor, 1963). *Diario mágico* (Magic Diary) (México: Ediciones UME, 1965). *Historias para Oscar Lewis* (Stories for Oscar Lewis) (México: Costa-Amic Editor, 1966). *Un Papa mexicano* (A Mexican Pope) (México: Costa-Amic Editor, 1969). *Los magos de la revolución* (The Wizards of the Revolution) (México: Costa-Amic Editor, 1972). *Los intelectuales* (The Intellectuals) (México: Costa-Amic Editor, 1978).

BIBLIOGRAPHY: Anon., "Almanaque sobre los Estados Unidos. La nueva obra de A. Quirozz,." in *Revista de la Semana* (Jan. 26, 1964): 3. John S. Brushwood and José Rojas Garcidueñas, *Breve historia de la novela mexicana* (México: de Andrea, 1959), p. 81. Alfredo Gamboa, *La novelística de Alberto Quirozz* (México: Imp. Juan Pablos, 1957). Ruth S. Lamb, *Bibliografía del teatro mexicano del siglo XX* (México: Eds. de Andrea, 1962), pp. 102-3. Luis Leal, *Bibliografía* del cuento mexicano (México: Eds. de Andrea, 1958), p. 116. José Luis Martínez, *Literatura* mexicana siglo XX, 1910-1949, vol. 1 (México: Ant. Libr. Robredo, 1949), p. 51; vol. 2 (1950), p. 58.

ALICIA G. WELDEN AND ELADIO CORTES

R

RABASA, Emilio (1856-1930). Born in Ocozocoautla, Chiapas, on May 22, 1856, Emilio Rabasa, born into a fairly well-to-do family, was educated at home until he was twelve. He furthered his studies at the Instituto de Ciencias y Artes in Oaxaca, receiving his law degree in 1878. He was elected to the state legislature in 1881 and, a year later, was named director of the Instituto de Chiapas. He also got married in 1882. For the next few years Rabasa served in civil and judicial capacities. Several of his earliest articles were published in *El Porvenir* and *El Liberal*, two local journals. By the time he moved to Mexico City in 1886, he had already established himself as a lawyer, politician, professor, and journalist.

Once in Mexico City, he began working as an agent and public defender for the Ministerio Público. He also taught political economics and seriously embarked on a career in journalism. With Reyes Spíndola, he founded *El Universal*. He also was the governor of Chiapas for four years (1891-1895), a senator (returning him to Mexico City), a teacher at the law school, and a member of the Real Academia de Jurisprudencia. He held membership in several other prestigious scientific, legal, and literary associations. He traveled widely throughout Europe and the United States during the early 1900s. He was also an important politician during the regime of Porfirio Díaz. In 1914, he served his government as a representative to a conference in Niagara Falls, then went to New York, where he lived for six years. He died in 1930.

Politically, in addition to his alliance with Porfirio Díaz, Rabasa was a liberal and a positivist, a follower of the ideas of Herbert Spencer, believing that the gradual adaptation to circumstances and the slow evolution of changes was the best possible course for Mexico. He viewed the Constitution as the supreme law, staunchly defending it as the only way of keeping order in the midst of change. He was considered the most knowledgeable Mexican about constitutional law, writing many books about it. A federalist, Rabasa recognized the sovereignty of the people and of individual states in the republic. With respect to Indian affairs, he took the point of view that the Indian was basically inferior and, therefore, needed protection. But, like José *Vasconcelos, he also saw promise in the mestizo as a productive member of society.

Rabasa began his literary career when he was only sixteen, publishing an ode to Emilio Castelar in *La Iberia*, the newspaper of Chiapas. He continued to contribute regularly in the journals noted above. In 1884, he dedicated "A Mercedes," a long poetic composition of fifty four sextets, to his wife. In 1886, he published an anthology of poets from Oaxaca, which included a prologue he had written.

Using the pseudonym Sancho Polo, Rabasa published four novels, attacking the pettiness, corruption, and apathy he saw rampant both in provincial towns and in the city. *La bola* (The Brawl) and *La gran ciencia* (Great Science) were both published in 1887. *El cuarto poder* (The Fourth Power) and *Moneda falsa* (Counterfeit Money) appeared in 1888. These were followed by a short fictional work, *La guerra de los tres años* (The Three-Year War), coming out in 1891.

La bola satirically deals with what happens when a small, local revolution breaks out in the imaginary town of San Martín de la Piedra, characterized by anonymity and broad generalizations. Such a revolution, in which a politician chooses to establish himself as the local boss, regardless of the opposition, property damage, and lives lost as a result of the skirmish, is termed a "bola." The story also contains an idyllic romance and an intrigue between a local unscrupulous chieftain, Cabezudo, and a young idealistic man, Quiñones, unaware of the nature of political intrigue.

La gran ciencia takes the action to the capital of the state, where intrigues on a larger scale get played out. In the work, Rabasa criticizes the opportunism of politicians whose "science" means how they stay in power, how they promote themselves and use the people around them to their advantage.

In *El cuarto poder*, the action is in Mexico City. The title refers to the press, which is seen as the terrible fourth power. Quiñones, a journalist and protagonist in all four novels, discovers that quite often newsmen invent the stories they print, both for personal enhancement and for increased sales. The somewhat idealistic Quiñones loses whatever idealism he had left by the end of the story, as he sees what reality is truly all about.

Moneda falsa deals with the return of Cabezudo and Quiñones to their small town as a result of their inability to adapt to the circumstances of the city. Apparently, Rabasa thought that in their provincial town, rather than in the devouring city, the characters could seek to improve social conditions and other aspects of society without changing its inherent structure.

Finally, *La guerra de tres años*, similar to *La bola*, takes place in a small town. Historically, the Mexican government during the Reform had prohibited external religious displays by the Church, what was called the "culto de la calle" (cult of the street). Despite the ban, people continued their traditions. In this short novel, Rabasa deals with the contradiction between officials who wish to enforce the Reform Laws and townspeople who insist upon maintaining their religious practices. In essence, Rabasa mocks the provincial customs and the false distances between Liberals and Conservatives.

Of these five works, *La bola* is the most well-known and best structured. They all deal with different aspects of public life. Since four of them also contain love intrigues, his novels are considered within the realm of romantic realism.

Emilio Rabasa was considered the best prose writer of his time. Yet, his period of literary creativity in fiction lasted for only a few years, almost as a juvenile escapade. Examining his novels, one finds them to be clearly written, easily read, and structurally well balanced. A master at characterization, he develops his literary figures as if sculpting a work of art. The episodes he narrates are also carefully detailed, without being monotonous. His work represents the first literary expression of Realism in the Mexican novel. He avoids the typical scenes of Romanticism and **costumbrismo**, favoring the new trend of the school of Realism, blending it at times with the classical touches of the old masters. He is considered the inventor of the political novel in Mexico as well as the first truly realistic novel.

With both a somber and humoristic tone, he deals primarily with the situations of the growing middle class, thus eliminating a more global vision of society. Indeed, he saw the middle class as the promise for the future. He did not prominently include the lower class in his works. Yet, he has been called "Rabasa Galdosiano" and has been compared to Emilia Pardo Bazán because both dealt with more varied social groups than did Rabasa. Like them, though, he took a social, but sometimes satirical, sometimes objective, approach to life and its problems. Elements of the picaresque are in some of his characters and situations, similar to the *Periquillo Sarniento* of Francisco *Lizardi. Rabasa relates the adventures of Quiñones, the journalist, through the four novels, in much the way that authors of picaresque novels have done.

In addition to his novelistic works, Rabasa also wrote many fine articles, essays, and books in the field of law. While his literary career was short-lived in comparison to his law career, Rabasa is honored as the first realistic novelist in Mexico, a distinction that guarantees him a permanent place in the annals of Mexican literature.

WORKS: Poetry: *A Mercedes* (México: n.p., 1884). *La mujer oaxaqueña. Colección de poesías escogidas de poetas oaxaqueños, formada y precedida de un prólogo de E. Rabasa* (The Woman of Oaxaca. Selected Poems by Poets from Oaxaca, Arranged by and with a Prologue by E. Rabasa) (Oaxaca: n.p., 1886). Studies and Essays: *El Artículo 14. Estudio Constitucional* (Article 14. Constitutional Study) (México: El Progreso Latino, 1906); 2nd ed., with *El Juicio Constitucional. Orígenes, teoría y extensión* (Constitutional Judgment. Origins, Theory, and Extension) (México: Porrúa, n.d.). *La Constitución y la dictadura. Estudio sobre la organización política en México* (The Constitution and the Dictatorship. A Study about Political Organization in Mexico) (México: Tip. de "Revista de Revistas," 1912), 2nd ed. (Madrid: Edit. América, 1917), 3rd ed. (México: Porrúa, 1956). *La acusación de don José Barros* (The Indictment of don José Barros) (México: n.p., 1912). *Comisiones unidas: Primera de puntos constitucionales y Primera de gobernación. Las cámaras de senadores* (United Commissions: The First about Constitutional Points and the First about Governance. The Senate Chambers) (México: n.p., 1913). *El juicio constitucional. Orígenes, teoría y extensión* (Constitutional Judgment. Origins, Theory, and Extension) (Paris and México: Libr. de la Vda. de Ch. Bouret, 1919). *La evolución histórica de México. Las evoluciones violentas. La evolución pacífica. Los problemas nacionales* (Mexico's Historic Evolution. Violent Evolutions. Peaceful Evolution. National Problems) (París and México: Libr. de la Vda. de Ch. Bouret, 1920), 2nd ed. (México: Porrúa, 1956). "La libertad de trabajo" (The Freedom of Work), in *Conferencias preliminares*, vol. 2 (México: Imp. Victoria, 1922). *Retratos y estudios* (Portraits and Studies) (México: UNAM, 1945). Novel: *La bola* (The Brawl) (México: Alfonso E. López, 1887), 2nd ed. (México: O. R. Spíndola, 1888), 3rd ed. (Paris and México: Libr. de la Vda. de Ch. Bouret, 1919). *La gran ciencia* (Great Science) (México: Alfonso E. López, 1887), 2nd ed. (Paris and México: Libr. de la Vda. de Ch. Bouret, 1919). *El cuarto poder* (The Fourth Power) (México: O. R. Spíndola, 1888), 2nd. ed. (Paris and México: Libr. de la Vda. de Ch. Bouret, 1919). *Moneda falsa* (Counterfeit Money) (México: O. R. Spíndola, 1888), 2nd ed. (Paris and México: Libr. de la Vda. de Ch. Bouret, 1919). *La Guerra de Tres Años* (The Three-Year War) (México: Edit. Cultura, 1931), 2nd ed., *La Guerra de Tres Años, seguido de poemas inéditos y desconocidos* (The Three-Year War, Followed by Unpublished and Unknown Poems) (México: Libro-Mex, 1955). *La bola y la gran ciencia* (The Brawl and the Great Science) (México: Porrúa, 1948). *El cuarto poder y la moneda falsa* (The Fourth Power and Counterfeit Money) (México: Porrúa, 1948).

BIBLIOGRAPHY: Víctor Abid, "Emilio Rabasa, novelista del hombre," in *Universidad de México* 8, 3 (Nov. 1953): 10. Fernando Alegría, *Nueva historia de la novela hispanoamericana* (Hanover, N.H.: Ediciones del Norte, 1986), pp. 41, 84-87, 91. Mariano Azuela, "Emilio Rabasa," in *Cien años de novela mexicana* (México: Botas, 1947), pp. 165-78. John S. Brushwood, *The Romantic Novel in Mexico* (Columbia: University of Missouri Studies, 1954), pp. 52-53. *Mexico in Its Novel* (Austin: University of Texas Press, 1966), pp. 122-23, 125-26, 128-31, 157-58, 162, 168. John S. Brushwood and José Rojas Garcidueñas, *Breve historia de la novela mexicana* (México: Eds. de Andrea, 1959), pp. 42-44. Emmanuel Carballo, Notes and prologue to *La Guerra de Tres Años*, (México: Edit. Cultura, 1931), pp. 9-23. "José López Portillo y Emilio Rabasa," in *Universidad de México* 9, 8, (April 1955): 1-2, 17-19; "La novela mexicana antes de después de la Revolución," in *La Cultura en México*, 100 (Jan. 15, 1964): ii-iv. David William Foster, *Handbook of Latin American Literature* (New York: Garland, 1987), pp. 358-60. Nemesio García Naranjo, "El Centenario de Rabasa," in *Novedades* (May 16, 1956): 4. Carlos González Peña, "Rabasa y sus novelas," in *Claridad en la lejanía*, (México: Edit. Stylo, 1947), pp. 211-18. Roland Grass, "Cómo se hace una revolución según Emilio Rabasa," in *Cuadernos Americanos* 5 (Sept.-Oct. 1965): 276-81. Manuel Gutiérrez Nájera, "*La bola*, de Sancho Polo," in *Obras. Crítica literaria* 1 (México: UNAM, 1959), pp. 301-3. Marcia A. Hakala, "Ignacio Altamirano y Emilio Rabasa: ¿Posible patrocinio?," in *Abside*, 37 (1973): 17-25. Juan B. Iguíniz, *Bibliografía de novelistas mexicanos* (México: Imp. de la Sría. de Relaciones, 1926), pp. 285-87. Julio Jiménez Rueda, *Letras mexicanas en el siglo XIX* (México: FCE, 1944), pp. 165-66. Luis Leal, *Panorama de la literatura mexicana actual* (Washingotn, D.C.: Unión Panamericana, 1968), pp. 9, 11, 64. Vicente Liévano, *Lic. Emilio Rabasa* (Tuxtla Gutiérrez: Edit. Palenque, 1946). Antonio Magaña Esquivel, "El realismo de Emilio Rabasa," in *El Nacional* (Dec. 17, 1964): 3. Joaquina Navarro, *La novela realista mexicana* (México: Cía. General de Ediciones, 1955), pp. 41-82. Alfonso Francisco Ramírez, "Emilio Rabasa," in *El Universal* (June 25, 1956): 3. Rodolfo Reyes, Prologue to *La Constitución y la dictadura* (México: Tip. de "Revista de Revistas," 1912), pp. v-xxv. Victoriano Salado Alvarez, Prologue to *La Guerra de Tres Años* (México: Edit. Cultura, 1931): iv-xvii. Sara Sefchovich, *México: país de ideas, país de novelas* (México: Grijalbo, 1987), pp. 59-62, 64, 66, 69, 96. Roy L. Tanner, "Palma, Rabasa y la intertextualidad," in *Crítica Hispánica* 9, 1-2 (1987): 51-67. María del Carmen Velázquez, "Rabasa y su visión porfiriana," in *Historia Mexicana* 6, 2 (Oct.-Dec. 1956): 278-81. Esperanza Velázquez Bringas and Rafael Heliodoro Valle, *Indice de escritores* (México: Talls. Gráf. de Herrero Hnos., 1928), pp. 135-38. Ralph E. Warner, *Historia de la novela mexicana en el siglo XIX* (México: Ant. Libr. de Robredo, 1953), pp. 92-95.

JEANNE C. WALLACE AND MIRTA BARREA-MARLYS

RAMIREZ, Ignacio (1818-1879). Ignacio Ramírez was born on June 22, 1818, in Guanajuato. Although he became a lawyer, his primary interests were in scientific endeavors; thus, he was very active in the scientific and other cultural associations of his time. In his entrance speech before the Academia de Letan, much to the consternation of the conservatives who were present, he argued positivistic ideas that God does not exist and nature is self-sustaining. Dedicating his life to politics and to the dissemination of his ideas, he sometimes used the pseudonym El Nicromante.

Very much in favor of political independence and against any foreign intervention in Mexican and Latin American affairs, Ramírez founded *El Clamor Progresista* (The Progressive Clamor) and *La Insurrección* (The Insurrection) to espouse his views. He was also deeply involved with other publications, such as *El Monitor Republicano* (The Republican Monitor) and *La Chinaca* (The Chicana), all of which became forums for his ideas. He was considered the apostle of the Reform in Mexico, periodically being imprisoned for his ideas and his actions. He contracted yellow fever while in one of the prisons, but later, despite his continuing calamities, used his experience to find ways to help those in need, via the establishment of pensions. He was a protestor, even protesting the execution of Maximilian as a useless gesture.

Ignacio Ramírez was also an economist, lobbying on behalf of the working class citizen, attempting to improve his lot in life, to deal with the problems created by a nascent capitalistic society. Able to discuss the latest scientific theories, Ramírez, a respected member of the Sociedad Mexicana de Geografía y Estadística, kept abreast of the changing times in virtually all disciplines. Also an educator, he taught law, literature, and philosophy, influencing many young people, including Ignacio M. *Altamirano, who became his best student. It was Altamirano who would be Ramírez's biographer and would continue his work both in and out of the classroom. Ramírez was also interested in the educational welfare of the indigenous population, helping to establish the means by which especially talented boys would receive a quality education, funded by the government. He also worked to achieve educational reforms that would make the system competitive with the best European ones at that time.

Except during the French domination in Mexico, which he spent in exile in California, Ramírez served his government in several capacities, including being a Supreme Court judge. He died suddenly on June 15, 1879, while in his second term as judge. His pseudonym stands for the liberal man of action who is dedicated to achieving Reformist ideals and to destroying any traditions which hinder the liberal. While his goals were clearly liberal, he could not forget his conservative heritage, particularly in his writings that demonstrate an indebtedness to the classics and other literary traditions of long standing. He was also considered one of the best poets of his era, composing both classical and nontraditional poems, although the former are more critically acclaimed than the latter.

WORKS: *Lecciones de literatura* (Lessons of Literature) (México: Imp. of Francisco Díaz de León, 1884). *Obras de Ignacio Ramírez* (Works by Ignacio Ramírez), 2 vols. (México: Ofna. Tip. de la Sría. de Fomento, 1889); 2nd ed. (México: Editora Nacional, 1952). *Discursos y artículos* (Speeches and Articles) (México: Imp. Victoria, 1917). *Ensayos* (Essays) (México: UNAM, 1944). *México en pos de la libertad* (Mexico in Pursuit of Freedom) (México: Empresas Editoriales, 1949).

BIBLIOGRAPHY: Ermilo Abreu Gómez, *Sala de retratos* (México: Edit. Leyenda, 1946), pp. 228-29. Ignacio M. Altamirano, "Los funerales del señor Ramírez," in *La Libertad* (México) 2, 141 (June 19, 1879): 1; and in *Obras completas* by Ignacio M. Altamirano, vol. 1 (México: SEP, 1949), pp. 204-10; "Biografía de Ignacio Ramírez," in *La literatura nacional*, vol. 2 (México: Porrúa, 1949), pp. 185-254. David R. Maciel, "Ideología y praxis. Ignacio Ramírez y el Congreso Constituyente, 1856-1857," in *Cuadernos Americanos* 221, 6 (Nov.-Dec. 1978): 119-29; *Ignacio Ramírez, ideólogo del liberalismo social en México* (México: UNAM, 1980): p. 220. Mauricio

Magdaleno, "Dos cabezas indias," in *El Libro y el Pueblo* 12, 1 (Jan. 1934): 1-12. José Martí, *La clara voz de México* (México: Imp. Universitaria, 1953): pp. 161-64. Porfirio Martínez Peñaloza,"Ideas estéticas y lingüísticas de Ignacio Ramírez. El Nigromante," in *Humanitas* 4 (1963): 357-72. Francisco Monterde, "Ignacio Ramírez, 'El Nigromante,'" in *Aspectos literarios de la cultura mexicana* (México: Universidad de Colima, 1987), pp. 55-63. Aurora M. Ocampo de Gómez and Ernesto Prado Velázquez, *Diccionario de escritores mexicanos* (México: UNAM, 1967), pp. 309-10. José Emilio Pacheco, *La poesía mexicana del siglo XIX* (México: Empresas Editoriales, 1965): pp. 203-4. María del Carmen Ruiz Castañeda, *Periodismo político de la Reforma en la ciudad de México, 1854-1861* (México: UNAM, 1954), pp. 163-68.

JEANNE C. WALLACE

RAMIREZ, José Agustín. See AGUSTIN, José.

RAMIREZ, José María (1834-1892), novelist. As a student of law and theology at San Ildefonso in Mexico City, Ramírez began his literary career by writing erotic poetry and sentimental "leyendas," or stories in verse, which he circulated among his classmates. Although he continued to write poetry throughout his life and occasional pieces made their way into local newspapers, Ramírez never achieved the fame he sought as a poet. Instead, he won recognition as the author of three romantic novels, *Una rosa y un harapo* (A Rose and a Rag), *Celeste* (Celestial), and *Los pícaros* (The Rogues). Ramírez was heavily influenced by French Romanticism, especially in terms of style. He cultivated a highly artificial, declamatory type of language which, according to Ignacio *Altamirano, made his novels inaccessible to the majority of Mexican readers. Despite this criticism, however, Ramírez was thought to have an original and promising talent. Today, he is looked at with less favor. Modern critics find him sentimental in the extreme, and they question the literary merit of his works.

WORKS: *Celeste* (Celestial) (Paris: Rosa y Bouret, 1865). *Los pícaros* (The Rogues) (Paris: Rosa y Bouret, 1866). *Una rosa y un harapo* (A Rose and a Rag) (México: F. Díaz de León, 1868).

BIBLIOGRAPHY: Ignacio Manuel Altamirano, *La literatura nacional*, vol. 1 (México: Porrúa, 1949), pp. 64-68. Carlos González Peña, *Historia de la literatura mexicana* (México: SEP, 1928), p. 345.

CYNTHIA K. DUNCAN

RAMIREZ Cabañas, Joaquín (1886-1945), pseudonym J. Pérez Lugo, Ramírez Cabañas was born in Coatepec, Veracruz, on August 23, 1886. When he was thirteen years old, he moved to the capital where he continued his studies in the Liceo Fournier and the National Preparatory School. Soon after, he abandoned his formal studies and began a long and oustanding career in journalism. He directed the magazine *Tiempo*, and contributed to many magazines and newspapers in Mexico City as well as other states; *Nosotros, Revista Moderna, El Universal Ilustrado, Revista de*

Revistas, El Heraldo, El Universal, etc. In 1915 Francisco *Gamoneda and Ramírez Cabañas founded the *Librería Biblios*, where many of the contemporary writers gathered to discuss literature and other topics of interest.

In 1921 he began his career as an educator, he taught history, language, and literature at the National Preparatory School and the Faculty of Arts and Letters until his death on January 2, 1945. He was considered a brilliant professor by his contemporaries. He wrote three volumes of poetry, *La sombra de los días* (The Shadow of the Days) (1918), *Remanso del silencio* (Dead Waters of Silence) (1922), *Esparcimiento* (Diversion) (1925), and a novel, *La fruta del cercado ajeno* (Other People's Fruit) (1921), which received a literary award. *La sombra de los días* consists of fifty sonnets written during his youth. In his last collection of poetry he describes the countryside and nature with an elegant language full of color and movement.

He produced many historical studies: chronicles, biographies, essays on religious, philosophical, economical, and sociological topics, such as the monographs "El pensador mexicano" (The Mexican Thinker), "El doctor Mora" (Doctor Mora), "El empréstito de México a Colombia" (The Mexican Loan to Colombia), "San Jerónimo Coatepec," and "Altamirano y el barón de Wagner" (Altamirano and the Baron of Wagner.) He developed an excellent reputation editing a number of valuable scholarly works of important Mexican authors for Robredo and Editorial Porrúa. He has been praised for the preparation of the editions of *Historia de las cosas de Nueva España* (The General History of the Things of New Spain), by Fray Bernardino de *Sahagún and *Historia verdadera de la conquista de la Nueva España* (The True History of the Conquest of New Spain), by Bernal *Díaz del Castillo. An eminent scholar, he contributed, through his writings, to the development of Mexican history, literature, and culture.

WORKS: Poetry: *La sombra de los días* (México: Imp. de José Ballesta, 1918). *Remanso del silencio* (México: América Latina, 1922). *Esparcimiento* (México: América Latina, 1925). Novel: *La fruta del cercado ajeno* (México: Talls. Tip. Don Quijote, 1921). Essays: *Estudios históricos* (México: Botas, 1935). *Gastón de Raousset, conquistador de Sonora* (México: Editorial Xóchitl, 1941). *La ciudad de Veracruz* (México: UNAM, 1943).

BIBLIOGRAPHY: Aurora M. Ocampo de Gómez and Ernesto Prado Velázquez, *Diccionario de escritores mexicanos* (México: UNAM, 1967), pp. 312-13. Ofelia Yarza C. "Ensayo biobibliográfico de don Joaquín Ramírez Cabañas," *Boletín del Instituto de Investigaciones Bibliográficas*, vols. 14-15 (1977-88): 561-81.

NORA ERRO-PERALTA

RAMIREZ de Asbaje (Asuaje), Juana. See CRUZ, Sor Juana Inés de la.

RAMOS, Raymundo (1934-   ). Born in Piedras Negras, Coahuila, on November 2, 1934, Ramos began school in his native city, continued in Monterrey, then did his preparatory school and university work at the National University of Mexico, where he received a *licenciatura* in Spanish letters. He has been a professor of sociology, and Mexican, Iberoamerican, and world literatures in secondary and preparatory schools. He has traveled several times to the United States.

Raymundo Ramos has produced poetry, short stories and essays; he has been awarded prizes and other distinctions in all three genres. In 1961, in New York, he was awarded the Ulysses Prize in Poetry for his poem *Canción inusitada*, and in 1963, the "Alfonso Reyes" essay prize awarded by the literary supplement to *Ovaciones*, for his critical work, *José María Velasco, pintor del Valle de México*. He has contributed to the literary supplements of *Ovaciones* and of *El Universal*; and to the journals *Impacto*, of Mexico City, and *Vida Universitaria*, of Monterrey.

WORKS: Poetry: *Paloma de sur a polo* (Dove from South to Pole), poem (México: Imp. Corona-Castillo, 1958). *Sonetos españoles*, (Spanish Sonnets) (México: Literary Supplement to the journal *Boletín*, 1960). *Martin Luther King*, viñetas de Francisco Mora (*Martin Luther King*, vignettes of Francisco Mora) (México: Talls. de la Impresora Saber, 1963). *Luz en las Segovias* (Light in the Segovias) (Monterrey, Nuevo León: Imp. de la Universidad de Monterrey, 1963). Short Stories: *Muerte amurallada, cuentos* (Walled-in Death, short stories) (México: Edit. Estaciones, 1958). *Enroque de verano* (Summer Castling), Cuadernos del Unicornio, 11 (México: n. p., 1958). Essay: *El testimonio autobiográfico en la literatura mexicana*, thesis, Facultad de Filosofía y Letras, UNAM (México: UNAM, 1966). "Prologue" in Gilberto Hernández Santana's: *Encarcelada ausencia* (México: Edit. Estaciones, 1958). *Memorias y autobiografías de escritores mexicanos* (México: UNAM, 1967).

BIBLIOGRAPHY: María Elvira Bermúdez, Review of *Muerte amurallada*, in *Diorama de la Cultura* (June 8, 1958): 4. Salvador Reyes Nevares, Review of *Muerte amurallada*, in *México en la Cultura* 471 (Mar. 23, 1958): 8. Carlos Valdés, Review of *Enroque de verano*, in *Universidad de México* 13, 5 (Jan. 1959): 30.

YOLANDA S. BROAD

RANGEL, Nicolás (1864-1935). Born on September 10, 1864, in León, Nicolás Rangel became a distinguished teacher and man of letters, who made a major contribution to Mexican literature with his massive research on Juan *Ruiz de Alarcón. He was also considered a master teacher of several generations of aspiring students and writers. His work on the life and works of Juan Ruiz de Alarcón was but one of his major endeavors. He also carefully studied and researched many other important historical and literary figures and events. A major work, *Antología del Centenario* (Anthology of the Centennial), a documented study of Mexican literature during the first century of independence, coedited with Pedro *Henríquez Ureña and Luis G. *Urbina, is a primary example of this research. Rangel worked for the Department of Public Education, and later was in charge of the *Boletín de la Biblioteca Nacional*. For many years he was responsbile for research for the nation's national archives. He taught Mexican history for almost twenty years, and was a founding member of the Academia Mexicana de la Historia, and a member of the Real Academia de Madrid, a distinguished association in which he was an active participant until his death on June 7, 1935.

WORKS: *Antología del centenario* (Anthology of the Centennial), ed. with Pedro Henríquez Ureña and Luis G. Urbina (México: Imp. de L. Sánchez, 1910). *Los estudios universitarios de don Juan Ruiz de Alarcón y Mendoza* (The University Studies of Juan Ruiz de Alarcón y Mendoza) (México: n.p., 1913). *Noticias biográficas del dramaturgo mexicano don Juan Ruiz de Alarcón y Mendoza* (Biographical Notes about the Mexican Playwright Juan Ruiz de Alarcón y Mendoza) (México: n.p., 1915). *Churubusco Huitzilopochco*, with Ramón Mena (México: UNAM, 1921). *Historia del toreo en México* (History of Bullfighting in Mexico) (México: Imp. de M. L. Sánchez, 1924). *Primer centenario de la Constitución de 1824* (First Centennial of the Constitution of 1824), with Pedro de Alba (México: Talls. Gráfs. Soria, 1924). *Documentos para la historia de la Independencia* (Documents for the History of the Independence), 2, with Ramón Mena (México: Publs. del Archivo General de la Nación, 1926). *Bibliografía de Juan Ruiz de Alarcón* (Bibliography of Juan Ruiz de Alarcón) (México: Sría. de Relaciones Exteriors, 1927). "Penosa vida de los peones del campo en el siglo XVIII" (The Hard Life of the Country Peons in the Eighteenth Century), in *Crisol* 1, 1 (Jan., 1929): 37-8. "El destierro de Fray Servando Teresa de Mier" (The Exile of Fray Servando Teresa de Mier), in *Crisol* 1, 2 (Dec., 1929): 29-33. *Los precursores ideológicos de la guerra de Independencia, 1789-1798* (The Ideological Precursors of the War for Independence, 1789-1798) (México: Talls. Gráfs. de la Nación, 1929). *Nuevos datos para la biografía de José María de Heredia* (New Information about José María de Heredia's Biography) (Havana: Imp. y Libr. El Universo, 1930). Edited and documented edition, Cristóbal Bernardo de la Plaza y Jaén, *Crónica de la Real Pontificia Universidad de México* (Chronicles of the Royal and Pontifical University of Mexico) (México: Talls. Gráfs. del Museo Nacional, 1931). *La vida colonial* (Colonial Life), 2 vols. (México: Talls. Gráfs. de la Nación, 1932). "Cuatro diálogos insurgentes" (Four Insurgent Dialogues), in *Boletín del Archivo General de la Nación*, vol. 3, 3 (México, 1932). *Album histórico Gráfico* (Graphic Historical Album), with Luis González Obregón (México: n.p., n.d.). *Los primeros evangelizadores de la Nueva España* (The First Evangelists in New Spain), conferences published by Grupo Ariel (México: Manuel León Sánchez, 1926)

BIBLIOGRAPHY: Aurora M. Ocampo de Gómez and Ernesto Prado Velázquez, *Diccionario de escritores nexicanos* (México: UNAM, 1967), pp. 312-13. Manuel Toussaint, "Documentos para la historia de la Independencia," in *Revista Mexicana de Estudios Históricos* 1, 1 (n. d.): 105-106. Rafael Heliodoro Valle, interview, in *Excelsior* (Nov. 1, 1931): 5B; and in *Revista del Museo Nacional de Guatemala* 3 (1947): 14-15. Esperanza Velázquez Bringas and Rafael Heliodoro Valle, *Indice de escritores* (México: Talls. Gráfs. de Herrero Hermanos Sucs., 1928), p. 233.

JEANNE C. WALLACE

RANGEL Guerra, Alfonso (1928-   ), critic. Born in Monterrey, Nuevo León, on November 16, 1928, Rangel Guerra received a law degree from the University of Nuevo León in 1953. In 1958 and 1959, he studied comparative literature and French literature at the University of Paris after receiving a fellowship from the French government. He also studied in the United States. He taught at the University of Nuevo León, served as director of the Escuela Preparatoria 1 and of the School of

Philosophy and Letters, and as rector of the University from 1955 to 1964. He served as president of the Instituto Internacional de Literatura Iberoamericana from 1963 to 1965 and as general executive secretary of the National Association of Universities. He has written extensively on literature and on higher education in Mexico.

Rangel Guerra is noted for his literary criticism. He has published numerous articles in journals as well as a number of books on literary and educational topics. In his books, he has proved himself an insightful and thorough critic.

WORKS: Essays and Studies: *Catálogo de índices de los libros de Alfonso Reyes* (Index Catalogue of the Books of Alfonso Reyes) (Monterrey: Universidad de Nuevo León, 1955). *La odisea de Alfonso Reyes* (The Odyssey of Alfonso Reyes), printed by the journal *Armas y Letras* (Jan.-Mar. 1960). *Imagen de la novela* (Image of the Novel) (Monterrey: Universidad de Nuevo León, 1964). *Historia de la literatura española* (History of Spanish Literature) (Monterrey: Ed. Delta, 1965). E. V. Niemayer, Jr., *General Bernardo Reyes*, prologue by Alfonso Rangel Guerra (Monterrey: Universidad de Nuevo León, 1966). *Agustín Yáñez* (México: Empresas Editoriales, 1969). *Manuel Gutierrez Nájera, Crónicas y Artículos sobre teatro* (Chronicles and Articles on Theater), edition and prologue by Alfonso Rangel Guerra (México: UNAM, 1974). Studies on Education: *The Provisional Universities of Mexico: An Analysis of Growth and Development* by Richard King with Alfonso Rangel Guerra, David Kline, and Noel F. McGinn (New York: Praeger, 1971). *Systems of Higher Education: Mexico* (New York: International Council of Economic Development, 1978). *La educación superior en México* (Higher Education in Mexico) (México: El Colegio de México, 1979).

BIBLIOGRAPHY: José Ma. Benítez, Review of *Imagen de la novela*, in *Revista Mexicana de Cultura* 912 (Sept. 20, 1964): 15. Heriberto García Rivas, *Historia de la literatura mexicana*, vol. 4 (México: Textos Universitarios, 1971), p. 566. José Antonio Montero, "La novela," in *Ovaciones* 147 (Oct. 18, 1964): 6. Aurora M. Ocampo de Gómez and Ernesto Prado Velázquez, *Diccionario de escritores mexicanos* (México: UNAM, 1967), p. 313. Gustavo Sáinz, Review of *Imagen de la novela*, in *México en la Cultura* 807 (Sept. 6, 1964): 9.

MARK FRISCH

THE REALISTIC NOVEL (1880-1910). The Mexican realistic novel owed a great debt to French and Spanish Realism, and could be summarized in Hippolyte Taine's dictum as "the methodical investigation of documents about human nature." Built on foundations laid by Honoré de Balzac, Gustave Flaubert, the Goncourt brothers, and Emile Zola in France, and first Pedro A. de Alarcón and Juan Valera, then later José María de Pereda, Benito Pérez Galdós, Emilia Pardo Bazán, and Leopoldo Alas, Clarín in Spain, Mexican realism was nevertheless distinct because of its growth during the seemingly endless dictatorship of Porfirio Díaz and its coexistence with Modernism in poetry. The Mexican so-called realistic novels of the *porfiriato* were generally romantic in conception, while the form was often that of the novel of manners. A belief in science as a cure-all was pervasive, while the themes were generally social or political, and like the European nineteenth-century realistic novel, the values extolled were clearly those of the bourgeoisie. Precursors of the realistic novel in Mexico are José Joaquín *Fernández de Lizardi (1776-1827), with his mordant observations about colonial society in *El Periquillo Sarniento* (Mangy Periquillo, 1816), *La Quijotita y su prima* (Quijotita and Her Cousin, 1819), and *Don Catrín de la Fachenda* (Don Dandy Showoff, 1820); Manuel *Payno (1810-1894) with *El fistol del diablo* (The Devil's Neckpin, 1845), and *Los bandidos de Río Frío* (The Bandits of Río Frío, 1891); Luis G. *Inclán (1816-1875) with *Astucia, el jefe de los hermanos de la Hoja o los charros contrabandistas de la Rama* (Astuteness, the Boss of the Hoja Brothers or the Charro Smugglers from La Rama, 1865); and José Tomás de *Cuellar (1830-1894), author of a series of twenty four novels published under the title *La linterna mágica* (The Magic Lantern, 1871-1892). The period of the realistic novel followed these precursors, and lasted almost exactly from 1880 to 1910, endinq abruptly with the cataclysmic outbreak of the Revolution and the landmark publication of Mariano *Azuela's *Los de abajo* (The Underdogs, 1910)--a novel from which all nineteenth-century trappings were absent, the first truly modern Mexican novel, realistic in a more literal sense of the word.

The realistic novel of the porfiriato, which comes between costumbrist predecessors and the novel of the revolution was best practiced by Emilio *Rabasa (1856-1930), Rafael *Delgado (1853-1914), José *López Portillo y Rojas (1850-1923), and Federico *Gambóa (1864-1939).

Rabasa, the least widely studied today of the four, produced in his youth a four-novel series using the same characters from the small town of San Miguel: *La bola* (The Brawl, 1887), a tale of political intrigue in the military involving Juan Quiñones and his beloved, Remedios; *La gran ciencia* (Great Science) (1887), about bureaucratic maneuverings in Mexico City, where Quiñones has followed Remedios; *El cuarto poder* (The Fourth Power) (1888), Quiñones' student life in Mexico; and *Moneda falsa* (Counterfeit Money) (1888), which tells of Quiñones' return to his village in pursuit of the ailing Remedios. Rabasa also authored a later novella in the same style, *La guerra de los tres años* (The Three Years' War), published one year after Rabassa's death, in 1931), again about political strife in the small town of San Miguel. Rabasa's writing style is direct, and above all else he seeks to move the action along quickly.

Rafael Delgado authored four novels; *La calandria* (The Lark) (1890), *Angelina* (1893), *Los parientes ricos* (Rich Relatives) (1901), and *Historia Vulgar* (Common Story) (1904). The novels all revolve around sentimental conflicts that give rise to social criticism, and the outlook is strictly secular, with none of the sentimental religiosity found in his contemporary, López Portillo y Rojas.

José López Portillos y Rojas' three important novels narrate three separate, significant periods of Mexican history: country life before the revolution in *La parcela* (The Plot of Ground) (1898); life in the provincial capital under the Reform in *Los precursores* (The Precursors) (1909), and porfirista society in the capital in *Fuertes y débiles* (The Strong and the Weak) (1919). All the novels include passages of religious devotion that color the landscape, especially the humble, rural ones.

Federico Gamboa authored short stories, *Del natural* (From the Natural) (1888), but is most famous for the novel *Santa* (1903), which tells the life of a courtesan, and follows the naturalistic example of Emilia Pardo Bazán.

Other minor realistic novelists of the period were Porfirio *Parra, Manuel *San Juan, Salvador *Cordero, Rafael *Ceniceros y Villareal, Angel del *Campo, and Salvador *Quevedo y Zubieta.

PATRICIA HART

REBOLLEDO, Efrén (1877-1929), poet, novelist, and diplomat. Efrén Rebolledo was born in Actopán, Hidalgo, on July 9, 1877. From an early age, he lived in Mexico City, where he studied law. He became known as a writer and poet within the group that founded the literary journal *Revista Moderna*. He later contributed to the journal *Pegaso* (1917). Along with Luis G. *Urbina and José Juan *Tablada, Rebolledo was one of the last "modernistas." In 1907 he joined the diplomatic corps and traveled to the Orient, where he would remain almost ten years; he published a book of poetry in Japan which reveals the influence of that environment. After returning to Mexico for a few years, he left again to represent his country in Norway. There, he published a volume that included a collection of poems and a novel, both inspired by the Nordic setting. When he died in Madrid on December ll, 1929, demonstrations were held in Mexico by his colleagues to express their grief.

Rebolledo was a prolific poet with an international dimension; his books were published in Guatemala, Paris, Japan, Norway, Chile, and Mexico. His verses were received with enthusiasm, as much for the quality of his poetry as for his eroticism, an uncommon characteristic of Mexican writers. He might have begun as a "modernist," and though very concerned with style, once he had found his course, he shed the artificial conventions of Modernism. This allowed him to achieve a brief collection of sonnets which because of their perfection and intensity, have earned him a place of distinction among Mexican poets. He was praised for his originality by his contemporaries Genaro *Estrada and José Juan *Tablada. Together with Tablada, Rebolledo is responsible for introducing Japanese characteristics to Mexican literature; their "japonismo" aroused curiosity and led many poets between 1922 and 1933 to write concrete poems and haikus. This style was short-lived, but Mexican poetry gained from it a capacity for conciseness and exactness that would be evident in later poets. Also, Rebolledo was one of the first to make Oscar Wilde and Rudyard Kipling known by translating them superbly into Spanish.

WORKS: *Obras completas* (Complete Works), introduction, edition, and bibliography by Luis Mario Schneider (México: INBA, 1968). Poetry: *Cuarzos* (Quartz) [1896-1901] (Guatemala: Arturo Siguere y Cía., 1902). *Hilo de corales* (A String of Coral) [1902-03] (Guatemala: Arturo Siguere y Cía., 1904). *Estela* [Poesía y prosa] (México: Ignacio Escalante, 1907). *Joyeles* (Petite Jewels), foreword by José Juan Tablada (París: Viuda de Charles Bouret, 1907). *Rimas japonesas* (Japanese Rhymes) (Tokyo: Shimbi Shoin, c. 1907, 1915). *Caro victrix* (México: Ignacio Escalante, 1916, 1918; México: Botas, 1918; México: Vargas Rea, 1944, 1955). *Libro de loco amor* (Book of Mad Love) (México: J. Ballesca, 1916). *Joyelero* (Jewel Maker) [Poesías completas] (Kristiania [Oslo, Norway]: Det Mallingske Bogtrykkeri, 1922; Buenos Aires: Juan Roldan y Cía., 1929). *Poemas escogidos* (Selected Poems), foreword by Xavier Villaurrutia (México: Ed. Cultura, 1939). Prose: *El enemigo* (The Enemy), 2nd ed. (México: Ignacio Escalante, 1908). *Más allá de las nubes* (Beyond the Clouds) (Guatemala: Arturo Siguere y Cía, 1908); republished in *Estela*. *Nikko* (México: Vda. de F. Díaz de León, 1910). *Hojas de bambú* (Bamboo Leaves) (México: Cía. Editora Nacional, 1910; Santiago de Chile: Imp. Universitaria, 1926). *El aguila que cae* (The Falling Eagle), tragedy, sketches by Jorge Enciso (Paris: Vda. de Ch. Bouret, 1916). *El desencanto de Dulcinea* (Dulcinea's Disenchantment) (México: J. Ballesca, 1916; Imp. de Murguía, 1919). *Salamandra* (Salamander) (México: Talls. Gráficos del Gobierno, 1919). *Saga de Sigrida la Blonda* (Saga of the Blond Sigrid) (Kristiania [Oslo, Noruega]: Det Mallingske Mogtrykkeri, 1922). *Salamandra, Caro victrix* (México: Premia Editora, 1979). Translations: Oscar Wilde, *El crimen de Lord Arturo Saville* (Lord Arthur of Saville's Crime) (México: J. Ballesca, 1916); *Intenciones* (Intentions) (México: J. Ballesca, 1916); *Salome* (México: Edit. Cultura, 1917). Maurice Maeterlinck, *La Muerte* (Death), in collaboration with Rafael Cabrera (Valencia, Spain: Edit. Prometeo, 1917). Rudyard Kipling, *Si* (If) (México: Imp. de Murguía, 1919).

BIBLIOGRAPHY: Antonio Castro Leal, *La poesía mexicana moderna* (México: FCE, 1952). Jorge Cuesta, *Antología de la poesía mexicana moderna* (México: Contemporáneos, 1928). Frank Dauster, *Breve historia de la poesía mexicana* (México: Eds. de Andrea, 1956). Enrique Díez-Canedo, "Efrén Rebolledo," in *Letras de América* (México: El Colegio de México, 1944), pp. 213-15. Genaro Estrada, *Poetas nuevos de México* (New Poets of Mexico) (México: Porrúa Hermanos, 1916). María Elena García Formenti, *Efrén Rebolledo, poeta parnasiano de México*, master's thesis, UNAM (México: UNAM, n. d.). Enrique González Martínez, "*Salamandra* de Efrén Rebolledo," in *El Heraldo de México*, (July 28, 1919): 3B. Carlos González Peña, "El príncipe caído," (The Fallen Prince) in *El Universal Ilustrado* (June 17, 1917): 5B; *Historia de la literatura mexicana* (México: Porrúa, 1954). Max Henríquez Ureña, *Breve historia del modernismo* (México: FCE, 1954). Juan B. Iguíniz, *Bibliografía de novelistas mexicanos* (México: Imp. de la Sría de Relaciones, 1926). Dalia Iñiguez, *Geografía poética de México* (México: n.p., 1959). Julio Jiménez Rueda, *Historia de la literatura mexicana* (México: Ediciones Botas, 1934). Ruth S. Lamb, *Bibliografía del teatro mexicano del siglo XX* (México: Eds. de Andrea, 1962). Luis Leal, *Bibliografía del cuento mexicano* (México: Eds. de Andrea, 1958). José Luis Martínez, *Literatura mexicana siglo XX* (México: Ant. Libr. Robredo, 1950). Carlos Monsiváis, *La poesía mexicana del siglo XX* (México: Empresas Editoriales, 1966), pp. 15-16, 233. Francisco Monterde, "Efrén Rebolledo," in *Revista de Revistas* (Feb. 2, 1930): 25-30. Amado Nervo, "*Cuarzos*, poesías de Efrén Rebolledo," in *Revista Moderna* 5, 7 (April 1902): 112. Salvador Novo, *Mil y un sonetos mexicanos* (A Thousand and One Mexican Sonnets) (México: Porrúa, 1963). Octavio Paz, *Anthologie de la poesie mexicaine* (Paris: Negel, 1952). Raúl Silva Castro, *Antología crítica del modernismo hispanoamericano* (New York: Las Americas, 1936). José Juan Tablada, "Mascaras. Efrén Rebolledo." in *Revista Moderna* 6, 12 (Sept., 1903): 97-99; "Capricho de Efrén Rebolledo," in *El Mundo Ilustrado* (Jun. 7, 1914): 7B. Arturo Torres-Rioseco, *Bibliografía de la novela mexicana* (Cambridge: Harvard University Press, 1933); *Bibliografía de la poesía mexicana* (Cambridge: Harvard University Press, 1934). Edna Worthley Underwood, *Anthology of Mexican Poets* (Portland: Mosher Press, 1932). Luis G. Urbina, "Esquela de luto. Efrén Rebolledo," in *El Universal* (Jan. 26, 1930): 5B. Xavier Villaurrutia, "La poesía de Efrén Rebolledo (I. Como leer a nuestros poetas [How to Read our Poets]. II. La tónica de Efrén Rebolledo [Efren Rebolledo's Pace])," *Poemas escogidos* (Rebolledo) (México: Editorial Cultura, 1939).

HERLINDA HERNANDEZ

REJANO, Juan (1903-1976), poet, critic, and translator. Juan Rejano was born in Puente Genil, Córdoba, Spain, on October 20, 1903. He was married to the poet, Luisa *Carnés. An established journalist when the Civil War began, he fought with the Loyalists and went into exile in Mexico in 1939. He founded various Mexican journals (*Romance, Ultramar,* and *Litoral*) and directed *Revista mexicana de Cultura,* the cultural section of *El Nacional,* from 1947 to 1957. He also translated two books of Polish poetry. He died in Mexico City on July 4, 1976, while making preparations to return to Spain.

Juan Rejano began writing poetry in the early years of his exile, and his nostalgia for Spain pervades his verse. Also, however, his Communist ideals converge with his artistic creativity in his poetry. Although he felt that the poet has the obligation to inspire the people to concrete political action, his poetry is also characterized by thematic balance, for not only did he treat political and revolutionary themes, but also more universal ones, such as love, solitude, death, nostalgia, and dreams. In addition to influences of other revolutionary poets, Rejano was influenced by the classic Spanish poetry, especially the Romancero tradition.

WORKS: *Fidelidad del sueño* (Faithfulness of Dreams) (México: Edit. Diálogo, 1943). *El Genil y los olivos* (Genil and the Olive Trees) (México: Edit. Litoral, 1944). *Víspera heróica* (Heroic Eve) (México: Edit. Gráfica Panamericana, 1947). *El oscuro límite* (Dark Limit) (México: Ediciones Cuadernos Americanos, 1948). *Noche adentro* (Into the Night) (México: Edit. Compañía Editora y Librera Ars, 1949). *Oda española* (Spanish Ode) (México: Edición Nuestro Tiempo, 1949). *Constelación menor* (Minor Constelation) (Morelia: Edit. La Espiga y el Laurel, 1950). Translation and poetic adaptation: *Poemas de la Nueva Polonia* (Poems of New Poland) (México: Eds. de la Embajada de Polonia, 1953). *Canciones a la paz* (Songs to Peace) (México: Eds. España y la Paz, 1955). Translation and poetic adaptation, *Poemas de Adam Mickiewicz* (Poems of Adam Mickiewicz) (México: Eds. de la Embajada de Polonia, 1957). *El río y la paloma* (The River and the Dove) (México: Eds. Ecuador, 1963). *El jazmín y la llama* (The Jazmine and the Flame) (México: Eds. Ecuador, 1965). *Alas de tierra* (Earth Wings) (México: UNAM, 1977).

BIBLIOGRAPHY: Max Aub, *La poesía española contemporánea* (México: Imp. Universitaria, 1954), pp. 216-17. Alberto Dallal, "Lo inasible y lo dócil," in *Cuadernos Americanos* 202, 5 (Sept.-Oct. 1975): 248-55. Horacio Espinosa Altamirano, "Juan Rejano o la dignidad desterrada," in *Boletín Bibliográfico de la Secretaría de Hacienda y Crédito Público* 290 (March 1, 1964): 10-11. Aurora M. Ocampo de Gómez and Ernesto Prado Velázquez, *Diccionario de escritores mexicanos* (México: UNAM, 1967), pp. 314-15. Mauricio de la Selva, "Homenaje a Juan Rejano." in *Cuadernos Americanos* 208, 5 (Sept.-Oct. 1976): 63-86.

KENNETH M. TAGGART

REQUENA Legarreta, Pedro (1893-1918). Born in Mexico City on January 13, 1893, he became a lawyer, then went to Washington, both to study and to work in the legal profession. At the same time, he wrote and published poetry. Aspiring to excellence, he distinguished himself for his ability to translate into Spanish the work of foreign poets. His untimely death in New York on December 15, 1918 produced quite a reaction in Mexico. His remains were returned to his homeland in 1920. Many of the

Mexican intellectuals of the day attended the burial ceremony, inasmuch as they admired and drew inspiration from Requena Legarreta.

Requena's most important work is the Spanish version of *Gitanjali* by Rabindranath Tagore, considered a masterful work and in which, according to Joaquín Méndez Rivas*, "Requena spent many hours studying the theological principles which inspired the primordial work...." He also did a poetic analysis of the *Gitanjali*. Another translation, published in New York, which gave him considerable fame was *El cancionero de la gran guerra*, a paraphrase of poems by French, Belgian, English and German authors, with reference to World War I. The three-volume collection was published just as the war ended. An anthology of it was made in Mexico. Some of Requena's original poems appeared in publications in the United States and Mexico, but many were not published until after his death, when Rafael López and José Luis Requena, the poet's father, each made anthologies.

WORKS: "Plegaria" and "Invocación a la muerte" (Prayer and Invocation to Death), poetic version of the concepts of Rabindranath Tagore, in *Revista Universal* (New York) (Sept. 1914). "Rembrandt," essay in *Revista Universal* (New York) (Oct. 1914). "Donde la fuente llora" (Where the Fountain Cries), poetry, in *Revista Universal* (New York) (Nov. 1914). "Himno de guerra" (War Hymn), in *Revista Universal* (New York) (Dec. 1914). "Los pétalos caen lentamente" (The Petals Fall Slowly), poetry, in *El Diluvio* (San Juan, Puerto Rico) (1915). "La última sonata de Beethoven" (Beethoven's Last Sonata), poetry, in *La Prensa* (New York) (July 24, 1915): 7. "Anacreóntica" (Anacreontic), poetry, in *Las Novedades* (New York) (1916): 12. "Al gran literato francés Anatole France, al alistarse como voluntario" (To the Great French Literary Figure Anatole France, upon His Voluntary Enlistment), poetry, in *Revista Universal* (New York) (May 1916). "Rabindranath Tagore en Nueva York," biography, in *Revista Universal* (New York) (Dec. 1916). "Sinfonía griega" (Greek Symphony), poetry, in *Juan Bobo* (San Juan, Puerto Rico) (April 14, 1917): 35-6. "Poesías," in *El Universal Ilustrado* 2, 85 (Dec. 20, 1918). *El cancionero de la gran guerra* (The Songbook of the Great War), 3 vols. (New York: n.p., 1918); parts published in *Antología de poetas muertos en la guerra* (Anthology of Poets Who Died in the War), vol. 10, 4 (México: Ed. Cultura, 1919). "Atado Prometeo a la roca implacable" (Prometheus Tied to the Implacable Rock), poetry in *Las Novedades* (New York) (1921): 10. "La copa de cristal" (The Crystal Glass), "Entre las sombras" (Among the Shadows) and "Púrpura y miel" (Purple and Honey), in *El Universal Ilustrado* 6, 270 (July 6, 1922): 7C. *Poesías líricas* (Lyrical Poems) (México: Miguel E. Castilleja & Sons, 1930).

BIBLIOGRAPHY: Anon., "Pedro Requena," in *The Saturday Evening Post* (New York) (Dec. 23, 1919). José D. Frías, *Antología de jóvenes poetas mexicanos* (Paris: Casa Edit. Franco-Iberoamericana, 1922). Angeles Mendieta Alatorre, "Las traducciones poéticas de Pedro Requena Legarreta," in *El Nacional* (June 1, 1966): 3. José Muñoz Cota, "Pedro Requena Legarreta," in *Revista Mexicana de Cultura* 894 (May 17, 1964): 5. Aurora M. Ocampo de Gómez and Ernesto Prado Velázquez, *Diccionario de escritores mexicanos* (México: UNAM, 1967), pp. 315-316. Thomas Walsh, "Pedro Requena Legarreta," in *The New York Times Review* (New York) (Jan. 21, 1923).

JEANNE C. WALLACE

RETES, José Ignacio (1918-), playwright. Born in Mexico City in 1918. He began his theatrical career in San Luis Potosí at the Teatro Universitario (University Theater), which he founded and later took to Mexico City. In the School of Philosophy and Letters at the Universidad Nacional Autónoma de México he studied with Rodolfo Usigli and with Seki Sano in his private academy. He has been a drama critic, acting teacher at the Instituto Cinematográfico de México (Cinematographic Institute of Mexico) and in the Academia de la Asociación Nacional de Actores (Academy of the National Association of Actors), director, actor, and dramatist. He has also written numerous documentaries and has directed theatrical series for television. *El aria de la locura* (The Aria of Madness), a three-act comedy opened at the Teatro del Caballito in 1953. *Una ciudad para vivir* (A City in Which to Live), a two-act comedy opened at the Sala Chopín on September 3, 1954 and was published two years later. In 1964 he directed a theatrical version of the novel *Juan Pérez Jolote* by Ricardo Pozas.

WORKS: Theater: *El día de mañana* (One of These Days), in *Revista Letras de Mexico* 5, 113 (July 1, 1945): 103-6. *Una ciudad para vivir* (A City in Which toLive), in Teatro mexicano del siglo XX 3 (México: FCE, 1956), pp. 612-78. Essays: "Teatro en el Seguro Social" (Theater at the Seguro Social) in *El teatro en México* 2, no editor (México: INBA, 1958-1964).

BIBLIOGRAPHY: Ruth S. Lamb, *Mexican Theatre of the Twentieth Century* (Claremont, CA: Ocelot Press, 1975), p. 105. José Luis Martínez, *Literatura mexicana del siglo XX, 1910-1949*, vol. 1 (México: Ant. Libr. Robredo, 1949), p. 86. Aurora M. Ocampo de Gómez and Ernesto Prado Velázquez, *Diccionario de escritores mexicanos* (México: UNAM, 1967), p. 316.

MARGARITA VARGAS

REVUELTAS, José (1914-1975), novelist, short story writer, poet and journalist. Born in Durango, Durango. Revueltas was the son of a miner and this family experience probably influenced his preoccupation with social topics. He comes from a well-known family of artists, including his brother Silvestre, who was a composer. When he arrived in Mexico City, he started to work as a journalist for *El Popular*, a local newspaper. During the sixties, he became a very strong anti-establishment political figure and was one of the leaders for the student movement in Mexico during and after the 1968 Olympics. He was incarcerated and not released until 1971.

Because of his inherently polemical nature and world view he got in trouble with Mexican authorities. His political beliefs were progressive and he wanted to portray social conditions prevalent in Mexican society. A member of the Mexican Communist party, he delved successfully into social protest in the series of novels and short stories that he published. He spent some time in the Islas Marías penitentiary for activities undertaken with the Communist party. This is a dreaded penitentiary on the Pacific Coast. These experiences are described in his first novel, *Los muros de agua* (The Walls of Water) (1941), which also deals with the bad treatment that political prisoners receive. It won him immediate fame. In 1943 he received the National

Literature Prize for his novel *El luto humano* (Human Mourning) (México: 1943), a powerful novel in which he narrates the struggles that the peasants have to go through in order to survive, and the failure of the Mexican Revolution to improve their condition. Technically it is a masterpiece in its interior monologues, which follow the influence of William Faulkner (1897-1962) and the new influences of cinematic technique. Other influences come from Malraux and Sartre. Themes that he develops almost obsessively are solitude, frustration, lack of hope, pessimism, bitterness, and finally death. *Los motivos de Caín* (Cain's Motives) (1957) deals with the cruelties perpetrated by United States soldiers during the World War II.

His influence has been important and his presence is still being felt in the works of younger writers who look for fuller commitments from society. Octavio *Paz has said of Revueltas, clearly an intellectual with leftist beliefs, that he is "one of the best writers of my generation and one of the purest men in Mexico." He has been tremendous in his portrayal of anguish and human suffering. He was willing to sacrifice himself and suffer persecution in order to preserve his social and human values.

WORKS: *Los muros de agua* (The Walls of Water) (México: Talleres de la Sociedad Cooperativa "Artes Gráficas Comerciales," 1941). *El luto humano* (Human Grieving) (México: Editorial México, 1943). (*The Stone Knife*. Translated by H.R. Hays. New York: Reynal and Hitchcock, 1947). *Dios en la tierra* (God on Earth) short stories (México: Ediciones "El Insurgente," 1944). *Israel*, drama (México: Sociedad General de Autores de México, 1947). *Los días terrenales* (Earthly Days) (México: Edit. Stylo, 1949). *La otra. Sobre una historia de Ryan James*, (filmscript with Roberto Gavaldón) (1949). *En algún valle de lágrimas* (In Some Valley of Tears) (México: Los Presentes, 1956). *Los motivos de Caín* (Cain's Motives) (México: Fondo de Cultura Popular, 1957). *Dormir entierra*, (Sleep Kills) short stories (Xalapa-Veracruz: Universidad Veracruzana, 1960). *Los errores* (Mistakes) (México: FCE, 1964). *Obra literaria* (Literary Works), 2 vols. (México: Empresas Editoriales, 1967. *Elapando* (México: Eds. Era, 1969), dedicated to Pablo Neruda. *Material de los sueños* (Material for Dreams) (México: Eds. Era, 1974). *Antología personal* (Personal Anthology) (México: FCE, 1975). And many more essays, short stories and dramas in different magazines.

BIBLIOGRAPHY: John S. Brushwood, *Mexico in Its Novel* (Austin: University of Texas Press, 1966). Seymour Menton, *The Spanish American Short Story: A Critical Anthology* (Los Angeles and Berkeley: University of California Press, 1975). Floyd F. Merrell, "Man and His Prisons: Evolving Patterns in José Revuelta's Narrative," *Revista de Estudios Hispánicos* 11 (1982): 233-250. María del Carmen Millán, *Antología de cuentos mexicanos*, vol. 1 (México: Editorial Nueva Imagen, 1977). Timothy Murad, "Before the Storm: José Revueltas and Beginnings of the New Narrative in Mexico," *Modern Language Studies* 8, 1 (1977-1978): 57-64. Luis A. Ramos, "Revueltas y el grotesco," *Texto Crítico* 2 (1975): 67-80. Publio O. Romero, "Los mitos bíblicos en *El luto humano*," *Texto Crítico* 2 (1975): 81-87. Jorge Ruffinelli, ed., *Conversaciones con José Revueltas* (Xalapa: Centro de Investigaciones Lingüístico-Literarias, Universidad Veracruzana, 1977). Monique Sarfati-Arnaud, "'*Dios en la tierra*': Lecture ideologique sur les Cristeros," *Les Langues Modernes* 75, 4 (1981): 440-448. Sam L. Slick, *José Revueltas* (Boston: Twayne, 1983).

OSCAR SOMOZA

REYES, Alfonso (1889-1959). Alfonso Reyes, one of Mexico's most distinguished citizens and man of letters, was born on May 17, 1889, in Monterrey. His father, General Bernardo Reyes, governer of the state of Nuevo León, profoundly influenced him, arousing his literary interests while he was still very young. His early life was spent in Monterrey, a city to which he always returned nostalgically.

In 1906 Reyes moved to Mexico City, becoming active with a group of young scholars who shared common interests. Promoting educational advancement and cultural renewal, they were known as the Centennial Generation, reflecting the 100-years since Mexican independence. The group, which included Antonio *Caso, José *Vasconcelos, Jesús T.* Acevedo, and Pedro* Henríquez Ureña, formed a literary society called the Ateneo de la Juventud. In 1912, they helped establish a school of higher studies, which became a division of the Universidad Nacional. There Reyes created the chair of Spanish language and literature. In 1911 he published his first volume of essays, *Cuestiones estéticas* (Aesthetic Questions) in Paris. He included an important essay on Góngora, which would help focus his later literary career.

Reyes' father died tragically in 1913 because of revolutionary turmoil, causing a tremendous impact on him. Going into voluntary exile to get away from the devastating circumstances of Mexican national life and his own personal tragedy, Reyes accepted an appointment as a secretary for the Mexican legation in France, thus launching a diplomatic career. Unfortunately, in 1914 he was forced to leave France when Germany invaded. Taking his family with him, he sought refuge in Spain, living in Madrid, under harsh conditions. Nonetheless, he continued relentlessly with his work, receiving several important literary commissions to prepare critical editions of Spanish classics and translations of several noted authors, such as Anton Chekhov, G. K. Chesterton, Laurence Sterne, and Robert Louis Stevenson. He prepared the culture section of *El Sol*, for José Ortega y Gasset. As a scholar, Reyes became a member of the philology section of the Center for Historical Studies directed by Ramón Menéndez Pidal. While World War I was being fought in Europe, he moved in literary and intellectual circles in Spain, studying, writing, and participating in the cultural life of Madrid.

He re-entered the Mexican diplomatic service in 1920, serving as a secretary of the legation in Spain. For the next four years he combined his literary and diplomatic careers in Spain. With the Mexican Revolution over, Reyes was able to concentrate his energies on establishing deeper cultural ties between Spain and Mexico, and later, between France and Mexico. Wherever he went, he fostered the causes of diplomacy, friendship, and culture.

As a writer, Reyes is known particularly for his poetry and his essays. His literary production was remarkable. Nostalgia for Mexico inspired a historical poetic essay, entitled *Visión de Anáhuac* (1917). A fusion of poetry and scholarship, the essay, stemming from the encounter between Cortés and Moctezuma, is a meditation on the destiny of Mexico, the blend of three civilizations. His dramatic poem *Ifigenia cruel* (1924) is a literary response to the author's sense of exile and search for liberation. This was successfully performed in both Mexico and Spain. His impressions of Spain were the focus of *Cartones de Madrid* (Sketches of Madrid) (1917) and *Horas de Burgos* (Hours in Burgos) (1932), both later collected in *Las vísperas de España* (The Twilight of Spain) (1937). While in Spain he published his first volume of verse, *Huellas* (Traces) (1922), and his first collected short stories, *El plano oblicuo* (The Oblique Plane) (1920). His many essays include, among other subjects, portraits of historical figures, philosophical meditations, and homey sketches of life. Articles he had written for various publications were grouped in the five volumes of *Simpatías y diferencias* (Affinities and Differences, 1921-1926). His literary studies of famous Spanish and Mexican writers, such as Miguel de Cervantes, Lope de Vega, Francisco de Quevedo (Spain) and Juan * Ruiz de Alarcón (Mexico) are hallmarks of excellence. One of his highest early achievements was the publication of his *Cuestiones gongorinas* (Questions Relating to Góngora) (1927), during the Góngora tercentenary.

In late 1924, Reyes was named minister of Mexico in France, serving there until 1927. Taking an active role in literary and cultural life, he formed fast friendships with many French writers, and he published various essays on a select group of writers, especially those in the vanguard movement.

Reyes was ambassador from Mexico twice, alternately in Argentina and Brazil from 1927 to 1939, where he was also a cultural missionary. He was quickly incorporated into the international literary circle, inspiring and providing leadership for the young Argentine poetic group. Ricardo Güiraldes, the noted Argentine writer, had died in Paris, and Reyes partially filled the void created by his loss. A special relationship was also established between Reyes and Borges, who was inspired to write tales of metaphysical fantasy. While Reyes was in Argentina, Federico García Lorca was assassinated in Spain. In response, Reyes wrote *Cantata en la tumba de Federico García Lorca* (Cantata at the Tomb of Federico García Lorca) (1937) performed with music, in Buenos Aires.

In Brazil, he felt an attraction to the capital, Río de Janeiro. He wrote the poetic volume *Romances de Río de Janeiro* (Songs of Rio de Janeiro) (1933), and a series of sketches and tales about Brazilian culture, later collected in *Quince presencias* (Fifteen Presences, 1955). He had numerous Brazilian friendships and became active in the cultural community there. While there, he wrote a series of portrait essays on great Europeans related to America. He also published a personal literary bulletin called *Monterrey*, after his native city in Mexico, to keep in touch with all his literary friends. Each number of *Monterrey* was signed with his personal emblem: a sketch of Monterrey with Cerro de la Silla (Saddle Mountain) in the background, plus a quotation about the beautiful view. The emblem appeared on many of his publications and on his tombstone.

During his stays in Buenos Aires and Rio de Janeiro, Reyes acted as the literary voice of Hispanic America, participating in a number of important conferences and other activities. He also made speeches, such as "Posición de América" (The Position of America) and "Notas sobre la inteligencia americana" (Thought on the American Mind), later collected as essays.

Around this time, Reyes was accused in Mexico of being too detached and universal. In response to this charge, he wrote "A vuelta de correo" (By Return Mail, 1932), indicating that he planned to write a series of essays with the theme "In Search of the National Soul," beginning with *Visión de Anáhuac*. He also maintained that he was exercising his right to be both Mexican and universal. He was still targeted for criticism throughout his life and even posthumously, since his writings did not all pertain to Mexican affairs.

In 1938 Reyes proposed that a cultural center open to exiled foreign scholars be founded. Upon his return to Mexico in 1939, he learned that the center would soon be a reality, with the name La Casa de España (The House of Spain), with Reyes as the director. He accepted the post, insisting that the name be changed to the more encompassaing El Colegio de México.

Reyes lived in Mexico until his death twenty years later. He housed his library (Capilla Alfonsina) in a new residence he had built. In 1945 Reyes cofounded El Colegio Nacional, where lectures by Mexico's most distinguished scholars, representing various specialties, were offered. Reyes, the "specialist in universals," was nicknamed the "Universal Mexican." In addition to his work with El Colegio de México and El Colegio Nacional, Reyes also taught classes at the Universidad de Morelia, Michoacán, and at the Universidad Nacional.

In 1945 he was named a delegate to the Interamerican Conference on War and Peace at Chapultepec, and in 1946-1947, he headed the Mexican delegation to the first UNESCO assembly in Paris. Also in 1945 he was awarded the National Prize in Literature. In 1955 the golden anniversary of his literary career was celebrated. While he never received the Nobel Prize for Literature, friends and colleagues made several attempts to have him nominated, catapulting him to greater international recognition. In 1957 he was elected director of the Mexican Academy of the Language. He died of a heart attack on December 27, 1959. There has been great interest in his literary production, with many studies being carried out by such notable critics as George Schade and James Willis Robb. Under government sponsorship, his family has continued on with the work of the Capilla Alfonsina.

WORKS: Poetry: *Obra poética* (Poetic Works) (México: FCE, 1952). *Homero en Cuernavaca* (Homer in Cuernavaca) (México: FCE, 1952). *Nueve romances sordos* (Nine Deaf Poems) (Huytlale, Talxcala: n.p., 1954). *Oración del 9 de febrero* (Prayer of the Ninth of February) (México: Eds. Era, 1963). "Oda nocturna a la esposa" (Nocturnal Ode to the Wife), in *Ovaciones* 180 (June 21, 1965): 8. Theater: *Ifigenia cruel* (Madrid: Edit. Calleja, 1924); in *Teatro mexicano del siglo XX*, edited by Antonio Magaña Esquivel (México: FCE, 1956), pp. 302-47; in *Antología de Alfonso Reyes*, no editor, (México: FCE, 1963). *Egloga de los ciegos* (Eclogue of the Blind), in *La Cultura en México* 108 (March 1964): 2-4. *Landrú-Opereta*, in *Cuarta antología de obras en un acto*, no editor (México: FCE, 1965). Prose: "Los *Poemas rústicos* de Manuel José Othón" (The *Rustic Poems* of Manuel José Othón), in *Conferencias de Ateneo de la Juventud* (México: Imp. Lacaud, 1910); 2nd ed. (México: UNAM, 1962). *Cuestiones estéticas* (Aesthetic Questions) (París: Sociedad de Ediciones Literarias y Artísticas, 1910-1911). *El paisaje en la poesía mexicana del siglo XIX* (The Landscape in 19th-Century Mexican Poetry) (México: Tip. de la Vda. de F. Díaz León, 1911). *El suicida* (The Suicide) (México: FCE, 1954). *Visión de Anáhuac* (Vision of Anáhuac) 4th ed. (México: El Colegio de México, 1954). *Cartones de Madrid (1914-1917)* (Sketches of Madrid, 1914-1917), 4, 6 (México: Ed. Cultura, 1917). *El cazador. Ensayos y divagaciones (1910-1921)* (The Hunter. Essays and Digressions, 1910-1921) (México: FCE, 1954). *Reloj de sol* (Sun Dial) (Madrid: Tip. Cervantes, 1926). *Simpatías y diferencias* (Affinities and Differences) 2nd edition and prologue by Antonio Castro Leal (México: Porrúa, 1945). *Cuestiones gongorinas* (Gongorine Questions) (Madrid: Espasa-Calpe, 1927). *El testimonio de Juan Peña* (The Testimony of Juan Peña) (Río de Janeiro: Vellas Boas, 1930). *Nervo* (Transit of Amado Nervo) (Santiago de Chile: Ercilla, 1937). *Ideas políticas de Goethe* (Political Ideas of Goethe) (México: I.C.I., 1937). *Las vísperas de España* (The Twilight of Spain) (Buenos Aires: Sur, 1937). *Mallarmé entre nosotros* (Mallarmé among Us) (Buenos Aires: Edit. Destiempo, 1938); (México: FCE, 1955). *Capítulos de literatura española* (Chapters of Spanish Literature), 1st series (México: El Colegio de México, 1939); 2nd. series (México: El Colegio de México, 1945). *La crítica de la edad ateniense*

(Criticism of the Athenian Age) (México: FCE, 1941). *Los siete sobre Deva* (The Seven on Deva) (México: FCE, 1942). *Ultima Tule* (Last Tule) (México: Imp. Universitaria, 1942). *La experiencia literaria* (Literary Experience) (Buenos Aires: Edit. Losada, 1942). *El deslinde* (The Demarcation) (México: El Colegio de México, 1944). *Dos o tres mundos* (Two or Three Worlds), prologue by Antonio Castro Leal (México: Letras de México, 1944). *La casa del grillo* (The Cricket's House), vignettes of Alberto Beltrán (México: FCE, 1945). *Calendario y Tren de ondas* (Calendar and Train of Waves) (México: FCE, 1945). *Panorama del Brasil* (Panorama of Brasil) (México: Sociedad Mexicana de Geografía y Estadística, 1945). *Juan Ruiz de Alarcón*, in *Homenaje a A. Schweitzer* (Cambridge, Mass.: n.p., 1945). *Los trabajos y los días* (Works and Days) (México: Eds. Occidente, 1945). "Las Letras Patrias" (Letters of the Country), in *México y la Cultura* (México: SEP, 1946), pp. 309-84. *Grata compañía* (Pleasant Company) (México: FCE, 1948). *Entre libros* (Among Books) (México: El Colegio de México, 1948). *De un autor censurado en el "Quijote": Antonio de Torquemada* (About an Author Censured in the "Quijote": Antonio de Torquemada) (México: Ed. Cultura, 1948). *Letras de la Nueva España* (Letters of New Spain) (México: FCE, 1948). *Sirtes* (México: FCE, 1949). *De viva voz* (In a Loud Voice) (México: Edit. Stylo, 1949). *Junta de sombras* (Gathering of Shadows) (México: El Colegio Nacional, 1949). *Tertulia de Madrid* (Gathering in Madrid) (Arentina: Espasa-Calpe, 1949). *Cuatro ingenios* (Four Talented Individuals) (Argentina: Espasa-Calpe, 1950). *El horizonte económico en los albores de Grecia* (The Economic Horizon in the Early Days of Greece) (México: El Colegio Nacional, 1950). *The Position of America* (New York: Alfred Knopf, 1950). *Verdad y mentira* (Truth and Falsehood) (Madrid: Aguilar, 1950). *En torno al estudio de la religión griega* (Concerning the Study of Greek Religion) (México: El Colegio Nacional, 1951). *Medallones* (Medallions) (Argentina: Espasa-Calpe, 1951). *Ancorajes* (Anchors) (México: FCE, 1951). *Trazos de historia literaria* (Bits of Literary History), 2 eds.(Argentina: Espasa-Calpe, 1951). *La X en la frente* (The X on the Forehead) (México: Porrúa y Obregón, 1952). *Marginalia*, 1st series, 1946-1951 (México: FCE, 1952); 2nd series 1909-1954 (México: Los Presentes, 1954); 3rd series, 1940-1959) (México: n.p., 1959). *Interpretación de las edades hesiódicas* (Interpretation of the Hesiodic Ages) (México: El Colegio Nacional, 1951). *Memorias de cocina y bodega* (Kitchen and Shop Memories) (México: FCE, 1953). *Dos comunicaciones* (Two Communications) (México: El Colegio Nacional, 1953). *A campo traviesa* (Crossing the Countryside) (México: FCE, 1954). *Parentelia* (México: Los Presentes, 1954); 2nd. ed. (México: FCE, 1959). *Crónica de Monterrey, I: Albores* (Chronicle of Monterrey, I: Dawn) (México: Edit. Libros de México, 1960). *Trayectoria de Goethe* (Trajectory of Goethe) (México: FCE, 1954). *Hipócrates y Asclepio* (México: El Colegio Nacional, 1954). *Los tres tesoros* (The Three Treasures) (México: FCE, 1955). *Quince presencias (1915-1954)* (Fifteen Presences, 1915-1954) (México: Eds. de Andrea, 1955). *Presentación de Grecia* (Presentation of Greece) (México: El Colegio Nacional, 1955). *Las burlas veras. Primer ciento* (The Real Jokes. The First Hundred) (México: FCE, 1957). *Las burlas veras. Segundo ciento* (The Real Jokes. The Second Hundred) (México: FCE, 1959). *Al Yunque (1944-1958)* (Stuck Out, 1944-1958) (México: FCE, 1959). *Los nuevos caminos de la lingüística* (New Roads of Linguistics) (México: Imp. Universitaria, 1960). *Antología de Alfonso Reyes* (Anthology of Alfonso Reyes) (México: FCE, 1963). *Antología de Alfonso Reyes*, 2nd series, vol. 1 (México: Costa-Amic, 1965). *Frente a la pantalla* (In Front of the Screen), with Martín Luis Guzmán and Federico Onís (México: UNAM, 1963). *Obras completas*, 17 Vols. (México: FCE, 1955-1965). *Diario: 1911-1930*

(Diary), prologue by Alicia Reyes (Guanajuato: Universidad de Guanajuato, 1969). *Antología personal* (Personal Anthology), prepared by Ernesto Mejía Sánchez (México: Martín Casillas Editores, 1983).

BIBLIOGRAPHY: Ermilo Abreu Gómez, *Sala de retratos* (México: Edit. Leyenda, 1946), pp. 242-45. Antonio Alatorre, "Un momento en la vida de Alfonso Reyes y una poesía suya inédita," in *La Gaceta* 220 (April 1989): 6-15. Enrique Anderson-Imbert, *Spanish American Literature*, vol. 2, 2nd ed., revised and updated by Elaine Malley (Detroit: Wayne State University Press, 1969), pp. 506-8, 553-56; "Teoría y práctica de la literatura," in *La Nación* (Buenos Aires, May 21, 1989): 1. Barbara Bockus Aponte, "El diálogo entre Ramón Gómez de la Serna y Alfonso Reyes," in *Insula* 210 (May 1964): 1, 4; "El diálogo entre Azorín y Alfonso Reyes," in *Insula* 219 (Feb. 1965): 1, 10; "A Dialogue Between Alfonso Reyes and José Ortega y Gasset," in *Hispania* 1 (March 1966): 36-43; *Alfonso Reyes and Spain* (Austin: University of Texas Press, 1972). María Teresa Babín, "Concha Meléndez y Alfonso Reyes," in *Sin Nombre* 14, 2 (Jan.-March 1984): 31-37. Félix Báez-Jorge, "Alfonso Reyes o la diplomacia de las letras," in *Plural* 213 (June 1989): 26-35. Angel J. Battistessa, "Alfonso Reyes: Aquí cerca y hace tiempo," in *La Nación* (Buenos Aires, May 21, 1989): 1-2. Olga Blondet, "Alfonso Reyes, bibliografía," in *Revista Hispánica Moderna* 22, 3-4 (July-Oct. 1956): 248-69. Emmanuel Carballo, *El cuento mexicano del siglo XX* (México: Empresas Editoriales, 1964), pp. 20-21, 28-29; *19 protagonistas de la literatura mexicana del siglo XX* (México: Empresas Editoriales, 1965), pp. 103-37. Emilio Carilla, "Un epistolario de excepción: Pedro Henríquez Ureña y Alfonso Reyes," in *Sur* 355 (July-Dec. 1984): 25-40. Eduardo Carranza, "Los tres mundos de Alfonso Reyes," in *Cuadernos Hispanoamericanos* 168 (Dec. 1963): 493-508. Adolfo Castañón, "El niño que fue Reyes," in *La Gaceta* (FCE) 224 (Aug. 1989): 48-49. Wilfrido Howard Corral and William Clamurro, "The Art of the Fragment in Spanish American Literature," in *Latin American Literature and Arts* 31 (Jan.-April 1982): 49-52. Frank Dauster, *Breve historia de la poesía mexicana* (México: Eds. de Andrea, 1956), pp. 143-45. Gabriella De Beer, "En torno al epistolario Henríquez Ureña--Alfonso Reyes," in *Cuadernos Americanos* 259, 2 (1985): 120-27. Christopher Domínguez Michael, "Alfonso Reyes y las ruinas de Troya," in *La Gaceta* (FCE) 220 (April 1989): 53-62. Fred Ellison, "Alfonso Reyes, Brazil, and the Story of a Passion," in *Los Ensayistas* 18-19 of Georgia Series on Hispanic Thought (Summer 1985): 55-63. José María Espinosa, "Alfonso Reyes, poeta," in *La Gaceta* (FCE) 220 (April 1989): 92-94. José María Ferández Gutiérrez, "Temas de la relación epistolar entre Díez-Canedo y A. Reyes," in *Revista de Estudios Extremeños* 42 (1986): 390-98. David William Forster and Virginia Ramos Foster, comp., *Modern Latin American Literature*, vol. 2 (New York: Frederick Ungar, 1975), pp. 237-45. Carmelo Gariano, "Los albores de lo hispánico según Alfonso Reyes," in *Explicación de Textos Literarios* 16, 1 (1987-1988): 38-47. Luis Garrido, *Alfonso Reyes* (México: Imp. Universitaria, 1954). Francisco Giner de los Ríos, "Invitación a la poesía de Alfonso Reyes," in *Cuadernos Americanos* 42, 6 (Nov.-Dec. 1948): 252-65. Antonio Gómez Robledo, "Alfonso Reyes, mexicano universal," in *Cuadernos Americanos* 2 (March-April 1965): 163-79. Manuel Pedro González, "Algunos libros de Alfonso Reyes," in *La Palabra y el Hombre* 31 (July-Sept. 1964): 417-528. Eduardo González Lanuza, "Alfonso Reyes o la conciencia del oficio," in *Cuadernos Americanos* 80, 2 (March-April 1955): 267-82. Martín Luis Guzmán, "Alfonso Reyes y las letras mexicanas," in *A orillas del Hudson* (México: Eds. Botas, 1920), pp. 47-72. Pedro Henríquez Ureña, *Seis ensayos en busca de nuestra expresión* (Buenos Aires and Madrid: Babel, 1927). Luisa Josefina Hernández, "Reyes y los veintes," review of the performance of *Landrú y la mano del comandante Arana*, in *Ovaciones* 114 (March 1, 1964): 8. Roberto Hozven, "Sobre la inteligencia americana de Alfonso Reyes," in *Revista Iberoamericana* 55, 148-49 (July-Dec. 1989): 803-17. Andrés Iduarte, Review of *Verdad y mentira*, in *Revista Hispánica Moderna* 20 (1954): 85. Andrés Iduarte, Eugenio Florit, and Olga Blondet, "El hombre y su mundo. La obra poética. Bibliografía," in *Revista Hispánica Moderna* 12, 3-4 (July-Oct. 1956): 197-269. Raimundo Lazo, *La personalidad, la creación y el mensaje de Alfonso Reyes* (La Habana: n.p., 1955). Luis Leal, *Breve historia del cuento mexicano* (México: Eds. de Andrea, 1956), pp. 90-91; *Bibliografía del cuento mexicano* (México: Eds. de Andrea, 1958), pp. 118-19. Raúl Leiva, *Imagen de la poesía mexicana contemporánea* (México: UNAM, 1959), pp. 49-61; Review of Reyes' anthology, in *Cuadernos de Bellas Artes* 4, 12 (Dec. 1963): 25-32. Manuel Lerín, "Apuntes sobre la poesía de Alfonso Reyes," in *Cuadernos Americanos* 81, 3 (May-June 1955): 212-26. Raymundo Lida, *Letras Hispánicas* (México: FCE, 1958), pp. 271-79. Luis Loayza, "París 1913-14: Una amistad difícil: Alfonso Reyes y Francisco García Calderín," in *La Gaceta* (FCE) 220 (April 1989): 16-22. Antonio Magaña Esquivel, "Mis recuerdos de Alfonso Reyes," in *Cuadernos de Bellas Artes* 4, 3 (March 1963): 21-28; *Teatro mexicano del siglo XX*, vol. 2 (México: FCE, 1956), pp. 300-301; *Medio siglo de teatro mexicano, 1900-1961* (México: INBA, 1964), pp. 74-75. Antonio Magaña Esquivel and Ruth S. Lamb, *Breve historia del teatro mexicano* (México: Eds. de Andrea, 1958), pp. 125, 131-132. Tomás Mallo, "El antipositivismo en México," in *Cuadernos Hispanoamericanos* 390 (Dec. 1982): 624-37. José Luis Martínez, "La prosa de Alfonso Reyes," in *Literatura mexicana siglo XX, 1910-1949*, vol. 1 (México: Libr. Robredo, 1949), pp. 280-83; vol. 2 (1950), pp. 101-5; "La obra de Alfonso Reyes," in *Cuadernos Americanos* 11, 1 (Jan.-Feb. 1952): 109-29; *El ensayo mexicano moderno* (México: FCE, 1958), pp. 266-69; "Alfonso Reyes," in *La Gaceta* (FCE) 220 (April 1989): 23-25. Robert G. Mead, *Breve historia del ensayo hispanoamericano* (México: Eds. de Andrea, 1956), pp. 106-11. Alfonso Méndez Plancarte, "La octava XI del Polifemo (Alfonso Reyes)," in *Cuestiúnculas gongorinas* (México: Eds. de Andrea, 1955), pp. 51-58. José Guilherme Merquior, "Asterisco sobre la posición de Alfonso Reyes," in *La Gaceta* (FCE) 220 (April 1989): 30-32. María del Carmen Millán, "La generación del Ateneo y el ensayo mexicano," in *Nueva Revista de Filología Hispánica* 15, 3-4 (1961): 634-35. Agustín Millares Carlo, Review of *La crítica en la edad ateniense*, in *Filosofía y Letras* 6 (April-June 1942): 271-73. Carlos Monsiváis, *La poesía mexicana del siglo XX* (México: Empresas Editoriales, 1966), pp. 26-27, 285-86. Jorge Luis Morales, *Alfonso Reyes y la literatura española* (Río Piedras: Editorial Universitaria, Universidad de Puerto Rico, 1980). Aurora M. Ocampo de Gómez and Ernesto Prado Velázquez, *Diccionario de escritores mexicanos* (México: UNAM, 1967), pp. 318-22. Manuel Olguín, *Alfonso Reyes, ensayista* (México: Eds. de Andrea, 1956). Julio Ortega, "La literatura mexicana y la experiencia comunitaria," in *Revista Iberoamericana* 55, 146-47 (Jan.-June 1989): 605-11. "On Alfonso Reyes," A symposium, in *Books Abroad* 19, 2 (1945): 111-24. Elda María Phillips, "Sendas de recuerdo: Evocación del paisaje español en dos escritores hispanoamericanos, Jorge Manach y Alfonso Reyes," in *Cuadernos de Aldeu* 1, 2-3 (May-Oct. 1983): 399-407. Alfonso Rangel Guerra, *Catálogo de índices de los libros de Alfonso Reyes* (Monterrey: Universidad de Nuevo León, 1955); *Las ideas literarias de Alfonso Reyes* (México: El Colegio de México, 1989). José Angel Rendón Hernández, *Alfonso Reyes, instrumentos para su estudio* (Monterrey: Universidad Autónoma de Nuevo León,

1980). Marcela del Río, "Una vision familiar de Alfonso Reyes: Mi tío Alfonso," in *Plural* 213 (June 1989): 22-25. James Willis Robb, *El estilo de Alfonso Reyes*, 2nd. ed., revised and enlarged (México: FCE, 1978); *Patterns of Image and Structure in the Essays of Alfonso Reyes* (Washington, D.C.: The Catholic University of America Press, 1958); *Repertorio bibliográfico de Alfonso Reyes* (México: UNAM, 1974); "Repertorio bibliográfico de Alfonso Reyes: Suplemento 1975-1977," in *Boletín del Instituto de Investigaciones Bibliográficas* (Mexico) 14-15 (1977-1978): 611-26; "Alfonso Reyes," in *Latin American Writers*, vol. 2, edited by Carlos A. Solé (New York: Charles Scribner's Sons, 1989), pp. 693-703; "Variedades de ensayismo en Alfonso Reyes y Germán Arciniegas," in *Thesaurus* 36 (1981); "'La cena' de Alfonso Reyes, cuento onírico: Surrealismo o realismo mágico," in *Thesaurus* 26 (1981); "En busca de la región más transparente del aire de Alfonso Reyes," in *Escolios* (Los Angeles) 4, 1-2 (May-Nov. 1979): 13-24; "Alfonso Reyes en busca de la unidad: Constancia y evolución," in *Revista Iberoamericana* 55, 148-49 (July-Dec. 1989): 819-37; "Variedades de ensayismo en Alfonso Reyes y Germán Arciniegas," in *Homenaje a Luis Alberto Sánchez* (Madrid: Insula, 1983); "Alfonso Reyes y Cecilia Meireles: Una amistad mexicano-brasileña," in *Hispania* 66, 2 (May 1983): 164-66; "José Vasconcelos y Alfonso Reyes: Anverso y reverso de una medalla," in *Los Ensayistas* 16-17 (March 1984): 55-65; "Alfonso Reyes y Eugenio Florit: De poeta a poeta," in *Revista Iberoamericana* 52, 137 (Oct.-Dec. 1986): 1015, 1041. George D. Schade, "Dos mexicanos vistos por sí mismos: Reyes y Abreu Gómez, in *Revista Iberoamericana* 55, 148-49 (July-Dec. 1989): 785-801. Mauricio de la Selva, Review of *Oración del 9 de febrero*, in *Cuadernos Americanos* 4 (July-Aug. 1963): 283. Guillermo Sheridan, "Correspondencia 1907-1914," in *Vuelta* 11, 128 (July 1987): 48-52. Walter Starkie, "A Memoir of Alfonso Reyes," in *Texas Quarterly* 2, 1 (1959): 67-77. Guillermo de Torre, *Tres conceptos de la literatura hispanoamericana* (Buenos Aires: Edit. Losada, 1963), 73-81, 227. Arturo Torres-Ríoseco, "Ultima entrevista con Alfonso Reyes," in *México en la Cultura* 566 (Jan. 17, 1960): 3-4. Elías Trabulse, "Las reflexiones de Alfonso Reyes sobre la historia de las ciencias: Si el hombre puede artificiosamente volar," in *La Gaceta* (FCE) 220 (April 1989): 33-38. Luis G. Urbina, "Madrid se despide de Alfonso Reyes. Dibujos de un menú," in *El Universal* 9 (May 11, 1924): 3-11. Rafael Heliodoro Valle, "Mi libro de estampas alfonsinas," in *Diorama de la Cultura* (Oct. 16, 1955). 3. Various, *Páginas sobre Alfonso Reyes*, vol. 1 (Monterrey: Eds. de Homenaje, Universidad de Nuevo León, 1955); vol. 2 (1957); *Libro jubilar de Alfonso Reyes* (México: UNAM, 1956); *Homenaje a Alfonso Reyes* (México: Ed. Cultura, 1965). Gabriel Zaid, "Una declaración desconocida de López Velarde," in *Vuelta* 12, 141 (Aug. 1988): 13-18. Serge Ivan Zaitzeff, "Las cartas madrileñas de Alfonso Reyes a Julio Torri," in *Revista Iberoamericana* 52, 135-36 (April-Sept. 1986): 703-59. David Zubatsky, ed., *Latin American Literary Authors: An Annotated Guide to Bibliographies* (Metchuen, N.J., and London: Scarecrow Press, 1986), pp. 209-11. Albert Zum Felde, *Indice crítico de la literatura hispanoamericana*, vol. 1 (México: Edit. Guaranía, 1954), pp. 549-56.

JEANNE C. WALLACE

REYES DE LA MAZA, Luis (1932-). Born in the city of San Luis Potosí on January 11, 1932, Luis Reyes de la Maza pursued studies in Spanish literature and language at the National Autonomous University of Mexico, and from 1956 on, was a researcher at the Institute of Research into Aesthetics. He has contributed to *El Nacional* with a theater column and other criticism on theater. He has also contributed to *Excelsior, Novedades, Anales del Instituto de Investigaciones Estéticas, Letras Potosinas,* and *Cuadrante.* The research that Luis Reyes de la Maza has done in the area of theater is an invaluable contribution to its history in Mexico. In his multivolume treatise, he has compiled documentation, consisting of programs and reviews, on plays performed from 1855 to 1900. With this work, he has made available to anyone interested in the history of theater in Mexico material that otherwise would have been inaccessible to scholars and the general public alike, and has proved himself to be the most knowledgeable scholar on the history of Mexican theater, thereby laying a solid base for future analysis and research. Besides his scholarly activities, Reyes de la Maza has been an active theater critic of performances in Mexico City.

WORKS: *El teatro en 1857 y sus antecedentes* (Theater in 1857 and Its Background), prologue by José Rojas Garcidueñas (México: Imp. Universitaria, 1956). *El teatro en México entre la Reforma y el Imperio [1858-1861]* (Theater in Mexico from the Reform to the Empire [1858-1861]) (México: Imp. Universitaria, 1958). *El teatro en México durante el segundo Imperio (1862-1867)* (Theater in Mexico during the Second Empire [1862-1867]) (México: Imp. Universitaria, 1959). *El teatro en México en la época de Juárez (1868-1872)* (Theater in Mexico in the Juárez Era [1868-1872]), (Mexico: Imp. Universitaria, 1961). *El teatro en México con Lerdo y Díaz (1873-1879)* (The Theater in Mexico with Lerdo and Díaz [1873-1879]) (México: Imp. Universitaria, 1963). *El teatro en México durante el porfirismo. I: 1880-1887* (Theater in Mexico during the Porfirist Period. I: 1880-1887) (México: Imp. Universitaria, 1964). *El teatro en México durante el porfirismo. II: 1888-1899* (Theater in Mexico during the Porfirist Period. II: 1888-1899) (México: Imp. Universitaria, 1965). Untitled article in *¿Qué Pasa con el teatro en México?* (México: Editorial Novaro, 1967): 53-58.

BIBLIOGRAPHY: Federico Alvarez, Review of *El teatro en México con Lerdo y Díaz,* en *La Cultura en México* 83 (Sept. 18, 1963): xix. Anon., "Bibliografía de Luis Reyes de la Maza," in *Bibliografía de los investigadores* 30, 2 (México) (1961): 205-8. Jesús Arellano, Review of *El teatro en 1857 y sus antecedentes,* in *Metáfora* 15 (July-Aug. 1957): 41. Huberto Batis, Review of *El teatro en México durante el porfirismo: II,* in *La Cultura en México* 202 (Dec. 29, 1965): xvi. Alberto Bonifaz Nuño, Review of *El teatro en 1857,* in Universidad de México 11, 6 (Feb. 1957). Frank Dauster, Review of *El teatro en México durante el segundo Imperio,* in *Revista Hispánica Moderna* 27, 3-4 (June-Oct. 1961). Ana Elena Díaz y Alejo, Review of *El teatro en México con Lerdo y Díaz,"* in *Letras Potosinas* 21, 149-50 (July-Dec. 1963): 1, 56. Juan García Ponce, Review of *El teatro en México entre la Reforma y el Imperio,* in *Universidad de México* 13, 3 (Nov. 1958): 30. Andrés Henestrosa, "La nota cultural," in *El Nacional* (Dec. 8, 1965): 3. Antonio Magaña Esquivel, Review of *El teatro en México durante el porfirismo, I,* in *El Nacional* (Oct. 6, 1964): 5; (Oct. 7, 1964): 5; (Oct. 8, 1964): 5. Aurora M. Ocampo de Gómez and Ernesto Prado Velázquez, *Diccionario de escritores mexicanos* (México: UNAM, 1967). Gustavo Sáinz, Review of *El teatro en México con Lerdo y Díaz,* in *México en la Cultura* 757 (Sept. 22, 1963): 9.

YOLANDA S. BROAD

REYES NEVARES, Salvador (1922-   ), essayist, short story writer, critic. Reyes Nevares was born in Durango on November 21, 1922. He completed his studies at the University of Mexico, where he earned a degree in law. Later he served in different commissions including the Labor Publishing House. He has also taught and lectured at various institutions among them the University of Guanajuato, the University of Veracruz, and the University of Nuevo León.

His literary activities included him as a member of the group Hiperión, he also helped found the editorial Los Epigrafes, which published adolescent stories. Other literary contributions included short stories, essays, and literary critiques in numerous magazines and newspapers including *Cuadernos de Bellas Artes*, *La Palabra y el Hombre*, *Estaciones*, and *Universidad de México*. He is most noted for his reviews (in *Novedades* and *Siempre!*) of the works of Mexican writers.

WORKS: *El amor en tres poetas (Antonio Machado, Pablo Neruda y Xavier Villaurrutia)* (Love in Three Poets [Antonio Machado, Pablo Neruda and Xavier Villaurrutia]) (México: Los Epigrafes, 1952). *El amor y la amistad en el mexicano* (Love and Friendship in the Mexican) (México: Ant. Libr. Robredo, 1952). *Frontera indecisa* (Vague Border) (México: Los Presentes, 1955). *Novelas selectas de Hispanoamérica* (Selected Novels of Spanish-America) (México: Labor, 1959).

BIBLIOGRAPHY: Anon., in *Anuario del Cuento Mexicano* (México: INBA, 1962), p. 200. Englantina Ochoa Sandoval, "Frontera indecisa," in *Metáfora* 5 (1955): 40-41. Guadalupe Rubens, "Sentido social de la novela mexicana," in *México en la Cultura* 36 (1949): 7.

SILKA FREIRE

REYES RUIZ, Jesús (1908-   ). Born in Aguascalientes, Jesús Reyes Ruiz is a lyrical poet with philosophical and mystical concerns. The poetry is contemporary mainly because of metric liberty and verse rythm. He has specialized in Sor Juana Inés de la *Cruz.

In *El centauro* (The Centaur), antagonistic forces (life-death, day-night, light-shadow) express the persistence of opposites, portraying the ambivalence of man in general and of the Mexican in particular. The book, stating the Centauric condition of the Mexican, is an anxious search for God.

WORKS: *Cuatro poemas* (Four Poems) (México: n.p., 1940). *Romance de Alfonso Ramírez "Calesero"* (The Ballad of Alfonso Ramírez "Calesero") (Durango: n.p., 1943). *Raíz y voz del libro* (Root and Voice of the Book) (México: n.p., 1946). *Discurso para un héroe* (Lecture for a Hero) (México: n.p., 1947). *La época literaria de Sor Juana Inés de la Cruz* (The Literary Times of Sor Juana Ines de la Cruz) (Monterrey: Universidad de Nuevo León, 1951). *Tres epistolas para hablar de tu ausencia* (Three Epistles to Speak of Your Absence) (México: Nueva Voz, 1953). *Casa en el recuerdo* (House in the Memory) (México: n.p., 1955). *Trinidad del hombre* (Poesía) (Trinity of Man) (México: Seminario de Cultura Mexicana, 1963). *El centauro* (The Centaur), Olympic Prize 1968 (México: Finisterre, 1968). *Casi entre sueños* (Almost in Between Dreams) (Sevilla: Editorial Católica Española, 1979).

BIBLIOGRAPHY: Anon., Bibliographical note in *Anuario de la poesía mexicana 1962* (México: INBA, 1963), p. 116. Antonio Castro Leal, *La poesía mexicana moderna* (México: FCE, 1953), p. 366. Alí Chumacero, "La poesía 1963," in *La Cultura en México* 99 (Jan. 8, 1964): 1. Elena Poniatowska, "¿Qué somos? ¿A dónde vamos? Tema del poema *Trinidad del hombre*, del embajador y poeta Jesús Reyes Ruiz," in *El Día* (Jan. 19, 1964): 4.

ALICIA G. WELDEN

RICO Cano, Tomás (1916-), poet, journalist, and teacher. Born in Uruapán, Michoacán, Tomás Rico Cano graduated with a degree in education from the University of Michoacán. He later enrolled in the San Nicolás de Hidalgo School, where he became a part of one of the more restless literary movements. From his youth, Rico Cano dedicated himself to literature. His literary group published many student newspapers to which he frequently contributed. Among the publications were *Juventud* (Youth), *La Chispa* (The Spark), *Voces* (Voices), *El Zumbido* (Humming), and *Clarinadas* (Trumpet Calls). He completed his studies at the School of Law and Social Sciences of Michoacán. He taought in various primary schools, and in 1940 he became an instructor at the Normal Urban School teaching economics, Spanish language and literature, and civics. He was also an instructor at the National School of San Nicolas. As a journalist he contributed to *La Voz de Michoacán* (The Voice of Michoacán), *Sol de Michoacán* (The Sun of Michoacán), *Diario de Michoacán* (Michoacan Daily), *El Centavo* (The Cent), and *El Nacional* (The National) among others.

His work consists of more than a dozen books of poetry, including one on the political and judicial thought of don José María Morelos y Pavón, and many collaborations in newspapers and magazines of Mexico City. His poetry is characterized by the love of his country and countrymen. In his sincere and emotional verses he expresses his desire for all that is good in his land.

WORKS: Poetry: *Esta niebla encendida* (This Inflamed Mist) (Morelia, Mich.: n.p., 1946). *De amor quince sonetos* (Fifteen Love Sonnets) (Morelia, Mich., n.p., 1948). *Diástole sin regreso* (Diastole with No Return) (Morelia: Ed. Campana de Coral, 1949). *Amando a tres ciudades* (Loving Three Cities) (Morelia: Ed. Tzinapu, Eds., 1952). *Un recado a mi madre* (A Message to My Mother) (Morelia, Mich.: n.p., 1957). *Un canto a la Revolución Mexicana* (An Ode to the Mexican Revolution) (Morelia: Eds. Tzinapu, 1960). *Tres romances morelianos* (Three Morelian Poems) (Moreli: Eds. Campana de Coral, 1964). *Un retablo purépecha* (Picture of a Pariah) (Morelia: Eds. SNTE, 1964. Essays: *Notas sobre el pensamiento político y jurídico de don José María Morelos y Pavón* (Notes on the Political and Judicial Thought of José María Morelos y Pavón) (Morelia: Universidad of Michoacán, 1950).

BIBLIOGRAPHY: Anon., "Autores michoacanos" in *El Centavo* 1, 9 (Oct. 30, 1956): 8; "Escaparate de libros," review of *Un retablo purpecha*, in *México en la Cultura* 827 (Jan. 24, 1965): 8. Thelma Nava, "Notas de poesía," review of *Un retablo purépecha*, in *El Día* (March 4, 1965): 9. Alfonso Reyes, "Testimonios sobre Rico Cano," in *El*

Centavo 1, 9 (Oct. 30, 1956): 8. Salvador Toscano, "Testimonios sobre Rico Cano," in *El Centavo* 9 (Oct. 30, 1956): 4.

DENISE GUAGLIARDO BENCIVENGO

RIESTRA, Gloria (1929-) poet and essayist. Born in Tampico, Tamaulipas, Gloria Riestra studied business at a young age. She began teaching while quite young and then took up journalism. She has written for a number of first-rate newspapers and journals. She has written four books of poetry and one collection of essays. Her poetry has been published in anthologies in Mexico as well as in other parts of the Spanish speaking world.

Riestra's literary writings have a marked mystical, religious bend. She has been compared with Emma *Godoy and San Juan de la *Cruz. Religious images run throughout her works. Her poetry sets up a contrast between unity, hope, and peace with God and solitude, loneliness, and despair without Him. *Según Tu Palabra* (According to Your Word) is a prose description and discussion of her religious experience, a defense of that experience in this age and the connection between language and religion.

WORKS: Poetry: *La soledad sonora* (The Sonorous Solitude) (México: Abside, 1950). *Celeste anhelo* (Celestial Yearnings) (México: Abside, 1952). *Al aire de su vuelo* (In the Air of Your Flight) (México: n.p. 1954). *La noche sosegada* (The Peaceful Night) (México: Editorial Jus, 1960). *Salmos de adoración* (Psalms of Adoration) (México: n.p., 1963). *Cena de amor* (Supper of Love) (México: n.p., 1964). *Lagar* (México: n.p., 1965). Prose: *Según Tu Palabra* (According to Your Word) (México: Jus, 1960).

BIBLIOGRAPHY: Anon., "Gloria Riestra y su *Lagar*," *Abside* 29, 2 (Jan.-April 1965): 246-47. Heriberto García Rivas, *Historia de la literatura mexicana*, vol. 4 (México: Textos Universitarios, 1971): p. 359-60. Aurora M. Ocampo de Gómez and Ernesto Prado Velázquez, *Diccionario de escritores mexicanos* (México: UNAM, 1967), p. 326. Miguel Sánchez Astudillo, "Gloria Riestra cumple 20 años," *Abside* 29, 3 (1965): 268-72. Alberto Valenzuela Rodarte, *Historia de la literatura mexicana* (México: Editorial Jus, 1961), p. 585-96.

MARK FRISCH

RIUS, Luis (1930-), poet and essayist. Luis Rius was born in Tarancón, Spain, on November 19, 1930. He has lived in Mexico since 1939 and has taught at various universities in Mexico including the UNAM. He has also contributed poems and essays to various periodicals such as *Cuadernos Americanos*, *Revista Mexicana de Literatura*, and the literary supplements of *Novedades*, *Excelsior*, *El Nacional*, and *Siempre!*.

WORKS: Poetry: *Canciones de vela* (Sail Songs) (México: Ed. Segrel, 1951). *Canciones de ausencia* (Forlorn songs) (México: Universidad de Guanajuato, 1954). *Canciones de amor y sombra* (Songs of Love and Shadows) (México: Ed. Era, 1965). *Canciones a Pilar Rioja* (Songs to Pilar Rioja) (México: Finisterre, 1970). Essays: *Los grandes textos de la literatura española hasta 1766* (Great Texts of Spanish Literature until 1700) (México: Ed. Pormaca, 1966). *León Felipe, poeta de barro* (León Felipe, Poet of Mud) (México: Promociones Editoriales Mexicanas, 1984).

BIBLIOGRAPHY: Angelina Muñiz, Review of *Canciones de amor y sombra*, in *Diorama de la Cultura* (Dec. 12, 1965): 4. José de la Colina, Review of *Canciones de ausencia*, in *Ideas de México* 11, 7-8 (Sept.-Dec. 1954): 48-50. Juan García Ponce, "1965, La poesía," in *La Cultura en México* 203 (Jan. 5, 1966): xiv.

NORA EIDELBERG

RIVA PALACIO y Guerrero, Vicente (1832-1896), novelist, short story writer, journalist, and poet. Born in Mexico City on October 16, 1832, Vicente Riva Palacio was the son of a well-knowm liberal lawyer, and the grandson of Mexico's Independence hero, Vicente Guerrero. He studied at the Colegio de San Gregorio, and received his law degree in 1854. Two years later, he was elected deputy to the National Congress, a position he held until 1861, when the French took control of Mexico City, and he was forced to resign. Riva Palacio abandoned the capital in 1862, and joined the Republican government of Benito Juárez in exile. He acted in both a military and administrative capacity, becoming first the governor of the state of Mexico in 1863 and, then, the governor of Michoacán in 1865. He was also appointed general of the central division of the Republican Army in 1865. He and his troops played an active role in the siege of Queretaro, which resulted in the capture and execution of the Emperor Maximilian in 1867. After the fall of the Empire, Riva Palacio returned to Mexico City, where he laid down his arms and took up his pen. In 1868, he completed the first of a series of historical novels, *Calvario y Tabor* (Calvary and Mt. Tabor), which would bring him recognition as one of Mexico's most popular and prolific nineteenth-century writers. Riva Palacio continued to be active in politics throughout the rest of his life. In 1874, he founded the satirical newspaper, *El Ahuizote* (The Nuisance), using it as a vehicle of attack against the government of Sebastián Lerdo de Tejada. He took part in the Revolution of Tuxtepec, winning for himself the position of Minister of Public Works when the revolution triumphed in 1878. Six years later, he was jailed for his verbal attacks against President Manuel González. The re-establishment of the Díaz government shortly afterwards brought Riva Palacio back into public life. He was appointed Magistrate of the Supreme Court, a position he held until 1886, when he became Mexico's minister plenipotentiary in Spain. He died in Madrid on December 22, 1896. Forty years later, his remains were brought to Mexico, and were placed in the Rotunda of Illustrious Men.

Riva Palacio is considered, by some critics, to be the creator of the historical novel in Mexico. He wrote without concern for literary merit, and openly declared that his only aim was to entertain his readers with dramatic, hair-raising adventures. He was more interested in the extraordinary twists and turns of the plot than in the careful construction of his sentences. He was not interested in the psychology of his characters but, rather, in their ability to move the plot along at a fast and lively pace.

His style, although sometimes choppy and abrupt, is easy to read and maintains reader interest through good use of dialogue. During his lifetime, Riva Palacio had a large reading public who devoured the pages of his novels as quickly as he could produce them. He used, as a source of inspiration for his many historical novels, his own recent experience in battle against the French and a vast private collection of archives and documents from Mexico's colonial past. The archives of the Inquisition in Mexico, in particular, provided him with a number of his plots. *Calvario y Tabor* (Calvary and Mt. Tabor), his first novel, appeared in 1868. Despite a rather misleading title, it deals with Mexico's struggle against the French during the years of Intervention. Ignacio *Altamirano wrote the prologue for the first edition, praising it for its treatment of a theme of national interest and its patriotic tone. The novel is, in essence, romantic. The characters are idealized, and military episodes are included only as a backdrop for love affairs. The book consists of a series of somewhat unrelated episodes dealing with orphans, secrets, rivalries, mistaken identity, unrequited love, and other standard ingredients of romantic fiction.

Monja y casada, virgen y martir (The Nun and the Married Woman, the Virgin and the Martyr) appeared in the same year. It is also romantic in tone and content. The women are either models of perfection or the embodiment of evil. The men are either heroes or villains. It is set in the year 1615 and attempts to portray life in colonial Mexico, although its main focus is on a series of fictionalized adventures and love affairs. *Martín Caratuza*, also published in 1868, is the sequel. It deals with many of the same characters and is set in the year 1623.

Las dos emparedadas (The Two Immured Women) appeared in 1869. It begins in Spain, in the court of Mariana of Austria after the death of Philip IV, but main characters are quickly transferred to Mexico, where they become embroiled in intrigues, jealous rivalries, and crimes of passion. *Los piratas del golfo* (The Pirates of the Gulf), which appeared in the same year, is generally regarded as one of Riva Palacio's better works. It deals with the famous English pirate John Morgan and a group of fictional Mexican characters who typically become involved in a number of romantic adventures.

La vuelta de los muertos (The Return of the Dead) was published in 1870. It presents the story of an Aztec prince, Tetzahuitl, and his mistress, doña Isabel, an Aztec woman who has been married to a Spaniard.

Memorias de un impostor, D. Guillén de Lampart, rey de México (Memoirs of an Impostor, D. Guillén de Lampart, King of Mexico) appeared in 1872. It is loosely based on a historical incident which involved the attempt of an Irish rogue to pass himself off as the illegitimate son of Felipe III and to claim Mexico as his kingdom in the seventeenth century. His capture and punishment by the Inquisition is the main focus of the book.

Riva Palacio also wrote a number of dramatic works, some of them in collaboration with Juan A. *Mateos. He either authored or coauthored *Borrascas de un sobretodo* (Dangers of an Overcoat) (1861); *Odio hereditario* (Hereditary Hate) (1861); and *Las liras hermanas* (The Twin Lyres) (1871). The plays were presented in Mexico City but never published. They have been lost, and little information is available about them today.

As a poet, Riva Palacio was not highly productive by nineteenth-century standards. His poetry occasionally appeared in newspapers at home and abroad, most notably in Altamirano's journal, *El Renacimiento* (The Renaissance). Later, his poems were collected in *Páginas en verso* (Pages in Verse) (1885) and in *Mis versos* (My Verses) (1893). "El Escorial," (The Escorial), "Al viento" (To the wind), and "La vejez" (Old Age) are generally considered to be his best poetic works. In them, he shows an unexpected restraint and a formal elegance which lend them a somber dignity.

Riva Palacio published many short stories in newspapers, literary journals, and as intercalated pieces in longer works. Most of these *cuentos* have never been collected. Riva Palacio's only published volume of short stories is the now famous *Cuentos del General* (The General's Stories), which consists of twenty-six tales. It was published in Spain in 1896, shortly before his death. Some critics see it as his single most important work, because of the high degree of literary polish, fine humor, and subtle irony which permeates the text. "El buen ejemplo" (The Good Example), "Un Stradivarius" (A Stradivarius), "La burra perdida" (The Lost Burro), "El divorcio" (The Divorce), and "La horma de su zapato" (He Met His Match) stand out as some of the best stories.

Riva Palacio's other work includes a biography of his contemporaries entitled *Los ceros. Galería de contemporáneos* (The Zeros. Gallery of My Contemporaries), which contains literary criticism on the work of numerous Mexican writers. Although Riva Palacio speaks openly and frankly about his fellow writers, the book is not as insulting as the title suggests, since he uses the term "zeros" more playfully than scornfully, and he includes himself in the ranks by stating that the book was written by "a zero." He also wrote *Historia de la administración de D. Sebastián Lerdo de Tejada* (The History of the Administration of D. Sebastián Lerdo de Tejada) (1875), a far from impartial look at the government of one of his political rivals, and he acted as general editor of the impressive five volume *México a través de los siglos* (Mexico Through the Centuries) (1884-1889), a detailed account of Mexican history from pre-Hispanic times up through the death of Juárez. Riva Palacio wrote volume 2, *El Virreinato* (The Viceroyalty), with much the same flamboyant style he used in his novels, although with more attention to detail and historical fact.

WORKS: *Calvario y Tabor* (Calvary and Mt. Tabor) (México: Manuel C. de Villegas, 1868; reprinted 1883, 1905, 1923). *Las dos emparedadas* (The Two Immured Women) (México: Manuel C. de Villegas, 1868; reprinted 1903, 1924); included in *La novela del México colonial*, edited by Antonio Castro Leal (México: Aguilar, 1964), pp. 605-844. *Monja y casada, virgen y martir* (The Nun and the Married Woman, the Virgin and the Martyr) (México: Manuel C. de Villegas, 1868; reprinted 1900, 1908, 1945, 1986); included in *La novela del México colonial*, edited by Antonio Casto Leal (México: Aguilar, 1964), pp. 349-604. *Los piratas en el golfo* (The Pirates in the Gulf) (México: Manuel C. de Villegas, 1869; reprinted 1946). *La vuelta de los muertos* (The Return of the Dead) (México: Manuel C. de Villegas, 1870). *Memorias de un impostor, D. Guillen de Lampart, rey de México* (Memoirs of an Impostor, D. Guillen de Lampart, King of Mexico) (México: Manuel C. de Villegas, 1872; reprinted 1946). Los ceros. *Galería de contemporáneos* (The Zeros. Gallery of My Contemporaries) (México: Imprenta de F. Díaz de León, 1882). *Páginas en versos* (Pages in Verse) (México: n.p., 1885). *México a través de los siglos* (Mexico Through the Centuries) (México: n.p., 1889; reprinted 1940, 1967). *Mis versos* (My Verses) (Madrid: Rivadeneyra, 1893). *Cuentos del general* (The General's Stories) (Madrid: Rivadeneyra, 1896; reprinted 1929, 1968). Antología de Vicente Riva Palacio (Anthology), edited by Clementina Díaz y de Ovando (México: UNAM, 1976).

BIBLIOGRAPHY: Carlos González Peña, *Historia de la literatura mexicana* (México: SEP, 1928), pp. 309-11. Luis Leal, *Breve historia del cuento mexicano* (México: Eds. de Andrea, 1956), pp. 57-58. María del Carmen Millán, *Literatura mexicana* (México: Edit. Esfinge, 1962), pp. 164-65. Carlos Monsiváis, "Vicente Riva Palacio: La evocación liberal contra la nostalgia reaccionaria," prologue to *Monja y Casada* (México: Edic. Oceano, 1986), pp. iii-xviii. John Lloyd Read, *The Mexican Historical Novel* (New York: Instituto de las Españas en los Estados Unidos, 1939), pp. 205-13. Pedro Serrano, *El general, silueta del excelentísimo señor don Vicente Riva Palacio con varias anotaciones* (México, n.p., 1934).

CYNTHIA K. DUNCAN

ROA Bárcena, José María (1827-1908), short story writer, poet, novelist, literary critic, and historian. Roa Bárcena was born in Jalapa, Veracruz, on September 3, 1827. The son of a well-to-do merchant, he learned in his youth to combine his interest in literature with a practical career in business, which he pursued throughout his adult life. In 1853, Roa Bárcena moved to Mexico City, where he began publishing articles in the conservative press. His poems and prose pieces appeared in *La Cruz* (The Cross), a Catholic journal edited by Joaquín *Pesado, *El Eco Nacional* (The National Echo), and *La Sociedad* (Society).

Although most young Mexican intellectuals of his generation supported the liberal cause, Roa Bárcena remained steadfastly loyal to the conservative party during the War of the Reform. He was a member of the Junta de Notables (Junta of Important Men) who voted in support of a monarchy in Mexico, and he formally welcomed the royal couple as they disembarked in Vera Cruz with his sonorous "Oda en la inauguración del segundo imperio" (Ode on the Inauguration of the Second Empire), which he had written especially for the occasion. He was one of the principal members of the Academia Imperial de Ciencias y Literatura, founded by Maximilian, and a frequent visitor to Chapultepec Palace in the early months of the Empire. However, Roa Bárcena soon came to realize that the emperor was not, at heart, a conservative, and that many of the emperor's planned reforms were similar to the goals of the Liberal party. Roa Bárcena then turned against Maximilian and the French, and began openly criticizing the Empire for not being conservative enough. He refused to participate in its administration and predicted its imminent downfall. In 1867, when Roa Bárcena's prediction came true and the emperor was put to death, the conservative author came under the critical eye of the newly reinstated Juárez government. He was sentenced to two years in prison for his anti-liberal views but, after several months, the sentence was reduced and Roa Bárcena was released. He retired from public life, and devoted his remaining time and energy to business and literary interests. He established a literary salon, which met on a regular basis for forty years and attracted other conservative writers. He continued to publish in *La Sociedad* (Society) and *La Cruz* (The Cross) and, later, following *Altamirano's advice that political differences should be put aside, in *El Renacimiento* (The Renaissance) and *La Universal* (The Universal). Some of his journalistic writings appear under the pseudonym Atenor, but they are immediately recognizable as the work of Roa Bárcena because of the strong religious, moral, and conservative political convictions found in them. A man of remarkable energy and discipline, he began to study Latin at the age of seventy, and soon thereafter translated the works of Virgil and Horace into Spanish. He became a member of the Academia Española de la Lengua and was one of the founding members of the Academia Mexicana de la Lengua. He died in Mexico City on September 21, 1908.

Roa Bárcena is best known for his work in the short story. Luis Leal claims that his stories are "some of the best that have been written in Mexico" because of the level of mastery in characterization, the development of themes, and the harmony of the various parts of the story. Most of Roa Bárcena's work originally appeared in print in local newspapers. In 1870, some of his early prose fiction was collected and published under the rather misleading title *Novelas originales y traducidas* (Original and Translated Novels). The only piece in the volume that is lengthy enough to be regarded as a novel in the modern sense of the word is *La quinta ideal* (The Model Villa). It is a novel of thesis that attacks liberal doctrines and exposes with subtle irony the tragic results of the Laws of the Reform. The work was written in 1857, during the War of Reform, and is heavily charged with emotion. In style, it is romantic, but the contents of the novel provide us with a realistic, although biased, portrait of the times. Other works in the collection might more properly be called short stories. They include "Buondelmonti," "Una flor en su sepulcro" (A Flower in Its Tomb), "Aminta Rovero," and a series of five interrelated tales under the general title "Noche al raso" (Night in the Open). "Buondelmonti" is set in Europe during the Middle Ages, and is a romantic work, focusing on a love affair between two young people whose families are involved in a political feud. "Una flor en su sepulcro" was one of Roa Bárcena's earliest prose pieces, written in 1849. It is loosely based on one of the author's own youthful love affairs, that ended with the girl's death. The story is sentimental in the extreme and represents a facet of Romanticism which Roa Bárcena later wholeheartedly rejected. "Aminta Rovero" was first published in *El Eco Nacional* (The National Echo) in 1857, and was probably written in 1853. Aminta represents the frivolous but ambitious middle-class woman who attempts to get ahead in the world by manipulating her suitors. "Noche al raso" is, by far, the best work in the collection. It deals with a group of travelers whose carriage breaks dowm at nightfall on the road between Puebla and Orizaba. To pass the time while they are waiting to be rescued, they make up stories. The results are five independent tales bound together by a narrative frame. They are entitled "El hombre del caballo rucio" (The Man with the Gray Horse), "El crucifijo milagroso" (The Miraculous Crucifix), "La docena de sillas para igualar" (A Dozen Chairs to Match), "El cuadro de Murillo" (The Painting by Murillo), and "A dos dedos del abismo" (Two Fingers Away from the Abyss). All of the stories, except "El hombre del caballo rucio" have some degree of social and political criticism. Nevertheless, despite their moral aim, they are lively, witty, and well-crafted narratives that easily hold the interest of the reader. The Spanish novelist, Juan Valera, described the "Noche al raso" stories as "a beautiful collection." He praised Roa Bárcena for his "cleverness, talent, and ability," and commented on the "naturalness, correctness, and charm" of his style.

Roa Bárcena's later work is indisputably his best. His short stories, "Lanchitas" (1878), "El rey y el bufón" (The King and the Clown) (1882), and "Combates en el aire" (Battles in the Air) (1892) are generally regarded as his most oustanding pieces. They appeared in a two-volume set entitled *Cuentos originales y traducidos* (Original and Translated Stories) in 1897, together with a reprinting of the five "Noche al raso" stories and "Buondelmonti." The collection also contained several stories by Charles Dickens and Ernest Theodor Hoffmann, which Roa Bárcena had translated into Spanish. "Lanchitas" is one of the first truly fantastic stories to be produced in Latin America. It takes as its point of departure a legend that has grown up in Mexico City around the figure of "Lanchitas," a priest who lived in the early years of the nineteenth century. The narrator, however, subtly transforms the legend into a spine-tingling ghost story that brings the supernatural element of the tale into the reader's own world. Elvira López Aparicio finds in this story a "perfect control of the language," and Leal notes that the story represents a "definite step forward in the evolution of the Mexican short story."

As a poet, Roa Bárcena is also well regarded. His poetic work is extensive and, generally, of a consistently high quality. His poetry is inclined to be somber and decorous, notable for its clear, correct use of language and a carefully controlled form. The themes most comunoly found in his verses are religion, love, nationalism, and philosophical reflection. His poems appeared regularly in local newspaper throughout the second half of the nineteenth century, and were collected in several volumes, including *Poesías líricas* (Lyric Poetry) (1859), *Leyendas mexicanas, cuentos y baladas del norte de Europa y algunos otros ensayos poeticos* (Mexican Legends, Stories, and Ballads from Northern Europe, with Some Other Attempts at Poetry) (1862), *Ultimas poesías líricas* (Recent Lyric Poetry) (1888), *Diana* (1892), and *Obras poéticas* (Poetic Works) (1913). He also translated into Spanish many of the poetic works of Schiller, Byron, and Tennyson, and edited a volume of Spanish poetry called *Acopio de sonetos castellanos* (Collection of Castilian Sonnets) (1887). In addition to his creative literary work, Roa Bárcena was an excellent scholar. He wrote biographies of the lives of José Joaquín Pesado and Manuel Eduardo *Gorostiza, which have been called "contributions of great value to Mexican literary history." He also wrote *Catecismo elemental de geografía universal* (Elementary Study of World Geography) (1861); *Catecismo de historia de México desde su fundación hasta mediados del siglo XIX* (Study of Mexican History from Its Beginnings to the Middle of the Nineteenth Century) (1888); *Ensayo de una historia anecdótica de México en los tiempos anteriores a la conquista* (Anecdotal History of Mexico in Pre-Conquest Times) (1862); and *Recuerdos de la invasión norteamericana* (Memoirs of the North American Invasion) (1902).

WORKS: *Flores de mayo* (May Flowers) (México: Imp. de Escalante y Cía, 1850). *Poesías líricas* (Lyric Poetry) (México: Imp. de Andrade y Escalante, 1859). *Catecismo elemental de geografía universal* (Elementary Study of World Geography) (México: Imp. de Santiago White, 1861). *Catecismo de historia de México desde su fundación hasta mediados del siglo XIX* (Study of Mexican History from Its Beginnings to the Middle of the Nineteenth Century) (México: Imp. de Santiago White, 1862). *Ensayo de una historia anecdótica de México en los tiempos anteriores a la conquista* (Anecdotal History of Mexico in Pre-Conquest Times) (México: Imp. Literaria, 1862). *Leyendas mexicanas, cuentos y baladas del norte de Europa y algunos otros ensayos poéticos* (Mexican Legends, Stories, and Ballads from the North of Europe with Some Other Attempts at Poetry) (México: Edit. Agustín Masse, 1862). *Compendio de historia profana* (Compendium of Profane History) (México: n.p., 1870). *Datos y apuntamientos para la biografía de Manuel Eduardo de Gorostiza* (Facts and Observations on the Biography of Manuel Eduardo de Gorostiza) (México: Imp. de Ignacio Escalante, 1870). *Novelas originales y traducidas* (Original and Translated Novels) (México: Imp. de Díaz León y White, 1870). *Biografía de don José Joaquín Pesado* (Biography of don José Joaquín Pesado) (México: Imp. de Ignacio Escalante, 1878). *Vasco Nuñez de Balboa* (México: José Ma. Sandoval, 1879). *Memorias de la Academia de la Lengua* (Memoirs of the Academy of the Language) (México: n.p.

1880). *Recuerdos de la invasión norteamericana* (Memoirs of the North American Invasion) (México: Librería Madrileña de Juan Buxd y Cía, 1883; reprinted 1947). *Varios cuentos* (Several Stories) (México: Tip. de Gonzalo A. de Esteva, 1883). Acopio de sonetos castellanos (Collection of Castilian Sonnets) (México: Imp. de Ignacio Escalante, 1887). *Ultimas poesías líricas* (México: Imp. de Ignacio Escalante, 1888). *Diana* (México: Imp. de Ignacio Escalante, 1892). *Antología de poetas mexicanos* (Anthology of Mexican Poets), editor (México: Oficina de la Sección de Fomento, 1894). *Cuentos originales y traducidos* (Original and Translated Stories) (México: Imp. de V. Agueros, 1897). *Obras poéticas* (Poetic Works) (México: Imp. de Ignacio Escalante, 1913). *Relatos* (Stories), edited by Julio Jiménez Rueda (México: UNAM, 1941). *Noche al raso* (Night in the Open), edited by Julio Jiménez Rueda (México: Imp. Universitaria, 1955).

BIBLIOGRAPHY: Carlos González Peña, *Historia de la literatura mexicana* (México: SEP, 1928), pp. 300-303. Julio Jiménez Rueda, Prologue to *Relatos* (México: UNAM, 1955), pp. vii-xxiv. Luis Leal, *Breve historia del cuento mexicano* (México: Eds. de Andrea, 1956), pp. 55-57. Elvira López Aparicio, *José María Roa Bárcena* (México: Edic. Metáfora, 1957). María del Carmen Millán, *Literatura Mexicana* (México: Edit. Esfinge, 1962), pp. 128, 159, 169. Ignacio Montes de Oca y Obregón, Prologue to *Obras poéticas* (México: Imp. de I. Escalante, 1913), pp. 1-169. Vicente Riva Palacio, *Los ceros. Galería de contemporáneos* (México: Imp. de F. Diaz de León, 1882), pp. 325-46.

                                                                CYNTHIA K. DUNCAN

ROBERTO SALAZAR. See BASILIO, Librado.

ROBLES, Antonio ("Antoniorrobles") (1897-?), short story writer and journalist. He was born on August 18, 1897, in Spain in Robledo de Chavela, where he lived until Franco came to power. He then noved to Mexico in 1938 and later became a Mexican citizen.

"Antoniorrobles" dedicated his life to writing children's literature for which he received several awards. His books are considered important to the education of young people. He taught teachers how to teach children's literature in the National School for Teachers. Even though he is noted for writing children's literature, he also wrote for adults, displaying a special sense of humor.

WORKS: *Cuentos de los juguetes vivos* (Tales of the Living Toys) (New York: n.p., n.d.). *¿Se comió el lobo a Caperucita?* (Did the Wolf Eat Little Red Riding Hood?) (México: America, 1942). *El barranco de los gitanos* (The Gypsies Gully) (Granada: Don Quijote, 1964). *El refugiado Centauro Flores* (The Refugee Centauro Flores) (México: Finisterre, 1965). *Le ravin des gitans* (Paris: Gallimard, 1965).

BIBLIOGRAPHY: Antonio Acevedo, "Anuncios y presencias," *Letras de México* 1 (1949): 1. María Luisa Cresta, *De literatura infantil a 50 respuestas de Antoniorrobles*

(México: Ateneo, 1966). M.M., "Antoniorrobles y su bruja doña Paz," *México en la Cultura* 745 (1963): 8. Luis Suárez, "Antoniorrobles," *Siempre!* 535 (1963): 39-41; "Antoniorrobles," *Siempre!* 598 (1963): 42-49.

SILKA FREIRE

ROBLES, Fernando (1887-?), novelist. Born in Guanajuato in 1897, Robles received his degree in philosophy and letters from King's College in London. He had temporary residences in Europe, North Africa, South America, and the United States (New York), and finally settled in Silao, Guanajuato.

He wrote numerous novels that carry historical themes of rebellion and revolution. These include *La virgen de los cristeros* (The Virgin of the Cristeros); *El santo que asesinó* (The Saint Who Murdered), which explains the assassination of General Obregón; and *Cuando el águila perdió sus alas* (When the Eagle Lost Its Wings), which describes the territorial losses suffered by Mexico in 1848 to the United States.

WORKS: *La virgen de los cristeros* (Buenos Aires: Claridad, 1934; La Prensa, n.d). *El santo que asesinó* (The Saint Who Murdered) (Buenos Aires: Perrotti, 1936). *Sucedió así* (It Happened So) (México: n.p., 1940). *Cuando el águila perdió sus alas* (When the Eagle Lost Its Wings) (México: n.p., 1951). *La estrella que no quiso vivir* (The Star That Didn't Want to Live) (México: FCE, 1957).

BIBLIOGRAPHY: Emmanuel Carballo, "*La estrella que no quiso vivir,*" *México en la Cultura* 410 (1957): 2. A.L. Palacios, "Cristeros, de Robles," *El Libro y el Pueblo* 10 (1934): 15-19. R.V., Review of *La virgen de los cristeros*, in *Letras de México* 4 (1937): 3.

SILKA FREIRE

RODRIGUEZ Beltrán, Cayetano (1866-1939), journalist, essayist, and writer of short stories. Rodríguez Beltrán was born in Tlacotalpan, State of Veracruz, on September 24, 1866. From an early age he worked as a journalist and as a teacher of literature in Jalapa's Secondary School. He used to sign his contributions to magazines with the anagram Onateyac. In 1908 Rodríguez Beltrán was elected a member of the Academia Mexicana de la Lengua (Mexican Academy of Language). He died in Jalapa on June 16, 1939.

After his short stories were published in four different collections, Rodríguez Beltrán was considered a "costumbrista" (person who writes about customs or habits). "El anonimo" (The Anonymous Letter) and "La gaviota" (The Sea Gull) are two short stories in which he portrays the customs and life of characters extracted from an environment that is very well known to him. The first deals with a middle-class couple; the second, with the unfortunate marriage of a fisherman of Veracruz. His book *Por mi heredad* (Through My Heritage) is a collection of essays about literature and about the works of Miguel de Cervantes.

WORKS: *Una docena de cuentos* (Twelve Short Stories), prologue by Rafael Delgado (México: Talls. de Ramón Araluce, 1900). *Atrevimientos literarios* (Literary Audacities), prologue by Rodolfo Menéndez (Tlacotalpán: Tip. La Reforma, 1901). *Perfiles del terruño* (Profiles of My Native Land) (México: Talls. de Ramón Araluce, 1902). *Cuentos costeños* (Short Stories of the Coast), prologue by José López Portillo y Rojas (Barcelona; Sopena, 1905). *Por mi heredad* (Through My Heritage) (México: Tip. La Europea, 1906). *Cuentos y tipos callejeros* (Short Stories and Street Characters) (Veracruz: Tip. del Gobierno del Estado, 1922).

BIBLIOGRAPHY: John S. Brushwood, *Mexico in its Novel* (Austin: University of Texas Press, 1966), p. 160. Rafael Delgado, prologue to *Una docena de cuentos de Cayetano Rodríguez Beltrán* (México: Talls. de Ramón Araluce, 1900), pp. 7-13. Julio Jiménez Rueda, *Historia de la literatura mexicana* (México: Botas, 1957), p. 306. José López Portillo y Rojas, prologue to *Cuentos Costeños de Cayetano Rodríguez Beltrán* (Veracruz: Talls. Gráficos del Gobierno del Estado, 1954), pp. 9-17.

BAUDELIO GARZA

RODRIGUEZ Chicharro, César (1930-), poet, essayist, university professor, and editor. Born in Madrid on July 11, 1930, Rodríguez Chicharro came to Mexico City in 1940 as an exile and adopted Mexican citizenship. He taught at the universities of Guanajuato (Mexico), Zulia (Venezuela), and at the Universidad Veracruzana, where he directs the magazine *La Palabra y el Hombre* (The Word and the Man). His book of poetry *Eternidad es barro* (Eternity Is Mud) protests war and men's indifference. His books of essays on literature have received various awards, among them the second prize of the Concurso Cervantino del Instituto Tecnológico y de Estudios Superiores of Monterrey, Nuevo León. His essays on the Mexican indigenous novel have received critical acclaim.

WORKS: Poetry: *Eternidad es barro* (Eternity Is Mud) (México: Los Presentes, 1955). *Aventuras del miedo* (Adventures of Fear) (Maracaibo: Universidad del Zulia, 1962). *Finalmente* (Finally) (México: Papel de Envolver, 1983). *En vilo* (In Suspense) (México: Universidad Autónoma de Chiapas, 1985). Essays: *Estudios literarios* (Literary Studies) (México: Universidad Veracruzana, 1963). *Escritura y vida: Ensayos cervantinos* (Writing and Life: Cervantian Studies) (México: UMAM, 1977). *Estudios de literatura mexicana* (Studies in Mexican Literature) (México: UNAM, 1983).

BIBLIOGRAPHY: Antonio de Espina, "Caminos de la poesía. *Eternidad es barro*," in *Tiempo* (June 6, 1955): 2. Manuel Lerín, Review of *Estudios literarios*, in *Revista Mexicana de Cultura* 891 (April 26, 1964): 15. Gustavo Sáinz, ìeview of *Estudios literarios*, in *México en la Cultura* 781 (March 8, 1964): 7.

NORA EIDELBERG

RODRIGUEZ Galván, Ignacio (1816-1842), poet, playwright, diplomat. Rodríguez Galván was born in Tizayuca, today the State of Mexico, on March 12, 1816. The poverty of his childhood and youth forced him to move to Mexico City, where he went to work in his uncle's bookstore. There he learned Latin and became familiar with the writers of his time. He began to translate and imitate French and Italian poets; he translated the classics; he read the Bible. However, he preferred Spanish literature. He was on his way to South America to represent his country when he made a stop in La Habana; there yellow fever took his life on July 25, 1842.

Rodríguez Galván has been recognized as an excellent romantic poet, but as a playwright he was not as good nor as successful; however, he gets credit for writing the first Mexican romantic play, *Muñoz, visitador de México* (Muñoz, Inspector of Mexico). At the age of nineteen he became a member of the Academia de San Juan. Both in his poetry and in his dramas Moctezuma and Cuauhtémoc have a prominent place. His poem "Profecía de Guatimoc" (Prophecy of Guatimoc) was considered by Marcelino Menéndez y Pelayo as "the masterpiece of Mexican romanticism." His favorite poetic themes were love, glory, fatherland, and faith. His brother, Antonio, published Ignacio's iyrical poems and plays in two volumes in 1851.

WORKS: Early Works: *Teatro escogido* (Selected Theater) (n.d.). *El Recreo de las familias* (Families' Recreation) (n.d.). "El Año nuevo" (New Year's) (n.d.). Poetry: "La profecía de Guatimoc" (Prophecy of Guatimoc) (n.d.). "El ángel caído" (The Fallen Angel) (n.d.). "Mora" (n.d.). "Eva ante el cadáver de Abel" (Eve before Abel's Dead Body) (n.d.). Narrative: "La hija del Oidor" (The Inspector's Daughter) (n.d.). "Manolito Pisaverde" (n.d.) "La procesión" (The Procession) (n.d.). "Tras un mal nos vienen ciento" (After One Evil, One Hundred More Come upon Us) (n.d.). Theater: *La capilla* (The Chapel) (1837). Muñoz, visitador de México (Muñoz, Inspector of Mexico), staged in Mexico (Sept. 27, 1838). *El privado del virrey* (The Viceroy's Favorite) (1842). Monterde mentions two more plays: *La Señorita* (The Young Lady) and *El teatro moderno* (Modern Theater) which, according to Antonio Magaña Esquivel, are fragments of an unfinished play *El Angel de la Guarda* (The Guardian Angel). Enrique de Olavarria y Ferrari mentions *El Precito*, which a friend of his saw.

BIBLIOGRAPHY: Carlos González Peña, *Historia de la literatura mexicana* (México: Porrúa, 1981), pp. 152-53. Raimundo Lazo, *Historia de la literatura hispano-americana, El siglo XIX* (México: Porrúa, 1976), pp. 14, 48, 49, 60, 269. Antonio Magaña Esquivel and Ruth S. Lamb, *Breve historia del teatro mexicano* (México: Eds. de Andrea, 1958), pp. 65-66. María del Carmen Millán, *Literatura mexicana* (México: Editorial Esfinge, 1962), pp. 139-40. Enrique de Olavarria y Ferrari, *Reseña histórica del teatro en México, 1538-1911* (México: Porrúa, 1961), vol. 1, pp. 366-407. Francisco Sosa, *Bibliografías de mexicanos distinguidos* (México: Oficina Tipográfica de las Secretaría de Fomento, 1884), pp. 902-05.

JOSEPH VELEZ

ROJAS Garcidueñas, José (1912-1981), critic. Rojas Garcidueñas was born in Salamanca in Guanajuato on November 16, 1912, and died in Mexico City on July 1, 1981. He received degrees in law and literature from UNAM and taught at various institutions of higher learning in Mexico as well as in the United States.

Rojas Garcidueñas also managed the Symphonic Orchestra of Mexico, was head of the Foreign Information Department of the Ministry of Foreign Relations, as well as consulting attorney for the general secretary for Borders and International Waters. He taught classes on Mexican, Spanish American, and Spanish literature, on art history, Mexican history, and world history. Rojas Garcidueñas was elected a regular member of the Academia Mexicana de la Lengua in 1961. Although his major interest was in the Colonial period in arts and letters, his best-known work was in collaboration with John S. Brushwood, *Breve historia de la novela mexicana* (A Brief History of the Mexican Novel).

WORKS : *El teatro de la Nueva España en el siglo XVI* (Theater in New Spain in the Sixteenth Century) (México: Imp. de Luiz Alvarez, 1935). *Don Carlos de Sigüenza y Góngora, erudito barroco* (Don Carlos de Sigüenza y Góngora, Barroque Genius) (México: Eds. Xochitl, 1945). *Gilberto Owen y su obra* (San Luis Potosí: S.L.I., 1954). *Bernardo de Balbuena. La vida y la obra* (México: Imp. Universitaria, 1958). *Breve historia de la novela mexicana* (A Brief History of the Mexican Novel), with John S. Brushwood (México: Eds. de Andrea, 1959). *El mar territorial y las aguas internacionales* (The Territorial Sea and International Waters) (México: Ediciones de la Paloma, 1960). *José Bernardo Couto* (Xalapa, Veracruz: Universidad Veracruzana, 1964). *Don Quijote en las artes de México* (Don Quijote in the Arts of Mexico) (México: n.p., 1968). *El Ateneo de la Juventud y la Revolucion* (The Ateneo de la Juventud and the Revolution) (México: n.p., 1979).

BIBLIOGRAPHY: Aurora M. Ocampo de Gómez and Ernesto Prado Velázquez, *Diccionario de escritores mexicanos* (México: UNAM, 1967), pp. 333-35. *Enciclopedia de México*, no editor (México: SEP, 1988), vol. 12, pp. 7011-12.

                                                        TERESA R. ARRINGTON

ROJAS González, Francisco (1904-1951), short story writer novelist, and critic, was born March 10, 1904, in Guadalajara, Jalisco. He was in the diplomatic service from 1920 to 1935 and was posted in Guatemala, as well as in the United States. He then returned to pursue his earlier interest in ethnography and published many studies on Mexican Indians. He was also an active contributor to many literary journals and was the editor of *Crisol*. He died in his native city on December 11, 1951.

Primarily a short story writer, Rojas González oriented his fiction toward themes involving Indians and the poor. His style is characterized by first-person narrative in the simple speech of his protagonists. In *El diosero* (Medicine Man), a collection of short stories published after his death, the title story examines the customs of an Indian medicine man, his efforts to influence nature (stop the rain), and also focuses on his marital customs with the eye of an anthropologist. Other stories deal with social customs of the poor (death rituals, for example), and government officials and clergy are often portrayed as unsympathetic characters. His novel *La negra Angustias* (Black Angustias) is important because of its portrayal of the role women played in the Mexican Revolution.

WORKS: *Historia de un frac* (Tale of a Formal Coat) (México: Libros Mexicanos, 1930). *Y otros cuentos* (And Other Stories) (Méico: Ediciones Libros Mexicanos,

1931). *Sed* (Thirst) (México: Editorial Libros Mexicanos, 1931). *El pajareador, Ocho cuentos* (Bird Hunter, Eight Stories) (México: A. del Bosque Impresor, 1934). *Chirrn y la celda 18, Viñetas de Oscar Frías* (Chirrn and Cell 18, Vignettes of Oscar Frías) (México: B. Costa-Amic, 1944). *La negra Angustias* (Black Angustias) (México: Edición y Distribución Ibero Americana de Publicaciones, 1944). "El cuento mexicano, su evolución y sus valores" (The Mexican Short Story, Its Development and Value), in *Tiras de Colores* 34-35 (Nov. 1944): 23-30. *Cuentos de ayer y de hoy* (Stories of Yesterday and Today) (México: Edit. Arte de América, 1946). *Lola Casanova* (Lola Casanova) (México: Edición y Distribución Ibero Americana de Publicaciones, 1947). *La última aventura de Mona Lisa* (The Last Affair of Mona Lisa) (México: n.p., 1949). *Antología del cuento americano contemporáneo*, (Anthology of the Contemporary Latin American Short Story) (México: SEP, 1952). *El diosero* (Medicine Man) (México: FCE, 1952). *Etnografía de México, Síntesis monográficas* (Ethnography of Mexico, Monographs) (México: UNAM, 1957.

BIBLIOGRAPHY: John S. Brushwood, *Mexico in Its Novel* (Austin: University of Texas Press, 1966), pp. 13-14, 228-29, 231. Raquel Chang-Rodríguez, "Trayectoria y símbolo de una revolucionaria: *La negra Angustias* de Francisco Rojas González," in - *Revista de Crítica Literaria Latinoamericana* 7, 13 (1981): 99-104. Jeanne Joanne Hochstatter, "Los cuentos y las novelas de Francisco Rojas González," thesis, UNAM, 1963. Francisco Monterde, "Los cuentos de Rojas González," in *Espiral* 122 (April 1972): 82-86. Aurora M. Ocampo de Gómez and Ernesto Prado Velázquez, - *Diccionario de escritores mexicanos* (México: UNAM, 1967), pp. 335-36. Joseph Sommers, *Francisco Rojas González: exponente literario del nacionalismo mexicano*, translated by Carlos Antonio Castro (Xalapa: Universidad Veracruzana, 1966).

KENNETH M. TAGGART

THE ROMANTIC THEATER IN MEXICO. The nineteenth century was a time of ideological, military, political, and economic turbulence, both in Europe and the New World, more particularly in Spanish America. In the first quarter of the nineteenth century most Hispanic colonies gained their independence from Spain. Among these colonies was Mexico, although it remained under some kind of absolutism throughout the rest of the century, with only brief periods of Republican government when the ideals of liberty and freedom prevailed. As Orlando Gómez Gil notes, it was during the times of greater political and revolutionary restlessness that romanticism appeared in Mexico, offering the appropriate means of literary expression to men who fought against tyranny, and suffered imprisonment or exile because of their political views.

The American countries share the universal romanticism triumphant in the Nineteenth Century. The new romantic conception of the world and life transcends all artistic works. Hugh Holman states that "the term designates a literary and philosophical theory which tends to see the individual at the very center of life and all experience." Most critics agree that it is almost impossible to define to everyone's satisfaction the term *romanticism*. However, two different considerations can throw some light on this matter. Holman asserts that the first consideration includes a series of contrasts of romanticism with other literary tendencies: its greater emphasis on character (as compared with emphasis on plot); its looser structure; its freer employment of imagination; its greater variety of style; its readiness to admit the humorous and even the grotesque. Then, Holman indicates that the second consideration includes opinions of renowned writers or critics such as Victor Hugo, for whom romanticism was "liberalism in literature"; or the German poet Heinrich Heine, who thought romanticism was a "revival of medievalism in art, letters, and life"; or the English critic Walter Pater, who thought that "the addition of strangeness to the beauty constituted the romantic temper"; or the American transcendentalist, Dr. F. H. Hedge, who was of the opinion that "the essence of romanticism was aspiration having its origin in wonder and mystery." In addition to these, romanticism has been defined as "the predominance of imagination over reason and formal rules and over the sense of fact or the actual."

With these principles in mind, it is important to remember that, at the beginning, romanticism in Hispanic America followed the general characteristics of European romanticism; the Mexican writers followed the same trends. The early influences on Mexican writers were English and Italian; later the Spanish playwrights influenced the Mexican dramatists, particularly the Duque de Rivas (Duke of Rivas), Antonio García Gutiérrez, and José Zorrilla, as noted by Julio Jiménez Rueda. Rodolfo *Usigli, a Mexican dramatist and critic, has said, "It is then that the young country leaps from the Middle Ages to Romanticism employing French and Byronian spurs for lyric poetry and Spanish spurs for the theater."

It was the good fortune of Ignacio *Rodríguez Galván (1816-1842) to be the initiator of romanticism in Mexico with his play *Muñoz, Inspector of Mexico* (September 27, 1832). "His opposite in life and works is Fernando *Calderón (1809-1845), a Romantic of the type who overdo themselves at the banquet table, adorned in French style with geographical exoticism and the author of *The Tournament* (June 18, 1839), *Herman, or The Return of the Crusade* [sic] (May 12, 1842), and *Ann Boleign* [sic]." On the other hand, Manuel José Othón (1858-1906) as a dramatist seems to be influenced by José Echegaray in works like *Herida en el corazón* (Wound in the Head) (November 14, 1877), *La sombra del hogar* (The Shadow of Home) (May 11, 1878), *Después de la muerte* (After Death) (October 14, 1886), *El último capítulo* (The Last Chapter) (October 9, 1905). It should be noted that romanticism appeared in Spain in the work of Larra (1834), and very slowly arrived in the old Colony at the time when it was about to disappear in the European countries that gave it birth: Germany, England, France, Italy. It is important to note that with the introduction of romanticism, a curious phenomenon takes place; this phenomenon will cause the existence of two camps in Mexico: the nationalist interpretation and the exotic expression. Rodriguez Galván's *Muñoz, Inspector of Mexico* and later Alfredo Chavero's *Xóchitl* and *Quetzalcóatl* may represent the nationalistic preferences, while Fernando Calderón's *The Tournament, Herman or The Return of the Crusader*, and *Anne Boleign* represent the exotic.

*Peón y Contreras, considered romantic nationalist and conservative, adapted to his theater themes similar to those used in his poetry: honor, chivalry, passions, religious remorse, ardent love, passionate reveries, and fatal disillusions, employing mechanisms similar to those used by European romantics.

This has been aptly pointed out by Antonio Magaña Esquivel and Ruth S. Lamb.

Concerning style, romanticism in Mexico shows two aspects that can be identified as neo-classic romanticism and neo-classic modernist romanticism. Here, too, Fernando Calderón and Rodríguez Galván represent the first aspect; José Peón Contreras and Manuel *Acuña, for instance, represent the second aspect.

The temperament of dramatists usually dictates the emphases they choose for their plays. Ignacio Rodríguez Galván stresses the facial features of his protagonist in *Muñoz, Inspector of Mexico* to such an extent that he falls into conventionalisms. José Peón y Contreras stresses honor and passion; José María *Vigil stresses romantic conflicts and sentimentality in, for instance, *El demonio del corazón* (The Heart's Demon); Isabel *Prieto de Landázuri, a Spanish woman raised in Mexico, describes the romantic melancholy, crying, sensitive poet Carlos in *Las dos flores* (The Two Flowers); Carlos Hipólito Serán shows an antiromantic attitude in *Ceros Sociales* (Social Zeroes). Julio *Jiménez Rueda considers Fernando Calderón and Ignacio Rodríguez Galván representatives of Mexican romaticism during its period of passionate exaltation; Fernando Calderón's play *The Tournament* is somber, but *Herman or the Return of the Crusader* is even more somber.

Other dramas with special emphases are: Pataleón *Tovar's *Una deshonra sublime* (Sublime Dishonor), with excessive sentimentalism, asides, tears and sobs; José Tomás *Cuéllar's *Deberes y Sacrificios* (Duties and Sacrifices), which stresses sentimental love and unfaithfulness. Antonio Magaña Esquivel considers this an "ultraromantic drama." Niceto *Zamacois' *El Jarabe* (The Syrup) adds a humorous emphasis. He describes his drama as "a work of Mexican customs, funny, pleasing, comical, satirical, and of laughter, written to do away with ill humour, a legacy left to us by our father Adam because he wanted to satisfy a foolish desire." Even Fernando Calderón's *A ninguna de las tres* (To None of the Three) criticizes, with a kind of healthy humor, poorly guided female education and imported fashions. It should be remembered that, at the end of the wars for independence, the country was left in extreme poverty, and after eleven years of political and military upheavals, the state of the arts was in a very poor condition. Perhaps because of this situation, the ideas normally associated with romanticism were embraced with enthusiasm, and after a few attempts at creating a national literature, a few dramas appeared expressing a renewed desire for freedom, as in Joaquín *Fernández de Lizardi's second part of *El Negro Sensible* (The Sensitive Black) (1825). However, it was in 1838, with the representation of Rodríguez Galván's *Muñoz, Inspector of Mexico*, that the romantic theater came into being. The very next year, Fernando Calderón's *The Tournament* (1839) represented the exotic element of the romanticism practiced in Mexico.

Other dramatists contributed to the development of the romantic theater: Guillermo *Prieto's *El Susto de Pinganillas* (Pinganillas' Scare), dramatic caprice with the students of Colegio de San Ildefonso (March 19, 1843); *A mi Padre* (To My Father), monologue in verse (Mexico, n.d.); *Patria y Honra* (Fatherland and Honor), drama in three acts (Mexico, n.d.); and *Alonso de Avila* (Teatro Principal, Mexico, May 1, 1842). Isabel Prieto de Landázuri's *Las dos flores* (The Two Flowers), drama in four acts and in verse (Mexico, 1861); and *Los Dos Son Peores* (The Two Are Worse), drama in three acts and in verse (Teatro Principal, Guadalajara, December 19, 1861); José T. Cuéllar's *Deberes y Sacrificios* (Duties and Sacrifices), drama in three acts and in verse (National Theater of Mexico, (October 18, 1855); Manuel Acuña's *El Pasado* (The Past), dramatic essay in three acts (Teatro Principal, May 9, 1872). José Peón y Contreras, the greatest Mexican romantic, belongs to the last part of romanticism, just like Manuel Acuña, and both produced romantic works in the last quarter of the nineteenth century. Peón y Contreras was a prolific writer, but only three of his plays will be mentioned here: *La Hija del Rey* (The King's Daughter) (National Theater of Mexico, April 27, 1876); *Antón de Alaminos* (Teatro Principal of Mexico, December 7, 1876); and *Gil González de Avila* (Teatro Principal of Mexico, February 20, 1876).

Alfredo Chavero was another prolific writer but only his most nationalistic plays are included here: *Xóchitl*, drama in three acts and in verse (Teatro Principal, September 26, 1877); *Quetzalcóatl*, tragic essay in three acts and in verse (Teatro Principal, March 24, 1878). The works by Manuel José Othón were presented mostly in San Luis Potosi; the following are only a few representative plays by this author: *Después de la muerte* (Ather Death), drama in three acts and in verse (Teatro Alarcón, San Luis Potosí, December 30, 1883); *Lo que hay detrás de la dicha* (What Lies behind Bliss), drama in three acts (Teatro Alarcón, San Luis, Potosi, October 14, 1886); and *El Ultimo Capítulo* (The Last Chapter), original work (Teatro de la Paz, San Luis Potosi, October 9, 1905).

It is significant that not a few of the romantic dramas were represented in Guadalajara, Zacatecas, San Luis Potosí, and even in Mérida, Yucatán. It seems clear that the period between 1838, the year of the representation of the first romantic play, and 1883, the representation of Manuel José Othón's play was a time of almost constant political and military struggle, either internally or internationally. Four events stand out: the War with the United States over Texas and other territories; the Juárez government and the Constitutional reforms; the short-lived Empire of Maximilian; and the Porfirio Díaz dictatorship, which lasted until 1910. Nevertheless, during the brief lapses of peace, the fine arts flourished and so did the Mexican romantic drama, except for the duration of the Empire when European authors were favored, and other genres gained popularity, such as the opera and *zarzuela*. These genres were also popular in the days of the Díaz dictatorship, at least in Mexico City.

Regarding, more specifically, themes and sources of inspiration, Mexican romantic playwrights seemed to go in two different directions, but not exclusively. That is to say, any given author might be inclined to follow European patterns and sources, but he might also exhibit some nationalistic tendencies. A good representative of this type of writing is Fernando Calderón, who was accused of not using national themes since he "dreamed of castles, minstrels, sturdy knights, tournaments and jousts, troubadours and well-guarded ladies inclined to love." This means that he was familiar with the French theater and he was knowledgeable of the Middle Ages; he sought for his theater, wherever he could find them, extraordinary subjects surrounded by the prestige of legend or history. It is not surprising, then, that his knightly plays deal with subjects typically romantic.

Orlando Gómez Gil, on the other hand, points out that "romanticism introduced American nature into the works; employed the Indians and the Mestizo (half-breed) as literary characters; and used local history as themes for some plays." This was the case of Guillermo *Prieto, who expressed his patriotic feelings, and those of many of his contemporaries, in plays such as *Patria y Honra* (Fatherland and Honor) and *Los tres boticarios* (The Three Pharmacists). Guillermo Prieto's life was as romantic as his literary production. He sided with Benito Juarez's cause, and fought for liberty and for a better Mexico.

Ignacio Rodríguez Galván "is a romantic because of his work and his very life; his desire for evasion, however, does not go beyond the borders of his Country." In this he is contrasted with Calderón, who took subjects from universal history, while Rodriguez Galván received his inspiration from legends, traditions, and colonial episodes which he adapted, freely, to the romantic taste. He viewed the American land and man as being rather consubstantial.

Another way to compare Calderón and Rodríguez Galván is by observing how they treat their subject matter. Calderón's *To None of the Three* places him inside and outside of romanticism, as if to make fun of it in a truly nationalistic discernment. On the other hand, Rodriguez Galván does not totally adhere to historical truth but allows his romantic fantasy to fly, thus creating dramatic situations of undeniable merit. Although he was "reported to be the initiator of romanticism in Mexico, he envelops this new soul of expression in a national and rhythmical body, and offers the first example of sober and controlled assimilation of a foreign school."

Other romantic writers fell into the excesses of the school; for instance, José María Vigil used native themes but in all of his works the action is expressed emphatically, and the romantic and sentimental conflict is exaggerated; José *Rosas Moreno deals with a controversial topic, the supposed love affair of Juana Inés de Asbaje--before becoming Sor Juana Inés de la Cruz--with the Count of Mancera, in his play *Sor Juana Inés de la Cruz*; then, in *Netzahualcóyotl, the Acolhuacan Poet*, he goes even farther back into history to find nationalistic themes for his romantic works. *Olavarría y Ferrari, in his *Reseña Histórica del Teatro en México* (Historical Review of the Theater in Mexico), devotes almost two-thirds of his three volumes to the review of operas and *zarzuelas* which were so popular, especially during the Díaz regime. There were many other attractions to distract the public, however, including American performers, circus functions, and the ascension of several men, at various times, in hot air balloons. Nevertheless, the romantic theater refused to die, although it was displaced from the capital and had to move to the provinces, as has been stated.

Several critics give different dates for the demise of the romantic theater. Perhaps it could safely be said that by 1886, the Mexican romantic theater came to its end. It is true that some romantic playwrights continued to produce quality plays, but it was time for another type of drama. Just as there were romantic writers who lived through the modernism period and were not affected by it, so Eduardo *Gorostiza lived through the romantic period without being affected in his works by it. Gorostiza has been credited with reviving the theater in Mexico, but he remained a classicist.

For Usigli, the romantics provided some sense of direction in the theatrical production during a period of chaos, which he describes as "thirty years of theatrical activity without any direction or any school, with the exception of the Romantics, in which some writers produce innumerable works which are not published and which are lost in the wanderings of the theatrical archives."

It is Octavio Valdés who best summarizes the role of romanticism in Mexico: "I have said that the forty years beginning with the death of Lizardi to the death of Maximiliam (1827-1867) represent the period or romantic rage in Mexico, but it is necessary to remember that this school had a long twilight, in Mexico and in all of the Iberian America. In fact, it extended itself-- atenuated--even into the end of the century."

BIBLIOGRAPHY: Emilio Carilla, *El romanticismo en la América Hispánica*, vol. 2 (Madrid: Editorial Gredos, 1975), p. 306. Guillermo Díaz-Plaja and Francisco Monterde, *Historia de la literatura española e historia de la literatura mexicana*, 7th ed. (México: Porrúa, 1968), p. 503. María Edmée Alvarez, *Literatura mexicana e hispanoamericana* (México: Porrúa, 1971), p. 232. Orlando Gómez Gil, *Historia crítica de la Literatura Hispanoamericana* (New York: Holt, Rinehart and Winston, 1968), p. 261. Manuel Pedro González, *Trayectoria de la novela en México* (México: Botas, 1951), p. 41. Carlos González Peña, *Historia de la literatura mexicana. Desde los orígenes hasta nuestros días* (México: Porrúa, 1981), p. 161. C. Hugh Holman, *A Handbook to Literature*, 4th ed. (Indianapolis: Bobbs Merrill Education Publishing, 1981), p. 394. Julio Jiménez Rueda, *Letras mexicanas en el siglo XIX* (México: FCE, 1944), p. 93. Antonio Magaña Esquivel and Ruth S. Lamb, *Breve Historia del Teatro Mexicano* (México: Eds. de Andrea, 1958). Francisco Monterde, *Bibliografía del Teatro en México* (New York: Bud Franklin, 1970), pp. i-iv. Enrique de Olavarría y Ferrari, *Reseña Histórica del Teatro en México*, vol. 1 (México: Porrúa, 1961), p. 181. Rodolfo Usigli, *Mexico in the Theater*, translated with an introduction by Wilder Scott (University, Miss.: Romance Monographs, Inc., 1976), p. 81.

JOSEPH VELEZ

ROMERO, José Rubén (1890-1952), poet, novelist, and short story writer. Romero was born in Cotija de la Paz, Michoacán. He worked for the newspaper *El Universal* in Mexico City and in 1930 was appointed Mexican consul in Barcelona. Later he became ambassador to Brazil (1937) and to Cuba (1939). *Apuntes de un lugareño* (Notes of a Villager) (1932) was his first novel. It is here that he firmly established his style in describing rural and small-town environments. This mode of writing has become known as regionalism. *Desbandada* (Disbandment) (1934) and *El pueblo inocente* (The Innocent Town) (1934) both are typical regionalist novels and show his preference for small-town backgrounds. Here people and their follies can be dissected more easily than in the big city where it is easier to hide from others.

Romero is well known for *La vida inútil de Pito Pérez* (The Futile Life of Pito Pérez) (1938), a novel that follows the picaresque tradition established by *El Lazarillo de Tormes* in Spain in 1554. Through the development of his picaresque anti-hero, and through the use of humor and cynicism, Romero gives us a frank and real view of the Mexico of his time. The action takes place in a small provincial town, Santa Clara del Cobo, where Pito Pérez is developed as the main character of the novel. The situation in which Romero places his character is within a town that is hermetic, ultra-religious, and very conservative. The protagonist wants the populace to show a more human side, but eventually he loses out and ends bitter and disappointed. He finds that it is very difficult to challenge and change tradition. The fact that the townspeople are together gives them assurance in their conservatism. They do not choose a new way out, proposed by an outsider who, just by appearance, cannot be trusted. Humor is one of the strongest elements in Romero's works, and this is what makes this particular novel easier and fun to read. Some feel that this is a novel of the Mexican Revolution because of the futility in trying to change a small town. Even after the Revolution, Mexican small towns still preserve their economic, moral, political, and religious conservatism, and their interest is basically the preservation of the status quo. It thus becomes a negative social comment on rural Mexico even after the Revolution.

The picaresque structure of the novel is basically the following. (1) The protagonist tells his own story in the first person, and in his own and very picturesque popular language. In his freedom of movement he cannot settle in one place long enough to gain a social position. (2) He is a vagrant. The purpose here is to be able to move more freely from one place and from one socio-economic level to another for the purpose of observing, and making critical comments on, people, customs, and institutions. (3) He is an individual who is not in agreement with the structured form of Mexican society of his time. Consequently, he lends himself very well to contrast of Mexican society of his time. Consequently, he lends himself very well to contrast and compare the several levels of Mexican society. (4) In a sense, he feels that society owes him something. Therefore, at any opportunity he takes whatever is at hand without even asking for it. He takes money, food, and he even has an affair with the pharmacist's wife. These acts cause the people around not to trust him, just as he does not trust them; there is such a tremendous gap between the values of Pito Pérez and those of the townspeople that at the end it is virtually impossible to bring them together. Hence, the mention of futility in the title. By this time Pito Pérez has become cynical.

Throughout his novels, Romero seems to have a knack for creating rural characters, so much so that at times he creates characters who come very close to caricatures representative of small-town inhabitants such as the typical mayor, pharmacist, priest, Spanish immigrant, zealous church people, etc.

Some of his contemporaries did not show much appreciation for Romero's writing skills. For instance, Salvador Novo, in an interview with Emmanuel Carballo, makes the following statement: "Among us, Romero was the maximun buffoon of the politicians. He believed that being a clown was equal to being a novelist." Rafael F. Muñoz, in a similar interview with Carballo says: "Romero gave me some of his novels, admirably well bound. Because of their physical beauty, they occupy a preferential place in my private library. I will confess to you, however, that I have not read them."

WORKS: *Cuentos rurales* (Rural Stories) (México: n.p., 1915). *Apuntes de un lugareño* (México: n.p., 1932); *Notes of a Villager*, translated by John Mitchell and Ruth Mitchell de Aguilar (N.Y.: Plover Press, 1988). *Mis amigos, mis enemigos* (My Friends, My Enemies) (México: n.p., 1921). *El pueblo inocente* (The Innocent Town) (México: n.p., 1934). *Desbandada* (Disbandment) (México: n.p., 1934). *Alvaro Obregón* (Biography) (México: n.p., 1935). *La vida inútil de Pito Pérez* (México: n.p., 1938); *The Futile Life of Pito Pérez*, unknown translator (Englewood Cliffs, N.J.: Prentice Hall, 1967). *Anticipación a la muerte* (Anticipation to Death) (México: n.p., 1939). *Una vez fui rico* (Once I was Rich) (México: n.p., 1939). *Mi caballo, mi perro y mi rifle* (My Horse, Ny Dog, and My Rifle) (Barcelona: n.p., 1936). *Breve historia de mis libros* (A Brief History of My Books) (Havana: n.p., 1942). *Algunas cosillas de Pito Pérez que se me olvidaron en el tintero* (A Few Things Related To Pito Pérez That I Forgot in my Inkwell) (México: n.p., 1945). *Rosenda* (México: n.p., 1946). *Obras completas* (Complete Works) (México: n.p., 1957). *Cuentos y poesías inéditos* (Unpublished Stories and Poetry), compiled by W. O. Cord (México: n.p., 1963)

BIBLIOGRAPHY: John S. Brushwood, *Mexico in Its Novel* (Austin: University of Texas Press, 1966). Emmanuel Carballo, *Diecinueve protagonistas de la literatura mexicana del siglo XX* (México: Empresas Editoriales, 1965). Howard Leslie Garrison, "The Genesis of a World View as a Function of Becoming in José Rubén Romero's *Los apuntes de un lugareño*," DAI 42, 8 (1982): pp. 3619A-20A. Tamara Holzapfel, "Soledad y rebelión en *La vida inútil de Pito Pérez*," *Hispania* 58 (1975): 851-63. Walter M. Langford, *The Mexican Novel Comes of Age* (Notre Dame: University of Notre Dame Press, 1971). Rand F. Morton, *Los novelistas de la Revolución Mexicana* (México: Editorial Cultura, 1949). Joseph Sommers, *After the Storm* (Albuquerque: University of New Mexico Press, 1968).

OSCAR SOMOZA

ROSADO Vega, Luis (1873-1958), poet, novelist, and dramatist. Born in Chemas, Yucatán, Luis Rosado Vega was director of the Atheneum of Arts and Sciences in Tlaxcala and of the Historical and Archaeological Museum in Mérida. He founded and directed the publication of *Tlaxcala*. Rosado Vega penned the words to the famous song "Peregrina", put to music by Ricardo Palmerín. In his modernist poetry, his early works show the influence of poets such as Rubén Darío, Amado *Nervo and José Santos Chocano and approach the inspiration of Jorge de Icaza and Luis *Urbina. His later style developed a pessimistic tone rendered in a quiet and simple expression. He also wrote numerous regionalist articles and essays, along with legends and traditions of his native soil. He was a contributor to such journals as *La Revista de Mérida*, *El Ateneo of Mérida*, *Revista de Revistas*, *Diario Yucateco*, *El Peninsular*, *El Eco del Comercio*, *La Revista de Yucatán*, *Arte y Letras*, *Pimienta y Mostaza*, *Arte de Mocorito*, and *Crónica* of Guadalajara. He authored a number of plays and two novels, one of which, *Claudio Martín*, deals with the exploitation of the chicle worker in Mexico.

WORKS: Novels: *María Clemencia* (Mérida: Imp. Gamboa Guzmán, 1912). *Claudio Martín, vida de un chiclero* (Claudio Martín, Life of a Chicle Worker) (México: Ed. SCOP., 1938). Poetry and Short Prose: *Sensaciones* (Sensations) (México: E. Sánchez, 1902). *Alma y sangre* (Soul and Blood) (Mérida: Gamboa Guzmán, 1906). *Libros de ensueño y de dolor* (Grief and Dream Books) (Mérida: Tip. de la Revista de Mérida, 1907). *Vaso espiritual* (Spiritual Vessel) (Havana: El Siglo XX, Sociedad Editorial Cuba Contemporánea, 1919). *El desastre* (The Disaster), Yucatan subjects (Havana: Siglo XX, Sociedad Editorial Cuba Contemporánea, 1919). *Parnaso de México* (Parnassus of Mexico) (México: Enrique Fernández Granados, 1919). *El sueño de Chichón* (Chichón's Dream) (México: Talls. Gráficos de la Nación, 1929). *Explotaciones cínicas. El falso intelectualismo y el caso típico de Luis de Oteyza* (Cynical Exploitations. False Intellectualism and the Typical Case of Luis de Oteyza) (Mérida: Gamboa Guzmán, 1930). *Bartolomé García Correa, ¿Cómo se hizo su campaña política?* (Bartolomé García Correa. How Was His Political Campaign Run?) (Mérida: Gamboa Guzmán, 1930). *El alma misteriosa del Mayab* (The Mysterious Soul of the Mayab), traditions and legends (México: Botas, 1934). *En los jardines que encantó la muerte* (In Death Enchanted Gardens) (México: Botas, 1936). *Poema de la selva trágica* (Poem of the Tragic Jungle) (México: Ed. SCOP, 1937). *Amerindamaya* (Stories of the Ancient Land of the Mayab) (México: Botas, 1938). *Un pueblo y un hombre* (A Town and a Man), history of Quintana Róo (México: A. Mijares y Hno, 1940). *Lo que ya pasó y aún vive* (What Happened Already and Is Still Around) (México: Edit. Cultura, 1947). *Romancero yucateco* (Yucatan Romances) (Mérida: Edit. Club del Libro, 1949). Theater: Unpublished: "Callejeras" (Streetwalkers). "La ofrenda a Venus" (The Gift to Venus). "Nictehó" (a Mayan musical). Published: *Payambó* (A Mayan opera) (México: Talls. Gráficos de la Nación, 1929).

BIBLIOGRAPHY: Anon., "Crónica bibliográfica," *Crónica* (Guadajara, Sept. 15, 1907); "Escritores mexicanos contemporáneos: Luis Rosado Vega," *Biblos* 2 (1920): 61-62. John S. Brushwood and José Rojas Garcidueñas, *Breve historia de la novela mexicana* (México: Ed. Andrea, 1959). Domingo Couoh Vázquez, "Otro poeta que se va: Luis Rosado Vega," *Bohemia Poblana* (Dec. 1958): 2. Frank Dauster, *Breve historia de la poesía mexicana* (México: Eds. de Andrea, 1956), p. 131. *Enciclopedia*

Yucatanense, vol. 5, pp. 301-2, 484-92, 561-64, 728-29; vol. 8, pp. 782-85. Genaro Estrada, *Poetas nuevos de México* (México: Porrúa, 1916), pp. 274-76. Max Henríquez Ureña, "Los de la nueva hora: Luis Rosado Vega," in *Crónica* (Guadalajara, Oct. 15, 1907): 7-10. Juan B. Iguániz, *Bibliografía de novelistas mexicanos* (México: Secretaría de Relaciones, 1926). Amado Nervo, "Sensaciones, por Luis Rosado Vega," *Revista Moderna* 5 (Sept. 1902): 286; reproduced in *Semblanzas y crítica literaria* (México: Imp. Universitaria, 1952), pp. 126-28, and in *Obras completas* (Madrid: Aguilar, 1962), p. 364. Sixto Osuna, "A propósito de un libro," *Arte* (Mocorito, Oct. 1, 1907): 17. Manuel Puga y Acal ("Brummel"), "Sensaciones, por Luis Rosado Vega," *Revista Ilustrada* (Guadalajara, Dec. 1902): 10-11.

BARBARA P. FULKS

ROSAS Moreno, José (1838-1883). Rosas Moreno was born in Lagos, in the state of Jalisco, on August 14, 1838. He was given a classical, humanist education in Lagos, then in León, Guanajuato, and continued it at the Colegio de San Gregorio in Mexico City. He embraced, however, the liberal cause of independence and suffered persecution during the conservative administration. The death of Juan *Valle, the blind poet of Guanajuato, forgotten and impoverished, particularly affected him during this period. During the republican restoration, however, he served as deputy to the General Congress. He founded several journals and served in other modest public positions. Near the end of his life, however, Rosas Moreno was also to suffer poverty and illness, barely eking out a living from texts he wrote for school.

Of his works, he is remembered most for his fables, which were adopted as texts in primary instruction for the Republic, and republished in 1985 together with fables of *Fernández de Lizardi. Gentle in tone but strong in moral content, they became part of the common heritage of Mexicans. For this work, Rosas Moreno was praised by Ignacio *Altamirano as "a notable personality" (who) "deserves our respectful attention." The guileless ease with which Rosas Moreno expressed himself found other outlets in poetry and drama, including *Sor Juana Inés de la Cruz* (Sor Juana Inés of the Cross), a drama in verse. Rosas Moreno also wrote Mexico's first theatrical works for children, including *Una lección de geografía* (A Geography Lesson) and *Amor filial* (Filial Love).

WORKS: *Poesías* (Poems) (México: n.p., 1864); 2nd ed. (México: Imp. Libr. de Murguía, 1891). *Ramo de violetas* (Cluster of Violets) (México: n.p., 1891). Theater: *Sor Juana Inés de la Cruz* (Sor Juana Inés of the Cross) (México: Ant. Imp. de Murguía, 1876). *Un proyecto de divorcio* (A Project of Divorce) (written in 1868) (México: Tip. y Lit. de Fiomeno Mata, 1883). *¡Pobre madre!* (Poor Mother!), in *El Tiempo* (Mexico) 4, 145 (April 29, 1894): 131-32. Many works of theater were not published; they are listed with only the date of performance: *Flores y espinas* (Flowers and Thorns) (1861-1862). *Nadie se muere de amor* (No One Dies of Love) (1862). *Una mentira inocente* (An Innocent Lie) (1863). *Los parientes* (The Relatives) (1872). *Amor filial* (Filial Love) (1874). *Una lección de geografía* (A Geography Lesson) (1874). Most of the following have no listed dates of publication: *El coronel Santibáñez* (Colonel Santibanez). *La mujer de César* (Caesar's Wife). *Alrededor de la* *cuna* (Around the Cradle). *Netzahualcóyotl, el bardo de Acolhuacán* (Netzahualcóyotl, the Bard of Acolhuacán). *El premio de la virtud* (Virtue's Reward). *La escuela del bello sexo* (The Fair Sex's School) (fragment). *Fábulas* (Fables) (México: Imp. de Ancona y Peniche, 1872); new ed., *Libro de fábulas* (Book of Fables) (México: Libro-Mex, editores, 1955). *Fábulas mexicanas* (Mexican Fables), includes fables of José Joaquín Fernández de Lizardi (México: Editorial Diana, 1985, 1987).

BIBLIOGRAPHY: Ignacio Altamirano, *La literatura nacional* (México: Porrúa, 1949), vol. 2, pp. 26-27, 43-66. Heriberto García Rivas, *Historia de la literatura mexicana* (México: Textos Universitarios, 1972), vol. 2, pp. 119, 173. Carlos González Peña, *History of Mexican Literature*, translated by Gusta Barfield Nance and Florene Johnson Dunstan (Dallas, Texas: Southern Methodist University Press, 1968), pp. 281-82, 329. Julio Jiménez Rueda, *Letras mexicanas en el siglo XIX* (México: FCE, 1944), pp. 147-48. Aurora M. Ocampo de Gómez and Ernesto Prado Velázquez, *Diccionario de escritores mexicanos* (México: UNAM, 1967), p. 340.

FILIPPA B. YIN

ROSS, María Luisa (188?-1945). Born in Tulancingo, Hidalgo, María Luisa Ross was educated at the state normal school, graduating as a teacher. She also pursued classes at the Escuela de Altos Estudios (School of Higher Studies) and at the Conservatorio Nacional (National Conservatory). A very talented, intellectual, and energetic person, Ross was involved in many social and civic endeavors. She founded, for instance, the Mexican Red Cross, the radio station for the department of public education, and the Unión Femenista Iberoamericana.

She visited the United States on several occasions for professional and educational reasons. She also went on a variety of cultural tours of Mexico. At one time, in the capacity of intellectual and educator, she went to Spain as a representative of the Mexican government, attending a few conferences.

In addition to her teaching and her cultural activities, Ross began a career in journalism in 1903, publishing articles in *El Mundo Ilustrado*. She was also a contributor to *El Imparcial* and *Revista de Revistas*, important journals of the day. For many years until her death in 1945, she worked laboriously for these and other papers, especially *El Universal*. At one time, she was the editor of this prestigious journal.

Many of the primary schools in Mexico benefited from her original readings and stories of didactic purpose by using her material as texts. She also wrote poetry and copied some of her favorite texts by Spanish-speaking authors. *Cuentos sentimentales* (Sentimental Stories), with such titles as "Ilusión de amor" (Illusion of Love), "El milagro," and "La novicia" was published in 1916. Several years later, in 1923, she published *Así conquista España* (That's How Spain Conquers), based on her experiences in Spain when she served at the aforementioned conferences. This is considered her most noteworthy book. It should not be overlooked, however, that she also translated several texts from Italian into Spanish. She also wrote several plays that were performed by student groups. Although not well known outside her social group, which included Luis Urbina, María Rosa Ross made a worthwhile contribution to Mexican life and letters.

WORKS: *Rosas de amor* (Roses of Love), scenic poem, performed in Teatro Arbeu, 1917. *Historia de una mujer* (Story of a Woman), four-act play, 1918. "Andrés Quintana Roo," in *Diez civiles notables de la historia patria* (México: Sría. de Instrucción Pública y Bellas Artes, 1914), pp. 65-81. *Cuentos sentimentales* (Sentimental Stories) (México: Tip. y Rayados El Arte, 1916). "Doña Leona Vicario," in *El Universal* (Mexico) (Sept. 1921). *Así conquista España* (That's How Spain Conquers) (México: Herrero, 1923). There are no dates for the next four plays: *El mundo de los niños* (The World of Children). *Memorias de una niña* (Memories of a Little Girl). *Lecturas selectas* (Selected Readings). *Lecturas instructivas y recreativas* (Instructive and Recreational Readings). Translations: Gabriel d'Annunzio, *La Gioconda* (México: Cía. Periodística Nacional, 1918). A. de Lorde and H. Bauche, *El laboratorio de las alucinaciones* (The Laboratory of Hallucinations), in *El Universal Ilustrado* 6, 264 (May 11, 1922): 3-6. Gustavo Lenotre, "Cuando Napoleón viajaba," in *El Universal Ilustrado* 6, 271 (July 13, 1922): 44-45.

BIBLIOGRAPHY: Anon., "Quién es quién en la ciudad de México y Distrito Federal," in *Directorio Comercial Murguía de la Ciudad de México*, no editor (México: Ed. Murguía, 1925-1926). Isabel Farfán Cano, "La musa del poeta Urbina," in *Todo* (Dec. 18, 1934): 10-11. Juan B. Iguíniz, *Bibliografía de novelistas mexicanos* (México: Imp. de la Sría. de Relaciones, 1926), pp. 328-29. Ruth S. Lamb, *Bibliografía del teatro mexicano del siglo XX* (México: Eds. de Andrea, 1962), p. 108. Luis Leal, *Bibliografía del cuento mexicano* (México: Eds. de Andrea, 1958), p. 129. Antonio Magaña Esquivel, *Medio siglo de teatro mexicano, 1900-1961* (México: FCE, 1956), pp. 26, 28, 36. Francisco Monterde, *Bibliografía del teatro en México* (México: Monografías Bibliográficas Mexicanas, 1933), pp. 477-78. Gerardo Sáenz, *Luis G. Urbina, vida y obra* (México: Eds. de Andrea, 1961), pp. 57-60.

ELADIO CORTES

RUBIN, Ramón (1912-), novelist and short story writer. Born in Mazatlán, Sinaloa, on June 14, 1912, Ramón Rubín and his family moved to Spain two years later, where he spent his childhood and adolescence. He later returned to Mazatlán for study, then went to Mexico City. From 1940 to 1970 he lived in Guadalajara, and since 1970 has lived in Autlán. Although he taught literature at the University of Sinaloa and that of Guadalajara, he is best known for his prose work, some of which has been adapted for stage and screen. Rubín has also edited several reviews, including *Revista de Revistas*, *El Informador*, and *El Occidental*.

Rubín's first book, *Cuentos del medio rural mexicano* (Stories about Mexican Rural Life), sets the theme for most of his later work: life and customs in the Mexican countryside. This theme is continued in collections of stories such as *Cuentos mestizos de México* (Mestizo Stories of Mexico), *Tercer libro de cuentos mestizos de México* (Third Book of Mestizo Stories of Mexico), *Cuentos de indios* (Stories about Indians), and *Las cinco palabras* (The Five Words).

WORKS: Short Stories: *Cuentos del medio rural mexicano* (Stories about Mexican Rural Life) (Guadalajara: Imp. Gráfica, 1942). *Cuentos mestizos de México* (Mestizo Stories of Mexico) (Guadalajara: Imp Gráfica, 1948). *Tercer libro de cuentos mestizos*

(Third Book of Mestizo Stories of Mexico) (Guadalajara: Imp Gráfica, 1948). *Diez burbujas en el mar, sarta de cuentos salobres* (Ten Bubbles in the Sea, a String of Salty Stories) (México: n.p., 1950). *Cuentos de indios* (Stories about Indians) (Guadalajara: Eds. Altiplano, 1954). *Cuentos de indios, segundo libro* (Stories about Indians, Second Book) (Guadalajara: Eds. Altiplano, 1958). *El hombre que ponía huevos* (The Man Who Laid Eggs) (Guadalajara: n.p., 1961). Novels: *Ese rifle sanitario* (That Sanitary Rifle) (Guadalajara: n.p., 1948). *El callado dolor de los Tzotziles* (The Silent Pain of the Tzotziles) (México: Authors Ed., 1948). *La loca* (The Crazy Woman) (México: n.p., 1950). *La canoa perdida* (The Lost Canoe) (Guadalajara: Eds. Altiplano, 1951). *El canto de la grilla* (The Song of the Cricket) (Guadalajara: Eds. Altiplano, 1952). *La bruma lo vuelve azul* (The Fog Makes Everything Blue) (México: FCE, 1954). *La sombra del Techincuagüe* (The Shadow of the Techincuagüe) (Guadalajara: Eds. Altiplano, 1955). *Cuando el Táguaro agoniza* (When the Táguaro Agonizes) (México: Ed. Azteca, 1960). *El seno de la esperanza* (The Bosom of Hope) (México: EDIMUSA, 1964), which was filmed in a co-production with the Soviet Union. *Donde la sombra se espanta* (Where My Shadow Is Afraid) (Xalapa: Universidad Veracruzana, 1964). *Las cinco palabras* (The Five Words) (México: n.p., 1969). *Pedro Zamora, historia de un violador* (Pedro Zamora, Story of a Rapist) (México: n.p., 1983). Essay: *Lago Cajititlán* (Cajititlán Lake) (Guadalajara: Jalisco en el Arte, 1960).

BIBLIOGRAPHY: Fernando Alegría, Historia de la novela hispanoamericana (México: Eds. de Andrea, 1966), p. 260. Enrique Anderson Imbert, *Historia de la literatura hispanoamericana* (México: FCE, 1954), p. 235. John S. Brushwood, *Mexico in Its Novel* (Austin: University of Texas Press, 1966), pp. 25-26, 48. Emmanuel Carballo, *19 protagonistas de la literatura mexicana del siglo XX* (México: Empresas Editoriales, 1965), pp. 11, 13, 15, 339-57. Manuel Pedro González, *Trayectoria de la novela en Mexico* (México: Botas, 1951), pp. 382-85. Luis Leal, *Historia del cuento hispanoamericano* (México: Eds. de Andrea, 1971), pp. 98, 99-100, 107, 158; *Breve historia del cuento mexicano* (México: Eds. de Andrea, 1956), p. 140. Kessel Schwartz, *A New History of Spanish American Fiction* (Coral Gables, Fla: University of Miami Press, 1971), vol. 2, 298-99.

TERESA R. ARRINGTON

RUEDA Medina, Gustavo (1905-1959). Rueda Medina was born in Aguascalientes in 1905 and died in Mexico City in 1959. He studied at the Vera Cruz Naval School and at the Submarine School in Cartagena, Spain, ultimately achieving the rank of rear admiral in the Mexican navy. He also served in the National Congress.

Rueda Medina's literary reputation is based on two novels: *¿Quién tiene un sacacorchos?* (Who Has a Corkscrew?) and his prize-winning *Las islas también son nuestras* (The Islands Are Also Ours). The former presents in a festive tone some serious problems associated with the Mexican navy. The latter reveals the unfortunate abandonment of México's coastal islands. In both cases, the social criticisms do not constitute the overriding thrust of the text, but are by-products of the plot. Although each novel exhibits flaws typical of novice authors, Rueda Medina's flowing style, graphic descriptions, and vitality are worthy of praise.

WORKS: *¿Quién tiene un sacacorchos?* (Who Has a Corkscrew?) (México: Porrúa, 1945). *Las islas también son nuestras* (The Islands Are Also Ours) (México: Porrúa, 1946).

BIBLIOGRAPHY: John S. Brushwood and José Rojas Garcidueñas, *Breve historia de la novela mexicana* (México: Eds. de Andrea, 1959), p. 122. Aurora M. Ocampo de Gómez and Ernesto Prado Velázquez, *Diccionario de escritores mexicanos* (México: UNAM, 1967), pp. 342-43.

ROBERT K. ANDERSON

RUIZ DE ALARCON, Juan (1580-1639), one of the major dramatists of the Spanish Golden Age, born in Taxco, Mexico. Ruiz de Alarcón began his studies at the Royal and Pontifical University in Mexico City, but obtained the title of *Bachiller* in Salamanca, Spain, in 1602. After a few years in Spain, he returned to his native Mexico in 1608 where he earned the degree of *Licenciado* in civil and canon law the following year. He also filed all the necessary papers for a doctorate, but it is not known if the degree was conferred. Although he failed to obtain a teaching position at the university while in Mexico City, his legal background helped him secure a position as assistant to the corregidor (mayor). Ruiz de Alarcón returned to Spain in 1613 where, thirteen years later, he became Royal Court reporter. This position gave him satisfaction and financial security. After this, he published two volumes of his works in Spain at his own expense. His first volume includes eight plays, and the second, twelve. He died in Seville.

Because Juan Ruiz de Alarcón was small, and physically deformed in his upper torso, he endured the derisive comments of some of Spain's prominent literary figures. Through his works and achievements, he equaled and, in some aspects, surpassed his critics. It was during those years of searching for a position of distinction that Ruiz de Alarcón wrote. When he finally reached his lifelong quest, being named court reporter, he apparently lost all incentive to write. He never wrote again.

Juan Ruiz de Alarcón's contribution to Golden Age theater is unique. According to critics, Spanish Golden Age drama is characterized by an emphasis on the action, a preoccupation with the themes of "honra" and "honor," and a lack of psychological insight. Ruiz de Alarcón's theater shares the first two characteristics, but it reveals greater psychological development of the characters. Also, Ruiz de Alarcón is said to be one of the first modern dramatists to deal with morality. Writers such as Agustín Moreto, Leandro F. de Moratín, Pierre Corneille, Molière, and Ignacio López de Ayala are indebted, in one way or another, to Ruiz de Alarcón's works.

Two of Ruiz de Alarcón's best known works are *La verdad sospechosa* (True Suspect), which explores the implications of lying, and *Las paredes oyen* (The Walls Have Ears), a play with obvious autobiographical elements: despite being poor, deformed, and unlucky, the protagonist succeeds.

WORKS: *Parte primera de las comedias de don Juan Ruiz de Alarcón y Mendoza.* (First Part of the Comedies of Don Juan Ruiz de Alarcón and Mendoza) (Madrid: n.p., 1628). The first part contains the following plays: *Los favores del mundo* (The

Favors of the World), *La industria y la suerte* (Industry and Fortune), *Las paredes oyen* (Walls Have Ears), *El semejante a sí mismo* (He Who Resembles Himself), *La cueva de Salamanca* (The Cave of Salamanca), *Mudarse por mejorarse* (A Change to Better Oneself), *Todo es ventura* (Everything Is Luck), *El desdichado en fingir* (The Unlucky Pretender). *Parte segunda de las comedias del Licenciado Don Juan Ruiz de Alarcón.* (Second part of the Comedies of Don Juan Ruiz de Alarcón) (Barcelona: n.p., 1634). The second part includes the following: *Los empeños de un engaño* (The Consequences of a Lie), *El dueño de las estrellas* (The Owner of the Stars), *La amistad castigada* (Friendship Punished), *La manganilla de Melilla* (The Scheme of Melilla), *La verdad sospechosa* (Truth Suspect), *Ganar amigos* (To Win Friends), *El Anticristo* (The AntiChrist), *El Tejedor de Sevilla* (The Weaver of Seville), *La prueba de las promesas* (The Proof of Promises), *Los pechos privilegiados* (The Privileged Ones), *La crueldad por el honor* (Cruelty on Account of Honor), *Examen de maridos* (An Examination for Husbands). *Comedias de don Juan Ruiz de Alarcón y Mendoza* (Comedies of Don Juan Ruiz de Alarcón), compiled by Juan Eugenio Hartzenbusch, in *Biblioteca de Autores Españoles*, vol. 20 (Madrid: Atlas, 1852); It includes all plays attributed to Alarcón. Agustín Millares Carlo, comp., *Obras completas de Juan Ruiz de Alarcón* (Complete Works of Juan Ruiz de Alarcón), 3 vols. (México: FCE, 1957). *The Truth Suspect,* translated by Julio del Toro and Robert V. Finney, in *Poet Lore* (Boston) 38 (1927), pp. 457-530. Translated by Robert C. Ryan, *Spanish Drama* (New York: Bantam Books, 1962), pp. 135-89. *La verdad sospechose* is the only work by Alarcón to be translated into English. *Las paredes oyen,* edited by Caroline B. Bourland, 1914 (New York: Holt, 1931). *La verdad sospechosa,* edited by Arthur L. Owen (Boston: Heath, 1928). *Comedia famosa de la prueba de las promesas,* edited by Frank O. Reed and Frances Eberling (New York: Crofts, 1942). *No hay mal que por bien no venga. Cuatro comedias,* edited by Mabel M. Harlan and John M. Hill, 1941 (New York: Norton, 1956), pp. 179-323. *Teatro completo de don Juan Ruiz de Alarcón,* edited by Ermilo Abreu Gómez (México: Cía Grl. de Ediciones, 1951). *Ruiz de Alarcón, Teatro,* edited by Alfonso Reyes, Clásicos Castellanos, vol. 37 (Madrid: La lectura, 1918).

BIBLIOGRAPHY: Ermilo Abreu Gómez, "Los graciosos en el teatro de Ruiz de Alarcón," *Investigaciones Lingistícas* 3 (1935): 189-201. Antonio Alatorre, "La mexicanidad de Ruiz de Alarcón," *Anuario de Letras* 6 (1964): 161-202. Antonio Castro Leal, *Juan Ruiz de Alarcón, su vida y su obra* (México: Cuadernos Americanos, 1943). José María Castro y Calvo, "El resentimiento de la moral en el teatro de D. Juan Ruiz de Alarcón," *Revista de Filología Española* 26 (1942): 282-97. Augusta M. Espantoso-Foley, "The Problem of Astrology and Its Use in Ruiz de Alarcón's *El dueño de las estrellas,*" *Hispanic Review* 32 (1964): 1-11. José Frutos Gómez de las Cortinas, "La génesis de *Las paredes oyen,*" *Revista de Filología Española* 35 (1951): 92-105. Julio Jiménez Rueda, *Juan Ruiz de Alarcón y su tiempo* (México: Porrúa, 1939). Miriam V. Melvin, "Influencia de Plauto y Terencio en el teatro de Ruiz de Alarcón," *Hispania* 11 (1928): 131-49. Walter Poesse, *Juan Ruiz de Alarcón* (New York: Twayne, 1972). Alice M. Pollin, "The religious motive in the plays of Juan Ruiz de Alarcón," *Hispanic Review* 29 (1961): 33-44. Dorothy Schons, "Alarcón's Reputation in Mexico," *Hispanic Review* 8 (1940): 139-44. Joseph H. Silverman, "El gracioso de Juan Ruiz de Alarcón y el concepto de la figura del donaire tradicional," *Hispania,* 35 (1952): 64-69.

ALFONSO GONZALEZ

RULFO, Juan (1918-1986), short story writer and novelist. Juan Rulfo was born May 16, 1918, in the small village of Apulco, near San Gabriel (now named Venustiano Carranza), in the municipality of Sayula, Jalisco. His father died when he was six; his mother, two years later. He completed his formal education while living in an orphanage in Guadalajara. He went to Mexico City at the age of fifteen, attended some university classes, but never obtained a degree. He worked at various jobs: in the Department of Immigration (1935-1945), with Goodrich (1947-1953), the Papaloapan Commission (1955-1956), as a movie scriptwriter and television producer (1959-1962), and at the Instituto Indigenista from 1962 until shortly before his death. In 1948, he married Clara Aparicio. They had four children. He suffered from lung cancer during the latter months of his life and died of a heart attack in Mexico City on January 7, 1986.

Although Rulfo's fiction consists of fewer than twenty short stories and one novel, he is considered one of the finest Latin American fiction writers of this century. He received Mexico's National Prize for Literature in 1970 and was admitted to the Mexican Academy of Language in 1980. In 1985, he received the prestigious Premio Cervantes (Cervantes Prize) in Spain in recognition of his life work. Most of the themes and innovative elements of style are present in his short stories, which were published as a collection under the title *El llano en llamas* (The Burning Plain) in 1953. His fame, however, rests upon his novel, *Pedro Páramo*, published in 1955. This work is a landmark in Mexican literature in that it marks the close of a major focus on the Mexican Revolution, and it is the forerunner of an entirely new type of fiction in Latin American literature. His themes which are very Mexican, yet universal, are hate, love, vengeance, violence, solitude, time, and the anguish of human existence. Social themes include the Revolution, religion and the clergy, and the cacique (regional boss) system. Themes, however, are secondary in importance to his portrayal of the authentic character of Mexican people and his desire to create a work of literary value. He evokes the reality of the Mexican **campesino**, to include his simple, yet poetic speech, and, in the process (as the critic John Brushwood has said), raises this character from a merely folkloric to a mythic plane of reality. His interest in visual imagery is seen not only in his prose, but also in his published collection of photographs *Inframundo*, whose stark scenes recall the imagery of his fiction. The structure of his novel is one of his most innovative elements of style. Narration is achieved through the fragmentary recollections of the dead inhabitants of Comala. Though there is no apparent order in the arrangement of the fragments, their totality presents a social mosaic of the town of Comala where the reality of life and death are one. The transcendent nature of his fiction has been demonstrated by the number of editions of his works (over twenty-five for the novel, more than a dozen for the short stories) and by the number of languages into which they have been translated (eighteen for the novel, nine for the short stories). He is reported to have left three novels unpublished: "La cordillera" (what was considered his perennially forthcoming novel) (The Mountain Range), "Los días sin flores" (Days without Flowers), and "En esta tierra no se ha muerto nadie" (In This Land No One Has Died).

WORKS: *El llano en llamas* (The Burning Plain) (México: Letras Mexicanas, 1953). *Pedro Páramo* (Pedro Páramo) (México: FCE, 1955). *Pedro Páramo*, translated by Lysander Kemp (New York: Grove Press, 1959). "Un pedazo de noche" (A Piece of Night), in *Revista Mexicana de Literatura* 3 (Sept. 1959): 7-14. "Hill of the Comadres," translated by Lysander Kemp in *Atlantic* 212 (March 1964): 102-5. "Matilde Arcángel," translated by M. C. Shedd, in *Kenyon Review* 28 (March 1966): 187-93. *The Burning Plain*, translated by George D. Schade (Austin: University of Texas Press, 1967). *Obra Completa* (Complete Works) (Caracas: Ed. Ayacucho, 1977). "La vida no es muy seria en sus cosas" (Life Is Not Very Serious in Its Bits and Pieces), in *Texto Crítico* 3, 7 (May-Aug. 1977): 172-75. *Antología personal* (Personal Anthology) (México: Ed. Nueva Imagen, 1978). *Inframundo, el México de Juan Rulfo* (Inner World, The Mexico of Juan Rulfo) (México: INBA, 1980). *El gallo de oro y otros textos para cine* (The Golden Cock and Other Movie Screenscripts) (México: Ed. Era, 1980). *Pedro Páramo*: treinta años después," in *Cuadernos Hispanoamericanos* 421-23 (July-Sept. 1985): 5-7.

BIBLIOGRAPHY: Bertie Acker, "Los temas de Rulfo en *El llano en llamas*," in *El cuento mexicano contemporáeo: Rulfo, Arreola y Fuentes; temas y cosmovisión* (Madrid: Editorial Playor, Colección Nova-Scholar, 1984). Nicolás Emilio Alvarez, *Análisis arquetípico, mítico y simbológico de Pedro Páramo* (Miami: Ediciones Universal, 1983). John S. Brushwood, *Mexico in its Novel* (Austin: University of Texas Press, 1966), pp. 18, 28, 20-34. John Joseph Deveny, Jr., "Narrative Techniques in the Short Stories of Juan Rulfo," Ph.D. Diss., University of Florida, 1973. Paul B. Dixon, "Three Versions of *Pedro Páramo*," in *Reversible Readings: Ambiguity in Four Modern Latin American Novels* (Alabama: University of Alabama Press, 1985), pp. 60-88. Margaret Virginia Ekstrom, "The Journey-Search Motif in the Works of Juan Rulfo," Ph.D. Diss., Indiana University, 1976. Marino Fernández-Cuesta, "Juan Rulfo: Bibliografía Anotada," Ph.D. Diss., University of New Mexico, 1983. Diane Hill Foltz, "The Presentation of Reality in *El llano en llamas* by Juan Rulfo," Ph.D. Diss., University of Pittsburgh, 1971. Carlos Fuentes, "Mugido, muerte y misterio: el mito de Rulfo," in *Revista Iberoamericana* 47, 116-17 (July-Dec. 1981): 11-21. Gabriel García Márquez, "Breves nostalgias sobre Juan Rulfo," in *Inframundo: el México de Juan Rulfo*, 2nd ed. (Hanover: Ediciones del Norte, 1983), pp. 23-25. Helmy F. Giacoman, cd., *Homenaje a Juan Rulfo, Variaciones interpretativas en torno a su obra* (Long Island City: L.A. Publishing Co., 1974). José Carlos González Boixo, "Bibliografía de Juan Rulfo," in *Cuadernos Hispanoamericanos* 421-23 (July-Sept. 1985): 469-90; "Bibliografía de Juan Rulfo: nuevas aportaciones," in *Revista Iberoamericana* 52, 137 (Oct.-Dec. 1986): 1051-59; Introduction, in *Pedro Páramo*, 4th ed. (Madrid: Ediciones Cátedra, 1986), 11-60. Donald Keith Gordon, "Juan Rulfo's Elusive Novel *La cordillera*," in *Hispania* 56, 4 (Dec. 1973): 1040-41). Nila Gutiérrez Marrone, *El estilo de Juan Rulfo: estudio lingüístico* (Jamaica: Bilingual Press/Editorial Bilinge, 1978). Luis Leal, Juan Rulfo (Boston: Twayne Publishers, 1983). Grace Marie Limán, "The Death Cult: Lyric and Symbolic Unity in the Works of Juan Rulfo," Ph.D. Diss., University of California, Los Angeles, 1975. Silvia Gladis Lorente-Murphy, "Juan Rulfo: realidad y mito de la revolución mexicana," Ph.D. Diss., University of Iowa, 1985. Ilse Adriana Luraschi, "Algunos recursos estilísticos en la obra de Juan Rulfo," Ph.D. Diss., University of Pitts-burgh, 1972. George R. McMurray, "Twentieth Anniversary of *Pedro Páramo*," in *Hispania* 58, 4 (Dec. 1975): 966-67. Luis Ortega Galindo, *Expresión y sentido de Juan Rulfo* (Madrid: Ediciones José Porrúa Turanzas, 1984). Violeta Peralta and Liliana Befumo Boschi, *Rulfo: la soledad creadora* (Buenos Aires: Fernando García Cambeiro, 1975). Marta Portal, *Análisis semiológico de Pedro Páramo* (Madrid: Narcea, 1981). Hugo Rodríguez Alcalá, *El arte de Juan Rulfo* (México: Ediciones de Bellas Artes, 1965). Alberto Ruy Sánchez, "Las muchas muertes de Juan Rulfo," in *Vuelta* 10, 112 (March 1986): 54. Joseph Sommers, ed., *La narrativa de Juan Rulfo, Interpretaciones críticas* (México: SepSetentas, 1974). Kenneth M. Taggart, "El tema de la muerte en Pedro Páramo," in *Yáñez, Rulfo y Fuentes: el tema de la muerte en tres novelas mexicanas* (Madrid: Ed. Playor, Colección Nova Scholar, 1983), pp. 127-91.

KENNETH M. TAGGART

S

SADA, Concepción (1899-?), dramatist. Born in Saltillo, Coahuila, on Aug. 20, 1899, Concepción Sada studied at the Colegio Inglés in that city. She continued her study of English in the United States at Tulane University in New Orleans and in Vancouver, Canada, at the British National School. She began writing plays at a very young age, and in 1932, she started using the pseudonym Diana Compecson whenever she published. She became a part of La Comedia Mexicana, and is credited with initiating the "teatro infantil" in México, which she organized at all levels. She translated and adapted a number of children's plays, founded the Escuela de Arte Teatral, and served in administrative roles directing the cultural events in México City. Her plays include strong and passionate female characters and follow the technical styles of the Spanish Theatre.

WORKS: Cinema: *Así era el mar* (The Sea Was Like This). Theater: *El tercer personaje* (The Third Character), written in 1935, first performed in 1936 (México: Unión Nacional de Autores, 1950). *La hora del festín* (The Hour of the Banquet), written in 1936 (México: Plycsa, 1937). *Como yo te soñaba* (Just the Way I Dreamt about You,) written in 1937, first performed in the Teatro Ideal in 1938, Act I was published in *Cuatro siglos de literatura mexicana*, pp. 512-26. *Un mundo para mí* (A World for Me), written in 1937, first performed in 1938; published in *Teatro mexicano del siglo XX*, vol. 2, selection and notes by Antonio Magaña Esquivel (México: FCE, 1956), pp. 444-509. *En silencio* (In Silence), written in 1941; first performed in 1942.

BIBLIOGRAPHY: Anon, Introduction to *El tercer personaje*, "Evolución del teatro," *Boletín Teatral* 2, 42 (Oct. 15, 1954). Alyce Golding Cooper, *Teatro mexicano contemporáneo*, 1940-1962, Diss. (UNAM, 1962), pp. 22, 47, 48, 130. Ruth S. Lamb, *Bibliografía del teatro mexicano del siglo xx* (México: Ed. de Andrea, 1962), p. 110. Antonio Magaña Esquivel, *Teatro mexicano del siglo XX*, vol. 2 (México: FCE, 1956), pp. 442-43; *Medio siglo de teatro mexicano, 1900-1961* (México: INBA, 1984), pp. 36, 41, 45, 85, 100, 104, 105, 106, 120. Antonio Magaña Esquivel and Ruth S. Lamb, *Breve historia del teatro mexicano* (México: Ed. de Andrea, 1958), pp. 112, 140-41. Aurora M. Ocampo de Gómez and Ernesto Prado Velázquez, *Diccionario de escritores Mexicanos* (México: UNAM, 1967), p. 348.

EDNA A. REHBEIN

SAHAGUN, Bernardo de (1500?-1590). One of the most important early missionary-chroniclers, Sahagún was born near the end of the fifteenth century in Sahagún, León, in Spain. He studied in Salamanca, and while still very young joined the order of St. Francis. He and nineteen other missionaries arrived in New Spain in 1529. He began studying Nahuatl on the journey to New Spain with some natives who had been taken to Spain by Cortés. He continued perfecting his knowledge of the language and the culture throughout the rest of his life, spent in Mexico. He traveled through many parts of Mexico and served in several capacities for his order, chief among which was as professor of Latin in the school for the Indian nobility, Santa Cruz de Tlaltelolco, from 1536 to 1540. He also spent the last twenty years of his life at this school in various capacities. He died in the cloister of San Francisco de México in 1590.

His many books written over a period of fifty years deal with three fields of study: religion, philology, and history. Few of these works are known today. The most famous and best-known is the *Historia general de las cosas de la Nueva España* (General History of the Things of New Spain), an encyclopedia of the indigenous civilization, a compilation of information written both in Nahuatl and Spanish. The first five of the twelve books deal with religion and superstitions; the sixth and seventh, intellectual life; the eighth, social life, the ninth, the economy, the tenth and eleventh, the vices and virtues of the people, and the plants, animals, and minerals of the country; and the twelfth, the story of the conquest. It is the first systematically prepared work on all aspects of the pre-Hispanic past of the new world.

WORKS: *Historia de las cosas de la Nueva España* (History of the Things of New Spain), 3 vols. (México: Editorial Nueva España, 1946); edition of Angel María Garibay (México: Editorial Porrúa, 1956); under the title of *Suma indiana,* edition of Mauricio Magdaleno, BEU 42 (México: UNAM, 1943).

BIBLIOGRAPHY: Arthur J. O. Anderson, "Aztec Hymns of Life and Love," in *New Scholar* 8, 1-2 (1982): 1-74. Munro S. Edmonson and Douglas W. Schwartz, *Sixteenth-Century Mexico: The Work of Sahagun* (Albuquerque: University of New Mexico Press, 1974). Joaquín García Icazbalceta, "Fr. Bernardino de Sahagún," *Obras de don Joaquín García Icazbalceta* (México: Imp. de V. Agüeros, 1896). Magda Marchetti, "Hacia una edición crítica de la historia de Sahagún," *Cuadernos hispanoamericanos* 396 (1983): 505-40. Marcelino Menéndez y Pelayo, *Antología de poetas hispano-americanos*, 4 vols. (Madrid, 1927). Paul Portuges, *Aztec Birth: The Turquoise Mockingbird of Light* (Santa Barbara: Inklings, 1979). Agustín Yáñez, *Crónicas de la Conquista de México* (México: UNAM, 1939).

ANITA K. STOLL

SAINZ, Gustavo (1940-), novelist, literary critic, journalist. One of Mexico's foremost contemporary novelists, Gustavo Sainz received the Xavier Villaurrutia Prize in 1974 for his novel *La Princesa del Palacio de Hierro* (The Princess of the Iron Palace). For several years Sainz was the director of the Literature Section of the Instituto Nacional de Bellas Artes, Mexico City. Born in Mexico City on July 13, 1940, Gustavo Sainz has taught at the Universidad Autónoma de México, at the Colegio de México, and in several North American universities. He was awarded Guggenheim and Tinker Foundation fellowships in 1976 and 1980, respectively. From 1981 until 1990 he held the position of professor in the Department of Modern and

Classical Languages at the University of New Mexico. He was recently appointed professor of Spanish by the University of California at Davis.

Sainz's early short stories appeared in the Annuals of the Instituto Nacional de Bellas Artes (1959-1962) and in Emmanuel Carballo's anthology, *El cuento mexicano del siglo XX*. His first novel, *Gazapo*, published in 1965, was an insightful work on middle- and lower-class adolescence in Mexico City. He was well acquainted with the work of Vicente *Leñero and Oscar Lewis, and in this first novel he demonstrated his ability to successfully manipulate various experimental narrative techniques, such as telling the story through the use of tape recordings, diaries, letters, and telephone conversations. In *Obsesivos días circulares* (Obsessive Circular Days) the action lasts as long as it takes the narrator to read James Joyce's *Ulysses*. The novel begins and ends with the takeoff and landing of a plane. *Fantasmas aztecas* (Aztec Ghosts) is a historical novel written in fragments; it is a novel that, like Mexican history itself, proceeds by ruptures. Each Mexican historical stage or period, according to Carlos *Fuentes' vision, negates and cancels the preceding one, and in so doing, it becomes vulnerable to secret contamination by those negated traditions. Thus, although the Christianity of the conquistadores negated the pre-Cortesian theogony's concept of circular time, the latter still persists in Mexico alongside occidental linear time. Like Baroque art, *Fantasmas aztecas* does not have a center; the novel's fragmentation and circularity are very well suited to express the character's internal agony and thought process and provide as well a more encompassing and realistic view of the world in which he lives. *Paseo en trapecio* (Tightrope Walk) is narrated by a ghost that goes around his city, forever lost to him, finding and weeping with old friends who have died. It is a book with a social and political commentary about personal and political impotency in contemporary Mexico through the life of the circus. It is an allegorical novel, some critics have said, about the impossibility of resurrection. But for Sainz, what matters most is not what is said, but how it is said.

Gustavo Sainz is an original voice within the American and European traditions. In his novels he has attempted to go beyond the limits of the strictly literary; he likes to tell stories which are untellable, to narrate with an anti-narrative language, and avoids all imitations and repetitions. His work questions the concept of reality and its perception; it plays with the concept of time, chronology, space, and narrative voices and techniques. Mexico City -- with all its idiosyncrasies, problems, histories, mythologies, laws, and vitality -- is an important preoccupation. Like some of the contemporary authors he admires, Pierre Guyotot, John Barth, Julieta *Campos, Carlos *Fuentes, Claude Simon, and Salvador *Elizondo among them, Sainz makes language the central reality of his work. He aspires to create a self-portrait from all his novels, for the author to become language itself.

WORKS: Novels: *Gazapo* (México: Joaquín Mortiz, 1965, rpt., 1966, 1967, 1970, 1972, 1975, 1976, 1978); edited by Jorge Alvarez (Buenos Aires: Colección Narradores, 1969); translated to English by Hardie St. Martin (New York: Farrar, Straus and Giroux, 1968); translated to French by Léonard Vergnes (Paris: Pavillons, Robert Laffont, 1968); translated to French by Hardie St. Martin (New York: Ace, 1969). *Gazapo e autobiografía*, translated into Italian by Enrico Cicogna (Milano: Saggiatore di Alberto Mandadori Editore, 1969). *Gazapo* (México: Ediciones Océano, 1982); (México: Ediciones Grijalbo, 1985). *Obsesivos días circulares* (México: Joaquín Mortiz, 1969); epilogue by David Decker (México: Best Sellers Ed. Grijalbo, 1979; tpt. 1980, 1981, 1982). *La Princesa del Palacio de Hierro*, winner of the Xavier

Villaurrutia Award 1974 (México: Joaquín Mortiz, 1974; rpt. 1975, 1976, 1978); (México: Ed. Grijalbo, 1985); *The Princess of the Iron Palace*, translated to English by Andrew Hurley (New York: Grove Press, 1987). *Compadre Lobo* (México: Ed. Grijalbo, 1977; rpt. 1977, 1978, 1981, 1982, 1987); recordings of Voz Viva de México (México: UNAM, 1978). *Kolezka Wilk*, translated to Polish by Andrzej Nowak (Krakow-Wroceaw: Wydawnictwo Literackie, 1985). *Fantasmas Aztecas* (México: Ed. Grijalbo, 1982; rpt. 1983, 1984, 1986); (México: Literatura Contemporánea Origen Planeta, 1985). *Paseo en trapecio* (México: Edivisión Compañía Editorial, 1985). *Muchacho en llamas* (México: Ed. Grijalbo, 1988). Autobiographies: *Gustavo Sainz*, introduction by Emmanuel Carballo (México: Empresas Editoriales, 1966). *Autorretrato con amigos*, in *Revista de Bellas Artes* 11 (México: Sept.-Oct. 1966): 30-43. *Autorretrato con amigos*, in *Los narradores ante el público* (México: Joaquín Mortiz, 1967). *Self-Portrait with Friends*, translated by John C. Murchison, in *The TriQuarterly Anthology of Contemporary Latin American Literature* (New York: José Donoso and William Henkin, 1969). *Self-Portrait with Friends*, translated by John C. Murchinson, in *Iowa Review* (Spring-Summer 1976); in *Writing from the World* (Iowa: Paul Engle and Hualing Nieh, 1976). Anthologies: *Los diez cuentos mexicanos*, in *México en la Cultura* (México: Novedades, 1962). *Antología de la poesía erótica*, notes by Miguel Donoso Pareja (México: Ed. Orientación, 1972). *Literatura y sociedad*, in *Revista Mexicana de Ciencia Política* (México: UNAM, 1974). *Cuentos de vampiros* (México: Pepsa Editores, 1975). *Cuentos del diablo* (México: Pepsa Editores, 1975). *Cuentos del futuro* (México: Pepsa Editores, 1975). *Jaula de palabras* (México: Ed. Grijalbo, 1980). *Corazón de palabras* (México: Ed. Grijalbo, 1981). *Homenaje Nacional a Alfonso Reyes* (México: INBA, 1981). *Los mejores cuentos mexicanos* (Madrid: Ed. Océano, 1982). *Ojalá te mueras y otras novelas clandestinas del México de hoy* (México: Ed. Océano, 1982). *Ritos de iniciación* (Madrid: Ed. Océano, 1982). Television and Movie Scripts: *La sorpresa*, directed by Jorge Fons, Diosa de Plata Award (Producciones Marte, 1968). *El quelite*, directed by Jorge Fons (Películas Naciones, 1970). *Temas Educativos*, produced by RTC, Channel 13 (1976). "Doce monólogos," *Para gente grande*, directed by Ricardo Rocha (1979).

BIBLIOGRAPHY: Grace Bearse, "More Mexican Writers to the Fore," in *Américas* 34, 4 (July-Aug., 1982): 59. Claude Bidon, *Mythe, Langage et Société ou l'étude de la classe moyenne à travers le roman de Gustavo Sainz, La Princes del Palacio de Hierro* (France: Université Paul Valery de Montpellier Maîtrise d'enseignement de Langues Vivantes et Etrangères, 1980). Fabianne Bradu, *Le nouvel art narratif dans le roman mexicain contemporain: Gustavo Sainz, Salvador Elizondo, Fernando del Paso* (France: Université de Paris, Sorbonne, Etudes Iberiques et Latino-américaines, 1978). James Brown, "*Gazapo*, modelo para armar," in *Nueva Narrative Hispánica* 3, 2 (1973): 237-44. David Decker, "The Circles and Obsessions of Gustavo Sainz," in *Review* 18 (1976): 44-47; "Gustavo Sainz and the Recent Mexican Novel," Ph.D. diss., Graduate School of the University of Kansas (1977); "*Obsesivos días circulares*: avatares de un voyeur," in *Texto Crítico* 9 (Universidad Veracruzana, 1977): 95-116. Harry J. Dennis, "*Fantasmas Aztecas*, de Gustavo Sainz," in *Explicación de Textos Literarios* 12, 1 (1983-1984): 92-93. Manuel Durán, "¿Quién le teme a Gustavo Sainz?," *INTI* 3 (University of Connecticut): 7-19. Dorothy Farrington Caram, "Gustavo Sainz: An Analysis of 'Obsesivos días circulares'," master's thesis, Rice University, Texas, 1974. Sharyl Sydney Ferguson, "Uncontrollable Reality in the Work of Gustavo Sainz," Ph.D. diss., University of Wisconsin, Madison, 1987. César Fernández Moreno, *América Latina en su Literatura* (México: Siglo XXI Editores, 1972), pp. 162-65. Lanin A. Gyurko, "Reality and Fantasy in *Gazapo*," in *Revista de Estudios Hispánicos* 8, 1 (Jan. 1974): 117-46. Joel Hancock, "The Narrator and His Craft: Artistic Impulse and Authorial Presence in Gustavo Sainz, *Compadre Lobo*," in *Crítica Hispánica* 4, 2 (1982): 149-55; "Gustavo Sainz' *Compadre Lobo*: A Dissection of the Creative Impulse," in *Revista Canadiense de Estudios Hispánicos* 7, 2 (Winter 1983): 291-96. Karen J. Hardy, "Gustavo Sainz' *La Princesa del Palacio de Hierro*: A Three-Hundred-Page Telephone Call," in *Revista de Estudios Hispánicos* 13, 2 (May 1979). Bella Josef, "A alternativa do humor em Gustavo Sainz," paper read at the ninth congress, Sociedade Brasiliera de Lingua e Literatura, 1978. Walter M. Langford, "Gustavo Sainz (1940)," in *The Mexican Novel Comes of Age* (Notre Dame: University of Notre Dame Press, 1971). Irving Leonard, "*Gazapo*," in *Review '68* (New York: Center of InterAmerican Relations, 1968), pp. 77-80. Lina Melero, *Le theme de la nuit dans le roman de Gustavo Sainz: 'Compadre Lobo'* (France: Maîtrise d'enseignement de Langues Vivantes et Etrangères, 1979). Carolyn Morrow, *The Challenge of a Changing Society: Mexican Literature of 1965-1980*, in *Latin American Digest* 15, 3-4 (Summer-Fall 1981): 4-7. Aurora M. Ocampo, *La crítica de la novela latinoamericana contemporánea* (México: Centro de Estudios Literarios, 1973). Aurora M. Ocampo de Gómez and Ernesto Prado Velázquez, *Diccionario de Escritores Mexicanos* (México: UNAM, 1967), p. 349. Marianna Pool Madrigal, "The Image of Limited God in Two Mexican Novels: 'Hasta no verte, Jesús mío,' and 'La Princesa del Palacio de Hierro'," master's thesis, Rice University, Texas, 1980. Emir Rodríguez Monegal, *El arte de narrar* (Caracas: Monte Avila Ed., 1968), pp. 255-68. Malkah Rabell, "De cosas simples a *Gazapo*," in *Diorama de la Cultura* (México: April 3, 1966): 3. Jorge Ruffinelli, "Sainz y Augustín: literatura y contexto social," in *Texto Crítico* 8 (Universidad Veracruzana, 1977): 155-64; "La novela mexicana en los últimos años," in *Cuadernos de Marcha* 3, 14 (July-Aug. 1982): 47-60. Pedro Trigo, "*Gazapo*," in his *Narrativa de un continente en transformación* (Caracas: Universidad Central de Venezuela, 1976). Raymond L. Williams, "The Reader and the Recent Novels of Gustavo Sainz," in *Hispania* 65, 2 (Sept. 1982): 383-87. Gero Von Wilpert and Ivar Ivask, *Literatura mundial moderna* (Madrid: Editorial Gredos, 1977).

ALINA CAMACHO-GINGERICH

SALAZAR de Alarcón, Eugenio (1530-1605?). Eugenio Salazar de Alarcón was born in Madrid about 1530, attended the universities of Alcalá and Salamanca, and received a degree in law from the University of Sigüenza. He first held posts in Spain and in the Canary Islands and then was sent to Santo Domingo as examiner and then to Guatemala and Mexico as prosecutor. Phillip III appointed him to the Council of the Indies in 1601. The date of his death is not known.

He was one of three Spanish poets who spent time in New Spain in the sixteenth century, bringing polished poetic forms and practices to the New World. He was a prolific poet, as demonstrated by over five hundred pages in the manuscript of his *Silva de varia poesía*. He is particularly praised for his descriptive poetry and his erotic poetry. His *Cartas* (Letters) are masterpieces of the genre and are prominent in epistolar anthologies. He is included in the *Catálogo de autoridades* (Catalog of Authorities) compiled by the Royal Spanish Academy.

WORKS: *Silvia de varia poesía* (Miscellany of Poetry), manuscript in the Academy of History, Madrid. *Cartas de Eugenio Salazar, vecino y natural de Madrid, escritas a muy particulares amigos suyos,* with a biography by Pascual de Gayangos (Madrid: Sociedad de Bibliófilos Españoles, 1886).

BIBLIOGRAPHY: Pedro Enríquez Ureña, *La cultura y las letras coloniales en Santo Domingo* (Buenos Aires: n.p., 1936). Joaquín García Icazbalceta, prologue in *Obras de Eugenio Salazar de Alarcón,* 4 vols., (México: V. Agüeros, 1897).

ANITA K. STOLL

SALAZAR Mallén, Rubén (1905-   ). Born in Coatzalcoalcos, Veracruz, on July 9, 1905, Salazar Mallén attended school in México City. He received his law degree from the National University. From an early age, he taught at the National Preparatory School, the School of Jurisprudence, and the National University. As a journalist, he contributed short stories and articles to some of México City's most eminent journals and reviews.

This staunchly committed writer, however, is known primarily for his novelistic production. Jorge *Cuesta, for example, considered him to be "the novelist of the 'Contemporáneos'." (*See* Vanguardist Prose Fiction in Mexico.) His first novel, *Cariátide* (Caryatides), the initial chapters of which were published in serial form in the journal *Examen,* led to his incarceration on the grounds of breaching the unwritten conventions of politeness and good taste. A court ruling in his favor constituted a victory for freedom of expression and paved the way for language experimentation by such writers as José *Agustín and Sergio *Elizondo.

Salazar Mallén's trademark is his tendency to focus upon the psychological development of his characters. In perhaps his best novel, *La soledad* (Solitude), for example, he describes the ruminations and feelings of an old man during the span of a single day.

WORKS: Novels: *¿Por qué perdió el cóndor?* (Why Did the Condor Lose?) (México: El Universal Ilustrado, 1924). *Cariátide* (Caryatides) (México, 1932). *Camino de perfección* (Way of Perfection) (México: Ed. del Autor, 1937). *Páramo* (High Barren Plain) (México: Ed. Stylo, 1944). *Ojo de agua* (Spring) (México: Ed. Stylo, 1949). *Ejercicios* (Exercises) (México: Talleres Gráficos del Departamento de Divulgación de la Secretaría de Educación Pública, 1952). *Camaradas* (Comrades) (México: Metáfora, 1959). *La iniciación* (The Initiation) (México: B. Costa-Amic, 1966). *¡Viva México!* (Long Live México!) (México: B. Costa-Amic, 1968). *Soledad* (Solitude) (México: UNAM, 1972). *La sangre vacía* (Empty Blood) (México: Ed. Oasis, 1982). *El paraíso podrido* (The Rotten Paradise) (Toluca: Universidad Autónoma del Estado de México, 1987). Stories: *Dos cuentos* (Two Stories) (México: Ed. Alcancía, 1932). *El sentido común* (Common Sense) (Xalapa: Universidad Veracruzana, 1960). Play: "Estampa" (Print), in *El Maestro Rural* 1, 15 (Oct. 1, 1932): 13-17. Other Works: *Alternativas del antimperialismo latinoamericano* (Alternatives of Latin American Anti-imperialism) (México: UNAM, 1935). *La democracia y el comunismo* (Democracy and Communism) (México, 1937). *Tres temas de la literatura mexicana* (Three Themes in Mexican Literature) (México: Secretaría de Educación Pública, 1947). *Apuntes para una biografía de Sor Juana Inés de la Cruz* (Notations for a Biography of Sor Juana Inés de la Cruz) (México: Ed. Stylo, 1952). *Las ostras; o, la literatura* (Oysters; or,

Literature) (México, 1955). *Desarrollo histórico del pensamiento político* (Historical Development of Political Thought) (México: B. Costa-Amic, 1962). *La polémica chino-soviética y la revolución proletaria* (The Chino-Soviet Polemic and Proletarian Revolution) (México: B. Costa-Amic, 1965). *El Hegel de Hegel y el Hegel de Marx* (The Hegel of Hegel and the Hegel of Marx) (México: B. Costa-Amic, 1966). *Don Quijote en el siglo XX* (Don Quijote in the Twentieth Century) (México: Ed. de los Estados, 1969). *El pensamiento político en América, desde la independencia política hasta nuestros días* (Political Thought, From Political Independence to Our Days) (México: Ed. Jus, 1973). *El estado coorporativo fascista* (The Cooperative Fascist State) (México: UNAM, 1977). *Reflexiones y objecciones* (Reflections and Objections) (México: Universidad Nacional Metropolitana, 1985).

BIBLIOGRAPHY: Emilio Abreu Gómez, Introduction, *Soledad*, by Rubén Salazar Mallén (México: UNAM, 1972), pp. 5-10. John S. Brushwood, *México in its Novel* (Austin: University of Texas Press, 1966), pp. 19-21 and 217-18. John S. Brushwood and José Rojas Garcidueñas, *Breve historia de la novela mexicana*, Manuales Studium, no. 9 (México: Eds. de Andrea, 1959), pp. 134-35. Marco Antonio Campos, Introduction, *La soledad*, by Rubén Salazar Mallén (Tlahuapán, Puebla: Premiá, 1985), pp. 7-11. Edward Mullen, "Rubén Salazar Mallén's 'Cariátide': A Forgotten Chapter in Mexican Literary History," in *In Honor of Boyd G. Carter: A Collection of Essays*, edited by George R. McMurray and Catherine Vera (Laramie: Department of Modern and Classical Languages, University of Wyoming, 1981), pp. 59-66. José Luis Ontiveros, Introduction, *Paraíso podrido*, by Rubén Salazar Mallén (Toluca: Universidad Autónoma del Estado de México, 1987), pp. 7-13; "Rubén Salazar Mallén: Proscrito de los Contemporáneos," *La palabra y el hombre* 53-54 (Jan.-June 1985): 97-100. Javier Sicilia, *Cariátide a destiempo y otros escombros* (Xalapa: Gobierno del Estado de Veracruz, 1980).

ROBERT K. ANDERSON

SAN JUAN, Manuel H. (1864-1917). Manuel H. San Juan was born on October 24, 1864 in Oaxaca. Although he became a lawyer, he was forced to cut short his career because of his opposition stance he voiced through the written word. As a journalist, he dedicated himself to dealing with many of the controversial issues of the day, thus arousing heated debate among his contemporaries. He was one of the founders of *El Universal* and actively contributed to a number of other journals. By 1890, he was living in Mexico City, the hub of political, cultural, and intellectual activity for him. He held several service positions, including working in an administrative capacity for the postal service. He died August 5, 1917.

San Juan wrote and published only one novel, *El señor Gobernador* (Mr. Governor), a satirical work with a political theme. Within the framework of a realistic novel, it deals with the customs, administrative follies and episodes and opportunistic characters of the century, set, nonetheless, in a pseudo-pleasant atmosphere. Although the novel never acquired much recognition, it is of value in the sense that, as a documentary piece, it illuminates some of the problems, the characteristics and the values of Mexican life in that time period.

WORKS: *El señor Gobernador* (Mr. Governor) (México: Imp. de M. Nava, 1901)

BIBLIOGRAPHY: Mariano Azuela, *Cien años de novela mexicana* (México: Eds. Botas, 1947). John S. Brushwood and José Rojas Garcisdueñas, *Breve historia de la novela mexicana* (México: de Andrea, 1959), pp. 54-55. Luis González Obregón, Prologue to *El señor Gobernador* (México: Imp. y Encuadernación de M. Nava, 1901), pp. iii-vi. Juan B. Iguíniz, *Bibliografía de novelistas mexicanos* (México: Imp. de la Sría. de Relaciones, 1926), pp. 339-41. Joaquina Navarro, *La novela realista mexicana* (México: Cía. Gral. de Ediciones, 1955), pp. 92-95. Aurora M. Ocampo de Gómez and Ernesto Prado Velázquez, *Diccionario de Escritores Mexicanos* (México: UNAM, 1967), p. 352. Victoriano Salado Alvarez, *Memorias de Victoriano Salado Alvarez*, vol. 1 (México: EDIAPSA, 1946), pp. 274-75.

JEANNE C. WALLACE

SANCHEZ Mármol, Manuel (1839-1912). Manuel Sánchez Mármol was born in Cunduacán, Tabasco, on May 25, 1839. He studied philosophy at the Conciliary Seminary in Mérida, Yucatán, and then studied for his law degree. His early journalistic endeavors included manuscript journals and a literary society. He was soon involved with national politics, and was appointed councillor of the municipal government of Mérida. With the French invasion, Sánchez Mármol returned to Tabasco, from which site he wrote vigorous defenses of national integrity and the liberal cause. He represented Tabasco in the sixth, seventh and eighth Congresses of the Union, and secretary of justice under President José María Iglesias. Although he suffered misfortune in the revolution of Tuxtepec, he was again honored under Porfirio Díaz, being elected federal deputy and senator. He was a member of the Mexican delegation to the Second Pan-American Conference (1902); professor of national history in the National Preparatory School; and a member of the Mexican Academy. He died on March 6, 1912, and his remains were entombed in the Rotunda of Illustrious Men in Mexico City.

His novels were published late in life, thus combining his liberal and romantic philosophy with what appear to be concessions to realist influences. *Juanita Souza* (1892) and *Previvida* (A Life Foretold) (1906) are examples of the foregoing; *Pocahontas* (published in 1882) is a political satire.

WORKS: *Poetas yucatecos y tabasqueños* (Yucatecan and Tabascan Poets), in collaboration with Alonso de Regil y Peón (Mérida, 1861). *El brindis de Navidad* (The Christmas Toast), in Album de Navidad (México: Imp. de Ignacio Escalante, 1871). *Pocahontas* (San Juan Bautista de Tabasco: Tip. Juventud Tabasqueña, 1882). *¡Ave Patria!* (Hail Our Country!) (San Juan Bautistas de Tabasco: Tip. de Juan S. Trujillo, 1889). *Juanita Souza*, 2nd ed. (México: Laso y Comp. Impresores y editores, 1901). *Las letras patrias* (Patriotic Studies) (México: Ballesacá, Sucs., 1902), and in *México, su evolución social*, vol. 1, Book 2 (México: J. Ballescá y Cía., Sucs., editor, 1902), pp. 603-66. *Antonio Pérez* (México: Imp. de Francisco Díaz de León, 1903). *Previvida* (A Life Foretold) (México: Imp. de Escalante, 1906; México: Premia Editora, 1982). *El misionero de la Cruz* (The Missionary of the Cross) and *Elogio del académico José Peón Contreras* (Eulogy for José Peón Contreras), in *Memorias de la Academia Mexicana* 6 (1910): 233-55. *Obras sueltas* (Collected Works) (Villahermosa, Tabasco: Cía. Edit. Tabasqueña, S.A., 1950), contains conferences, political and literary articles, essays, and short stories.

BIBLIOGRAPHY: Heriberto García Rivas, *Historia de la literatura mexicana* (México: Textos Universitarios, S.A., 1972), vol. 2, pp 143, 207. Carlos González Peña, *History of Mexican Literature*, translated by Gusta Barfield Nance and Florene Johnson Dunstan (Dallas, Texas: Southern Methodist University Press, 1968), p. 327. Aurora M. Ocampo de Gómez and Ernesto Prado Velázquez, *Diccionario de escritores mexicanos* (México, UNAM, 1967), pp. 353-54.

FILIPPA B. YIN

SANSON Flores, Jesús (1909-1966), poet and journalist. Born in Morelia, Sanson Flores was a student at the Colegio de San Nicolás de Hidalgo. He worked with President Lazaro Cardenas in implemening the Agrarian Reform and was first secretary of the Mexican Embassy with the Spanish Republican government. Sanson Flores directed *Juventud* and *Redención*, workers' newspapers and was a member of the Carlos Gutiérrez Cruz poetic group. Jis interests were social, popular, and even revolutionary.

WORKS: Poetry: *¡Clarinadas . . .!* (Clarion Beat) (Morelia: 1928). *Puños en alto* (Fists Up) (México: n.p., 1932). *El niño proletario* (The Proletarian Boy) (México: Camara de Diputados, 1936). *Canción del odio* (Song of Hate) (México: El Mundo, 1938). *Bajo el sol de España* (Under the Sun of Spain) (México: n.p., 1939). *Hampa* (Underworld) (México: n.p., 1941). *El camino perdido* (The Lost Path) (México: n.p., 1954).

BIBLIOGRAPHY: Antonio Castro Leal, *La poesía mexicana moderna* (México: FCE, 1953), p. 370. José Luis Martínez, *Literatura mexicana siglo xx, 1910-1949*, vol. 1 (México: Ant. Libr. Robredo, 1949), p. 51; vol. 2 (1950), p. 112. Juan de Onís, "Los libros del mes," review of *Hampa*, in *Norte* 72 (México, 1942): 7. Rafael Vázquez Solorio, "Sanson Flores, bohemio transhumante," in *Siempre!* 671 (May 4, 1966): 8.

DELIA GALVAN

SANTACILIA, Pedro (1826-1910). Born on June 24, 1826, in Santiago de Cuba, Pedro Santacilia, as a child, went into exile in Spain with his father where he began his education and wrote some of his first literary compositions. He returned to Cuba in 1845 and contributed to several Cuban publications; he, along with others, founded the magazine *Ensayos Literarios*, in which he became known for his writings in poetry and prose. He was incarcerated in 1851 for his pro-independence activities in Cuba and was deported to Spain the following year. He lived in Sevilla, but shortly had to flee in 1853, traveling to New York via Gibraltar. Once in the United States he dedicated his energies both to the revolution as well as to literary endeavors. He translated the psalm of David, *Super flumina Babilonys illic flevimus . . .*, the prophet's lament for the enslavement of Israel by Babylonian tyranny. His ode "A España" (To Spain) is a continuation of his "Canto de Guerra" (Song of War), in which he shows hate for colonial despotism. He also published in the United States an annotated translation of the Italian Mazzini, *El Papa en el siglo XIX* (The Pope in the Nineteenth Century), as well as a collection of poetry entitled *El arpa del proscripto* (The Proscribed Harp) in 1856. He moved to New Orleans where he became acquainted with Juárez, at the time of his exile, and was his partisan against French imperialism of the Second Empire. Upon the triumph of the Republic, Santacilia went to Mexico, where he held many high offices, among them secretary to President Benito Juárez. Santacilia later married Juárez's daughter. Because of his influence and work for the Cuban insurgents, he was named a revolutionary agent when the Yara revolt began.

Santacilia was a man of great literary and historical knowledge. His treatise entitled *Del movimiento literario en México* (1868) became a major contribution to Mexican history. In it, Santacilia's intent is to show that the rebirth of the Republic meant a new life for literature in general.

WORKS: *Ensayos literarios* (Literary Essays), by José Joaquín Hernández and Francisco Baralt (Santiago de Cuba: La Real Sociedad Económica, 1846). *Instrucción sobre el cultivo del cacao* (Instructions on Cultivating Cocoa) (Puerto Príncipe: Imp. Fanal, 1849). José Mazzini, *El Papa en el siglo XIX* (The Pope in the Nineteenth Century), translation and notes by P. Santacilia, 2nd ed. (New Orleans: Imp. Sherman, Wharton and Co., 1855). *El arpa del proscripto* (The Proscribed Harp) (New York: L. Hansen, 1856; J. Durand, 1864). "Salmo de David" (The Psalm of David), in José María Chacón y Calvo, *Las cien mejores poesías cubanas* (Madrid: Edit. Reus, 1922), pp. 177-78; and in Rafael Stenger, *Cien de las mejores poesías cubanas*, 2nd ed. (Havana: Eds. Miraflor, 1948), pp. 170-71). *El laúd del desterrado* (The Exiled's Lute) (New York, 1858). *El genio del mal* (The Evil Genius) (México: Nabor Chávez, 1861). *Observaciones al discurso de don Joaquín Pacheco* (Observations on the Discourse of don Joaquín Pacheco) (México: Juan Abadiano, 1862). *Apólogos* (Apologues) (México: J. Fuentes and Co., 1867). *Del movimiento literario en México* (On the Literary Movement in Mexico) (México: Govt. Publ., José M. Sandoval, 1868); reprinted en *Las L.P.* (Jan.-March 1954), with prologue and bibliography by Aquiles Fuentes. *Juárez y César Cantú* (Juárez y César Cantu) (México: Govt. Publ., 1885).

BIBLIOGRAPHY: *Archivos privados de don Benito Juárez y don Pedro Santacilia* (México: SEP, 1928). José María Carbonell, "Pedro Santacilia, su vida y sus versos," in *Anales de la Academia de Artes y Letras* (La Habana) 3 (1924): 156-81. Benjamín Jarnés, *Enciclopedia de la Literatura*, vol. 5, p. 562. Raimundo Lazo, *La literatura cubana* (México: UNAM, 1965), pp. 103-6. Otto Olivera, *Breve Historia de la literatura antillana* (México: de Andrea, 1957), pp. 42, 43. Juan J. Remos, *Historia de la literatura cubana*, vol. 2 (La Habana: Cárdenas y Cía, 1945), pp. 263-70.

DENISE GUAGLIARDO BENCIVENGO

SANTULLANO, Luis A. (1879-1952), novelist, teacher, and scholar. Santullano was born in Oviedo, Asturias (Spain), on December 8, 1879, and he died in Mexico City on May 12, 1952. He studied law in Oviedo and later moved to Madrid, where he took up teaching and journalism. He collaborated in many of Madrid's newspapers, among them *El Sol*, *El Imparcial*, *La Esfera*, and *Nuevo Mundo*. He then traveled through France, England, Belgium, and finally Switzerland, where he lived a long time. Later, in the Spanish zone of Morocco he aided in the organization of schools. Like many other Spanish intellectuals, he left Spain due to the Civil War. He first went to Columbia University where he taught Spanish literature between 1939 and 1940; then he transferred to the Polytechnical Institute of Puerto Rico and remained there from 1940 to 1944. Once in Mexico, he became an official of the Colegio de México from 1944 until his death in 1952.

Santullano was a gifted writer, preoccupied with human concerns. Besides his novels, he left pedagogical essays and articles on literary criticism, as well as translations of universal masterpieces and editions of some classic Castillian authors.

WORKS: Novels: *Carrocera, labrador*, published later with the title of *Don Felipete, o la candidez* (Don Felipete or Candor) (Madrid: n.p., 1926). *Piñón* (n.d.). *Paxarón, o la fatalidad* (Big Bird or Fatality) (Madrid: Biblioteca Nueva, 1932). *Bartolo o la vocación* (Bartolo: Vocation) (Madrid: Espasa-Calpe, 1936). *Tres novelas asturianas* (Three Novels from Asturias) (México: Edit. Centauros, 1945). It includes *Paxaron, o la fatalidad*; *Telva, o el puro amor* (Telva or Pure Love); and *Don Felipete, o la candidez*. Essays: *Mirada al Caribe: Fricción de culturas en Puerto Rico* (View of the Caribbean: Friction between Cultures in Puerto Rico) (México: El Colegio de México, 1945). *Padres, hijos y maestros: Antipedagogía* (Parents, Children, and Teachers: Against Pedagogy) (México: Edit. México, 1945). *El pensamiento vivo de Cossío* (Cossío's Philosophy) (México: n.p., 1946). *Los estudiantes* (The Students). *Hacia una escuela mejor* (Toward a Better School). *De la escuela a la Universidad* (From School to the University). Foreword to Pedro Calderón de la Barca, *Teatro* (Theatre), 1945. Foreword and compiler, Tirso de Molina, *El vergonzoso en Palacio* (The Shy One at the Palace), and *El burlador de Sevilla y convidado de piedra* (Legend of Don Juan of Seville) (México: Col. Literaria Cervantes, no. 12, 1945). Editor and compiler, *Las mejores páginas del "Quijote"* (The Best Pages of "Don Quixote") (México: M. Aguilar, 1948). Editor, *Romancero español* (Spanish "Romancero") (Madrid: M. Aguilar, n.d.). Editor, *Obras completas de Santa Teresa* (The Complete Works of Saint Theresa) (Madrid: Aguilar, n.d.); includes a study of mysticism. Editor, *Místicos españoles* (Spanish Mystics) (Madrid: Biblioteca Literaria del Estudiante, n.d.). Editor, *Jovellanos, siglo XVIII* (Jovellanos, Eighteenth Century) (Madrid: M. Aguilar, n.d.). Translations: *La Eneida*, *La Iliada*, *La Odisea* (The Aeneid, The Iliad, The Odyssey); these are abbreviated versions.

BIBLIOGRAPHY: *Diccionario Enciclopédico UTEAH*, vol. 9 (México: n. p., 1952), p. 498. Eugenio G. de Nora, *La novela española contemporánea* (Contemporary Spanish Novel), 2 vols. (Madrid: Edit. Gredos, 1962), vol. 2, pp. 47-49. Federico Carlos Saínz de Robles, *Ensayo de un diccionario de la literatura* (Toward a Dictionary of Literature), 2 vols., 2nd ed. (Madrid: Aguilar, 1953), vol. 2, p. 1030.

HERLINDA HERNANDEZ

SARMIENTO, Justino (1885-1937). Justino Sarmiento was born in Tlacotepec, Veracruz, September 26, 1885. He studied in Veracruz, Jalapa, where he taught and was director of the José Miguel Macías school. He died in Veracruz on October 13, 1937.

He contributed poetry and short stories to *El Dictamen* (Veracruz) and *Revista de Revistas* (México). His best known work is a regional novel, *Las perras* (1833), where he presents the life and customs of his native state in its vernacular language.

WORKS: *Las perras* (n.p.: n.p., 1833).

BIBLIOGRAPHY: John B. Brushwood and José Rojas Garciadueñas, *Breve historia de la novela mexicana* (Mexico City: Ediciones de Andrea, 1959), p. 77. Aurora M. Ocampo de Gómez and Ernesto Prado Velázquez, *Diccionario de escritores mexicanos* (México: UNAM, 1967), pp. 356-57.

NORA ERRO-PERALTA

SARTORIO, José Manuel (1746-1829), poet and pulpit orator. Born to a poor family in Mexico City on April 17, 1746, Sartorio distinguished himself at an early age as a brilliant student of languages. After pursuing his studies at the Jesuit school of San Ildefonso until the Society's expulsion in 1767, he continued his religious training in the years that followed and was admitted to the priesthood. During his career, Sartorio occupied numerous positions within the lower ranks of the Church, among them the ecclesiastical censor of literary and dramatic works, and he refused to use his ability as a persuasive preacher to support the further dominance of Spain in the viceroyalty. As a member of the Provisional Assembly after independence, he signed the emancipation document and spoke in the national cathedral when the liberation force arrived in Mexico City. Although he was a friend of Iturbide, from whom he had received the Cross of Guadalupe, he was permitted to spend the rest of his life in Mexico without being forced into exile.

Sartorio wrote a vast number of religious works, such as sermons and prayers, and a limited number of lyric poems on secular themes. His literary production is characterized by mediocrity with the exception of his poetry honoring the Virgin Mary. It reveals a genuine sincerity on the part of the poet and is noted for its mystical qualities.

WORKS: *La parte debida a las benditas almas de los sacerdotes* (The Debt Owed to the Blessed Souls of the Priests) (México: Imprenta de los Herederos del Licenciado Don Joseph de Jiuregui, 1785). *La felicidad de México en el establecimiento de la V. Orden Tercera de Siervos de María* (The Joy of Mexico in the Establishment of the Third Order of the Servants of Mary) (México: Imprenta de Don Felipe de Zúñiga y Ontiveros, 1792). *La imagen de María triunfante de las aguas* (The Image of Triumphant Mary of the Waters) (México: Imprenta de Don Mariano Joseph de Zúñiga y Ontiveros, 1797). *Poesías sagradas y profanas* (Sacred and Profane Poems) (Puebla: Imprenta del Hospital de San Pedro, 1832).

BIBLIOGRAPHY: Carlos González Peña, *History of Mexican Literature*, translated by Gusta Barfield Nance and Florene Johnson Dunstan (Dallas: Southern Methodist University Press, 1968), pp. 119-21. Pedro Henríquez Ureña, *Estudios mexicanos*

(México: FCE, 1984), pp. 153-56. Francisco Pimentel, *Historia crítica de la Poesía en México* (México: Oficina Tip. de la Secretaría de Fomento, 1892), pp. 362-88.

JULIE GREER JOHNSON

SCHMIDHUBER de la Mora, Guillermo (1943-), playwright, essayist. Schmidhuber was born in Mexico City on October 27, 1943. He studied in Guadalajara and lived for several years in Monterrey, where he continued his education. In 1969, he went to study business administration at the Wharton School of the University of Pennsylvania in Philadelphia. He abandoned business to study literature at the University of Cincinnati, where he earned his doctorate in Hispanic literatures in 1989. He was recipient of scholarships both at the University of Cincinnati and at the University of Kansas.

Schmidhuber has been the recipient of many honors and prizes, among them the Nezahualcoyotl Award given by the Mexican Writers' Guild for his play *La catedral humana* (The Human Cathedral), the Ramón López Velarde Prize (1980) from the Government of Zacatecas for *The Heirs of Segismundo*, a play which gave him the National Award for Drama from INBA. Also in 1987, he was honored with the Letras de Oro Prize for the best play of the year for his *Por las tierras de Colón*.

In 1984, he was appointed a member of the Arts Council of the State of Nuevo León. Schmidhuber considers himself a provincial writer, referring to his years of literary formation and personal development. Yet, living in the United States, the distinguished author sees life with different colors, different nuances, which he seeks to capture in his writing. He gives conferences on the theater in various universities. He attended and participated in the Conferencia de Intelectuales de Valencia and the inaugural events of the Festival de Teatro Clásico de Mérida, both in 1987.

His first play, unpublished, was *La parábola de la mala posada* (The Parable of the Bad Inn), written in 1968. In 1974, he published *La catedral humana*, thus establishing his theatrical career. The play is distinguished by its dialogue and rich imagery. Another publication in the same year was *Nuestro Señor Quetzalcoatl* (Our Lord Quetzalcoatl), presented at the Ninth Tirso de Molina Award in Madrid. It was one of the finalists. As of 1989, Schmidhuber published some nineteen plays, many of them having been critiqued and performed.

A notable example of his work in the early 1980s is *Felicidad Instantánea* (Instant Happiness). Reminiscent of Carballido's *La zona intermedia*, the play is a moral tale, in which individual destinies are played out in a world seemingly without ethical values. The play is cathartic, in that the audience or reader can feel true empathy for the characters who undergo intensive transformations in their lives, emerging as more spiritual beings.

In 1985, *Cuarteto de mi gentedad* (Quartet of My People) was published, with a presentation made by Vicente *Leñero. It is a set of four short plays, in which the elements of fire, water, wind, and earth are motifs that unify the work. The author is concerned with moral and existential questions, as is evident in many of his other plays.

WORKS: Theater: *Nuestro Señor Quetzalcoatl* (Our Lord Quetzalcoatl) (México: Sierra Madre, 1979). "Los héroes inútiles," in *La Cabra* (UNAM) 30-32 (1981): 1-16. *Los herederos de Segismundo* (The Heirs of Segismund), introduction by Rafael

Solana (México: Fonapaz, 1982); also with an introduction by Fernando de Ita (Oásis, 1982). *Teatro de Guillermo Schmidhuber* (Theater of . . .), three plays: *Los héroes inútiles, Todos somos el rey Lear,* and *Lacandonia* (México: Eds. Cerda, 1982). "Perros Bravos" (Fierce Dogs), in *Repertorio* (University of Querétaro) 2, 2 (1982): 23-34. "Juegos Centrífugos" (Centrifugal Games), in *Repertorio* (Univ. of Querétaro) 2/2, 1982, pp. 35-66. "El robo del penacho de Moctezuma" (The Robbery of Montezuma's Plume) in *Repertorio* (University of Querétaro) 1982, pp. 42-73; also (Caracas: Cuadernos de Dramaturgia, 1987). *Felicidad instantánea/ Instant Happiness,* introduction by Alfredo Gracia Vicente (México: Author's Ed., 1983). "Fuegos Truncos," (Dead Fires), in *Fuego: valores contemporáneos* (México: Cerillera la Central, 1984). *La catedral humana* (The Human Cathedral) (México: Sierra Madre, 1984). "María Terrones," in *Estaciones* 1, 1 (Summer 1984). *Cuarteto de mi gentedad,* four short plays: "Fuegos Truncos," "María Terrones," "La ventana," and "Perros Bravos," introduction by Vicente Leñero (México: Oásis, 1985). *El día que Monalisa dejó de sonreir* (The Day Monalisa Stopped Smiling), introduction by Fernando de Toro (México: Oásis, 1987), also in English translation as *The Day Monalisa Stopped Smiling,* in *Modern International Drama* 23, 2 (Spring 1990): 79-105. "Por las tierras de Colón," in *El Porvenir* (Monterrey, N.L., Aug. 27-30, 1987). *Por las tierras de Colón* (On Columbus' Lands), introduction by Osvaldo Obregón (Chile: Eds. LAR, 1988); also (Barcelona: Salvat, 1988). Not published: "La parábola de la mala posada" (The Parable of the Evil Inn), 1968. "La mano del hombre" (The Man's Hand), 1977. "El teatro en un baúl" (The Theater in a Trunk), 1985. "El Cíclope" (The Cyclop), 1987. "El armario de las abuelas" (The Grandmothers' Closet), 1990. "El quinto viaje de Colón" (Columbus' Fifth Voyage), 1990. Essays: *La magia de la escena, 5000 años de teatro* (The Magic of the Scene, 5,000 Years of Theater), with Victor Tinoco (México: Centro Cultural Alfa, 1985). *El advenimiento del teatro mexicano* (The Advent of the Mexican Theater) (México: INBA, 1990). "Museos de México, museos y patrimonio histórico" (Museums of Mexico, Museums and Historical Patrimony), in *Museums* (UNESCO) 33, 3 (1980). "V Festival de Teatro de Caracas 81," in *La Cabra* (UNAM) 37 (1981): 21-27. "Encuentro teatral America Latina-España," in *Latin American Theater Review* 15, 2 (1982): 55-57. "Nueva dramaturgia mexicana," in *Latin American Theater Review* 17, 2 (Fall 1984). "El riesgo de ser dramaturgo," in *Journal of the Pape Museum (MBP)* (Monclova, Mexico) 1, 3 (April-June 1984): 83-88. "Teatro mexicano contemporáneo," in *Deslinde* 4, 10-11 (May-Dec. 1985). "El teatro mexicano y la provincia," in *Latin American Theater Review* 18, 2 (Spring 1985): 23-27; also in *Jalisco en el arte* 2-3 (Spring-Summer 1987): 17-19. "Dramaturgia, arte y riesgo," in *Deslinde* 5, 12 (Jan.-April 1986). "Buero Vallejo: dos teatros y un abismo," in *Estreno* 12, 2 (Fall 1986): 6-8. "Homenaje a Guillermo Ugarte Chamorro," in *Latin American Theater Review* 21, 1 (Fall 1987): 74. "Los viejos y la dramaturgia mexicana," in *Le cahiers du Criar* (Rouen, France) 727-7 (1987): 127-33. "Rincón Latinoamericano," in *Estreno* 14, 1 (Spring 1988). "Rincón Hispanoamericano 1988," in *Estreno* 14, 2 (Fall 1988). "Francisco Ruiz Ramón, dramaturgo premiado," in *Estreno* 15, 1 (Spring 1989). "El Teatro Hispanoamericano durante el Modernismo," in *Revista Iberoamericana* 54, 145 (Oct.-Dec. 1988).

BIBLIOGRAPHY: Anon., "Eligen a Guillermo Schmidhuber el mejor dramaturgo de México," in *El Diario de Monterrey* (Nov. 13, 1984). *Dramaturgos nacionales y sus obras premiadas por Bellas Artes* (México: Universidad Autónoma Metropolitana, 1984). "Mexican Playwright's Hobby Turns to Drama," in *Cincinnati Inquirer* (Jan. 20,

1987). "Entregaron Premios 'Letras de Oro'," in *Diario de las Américas* (Miami: Literary Section, Jan. 24, 1987). "Premio internacional al dramaturgo Guillermo Schmidhuber," in *Revista Proceso* (April 29, 1987). "Protagonistas del Arte: Guillermo Schmidhuber," in *Jalisco en el Arte* 2, 3 (Spring-Summer 1987): 48-54; *International Authors and Writers Who's Who* (London: International Biogra- phic Center, 1988); "Triana y Schmidhuber" and "Un mexicano en Cincinnati," in *Dramaturgos* 2, 1 (Jan.-Feb. 1988). Elida Avalos, "El premio Bellas Artes de Literatura 1980," in *Novedades* (Nov. 23, 1980). Angelina Camargo Breña, "Nuestro teatro tiene gran poderío," in *Excelsior* (Sept. 15, 1987). Christine Dziwura Martínez, "Guillermo Schmidhuber: el teatro y la cuestión de la existencia humana," in *Aleph* (Pennsylvania State University) 1 (1986): 17-26. María Idalia, "Guillermo Schmidhuber abandona nuestro país," in *Excelsior* (Aug. 2, 1986). "'Letras de Oro' para Guillermo Schmidhuber," in *Excelsior* (Feb. 12, 1987). Fernando de Ita, "*Los herederos de Segismundo* es una obra que busca poner al día *La vida es sueño*," in *Unomasuno* (Aug. 8, 1981). Andrea G. Labinger, "*El teatro de Guillermo Schmidhuber* and *Instant Happiness*," in *Latin American Theater Review* 19, 1 (Fall 1985): 105-07. "*Cuarteto de mi gentedad*," in *Latin American Theater Review* 20, 2 (Spring 1987). Rafael Martínez, "Entrevista a Guillermo Schmidhuber," in *Los Juglares* (Monterrey, June 1985). Lourdes Meluza, "Certamen Literario rebela diversidad," in *Miami Herald* (Jan 27, 1987). Margarita Mendoza López, *Teatro mexicano del siglo XX* (México: Inst. Mex. del Seguro Social, 1987), pp. 241-44, 410-28. Malkah Rabel, "Monterrey, ciudad de mucha pintura y poco teatro: Guillermo Schmidhuber," in *El Día* (May 5, 1980); "Nace un dramaturgo nacional," in *El Gallo Ilustrado* (Oct. 2, 1980); "Dos premios nacionales al mismo dramaturgo," in *El Día* (Nov. 11, 1980). Joaquín Roy, "Escribir en español en Norteamérica," in *El Periódico* (Barcelona, Jan. 25, 1987). Rafael Solana, "Schmidhuber," in *Siempre!* (May 20, 1981); "Teatro," review of *Los herederos de Segismundo*, in *Siempre!* 1469 (Aug. 19, 1981); "Teatro," review of *Los héroes inútiles*, in *Siempre!* 1505 (Apr. 28, 1982); "El premio 'Letras de Oro' a Guillermo Schmidhuber," in *El Universal* (Feb. 14, 1987). Jaime Vázquez, "El teatro, homenaje a la libertad y canto a la humana tontería: Schmidhuber," in *Excelsior* (Dec. 22, 1984). George Woodyard and Lucía Garabito, "Rincón hispanoamericano," in *Estreno* 7, 2 (Fall 1981): 29. Phyllis Zatlin, "The Contemporary Spanish and Mexican Stages: Is There a Cultural Exchange?," in *Latin American Theater Review* 19, 1 (Fall 1985): 43-47.

ELADIO CORTES

SEGALE, Atenógenes (1868-1903), novelist, dramatist and poet. Segale was born in Zamora, Michoacán, on December 10, 1868. He began preparatory school in the Catholic Seminary of Zamora and later continued his studies in theology at the Conciliary Seminary of Mexico City. Segale was ordained a Catholic priest in 1892. For the next eleven years he was chaplain of the Vizcaine School and of the Sanctuary of Our Lady of the Remedies in Mexico City. He died in Toluca on July 16, 1903.

Segale's first novel, *La estatua de Psiquis* (The Statue of Psyche), was published in 1892 by *El Tiempo*. The same newspaper published *Del campo contrario* (From the Opposing Camp), a collection of short stories, in 1897. Modern criticism pays more attention to Segale's poetry than to his narrative fictions and dramatic works. His humanistic education and his knowledge of classical languages and cultures are shown, together with his delicate and balanced sensitivity, in most of his works. In poetry, Segale cultivated the sonnet of religious tone, as in *El primer viático* (The First Viaticum), and that of modernistic style in, *A una pecadora* (To a Woman Sinner) and *A un amante novel* (To an Inexperienced Lover). Segale is considered a Neoclassical poet next to Joaquín *Arcadio Pagaza and Ignacio *Montes de Oca y Obregón.

WORKS: Novel: *La estatua de Psiquis* (The Statue of Psyche) (México: El Tiempo, 1892). *Del campo contrario* (From the Opposing Camp) (México: Author's edition, 1897). Poetry: *Preludios* (Preludes) (México: Imp. de la Voz de México, 1893). *Del fondo del alma* (From the Bottom of the Soul) (México: Imp. Gutemberg de Miguel Terrazas, 1895). *Versos perdidos* (Lost Verses) (México: Imp. La Europea, 1897). Drama: *El principe de Viana* (The Prince of Viana) (México: Imp. de Murgía y Rivera, 1894).

BIBLIOGRAPHY: Jesús García Gutiérrez, "Carta a Fabio," in *Obras completas de Atenógenes Segale*, vol. 1 (México: Librería de José L. Vallejo, 1901). Perfecto Méndez Padilla, "Su vida en su poesía," in *Abside* 3 (1939). Octaviano Valdes. "Introduction," *Poesía neoclásica y académica*, BEU, no. 69 (México: UNAM, 1946), pp. xl-xli; 155-59.

                                                                          BAUDELIO GARZA

SEGOVIA, Tomás (1927-), poet, essayist, dramatist and novelist. Born in Valencia, Spain, Segovia moved to Mexico in 1940. He worked as general editor of publications for the National University of Mexico. He began writing poetry in his teens. He has published widely in journals and has been very prolific. His writings are oriented around polarities.

  Segovia draws on images such as light and darkness, day and night, and sun and clouds in much of his poetry. He has been willing to experiment with different forms at times. His work *Poesía 1943-76* (Poetry 1943-76) offers a thorough and balanced look at the evolution of his poetry and his vision. The theme of exile figures centrally in that vision, and he alternates between the hope and despair that the exiled life offers. His 1982 collection of poems includes *Cuaderno del nómada* (Notebook of a Nomad), which offers some insights into the nature and the problems of the exile experience and achieves a universalization of that experience.

WORKS: Poetry: *La luz provisional* (The Provisional Light) (México: Hoja, 1950). *Siete Poemas* (Seven Poems) (México: Los Presentes, 1955). *Apariciones* (Apparitions) (México: Cuadernos de la Revista Mexicana de Literatura, 1957). *Luz de aquí* (Light from Here) (México: Colección Tezontle, 1958). *El sol y su eco* (The Sun and Its Echo) (Xalapa: Universidad Veracruzana, 1960). *Anagnorisis* (Anagnorisis) (México: Siglo XXI, 1967). *Historias y poemas* (Tales and Poems) (México: Era, 1968). *Terceto* (Tercet) (México: J. Mortiz, 1972). *Figura y Secuencias* (Figure and Sequences) (México: Premia, 1979). *Bisutería* (Costume Jewelry) (México: UNAM, 1981). *Poesía: 1943-1976* (Poetry: 1943-1976) (México: FCE, 1982). *Partición 1976-82* (Partition)

(Valencia: Pretextos, 1983). *Poética y profética* (Poetic and Prophetic) (México: FCE, 1985). *Lapso* (Lapse) (Valencia: Pretextos, 1986). *Cuaderno inoportuno* (Inappropriate Notebook) (México: FCE, 1987). Novel: *Primavera muda* (Mute Spring) (México: Los Presentes, 1954). Prose: *Actitudes* (Attitudes) (Guanajuato: Universidad de Guanajuato, 1970). *Contracorrientes* (Crosscurrents) (México: UNAM, 1973). *Trizadero* (México: FCE, 1974). *Personajes mirando una nube* (Characters Watching a Cloud) (México: J. Mortiz, 1981). Drama: *Zamora bajo los astros* (Zamora under the Stars) (México: Imprenta Universitaria, 1959). Essays: *Aproximación al pensamiento de Fourier* (Understanding the Thought of Fourier) (Madrid: M. Castellote, 1973). (Translation: *André Breton, Antología 1913-1966* (André Breton, Anthology), edited by Marguerite Bonne translated by Tomás Segovia (México: Siglo Veintuno, 1979).

BIBLIOGRAPHY: Aurelio Asiain, "Ese que cuenta como su fortuna varios ruidos de silabas sin peso," *Revista de la Universidad de México* 36, 4 (Aug. 1981): 40-41; Review of *Figura y secuencias* by Tomas Segovia, *Vuelta* 4, 44 (July 1980): 34-36. Frank Dauster, *The Double Strand: Five Contemporary Mexican Poets* (Lexington: The University of Kentucky Press, 1987), p. 30. Enrique de Rivas "Zamora bajo los astros," *Revista de la Universidad de México* 14, 6 (Feb. 1960): 31. Luis Fernando Lara, "Poética y Profética," *Vuelta* 10, 114 (May 1986): 39-40. Heriberto García Rivas, *Historia de la literatura mexicana*, vol. 4 (México: Textos Universitarios, 1971), p. 357. Manuel Mejía Valera, "Narradores mexicanos contemporaneos," *Cuadernos Americanos* 212, 3 (May-June 1977): 266-70. Emilio Miró, "Dos Poetas: Manuel Vázquez Montalbón y Tomás Segovia, en una colección," *Insula* 38, 434 (Jan. 1986): 6. Aurora M. Ocampo de Gómez and Ernesto Prado Velázquez, *Diccionario de escritores mexicanos* (México: UNAM, 1967), p. 358. José Miguel Oviedo, "Literatura mexicana: límites de un concepto," *Tinta* 1, 5 (Spring 1987): 59-62; "Trizadero de Tomás Segovia: quién escribe qué?," *Texto Crítico* 1, 1 (Jan.-June 1975): 61-69. Guillermo Sheridan, review of El cuaderno del nómada by Tomás Segovia," *Vuelta* 3, 27 (Feb. 1979): 40-41. Pedro Shimose, ed., *Diccionario de autores iberoamericanos* (Madrid: Ministerio de Asuntos Exteriores, 1982), p. 396.

MARK FRISCH

SEGURA, José Sebastián (1822-1889). Segura was born in Córdoba, Veracruz, on January 20, 1822. As a young man, he enrolled at the School of Mining, where he studied engineering. He did his internship in the mines of Monte in Pachuca for two years and in 1844 received his degree. As a student, he always felt drawn to literature. His first poetic essays appeared in literary publications of the day, such as *La Aurora* (The Dawn), *El Año Nuevo* (The New Year), and *Presente Amistoso* (Friendly Present). He traveled to Europe and returned at year's end of 1866. When his wife died, he shirked social life and became drawn to the ecclesiastical life. He received his sacred orders in February of 1888 and in March of that year conducted his first mass at the church of San Cosme. Segura died the following year on February 14, 1889.

A poet of sublime inspiration, Segura wrote romantic verses as a young man, but later religious themes predominated. He was brother-in-law and disciple of Pesado who belonged to the same literary group. Segura was interested in biblical poetry and translated several psalms and verses from the Prophets. He also translated the first three cantos of *The Divine Comedy*, several odes of Homer, eclogues of Virgil, war hymns by Tirteo, and the Invocation of *Paradise Lost* by John Milton. He also translated several poems by Johann Schiller in *El Renacimiento* (Renaissance) in 1869. These included "Canción de la campana" (Song of the Bell), "El guante" (The Glove), "El caballero de Toggenburgo" (The Gentleman of Toggenburg), "El buzo" (The Diver), "La joven forastera" (The Young Stranger), and "Fantasía fúnebre" (Mournful Fantasy). He also translated some parables by Krummacher (*El Renacimiento*, 1869), which included "El sueño de Caín" (Cain's Dream), "La rosa y el lirio" (The Rose and the Lily), "Adam y el querubín" (Adam and the Cherubim), "La rosamusgo" (The Musk Rose), "Muerte y sueño" (Death and Sleep), and "Lamentos de Caín" (Laments of Caín), among others. Segura was greatly influenced by the Italian poets and other academicians of his time. Pesado's influence is also present especially in some of Segura's original compositions and even in some of the translations that he chose. He poetry is characterized by great care and elegance.

WORKS: *Observaciones que a la iniciative presentada por el actual señor Ministro de Hacienda Manuel Payno en su exposición hace el ciudadano J. Sebastián Segura* (Proposed Laws by Citizen J. Sebastián Segura to the Secretary of the Treasury, Mr. Manuel Payno) (México: Imp. Murguía, 1850). *Boletín de las leyes del Imperio Mexicano o sea Código de la Resauración; colección completa de las leyes y demás disposiciones dictadas por la intervención francesa, por el Supremo Poder Ejecutivo Provisional, y por el Imperio Mexicano, con un apéndice de los documentos oficiales más notables y curiosos de la época* (Bulletin of the Laws of Imperial Mexico or The Code of Restoration, with Appendix) (México: Imp. Literaria, 1863-1865). *Respuestas breves y familiares a las objeciones más vulgares contra la religión, por el Ilmo. señor L. G. Segur; traducidas del francés por el señor don José Segura* (Brief and Familiar Answers to the Most Common Ojections against Religion by L. G. Segur, Translated from the French by José Segura) (Orizaba: Ed. de la Biblioteca de la Verdad Católica, Tip. del Ferro-Carril, 1869). *Poesías* (Poetry) (México: Imp. de I. Escalante, 1872; other edition by Librerías La Ilustración, Veracruz-Puebla, A. Donnamette, Paris, 1884). *Ambición y coquetismo* (Ambition and Flirtation), comedy in three acts, premiered at the Teatro Principal in Mexico on Aug. 10, 1876. *Hermosura y vanidad* (Beauty and Vanity) (México: Ant. Imp. Murgía, 1881). *Los caballeros de industria* (Gentlemen of Industry), comedy in verse (n.d., n.p.). *Susana* (Susan), poem in five cantos (n.d., n.p.). "Los carácteres de la poesía romántica, pagana y hebrea" (Characters of Romantic Poetry, Pagan and Hebrew), in *La Ilustración Mexicana*, vol. 1. *Novisima gramática francesa* (New French Grammar) (México: Ant. Imp. Murgía, 1885). "Acción de gracias el día último del año 1887, sermón predicado por el diácono Sr. D. José Sebastián Segura en el templo de San Bernardo, de esta capital, la noche del 31 de diciembre de 1887" (A Sermon of Thanksgiving Given by the Deacon José Sebastián Segura on 31 December 1887 at the Church of San Bernardo in Mexico City), in *El Tiempo* 5, 1301.

BIBLIOGRAPHY: Victoriano Agüeros, *Escritores mexicanos . . .* (n.p.), pp. 57-63. Alberto María Carreño, *Memorias de la Academia*, vol. 7 (n.p., 1945), pp. 222-23; vol. 8 (n.p., 1946), pp. 306-7. Jesús García Gutiérrez, *La poesía religiosa . . .* (n.p., n.d.), p. 146. Gabriel Méndez Plancarte, *Horacio en México* (México: UNAM, 1937), pp.

107-10. Marcelino Menéndez y Pelayo, *Historia* . . ., *vol. 1* (n.p., n.d.), pp. 172-73. Francisco Monterde, *Bibliografía de teatro* . . . (n.p., n.d.), p.342. Octaviano Valdés, *Poesía neoclásica* . . . (n.p., n.d.), pp. xxi-xxii. Emeterio Valverde Téllez, *Bio-bibliografía eclesiástica mexicana*, vol. 3 (n.p., n.d.), pp. 422-26.

DENISE GUAGLIARDO BENCIVENGO

SELVA, Mauricio de la (1930-), poet, short-story writer, essayist, and literary critic. Born in Villa de Soyapango, El Salvador, Selva has lived in Mexico since 1951. His poetry deals with a variety of subjects - death, loneliness, happiness - and uses varied techniques. His essays reveal the scorching problems that pertain to Latin America as reflected in its literature. He has contributed critical essays to many periodicals such as *Cuadernos Americanos, Americas*, etc.

WORKS: Poetry: *Nuestro canto a Guatemala* (Our Song to Guatemala) (México: n.p., 1954). *Palabra* (Word) (México: Los Presentes, 1956). *Dos Poemas* (Two Poems) (S. Salvador: 1958). *La fiebre de los párpados* (The Fever of the Eyelids) (México: Ecuador, 1963). *Las noches que le faltan a mi muerte* (Nights Waiting until My Death) (México: Ecuador, 1966). *Contribución al paraíso* (Contribution to Paradise) (México: Ecuador, 1968). *Algunos poetas mexicanos*, 1 ed. (México: Finisterre, 1971). Essays: *Ensayo biográfico-político sobre Sandino* (Essay on Sandino) (México: Tribuna de México, 1954). *Diálogos con América* (Dialogues with America), in *Cuadernos Americanos* (México: Cuadernos americanos, 1964).

BIBLIOGRAPHY: Federico Alvarez, Review of *Diálogos con América*, in *La Cultura en México* 159 (March 3, 1965): 16, 17. Anon., Review of *La fiebre de los párpados*, in *Cuadernos de Bellas Artes* 4, 7 (July 1963): 91.

NORA EIDELBERG

SELVA, Salomón de la (1893-1959). Selva was born in León, Nicaragua, on March 20, 1893, but Mexico was his adopted home. Recipient of a scholarship at age twelve, Selva studied in the United States, and later held a variety of positions in New York and other places, including a professorship in literature at Cornell University. His first published work was an English rendition of Rubén Darío's poetry. In 1918 he also published a poetic volume, *Tropical Town and Other Poems*, in English. Later that year, he joined the British army, which would have a significant impact on his life and work. During the final days of World War I, he wrote a book of intense poems, *El soldado desconocido* (The Unknown Soldier), which was published in Mexico in 1922. After the war, Selva adopted Mexico as his second homeland, dedicating himself to journalism, teaching, and traveling. He published a variety of works under his own name and under the pseudonym Juan del Camino, among others. He received a literary prize for his poem "Evocación de Horacio" (Evocation of Horace) at the Juegos Florales del Centenario de la fundación de Mérida, Yucatán. A contributor to several literary publicaciones, such as *América, Letras de México*, and others, Selva was distinguished as an honorary member of the Academia Mexicana de la Lengua in 1952. A few months before his death, he had accepted a diplomatic post in Europe, offered to him by the government of Nicaragua. He died prematurely in Paris in 1959.

Although Selva's first publications were in English, he evokes the memory of his childhood in Nicaragua in his writings. His later works were influenced largely by his unhappy wartime experiences in the trenches of Europe. For example, *El soldado desconocido* (1922) is a wrenching and bitter poem whose backdrop is represented by those very trenches where the soldier becomes anonymous.

Selva also was a novelist. In his first endeavor, *La vida de San Adefesio* (The Life of Saint Adefesio) (1932), the action occurs in León, Nicaragua, a familiar place to the author. The protagonist, an introspective seminary student, resembles his creator.

Another one of his poetic works, *Evocación de Horacio* (1949), was critically acclaimed as the work of a more mature, original poet. He also wrote essays on North American, European, and Spanish thought with regard to the movements for independence in Latin American, published posthumously, as was an additional volume of poetry.

WORKS: Poetry: *Tropical Town and Other Poems* (London: John Lane, 1918). *A Soldier Sings* (London: Bodley Head, 1919). *El soldado desconocido* (The Unknown Soldier) (México: Cultura, 1922). *Las hijas de Erectheo* (Erectheo's Daughters) (Panama: Andrese, 1933). *Romance que dice: "¡Qué abrileña que has llegado!"* (A Romance Which Says: How Like April You Have Arrived!) (México: n.p., 1949). *Evocación de Horacio, Canto a Mérida, Yucatán* (Evocation of Horacio, Song to Mérida, Yucatán) (México: Talls. Gráfs. de la Nación, 1949). *Tres poesías a la manera de Rubén Darío* (Three Poetry Pieces Similar to Those of Rubén Darío) (México: Depts. de Divulgación de la Secretaría de Educacón Pública, 1951). *Canto a la Independencia nacional de México* (Song to Mexico's National Independence) (México: Imp. Arana, 1955). *Evocación de Pindaro* (Evocation of Pinaro) (El Salvador: Depto. Edit. del Ministerio de Cultura de San Salvador, 1957). *Acolmixtli Nezahualcóyotl* (México: Talls. Gráfs. Editorial Comaval, 1958). *Versos y versiones nobles y sentimentales* (Verses and Noble and Sentimental Versions) (Managua: Fondo de Promoción Cultural, Banco de América, 1975). Novels: *La vida de San Adefesio* (The Life of Saint Adefesio) (Costa Rica: Joaquín García Monge, 1932). *La ilustre familia* (The Illustrious Family) (México: Eds. de la Revista América, 1954). Essay: "Ideas de la emancipación norteamericana y de la independencia de Hispanoamérica," in *BNBD* 18 (July-Aug. 1977): 45-65.

BIBLIOGRAPHY: Mariano Fiallos Gil, "Salomón de la Selva, poeta de la humildad y la grandeza, in *Cuadernos Universitarios* 22 (Nicaragua, Feb. 1963). Aurora M. Ocampo de Gómez and Ernesto Prado Velázquez, *Diccionario de Escritores Mexicanos* (México: UNAM, 1967). José Emilio Pacheco, *Nota sobre la otra vanguardia*, in *Casa de las Américas* (Jan.-Feb. 1980): 103-7. Manuel Rodríguez Vizcarra, Jr., ed., *"Mi primer judío" por Salomón de la Selva* (Monterrey, México: Eds. Sierra Madre, 1969).

JEANNE C. WALLACE

SEPULVEDA, Irma Sabina (1930-   ), playwright and short story writer. Born in Nuevo León on March 28, 1930, Irma Sabina Sepúlveda studied theater at the INBA (Instituto Nacional de Bellas Artes in México). She started writing in 1961, and in

1962, she won first prize at the Concurso Latinoamericano, sponsored by the periodical *Hoy*, with her short story *El pajarito triste* (The Sad Bird), ln 1963, some of her plays were staged in Monterrey. She has contributed to *La Tribuna* and *El Sol* in San Luis Potosí, and *México en la Cultura*, *Unica*, and other periodicals in México. In her stories and plays, she re-creates popular themes of northwest Mexico. Her collection, *Agua de las verdes matas* (Water from the Green Shrubs), has seven stories dealing with Indian themes.

WORKS: Short Stories: *Agua de las verdes matas* (Monterrey: Ed. Vallarta, 1963). *Los cañones de Pancho Villa* (The Cannons of Pancho Villa) (Monterrey: Sistemas de Servicios Técnicos, 1969). Theater: *El Agiotista* (The Stockjobber) (Monterrey: Sistemas de Servicios Técnicos, 1970). Sepúlveda has other plays that have been staged but have remained unpublished, such as *La luna buena* (The Good Moon), *Hay sombras que secan nopaleras* (There Are Shadows That Dry Cacti), *El príncipe feo* (The Ugly Prince), *El pajarito triste* (The Sad Little Bird) and others.

BIBLIOGRAPHY: Federico Alvarez, Review of *Agua de las verdes matas*, in *La Cultura en México* 77 (Aug. 7, 1963). Anon., "Autores Nuevoleoneses. Irma Sabina Sepúlveda González," in *Inter Folia* 112 (Oct. 31, 1973): 1, 3.

NORA EIDELBERG

SERRANO Martínez, Celedonio (1913-), teacher, poet, and essayist. Born March 3, 1913, in Puerta Arriba, Guerrero, Serrano Martínez has been a professor of Spanish language and literature as well as a writer. His best known work, a revolutionary *corrido* entitled *El Coyote* (The Coyote), was inspired by the revolutionary leader Nabor Mendoza.

WORKS: *Romancero de Balsas* (Ballad Book of Balsas) (México: Editorial Vértice, 1944). *El Coyote*: *Corrido de la Revolución* (The Coyote: Ballad of the Revolution) (México: SEP, 1951). *Ignacio Manuel Altamirano: Breve asomo a su vida y a su obra* (Ignacio Manuel Altamirano: A Brief Look at His Life and Work) (Toluca: Ediciones del Instituto Científico y Literario Autónomo del Estado de México, 1952). *Voces del campo* (Voices of the Countryside) (México: Self-published, 1953). *Nuevo diálogo de la lengua* (New Conversation about Language) (México, 1957). *El corrido mexicano no deriva del romance español* (The Mexican Ballad Is Not Derived from the Spanish Ballad) (México: Centro Cultural Guerrerense, 1963).

BIBLIOGRAPHY: Frank Dauster, *Breve historia de la poesía mexicana* (México: de Andrea, 1956), p. 183. José Luis Martínez, vol. 1, *Literatura mexicana del siglo XX*, *1910-1949* (México: Ant. Libr. Robredo, 1949), p. 84. Vol. 2 (1950), p. 113. Aurora M. Ocampo de Gómez and Ernesto Prado Velázquez, *Diccionario de escritores mexicanos* (México: UNAM, 1967), p. 361.

TERESA R. ARRINGTON

SHELLEY, Jaime Augusto (1939-). Shelley was born on August 7, 1939, in Mexico City, where he received his education. A student of letters, law, and anthropology, he was awarded a scholarship in 1961 to the Centro Mexicano de Escritores. He

634   SHELLEY, Jaime Augusto

widely published some of his early poetry in such reviews as *La palabra y el hombre*, *El rehilete*, *Situaciones*, *Revista mexicana de literatura*, and *Pájaro cascabel*.

Shelley's major publications include "La rueda y el eco" (The Wheel and the Echo), part of the collected works found in *La Espiga Amotinada* (1960); *La Gran Escala* (The Great Scale) (1961); *Canción de las ciudades* (Song of the Cities) (1963); *Hierro Nocturno* (Nocturnal Iron), found in *Ocupación de la Palabra* (1965); *Hierofante* (1967); *Himno a la Impaciencia* (Hymn to Impatience) (1971); *Por Definición* (By Definition) (1976); *Avidos Rebaños* (Greedy Herds) (1981); and *Victoria* (1983).

Regarding his own literary production, Shelley stated that his poems formed a small odyssey, reflecting on daily life. He has been lauded for the wealth and variety of his poetic attributes. Handling his verse in a dynamic and expressive manner, he reveals refreshing and insightful lyrical qualities. Moved especially by the plight of the downtrodden, Shelley addresses the many disturbing social situations that he witnesses in daily life in an anguished, yet beautifully expressive, cry. In his work, *Himno a la impaciencia*, for instance, he voices his social concerns, conveying a profound level of feeling.

WORKS: "La rueda y el eco" (The Wheel and the Echo), in *La Espiga Amotinada* (México: FCE, 1960). *La Gran Escala* (The Great Scale) (México: Universidad Veracruzana, 1961). *Canción de las ciudades* (Song of the Cities) (México: Papeles de la Ciudad, 1963). *Ocupación de la Palabra*, works of Jaime Augusto Shelley, Luis Buñuelos, Jaime Labastida, Oscar Oliva, and Eraclio Zepeda (México: FCE, 1965). *Hierofante* (México: n.p., 1967). *Himno a la Impaciencia* (Hymn to Impatience) (México: Siglo XXI, 1971). *Por Definición* (By Definition) (México: 1973). *Avidos Rebaños* (Greedy Herds) (México: 1981). *Victoria* (México: Martín Casilla, 1983).

BIBLIOGRAPHY: Ricardo Aguilar Melantzón, "Efraín Huerta and the New School of Mexican Poets," *Latin American Literary Review* 11 (1983): 41-56. Federico Alvarez, Review of *Ocupación de la palabra*, in *Revista de Bellas Artes* 3 (May-June 1965): 91-95. Jesús Arellano, "Las ventas de Don Quijote," review of *Ocupación de la palabra*, in *Nivel* 33 (Sept. 25, 1965): 5. Angel Bárcenas, "Degeneración de la poesía," review of *Ocupación de la palabra*, in *Revista Mexicana de Cultura* 968 (Oct. 17, 1965): 15. Eduardo César, "Sobre *La espiga amotinada*," *Lugar de encuentro*, edited by Norma Klahn and Jesse Fernández (México: Editorial Katún, 1987), pp. 191-204. David William Foster, *A Dictionary of Contemporary Latin American Authors* (Phoenix: Publishers Press, 1975), pp. 95-96. Isabel Frayre, "Cinco poetas," review of *Ocupación de la palabra*, in *Revista de la Universidad de México* 20, 2 (Oct. 1965): 28. Carlos González Peña, "Nuevos poetas," *Historia de la literatura mexicana*, 15th ed. (México: Porrúa, 1984), pp. 300-302. Porfirio Martínez Peñalosa, *Los cinco poetas de La espiga amotinada*, vol. 2 (México: Instituto Cultural Mexicano Israelí, 1966). Thelma Nava and Miguel Donoso, "Otra vez la espiga amotinada," in *El Gallo Ilustrado* 162 (Aug. 1, 1965): 1-3. Octavio Paz et al., eds., *New Poetry of Mexico* (New York: Dutton, 1970), pp. 44-47. Aurora M. Ocampo de Gómez and Ernesto Prado Velázquez, *Diccionario de Escritores Mexicanos* (México: UNAM, 1967), p. 361. Mauricio de la Selva, Review of *Ocupación de la palabra*, in *Cuadernos Americanos* 5 (1965): 295-300. Ramón Xirau, Review of *Ocupación de la palabra*, in *Diálogos* 6 (1965): 43.

                                                JEANNE C. WALLACE

SIERRA, Justo (1848-1912), poet, historian, educator, short story writer. The son of a well-known doctor, jurist, and novelist himself (Justo *Sierra O'Reilly, 1814-1861), Sierra was born in Campeche on January 26, 1848, and began his studies in Merida, but from there went to the Colegio de San Ildefonso in Mexico, where his poetic gift was quickly noted, and where he made friends with his fellow students, including future poets Manuel *Acuña and Agustín *Cuenca. As a young man, Sierra contributed to the periodicals *El Renacimiento* and *El Monitor*, and later he became an important educator, sociologist, and historian. As a political figure, he was a congressman, a maqistrate of the Supreme Court, subsecretary and minister of public education, minister of fine arts, and most importantly, founder of the National University. He died in Madrid on September 13, 1912, where he was serving as plenepotentiary Minister to Spain.

Sierra's youthful poetry was postromantic, very much influenced by his reading of Victor Hugo and Gustavo Adolfo Becquer. The most famous of these verses, "Playeras" (Beach Rhymes), has been called an antici-pation of modernism by Enrique Anderson Imbert; other poems by him often anthologized are, "A Dios" (To God) and "El beato Calasanz" (Pious Calasanz). Positive aspects of his poetry are the imagina-tive images and the discipline of the verses, while detractors (and there are many of these) point to his overuse of neologism, his obscure phraseology, and somewhat "frenchified" spirit. His *Cuentos romanticos* (Romantic Stories), again influenced by Becquer, show his side as historian and reformer as well. Remembered as a practical man of action, Sierra always put his prose and poetry to the service of his positive ideals, if in romantic dress.

WORKS: *Obras completas del maestro Sierra* (Complete Works of the Master Sierra) (México: UNAM, 1948). Novel: *El angel del porvenir* (The Angel of the Future) (México: Francisco de León and Santiago White, 1873). Stories and Other Prose: Old political tracts and articles. *Prosas* (Prose) (México: Cultura, 1873). *Cuentos romanticos* (Romantic Stories), México: Porrúa, 1946). Poetry: *Poesías, 1848-1912* (Poetry, 1848-1912) (México: Editorial de la Universidad Nacional, 1937). In addition, Sierra wrote a number of historical treatises, prologues, and political tracts and articles.

BIBLIOGRAPHY: Carlos G. Amezaga, *Poetas mexicanos* (Buenos Aires: Pablo E. Coni and Sons, 1896). José Joaquín Blanco, *Crónica de la poesía mexicana* (México: Libro de Bolsillo, 1983), p. 26. Wilberto Cantón, *Posiciones* (México: Serie Letras, 1950), pp. 9-34. William Rex Crawford, *A Century of Latin American Thought* (Boston: Harvard University Press, 1944). Frank Dauster, *Breve historia de la poesía mexicana* (México: Andrea, 1956), p. 79. Balbino Dávalos, "Sierra y sus versiones de Heredia," in Ofrenda (March 3, 1947): 183-93; "Las revistas políticas de don Justo Sierra," in *El Universal* (México, May 10, 1948): 3. Hilarion Frías y Soto, "Cuentos románticos por Justo Sierra," in *El siglo XIX* (México, May 2, 1896). Heriberto García Rivas, *Historia de la literatura mexicana*, vol. 2 (México: Porrúa, 1972), pp. 90, 212, 217. Carlos González Peña, *History of Mexican Literature* (Dallas: Southern Methodist University Press, 1968), pp. 28, 102, 153, 195, 202, 224, 261, 263, 264, 271-74, 291, 292, 295, 333, 344-45, 348, 353, 357, 363-65, 388, 433. Sergio Howland Bustamante, *Historia de la literatura mexicana* (México: F. Trilas, 1967), pp. 180, 181, 188, 242, 245, 262, 264-65. Aurora M. Ocampo de Gómez and Ernesto Prado Velázquez, *Diccionario de escritores mexicanos* (México: UNAM, 1967), pp. 361-64.

Edmundo O'Gorman, *Justo Sierra y los de la Universidad de México, 1910* (México: Centro de Estudios origenes de la Universidad de México, 1910; México: Centro de estudios filosóficos, 1950). Enrique de Olavarría y Ferrari, *El arte literario en México* (Málaga: Imprenta de la Revista Andalucia, 1877), pp. 80-92; *Poesías líricas mexicanas* (Madrid: Espinoza y Bautista, 1882), pp. 62-63. José Emilio Pacheco, *La poesía mexicana del siglo XIX* (México: Empresas Editoriales, 1965), pp. 297-302. Bernard John Pankow, "Justo Sierra, prosista," thesis (México: UNAM/Escuela de Verano, 1954). Alejandro Quijano, "Mi maestro Sierra," in *El Mundo Ilustrado* (México, Sept. 22, 1912). Francisco Sosa, *Los contemporáneos* (México: Gonzalo A. Esteva, 1884), pp. 245-58. Ralph E. Warner, "Justo Sierra's El angel del porvenir," in *Hispanic Review* 16 (July 1948): 242-44. Agustín Yáñez, "El ideario educativo de Justo Sierra," in *Cuadernos Americanos* 7, 4 (Mexico, July-Aug. 1948): 188-207.

PATRICIA HART AND JOSEF HELLEBRANDT

SIERRA O'REILLY, Justo (Justo Sierra the Elder) (1814-1861), jurist, educator, and novelist; father of Justo *Sierra. Born on September 24, 1814 in Sotuta, in the Yucatán, Sierra did his studies at a Seminary in Merida, where he was later appointed librarian and then secretary. He later studied and practiced law, and in 1841 in Campeche founded his first newspaper, *El Museo Yucateco*, in which he published historical and biographical articles, as well as some of his own fiction. In 1842 he married Concepción Mendez, with whom he had five children, including the well-known novelist, Justo, and another writer, Santiago, who was killed in a duel. In 1845 he founded the newspaper *Registro Yucateco*, which appeared sporadically until 1849. His third paper, *El Fenix*, came out in Campeche from 1848 to 1951, and it was there that he published his novel *La hija del judío* (The Jew's Daughter) in installments (1848-1849). Sierra subsequently occupied several government posts and founded one last newspaper, *La Unión Liberal* (1855-1857), before his death in Mérida on January 15, 1861.

In addition to his journalistic writings, biographical sketches, letters, and editorials, Sierra is remembered for his stories and leqends, and for his two romantic novels strongly influenced by Alexandre Dumas and Eugène Sue, *La hija del judío* (The Jew's Daughter) and *Un año en el hospital de San Lázaro* (A Year in Saint Lazarus' Hospital). On the basis of these two regional novels, he is sometimes considered the first historical novelist in México. The stories reached carefully achieved episodic suspense, designed to heighten their attractiveness for publication in installmemts.

WORKS: *El filibustero* (The Buccaneer), in *El Museo Yucateco* (Campeche, serialized 1841); as book (Mérida: Editorial de la Revista Yucatán, 1923). *Un año en el hospital de San Lázaro* (A Year in Saint Lazarus' Hospital), in *Registro Yucateco* (Mérida, serialized 1845-1846). *La hija del judío* (The Jew's Daughter), in *El Fenix* (Campeche, serialized 1848-1849); as book (Mérida: J. G. Corrales, 1874). *Obras del doctor don Justo Sierra* (Works of Doctor Justo Sierra) (México: Agüeros, 1905). Sierra O'Reilly also authored articles on travel and jurisprudence.

BIBLIOGRAPHY: Crescencio Carrillo y Ancona, Prologue to *La hija del judío* (Mérida: J. G. Corrales, 1874). Antonio Castro Leal, Prologue to *La hija del judío*

(México: Porrúa, 1959). Genaro Fernández MacGregor, "Don Justo Sierra O'Reilly," in *El Universal* (México, February 22, 1954): 3. Heriberto García Rivas, *Historia de la literatura mexicana*, vol. 2 (México: Porrúa, 1972), pp. 51, 120, 131, 212. Carlos Gonzalez Peña, *History of Mexican Literature* (Dallas: Southern Methodist University Press, 1968), pp. 241, 249. Matilde Guerra Peón, *Justo Sierra O'Reilly y los orígenes de la novela en Yucatán*, thesis (México: UNAM /Facultad de Filosofía y Letras, 1963). Sergio Howland Bustamante, *Historia de la literatura mexicana* (México: F. Trillas, 1967), p. 180. Francisco Sosa, *Biografías de mexicanos distinguidos* (México: Secretaría de Fomento, 1885).

PATRICIA HART

SIGÜENZA, Silvia (1943-), poet. Born in Jalapa, Veracruz, Silvia Sigüenza studied Spanish literature, history and pedagogy, although she has not received a degree. She has worked in education, research, and journalism. Her poetic work, although of limited circulation, is beginning to be recognized by both critics and the public. Among other subjects, she deals with questions of intimacy, the sterility of life, and the breakdown of justice. In her more extensive book, *Camino al corazón oscuro y enemigo* (Route to the Dark and Enemy Heart), and in *El hecho y sus silencios* (The Fact and Its Silences), she gives the reader centerstage to experience those images and emotions she wishes to convey.

WORKS: *Poemas* (Poems) (Barcelona: n.p., 1967). *Estoy lejos de mi como al principio* (I Am Far Away from Me as at the Beginning) (Jalapa: Ed. del Caballo Verde, 1974). *Camino al corazón oscuro y enemigo* (Route to the Dark and Enemy Heart) (Jalapa: Ed. Amate, 1980). *Retorno a la palabra* (Return to the Word) (Jalapa, Ed. Papel de Envolver, 1983). *El hecho y sus silencios* (The Fact and Its Silences) Col. Los Libros del Fakir, no. 41 (México: Ed. Oasis, 1984).

BIBLIOGRAPHY: Esther Hernández-Palacios and Angel José Fernández, *La poesía veracruzana* (Jalapa: Universidad Veracruzana, 1984).

ESTHER HERNANDEZ-PALACIOS

SILVA Villalobos, Antonio (1929-). Silva Villalobos was born on November 21, 1929 in México. He studied at first at the Universidad Michoacana de San Nicolás de Hidalgo, and then at the National University, where he studied anthropology and political science. He founded and edited a number of literary journals including *Remanso de Ensueños, Espiral,* and *Espiral y El Nicolaita.*

Silva Villalobos has not been extremely prolific, but his poetry is searching and sensitive. *Asombro* (Astonishment) and *Sedienta cal* (Dry Lime) employ some unique metaphors and express an original poetic vision.

WORKS: Poems: *Gajo de Sombra* (Branch of Shade) (México: Viñeta de Mariano Rechy, 1954). *Asombro* (Astonishment) (México: Ed. Metáfora, 1956). *Sedienta cal* (Dry Lime) (México: Ed. Metáfora, 1960). Essay: *Acusación política* (México: Ed. Metáfora, 1958).

638   SOLANA, Rafael

BIBLIOGRAPHY: Jesús Arellano, "Poesía mexicana en 1956," in *Metáfora* 14 (May-June 1957): 10-16. Heriberto García Rivas, *Historia de la literatura mexicana*, vol. 4 (México: Textos Universitarios, 1971), p. 360. Aurora M. Ocampo de Gómez and Ernesto Prado Velázquez, *Diccionario de escritores mexicanos* (México: UNAM, 1967), p. 367.

MARK FRISCH

SOLANA, Rafael (1915-   ), poet, short story writer, novelist, playwright, and radio and television scriptwriter. Solana was born in Veracruz on August 4, 1915. He studied in the schools of law and Filosofía y Letras in México. Journalism has been his principal employment. He has traveled in the United States, Europe, the north of Africa, and parts of Asia. Aside from his diverse literary production, he has studied acting at the University of México, and has written critical articles on the theater for various newspapers. He was private secretary to Jaime *Torres Bodet in the Secretaría de Educacion Pública (1958-1964) and has been director of Relaciones Públicas de la Televisión. Apart from his work as writer of diverse genres, Solana has been producer and director of theater and television productions. As a poet, he was part of the group that published the literary magazine *Taller*. His theatrical works as well as his poetry and stories are characterized by examples of the fantastic and reveal a subtle sense of humor; a thematic interest in his works is the world of the celebrity.

WORKS: Poetry: *Ladera* (Hillside) (México: Editorial "La Cultura," 1934). *Los espejos falsarios* (False Mirrors) (México: Géminis, 1944). *Alas* (Wings), sonnets (México: Ed. Estaciones, 1968). *Todos los sonetos* (All the Sonnets) (México: Ed. Ecuador, 1963). *Pido la palabra* (I Ask for the Floor) (México: Eds. Pájaro Cascebel, 1964). *Las torres más altas* (The Tallest Towers) (México: Pájaro Cascebel, 1964). *Las torres más altas* (The Tallest Towers) (México: Ediciones Oasis, 1970). *Bosque de estatuas* (Forest of Statues) (México: Federación Editoral Mexicana, 1971). *Medusa* (México: Aguilar, 1974). *Salgo* (I'm Leaving) (México: UNAM, 1981). Essays: *El crepúsculo de los dioses* (Twilight of the Gods) (México: Ediciones de "Multitudes," 1943; Private ed., 1962). *Momijigari, journalistic chronicle of a trip to Japan* (México, 1964). "El teatro comercial en México" (The Commercial Theater in Mexico) in *El teatro en México*, vol. 2: *1958-1964* (México: INBA, 1965). *Musas Latinas: Leyendo a Loti, Leyendo a Queiroz, Oyendo a Verdi* (Latin Muses: Reading Loti, Reading Queiroz, Listening to Verdi) (México: FCE, 1969). "Ser o no ser, análisis de *Palindroma*." (To Be or Not to Be, Analysis of *Palindroma*), in *Vida Literaria* 17-18 (1971): 19-21. "Su vida." (His Life, tribute to Don Juan Tablada), in *Vida Literaria* 13 (1971): 6-13. "Omnibus por cantidad, minibus por calidad." (Omnibus for Quantity, Minibus for Quality) (analysis of *Omnibus de la poesía mexicana*), in *Vida Literaria* 19 (1972): 22. "Un libro inquietante." (analysis of *El Padre Prior*), in *Vida Literaria* 20 (1972): 16-17. *Teatro mexicano 1968* (Mexican Theater 1968) (México: Aguilar, 1974). Narrative: *El envenenado* (The Poisoned One) (México: Eds. Taller, 1939). *La trompeta* (México: 1941). *La música por dentro* (The Music Within) (México: Geminis, 1943). *Los santos inocentes* (The Innocent Saints) (México: Geminis, 1944). *El crimen de tres bandas* (The Three Gang Crime), introduction by Henrique González Casanova, no. 13 (México: B. Costa-Amic, 1945). *El sol de octubre* (The October Sun)

(México: FCE, 1959); (México: Ed. Diana, 1968). *La casa de la Santísima* (The House of the Santisima) (México: Eds. Oasis, 1960). *El Oficleido y otros cuentos* (The Ophicleide and Other Stories) (México: Libro Mex Eds., 1960). *El Palacio Maderna* (Maderna's Palace) (México: Eds. Oasis, 1960). *Todos los cuentos de Rafael Solana* (All the Stories by Rafael Solana) (México: Eds. Oasis, 1961). *Viento del sur* (South Wind) (México: Eds. Oasis, 1970). *Juegos de invierno* (Winter Games) (México: Eds. Oasis, 1970). *Real de catorce* (Fourteen in Camp) (México: Ed. Grijalbo, 1979). Theater: *Las islas de oro* (Islands of Gold), comedy in three acts, premiere 1952 (México: Col. Teatro Mexicano, 1954). *Estrella que se apaga* (Extinguished Star), comedy in three acts, premiere 1953 (México: Col. Teatro Mexicano, 1953). *Sólo quedaban las plumas* (Only the Feathers Were Left), comedy in three acts, premiere 1953 (México: Gráficas Menhir, 1961). *La ilustre cuna* (The Distinguished Cradle), comedy in three acts, premiere 1954, in *Panorama del Teatro en México* 1, 6 (Jan. 1955): 19-46. *Debiera haber obispas* (There Should Have Been Women Bishops), comedy in three acts, premiere 1954, in *Teatro mexicano del siglo XX*, vol. 3, introduction, notes, and edition by Celestino Gorostiza, no. 27 (México: FCE, 1956), pp. 480-542; Laudatory ed., Ger. trans. (México, 1963; México: Eds. Oasis, 1970). *Lazaro ha vuelto* (Lazarus Has Returned), premiere 1955; with *El arca de Noé* (Noah's Ark) (México, 1965). *La edad media* (The Middle ages), comedy in three acts, premiere 1955, entitled *El Plan de Iguala* (The Iguala Plan). *A su imagen y semejanza* (To Her Image and Likeness), premiere 1957, edited by author, with *Espada en mano* (Sword in Hand) (México, 1960); German translation, *El Círculo cuadrado* (The Squared Circle), comedy, premiere 1957. *Ni lo mande Dior* (Not Even Dior Sends It) (México: Teatro de Bolsillo, 1958); in *Antología de obras en un acto*, vol. 1, pp. 115-44. *La casa de la Santísima*, theatrical version of the novel, premiere 1960 (México: Col. Teatro Mexicano, 1960). *Ensalada de Nochebuena* (Christmas Eve Salad) premiere in 1963, entitled *Una vez al año* (Once a Year) (México: Teatro Mexicano, 1964); in *Teatro mexicano, 1963*, introduction and edition by Antonio Magaña Esquivel (México: Col. Aguilar, 1965), German translation, with *El arca de Noé*; with *Lázaro ha vuelto* (México, 1965). *La guerra de las gordas* (War of the Fat Women) (México: Aguila, 1965). *Vestida y alborotada* (All Dressed Up and No Place to Go) (México: Eds. Finisterre, 1965). *El día del juicio* (Judgement Day) (México: 1967). *Los lunes, salchichas* (Sausages on Mondays) (México: R. Peregrina, 1967). *Comedias* (Comedies) (México: Porrúa, 1970). *Camerino de segundas* (The Understudies' Dressing Room) (México: UNAM, Unidad Xochimilco, 1987). Chronicles: "Noches de estreno" (First Nights), chronicles of Mexican Authors, in *¡Siempre!* (México: Eds. Oasis, 1963).

BIBLIOGRAPHY: H.A., "Rafael Solana. En Europa el teatro es artículo de primera necesidad," in *México en la Cultura* 692 (June 17, 1962): 2. José Alameda, "Unas cuantas palabras sobre los sonetos de Rafael Solana," in *¡Siempre!* 543 (Nov. 20, 1963): 42. Federico Alvarez, Review of "Noches de estreno," in *La Cultura en México* 98 (Jan. 1, 1964): xviii. Anon., "Escaparate," review of "Todos los cuentos," in *México en la cultura* 668 (Dec. 31, 1961): 9; Biobibliographic note in *Anuario del cuento mexicano 1962* (México: INBA, 1963), p. 283; Review of Oyendo a Verdi, in *Tiempo* 42, 1087 (Mar. 4, 1963): 63; Review of *Debiera haber obispas*, in *Cuadernos de Bellas Artes* 4, 8 (Aug. 1963): 100-101; "Pasa al libro una pugna que se inició en las tablas," review of Ensalada de Nochebuena, in *Revista de la Semana* (Feb. 2, 1964): 3; "Un nuevo libro de Rafael Solana," review of *Pido la palabra*, in *Revista de la Semana*

(April 19, 1964): 3; Review of *Momijigari*, in *Revista de la Semana* (Dec. 6, 1964): 3; "Dos piezas de tema bíblico ha publicado Rafael Solana" (*Lázaro ha vuelto* and *El arca de Noé*), in *Revista de la Semana* (Dec. 13, 1964): 3. Angel Bercenas, "Edición homenaje a Solana," in *Revista mexicana de cultura* 864 (July 7, 1963): 15; "Noches de estreno," in *Revista mexicana de cultura* 864 (Oct. 20, 1963): 15; Review of *Todos los sonetos*, in *Revista mexicana de cultura* 872 (Dec. 15, 1963): 15; Review of *Experiencia transcendente en la obra de Rafael Solana*, by Chester C. Christian, in *Revista mexicana de cultura* 878 (Jan. 6, 1964): 155; Review of *Ensalada de Nochebuena*, in *Revista mexicana de cultura* 882 (Feb. 23, 1964): 15. María Elvira Bermúdez, "Tres libros de Rafael Solana," in *Diorama de la Cultura* (Apr. 1, 1962): 2, 3. Emmanuel Carballo, "Cataño Morlet y la Sociedad de Geografía plagian a Rafael Solana," in *La cultura en México* 160 (Mar. 10, 1965): xv-xvi. Fausto Castillo, "Solana," Review of *La casa de la Santísima*, in *México en la cultura* 600 (Sept. 11, 1960): 8. Catay, "Teatro mexicano en Alemania," in *El Gallo* ílustrado (July 10, 1964): 4. Chester C. Christian, Jr., "Experiencia transcendente en la obra de Rafael Solana," thesis, College of Arts, Texas Western College; Bilingual ed. by Rafael Solana (México, 1963). Alí Chumacero, Review of *La música por dentro*, in *El Hombre y la Palabra* 3 (1944): 120. Frank Dauster, *Breve historia de la poesía mexicana*, Manuales Studium, no. 4 (México: Ed. de Andrea, 1956), p. 176. Hector Fontanar, "Hombres de México. Rafael Solana, escritor," in *El Día* (July 10, 1964): 9. Ramón Gálvez, Review of *Todos los sonetos*, in *El Libro y el Pueblo* 4, 5 (Sept. 1963): 18-19. María Teresa Gómez Gleason, "Rafael Solana ante su público," in *Revista Mexicana de Cultura* 970 (Oct. 31, 1965): 6-7. Celestino Gorostiza, *Teatro mexicano del siglo xx*, vol. 3, introduction and editon, no. 27 (México: FCE, 1956), p. 479. Miguel Guardia, Review of *Estrella que se apaga*, in *México en la cultura* 205 (Feb. 22, 1953): 4; "El teatro en México: El Plan de Iguala," in *México en la cultura* 339 (Sept. 1955): 4; Review of *La casa de la Santísima*, in *México en la cultura* 600 (Sept. 11, 1960): 8. Ruth S. Lamb, *Bibliografía del teatro mexicano del siglo xx*, no. 33 (México: Eds. de Andrea, 1962), pp. 113-14. Luis Leal, *Breve historia del cuento mexicano*, Manuales Studium, no. 2 (México: Eds. de Andrea, 1956), pp. 136-37; *Bibliografía del cuento mexicano*, Col. Studium, no. 21 (México: Eds. de Andrea, l958), p. 139. Alfredo Leal Cortés, "Ambición y fracaso de Solana," review of *El sol de octubre*, in *México en la cultura* 538 (July 5, 1959): 4. Antonio Magaña Esquivel, "Rafael Solana triunfa con su comedia, *Debiera haber obispas*," in *El Nacional* (May 3, 1954); "El teatro mexicano en Alemania" (Dealing with *A su imagen y semejanza*, translated and produced as *Das Konzert der Marionette*), in *México en la cultura* 706 (Sept 23, 1962): 4; "Una comedia mexicana en versión de Hans y Fritz," in *Revista mexicana de cultura* 848 (June 30, 1963): 11; "Tres comedias humorísticas," review of *Una vez al año*, in *Revista mexicana de cultura* 863 (Oct. 13, 1963): 11; "En el extranjero triunfa el teatro mexicano," *Ensalada de Nochebuena*, under the title of *Nier einmal ins Jahr*, in *Revista mexicana de cultura* 896 (May 31, 1964): 11; *Medio siglo de teatro mexicano, 1900-1961* (México: INBA, 1964), pp. 122, 124, 146, 148-49, 165. Antonio Magaña Esquivel and Ruth S. Lamb, *Breve historia del teatro mexicano*, Manuales Studium, no. 8 (México: Eds. de Andrea, 1958), pp. 147-49. Mauricio Magdaleno, "Aguinaldos de Rafael Solana," review of *Oyendo a Verdi*, in *México en la cultura* 725 (Feb. 10, 1963): 11. José Luis Martínez, *Literatura mexicana siglo XX, 1910-1949*, Clásicos y Modernos, no. 4 (México: Ant. Libr. Robredo, 1950), vol. 1, pp. 78, 79, 181, 342; vol. 2, p. 114. Porfirio Martínez Peñaloza, Review of *El sol de octubre*, in *Estaciones* 4, 14 (Summer 1959): 250-51. María Luisa Mendoza, Review of *Debiera haber obispas*, in *El Gallo*

Ilustrado 552 (June 23, 1963): 4. Marco Antonio Millán, Review of *Todos los sonetos*, in *México en la cultura* 765 (Nov. 17, 1963): 3. Juan Miguel de Mora, Review of *Una vez al año*, in *Ovaciones* 93 (Oct. 6, 1963): 6. Mauricio Navarrete, Review of *Una vez al año*, in *México en la cultura* 759 (Oct. 6, 1963): 4. Octavio Novarro, Carmen Galindo, Mada Carreño, Salvador Reyes Nevares, and Wilberto Cantón, commentaries in *Vida literaria* (1970): 4-20. Aurora M. Ocampo de Gómez and Ernesto Prado Velázquez, *Diccionario de escritores mexicanos* (México: UNAM, 1967). Jorge Olmo, Review of *El sol de octubre*, in *Universidad de México* 13, 11 (July 1959): 31. Mara Reyes, "Diorama teatral," review of *Debiera haber obispas*, in *Diorama de la Cultura* (July 7, 1963): 7. Salvador Reyes Nevares, review of *Ni lo mande Dior*, in *México en la Cultura* 496 (Sept. 24, 1958): 4; Review of *El oficleido y otros cuentos* in *México en la Cultura* 570 (Feb.15, 1960): 4; Review of *La casa de la Santísima*, in *México en la Cultura* 597 (Aug. 21, 1960): 7; "Dos libros de Rafael Solana," review of *Todos sus cuentos* and *Leyendo a Queiroz*, in *Cuadernos de Bellas Artes* 3, 21 (Feb., 1962): 61-62. Antonio Robles, Review of *Veinte lecturas*, in *Diorama de la Cultura* (June 28, 1964): 7. Antonio Rodríguez, "Portugal rinde cálido homenaje a Rafael Solana por su libro sobre Eça de Queiroz," in *¡Siempre!* 576 (July 8, 1964): 40, 118. José Natividad Rosales, "Rafael Solana. Un triunfador en el foro de Bertold Brecht," in *¡Siempre!* 509 (Mar. 27, 1963): 10-11; (May 15, 1963): 7. Mauricio de la Selva, "Asteriscos," review of *Todos los sonetos*, in *Diorama de la Cultura* (Dec. 15, 1963). Rafael Solana, "Autocrítica de *A su imagen y semejanza*," in *Novedades* (Jan. 18, 1957); in *¡Siempre!* (Jan. 23, 1957); "Rafael Solana," in *Los narradores ante el público*, pp. 11-19. Juan Tomás, "*A su imagen y semejanza*, como todo lo de Solana: desigual," in *Esto* (Jan 24, 1957). Carlos Valdéz, Review of *Las islas de oro*, in *México en la cultura* 324 (June 5, 1955): 2. Various, "Homenaje a sus 30 años de escritor," in *El Centavo* 2, 27 (Sept. 1959). Francisco Zendejas, Review of *El sol de octubre*, in *El Libro y el Pueblo* 3, 1 (July-Sept.): 102-3.

JOAN SALTZ

SOLARES, Ignacio (1945-   ), journalist, playwright, and novelist. Ignacio Solares was born in the city of Chihuahua. Between 1966 and 1976, while writing for the Mexico City daily *Excelsior*, Solares edited journals such as *Revista de Revistas* and *Plural*. At present he teaches at the National University. Ignacio Solares' interest in parapsychology, religion, telepathy, dreams, and metamorphosis as man's reactions to the inexplicable fears and limitations that dictate his behavior is apparent in all his work. He has authored six novels, two plays, and an essay on alcoholism. His novel *Casas de encantamiento* (Houses of Enchantment) won the prize Novedades in 1988. Solares' novels have the simplicity of a fairy tale and the complexity of a metaphysical treatise. The author's ability to capture and hold the reader's interest is one of his main assets. He is one of contemporary Mexico's best novelists.

WORKS: *El hombre habitado* (The Inhabited Man) (México: Ed. Samo, 1975). *Puerta del cielo* (Door to Heaven) (México: Grijalbo, 1976). *Delirium Tremens* (México: Cossed, 1979). *Anónimo* (Anonymous Note) (México: Cía. Gral. de Ediciones, 1979). *El árbol del deseo* (The Wish Tree) (México: Cía. Gral. de Ediciones, 1980). *El problema es otro* (This is not the Problem) and *Desenlace* (Outcome) (México:

UAEM, 1983). *Serafín* (Seraph) (México: Diana, 1985). *Casas de encantamiento* (Houses of Enchantment) (México: Plaza y Valdés, 1987).

BIBLIOGRAPHY: Aída M. Beaupied, "La teoría de lo fantástico de Todorov en *Anónimo* de Ignacio Solares," in *Chasqui* 9, 2-3 (1980): 59-64. John S. Brushwood, "La realidad de lo fantástico: Las novelas de Ignacio Solares," in *La Semana de Bellas Artes* (Aug. 27, 1980): 10-12. Ignacio Trejo Fuentes, "Despertar siendo otro," in *La Semana de Bellas Artes* (Sept. 26, 1979): 8, 9.

ALFONSO GONZALEZ

SOLORZANO, Carlos (1922-   ). Born in Guatemala City on May 1, 1922, Carlos Solórzano moved to Mexico in 1939, making it his permanent home. Graduating from the Universidad Nacional Autónoma de México with both his master's and his doctorate, Solórzano also received his doctorate in dramatic arts from the Sorbonne in 1951, having spent several postwar years in France. Upon his return to Mexico, he was named director of the Teatro Universitario of UNAM, a post he held for ten years. At the same time, he organized student theatrical groups that performed plays by some of the most outstanding European playwrights of the twentieth century. He has had a number of theatrical successes with his own work and has also participated in conferences and theatrical festivals, mostly in the United States and France.

Solórzano began writing plays in 1951, publishing first *Doña Beatriz, la sin ventura* (Doña Beatriz, the Unfortunate One). A work of historical character, *Doña Beatriz* was inspired by Albert Camus' *Calígula* and an actual incident in which Doña Beatriz de la Cueva died in a flood in Guatemala. This first play was followed by *El hechicero* (The Sorceress) in 1954.

Las manos de Dios (The Hands of God), a 1956 play, is a more abstract work, using ideas and concepts to illustrate the conflict and differences between active rebellion and its opposite, submission. Characters tend to be symbolic or generic, which allows space for the exposition of philosophical ideas. Using a wide variety of themes, techniques, and approaches, Solórzano experiments with the theater, especially the theater of the grotesque and the vanguard.

Religion has played a significant role in Solórzano's life. As a child, he was exposed to a religious philosophy, which he later rejected, choosing to become a nonbeliever. But the eternal questions of an afterlife and related issues remain. Mexico's colonial past, with its paternalistic system of government, also is a factor in his writings, in that he speaks of the oppressors and the oppressed. He sees freedom as being good and oppression as being evil. But he also believes that, to a great extent, those who have had little democratic preparation often prefer to remain oppressed. This belief is evident in some of his plays.

In an interview with Teresa Méndez-Faith, Solórzano noted that a major concern for him, transformed into a theme, is that the world is hostile and man must somehow reconcile himself with it, which is very difficult to do. He sees the world as ruled by fate, without laws or logic. His intellectual pessimism, fatalism, and generally gloomy outlook were intensified by reality when his twenty-two-year-old son, who was pursuing his doctorate in the United States, was killed in a hunting accident. For the two years following the death of his son, Solórzano was unable to write, withdrawing into an introspective silence.

When he returned to writing, he put aside the theater in favor of the novel, publishing *Los falsos demonios* (The False Demons) (1966), which focuses on both the political and the psychological problems of a nation's citizens, as evidenced in Guatemala. He shows how tyrannical political rule deeply and negatively affects the ordinary citizen's private life. He also wrote *Las celdas* (The Jail Cells), based on a real incident in Mexico.

Also a theater critic, Solórzano wrote for a number of journals, including the French *Rendezvous de Theatre*, as well as for others in Mexico, Argentina, Guatemala, Puerto Rico, the United States, and Spain. In the field of the essay, he published *Teatro latinoamericano del siglo XX* (Latin American Theater of the Twentieth Century) in 1961 and *Antología del teatro hispanoamericano contemporáneo* (Anthology of Contemporary Spanish American Theater) in 1964.

WORKS: Theater: *Doña Beatriz, la sin ventura* (Doña Beatriz, the Unfortunate One), performed in 1952; in *Cuadernos Americanos* (Sept.-Oct. 1951): 215-61; (translated to French 1954). *El hechicero* (The Sorceress), performed in 1954; in *Cuadernos Americanos* 40 (México, 1955) (translated to French). *Las manos de Dios* (The Hands of God), performed in 1956 (México: Edit. Costa-Amic, 1957) (translated to French, English, and Russian). *El crucificado* (The Crucified), in *Dos obras de Carlos Prieto y Carlos Solórzano*, Col. Teatro Mexicano (México: n.p., 1957), pp. 23-39; (México: Libros del Unicornio, 1959) (translated to French). *Los fantoches* (The Puppets), performed in 1958; (México: Libros del Unicornio, 1959) (translated to French, English and German). *Cruce de vías* (Crossroads), 1958 (México: Libros del Unicornio, 1959) (translated to English). *Tres actos* (Three Acts), contains *Los fantoches*, *Cruce de vías*, and *El crucificado* (México: n.p., 1959). *El sueño del ángel* (The Angel's Dream), in *Antología de obras en un acto*, vol. 3 (México: Col. Teatro Breve Mexicano, 1960), pp. 43-52. *La muerte hizo la luz* (Death Created the Light), in *Revista de Guatemala*, 1951. *El censo* (The Census), 1962. *Los falsos demonios* (The False Demons), 1963, performed in Paris, 1964. *Los fantoches* (The Puppets), in *1, 2, 3 [Uno, dos, tres]: tres dramas mexicanos en un acto* (New York: Odyssey Press, 1971). Essay: *Del sentimiento plástico en la obra de Unamuno* (Of Plastic Sentiment in the Works of Unamuno) (México: n.p., 1944). *Unamuno y el existencialismo* (Unamuno and Existentialism) (México: n.p., 1946). *Espejo de novelas* (Mirror of Novels) (México: n.p., 1945). *Novelas de Unamuno* (Unamuno's Novels) (México: n.p., 1948). *Teatro latinoamericano del siglo XX* (Latin American Theater of the Twentieth Century) (Buenos Aires: Eds. Nueva Visión, 1961); 2nd ed., enlarged (New York: Collier Books, 1964). *El Teatro de la posguerra en México* (Postwar Theater in Mexico), offprint of *Hispania* 47, 4 (Dec. 1964): 693-97. *Testimonios teatrales de México* (México: UNAM, 1973). Anthology: *Antología del teatro hispanoamericano contemporáneo* (Anthology of Contemporary Spanish American Theater), 2 vols., selection, prologue, and notes (México: FCE, 1964). Novel: *Los falsos demonios* (False Demons) (México: Ed. Joaquín Mortiz, 1966).

BIBLIOGRAPHY: Demetrio Aguilera Malta, "La visión continental de Solórzano," review of his *Antología* . . ., in *El Gallo Ilustrado* 136 (Jan. 31, 1965): 4. Angel de las Bárcenas, Review of *El hechicero*, in *México en la Cultura* 340 (Sept. 25, 1955): 2; Review of *Las manos de Dios*, in *Diorama de la Cultura* (Nov. 24, 1957). Huberto Batis, Review of *Anthología* . . ., in *La Cultura en México* 162 (March 24, 1965): xv. Emmanuel Carballo, "El inconforme escribe con la esperanza de que el mal

644 SOLORZANO, Carlos

denunciado sea resuelto," review of *Antología* . . ., in *La Cultura en México* 161 (March 17, 1965): xv. Rosario Castellanos, "El engendrado del despotismo," in *La Cultura en México* 229 (July 6, 1966): xiii-xiv. Rosa Castro, "Tiempo del teatro. Una entrevista con Carlos Solórzano," in *México en la Cultura* 261 (March 21, 1954): 3. José de la Colina, "Defensa de tres obras de Solórzano," in *México en la Cultura* (Nov. 2, 1958). Frank Dauster, "Carlos Solórzano," in *México en la Cultura* 485 (June 29, 1958): 9; "Hacia el teatro nuevo: un novel autor dramático," in *Hispania* 41 (1958): 70-72; "El teatro vanguardista de Carlos Solórzano," in *La Cultura en México* 87 (Oct. 16, 1963): xiv-xv; "The Drama of Carlos Solórzano," in *Modern Drama* 7 (1964): 89-100. Juan García Ponce, Review of *Tres actos*, in *Universidad de México* 13, 3 (Nov. 1959): 27. Henrique González Casanova, "Personas y lugares. Teatro," review of *Los fantoches*, in *La Cultura en México* 51 (Feb. 6, 1963): xvii. Carlos González Peña, Review of *Doña Beatriz, la sin ventura*, in *El Universal* (Oct. 30, 1952). Miguel Guardia, "Musset y Solórzano," in *México en la Cultura* 280 (Aug. 1, 1954): 5; "Teatro en México," review of *Las manos de Dios*, in *México en la Cultura* 390 (Sept. 9, 1956): 5; "Teatro hispanoamericano," in *Diorama de la Cultura* (Feb. 7, 1965): 4. Juan Guerrero Zamora, "Dramaturgos mexicanos vistos desde Europa," in *México en la Cultura* 757 (Sept. 22, 1963): 4. Ruth S. Lamb, *Bibliografía del teatro mexicano del siglo XX* (México: Eds. de Andrea, 1962), p. 114. Raúl Leiva, "Drama entre la rebelión y la sumisión," review of *Las manos de Dios*, in *México en la Cultura* 390 (Sept. 8, 1956): 5; Review of *La Antología* . . ., in *México en la Cultura* 829 (Feb. 7, 1965): 9; "Una novela de Carlos Solórzano. *Los falsos demonios*," in *México en la Cultura* 899 (June 12, 1966): 6. Antonio Magaña Esquivel, *Medio siglo de teatro mexicano, 1900-1961* (México: INBA, Dept. de Lit., 1964), pp. 145-47. Armando de María y Campos, Review of *Doña Beatriz, la sin ventura*, in *Novedades* (Oct. 7, 1952); Review of *El hechicero*, in *México en la Cultura* 331 (July 24, 1955); Review of *Las manos de Dios*, in *Novedades* (Sept. 5, 1956); Review of *Tres obras en un acto*, in *Novedades* (Oct. 28, 1958). Teresa Méndez-Faith, "Dos tardes con Carlos Solórzano," in *Latin American Theatre Review* 18, 1 (Fall 1984): 103-10. María Luisa Mendoza, Review of *Antología* . . ., in *La Cultura en México* 157 (Feb. 17, 1965): xiv-xv. Margarita Nelken, "Fuentes de plasticidad escénica," review of *Tres obras en un acto*, in *Diorama de la Cultura* (Nov. 2, 1958). Aurora M. Ocampo de Gómez and Ernesto Prado Velázquez, *Diccionario de Escritores Mexicanos* (México: UNAM, 1967), pp. 369-70. Elena Poniatowska, Interview with Carlos Solórzano, in *El Día* (Sept. 1, 1964): 11. L. Howard Quackenbush, "El antiradicalismo religioso del teatro centroamericano actual," in *Chasqui* 9, 2-3 (1980): 14-17. Salvador Reyes Nevares, "Teatro de Carlos Solórzano," in *México en la Cultura* (Dec. 13, 1959). Esteban Rivas, *Carlos Solórzano* (México: Anáhuac, 1970). Cipriano Rivas Xerif, Review of *Las manos de Dios*, in *Revista Mexicana de Cultura* (Sept. 30, 1956). John R. Rosenberg, "The Ritual of Solórzano's *Las manos de Dios*," in *Latin American Theatre Review* 17, 2 (Spring 1984): 39-40. Rubén Salazar Mallen, "Otro Prometeo," review of *Las manos de Dios*, in *Mañana* (Dec. 21, 1957); "Tres piezas mexicanas," in *Mañana* (Nov. 15, 1958). Agustín del Saz, "*El teatro latinoamericano del siglo XX*, de Carlos Solórzano," in *Papeles de Son Armadans* 116 (Nov. 1965): 209-12; "La obra de Carlos Solórzano juzgada en España," in *La Cultura en México* 201 (Dec. 22, 1965): viii. Peter Schoenbach, "La libertad en *Las manos de Dios*," in *Latin American Theatre Review* 3, 2 (Spring 1970): 21-29. Carlos Solórzano, "El teatro latinoamericano contemporáneo" (answer to "Teatro de vanguardia de Carlos Solórzano," by Frank Dauster and George Wing), in *Diorama de la Cultura* (Sept. 15, 1963): 3. Edmundo

Valdés, "Tertulia literaria," review of *Las manos de Dios*, in *Novedades* (Nov. 12, 1957). Elvira Vargas, "Multicosas," in *Novedades* (Oct. 25, 1955); Review of *Las manos de Dios*, in *Novedades* (Nov. 11, 1957). George Wing, "El teatro de Solórzano y el mito," in *México en la Cultura* 758 (Sept. 29, 1963): 4. Francisco Zendejas, "Multilibros," review of *Las manos de Dios*, in *Excelsior* (Nov. 15, 1957).

JEANNE C. WALLACE

SOSA, Francisco (1848-1925), poet, historian, biographer. Born in San Francisco de Campeche on April 2, 1848, Sosa was taken early to Mérida, where he did his first studies, and published poems in the newspaper *La Esperanza*. Later in Mexico City he occupied several public posts, and was eventually named prefect to Coyoacan, where he settled. In 1892 he traveled to Spain for the Four Hundreth Anniversary of the Discovery of America, and was there elected a member of the Royal Academy of the Spanish Language. Besides writing poetry throughout his life, he was a frequent contributor to various liberal publications, and also served as a member of the Mexican Academy of the Language, and as director of the National Library until 1912. He died in his home in Coyoacan on February 9, 1925.

Although Sosa dabbled in many genres, his literary reputation is derived mainly from his poetry--romantic lyrics typified in his often anthologized *A Lelia* and *A Clementina* (dedicated to actress Clementina Vere). More important than his poetry was his historical writing, and he was particularly noted as an impartial, acute biographer of famous Mexican historical figures. Public praise of his work in his lifetime came in the form of elegies delivered by contemporaries Juan de Dios *Peza and Vicente *Riva Palacio.

WORKS: History and Biography: *Manual de biografía yucateca* (Manual of Yucatecan Biography) (Mérida: J. D. Espinosa and Sons, 1866). *El doctor Cupido* (Doctor Cupido) (México: Aguilar and Ortiz, 1873). *Ensayo biográfico y crítico de don Wenceslao Alpuche* (Biographical and Critical Essay on Wenceslao Alpuche) (México: Imprenta del Comercio de Nabor Chávez, 1873). *El monumento de Colón* (The Monument to Columbus) (México: Jens y Zapiain, 1877). *El episcopado en México* (The Mexican Bishopric) (México: Jens y Zapiain, 1877). *Efimérides históricas y biográficas* (Ephemeral Historical and Biographical Notes) (México: Gonzalo A. Esteva, 1883). *Bioqrafías de mexicanos distinguidos* (Biographies of Distinguished Mexicans) (México: Secretaría de Fomento, 1885). *Biografía del Sr. Licenciado Manuel Larrainzar* (Biography of the Lawyer Manuel Larrainzar) (México: Barbedillo, 1884). *Los contemporáneos* (The Contemporaries) (México: Gonzalo A. Esteva, 1884). *Annuario biográfico nacional* (National Bioqraphic Annuary) (México: La Libertad, 1884). *Apuntamientos para la historia del monumento de Cuauhtémoc* (Notes on the History of the Monument to Cuauhtemoc) (México: Secretaría de Fomento, 1887). *Epístola a un amigo ausente* (Epistle to an Absent Friend) (México: Secretaría de Fomento, 1888). *Noticias biográficas de don Juan José de Vertiz y Salcedo, segundo virrey de Buenos Aires* (Bioqraphical Notices on Juan José de Vertiz y Salcedo, Second viceroy to Buenos Aires) (México: Secretaría de Fomento, 1889). *Bosquejo histórico de Coyoacán* (Historical Outline of Coyoacan) (México: Secretaría de Fomento, 1890). *Noticias biográficas de D. Ponciano Arriaga* (Biographic Notices about Ponciano Arriaga) (México: Secretaria de Fomento, 1900). *Las estatuas de la Reforma* (Statues along La Reforma) (México: Secretaria de Fomento, 1900). *Conquistadores antiguos y modernos* (Ancient and Modern Conquerors) (México: J. Aguilar Vera, 1901). *Recuerdos de Italia* (Memories of Italy) (México: Tipografía Económica, 1903). *Apuntamientos biograficos del señor Licenciado don Manuel Sánchez Marmol* (Biographical Notes about Lawyer Manuel Sanchez Marmol) (México: Internacional, 1912). *Carta hidrográfica de la República Mexicana* (Hydrographic Chart of the Mexican Republic) (México: Manuel Orozco y Berra, 1912). Poetry: *Ecos de gloria* (Echos of Glory) (México: Francisco Díaz de León, 1885). *Recuerdos* (Memories) (México: Dublin, 1888). Stories and Legends: Magdalena (México: Francisco Diaz de León and Santiago White, 1871). *Una venganza* (Revenge) (México: Aguilar, 1874). *Doce leyendas de Francisco Sosa* (Twelve Legends by Francisco Sosa) (México: Ireneo Paz, 1877). Criticism and Literary Scholarship: *Versiones castellanas de "La Jersualem Libertada"* (Castillian Versions of "La Jerusalem Libertada") (México: Secretaria de Fomento, 1885). *Escritores y poetas sudamericanos* (South American Writers and Poets) (México: Secretaria de Fomento, 1890). *Elogio del ilustro poeta don Casimiro del Collado* (Praise for the Illustrious Poet Casimiro del Collado) (México: Francisco Díaz de León and Santiago White, 1898). In addition, Sosa published a myriad of historical articles, editorials, speeches, and prologues.

BIBLIOGRAPHY: Carlos G. Amezaga, *Poetas mexicanos* (Buenos Aires: Pablo E. Coni and Sons, 1896), p. 142. Alberto Maria Carreño, Prologue to *El episcopado mexicano* (México: Jens y Zapiain, 1877). "Francisco Sosa, historiador, biógrafo, poeta, periodista," *Enciclopedia yucatense* (México: Editorial Oficial del Gobierno de Yucatán, 1944). Frank Dauster, *Breve historia de la poesía mexicana* (México: Andrea, 1956), p. 95. Heriberto García Rivas, *Historia de la literatura mexicana*, vol. 2 (México: Porrúa 1972), p. 123. Carlos González Peña, *History of Mexican Literature* (Dallas: Southern Methodist University Press, 1968), P. 356. Aurora M. Ocampo de Gómez and Ernesto Prado Velázquez, *Diccionario de escritores mexicanos* (México: UNAM, 1967), pp. 370-72. Ireneo Paz, *Los hombres prominentes de México* (México: La Patria, 1888).

PATRICIA HART AND JOSEF HELLEBRANDT

SOTOMAYOR, Arturo (1913-), poet, essayist, short story writer. Born in the port of Veracruz, Sotomayor studied law at the National Autonomous University in Mexico City. By profession he is a journalist and a professor of Mexican history.

Sotomayor's poetry is direct, clear, simple, and objective. His themes are woman, the sea, color, and nature. In his work woman, land, and poetry are seen as one.

WORKS: Poetry: *Vértigo azul, poemas* (Blue Vertigo, Poems) (México: Letras de México, 1947). *El ángel de los goces* (The Angel of Pleasures) Los Presentes, no. 30 (México, 1955). *En esta tierra, poema* (On This Earth, Poem) (México: Privately published, 1956). Essay: *Nuestros niños héroes: Biografía de una noticia* (Our Boy Heroes: Biography of a News Report) (México: Talleres Gráficos de la Nación, 1947). *Sombras bajo la luna: ensayos y relatos* (Shadows under the Moon: Essays and Stories) (México: Editorial Manuel Porrúa, 1948). *Dos sepulcros en Bonampak* (Two

Tombs in Bonampak) (México: Librería del Prado, 1949). *Los bárbaros sobre la ciudad de México: ensayo* (The Barbarians over Mexico City: Essay) (México: Col. Panoramas, Costa-Amic, 1960). *Viajes al pasado de México* (Journeys to the Mexican Past) (México: Instituto de Antropología e Historia, 1963).

BIBLIOGRAPHY: Ermilo Abreu Gómez, "El libro de hoy: *Viajes al pasado de México*," *Revista Mexicana de Cultura* 881 (Feb. 16, 1964): 5. Anon., Biobibliographical note in *Anuario del cuento mexicano 1961* (México: Dept. of Literature, INBA, 1962), p. 217. Jesús Arellano, "Las ventas de Don Quijote," *Nivel* 20 (Aug. 25, 1964): 5. Luis Leal, *Bibliografía del cuento mexicano* (México: Ediciones de Andrea, 1958), p. 140. Raúl Leiva, Review of *El ángel de los goces*, in *México en la Cultura* 365 (March 18, 1956): 2. José Luis Martínez, *Literatura Mexicana Siglo XX*, vol. 2, p. 114. Aurora M. Ocampo de Gómez and Ernesto Prado Velázquez, *Diccionario de Escritores Mexicanos* (México: UNAM, 1967), p. 372.

PETER G. BROAD

SOUTO Alabarce, Arturo (1930-   ), short story writer, essayist, critic, book editor, and university professor. Born in Madrid on January 17, 1930, Souto Alabarce has lived in México since 1942. He has traveled in Europe and in the United States and taught in the latter country. Souto founded and contributed to the following periodicals: *Ensayos Científicos*, *Clavileño*, *Segrel*, and *Ideas de México*. In his short story collection, *La plaga del crisántemo* (The Plague of the Chrysanthemum), he has seven stories, two of which, "Coyote 13" and "El pinto" (The Speckled One), have been translated to several languages and included in various anthologies. He has written a number of essays on literature and prologues to books as well as film criticism and translations of English and French books.

WORKS: *La plaga del crisántemo* (The Plague of the Chrysanthemum) (México: Imp. Universitaria, UNAM, 1960). Essays: *El romanticismo* (Romanticism (México: Ed. Patria, 1955). *Grandes textos creativos de la literatura española* (Great Creative Texts of Spanish Literature) (México: Pormaca, 1967). *El Ensayo* (The Essay) (México: Asociación Nacional de Universidades e Institutos de Enseñanza Superior, 1973). Prologues: *Emilio Castelar, Discursos* (Speeches) (México: Porrúa, 1980). *Diego de San Pedro: Cárcel de amor* (Prison of love) (México: Porrúa, 1981). *José María Gabriel y Galán. Obras completas* (Complete Works) (México: Ed. Porrúa, 1981). León Felipe, *Antología de Poesía* (Selected Poems) (México: INBA, 1985).

BIBLIOGRAPHY: José de la Colina, Review of *El romanticismo*, in *Universidad de México* 10, 7 (Mar. 1956): 30. Salvador Reyes Nevares, "Los libros al día," review of *La plaga del crisántemo*, in *México en la Cultura* 621 (Feb. 5, 1961): 2. Gustavo Sainz, "Temática," about the story "Coyote 13," in *México en la Cultura* 764 (Nov. 10, 1963): 2.

NORA EIDELBERG

SPERATTI PIÑERO, Emma Susana (1919-   ). Born in Buenos Aires, Argentina, on October 31, 1919, Emma Susana Speratti Piñero became a teacher of Spanish and of literature, receiving her doctorate from UNAM. She made her permanent home in Mexico. She has been a professor in several colleges and universities, including Mexico City College, the Universidad de San Luis Potosí, and the Middlebury Summer School in Vermont. The recipient of a scholarship in 1951 from the government of Spain, she also was awarded one by El Colegio de México, where she worked as a researcher from 1953 to 1960. She has traveled widely throughout Mexico, the United States, and Europe. A frequent speaker at conferences and symposiums, Speratti Piñero is best known for her work as an essayist, researcher, and translator. It is apparent from her published works that she has an interest in biblical materials. She also is adept at translating works in English, French, and Russian. She has prepared editions of various works and written prologues.

WORKS: Essays: *Hacia una cronología de Horacio Quiroga* (Toward a Chronology of Horacio Quiroga), offprint of the *Nueva Revista de Filología Hispánica* 9, 4 (1955): 367-82. *La literatura fantástica en Argentina* (Fantastic Literature in Argentina), in collaboration with Ana María Barrenechea (México: Imp. Universitaria, 1957). *La elaboración artística en "Tirano Banderas"* (Artistic Elaboration in *Tirano Banderas*) (México: Publs. de la *Nueva Revista de Filología Hispánica*, 1957). *Temas bíblicos y greco-romanos en la poesía de Concha Urquiza* (Biblical and Greco-Roman Themes in the Poetry of Concha Urquiza), offprint of the *Revista de la Facultad de Humanidades de la Universidad Nacional Autónoma de San Luis Potosí* 1, 2 (1959): 99-116. Translations: Edmond Wilson, *Los rollos del Mar Muerto* (The Dead Sea Scrolls) (México: FCE, 1957). Millar Burrow, *Los rollos del Mar Muerto* (The Dead Sea Scrolls) (México: FCE, 1958). Marc Slonim, *La literatura rusa* (Russian Literature) (México: FCE, 1962). Norbert Dufourcq, *Breve historia de la música* (Short History of Music) (México: FCE, 1963). Michael Harrington, *La cultura de la pobreza en los Estados Unidos* (The Culture of Poverty in the United States) (México: FCE, 1963). T. R. Batten, *Las comunidades y su desarrrollo* (Communities and Their Development) (México: FCE, 1964). Other: Editions, prologues, and stories.

BIBLIOGRAPHY: Enrique Anderson-Imbert, *Spanish American Literature*, vol. 2 (Detroit: Wayne State University Press, 1969), p. 741. José de la Colina, Review of *La literatura fantástica en Argentina*, in *Universidad de México* 11, 10 (June 1957): 30. Orlando Gómez-Gil, *Historia crítica de la Literatura Hispanoamericana* (New York: Holt, Rinehart and Winston, 1968), p. 733. Aurora M. Ocampo de Gómez and Ernesto Prado Velázquez, *Diccionario de Escritores Mexicanos* (México: UNAM, 1967), pp. 373-74.

MICHELE MUNCY

SPOTA, Luis (1925-). Born on July 13, 1925 in Mexico City, Luis Spota attended only elementary school, then went to work in a variety of different jobs, mostly as a reporter. In that capacity, he has traveled widely throughout much of the world. He has also published quite a few novels, using his experiences as an investigative reporter to produce excellent narratives. Called a self-made novelist, publishing a novel almost every other year from 1947 to the early 1970s, Spota is a gifted writer, with a flair for the controversial. His novels are often bestsellers, the first few being highly autobiographical, as he capitalized on his own experiences. His first novel, *El coronel fue echado al mar* (The Colonel Was Tossed to the Sea), published in 1947, resulted partly from Spota's first job on a merchant steamship.

In many of his novels, Spota reveals himself to be sharply cynical, portraying seamy and sordid characters and situations from all walks of life. Most of his novels are set principally in Mexico City; thus, he portrays the urban sector more than any other. Walter Langford points out that most of his characters lack a sense of morality and Spota usually kills off one or two of them near the end of the stories. Spota's later works are considered more mature, more well developed, depending less on special effects and other devices typical to newspaper reporters. He creates characters that are more plausible, more reliable. His later novels appear more balanced, more finely structured than the first ones. Despite his increasing success as a novelist, many of his works have been unfavorably reviewed or totally ignored by some critics, partly because of what he writes about and partly because of his abrasive personality.

Walter Langford sums up some of Spota's characteristics as a writer when he says: "he approaches his writing in a manner that is uninhibited, imaginative, sometimes 'flashy' and sensational, usually brash or brazen. He brings to his writing a mixture of cynicism, irreverence regarding just about all things and persons, an aversion toward insincerity wherever he sees it, impatience with the national ills, and a crusader's instincts."

WORKS: Prose: *José Mojica, hombre, artista y fraile* (José Mojica, Man, Artist, and Friar) (México: Ed. Tollocan, 1943). *Biografía del licenciado Alemán* (Biography of the Lawyer Alemán) (México: Talls. Gráfs. de la Nación, 1946). Stories: *De la noche al día* (From Night to Day). Theater: *Dos obras de teatro. Ellos pueden esperar y Dos veces la lluvia* (Two Theatrical Works. They Can Wait and Twice the Rain) (Mexico, 1949). *El aria de los sometidos* (The Aria of the Subjected) (México: Costa-Amic, 1962). Novels: *El coronel fue echado al mar* (The Coronel Was Tossed to the Sea) (México: Talls. Gráfs., 1947). *Murieron a mitad del río* (They Died in the Middle of the River) (México: Porrúa, 1948). *Más cornadas da el hambre* (The Wounds of Hunger) (México: Porrúa, 1950). *Vagabunda* (Vagabond Lady) (México: Talls. Gráfs., 1950). *La estrella vacía* (The Empty Star) (México: Porrúa, 1950). *Las grandes aguas* (The Big Waters) (México: Porrúa, 1954). *Casi el paraíso* (Almost Paradise) (México: FCE, 1956). *Las horas violentas* (The Violent Hours) (México: Costa-Amic, 1958). *La sangre enemiga* (The Enemy Blood) (México: FCE, 1959). *El tiempo de la ira* (The Time of Wrath) (México: FCE, 1960). *La pequeña edad* (The Little Age) (México: FCE, 1964). *La carcajada del gato* (The Cat's Guffaw) (México: Joaquín Mortiz, 1964). *Los sueños del insomnio* (The Dreams of Insomnia) (México: Joaquín Mortiz, 1966). *Lo de antes* (The Same As Before) (México: Joaquín Mortiz, 1968).

BIBLIOGRAPHY: Joel R. Bollinger, "El arte narrativo de Luis Spota," *DAI* 33 (1973): 6340A-41A. Donald F. Brown, "'Germinal's' Progeny," in *Hispania* 51 (Sept. 1968): 424-32. John S. Brushwood, *Mexico in its Novel* (Austin: University of Texas Press, 1966), pp. 28, 35. John S. Brushwood and José Rojas Garciadueñas, *Breve historia de la novela mexicana* (México: Eds. de Andrea, 1959). Jorge Campos, "Letras de América. El México de Luis Spota," in *Insula* 220 (March 1965): 15. Fernando García Núñez, "Notas sobre la frontera norte en la novela mexicana," in

Cuadernos Americanos 2, 4 (1988): 159-68. Felipe Garrido, "Spota Kid vs. los intelectuales," in *Novedades* (Feb. 14, 1965): 2-4. Manuel Pedro González, "Luis Spota, gran novelista en potencia," in *Revista Hispánica Moderna* 26 (Jan.-April 1960): 102-6. Walter M. Langford, *The Mexican Novel Comes of Age* (Notre Dame, Ind.: University of Notre Dame Press, 1971), pp. 103-26. Carlos Monsiváis, "Luis Spota: novelista del futuro," in *Universidad de México* 14 (Jan. 1960): 37. Aurora M. Ocampo de Gómez and Ernesto Prado Velázquez, *Diccionario de Escritores Mexicanos* (México: UNAM, 1967), pp. 374-75. Carlos Ramos Gutiérrez, Review of *Casi el paraíso*, in *Metáfora* 12 (Jan.-Feb. 1957): 8-10. Jorge Ruffinelli, "Código y lenguaje en José Agustín," in *PH* 13 (1972): 57-62. León E. Seamon, "Analysis of Social Criticism, Abnormal Psychology and Style in the Novels of Luis Spota," *DAI* 33 (1973): 5198A. Luis Spota, "Luis Spota," in *Los narradores ante el público*, pp. 69-86. Francisco Zendejas, Review of *La sangre enemiga*, in *El Libro y el Pueblo* 3, 1 (July-Sept. 1959): 103-5.

MICHELE MUNCY

T

TABLADA, José Juan (1871-1945), poet and journalist. José Juan de Aguilar Acuña Tablada y Osuna was born in Mexico on April 3, 1871. His early studies were completed in a private school; he then continued in a military school. A versatile man, he took painting lessons and was interested in gymnastics. When he was twenty-one, he first published in *El universal*. His work was published by magazines and newspapers in Mexico, Havana, Caracas, Bogota, Madrid, New York and San Juan. By the time of his death, he had published well over 10,000 articles in different magazines and newspapers, having used more than fifteen pseudonyms.

Starting as a modernist, he founded *La revista moderna*. Among those in the Mexican modernist movement, he was the one most influenced by Charles Baudelaire. For several years, Tablada lived an active bohemian lifestyle, part of the intellectual core of the Porfirio era. A trip to Japan in 1900 had strong repercussions in his next period of literary production.

Later, in 1911-1912, he lived awhile in Paris, returning to Mexico shortly thereafter. A collaborator of Victoriano Huerta, he was forced into exile and went to New York in 1914. When order was restored by Carranza, Tablada was named by the new leader a member of the diplomatic service in Colombia and Venezuela. He quickly resigned, however, and returned to New York in 1920. In 1935, he returned to Mexico. Several years later, debilitated by heart disease, he went to New York again, where he died of a heart attack on August 2, 1945.

Tablada cultivated virtually all the literary genres. As a poet, he is of major importance for having introduced the Japanese poetry form, Hai-Ku, with *Un día* (One Day). Another significant accomplishment is his collection *Li-Po y otros poemas* (Li-Po and Other Poems), containing ideographic poetry coinciding with Apollinaire.

An erudite man, Tablada was strongly influenced by French and English culture. He had a profound interest in such topics as pre-Hispanic art, oriental fine arts, and theosophy, which are reflected in the excellent prose of his chronicles, essays, novels, his two books of memoirs, his diary, and his literary criticism.

WORKS: Poetry: *El florilegio* (Anthology) (México: Ed. Escalante, 1899); 2nd ed., enlarged and amplified by Jesús E. Valenzuela (Paris and Mexico: Libr. de Vda. de Ch. Bouret, 1904). *Al sol y bajo la luna* (To the Sun and under the Moon), preliminary note by Leopoldo Lugones (Paris and Mexico: Vda. de Ch. Bouret, 1918). *Un día . . . Poemas sintéticos* (One Day . . . Synthetic Poems) (Caracas: Ed. Bolivar, 1919). *Li-Po y otros poemas, poemas ideográficos* (Li-Po and Other Poems, Ideographic Poems) (Caracas, Ed. Bolivar, 1920). *Retablo a la memoria de Ramón López Velarde* (Altar-piece to the Memory of Ramón López Velarde) (New York: n.p., 1921). *El jarro de flores* (The Jug of Flowers) (New York: Escritores Sindicatos, 1922). *La feria, poemas mexicanos* (The Fair, Mexican Poems) (New York: Ed. F.

Mayans, 1928). *Los mejores poemas de José Juan Tablada* (The Best Poems of José Juan Tablada), several previously unpublished (México: Ed. Surco, 1943). Narrative: *Hiroshigue, el pintor de la nieve y la lluvia, de la noche y la luna* (Hiroshigue, the Painter of the Snow and the Rain, of the Night and the Moon) (México: Monografías Japonesas, 1914). *Los días y las noches de París* (Days and Nights of Paris) (Paris and Mexico: Vda. de Ch. Bouret, 1918). *Cultura mexicana artes plásticas* (Mexican Culture Fine Arts) (Caracas: conf. of *Universal*, 1920). *La resurrección de los ídolos* (The Idols' Resurrection) (México: Novela Americana, Ed. of *El universal ilustrado*, 1920). *El Arca de Noé* (Noah's Ark) (México: Ed. Aguilas, 1926). *Historia del arte mexicano* (History of Mexican Art) (México: Ed. Aguilas, 1927). *La feria de la vida* (The Fair of Art) (México: Ed. of Botas, n.d.). *Del Horismo a la Carcajada* (From Horismo to Laughter) (México: Ed. Mexicana, 1944). Other Prose: *La defensa social, historia de la campana de la división del Norte* (Social Defense, History of the North Division Campaign) (México: Imp. of the Federal Government, 1903). La epopeya nacional, Porfirio Díaz (The National Epic, Porfírio Díaz) (México: Talleres Linotipo of *El mundo ilustrado*, 1909). *Madero, Chantecler* (México: Imp. de Antonio Enríquez, 1910). *Tiros al Blanco* (Target Practice) (México: Imp. de Manuel León Sánchez, 1910). "Bibliografías de Secretarios de Relaciones Exteriores," in *Boletín*, 1909-1912 (México). "Calles" (*Calles*), in *Del México actual* (México: Sría. de Relaciones Exteriors, 1933), no. 6, pp. 16-46.

BIBILIOGRAPHY: Carlos G. Amezaga, *Poetas mexicanos* (Buenos Aires: Imp. de Pablo E. and Sons, 1896). Anon., "Mexican Writers: D. José Juan Tablada," in *Biblos* 2, 62 (1920): 45-46. Octavio G. Barreda, "Memorias," review of *La feria de la vida*, in *Letras de México* 1, 19 (Nov. 16, 1937): 3. Nina Cabrera de Tablada, *José Juan Tablada en la intimidad* (México: UNAM, 1957). Antonio Castro Leal, *La poesía mexicana moderna* (México: Academia Mexicana de la Cultura, 1953), pp. 128-37. Gloria Ceide Echeverría, *El Haikai en la lírica mexicana* (México, Eds. Andrea, 1967), pp. 23-57. Juan Gustavo Cobo Borda, "José Juan Tablada: su poesía ideográfica," in *Sábado*, supplement of *Unomásuno* 529 (Nov. 21, 1987): 5. Ciego Córdoba, "José Juan Tablada y el Haikai," in *Revista mexicana de cultura* 2, 254 (1963). Jorge Cuesta, *Antología de la poesía mexicana moderna* (México: Ed. Cultura, 1928), p. 62. Enrique Díez-Canedo, "Tablada y el Haikai," in *Letras de América, estudios sobre las literaturas continentales* (México: Colegio de Mexico, 1944), pp. 216-21; 2nd ed. (México: FCE, 1983), p. 190.   Max Enríquez Ureña, *Breve historia del modernismo* (Mexico, FCE, n.d.), pp. 473-76. Genaro Fernández McGregor, "El periplo de Tablada," in *El universal* (Nov. 11, 1946): 3. Merlin H. Forster, *Historia de la poesía hispanoamericana,* in *American Hispanist* (Indiana) (1981): 101-3; Bibliography on and about Tablada, in *Sábado* (1987): 318-19. Federico Gamboa, *Mi diario* (Mexico, Ed. Botas, 1938), pp. 177-81. José María González de Mendoza, *Ensayos selectos* (Mexico, FCE, 1970); "José Juan Tablada," in *Letras en México* 1, 16 (Oct. 1, 1937): 1-2; "Universalidad de la poesía de José Juan Tablada," in *Revista de Revistas* 26, 1390; "Los mejores poemas de José Juan Tablada" (México: Ed. cit.); *Los cuatro poetas*, in *Rueca* 20 (1951-1952): 41-47; "Trayectoria de José Juan Tablada," in *Nivel* 26 (1965): 1-2. Emiliano Hernández, "*El florilegio*, versos de José Juan Tablada," in *Revista Moderna* (1904): 74-75. Esther Hernández Palacios, "Tablada o el crisol de las sorpresas," in *Texto crítico* 4 (1984). Rafael Lozano, "Dos formas de la poesía japonesa: La Tanka, y el Haikai," in *Papel literario*, supplement to *Nacional* (Caracas, Oct. 8, 1853). Manuel Maple Arce, *Recordación de José Juan Tablada* (Tokyo:

Universal Fraternity, 1957); Incitaciones y valoraciones (México: Ed. Cultura, 1956). Amanda Marical Acosta, *La poesía de Juan José Tablada* (Mexico, thesis, 1949). Carlos Monsiváis, *La poesía mexicana del siglo XX* (México: Empresas Editoriales), pp. 27-28, 239. Francisco Monterde, "Anecdotario, epigrama de José Juan Tablada," in *Antena* 2: 10-11; *Itinerario contemplativo,* eulogy of J. J. Tablada (México: Ed. Cultura, 1923). Amado Nervo, "Claro-Oscuro, Patricio Lírico" (Madrid: Ed. Aguilar, 1962), vol. 2, pp. 339-40; *"El florilegio,"* in *Obras completas* (Madrid: Ed. Aguilar, 1962), vol. 2, p. 343. José de Jesús Núñez y Domínguez, *José Juan Tablada* (México: Ed. Galatea, 1951), paper read before the Mexican Academy. Octavio Paz, "Estela de José Juan Tablada," in *Letras de México* (Oct. 1945); in *Las peras del olmo* (México: Imp. Universitaria, 1957), pp. 76-85. Allen W. Phillips, "Una amistad literaria, Tablada y López Velarde," in *Nueva revista de filosofía hispánica* 15, 3-4 (July-Dec. 1961): 505-616. Antonio Quevedo Escobedo, *Los cuatro poetas: Gutiérrez Nájera, Urbina, Icaza, Tablada,* in *El hijo pródigo* 9 (1945): 135-43. Guillermo Sucre, *La máscara y la transpariencia. Ensayos sobre poesía hispanoamericana,* 2nd ed. (Mexico, FCE, 1985), p. 79. Jaime Torres Bodet, "José Juan Tablada," in *Educación y concordia internacional* (México: Ed. Colegio de Mexico, 1948), pp. 96-97. Luis G. Urbina, "Florilegio de José Juan Tablada," in *Revista moderna* 2, 10 (Oct. 1899): 305-6; and in *Hombres y libros,* pp. 197-203; "José Juan Tablada," in *Revista Moderna* 6 (Feb. 1903): 51-52. Jesús E. Valenzuela, "Para un libro de Tablada," in *Revista Moderna* 5 (Feb. 1904): 373-76. Ramón Xirau, "Del modernismo a la modernidad," in *Lecturas, ensayos sobre la literatura española e hispanoamericana,* in *Sábado* (UNAM), 529 (1983): 72.

ESTHER HERNANDEZ-PALACIOS

TAPIA DE CASTELLANOS, Esther (1842-1897). Esther Tapia de Castellanos was born in Morelia, in the state of Michoacaán, on March 9, 1842. She completed her studies and lived in Morelia, although her works were also published in other places, including Guadalajara, Mexico, and Spain. Tapia de Castellanos began publishing poetry as a youth, deeply impressed by the tragedy of the Martyrs of Tacubaya in 1859.

Her first book of collected works, *Flores silvestres* (Wildflowers), was published in 1871. She was esteemed for her facile versification and for a marked interest in maternal themes, which carried her poetry beyond the immediate context. Many individual poems were published in journals of the capital and in other cities. She died in Guadalajara on January 8, 1897.

WORKS: *Flores Silvestres* (Wildflowers) (México, 1871). *Cánticos de los niños* (Children's Songs) (Guadalajara, 1881). *Obras poéticas* (Poetic Works), 2 vols. (Guadalajara, 1905).

BIBLIOGRAPHY: Carlos G. Amezaga, *Poetas mexicanos* (Buenos Aires: Imp. de Pablo E. Coni e hijos, 1896), pp. 303-16. Heriberto García Rivas, *Historia de la literatura mexicana* (México: Textos Universitarios, 1972), vol. 2, pp. 91, 171, 217. Aurora M. Ocampo de Gómez and Ernesto Prado Velázquez, *Diccionario de escritores mexicanos* (México: UNAM, 1967), p. 377. Laureana Wright de Kleinhans, *Mujeres notables mexicanas* (México: Tip. Económica, 1910), pp. 497-504.

                                                                    FILIPPA B. YIN

TARIO, Francisco. See, PELAEZ, Francisco.

TEJEDA DE TAMEZ, Altaír (1926-   ). Born on October 23, 1926, in Ciudad Victoria, Tamaulipas, Altaír Tejeda de Tamez has achieved recognition as a poet, short story writer, journalist, playwright, and novelist. She spent her childhood in Ciudad Victoria, attending local schools. She got her teaching credentials in the Escuela Nacional de Maestros in Mexico City, later receiving her master's degree in Spanish language and literature from the Universidad de Coahuila. She has been teaching sporadically in different schools and universities since 1958, also holding several positions in cultural institutions in Tamaulipas. Today she is the coordinator of Cultural Services for Public Education of the State of Tamaulipas.

Tejeda de Tamez began writing at a very early age. When she was only nine, the magazine *Aladino* of Mexico City published her first short stories. At age fourteen, under the direction of the famous educator Francisco de P. Arreola, she started writing poetry. In 1952, she published her first book of poems, *XXX minutos* (Thirty Minutes), in Saltillo, Coahuila, and in 1958, her first book of short stories came out. Since then she has published a book almost every year, receiving many awards, national and local, the first one in 1948 for her short story "Golondrina." In 1951, she received the María Enriqueta Prize for her poem "Dolor de Navidad." The most important was given to her by INBA in 1958 for *Canasta*, judged the best play in the Northeast of Mexico. The next year, she received the National Prize for Theater for her *Otoño muere en primavera* (Autumn Dies in the Spring). She has also been the recipient of diverse honors for her journalistic work in several of the newspapers and magazines of Tamaulipas.

Altaír Tejeda's theater is an accurate reflection of the way people really live. She captures their essence, their mannerisms and habits. Witty at times, convincing in her realistic character portrayal, she creates and sustains situations that spark the imagination of the audience. Many of her plays have been successfully staged, among them, one of the early ones, *Canasta*. It is a simple, interesting, and human work that revolves around some frivolous women playing canasta while their families suffer from their absence. The child of one of them actually dies as the game goes on. The lively portrayal of the women enjoying their card game is a vivid contrast to the tragic situation unfolding elsewhere. *Yerbabuena*, probably her best and most powerful drama, is based on the actual, but somewhat minimized tragic facts which took place in a small locality of Tamaulipas, Yerbabuena. Witchcraft and superstitions constitute the background of the play that focuses on the ritualistic behavior of some of the poor people who take hallucinogenic drugs and practice human sacrifice. Many die in the resulting massacre, while others are condemned to languish in prison for seventeen years. The death of the "curandero" (witch doctor) is the play's climax, when the Indians convert him into a god.

A dynamic, astute observer of reality, Altaír Tejeda writes with equal dexterity about a wide variety of subjects. She possesses an innate creative intelligence, recognized by critics throughout Mexico. Some of her major influences are Jorge *Ibargüengoitia, Vicente *Leñero and Emilio *Carballido.

Known also as a very forceful and spontaneous poet, Altaír Tejeda offers the reader a poetic vision that is simple, yet elegant, fresh and, at times, nostalgic. She has published several important works, *Acroama* (1961), *Palabras sencillas* (Simple Words) (1975), *Azares de Amor y Muerte* (Love and Death Perils) (1979), and *La Jaula de oro* (The Gold Cage) (1986).

Love in all its dimensions, tenderness, and hope are some of her most frequently expressed themes. Her poetry includes romantic poems, such as those of "Adiós, mi amor . . .," where she writes about the distancing effect upon two lovers who are parted, and melancholy poems, particularly when she expresses what has been lost and is now only a memory. Several important critics have favorably assessed her poetry and its impact on the letters of Northeast Mexico.

The clear and direct technique which charaterizes her poems is reflected in her short stories and chronicles published in six volumes whose great variety of themes treated includes fantasy, mystery, and social concerns. Many are written in first person, and several of them are autobiographical. *Ochenta ventanas para asomarse al mundo* (80 Windows to Look at the World) (1983), *Crónicas y cuentos* (Chronicles and Short Stories) (1985), and *Buenos Días Victoria* (Good Morning, Victoria) (1987) are collections of the articles she has published weekly during several years in her column Ventana dominical (Sunday Window) of *El Diario de Ciudad Victoria*. She has just published a novel, *Ménage à Trois* (1990), which reflects a comic-picaresque tendency, already present in some of her most recent short stories.

WORKS: *XXX Minutos* (30 Minutes) (Saltillo: n. p., 1952). *El perro acomplejado* (The Dog with a Complex) (México: Los Presentes, 1958). *Acroama* (Monterrey: Univ. of Nuevo León, 1960). *Fuensanta* (Saltillo, Coah.: Mástil, 1966). *Palabras sencillas* (Simple Words) (Ciudad Victoria, Tam.: Gobierno de Tamaulipas, 1975; México: Fed. Ed. Mexicana, 1980). *Imágenes* (Images) (Saltillo, Coah.: Ed. Espigas, 1977). *Saltillo 400* (Monterrey: Ed. Alfonso Reyes, 1977). *Azares de amor y muerte* (Love and Death Perils) (Ciudad Victoria: Universidad Autóctona de Tamaulipas, 1978). *El Péndulo* (The Pendulum) (Ciudad Victoria: Universidad Autóctona de Tamaulipas, 1980). *El cementerio de las palabras* (The Words' Graveyard) (México: Fed. Ed. Mexicana, 1980). *Yerbabuena y otras piezas* (Yerbabuena and Other Plays) (México: Fed. Ed. Mexicana, 1983). *Ochenta ventanas para asomarse al mundo* (80 Windows to Look at the World) (México: Fed. Ed. Mexicana, 1983). *Los Mutantes y otras piezas* (The Mobile Ones and Other Plays) (México: Fed. Ed. Mexicana, 1985). *Cuentos y crónicas* (Short Stories and Chronicles) (México: Fed. Ed. Mexicana, 1985). *La Jaula de oro* (The Gold Cage) (Ciudad Victoria: Gobierno de Tamaulipas, 1986). *Buenos días, Victoria* (Good Morning, Victoria) (México: Fed. Ed. Mexicana, 1987). *Estrategia* (Strategy) (México: Fed. Ed. Mexicana, 1989). *Ménage à Trois* (México: Fed. Ed. Mexicana, 1990).

BIBLIOGRAPHY: Pedro Alonzo Pesina, "Altaír Tejeda de Tamez es una de las grandes escritoras," in *Estilo* (July 17, 1984): C-1. Anon., "*Yerbabuena*," in *El Mercurio* (Sept. 21, 1988): 5A. Patricia Avila Loya, "Del Costumbrismo a la Vanguardia," in *El Financiero* (March 7, 1990): 76. Horoamté Crecido Gaertero, "Altaír Tejeda,

Escritora," in *Vanguardia* (Saltillo, June 1977): n.p. Carlos González Salas, *"Azarez de amor y muerte,"* in *Vida universitaria* (Feb. 21, 1980); "Altaír Tejeda, dramaturga," in *El Bravo* (Oct. 6, 1982): 1, 10. *La poesía Femenina Contemporánea en México, 1941-1968* (Ciudad Victoria: Inst. Tam. de Cult., 1990), pp. 320-22. Juan Francisco Ipiña, "Proscenio," in *El Diario de Ciudad Victoria* (July 9, 1988): 3C. Azabel Jaramillo, "El buen escritor se hace: Altaír Tejeda de Tamez," in *El Diario de Ciudad Victoria* (Oct. 4, 1990): 1C. Elias Laborie, "VI Congreso Nacional de Teatro Amateur," in *La Afición* (Mar. 7, 1990): 15C. Ana Lucía Maldonado, "Es obra difícil y buena," review of *Los Mutantes,* in *El Norte* (Oct. 31, 1987). Michèle Muncy, "Altaír Tejeda de Tamez," in *En la Cultura* 6 (Apr. 1990): 20-29. Guillermo Murray Prisant, "Amor Teatral," in *El Universal* (Mar. 9, 1990): 4C. Miguel Angel Pineda Muñoz, "Brindan mayor apoyo al teatro tamaulipeco," in *El Nacional* (Mar. 8, 1990): 18E. Roger Pompa, "Triunfo de *Canasta* en el Montoya," in *El Porvenir* (1959): 6, 9. Francisco Ramos, "Altaír Tejeda, Poetisa de la frontera norte," in *El Diario* (Aug. 17, 1986): C. Carlos David Santamaría, "Reconocimiento a Altaír Tejeda de Tamez," in *La Verdad* (June 14, 1989): n.p. Rafael Solana, *"Yerbabueba,"* in *Siempre!* (Aug. 6, 1982): n.p.

                                                                    ELADIO CORTES

TELLEZ Rendón, María Nestora (1828-1890). Born on February 26, 1828, in Querétaro, María Nestora Téllez Rendón was blinded by disease as an infant. Of extraordinary mental capacity, Téllez Rendón was educated primarily by her father, who refused to allow her visual impairment to handicap her life. She was especially adroit in the fields of philosophy, Latin studies, and religion, the latter being the focus of her literary attention. After her father's death, her mother, also an educator, became her primary mentor, encouraging her intellectual growth. Hired first as an assistant, Téllez Rendón took her mother's place upon her death, and soon was the director of a private school which, under her administrative guidance, became very prestigious. Following her success in her own professional exams in 1866, she was awarded the much-coveted Cruz de la Orden Imperial de San Carlos. She lived almost thirty years longer, dedicating her life to the service of others in her chosen field of education. She died in Guanajuato on December 19, 1890.

Her only literary work, the novel *Staurófila,* was apparently coauthored with several of her contemporaries. A parable in which the love of Jesus Christ is symbolized by the imagery of the devoted soul, *Staurófila* stands out as a tribute to one who was able to overcome successfully a personal tragedy, that of her blindness, to focus instead on her well-developed intellectual capacity and scholarship.

WORKS: *Staurófila* (Querétaro: Imp. de Luciano Frías y Soto, 1889); 3rd ed. (México: Libr. Católica del Sagrado Corazón de Jesús, de José I. Gloria, 1903); 6th ed. (París and México: Libr. de la Vda. de Ch. Bouret, 1919); and Col. Económica Libros de Bolsillo, No. 349 (México: Editora Nacional, 1958).

BIBLIOGRAPHY: Juan B. Iguíniz, *Bibliografía de novelista mexicanos* (México: Imp. de la Sría. de Relaciones, 1926), pp. 364-67. Aurora M. Ocampo de Gómez and Ernesto Prado Velázquez, *Diccionario de Escritores Mexicanos* (México: UNAM,

1967), p. 377. Arturo Torres-Rioseco, *Bibliografía de la novela mexicana* (Cambridge, Mass.: Harvard University Press, 1933), p. 54.

MICHELE MUNCY

TEODORO DE ORONTOBOLO. See BASILIO, Librado.

TERRAZAS, Francisco de (1525?-1600). Terrazas was the son of the conquistador of the same name who came to New Spain with Cortés as his majordomo. His date of birth is unknown, and it is supposed that he died around the end of the sixteenth century. What remains of his works are nine sonnets, an epistle in tercets, ten decimas, and fragments of an epic poem entitled *Nuevo mundo y conquista* (New World and Conquest). His poetry shows influence of the Sevillan school, and it is suggested that he could have been a friend of Gutierre de *Cetina during his stay in the New World. His best work is said to be the sonnet that begins "Dejad las hebras de oro ensortijado . . . (Forsake the golden ringlets . . .). In *Nuevo mundo y conquista*, a work of only mediocre quality, he apparently intended to tell of the expeditions of Hernández de Córdoba y Juan de Grijalva, the trip of Cortés, and the conquest of Mexico.

WORKS: *Poesías de Francisco de Terrazas* (Poems of Francisco de Terrazas), edition, prologue, and notes by Antonio Castro Leal (México: Porrúa, 1941).

BIBLIOGRAPHY: Prologue of edition cited above, Pedro Henríquez Ureña, "Nuevas poesías atribuidas a Terrazas," *Revista de Filología Española* (Madrid, 1918): 49-56). J. Amor y Vázquez, "Terrazas y su *Nuevo mundo y conquista* en los albores de la mexicanidad" in *Nueva revista de Filología hispánica* 16 (1962): 395-415.

ANITA K. STOLL

THEATER IN COLONIAL MEXICO. The theater in Mexico flourished during the colonial period like few other art forms. Fueled by the existence of a pre-Hispanic theatrical tradition and by the missionaries' zeal to teach the Catholic faith, a form of religious theater, in Indian or Spanish languages, was in operation a few years after the conquest of Mexico in 1521. Though secular theater appears as early as 1539, the nonreligious plays that have survived date from the 1560s. A more scholarly type of theater was that written in Spanish and/or in Latin by students and faculty at the Jesuit schools after 1572. All three manifestations of theater were written and staged throughout the Spanish domination of Mexico.

The first Mexican theatrical representations in Indian dialects and in Spanish were *autos*, religious dramatic allegories. Directed for the most part by the priests and represented by the Indians and/or Spaniards, these *autos* were very popular among the Indian population during the Spanish rule. Indians represented biblical characters, allegorical figures, or themselves. The resulting performances, as described by the chroniclers, were funny, inspirational, and quite different from anything that a cast of Spaniards alone might have produced. Almost all *autos*, in Spanish or in an native language, ended with a *Tocotín*, an Indian dance accompanied by indigenous instruments. These *autos* not only instructed, but also entertained their audience. Short farces, jokes, songs, dances, or one-act secular compositions often were performed at the beginning or the end of the play or both, and between acts. An example of this type of play is *The Final Judgement*, written by Andrés de Olmos during the first half of the sixteenth century. These plays were staged in the *atrio*, or courtyard, of a church in order to accommodate a large number of spectators.

Though the handwriting, vocabulary, and historical facts found in several of these *autos* clearly place them in the sixteenth or seventeenth century, several of them were not printed or translated into Spanish and other languages until the eighteenth century and in some instances, the nineteenth and twentieth centuries. An example is *The Sacrifice of Isaac*, written by Bernabé Vásquez in the second half of the eighteenth century, and translated into Spanish in 1899. *The Merchant*, a secular play written by Don José Gaspar in 1687, was translated into English in 1970.

The first known play by an American born playwright is Juan Pérez Ramírez' *Desposorio espiritual entre el pastor Pedro y la iglesia mexicana* (Spiritual Wedding of the Shepherd Peter and the Mexican Church). It was written and performed in Spanish in order to celebrate the presentation of the archbishop's pallium to don Pedro Moya de Contreras in 1574. It is a pastoral play "a lo divino" in which the characters have allegorical biblical roles. The son of a Spanish soldier and an Indian woman, Pérez Ramírez was a priest who knew Nahuatl, Spanish, and Latin. His play is an example of missionary theater not aimed directly at the natives of the New World, but also prevalent in colonial Mexico.

The first nonreligious drama that we have notice of was presented in 1539: *La conquista de Rodas* (The Conquest Of Rhodes), to celebrate the peace treaty between Charles V of Spain and Francis I of France. During the second half of the sixteenth century, livelier, more popular forms of theater appeared. These were the *entremeses*, *sainetes*, and *coloquios*. The first two were one-act plays, with or without music, in which local affairs were addressed. The *coloquios* varied in length from one to seven acts and were concerned with current historical events, biblical themes, and local mores. The short dramas were presented at the beginning, between acts, or at the end of longer, more serious plays, as in the case of the *autos*. Since they were meant as an element of comic relief, they were not taken very seriously and were therefore not published. Only a few have survived. Fernán *González de Eslava, a Spaniard who came to the New World in 1558, excelled in these short dramatic genres.

With the arrival of the Jesuits in 1572, a more frequent and scholarly kind of theater appeared. As a rule they had dramatical representations at the beginning and at the end of the school term, during the festivities of Corpus Christi and its patron saints, and for celebration of important events, such as the arrival of a new viceroy or the birth of a child to the queen or the vicereine. Students were required to write and act out dialogues, eclogues, and longer plays in Latin or Spanish at the main *colegios* and *universidades* of Mexico. These plays, also written by faculty, were based on classical models. For the most part they were rhetorical exercises that catered to small audiences. One such play is *El triunfo de los Santos* (The Triumph of the Saints), written by Pedro Morales in 1579 to celebrate the arrival of some important Catholic relics; another one is the *Dialogus in adventu inquisitorium factus* (Dialogue upon the Arrival of the Inquisitors), written by Bernardino de Llanos in 1589 to honor the visit of the Inquisitors.

Mexico was the first Spanish colony in the Americas to have commercial theater. Professional actors were imported as early as 1574, and by the end of the sixteenth century there were two Corrales de comedias (Theater Houses) in operation: one, next door to the Hospital de Nuestra Señora, and the other in the patio of the Hospital Real de Indios. As in Spain, hospitals in Mexico supplemented their income by renting out space for theatrical presentations. Gonzalo de Riancho was the first lay director hired to oversee and stage plays during religious festivities and at other times. He served in this capacity from 1595 to 1618.

The seventeenth century is highlighted by a playwright who was known mainly in Spain, Juan *Ruiz de Alarcón, and by a Hieronymite nun, Sor Juana Inés de la *Cruz. Ruiz de Alarcón, a major Golden Age author, is considered to be one of the first Western writers preoccupied with the psychological development of his characters, and with morality. *La verdad sospechosa* (Truth Suspect) deals with the moral and psychological implications of lying. He is said to be the founder of the comedy of character. Writers such as Moreto, Moratín, Corneille, Molière, and López de Ayala are indebted, in one way or another, to Juan Ruiz de Alarcón.

Although better known for her poetry and feminist views, Sor Juana Inés de la Cruz's contribution to Mexican theater is significant. She wrote mainly one-act plays (*loas, coloquios, entremeses*, sainetes). She also wrote one comedy, *Los empeños de una casa* (The Travails of a Household). It is an entertaining play in which one of the characters, doña Leonor, shares some the characteristics of the author. She is an educated, eloquent, and independent woman. Sor Juana's success seems to have made an impact in the way men regarded women for, in 1687, María de Celi, an actress, was named director of the Coliseo, the official theater house, by the viceroy. During the eighteenth century several women held this post.

Other seventeenth century playwrights include Cristóbal Gutiérrez de Luna, who wrote a play about the Christianization of the Indian nobility, *Coloquio de la nueva conversión y bautismo de los últimos reyes de Tlaxcala* (Colloquy of the New Conversion and Baptism of the Last Kings of Tlaxcala). Matías de *Bocanegra wrote a fictionalized account of St. Francis of Borja's life in 1640, *Comedia de San Francisco de Borja* (Play of Saint Francis of Borja). Francisco de Acevedo wrote *El pregonero de Dios y patriarca de los pobres* (The Announcer Of God and Patriarch of the Poor). It is a comedy about the life of St. Francis of Assisi which was censured by the Inquisition for not adhering to historical truth.

The first half of eighteenth-century Mexican secular theater is dominated by Eusebio Vela, an actor, director, and playwright who came to the New World in 1713 to work in his brother's theatrical company. Only three of fourteen works that he reportedly wrote have reached us: *Si el amor excede al arte* (If Love Exceeds Art), *La pérdida de España* (The Loss of Spain), and *Apostolado de las Indias y martirio de un cacique* (Apostolate of the Indies And Martyrdom of a Cacique). Vela paid more attention to scenography than to poetry, ideas, or didacticism. He had a penchant to awe and terrify his audience by having, onstage, representations of rocks that turned into mythological monsters such as the Furies, or the Devil riding a dragon to meet St. James on a white stallion. There were thunders in the dark, screams, the sound of chains being dragged, foul smells. Because of his scenography and his intent to shock his audience, he may well be regarded as an early romantic. Ana María de Castro assumed directorship of the Coliseo after Vela's death in 1737.

During this same period, Cayetano Javier de Cabrera y Quintero, a Bethlehem Hospitaller priest, distinguished himself as a playwright and a poet. He wrote several short dramatic compositions, an example of which is *Los empeños de la casa de sabiduría* (The Travails of the House of Wisdom), written as an introduction to the presentation of Sor Juana's *Los empeños de una casa* (The Travails of a Household). One of his longer dramatic works that have survived is *El iris de Salamanca* (The Iris of Salamanca), which deals with the life of St. John Sahagun. His narrative work, *Escudo de Armas* (Coat of Arms), was censured in 1746. In it, he documents the Virgin of Guadalupe's right to be called the Patron Saint of Mexico, but he also derides the Indians, the medical profession, and the royalties that city hall received from *pulque*, a pre-Hispanic alcoholic drink.

The period from the second half of the eighteenth century up to the Mexican Independence in 1821 witnessed the rise of secular popular theater and somewhat of a decline of religious dramas. Recently imported ideas from the United States and France were discussed, and new theaters were built in Mexico City (1753) and in Puebla (1760). Of many "pantomime dances" by Juan de Medina, two written in 1796 have survive:. *Los juegos de Eglea* (The Games of Eglea) and *Muerte trágica de Muley-Eliacid, emperador de Marruecos* (The Tragic Death of Muley-Eliacid, Emperor of Morocco).

Also, a more nationalistic type of theater began to emerge. Fernando Gavila, sometimes known as Fernando de Dávila, wrote and had staged *La mexicana en Inglaterra* (The Mexican Woman in England) in 1792. He also wrote *La lealtad americana* (American Loyalty) in 1796, and the *zarzuela*, a short musical dramatic composition, *La linda poblana* (The Beautiful Girl from Puebla) in 1802. José Agustín de *Castro is the author of "loas," "autos," and two one-act plays: *El charro* (The Cowboy) and *Los remendones* (The Shoemakers). The first is a monologue by a "charro," a not so bright prototype of masculinity, who finds himself in the patio of a convent. The second is a light satire on the empty claims to nobility by two poverty-stricken shoemakers. Typical Mexican dances such as the "Jarabe" and the "Bamba poblana" were featured in place of the more traditional "entremeses."

Religious drama, though not as prevalent as before, was still popular among certain audiences. Manuel Quiroz Campo Sagrado's *Certamen poético en argumentos entre los cinco sentidos* (Poetic Contest in Dialogues among the Five Senses), a dramatic panegyric of the Virgin Mary, is an example.

The outstanding literary figure during the Wars of Independence (1810-1821) is José Joaquín *Fernández de Lizardi, a journalist who began writing stories, novels, and dramas after his newspaper, *El Pensador Mexicano* (The Mexican Thinker), was shut down. His dramatic production during these years includes *El fuego de Prometeo* (The Fire of Prometheus), *Auto mariano* (Auto of the Virgin Mary), *La noche más venturosa* (The Most Fortunate Eve), and *Todos contra el payo* (Everyone against the Simpleton).

Around the end of the eighteenth century the *autos* and *coloquios* dealing with the Nativity evolved into what is known as *pastorelas*. The *pastorela* includes songs, music, and dramatic presentations. As in the case of its two predecessors, the *pastorelas* were staged in all of New Spain domains from New Mexico to Central America. Local priests were mainly responsible for staging these works. Some of the *pastorelas* written during this period include Fernández de Lizardi's *La noche más venturosa*. Throughout the nineteenth century they became so popular that they were featured regularly, during Christmas time, at the main theaters. Today, in the waning years of the twentieth century, it is not uncommon to find in December *pastorelas* performed by professionals or amateurs.

MAIN WORKS OF THE PERIOD: Francisco de Acevedo, *El pregonero de Dios y Patriarca de los pobres* (The Announcer Of God And Patriarch Of The Poor), edited by Julio Jiménez Rueda (México: Imp. Universitaria, 1945), first staged in 1684. *Auto de la adoración de los Reyes Magos* (Auto of the Worship of the Three Wise Men), translated by Francisco del Paso Troncoso. Cid Prez and Martí de Cid 61-82. *Auto de la destrucción de Jerusalén* (Auto of the Destruction of Jerusalem), translation by Francisco del Paso Troncoso (Florence: Salvador Landi, 1907); reprinted in Rojas Garcidueñas, *Autos y coloquios*, 1-36; Also in English translation by Marylin Ekdahl Ravicz. Matías de Bocanegra, *Comedia de San Francisco de Borja* (Comedy of St. Francis of Borja), 1640, in Rojas Garcidueñas and Arróm, 221-379. Cayetano Javier de Cabrera y Quintero, *Obra dramática: Teatro novohispano del siglo XVIII* (Theatrical Works: Theater of New Spain in the Eighteenth Century), edited by Claudia Parodi (México: UNAM, 1976). José Agustín de Castro, *Los remendones* (The Shoemakers) and *El charro* (The Cowboy), in *Poesías sagradas* (México, 1809). Francisco Cervantes de Salazar, *Tres diálogos latinos* (Three Latin Dialogues), translated by Joaquín García Icazbalceta (México, 1875); reprinted as *México en 1554 y Túmulo imperial*, edited by Edmundo O'Gorman (México: Porrúa, 1985); also as *México en 1554*, edited by Margarita Peña (México: Trillas, 1986). Sor Juana Inés de la Cruz, *Inundación castálida* (Castillian Flood) (Madrid, 1689); *Fama y obras póstumas* (Fame and Posthumous Works) (Madrid, 1700); *Obras de Sor Juana Inés de la Cruz* (Works Of Sor Juana Inés De La Cruz) (Sevilla: 1692); *Obras completas* (Complete Works), edited by Francisco Monterde (México: Porrúa, 1981). Fernández de Lizardi and José Joaquín, *Obras II. Teatro* (Works II. Theater), edited by Jacobo Chencinsky (México: UNAM, 1965). José Gaspar, *The Merchant*, translated by Byron McAffee. Ravicz 99-118; first staged in the sixteenth century. Fernán González de Eslava, *Coloquios espirituales y sacramentales* (Spiritual And Religious Colloquies), edited by Rojas Garcidueñas, 2 vols. (México: UNAM, 1972); "Coloquio de los cuatro doctores de la iglesia" (Colloquy of the Four Doctors of the Church), in Rojas Garcidueñas, *Autos y coloquios* 81-115; "Coloquio del Conde de la Coruña" (Colloquy of the Count of La Coruña), in Rojas Garcidueñas, *Autos y coloquios* 117-73. Gutiérrez de Luna, "Coloquio de la nueva conversión y bautismo de los cuatro últimos reyes de Tlaxcala" (Colloquy of the New Conversion and Baptism of the Last Four Kings of Tlaxcala), in Rojas Garcidueñas and Arróm 183-220, first staged circa 1619. Diego Juárez, *La caída del hombre* (The Fall of Man), lost, first staged on July 15, 1575; *La conquista de Roda* (The Conquest of Rhodes), lost, first staged in 1539. Bernardino de Llanos, *Pro patris Antonii de Mendoza adventu* (Eclogue Upon the Arrival of Father Antonio de Mendoza), 1585, translated by José Quiñones Melgoza as *Egloga por la llegada del padre Antonio de Mendoza* (México: UNAM, 1975), first staged at the Colegio de San Idelfonso in 1585; *Dialogus in adventu inquisitorium* (Dialogue Upon The Arrival Of The Inquisitors ...) (México, 1589), translated by José QuiÑones Melgoza as *Diálogo en la visita de los inquisidores* (Dialogue upon the Visit of the Inquisitors) (México: UNAM, 1982), first staged at the Colegio de San Idelfonso in 1589. Pedro Morales, "Tragedia del triunfo de los santos" (Tragedy of the Triumph of the Saints) (México, 1579);.reprinted in Rojas Garcidueñas and Arróm, 1-148; "An Edition of 'Triunfo de los santos' with a consideration of Jesuit Plays in Mexico before 1650," edited by Harvey L. Johnson,

Diss., University of Pennsylvania, 1941; first staged on November 1, 1578. Fray Andrés de Olmos, *Auto del juicio final* (Auto of the Final Judgment), translated by John J. Cornyn and Byron McAfee. Ravicz 143-57; first staged at the Chapel of San José de los Naturales in Mexico circa 1540. Juan Pérez Ramírez, "Desposorio del pastor Pedro y la Iglesia Mexicana" (Wedding Of The Shepherd Peter And The Mexican Church), translation by Francisco del Paso Troncoso, in Rojas Garcidueñas, *Autos y coloquios*, 37-77; first staged in 1574. Juan Ruiz de Alarcón, *Parte primera de las comedias de don Juan Ruiz de Alarcón y Mendoza* (First Part of the Comedies of) (Madrid, 1628); *Parte segunda de las comedias de don Juan Ruiz de Alarcón y Mendoza* (Second Part of the Comedies of) (Barcelona, 1634). All of these comedies were staged in Spain after Alarcón's second trip in 1614. The first part contains eight works, and the second twelve. *Primera parte . . .* and *Segunda parte . . .* (First Part . . . and Second Part . . .), edited by Alva Ebersole (Valencia: Artes Gráficas Soler, Hispanófila, 1966); *La verdad sospechosa* (The Truth Suspect), translated by Julio del Toro and Robert Finney, in *Poet Lore* (Boston), 38 (1927): 457-530; translated by Robert C. Bryan, in *Spanish Drama* (New York: Bantam Books, 1962): pp. 135-89. This is the only play by Ruiz de Alarcón to be translated into English. Manuel de los Santos y Salazar, *Invención de la Santa Cruz por Santa Elena* (How the Blessed St. Helen Found the Holy Cross), 1714, translated by Francisco Paso y Troncoso (México, 1890): rerpinted and translated as *How The Blessed St. Helen Found The Holy Cross*, translated by Byron McAfee, in Ravicz, 160-178. *Souls and Testamentary Executors*, translated by Byron McAfee and John H. Cornyn, in Ravicz 211-34. Manuel Quiroz Campo Sagrado, *Certamen poético en argumentos entre los cinco sentidos. Colección de varias poesías de arte menor y mayor* (México: AGN/INBA, 1984), pp. 158-203. Eusebio Vela, *Tres comedias de Eusebio Vela*, edited by Jefferson Rea Spell and Francisco Monterde (México: Imp. Universitaria, 1948). Manuel Zumana, *Parónope* (México, 1711), lost; *El Rodrigo* (México, 1711), lost.

BIBLIOGRAPHY: Juan José Arróm, *El teatro de Hispanoamérica en la época colonial* (La Habana: Anuario Bibliográfico Cubano, 1956). David G. Brinton, ed., *The "Gegence," A Comedy Ballet in the Nahuatl Spanish Dialect of Nicaragua* (Philadelphia, 1883). Antonio Castro Leal, *Juan Ruiz de Alarcón: Su vida y su obra* (México: Cuadernos Americanos, 1943). José Cid Pérez and Dolores Martí de Cid, Introduction, *Teatro indoamericano colonial* (México: Aguilar, 1970). Genaro García, *Documentos inéditos . . .*, vol. 15 (México, 1907). Joaquín García Icazbalceta, "Representaciones religiosas en el siglo XVI," *Obras: Opúsculos varios*, vol. 1 (México: 1896). Irving A. Leonard, *Baroque Times in Old Mexico* (Ann Arbor: University of Michigan Press, 1959); "The 1790 Theater Season in the Mexico City Coliseo," *Hispanic Review* 19 (1951): 104-20; "The Theater Season of 1791-1792 in Mexico City," *Hispanic American Historical Review* 31 (1951): 349-64; "La temporada teatral de 1792 en el Nuevo Coliseo de Mxico," *Nueva Revista de Filología Hispánica* 5 (1951): 349-410. Armando de María y Campos, *Representaciones teatrales en la Nueva España: Siglos XVI al XVIII* (México: Costa-Amic, 1959); *Pastorelas mexicanas: Su origen, historia y tradición* (México: Diana, 1985). Sister Joseph Marie, *The Role of the Church and the Folk in the Development of the Early Drama in New Mexico* (Philadelphia: University of Pennsylvania, 1948). Byron McAfee, and R. H. Barlow, trans. and ed., "Un cuaderno de marqueses," *El México antiguo* 6, 9-12 (1947): 392-404. Marianne Oeste de Bopp, "Autos mexicanos del siglo XVI," *Historia Mexicana* 3, 9 (1953): 112-23. Walter Poesse, *Juan Ruiz de Alarcón* (New York:

Twayne, 1972). Marylin Ekdahl Ravicz, Introduction, *Early Colonial Religious Drama in Mexico: From Tzompantli to Golgotha* (Washington: The Catholic University of America Press, 1970). Alfonso Reyes, *Letras de la Nueva España* (México: Fondo de Cultura Económica, 1948). Winston A. Reynolds, "El demonio y Lope de Vega en el manuscrito mexicano Coloquio de la nueva conversión y bautismo," in *Cuadernos Americanos* 163, 2 (1969): 172-84. Stanley L. Robe, Introduction, *"Coloquios de pastores" from Jalisco* (Berkeley: University of California Press, 1954). José Rojas Garcidueñas, Introduction, *Autos y coloquios del siglo XVI* (México: Uiversidad Nacional Autónoma de México, 1972); *El teatro de Nueva España en el siglo XVI* (1935; México: Sep-Setentas, 1973). José Rojas Garcidueñas and José J. Arróm, Introductions, *Tres piezas teatrales del virreinato* (México: Universidad Nacional Atónoma de México, 1976), pp. 1-34, 149-82, 221-36. Hildburg Schilling, *Teatro profano en la Nueva España* (México: Imp. Universitaria, 1958). Jefferson R. Spell, "The Theater in Mexico City, 1805-1806," *Hispanic Review* 1 (1933): 55-65. Carlos Miguel Suárez Radillo, *El teatro barroco hispanoamericano*, vol. 1 (Madrid: José Porrúa Turanzas, 1981). J. Luis Trenti Rocamora, *El teatro en la América colonial* (Buenos Aires: Huarpes, 1947). Frida Weber de Kurlat, *Lo cómico en el teatro de Fernán González de Eslava* (Buenos Aires: University of Buenos Aires, Filosofía y Letras, 1963).

ALFONSO GONZALEZ

TORRES, Teodoro (1891-1944), novelist, journalist, historian, humorist. Born in Villa de Guadalupe, San Luis Potosí, Teodoro Torres moved to Mexico City where he started first as a journalist. He also lived nine years in San Antonio, Texas, where he was editor of *La Prensa*, a well-known newspaper published in Spanish. This experience in San Antonio was very useful for his descriptions in *La patria perdida* (The Lost Motherland) (1935). Other publications that he worked for were newspapers and cultural publications, such as *Excelsior, Revista de Revistas, México al Día*, and *Saber*. He founded the first school of journalism in Mexico. In 1941 he was elected as a Mexican representative of the Spanish Royal Academy.

La patria perdida is a novel that deals with exile in a very critical period of Mexican history, the Mexican Revolution. Luis Alfaro, the main character of the novel and a former officer of the Federal Army, "voluntarily" exiles to the United States during the Revolution. Revolutions place a very heavy burden on people. Here it becomes a great opportunity for Torres, as a fiction writer, to place his characters within this critical framework. He can highlight the problems upon discovering the cultural and linguistic differences found in the new country. Although San Antonio, even now, seems to have much influence from Mexico, the differences can still be emphasized. As time goes by, Alfaro, in his new country, realizes that Mexico has gone through changes. Personally, he realizes that he himself has changed. There is a strong feeling of loneliness away from his country of origin, and it is very difficult for him to adapt to the new environment. The feeling of loneliness is not limited to Alfaro's personal situation, but by extension, there is a feeling of loneliness in general. This is a very common theme in the Mexican novel of the 1930s and 1940s. It also appears very markedly in contemporary Chicano novels, such as *Pocho* (1959), *Barrio Boy* (1971), and *Peregrinos de Aztlán* (1974), to name just a few.

WORKS: *La patria perdida* (The Lost Motherland) (México: Premi Editora, S.A., 1935). *Golondrina* (México: 1945). Also a biography of Pancho Villa, a book on humor, and a collection of journalistic anecdotes.

OSCAR SOMOZA

TORRES Bodet, Jaime (1902-1974), poet, novelist, educator, essayist, and diplomat. Born in Mexico City, Torres Bodet was one of the founding fathers of the group known as the Contemporáneos in 1928. A diplomat since 1929, Torres Bodet was ambassador of Mexico to France (1954-1958), and director general of UNESCO (1948-1952). He served as secretary of public education during two terms, 1943-1946 and 1958-1964. He was a member of the Academia Mexicana de la Lengua and the Colegio Nacional. Torres Bodet received the Premio Nacional de Letras (National Award for Literature) in 1966. He was a writer committed to both aesthetic and social concerns.

WORKS : Poetry: *Fervor* (Fervor) (México: Ballesca, 1918). *El corazón delirante* (The Delirious Heart) (México: Porrúa, 1922). *Canciones* (Songs) (México: Ed. Cultura, 1922). *Nuevas canciones* (New Songs) (Madrid: Saturnino Calleja, 1923). *La casa: Poema* (The House: Poem) (México: Herrero Hnos., 1923). *Los días* (The Days) (México: Herrero Hnos., 1923). *Poemas* (Poems) (México: Herrero Hnos., 1924). *Biombo* (Screen) (México: Herrero Hnos., 1925). *Destierro* (Exile) (Madrid: Espasa Calpe, 1930). *Cripta* (Crypt) (México: Loera y Chávez, 1937). *Sonetos* (Sonnets) (México: Gráfica Panamericana, 1949). *Fronteras* (Frontiers) (México: FCE, 1954). *Sin tregua* (Without Truce) (México: FCE, 1957). *Trébol de cuatro hojas* (Four Leaf Clover) (Jalapa: Universidad Veracruzana, 1960), published earilier by the author in Paris. *Poemas* (Poems) (París: Gallimard, 1960). *Selected Poems of Jaime Torres Bodet*, edited and translated by Sonja Karsen (Bloomington: Indiana Univeristy Press, 1964). *Obra poética* (Poetic Works), introduction by Rafael Solana (México: Porrúa, 1967). *Song of Serene Voices*, translated by J. C. R. Green (Portree, Isle of Skye: Aquila [Phaeton Press], 1982). Essays: *Contemporáneos: Hojas de crítica* (Contemporáneos: Papers on Criticism) (México: Herrero Hnos., 1928). "Perspectiva de la literatura mexicana actual 1915-1928" (Perspective on Contemporary Mexican Literature 1915-1928), in *Contemporáneos* 2 (1928): 1-33. "*Paisaje de Garcilaso.*" *Tres ensayos de amistad para Garcilaso* (Garcilaso's Landscape: Three Friendship Essays for Garcilaso) (México: Taller poético, 1936). *Educación mexicana: Discursos, entrevistas, mensajes* (Mexican Education: Speeches, Interviews, Messages) (México: SEP, 1944). *La obra educativa en el sexenio 1940-1946* (Education during the 1940-1946 Administration) (México: SEP, 1946). *Educación y concordia internacional: Discursos y mensajes (1941-1947)* (Education and International Harmony: Speeches and Messages) (México: El Colegio de México, 1948). *El escritor en su libertad* (The Writer in His Liberty) (México: El Colegio de México, 1953). *Tres inventores de la realidad: Stendhal, Dostoiewski y Perez Galdós* (Three Inventors of Reality: Stendhal, Dostoyevski, and Pérez Galdós) (México: Imp. Universitaria, 1955). *Balzac* (Balzac) (México: FCE, 1959). *Maestros venecianos* (Venetian Masters) (México: Porrúa, 1961). *León Tolstoi: Su vida y su obra* (Leon Tolstoi: Life and Works) (México: Porrúa, 1965). *Discursos (1941-1964)* (Speeches: 1941-1964) (México: Porrúa, 1965). *Rubén Darío: Abismo y cima* (Ruben Darío: Abyss and Zenith). (México: FCE,

1966). *Tiempo y memoria en la obra de Proust* (Time and Memory in the Works of Proust) (México: Porrúa, 1967). Novels: *Margarita de niebla* (Margaret in the Fog) (México: Ed. Cultura, 1927). *La educación sentimental* (Sentimental Education) (Madrid: Espasa Calpe, 1929). *Proserpina rescatada* (Proserpine Rescued) (Madrid: Espasa Calpe, 1931). *Estrella de día* (Day Star) (Madrid: Espasa Calpe, 1933). *Primero de enero* (January First) (Madrid: Ed. Literatura, 1935). *Sombras* (Shadows) (México: Cultura, 1937). Short Stories: *Nacimiento de Venus y otros relatos* (The Birth of Venus and Other Stories) (México: Cultura, 1941). Memoirs: *Tiempo de arena* (Sand Time) (México: FCE, 1955). *Sin tregua* (Without Truce) (México: FCE, 1957). *Años contra el tiempo* (Years against Time) (México: Porrúa, 1969). *Memorias II: La victoria sin alas* (Memoirs II: Victory without Wings)(México: Porrúa, 1970). *El desierto internacional* (The International Desert) (México: n.p., 1971). *La tierra prometida* (The Promised Land) (México: n.p., 1972). *Equinoccio* (Equinox) (México: n.p., 1974).

BIBLIOGRAPHY: Alicia G. R. Aldaya, *Tres poetas Hispanoamericanos* (Madrid: Playor, 1978), pp. 14-39. Antonio Brambila, "Melancolía por el suicidio," *Abside* 38 (1974): 79-84. Fernando Burgos, *De la crónica a la nueva narrativa hispanoamericana: Coloquio sobre literatura mexicana* (Oaxaca [México]: Oasis, 1986), pp. 139-49. Jorge Campos, "El Ruben Darío de Torres Bodet," *Insula* 22 (1967): 9. Emmanuel Carballo, "Jaime Torres Bodet (1902-1974)." *19 Protagonistas de la literatura mexicana* (México: SEP [Lecturas Mexicanas], 1986), pp. 266-301. Frank Dauster, *Ensayos sobre poesía mexicana. Asedio a los "Contemporáneos"* (México: De Andrea, 1963). Merlin H. Forster, *Los Contemporáneos (1920-1932): Perfil de un experimento vanguardista* (México: De Andrea, 1964); "Three Versions of a Poem by Jaime Torres Bodet," in *Romance Notes* 10 (1968): 32-36. Harry S. Gillespi, "Thematic Recurrence in Jaime Torres Bodet's Poetry," *DAI* 33 (1973): 5174A, University of Missouri, Columbia; "A Fourth Version of Jaime Torres Bodet's 'Buzo'," in *Romance Notes* 18 (1977): 28-31. Marta R. Gómez, *Jaime Torres Bodet en quince semblanzas* (México: Oasis, 1965). Jane Eiland Hamilton, "The World View of Jaime Torres Bodet in *Fronteras* and *Sin tregua*," *DAI* 38 (1978): 6754A, University of Arizona. José Hernández Vargas, "Los vasos comunicantes: Realidad e irrealidad," *Cuadernos Americanos* 317 (1976): 327-53. Sonja Karsen, ed. and trans., *Selected Poems of Jaime Torres Bodet* (Bloomington: Indiana Univeristy Press, 1964); *Jaime Torres Bodet* (New York: Twayne, 1971). Beth Miller, *La poesía constructiva de Jaime Torres Bodet* (México: Porrúa, 1974); compiler, *Ensayos contemporáneos sobre Torres Bodet* (México: UNAM, 1976); "Jaime Torres Bodet and Autobiography," *Auto/Biography Studies* (New York) 34 (1988): 37-47. Judy Held Miller, "The Development of Cinematographic Techniques in Three Novels of Jaime Torres Bodet," *DAI* 36 (1975): 2791A, University of New York, Albany. Joaquim Montezuma de Carvalho, "Jaime Torres Bodet Proust," *Norte: Revista Hispano Americana* 267 (1975): 61-65. Douglas Morgenstern, Douglas, "Death and Time in Three Poems by Jorge Carrera Andrade, Jaime Torres Bodet, and José Gorostiza," *Kentucky Romance Quarterly* 23 (1976): 63-75. Edward J. Mullen, "Nota sobre un poema no estudiado de Jaime Torres Bodet," *Duquesne Hispanic Review* 8, 2 (1969): 1-6; "Poetic Revision in Jaime Torres Bodet's 'Canción de cuna'," *Papers on Language and Literature* 6 (1970): 180-87; "Destierro y la visión superrealista de Jaime Torres Bodet," *Hispanófila* 50 (1974): 85-98. Ollie Olympo Oviedo, "The Reception of the Faust Motif in Latin American Literature: Archetypal Transformations in Works by Estanislao del Campo, Alberto Gerchunoff, Joao Guimaraes Rosa, Carlos

Fuentes, and Jaime Torres Bodet," *DAI* 48 (1988): 2867A, New York University. Margaret S. Peden, "Una nota sobre la muerte del modernismo: *Nacimiento de Venus de don Jaime Torres Bodet*," *Cuadernos Hispanoamericanos* 284 (1974): 431-35. Gustavo Pérez Firmat and Gregorio Martin, eds., "Jaime Torres Bodet's *Margarita de niebla* and the Problem of Fictional Characterization," *Selected Proceedings: 32nd Mountain Interstate Foreign Language Conference* (Winston-Salem, N.C.: Wake Forest University, 1984), pp. 247-54. Mercedes Ruiz García, *La obra novelística de Jaime Torres Bodet* (México: Sec. de Hacienda y Crédito Público, 1971; Fort Worth: Texas Christian University Press, 1977). Arturo Torres Rioseco, "Fronteras de Jaime Torres Bodet," *Revista Iberoamericana* 38 (1954): 384-87.

MIRTA A. GONZALEZ

TORRI, Julio (1889-1970). Born in Saltillo, Coahuila, on June 27, 1889, Torri spent his early years in his native city. In 1908, he went to Mexico City and received his law degree in 1913. In addition to being a member of the prestigious Ateneo de la Juventud, Torri occupied several important educational positions in the city. He was, for instance, the founder and head of the Departamento de Bibliotecas, which would become an important institution. He also worked extensively in the publishing field, helping to disseminate not only the important books of his time, but also the classics. One of José *Vasconcelos' close associates, he collaborated with him in several capacities over time. Traveling on behalf of Mexico, serving on important educational committees, and investing himself in his own literary production kept Torri very active. Twice, in the capacity of visiting professor, he gave summer classes at the University of Texas. A trip to Europe in 1952 inspired some of his prose writing. He taught Spanish and French literature at the Escuela Nacional Preparatoria for thirty-six years, and elsewhere until 1964. In 1933, he earned a doctorate in Literature. Several years later, in 1942, he became a member of the Academia Mexicana de la Lengua.

Although of limited literary production, Julio Torri is considered one of the best prose writers of his generation. He wrote three short books of essays, a manual of Spanish literature and a few critical studies. Influenced by Baudelaire, Horace, and Boccaccio, among others, he wrote straightforward and technically artistic prose. He was opposed to the verbal extravagance and some of the literary innovations of his time, yet he was quite original in his own work. He strove to keep his prose simple but elegant, complex perhaps in content, but not in form. In particular, some of Torri's essays are thought to be refreshing and authentic vignettes of life. He also wrote short stories that reveal his talent to subtly integrate humor with emotion in a fluid writing style. He is also credited with popularizing the poem in prose.

His death in 1970 spurred many eulogies about his life, his works, and his impact on Mexican literature.

WORKS: *Ensayos y poemas* (Essays and Poems) (México: Edit. Porrúa, 1917); shorter edition, *Ensayos y fantasías* (Essays and Fantasies). Goethe, *Hermann y Dorotea* (Hermann and Dorothy), prologue (México: Editorial Cultura, 1917). *El Convivio* (San José de Costa Rica: Imp. Alsina, 1918); 2nd ed. (México: Edit. Porrúa

1937). Enrique Heine, *Las noches florentinas* (Florentine Nights), translation, in *Cultura* 7, 3 (México, 1918): 14-88; 2nd ed. (Buenos Aires: Editorial Bable, 1923). *Romances viejos* (Old Romances), prologue (México: Editorial Cultura, 1918). Aeschylus, *Tragedias* (Tragedies), prologue (México: UNAM, 1921). *Ensayos y poemas* (Essays and Poems) (México: Porrúa, 1937). *El convivio*, translation by Dorothy Margaret Kress (New York: Institute of French Studies, 1938). *De fusilamientos* (About Executions) (México: La Casa de España en México, 1940). Pascal, *Discursos sobre las pasiones del amor* (Discourses on the Passions of Love), translation (México: Editorial Séneca, 1942). *Sentencias y lugares comunes* (Judgments and Common Places), Pajaritas de Papel (México: PEN Club de Mexico, 1945); 2nd ed., *La pajarita de papel, 1924-1925* (México: INBA, 1965). "Recuerdos de Pedro Henríquez Ureña" (Memories of Pedro Henríquez Ureña), in *Filosofía y Letras* 23 (1946): 99-102. *Grandes cuentistas* (Great Story Writers), selection, preliminary study, and bibliographical notes (Buenos Aires: W. M. Jackson, 1949). Luis G. Urbina, *Crónicas* (Chronicles), prologue and selection (México: UNAM, 1950). Luis Rius, *Canciones de vela* (Songs of Wakefulness), epilogue (México: Eds. Segrel, 1951). *La literatura española* (Spanish Literature) (México and Buenos Aires: FCE, 1952); 2nd ed., revised (1955); 3rd ed. (1960); 4th ed. (1964). "La *Revista Moderna de México*" (México: Ed. Jus, 1954); also in *Memorias de la Academia Mexicana Correspondiente de la Española* (Memories of the Academia Mexicana Respective to the Academia Española) 14 (1956): 311-22. *Antología* (Anthology), selections (México: Costa-Amic, n.d. [1959?]). *Raquel Banda Farfán, Un pedazo de vida* (A Piece of Life), stories, prologue (México: Editorial Comaval, 1959). *Tres libros* (Three Books) (México: FCE, 1964). *Julio Torri* (México: FCE, 1980). *[Selecciones] Diálogo de los libros* (Selections: Dialogue of Books) (México: FCE, 1980). *De fusilamientos, y otras narraciones* (About Executions and Other Narrations) (México: Secretaria de Educación Pública, 1984). *El ladrón de ataúdes* (The Coffin Thief) (México: FCE, 1987). *Ensayos y notas* (Essays and Notes) (México: UNAM, 1988).

BIBLIOGRAPHY: Ermilo Abreu Gómez, "Retrato de Julio Torri," in *Vida Literaria* 5, 6 (1970): 38-39. Demetrio Aguilera Malta, "Julio Torri, orfebre de la prosa," in *El Gallo Ilustrado* (Aug. 16, 1964): 4. Jesús Arellano, Review of *Antología*, in *Metáfora* 14 (May-June 1957): 43. Huberto Batis, Review of *Tres libros*, in *La Cultura en México* (Sept. 2, 1964): xix. Mario Calleros, "Las mesas de plomo. Julio Torri," in *Ovaciones* (Aug. 25, 1963): 2. Emmanuel Carballo, "Julio Torri," in *México en la Cultura* (March 16, 1958): 2; "Entrevista con Julio Torri," in *Ovaciones* (June 7, 1964): 2-5; "Elogio ininterrumpido de Julio Torri," in *La Cultura en México* (Aug. 26, 1964): xvi; *El cuento mexicano del siglo XX* (México: Empresas Editoriales, 1964), pp. 18-20; Review of *Tres libros*, in *La Cultura en México* (Jan. 6, 1965): iv; "Carta a Manuel Pedro González," in *La Cultura en México* (Oct. 27, 1965): xv; *19 protagonistas de la literatura mexicana del siglo XX* (México: Empresas Editoriales, 1965), pp. 141-51; "Innovador desconocido," in *Vida Literaria* 5, 6 (1970): 44-45. Jorge Cervera Sánchez, "Julio Torri, escritor y maestro," in *México en la Cultura* (June 26, 1949): 2, 6. Hugo Covantes, "Julio Torri, hombre y maestro," in *México en la Cultura* (Jan. 31, 1964): 9. Esteban Durán Rosado, Review of *Tres libros*, in *Revista Mexicana de Cultura* (Aug. 30, 1964): 15. Jorge González Durán, "El héroe fugaz," review of *De fusilamientos*, in *Tierra Nueva* (Jan.-April 1941): 85-91. Andrés Henestrosa, Review of Prosas dispersas," in *El Nacional* (May 20, 1964): 3; "Tránsito de Julio Torri," in *Vida Literaria* 5, 6 (1970): 43. Benjamín Jarnés, "Agudez, pasto del alma," in *Vida*

Literaria 5, 6 (1970): 36-38. Dolores M. Koch, "El micro-relato en México: Torri, Arreola, Monterroso y Aviles Fabila," in *Hispamérica* (Dec. 1981). Luis Leal, *Panorama de la literatura mexicana actual* (Washington, D.C.: Unión Panamericana, 1968), pp. 20, 111. José Luis Martínez, "Julio Torri," in *Vida Literaria* 5, 6 (1970): 39-41. Ernesto Mejía Sánchez, "Opiniones," in *Vida Literaria* 5, 6 (1970): 26-34; "Una carta de Alfonso Reyes," in *Vida Literaria* 5, 6 (1970): 41-42; "Anversos y reversos de Julio Torri," in *Revista de Letras* 4 (1970): 234-40. Aurora M. Ocampo de Gómez and Ernesto Prado Velázquez, *Diccionario de Escritores Mexicanos* (México: UNAM, 1967), pp. 382-83. José Emilio Pacheco, Review of *Tres libros*, in *Diálogos* 1, 1 (Nov.-Dec. 1964): 31. Salvador Reyes Nevares, Review of "Prosas dispersas," in *La Cultura en México* (May 20, 1964): xx. Manuel J. Rodríguez Tejada, *Antología de poetas y escritores coahuilenses* (Paris: Les presses Universitaires de France, 1926). Sara Sefchovich, *México: país de ideas, país de novelas* (México: Editorial Grijalbo, 1987), pp. 83, 161, 168, 173. Mauricio de la Selva, Review of *Tres libros*, in *Diograma de la Cultura* (Aug. 16, 1964): 4; *Cuadernos Americanos* 5 (Sept-Oct. 1964): 287-89. Teodoro Torres, *El humorismo y la sátira en México* (México: FCE, 1943); *El trato con escritores* (México: INBA, 1961), pp. 120, 121, 124, 127, 183; *El trato con escritores*, 2nd series (México: INBA, 1964), pp. 61, 122, 124, 127, 183. Ramón Xirau, "Julio Torri y el significado de la brevedad," in *Vida Literaria* 5, 6 (1970): 41-42. Serge I. Zaitzell, "Julio Torri, originalidad y modernidad," in *Texto Crítico* 11 (Universidad Veracruzana, 1978); "Julio Torri y el cuento mexicano actual," in *Tinta* (May 1983): 21-25; "Julio Torri, precursor de Julio Cortázar," in *Coloquio internacional: lo lúdico y lo fantástico en la obra de Cortázar*, vol. 1 (Madrid: Fundamentos, 1986), pp. 25-31; "Las cartas madrileñas de Alfonso Reyes a Julio Torres," in *Revista Iberoamericana* (Apr.-Sept. 1986): 703-59.

JEANNE C. WALLACE

TOSCANO, Carmen (1910-1988), poet, essayist, playwright, and filmmaker. The daughter of the filmmaker Salvador Toscano, Carmen Toscano earned a doctorate in literature from UNAM. She did the editing work of the documentary *Memorias de un mexicano* (Memories of a Mexican), and she promoted the founding a film library in the 1950s and 1960s. She has also worked for television. With María del Carmen Millán, she founded *Rueca*.

Toscano was a regular contributor to *Taller poetico*, *America*, and *Universidad de México*. She produced the film *Ronda de Revolución* (Revolution Circle), and she worked for television and traveled extensively. She was awarded a prize by Talleres Gráficos de la Nación for her biography on Acuña's *Rosario*. Her one-act play *La llorona* has also been praised. Frank Dauster says that her pure voice shows disillusioned, subtle tenderness.

WORKS: Poetry: *Trazo incompleto* (Incomplete Stroke) (México: 1934). *Inalcanzable y mío* (Unreachable and Mine) (México: 1936). Biography: *Rosario la de Acuña* (Acuña's Rosario). *¿Mito romantico?* (Romantic Myth?) (México: 1948). Theater: *El huesped* (The Guest), *El amor de la tia Cristina* (Aunt Cristina's Love), and *Cierto dia* (A Certain Day), in *America* 62 (Jan. 1950): 231-62. *Leyendas de México colonial*

(Legends of Colonial Mexico) (México: Libros-Mex, 1955). *La llorona* (The Weeping Woman) (México: FCE, 1959). Prose: *Las senadoras suelen guisar* (Women Senators Usually Cook) (México: 1964).

BIBLIOGRAPHY: Antonio Castro Leal, La poesía mexicana moderna (México: FCE, 1953), p. xxx, 377. Frank Dauster, *Breve historia* de la poesía mexicana (México: Eds. de Andrea, 1956), p. 178. Alyce Golding Cooper, Teatro mexicano contemporáneo (México: UNAM, 1962), pp. 53, 55, 131. Ruth S. Lamb, *Bibliografía del teatro mexicano del siglo xx* (México: Eds. de Andrea, 1962), p. 118. José Luis Martínez, *Literatura mexicana siglo xx* (México: Ant. Libr. Robredo, 1949), vol. 1, p. 78; v. 2 (1950), p. 119. Salvador Reyes Nevares, Review of *La llorona* in *Mexico en la Cultura* 570 (Feb. 15, 1960): 4. Emilia Romero, Review of *La llorona*, in *Nivel* 16 (April 25, 1960): 5. Carmen Toscano, "*Rueca*," in *Las revistas literarias de México* (México: INBA, 1963):, pp. 99-112.

DELIA GALVAN

TOUSSAINT, Manuel (1890-1955). Born in Mexico City on May 29, 1890, Manuel Toussaint was a highly educated man who founded the art history chair at the Nueva España school, a post which he held for many years. He was one of the founders of the publishing house México Moderno in 1919. Later, in 1934, he founded what would later become the Institute of Aesthetics Research at the University of Mexico. He was the institute director until his untimely death in New York, on November 22, 1955, while on an art mission to Venice. During his many years as the institute's director, he traveled extensively to promote Mexico's advances in art studies. He also held a number of other important positions, such as the director of the Escuela Nacional de Bellas Artes (1928-1929), and the secretary of José *Vasconcelos; he also served as a member of several well-known fine arts and history academies and the Academia Mexicana de la Lengua.

With regard to his literary production, most of his work centered on studies of Mexican art. He wrote such books as *La pintura en México durante el siglo XVI* (Painting in Mexico during the Sixteenth Century) (1936), *La catedral de México y el Sagrario Metropolitano. Su historia, su tesoro, su arte* (The Cathedral of Mexico and the Metropolitan Sanctuary. Its History, Treasure and Art) (1948), and *Pintura colonial en México* (Colonial Painting in Mexico) (1965). The last is considered the first major history of Mexican paintings from the early sixteenth century to the early nineteenth century. Along with Salvador Toscano and Justino Fernández, he coauthored *Historia del arte en México* (History of Art in Mexico), having sole responsibility for the main volume: *Arte colonial en México* (Colonial Art in Mexico).

In addition to many articles published in newspapers and journals, he wrote extensively and published texts of important literary figures, such as Sor Juana Inés de la *Cruz and Ignacio *Altamirano, providing introductory studies for their works. His creative works include *Las aventuras de Pipiolo en el Bosque de Chapultepec* (Pipiolo's Adventures in Chapultepec) (1954), stories for children written under the pseudonym Santos Caballero, and *Viajes alucinados* (Deceptive Journeys) (1924), Manuel Toussaint enjoyed a well-deserved reputation in both art and literature.

670 TOUSSAINT, Manuel

WORKS: *Las cien mejores poesías líricas mexicanas* (The One Hundred Best Mexican Lyrical Poems), in collaboration with Antonio Castro Leal and Alberto Vázquez del Mercado (México: Porrúa, 1914). *Poesías escogidas de Sor Juana Inés de la Cruz* (Selected Poems of Sor Juana Inés de la Cruz), selection and prologue, in *Cultura* 1, 6 (Mexico, 1916). *Los mejores poemas de José Asunción Silva* (The Best Poems of José Asunción Silva), selection and prologue, in *Cultura* 5, 5 (Mexico, 1917). Guillermo Valencia, *Poemas selectos* (Selected Poems), introduction, in *Cultura* 2, 6 (Mexico, 1917). *El tesoro de Amiel, selección del "Diario Intimo"* (The Treasure of Amiel, Selection of the "Intimate Diary"), prologue, in *Cultura* 9, 3 (Mexico, 1918). Luis G. Urbina, *Poemas selectos* (Selected Poems), critical comments, in *Cultura* 2, 4 (Mexico, 1919). Agustín F. Cuenca, *Poemas selectos* (Selected Poems), prologue (México: Mexico Moderno, 1920). *Los cien mejores poemas de Enrique González Martínez* (The One Hundred Best Poems of Enrique González Martínez), study, in *Cultura* 11, 6 (Mexico, 1920). *Viajes alucinados, rincones de España* (Deceptive Journeys, Corners of Spain) (México: Editorial Cultura, 1924). *Poemas inéditos, desconocidos y muy raros de Sor Juana Inés de la Cruz, la Décima Musa* (Unpublished, Unknown and Very Rare Poems by Sor Juana Inés de la Cruz, the Tenth Muse), discovered and compiled (México: Manuel León Sánchez, 1926). *Obras escogidas de Sor Juana Inés de la Cruz, Respuesta a Sor Philotea de la Cruz, Poesías* (Selected Works of Sor Juana Inés de la Cruz, Answer to Sor Philotea de la Cruz, Poems), edition and prologue (México: Editorial Cultura, 1928). Vicente Riva Palacio, *Cuentos del general* (The General's Stories), edition and prologue (México: Editorial Cultura, 1929). *Discursos patrióticos de Ignacio Manuel Altamirano* (Patriotic Speeches by Ignacio Manuel Altamirano), edition and prologue (México: Editorial Cultura, 1932). *La litografía en México en el siglo XIX; sesenta facsimiles de las mejores obras con un texto de Manuel Toussaint* (México: Estudios neolitho, M. Quesada B., 1934). "Genaro Estrada, bibliófilo y coleccionista" (Genaro Estrada, Bibliophile and Collector), in *Letras de México* 1, 18 (Nov. 1938): 3. "Evocando a don Luis González Obregón" (Evoking Luis González Obregón), in *Letras de México* 1, 31 (Sept. 1938): 1. "El periodismo mexicano en los albores de la Independencia (1821-1835)" (Mexican Journalism in the Early Days of Independence [1821-1835]), in *IV Centenario de la imprenta en México, la primera en América* (México: Asociación de Libreros de México, 1939), pp. 281-91. "La importancia de Heredia en la literatura mexicana de su tiempo" (Heredia's Importance in the Mexican Literature of His Time), in *Revista de Estudios Universitarios* 1 (July-Sept. 1939). "Pagaza, traductor de Virgilio" (Pagaza, Virgil's Translator), in *Abside* 3, 3 (1939): 38-50. *El libro de las charrerías por Luis Inclán* (The Book of Tawdriness, by Luis Inclán), edition and prologue (México: Porrúa, 1940). "Nuevos aspectos de la biografía de Fray Manuel Navarrete" (New Aspects of Fray Manuel Navarrete's Biography), in *Revista de Literatura Mexicana* 2 (Oct.-Nov. 1940): 226-34. *Compendio bibliográfico del "Triunfo Parténico" de don Carlos de Sigüenza y Góngora* (Bibliographic Compendium of the "Parthenic Triumph" of Carlos de Sigüenza y Góngora), compiled (México: UNAM, 1941). "Francisco Pérez Salazar," in *Anales del Instituto de Investigaciones Estéticas* 2, 8 (1942). "Un excelente libro sobre Ruiz de Alarcón" (An Excellent Book about Ruiz de Alarcón), in *Cuadernos Americanos* 9, 3 (May-June 1943): 238-41. "Anecdotario de don Artemio (de Valle Arizpe)" (Book of Anecdotes of don Artem [de Valle Arispe]), in *Nuestro México* 7 (Sept. 1945): 25. "Una nota bibliográfica sobre *El Pensador Mexicano*" (A Bibliographical Note about *The Mexican Thinker*), in *Nuestro México* 8 (Sept. 1945): 24-25. "Sor Juana Inés de la Cruz," in *Homenaje a don Francisco*

Gamoneda (Homage to Francisco Gamoneda) (México: Imp. Universitaria, 1946), pp. 483-88. "Simona Weill, una mística contemporánea" (Simona Weill, a Contemporary Mystic), in *México en la Cultura* 55 (Feb. 19, 1950): 3. "La poesía de Enrique González Martínez" (The Poetry of Enrique González Martínez), in *La obra de Enrique González Martínez* (México: El Colegio Nacional, 1951), pp. 60-67. *Homenaje del Instituto de Investigaciones Estéticas a Sor Juana Inés de la Cruz, en el tercer centenario de su nacimiento* (Homage of the Institute of Esthetic Research to Sor Juana Inés de la Cruz, on the Third Centennial of Her Birth), study (México: Imprenta Universitaria, 1952). *Bibliografía mexicana de Heredia* (Mexican Bibliography of Heredia) (México: Talls. Gráfs. de la Nación, 1953). "Nuevos datos sobre Arias de Villalobos" (New Information on Arias de Villalobos), in *Anales del Instituto de Investigaciones Estéticas* 6, 21 (1953): 92-94. *Las aventuras de Pipiolo en el bosque de Chapultepec* (The Adventures of Pipiolo in Chapultepec Park), story for children written by Santos Caballero, pseudonym of Manuel Toussaint (México: Ancora, 1954). "Las bucólicas VIII and X de Virgilio, traducidas por el padre Diego José Abad" (Virgil's Pastoral Poems VII and X, translated by Father Diego José Abad), in *Homenaje de El Colegio Nacional a Alfonso Reyes* (México: El Colegio Nacional, 1956), pp. 181-205. "Cinco poemas de Manuel Toussaint" (Five Poems by Manuel Toussaint), in *México en la Cultura* 355 (Jan. 8, 1956): 3. "Epístola moral a Fabio" (Moral Epistle to Fabio), in *Memorias de la Academia Mexicana* 15 (1956): 125-36. *Pintura Colonial en México* (México: UNAM, Instituto de Investigaciones Estéticas, 1965). *Colonial Art in Mexico*, translated and edited by Elizabeth Wilder Weismann (Austin: University of Texas Press, 1967). *Tasco: guía de emociones* (Tasco: Guide of Emotions), with woodcuts by Díaz de León (México: FCE, 1967).

BIBLIOGRAPHY: Juan Almela Meliá, *Guía de personas que cultivan la historia de América* (México: Edit. Galatea, 1951), p. 423. Anon., "Bibliografía de Manuel Toussant," in *Letras de México* 13 (Jan. 15, 1940): 2. José Bravo Ugarte, "Necrología. Doctor don Manuel Toussaint," in *Memorias de la Academia Mexicana de la Historia* 15, 1 (Jan.-March 1956): 5-6. Alfred Cardona Peña, "Charla con Manuel, Toussaint," in *Vida universitaria* 213 (1955): 2; "Mal año se fue," in *Vida universitaria* 249 (1956): 16-17. Manuel Carrera Stampa, "Bibliografía de don Manuel Toussaint," in *Boletín bibliográfico de la Secretaria y Hacienda y Crédito Público* 49 (Dec. 1955): 4-6; 50 (Jan. 1956): 4; 51 (Jan. 1956): 4; 52 (Feb. 1956): 4-5. Antonio Castro Leal, "Manuel Toussaint," in *Letras de México* 13 (Jan. 1940): 1-2. Genaro Fernández MacGregor, "La Aparición de Santos Caballero en la literatura mexicana," in *El Universal* (Jan. 1955): 3. Francisco Javier Hernández, "Espejo del tiempo," in *México al Día* 434 (Jan. 1947): 6. José Luis Martínez, *El ensayo mexicano moderno*, 2nd ed. (México: FCE, 1971). Vicente T. Mendoza, *El papel de Manuel Toussaint en el folklore de México*, Anuario de la Sociedad Folklórico 11 (Mexico, 1937). Adolfo Menéndez Samará, "Manuel Toussaint," in *Letras de México* 3 (Feb. 15, 1937): 4; "Atentas contraobjeciones al señor Toussaint," in *Letras de México* 7 (May 1937): 4. Renato Molina Enríquez, "Evocación de Manuel Toussaint y Ritter," in *Boletín bibliográfica de la Secretaría de Hacienda y Crédito Público* 49 (Dec. 15, 1955). Aurora M. Ocampo de Gómez and Ernesto Prado Velázquez, *Diccionario de Escritores Mexicanos* (México: UNAM, 1967), pp. 383-85. Alejandro Quijano, answer to Manuel Toussaint, in *Memorias de la Academia Mexicana* 15 (1956): 137-40. James Willis Robb, "Caminos cruzados de Manuel Toussaint y Alfonso Reyes," in *Diálogos* (May-June 1980): 4-9. Pedro Rojas Rodríguez, "Semblanza de don Manuel Toussaint," in *Revista de la Universidad de México* 8, 2 (Oct. 1953): 8, 28. Octaviano Valdés, "El barroco, espíritu y forma del arte de México," in *Memorias de la Academia Mexicana* 15 (1956): 302-21. Various, *México en la Cultura* 355, homage to Manuel Toussaint (Jan. 8, 1956); *Anales del Instituto de Investigaciones Estéticas* 6, 25, homage to Manuel Toussaint (México: UNAM, 1957).

JEANNE C. WALLACE

TOVAR, Juan (1941-). Born October 23, 1941, in Puebla and educated in Mexico City, Tovar became a chemical engineer, but he began writing and publishing extensively at a fairly young age, contributing to literary publications such as *Siempre!*, *Ovaciones*, *El cuento*, *El día*, and *Casa de las Américas*. He has been the recipient of several distinguished awards. He also has worked as a translator and a literary critic.

His first collection of stories, *Hombre en la oscuridad* (Man in the Darkness) (1965), is characterized by an objective and starkly realistic depiction of oppressive social conditions in a Mexican village. He received a prize awarded by the journal *La Palabra y el Hombre* for his next book, *Los misterios del reino* (The Mysteries of the Realm) (1966), a collection mostly of short stories. Although it is written with greater narrative diversity, Tovar maintains the same thematic thread revolving around the deficits of modern life, such as lack of communication and the search for self. Nonetheless, he tempers his narrative with humor and tenderness. Another story, "La plaza," published in the journal *El Cuento*, was awarded first prize by the Instituto Nacional de la Juventud Mexicana.

In his two novels, *El mar bajo la tierra* (The Sea under the Land) (1967) and *La muchacha en el balcón o la presencia del coronel retirado* (The Girl on the Balcony or the Presence of the Retired Colonel) (1970), Tovar experiments with some of the now more common literary techniques, such as the flashback, blurring and fusion of time and space, and multiple viewpoints, thus demonstrating an ability to weave technically complex narratives in an insightful and expressive manner.

His filmscript "Pueblo fantasma," in collaboration with Ricardo Vinós and Parménides García Saldaña based on Tovar's story, "Final feliz," won third prize in the Concurso de Argumentos de Cine. Dream sequences, flashbacks, and other contemporary technical devices are used to contrast adolescent daydreams with harsh reality.

Tovar has also written some theatrical pieces, including a one act play, *Coloquio de la rueda y su centro* (Discussion of the Wheel and Its Center), an imaginative rendition of the legend of Santa Catalina de Alejandría. It is a contemporary version, based on the medieval miracle play. *La madrugada* (The Dawn) (1979), an overly sentimental tribute to General Francisco Villa, deals with the folk hero's assassination. Finally, a short play, *De paso* (In Passing) (1985), written in collaboration with Beatriz Novaro, is found in *Tramoya*, a journal of original theatrical pieces.

WORKS: *Hombre en la oscuridad* (Man in the Darkness) (México: Universidad Veracruzana, 1965). *Los misterios del reino* (The Mysteries of the Realm) (México: Universidad Veracruzana, 1966). *Diez cuentos mexicanos contemporáneos* (Ten Contemporary Mexican Stories), edited by Joffre de la Fontaine (México:

Universidad Veracruzana, 1967). "Pueblo fantasma" (Ghost Town), with Ricardo Vinos and Parménides García Saldaña, filmscript adaptation of a Tovar story (Universidad Veracruzana, Jan.-March 1967), pp. 149-175; "*Inventando que sueño* de José Agustín" (José Agustín's *Inventing That I Dream*), *Revista de Bellas Artes* 22 (1968): 59-60. "Cuide su vida" (Take Care of Your Life), story in *Narrativa joven de hoy* (México: Siglo XXI Editores, 1969), pp. 22-32. "Final feliz" (Happy Ending), story from *Los misterios del reino* in *Narrativa mexicana de hoy* (Madrid: Alianza Editorial, 1969), pp. 208-19. *Coloquio de la rueda y su centro* (Discussion of the Wheel and Its Center) (Monterrey: Ediciones Sierra Madre, 1970). "Algún gesto, no sabe uno de quién" (Some Gesture, No One Knows Whose), *Vidal* 27 (1972): 19-20. *Markheim, paráfrasis escénicas del cuento de Robert Louis Stevenson* (Markheim, Scenic Paraphrases of Robert Louis Stevenson's Story), in *Teatro joven de México. 15 obras presentadas por Emilio Carballido* (México: Navaro, 1973). "[*La mirada en el centro*]" (The Glance in the Center) *Vuelta* 11 (1977): 38-39. *La madrugada* (The Dawn) (México: Editorial Latitudes, 1979). *De paso* (In Passing), a play in collaboration with Beatriz Novaro, in *Tramoya* 3 (July-Sept. 1985): 3-15. "La niña junto al estanque" (The Girl next to the Pond), story in *Narrativa hispanoamericana 1816-1981* 6 (México: Siglo XXI Editores, 1985), pp. 124-69.

BIBLIOGRAPHY: José Agustín, "Con Juan Tovar," in *Diorama de la Cultura* (Nov. 6, 1966): 3, 6. Anon., "Juan Tovar, premiado por *La Palabra y el Hombre*," in *Revista de la Semana* (May 22, 1966): 3. Huberto Batis, "Premio cuento de la Universidad Veracruzana," in *El Heraldo Cultural* 29 (May 29, 1966): 14. Beatriz Bueno, "Cine principiantes. Once recomendados," in *Diorama de la Cultura* (Oct. 9, 1966): 3. Emilio Carballido, note on the cover of *Los misterios del reino* (México: Universidad Veracruzana, 1966). Emmanuel Carballo, "Novela y cuento," review of *Hombre en la oscuridad*, in *La Cultura en México* 203 (Jan. 5, 1966): vi. Xorge del Campo, Biographical sketch in *Narrativa joven de hoy* (Madrid: Alianza Editorial, 1969), pp. 19-21. Angel Flores, Biographical sketch in *Narrativa hispanoamericana 1816-1981* (México: Siglo XXI, 1985), pp. 123-24. David William Foster, *A Dictionary of Contemporary Latin American Authors* (Phoenix: Publishers Press, 1975), pp. 101-2. Carlos González Peña, *Historia de la literatura mexicana*, 15th ed. (México: Porrúa, 1984), p. 322. Aurora M. Ocampo de Gómez and Ernesto Prado Velázquez, *Diccionario de Escritores Mexicanos* (México: UNAM, 1967), pp. 385-86. Gustavo Sainz, Review of *Hombre en la oscuridad*, in *México en la Cultura* 856 (Aug. 15, 1965): 6. Oscar Villegas, "Juan Tovar y *Los misterios del reino*," interview, in *La Cultura en México* 245 (Oct. 26, 1966): xv.

JEANNE C. WALLACE

TOVAR, Pantaleón (1828-1876). Born in Mexico City on July 27, 1828, Pantaleón Tovar, despite a rudimentary education, had a highly developed intellectual capacity. A great patriot, he fought against foreign intervention in both 1847 and 1862. His writings reveal a man with liberal, democratic ideals, ideals for which he was sometimes persecuted. Partly as a result of his political inclinations, he periodically suffered the extremes of poverty. As a young man, he wrote his first dramatic essay,

Misterios del corazón (Mysteries of the Heart), focusing on the portrayal of customs and manners. It was performed in Toluca in 1848.

The political turmoil took its toll on Tovar, so he left Mexico for Cuba, settling in Havana, where he published *La hora de Dios* (God's Hour) (1865), a novel whose point of departure revolves around a variety of Mexican customs, and *Horas de ostracismo* (Hours of Ostracism), which reflects his period of exile. From Havana he went to New York and was a self-supporting translator, a position for which he was quite well suited. Returning to Mexico, he served briefly under then General Porfirio Díaz. He also served in an editorial capacity for several journals, including *El Guardia Nacional* and *El Federalista*. He later held a governmental administrative post and was the editor for Siglo XIX. Despite holding positions of public service, he found himself again in poverty by 1872. Undeterred by his circumstances, however, he dedicated the remainder of his life to journalism and politics. He died on August 22, 1876.

Tovar's work was a combination of the Romantic style and Realism. A well-known writer and orator and very enmeshed with the concerns of the lower classes, he spoke to the people through his plays, novels, and essays, and through his political speeches, especially those having to do with patriotic themes. Among other writings, he published biographical portraits of famous Mexicans, including those of pre-Hispanic cultures, in *Hombres ilustres mexicanos*, a well-known and respected documentary publication of the time. Pantaleón Tovar belonged to several literary and scientific associations and used their congresses and other meetings as a forum for expressing his ideas.

Tovar's work has not received much critical acclaim; on the contrary, according to Ignacio *Altamirano, it has been deemed scarred by the writer's pessimistic outlook on life. His novel of intrigue, *Ironías de la vida* (Life's Ironies), containing five plots and several subplots, is an exposition of the many deficiencies of society, especially those that lead to criminal behavior and immorality. Nonethless, his work does contain considerable merit. He was successful in weaving a complex novel, in creating an occasional strong character, and in addressing the many social issues of the day, particularly of the lower class. Despite his shortcomings as a writer, Pantaleón Tovar did advance the Mexican narrative.

WORKS: "Discurso Cívico que pronunció la noche del 15 de septiembre de 1850, en conmemoración del glorioso Grito de Dolores, el ciudadano Pantaleón Tovar" (Civic Speech Which the Citizen Pantaleón Tovar Gave the Evening of September 15, 1850, Commemorating the Glorious Grito de Dolores), in *Colección de composiciones en prosa y verso* (Collection of Compositions in Prose and Verse) (México: Imp. de Cumplido, 1850), pp. 13-21. "Discurso cívico que el ciudadano Pantaleón Tovar, nombrado orador por la Junta Patriótica de Tlalpan, pronunció en esa ciudad el 27 de septiembre de 1857, aniversario de nuestra gloriosa Independencia" (Civic Speech Which Citizen Pantaleón Tovar, Named Orator by the Junta Patriótica de Tlalpan, Gave in That City on September 27, 1857, the Anniversary of Our Glorious Independence), in *Corona cívica* (Civic Crown) (México: Imp. de M. Murguía, 1857). *Horas de ostracismo* (Hours of Ostracism) (Havana: Villa y Hno. Impresores, 1865). *Historia parlamentaria del Cuarto Congreso Constitucional* (Parlimentary History of the Fourth Constitutional Congress), 4 vols. (México: Imp. de I. Cumplido, 1872-1874). "Huitzilíhuitl, segundo rey de México" (Huitzilíhuitl, Second King of Mexico), in *Hombres ilustres mexicanos*, vol. 1, pp. 49-68. "Motecuhzoma II, Xocoyotzín, sexto emperador de México) (Montezuma II, Xocoyotzín, Sixth Emperor of Mexico), in *Hombres ilustres mexicanos*, vol. 1, pp. 233-53. "Don Juan Ruiz de Alarcón y Mendoza," in *Hombres ilustres mexicanos*, vol. 2, pp. 283-330. "Don Miguel Bustamante y Septiem," in *Hombres ilustres mexicanos*, vol. 3, pp. 207-14. Novel: *Ironías de la vida* (Ironies of Life) (México: Imp. J. M. Lara, 1851). *La hora de Dios* (The Hour of God) (Havana: Villa y Hno. Impresores, 1965). Theater: *Misterios del corazón* (Mysteries of the Heart), performed in Toluca, 1848. *Justicia del cielo* (Heaven's Justice), performed in Toluca, 1849. *La Catedral de México* (The Cathedral of Mexico), performed in the Gran Teatro Nacional, Dec. 1850. *La conjuración de México* (The Conspiracy of Mexico), 1851 or 1852. *Una deshonra sublime* (A Sublime Dishonor), performed in the Teatro Nacional de México, Dec. 10, 1853 (México: Est. Tip. de Andrés Boix, 1854; México: F. Díaz de León and Santiago White, 1870). *Risa de llanto* (Laughter of Crying), performed in 1856. *La gloria del dolor* (The Glory of Pain), 1857. *¿Y para qué?* (And For What?), n.d. *La toma de Oaxaca por Morelos* (The Capture of Oaxaca by Morelos), n.d. *El rostro y el corazón* (The Face and the Heart), n.d. *Don Quijote de la Mancha*, n.d.

BIBLIOGRAPHY: Ignacio M. Altamirano, *Artículos literarios* (México: Victoriano Agüeros, 1899), p. 406; *La literatura nacional*, vol. 1 (México: Edit. Porrúa, 1949), p. 49. John S. Brushwood, *The Romantic Novel in Mexico* (Columbia, Missouri, 1954), pp. 25-26, 90-91; *Mexico in Its Novel* (Austin: University of Texas Press, 1966), pp. 78-80, 84, 85, 99, 134. John S. Brushwood and José Rojas Garcidueñas, *Breve historia de la novela mexicana* (México: Eds. de Andrea, 1959). Juan B. Iguínez, *Bibliografía de novelistas mexicanos* (México: Imp. de la Sría de Relaciones, 1926), pp. 372-74. Antonio Magaña Esquivel and Ruth S. Lamb, *Breve historia del teatro mexicano* (México: Eds. de Andrea, 1958), p. 68. Porfirio Martínez Peñaloza, "La figura romántica de Pantaleón Tovar," in *Revista Mexicana de Cultura* 845 (June 9, 1963): 1-2. Francisco Monterde, *Bibliografía del teatro en México* (México: Monografía Bibliográficas Mexicanas, 1933), pp. 358-59. Aurora M. Ocampo de Gómez and Ernesto Prado Velázquez, *Diccionario de Escritores Mexicanos* (México: UNAM, 1967), pp. 385-86. Francisco Pimentel, *Obras completas de D. Francisco Pimentel*, vol. 5 (México: Tip. Económica, 1903-1904), pp. 156-57, 337. Francisco Sosa, *Biografías de mexicanos distinguidos* (México: Ed. de la Sría. de Fomento, Ofna. Tip. de la Sría. de Fomento, 1884), pp. 1015-20. Ralph E. Warner, *Historia de la novela mexicana en el siglo xix* (México: Ant. Libr. Robredo, 1953), p. 21. José Zorrilla, *México y los mexicanos (1855-1857)* (México: Eds. de Andrea, 1955), pp. 131-33.

JEANNE C. WALLACE

TRAVEN, B. [Bruno?] (1890-1969), German born novelist. Traven published twelve novels in more than 500 editions in thirty-six languages, but only five novels had been published in the United States up to 1967. Although his technical writing is somewhat deficient, his ability to tell a story and his use of irony are very powerful. The identity of Traven, known in the United States mainly for *The Treasure of the Sierra Madre*, has been a mystery even several years after his death. A long-time resident of Mexico, he went by several different names to avoid publicity. He did not feel comfortable being in the limelight through the fame that his novels had given him. So he became known by several pseudonyms, including Ret Marut, Richard Maurhut, Berick Traven Torsvan, and Hal Croves. The latter supposedly was his literary agent. There were even some rumors that he was the son of Kaiser Wilhelm II. He just wanted to be known as a writer who cared more about his subjects. In a 1966 interview with Judy Stone he states: "Forget the man! What does it matter if he is the son of a Hohenzollern prince or anyone else? Write about his works. Write how he is against anything which is forced upon human beings." He was trying to avoid publicity, some critics claim, because of his direct participation in the Bavarian Revolution (1918-1919) under the name Ret Marut. He did not want to be associated with this revolution because it was due to its failure that Adolph Hitler seized the opportunity to rise to power.

The Treasure of the Sierra Madre (1927) is a tale of adventure and suspense. Three American men look for gold in Mexico. As the novel progresses, we find that their characters change. They lose trust in each other, especially when they find the gold. It is a novel of greed and uselessness as they see, in the end, the gold dust blown away. Only one character, the old man Howard, can find some relief and keep a sane perspective on the final outcome. He justifies it as a "joke" that the gods had played on the men. Some of his other novels, such as *Government* (1931) and *The Rebellion of the Hanged* (1936), show the excessive abuses of landlords and the call for uprisings on the part of the peasants and Indians. Specifically, he wanted to show some of the reasons for the Revolution of 1910 and some of the ways the downtrodden fought against abuses committed by the Porfirio Díaz regime.

WORKS: *The Death Ship* (Berlin: 1926). *The Cotton Pickers* (Berlin: 1926). *The Treasure of the Sierra Madre* (Berlin: 1927). *The Bridge in the Jungle* (Berlin: 1929). *The White Rose* (Berlin: 1929). *The Carreta* (Berlin: 1931). *Government* (Berlin: 1931). *The March to Caobaland* (Zurich, Wien, Prague: 1933). *The Rebellion of the Hanged* (Zurich, Prague 1936). *The Creation of the Sun and the Moon* (1936). *The General from the jungle* (Amsterdam: 1940). *Macario* (Zurich: 1950). *Stories by the Man Nobody Knows* (Evanston, Ill.: 1961). *The Night Visitor and Other Stories* (New York: 1966).

BIBLIOGRAPHY: Michael L. Baumann, *B. Traven, An Introduction* (Albuquerque: University of New Mexico Press, 1976). Donald O. Chankin, *Anonymity and Death: The Fiction of B. Traven* (The Pennsylvania State University Press, 1975). Manfred George, "B. Traven's Identity," *New Republic* (March 24, 1987). Walter M. Langford, *The Mexican Novel Comes of Age* (Notre Dame: University of Notre Dame Press, 1971). Luis Spota, "*Mañana* descubre la identidad de B. Traven," *Mañana* (August 7, 1948). Judy Stone, *The Mystery of B. Traven* (Los Altos, Calif.: William Kaufmann, 1977). Luis Suárez, "Traven y ¡Siempre! Una polémica en Europa!" ¡*Siempre*! (Nov. 16, 1966).

OSCAR SOMOZA

TREJO, Blanca Lydia (1906-1970). Trejo was born in Comitán de las Flores, Chiapas, on February 25, 1906, and died in México City on September 27, 1970.

After completing her primary education in her hometown, she studied at Guatemala's Casa Central and at Mexico City's National Autonomous University. From an early age, she became involved in journalism, contributing articles to a number of regional, national, and foreign newspapers and journals, including the renowned *Revista de Occidente*. During the Spanish Civil War, she served in Barcelona as Mexico's minister of foreign affairs.

Trejo was recognized as one of Mexico's foremost writers, scholars, and proponents of literature for children. Throughout her life, this award-winning writer campaigned to develop a program of children's literature for her country's schools and libraries. She wrote many stories, all beautifully illustrated in color. Her stories--all of which contain morals--have a threefold purpose: to entertain; to instill within the child a sense of social responsibility and goodness; and to educate aesthetically. Also a scholar of Spanish American legends and traditions, she has published two important studies: *La literatura infantil en México desde los aztecas hasta nuestros días* (Children's Literature in México from the Aztecs to the Present) and *Leyendas mexicanas* (Mexican Legends).

WORKS: Stories: *La marimba* (The Marimba) (México: Secretaría de Educación Pública, 1935). *El ratón Panchito Roe-libros* (Pancho Book-Knawer, the Rat) (México: Talleres Gráficos de la Nación, 1935). *El héroe de Nacozari* (The Hero of Nacozari) (México: Ed. Bolívar, 1936). *Paradojas-contrastes* (Paradoxes-Contrasts) (México: Cámara de Diputados, 1937). *Lecturas de juventud* (Readings of Youth) (Toluca: Talleres de la Escuela de Artes y Oficios, 1941). *El congreso de los pollitos* (The Congress of the Chicks) (México: Ed. Bolívar, 1945). *Lo que sucedió al nopal*, (What Happened to the Prickly Pear) (México: Ed. Bolívar, 1945). *Cuentos para niños* (Stories for Children) (México: 1947). *Maravillas de un colmenar* (The Wonders of a Beehive) (México: 1954). *Copo de algodón* (Bundle of Cotton) (México: 1955). *El quetzal* (México: 1955). *Leyendas mexicanas* (Mexican Legends) (México: Ed. Universitaria, 1959). *Limones para Mr. Nixon y otros más* (Lemons for Mr. Nixon and Others) (México: Talleres Tipográficos Plus, 1960). *La pícara sábelotodo* (The Wise Guy Rogue) (México: 1965). Novels: *Un país en el fango* (A Country in the Mire) (México: Ed. Polis, 1942). *El padrastro* (The Stepfather) (México: Ed. Bolívar, 1944). Other works: *Cantos a la madre* (Songs for Mother) (México: Secretaría de Educación Pública, 1936). *Convenciones y convencionalistas* (Conventiones and Conventionalists) (Barcelona: J. Pugés, 1938). *Lo que vi en España* (What I Saw in Spain) (México: Ed. Polis, 1940). *La literatura infantil en México desde los aztecas hasta nuestros días* (Children's Literature in México from the Aztecs to the Present) (México: 1950).

BIBLIOGRAPHY: Octavo Gordillo y Ortiz, *Diccionario biográfico de Chiapas* (México: B. Costa-Amic, 1977), pp. 247-48. Julia Hernández, *Novelistas y cuentistas de la revolución* (México: Unidad Mexicana de Escritores, 1960), pp. 245-46. Luis Leal, *Breve historia del cuento mexicano*, Manuales Studium, no. 2 (México: Eds. de Andrea, 1956), p. 145. Mercedes Maiti, Introduction, *Limones para Mr. Nixon y otros más*, by Blanca Lydia Trejo (México: Talls. Tipográficos Plus, 1960), pp. 5-10. Isabel Schon, *México and Its Literature for Children and Adolescents* (Tempe: Arizona State University Center for Latin American Studies, 1977), pp. 31-33.

ROBERT K. ANDERSON

TRUEBA, Eugenio (1921-), educator, short story writer, playwright, and novelist. Born in Silao, Guanajuato, Eugenio Trueba has served at the university of his native state as president and as chairman and professor of the law school.

WORKS: Short Story: *Cuentos* (Stories) (México: *Cuadernos del Gallo pitagórico*, 1951). *Antesala* (Antechamber) (México: Los presentes, 1956). *La Pupila del gato* (The Cat's Pupil) (Guanajuato: Eds. Llave, 1957). Theater: *Los intereses colectivos* (The Collective Interests) (Guanajuato: Universidad de Guanajuato, 1960). Novel: *La turbia imagen* (The Tainted Image) (México: Ed. Llave, 1962). Essays: *Derecho y Persona humana* (The Law and the Human Being) (México: Ed. Jus, 1966).

BIBLIOGRAPHY: Emmanuel Carballo, Review of *Antesala*, in *México en la Cultura* 365 (1956): 2. Sister Grace Marie, Review of *La turbia imaqen*, in *Books Abroad* (Winter 1964): 58. Luis Leal, Bibliografía del cuento mexicano (México: De Andrea, 1958), pp. 145-46.

ALFONSO GONZALEZ

U

URQUIZA, Concha (1910-1945), mystic poet. Born in Morelia, Concha Urquiza had a passionate and tormented personality. She was attracted by the sea, where she died; she probably committed suicide. After embracing, then rejecting, atheism and Marxism, she entered a convent but took no vows. She lived for a time in New York. Urquiza taught literature and history in San Luis Potosí; she studied literature at UNAM and had accepted a teaching position in Ensenada when she died. She has been compared to Sor Juana Inés de la *Cruz for her intense lyrical impulse, especially in her five erotic sonnets and her biblical sonnets. "Nox," her last poem, synthesizes hope and pain; "La cita" reflects the mystic experience, "Job" has an erotic, divine quality. Urquiza wrote poems at age twelve that were published in *Revista de Revistas*; later she published in *Abside, Lectura, Rueca, México al Día, Juventud y Saber, Lagos*, and *Aula*. Her roots were in the Spanish classics: Gonzalo de Berceo, Fray Luis de León, San Juan de la Cruz. She connected old Spanish Romance verse to Lorca-style Romance. She wrote biblical as well as erotic poetry; her religious, mystic poetry shows her inner spiritual struggle, her anguish and hope. Urquiza's poems were published posthumously.

WORKS: *Obras, poemas y prosas de Concha Urquiza* (Works, Poems and Prose of Concha Urquiza), edited with an introduction by Gabriel Méndez Plancarte (México: Abside, 1946).

BIBLIOGRAPHY: Alejandro Aviles, *Antología de la poesía de Concha Urquiza* (México: Jus, 1975). Rosario Castellanos, "Presencia de Concha Urquiza" in *Las Letras Patrias* 5 (1957): 146-52. Frank Dauster, *Breve historia de la poesía mexicana* (México: Ed. de Andrea, 1956), p.178. Carlos González Peña, *Historia* de la literatura mexicana (México: Porrúa, 1966), p. 294. John H. Hammond, "Concha Urquiza: Veinticinco años después" in *South Central Bulletin* 31 (1971): 183-87. Raul Leiva, *Imagen de la poesía mexicana contemporánea* (México: UNAM, 1959), pp. 193-200, 363. Guillermina Llach, "En torno a un recuerdo," in *Horizontes* 14, 15 (Oct. 1960): 3-4. José Luis Martínez, *Literatura mexicana siglo XX*, vol. 1 (México: Ant. Libr. Robredo, 1949), p. 83; vol. 2 (1950), p. 121. María del Carmen Millán,"Tres escritoras mexicanas del siglo XX," in *Cuadernos Americanos* 202 (1975): 163-81. José Antonio Montero, "Concha Urquiza," in *Horizontes* 14-15 (Oct. 1960): 5-6. Emma Susana Speratti, "Temas bíblicos y grecorromanos en la poesía de Concha Urquiza," in *Revista de la Facultad de Humanidades* (San Luis Potosí, Apr.-June 1959): 99-115. Juan Ignacio Valdés, "Poemas de Concha Urquiza," in *Ideas de México* 1, 1 (July-Aug. 1953): 47. Elda B. Wilmot, "Pensamiento y poesía de Concha Urquiza," in *DAI* 29, 9 (1968): 1238A-39-A.

DELIA GALVAN

URQUIZO, Francisco L. (1891- ?). Born October 4, 1891, in Coahuila Urquizo was a farmer until the outbreak of the Mexican Revolution. Serving in a variety of important military capacities, he mainly supported Venustiano Carranza. Following Carranza's assassination, Urquizo traveled to Europe and to different parts of America. A patriotic man, he also worked for the defense department of Mexico and in other capacities as well.

A contributor to a number of important literary journals and reviews, he began writing at a very young age. Owing to his political proclivities, much of his literary focus after 1914 was on the military. He wrote *Honor Militar* (Military Honor) and *Blockhouses de alta luz* (Brightly Lit Blockhouses), both for the film industry.

Drawing on his lengthy travel experiences, he penned several books about his various journeys, including *Europa Central en 1922* (Central Europe in 1922), *Cosas de la Argentina* (Things about Argentina), and *Madrid de los años veinte* (Madrid in the 1920s).

Urquizo published his first novel in Madrid in the 1920s, *Lo incognoscible* (The Unknowable), a youthful literary venture. His real storytelling talent would be revealed in later works, in which he capitalized on his own personal experiences as a soldier in the Revolution, with the intent of presenting a particular viewpoint. General Venustiano Carranza inspired several of his books, including *México Tlaxcalantongo* (1932), a historical novel about the general's last days. *Venustiano Carranza, el hombre, el político, el caudillo* (Venustiano Carranza, the Man, the Politician, the Leader) (1935) and *Siete años con Carranza* (Seven Years with Carranza) (1959), both of which portray Carranza in a very human way, are valuable biographical studies of one of the most important men of the Revolution. Other biographical works are *Morelos, genio militar de la Independencia* (Morelos, Military Genius of the Independence Movement) (1945) and *Un pedazo de historia de la Revolution, vida del general Federico Montes* (A Slice of History about the Revolution, the Life of General Federico Montes) (1959). Urquizo also wrote several short stories and novelized narrations, which are primarily sketches and memories of his days as a soldier. His work is considered an invaluable source of documentary and historical character. His ease in writing, use of personal anecdotes, and realism characterize much of his work. Critics believe that Urquizo has earned the title "novelist of the soldier" for his brilliant character portrayals in the novels, especially in *Tropa vieja* (Old Troop), considered one of the best novels of the Revolution.

WORKS: *La caballería constitucionalista, su organización e instrucción* (The Constitutionalist Cavalry, Its Organization and Instruction) (Saltillo: Gobierno del Estado, 1914). *Guía del mando* (Command Guide) (n.p., 1915). *Colonias militares* (Military Colonies) (México: Tall. Gráf. de la Sec. de Guerra y Marina, 1916). *Organización del Ejército Constitucionalista* (Organization of the Constitutionalist Army) (México: Tall. Gráf. de la Sec. de Guerra y Marina, 1916). Alvaro Obregón's *Ocho mil kilómetros en campaña* (Eight Thousand Kilometers on the Campaign), preliminary study (México: FCE, 1917). *Almanaque militar* (Military Almanac) (México: Dir. de Tall. Gráf., 1919). *Proyecto para la formación del Estado Mayor del Ejército* (Project for the Formation of the Great State of the Army) (México: Dir. de Tall. Gráf., 1919). *Manual del oficial constitucionalista, Infantería* (Manual of the Contistutionalist Official, Infantry) (México: Dir. de Tall. Gráf., 1920). *México Tlaxcalantongo: Mayo de 1920* (México Tlaxcalantongo: May 1920) (México: Editorial Cultura, 1932); 2nd ed. (México: Editorial Cultura, 1943). *Europa Central en 1922*

(Central Europe in 1922) (Madrid: V. H. Sanz Calleja, 1922). *Lo incognoscible* (The Unknowable), novel (Madrid: V. H. Sanza Calleja, 1923). *De la vida militar mexicana* (About Mexican Military Life), stories (México: Herrero Hnos., 1930). *El primer crimen* (The First Crime) (México: Editorial Cultura, 1933). *Mi tío Juan* (My Uncle John), novel (México: Editorial Claret, 1934). *Recuerdo que . . .* (I Recall That . . .) (México: Botas, 1934); 2nd ed. (México: Publs. Mundiales, 1937). *Hay de todo un poco* (There's a Little Bit of Everything), (México: OFMSA, 1935). *Don Venus- tiano Carranza: el hombre, el político, el caudillo* (Don Venustiano Carranza: The Man, the Politician, the Leader) (Pachuca: Eds. del Instituto Científico y Literario del Estado de Hidalgo, 1935); 6th ed. (México: Editorial Muñoz, 1957). *Charlas de sobremesa* (After-Dinner Talks) (Pachuca: Talleres Linotip. del Gobierno del Estado de Hidalgo, 1937). *Tropa vieja* (Old Troop), novel (México: Talleres Gráficos del Departamento de Publicidad y Propaganda, 1943; (México: Ed. Populibros, 1955). *Morelos, genio militar de la Independencia* (Morelos, Military Genius of Independence) (México: Ed. Xóchitl, 1945). *Cuentos y leyendas* (Stories and Legends) (México: Ed. Cultura, 1945). *Al viento* (To the Wind) (México: Ed. Marte, 1953). *¡Viva Madero!* (Long Live Madero!) (México: Ed. Marte, 1954); 2nd ed. (México: Populibros, 1957). *3 de diana* (Three of Diana), 11th ed. (México: n.p., 1955). *Páginas de la Revolución* (Pages of the Revolution) (México: Bibl. del Instituto Nacional de Estudios Históricos de la Revolución, 1956). *Un pedazo de historia de la Revolución. Vida del general Federico Montes* (A Slice of History of the Revolution. The Life of General Federico Montes) (México: Costa-Amic, 1959). *Siete años con Carranza* (Seven Years with Carranza) (México: n.p., 1959). *Polvo del camino* (Dust of the Road) (México: n.p. 1959). *Madrid de los años veinte* (Madrid in the 1920s) (México: Costa-Amic, 1961). *Breviario humorístico* (Humoristic Breviary) (México: Costa-Amic, 1963). *El desván* (The Loft) (México: Costa-Amic, 1964). *Símbolos y números* (Symbols and Numbers) (México: Costa-Amic, 1965). *La Ciudadela quedó atrás* (The Citadel Stayed Behind) (México: Costa-Amic, 1965). *Aquellos vientos* (Those Winds) (México: Costa-Amic, 1965). *Fui soldado de levita de esos de caballería* (I Was a Levite Soldier Like Those of Chivalry) (México: FCE, 1967).

BIBLIOGRAPHY: Miguel Alessio Robles, *Historia política de la Revolución Mexicana* (México: Eds. Botas, 1938). Huberto Batis, Review of *La Ciudadela quedó atrás*, in *El Heraldo Cultural* 6 (Dec. 19, 1965): 15. Esteban Durán Rosado, Review of *Breviario humorístico*, in *Revista Mexicana de Cultura* 876 (Jan. 12, 1964): 15; Review of *El desván*, in *Revista Mexicana de Cultura* 889 (April 12, 1964): 15. Gastón García Cantú, Review of *Tropa vieja*, in *México en la Cultura* 392 (Sept. 23, 1956): 2. Ernest Moore, "A General Writes of the Mexican Revolution," in *Romantic Review* 28, 3-4 (1936): 305-7. Javier Morente, Review of *Breviario humorístico*, in *Diograma de la Cultura* (Dec. 22, 1963): 4. Aurora M. Ocampo de Gómez and Ernesto Prado Velázquez, *Diccionario de Escritores Mexicanos* (México: UNAM, 1967), pp. 390-92. Salvador Reyes Nevares, Review of *Símbolos y números*, in *La Cultura en México* 208 (Feb. 9, 1966): xvi. Carlos Valdés, Review of *Tropa vieja*, in *Revista de la Universidad de México* 10, 4 (Dec. 1955): 30.

JEANNE C. WALLACE

URUETA, Margarita (1913 or 1918-   ), playwright and fiction writer. Margarita Urueta was born in Mexico City on November 13, 1913 or 1918. Her father was the

well-known writer and politician Jesús Urueta. In 1945 she became president of the
Teatro de México. For a while she wrote soap operas and programs for television,
then she traveled throughout Europe, studied, and wrote new plays. Upon her return
to Mexico in 1963, she put on her own plays and built her own theater, which she
appropriately named "Jesús Urueta." Her play *Duda infinita* (Infinite Doubt) opened
in 1959 at the Teatro Ródano. In 1964, with *La mujer transparente* (The Transparent
Woman) she became affiliated with avant-garde theater. In the sixties, several of her
plays were staged: the children's play *Juanito Membrillo*, *La Pastorela de las tres
Marias* (The Shepherd's Song of the Three Marys), and *El hombre y su máscara* (The
Man and His Mask), all in 1964; *Poderoso caballero es don dinero* (A Powerful
Gentleman Is Sir Money), in 1965; and *La muerte de un soltero* (The Death of a
Single Man) in 1966.

WORKS: Biographies: *Jesús Urueta: la historia de un gran desamor* (Jesús Urueta:
The Story of a Great Non-Love) (México: 1964). Novel: *Hasta mañana, compadre*
(See You Tomorrow, Old Buddy) (México: B. Costa-Amic, 1975). Short Stories:
Almas de perfil (Souls in Profile) (México: 1933 or 1934?). *Una conversación sencilla*
(A Simple Conversation) (México: 1934 or 1936?). *El mar la distraía* (The Sea
Entertained Her) (México: Col. Mirasol, no. 3, 1940). *Mediocre* (México: 1947).
Espia sin ser (A Spy Without Being) (México: 1961). *Amor en 13 Dimensiones* (Love
in Thirteen Dimensions) (México: Ed. Novaro, 1970). Theater: *San lunes. Una hora
de vida y Mansión para turistas* (Saint Monday, One Hour to Live, and Mansion for
Tourists) (México: Ed. Quetzal, 1943). *Ave de sacrificio* (Sacrificial Bird) (México:
Letras de México, 1945). *Teatro nuevo: Las máquinas devoran a una señorita llamada
Rivela, o El dios laico: Graju: La mujer transparente: Angel de justicia, o el señor perro*
(New Theater: The Machines Devour a Young Woman Named Rivela, or The
Secular God; Graju; The Transparent Woman; Angel of Justice or Mr. Dog)
(México: Joaquín Mortiz, 1963).

BIBLIOGRAPHY: Herbert H. Hoffman, *Cuento Mexicano Index* (Newport Beach,
Calif: Headway Publications, 1978). Aurora M. Ocampo de Gómez and Ernesto
Prado Velázquez, *Diccionario de escritores mexicanos* (México: UNAM, 1967), pp.
392-93. Ralph E. Warner, *Historia de la novela mexicana en el siglo XIX* (México:
Antigua Librería Robredo, 1953).

                                                        MARGARITA VARGAS

USIGLI, Rodolfo (1905-1979). Usigli was born in México City on November 17,
1905, and died there on June 8, 1979. He studied at the National Conservatory and
at Yale University's School of Dramatic Arts. He taught theatrical history and
dramatic theory at the National Autonomous University and lectured widely on these
topics. He also served as director of theater for the National Institute of Fine Arts
and founded the Teatro Media Noche (Midnight Theater), for which he translated
a number of foreign plays. Between 1944 and 1973, he periodically held diplomatic
posts in Britain and France, as well as ambassadorships in Norway, Lebanon, and
Belgium.

A poet, novelist, and essayist, Usigli is known primarily for his contributions to the Mexican theater. Usigli began writing and staging his plays during the era of the Contemporáneos, but unlike its experimentalist members, he emphasized the uniqueness of the theater of each country. (*See* Vanguardist Prose Fiction in Mexico.) In his opinion, plays written by his countrymen should reflect Mexican society and educate its public through criticism and through the presentation of models for national greatness.

Usigli also expressed a preference for a poetic theater. However, because he was convinced that Mexican theater required a solid base in realism prior to adapting a nonrealistic mode, initially he avoided writing in a poetic fashion. Many years later, the publication of his first full-length poetic play, *Corona de fuego* (Crown of Fire), was seemingly a sign that he believed his country had achieved self-knowledge and that its dramatists were ready to experiment with new styles, including poetic theater.

While Usigli's plays stress meaningful national themes, they also transcend México's national boundaries in certain areas. Some of them reflect foreign influences: Shaw's views on the purpose of theater, Friedrich Nietzsche's ideas on the spirit of tragedy, and Hegel's concept of myth formation, as well as themes from writers like Molière, the classical Greeks, and the Spanish Golden Age masters. Also, because he believed that the essential material of the theater was human passions and ideas, his plays often communicate universal human phenomena. Nevertheless, as mentioned above, said plays also depict his countrymen and their cultural idiosyncrasies.

Many of Usligi's dramatic works fall into one or more of three broad categories: social or political satire, psychological problems and dramatic episodes of Mexican history. Three of his classics, *El gesticulador* (The Gesticulator), *El niño y la niebla* (The Child and the Fog), and *Corona de sombra* (Crown of Shadows), respectively, constitute prime illustrations of this proclivity.

In addition to gaining fame throughout the world for his dramatic production, Usigli helped train actors and dramatists for the Mexican stage. Some of the most well known of his students were Emilio *Carballido, Luisa Josefina *Hernández and Sergio *Magaña. As a result of his creative and instructional endeavors, he received the prestigious National Prize for Letters in 1972 and was publicly recognized at that time as the creator of modern Mexican theater and as one of Spanish America's leading dramatists.

WORKS: Plays: Most of the plays listed below can be found in Usigli's *Teatro completo* (Complete Theater), 2 vols. (México: FCE, 1963 and 1966). The year that appears to the right of the title in English translation refers to the play's debut. *El apóstol* (The Apostle, 1931), in *Teatro completo*, vol. 1, pp. 13-59. *Falso drama* (False Drama, 1932), in *Teatro completo*, vol. 1, pp. 60-67. *4 Chemins 4* (4 Road 4, 1932), in *Teatro completo*, vol. 1, pp. 68-120. *Noche de estío* (Summer Evening, 1933), in *Teatro completo*, vol. 1, pp. 170-216. *El presidente y el ideal* (The President and the Ideal, 1935), in *Teatro completo*, vol. 1, pp. 217-350. *Estado de secreto* (State of Secrecy, 1935), in *Teatro completo*, vol. 1, pp. 351-403. *La última puerta* (The Last Door, 1934), in *Teatro completo*, vol. 1, pp. 404-11. *Alcestes* (Alcestes, 1936), in *Teatro completo*, vol. 1, pp. 121-69. *El niño y la niebla* (The Child and the Fog, 1936), in *Teatro completo*, vol. 1, pp. 442-92. *Medio tono* (Half Tone, 1937), in *Teatro completo*, vol. 1, pp. 493-564. *Otra primavera* (*Another Springtime*, 1937), in *Teatro completo*, vol. 1, pp. 217-350. *Another Springtime*, translated by Wayne Wolfe (New York: Samuel French, 1961). *Mientras amemos* (While We Love, 1937), in *Teatro completo*, vol. 1, pp. 493-564. *La mujer no hace milagros* (The Woman Doesn't Do Miracles, 1938), in *Teatro completo*, vol. 1, pp. 803-92. *Aguas estancadas* (Stagnant Waters, 1938), in *Teatro completo*, vol. 1, pp. 619-74. *El gesticulador* (*The Gesticulator*, 1938), in *Teatro completo*, vol. 1, pp. 803-92. *The Gesticulator*, in Annabel Clark, "An English Translation of Three Modern Mexican Plays by Rodolfo Usigli," Ph.D. Diss., University of Denver, 1971. *La crítica de "La mujer no hace milagros"* (The Criticism of "The Woman Doesn't Do Miracles," 1939), in *Teatro completo*, vol. 1, pp. 883-914. *Vacaciones I* (Vacation I, 1940), in *Teatro completo*, vol. 2, pp. 22-47. *Sueño de día* (Daydream, 1940), in *Teatro completo*, vol. 2, pp. 7-21. *La familia cena en casa* (The Family Dines at Home, 1942), in *Teatro completo*, vol. 2, pp. 69-146. *Dios, Batidillo y la mujer*, (God, Batidillo and the Woman, 1943), in *Teatro completo*, vol. 2, pp. 223-25. *Corona de sombra* (*Crown of Shadows,* 1943), in *Teatro completo*, vol. 2, pp. 147-222. *Crown of Shadows*, translated by William F. Stirling (London: A. Wingate, 1946). *Vacaciones II* (Vacation II, 1945), in *México en la Cultura* (Feb. 5, 1956): 2, 4. *La función de despedida* (The Good-Bye Party, 1949), in *Teatro completo*, vol. 2, pp. 236-51. *Las madres* (The Mothers, 1949), in *Teatro completo*, vol. 2, pp. 631-737. *Los fugitivos* (The Fugitives, 1950), in *Teatro completo*, vol. 2, pp. 335-87. *Jano es una muchacha* (Jano Is a Girl, 1952), in *Teatro completo*, vol 2, pp. 388-459. *Jano Is a Girl*, in Annabel Clark, "An English Translation of Three Modern Mexican Plays by Rodolfo Usigli," Ph.D. Diss., University of Denver, 1971. *Un día de estos* (*One of These Days*, 1953), in *Teatro completo*, vol. 2, pp. 460-544. *One of These Days*, in *Two Plays: Crown of Light. One of These Days*, translated by Thomas Bledsoe (Carbondale: Southern Illinois University Press, 1971). *La exposición* (The Exposition, 1955), in *Teatro completo*, vol. 2, pp. 545-630. *La diadema* (The Diadem, 1960), in *Teatro completo*, vol. 2, pp. 738-73. *Corona de fuego* (Crown of Fire, 1960), in *Teatro completo*, vol. 2, pp. 774-840. *Un navío cargado de . . .* (A Ship Loaded with . . ., 1961), in *Tres comedias inéditas* (México: Ecuador, 1967), pp. 9-68. *El testamento y el viudo* (The Will and the Widower, 1962), in *Tres comedias inéditas* (México: Ecuador, 1967), pp. 69-100. *El encuentro* (The Encounter, 1963), in *Tres comedias inéditas* (México: Ecuador, 1967), pp. 101-32. *Corona de luz* (*Crown of Light*, 1963), in *Teatro completo*, vol. 2, pp. 841-917. *Crown of Light*, in *Two Plays: Crown of Light. One of These Days*, translated by Thomas Bledsoe (Carbondale: Southern Illinois University Press, 1971); *Crown of Light*, in Annabel Clark, "An English Translation of Three Modern Mexican Plays by Rodolfo Usigli," Ph.D. Diss., University of Denver, 1971. *Carta de amor* (Love Letter, 1968), in *Revista de la Universidad de México* 22 (June 1968): 9-14. *El gran circo del mundo* (The Great Circus of the World, 1968), in *Cuadernos Americanos* 28 (Jan.-Feb. 1969): 95-106; 28 (Mar.-Apr. 1969): 38-96. *Los viejos: diálogo imprevisto en un acto* (The Old Ones: Unforeseen Dialogue in One Act) (México: Finesterre, 1971). *¡Buenos días, señor Presidente!* (Good Morning, Mr. President!) (México: Joaquín Mortiz, 1972). Poetry: *Conversación desesperada* (Desperate Conversation) (México: Cuadernos de México Nuevo, 1938). Novels: *Ensayo de un crimen* (Rehearsal of a Crime) (México: Ed. Nacional, 1944). Story: *Obliteración* (Obliteration) (México, 1973). Other Works: *México en el teatro* (*México in the Theater*) (México: Imprenta Mundial, 1932); *México in the Theater*, translated by Wilder P. Scott (University, Miss.: Romance Monographs, University of Mississippi Press, 1976). *Caminos del teatro en México* (Pathways of the Theater in México) (México: Secretaría de Relaciones Exteriores, 1933). *Itinerario del autor dramático* (Itinerary of the Playwright) (México: La Casa de España en México, 1940). *Anatomía del teatro* (Anatomy of the Theater) (México:

Ecuador, 1967). *Juan Ruiz Alarcón en el tiempo* (Juan Ruiz Alarcón in Time) (México: Secretaría de Educación Pública, 1967). *Voces--Diario de Trabajo (1932-1933)* (Voices--An Account of Work) (México: Seminario de Cultura Mexicana, 1967). *Imagen y prisma de México* (Image and Prism of México) (México: Eds. del Seminario de Cultura Mexicana, 1972). *Conversaciones y encuentros* (Conversations and Encounters) (México: Organización Editorial Novaro, 1974). *Teoría y praxis del teatro en México* (Theory and Praxis of the Mexican Theater), edited by Sergio Jiménez and Edgar Ceballos (México: Grupo Editorial Gaceta, 1982).

BIBLIOGRAPHY: Peter R. Beardsell, "Insanity and Poetic Injustice in Usigli's 'Corona de sombra,'" *Latin American Theatre Review* 10, 1 (1976): 5-14. Vera F. Beck, "La fuerza motriz en la obra dramática de Rodolfo Usigli," *Revista Iberoamericana* 18, 36 (Sept. 1953): 369-83. Edgar Ceballos, "Usigli, ese desconocido," in *Escenarios de dos mundos* 3, 0183: 3-10. Helia D'Acosta, *Veinte hombres y yo* (México: Editores Asociados, 1972), pp. 286-313. Eunice Joiner Gates, "Usigli As Seen in His Prefaces and Epilogues," *Hispania* 37, 4 (1954): 432-39. Consuelo Howatt, "Rodolfo Usigli," *Books Abroad* 24, 2 (Spring 1950): 127-30. William Knapp Jones, *Behind Spanish American Footlights* (Austin: University of Texas Press, 1966), pp. 502-4. Leonard S. Klein, ed., *Latin American Literature in the Twentieth Century: A Guide* (New York: Ungar, 1986), pp. 189-92. John W. Kronik, "Usigli's 'El gesticulador' and the Fiction of Truth," *Latin American Theatre Review* 11, 1 (Fall 1977): 5-16. Mario Marcelese, "The Hispanoamerican Author in Action: Rodolfo Usigli," *American Literary Accents* 2, 8 (1965): 15-23. Arthur A. Natella, "Christological Symbolism in Rodolfo Usigli's *El Gesticulador*." in *DL* 5 (1988): 455-61. Gordon Ragle, "Rodolfo Usigli and His Mexican Scene," *Hispania* 46, 2 (May 1963): 307-11. Donald L. Rosenberg, "The Dramatic Theory of Rodolfo Usigli: The Poetry of Selective Realism," Ph.D. Diss., Iowa State University, 1962. Ronald Vance Savage, "The Mexican Theatre of Rodolfo Usigli: Theory and Practice," Ph.D. Diss., University of Oregon, 1969; "Rodolfo Usigli's Idea of Mexican Theatre," *Latin American Theatre Review* 4, 2 (Spring 1971): 13-20. Wilder P. Scott, "A Critical Study of the Life and Dramatic Works of Rodolfo Usigli," Ph.D. Diss., University of Georgia, 1969; "Rodolfo Usigli and Contemporary Dramatic Theory," *Romance Notes* 11, 3 (Spring 1970): 526-30; "Toward an Usigli Bibliography," *Latin American Theatre Review* 6, 1 (1972): 53-62. Donald L. Shaw, "Dramatic Technique in Usigli's 'El gesticulador,'" *Theatre Research International* 1, 2 (Feb. 1976): 125-33. Gerard J. Sheridan, "'Lo mexicano' in the Theatre of Rodolfo Usigli," Ph.D. Diss., St. John's University, 1965. Solomon H. Tilles, "Rodolfo Usigli's Concept of Dramatic Art," *Latin American Theatre Review* 3, 2 (Spring 1970): 31-38. Ellis Eugene Williams, "Character and Characterization in the Early Plays of Rodolfo Usigli," PhD. Diss., University of Georgia, 1971; "Abnormal Psychology in Some of Usigli's Works," *Specialia* 1 (1969): 1-8. Francisco Zendejas, "Una entrevista con Rodolfo Usigli," *Diorama de la Cultura* (Aug. 2, 1964): 3.

ROBERT K. ANDERSON

V

VALADES, Edmundo (1915-). Born in Guaymas, Sonora, Edmundo Valadés later went to Mexico City, where he established himself as a journalist writing for several newspapers and magazines. Since 1964 he has very successfully edited the literary periodical *El cuento* (The Short Story), which publishes short stories from all over the world. He has also published critical essays on the short story and on the novel of the Mexican Revolution. Known mainly as a short story writer, Valadés develops a combination of themes within several different backgrounds, ranging from childhood to old age, from the city to the rural area; themes such as adolescence, erotic love, the dehumanizing spirit in the big city, the separation and coming together of dreams and reality. *La muerte tiene permiso* (Death Has Permission) (1955) is a collection of short stories, some of which had been previously published elsewhere. The short story that gives its title to the collection is outstanding. It contains a very interesting turn of events and self-deception on the part of the powerful politicians and landowners in a Mexican rural environment. The peasants in a small rural community are concerned about the abuses of a local mayor. He feels all-powerful and thinks that he can do whatever he wished. As the narration develops, the peasants are in front of a regional commission asking for advice and justice from its members. After several exchanges and questions from the peasants' representative, they get their request approved. So, the peasants, having obtained the support of the authorities by a trick in verbal exchange, inform them that they have already killed the mayor. The surprising and clever turn of events here is that justice is served, although the commission members did not intend it to be so. This is typical of Valadés as he searches for creative solutions for his characters, who find themselves in delicate and, sometimes, desperate situations. Other representative stories by Valadés are *La infancia prohibida* (The Forbidden Childhood), *Asunto de dedos* (A Matter for the Fingers), and *En cualquier ciudad del mundo* (In Any City of the World). Valadés' narrative styles include narration in the third person, interior monologues, flashbacks, cinematic techniques, and experimentation with language. All of these qualities define a writer who is in the process of experimenting with narrative techniques in search of his place in the world of short story writers.

WORKS: Short Stories: *La muerte tiene permiso* (Death Has Permission) (México: FCE, 1955). *Antípoda* (Antipode) (México: 1961). *Las dualidades funestas* (Ill-Fated Dualities) (México: 1966). Editor of *El libro de la imaginación* (The Book of Imagination) (México: FCE, 1976). Other Prose: With Luis Leal, *La Revolución y las letras* (México: INBA, 1960).

BIBLIOGRAPHY: Josef Bella, "Valadés: A Renovaçao De Conto Urbano Mexicano" (Minas Gerais: Suplemento Literário, 12 April), p. 4. Paulo Kruel de Almeida, "Os

12 Años da El Cuento por su Criador, Edmundo Valadés," *Escrita* 13: 23-25 (interview). María del Carmen Millán, *Antología de cuentos mexicanos*, vol. 1 (México: Editorial *Nueva Imagen*, 1977).

OSCAR SOMOZA

VALDES, Carlos (1928-   ), short story writer, novelist, poet, essayist and translator. Born in Guadalajara, Jalisco, Carlos Valdés affiliated himself with the Parnassion school and tried to edit a journal, *Dada*, which failed. He published some literary pieces in *El Informado*, (The Informer), and had a hand in the success of the Guadalajara journal, *Ariel*. In 1953, he moved to Mexico and served as editor of *Universidad de México* and as a scholar at the Colegio de México.

Valdés has published several collections of short stories, a chronicle, two novels, and an essay. His short stories bring together different planes of reality. The harsh world of everyday life coexists with the imaginative or the fantastic. His style is polished and terse. His characters achieve a psychological depth that helps bring them to life. His first novel, *Los antepasados* (*The Ancestors*), is set in the village of Tonantlan. Like writers such as William Faulkner, Agustín *Yáñez, and Gabriel García Márquez, he uses the village as a structure to flesh out his themes and characters. His novel *Voz de la tierra* (Voice of the Land) is set in the same village. He makes subtle and effective use of the images and myths of the *Passion* story in relating the killing of Pascual Gutierrez. His *Crónicas del vicio y la virtud* (Chronicles of Vice and Virtue) give insightful and at times humorous comments on everyday life. He has done translations and recordings, also.

WORKS: Short Stories: *Ausencias* (Absences) (Mexico City: Los Presentes, 1955). *Dos ficciones* (Two Fictions) (Mexico City: Cuadernos de El Unicornio, 1958). *Dos y los muertos* (Two and the Dead) (México: Imprenta Universitaria, 1960). *El nombre es lo de menos* (The Name Is the Least of It) (Mexico City: Letras mexicanas, no. 70, 1961). Novels: *Los antepasados* (The Ancestors) (Mexico City: Cuadernos del Viento, 1963). *La voz de la tierra* (The Voice of the Land) (Mexico City: Letras mexicanas, no. 107, 1972). Chronicles: *Crónicas del vicio y la virtud* (Chronicles of Vice and Virtue) (Mexico City: Era, 1963). Essay: *José Luis Cuevas* (México: UNAM, 1966). Translations: Ernest Becker, *La estructura de mal: un ensayo sobre la unificación de la ciencia del hombre* (The Structure of Evil: An Essay on the Unification of the Science of Man), translated by Carlos Valdés (México: FCE, 1980). Oscar J. Martínez, *Ciudad Juárez*, translation of *Border Room Town* by Carlos Valdés (México: FCE, 1982).

BIBLIOGRAPHY: Federico Alvarez, "Cronicas del vicio y la virtud," *La Cultura en México* 71 (June 26, 1963): xx. Jesús Arellano, "Las ventas de Don Quijote," *Nivel* 13 (Jan. 25, 1964): 5. Huberto Batis, "Entrevista con Carlos Valdés", *Cuadernos del Viento* 37-38 (Aug.-Dec. 1963): 601-3. Alberto Bonifaz Nuño, Review of *El nombre es lo de menos*, in *Cuadernos del Viento* 18 (Jan. 18, 1962): 287. Heriberto García Rivas, *Historia de la literatura mexicana*, vol. 4 (México: Textos Universitarios, 1971), p. 519. Henrique González Casanova, "Personas y lugares," *La Cultura en México* 100 (Jan. 15, 1963). Carlos González Peña, *History of Mexican Literature*, translated by

Gusta Barfield Nance and Florene Johnson Dunstan (Dallas: Southern Methodist University Press), p. 450. Manuel Mejía Valera, Review of *El nombre es lo de menos*, in *Revista Interamericana de Bibliografía* 12, 4 (Oct.-Dec. 1962): 462. Aurora M. Ocampo de Gómez and Ernesto Prado Velázquez, *Diccionario de escritores mexicanos* (México: UNAM, 1967), pp. 396-97. Carlos Valdés, "Veinte años después" (interview), *Revista de la Universidad de México* 32, 8 (April 1978): 30- 31.

MARK FRISCH

VALDES, Octaviano (1901-   ), poet, essayist, novelist, and translator. Octaviano Valdés was born in Cacalomacin, Estado de México. He studied at the Universidad Gregoriana de Roma (1922-1929), from which he received the degree of doctor of philosophy and theology. Valdés became a priest in 1927 and has taught at the Seminario Conciliar de México since 1930. He became a member of the Academia Mexicana de la Lengua in 1956. He regularly contributes poems and essays to *Abside*.

WORKS: Poetry: *El pozo de Jacob* (The Well of Jacob) (México: E. Tipográfica Salesiana, 1933). *Bajo el ala del angel* (Under the Wing of the Angel) (México: *Abside*, 1952). Essays: *El prisma de Horacio* (Horatios Prism) (México: UNAM, 1937). *El padre Tembleque: Biografía del constructor del acueducto de Zempoala y Otumba* (México: Jus, 1945), edition and introduction. *Poesía neoclásica y académica* (México: UNAM, 1946). *El barroco, espíritu y forma del arte de México* (The Baroque, Spirit and Form of the Art in Mexico) (México: *Abside*, 1956). Translations: *Por los campos de México* (Through the Fields of Mexico) (México: UNAM, 1942); prose translation of Rafael Landívar's poem, *Rusticatio Mexicana*. Novel: *La cabellera de Berenice* (Berenice's Hair) (México: Jus, 1968).

BIBLIOGRAPHY: Emma Godoy, "El autor de La cabellera de Berenice," *Abside* 33 (1969): 43-56. Raymond L. Grismer and Mary McDonald,   *La vida y obras de escritores mexicanos* (La Habana: Ed. Alfa, 1945), pp. 153-55.

MIRTA A. GONZALEZ

VALENZUELA, Jesús E. (1856-1911). Born in Guanaceví, Durango, on December 24, 1856, Jesús E. Valenzuela pursued a career in law, serving in many capacities during his lifetime, including that of deputy to the national congress for several years. He was also very involved with educational development in Mexico during the latter part of the nineteenth century. He achieved international distinction in both Chile and Italy for his dedicated and far reaching work.
   In 1898, he founded *Revista Moderna*, an important literary journal of which he was the editor until his death in 1911. Although he himself had only a few publications, mostly poetry, Valenzuela was the inspiration, the motivation, and the driving force behind many of the writers of his time. An enthusiastic and dedicated editor and educator, he used his position to enhance and direct the careers of some of the finest writers.

The author of three books of poetry, *Almas y cármenes* (Souls and Verses), *Lira libre* (Free Verse), and *Manojo de rimas* (Handful of Rhymes), Valenzuela generated a favorable response to his works, although they are not especially polished pieces.

WORKS: *Almas y cármenes* (Souls and Verses) (México: Escalante, 1904). *Lira libre* (Free Verse) (México: Escalante, 1906). *Manojo de rimas* (Handful of Rhymes) (México: Talls. Gráfs. de Eduardo Aguirre, 1907). *Miserias humanas* (Human Miseries) (París and México: Libr. de la Vda. de Ch. Bouret, n.d.). "Mis recuerdos" (My Memories), in *Excelsior* (Aug. 27, 1945 - Feb. 12, 1946).

BIBLIOGRAPHY: Rubén M. Campos, "Almas y cármenes," in *Revista Moderna* (July 1905): 270-74; *El folklore literario de México* (México: Talls. Gráficos de la Nación, SEP, 1929), pp. 552, 554, 558, 559. Genaro Estrada, *Poetas nuevos de México* (México: Eds. Porrúa, 1916), pp. 318-21. Max Henríquez Ureña, *Breve historia del modernismo* (México and Buenos Aires: FCE, 1954), p. 465. Joaquín Márquez Montiel, *Hombres célebres de Chihuahua* (México: Edit. Jus, 1955), pp. 85-91. Amado Nervo, "Jesús E. Valenzuela," in *Obras completas*, vol. 2 (Madrid: Aguilar, 1962), pp. 22-23; "*Almas y cármenes*," ibid., pp. 384-85. Aurora M. Ocampo de Gómez and Ernesto Prado Velázquez, *Diccionario de Escritores Mexicanos* (México: UNAM, 1967), pp. 397-98. Victoriano Salado Alvarez, "Carta de don Jesús E. Valenzuela," in *De mi cosecha* (Guadalajara: Imp. de Ancira y Hno. A. Ochoa, 1899), pp. 21-30. Justo Sierra, "Jesús E. Valenzuela," in *Revista Moderna* (June 1911): 168-69. José Juan Tablada, *La feria de la vida* (México: Eds. Botas, 1937), pp. 433-40, 450-56. Luis G. Urbina,"Los libros del año: *Lira libre*," in *Revista Moderna* (Feb. 1907): 345; *Hombres y libros* (México: El Libro Francés, 1923), pp. 231-32.

JEANNE C. WALLACE AND MIRTA BARREA-MARLYS

VALLE, Juan (1838-1864 or 1865?). Juan Valle was born in the city of Guanajuato on July 4, 1838. Becoming blind at the age of four or five, he obtained his literary education through readings by his brother, which were drawn from biblical and classical sources, the Spanish poets of the sixteenth century and the Mexican national poets. At an early age he began to write poetry, composing it mentally and then dictating it. His first play, *Misterios sociales,* was presented in Guanajuato when Valle was seventeen years old.

Valle espoused the liberal cause during the civil war, and for this political stance he was persecuted, jailed, and exiled. During this period he became acquainted with Esther *Tapia and Guillermo *Prieto, among other writers. Returning to Guanajuato after this period, he was again forced to flee during the French invasion. During this period in Guadalajara he married Doña Josefa Aguiar, a childhood friend, with whom he had one daughter. He died in Guadalajara, on December 31, 1864, or in January of 1865, after a grave illness.

Valle's poetry was liberal and romantic in its subject matter and feeling, although it maintained certain links with his classical education. In Valle's civic poems he was without peer among the poets of his time, becoming known as the "Tyrtaeus of liberty." He also shows considerable quality in his works of autobiographic or subjective origin, touching themes of religious, historic, and personal value.

WORKS: *Poesías* (Poems) (México: Imp. de I. Cumplido, 1862). *Misterios sociales* (Social Mysteries), in *Poesías* (México: Imp. de I. Cumplido, 1962). *Flores y abrojos* (Flowers and Thorns), not published.

BIBLIOGRAPHY: Heriberto García Rivas, *Historia de la literatura mexicana* (México: Textos Universitarios, S.A., 1972), vol. 2, p. 115. Carlos González Peña, *History of Mexican Literature*, translated by Gusta Barfield Nance and Florene Johnson Dunstan (Dallas: Southern Methodist University Press, 1968), pp. 220-22. Julio Jiménez Rueda, *Letras mexicanas en el siglo XIX* (México: FCE, 1944), p. 95. Aurora M. Ocampo de Gómez and Ernesto Prado Velázquez, *Diccionario de escritores mexicanos* (México: UNAM, 1967), p. 398. Francisco Zarco, Prologue to *Poesías*, ed. cit., pp. i-xv.

FILIPPA B. YIN

VALLE, Rafael Heliodoro (1891-1959). A Honduran diplomat, journalist, historian, poet, and essayist, Rafael Heliodoro Valle was born in Tegucigalpa on July 3, 1891. He studied in his native city, then went to Mexico on a scholarship, where he continued his academic life at the Escuela Normal de Tacuba, graduating as a teacher. By this time, he had already published articles in newspapers. His first significant publication was a book of poems, *El rosal del ermitaño* (The Hermit's Rosebush) (1911).

Valle returned to Honduras in 1912 and founded, along with Alfonso Guillén Zelaya and Salatiel Rosales, El Ateneo de Honduras (The Honduras Atheneum), a group noted for its scholarly discussions. He was interesting in improving the educational system in Honduras and in raising the literacy level. He was named undersecretary in the Ministry of Education, enabling him to implement educational ideas brought from Mexico. He was then named Honduran consul in Mobile, Alabama, in 1913, a post which gave him the opportunity to learn English. He also published *Como la luz del día* (Like the Light of Day) in 1913.

In 1915 he published a well-received book of essays, *Anecdotario de mi abuelo* (My Grandfather's Anecdotes). That same year, he also wrote a popular poem, "Jazmines del cabo" (Jasmines of the Cape), extolling romantic love and the lush physical beauty of his native land. This was followed by *El perfume de la tierra natal* (The Perfume of the Native Land) in 1917, and *Anfora sedienta* (The Thirsty Urn) in 1922. Valle wrote in a modernist style musical poems that were direct and celebrated romantic love, nature, and especially nature in Honduras.

He was a member of many cultural institutions, including the Sociedad de Geografía e Historia de Honduras, the Sociedad Mexicana de Georgrafía y Estadística, the Academia Colombiana de la Historia. He was the founder of the Academia de la Lengua in Honduras. He was a consul in Belize in 1916. He gave conferences in various universities, including Columbia, Stanford, Louisiana, Tulane, Texas, Rutgers, and Georgetown.

In 1919 Valle was sent to Washington, D.C., on a special mission. He then went to New York City, where he became friends with Luís Muñoz Marín, Salomón de la Selva, and Katherine Anne Porter. He returned to Mexico in 1921, to become active in journalism and to write historical and bibliographic projects. He worked for the

Mexican Ministry of Education, under José *Vasconcelos, and wrote essays for *El Universal*, *El Universal Ilustrado*, and *Excélsior*. He also worked as a consultant for the Museo Nacional and taught classes at a local military college. He began a most ambitious historical compilation, *La anexión de Centroamérica a México* (Central America's Annexation to Mexico). He collected everything leading to the annexation and published it with an introduction. The first volume appeared in 1924 and the sixth in 1949. Other historical studies during this period include *Cómo era Iturbide* (What Iturbide Was Like) in 1922, *La nueva poesía de América* (The New Poetry of America) in 1923, *El convento de Tepotzotlán* (The Tepotzotlan Convent) in 1924, *San Bartolomé de las Casas* in 1926, and *Bibliografía de don José Cecilio del Valle* in 1934.

During the 1920s, Valle's ideas were influenced by those of the Mexican writers Ramón *López Velarde and Enrique *González Martínez, as well as by the Colombian Porfirio Barba-Jacob, whose biography he wrote. He also prepared a complete bibliography of Barba-Jacob's works.

Valle returned to Washington for a few months in 1930, as a member of the Honduran delegation to the Conference on the Border Question between Honduras and Guatemala. He then spent most of the 1930s in Mexico and continued writing for many major newspapers, both Mexican and international, becoming the most widely known Latin American journalist of the time. In 1942 he published a bibliography on Latin American journalism entitled *La bibliografía del periodismo en la América española* (The Bibliography of Journalism in Spanish America). He also wrote *El periodismo en Honduras: Notas para su historia* (Journalism in Honduras: Historical Notes), published posthumously in 1960.

In 1938 he married Laura Alvarez, a Honduran who had inspired him, and they went to Stanford University, where he was a visiting lecturer. In 1940 he was awarded the Marie Moors Cabot Prize for Journalism at Columbia University. He was later honored at the Pan American Union, and he was received in Washington by President Franklin D. Roosevelt.

Widowed shortly after his first marriage, Valle married the Peruvian poet Emilia Romero in 1941. The two undertook an extensive lecture tour throughout South America. In 1945 Valle, invited by President Juan José Arévalo, was awarded an honorary doctorate at the Universidad de San Carlos in Guatemala. In *Excélsior* and in *La Opinión*, he published his famous interview with President Arévalo in which the Guatemalan president talked about the problems facing Guatemala. Valle wrote additional articles about Arévalo, praising him as a great statesman and concerned citizen. Valle also sought to raise the political consciousness of his countrymen and used his pen as his weapon of choice.

In the 1940s, Valle was more active politically, but he was returned to teaching. He completed a doctorate in history at UNAM in 1948. His dissertation, published in 1950, dealt with Cristóbal de Olid, conquistador of Mexico and Honduras. In 1942 Valle edited a volume of correspondence between Jeremy Bentham and José Cecilio del Valle. He wrote essays on cultural history, such as *Imaginación de México* (México's Imagination) (1945), which focused on the rich legacy of pre-Columbian legends and myths, and *Semblanza de Honduras* (Hondura's Face) (1947), which analyzed the cultural history of his native land. He published works dealing with some major nineteenth-century Spanish-American figures as well as numerous bibliographies. In 1949 he completed the last volume of six on the annexation of Central America. He also turned to politics.

Valle believed that the Liberal and Conservative parties of Honduras differed very little. He favored political union for the five countries of Central America, believing the peace would come only if the countries were united. Valle was involved in numerous attempts to achieve this goal, but was always thwarted.

In 1947, Valle and a group of Hondurans in Mexico formed the Liberal Democratic Committee of Honduras. In 1949, Valle was named ambassador to Washington by the new Honduran president. While there, he, along with several other prominent Latin Americans, founded the Latin American Atheneum of Washington, ushering in a golden age for Latin American culture in Washington during the 1950s. Conferences and lectures were held at Georgetown University. Valle tried to acquaint North Americans with Spanish-American culture. Valle's ambassadorship came to an abrupt halt when on March 1, 1955, he received a telegram from his Foreign Office asking for his resignation. The new Honduran president was reacting to criticism about some of Valle's articles about border disputes between Honduras and Nicaragua.

Valle spent many months trying to defend himself from insinuations and rumors that intimated that he might have had dealings with President Anastasio Somoza of Nicaragua, and the travail began to affect his health. In 1957 the Mexican Writers' Center organized a banquet to honor Valle's literary and journalistic achievements, an event attended by many of the important literary and political figures of the continent.

Valle died in Mexico City on July 29, 1959. Two years before, his wife had edited a commemorative volume about his work entitled *Recuerdo a Rafael Heliodoro Valle en los cincuenta años de su vida literaria* (Honoring the Fiftieth Anniversary of Rafael Heliodoro Valle's Literary Career). As a posthumous homage, the Mexico government honored his mortal remains with the Aztec Eagle. He was considered a postmodernist poet. His historic essays reveal a constant concern about American figures and themes.

Perhaps the book that best represents Valle's ideas and ideology is his *Historia de las ideas contemporánea en Centro-América* (History of Contemporary Thought in Central America), published posthumously in 1960. In it he dealt with topics such as democracy and dictatorship, religion and the state, humanism versus materialism, philosophy, economics, culture, and literary criticism. He assessed accurately the strengths and weaknesses of Central America and analyzed in depth the work of most of its prominent writers and thinkers. Above all he castigated those who tried to blame all the ills that befell Central American on outside forces. Valle held that the citizens' own lack of willingness to work for democracy was the root of backwardness and lack of progress. The work stands as a major contribution to Central American thought.

Valle was a man for all seasons, a versatile intellectual, a poet rich in stylistic resources, a phenomenal bibliographer who saw the need to place research aids at the scholar's disposal, a historian who possessed encyclopedic knowledge and recognized the importance of preserving the past accurately, and a masterful and dedicated journalist. Valle brought his erudition, learning, and graceful poetry and prose to the service of his country as a diplomat, and to the entire hemisphere while serving in cultural and diplomatic missions for Honduras, Mexico, the United Nations, and the Organization of American States.

Valle's contributions to education were a lifetime endeavor. He lived the greater part of his life in Mexico, but was still a Honduran. Through his own life, devoted to poetry, scholarship, journalism, and public service, Valle demonstrated that even while living away, one could remain active in civic and intellectual life.

He was called one of the "distinguished journalists of this century" by Carl W. Ackerman, dean of the graduate school of journalism at Columbia University. Valle's numerous publications and diverse accomplishments form a solid and substantial whole, leaving behind the legacy of a tireless journalist, inspired poet, educator, and man of letters, who above all wanted to bring order and progress, and expand the cultural horizon of his fellow Spanish Americans.

WORKS: Poetry: *El rosal del ermitaño* (The Hermit's Rosebush) (México: n.p., 1911; San José de Costa Rica: n.p., 1920). *Como la luz del día: poemas de pasión, amor, y sacrificio* (Like the Light of Day: Poems of Passion, Love and Sacrifice) (Tegucigalpa: n.p., 1913). *Anfora sedienta* (The Thirsty Urn) (México: M. León Sánchez, Sucs., 1922). *Unísono amor* (Unison Love) (México: 1940). *Contigo* (With You) (México: Eds. R. Loera y Chávez, 1943). *La sandalia de fuego* (The Sandal of Fire) (Managua: Col. Poesía de América, 1952). *La sonrisa de Italia* (The Smile of Italy), in *Abside* 16, 2 (April-June 1952): 213-25. *Poemas* (Tlaxcala: Talls. Gráfs. de Tlaxcala, 1954). *La rosa intemporal* (The Never-Changing Rose) (México: Private Ed., 1964). Anthologies and Prologues: *Poetas de América* (Poets of America) (México: El Universal Ilustrado, 1922). *La nueva poesía de América* (The New Poetry of America) (México: n.p., 1924). Rafael Landívar, *Geórgicas mexicanas* (Mexican Chants), biobibliographical note (México: SEP, 1924). *La anexión de Centro América a México* (The Annexation of Central America to Mexico), 6 vols. (México: Sría. de Relaciones Exteriores, 1924-1949). Gabriel López Chiñas, *Vinnigulasa: Cuentos de Juchitán*, prologue (México: Ed. Neza, 1940). Eduardo Enrique Ríos, *Fray Margil de Jesús, apóstol de América* (Friar Margil de Jesús, Apostle from America), prologue (México: Talls. Gráfs. de la Nación, 1941). *José Cecilio del Valle*, prologue and selection (México: SEP, 1943). *Cartas hispanoamericanas* (Spanish American Letters), prologue and selection (México: SEP, 1945). Margarita Paz Paredes, *Voz de la tierra* (Voice of the Earth), prologue (México: Ed. Firmamento, 1946). *Tres pensadores de América* (Three American Thinkers [Bolívar, Bello, Martí]), prologue and selection (México: SEP, 1946). John Tate Lanning, *Reales cédulas de la Real y Pontífica Universidad de México de 1551-1816* (Royal Decrees from the Royal and Pontificate University of Mexico from 1551-1816), preliminary study (México: UNAM, 1946). *Semblanza de Honduras* (Portrait of Honduras), compiler (Tegucigalpa: n.p., n.d. [1947]). Enrique Cordero y Torres, *Historia del periodismo en Puebla* (History of Journalism in Puebla), prologue (México: n.p., 1947). Gabriel López Chiñas, *Canto del hombre a la tierra* (Man's Song to the Earth), prologue (México: Edit. Firmamento, 1951). Salvador Toscano, *Cuauhtémoc*, prologue (México: FCE, 1953). *Flor de Mesoamérica* (Flower of Mesoamérica) (San Salvador, El Salvador: Ministerio de Cultura, 1955). Essays: *Cómo era Iturbide* (What Iturbide Was Like) (México: Museo Nacional de Arqueología, Historia y Etnografía, 1922). *Ephraim George Squier* (México: Sociedad Científica "Antonio Alzate," 1922). *El convento de Tepotzotlán* (The Convent of Tepotzotlán) (México: Museo Nacional de Arqueología, Historia y Etnografía, 1924). *Indice de la nueva poesía americana* (Index of the New American Poetry) (Buenos Aires: n.p., 1926). *Indice de escritores* (Index of Writers), with Esperanza Velázquez Bringas (México: Herrero, 1928)."La lección de Landívar" (The Lesson of Landívar), in *Excélsior* (Oct. 27, 1931). "Figuras de Landívar en el agua" (Figures of Landívar in the Water), in *Revista de Revistas* (Nov. 1, 1931).

"Bibliografía de Martí en México," in *El Libro y el Pueblo* 10, 9 (Nov. 1932): 28-31. *Bibliografía mexicana* (México: n.p., 1933). "El Renacimiento, de Altamirano" (The Renaissance, of Altamirano), in *El Libro y el Pueblo* 12, 11 (1934): 530-35. *Bibliografía de don José Cecilio del Valle* (México: n.p., 1934). *México imponderable* (Santiago de Chile: Col. Contemporáneos, 1936). *El espejo historial* (The Historical Mirror) (México: n.p., 1937). *Bibliografía de Ignacio Manuel Altamirano* (México: DAPP, 1939). *Cronología de la cultura* (Chronology of Culture) (Monterrey, México: n.p., 1939). *Tierras de pan llevar* (Taking Bread Lands) (Santiago de Chile: n.p., 1939). *Indice de la poesía centroamericana* (Index of Central American Poetry) (Santiago de Chile: Bibl. América, 1941). *Bibliografía del periodismo de América española* (Bibliography of Spanish-American Journalism) (Cambridge, Mass.: n.p., 1942); in *Handbook of Latin American Studies: 1941*, no. 7 (Cambridge, Mass.: n.p., 1942), pp. 559-91. *Cartas de Bentham a José del Valle* (Letters from Bentham to José del Valle) (México: n.p., 1942). *Visión del Perú* (Vision of Peru) (México: n.p., 1943). *Iturbide, varón de Dios* (Iturbide, Man of God) (México: Xóchitl, 1944). *Imaginación de México* (Buenos Aires: Espasa Calpe, 1945). *Santiago en América* (México: Ed. Santiago, 1946). *Bolívar en México* (México: n.p., 1946). "Enrique González Martínez," in *Suma bibliográfica* (México: n.p., 1946). *Animales de América antigua* (Animals of Ancient America) (México: SEP, 1947). *Héroes de 1847* (México: SEP, 1947). *Un diplomático mexicano en París* (A Mexican Diplomat in Paris) (México: n.p., 1948). *Cristóbal de Olid, conquistador de México y Honduras* (México: SEP, 1948). *Bibliografía cervantina en la América española* (A Cervantine Bibliography in Spanish America), with Emilia Romero (México: Ed. de la Academia Mexicana de la Lengua, Imp. Universitaria, 1950). "Saludo a Landívar" (Greetings to Landívar), in *Abside* 16, 2 (1952): 223-34. "Las cartas de Cortés" (Cortés' Letters), in *Historia mexicana* (El Colegio de México) 2, 4 (April-June 1953): 549-63. *Bibliografía de Hernán Cortés* (México: Sociedad de Estudios Cortesianos, 1953). *Bibliografía de Sebastián de Aparicio* (México: n.p., 1953). *Bibliografía de Rafael Landívar* (Bogotá: Instituto Caro y Cuervo, 1953). "Más sobre Díaz Mirón" (More about Díaz Mirón), in *Las Letras Patrias* 1 (Jan.-March 1954): 65-70. *Jesuitas de Tepoztotlán* (Bogotá: Instituto Caro y Cuervo, 1955). *El periodismo en Honduras: notas para su historia* (Journalism in Honduras: Notes for Its History), offprint of the *Revista de Historia de América* (Instituto Panamericano de Geografía e Historia): 48 (Dec. 1959): 517-600. "Evocación de García Monge," in *Nivel* 1 (Jan. 1959). *Viajero feliz* (Happy Traveler) (San Salvador, El Salvador: Ministerio de Cultura, 1959). *Historia de las ideas contemporáneas en Centro-América* (History of Contemporary Thought in Central America) (México: FCE, 1960). *Bibliografía de Porfirio Barba-Jacob*, posthumous work arranged by Emilia Romero de Valle (Bogotá: Instituto Caro y Cuervo, 1961).

BIBLIOGRAPHY: Ermilo Abreu Gómez, *Sala de retratos* (México: Edit. Leyenda, 1946), pp. 276-78; Review of *La rosa intemporal*, in *México en la Cultura* 823 (Dec. 27, 1964): 11. Oscar Acosta, *Rafael Heliodoro Valle: Vida y obra, biografía, estudio crítico, bibliografía y antología de un intelectual hondureño* (Tegucigalpa: n.p., 1973). Roberto Brenes-Mesen, *Crítica americana* (San José, Costa Rica: Eds. del Convivio, 1936), pp. 111-26. Wilberto Cantón, "Personalidad de Rafael Heliodoro Valle," in *Bohemia Poblana* 120 (May 1953). Alfredo Cardona Peña, "Rafael Heliodoro Valle," in *Nivel* 8 (Aug. 25, 1959): 3. Oscar Casteñeda Batres, "Conciencia de México: Rafael Heliodoro Valle," in Boletín bibliográfico de la Secretaría de Hacienda y Crédito Público 160 (Aug. 1, 1959): 1, 7. *Diccionario de la Literatura Latinoamericana.*

696   VALLE-ARIZPE, Artemio de

América Central, vol. 2 (Washington, D.C.: Unión Panamericana, 1963), pp. 180-83. Georgette M. Dorn, "Rafael Heliodoro Valle," in Esteban Durán Rosado, "Antología poética de Rafael Heliodoro Valle," in *Revista Mexicana de Cultura* 920 (Nov. 15, 1964): 4. Max Henríquez Ureña, *Breve historia del modernismo* (México and Buenos Aires: FCE, 1954), p. 399. Enrique Labrador Ruiz, "Requiem para Rafael Heliodoro," in *La Nueva Democracia* (New York, Jan. 1960): 20-21. César Lizardi Ramos, "Coronas para Heliodoro Valle," in *Diorama de la Cultura* (Jan. 17, 1965): 4. Juan Marín, "Presencia de Rafael Heliodoro Valle," in *La Nueva Democracia* (New York, April 1960): 30-34. Aurora M. Ocampo de Gómez and Ernesto Prado Velázquez, *Diccionario de Escritores Mexicanos* (México: UNAM, 1967), pp. 398-400. Emilia Romero de Valle, comp., *Recuerdo a Rafael Heliodoro Valle en los cincuenta años de su vida literaria* (México: Morales Hnos., 1957). Gustavo Sainz, Review of *La rosa intemporal*, in *México en la Cultura* 807 (Sept. 6, 1964): 9. Luis Mario Schneider, "*La rosa intemporal* de Rafael Heliodoro Valle," in *Nivel* 22 (Oct. 25, 1964): 11. José Manuel Topete, "Rafael Heliodoro Valle y el Ateneo Americano de Washington," in *Revista Iberoamericana* (Jan.-June 1957): 125-31. Various, *Homenaje*, in *Universidad de Honduras* (Tegucigalpa, 1959). *Homenaje a Rafael Heliodoro Valle*, in *El Centavo* 3, 31 (Feb. 1960). *Homenaje*, in *Nivel* 29 (May 25, 1965). Esperanza Velázquez Bringas and Rafael Heliodoro Valle, *Indice de escritores* (México: Herrero Hnos., 1928), pp. 303-5. Manuel A. Woolrich B., "Fichas para una bibliografía de Rafael Heliodoro Valle," in Boletín bibliográfico de la Secretaría de Hacienda y Crédito Público 160 (Aug. 1, 1959): 4-6.

JEANNE C. WALLACE

VALLE-ARIZPE, Artemio de (1888-1961). Born in Saltillo, Coahuila, on January 25, 1888, Artemio de Valle-Arizpe studied first under the Jesuits. He then went to the univeristy in Mexico City, graduating as a lawyer in 1910. He had a very short-lived period as a politician, serving in the Congreso de la Unión in 1911 for his local district. His next stop was San Luis Potosí, where he decided to work in his chosen legal field. A few years later, in 1919, he entered the Mexican diplomatic corps, living abroad in Spain, Belgium, and Holland for nine years. While in Madrid, he published some of his first works. He returned home to Mexico in 1928, this time dedicating himself to literature and historical studies. He joined the most important academies and cultural organizations, including the Academia Mexicana de la Lengua and the Academia de la Historia. On February 10, 1942, he was named the "Chronicler of Mexico City," an honor bestowed upon him in recognition of his many achievements. After serving his country for many years both as a diplomat and as a writer, Artemio de Valle-Arizpe died in Mexico City on November 15, 1961.

Most of Valle-Arizpe's work deals with the colonial period. His novels, stories, and accounts of the past are characterized by his very original style, a combination of archaic language, classical portraits of characters, and other elements that mimic the literature of the colonial period with occasional modern touches, even in those same characteristics just mentioned. He wrote about court figures, members of the viceroyalty, explorers and conquerors, and the common people of the colony. Using jest, sardonic humor, and other picaresque elements in some of his works, Valle-Arizpe attempted to re-create the past, as if it were still that way. His vast erudition and scholarly methods of writing led him to produce a wealth of historical fiction that portrays a genuine saga of early Mexico.

WORKS: Anthology: *La gran ciudad de México Tenustitlán, perla de la Nueva España, según relatos de antaño y ogaño* (The Great City of Mexico Tenochtitlán, Pearl of New Spain, According to Stories of Yesteryear and Nowadays) (México: Tip. Murguía, 1918). *Ejemplo* (Example), novel (Madrid: Tip. Artística, 1919). *Vidas milagrosas* (Miraculous Lives) (Madrid: Tip. Artística, 1921). *Doña Leonor de Cáceres y Acevedo y Cosas tenedes* (Madrid, Tip. Artística, 1922). *La muy noble y leal ciudad de México, según relatos de antaño y ogaño* (The Very Noble and Royal City of Mexico, According to Stories of Yesteryear and Nowadays) (México: Ed. Cultura, 1924). *Del tiempo pasado* (Of Time Past) (Madrid: Biblioteca Nueva, 1932. *Amores y picardías* (Loves and Roguishness) (Madrid: Biblioteca Nueva, 1932). *Virreyes y virreinas de la Nueva España* (Viceroys and Vicereines of New Spain) (Madrid: Biblioteca Nueva, 1933). *Libro de estampas* (Book of Portraits) (Madrid: Biblioteca Nueva, 1934). *Historia de vivos y muertos* (Stories about the Living and the Dead) (Madrid: Biblioteca Nueva, 1936). *El Palacio Nacional de México* (The National Palace of Mexico) (México: Imp. de la Sría. de Relaciones Exteriores, 1936). *Tres nichos y un retablo* (Three Niches and an Altar-Piece) (México: Eds. Botas, 1936). *Por la vieja calzada de Tlacopan* (By the Old Causeway in Tlacopan) (México: Talls. de Tostado, 1937). *Lirios de Flandes* (Lilies of Flanders) (México: Edit. Polis, 1938). *Historia de la ciudad de México, según relatos de sus cronistas* (History of Mexico City, According to Accounts by Its Chroniclers) (México: Edit. Pedro Robredo, 1939). *Cuentos del México antiguo* (Stories from Old Mexico) (México and Buenos Aires: Espasa-Calpe, 1939). *Andanzas de Hernán Cortés y otros excesos* (Adventures of Hernán Cortés and Other Excesses) (Madrid: Biblioteca Nueva, 1940). *El Canillitas* (México: Edit. Polis, 1941). *Notas de platería* (Notes about the Silversmith Shop) (México: Edit. Polis, 1941). *Leyendas mexicanas* (Mexican Legends) (México and Buenos Aires: Espasa-Calpe, 1943). *Cuadros de México* (Sketches of Mexico) (México: Edit. Jus, 1943). *Jardinillo seráfico* (Angelic Little Garden) (México: Edit. Jus, 1944). *La movible inquietud* (The Movable Anxiety) (México: EDIAPSA, 1945). *Amor que cayó en castigo* (Love Which Became Punishment) (México: Col. Lunes, 1945). *En México y en otros siglos* (In Mexico and in Other Centuries) (México and Buenos Aires: Espasa-Calpe, 1950). *La Güera Rodríguez* (The Blond Rodriguez) (México: Cía. Gral. de Ediciones, 1949). *Calle vieja y calle nueva* (Old Street and New Street) (México: Cía. Gral. de Ediciones, 1949). *Espejo del tiempo* (Mirror of Time) (México: Edit. Patria, 1951). *Lejanías entre brumas* (Distances between Mists) (México: Edit. Patria, 1951). *Sala de tapices* (Room of Tapestries) (México: Edit. Patria, 1951). *Fray Servando* (México and Buenos Aires: Espasa-Calpe, 1951). *Coro de sombras* (Choir of Shadows) (México: Edit. Patria, 1951). *Inquisición y crímenes* (Inquisition and Crimes) (México: Edit. Patria, 1952). *Piedras viejas bajo el sol* (Old Stones under the Sun) (México: Edit. Patria, 1952). *Juego de cartas* (Card Game) (México: Edit. Patria, 1953). *Personajes de historia y de leyenda* (Personages from History and from Legend) (México: Edit. Patria, 1953). *De la Nueva España* (Of New Spain) (México and Buenos Aires: Espasa-Calpe, 1956). *Papeles amarillentos* (Yellowed Papers) (México: Edit. Patria, 1954). *Horizontes iluminados* (Illuminated Horizons) (México: Edit. Patria, 1954). *Engañar con la verdad* (To Deceive with the Truth) (México: Eds. Los Presentes, 1955). *Deleite para indiscretos* (Crime for the Indiscreet) (México: Edit. Patria, 1955). *Cuando había virreyes* (When There Were

Vicerroys) (México: Edit. Patria, 1956). *Gregorio López, hijo de Felipe II* (Gregorio López, Son of Felipe II) (México: Cía. Gral. de Ediciones, 1957). *De la otra edad que es esta edad* (From the Other Age Which Is This Age) (México: Edit. Patria, 1957). *Obras completas* (Complete Works), vol. 1 (México: Eds. de Libreros Unidos Mexicanos, 1959); vol. 2 (1962).

BIBLIOGRAPHY: Ermilo Abreu Gómez, *Sala de retratos* (México: Edit. Leyenda, 1946), pp. 279-81. Enrique Anderson-Imbert, *Spanish American Literature*, vol. 2 (Detroit: Wayne State University Press, 1969), pp. 512-13. John S. Brushwood and José Rojas Garcidueñas, *Breve historia de la novela mexicana* (México: Eds. de Andrea, 1959), pp. 88-90. Emmanuel Carballo, *19 protagonistas de la literatura mexicana del siglo XX* (México: Empresas Editoriales, 1965), pp. 155-66. Alfredo Cardona Peña, *Semblanzas mexicanas* (México: Libro-Mex, 1955), pp. 135-39. Genaro Fernández MacGregor, *Carátulas* (México: Eds. Botas, 1935), pp. 129-45. Luis Leal, *Breve historia del cuento mexicano* (México: Eds. de Andrea, 1956), pp. 95-96; *Bibliografía del cuento mexicano* (México: Eds. de Andrea, 1958), pp. 150-52. Francisco Monterde, "Don Artemio de Valle-Arizpe se fue," in *Universidad de México* 16, 5 (Jan. 1962): 31. Aurora M. Ocampo de Gómez and Ernest Prado Velázquez, *Diccionario de Escritores Mexicanos* (México: UNAM, 1967), pp. 400-402. Eglantina Ochoa Sandoval, Review of *Deleite para indiscretos*, in *Metáfora* 6 (Jan.-Feb. 1956): 37-38. Various, "Homenaje a Don Artemio de Valle-Arizpe," in *Revista Mexicana de Cultura* 765 (Nov. 26, 1961); "Homenaje a Artemio de Valle-Arizpe," in *Bohemia Poblana* 115 (1952): 1-10; "Homenaje póstumo," in *Bohemia Poblana* 211 (Dec. 1961).

JEANNE C. WALLACE

VANGUARDIST PROSE FICTION IN MEXICO. The 1920s and 1930s brought many changes to Mexican literature that were a reaction to both the turmoil and ideology of the Mexican Revolution of 1910 and to the increased industrialization ocurring in Europe at the turn of the century. Two literary groups arose in Mexico which responded by breaking from the traditional narrative of the nineteenth century and experimenting with techniques and topics that better represented their experience. These groups have come to be known as the Contemporáneos and the Estridentistas. Independently of one another, they formed literary groups that helped stimulate creative, innovative activity among their members. Because the two held diverse views about art, the creative process, and its function, they were often at odds with one another, and therefore, they did not produce any collective works. The groups were comprised not only of poets and prose writers, but of artists in the visual arts as well. Because the best-known works and the majority of the literary activity during this time involved poetry, the vanguard in Mexico, as in the rest of Latin America, is primarily known for its poetic contributions, while its prose fiction work has for the most part been neglected or rejected as either insignificant or of bad quality. Nevertheless, there were significant and noteworthy attempts by members of both literary groups to break with the old narrative and to introduce an innovative style of prose fiction. Because of the different goals and approaches by both groups, their works need to be considered separately.

Estridentismo: The Estridentista movement, while interested in literary innovation, was also highly committed to social concerns and it is primarily this social orientation that separated it from the Contemporáneos. The group, which remained active from 1921 through 1927, is generally considered to be a reaction to the Mexican Revolution and the struggle between the social classes in Mexico. Many of the young writers who participated in the group had witnessed the fighting that had occurred during the Revolution and proceeded to react to it.

The poet Manuel *Maples Arce is considered the initiator of the Estridentista movement because he wrote and promulgated the group's manifestos, *Actual No. 1, Actual No. 2,* and *Actual No. 3,* modeled after the Italian Futurist manifesto. The manifestos strongly attacked traditional literature and established thought, proclaimed that literature is cosmopolitan rather than nationalistic, recognized the difficulty and elitist nature of the literature, and called for the creation of "pure poetry" eliminating all anecdote and incorporating a new syntax. Among its other participants and contributors were Germán List Arzubide, Luis Quintanilla, Salvador Gallardo, the painter Alva de la Canal, and the prose fiction writers Xavier *Icaza, and Arqueles *Vela. Although at first the group was not well received, it did draw the attention it wanted. The group, highly interested in the latest machinery and technology, tried to incorporate these advancements in their literature. The group attempted to combine terms that were different from one another in order to produce surprise or shock, but thematic unity was still very important. These works are full of references to electricity, speed, motors, power, airplanes, cars, metal, skyscrapers, cinema, geometry, and mathematical terminology. Their interest in surrealism and in Freudian psychology manifests intself in the frequent inclusion of dream and hallucinatory sequences from which emerges a sense of ambiguity in the text and which invite the reader to participate in order to decipher the meaning of the work. The Estridentistas unlike the Contemporáneos, used humor to stress certain societal and political concerns. This is another major difference between the two groups.

Some of the first works by the group were published in *El Universal Ilustrado.* Together, they organized and published a number of magazines that included art, literature, and literary pronouncements. *Ser* was published in 1922 in Puebla, *Irradiador* appeared in 1923, and *Horizonte,* published by Germán List Arzubide and the primary vehicle for the diffusion of Estridentismo, was printed from 1926 through 1927.

Among the Estridentistas who experimented with prose fiction were Arqueles Vela and Xavier Icaza. Vela wrote the short novels, *La señorita etcétera* (Miss Etcetera) (1922), *Un crimen provisional (A Provisional Crime)* (1924), *El café de nadie* (Nobody's Café) (1926), and *El intransferible* (The Not Transferable) (1927). Xavier Icaza wrote a number of short narrative works during the time the group was together, including *Dilema* (Dilemma) (1921), *La hacienda, novela mexicana* (The Hacienda, Mexican Novel) (1921), *Gente mexicana* (Mexican People) (1924), *Magnavoz* (Magnabox) (1926), *Discurso Mexicano* (Mexican Discourse) (1926), and *Panchito Chapopote, retablo tropical o relación de un extraordinario sucedido de la heróica Veracruz* (Panchito Chapopote, Tropical Altar-Piece or Story of an Extraordinary Happening of the Heroic Veracruz) (1928). Most of these works were rather short, fragmented, and episodic.

Vela's best-known narrative is *El café de nadie* (1926), in which he incorporates a number of the techniques already mentioned. The short novel centers around a cafe from which the work gets its name, and which was a place that was actually frequented by the Estridentistas. The *nadie* of the title suggests the fact that the people in the cafe are all faceless and lack identity. Vela is able to convey the dehumanization and lack of identity that people experience in the rapid-paced society of which he is a part. Vela makes several references to cinema and to movie actors, at times blending these movie characters and scenes with those of the narrative being presented in the text. He relies on mathematical and scientific terminology to suggest the multiplicity of personalities and intentionally maintains a sense of ambiguity to communicate the lack of identity of his characters.

Xavier Icaza's noteworthy narrative is *Panchito Chapopote* (1928). It tells of the turmoil caused by foreign investors and by the onset of the Mexican Revolution. Icaza communicates the chaos caused by the fighting by fragmenting his text, and time and space. The work is highly episodic and is like a play in that it includes very little background narrative; instead it includes short, cryptic descriptions that are similar to stage or movie set directions. The narrative also includes titles or headings of the people who speak, including the "implied author" and a chorus.

Contemporáneos: During the same time period as the Estridentista experiments, a group of writers in the Mexico City area formed what came to be known as the Contemporáneos. Origins of this group date back prior to 1920 when Jaime *Torres Bodet, Ortiz de *Montellano, Enrique *González Rojo, Carlos *Pellicer, and José *Gorostiza met while students at the Escuela Nacional Preparatoria. They continued school together at the Escuela de Altos Estudios and the Facultad de Jurisprudencia at the Universidad Nacional where they were influenced by Alfonso *Caso and Enrique *González Martínez, members of the Ateneo de México. Inspired by this group, Torres *Bodet and Ortiz de *Montellano formed the Nuevo Ateneo de la Juventud in 1918. The young writers published some of their early works in the magazine *Pegaso* (1917) and the student journal *San-Ev-Ank* (1918). These writers were later joined by Salvador *Novo and Xavier *Villaurrutia in 1921. And later, Jorge *Cuesta and Gilberto *Owen became part of the group. The group received a great deal of backing from the government when Alvaro Obregón was president and José *Vasconcelos became part of his cabinet.

These writers began writing in magazines and literary newspapers. The first magazine the group published was *México Moderno*. Between December 1922 and October 1923, Torres Bodet and Ortiz de Montellano directed the publication of *La Falange*. Novo, Villaurrutia, Cuesta, and Owen organized the magazine *Ulises*, which was published from May 1927 through February 1928. The magazine *Contemporáneos*, for which the group is best known, began publication in 1928. It had the longest-running publication, from June 1928 through December 1931, and unlike some of the other magazines, it was printed on fine quality paper and included a number of sketches and photographs. This magazine included works by many of the members of the group, but also those of some established Mexican, Spanish American, and Spanish writers, and translations of other well-known works.

The group's ideology and purpose are explained by their goals for their magazine, which was the "representation of contemporary universal culture." They discussed their concerns about the relationship between Mexicoan art and literature and European and Spanish art and literature, and tried to bring Mexican literature to the forefront.

This group was strongly influenced by many European writers, but primarily by André Gide, whose works they knew very well, and Marcel Proust, whom they admired because he had created a new way of perceiving man's environment. As a result, these writers did away with anecdote and tried to describe and develop an extended concept or image. They thus fragmented time and space, creating their own order, one that best conveyed the concept being communicated by the entire text. The group used metaphors extensively; often the work itself is one extensive metaphor.

Because of the complex imagery, metaphors, and topics, the Contemporáneos were often accused of being escapists and elitist. They were sometimes accused of writing literature which was not "virile." Indeed, this is another of the differences between the Estridentistas, who consciously chose social and political topics, and the Contemporáneos, who stayed away from social themes to concentrate on more literary and philosophical ideas.

Among the Contemporáneos who experimented with prose fiction were Salvador Novo, Gilberto Owen, Javier Villaurrutia, and Jaime Torres Bodet. All with the exception of Torres Bodet wrote but a few prose works. Novo's short novel is *El joven* (The Young Man) (1928); Owen's are *La llama fría* (The Cold Flame) (1925) and *Novela como nube* (Novel like a Cloud) (1928); Villaurrutia's is *Dama de corazones* (Lady of Hearts) (1928); and Torres Bodet's are *Margarita de niebla* (Margarita of Fog) (1927), *Educación sentimental* (Sentimental Education) (1929), *Proserpina rescatada* (Ransomed Proserpina) (1931), *Estrella de día* (Day-Time Star) (1933), *Primero de enero* (January First) (1935), and a collection of short stories, *Nacimiento de Venus, y otros relatos* (Birth of Venus and Other Tales) (1941).

Novo's *El joven*, though published in 1928, was written in 1923, before the author began his association with the Contemporáneos. As a result, the work -- which is similar to the works of the Contemporáneos group with respect to its experimentation with techniques such as fragmentation of time and space and the blending of the character, narrator, and the implied author -- is thematically similar to the works of the Estridentistas. The work centers around the impressions of a young man, the *joven* of the title, who is reintroduced to Mexico City after a period of convalescense. His reactions and comments become a form of collective self-criticism of Mexican people and society.

Owen's *Novela como nube* is a highly complex, extended metaphor that the author uses to question reality as perceived by the individual, while also reflecting on the creative process itself. In true Contemporáneo fashion, Owen's narrative includes a number of dream sequences, blends the characters in the text with the action on the movie screen, describes minute details of picturesque scenes that become almost like paintings, and succeeds in leading the reader to question this "reality" which has been created in the text. The story line parallels the ancient myth of Ixion who falls in love with Juno, Jupiter's wife, and as his punishment is banished to dwell in Hades forever. Juno is changed into a cloud, thus the *nube* of the title. Because of the work's complexity, it has long been overlooked and misunderstood, but deserves re-examination.

Villaurrutia's *Dama de corazones*, like Owen's narrative, also questions reality. The story centers around two young sisters, who like the two faces of the Queen of Hearts in a card deck, the *dama* of the title, are opposites, yet connected to one another. The narrative describes the young women entirely from the narrator's perspective, so the reader is left to decide whether or not the young man is a reliable narrator.

Torres Bodet is the only one of the group who wrote extensively. His novels incorporate a number of technical innovations, including fragmentation of time and space, and psychological analysis of the characters. Many of his novels are presented

702 VARGAS Martínez, Ubaldo

from a single perspective, from the point of view of an innocent young man who is in love and confused. In *Estrella de día,* he, like Owen, also experiments with scenes in which the action of the narrative is blended with action that occurs on a movie scene. *Margarita de niebla* questions the reliability of the narrator while also depicting the psychological complexity of his characters.

BIBLIOGRAPHY: Ermilo Abreu Gómez, "Contemporáneos," *Las revistas literarias de México* (México: Instituto Nacional de Bellas Artes, 1963), pp. 165-84. Gabriela Becerra, comp., *Estridentismo: memoria y valoración,* introduction by Esther Hernández Palacios (México: Fondo de Cultura Económica, 1983). John S. Brushwood, "Las bases del vanguardismo en Xavier Icaza," *Texto Crítico* 24-25 (1984): 161-70. Peter Burger, *Theory of the Avant-Garde,* translated by Michael Shaw, foreword by Jochen Schulte-Sasse (Minneapolis: University of Minnesota Press, 1984). Fernando Burgos, ed., *Prosa hispánica de vanguardia* (Madrid: Editorial Orígenes, 1986). Oscar Collazos, ed., *Los vanguardismos en la América Latina* (1970; Barcelona: Ediciones de Bolsillo, 1977). Juan Coronado, "*Novela como nube*: prosa como poesía (un acercamiento a Owen," *Los Empeños: La Vida Literaria* 1 (April-June 1981): 139-48. Sergio Fernández, director, *Los Empeños: La Vida Literaria,* 1 (April-June 1981). Merlin H. Forster, *Los "Contemporáneos" 1920-1932: perfil de un experimento vanguardista mexicano* (México: Ediciones de Andrea, 1964). Germán List Azurbide, *El movimiento estridentista* (Xalapa, Veracruz: Ediciones de Horizonte, 1926). Manuel Maples Arce, "El origen del vanguardismo en México," *La Cultura en México* 276 (May 31, 1967): 2-6. Nelson Osorio Tejeda, "Contribución a una bibliografía sobre el vanguardismo hispanoamericana," *Revista de Crítica Literaria Latinoamericana* 15 (First Semester 1982): 141-50. Gustavo Pérez Firmat, *Idle Fictions: The Hispanic Vanguard Novel, 1926-1934* (Durham, N.C.: Duke University Press, 1982. Edna Aguirre Rehbein, "Vanguardist Techniques in Mexican Prose Fiction: 1923-1964," Diss., University of Texas, 1988. Luis Mario Schneider, ed., *El estridentismo -- México 1921-1927* (México: UNAM, Imprenta Universitaria, 1985); *El estridentismo o una literatura de la estrategia* (México: Ediciones de Bellas Artes, 1970). Guillermo Sheridan, *Los Contemporáneos ayer* (México: FCE, 1985); editor, *Homenaje Nacional a los Contemporáneos, monólogos en espiral, antología de narrativa* (México: INBA, 1982). Hugo J. Verani, *Las vanguardias literarias en Hispoamérica, manifiestos, proclamas y otros escritos* (Roma: Bulzoni Editores, 1986).

EDNA A. REHBEIN

VARGAS Martínez, Ubaldo (1913-). Vargas Martínez was born on October 7, 1913 in Mexico City. He studied both at the National Preparatory School and in the Faculties of Philosophy and Letters and Law at the National Autonomous University of Mexico. He earned his law degree in 1940. In 1943 he traveled to the University of North Carolina at Chapel Hill with a scholarship from the United States government. There he earned a degree in English language and literature. On his return he was made professor of English language and literature in the secondary schools of the Department of Education, and of world literature in the schools associated with the National University of Mexico. Beginning in 1963 he was a researcher with the Center for Literary Studies of that university.

Vargas Martínez, who has dedicated his life to teaching and research, is best known as a careful, erudite, and pleasing biographer. His biographies have won him several prizes.

WORKS: Studies: Prologue to Tirso de Molina, *La prudencia en la mujer*, BEP, no. 405 (México, 1948). Prologue to José Joaquín Fernándea de Lizardi, *Obras. II Teatro* (Works: II Theater) (México: Centro de Estudios Literarios, UNAM, 1965), pp. 7-31. Biographies: *La ciudad de México 1325-1960* (Mexico City 1325-1960) (México: Premio Ciudad de México, Depto. Central, 1961). *Morelos, siervo de la nación* (Morelos, Servant of the Nation), prologue by Antonio Díaz Soto y Gama (México: SEP, 1963); 2d ed., Col. Sepan Cuantos, no. 55 (México: Porrúa, 1966). *Hermenegildo Galeana: paradigma del héroe* (Hermenegildo Galeana, Paradigm of the Hero) (México: SEP, 1964).

BIBLIOGRAPHY: Anon., "Exaltación de un héroe, premiada en un concurso," review of *Morelos, siervo de la nación*, in *Revista de la Semana*, (Nov. 3, 1963): 3; "Tres grandes conmemoraciones," review of the biography of Galeana, in *El Universal* (Aug. 2, 1964). Huberto Batis, review of *Obras. II Teatro* of Fernández de Lizardi, *La Cultura en México* 203 (Jan. 5, 1966): ii. Antonio Díaz Soto y Gama, Prologue to *Morelos, siervo de la nación* (México: SEP, 1963). Isidoro Enríquez Calleja, "*Morelos, siervo de la nación*," *El Universal* (Oct. 9, 1966). Ramón Gálvez, "*Morelos, siervo de la nación*," *El Libro y el Pueblo* 4, 8 (Dec. 1963): 11-13. Henrique González Casanova, "Personas y lugares: Actualidad del Pensador Mexicano," *La Cultura en México* 166 (Apr. 21, 1965): xv. S.H.U., "La Tarea editorial," review of *Obras II* of Fernández de Lizardi, in *La Cultura en México* 190 (Oct. 6, 1965): xvii. Andrés Henestrosa, "Defensa de José J. Fernández de Lizardi," *México en la Cultura* 888 (March 27, 1966): 1. Armando de Maria y Campos, "Cómo fue la rendición del insurgente Mariano Matamoros," *Revista Mexicana de Cultura* 872 (Dec. 15, 1963): 4-5. Fernando Medina Ruiz, "Morelos, héroe representativo de los países centroamericanos," *El Universal Gráfico* (Aug. 26, 1961): 2, 4. Javier Morente, "Sala de lectura," review of the 2d edition of *Morelos . . .*, *Diorama de la Cultura* (Oct. 2, 1966): 4. J. R. Spell, Review of *Obras II* of Fernández de Lizardi, *Hispania* 1 (March 1965): 183-84. Aurora M. Ocampo de Gómez and Ernesto Prado Velázquez, *Diccionario de Escritores Mexicanos* (México: UNAM, 1967), pp. 402-3.

                                                        PETER G. BROAD

VASCONCELOS, José (1881-1959). José Vasconcelos, a great and representative Mexican writer, was born in the city of Oaxaca on February 27, 1881. His intellectual formation began in the Mexican capital where he graduated from law school in 1907. In 1910, Vasconcelos vehemently attacked what he considered the "shortsighted" philosophy of Positivism and followed the new road of Mexican thought. He was to remain vehement about his beliefs throughout his life.

When Mexico was celebrating its centenary, Vasconcelos published his first important work: *Gabino Barreda y las ideas contemporáneas* (Gabino Barreda and Contemporary Ideology). In 1914, the Mexican president, Eulalio Gutierrez, named him secretary of education, and Vasconcelos became the bridge that would take the "Revolution" from the political to the teaching sphere. Two years later, because of a disagreement with the government, he left the country and traveled to Peru. His brief absence from the national scene ended, however, when he was named president of Mexico's National University. In that position, he was very successful in getting the university to address the people's ideals and aspirations.

In 1921, he was asked once again to head the Department of Education. In that capacity, he utilized missionaries to teach the peasants to read and write; he made it possible for the people to become familiar with classical authors (Homer, Plato, Dante, Cervantes, Goethe, etc.); and he placed those Latin American writers who were becoming classical--José Santos Chocano, Gabriela Mistral, Manuel Ugarte, etc.- in the tribunals and teaching institutions. He founded schools, libraries, and institutes; he encouraged new painters. Thus, Mexico's preoccupation with culture and education was at the forefront.

During the presidency of his political rival, Plutarco Elias Calles, who came to power in 1924, Vasconcelos traveled throughout Europe and the United States. He returned to Mexico at the end of 1927, and in 1929 became a presidential candidate. He had already published his two principal works in Europe: *La raza cósmica* (The Cosmic Race) (1925) and *Indología* (Indology) (1929). Defeated in the presidential election, he began the sad years that were to become his most productive decade. His philosophical works, which have been described as deficient and imperfect by some critics, appeared then. His *Metafísica* (Metaphysics) (1929), his *Etica* (Ethics) (1931), and his *Estética* (Aesthetics) (1935) all reveal improvised solutions that seek to placate the American hunger for a philosophy of its own. Later he was to write his transparent autobiography: *Ulises Criollo* (Ulises, the Creole) (1936), *La tormenta* (The Tempest) (1936), *El desastre* (The Disaster (1938), and *El proconsulado* (The Proconsulate) (1939). And while he weaves his long history in books, he writes a short one for Mexico--*Breve Historia de México* (A Short History of Mexico).

Fifteen years had passed since *La raza cósmica* was first published and, now, he filled he remaining nineteen years of his life with more philosophical and historical writings. Among other works, he published in 1940 his *Manual de Filosofía* (A Philosophy Manual), then *Hernán Cortés* (1941), *Apuntes para la Historia de Mexico* (Notes for the History of Mexico) (1945), *Todología* (About All) (1952), *Temas contemporáneos* (Contemporary Themes) (1955), and *En el ocaso de mi vida* (At the End of My Life) (1957). He died in Mexico City on June 30, 1959. For a posthumous publication, he left *La flama: los de arriba en la revolución* (The Flame: The "Winners" in the Revolution). There is a hint of contradiction and bitterness in the last period of Vasconcelos' life. But rather than a reactionary--as some of his fellow countrymen described him--Vasconcelos is an indisputable and marvelous example of the best of America's writers.

WORKS: *Education in Mexico: Present Day Tendencies* (Washington, D.C.: Government Printing Office, 1923). *Aspects of Mexican Civilization: Lectures on the Harris Foundation by J. Vasconcelos and Manuel Gamio* (Chicago: University of Chicago Press, 1926). *Páginas escogidas* (Selected Pages), selection and forward by Antonio Castro Leal (México: Ediciones Botas, 1940). *Vasconcelos*, foreword and selection by Genaro Fernández Mac Gregor (México: SEP, 1942). *El viento de Bagdad: cuentos y ensayos*, selection by Antonio Castro Leal (México: Letras de México, 1945). *La sonata mágica: cuentos y relatos*, 2nd ed. (Buenos Aires: Espasa-

Calpe, 1950). Obras completas (Complete Works), 4 vols. (México: Libreros Unidos Mexicanos, 1957-1959), include bibliographies.

BIBLIOGRAPHY: R. Bonifaz Nuño, "Imagen de Vasconcelos," in *Abside* 27 (1964). Antonio Castro Leal, "José Vasconcelos," in *Revista de las Indias* (Bogotá) 4 (Nov. 1939). Max Henríquez Ureña, "Perfil de Jose Vasconcelos," in *Carteles* (La Habana, Cuba) 40, 28 (July, 1959). Pedro Henríquez Ureña, "Discurso en homenaje a Vasconcelos," in *Nosotros* (Buenos Aires, Oct. 1922). *Homenaje del Colegio Nacional a Samuel Ramos y José Vasconcelos* (México: Colegio Nacional, 1960). José Luis Martínez, "La obra literaria de José Vasconcelos," in *Filosofía y Letras* (Mexico) 13 (1947). Gabriela Mistral, "La indología de Vasconcelos," in *Revista de Filosofía* (Buenos Aires) 13, 5 (1927). William H. Pugh, *José Vasconcelos y el despertar del Mexico moderno,* translated by Pedro Vázquez Cisneros (México: Ed. Jus, 1958). Jesús Silva Herzog, "Vasconcelos," in *Nivel* 8 (Aug. 25, 1959). Gabriella De Beer, *José Vasconcelos and His World* (New York: Las Americas, 1966). John Herbert Maddox, *Vasconcelos of México, Philosopher and Prophet* (Austin: University of Texas Press, 1967). Josefina Oseguera Jurado, "Un mexicano singular," in *El Libro y el Pueblo* 45 (1968). Antonio Sacoto, "Aspectos indigenistas en la obra literaria de José Vasconcelos (1891-1959)," in *Cuadernos Americanos* 28, 2 (1969).

HERLINDA HERNANDEZ

VAZQUEZ, Jorge Adalberto (1886-1959). Born in Alquines, San Luis Potosí, on October 8, 1886, Vazquez studied in the capital and began publishing poetry in 1906. In 1916 he became a professor of literature at the National University of San Luis Potosí. In 1918 he moved to México City, to work for the Department of Fine Arts, then for the library, and from 1925 to 1932 he worked in the Secretariat of Public Education. He was a founding member of the Academy of Arts and Sciences in San Luis de Potosi.

His works include short stories, essays, and above all poetry, which, during his long career, displayed many different styles. His poetry acquired purity and technical expertise. He died in Mexico City on August 8, 1859.

WORKS: Poetry: *Rincón del olvido* (The Corner of Oblivion) (San Luis Potosí: n.p., 1912). *El espíritu intacto* (The Untouched Spirit) (México: León Sánchez, 1923). *La sombra invisible* (The Invisible Shadow) (México: Editorial Mexicana, 1944). Essays and Short Stories: *Por campos ubérrimos* (Through Abundant Fields) (México: Porrúa, 1940).

BIBLIOGRAPHY: José Luis Martínez, *Literatura mexicana siglo XX (1910-1949),* vol. 2 (México: Ant. Librería Robredo, 1949), p. 126. Aurora M. Ocampo de Gómez and Ernesto Prado Velázquez, *Diccionario de escritores mexicanos* (México: UNAM, 1967), pp. 404-5.

NORA ERRO-PERALTA

VELA, Arqueles (1899- ?) poet, short story writer, and critic. Arqueles Vela was born in Tapachula, Chiapas, on December 2, 1899. He began his writing career as a journalist for *El Demócrata* in 1920. In 1921, he worked for *El Universal Ilustrado* and also published his first collection of poetry, *El sendero gris y otros poemas* (The Gray Path and Other Poems). This is also the year that the Estridentista movement of which Vela became a part, was begun by Manuel *Maples Arce. (*See* Vanguardist Prose Fiction in Mexico.) Vela's first short novel, *La señorita Etcétera* (Miss Etcetera), was published in 1922 as part of the literary segment "Novela Semanal" of *El Universal Ilustrado*.

He traveled and studied throughout Europe and the Orient from 1925 through 1933, when he returned to México. He began directing the literary supplement of *El Nacional*, and together with Germán Cueto, Lola Velázquez, and Ermilo *Abreu Gómez, he formed the first theater groups for youth. Vela became very active in education and in providing opportunities for study to all. Together with Agustín *Yáñez, he participated in broadcasting classes over the radio. In 1935, he taught art history and literature at the Escuela Nacional de Maestros, and also taught at the Universidad Nacional. He began a program of evening art courses for workers, and served on a number of education commissions. In 1936, he helped start the Escuela Normal Superior. Between 1939 and 1958, he served as director of the Escuela Secundaria Nocturna, then of the Escuela Secundaria Experimental, and later of the Escuela Normal Superior.

Arqueles Vela's works became known in *El Universal Ilustrado*, where he published his first articles, stories, and poems, using the pseudonym Silvestre Paradox. His poetry is characteristic of the literary movement, the Estridentistas, of which he was an active member. But starting in 1945, with the publication of his first noteworthy short story collection, *Cuentos del día y de la noche* (Stories of Day and Night), Vela became recognized as a serious contributor to contemporary Mexican prose. He also published a number of critical and theoretical essays on art and literature in well-known journals and newspapers.

WORKS: Poetry: *El sendero gris y otros poemas* (The Gray Path and Other Poems), 1919-1920 (México, 1921). *Cantada a las muchachas fuertes y alegres de México* (Cantata to the Strong and Happy Girls of México) (México, 1940). *Poemontaje* (Poem Montage) (México: Ediciones de Andrea, 1968). Short Story, Sketch, and Novel: *La señorita etcétera* (Miss Etcetera) (México: *El Universal Illustrado*, 1922). *El café de nadie y Un crimen provisional* (Nobody's Café and A Provisional Crime), novels (Xalapa, Veracruz: Horizonte, 1926). *El viaje redondo* (The Round Trip) (México: Revista de Revistas, 1929); 2nd., edition with *Cuentos del día y de la noche* (Stories of Day and Night) (México: Ediciónes Botas, 1962). *Cuentos del día y de la noche* (Stories of Day and Night) (México: Editorial Don Quijote, 1945); 2nd ed. incremented and corrected, *Cuentos del día y de la noche y El viaje redondo* (México: Edición Botas, 1962). *La volanda* (In the Air), novel (México, 1956). *El picaflor* (The Hummingbird) novel, (México: Costa-Amic, 1961); 2nd ed. (1965). *Luzbela* (México: Costa-Amic., 1966). Essays: *Introducción, organización, interpretación y dirección del teatro de muñecos* (Introduction, Organization, Interpretation and Direction of a Puppet Theater) (México, 1936). *Historia materialista del arte* (Materialistic History of Arts) (México, 1936). *Evolución histórica de la literatura universal* (Historical Evolution of the Universal Literature) (México, 1941); 2nd ed., complemented, reformed, and corrected under the title of *Literatura Universal* (Universal Literature) (México: Ediciónes Botas, 1951). *El arte y la estética* (Art and Aesthetic), general theory of art (México, 1945). *El trabajo y el amor* (The Job and Love) (México, 1945). *Teoría literaria del Modernismo* (Literary Theory of Modernism) 2nd ed. (México:

Ediciónes Botas, 1940). *Elementos del lenguaje y didáctica de la expresión* (Elements of the Language and Didactic of Expression) (México, 1953). *Fundamentos de la literatura mexicana* (Fundamentals of Mexican Literature) (México, 1953). *Fundamentos de la historia del arte* (Fundamentals of Art History) (México, 1953). *Análisis de la expresión literaria* (Analysis of Literary Expression) Col. Studium, no 51 (México: Ed. de Andrea, 1965).

BIBLIOGRAPHY: Ermilio Abreu Gòmez, "Los libros y otros engaños. Arqueles Vela y sus Fantasías," *Revista Mexicana de Cultura* 856 (Aug. 25, 1963): 7. Demetrio Aguilera Malta, "Arqueles Vela busca nuevos horizontes," *El Gallo Ilustrado* 79 (Dec. 25, 1963): 4; "La rosa de los vientos. El lenguaje artístico," review of *Análisis de la expresión literaria, El Gallo Ilustrado* 147 (April 18, 1965): 4; Review of *El picaflor*, in *El Gallo Ilustrado* 178 (Nov. 21, 1965): 4. Anon., Bibliographic review in *Biblos* 4, 186 (Aug. 12, 1922): 121-22; review of *El picaflor*, in *Cuadernos de Bellas Artes* 2, 7 (July 7, 1961): 79; 8 (August, 1961): 47; Review of *Cuentos del día y de la noche*, in *Cuaderno de Bellas Artes* 4, 1 (Jan. 1963): 92. "Nueva edición de la novela *El picaflor*," *Revista de la Semana* (Feb. 6, 1966): 3; "Novela estridentista: *Luzbela*," *Revista de la Semana* (July 31, 1966): 3. Gabriela Becerra, *Estridentismo: Memoria y valoración* (México: FCE, 1983). José María Benítez, "El Estridentismo, El Argorismo, Crisol," *Las revistas literarias de México* (México: INBA, 1963), pp. 145-64. John Brushwood, *Mexico in Its Novel*, lst ed., 1966 (Austin: University of Texas Press, 1975), pp. 192-94; and *The Spanish American Novel* (Austin: University of Texas Press, 1975), pp. 52-55. Miguel Bustos Cereceda, "Estridentistas en la sombra," in *Estridentismo: Memoria y valoración*, edited by Gabriel Becerra (México: FCE, 1983), pp. 260-86. Rómulo Cosse, "*El Café de nadie* y las Vanguardias Hispanoamericanas," in *Estridentismo: Memoria y valoración*, edited by Gabriela Becerra (México: FCE, 1983), pp. 176-78. Carmen de la Fuente, "Capítulos para el estudio de la literatura mexicana," *Boletín bibliográfico de la Secretaría de Hacienda y Crédito Público* (México) 320 (June 1, 1965): 15-17. Merlin H. Forster, *Historia de la poesía hispanoamericana* (Clear Creek, Ind.: American Hispanist, 1981), p. 136. Carlos González Peña, *Historia de la literatura mexicana, 1928* (México: Porrua, 1966), p. 307. Manuel Gónzalez Ramírez, "El modernismo," review of *Teoría literaria del Modernismo*, in *México en la Cultura* 38 (Oct.23, 1949): 7. Andrés Henestrosa, "La nota cultural," review of *Análisis de la expresión literaria*, in *El Nacional* (April 17, 1965): 3. Luis Leal, *Breve historia del cuento mexicano*, Manuales Studium, no. 3 (México: Ediciones de Andrea, 1956), p. 123; *Bibliografía del cuento mexicano*, Col. Studium, no. 21 (México: Ediciones de Andrea, 1958), p. 154; "El movimiento estridentista," *Los vanguardismos en la América Latina*, edited by Oscar Collazos (Barcelona: Ediciones Península, 1977), pp. 105-16. Raúl Leiva, "Escaparates de libros," review of 2nd edition of *El picaflor*, in *México en la Cultura* 863 (Nov. 7, 1965) p. 9; "Escaparate de libros," review of *Análisis de la expresíon literaria*, in *México en la Cultura* 976 (Jan. 2, 1966): 7; Review of *Luzbela*, in *México en la Cultura* 911 (Sept. 4, 1966): 6. Hortensia Lénica Pyhol Vda. de Vela, "La narrativa estridentisa del intransferible Arqueles Vela," in *Estridentismo: Memoria y valoración*, edited by Gabriela Becerra, (México: FCE, 1983), pp. 189-212. Germán List Azurbide, *El movimiento estridentista* (Xalapa, Veracruz: Ediciones de Horizonte, 1926). Velia Márquez, "Arqueles Vela, su nuevo libro, la literatura hispanoamericana y el movimiento estridentista," in *México en la Cultura* 774 (Jan. 19, 1964): 5. José Luis Martínez, *Literatura mexicana del siglo xx, 1910-1949*, vol. 1, Clásicos y Modernos, no. 3 (México: Antigua Librería Robredo, 1949), p. 29;

vol. 2, no. 4 (1950), pp. 126-27. Carlos Monsivais, "Los estridentistas y los agoristas," *Los vanguardismos en la América Latina*, edited by Oscar Collazos (Barcelona: Ediciones Península, 1977), pp. 117-22. Aurora M. Ocampo de Gómez and Ernesto Prado Velázquez, *Diccionario de escritores Mexicanos* (México: UNAM, 1967), pp. 405-6. Renato Prada Oropeza, "Texto y proyección: los relatos de Arqueles Vela," in *Estridentismo: Memoria y valoración*, edited by Gabriela Becerra (México: FCE, 1983), pp. 159-75. Edna Aguirre Rehbein, "Vanguardist Techniques in Mexican Prose Fiction: 1923-1964," Ph.D. Diss., University of Texas, 1988, pp. 130-43. Luis Mario Schneider, *El Estridentismo -- México 1921-1927* (México: UNAM, 1985); *El Estridentismo o una literatura de la estrategia* (México: Ediciones de Bellas Artes, 1970). Ida Vitale, "*El intransferible* de Arqueles Vela," *Vuelta* 12 (1977): 43-45. Jesús Zavala, Review of *Cuentos del día y de la noche*, in *Letras de México* 5, 4 (April 1946).

EDNA A. REHBEIN

VERA, Agustín (1889-1946). Born on October 22, 1889, in Acámbaro, Guanajuato, Agustín Vera lived in San Luis Potosí from 1900 until his death in 1946. Educated at the university there, he became a lawyer in 1914. A state judge, he also taught international law at the law school.

With regard to his literary career, Agustín Vera wrote novels, stories and legends, poetry, and theater. Perhaps most well-known and loved are his *Leyendas potosinas* (Legends of Potosí), which are spiced with local lore and color. Although the fact was largely unknown at first, he also was a novelist of the Revolution and his work, *La revancha* (The Revenge), is a characteristic example of the episodic and regional novel of that time. He narrates events that occurred in the San Luis Potosí area from 1914 to 1917, using a love entanglement as a point of departure. The local environment, historical personalities, and typical customs all serve to enhance the realistic quality of *La revancha*. Although he did not write or publish extensively, his contribution is, nonetheless, significant.

WORKS: *En la profunda sombra* (In the Deep Shadow), novel (San Luis Potosí: Manuel Sancho Editor, 1916). *La revancha* (The Revenge), novel (San Luis Potosí: Talls. Linotip. de la Acción, 1930). *Leyendas potosinas* (Legends of Potosí) (San Luis Potosí: Talls. Linotip. de la Acción, n.d.). *Como en los cuentos* (Like in Stories), theater (San Luis Potosí: Talls. Gráficos de la Escuela Industrial Militar Benito Juárez, n.d.).

BIBLIOGRAPHY: Manual Pedro González, "Una novela desconocida," in *Cuadernos Americanos* (Nov.-Dec. 1950): 290-97. Antonio Magaña Esquivel, "Un novelista desconocido: Agustín Vera," in *El Nacional* March 11, 1965): 3. María del Carmen Millán, "Una novela de la Revolución," in *Letras Potosinas* 13, 118 (Oct.-Dec. 1955): 118; in *Acta Politécnica Mexicana* 13, 13 (July-Aug. 1961): 81-84. Aurora M. Ocampo de Gómez and Ernesto Prado Velázquez, *Diccionario de Escritores Mexicanos* (México: UNAM, 1967), p. 406. Francisco Palán Navarro, "Agustín Vera," in *Estilo* 7 (July-Sept. 1947): 169-73. Rodolfo B. Ruiz, *Del lírico vergel potosino* (San Luis Potosí: Talls. Tip. de la Escuela Militar Benito Juárez, 1919).

JEANNE C. WALLACE

VICENS, Josefina (1915-), novelist, reporter, and bullfight chronicler. Vicens was born in Villahermosa, Tabasco, on November 23, 1915. She completed all of her studies in Mexico City, where she has resided since 1919. She has traveled in various European countries, as well as the United States. Vicens has worked in theHouse of Deputies and the Senate, and has been secretary ofaction for the Confederación Nacional Campesina, head of feminist action for the Confederación Nacional Campesina, head of the women's agrarian section of the Partido Revolucionario Mexicano, contributor to various weeklies in which she wrote on political affairs, senior official of the technical section of the Sindicato de Cinematografistas, and scriptwriter and film editor.

Vicens has published only two novels, *El libro vacío* (The Empty Book) (1958), and *Los años falsos* (The False Years) (1981). Since the writing of her last novel, Vicens has become blind. The central problem of *El libro vacío* is that of José García, who wants to write a novel of merit, but who is convinced that neither his experiences nor his skills as a writer will enable him to create the work he envisions. *El libro vacío* is written with a simplicity of style and a sensitivity that resulted in its receiving the Villarrutia Prize for narrative fiction in 1958. *Los años falsos* is a novel that criticizes a corrupt political system, the ramifications of which penetrate relationships at a personal level.

WORKS: Novels: *El libro vacío* (México: Cía. General de Eds. 1958; México: Gob. del Est. de Tabasco, 1965; México: Sept., 1966); French translation, *Le cahier clandestin*, introduction by Octavio Paz (Paris: Julliard, 1964). Theater: *Un gran año*, in *Cuadernos de Bellas Artes* 3, 2 (Feb. 1965).

BIBLIOGRAPHY: L. Amado Blanco, Review of *El libro vacío*, in *Información* (Havana) (Nov. 23, 1958); *El libro lleno*, in *Información* (Havana) (Nov. 27, 1958). Barbara B. Aponte, "Los años falsos y Espacio de una soledad," in *Explicación de Textos Literarios* 16, 1 (1987-1988): 86-93. Roberto Blanco Moreno, Review of *El libro vacío*, in *Claridades* (Nov. 23, 1958). María Elvira Bermúdez, Review of *El libro vacío*, in *Diorama de la Cultura* (Mar. 8, 1959). J.C., Review of *El libro vacío*, in *Jueves de Excelsior* (Nov. 5, 1958). Emmanuel Carballo, "1958, El año de la novela," in *México en la Cultura* 511 (Dec. 28, 1958): 1, 11; "Jorge López Páez y Josefina Vicens," in *México en la Cultura* 514 (Jan. 18, 1959): 2. Rosario Castellanos, *La novela mexicana contemporanea y su valor testimonial,* in *Hispania* 47, 2 (May 1964): 223-24, 229. Florencia Castillo, Guadalupe Chiunti, Sara Luz Páez, Angélica Prieto, Azucena de Alba Vásquez, "Sentido e interpretación en *El libro vacío*," in *Semiosis* 18 (Jan.-June 1987): 149-97. Rosalía de Chumacero, "Perfil y pensamiento de Josefina Vicens," in *Zocalo* (Nov. 6, 1959). Sergio Fernández, Review on tbe jacket of *El libro vacío* (México: Cía. General de Eds. 1958). Rlaide Foppa, "La verdad sobre Josefina Vicens," in *El Imparcial* (April 17, 1959). Socorro Garcìa, "Josefina Vicens," in *México en la Cultura* 496 (Sept. 14, 1958): 1, 11. Jaime García Torres, "La feria de los dioses," review of *El libro vacío*, in *Universidad de México* 13, 2 (Oct. 1958): 3. Porfirio Martínez Peñaloza, Review of *El libro vacío*, in *Afirmaciones* (Sept.-Oct. 1958). Aurora M. Ocampo de Gómez and Ernesto Prado Velázquez, *Diccionario de escritores mexicanos* (México: UNAM, 1967), pp. 406-7. Octavio Paz, "Josefina Vicens," in *México en la cultura* 496 (Sept. 14, 1958): 1. Margarita Peña, Review of *Le cahier clandestin*, in *El Rehilete* 10 (Feb. 1964): 51-52. Margarita Ponce, Review of *El libro vacío*, in *Jueves de Excelsior* (Sept. 17, 1959). Elena Poniatowska, Review of *El libro vacío*, in *Novedades* (Nov. 16, 1958). Salvador Reyes Nevares, Review of *El libro vacío*, in *México en la cultura* 498 (Sept. 7, 1958): 4. Marcela del Río, Review of *El libro vacío*, in *Excelsior* (Nov. 16, 1958); *La mujer en la cultura*, talk with Josefina Vicens, in *Boletín bibliográfico de la Secretaría de Hacienda y Crédito Público* 203 (Dec. 3, 1960): 2. Emma Susana Speratti, Review of *El libro vacío*, in *Revista Mexicana de Literatura* (Jan.- March 1959).

JOAN SALTZ

VIGIL, José María (1829-1909). Born in Guadalajara, Jalisco, on October 11, 1829, José María Vigil chose a career in literature and journalism, becoming a writer, teacher, and librarian. Essays, plays, and poetry comprise most of his original work. He saw his first works published in *El Ensayo Literario*, the journal of La Falange de Estudio, a literary society of which he was a member. With regard to his poetry, he was considered only mediocre; his poetic attempts seen lacking in lyrical qualities. He was, however, much more applauded for his dramatic work, some of which was performed in the theater in Guadalajara. The plays *Dolores*, *La hija del carpintero* (The Carpenter's Daughter), and *Un demócrata al uso* (A Contemporary Democrat) are examples of his dramatic work.

Vigil taught Latin and philosophy at the state boys' schools from 1855 to 1858 and also became involved at the administrative level with *El País*, an official newspaper. He created a public library using books that had been ecclesiastically censored and suppressed. A firm believer in democratic ideals, Vigil took refuge in the United States during the French rule in Mexico. He worked arduously to support the cause of Mexican independence and self-rule. Following the demise of the Maximilian puppet government, he returned to Mexico in triumph, serving as a deputy for five terms. He resumed his teaching career for a while and served his country also as a judge. He became director of the Biblioteca Nacional in 1879, a post he held until his death on February 18, 1909, having reorganized the library system, thus making it more efficient and up-to-date. José María Vigil made a valuable contribution to his country through his teaching, his library work, and his patriotic service.

WORKS: Theater and Poetry: *Dolores, o una pasión* (Dolores, or a Passion), drama (Guadalajara: Imp. de J. Camarena, 1851). *La hija del carpintero* (The Carpenter's Daughter), drama (México: Imp. de Juan B. Navarro, 1854). *Realidades y quimeras* (Realities and Fancies), poetry (Guadalajara: Eds. de El País, 1857). *Flores de Anáhuac* (Flowers of Anáhuac), vol. 2, drama [contains *Dolores, o una pasión*, *La hija del carpintero*, *Víctimas y verdugos*, and *El demonio del corazón*] (Guadalajara: Tip. de J. M. Brambila, 1867). *Un demócrata al uso* (A Contemporary Democrat), drama (México: Imp. de I. Cumplido, 1872). Studies and Biography: "Algunas observaciones sobre la literatura nacional" (Some Observations about National Literature), in *El Eco de Ambos Mundos* (Mexico, May 12, 1872): 1-2. "Sor Juana Inés de la Cruz," in *Composiciones leídas en la velada literaria que consagró el Liceo Hidalgo a la memoria de Sor Juana Inés de la Cruz* (México: Imp. de El Porvenir, 1874); in *El Federalista*, vol. 6 (Mexico, 1874). "Juan Valle," speech, in *El Porvenir* (June 16, 1875). "Algunas consideraciones sobre la literatura mexicana" (Some Considerations on Mexican Literature), in *El Federalista* (Mexico, Sept.-Oct. 1876; in *Revista Mensual Mexicana*

(Mexico, 1877); and in *Las Letras Patrias* 5 (1957): 17-51. "La señora doña Isabel Prieto de Landázuri, estudio biográfico y literario" (Isabel Prieto de Landázuri, Biographical and Literary Study), in *Memorias de la Academia Mexicana* 2, 2 (1882): 140-245; also as prologue to *Obras poéticas* (Poetic Works) of Isabel Prieto de Landázuri (México: Imp. de Ireneo Paz, 1883). "*El Romancero Nacional* de Guillermo Prieto," in *La República Literaria*, Guadalajara, 1887. "Cantares mexicanos" (Mexican Songs), in *Revista Nacional de Letras y Ciencias*, Mexico, 1889. Prologue to *Poetisas mexicanas* (Mexican Poetesses) (México: Ofna. Tip. de la Srtía. de Fomento, 1893). "Reseña histórica de la poesía mexicana" (Historic Review of Mexican Poetry), introduction for *Antología de poetas mexicanos* (México: Academia Mexicana de la Lengua, Ofna. Tip. de la Sría. de Fomento, 1894). "Carta a Amado Nervo" (Letter to Amado Nervo), in Amado Nervo, *El Bachiller* (México: Tip. de *El Nacional*, 1896). *Lope de Vega* (México: Tip. y Lit. La Europea de J. Aguilar Vera y Cía., 1904); and in *Memorias de la Academia* 5 (1905): 1-210. *Reseña histórica de la literatura mexicana* (Historic Review of Mexican Literatura), incomplete (México: n.p., 1909). *Nezahualcóyotl, el rey-poeta* (Nezahualcóyotl, the Poet-King) (México: Eds. de Andrea, 1957); previously published in *Hombres ilustres mexicanos*, vol. 2 (México: Eduardo L. Gallo), pp. 67-205. Prologues: Pablo J. Villaseñor, *Leyendas históricas y tradicionales* (Traditional and Historical Legends) (Guadalajara: Tip. de Dionisio Rodríguez, 1853). Joaquín Téllez, *Ratos perdidos* (Lost Time) (México: Imp. de El Porvenir, 1871). Esther Tapia de Castellanos, *Flores silvestres* (Wild Flowers) (México: Imp. de I. Cumplido, 1871). Clemente Villaseñor, *Ensayos poéticos* (Poetic Essays) (México: Imp. de J. A. Bonilla, 1874). Agapito Silva, *Poesías* (Poems) (México: Imp. del Hospicio de San Nicolás, 1875); and in *Sueños y realidades* (Dreams and Realities) (México: Imp. de I. Cumplido, 1885). Juan Pablo de los Ríos, *Gencianas y madreselvas* (Gentian and Honeysuckle) (México: Tip. de Ireneo Paz, 1882). Anthologies and Editions: Fray Bartolomé de las Casas, *Historia de las Indias*, edited by José María Vigil (México: Imp. de Ireneo Paz, 1877). *Poetisas mexicanas, siglos XV, XVII, XVIII y XIX* (Mexican Poetesses, Fifteenth, Seventeenth, Eighteenth and Nineteenth Centuries) (México: Ofna. Tip. de la Sría. de Fomento, 1893). Book Reviews: Diego Bas, "La belleza y el arte" (Beauty and Art), in *Boletín de la Biblioteca Nacional* (Jan. 31, 1905). Joaquín Casasús, *Las elegías de Tíbulo, de Ligdamo y de Sulpicia, traducidas en verso castellano* (The Elegies of Tíbulo, Ligdamo and Sulpicia, Translated to Spanish Poetry), in *Boletín de la Biblioteca Nacional* (May 31, 1905). "Bibliográfica," in *Boletín de la Biblioteca Nacional* (Nov. 30, 1905). Translations: *Sátiras de Persio, traducidas del latín en verso castellano* (Satires of Perseus, Translated from Latin to Spanish Poetry), bilingual ed. (México: Tip. de Gonzalo A. Esteva, 1879). Schiller, *La repartición de la tierra* (The Distribution of Land), in *La Familia* (Mexico, March 24, 1884). Washington Irving, *Un poeta rey* (A Poet King), in *La Familia* (Nov. 1, 8, 1884). F. Ponsard, *Carlota Corday, tragedia en 5 actos y un prólogos* (Carlota Corday, Tragedy in Five Acts and a Prologue) (México: Ofna. Tip. de la Sría. de Fomento, 1895). *XXX epigramas de Marcial, traducidos del latín en verso castellano* (Thirty Epigrams by Martial, Translated from Latin to Spanish Poetry) (México: Ofna. Tip. de la Sría. de Fomento, 1899). Honoré de Balzac, *La misa del ateo* (The Atheist's Mass), in *El País*, Guadalajara. "Estudios filosóficos" (Philosophical Studies), in *El Eco de Ambos Mundos* (May-Nov. 1871). *Ensayo histórico del Ejército de Occidente* (Historical Essay on the Western Army), in collaboration with Juan B. Híjar y Haro (México: Imp. de I. Cumplido, 1874). *Revista filosófica* (Journal of Philosophy) (México: Imp. de Ireneo Paz, 1882).

"Polémica con el Sr. D. Carlos Selva sobre apreciaciones históricas" (Polemic with Carlos Selva on Historical Assessments), in *La Patria* (Mexico, Sept.-Oct. 1883). "Fray Martín Durán," in *La República Literaria*, Guadalajara, 1888. "Historia de la Reforma, de la Intervención y del Imperio" (History of the Reform, the Intervention and the Empire), in *México a través de los siglos*, vol. 5 (Barcelona: Espasa y Cía., Editores, 1889). "Discurso en conmemoración de Manuel Orozco y Berra" (Speech in Commemoration of Manuel Orozco y Berra), in *Revista Nacional de Letras y Ciencias*, Mexico, 1890. "Polémica sobre filosofía con el Dr. don Porfirio Parra" (Polemic on Philosophy with Dr. Porfirio Parra), in *El Universal* (Mexico, Feb. 20, 21, and March 6, 1891). "Discurso del Sr. D. José Ma. Vigil en la muerte de Joaquín García Icazbalceta" (Speech by José María Vigil upon the Death of Joaquín García Icazbalceta), in *Memorias de la Academia Mexicana* 4, 1 (1895): 22-43.

BIBLIOGRAPHY: Alberto María Carreño, *Memorias de la Academia Mexicana Correspondiente de la Española*, vol. 7 (México: Edit. Jus, 1945), pp. 151-52; vol. 8 (México: Edit. Jus, 1946), pp. 338-47. Antonio Caso, *México, Apuntamientos de cultura patria* (México: Imp. Universitaria, 1943), p. 89. Jesús García Gutiérrez, *La poesía religiosa en México*, vol. 11, no. 1 (México: Ed. Cultura, 1919), p. 175. Luis González Obregón, *La Biblioteca Nacional de México. Reseña histórica (1833-1910)*, Ch. 8 (Mexico, 1910), pp. 57-65. Luis Leal, Review of *Nezahualcóyotl*, in *Revista Iberoamericana* 23, 46 (July-Dec. 1958): 465-67. Ricardo López Méndez, "Lope de Vega y José María Vigil," in *Excelsior* (Sept. 24, 1962): 6, 9. José López Portillo y Rojas, "Oración fúnebre pronunciada en el Panteón de Dolores, en los funerales del señor José Ma. Vigil el 20 de febrero de 1909," in *Boletín de la Biblioteca Nacional* (Feb. 1909): 10-12. Antonio Magaña Esquivel and Ruth S. Lamb, *Breve historia del teatro mexicano* (México: Eds. de Andrea, 1958), pp. 68-69. Daniel Muñoz y Pérez, "Retratos de la sala iconográfica," in *El Universal* (Nov. 6, 1959). Aurora M. Ocampo de Gómez and Ernesto Prado Velázquez, *Diccionario de Escritores Mexicanos* (México: UNAM, 1967), pp. 407-8. José Pascual Buxó, *Góngora en la poesía novohispana* (México: UNAM, 1960), pp. 10-11. Carlos J. Sierra, *José María Vigil* (México: Club de Periodistas de México, Bibl. del Periodista, 1963); "Apuntes hemerográficos de José María Vigil," lst part, in *Boletín de la Biblioteca Nacional* 289 (Feb. 15, 1964): 12-19; 2nd part, 290 (March 1, 1964): 12-16, 3rd part, 291 (March 15, 1964): 12-17. Francisco Sosa, *Los contemporáneos* (México: Imp. de Gonzalo A. Esteva), pp. 209-233.

JEANNE C. WALLACE

VILALTA, Maruxa (1932-   ). Born in Barcelona, Spain, on September 23, 1932 (Hopzafel places her year of birth at 1931), Maruxa Vilalta emigrated to Mexico along with other exiled Republicans and became a Mexican citizen. It was in Mexico that she received her training in newspaper work and in literary writing. She took classes at the Franco-Mexican lycée, at the School of Philosophy and Letters of the UNAM, and at Cambridge University. She has been a reporter for the daily *Excelsior*, and has directed television programs such as "Mujeres que trabajan" (Women Who Work), and also has done commentary on politics, theater, and entertainment. She has traveled to Europe, the United States, and Canada.

Maruxa Vilalta began by writing novels and short stories, and the latter have been published in various dailies and journals, but it is in the theater that she has known her greatest successes. Her first work was the adaptation of one of her novels: *Los desorientados*, an accusation directed against present-day youth, whose lives and interests wind up being destroyed and impaired by the imcomprehension of their parents, and by their own egotism and overblown ambitions. Her second work, *Un país feliz*, develops the problem of propaganda versus reality in countries run by dictators. *El 9* is a play about the mechanization of humanity. *Cuestión de narices* and *La última letra* both treat, in absurdist terms, the problem of people whose words express love for one another, while their speech and other actions are hostile and violent. *Un día loco* is a monologue by an older woman who is concerned with recapturing the experience and message of a phone call she has received. In *Esta noche juntos, amándonos tanto*, a couple in an enclosed room receives--and accepts-- "newspeak" reports of state terrorism, while "tuning out" attempts at contact and straighter information from a neighbor. *Historia de él* is about the rise of a dictator; *Una mujer, dos hombres y un balazo* is a parodic version of four different types of spectacle: a melodrama, a musical comedy, an absurdist play, and a surrealistic one; *Pequeña historia de horror* is a lyrically distorted version of popular, soap opera style entertainment.

In general, Maruxa Vilalta's theater is characterized by her concerns for society and by a great mastery of theatrical form. Sganarelli describes her work as "sometimes essentially naturalistic, at others mostly absurd." Her theatre is also frequently marked by violence, if not physical, at least psychological. It is consistently sociopolitical, protesting the contemporary condition of mankind, but there is an underlying recognition that the sociopolitical problems are products of the individuals who also create them. Her works are often circular, ending where they began with no apparent progress or resolution for the problems presented, and thus they reinforce the notion that we cannot improve society without changing the individual, and conversely we cannot alter the individual without revamping society, in a never-ending vicious circle of inertia.

WORKS: Novels: *El castigo* (The Punishment) (México: Edit. La Prensa, 1957). *Los desorientados* (The Confused) (México: Eds. Selecta, 1958); 2nd ed. (1958); 3rd ed. (Libro-Mex, 1960). *Dos colores para el paisaje* (Two Colors to the Landscape) (México: Libro-Mex, 1961). Short Stories: *El otro día, la muerte* (The Other Day, Death) (México: Ed. Joaquín Mortiz, 1974). Theater: *Los desorientados* (The Confused), premiered en Mexico in 1960; 2nd stage performance, 1965 (México: Col. Teatro Mexicano, 1958); 2nd ed. (Libro-Mex, 1960); 3rd ed. (Eds. Ecuador, 1965); (México: FCE, 1972). *Un país feliz*, (A Happy Country), premiered in 1963 (México: Eds. Ecuador, 1964). *La última letra* (The Last Letter) (México: Costa Amic, 1960; México: FCE, 1972). *Soliloquio del tiempo* (Soliloquy of Time) (México: Eds. Ecuador, 1964; México: FCE, 1972). *Trío* ("Soliloquio del tiempo," "Un día loco" [a Crazy Day] and "La última letra"), one-act plays, premiered in 1964 (México: Col. Teatro Mexicano, no. 23, 1965). *El 9* (The 9), premiered in 1965 (México: Eds. Ecuador, 1965; Mexico: FCE, 1972). *Cuestión de narices* (A Matter of Noses), premiered in 1966 (México: FCE, 1972). *Esta noche amándonos todos* (Tonight, All of Us Loving Each Other) (México: FCE, 1972). *Teatro* (Theater) (México: Ed. Joaquín Mortiz, 1981). *Nada como el piso* (Nothing like a Flat) (México: Ed. Joaquín Mortiz, 1984). Anthologies and Prologues: *Antologías de obras en un acto*, selection

714   VILALTA, Maruxa

and prologue, 3 vols. (México: Col. Teatro Mexicano, 1959, 1960, and 1965).
Translation: Albert Husson, *El sistema Fabrizzi*, translated from the French by
Maruxa Vilalta, premiered in Mexico under the direction of Maruxa Vilalta, in 1966.

BIBLIOGRAPHY: Anon., Review of *Dos colores para el paisaje*, in *Cuadernos de
Bellas Artes* 2, 8 (Aug. 1961): 46-47; "Maruxa Vilalta ha publicado un nuevo volumen
de teatro," review of *Trío*, in *Revista de la Semana* (Mar. 28, 1965): 3; "Tercera
edición de una obra dramática de Maruxa Vilalta," in *Revista de la Semana* (Oct 3,
1965): 3; "Otra pieza teatral de la escritora Maruxa Vilalta," in *Revista de la Semana*
(Dec. 5, 1965): 3. Francois Baguer, "Escena," review of *Un país feliz*, in *Excelsior* (Jan.
17, 1964). Grace Bearse and Lorraine Elena Roses, "Maruxa Vilalta: Social
Dramatist," in *Revista de Estudios Hispánicos* 18, 3 (Oct. 1984): 399-406. Joan Rea
Boorman, "Contemporary Latin American Woman Dramatists.," in *Rice University
Studies* 64 (1978): 69-80. Jeanine S. Gaucher-Shultz, "La temática de dos obras
premiadas de Maruxa Vilalta," in *Latin American Theatre Review* 12, 2 (1979): 87-90.
Sigfredo Gordon, "La escena," review of *Un país feliz*, in *Ultimas Noticias* (Jan. 18,
1964). Tamara Holzapfel, "The Theatre of Maruxa Vilalta: A Triumph of Versatility,"
in *Latin American Theatre Review* 14, 2 (Spring 1981): 11-18. Antonio Magaña
Esquivel, Review of *Un país feliz*, in *El Nacional* (Aug. 15, 1964): 3; "Maruxa Vilalta
busca su segundo triunfo," in *Revista Mexicana de Cultura* 908 (Aug. 23, 1964): 11;
Medio siglo de teatro mexicano, 1900-1961 (México: INBA, 1964), pp. 124, 163;
"Reposición de *Los desorientados*," in *El Nacional* (Mar. 12, 1965): 5; (Mar. 13, 1965):
5; "Buen momento del teatro mexicano," in *Revista Mexicana de Cultura* 939 (Mar.
28, 1965): 11; Review of *Trío*, in *Revista Mexicana de Cultura* 962 (Sept. 5, 1965): 11;
Review of *El 9*, in *El Nacional* (Oct. 15, 1965): 5; in *Revista Mexicana de Cultura* 970
(Oct. 31, 1965): 11. Sharon Magnarelli, *The Lost Rib* (Lewiston, Penn.: Bucknell
University Press, 1985); "Esta noche juntos, amándonos tanto, de Maruxa Vilalta," in
Plural (Revista Cultural de *Excelsior*) 1, 205 (Oct. 18, 1988): 30-32; "Discourse as
Content and Form in the Works of Maruxa Vilalta," in *Hispanic Journal* 9, 2 (Spring
1988): 99-111; "Contenido y forma en la obra de Maruxa Vilalta," in *Plural* 12, 192
(Sept. 16, 1987): 77-78. María Luisa Mendoza, "Dos damas de vanguardia," in *El
Gallo Ilustrado* 173 (Oct. 17, 1965): 4; Review of *Cuestión de narices*, in *El Gallo
Ilustrado* 222 (Sept. 25, 1966): 4. Beth Miller and Alfonso González, eds., "Maruxa
Vilalta," in *26 autoras del México actual* (México: Costa Amic, 1978), pp. 405-17. Juan
Miguel de Mora, Review of Vilalta's directing of *Album de familia* by Ustinov, in *El
Heraldo Cultural* 25 (Apr. 30, 1966): 11; "Un Fausto gimnasta y unas narices
ministeriales," in *El Heraldo Cultural* 46 (Sept. 25, 1966): 11. Gloria V. Morales,
"Maruxa Vilalta: Un teatro que rompe con lo tradicional," in *Plural* 12, 192 (Sept.
1987): 72-75. Kirsten F. Nigro et al., eds., "*Esta noche juntos, amándonos tanto,* de
Maruxa Vilalta: texto y representación," in *Actas del Sexto Congreso Internacional de
Hispanistas celebrado en Toronto del 22 al 26 agosto de 1977*, edited by Alan M.
Gordon (Toronto: Department of Spanish, 1979). Elda Peralta, "Entrevista con
Maruxa Villalta," in *Plural* 8, 91 (1979): 40-46. Elena Poniatowska, "Habla la autora
teatral Maruxa Vilalta," in *El Gallo Ilustrado* 225 (Oct. 16, 1966): 2-3. L. H.
Quackenbush, "Cuestión de vida y muerte: Tres dramas existenciales," in *Latin
American Theatre Review* 8, 1 (1974): 49-56. Mara Reyes, "Diorama teatral," review
of *Trío*, in *Diorama de la Cultura* (Aug. 16, 1964): 4; Review of *Cuestión de narices*,
in *Diorama de la Cultura* (Sept. 18, 1966): 5. Marcela del Río, "Maruxa Vilalta,
directora teatral," in *Diorama de la Cultura* (June 13, 1965): 7, 8. Antoniorrobles,

"Contenido social en la nueva pieza de Maruxa Vilalta," in *¡Siempre!* 693 (Oct. 5, 1966): 39. Lorraine Roses, "La espresión dramática de la inconformidad social en cuatro dramaturgas hispanoamericanas," in *Plaza* 5-6 (Fall-Spring 1981-1982): 97-114. Fernando Sánchez Mayans, "Notas bibliográficas," review of *Trío*, in El Libro y el Pueblo 3 (Apr. 1965): 19-20. Mauricio de la Selva, "Asteriscos," review of *Un país feliz*, in *Diorama de la Cultura* (Aug. 9, 1964): 7. Carlos Solórzano, "Marcela del Río y Maruxa Vilalta, dos jóvenes que prometen," in *La Cultura en México* 195 (Nov. 10, 1965): xix; "El teatro de Maruxa Vilalta," in *Latin American Theatre Review* 18, 2 (Spring 1985): 83-87. Carlos Solórzano, Salvador Reyes Nevares and José Antonio Alcáraz, "Análisis de Teatro de Maruxa Vilalta," in *Vida Literaria* 25 (1972). Carmen G. de Tapia, "El teatro en acción," review of *Un país feliz*, in *El Universal Gráfico* (Jan. 22, 1964). Victor M. Valenzuela, *Siete comediografas hispanoamericanas* (Bethlehem, Penn.: Lehigh University Press, 1975). Daniel Zalacaín, *Teatro absurdista hispanoamericano* (Chapel Hill, N.C.: Albatros Hispanófila, 1985).

PETER G. BROAD

VILLASEÑOR, Eduardo (1896- ?), prose writer, playwright, and diplomat. Villaseñor was born in Anganacutiro, Michoacán, on November 19, 1896. After finishing his studies in law and in philosophy and letters at the National University, he held several diplomatic and banking positions, including subsecretary of Hacienda (1938) and director of the Bank of Mexico (1940).

He contributed to newspapers and magazines both Mexican and foreign; and many of his works, which reflect his knowledge of economics and of the social situation of Mexico, appear in numerous anthologies. His style is both simplistic and unconstrained, and he offers a variety of themes.

WORKS: *Ensayos interamericanos* (Interamerican Essay) (México: Cuadernos americanos, 1844). *The English. Are They Human?* (México: Institute Angloamerican, 1953. *Los recuerdos y los días* (The Memories and the Days) (México: FCE, 1960).

BIBLIOGRAPHY: Anon., Bibliographical note in *Anuario de la poesía mexicana* (México: Inst. de Bellas Artes, 1962), p. 127. Ruth S. Lamb, *Bibliografía del teatro mexicano del siglo XX*, Manuales Studium, no. 33 (México: Eds. de Andrea, 1962), pp. 126-27.

SILKA FREIRE

VILLAURRUTIA, Xavier (1903-1950), playwright and essay writer. Villaurrutia was born in Mexico City on March 27, 1903. He studied at the French High School of Mexico and later attended the Preparatoria. There he met Salvador *Novo, *Torres Bodet, Jorge *Cuesta, and other classmates who later would be recognized men of letters. He tried to study law, but abandoned it for writing. In 1927, he founded the journal *Ulises* with Novo, and when it ceased publication, the two friends founded *Contemporáneos*. These two magazines had a great impact on Mexican letters in that they attracted a group of very good young writers that formed the Ulises and the

Orientación associations which aspired to revitalize the Mexican theater. Although Villaurrutia can be considered a poet, his work on the theater and as an essay writer is very important. In 1935 and 1936, thanks to a Rockefeller Scholarship, he attended Yale University, where he studied theater, acting, and dramatic theory. Upon his return to Mexico, he taught literature at the UNAM and directed the theater section of the INBA. He contributed to many magazines and literary journals, among them *Letras de México*, *El hijo pródigo*, *Antena*, and *Revista de Bellas Artes*.

Villaurrutia's work in the Teatro Ulises and Grupo Orientación, along with the efforts of Celestino *Gorostiza and Julio Bracho, contributed to complete change of the theater. New plays by foreign authors were staged, new points of view expressed, and the domination of the commercial theater came to an end with the foundation of a number of small experimental theaters.

As part of the Contemporáneos group, his poetry was instrumental in renewing the genre. His first book, *Reflejos* (Reflexions), showed his affinity with *López Velarde, but soon he changed, influenced by Juan Ramón Jiménez and others. *Nostalgia de la muerte* (Nostalgia of Death), considered to be his best book, represented the peak of his poetry. The concept of death evolves from the common idea of the end of life to a more sophisticated idea considering it as something symbolic. Following Rilke's concept of death as an integral part of one's life, Villaurrutia enlarges his poetic subjects to include the existence of God, love, darkness, and the idea of life after death, as can be seen in his *Décima muerte* (Tenth Death).

Villaurrutia's first published essay was "La poesía de los jóvenes en México" (Poetry of the Young Generation in Mexico) (1921). It is an excellent exposition and study of the new poetry, of which he was a significant part. This essay was followed by *Textos y pretextos*, a collection of different studies of literary criticism of foreign as well as national writers.

Villaurrutia died at age forty-seven, on December 25, 1950.

WORKS: *Reflejos* (Reflexions) (México: Cultura, 1926). *Nocturnos* (Nocturnes) (México: Fábula, 1933). *Nocturno de los ángeles* (Nocturne of the Angels) (México: Ed. Hipocampo, 1936). *Nocturno mar* (Sea Nocturne) (México: Ed. Hipocampo, 1937). *Nocturno rosa* (Pink Nocturne) (México: Ed. Angel Chápero, 1937). *Nostalgia de la Muerte* (Nostalgia of Death) (Buenos Aires: Ed. Sur, 1938; México: Ed. Mictlán, 1946). *Décima muerte y otros poemas no coleccionados* (Tenth Death and Other Uncollected Poems) (México: Nueva Voz, 1941). *Canto a la primavera y otros poemas* (Spring Song and Other Poems) (México: Nueva Floresta, 1948). Novel: *Dama de corazones* (Queen of Hearts) (México: Ed. de Ulises, 1928). Theater: *Parece mentira* (It Seems Untrue) (México: Imp. Mundial, 1934). *¿En qué piensas?* (What Are You Thinking About?) (México: Ed. Letras de México, 1938). *Sea usted breve* (Be Brief) (México: Cuadernos de México Nuevo, 1938). *El ausente* (The Absent One) in *Tierra nueva* 3, 13-14)Jan.-Apr. 1942): 35-50. *La mulata de Córdoba* (The Mulatto Woman from Cordoba), in *El Hijo Pródigo* 24 (Mar. 1945): 166-83. *Invitación a la muerte* (Invitation to Death), in *El Hijo Pródigo* 6 (Sept. 1943): 355-362; 7 (Oct. 1943): 41-50; 8 (Nov. 1943): 10-111; (México: Ed. Letras de México, 1947). *La hiedra* (The Ivy), in *Collection Nueva Cultura* 2, 1 (1941). *La mujer legítima* (The Wife) (México: Ed. Rafael Loera y Chávez, 1943). *Autos profanos* (Secular Plays) (México: Ed. Letras de México, 1943). *El hierro candente* (The Red Iron) in *El Hijo Pródigo* 19 (Oct. 1944): 44-57; 20 (Nov. 1944): 110-120; (México: Ed. Letras de México, 1945). *Juego peligroso* (Dangerous Game) (México: n.p., 1949). *Poesía y teatro completo* (México: FCE,

1953). Essays: *Textos y pretextos* (Texts and Pretexts) (México: La casa de España, 1940). *Cartas de Xavier Villaurrutia a Novo* (Correspondence: Xavier Villaurrutia's Letters to Novo), translation by André Gide (México: INBA, 1966). *La escuela de las mujeres* (México: Ed. La Razón, 1931).

BIBLIOGRAPHY: Ermilo Abreu Gómez, *Sala de retratos (México: Edit. Leyenda, 1946),* p. 292-93. Antonio Acevedo Excobedo, "Acerca de Villaurrutia," in *EL Nacional* (May 8, 1966): 3. Enrique Anderson Imbert, *Historia* de la literatura hispanoamericana (México: FCE, 1954), vol. 2, pp. 19, 158, 159, 161-63. Enrique Anderson Imbert and Eugenio Florit, *Literatura hispanoamericana* (New York: Holt, Rinehart and Winston), pp. 665-66. Max Aub, "Teatro," review of *Autos profanos,* in *Letras de México* 2 (Feb.15, 1943): 7; "Xavier Villaurrutia," in *México en la Cultura* 266 (Arpil 25, 1964): 3. Angel de las Bárcenas, "Villaurrutia y la crítica", in *México en la Cultura* 304 (Jan. 16, 1955): 2. Luis G. Basurto, "El teatro y la amistad in Xavier Villaurrutia", in Cuadernos de Bellas Artes 1, 5 (Dec. 1960). Fabienne Bradu, "Presencia y figura de Xavier Villaurrutia en la critica mexicana," in *Vuelta* 12, 137 (Apr. 1988): 55-57. John S. Brushwood and José Rojas Garcidueñas, B*reve historia de la novela mexicana* (México: Eds. de Andrea), p. 132. Armando Cámara, "Cartas de Villaurrutia a Novo," in *Revista de Bellas Artes* 10 (July-Aug. 1966), p. 101. Wilberto Cantón, "Opina Villaurrutia: El INBA no ha hecho por el teatro mexicano lo que debería hacer," in *México en la Cultura* 57 (March 5, 1950): 7.   Miguel Capistrán, "Villaurrutia a Novo, Epistolario," in *Diorama de la Cultura* (Aug. 14, 1966): 3, 6. Alfredo Cardona Peña, *Semblanzas mexicanas* (México: Eds. Libro-Mex), pp. 144-50. A. Casa Beltrán, "*Yerro candente,* una comedia que ofrece nuevas, nobles, bellísimas posibilidades al teatro," in *Así* (April 22, 1944): 37. Eduardo Colín, "Xavier Villaurrutia, poeta," in *Rasgos* (México: Imp. Manuel León Sánchez, S.C.L.), 127-34. J. Crespo de la Serna, "Las ideas y las formas. Villaurrutia, crítico de arte," in *Excelsior* (Dec. 31, 1950). Jorge Cuesta, Review of *Reflejos,* in *Ulises* 1, 1 (May 1927): 28-29; in *Poemas y ensayos* (México: UNAM, 1964), vol. 2, pp. 29-31; *Antología de la poesía mexicana moderna* (México: Eds. Contemporáneos, 1928); "Xavier Villaurrutia," in *Romance* 1, 11 (July 1940); with others, "Homenaje a Xavier Villaurrutia," in *México en la Cultura* 102 (Jan. 14, 1951). Fernando Charry Lara, "Tres poetas mexicanos, II Villaurrutia", in *Un. de M.,* vol. XI, no. 4, December, 1956, pp. 17-18. Alí Chumacero, "La poesía de Xavier Villaurrutia," in *México en la Cultura* 197 (Dec. 28, 1952), p. 3; Prologue to *Poesía y teatro completos,* ed. cit.; prologue to *Obras,* ed. cit., pp. ix-xxx. Alberto Dallal, "Nostalgia de Villaurrutia", in Universidad de México 20, 12 (Aug., 1966): 51. Frank Dauster, "La poesía de Xavier Villaurrutia," in *Revista Iberoamericana* 18, 36 (Jan.-Sept. 1953); "El teatro de Xavier Villaurrutia," in *Estaciones* 1, 4 (winter 1956): 479-87; *Breve historia de la poesía mexicana* (México: Eds. de Andrea, 1956), pp. 157-60; *Ensayos sobre poesía mexicana* (México: Eds. de Andrea, 1963), pp. 5-29. Merlin H. Forster, *Los Contemporáneos* (México: Eds. de Andrea, 1964), pp. 83-91, 125-26, 141-44. Juan García Ponce "La noche y la llama," in *Universidad de México,* 21, 5 (Jan. 1967): 4-11. Enrique González Rojo, Review of *Dama de corazones,* in *Contemporáneos* 1, 3 (Aug. 1928): 319-21. Celestino Gorostiza, "El teatro de Xavier Villaurrutia," in *Cuadernos Americanos* 11, 2 (March-April 1952): 287-90; "Lo Blanco y lo negro. Carta a Xavier Villaurrutia," in *Letras de México* 1 (Jan. 15, l943): 6, 8.   Miguel Guardia, Review of *Juego peligroso,* in *México en la Cultura* 73 (June 25, 1950): 4; Review of *La mujer legítima,* in *México en la Cultura* 144 (Nov. 4, 1951): 4. Andrés Henestrosa, "La nota cultural," Review of Los 25 años

718 VILLAURRUTIA, Xavier

de la antología *Laurel,* in *El Nacional* (Aug. 13, 1966): 3; Review of *Las Cartas de Villaurrutia a Novo,* in *El Nacional* (June 24, 1966): 3. Andrés Iduarte, Review of *Autos profanos,* in *Revista Hispánica Moderna* (July-Oct. 1946): 281. Ruth S. Lamb, Bibliografía del teatro mexicano del siglo xx *(México: Eds. de Andrea, 1962),* pp. 127-28. Agustín Lazo, "Presencia de Villaurrutia," in *Excelsior* (Dec. 31, 1950); in *Revista de Guatemala* 1 (1951). Luis Leal, "Xavier Villaurrutia, crítico," in *Estaciones* 4, 13 (1959). Raúl Leiva, "Xavier Villaurrutia," in *Los sentidos y el mundo* (Guatemala: n.p., 1952); *Imagen de la poesía mexicana contemporánea* (México: UNAM, 1959), pp. 151-63, 363. Eduardo Lizalde, Review of *Poesía y teatro completos,* in Universidad de México 8, 7 (March 1954): 31. Alberto R. López, "La Poesía de Xavier Villaurrutia," sobretiro de la *Memoria del Segundo Congreso International de Catedráticos de la Literatura Iberoamericana* (Los Angeles, Calif., 1940). Antonio Magaña Equivel, *Imagen del teatro* (Letras de México, 1940); *Teatro mexicano del siglo xx* (México: FCE, 1956), vol. 2, pp. 244-46; "Xavier Villaurrutia, dramaturgo," in *El Nacional* (Sept. 10, 1964): 5; "Teatro. Las piezas mayores de Xavier Villaurrutia," in *El Nacional* (Sept. 12, 1964): 5; "Homenje a Xavier Villaurrutia como dramaturgo," review of *Juego peligroso,* in *Revista Mexicana de Cultura* 912 (Sept. 20, 1964): 11; Medio siglo de teatro mexicano, 1900-1961 (México: INBA, 1964), pp. 56-61, 73-74. Antonio Magaña Esquivel and Ruth S. Lamb, *Breve historia del teatro mexicano* (México: Eds. de Andrea, 1958), pp. 129-31. Jorge A. Marban, "El ritmo dramático: Clave interpretativa en *Invitación a la muerte.*" in *Explicación de Textos Literarios* 14, 2 (1985-1986): 3-9. Manuel Martín-Rodríguez, "El fondo angustiado de los 'Nocturnos' de Xavier Villaurrutia," in *Revista Iberoamericana* 55, 148-49 (July- Dec. 1989): 1119-28. José Luis Martínez, "Con Xavier Villaurrutia," in *Tierra Nueva* 1, 2 (April-May 1940); "Carta a Xavier Villaurrutia a propósito de su teatro," in *El Universal* (Nov. 28, 1942): 4, 13; Literatura mexicana siglo xx, *1910-1949,* vol. 1 (México: Ant. Libr. Robredo, 1949), pp. 140-42; vol. 2 (1950), pp. 127-28; El ensayo mexicano moderno, vol. 2 (México: FCE, 1958), 31-63. Ma. Luisa Mendoza, "El Teatro," review of *Juego peligroso,* in *El Gallo Ilustrado* 117 (Sept. 20, 1964): 4. Carlos Monsiváis, *La poesía mexicana del siglo xx* (México: Empresas Editoriales, 1966), pp. 31-34, 44-46, 465. José Moreno Villa, "Amistades literarias mexicanas. Xavier Villaurrutia," in *México en la Cultura* 101 (Jan. 7, 1951): 7. Elías Nandino, "Xavier Villaurrutia," in *Letras de México* 32 (Aug. 1, 1938); "La poesía de Xavier Villaurrutia," in *Estaciones* 1, 4 (1956): 460-68. Salvador Novo, "Xavier Villaurrutia, epigramático," in *México en la Cultura* 873 (Dec. 12, 1965): 2. Gilberto Owen, "Xavier Villaurrutia: *Invitación a la muerte,*" in *El Hijo Pródigo* 4, 13 (April 1944): 59-60. Octavio Paz, "Cultura de la muerte," in *Letras de México* 33 (Nov. 1, 1938); "Laurel y poesía moderna," in *Quimera* 27, 27 (Dec. 1982): 10-19; (Jan. 1983): 12-22. Mara Reyes, "Diorama teatral," review of *Juego peligroso,* in *Diorama de la Cultura* (Sept. 13, 1964): 7. Salvador Reyes Nevares, *El amor en tres poetas* [Machado, Neruda, Villaurrutia] (México: Los Epígrafes, 1951). Oscar Rivera-Rodas, "Para una semiótica proxémica en Villaurrútia," in *Revista Iberoamericana* 55, 148-49 (July-Dec. 1989): 1239-59. César Rodríguez Chicharro, "Disemia y paronomasia en la poesía de Xavier Villaurrutia," in *La Palabra y el Hombre* 30 (June-Aug. 1964); "Correlación y paralelismo en la poesía de Xavier Villaurrutia," in *La Palabra y el Hombre* 37 (Jan.-Mar. 1966): 81-90. José Rojas Garciadueñas, "Xavier Villaurrutia, crítico," in *Nivel* 25 (Jan. 25, 1961): 1, 4. Rubén Salazar Mallén, Review of "Los Autos profanos," in *El Universal* (April 29, 1945); "Xavier Villaurrutia," in *Excelsior* (Dec. 27, 1950). Luis Mario Schneider, "Bibliografía de Xavier Villaurrutia," in *Obras* ..., pp. xxxi-lxxi.

Guillermo Schmidhuber, "Díptico sobre el teatro mexicano de los treinta: Bustillo y Magdalena, Usigli y Villaurrutia," in *Revista Iberoamericana* 55, 148-49 (July-Dec. 1989): 1221-37. Tomás Segovia, "El mundo de Xavier Villaurrutia," in *Universidad de México* 8, 10 (June 1954): 1-2, 21-22.; Villaurrutia desde aquí," in *Nivel* 36 (Dec. 25, 1961): 1, 2, 6. Donal L. Shaw, "Pasión y verdad en el teatro de Villaurrutia," in Revista Iberoamericana 28, 54 (July-Dec. 1962): 337-46. Octavio de la Suaree, Jr., "Algunas consideraciones sobre el teatro poético de Xavier Villaurrutia," in Festschrift José Cid Perez, edited by Alberto Gutiérrez de la Solana and Elio Alba-Buffill (New York: Senda Nueva de Eds., 1981), pp. 159-66. Jaime Torres Bodet, *Contemporáneos: notas de crítica* (México: n.p., 1928). Arturo Torres-Rioseco, "Xavier Villaurrutia," in *Ensayos sobre la literatura latinoamericana* (México: FCE, 1953), pp. 204-7; "Xavier Villaurrutia," in *Nivel* 30 (June 25, 1965): 4. Rodolfo Usigli, "Xavier Villaurrutia," in *Letras de México* (Mar. 15, 1943); "Estética de la muerte," in *El Hijo Pródigo* (July 15, 1946). Edmundo Valadés, "Nostalgia de Xavier Villaurrutia," in *México en la Cultura* 176 (July 1952): 3. Carlos Valdés, Review of *El solterón*, in *Universidad de México* 10, 1 (Sept. 1955): 31. Juan Villegas, "La hiedra de Xavier Villaurrutia y la imagen de la sociedad mexicana," in *Explicación de Textos Literarios* 16, 1 (1987-1988): 18-27. Hanya Wozniak-Brayman, "The Literary World of Xavier Villaurrutia: Search for Aesthetic Unity," in *Dissertation Abstracts International* 41, 8 (Feb. 1981): 3600A. Ramón Xirau, *Tres poetas de la soledad* (México: Ant. Lib. Robredo, 1955). Agustín Yañez, Review of *Dama de corazones*, in *Bandera de provincias* (Sept. 1929). Francisco Zendejas, "Carta a Rodolfo Usigli, Xavier Villaurrutia y Agustín Lazo," in *México en la Cultura* (Nov. 20, 1949); Review of *Poesía y teatro completos*, in *México en la Cultura* 255 (Feb. 7, 1954): 2; "Multilibros," Review of *Obras*, in *Excelsior* (Nov. 24, 1966): 1, 9.

MICHELE MUNCY

VILLEGAS, Oscar (1943-), playwright. Oscar Villegas was born in Ciudad del Maíz, San Luis Potosí. He started writing short stories from a very early age, and at age fifteen he wrote short plays for school. After moving to México, he studied fine arts at the Academia de San Carlos, theory and dramatic composition at the UNAM, and stage directorship at the Theater School of the INBA. He also attended the famous Taller Mester directed by Juan José *Arreola. He also worked as a ceramic master at an experimental ceramic workshop in México. In 1967 he published his first formal play, *La paz de la buena gente* (The Peace of Good People), which won the prestigiuos Premio Ruiz de Alarcón in 1980 for the best Mexican play. Also in 1967 he published *El renacimiento* (The Rebirth), and in 1969 he wrote *Santa Catarina* (Saint Catherine). For the latter he was given the Premio SEP in 1969. Not much later, in 1976, he was awarded the Premio Protea for *Atlántida*. He contributed to *El Heraldo de México*, writing for the section Crítica de Teatro from 1968 to 1972.

   In his theater, Oscar Villegas demonstrates a marked preference for the themes of love, sex, and myth, all of which are presented in one-act plays divided into multiple scenes. His characters are simple but solid in their convictions, and he skillfully manipulates language to complete the characterization of his personages.

   In *La paz de la buena gente*, Villegas tries to discover truth within his characters, who, powerless to effect changes, seem to suffer from the unavoidable passage of time. In the following plays, the author works with concepts and topics such as sex, youth, and homosexuality. In *Atlántida*, considered his best play, Villegas presents the life of young people living in a poor neighborhood, void of meaning, lacking in moral values. Failure to communicate effectively and loss of self are two painful problems for the adolescents who want to emulate the values of the old and chimeric Atlántida, but are powerless to change their own circumstances by themselves.

WORKS: *La paz de la buena gente* (The Peace of Good People) (México: INBA, Rev. de Bellas Artes, 1967; 2nd ed. UAM, 1982). *El renacimiento* (The Rebirth) (Xalapa: Universidad Veracruzana, 1967). *El señor y la señora* (The Gentleman and the Lady) (México: INJUVE, 1969). *Marlon Brando es otro* (Marlon Brando Is Somebody Else) (México: INJUVE, 1969); 2nd ed. (Novaro, 1973). *La pira* (The Pyre) in *Tramoya* (1st epoch) 9 (Oct.-Dec. 1977): 4-21. *Santa Catarina* (Saint Catherine) (México: Ed. Extemporáneos, 1977); 2nd ed. (UNAM, 1982). *Atlántida*, in *Tramoya* (1st epoch), 2 (Jan.-Mar. 1976): 27-86. *El reino animal* (Animal Kingdom), in *Tramoya* (1st epoch), 23 (Jan.-Mar. 1982): 108-15. *Mucho gusto en conocerlo* (Plased to Have Met You), in *Tramoya* (2nd epoch), 1 (Jan.-Mar. 1985): 7- 56. *Mucho gusto en conocerlo y otras obras*, volume with *La paz de la buena gente*, *Santa Catarina*, *Atlántida*, and *Mucho gusto en conocerlo* (México: Editores Mexicanos Unidos, 1985). *Acá entre dos* (Here Between Two), in *Tramoya* (2nd epoch), 21 (Oct.-Dec. 1989): 117-19. *El refugio de las zorras* (The Shelter of the Foxes), in *Tramoya* 25b (Oct.-Dec. 1990): 3-12. *Lo verde de las hojas* (The Greenness of the Leaves), in *Tramoya* 25b (Oct.-Dec. 1990): 13-22. Essays: "El rey se muere... asesinado," in *El Heraldo de México* 119 (Feb. 1968). "Ninón de la vida diaria," in *El Heraldo de México* 200 (Sept. 1969). "El turno de la juventud," in *El Heraldo de México* 218 (Jan. 1970). "De escándalo a escándalo," in *El Heraldo de México* 350 (July 1972). "Ninón de la vida diaria," in *Tramoya* (1st epoch), 11 (Apr.-Jun. 1978): 54-61. "Igualmente, Tomás," in *Tramoya* (2nd epoch), 1 (Jan.-Mar. 1985): 57-61. "Y pensar que pudimos," in *Tramoya* (2nd epoch), 23 (Apr.-June 1989): 5-8.

BIBLIOGRAPHY: Tomás Espinosa, "Oscar Villegas es otro," in *La semana de Bellas Artes* 61 (Jan. 1979). "Mucho gusto en conocerlo," in *Tramoya* (2nd epoch), 1 (Jan.-Mar. 1985): 3-6. George Woodyard, "El teatro de Oscar Villegas: experimentación con la forma," in *Teatro Crítico* (Universidad Veracruzana) 10 (1978), also in the edition of *Mucho gusto en conocerlo y otras obras*.

ELADIO CORTES

W

WRIGHT DE KLEINHANS, Laureana (1846-1896), poet, early feminist writer. Laureana Wright was born in Taxco, Guerrero, on July 14, 1846, and studied in Mexico City, where in 1865 she published her first poems. After marriage to Sebastian Kleinhans in 1868, she participated in a number of literary organizations, including the Sociedad Netzalhualtín Cuenca. She was a *coyotl*, along with Manuel *Acuña and Agustín *Cuenca, and she was also an honorary member in the Liceo Mexicano. Wright de Kleinhans is best known not for her youthful verses, but rather for her writings in favor of the emancipation of the Mexican woman. She was the director of the magazine *Violetas del Anáhuac* from 1887 to 1889, a precursor of Mexican feminist publications, and left finished her most important work, *Mujeres notables de México*, on her death in Mexico City on September 22, 1896.

WORKS: "Sor Juana Inés de la Cruz," *Violetas del Anáhuac* (México: Feb. 12, 1888). *La emancipación de la mujer por medio del estudio* (The Emancipation of Woman through Study) (México: Imprenta Nueva, 1891). *Educación errónea de la mujer y medios practicos para corregirla* (Erroneous Education of Women and Practical Means of Correction) (México: Gaceta Popular, Imprenta Nueva, 1892). *Mujeres notables mexicanas* (Notable Mexican Women) (México: Secretaría de Bellas Artes, 1910).

BIBLIOGRAPHY: Heriberto Garcia Rivas, *Historia de la literatura mexicana* (México: Porrúa, 1972), p. 190. Obituary, *El Partido Liberal* (México, Sept. 25 1896). Aurora M. Ocampo de Gómez and Ernesto Prado Velázquez, *Diccionario de escritores mexicanos* (México: UNAM, 1967), pp. 412-13.

PATRICIA HART AND JOSEF HELLEBRANDT

Y

YAÑEZ, Agustín (1904-1980), novelist, short story writer, essayist, and critic. Born May 4, 1904 in Guadalajara, Jalisco, Agustín Yáñez distinguished himself as an educator, statesman, politician, and journalist. Beginning at age fifteen, he held posts in various educational institutions in Guadalajara, eventually becoming a professor at the National University. He served as his country's representative to national and international educational meetings, and his career as a statesman included posts as ambassador to Argentina and UNESCO. His most significant accomplishments in politics were his service as governor of Jalisco (1953-1959), advisor to President López Mateos, and secretary of education in the administration of Gustavo Díaz Ordaz. His career in journalism included service as editor of three journals: *Bandera de Provincias* in Guadalajara (1929-1930), *Occidente* in Mexico City (1944-1945), and *Filosofía y Letras* (1946-1947). He served also on the editorial boards of several other journals. He died in Mexico City on January 17, 1980.

The contributions of Yáñez to the development of Mexican literature are manifested most clearly in his novel, *Al filo del agua* (The Edge of the Storm). This psychological novel presents a new perception of Mexican reality and marks a major innovation in the development of the Mexican novel. Though highly critical of the closed pre-Revolution society, it is much more than a novel of social protest. It represents an incisive portrayal of Mexican character. The images drawn transcend time and place of focus, thus surpassing the traditonal Mexican historical novel. Equally important, the portrayal is achieved with consummate artistry. The style is highly poetic, rhythmic, rich in imagery, yet unobstrusive. He makes extensive use of interior monologue, multiple planes of narration, flashbacks, and thematic counterpoint. His innovative blending of past and present set a pattern for later writers. His literary accomplishment consists of more than twenty major works of fiction and nonfiction and spans over thirty years. Like Honoré de Balzac, Yáñez draws a detailed picture of his contemporary society, with a realistic assessment of its strengths and weaknesses. The sociohistorical value of his works, although highly significant, is exceeded in importance by their literary qualities.

WORKS: "Baraliptón" (Syllogism), in *Ocampo: Revista bimestral* 1, 3 (March-April 1931): 174-97. *Espejismo de Juchithn* (Illusions of Juchithn) (México: Imprenta Universitaria, 1940). *Flor de juegos antiguos* (Remembrances of Childhood Games) (Guadalajara: Eds. de la Universidad de Guadalajara, 1941). *Pasión y convalescencia* (Passion and Convalescence) (México: *Abside*, 1943). *Archipielago de mujeres* (Archipelago of Women) (México: UNAM, 1943). *El Contenido Social de la Literatura Iberoamericana* (Social Elements in Latin American Literature) (México: El Colegio de México, 1944). *Melibea, Isolda y Alda en tierras cblidas* (Melibea, Isolda, and Alda In Torrid Lands) (Buenos Aires: Espasa-Calpe, 1946). *Yahualica*

(Yahualica) (México: Eds. Cámara de Diputados, 1946). *Al filo del agua* (The Edge of the Storm) (México: Editorial Porrúa, 1947). *Don Justo Sierra: su vida, sus ideas y sus obras* (Justo Sierra: His Life, Ideas, and Works) (México: UNAM, 1950). *La creación* (Creation) (México: FCE, 1959). *Ojerosa y pintada: la vida en la ciudad de Mexico* (Drawn and Haggard: Life in Mexico City) (México: Libro Mex, 1960). *La tierra pródiga* (The Prodigal Land) (México: FCE, 1960). "Cómo escribí La tierra pródiga," (How I Wrote "The Prodigal Land"), in *¡Siempre!* 452 (Feb. 21, 1962):. 5. *Las tierras flacas* (The Lean Lands) (México: Editorial Joaquín Mortiz, 1962). The Edge of the Storm (*Al filo del agua*), translated by Ethel Brinton (Austin: University of Texas Press, 1963). *Tres cuentos* (Three Short Stories) (México: Editorial Joaquin Mortiz, 1965). *Los sentidos al aire* (Feelings in the Wind) (México: INBA, 1964). "Antonio López de Santa Anna: Espectro de una sociedad," in *Cuadernos Americanos* 179, 6 (Nov.-Dec. 1971): 155-59. *Las vueltas del tiempo* (Cycle of Time) (México: Edit. Joaquín Mortiz, 1973). "La barca," in *Cuadernos Americanos* 201, 4 (July-Aug. 1975): 249-60.

BIBLIOGRAPHY: Manuel Altolaguirre, "Sobre Al filo del agua," in *Nivel* 13 (Jan. 25, 1964): 2, 4. John S. Brushwood, *Mexico in Its Novel, A Nation's Search for Identity* (Austin: University of Texas Press, 1966), pp. 7-12, 18, 39, 45-48, 50, 63, 222, 225, 232-233; "La arquitectura de las novelas de Agustín Yañez," in *Revista Iberoamericana* 36, 72 (July-Sept. 1970): 437-51. Eileen Connolly, "La centralidad del protagonista en *Al filo del agua*," in *Revista Iberoamericana* 32 (1966): 275-80. Donald William Davey, "Catholicism and the Bible in *Al Filo del agua* and *Las tierras flacas* by Agustín Yáñez," Ph.D. Diss., University of Florida, 1974. Gilbert Edward Evans, "El mundo novelístico de Agustín Yáñez," Ph.D. Diss., Yale University 1965. John J. Flasher, *México Contemporáneo en las novelas de Agustín Yáñez* (México: Porrúa, 1969). Thomas Rudy Franz, "Three Hispanic Echoes of Tolstoi at the Close of World War II," in *Hispanic Journal* 6, 1 (Fall 1984): 37-51. Helmy F. Giacoman, ed., *Homenaje a Agustín Yáñez, Variaciones interpretativas en torno a su obra* (Long Island City: Las Americas, 1973). Barbara Jeannette Graham, "Social and Stylistic Realities in the Fiction of Agustín Yáñez," Ph.D. Diss., University of Miami, 1969. Elaine Haddad, "The Structure of *Al filo del agua*," in *Hispania* 47 (1964): 522-29. Joel Hancock and Ned J. Davison, "*Al filo del agua* revisited: A Computer-aided Analysis of Theme and Rhythm in the 'Acto Preparatorio," in *Chasqui* 8, 1 (Nov. 1978): 23-42. Ramona B. Lagos, "Las tierras flacas: capitalismo agrícola e ideología," in *Nueva Narrativa Hispanoamericana* 4, 1-2 (Jan.-Sept. 1974): 145-70. Walter M. Langford, "Agustín Yáñez: A Quantum Jump for the Mexican Novel," in *The Mexican Novel Comes of Age* (Notre Dame: University of Notre Dame Press, 1971), pp. 71-87. Luis Leal, "Agustín Yáñez y la novela mexicana: rescate de una teoría," in *Revista Iberoamericana* 48, 118 (Jan.-June 1982): 112-29. María del Refugio Llamas Jiménez, *Trilogía de personajes femeninos en Al filo del agua* (México: Edit. Porrúa, 1971). María del Carmen Millán, "En memoria de Agustín Yáñez," in *La Palabra y el Hombre* 37 (Jan.-March 1981): 89-91. Samuel J. O'Neil, "Interior monologue in *Al filo del agua*," in *Hispania* 2 (1968): 447-55. Barbara Marie Quevedo, "The Myth of Unattainable Love in the Fiction of Agustín Yáñez," Ph.D. Diss., University of California at Berkely, 1977. Frank Douglas Robertson, "Archetypes in the Fiction of Agustín Yáñez," Ph.D. Diss., University of California at Irvine, 1986. John Skirius, "The Cycles of History and Memory: *Las vueltas del tiempo*: A Novel by Agustín Yáñez," in *Mester* 12, 1-2 (May 1983): 78-100. Joseph Sommers, "Génesis de la novela: Agustín Yáñez," in *Yañez, Rulfo, Fuentes: La novela mexicana moderna* (Caracas: Monte Avila Editores, 1969), pp. 57-91. Luis Suárez, "Agustín Yáñez. Un intelectual en el poder," in *México en la Cultura* (Feb. 15, 1959): 1, 12. Kenneth M. Taggart, "El tema de la muerte en *Al filo del agua*," in *Yáñez, Rulfo y Fuentes: el tema de la muerte en tres novelas mexicanas* (Madrid: Ed. Playor, Colección Nova Scholar, 1983), pp. 73-126. Stella Teichert Clark, "El estilo y sus efectos en la prosa de Agustín Yáñez," Ph.D. Diss., Universioty of Kansas, 1971. Linda M. Van Conant, *Agustín Yáñez, Interprete de la novela mexicana moderna* (México: Edit. Porrúa, 1969). John Walker, "Timelessness through Memory in the Novels of Agustín Yañez," in *Hispania* 57, 3 (Sept. 1974): 445-51. Richard A. Young, "Perspectivas autobiográficas en Flor de juegos antiguos de Agustín Yáñez," in *Abside* 40, 3 (July-Sept. 1976): 247-69.

KENNETH M. TAGGART

Z

ZAMACOIS, Niceto de (1820-1885). Although born in Spain in 1820, Niceto de Zamacois, a historian, novelist, and poet, moved to Mexico while he was quite young. During a period of politic turmoil and hostility toward Spaniards, he returned to Spain in 1858, contributing his literary work to *El Museo Universal* and other journals. He went back and forth between Spain and Mexico several times.

While in Spain, he began work on his twenty-volume *Historia de México* (History of Mexico), with special emphasis on clarifying many controversial issues and using hitherto unpublished manuscripts and documents, such as those found in convents, in the national archives, and other places. Zamacois never renounced his Spanish citizenship; he could not, therefore, participate in Mexican political affairs or hold governmental posts, although many of his contemporaries wanted him to do so.

His other literary production is comprised of essays, poetry, plays and novels. The above-mentioned historical work was a service to Mexico and a source of respectable, reliable information, especially with reference to those events to which the author was a witness, since he had met and dealt with many of the people mentioned in the work.

He also wrote *El testamento del Gallo Pitagórico* (The Will of the Pythagorian Cock), a satirical work designed to bring laughter at the expense of the vagabond or rogue in society, thus elevating others of more honor. *El jarabe* (Syrup) is another satire, a pleasantly humorous play depicting Mexican local customs. Some of his plays are based on or are similar to the Spanish zarzuela, with which Zamacois was quite familiar.

WORKS: *El sitio de Monterrey* (The Siege of Monterrey), play, performed in July 1846. *Los ecos de mi lira* (The Echoes of My Lyre), poems (México: n.p., 1849). *Los misterios de México* (The Mysteries of Mexico), theater, in *El Español* 1, 15 (Nov. 8, 1851). "La casera" (The Landlady) and "El criado" (The Servant), in *Los mexicanos pintados por sí mismos* (México: Imp. de Murguía, 1855; Biblioteca Nacional, 1935; Edit. Símbolo, 1946). "La plaza de San Juan" (The Plaza of San Juan), in *México y sus alrededores*, 1855. *El testamento del Gallo Pitagórico* (The Will of the Pythagorian Cock) (México: n.p., 1855). *El jarabe* (Syrup) (México: Imp. de V. Segura, 1860); 2nd ed. (México: Imp. de Luis Inclán, 1861). *El Capitán Rossi* (Captain Rossi) (México: Imp. Literaria, 1864). *El mendigo de San Angel* (The Beggar of San Angel), novel (México: Imp. Literaria, 1864-1865). Translation of Bulwer Lytton, *La destrucción de Pompeya* (The Destruction of Pompei) (México: Imp. de I. Cumplido, 1871). *Historia de México* (History of Mexico), 18 vols. in 20 vols. (Barcelona: J. Parres y Cía, 1876-1882). *La herencia de un barbero* (A Barber's Inheritance), play (México: Imp. y Libr. de Aguilar e Hijos, 1879). *Un ángel desterrado del cielo* (An Angel Exiled from Heaven), legend (México: n.p., 1885).

BIBLIOGRAPHY: Francisco Monterde, *Bibliografía del teatro en México* (México: Monografías Bibliográficas Mexicanas), pp. 385-86. Aurora M. Ocampo de Gómez and Ernest Prado Velázquez, *Diccionario de Escritores Mexicanos* (México: UNAM, 1967), pp. 417-18. Juan de Dios Peza, *Poetas y escritores modernos mexicanos*, 2nd ed. (México: Eds. de *El Libro y el Pueblo*, 1965), p. 53. Arturo Torres Rioseco, *Bibliografía de la novela mexicana* (Cambridge: Harvard University Press, 1933), p. 58.

JEANNE C. WALLACE

ZARCO Mateos, Francisco (1829-1869), journalist, historian. Born December 4, 1829, in Durango, Zarco was primarily a self-educated man who, nevertheless, came to be recognized in his short lifetime as one of Mexico's leading journalists and statesmen. He began his political career in 1848 when he was named chief secretary to the minister of foreign relations. Soon afterwards, he began to publish articles in *El Siglo XIX* (The Nineteenth Century); in 1849, he became editor of this journal, and remained affiliated with it throughout most of his life. He founded *Las Cosquillas* (The Tickler), a satirical review, around mid-century, and he contributed to *El Presente Amistoso* (The Friendly Present), *La Ilustración mexicana* (Mexican Enlightenment), *El Demócrata* (The Democrat), and journals in Chile, Argentina, Colombia, and Venezuela. Most of his writing is in a political vein, in defense of the liberal cause, although he was an independent thinker and spoke out against all forms of injustice, regardless of the party involved. As a member of Congress in 1856-1857, he achieved fame as an orator and drew large audiences of liberal-minded youths who applauded his speeches. His *Historia del congreso extraordinario constituyente 1856-1857* (History of the Extraordinary Constitutional Congress 1856-1857) is still regarded as an important text for the study of constitutional law in Mexico today.

During the political instability of 1860, Zarco was persecuted and imprisoned by the conservatives for his inflammatory pamphlet, *Los Asesinatos de Tacubaya* (The Murders of Tacubaya). Soon after his release in 1861, he was named a member of the Juárez cabinet and accompanied the Juárez government into exile in San Luis Potosi and Saltillo, There he founded the liberal newspapers *La Independencia mexicana* (Mexican Independence) and *La Acción* (Action).

When Juárez was restored to power in 1867, Zarco was named to a diplomatic post in New York City. He quickly became disenchanted with the Juárez government, however, and resigned his position. He returned to Mexico City, where he died in poverty on December 22, 1869. Despite the controversy that surrounded him in life, his death was publically mourned by Mexico's leading men of letters.

Zarco published about fifty costumbristic sketches between 1851 and 1854, under the pseudonym Fortu. Because of the melancholy and pessimistic tone of his writing, he has been called "The Mexican Larra." Zarco's style is simple and clear, but elegant, showing a great satirical wit. He is also remembered as a leading spirit behind the Hidalgo Lyceum, a political and literary society that he founded in the late 1850s.

WORKS: *Comentarios de Francisco Zarco sobre la intervención francesa* (Commentaries of Francisco Zarco about French Intervention) (México: Pub. de La Secretaría de Relaciones Exteriores, 1929). *Historia del congreso extraordinario constituyente 1856-1857* (History of the Extraordinary Constitutional Congress 1856-1857) (México: El Colegio de México, 1956). *Crónica del congreso extraordinario constituyente 1856-1857* (Chronicle of the Extraordinary Constitutional Congress 1856-1857) (México: El Colegio de México, 1957). *Textos políticos* (Political Texts) (México: UNAM, 1957). *Francisco Zarco ante la intervención francesa y el Imperio* (Francisco Zarco on French Intervention and the Empire) (México: Secretaría de Relaciones Exteriores, 1958). *Escritos Literarios* (Literary Writings) (México: Porrúa, 1968). *Castillos en el aire y otros textos mordaces* (Castles in the Air and Other Witty Texts) (México: INBA, 1984).

BIBLIOGRAPHY: Oscar Castañeda Batres, Prologue, *Francisco Zarco* (México: Club de periodistas, 1961), pp. 13-116. Luis Leal, *Breve historia del cuento mexicano* (México: de Andrea, 1956), p. 47. Marta del Carmen Millán, *Literatura mexicana* (México: Edit. Esfinge, 1962), p. 170. Antonio de la Peña y Reyes, Prologue, *Comentarios de Francisco Zarco sobre la intervención francesa* (México: Secretaría del Relaciones Exteriores, 1929), pp. vii- xxxv. Jefferson R. Spell, "The Costumbrista movement in Mexico," *PMLA* 50 (1935): 290-315. Xavier Tavera Alfaro, Prologue, Textos políticos (México: UNAM, 1957), pp. v-xxvi.

CYNTHIA K. DUNCAN

ZAYAS ENRIQUEZ, Rafael de (1848-1932), dramatist, poet, journalist. Born in Veracruz on July 24, 1848, Zayas Enríquez studied early on in Germany, and later returned to Mexico, where he lived first in Medellin and later in Veracruz. In Veracruz he published his first articles in *El Eco del Comercio* and *El Ferrocarril*, and around 1869 he founded with others a literary magazine called *Las violetas*. In 1869 his first play, a romantic verse-drama called *Paula*, premiered in the Teatro Principal de Veracruz. In 1876 he moved to Campeche, where he received a law deoree and practiced for a time, but later he returned again to Veracruz, where for political reasons he was once more forced to leave abruptly. In 1889 he traveled to Barcelona in an attempt to publish works there, and on his return to Mexico he held several public posts and wrote a number of editorials. Zayas Enriquez died on June 9, 1932.

The historical works of Zayas Enriquez were widely read and translated during his life. He was also a novelist, publishing his first two novels himself: *Remordimiento* (Remorse) and *Oceánida* (The Australiad). He is better remembered for *El teniente de los gavilanes* (The Lieutenant of the Sparrow Hawks), which narrates in detail the amorous adventures of the bandit protagonist. His mixture of realism and romanticism is typical of end-of-century writing. Most of his poetry was lyric or erotic, and he also published works of literary criticism.

WORKS: Drama: *Paula*, unpublished, produced in Veracruz in 1871. *El expósito* (The Foundling), unpublished, produced in Veracruz in 1874. *El Conde de Villamediana* (The Count of Villamediana), unpublished produced in the Teatro Arbeu in 1902. Novels: *Oceánida* (The Australiad) (Veracruz: Rafael de Zayas, 1881). *Remordimiento* (Remorse) (Veracruz: Rafael de Zayas, 1881). *El teniente de los gavilanes* (The Lieutenant of the Sparrow Hawks) (New York: Appleton, 1902). Poetry: *Tropicales* (Tropical Verses) (Veracruz: Rafael de Zayas, 1883). *Poemas sudras* (Sudra

Poems)(México: Tipografía Artística, 1903). *Epicas* (Epics) (Paris: Le Livre Libre, 1929). Biography: *Benito Juárez, su vida, su obra* (Benito Juárez, His life, His works) (México: Francisco Díaz de León, 1906). He also co-authored *El dieciocho de julio de 1906: a la imperecedera memoria del mejor de los hijos de México, del buen ciudadano, Benito Juárez* (The Eighteenth of July of 1906: To the Imperishable Memory of the Best of Mexico's Sons, the Good Citizen Benito Juárez) (Pachuca: Luis B. García, 1906). He also wrote a number of historical and political articles, tracts, and editorials, many of which he published himself.

BIBLIOGRAPHY: Ricardo Domínguez, *Los poetas mexicanos* (México: Pedro J. García, 1888). Hilarión Frías y Soto, "Nubes de gloria. Rafael de Zayas Enríquez," *El siglo XIX* (México, June 30, 1894). Carlos González Peña, *History of Mexican Literature* (Dallas: Southern Methodist University Press, 1968), pp. 327, 334. Aurora M. Ocampo de Gómez and Ernesto Prado Velázquez, *Diccionario de escritores mexicanos* (México: UNAM, 1967). Juan de Dios Peza, *Poetas y escritores mexicanos modernos* (México: El Anuario Mexicano, 1878), p. 41.

PATRICIA HART AND JOSEF HELLEBRANDT

ZENDEJAS, Francisco (1917-   ). Zendejas was born in Mexico CIty on June 10, 1917. He studied at the National School of Economics at the UNAM, at the Schools of Economics at the University of Columbia and the University of Washington. He was a professor of languages for the Office of Education; a private secretary to the minister of the Office of Employment; the head of the Department of Publicity and Shows for the National Institute of Fine Arts in 1943; an editor for the magazine *Artes de México* (Mexican Arts); the Mexican representative to London for the First Congress on Mental Health in 1947; founder of and spokesman for the Xavier Villaurrutia Prize in Literature since 1955. He has contributed to many magazines and newspapers in Mexico City, nationwide and abroad. Zendejas has traveled to the United States, Europe, South America, and the Mideast.

His works, which include essays, theatrical pieces, stories, and articles, are characterized by their humor, wit, and liveliness. He began his writing career with the publication of critical essays in *El Nacional* (The National) in 1937. He also wrote essays for *El Hijo Pródigo* (The Prodigal Son), *Letras de México* (Mexican Letters), *Cuadernos Americanos* (American Notebooks), *Las Hoy* (Today), and *Cuadernos* (Notebooks) of Paris, among others. He published his own literary magazine entitled *Prometeus* (Prometheus) in 1949, to which young Mexican and Hispanic poets and prose writers contributed. In *Prometeus* Zendejas published fragments of his own novel, *El amor ideologico* (Ideologic Love), as well as translations of poems and other general prose articles. Zendejas wrote a daily column for several years in the daily newspaper *Excelsior* entitled "Multilibros" (Many Books), a Mexican bibliography. He has also worked on radio and television and has been director for several art galleries.

WORKS: Theater: *Teatro político* (Political Theatre) (Durango: Ed. del Dept. of Continuing University Education of the University of Juárez, 1965), contains "La hoz y el martillo" (The Hammer and Sickle), "Gerónimo" (Geronimo), and "Cuando el príncipe muere" (When the Prince Dies), Poetry: *Hacía la décima flor* (Near the

Tenth Flower) (Mexico, 1966). Narrative: *Novelas cortas y cuentos dialogados* (Short Novels and Dialogued Stories), by Luciano de Samosata (México: Ed. Jus, 1966).

BIBLIOGRAPHY: Andrés Henestrosa, "La nota cultural," *El Nacional* 13 (Feb. 1965): 3; "La nota cultural," review of Zendejas's thirty years as a journalist, *El Nacional* (Nov. 10, 1966): 3. Ruth S. Lamb, *Bibliografía del teatro mexicano del siglo XX* (México: Eds. de Andrea, 1962), p. 156. Carlos Solórzano, "Teatro político," *Diorama de la Cultura* 6 (June 1965): 7.

DENISE GUAGLIARDO BENCIVENGO

ZEPEDA, Eraclio (1937). Born in Tuxtla Gutiérrez, Chiapas, on March 24, 1937, Eraclio Zepeda completed his basic studies in his native city. He went to the Universidad Veracruzana, then worked there as a literature professor. His very early poetry and short stories first appeared in the literary journals, *Situaciones* and *La Palabra y el Hombre* in Jalapa, and in *México en la Cultura* and *Revista Mexicana de Literatura* in Mexico City.

A student of social anthropology, literature, history, and the indigenous narrative, Zepeda has exercised his many gifts and talents as a teacher, writer, actor, and popular television personality. He has traveled extensively and has also been a political activist. It is not surprising that most of his work has a social orientation. Zepeda, in the capacity of reporter and professor of literature, has traveled and lived in Cuba, the Soviet Union, China, several European countries, and Central America. He even followed the route of Marco Polo, going from Beijing to Jerusalem. After several years of such extensive travels, he returned to Mexico and headed several cultural programs, most in an effort to recapture the indigenous cultures. On two occasions, he has given screen portrayals of General Francisco Villa. He is, furthermore, an authentic cultivator of the oral tradition, listening to and interpreting tales that he eventually turns into published stories.

Eraclio Zepeda is considered the premier contemporary story writer/teller in Mexico, focusing principally on the world of the indigenous people of Chiapas. His texts arise primarily from all aspects of nature, but are not limited to it. Modern life provides a framework for many of his narratives, which tell of man's most basic needs.

Zepeda began his writing career when he was twenty-two, with the publication of a book of stories, *Benezulul*, in 1959. The well-received book gave Zepeda national recognition as a writer. The stories that comprise the volume have been anthologized and reproduced in several different languages. The Indian belief system, with its charms, incantations, magic, and miracles, provides Zepeda with an anthropological point of view that he employs as an integral part of his prose. *Benezulul*, set in Chiapas, is perhaps his most significant collection of stories. In it, he concentrates on primitive aspects of Indian psychology, set against a background of stunning natural beauty. As critic Barbara Brodman notes, the distinctions between man and nature and between life and death are often blurred in the book, all becoming part of a circular life cycle in which man is constantly faced with death. Both the living and the dead are characters in the stories, reflecting the Mexican and pre-Conquest cult of death.

Also a noted poet and member of La Espiga Amotinada, Zepeda published in the collection, *La espiga amotinada*, along with Luis *Buñuelos, Oscar *Oliva, Jaime

*Labastida and Jaime Augusto *Shelley. He also produced a poetic volume in Havana, shortly following the Cuban Revolution. Although he is known mainly for his stories, he has continued to write poetry ever since. Zepeda's poetry is influenced largely by the forces of nature and also has a social orientation. *Relación de travesía* (1960) (Crossroad Tale) includes his poetry from 1960-1965. In it, he remarks: "I believe that poetry ought to be simple, clear, almost like talking to a friend . . .. I also believe that poetry ought to be the bearer of an idea, vehicle of a feeling, whether it be personal or collective."

In 1967, he published a volume of stories, *Trejito*, followed by *Asalto nocturno* (1973) (Nocturnal Assault), and the book for which he received the Premio Xavier Villaurrutia, *Andando el tiempo* (1982) (Time Marching On).

Asalto Nocturno, winner of the Premio Nacional del Cuento 1974, combines the unusual and the fantastic with a deep sense of humanity rooted in tradition. The tales that comprise the book are clearly didactic, urging man to dissolve the boundaries that alienate people. Zepeda demonstrates a high degree of literary creativity, enhanced by the use of simple, refreshing language and effective structural techniques.

In *Andando el tiempo*, Zepeda demonstrates his qualifications as the writer most able to understand and convey the indigenous world of Mexico today. Aesthetically creating realistic indigenous characters and situations, Zepeda writes poetry and prose that is almost magical, with myth and legend pervading the atmosphere.

In 1985, *Confrontaciones* (Confrontations), a very important dialogue, was published. A participant of the cycle of conferences, "Confrontaciones. El creador frente al público," Eraclio Zepeda sustained a long talk with the students, the teachers, the workers of the UAM-Azcapotzalco on November 29, 1984. Speaking freely on a wide variety of subjects, Zepeda, the man-of-letters, the militant, the actor, and the teacher, brought to the fore many of his ideas on issues of contemporary life. In *Confrontaciones*, he describes what the art of writing is to him, the result of long periods of talking, of chatting with others, of seeking out the experiences that support what is to be written. Writing is the culmination of all that verbally and experientially precedes it. Thus, Eraclio Zepeda, an acclaimed author, actor, and teacher, continues to make a powerful and positive impact, having gained both national and international respect and recognition.

WORKS: *Benzulul*, stories (Jalapa: Universidad Veracruzana, 1959); 2nd ed. (1981). *El tiempo y el agua* (Time and Water), theater, 1960, staged in Chiapas in 1965. "Los soles de la noche" (The Suns of Night), poetry, in *La espiga amotinada* (México: FCE, 1960). *Tres cuentos* (Three Short Stories) (Xalapa: Federación Estudiantil, 1960). Poetry selection in *Revista Mexicana de Literatura* 7-8 (July-Aug. 1963): 59-61. *Asela*, poetry (Cuba: UNEAC, 1964). *Ocupación de la palabra* (Use of the Word) (México: FCE, 1965). *Compañía de combate* (Combat Company) story (La Habana: Ed. Unión, 1965). *Trejito*, story (Chiapas: Editorial Renovación, 1967). Story "Vientooo" from *Benzulul* in *Narrativa mexicana de hoy*, prologue, selection, and notes by Emmanuel Carballo (Madrid: Alianza Editorial, 1969), pp. 182-98. Poem in *La muerte en la poesía mexicana*, 1st ed., prologue and selection by Merlin H. Forster (México: Editorial Drogenes, 1970), p. 43. *Asalto nocturno* (Nocturnal Assault) (México: Joaquín Mortiz, 1973). *Andando el tiempo* (Time Marching On) (México: M. Casillas Editores, FONAPAS, 1982). *Relación de travesía* (México: Editorial Villicaña, 1985). *Confrontaciones* (Confrontations) (Azcapotzalco: UAM, 1985).

BIBLIOGRAPHY: Ricardo Aguilar Melantzón, "Efraín Huerta and the New School of Mexican Poets," in *Latin American Literary Review* 11, 22 (Spring-Summer 1983). Barbara L. C. Brodman, *The Mexican Cult of Death in Myth and Literature* (Gainesville: University Presses of Florida, 1976), pp. 76-82. Rosario Castellanos, Review of *Benzulul*, in *México en la Cultura* 572 (Feb. 28, 1960): 4. Eduardo César, "Sobre *La espiga amotinada*," in *Lugar de encuentro*, edited by Norma Klahn and Jesse Fernández (México: Editorial Katún, 1987), pp. 191-204. Frank Dauster, *The Double Strand* (Lexington: University Press of Kentucky, 1987), p. 33. J. Ann Duncan, *Voices, Visions, and a New Reality   Mexican Fiction since 1970* (Pittsburgh: University of Pittsburgh Press, 1986), pp. 25, 195. David William Foster, comp., *A Dictionary of Contemporary Latin American Authors* (Tempe: Center for Latin American Studies, Arizona State University, 1975), p. 110. Carlos González Peña, *Historia de la literatura mexicana* (México: Porrúa, 1984), pp. 300-302. Luis Leal, *Panorama de la literatura mexicana actual* (Washington, D.C.: Unión Panamericana, Sría. General de la OEA, 1968), p. 143. Juan Manuel Marcos, Review of *Andando el tiempo*, in *Revista iberoamericana* 51, 130-31 (Jan.-June 1985). Porfirio Martínez Peñaloza, *Los cinco poetas de La espiga amotinada* (México: Publs. del Instituto Cultural Mexicano-Israelí, 1966). Thelma Nava and Miguel Donoso Pareja, "Otra vez la espiga amotinada," in *El Gallo Ilustrado* 162 (Aug. 1, 1965): 1-3. Aurora M. Ocampo de Gómez and Ernesto Prado Velázquez, *Diccionario de Escritores Mexicanos* (México: UNAM, 1967), p. 421. Pedro Orgambide, "Narradores latinoamericanos--1982," in *Plural* 135 (Dec. 1982): 18. Salvador Reyes Nevares, Review of *Benzulul*, in *México en la Cultura* 568 (Jan. 31, 1960). Joseph Sommers, "El ciclo de Chiapas: nueva corriente literaria," in *Cuadernos Americanos* 2 (March-April 1964): 246-61; "Eraclio Zepeda y el oficio de narrar," *La brújula en el bolsillo* (Mexico, Sept. 1982): 14-25.

JEANNE C. WALLACE

ZUCKERMANN, Lydia (1919-), novelist, critic, and author of short stories. Lydia Zuckermann was born on February 17, 1919, in Paris, France. She obtained her bachelor's degree from the Sorbonne, where she majored in Russian language and literature, and from 1939 to 1942 she taught literature at the Lycèe Victor Duruy. She first visited Mexico in 1942, returning in 1948 to Europe, where she lived in her husband's native Germany for four years. She returned to México to take up permanent residence there in 1952. She has published a variety of articles and short stories in journals and newspapers in several countries, especially in France and Germany. Among other things, her articles have dealt with the work of Jean Cocteau and Bertolt Brecht. In addition to her own name, she has written under the pseudonyms Lydia Lambert and Michelín Lapouse. It was Zuckermann's first book, *Pushkin, poeta y amante* (Pushkin, Poet and Lover), that initially won recognition for her in the literary world. Written as a biographical novel, it was translated and published abroad and was particularly successful in England and the United States. Her subsequent novels were psychological in nature and served to establish her more firmly in Mexican literary circles.

WORKS: *Pushkin, poeta y amante* (London: Francis Aldor, 1946). *Anoche tuve un sueño extraño* (Last Night I Had a Strange Dream) (México: Ed. Pax, 1962). *La mujer que habla latín* (The Woman Who Knew Latin) (México: Federación Editorial Mexicana, 1973), in *Tiempo* (Aug. 20, 1962). *Triste columpio* (Sad Swing) (México: Joaquín Mortiz, 1964).

BIBLIOGRAPHY: Anon., Review of *Triste columpio*, in *México en la Cultura* 801 (July 26, 1964), p. 7; Review of *Triste columpio*, in *Cuadernos de Bellas Artes* 5, 10 (Oct. 1964): 80. Huberto Batis, Review of *Triste columpio*, in *La Cultura en Mexico* 137 (Sept. 30, 1964): xviii. Enrique Jaramillo Levi, "*La mujer que sabía latín*," in *Cuadernos Hispanoamericanos* 300 (1975): 724-26. Marta Luisa Mendoza, "Aquella vieja infancia olvidada. Lydia Zuckermann descubre la novela analítica," in *El Día* (Sept. 13, 1964): 4. Aurora M. Ocampo de Gómez and Ernesto Prado Velázquez, *Diccionario de Escritores Mexicanos* (México: UNAM, 1967), pp. 421-22. Gustavo Sainz, "No se puede desterrar el psicoanálisis de la novelística moderna, dice Lydia Zuckermann," in *México en la Cultura* 706 (Sept. 23, 1962): 3.

                                                                              JANIS L. KRUGH

ZUÑIGA, Olivia (1916-). Olivia Zúñiga was born in Purificación, Jaliso, on August 21, 1916. She has contributed to many publications such as *México en la Cultura* (Culture in Mexico), *Ariel* (Ariel), *Summa*, *Et Caetera*, *La Palabra y el Hombre* (Word and Man), and *Xalixtlico* among others. In 1951, she received the Jalisco Award for the Novel for her work *Retrato de una niña triste* (Portrait of a Sad Child), and in 1958 she received the José María Vigil Medal.

   She became known in literature as a poet. In her first book of verses, *Amante imaginado* (Imaginary Lover), published in 1947, she deals with intimate communication and the predominace of pain. In 1953 she published her second book of poetry, which was centered around the artistic ideas of sculptor Mathías Goeritz. Her first novel, *Retrato de una niña triste* (1951), was composed with her own childhood memories. In it she achieves a coherence between emotion and literary device. Zúñiga resurrects her own bitter childhood world. Her second novel, *Entre el infierno y la luz* (Between Hell and Light), published in 1953, is the anguished story of a woman's life lost without her beloved. Her third work in prose, *La muerte es una ciudad distinta* (Death Is a Different City), published in 1959, is not actually a novel but a simple fantasy of the author in which she weaves memories, dialogues, and political discourses in an intellectualized world that goes from the objective to the subjective and sentimental. She has also published a biography, stories, and poems in magazines and anthologies, and complied *Antología universal de lecturas infantiles* (Anthology of Children's Stories), published in 1952.

WORKS: Poetry: *Amante imaginado* (Imaginary Lover) (Guadalajara, Jalisco: n.p., 1947). *Los amantes y la noche* (Lovers and the Night), poetry about the sculptor Mathías Goeritz, and illustrated by Mathías Goerity (México: Eds. El Eco, 1953). Novels: *Retrato de una niña triste* (Portrait of a Sad Child) (Guadalajara: Eds. Et Caetera, 1951). *Entre el infierno y la luz* (Between Hell and Light), introduction by Arturo Rivas Sainz (Guadalajara: Instituto Tecnológico de Guadalajara, 1953). *La muerte es una ciudad distinta* (Death Is a Different City) (México: Libros del Unicornio, 1959). Anthology: *Antología universal de lecturas infantiles* (Universal

Anthology of Children's Stories) (México: Edit. Patria, 1952). Biography: *Mathías Goeritz* (Mathías Goeritz) (México: Edit. Intercontinental, 1963).

BIBLIOGRAPHY: Emilio Carballido, Review of *Amante imaginado*, in *Fuensanta* 1, 11 (Oct. 31, 1949); Review of *Retrato de una niña triste*, in *Revista Mexicana de Cultura* 220 (June 17, 1951): 11. Ramón de Ertze, "Mathías Goeritz en el templo de San Lorenzo," in *Diograma de la Cultura* (Nov. 10, 1963): 1, 4. Sergio Fernández, Review of *Mathías Goeritz* in *La Cultura en México* 93 (Nov. 27, 1963): xvii. Margarita Peña, "Olivia Zúñiga y sus libros," in *Ovaciones* suppl. no. 98 (Nov. 10, 1963): 8. Salvador Reyes Nevares, Review of *La muerte es una ciudad distinta*, in *México en la cultura* 568 (Jan. 31, 1960): 4. José Zapata Vela, "Carta a Olivia Zúñiga con motivo de su libro: *Retrato de una niña triste*," in *Revista Mexicana de Cultura* 229 (Aug. 19, 1951): 10.

DENISE GUAGLIARDO BENCIVENGO

Bibliography

ABREU GOMEZ, Ermilo. *Sala de retratos, Intelectuales y artistas de mi época* (México: Edit. Leyenda, S. A., 1946).

_____, et al. *Cuatro siglos de literatura mexicana*, selections (México: Edit. Leyenda, S.A., 1946).

ACEVEDO Escobedo, Antonio. *Rostros en el espejo* (México: Seminario de Cultura Mexicana, 1974).

AGRAZ García de Alba, Gabriel. *Bibliografía de los escritores de Jalisco*, 2 vols. (México: UNAM, 1980).

AGUEROS, Victoriano. *Escritores mexicanos contemporáneos*, (México: Imp. de Ignacio Escalante, 1880).

AGUILAR Camín, Hector, et al. *Interpretaciones de la Revolución mexicana*, 2 vols. (México: UNAM-Nueva Imagen, 1970)

AGUIRRE, Ramiro. *Panorama de la literatura mexicana del siglo XX* (México: UME, 1968).

ALBORG, Juan Luis. *Hora actual de la novela española*, 2 vols. (Madrid: Eds. Taurus, 1958, 1962).

ALEGRIA, Fernando. *Novelistas contemporáneos hispanoamericanos* (Boston: D. C. Heath, 1964).

_____. *Breve historia de la novela hispanoamericana* (México: Eds. de Andrea, 1959).

_____. *Historia de la novela hispanoamericana* (México: Eds. de Andrea, 1965).

ALMADA, Francisco R. *Diccionario de historia, geografía y biografía chihuahuenses*, (Chihuahua: n.p., 1927).

_____. *Diccionario de historia, geografía y biografía sonorenses* (Chihuahua: n.p., 1952).

ALTAMIRANO, Ignacio M. *La literatura nacional, revistas, ensayos,biografías y prólogos*, edition and prologues by José Luis Martínez, 3 vols. (México: Edit. Porrúa, 1949).

AMEZAGA, Carlos G. *Poetas mexicanos*, (Buenos Aires: Imp. de Pablo E. Coni e hijos, 1896).

ANDERSON IMBERT, Enrique. *Historia de la literatura hispanoamericana*, vol. 1 (México: FCE, 1954); 2nd. ed. (1957); 3rd. ed. (1961); 4th. ed. (1964).

_____. *Historia de la literatura hispanoamericana*, 2 vol. (México: FCE, 1957); 2nd. ed. (1961); 3rd. ed. (1964).

_____. and Eugenio FLORIT. *Literatura hispanoamericana, antología e introducción histórica* (New York: Holt, Rinehart and Winston, 1960).

ANDRADE, Cayetano. *Antología de escritores nicolaítas 1540-1940* (México: Talls. Gráficos de la Nación, 1941).

ARANDA Pamplona, Hugo. *Bibliografía de los escritores del estado de México* (México: UNAM, 1978).

ARELLANO, Jesús. *Antología de los 50 poetas contemporáneos de México* (México: Eds. Alatorre, 1952).
_____. *Poetas jóvenes de México* (México: Eds. Libro-Mex, 1955).
ARGUDIN, Yolanda. *Historia del teatro en México* (México: Panorama Editorial, 1985).
ARROM, José Juan. *Esquema generacional de las letras hispanoamericanas, ensayo de un método* (Bogotá: Instituto Caro y Cuervo, 1963).
ARRONIZ, Marcos. *Manual de biografía mexicana o galería de hombres célebres de México* (París: Libr. de Rosa Bouret y Cía., 1857).
AUB, Max. *Poesía mexicana, 1950-1960* (México: Aguilar, 1960).
AYALA Blanco, Jorge *La búsqueda del cine mexicano* (México: UNAM, 1974).
AZUELA, Mariano. *Cien años de novela mexicana* (México: Eds. Botas, 1947).
AZUELA, Salvador. *Gente de letras* (Toluca: Estado de México, 1979).
BATIS, Huberto. *Indices de El Renacimiento, Semanario literario mexicano (1869)* (México: UNAM, 1963).
BENEDETTI, Mario. *Letras del continente mestizo* (Montevideo: Arca, 1967).
BERISTAIN DE SOUZA, José Mariano. *Biblioteca Hispano Americana Septentrional*, 5 vols., 3rd ed. (México: Eds. Fuente Cultural, 1947).
BERMUDEZ, Maria Elvira. *Los mejores cuentos policiacos mexicanos* (México: Libro-Mex, 1955).
BLANCO, José Joaquín. *Crónica de la poesía mexicana* (Culiacán: UAS, 1981).
BOLIO, Edmundo. *Diccionario histórico, geográfico y biográfico de Yucatán* (México: n.p., 1945).
BRADING, David. *Los orígenes del nacionalismo mexicano* (México: Era, 1981).
_____. *Prophecy and Myth in Mexican History* (Cambridge: CLAS, n. d.).
BRAVO, Roberto. *Itinerario inicial* (La joven narrativa de México) (Tuxtla Gutierrez: Universidad Autónoma de Chiapas, 1985).
BRUSHWOOD, John S. *The Romantic Novel in Mexico* (Columbia, Missouri: n.p., 1954).
_____. *Mexico in Its Novel, A Nation's Search for Identity* (Austin: University of Texas Press, 1966).
_____. *La novela mexicana 1967-1982* (México: Grijalbo, 1984).
_____. and José ROJAS GARCIDUEÑAS. *Breve historia de la novela mexicana* (México: Eds. de Andrea, 1959).
BUSTOS Cerecedo, Miguel. *La creación literaria en Veracruz*, 2 vols. (Xalapa: Gobierno de Veracruz, 1977).
CAMPBELL, Federico. *Conversaciones con escritores* (México: Diana, 1981).
CAMPOS, Julieta. *Oficio de leer* (México: FCE, 1971).
CARBALLIDO, Emilio. *Teatro joven de México*, 9th ed. (México: EDIMUSA, 1985).
_____. *Nueve obras jóvenes* (México: EDIMUSA, 1985).
_____. *Avanzada. Más teatro joven de México* (México: EDIMUSA, 1985).
_____. *Teatro para adolescentes* (México: EDIMUSA, 1985).
CARBALLO, Emmanuel. *Cuentistas mexicanos modernos*, 2 vols. (México: Eds. Libro-Mex, 1956).
_____. *El cuento mexicano del siglo XX* (México: Empresas Editoriales S.A., 1964).
_____. *19 protagonistas de la literatura mexicana del siglo XX* (México: Empresas Editoriales, S.A., 1965).
_____. *Protagonistas de la Literatura Mexicana* (México: Consejo Nacional de Fomento Educativo, 1986).

CARDONA PENA, Alfredo. *Semblanzas mexicanas, artistas y escritores del México actual* (México: Eds. Libro-Mex, 1955).

CARREÑO, Alberto María. *Memorias de la Academia Mexicana Correspondiente de la Española*, vols. 7-17, (México: Edit. Jus. 1945-1960).

_____. *Semblanzas*, 1st part, Colección de Obras Diversas, vol. 2 (México: Eds. Victoria, 1939).

_____. *Semblanzas*, 3rd part, Colección de Obras Diversas, vol. 8 (México: Eds. Victoria, 1939).

CARTER, Boyd G. *Las revistas literarias de Hispanoamérica, breve estudio y contenido* (México: Eds. de Andrea, 1959).

CASTELLANOS, Rosario. *Juicios sumarios*, ensayos (Xalapa: Universidad Veracruzana, 1966).

CASTILLO, Gerónimo D. *Diccionario histórico biográfico y monumental de Yucatán* (México: Imp. de Castillo y Cía., 1866).

CASTILLO NEGRETE, Emilio del. *Galería de oradores de México en el siglo XIX*, vol.1 (México: Tip. de Santiago Sierra, 1877); vol. 2 (México: Tip. de R. I. González e Hijos, 1878); vol. 3 (México: Imp. de J. Guzmán Hnos., 1880).

CASTRO LEAL, Antonio. *La poesía mexicana moderna* (México: FCE, 1953).

_____. *La novela del México colonial* (México: Aguilar, 1964).

_____. *La novela de la Revolución*, 2 vols. (México: Edit. Aguilar, 1965).

_____. *Repasos y defensas* (México: Colegio Nacional, 1984).

CERNUDA, Luis. *Estudios sobre la poesía española contemporánea* (Madrid: Eds. Guadarrama, 1957).

COBO Borda, Juan Gustavo *Antología de la poesía hispanoamericana* (México: FCE, 1985).

COHEN, Sandro. *Palabra nueva. Dos décadas de Poesía en México* (México: Premiá, 1981).

COLIN, Eduardo *Verbo selecto, crítica hispanoamericana*, (México: Eds. Mexico, Moderno, 1922).

_____. *Rasgos* (México: Imp. Manuel León Sánchez, S.C.L., 1934).

CONGRAINS Martín, Enrique. *Antología contemporánea del cuento mexicano* (México: ILAVC, 1963).

CORDERO Y TORRES, Enrique. *Poetas y escritores poblanos, 1900-1943* (Puebla: Casa Editora Nieto, S.A., 1943).

_____. *Diccionario General de Puebla*, 3 vols. (Puebla: Centro de Estudios Históricos de Puebla, n. d.).

CORTES, Eladio. *De literatura hispánica* (México: EDIMUSA, 1989).

CORTES, Jaime Erasto. *El cuento: siglos XIX y XX* (México: PROMEXA, 1985).

CUESTA, Jorge. *Antología de la poesía mexicana moderna* (México, Contemporáneos, 1928); 2nd ed. (FONAPAS, 1980); 3rd ed. (FCE-SEP, 1985).

_____. *Poemas y ensayos*, 4 vols., Colección Poemas y Ensayos (México: UNAM, 1964).

DAUSTER, Frank. *Breve historia de la poesía mexicana* (México: Ed. de Andrea, 1956).

_____. *Ensayos sobre poesía mexicana, asedio a los contemporáneos* (México: Ed. de Andrea, 1963).

_____. *Historia del teatro hispanoamericano, siglos XIX y XX* (México: Ed. de Andrea, 1966).

_____. *Ensayos sobre teatro hispanoamericano* (México: SepSetentas, 1975).

_____. *The Double Strand* (Lexington, KY: The University Press of Kentucky, 1987).

DESSAU, Adalbert. *La novela de la Revolución mexicana* (México: FCE, 1972).

DIAZ-PLAJA, Guillermo and Francisco MONTERDE. *Historia de la literatura española e historia de la literatura mexicana* (México: Edit. Porrúa, S.A., 1955).

DIAZ Y ALEJO, Ana Elena. *La prosa en la Revista Azul (1894-1896)*, thesis (México: UNAM, 1965).

DIAZ Y ALEJO, Ana Elena, Aurora OCAMPO ALFARO, and Ernesto PRADO VELAZQUEZ. *Indices de El Domingo, revista literaria mexicana (1871-1873)* (México: UNAM, 1959).

DIAZ Y ALEJO, Ana Elena and Ernesto PRADO VELAZQUEZ. *Indices de El Nacional, periódico literario mexicano (1880-1884)* (México: UNAM,1961.

DIEZ-CANEDO, Enrique. *Letras de América* (México: FCE, 1944).

EARL, Peter G. and Robert G. Mead. *Historia del ensayo hispanoamericano* (México: de Andrea, 1974).

ECHANOVE Trujillo, Carlos A., et al. *Enciclopedia jucatense*, 8 vols. (México: Gobierno de Yucatán, 1944-1947).

ELIZONDO, Salvador. *Museo Poético* (México: UNAM, 1974).

ESQUIVEL Pren, José. *Historia de la literatura en Yucatán* (México: Eds. de la Universidad de Yucatán, 1981).

ESTRADA, GENARO. *Poetas nuevos de México* (México: Eds. Porrúa, 1916).

FELL, Claude. *Estudios de literatura hispanoamericana contemporánea* (México: SEP, 1976).

FERNANDEZ, Josefina I. de. *Antología de la Novela Moderna y Contemporánea en México* (México: UNAM, 1975).

FERNANDEZ LEDEZMA, Enrique. *Galería de fantasmas, años y sombras del siglo XIX*, (México: Edit. México Nuevo, 1939).

FERNANDEZ MACGREGOR, Genaro. *Carátulas* (México: Eds. Botas, l935).

FLORES, Angel. *El realismo mágico en la ficción narrativa hispanoamericana* (Guadalajara: Eds. Caetera, 1958).

_____. *Historia y antología del cuento y la novela en Hispanoamérica* (New York: Las Américas Publishing Company, 1959).

_____. *Bibliografía de escritores hispanoamericanos 1609-1974* (New York: Gordian Press, 1975).

_____. *Narrativa hispanoamericana 1816-1981*, 8 vols. (México: Siglo XXI Eds., 1985).

_____ and Raul Silva Cáceres. *La novela hispanoamericana actual* (New York: Las Américas, 1971).

FORSTER, Merlin H. *Los Contemporáneos, 1920-1932, perfil de un experimento vanguardista mexicano* (México: Eds. de Andrea, 1964).

_____. *An Index to Méxican Literary Periodicals (1920-1960)* (New York: The Scarecrow Press, 1966).

FRANCO, Jean. *Historia de la literatura hispanoamericana* (Barcelona: Ariel, 1975).

_____. *La cultura moderna en América Latina* (México: Grijalbo, 1985).

FUENTES, Carlos. *La nueva novela hispanoamericana* (México: Mortiz, 1976).

GALLO, Eduardo L., ed. *Hombres ilustres mexicanos, biografías de los personajes notables desde antes de la Conquista hasta nuestros días* (México: Imp. de I. Cumplido, 1873-1874).

GALLY, Hector. *30 cuentos de autores mexicanos jóvenes* (México: Ed. Pax, 1967).

GARCIA CUBAS, Antonio. *Diccionario geográfico, histórico y biográfico de los Estados Unidos Mexicanos*, vol. 1 (México: Imp. de Murguía, 1888); vols. 2-5 (Ofna. Tip. de la Sría. de Fomento, 1888-1891).

GARCIA GRANADOS, Rafael. *Diccionario biográfico de historia antigua de Méjico*, 3 vols. (México: Edit. Jus, S.A., 1952-1953).

GARCIA ICAZBALCETA, Joaquín. *Bibliografía mexicana del siglo XVI*, 1st ed., 1886; new ed. by Agustín Míllares Carlo (México: FCE, 1954).

GARCIA MORAL, Concepción. *Antología de la poesía mexicana* (Madrid: Editora Nacional, 1975).

GARCIA RIERA, Emilio. *Historia documental del cine mexicano*, 9 vols. (México: Era, 1969-1978).

GARCIA RIVAS, Heriberto. *150 biografías de mexicanos ilustres* (México: Edit. Diana, S.A., 1964).

_____. *Historia de la literatura mexicana*, 4 vols. (México: Manuel Porrúa, 1971-1974).

GARIBAY K, Angel María, et al. *Diccionario Porrúa, de historia, biografía y geografía de México* (México: Edit. Porrúa, S.A., 1964).

GILLY, Adolfo, et al. *Interpretaciones de la Revolución mexicana* (México: UNAM, 1979).

GLANZ, Margo *Onda y escritura en México* (México: Siglo XXI, 1971).

_____. *Repeticiones. Ensayos sobre literatura mexicana* (Xalapa: Universidad Veracruzana, 1979).

_____ and Xorge del Campo. *Narrativa joven de México* (México: Siglo XXI, 1969).

GOLDING COOPER, Alyce. *Teatro mexicano contemporáneo, 1940-1962*, thesis (México: UNAM, 1962).

GOMEZ-GIL, Orlando. *Historia crítica de la literatura hispanoamericana* (New York: Holt, Rinehart and Winston, 1968).

_____. *Literatura hispaniamericana. Antología crítica*, 2 vols. (New York: Holt, Rinehart and Winston, 1972, 1971).

GONZALEZ, Héctor. *Siglo y medio de cultura nuevoleonesa* (México: Eds. Botas, 1946).

GONZALEZ, Manuel Pedro. *Trayectoria de la novela en México* (México: Eds. Botas, 1951).

GONZALEZ CASANOVA, Pablo, et al. *México hoy* (México: Siglo XXI Eds., 1977).

_____ and Hector AGUILAR CAMIN. *México ante la crisis* (México: UNAM, 1985).

GONZALEZ DE LEON, Jorge. *Poetas de una generación (1940-1949)* (México: UNAM, 1981).

GONZALEZ OBREGON, Luis. *Breve noticia de los novelistas mexicanos en el siglo XIX* (México: Tip. de O. R. Spíndola, 1889).

GONZALEZ PEÑA, Carlos *Historia de la literatura mexicana* (México: Edit. Porrúa, S.A., 1966); Translated into English by Gusta Barfield Nance and Florene Johnson Dunstan (Dallas: Southern Methodist University Press, 1943), 4th ed. (1969).

_____. *Gente mía* (México: Edit. Stylo, 1946).

_____. *Claridad en la lejanía* (México: Edit. Stylo, 1947).

GOROSTIZA, Celestino. *Teatro mexicano del siglo XX*, vol. 3 (México: FCE, 1956).

GRISMER, Raymond L. and Mary B. MACDONALD. *Vida y obras de autores mexicanos* (La Habana: Edit. Alfa, 1945).

GUTIERREZ NAJERA, Manuel. *Obras. Crítica literaria*, vol. 1 (México: UNAM, 1959).

HALE, Charles A. *El liberalismo mexicano en la época de Mora 1821-1853* (México: Siglo XXI, 1976).

HENRIQUEZ UREÑA, Max. *Breve historia del modernismo* (México and Buenos Aires: FCE, 1954).

HENRIQUEZ UREÑA, Pedro. *Historia de la cultura en la América hispánica* (México: FCE, 1947); 2nd ed. (1961).

_____. *Las corrientes literarias en la América hispánica* (México: FCE, 1949).

HERNANDEZ, Julia. *Novelistas y cuentistas de la Revolución mexicana* (México: Unidad Mexicana de Escritores, 1960).

HERNANDEZ Palaciós, Esther and Angel José FERNANDEZ. *La poesía veracruzana. Antología* (Xalapa: Universidad Veracruzana, 1984).

HIGUERA, Ernesto. *Antología Sinaloense*, vol. 1 (Culiacán: Eds. Culturales del Gobierno del Estado de Sinaloa, 1958).

_____. *Antología de prosistas sinaloenses*, vol. 2 (Culiacán: Eds. Culturales del Gobierno del Estado de Sinaloa, 1959).

HILTON, Ronald, ed. *Who's Who in Latin America*, Part I: *Mexico* (Stanford, Calif.: Stanford University Press, 1946).

HOWLAND BUSTAMANTE, Sergio. *Historia de la literatura mexicana* (México: Edit. F. Trillas, S.A., 1961).

IGUINIZ, Juan B.. *Bibliografía de novelistas mexicanos* (México: Imp. de la Sría. de Relaciones Exteriores, 1926).

_____. *Bibliografía biográfica mexicana* (México: Imp. de la Sría, de Relaciones Exteriores, 1930).

ILLESCAS, Francisco R. and Juan Bartolo HERNANDEZ. *Escritores veracruzanos, reseña biográfico-antológica* (Veracruz, Ver.: Universidad Veracruzana, 1945).

JARAMILLO Levi, Enrique. *El cuento erótico en Mexico* (México: Diana, 1973; Eds. del Valle de Mexico, 1978).

_____. *Poesía erótica mexicana 1889-1980* (México: Eds. Domés, 1982).

JIMENEZ, Sergio and Edgar CEBALLOS. *Teoría y praxis del teatro en México* (México: Ed. Gaceta, 1982).

JIMENEZ RUEDA, Julio. *Historia de la literatura mexicana*, 6th. ed. (México: Eds. Botas, 1957).

_____. *Letras mexicanas en el siglo XIX*, Colección Tierra Firme, no. 3 (México, FCE, 1944).

JONES, Willis Knapp. *Breve historia del teatro latinoamericano* (México: Ed. de Andrea, 1956).

KRAUSS ACAL, Irma. *La poesía en la Juventud Literaria, semanario mexicano (1887-1888)*, thesis (México: UNAM, 1965).

LAMB, Ruth S. *Bibliografía del teatro mexicano del siglo XX* (México: Eds. de Andrea, 1962).

LANGFORD, Walter M. *The Mexican Novel comes of age* (Notre Dame: Univ. of Notre Dame Press, 1972).

_____. *La novela mexicana. Realidad y valores* (México: Diana, 1975).

LAZO, Raimundo. *Historia de la literatura hispanoamericana. Siglo XIX* (México: Porrúa, 1976).

LEAL, Luis. *Breve historia del cuento mexicano* (México: Eds. de Andrea, 1956).

_____. *Antología del cuento mexicano* (México: Eds. de Andrea, 1957).

_____. *Bibliografía del cuento mexicano* (México: Eds. de Andrea, 1958).

_____. *El cuento veracruzano* (Xalapa: Universidad Veracruzana, 1966).

_____. *Historia del cuento hispanoamericano* (México: Eds. de Andrea, 1966); 2nd ed. (1971).

_____. "Literatura mexicana 1940-1963", in *Panorama das literaturas das Américas*, edited by Joaquim de Montezuma de Carvalho, vol. 4 (Nova Lisboa, Brazil: Municipio de Nova Lisboa, 1965), pp. 1997-2050.

_____. *Panorama de la literatura mexicana actual* (Washington, D.C.: Unión Panamericana, 1968).

_____. *Breve historia de la literatura hispanoamericana* (New York: Alfred A. Knopf, 1971).

LEDUC, Alberto, Luis LARA PARDO, and Carlos ROUMAGNAC. *Diccionario de geografía, historia y biografía mexicanas* (París and México: Libr. de la Vda. de Ch. Bouret, 1910).

LEIVA, Raúl. *Imagen de la poesía mexicana contemporánea* (México: UNAM, 1959).

_____. *Iluminaciones* (México: Ed. Letras, 1973).

LEON, Nicolás. *Hombreas ilustres y escritores michoacanos, galería fotográfica y apuntamientos biográficos* (Morelia: Imp. del Gobierno, 1884).

LEON-PORTILLA, Miguel. *Los antiguos mexicanos* (México: FCE-SEP, 1985).

LERIN, Manuel, and Marco Antonio MILLAN. *29 cuentistas mexicanos actuales* (México: Eds. de la Revista América, 1945).

LIST ARZUBIDE, Germán. *El movimiento estridentista* (Jalapa: Eds. Horizonte, 1927).

LOPEZ CAMARA, Francisco. *La génesis de la conciencia liberal en México* (México: UNAM, 1969).

MAGAÑA ESQUIVEL, Antonio. *Teatro mexicano del siglo XX*, vols. 2, 4, 5 (México: FCE, 1956, 1970).

_____. *Medio siglo de teatro mexicano, 1900-1961* (México: INBA, 1964).

_____. *La novela de la Revolución*, 2 vols. (México: Porrúa, 1964, 1974).

_____. *Medio siglo de teatro mexicano 1900-1961* (México: INBA, 1964).

_____ and Ruth S. LAMB. *Breve historia del teatro mexicano* (México: Eds. de Andrea, 1958).

MANCISIDOR, José. *Cuentos mexicanos del siglo XIX*, 2nd ed. (México: Edit. Nueva España, S.A., [1946]).

_____. *Cuentos mexicanos de autores contemporáneos* (México: Edit. Nueva España, S.A., [1946]).

MANRIQUE, Jorge Alberto, et al. *Historia General de México*, 4 vols., 2nd ed. (México: El Colegio de México, 1977).

MANZANO C., Teodomiro. *Diccionario biográfico del Estado de Hidalgo* (Pachuca de Soto, Hgo., n. p., 1948).

MARINELLO, Juan. *Contemporáneos. Noticia y memoria* (Las Villas, Cuba: Universidad Central de las Villas, 1964).

MARQUEZ, Javier. *Pensamiento de México en los periodicos* (México: Eds. Tecnos, 1976).

MARQUEZ MONTIEL, Joaquín. *Hombres célebres de Puebla*, 2 vols. (México: Edit. Jus, 1952, 1955).

_____. *Hombres célebres de Chihuahua* (México: Edit. Jus, 1953).

MARRA LOPEZ, José R. *Narrativa española fuera de España (1939-1961)* (Madrid: Eds. Guadarrama, 1963).

MARTIN, Dolores Moyano, ed. *Handbook of Latin American Studies* (Austin: University of Texas Press, 1989).
MARTINEZ, José Luis. *Literatura mexicana siglo XX, 1910-1949* (México: Ant. Libr. Robredo, 1949, 1950).
_____. *La expresión nacional, letras mexicanas del siglo XLX* (México: Imp. Universitaria, 1955).
_____. *El ensayo mexicano moderno*, 2 vols. (México: FCE, 1958).
MEAD, Robert G. *Breve historia del ensayo hispanoamericano* (México: Eds. de Andrea, 1956).
MEDINA ROMERO, Jesús. *Antología de poetas contemporáneos, 1910-1953* (San Luis Potosí: Universidad Autónoma de San Luis Potosí, 1953).
MELENDEZ, Concha. *La novela indianista en Hispanoamérica (1832-1889)* (Madrid: n. p., 1934).
MELGORZA, Arturo. *Modernizadores den la narrativa mexicana* (México: SEP-Katún, 1984).
Memorias de la Academia Mexicana Correspondiente de la Real Española, 6 vols., (México: Academia Mexicana, 1876-1910).
Memorias de la Academia Mexicana Correspondiente de la Española, 11 vols., from 7 to 17 (México: Academia Mexicana, 1945-1960).
Memorias de los congresos del Instituto Internacional de Literatura Iberoamericana, 20 vols. one per year (Diferent cities: Instituto Internacional de Literatura Iberoamericana, 1938-1981).
MENDEZ PLANCARTE, Alfonso. *Poetas novohispanos, primer siglo (1521-1621)* (México: UNAM, 1942); 2nd ed. (1964).
_____. *Poetas novohispanos, segundo siglo (1621-1721)* (México: UNAM, 1944).
_____, *Poetas novohispanos, segundo siglo (1621-1721)* (México: UNAM, 1945).
MENDEZ PLANCARTE, Gabriel. *Humanistas del siglo XVIII* (México: UNAM, 1941); 2nd ed. (1962).
_____. *Horacio en México* (México: UNAM, 1937).
MENENDEZ Y PELAYO, Marcelino. *Historia de la poesía hispanoamericana* (Madrid: Libr. Gral. de Victoriano Suárez, Madrid, 1911).
MENTON, Seymour. *El cuento hispanoamericano, antología crítico-histórica*, 2 vols. (México and Buenos Aires: FCE, 1964).
MEYER, Doris and Margarite FERNANDEZ OLMOS, eds. *Contemporary Women Authors of Latin America* (New York: Brooklyn College Press, 1983).
MICHELENA, Margarita. *Notas en torno a la poesía mexicana contemporánea* (México: Asociación Mexicana por la Libertad de la Cultura, 1959).
MILLAN, María del Carmen. *El paisaje en la poesía mexicana* (México: Imp. Universitaria, 1952).
_____. *Literatura mexicana* (México: Edit. Esfinge, 1962); 5th ed. (1970).
_____. *Antología de cuentos mexicanos*, 3 vols. (México: SEP, 1976); 2nd ed. 2 vols. (México: Nueva Imagen, 1977).
MILLER, Beth and Alfonso GONZALEZ. *26 autores del México actual* (México: Costa-Amic, 1978).
MONSIVAIS, Carlos. *La poesía mexicana del siglo xx* (México: Empresas Editoriales, 1966).
_____. *Antología de la crónica en México* (México: UNAM, 1979).
MONTERDE, Francisco. *Bibliografía del teatro en México* (Mexico, Secretaría de Relaciones Exteriores, 1933).

_____. *Cultura mexicana, aspectos literarios* (México: Editora Intercontinental, 1946).

_____. *Teatro mexicano del siglo XX*, vol. 1 (México: FCE, 1956).

MONTES DE OCA, Francisco. *Ocho siglos de poesía en lengua española* (México: Porrúa, 1961).

_____. *Poesía mexicana. Antología* (México: Porrúa, 1968; 1971).

MOORE, Ernest R. *Bibliografía de novelistas de la Revolución Mexicana* (Mexico, n.p., 1941).

MORTON, F. Rand. *Los novelistas de la Revolución Mexicana* (México: Edit. Cultura, 1949).

NAVARRO, Joaquina. *La novela realista mexicana* (México: Compañía General de Ediciones, 1955).

NORIEGA, Alfonso. *El pensamiento conservador y el conservadurismo mexicano* (México: UNAM, 1972).

NORIEGA, Elio, et al. *Estudios de historia moderna y contemporánea de México* (México: UNAM, 1979).

NOVO, Salvador *La vida en México en el periodo presidencial de Lázaro Cárdenas* (México: Empresas Editoriales, 1964).

_____. *La vida en México en el periodo presidencial de Manuel Avila Camacho* (México: Empresas Editoriales, 1965).

_____. *La vida en México en el periodo presidencial de Miguel Alemán* (México: Empresas Editoriales, 1967).

NUÑEZ Y DOMINGUEZ, José de J. *Los poetas jóvenes de México y otros estudios literarios nacionalistas* (París and México: Libr. de la Vda. de Ch. Bouret, 1918).

OCAMPO, Aurora M. *Literatura mexicana contemporánea* (México: UNAM, 1965).

_____. *La crítica de la novela iberoamericana contemporánea. Antología* (México: UNAM, 1973); 2nd. ed. (1974).

_____. *Cuentistas mexicanas siglo XX. Antología* (México: UNAM, 1976).

_____. et al. *La crítica de la novela mexicana contemporánea* (México: UNAM, 1981).

_____ and Ernesto Prado Velázquez, *Diccionario de Escritores mexicanos* (México: UNAM, 1967).

O'GORMAN, Edmundo, et al. *Mexico. Cincuenta años de Revolución* (México: FCE, 1963).

OLAVARRIA Y FERRARI, Enrique *El arte literario en Mexico*, 2nd ed. (Madrid: Espinosa y Bautista, 1878).

_____. *Poesías líricas mexicanas*, 3rd ed. (Madrid: Perlado, Páez y Cía., 1910).

OLIVO LARA, Margarita. *Biografías de veracruzanos distinguidos*, (México: Museo Nacional de Arqueología, Historia y Etnografía, 1931).

ONIS, Federico de. *Antología de la poesía española e hispanomaericana (1881-1932)* (Madrid: Publs. de la Revista de Filología Española, 1934).

OROZCO Y BERRA, Manuel. *Diccionario universal de historia y de geografía*, 10 vols. (México: n.p. 1853-1856).

ORTEGA, Julio. *La contemplación y la fiesta* (Caracas: Monte Avila, 1969).

_____. *Convergencias/Divergencias/Incidencias* (Barcelona: Tusquets, 1973).

ORTEGA HERNANDEZ, Gregorio. *Hombres, mujeres*, prólogue by José Vasconcelos (México: Aztlán, 1926); 2a. ed. (México: INBA, 1966).

OSORIO, Luis Enrique. *La novela hispanoamericana* (Bogotá: Edit. La Idea, 1965).

PACHECO, José Emilio. *La poesía mexicana del siglo XIX* (México: Empresas Editoriales, S.A., 1965).

PALAU Y DULCET, Antonio. *Manual del librero hispanoamericano*, 7 vols., 2nd ed. (Barcelona: Libr. Anticuaria de A. Palau, 1948).

Panorama das literaturas das Américas (De 1900 a actualidade) 4 vols., edited by Joaquim de Montezuma de Carbalho (Nova Lisboa: Municipio de Nova Lisboa, 1963).

PAYRO, Roberto P. *Historias de la literatura americana, guía bibliográfica* (Washington, D.C.: Unión Panamericana, 1950).

PAZ, Ireneo. *Los hombres prominentes de México* (México: Imp. y Lit. de La Patria, 1888).

PAZ, Octavio. *El laberinto de la soledad*, 3rd ed. (México: FCE, 1963).

_____. *Las peras del olmo* (México: Imp. Universitaria, 1957); 2nd ed. UNAM, 1965).

_____. *Puertas al campo* (México: UNAM, 1966).

_____. Alí CHUMACERO, José Emilio PACHECO, and Homero ARIDJIS. *Poesía en movimiento. Mexico, 1915-1966*, prólogue by Octavio Paz (México: Siglo XXI, 1966).

PERAL, Miguel Angel. *Diccionario biográfico mexicano*, 3 vols. (México: Edit. P.A.C., [ca. 1944]).

PEREZ MINIK, Domingo. *Novelistas españoles de los siglos XIX y XX* (Madrid: Guadarrama, 1957).

PERUS, Françoise. *Literatura y sociedad en América Latina* (México: Siglo XXI, 1976).

PEZA, Juan de Dios. *Poetas y escritroes modernos mexicanos, en El anuario mexicano de Filomeno Mata* (México: Filomeno Mata, 1878); 2nd. ed. (México: SEP, 1965).

PHILLIPS, Allen W. *Estudios y notas sobre literatura hispanoamericana* (México: Ed. Cultura, 1965).

_____. *Cinco estudios sobre literatura mexicana moderna* (México: SEP, 1974).

PIMENTEL, Francisco *Historia crítica de la literatura y de las ciencias en México desde la Conquista hasta nuestros días. Poetas*, 2nd ed. (México: Libr. de La Enseñanza, 1890).

_____. *Historia crítica de la poesía en México* (México: Ofna. Tip. de la Sría. de Fomento, 1892).

_____. *Obras completas de D. Francisco Pimentel*, 5 vols. (México: Tip. Económica, 1903-1904).

PORTAL, Marta. *Proceso narrativo de la Revolución Mexicana*, 2nd ed. (Madrid: Cultura Hispánica, 1980).

PRADO VELAZQUEZ, Ernesto *La poesía en la Revista Azul (1894-1896)*, thesis, (México: UNAM, 1965).

PRIETO, Guillermo. *Memorias de mis tiempos*, vol. 1; *1828-1840*, vol. 2; *1840-1853* (París-México: Libr. de la Vda. de Ch. Bouret, 1906).

RAMA, Angel *Novísimos narradores hispanoamericanos en Marcha. 1964-1980* (México: Marcha Ed., 1981).

RAPP, Helen Louis. *La novela del petróleo en Mexico* (México: UNAM, 1957).

READ, John Lloyd. *The Mexican Historical Novel, 1826-1910* (New York: Instituto de las Españas, 1939).

Las Revistas Literarias de México (México: INBA,1963).

Las Revistas Literarias de México, 2nd. series (México: INBA, 1964).

REYES, Alfonso. *Obras Completas*, 20 vols. to 1965 (México:FCE, 1955-1980).

REYES NEVARES, Salvador. "La literatura mexicana en el siglo XX. I (1900-1930)," in *Panorama das Literaturas das Américas (De 1900 a actualidade)*, vol. 4, edited by Joaquim de Montezuma de Carvalho (Nova Lisboa: Município de Nova Lisboa, Angola, 1963), pp. 1937-1995.

RIO, Angel del. *Historia de la literatura española*, rev. ed., 2 vols. (New York: Holt, Rinehart and Winston, 1963).

RIO, Rafael del. *La poesía mexicana contemporánea y otros ensayos* (Torreón, Coah.: Eds. Revista Cauce, 1955).

RIVA PALACIO, Vicente. *Los Ceros, Galería de contemporáneos, por Cero* (México: Imp. de F. Díaz de León, Editor, 1882).

ROBLES, Martha. *La sombra fugitiva*, 2 vols. (México: UNAM, 1986).

RODRIGUEZ MONEGAL, Emir. *Narradores de esta América* (Montevideo: Alfa, 1974).

RODRIGUEZ PLAZA, Joaquina. *De poetas, cronistas y novelistas en los siglos mexicanos*, 4 vols. (México: UAM, 1983).

ROGGIANO, Alfredo L. *En este aire de América* (México: Cultura, 1966).

ROUAIX, Pastor. *Diccionario geográfico, histórico y biográfico del Estado de Durango* (México: Edit. Cultura, 1946).

RUFFINELLI, Jorge. *El otro México. México en la obra de B. Traven, D. H. Lawrence y Malcolm Lowry* (México: Nueva Imagen, 1978).

RUIZ, Bernardo. *La rosa de los vientos. Antología de prosa y poesía* (México: UAM-Azcapotzalco, 1979).

SABATO, Ernesto. *El escritor y sus fantasmas, Ensayistas hispánicos* (Buenos Aires: Edit. Aguilar, 1963).

SAINZ, Gustavo. *Jaula de palabras* (México: Grijalvo, 1980).

_____. *Corazón de palabras* (México: Grijalbo, 1981).

_____. *Los mejores cuentos mexicanos* (México: Océano, 1982).

_____. *Narrativa Hispanoamericana, 1819-1981*, 8 vols. (México: Siglo XXI, 1985).

SAINZ DE ROBLES, Federico Carlos. *Ensayo de un diccionario de la literatura*, vol. 2 (Madrid, Aguilar, 1953).

SALADO ALVAREZ, Victoriano. *Memorias de Victoriano Salado Alvarez*, vol. 1; *Tiempo viejo*; vol. 2; *Tiempo nuevo* (México: EDIAPSA, 1946).

SANCHEZ, Luis Alberto. *Proceso y contenido de la novela hispanoamericana* (Madrid: Ed. Gredos, 1953).

SANCHEZ VAZQUEZ, Adolfo. *Filosofía de la praxis* (México: Grijalbo, 1967).

SAZ, Agustín del. *Teatro hispanoamericano*, 2 vols. (Barcelona: Edit. Vergara, 1964).

SCHNEIDER, Luis Mario. *El estridentismo o una literatura de la estrategia* (México: INBA, 1970).

_____. *Ruptura y continuidad, la literatura mexicana en polémica* (México: FCE, 1975).

_____. *El estridentismo* (México: UNAM, 1985).

SEFCHOVICH, Sara, et al. *Mujeres en espejo*, vol. 1 (México: Folios, 1983).

SILVA HERZOG, Jesús. *Breve historia de la Revolución mexicana*, vol. 1, 3rd. ed. (México: FCE, 1964).

_____. *Biografías de amigos y conocidos* (México: Editorial de Cuadernos Americanos, 1980).

SKIRIUS, John. *El ensayo hispanoamericano del siglo XX* (México: FCE, 1981).

SOLDEVILLA DURANTE, Ignacio. *La novela desde 1936* (Madrid: Alhambra, 1980).

SOMMERS, Joseph. *After the Storm, landmarks of the Modern Mexican Novel* (Albuquerque: Univ. of New Mexico Press, 1968).

SOSA, Francisco. *Los contemporáneos* (México: Imp. de Gonzalo A. Esteva, 1884).

_____. *Biografías de mexicanos distinguidos* (México: Ed. de la Sría. de Fomento, 1884).

SPOTA, Luis. *¿Qué pasa con la novela en México?* (Monterrey: Ed. Sierra Madre, 1972).

STARR, Frederick. *Readings from Modern Mexican Authors* (Chicago: The Open Court Publishing Company, 1904).

STEIN, Stanley and Bárbara STEIN. *La herencia colonial de América Latina* 14th ed. (México: Siglo XXI, 1982).

TORRENTE BALLESTER, Gonzalo. *Panorama de la literatura española contemporánea* (Madrid: Eds. Guadarrama, 1971).

TORRES, Vicente Francisco. *El cuento policial mexicano* (México: Diógenes, 1982).

TORRES-RIOSECO, Arturo. *Bibliografía de la novela mexicana* (Cambridge: Harvard University Press, 1933).

_____. *Antología de la literatura hispanoamericana* (New York: F.S. Crofts & Co., 1939); 2nd ed. (1947).

_____. *Nueva historia de la gran literatura iberoamericana*, 4th. ed. (Buenos Aires: EMECE, 1961).

_____. *Historia de la literatura iberoamericana* (New York: Las Americas, 1965).

_____ and WARNER, Ralph E. *Bibliografía de la poesía mexicana* (Cambridge: Harvard University Press, 1934).

El trato con escritores (México: INBA, 1961).

El trato con escritores, 2nd. series (México: INBA, 1964).

TREVIÑO, Julio C. *Antología mascarones* (México: Imp. Universitaria, 1954).

URBINA, Luis G.. *Hombres y libros* (México: El libro francés, S.A., [1923]).

_____. *La vida literaria de Mexico*, Madrid, 1917.

_____. *La vida literaria de Mexico y La literatura mexicana durante la guerra de la Independencia* (México: Ed. Porrúa, 1946).

VALBUENA BRIONES, Angel. *Historia de la literatura española*, vol. 4, literatura hispanoamericana (Barcelona: Edit. Gustavo Gili, S.A., 1962).

VALDES, Héctor. *Introducción al estudio de la Revista Moderna (1898-1903)*, thesis (México: UNAM, 1963).

_____. *Poetisas mexicanas siglo XX. Antología* (México: UNAM, 1976).

VALDEZ, Octaviano. *Poesía neoclásica y académica* (México: UNAM, 1946).

VALENZUELA RODARTE, Alberto. *Historia de la literatura en México* (México: Edit. Jus, 1961).

VALVERDE, José María. *Historia de la Literatura latinoamericana*, 2 vols. (Barcelona: Planeta, 1974).

VALVERDE TELLEZ, Emeterio *Bio-bibliografía eclesiástica mexicana (1821-1943)*, 3 vols., Direction and prólogue by José Bravo Ugarte (México: Edit. Jus, 1949).

_____. *Apuntaciones históricas sobre la filosofía en México* (México: Herrero Hnos., 1896).

_____. *Bibliografía filosófica mexicana*, 2 vols., 2nd. ed., (León, Gto.: Imp. de Jesús Rodríguez, 1913).

VAZQUEZ, Jorge Adalberto. *Perfil y esencia de la poesía mexicana* (México: n. p., 1955).

VELA, Arqueles. *Fundamentos de la literatura mexicana* (México: Patria, 1966).

VELAZQUEZ BRINGAS, Esperanza, and Rafael Heliodoro VALLE. *Indice de escritores*, (México: Talls. Gráf. de Herrero Hermanos Sucs., 1928).

VELAZQUEZ CHAVEZ, Agustín. *Jardín de la poesía mexicana. Siglos XV al XX.* (México: Ed. Casas, 1966).

VIGIL, José María. *Poetisas mexicanas, Siglos XV, XVI, XVII, XVIII and XIX* (México: Ofna. Tip. de la Sría. de Fomento, 1893).

VILLAURRUTIA, Xavier. *Obras* (México: FLB, 1966).

VILLEGAS, Abelardo. *Autognosis, el pensamiento mexicano en el siglo XX* (México: Instituto Panamericano de Geografía e Historia, 1985).

_____. *México en el horizonte liberal* (México: UNAM, 1981).

VILLORO, Luis. *El proceso ideológico de la revolución de independencia* (México: UNAM, 1983).

VOGT, Wolfgang. *El pensamiento latinoamericano del siglo XIX* (Guadalajara, Jal: UAG, 1982).

WARNER, Ralph E. *Historia de la novela mexicana en el siglo XIX* (México: Ant. Libr. Robredo, 1953).

WONG, Oscar. *Nueva Poesía de Chiapas* (México: KAtún, 1983).

WRIGHT DE KLEINHANS, Laureana. *Mujeres notables mexicanas* (México: Tip. Económica, 1910).

XIRAU, Ramón. *Mito y poesía, Ensayo sobre literatura contemporánea de lengua española* (México: UNAM, 1973).

ZAID, Gabriel. *Omnibus de poesía mexicana* (México: Siglo XXI, 1971; 8th ed. 1980).

_____. *El progreso improductivo* (México: Siglo XXI, 1976).

_____. *Asamblea de poetas jóvenes de México* (México: Siglo XXI, 1980).

ZEA, Leopoldo. *Latinoamérica en la encrucijada de su historia* (México: UNAM, 1981).

_____. "Prefacio de 1943" in *El positivismo en México* (México: FCE, 1981).

ZORRILA, José. *México y los mexicanos (1855-1857)* (México: Eds. de Andrea, 1955).

ZUM FELDE, Alberto. *Indice crítico de la literatura hispanoamericana*, vol. 1; *El ensayo y la crítica*; vol. 2; *La narrativa* (México: Edit. Guaranía, 1954, 1959).

_____. *Indice crítico de la literatura hispanoamericana, La narrativa* (México: Edit. Guaranía, 1959).

Index

This index includes references to names or pseudonyms of writers, themes, and some early literary works, important foreign literary figures and major movements, groups and influences. Writers listed as individual entries appear with their first last names in capital letters. Occasionally both last names are capitalized when the writer is publicly known accordingly, e.g., ABREU Gómez, Ermilo or CASTRO LEAL, Antonio. Influences noted in entries are listed alphabetically by the accepted last name. Mexican writers mentioned within the context of the entries have been omitted from the index. Page references to main entries appear in bold typeface.

768   INDEX

DUE